Essentials of
Programming Languages

Daniel P. Friedman
Mitchell Wand
Christopher T. Haynes

Foreword by Harold Abelson

Essentials of
Programming Languages

The MIT Press
Cambridge, Massachusetts London, England

McGraw-Hill Book Company
New York St. Louis San Francisco Montreal Toronto

This book was edited and produced by The MIT Press under a joint production-distribution arrangement with the McGraw-Hill Book Company.

Ordering Information:

North America
Text orders should be addressed to the McGraw-Hill Book Company. All other orders should be addressed to The MIT Press.

Outside North America
All orders should be addressed to The MIT Press or its local distributor.

This book was typeset by the authors using TEX 3.0. Camera-ready copy was generated off a L300 phototypesetter by Chiron, Inc.

This book was printed and bound in the United States of America.

Library of Congress Cataloging-in-Publication Data

Friedman, Daniel P.

    Essentials of programming languages / Daniel P. Friedman, Mitchell
Wand, Christopher T. Haynes.

      p.   cm.

    Includes bibliographical references and index.

    ISBN 0-262-06145-7 (MIT Press) (hb)

    ISBN 0-07-022443-9 (McGraw-Hill)

    1. Programming languages (Electronic computers)

I. Wand, Mitchell. II. Haynes, Christopher Thomas. III. Title.

QA76.7.F73   1992

005.13—dc20   91-23373

                                                                       CIP

Contents

1

Tools for Symbolic Programming *1*

2

Induction, Recursion, and Scope *31*

3

4

5

Contents

6

7

8

9

Continuation-Passing Interpreters *291*

10

Imperative Form and Stack Architecture *335*

11

Scanners and Parsers *375*

12

Contents

List of Figures

List of Figures

List of Figures

List of Figures

Foreword

This book brings you face-to-face with the most fundamental idea in computer programming:

> The interpreter for a computer language is just another program.

It sounds obvious, doesn't it? But the implications are profound. If you are a computational theorist, the interpreter idea recalls Gödel's discovery of the limitations of formal logical systems, Turing's concept of a universal computer, and von Neumann's basic notion of the stored-program machine. If you are a programmer, mastering the idea of an interpreter is a source of great power. It provokes a real shift in mindset, a basic change in the way you think about programming.

I did a lot of programming before I learned about interpreters, and I produced some substantial programs. One of them, for example, was a large data-entry and information-retrieval system written in PL/I. When I implemented my system, I viewed PL/I as a fixed collection of rules established by some unapproachable group of language designers. I saw my job not as to modify these rules, or even to understand them deeply, but rather to pick through the (very) large manual, selecting this or that feature to use. The notion that there was some underlying structure to the way the language was organized, and that I might want to override some of the language designers' decisions, never occurred to me. I didn't know how to create embedded sub-languages to help organize my implementation, so the entire program seemed like a large, complex mosaic, where each piece had to be carefully shaped and fitted into place, rather than as a cluster of languages, where the pieces could be flexibly combined. If you don't understand interpreters, you can still write programs; you can even be a competent programmer. But you can't be a master.

There are three reasons why as a programmer you should learn about interpreters.

First, you will need at some point to implement interpreters, perhaps not interpreters for full-blown general-purpose languages, but interpreters just the same. Almost every complex computer system with which people interact in flexible ways—a computer drawing tool or an information-retrieval system, for example—includes some sort of interpreter that structures the interaction. These programs may include complex individual operations—shading a region on the display screen, or performing a database search—but the interpreter is the glue that lets you combine individual operations into useful patterns. Can you use the result of one operation as the input to another operation? Can you name a sequence of operations? Is the name local or global? Can you parameterize a sequence of operations, and give names to its inputs? And so on. No matter how complex and polished the individual operations are, it is often the quality of the glue that most directly determines the power of the system. It's easy to find examples of programs with good individual operations, but lousy glue; looking back on it, I can see that my PL/I database program certainly had lousy glue.

Second, even programs that are not themselves interpreters have important interpreter-like pieces. Look inside a sophisticated computer-aided design system and you're likely to find a geometric recognition language, a graphics interpreter, a rule-based control interpreter, an object-oriented language interpreter, all working together. One of the most powerful ways to structure a complex program is as a collection of languages, each of which provides a different perspective, a different way of working with the program elements. Choosing the right kind of language for the right purpose, and understanding the implementation tradeoffs involved: that's what the study of interpreters is about.

The third reason for learning about interpreters is that programming techniques that explicitly involve the structure of language are becoming increasingly important. Today's concern with designing and manipulating class hierarchies in object-oriented systems is only one example of this trend. Perhaps this is an inevitable consequence of the fact that our programs are becoming increasingly complex—thinking more explicitly about languages may be our best tool for dealing with this complexity. Consider again the basic idea: the interpreter itself is just a program. But that program is written in some language, whose interpreter is itself just a program written in some language whose interpreter is itself . . .. Perhaps the whole distinction between program and programming language is a misleading idea, and that future programmers will see themselves not as writing programs in particular, but as creating new languages for each new application.

Friedman, Wand, and Haynes have done a landmark job, and their book will change the landscape of programming-language courses. They don't just *tell* you about interpreters; they *show* them to you. The core of the book is a tour de force sequence of interpreters starting with an abstract high-level language and progressively making linguistic features explicit until we reach a state-machine with a parser and compiler. You can actually run this code, study and modify it, change the way these interpreters handle scoping, parameter-passing, control structure.

Part of the reason for the appeal of this approach is that the authors have chosen a good tool—the Scheme language, which combines the uniform syntax and data-abstraction capabilities of Lisp, with the lexical scoping and block structure of Algol. The result is a language that is high-level enough so that an interpreter can be expressed in a single page of code, yet explicit enough to deal with control flow and register allocation. But a powerful tool becomes most powerful in the hands of masters. The sample interpreters in this book are outstanding models. Indeed, since they are *runnable* models, I'm sure that these interpreters will find themselves at the cores of many programming systems over the coming years.

This is not an easy book. Mastery of interpreters does not come easily, and for good reason. The language designer is a further level removed from the end user than is the ordinary application programmer. In designing an application program, you think about the specific tasks to be performed, and consider what features to include. But in designing a language, you consider the various applications people might want to implement, and the ways in which they might implement them. Should your language have static or dynamic scope, or a mixture? Should it have inheritance? Should it pass parameters by reference or by value? Should continuations be explicit or implicit? It all depends on how you expect your language to be used, on which kinds of programs should be easy to write, and which you can afford to make more difficult.

Also, interpreters really *are* subtle programs. A simple change to a line of code in an interpreter can make an enormous difference in the behavior of the resulting language. Don't think that you can just skim these programs—very few people in the world can glance at a new interpreter and predict from that how it will behave even on relatively simple programs. So study these programs. Better yet, *run* them—this is working code. Try interpreting some simple expressions, then more complex ones. Add error messages. Modify the interpreters. Design your own variations. Try to really master these programs, not just get a vague feeling for how they work.

Foreword

If you do this, you will change your view of your programming, and your view of yourself as a programmer. You'll come to see yourself as a designer of languages rather than only a user of languages, as a person who chooses the rules by which languages are put together, rather than only a follower of rules that other people have chosen.

Hal Abelson
Cambridge, MA

Preface

The goal of this book is to give students a deep, hands-on understanding of the essential concepts of programming languages, using Scheme as an executable metalanguage. Because Scheme is a wide-spectrum language, it enables us to write both at the very high level needed to produce a concise, comprehensible interpreter and at the much lower level needed to understand how that interpreter might be coded in assembly language, or transformed into a compiler. Because of Scheme's excellent abstraction facilities, we can write substantial language-processing systems that are nevertheless compact enough for students to understand and manipulate with a reasonable amount of effort. This is a hands-on book: everything discussed in the book may be programmed by students.

Many texts are descriptive in nature and may be of use to the casual reader. Not this one. Our approach is analytic. Though we make little use of mathematical notation, our Scheme programs often play the same role. As with analytic texts in any discipline, this book requires careful reading with attention to detail. Before the material is mastered, it will frequently require rereading and reflection. Deep concepts are only absorbed with active participation. Their power must be experienced, not passively viewed.

Though we believe Scheme is an excellent metalanguage, this book is about the essentials of programming languages in general, *not* Scheme in particular. To emphasize this, we have given the interpreted language developed in this book a syntax very different from that of Scheme. This interpreted language is designed only for our pedagogic purposes and is not intended for other use. It is composed of a number of pieces, introduced throughout the text, which are not necessarily designed to form a coherent whole. Indeed, as we build new interpreters we often use the same concrete syntax with different semantics.

Beyond the use of Scheme, we use four major strategies:

1. The first strategy is the use of interpreters to explain the run-time behavior of programs in a given language. Interpreters express language design decisions in a manner that is both formal (unambiguous and complete) and executable. Furthermore, our interpreters are generally expressed in a fashion consistent with the principles of denotational semantics; they express key ideas of denotational semantics in a concrete way.

2. Instead of relying on mere descriptions, using English, diagrams, or some abstract notation, we present each principle using Scheme programs that implement it. The use of Scheme enables the student to understand these programs without drowning in a sea of irrelevant detail. The exercises allow the student to experiment with alternatives in design and implementation.

3. We emphasize the systematic derivation of low-level implementations from their high-level abstractions. We show how simple algebraic manipulation can be used to derive program properties and correctness-preserving program transformations. In particular, we use these techniques to derive stack-management protocols and to transform an interpreter into a compiler.

4. Finally, we use data abstraction, expressed as a modular coding style, to separate algorithms from the representation of the underlying quantities. In this way, we can change data representation without changing programs. In the case of interpreters, we use this technique to investigate different implementation strategies.

Through the use of these strategies, we are able to give students several working models, ranging from very high-level (almost formal semantics) to very low-level (almost assembly language), and to demonstrate a clear connection between these models.

Such depth must come at the expense of breadth. We make no attempt to survey existing languages, though we occasionally point out the design choices used in common languages. Although our approach is largely motivated by the developments in programming language semantics over the last 20 years, we do not address a number of important research areas, such as type checking and inference, logic programming, parallelism, and verification. We believe, however, that a command of the essentials will allow the student to study these topics. For example, an understanding of the mechanics of logic programming certainly requires understanding of continuations, dynamic binding, and the distinction between a variable's name, its binding, and the value of its binding.

Preface

Organization

The chart below represents the organizational structure of the book. The squares on the organizational chart represent chapters where syntax is introduced.

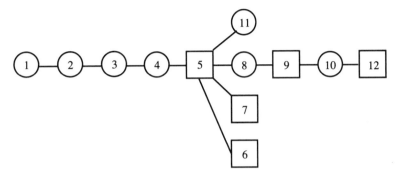

The first four chapters provide the foundations for a careful study of programming languages. Chapter 1 introduces most of the features of Scheme that are required in later chapters, along with some basic terminology. Readers who have prior experience with Scheme or other Lisp dialects may wish to skim this chapter and refer to it as necessary. Chapter 2 emphasizes the connection between inductive data specification and recursive programming, and introduces several notions related to the scope of variables. A set of exercises is provided to develop facility with recursive programming. Chapter 3 introduces some commonly used syntactic abstractions, including a variant record facility. This leads to a discussion of data abstraction and examples of representational transformations of the sort used in subsequent chapters. Chapter 4 introduces, in the context of the lambda calculus, several rewrite rules that are basic program transformations and provides a brief review of imperative programming.

The next three chapters show how these foundations may be used to describe the semantics of programming languages. Chapter 5 introduces interpreters as mechanisms for explaining the run-time behavior of languages and develops an interpreter for a simple, lexically scoped language with first-class procedures and variable assignment. This interpreter is the basis for most of the material in the remainder of the book. The chapter goes on to explore static and dynamic scoping and the implementation of recursion. Chapter 6 explores some parameter-passing mechanisms. Chapter 7 presents varieties of object-oriented facilities. These include several characterizations of inheritance and meta-classes. These two chapters can be studied in either order.

Chapters 8–10 show how the use of continuation-passing style enables us to transform our high-level interpreters into a flowchart-like form. Chapter 8 introduces continuation-passing style as a technique for expressing recursion by iteration. Using algebraic techniques, chapter 9 transforms our interpreter into continuation-passing style, and applies the techniques of chapter 3 to develop data structure representations of continuations. Data abstraction techniques then allow us to explore alternative representation strategies for the data manipulated by our interpreters. This includes the ability to make continuations accessible to the programmer as first-class objects of computation. In chapter 10 we complete the task of transforming our interpreter to a set of data structures manipulated by a finite-state controller. This gives us an interpreter that can be implemented in any low-level language. We then show how these data structures can be represented in a single stack with static and dynamic links. This development provides a solid understanding of stack-based language architectures, and also illustrates the power of algebraic reasoning techniques.

Finally, chapters 11 and 12 apply our techniques to the development of scanners, parsers, and compilers. Chapter 11 introduces lexical scanning and parsing techniques. Program transformations clarify the relationship between recursive descent and table-driven parsers. We show in chapter 12 how to start with a high-level functional specification of a language and, by choosing suitable representations of our data abstractions, derive both a virtual machine and a compiler that translates the high-level language to code for the virtual machine.

Chapters 5 through 10 are the heart of this book. The derivation of a sequence of interpreters ranging from very high- to very low-level does more than provide a solid, hands-on understanding of programming language semantics and a disciplined approach to language implementation. It also teaches an approach to programming that starts with a high-level operational specification, which also serves as a rapid prototype, and ends with what is effectively assembly language. We believe the programming transformation techniques used in this process should be in the toolbox of every computer scientist.

Usage

This text has been used in various forms to teach students from the sophomore to the graduate level, and in continuing education classes for professional programmers. It also has much to offer the dedicated computer scientist through self-study.

Preface

We assume the reader has at least one year of programming experience, including experience with a high-level language and assembly language and an introduction to data structures. Previous exposure to Lisp or Scheme is helpful but not required. This course might be followed by one in compiler construction or formal semantics of programming languages.

It is unlikely that all the material in this book can be covered in a single semester. Undergraduate students without some background in Scheme or Lisp will need to start with chapter 1 and can cover the material through chapter 5 or 6 in a semester. Undergraduate students who already know Scheme can quickly review the material in the first three chapters and cover chapters 4 through 10 in a semester. Well-prepared graduate students can reach chapter 12.

Not all of the material in each chapter need be covered. Much of the material in chapter 4, material at the end of chapters 5, 6, and 9, and all of chapters 7, 11, and 12 may be omitted as necessary. In chapter 8, a good introduction to the subject can be obtained by reading sections 8.1 and 8.2 and going through the examples in section 8.5.

The entire scanner, parser, and grammar for the interpreted language is given in the appendices. This facilitates the use of the syntax in exercises beginning with chapter 5, even though the parser technology is not developed until chapter 11. Those who prefer not to deal with the character syntax can use list structure syntax. This allows exercises to be done using the simple recursive descent parser, which is also given in the appendices. In order to study chapter 6, chapter 7, sections 9.3 through 9.6, or chapter 12, you need the appropriate parser for that chapter as well as the parser for the syntax of chapter 5.

Exercises are a vital part of the text and are scattered throughout. They range in difficulty from being trivial (if related material is understood) to requiring many hours of thought and programming work. We regard certain exercises as fundamental to mastery of the material. We introduce these with a bullet • instead of a circle ∘ and encourage readers to attempt them all.

Acknowledgments

Ten years ago, when we were all together at Indiana University, we decided to write a book based on the undergraduate programming languages course, C311. We had all taught it and felt that we had a way to unify its presentation. Eugene Kohlbecker, who had come to believe in our approach, was also an author. Eugene contributed many hours and hundreds of draft pages at the early stages, and without his taking charge in those early days, we would likely never have gotten started. We owe much to Eugene and use this forum to thank him. About the same time, Will Clinger arrived in Bloomington and he suggested that we change the course from using Lisp to using Scheme. He developed the Scheme 311 compiler, an ancestor of MacScheme, and the course has never been the same. For this and his time as an early author of the book, we thank him.

We very much appreciate having had the opportunity to course-test the book. We thank Claude Anderson, John Casey, Bruce Duba, Matthias Felleisen, Max Hailperin, Richard Kelsey, Dino Oliva, Jeff Perotti, and Richard Salter for trying out the book and for their comments. We particularly want to acknowledge Max for his insights, which greatly improved the material on parameter passing in chapter 6. We are grateful to Matthias for pointing out a bug in the implementation of recursive environments of chapter 5 and for his comments on chapter 4, which helped us improve the focus of that chapter. In addition, his concern for the lack of examples using continuations led to more material on them in chapter 9. We are grateful to Richard Kelsey for pointing out that chapter 11 should come after teaching continuation-passing style, rather than before understanding interpreters. His concern that it was too difficult for someone with little or no background using continuations helped us see the structure of the book more clearly.

We are grateful for the words of wisdom, criticism, and encouragement from Harold Abelson, Olivier Danvy, Kent Dybvig, Jim Miller, John Nienart, George Springer and Guy Steele. We particularly appreciate Hal for his suggestion of collecting the grammar rules in an appendix. This decision led to changes that significantly improved the book's overall clarity. In addition, Hal's criticism led to the inclusion of the implementation of the CPS algorithm in chapter 8 and to the inclusion of dynamic winding in chapter 9. We want to thank Kent for carefully reading the entire book and for making many suggestions that improved its clarity. Especially we want to thank him for his help in correcting our presentation of proper tail recursion. John's insight as a long-time practitioner of object-oriented programming led to what is now chapter 7. Without our discussions, it is unlikely that it would have its current, unified form. George taught us much about what freshmen could understand. This led to a clearer understanding of what sophomores and juniors should be able to understand. Furthermore, it helped clarify what it was that we really wanted to discuss in this book. We are also grateful to him for his words of encouragement. Jim Miller spent many hours of late-night phone conversations helping us conform to the Scheme standards. We thank all these hardy souls for their good suggestions; any mistakes or deficiencies are of course our own.

During the course of this book's development, it has been read by many students. In addition, some of the students helped solve some typesetting problems. We particularly appreciate the suggestions of David Boyer, Venkatesh Choppella, Peter Harlan, Bob Hieb, Haydn Huntley, Jim Marshall, Jacqueline Pulliam, Jon Rossie, Shing Shong (Bruce) Shei, Raja Thiagarajan, Sho-Huan (Simon) Tung, and Kiran Wagle. Jon discovered a subtle bug in an earlier version of our CPS algorithm. Venky's help on chapter 10 was greatly appreciated. David, Peter, and Haydn helped with their comments on chapter 12. Jacque and Raja rekindled our interest in inheritance in object-oriented programming. Simon commented on chapters 7 and 12, and Bob commented on chapter 8. Bruce and Kiran helped with some subtle aspects of typesetting.

We would like to thank Julia Lawall, Shinnder Lee, and John Simmons for their endless testing and retesting of the programs in this book. In addition, they have offered improvements at every step of the way. Julia's observation that our terminology in chapter 8 was inconsistent with her intuition led to major improvements in that chapter. Her efforts in chapter 12 enabled us to include a compiler that generated properly tail-recursive code. She also developed the streams solution of appendix F when we realized that conventional streams would not work for interactive systems. Julia, Shinnder, and John have uncovered the subtlest of errors and greatly improved the clarity of many of the programs in this book. For all of these contributions, we thank them.

Designing and drawing diagrams are difficult tasks. For helping design the diagrams, showing us how to use the drawing tool, and then drawing the actual diagrams, we would like to thank Venkatesh Choppella, Julia Lawall, John Simmons, and Kiran Wagle.

What wonderful software tools we have. These are especially impressive tools to those of us whose first programs used plugboards or punched cards. We would like to thank Richard Stallman and the Free Software Foundation for GNU Emacs, Donald Knuth for TeX, Gerald Sussman and Guy Steele for originating Scheme, Will Clinger for the Scheme 311 compiler, and Kent Dybvig for Chez Scheme. We are also grateful to the designers and implementors of the Internet who made it possible to work together across vast distances.

We are grateful to our respective academic homes, Indiana University and Northeastern University for encouraging us at every step of this project. We also want to thank the National Science Foundation for support of research that led to ideas presented in this book.

Working with Teresa Ehling at MIT Press has been a pleasure. She has made the process a most satisfying experience.

Every attempt has been made to acknowledge those who have helped us. We regret any oversight.

Last, we would like to thank those around us whose presence constantly reminds us of what is most important. They are our wives, Mary, Barbara and Janice, and our children, Brian, Robert, Rebecca, Jennifer, and Joshua. They deserve admiration for their patience, love, and understanding throughout the long gestation of this book.

Dan Friedman
Mitch Wand
Chris Haynes

Acknowledgments

Essentials of
Programming Languages

1 Tools for Symbolic Programming

You are about to begin the study of programming languages. It would be convenient if all the concepts behind programming languages could be explained using only natural language. Unfortunately, many aspects of programming languages require a high degree of precision, and natural language is not precise enough. In addition, we want to do more than just describe programming languages: we want to show how they are implemented. To fulfill these purposes, we use three different modes of expression:

1. For motivation and explanation, we use ordinary English.
2. When we need to be precise, we use the language of elementary mathematics: sets, functions, and elementary algebra.
3. When we need to display actual algorithms and implementations, we use the programming language Scheme.

The first two chapters of this book are designed to familiarize you with reading and writing Scheme programs. This includes a number of techniques for manipulating symbolic information of the kind found in programs and their run-time data structures. Particular emphasis is placed on techniques for *functional programming,* especially *recursion.* Along the way, we also introduce several fundamental concepts that allow us to talk precisely about programming languages. These are the basics you need to understand the rest of the book.

We begin in section 1.1 by introducing several basic ways of building Scheme expressions. Section 1.2 introduces a few primitive data types that taken together make Scheme especially suitable for symbolic programming. This is followed in section 1.3 by a discussion of procedures, which may be used with more flexibility in Scheme than in most other languages.

For every form of expression (or other component of a program) it is useful to distinguish between its *syntax,* which refers to rules governing how it is formed, and its *semantics,* which refers to rules that specify its meaning.

If you are already familiar with Scheme or another dialect of LISP, you may wish to skim this chapter quickly, taking note of any unfamiliar terminology (indicated by *italics*), and later refer to this chapter for specific information on Scheme. We introduce only those features of Scheme that are used later in this book.

1.1 Simple Expressions

A *statement* is a programming language construct that is evaluated only for its effect. Examples include assignment statements, input/output statements, and control statements (`while` loops, `if` statements, etc.). Programs in most languages are composed primarily of statements; such languages are said to be *statement oriented.*

Programming language constructs that are evaluated to obtain values are called *expressions.* Arithmetic expressions are the most common example. Expressions may occur as parts of statements, as in the right-hand side of an assignment statement. The data that may be returned as the values of expressions constitute the *expressed values* of a programming language. Expressions that are evaluated solely for their value, and not for any other effects of the computation, are said to be *functional.*

Some programming languages, such as Scheme, are *expression oriented:* their programs are constructed of definitions and expressions; there are no statements. This section reviews basic techniques for constructing expressions in Scheme.

1.1.1 Literals, Procedure Calls, and Variables

The simplest form of expression is a *literal* (or *constant*), which always returns the indicated value. For example, the result of evaluating the *numeral* 2 is a value denoting the number two, which has the printed representation 2. Other literals we shall have occasion to use include *strings,* such as "This is a string.", the *boolean* values #t (true) and #f (false), and *characters,* such as #\a and #\space. We discuss these and other Scheme data types in the next section.

The next simplest form of expression is a *variable reference.* The value of a variable reference is the value currently associated with, or *bound to,* the variable. A variable is said to *denote* the value of its *binding.* The data that can be bound to variables constitute the *denoted values* of a programming language. Since all variable references in Scheme are also expressions, and the value of any expression may be bound to a variable, the denoted values and the expressed values of Scheme are the same, at least in the absence of variable assignment (section 4.5).

Variables are represented by *identifiers*. As in most languages, sequences of letters and digits (not starting with a digit) may be used as identifiers, for example: x, x3, foo, and longidentifier. Scheme is more permissive than most languages in the use of special characters to form identifiers. For example, the following are all identifiers: +, /, two+three, zero?, long_identifier, an-even-longer-identifier. Some special characters, such as parentheses and spaces, are not allowed in identifiers. Digits may generally be used in identifiers, *e.g.* x3, but not as the first character. A few identifiers, such as define and if, are reserved for use as *keywords* and should generally not be used as variables.

Scheme provides standard bindings for a number of variables. For example, + is bound to the addition procedure and zero? is bound to a boolean procedure, or *predicate,* that tests whether its argument is zero. Other standard bindings will be introduced as they are needed. We call procedures that are the values of standard bindings *standard procedures.* (See appendix I.)

If a value is the binding of some variable, it is often convenient to refer to the value by the name of the variable. However, the distinction between the name of a variable and the value of its binding is very important. In this book we observe this distinction by using different fonts. When referring to the variable named "x" as a part of a program, we use the standard typewriter-style font: x. When referring to the value of the variable x, we use an italic font: *x*. Thus we use "zero?" instead of "the value of the variable zero?" when referring to the numeric zero predicate.

Statement-oriented languages usually distinguish between *functions,* which return values and are used in expressions, and *procedures,* which do not return values and are invoked by *procedure call* statements. Though function calls and procedure calls often look the same, syntactically they are distinct: function calls are expressions, while procedure calls are statements. However, since Scheme does not have statements, it does not make this distinction. In fact, Scheme functions are usually called procedures, and Scheme function calls are then referred to as procedure calls. We use the term "function" to refer only to abstract mathematical functions.

The syntax of procedure calls in Scheme is not typical of other programming languages. For example, a call to the procedure *p* with arguments 2 and 3 is written in Scheme as (p 2 3), instead of p(2,3). Parentheses surround the entire procedure call, and its components are separated by spaces. We say that the procedure *p* is *applied* to the arguments 2 and 3. Procedure (or function) calls are sometimes referred to as *applications* or *combinations*.

The general syntax of procedure calls is

$$(operator \ operand_1 \ ... \ operand_n)$$

The ellipsis "..." indicates possible repetition. There may in general be any number of operands, or possibly none at all ($n = 0$). The *operator* and each *operand* are components that are themselves expressions. They are called *subexpressions.* The operator subexpression is evaluated to obtain a procedure, while the operand subexpressions are evaluated to obtain the *arguments* of the call before invoking the procedure. (Arguments are also referred to as *actual parameters,* or simply *parameters.*) In Scheme, the order in which the operator and operand subexpressions are evaluated is not specified, but in some languages it is guaranteed to be left to right and in others it is always right to left.

Any expression may be used as an operand in a procedure call. For example, the procedure call

```
(+ x (p 2 3))
```

contains the operand (p 2 3), which is itself a procedure call. If the value of (p 2 3) is 6 and x is 3, then (+ x (p 2 3)) is 9. (More precisely, "the value of (+ x (p 2 3)) is 9." Since a compound expression's value is not likely to be confused with the expression itself, in such cases we shall often omit the phrase "the value of.")

Operators may also be arbitrarily complex, as long as they return procedures. Thus if *g* were a procedure that when applied to 2 returned the addition procedure, then

```
((g 2) 3 4)
```

would return 7. Procedures that return procedures are called *higher-order procedures,* and expressions that return procedures are called *higher-order expressions.* They may be unfamiliar, but much will be accomplished with them later.

1.1.2 Definitions, Programs, and the Read-Eval-Print Loop

Most operations can be expressed as procedure calls. For those that cannot, a small number of *special forms* are required.

Consider the operation of binding the variable x to 3. We would like to accomplish this by saying

```
(define x 3)
```

The general definition syntax we use is

```
(define variable expression)
```

where *variable* and *expression* indicate an arbitrary variable and expression. If this were a procedure call, with the variable `define` bound to some procedure, *variable* would be evaluated as an argument and its value passed to the procedure. But *variable* may be unbound, in which case it cannot be evaluated. Even if the variable were already bound, say `x` was bound to 7, it still would not do to evaluate the variable. The special form `define` must modify the binding of `x`, which would not be possible if it were simply passed the value 7.

The solution is to declare that the above syntactic form is special—distinct from a procedure call. Each special form is indicated by an identifier, in this case `define`, that should not be used as a variable. These special form identifiers are called *keywords*. Each special form has its own sequencing rule, that is order of evaluation of subexpressions. In this case *expression* is evaluated first, and then *variable* is bound to the value of *expression*.

A Scheme program consists of a sequence of definitions and expressions that are executed in order by the Scheme system. These definitions and expressions are said to be at *top level*. We next discuss a few features of typical *programming environments* in which the Scheme language is used. It should be borne in mind that these are not features of the language itself.

Programs may be stored in a file for convenient loading, or they may be entered interactively. In the *interactive* mode, you enter a definition or expression, which is evaluated as soon as it is complete. When an expression is entered, its value is printed. The system then prints an input prompt and the cycle repeats. This repetitive action is often called the *read-eval-print loop*. The transcript of a brief interactive session follows.

```
> 3
3
> *     ; evaluates to the standard multiplication procedure
#<Procedure>
> (* 2 3)
6
> (define x 3)
> x
```

```
3
> (+ x (* 2 3))
9
```

In this case the Scheme prompt is ">." A semicolon ";" and anything following it on the same line is ignored by Scheme so that comments may be inserted in programs and transcripts. In general, procedures cannot be printed. Thus the system simply prints some indication that a procedure has been returned. In this book "#<Procedure>" is that indicator.

Following a definition, many Scheme systems print the name of the variable defined. As the transcript illustrates, however, we choose not to print anything following a definition. This emphasizes that, in general, definitions do not have values. In this respect they are like statements, but their use is more limited. In this book define is used only at top level.

A final note about definitions: the value of a variable may be *redefined*. That is, the value of an already defined variable may be changed with another definition.

```
> (define x 2)
> x
2
> (define x (+ 1 x))
> x
3
```

Redefinition is allowed simply to make software development more convenient. In Scheme the values of variables with standard bindings, such as +, can be redefined. This is occasionally useful, for example, if you wish to keep track of how many times + is invoked with a negative argument. Redefinition of standard procedures, however, is risky; others may depend on them in unexpected ways.

The interactive nature of Scheme aids program development. It is also helpful in learning Scheme, because it makes it easy to try things out if you wish to test your understanding or discover what will happen. Transcripts of interactions with Scheme are also a convenient way of providing examples. We use them frequently. You are urged to study our examples carefully to be sure you understand why Scheme behaves as it does. Sometimes definitions made in one transcript will be used in other transcripts that follow.

- *Exercise 1.1.1*

Start interacting with Scheme today! ☐

Tools for Symbolic Programming

Read-eval-print loops and redefinitions may not be appropriate in some programming environments. For example, a Scheme implementation might be designed to compile Scheme programs on one machine for execution at a later time on other machines. In this case a read-eval-print loop would be meaningless and redefinition would probably be undesirable. By making a clear distinction between a programming language and programming environments that support it, we treat the language itself as an abstraction. Such language abstraction is important, for it allows the same language to be used in many different environments.

1.1.3 Conditional Evaluation

We have seen that Scheme definitions cannot be expressed with an application, so a special form must be used. Conditional expressions are a second situation in which a special form is required. The basic conditional expression in Scheme has this syntax:

$$(\text{if } \textit{test-exp} \quad \textit{then-exp} \quad \textit{else-exp})$$

The expression *test-exp* is evaluated first. If its value is true, *then-exp* is evaluated, and its value is returned as the value of the entire if expression. If the value of *test-exp* is false, *else-exp* is evaluated to obtain the value of the if expression.

```
> (if #t 1 2)
1
> (zero? 5)
#f
> (if (zero? 5) 1 (+ 1 2))
3
> (define true #t)
> (define false #f)
> (if (zero? 0)
      (if false 1 2)
      3)
2
> (if (if true false true) 2 3)
3
```

The special form if cannot be implemented as a procedure. For one thing, only one of *then-exp* or *else-exp* should be evaluated, and it would be inefficient to evaluate both; but there is an even more compelling reason. An important use of conditionals is to prevent an expression from being evaluated when it is unsafe to do so. For example, we might write

```
(if (zero? a) 0 (/ x a))
```

to make sure that `a` is nonzero before dividing. In this situation, we say the test *guards* the division. Were `if` a procedure, its arguments would be evaluated before being applied, so the division-by-zero we were trying to avoid would be performed before it could be stopped.

Several other special forms will be introduced later as they are needed, but `define` and `if` are enough to get us started.

1.2 Data Types

In this section we explore some of the data types in Scheme. Scheme implementations vary somewhat in the range of data types they support, and the repertoire of operations on the data types also varies. We discuss only those data types and operations that are required in this book. They should be part of every implementation.

For each data type, we shall be concerned with three things:

1. The set of values of that type.

2. The procedures that operate on that type.

3. The representation of values of that type when they appear internally as literals in programs or externally as characters that are read or printed.

For example, in mathematics the data type of sets consists of the sets themselves, the well-defined operations on these sets (such as union, intersection, and set-difference), and the notation used to represent sets.

It is an error to pass a standard procedure a value that is not of the expected type. For example, it does not make sense to try to add a number to `#t`. *Type checking* is required to detect such *type errors*. If these checks are performed at run time when standard procedures are invoked, as is generally the case for Scheme implementations, we have *dynamic type checking*. In many languages, an analysis is performed at compile time to detect potential type errors. This analysis, which must be based only on the text of the program and not run-time values, is called *static type checking*. It has the advantage of catching errors earlier but requires more complicated and restrictive rules for determining if a program is correctly typed.

1.2.1 Numbers, Booleans, Characters, Strings, and Symbols

We have already used two data types: *number* and *boolean*. Numbers may be included in Scheme programs in the usual way. The operations on numbers include the standard arithmetic operations, such as +, -, *, and /. The type predicate `number?` takes an arbitrary value and returns true if its argument is a number and false otherwise. The equality predicate for numbers is =.

The boolean data type has only two values, true and false, represented by #t and #f, respectively. Booleans are used primarily in conditional expressions. The type predicate `boolean?` tests an arbitrary value to see if it is a boolean, boolean values may be compared for equality using the predicate `eq?`, and the standard procedure `not` performs logical negation.

```
> (eq? (boolean? #f) (not #f))
#t
```

Characters that are visible when they print are represented as literals by preceding them with #\, for example #\a and #\%. Some nonprinting characters also have literal representations, such as #\space and #\newline. The character type, equality, and order predicates are `char?`, `char=?`, and `char<?`, respectively, and `char->integer` takes a character and returns an integer representation of the character. The predicates `char-alphabetic?`, `char-numeric?`, and `char-whitespace?` are used to determine the class of a character. The predicate `char-whitespace?` returns true when its argument is a space, return or linefeed character.

```
> (char? #\$)
#t
> (char=? #\newline #\space)
#f
> (char<? #\a #\b)
#t
```

Strings are sequences of characters that are represented by surrounding the characters with double quote marks. The string type predicate is `string?`. The procedure `string-length` takes a string and returns an integer indicating the number of characters in the string. The procedure `string-append` concatenates its arguments to form a new string. The procedures `string->symbol`, `string->number`, and `string->list` convert a string into a symbol, number, and list of characters, respectively. (Symbols and lists will be discussed soon.) The procedure `string` takes any number of arguments, which must be characters, and returns a string of these characters. The procedure *string-ref* takes a string and a nonnegative integer less than the length of the string and returns the character indexed by the integer. Indexing is *zero based,* meaning that the characters are numbered starting with zero.

```
> (define s "This is a.")
> (define ss (string-append s "longer string"))
> (string? s)
#t
> (string-length s)
10
> (string-length ss)
23
> (string-ref s 2)
#\i
> (string #\a #\b)
"ab"
> (string->symbol "abc")
abc
> (string->list s)
(#\T #\h #\i #\s #\space #\i #\s #\space #\a #\.)
```

Programs that process other programs, such as many in this book, frequently manipulate identifiers. Identifiers are central to a number of other kinds of programming, such as artificial intelligence and database applications. In fact, identifiers play an important role in most programs that are not primarily concerned with manipulating numbers. When identifiers are treated as values in Scheme, they are called *symbols*. The manipulation of symbols is greatly facilitated by providing a distinct data type for them.

Just as strings must be surrounded with quote marks to distinguish them from the rest of a program, symbolic literals must be specially marked, for otherwise they would be indistinguishable from variable references. Thus another special form is needed to introduce symbols into programs:

(quote *datum*)

Here *datum* may be a symbol or any other standard external (printed) representation for Scheme data. The value of a quoted literal expression is the associated data value.

```
> (define x 3)
> x
3
> (quote x)
x
> 99
99
> (quote 99)
99
```

Such expressions are used so often that there is an abbreviation for them. The form (quote *datum*) may also be written

$$' datum$$

utilizing the single-quote character. Most languages have quoting mechanisms of some sort to avoid confusion between literals and other program elements. The only literals that are "self-quoting," meaning that they may be used directly as expressions without being enclosed in a quote expression, are numbers, booleans, strings, and characters.

Two basic operations on symbols are the symbol type predicate, *symbol?*, and the predicate for testing equality of two symbols, *eq?*,

```
> (define x 3)
> (number? x)
#t
> (symbol? x)
#f
> (number? 'x)
#f
> (symbol? 'x)
#t
> (eq? 'x 'x)
#t
> (eq? 'x 'y)
#f
> (define y 'apple)
> y
apple
> (eq? y (quote apple))
#t
> (eq? y 'y)
#f
```

1.2.2 Lists

A *list* is an ordered sequence of *elements,* which may be of arbitrary types. Lists are a flexible way of combining multiple values into a single *compound* object. Scheme provides convenient facilities for creating and manipulating lists. These facilities, along with most other Scheme data types, are derived from the much older language LISP. (The name stands for LISt Processing.)

A list is represented by surrounding representations of its elements with a pair of parentheses. For example, (a 3 #t) represents a list consisting of three elements: the symbol a, the number three, and the value true. Here are a few more lists

()	the *empty list*
(a)	a list of length 1
((b c d))	a list of length 1 that contains a list of length 3

Just as quote is necessary to distinguish between symbolic literals and variables, it is also necessary to avoid confusing literal lists with procedure calls or special forms. The expression (quote (a b c)) yields the list (a b c) as its value. However, the expression (a b c) is a procedure call whose value depends on the values of the variables a, b, and c; or perhaps it is a special form where a is a keyword.

There are several standard procedures that build new lists. Here we consider the most important ones, *list* and *cons*. The standard procedure *list* may be applied to any number of arguments. It forms a list of their values. (Most procedures take a fixed number of arguments, but *list*, *string* and *string-append* are exceptions.)

```
> (list 1 2 3)
(1 2 3)
> (define x 3)
> (define y 'apple)
> (list x y)
(3 apple)
> (define list-1 '())
> (define list-2 '(a))
> (define list-3 '((b)))
> (list list-1 list-2 list-3 '(((c))))
(() (a) ((b)) (((c))))
> (list)
()
```

The second important list-building procedure, *cons*, always takes two arguments. The first may be any Scheme value, and the second must (for the moment) be a list. If its first argument is the value v and its second argument is the list $(v_0 \ v_1 \ \ldots \ v_{n-1})$, then *cons* returns the list $(v \ v_0 \ v_1 \ \ldots \ v_{n-1})$. The returned list is always one longer than the second argument. The name cons stands for *cons*truct, because *cons* constructs a new compound object. (Actually *cons*'s second argument may be anything. But if it is not a list, the value returned will not be a list either. We discuss this further in section 1.2.3.) Study the following examples carefully; they illustrate several important features of *cons*.

```
> (cons 'a '(c d))
(a c d)
> (list 'a '(c d))
(a (c d))
> (cons '(a b) '(c d))
((a b) c d)
> (cons '() '(c d))
(() c d)
> (cons 'a '())
(a)
> (cons '(a b) '())
((a b))
> (define y 'apple)
> (cons y list-2)
(apple a)
> (define list-4 (cons list-1 list-2))
> list-4
(() a)
> (cons list-4 list-3)
((() a) (b))
```

Observe in these examples that if the first element to *cons* is a list, that list becomes an element of the value returned by *cons*. To add all elements of a list to the front of another list (in the same order), the procedure *append* should be used.

```
> (append '(a b) '(c d))
(a b c d)
> (append '() '(c d))
(c d)
> (append '(a b) '())
(a b)
```

Compare these results with those obtained by passing the same arguments to
cons.

The simplest way to divide a list is between the first element and the rest
of the list. For historical reasons, the first element of a list is known as its *car*
and the rest of the list is known as its *cdr*. The standard procedures car and
cdr select these components of a list. Thus if l is the list $(v_0\ v_1\ \ldots\ v_{n-1})$,
then $(car\ l) = v_0$ and $(cdr\ l) = (v_1\ \ldots\ v_{n-1})$. It is an error to call car or
cdr with the empty list.

```
> (car '(a b c))
a
> (cdr '(a b c))
(b c)
> (car (cdr '(a b c)))
b
> (cdr '(a))
()
```

Clearly car and cdr undo what cons does. The exact relationship between
car, cdr, and cons is expressed by the equations

$$(car\ (cons\ v\ l)) = v$$
$$(cdr\ (cons\ v\ l)) = l$$

where v is any value, l is any list, and $=$ indicates identical values.

Nested calls to car and cdr are so common that Scheme provides an assort-
ment of procedures that take care of the more frequent cases. For example,
the procedures *cadr* and *caddr* are defined such that

$$(cadr\ l) = (car\ (cdr\ l))$$
$$(caddr\ l) = (car\ (cdr\ (cdr\ l)))$$

The sequence of as and ds surrounded by c and r in the procedure name
determines the cars and cdrs and their ordering. The rightmost a/d (car/cdr)
is performed first, just as the innermost procedure call is done first.

```
> (cadr '(a b c))
b
> (cddr '(a b c))
(c)
> (caddr '(a b c))
c
```

Empty lists are always represented by the same object, called the *empty list*. (For historical reasons, it is sometimes called the *null* object.) The predicate null? tests if its argument is the empty list.

```
> (null? '())
#t
> (define list-2 (list 'a))
> list-2
(a)
> (null? list-2)
#f
> (null? (cdr list-2))
#t
```

o *Exercise 1.2.1*
Fill in the blank lines of the following transcript.

```
> (define x '(a b ((3) c) d))
> (car (cdr x))

> (caddr x)

> (cdaddr x)

> (char? (car '(#\a #\b)))

> (cons 'x x)

> (cons (list 1 2) (cons 3 '(4)))

> (cons (list) (list 1 (cons 2 '()))))
```

▯

1.2.3 Pairs

Most of the time it is desirable to view lists abstractly as we have just done, however, it is sometimes necessary to understand how lists are constructed.

In Scheme, nonempty lists are represented as *pairs*. A pair (sometimes called a *dotted pair* or *cons cell*) is a structure with two fields, called *car* and *cdr*. The procedure *cons* creates a new pair with the car and cdr fields

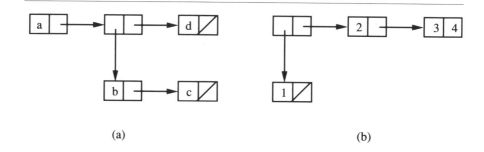

(a)   (b)

Figure 1.2.1   Box diagrams

initialized to the values of its first and second arguments, respectively. The procedures *car* and *cdr* access the two fields. This explains the behavior introduced in the last section. The type predicate for recognizing pairs is *pair?*.

The structure of values built from pairs is conveniently illustrated by diagrams in which pairs are represented by boxes. Each of these boxes has a left and a right half, representing the car and cdr fields, respectively. Each half contains a pointer to another box if the value of the corresponding field is another pair. If the field value is the empty list, this is represented by a slash through the box. Finally, if the field value is a symbol, number, or boolean, its printed representation is written in the corresponding half of the box. The list (a (b c) d) is represented in figure 1.2.1 (a).

If a list has length n, the result of taking the cdr of the list n times must be the empty list. Thus a list is represented by either the empty list or a chain of pairs, linked by their cdr fields, with the empty list in the cdr field of the last pair of the chain. A cdr-linked chain of cons cells that does not end in the empty list is called an *improper list,* even though it is not a list at all. Figure 1.2.1 (b) illustrates such a data structure. We can denote such data structures in a linear format by writing (*a . d*) for a pair whose car is *a* and whose cdr is *d*. (Hence the term *dotted pair.*) The data structures in figure 1.2.1 (a) and (b) might be written as

$$(a . ((b . (c . ())) . (d . ())))$$

and

$$((1 . ()) . (2 . (3 . 4)))$$

respectively. Either of these might appear quoted in a Scheme program. This *dot notation* may be intermixed with conventional list notation, so the second structure might also be written

$$((1)\ 2\ 3\ .\ 4)$$

Dot notation is required only when writing improper lists.

The predicate *eq?* may be used to compare pairs as well as symbols. In fact, *eq?* may be used to test if any two objects are the same object. The behavior of *eq?* on symbols, booleans, characters, and the empty list is straightforward: if they have the same written representation, they are the same object. This is not necessarily true for numbers, pairs, and strings. The behavior of *eq?* on numbers is implementation dependent. If *eq?* is presented with two pairs (or strings), it returns true if and only if they are the *same* pair (or string). Since *cons* creates a new pair every time it is called, *eq?* must be used with caution on lists.

```
> (define a (cons 3 '()))
> (define b (cons 3 '()))
> a
(3)
> b
(3)
> (eq? a a)
#t
> (eq? a b)
#f
> (eq? (cons 1 2) (cons 1 2))
#f
> (eq? '() '())
#t
```

In this example a and b are different pairs, even though they both print as (3), so they are not "*eq* to each other." However, every reference to the variable a returns the same pair, so (eq? a a) is true.

Pairs may be *shared*. That is, the same pair may be referred to by different variable bindings and pair fields.

```
> b
(3)
> (define c b)
> (eq? b c)
```

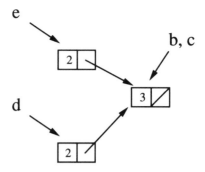

Figure 1.2.2 Box diagram with sharing

```
#t
> (define d (cons 2 c))
> (define e (cons 2 c))
> d
(2 3)
> e
(2 3)
> (eq? d e)
#f
> (eq? (cdr d) (cdr e))
#t
```

Here *b*, *c*, the cdr of *d*, and the cdr of *e* are all the same pair, though *d* and *e* are different pairs. Standard printed notation does not represent sharing, but box diagrams do, as figure 1.2.2 illustrates. The sharing of literals is not specified; for example, (eq? '(3) '(3)) could be true or false.

There are procedures for assigning new values to the car and cdr fields of an existing pair, which will be discussed in section 4.5. When a pair is modified by one of these procedures, the change is noted in all data structures that share the pair.

The only other way to detect sharing of pairs is by using *eq?*.

• *Exercise 1.2.2*
Fill in the blank lines of the following transcript.

```
> (define x1 '(a b))
> (define x2 '(a))
```

```
> (define x3 (cons x1 x2))
> x1

> (eq? x3 (cons x1 x2))

> (eq? (cdr x3) x2)

> (eq? (car x1) (car x2))

> (cons (cons 'a 'b) (cons 'c '()))

> (cons 1 (cons 2 3))
```

☐

1.2.4 Vectors

So far we have seen one means for building compound data objects in Scheme:
the cons cell. These cells may be used to construct lists of arbitrary length.
Lists are a *derived* data type because they are built using *primitive* data types:
the cons cell and the empty list. The advantage of lists is the ease with which
new lists may be formed by adding elements to the front of existing lists.
However, lists do not provide names for all their elements or random access to
them. Compositions of invocations of `car` and `cdr`, also called car/cdr chains,
are an awkward way of referring to the first few list elements. It is possible to
access list elements via an index number, but with conventional lists access
time increases linearly with the index, since to reach a given element it is
necessary to traverse the cdr pointers of all the elements that appear earlier
in the list.

Neither cons cells nor lists correspond to the two ways to build compound
data objects that are most commonly provided by programming languages:
records and arrays. Record elements are selected by *field names.* Records
are also *heterogeneous,* meaning that their elements may differ in their type.
Arrays, on the other hand, are *homogeneous,* in the sense that each of their
components must be of the same type, and array components are selected by
an index number (or multiple index numbers in the case of multidimensional
arrays). Both records and arrays provide *random access* to their components;
that is, each component may be accessed in the same amount of time.

Scheme does not provide arrays or records directly. Instead it supplies
vectors, which may be used in place of arrays and records. Vectors provide

random access via index numbers (like arrays) and may be heterogeneous (like records).

The standard procedure *vector* takes an arbitrary number of arguments, such as *list* and *string*, and constructs a vector whose elements contain the argument values. Vectors are written like lists, but with a hash (#) immediately preceding the left parenthesis. By convention, vectors must also be quoted when they appear in programs as literals.

```
> (define v1 (vector 1 2 (+ 1 2)))
> v1
#(1 2 3)
> (define v2 (quote #(a b)))
> v2
#(a b)
> (vector v1 v2)
#(#(1 2 3) #(a b))
> '#(#(a nested vector) (and a list) within a quoted vector)
#(#(a nested vector) (and a list) within a quoted vector)
```

The number of elements in a vector is its *length,* which may be determined with the standard procedure *vector-length*. The type predicate for vectors is *vector?*. The selector *vector-ref* takes a vector and a zero-based index and returns the value of the element indicated by the index. Thus the indices for a given vector are natural numbers in the range from zero through one less than the length of the vector. There are procedures, *vector->list* and *list->vector*, for transforming one compound data type into the other.

```
> (define v3 '#(first second last))
> (vector? v3)
#t
> (vector-ref v3 0)
first
> (vector-length v3)
3
> (vector-ref v3 (- (vector-length v3) 1))
last
> (vector-ref '#(another #((heterogeneous) "vector")) 1)
#((heterogeneous) "vector")
> (vector->list v3)
(first second last)
```

Of course it is an error to pass `vector-ref` an index number that is not a valid index for the given vector.

We use a data structure called a *cell*, a "one-element" vector. In addition to the procedure `make-cell`, which constructs a cell, there is a procedure for referencing a cell, `cell-ref` and one that determines if its argument is a cell, `cell?`. Cells will be useful in chapter 5 for characterizing languages with side effects and in chapter 6 for describing various parameter-passing mechanisms. See exercise 1.3.2 for an implementation of cells.

The procedure `eq?` may again be used to test whether two objects are the *same* vector. An assignment operation for changing the value of a vector element is introduced in section 4.5. As was the case with pairs, the sharing of vectors in data structures may be revealed using `eq?` or assignment.

○ *Exercise 1.2.3*
Fill in the blank lines of the following transcript

```
> (define v1 (vector (cons 1 2) 3))
> (define v2 (vector 'a v1))
> v2

> (define v3 '#(a #((1 . 2) 3)))
> (eq? v1 v3)

> (eq? v1 (vector-ref v2 1))

> (eq? (vector-ref v1 0)
       (vector-ref (vector-ref v2 1) 0))

```

▯

1.3 Procedures

As you might expect, `procedure?` is a Scheme type predicate for procedures. The following transcript illustrates this as well as demonstrating that procedures can be treated as values.

```
> (procedure? 'car)
#f
> (procedure? car)
#t
```

```
> (procedure? (car (list cdr)))
#t
```

The first two examples distinguish between the symbol car and the procedure
car. The second and third illustrate passing a procedure as an argument to
another procedure. In the third, the procedure cdr is also stored in a data
structure and returned as the value of another procedure, car. Here are some
more complicated examples

```
> (if (procedure? 3) car cdr)
#<Procedure>
> ((if (procedure? 3) car cdr) '(x y z))
(y z)
> (((if (procedure? procedure?) cdr car)
     (cons car cdr))
   '(car in the car))
(in the car)
> (((if (procedure? procedure?) car cdr)
     (cons car cdr))
   '(x y z))
x
```

Procedures are normally called using the application form, as in (+ 1 2),
but sometimes we need to call a procedure with argument values that have
already been assembled into a list. The standard procedure apply is provided
for this purpose. It takes a procedure and a list and returns the result of calling
the procedure with the values given in the list.

```
> (apply + '(1 2))
3
> (define abc '(a b c))
> (apply cons (cdr abc))
(b . c)
> (apply apply (list procedure? (list apply)))
#t
```

1.3.1 lambda

We have seen that Scheme supplies a number of standard procedures. It is
also possible for the user to create new procedures, which may not be bound
to variables. The special form for creating new procedures is lambda. Its most
common syntax is

$$\text{(lambda } formals \; body)$$

Here *formals* is a (possibly empty) list of variables, and *body* is any expression. The listed variables are said to be *formal parameters,* or *bound variables,* of the procedure. In many languages, type information must be provided for formal parameters. However, Scheme automatically keeps track of types at run time, so type declarations are not required. (This is more flexible and simplifies code, but has the disadvantage that type errors are not detected until run time, increasing run-time overhead. We shall have more to say about types in chapter 3.) When the procedure is called, the formal parameters (if any) are first *bound to* (associated with) the arguments, and then the body is evaluated. Within the body, the argument values may be obtained by variables that correspond to the formal parameters. Lambda bindings are not accessible outside the body of the procedure: they are said to be *local* to the procedure's body.

For example, a procedure that adds two to its argument may be created by evaluating the expression:

$$\text{(lambda (n) (+ n 2))}$$

This expression does not give the procedure a name. Naming is accomplished by another expression, such as a `define` expression, if desired, however, a procedure may be applied immediately, passed as an argument, or stored in a data structure without ever being named.

```
> ((lambda (n) (+ n 2)) 4)
6
> (list (lambda (n) (+ n 2)) 6)
(#<Procedure> 6)
> (define add2 (lambda (n) (+ n 2)))
> (add2 6)
8
> (define select
    (lambda (b lst)
      (if b
          (car lst)
          (cadr lst))))
> (select #f '(a b))
b
> ((select #t (list cdr car))
   '(a b c))
(b c)
```

Procedures without names, which are not the binding of a variable, are said to be *anonymous*. In most other languages, procedures are never anonymous: they may be created only via declarations that name them. (Of course anonymity is relative to context: if an anonymous procedure is bound to a parameter via procedure call, it is not anonymous in the context of the called procedure.)

Anonymous procedures are often used as arguments. We illustrate this using the procedures `map` and `andmap`, which generally take two arguments: a procedure and a list. The list may be of any length, and the procedure must take one argument. The procedure `map` builds a new list whose elements are obtained by calling the procedure with the elements of the original list. The procedure `andmap` applies the procedure to each element of the list and returns true if all are true. Otherwise it returns false.

```
> (map (lambda (n) (+ n 2)) '(1 2 3 4 5))
(3 4 5 6 7)
> (define add2
    (lambda (n)
      (+ n 2)))
> (map add2 '(1 2 3 4 5))
(3 4 5 6 7)
> (andmap number? '(1 2 3 4 5))
#t
> (map null? '((a) () () (3)))
(#f #t #t #f)
> (andmap null? '((a) () () (3)))
#f
> (map car '((a b) (c d) (e f)))
(a c e)
> (map list '(a b c d))
((a) (b) (c) (d))
> (map (lambda (f) (f '(a b c d)))
       (list car cdr cadr cddr caddr))
(a (b c d) b (c d) c)
```

1.3.2 First-Class Procedures

A value is said to be *first class* if it may be passed to and returned from procedures and stored in data structures. In Scheme, *all* values are first class, including procedures. In other languages, simple values such as numbers are first class, compound values such as records and arrays are sometimes first class, and procedures are almost never first class. Though it is usually possible to pass procedures as arguments, it is often impossible to return them as values or store them in data structures. (See chapter 10 for a discussion of the implementation of such languages.) First class procedures contribute greatly to the expressive power of a language.

For an example of a procedure that takes procedural arguments and returns a procedural result, consider the problem of defining a procedure that performs functional composition. Assume that f and g are two functions of one argument such that $\text{Range}(g) \subseteq \text{Domain}(f)$. Then the *composition* of f and g, $f \circ g$, is defined by this equation:

$$(f \circ g)(x) = f(g(x)).$$

The assumption about the range of g and the domain of f ensures that every possible result from g is a possible argument to f. It is straightforward to define composition in Scheme.

```
> (define compose
    (lambda (f g)
      (lambda (x)
        (f (g x)))))
> (define add4 (compose add2 add2))
> (add4 5)
9
> ((compose car cdr) '(a b c d))
b
> ((compose list (compose cdr cdr))
    '(a b c d))
((c d))
```

● *Exercise 1.3.1*
What is unusual about the following expression?

```
((lambda (x)
   (list x (list (quote quote) x)))
 (quote (lambda (x)
          (list x (list (quote quote) x)))))
```

Try to figure out what it does without typing it into a Scheme system. Can similar behavior be achieved without using `list`? □

- *Exercise 1.3.2*

  Here is an implementation of cells.

  ```
  (define cell-tag "cell")

  (define make-cell
    (lambda (x)
      (vector cell-tag x)))

  (define cell?
    (lambda (x)
      (if (vector? x)
          (if (= (vector-length x) 2)
              (eq? (vector-ref x 0) cell-tag)
              #f)
          #f)))

  (define cell-ref
    (lambda (x)
      (if (cell? x)
          (vector-ref x 1)
          (error "Invalid argument to cell-ref:" x))))
  ```

  Fill in the values of the following transcript.

  ```
  > (define c (make-cell 5))
  > c

  > (cell? c)

  > (cell-ref c)
  ```

  ☐

- *Exercise 1.3.3*

  Consider two or three other languages you know or for which you can find doc-
  umentation. What restrictions, if any, are imposed on procedures that keep
  them from being first class? Is it possible to create anonymous procedures? ☐

  Here is an example of a procedure that takes a numeric value and returns
  a procedure.

```
(define f
  (lambda (x)
    (lambda (y)
      (+ x y))))
```

When f is passed a number x it returns a procedure that takes a number and adds x to it.

```
> (define new-add2 (f 2))
> (new-add2 4)
6
```

Here *new-add2* has the same behavior as the *add2* procedure defined earlier. So what is the point of defining f? If a computation requires generating many of these add-n procedures for different values of n, or if the values of n are unknown at the time the program is written, then a procedure like f is called for.

```
> (define add3 (f (+ 1 2)))
> (add3 5)
8
> ((f 5) 6)
11
> (define g
    (lambda (a)
      (lambda (d)
        (cons a d))))
> ((g 'a) '(b c))
(a b c)
> (map (g 'a) '((b c) (1 2)))
((a b c) (a 1 2))
```

Having functions of more than one argument is certainly convenient, but it is not absolutely necessary. Using the technique just illustrated, any procedure p of $n \geq 2$ arguments can always be transformed into a procedure p' of one argument that returns a procedure of $n - 1$ arguments such that

$$((p' \, x_1) \, x_2 \, \ldots \, x_n) = (p \, x_1 \, \ldots \, x_n)$$

By repeating this transformation $n - 1$ times, we obtain a procedure p'' such that

$$(\ldots ((p'' \, x_1) \, x_2) \, \ldots \, x_n) = (p \, x_1 \, x_2 \, \ldots \, x_n)$$

This transformation is known as *currying*. The procedures *f* and *g* above are curried versions of the addition and *cons* procedures, respectively. Of course if an existing procedure is to be replaced by a curried version, all calls to the procedure must be changed.

A curried version of a procedure normally takes the first argument first, but this is not always what is desired. The following example illustrates the use of a "reverse-curried" version of *cons*.

```
> (define h
    (lambda (d)
      (lambda (a)
        (cons a d))))
> ((h '(b c)) 'a)
(a b c)
> (map (h '(b c)) '(a 1 2))
((a b c) (1 b c) (2 b c))
```

• *Exercise 1.3.4*

Write a procedure *curry2* that takes a procedure of two arguments and returns a curried version of the procedure that takes the first argument and returns a procedure that takes the second argument. For example,

```
> (((curry2 +) 1) 2)
3
> (define consa ((curry2 cons) 'a))
> (consa '(b))
(a b)
```
▯

○ *Exercise 1.3.5*

Write a curried version of *compose*. Can you think of a use for it? ▯

○ *Exercise 1.3.6*

A language could be designed like ML, so that if a procedure is passed fewer arguments than it expects, it simply returns a procedure that takes the rest of the arguments. Thus procedures are "automatically" curried. What are the advantages and disadvantages of this feature? ▯

1.3.3 Variable Arity Procedures

The *arity* of a procedure is the number of arguments that it takes. Most procedures, including those that result from evaluating lambda expressions of the form introduced so far, have fixed arity. An error message results if a fixed arity procedure is invoked with the wrong number of arguments. Examples of procedures that can take a variable number of arguments are the standard procedures `list`, `vector`, and `string`. It is occasionally necessary to define new procedures of variable arity. This is accomplished with a lambda expression of the form

$$\text{(lambda } formal \; body)$$

where *formal* is a single variable. When the resulting procedure is invoked, this variable is bound to a list of the argument values. The simplest example is (lambda x x), which is equivalent to `list`. A more interesting example is the following procedure, which may be invoked with two or more arguments, in which case it behaves like `+`, or with one argument, in which case it behaves like a curried `+`.

```
> (define plus
    (lambda x
      (if (null? (cdr x))
          (lambda (y) (+ (car x) y))
          (apply + x))))
> (plus 1 2)
3
> ((plus 1) 2)
3
```

• *Exercise 1.3.7*

Define a version of compose that takes as arguments either two or three procedures (of one argument) and composes them. The composition of three procedures is specified by this equation:

$$\text{(compose f g h)} \Rightarrow \text{(compose f (compose g h))}$$

☐

Scheme programs consist mainly of expressions, which are evaluated for their value, rather than statements, which are evaluated only for their effect on the computation. Variable references and literals are the simplest forms of expression; they do not contain subexpressions, as other forms do. Procedure call expressions are the most common expressions in Scheme.

Programs are composed of definitions, introduced by the keyword `define`, and expressions. A read-eval-print loop provides a convenient interactive programming environment, but such programming environment features are generally not part of a language specification.

The special form `if` provides conditional evaluation. It cannot be a procedure, because it is improper to evaluate both its "then" expression and "else" expression.

Scheme supports a number of primitive data types, including numbers, booleans, characters, symbols, pairs, strings, and vectors. Pairs and vectors are compound data types that contain data elements. Lists are an important type derived from pairs and the empty list. New procedures are created by the `lambda` special form.

Procedures, and all other data objects in Scheme, are first class: they may be stored in data structures and returned from procedures as well as passed to procedures. They may also be anonymous: they need not be bound to a variable at the point of their creation.

2   Induction, Recursion, and Scope

This chapter introduces the fundamental technique of recursive programming, along with its relation to the mathematical technique of induction. The notion of scope, which plays a primary role in programming languages, is also presented. Finally, the material in this chapter will improve your facility with the tools introduced in chapter 1. Section 2.1 and section 2.2 introduce techniques for inductively specifying data structures and show how such specifications may be used to guide the construction of recursive programs. Section 2.3 then introduces the notions of variable binding and scope.

The programming exercises are the heart of this chapter. They provide experience that is essential for mastering the technique of recursive programming upon which the rest of this book is based.

2.1   Inductively Specified Data

We have already seen a number of data types in Scheme. What is a data type in general? For our purposes, it is enough to say that a data type consists of a set of values along with a set of operations on those values. Every time we decide to represent a certain set of quantities in a particular way, we are defining a new data type: the data type whose values are those representations and whose operations are the procedures that manipulate those entities.

When writing code for the operations on a new data type, it is important to know precisely what values may occur as members of the type. In this section we introduce formal techniques for specifying the set of values that belong to a data type.

2.1.1 Inductive Specification

Inductive specification is a powerful method of specifying a set of values. To illustrate this method, we use it to describe a certain subset of the natural numbers:

Define the set S to be the smallest set of natural numbers satisfying the following two properties:

1. $0 \in S$, and
2. Whenever $x \in S$, then $x + 3 \in S$.

"The smallest set" is the one that is a subset of all the sets satisfying properties 1 and 2.

Let us see if we can describe some partial information about S to arrive at a noninductive specification. We know that 0 is in S, by property 1. Since $0 \in S$, by property 2 it must be that $3 \in S$. Then since $3 \in S$, by property 2 we conclude that $6 \in S$, and so on. So we see that all the multiples of 3 are in S. If we let M denote the set of all multiples of 3, we can restate this conclusion as $M \subseteq S$. But the set M itself satisfies properties 1 and 2. Since S is a subset of every set that satisfies properties 1 and 2, it must be that $S \subseteq M$. So we deduce that $S = M$, the set of multiples of 3. This is plausible: we know all the multiples of 3 must be in S, and anything else is extraneous.

This is a typical inductive definition. To specify a set S by induction, we define it to be the smallest set satisfying two properties of the following form:

1. Some specific values must be in S.
2. If certain values are in S, then certain other values are also in S.

Sticking to this recipe guarantees that S consists precisely of those values inserted by property 1 and those values included by repeated application of property 2. As stated, this recipe is rather vague. It can be stated more precisely, but that would take us too far afield. Instead, let us see how this process works on some more examples.

The data type list-of-numbers is the smallest set of values satisfying the two properties:

1. The empty list is a list-of-numbers, and
2. If l is a list-of-numbers and n is a number, then the pair $(n \ . \ l)$ is a list-of-numbers.

From this definition we infer the following:

1. () is a list-of-numbers, because of property 1.

2. (14 . ()) is a list-of-numbers, because 14 is a number and () is a list-of-numbers.

3. (3 . (14 . ())) is a list-of-numbers, because 3 is a number and (14 . ()) is a list-of-numbers.

4. (-7 . (3 . (14 . ()))) is a list-of-numbers, because -7 is a number and (3 . (14 . ())) is a list-of-numbers.

5. Nothing is a list-of-numbers unless it is built in this fashion.

Converting from dot notation to list notation, we see that (), (14), (3 14), and (-7 3 14) are all members of list-of-numbers.

2.1.2 Backus-Naur Form and Syntactic Derivations

The previous example was fairly straightforward, but it is easy to imagine how the process of describing more complex data types might become quite cumbersome. To remedy this, a notation has been developed to express the same ideas more concisely: *Backus-Naur Form,* or *BNF.* We frequently use it to describe the structure of a data type. BNF is also widely used in specifying the syntax of programming languages.

BNF can be used to inductively define a number of sets at once. These sets are called *syntactic categories,* or sometimes *nonterminals,* and are customarily written with angle brackets around the name of the set: ⟨list-of-numbers⟩. (When no ambiguity results, we shall sometimes refer informally to syntactic categories without using angle brackets or dashes: "list of numbers.") Each syntactic category is defined by a finite set of *rules,* or *productions.* Each rule asserts that certain values must be in the syntactic category.

The BNF definition of list-of-numbers has two rules that correspond to the two properties.

⟨list-of-numbers⟩ ::= ()
⟨list-of-numbers⟩ ::= (⟨number⟩ . ⟨list-of-numbers⟩)

The first rule says that the empty list is in ⟨list-of-numbers⟩, and the second says that if n is in ⟨number⟩ and l is in ⟨list-of-numbers⟩, then $(n . l)$ is in ⟨list-of-numbers⟩.

Each rule begins by naming the syntactic category being defined, followed by ::= (read *is*). The right-hand side of each rule specifies a method for constructing members of the syntactic category in terms of other syntactic categories and *terminal symbols,* such as the left and right parentheses, and the period in the previous example.

Often some syntactic categories mentioned in a BNF rule are left undefined, such as ⟨number⟩. Defining all categories would needlessly complicate the rule if it is safe to assume the reader knows what some of the categories are.

BNF is often extended with a few notational shortcuts. One can write a set of rules for a single syntactic category by writing the left-hand side and ::= just once, followed by all the right-hand sides separated by the special symbol | (vertical bar, read *or*). A ⟨list-of-numbers⟩ can then be defined by

⟨list-of-numbers⟩ ::= () | (⟨number⟩ . ⟨list-of-numbers⟩)

Another shortcut is the *Kleene star,* expressed by the notation {...}*. When this appears in a right-hand side, it indicates a sequence of any number of instances of whatever appears between the braces. This includes the possibility of no instances at all. Using the Kleene star, the definition of ⟨list-of-numbers⟩ in list notation is simply

⟨list-of-numbers⟩ ::= ({⟨number⟩}*)

If there are zero instances, we get the empty list. A variant of the star notation is *Kleene plus* {...}+, which indicates a sequence of *one* or more instances. Substituting + for * in the above example would define the syntactic category of nonempty lists of numbers. These notational shortcuts are just that—it is always possible to do without them by using additional BNF rules.

If a type is specified using BNF rules, a *syntactic derivation* may be used to prove that a given data value is a member of the type. Such a derivation starts with the nonterminal corresponding to the type. At each step, indicated by an arrow ⇒, a nonterminal is replaced by the right-hand side of a corresponding rule, or with a known member of its syntactic class if the class was left undefined. For example, the previous demonstration that (14 . ()) is a list of numbers may be formalized with the following syntactic derivation:

    ⟨list-of-numbers⟩
⇒ (⟨number⟩ . ⟨list-of-numbers⟩)
⇒ (14 . ⟨list-of-numbers⟩)
⇒ (14 . ())

The order in which nonterminals are replaced is not significant. Thus another possible derivation of (14 . ()) is

Induction, Recursion, and Scope

⟨list-of-numbers⟩
⇒ (⟨number⟩ . ⟨list-of-numbers⟩)
⇒ (⟨number⟩ . ())
⇒ (14 . ())

○ *Exercise 2.1.1*

Write a syntactic derivation that proves (-7 . (3 . (14 . ()))) is a list of numbers. □

2.1.3 Using BNF to Specify Data

The term *datum* refers to any literal data representation. BNF may be used to specify concisely the syntactic category of data in Scheme. We have seen that numbers, symbols, booleans, and strings all have literal representations, which we associate with the syntactic categories ⟨number⟩, ⟨symbol⟩, ⟨boolean⟩, and ⟨string⟩, respectively. Section 1.2 informally introduced representations for lists, improper lists (which end with dotted pairs), and vectors. These compound data types contain components that may be numbers, symbols, booleans, strings, or other lists, improper lists or vectors. This is formally specified by the following BNF rules

---

$$\langle\text{list}\rangle ::= (\{\langle\text{datum}\rangle\}^*)$$
$$\langle\text{dotted-datum}\rangle ::= (\{\langle\text{datum}\rangle\}^+ . \langle\text{datum}\rangle)$$
$$\langle\text{vector}\rangle ::= \#(\{\langle\text{datum}\rangle\}^*)$$
$$\langle\text{datum}\rangle ::= \langle\text{number}\rangle \mid \langle\text{symbol}\rangle \mid \langle\text{boolean}\rangle \mid \langle\text{string}\rangle$$
$$\mid \langle\text{list}\rangle \mid \langle\text{dotted-datum}\rangle \mid \langle\text{vector}\rangle$$

These four syntactic categories are all defined in terms of each other. This is legitimate because there are some simple possibilities for data that are not defined in terms of the other categories.

To illustrate the use of this grammar, consider the following syntactic derivation proving that (#t (foo . ()) 3) is a datum.

⟨list⟩
⇒ (⟨datum⟩ ⟨datum⟩ ⟨datum⟩)
⇒ (⟨boolean⟩ ⟨datum⟩ ⟨datum⟩)
⇒ (#t ⟨datum⟩ ⟨datum⟩)
⇒ (#t ⟨dotted-datum⟩ ⟨datum⟩)

$\Rightarrow$ (#t ({⟨datum⟩}$^{+}$. ⟨datum⟩) ⟨datum⟩)

$\Rightarrow$ (#t (⟨symbol⟩ . ⟨datum⟩) ⟨datum⟩)

$\Rightarrow$ (#t (foo . ⟨datum⟩) ⟨datum⟩)

$\Rightarrow$ (#t (foo . ⟨list⟩) ⟨datum⟩)

$\Rightarrow$ (#t (foo . ()) ⟨datum⟩)

$\Rightarrow$ (#t (foo . ()) ⟨number⟩)

$\Rightarrow$ (#t (foo . ()) 3)

All three elements of the outer list were introduced at once. This shortcut was possible because the grammar uses a Kleene star. Of course, the Kleene star and plus notation could be eliminated by introducing new nonterminals and productions, and the three list elements would then be introduced with three derivation steps instead of one.

○ *Exercise 2.1.2*

Rewrite the ⟨datum⟩ grammar without using the Kleene star or plus. Then indicate the changes to the above derivation that are required by your grammar. □

○ *Exercise 2.1.3*

Write a syntactic derivation that proves (a "mixed" #(bag (of . data))) is a datum, using either the grammar in the book or your grammar from the last exercise. What can you say about (a . b . c)? □

Let us consider the BNF definitions of some other useful data types. Many symbol manipulation procedures are designed to operate on lists that contain only symbols and other similarly restricted lists. We formalize this notion with these rules:

$$\langle\text{s-list}\rangle ::= (\{\langle\text{symbol-expression}\rangle\}^*)$$
$$\langle\text{symbol-expression}\rangle ::= \langle\text{symbol}\rangle \mid \langle\text{s-list}\rangle$$

The literal representation of an s-list contains only parentheses and symbols. For example

```
(a b c)
(an (((s-list)) (with lots) ((of) nesting)))
```

A binary tree with numeric leaves and interior nodes labeled with symbols may be represented using three-element lists for the interior nodes as follows

$$\langle\text{tree}\rangle ::= \langle\text{number}\rangle \mid (\langle\text{symbol}\rangle \ \langle\text{tree}\rangle \ \langle\text{tree}\rangle)$$

Examples of such trees follow:

```
1
2
(foo 1 2)
(bar 1 (foo 1 2))
(baz (bar 1 (foo 1 2)) (biz 4 5))
```

BNF rules are said to be *context free* because a rule defining a given syntactic category may be applied in any context that makes reference to that syntactic category. Sometimes this is not restrictive enough. For example, a node in a binary search tree is either empty or contains a key and two subtrees

⟨bin-search-tree⟩ ::= () | (⟨key⟩ ⟨bin-search-tree⟩ ⟨bin-search-tree⟩)

This correctly describes the structure of each node but fails to mention an important fact about binary search trees: all the keys in the left subtree are less than (or equal to) the key in the current node, and all the keys in the right subtree are greater than the key in the current node. Such constraints are said to be *context sensitive*, because they depend on the context in which they are used.

Context-sensitive constraints also arise when specifying the syntax of programming languages. For instance, in many languages every identifier must be declared before it is used. This constraint on the use of identifiers is sensitive to the context of their use. Formal methods can be used to specify context-sensitive constraints, but these methods are far more complicated than BNF. In practice, the usual approach is first to specify a context-free grammar using BNF. Context-sensitive constraints are then added using other methods, usually prose, to complete the specification of a context-sensitive syntax.

2.1.4 Induction

Having described data types inductively, we can use the inductive definitions in two ways: to prove theorems about members of the data type and to write programs that manipulate them. Writing the programs is the subject of the next two sections; here we present an example of such a proof.

Theorem. *Let $s \in$ ⟨tree⟩. Then s contains an odd number of nodes.*

Proof. The proof is by induction on the size of s, where we take the size of s to be the number of nodes in s. The induction hypothesis, $IH(k)$, is that any tree of size $\leq k$ has an odd number of nodes. We follow the usual prescription for an inductive proof: we first prove that $IH(0)$ is true, and we then prove that whenever k is a number such that IH is true for k, then IH is true for $k + 1$ also.

i. There are no trees with 0 nodes, so $IH(0)$ holds trivially.

ii. Let k be a number such that $IH(k)$ holds, that is, any tree with $\leq k$ nodes actually has an odd number of nodes. We need to show that $IH(k+1)$ holds as well: that any tree with $\leq k+1$ nodes has an odd number of nodes. If s has $\leq k+1$ nodes, there are exactly two possibilities according to the BNF definition of ⟨tree⟩:

   a. s could be of the form n, where n is a number. In this case, s has exactly one node, and one is odd.

   b. s could be of the form ($sym\ s_1\ s_2$), where sym is a symbol and s_1 and s_2 are trees. Now s_1 and s_2 must have fewer nodes than s. Since s has $\leq k+1$ nodes, s_1 and s_2 must have $\leq k$ nodes. Therefore they are covered by $IH(k)$, and they must each have an odd number of nodes, say $2n_1 + 1$ and $2n_2 + 1$ nodes, respectively. Therefore the total number of nodes in the tree, counting the two subtrees and the root, is

$$(2n_1 + 1) + (2n_2 + 1) + 1 = 2(n_1 + n_2 + 1) + 1$$

which is once again odd.

This completes the proof of the claim that $IH(k+1)$ holds and therefore completes the induction. □

The key to the proof is that the substructures of a tree s are always smaller than s itself. Therefore the induction might be rephrased as follows:

1. IH is true on simple structures (those without substructures).

2. If IH is true on the substructures of s, then it is true on s itself.

2.2 Recursively Specified Programs

In the previous section, we used the method of inductive definition to characterize complicated sets. Starting with simple members of the set, the BNF rules were used to build more and more complex members of the set. We now use the same idea to define procedures for manipulating those sets. First we define the simple parts of a procedure's behavior (how it behaves on simple inputs), and then we use this behavior to define more complex behaviors.

Imagine we want to define a procedure to find powers of numbers, *e.g.* $e(n, x) = x^n$, where n is a nonnegative integer and $x \neq 0$. It is easy to define a sequence of procedures that compute particular powers: $e_0(x) = x^0$, $e_1(x) = x^1$, $e_2(x) = x^2$:

$$e_0(x) = 1$$
$$e_1(x) = x \times e_0(x)$$
$$e_2(x) = x \times e_1(x)$$
$$e_3(x) = x \times e_2(x)$$

In general, if n is a positive integer,

$$e_n(x) = x \times e_{n-1}(x).$$

At each stage, we use the fact that the problem has already been solved for smaller n. We are using mathematical induction. Next the subscript can be removed from e by making it a parameter.

1. If n is 0, $e(n, x) = 1$.

2. If n is greater than 0, we assume it is known how to solve the problem for $n - 1$. That is, we assume that $e(n - 1, x)$ is well defined. Therefore, $e(n, x) = x \times e(n - 1, x)$.

To prove that $e(n, x) = x^n$ for any nonnegative integer n, we proceed by induction on n:

1. (Base Step) When $n = 0$, $e(0, x) = 1 = x^0$.

2. (Induction Step) Assume that the procedure works when its first argument is k, that is, $e(k, x) = x^k$ for some nonnegative integer k. Then we claim that $e(k + 1, x) = x^{k+1}$. We calculate as follows

$$e(k + 1, x) = x \times e(k, x) \qquad \text{(definition of } e)$$
$$= x \times x^k \qquad \qquad (\textit{IH at } k)$$
$$= x^{k+1} \qquad \text{(fact about exponentiation)}$$

This completes the induction.

We can write a program to compute e based upon the inductive definition

```
(define e
  (lambda (n x)
    (if (zero? n)
        1
        (* x
           (e (- n 1) x)))))
```

The two branches of the `if` expression correspond to the two cases detailed in the definition.

If we can reduce a problem to a smaller subproblem, we can call the procedure that solves the problem to solve the subproblem. The solution it returns for the subproblem may then be used to solve the original problem. This works because each time we call the procedure, it is called with a smaller problem, until eventually it is called with a problem that can be solved directly, without another call to itself.

In the above example, we used induction on integers, so the subproblem was solved by recursively calling the procedure with a smaller value of n. When manipulating inductively defined structures, subproblems are usually solved by calling the procedure recursively on a substructure of the original.

When a procedure calls itself in this manner, it is said to be *recursively defined*. Such *recursive calls* are possible in Scheme and most other languages. The general phenomenon is known as *recursion,* and it occurs in contexts other than programming, such as inductive definitions. Later we shall study how recursion is implemented in programming languages.

2.2.1 Deriving Programs from BNF Data Specifications

Recursion is a powerful programming technique that is used extensively throughout this book. It requires an approach to programming that differs significantly from the style commonly used in statement-oriented languages. For this reason, we devote the rest of this section to this style of programming.

A BNF definition for the type of data being manipulated serves as a guide both to where recursive calls should be used and to which base cases need to be handled. This is a fundamental point: *when defining a program based on structural induction, the structure of the program should be patterned after the structure of the data.*

A typical kind of program based on inductively defined structures is a predicate that determines whether a given value is a member of a particular data type. Let us write a Scheme predicate, `list-of-numbers?` that takes a datum and determines whether it belongs to the syntactic category ⟨list-of-numbers⟩.

```
> (list-of-numbers? '(1 2 3))
#t
> (list-of-numbers? '(1 two 3))
#f
> (list-of-numbers? '(1 . 2))
#f
```

Recall the definition of ⟨list-of-numbers⟩:

⟨list-of-numbers⟩ ::= () | (⟨number⟩ . ⟨list-of-numbers⟩)

We begin by writing down the simplest behavior of the procedure: what it does when the input is the empty list.

```
(define list-of-numbers?
  (lambda (lst)
    (if (null? lst)
        ...
        ...))))
```

By definition, the empty list is a ⟨list-of-numbers⟩. Otherwise, lst is not a ⟨list-of-numbers⟩ unless it is a pair.

```
(define list-of-numbers?
  (lambda (lst)
    (if (null? lst)
        #t
        (if (pair? lst)
            ...
            #f)))))
```

(Throughout this book, bars in the left margin indicate lines that have changed since an earlier version of the same definition.) If lst is a pair, there are two alternatives: either the first element is a number, or it is not. If not, the original value cannot be a list of numbers, so we write

```
(define list-of-numbers?
  (lambda (lst)
    (if (null? lst)
        #t
        (if (pair? lst)
            (if (number? (car lst))
                ...
                #f)
            #f)))))
```

The only case left to consider is when the first element of the list in question passes the *number?* test. According to the definition of ⟨list-of-numbers⟩, a nonempty list belongs to ⟨list-of-numbers⟩ if and only if its first element is a number and its cdr belongs to ⟨list-of-numbers⟩. Since we already know that *lst* is nonempty and its car is a number, we can deduce that *lst* is a list of numbers if and only if its cdr is a list of numbers. Therefore we write

```
(define list-of-numbers?
  (lambda (lst)
    (if (null? lst)
        #t
        (if (pair? lst)
            (if (number? (car lst))
                (list-of-numbers? (cdr lst))
                #f)
            #f))))
```

To prove the correctness of *list-of-numbers?*, we would like to use induction on the length of *lst*. However, the argument to *list-of-numbers?* may not be a list at all. This prompts us to define the *list-size* of a datum to be zero if the datum is not a list and its length if it is a list. We now proceed by induction on the list-size:

1. *list-of-numbers?* works on data of list-size 0, since the only list of length 0 is the empty list, for which the correct answer, true, is returned, and if *list-of-numbers?* is not a list, the correct answer, false, is returned.

2. Assuming *list-of-numbers?* works on lists of length k, we show that it works on lists of length $k + 1$. Let *lst* be such a list. By the definition of ⟨list-of-numbers⟩, *lst* belongs to ⟨list-of-numbers⟩ if and only if its car is a number and its cdr belongs to ⟨list-of-numbers⟩. Since *lst* is of length $k + 1$, its cdr is of length k, so by the induction hypothesis we can determine the cdr's membership in ⟨list-of-numbers⟩ by passing it to *list-of-numbers?*. Hence *list-of-numbers?* correctly computes membership in ⟨list-of-numbers⟩ for lists of length $k + 1$, and the induction is complete.

The recursion terminates because every time *list-of-numbers?* is called, it is passed a shorter list. (This assumes lists are finite, which will always be the case unless the list mutation techniques introduced in section 4.5.3 have been used.)

As a second example, we define a procedure *nth-elt* that takes a list *lst* and a zero-based index *n* and returns element number *n* of *lst*.

Induction, Recursion, and Scope

```
> (nth-elt '(a b c) 1)
b
```

The procedure `nth-elt` does for lists what `vector-ref` does for vectors. (Actually, Scheme provides the procedure `list-ref`, which is the same as `nth-elt` except for error reporting, but we choose another name because standard procedures should not be tampered with unnecessarily.)

When n is 0, the answer is simply the car of `lst`. If n is greater than 0, then the answer is element $n - 1$ of `lst`'s cdr. Since neither the car nor cdr of `lst` exist if `lst` is the empty list, we must guard the `car` and `cdr` operations so that we do not take the car or cdr of an empty list.

```
(define nth-elt
  (lambda (lst n)
    (if (null? lst)
        (error "nth-elt: list too short")
        (if (zero? n)
            (car lst)
            (nth-elt (cdr lst) (- n 1))))))
```

The procedure `error` signals an error by printing its arguments, in this case a single string, and then aborting the computation. (`error` is not a standard Scheme procedure, but most implementations provide something of the sort. See appendix D and check your Scheme language reference manual for details.) If error checking were omitted, we would have to rely on `car` and `cdr` to complain about being passed the empty list, but their error messages would be less helpful. For example, if you receive an error message from `car`, you might have to look for uses of `car` throughout your program. Even this would not find the error if `nth-elt` were provided by someone else, so that its definition was not a part of your program.

Let us try one more example of this kind before moving on to harder examples. The standard procedure `length` determines the number of elements in a list.

```
> (length '(a b c))
3
> (length '((x) ()))
2
```

We write our own procedure, called `list-length`, to do the same thing. The length of the empty list is 0.

```
(define list-length
  (lambda (lst)
    (if (null? lst)
        0
        ...)))
```

The blank is filled in by observing that the length of a nonempty list is one
more than the length of its cdr.

```
(define list-length
  (lambda (lst)
    (if (null? lst)
        0
|       (+ 1 (list-length (cdr lst)))))))
```

○ *Exercise 2.2.1*

The procedures `nth-elt` and `list-length` do not check whether their arguments are of the expected type. What happens on your Scheme system if they
are passed symbols when a list is expected? What is the behavior of `list-ref`
and `length` in such cases? Write your own versions that guard against these
situations. Is it always necessary to signal errors when this occurs, or can a
sensible value sometimes be returned? When is it worth the effort to check
that arguments are of the right type? Why? □

2.2.2 Three Important Examples

In this section, we present three simple recursive procedures that will be used
as examples later in this book. As in previous examples, they are defined
so that (1) the structure of a program reflects the structure of its data and
(2) recursive calls are employed at points where recursion is used in the data
type's inductive definition.

The first procedure is *remove-first*, which takes two arguments: a symbol,
s, and a list of symbols, *los*. It returns a list with the same elements arranged
in the same order as *los*, except that the first occurrence of the symbol *s* is
removed. If there is no occurrence of *s* in *los*, then *los* is returned.

```
> (remove-first 'a '(a b c))
(b c)
> (remove-first 'b '(e f g))
(e f g)
```

```
> (remove-first 'a4 '(c1 a4 c1 a4))
(c1 c1 a4)
> (remove-first 'x '())
()
```

Before we start on the program, we must complete the problem specification by defining the data type ⟨list-of-symbols⟩. Unlike the s-lists introduced in the last section, these lists of symbols do not contain sublists.

⟨list-of-symbols⟩ ::= () | (⟨symbol⟩ . ⟨list-of-symbols⟩)

A list of symbols is either the empty list or a list whose car is a symbol and whose cdr is a list of symbols. If the list is empty, there are no occurrences of s to remove, so the answer is the empty list.

```
(define remove-first
  (lambda (s los)
    (if (null? los)
        '()
        ...)))
```

If *los* is nonempty, is there some case where we can determine the answer immediately? If *los* = (s s_1 ... s_{n-1}), the first occurrence of s is as the first element of *los*. So the result of removing it is just (s_1 ... s_{n-1}).

```
(define remove-first
  (lambda (s los)
    (if (null? los)
        '()
        (if (eq? (car los) s)
            (cdr los)
            ...))))
```

If the first element of *los* is not s, say *los* = (s_0 s_1 ... s_{n-1}), then we know that s_0 is not the first occurrence of s. Therefore the first element of the answer must be s_0. Furthermore, the first occurrence of s in *los* must be its first occurrence in (s_1 ... s_{n-1}). So the rest of the answer must be the result of removing the first occurrence of s from the cdr of *los*. Since the cdr of *los* is shorter than *los*, we may recursively call *remove-first* to remove s from the cdr of *los*. Thus using (cons (car los) (remove-first s (cdr los))), the answer may be obtained. With this, the complete definition of *remove-first* follows.

```
(define remove-first
  (lambda (s los)
    (if (null? los)
        '()
        (if (eq? (car los) s)
            (cdr los)
            (cons (car los) (remove-first s (cdr los)))))))
```

- *Exercise 2.2.2*

  In the definition of *remove-first*, if the inner if's alternative (cons ...) were
  replaced by (remove-first s (cdr los)), what function would the resulting
  procedure compute? ▯

The second procedure is *remove*, defined over symbols and lists of symbols.
It is similar to *remove-first*, but it removes all occurrences of a given symbol
from a list of symbols, not just the first.

```
> (remove 'a4 '(c1 a4 d1 a4))
(c1 d1)
```

Since *remove-first* and *remove* work on the same input, their structure is
similar. If the list *los* is empty, there are no occurrences to remove, so the
answer is again the empty list. If *los* is nonempty, there are again two cases
to consider. If the first element of *los* is not *s*, the answer is obtained as in
remove-first.

```
(define remove
  (lambda (s los)
    (if (null? los)
        '()
        (if (eq? (car los) s)
            ...
            (cons (car los) (remove s (cdr los)))))))
```

If the first element of *los* is the same as *s*, certainly the first element is not to
be part of the result. But we are not quite done: all the occurrences of *s* must
still be removed from the cdr of *los*. Once again this may be accomplished
by invoking *remove* recursively on the cdr of *los*.

Induction, Recursion, and Scope

```
(define remove
  (lambda (s los)
    (if (null? los)
        '()
        (if (eq? (car los) s)
            (remove s (cdr los))
            (cons (car los) (remove s (cdr los)))))))
```

- *Exercise 2.2.3*

In the definition of `remove`, if the inner `if`'s alternative (cons ...) were replaced by (`remove s (cdr los)`), what function would the resulting procedure compute? □

The last of our examples is *subst*. It takes three arguments: two symbols, *new* and *old*, and an s-list, *slst*. All elements of *slst* are examined, and a new list is returned that is similar to *slst* but with all occurrences of *old* replaced by instances of *new*.

```
> (subst 'a 'b '((b c) (b d)))
((a c) (a d))
```

Since *subst* is defined over s-lists, its organization reflects the definition of s-lists

$$\langle\text{s-list}\rangle ::= (\{\langle\text{symbol-expression}\rangle\}^*)$$
$$\langle\text{symbol-expression}\rangle ::= \langle\text{symbol}\rangle \mid \langle\text{s-list}\rangle$$

If the list is empty, there are no occurrences of *old* to replace.

```
(define subst
  (lambda (new old slst)
    (if (null? slst)
        '()
        ...)))
```

If *slst* is nonempty, its car is a member of ⟨symbol-expression⟩ and its cdr is another s-list. Thus the program branches on the type of the symbol expression in the car of *slst*. If it is a symbol, we need to ask whether it is the same as the symbol *old*. If it is, the car of the answer is *new*; if not, the car of the answer is the same as the car of *slst*. In either case, to obtain the answer's cdr, we need to change all occurrences of *old* to *new* in the cdr of *slst*. Since the cdr of *slst* is a smaller list, we may use recursion.

```
(define subst
  (lambda (new old slst)
    (if (null? slst)
        '()
        (if (symbol? (car slst))
            (if (eq? (car slst) old)
                (cons new (subst new old (cdr slst)))
                (cons (car slst) (subst new old (cdr slst))))
            ...))))
```

In the final case to be considered the car of *slst* is a list. Since the car and
cdr of *slst* are both lists, the answer is obtained by invoking *subst* on both
and consing the results together.

```
(define subst
  (lambda (new old slst)
    (if (null? slst)
        '()
        (if (symbol? (car slst))
            (if (eq? (car slst) old)
                (cons new (subst new old (cdr slst)))
                (cons (car slst) (subst new old (cdr slst))))
            (cons (subst new old (car slst))
                  (subst new old (cdr slst)))))))
```

This definition has been completed by following the structure of ⟨s-list⟩ and
then ⟨symbol-expression⟩ and checking for *old* when dealing with symbols.

The subexpression (subst new old (cdr slst)) appears three times in the
above definition. This redundancy can be eliminated by noting that when
slst is nonnull, the answer's car and cdr may be independently computed and
then combined with *cons*. The answer's cdr is obtained by invoking *subst*
on the cdr of *slst*. The answer's car is obtained by substituting *new* for *old*
in the car of *slst*, but the type of *slst*'s car is ⟨symbol-expression⟩, not
⟨s-list⟩, so *subst* cannot be used directly. The solution is to make a separate
procedure for handling substitutions on members of ⟨symbol-expression⟩.

```
(define subst
  (lambda (new old slst)
    (if (null? slst)
        '()
        (cons (subst-symbol-expression new old (car slst))
              (subst new old (cdr slst))))))
```

```
(define subst-symbol-expression
  (lambda (new old se)
    (if (symbol? se)
        (if (eq? se old) new se)
        (subst new old se))))
```

Since we have strictly followed the BNF definition of ⟨s-list⟩ and ⟨symbol-expression⟩, this recursion is guaranteed to halt. Observe that *subst* and *subst-symbol-expression* call each other recursively. Such procedures are said to be *mutually recursive*.

- *Exercise 2.2.4*
  In the last line of `subst-symbol-expression`, the recursion is on *se* and not a smaller substructure. Why is the recursion guaranteed to halt? □

- *Exercise 2.2.5*
  Write *subst* using `map`. □

The decomposition of *subst* into two procedures, one for each syntactic category, is an important technique. It allows us to think about one syntactic category at a time, which is important in more complicated situations.

There are many other situations in which it may be helpful or necessary to introduce auxiliary procedures to solve a problem. Always feel free to do so. In some cases the new procedure is necessary in order to introduce an additional parameter. As an example, we consider the problem of summing all the values in a vector.

Since vectors require a program structure that differs from the ones we have used for lists, let us first solve the problem of summing the values in a list of numbers. This problem has a natural recursive solution because nonempty lists decompose naturally into their car and cdr components. We return 0 as the sum of the elements in the empty list.

```
(define list-sum
  (lambda (lon)
    (if (null? lon)
        0
        (+ (car lon)
           (list-sum (cdr lon))))))
```

It is not possible to proceed in this way with vectors, because they do not decompose as readily. Sometimes the best way to solve a problem is to solve a more general problem and use it to solve the original problem as a special case. For the vector sum problem, since we cannot decompose vectors, we generalize the problem to compute the sum of part of the vector. We define `partial-vector-sum`, which takes a vector of numbers, *von*, and a number, *n*, and returns the sum of the first *n* values in *von*.

```
(define partial-vector-sum
  (lambda (von n)
    (if (zero? n)
        0
        (+ (vector-ref von (- n 1))
           (partial-vector-sum von (- n 1)))))))
```

Observe that *von* does not change. In the next chapter we shall see how the conceptual overhead of passing such parameters may be avoided. Since *n* decreases steadily to zero, a proof of correctness for this program would proceed by induction on *n*. It is now a simple matter to solve our original problem

```
(define vector-sum
  (lambda (von)
    (partial-vector-sum von (vector-length von))))
```

○ *Exercise 2.2.6*
Prove the correctness of `partial-vector-sum` with the following assumption: $0 \leq n < length(von)$. □

Getting the knack of writing recursive programs involves practice. Thus we conclude this section with a number of exercises.

● *Exercise 2.2.7*
Define, test, and debug the following procedures. Assume that *s* is any symbol, *n* is a nonnegative integer, *1st* is a list, *v* is a vector, *los* is a list of symbols, *vos* is a vector of symbols, *slst* is an s-list, and *x* is any object; and similarly *s1* is a symbol, *los2* is a list of symbols, *x1* is an object, etc. Make no other assumptions about the data unless further restrictions are given as part of a particular problem. You do not have to check that the input matches the description; for each procedure, assume that its input values are members of the specified data types.

To test your procedures, at the very minimum try all of the given examples. You should also use other examples to test your procedures, since the given examples are not adequate to reveal all possible errors.

1. (duple n x) returns a list containing n copies of x.

```
> (duple 2 3)
(3 3)
> (duple 4 '(ho ho))
((ho ho) (ho ho) (ho ho) (ho ho))
> (duple 0 '(blah))
()
```

2. (invert lst), where lst is a list of 2-lists (lists of length two), returns a list with each 2-list reversed.

```
> (invert '((a 1) (a 2) (b 1) (b 2)))
((1 a) (2 a) (1 b) (2 b))
```

3. (list-index s los) returns the zero-based index of the first occurrence of s in los, or −1 if there is no occurrence of s in los.

```
> (list-index 'c '(a b c d))
2
> (list-ref '(a b c) (list-index 'b '(a b c)))
b
```

4. (vector-index s vos) returns the zero-based index of the first occurrence of s in vos, or −1 if there is no occurrence of s in vos.

```
> (vector-index 'c '#(a b c d))
2
> (vector-ref '#(a b c) (vector-index 'b '#(a b c)))
b
```

5. (ribassoc s los v fail-value) returns the value in v that is associated with s, or fail-value if there is no associated value. If the first occurrence of s in los has index n, the value associated with s is the nth value in v. There is no associated value for s if s is not a member of los. You may assume that los and v are the same length.

```
> (ribassoc 'b '(a b c) '#(1 2 3) 'fail)
2
> (ribassoc 'c '(a b foo) '#(3 squiggle bar) 'fail)
fail
> (ribassoc 'i '(a i o i) '#(fx (fz) () (fm fe)) 'fail)
(fz)
```

6. (filter-in p lst), where *p* is a predicate, returns the list of those elements
   in *lst* that satisfy the predicate.

```
> (filter-in number? '(a 2 (1 3) b 7))
(2 7)
> (filter-in symbol? '(a (b c) 17 foo))
(a foo)
```

7. (product los1 los2) returns a list of 2-lists that represents the Cartesian
   product of *los1* and *los2*. The 2-lists may appear in any order.

```
> (product '(a b c) '(x y))
((a x) (a y) (b x) (b y) (c x) (c y))
```

8. (swapper s1 s2 slst) returns a list the same as *slst*, but with all occurrences of *s1* replaced by *s2* and all occurrences of *s2* replaced by *s1*.

```
> (swapper 'a 'd '(a b c d))
(d b c a)
> (swapper 'x 'y '((x) y (z (x))))
((y) x (z (y)))
```

9. (rotate los) returns a list similar to *los*, except that the last element of
   los becomes the first in the returned list.

```
> (rotate '(a b c d))
(d a b c)
> (rotate '(notmuch))
(notmuch)
> (rotate '())
()
```

☐

- *Exercise 2.2.8*
  These are a bit harder.

  1. (down lst) wraps parentheses around each top-level element of *lst*.

     ```
     > (down '(1 2 3))
     ((1) (2) (3))
     > (down '(a (more (complicated)) object))
     ((a) ((more (complicated))) (object))
     ```

  2. (up lst) removes a pair of parentheses from each top-level element of *lst*. If a top-level element is not a list, it is included in the result, as is. The value of (up (down lst)) is equivalent to *lst*, but (down (up lst)) is not necessarily *lst*.

     ```
     > (up '((1 2) (3 4)))
     (1 2 3 4)
     > (up '((x (y)) z))
     (x (y) z)
     ```

  3. (count-occurrences s slst) returns the number of occurrences of *s* in *slst*.

     ```
     > (count-occurrences 'x '((f x) y (((x z) x))))
     3
     > (count-occurrences 'w '((f x) y (((x z) x))))
     0
     ```

  4. (flatten slst) returns a list of the symbols contained in *slst* in the order in which they occur when *slst* is printed. Intuitively, *flatten* removes all the inner parentheses from its argument.

     ```
     > (flatten '(a b c))
     (a b c)
     > (flatten '((a b) c (((d)) e)))
     (a b c d e)
     > (flatten '(a b (() (c))))
     (a b c)
     ```

  5. (merge lon1 lon2), where *lon1* and *lon2* are lists of numbers that are sorted in ascending order, returns a sorted list of all the numbers in *lon1* and *lon2*.

```
> (merge '(1 4) '(1 2 8))
(1 1 2 4 8)
> (merge '(35 62 81 90 91) '(3 83 85 90))
(3 35 62 81 83 85 90 90 91)
```
□

- *Exercise 2.2.9*

These are harder still:

1. (path n bst), where *n* is a number and *bst* is a binary search tree that contains the number *n*, returns a list of Ls and Rs showing how to find the node containing *n*. If *n* is found at the root, it returns the empty list.

```
> (path 17 '(14 (7 () (12 () ()))
                (26 (20 (17 () ())
                        ())
                    (31 () ()))))
(R L L)
```

2. (car&cdr s slst errvalue) returns an expression that, when evaluated, produces the code for a procedure that takes a list with the same structure as *slst* and returns the value in the same position as the leftmost occurrence of *s* in *slst*. If *s* does not occur in *slst*, then *errvalue* is returned.

```
> (car&cdr 'a '(a b c) 'fail)
(lambda (lst) (car lst))
> (car&cdr 'c '(a b c) 'fail)
(lambda (lst) (car (cdr (cdr lst))))
> (car&cdr 'dog '(cat lion (fish dog) pig) 'fail)
(lambda (lst) (car (cdr (car (cdr (cdr lst))))))
> (car&cdr 'a '(b c) 'fail)
fail
```

3. (car&cdr2 s slst errvalue) is like the previous exercise, but it generates procedure compositions.

```
> (car&cdr2 'a '(a b c) 'fail)
car
> (car&cdr2 'c '(a b c) 'fail)
(compose car (compose cdr cdr))
> (car&cdr2 'dog '(cat lion (fish dog) pig) 'fail)
(compose car (compose cdr (compose car (compose cdr cdr))))
> (car&cdr2 'a '(b c) 'fail)
fail
```

Induction, Recursion, and Scope

4. (compose p1 ... pn), where *p1*, ..., *pn* is a sequence of zero or more procedures of one argument, returns the composition of all the procedures. The
   composition of zero procedures is the identity procedure, the composition
   of one procedure is the procedure itself, and the composition of two or more
   procedures is specified by this equation:

$$((\texttt{compose p1 p2 ...) x}) \Rightarrow (\texttt{p1 ((compose p2 ...) x)})$$

```
> ((compose) '(a b c d))
(a b c d)
> ((compose car) '(a b c d))
a
> ((compose car cdr cdr) '(a b c d))
c
```

5. (sort lon) returns a list of the elements of *lon* in increasing order.

```
> (sort '(8 2 5 2 3))
(2 2 3 5 8)
```

6. (sort predicate lon) returns a list of elements determined by the predicate.

```
> (sort < '(8 2 5 2 3))
(2 2 3 5 8)
> (sort > '(8 2 5 2 3))
(8 5 3 2 2)
```
☐

2.3 Static Properties of Variables

Those properties of a program that can be determined by analyzing the text
of a program are said to be *static*, as opposed to the *dynamic* properties that
are determined by run-time inputs. It is important to determine if a property
is static, because static properties can be analyzed by a compiler to detect
errors before run time and to improve the efficiency of object code.

In Scheme, as in most other languages, the relation between a variable
reference and the formal parameter to which it refers is a static property. In
this section we focus on this relation and some of its important consequences.

2.3.1 Free and Bound Variables

In order to focus on variable binding with a minimum of distraction, we initially study it in the most abstract context possible. For this purpose we introduce a language that has only variable references, `lambda` expressions with a single formal parameter, and procedure calls.

⟨exp⟩ ::= ⟨varref⟩
    | (`lambda` (⟨var⟩) ⟨exp⟩)
    | (⟨exp⟩ ⟨exp⟩)

This language is called the *lambda calculus*. Although quite concise, its concepts generalize easily to most programming languages. For these reasons, the lambda calculus is the formal basis for much of the theory of programming languages.

The traditional syntax for procedures in the lambda calculus uses the Greek letter λ (lambda), replacing the second alternative in the above grammar with

$$\lambda \langle \text{var} \rangle \, . \, \langle \text{exp} \rangle$$

We use the keyword `lambda` and the extra parentheses so that these expressions look like Scheme expressions. Furthermore, since elements of ⟨exp⟩ are lists, it is convenient to write programs that manipulate them.

A variable reference is said to be *bound* in an expression if it refers to a formal parameter introduced in the expression. A reference that is not bound to a formal parameter in the expression is said to be *free*. Thus in

$$((\texttt{lambda (x) x) y}) \qquad\qquad (*)$$

the reference to x is bound and the reference to y is free. A variable is said to *occur bound* in an expression if the expression contains a bound reference to the variable. Similarly, a variable is said to *occur free* in an expression if the expression contains a free reference to the variable.

All variable references must have some associated value when they are evaluated at run time. If they are bound to a formal parameter, they are said to be *lexically bound*. Otherwise, they must either be bound at top level by definitions or be supplied by the system. In this case, they are said to be *globally bound*. It is an error to reference a variable that is neither lexically nor globally bound.

The value of an expression depends only on the values associated with the variables that occur free within the expression. The context that surrounds the expression must provide these values. For example, the value of (*) depends on the value of the free variable y. If (*) were embedded in the body of a lambda expression with formal parameter y, as in

$$\texttt{(lambda (y) ((lambda (x) x) y)),} \qquad (**)$$

then the binding of this parameter would provide the value for the reference to variable y. Thus a variable reference that is free in one context, such as (*), may be bound in a larger surrounding context, such as (**).

The value of an expression is independent of bindings for variables that do not occur free in the expression. For example, the value of (*) is independent of any bindings that might exist for x at the time that (*) is evaluated. By the time the free occurrence of x in the body of (lambda (x) x) is evaluated, it will have a new binding (in (*), the value associated with y).

The meaning of (lambda (x) x) is always the same: it is the identity function that returns whatever value it is passed. Other lambda expressions without free variables also have fixed meanings. For example, the value of

```
(lambda (f)
  (lambda (x)
    (f x)))
```

is a procedure that takes a procedure, f, and returns a procedure that takes a value x, applies f to it, and returns the result. Lambda expressions without free variables are called *combinators*. A few combinators, such as the identity function and the above application combinator, are useful programming tools. We shall use more elaborate combinators in the procedural representation of data types, beginning in section 3.6.

Free and bound occurrences may be defined formally as follows:

A variable x *occurs free* in an expression E if and only if

1. E is a variable reference and E is the same as x; or
2. E is of the form $(E_1 \ E_2)$ and x occurs free in E_1 or E_2; or
3. E is of the form (lambda $(y) \ E'$), where y is different from x and x occurs free in E'.

A variable x *occurs bound* in an expression E if and only if

1. E is of the form $(E_1 \ E_2)$ and x occurs bound in E_1 or E_2; or
2. E is of the form (lambda $(y) \ E'$), where x occurs bound in E' or x and y are the same variable and y occurs free in E'.

No variable occurs bound in an expression consisting of just a single variable.

- *Exercise 2.3.1*

  Write a procedure *free-vars* that takes a list structure representing an expression in the lambda calculus syntax given above and returns a set, a list without duplicates, of all the variables that occur free in the expression. Similarly, write a procedure *bound-vars* that returns a set of all the variables that occur bound in its argument.

  Hint: The definitions of occurs free and occurs bound are recursive and based on the structure of an expression. Your program should have a similar structure. □

- *Exercise 2.3.2*

  Write predicates *free?* (respectively, *bound?*) that determines if an expression contains a free (respectively, bound) instance of a particular variable. □

- *Exercise 2.3.3*

  Give an example of a lambda calculus expression in which the same variable occurs both bound and free. □

- *Exercise 2.3.4*

  Give an example of a lambda calculus expression in which a variable occurs free but which has a value that is independent of the value of the free variable. □

- *Exercise 2.3.5*

  Scheme lambda expressions may have any number of formal parameters, and Scheme procedure calls may have any number of operands. Modify the definitions of occurs free and occurs bound to allow lambda expressions with any number of formal parameters and procedure calls with any number of operands. □

- *Exercise 2.3.6*

  Extend the formal definitions of occurs free and occurs bound to include if expressions. □

○ *Exercise 2.3.7*

What effect does `quote` have on the set of free and bound variables? ☐

2.3.2 Scope and Lexical Address

Associated with each declaration of a variable (as in a formal parameter list) is a *region* of text within which the declaration is effective. The region depends on the form of declaration. For example, in Scheme the region of a formal parameter is the body of the lambda expression, and the region of a top-level definition is the entire program (all text entered at top level). The *scope* of a variable declaration is the text within which references to the variable refer to the declaration. Alternatively, we may speak of the declarations that are *visible* at the point of a variable reference, meaning those that contain the variable reference within their scope. The region and scope of a variable may be the same, but we shall see that the scope does not include the entire region.

Declarations have a limited scope so that the same variable name may be used for different purposes in different parts of a program. For example, in this chapter we have repeatedly used `1st` as a formal parameter, and in each case its scope was limited to the body of the corresponding lambda expression.

In most languages, including Scheme, a declaration's region and scope can be determined statically. Such languages are said to be *lexically* or statically scoped. Most modern languages allow regions to be *nested* within each other, as when one lambda expression appears in the body of another. Regions are sometimes called *blocks,* and such languages are said to be *block structured.*

Block-structured languages do not allow declarations that use the same variable name to be associated with the same region. For example, the expression (`lambda (x x)` ...) is illegal. Declarations using the same variable name, however, may be nested. In this case the intention is clearly that the inner declaration supersedes the outer one. Thus the inner one creates a *hole* in the scope of the outer one. For example, consider

```
> (define x
    (lambda (x)
      (map (lambda (x) (+ x 1)) x)))
> (x '(1 2 3))
(2 3 4)
```

The region of the `x` declared on the first line is the read-eval-print loop's top level, which includes the body of the definition: however, its scope does not include the body of the defined procedure. The scope of the formal parameter x in the third line is the lambda expression's body, (+ x 1). This formal parameter creates a hole in the scope of the formal parameter x in the second line. The scope of the x in the second line includes the reference to x as the second argument to map, but not the reference to x as the first argument to +. The inner declarations of x *shadow* the outer declarations of x.

Thus the scope of a declaration is the region of text associated with the declaration, excluding any inner regions associated with declarations that use the same variable name. Put another way, the declaration of a variable v has a scope that includes all references to v that *occur free* in the region associated with the declaration. Those references to v that *occur bound* in the region associated with its declaration are shadowed by inner declarations.

There is a simple algorithm for determining to which declaration a variable reference refers. Search the regions enclosing the reference, starting with the innermost. As each successively larger region is encountered, check whether a declaration of the given variable is associated with the block. If one is found, that is the declaration of the variable. If not, proceed to the next enclosing region. If the outermost (top-level or global) region is reached and no declaration is found, the variable reference is unbound.

- *Exercise 2.3.8*

In the following expressions, draw an arrow from each variable reference to its associated formal parameter declaration.

```
(lambda (x)
  (lambda (y)
    ((lambda (x)
       (x y))
     x)))

(lambda (z)
  ((lambda (a b c)
     (a (lambda (a) (+ a c)) b))
   (lambda (f x)
     (f (z x)))))
```


○ *Exercise 2.3.9*

Repeat the above exercise with programs written in another block-structured language. □

Induction, Recursion, and Scope

It is sometimes more helpful to picture the borders of regions, rather than the interiors of regions. These borders are called *contours*. Execution of the above algorithm may then be viewed as a journey outward from a variable reference. In this journey a number of contours may be crossed before arriving at the associated declaration. The number of contours crossed is called the *lexical* (or *static*) *depth* of the variable reference. For example, in

```
(lambda (x y)
  ((lambda (a)
     (x (a y)))
   x))
```

the reference to x on the last line and the reference to a both have lexical depth zero, while the references to x and y in the third line both have lexical depth one.

The declarations associated with a region may be numbered in the order of their appearance in the text. Each variable reference may then be associated with two numbers: its lexical depth and the position of its declaration in the declaring contour (its *declaration position*). Taken together, these two numbers are the *lexical address* of the variable reference.

To illustrate lexical addresses, we may replace every variable reference v in an expression by

$$(v : d\ p)$$

where d is its lexical depth and p is its declaration position. Using zero-based indexing for both d and p, the above example becomes

```
(lambda (x y)
  ((lambda (a)
     ((x : 1 0) ((a : 0 0) (y : 1 1))))
   (x : 0 0)))
```

Since the lexical address completely specifies each variable reference, variable names may be considered superfluous! That is, variable references could be replaced by expressions of the form (: $d\ p$), and formal parameter lists could be replaced by their length, as in

```
(lambda 2
  ((lambda 1
     ((: 1 0) ((: 0 0) (: 1 1))))
   (: 0 0)))
```

Variable names are certainly a great help in understanding programs, but they are not absolutely necessary in writing programs.

Compilers routinely calculate the lexical address of each variable reference. Once this has been done, the variable names may be discarded unless they are required to provide debugging information.

• *Exercise 2.3.10*

Consider the subset of Scheme specified by the BNF rules

⟨exp⟩ ::= ⟨varref⟩
     | (if ⟨exp⟩ ⟨exp⟩ ⟨exp⟩)
     | (lambda ({⟨var⟩}*) ⟨exp⟩)
     | ({⟨exp⟩}+)

Observe that a `lambda` expression can have zero formal parameters.

Write a procedure *lexical-address* that takes any expression and returns the expression with every variable reference v replaced by a list $(v : d\ p)$, as above. If the variable refers to a free variable, like `eq?` and `cons`, imagine that the entire expression is wrapped within a lambda that binds it. In the example below, it would be (lambda (eq? cons) (lambda (a b c) ...)).

```
> (lexical-address '(lambda (a b c)
                      (if (eq? b c)
                          ((lambda (c)
                             (cons a c))
                           a)
                          b)))
(lambda (a b c)
  (if ((eq? : 1 0) (b : 0 1) (c : 0 2))
      ((lambda (c)
         ((cons : 2 1) (a : 1 0) (c : 0 0)))
       (a : 0 0))
      (b : 0 1)))
☐
```

• *Exercise 2.3.11*

What is wrong with the following lexical-address expression?

```
(lambda (a)
  (lambda (a)
    (a : 1 0)))
☐
```

- *Exercise 2.3.12*

Write a Scheme expression that is equivalent to the following lexical-address expression from which variable names have been removed.

```
(lambda 1
  (lambda 1
    (: 1 0)))
```
☐

○ *Exercise 2.3.13*

Write the procedure un-lexical-address, which takes lexical-address expressions with formal parameter lists and with variable references of the form (: *d p*), and returns an equivalent expression formed by substituting standard variable references for the lexical address information, or #f if no such expression exists.

```
> (un-lexical-address '(lambda (a)
                          (lambda (b c)
                            ((: 1 0) (: 0 0) (: 0 1)))))
(lambda (a) (lambda (b c) (a b c)))
> (un-lexical-address '(lambda (a) (lambda (a) (: 1 0))))
#f
```
☐

2.3.3 Renaming Variables

Since variable names are not strictly necessary, as we have just seen, the behavior of a procedure must surely be independent of the choice of its formal parameter names. Thus (lambda (*var*) *var*) is the identity combinator, regardless of what identifier *var* is chosen for its formal parameter.

From this observation we wish to obtain a general program transformation rule. (Other transformation rules will be introduced in chapter 4.) The general idea is that the meaning of a lambda expression is unchanged if the name of a formal parameter is changed along with all references to the parameter, however, there are two difficulties that must be avoided. First, the new variable name should not conflict with any other variable names used in that part of the program. Such a conflict occurs exactly in those cases where the new name is the same as the name of a variable that occurs free in the body of the original lambda expression. For example,

```
(lambda (x) (cons x '()))
```

is not the same as

```
(lambda (cons) (cons cons '()))
```

In this case the new binding of `cons` is said to *capture* the existing reference to another binding of `cons`.

The second difficulty occurs if an inner formal parameter declaration creates a hole in the scope of the outer formal parameter: the references to the inner declaration should not be changed. For example,

```
(lambda (x)
  ((lambda (x) (cons x '()))
   (cons x '())))
```

might be transformed to

```
(lambda (y)
  ((lambda (x) (cons x '()))
   (cons y '())))
```

but should not become

```
(lambda (y)
  ((lambda (x) (cons y '()))
   (cons y '())))
```

The result of substituting an expression y for all free occurrences of a variable x in an expression exp is written $exp[y/x]$ (or by some authors $[y/x]exp$ or $exp[x \leftarrow y]$), and may be read "exp with y for x." With this notation the general variable renaming rule for lambda expressions with one formal parameter may be expressed as

$$\texttt{(lambda } (var) \; exp) = \texttt{(lambda } (var') \; exp[var'/var])$$

where var' is any variable that does not occur free in exp. In the lambda calculus this called α-*conversion*. Generalizing this rule to procedures with multiple formal parameters is straightforward.

Induction, Recursion, and Scope

o *Exercise 2.3.14*

Write a procedure `rename` that takes a lambda calculus expression `exp` and two variables `var1` and `var2` and returns `exp[var1/var2]` if `var1` does not occur free in `exp` and `#f` otherwise.

```
> (rename '(lambda (b) (b a)) 'c 'a)
(lambda (b) (b c))
> (rename '((lambda (x) x) x) 'y 'x)
((lambda (x) x) y)
> (rename '(a b) 'a 'b)
#f
```

☐

o *Exercise 2.3.15*

Use `rename` to write a procedure `alpha-convert` that takes a lambda expression `exp` of the form `(lambda (var) exp)`, and a variable `v`, and returns `(lambda (v) exp[v/var])`, or `#f` if `v` occurs free in `exp`.

```
> (alpha-convert '(lambda (a) (lambda (b) (b a))) 'c)
(lambda (c) (lambda (b) (b c)))
> (alpha-convert '(lambda (x) ((lambda (x) x) x)) 'y)
(lambda (y) ((lambda (x) x) y))
> (alpha-convert '(lambda (x) (y x)) 'y)
#f
```

☐

2.4 Summary

Induction provides a powerful tool for specifying data. Backus-Naur Form, or BNF, is a convenient shorthand for expressing context-free inductive definitions. The structure of data can often be expressed concisely using BNF, as can the structure of programs. Structural induction is a technique for basing proofs on inductive data specifications.

Procedures may contain calls to themselves. Such procedures are said to be recursive. Many recursive procedures may be derived systematically from inductive specifications of their data. The structure of recursion in such procedures matches the inductive structure of the data definitions. Three examples, `remove-first`, `remove`, and `subst`, illustrate the use of inductive specifications, and will be the basis for later examples.

A variable reference may either be free in the context of a particular expression, or it may be bound to some formal parameter in the expression. Associated with each declaration is a region within which it has effect and a scope within which variable references using the same name refer to the variable introduced by the declaration. Regions may be nested in block-structured languages. The boundary of a region is called its contour.

Each variable reference is completely characterized by its lexical address. This consists of its lexical depth, the number of contours that separate it from its associated declaration, and the position of the declaration among others of the same contour.

Variable names may be systematically changed without changing the meaning of a program, provided the new name does not conflict with variables occurring free in the region of the renamed variable, and only references in the scope of the renamed variable are changed. This is called α-conversion.

3 Syntactic Abstraction and Data Abstraction

In this chapter we present several special forms that are precisely equivalent to syntactic patterns that are expressible in terms of existing forms. They are examples of *syntactic abstraction,* since they abstract common syntactic patterns. They are informally known as *syntactic sugar,* since they make a language more pleasant to use but add nothing of substance. First we introduce syntactic abstractions that are useful for creating local bindings and performing multi-way branches. We then present a record facility for Scheme that may be implemented via two more syntactic abstractions.

Our implementation of records hides details of how records are implemented. This provides an example of *data abstraction* and leads to a general discussion of *abstract data types.* These data types allow the development of programs that are independent of how their data is represented. One of the benefits of such *representation independence* is that data that is first represented, for simplicity, as first-class procedures may later be represented, for efficiency, as records or other more specialized data representations. The last section illustrates such transformations of data representation, which are extensively used throughout the rest of this book.

3.1 Local Binding

So far we have seen two ways to create bindings in Scheme. Definitions, as we use them, create *top-level* bindings whose region is the entire program. Lambda expressions, which yield procedures, create local bindings for their parameters when invoked. The region of these bindings is restricted to the body of the procedure. There is frequently a need to create local bindings for immediate use, rather than for use when a procedure is invoked. This section introduces two special forms for creating such bindings.

3.1.1 let

Consider the `if` expression of the first *subst* definition in section 2.2.2.

```
(define subst
  (lambda (new old slst)
    ...
    (if (symbol? (car slst))
        (if (eq? (car slst) old)
            (cons new (subst new old (cdr slst)))
            (cons (car slst) (subst new old (cdr slst))))
        (cons (subst new old (car slst))
              (subst new old (cdr slst))))
    ... ))
```

The expression (subst new old (cdr slst)) appears three times, and its value is always needed if *slst* is not null. It would be clearer if this value could be computed and bound to a variable, say `cdr-result`, before the expression is evaluated and then simply referred to by this name. Since this binding has no significance outside of this expression, the binding should be local to the expression. One way to accomplish this is to use a lambda expression whose body is the expression and invoke the resulting procedure immediately.

```
((lambda (cdr-result)
   (if (symbol? (car slst))
       (if (eq? (car slst) old)
           (cons new cdr-result)
           (cons (car slst) cdr-result))
       (cons (subst new old (car slst))
             cdr-result)))
 (subst new old (cdr slst)))
```

We treat (car slst) similarly, since it appears four times.

```
((lambda (car-value cdr-result)
   (if (symbol? car-value)
       (if (eq? car-value old)
           (cons new cdr-result)
           (cons car-value cdr-result))
       (cons (subst new old car-value)
             cdr-result)))
 (car slst)
 (subst new old (cdr slst)))
```

The original expression has now been simplified considerably. Furthermore, in the original expression (car slst) is evaluated two or three times (depending on which if branches are taken), whereas in the version above it is evaluated only once. This illustrates another advantage of local bindings: they can reduce the amount of computation. In our example, the amount of computation involved in taking the car of *slst* is small enough that this is of little significance, however, sometimes expressions that appear repeatedly involve a great deal of computation.

You probably sense the problem with the approach taken above: it is difficult for the eye to match the formal parameters with their associated operands. Looking at the expression above, it is not obvious that *cdr-result* is the value of (subst new old (cdr slst)). The let special form is provided to solve this problem. Using let, the definition of *subst* becomes

```
(define subst
  (lambda (new old slst)
    (if (null? slst)
        '()
        (let ((car-value (car slst))
              (cdr-result (subst new old (cdr slst))))
          (if (symbol? car-value)
              (if (eq? car-value old)
                  (cons new cdr-result)
                  (cons car-value cdr-result))
              (cons (subst new old car-value)
                    cdr-result)))))))
```

In general, let expressions have the form

$$(\text{let } ((var_1 \ exp_1)$$
$$\dots$$
$$(var_n \ exp_n))$$
$$body)$$

The region associated with the declarations of $var_1, \ldots, var_n$ is *body*. Each of the expressions $exp_1, \ldots, exp_n$ is evaluated, the variables $var_1, \ldots, var_n$ are bound to their values, and finally the expression *body* is evaluated and its value is returned. Thus the above form is precisely equivalent to

$$((\text{lambda } (var_1 \ \dots \ var_n) \ body)$$
$$exp_1 \ \dots \ exp_n)$$

In fact, when some Scheme compilers see a `let` expression, they immediately translate it into this form. (They also typically implement `let` or the equivalent form efficiently by avoiding the creation of a procedure, as in figure 5.3.2.)

Sometimes when two local bindings are required, the value of one of them depends on the value of the other. In this case nested `let` expressions must be used. For example,

```
(let ((x 3))
  (let ((y (+ x 4)))
    (* x y)))
```

is *not* equivalent to

```
(let ((x 3)
      (y (+ x 4)))
  (* x y))
```

since in the latter expression the region of the new declaration of x is the body of the `let` expression and does *not* include the expression (+ x 4) used to define y. The `let` expression is equivalent to this lambda expression:

```
((lambda (x y) (* x y))
 3
 (+ x 4))
```

It is clear that (+ x 4) is not in the scope of the formal parameter x. Nested `let` expressions may also be used to create bindings for the same variable:

```
(let ((x 3))
  (let ((x (* x x)))
    (+ x x)))
```

Here the inner `let` creates a *hole* in the scope of the outer binding of x, but the hole does not include the expression (* x x). Thus the expression has value 18. If this is not clear, try replacing each `let` expression by the equivalent application of a procedure created by `lambda`.

- *Exercise 3.1.1*

What are the values of the following two expressions?

Syntactic Abstraction and Data Abstraction

```
(let ((x 5) (y 6) (z 7))
  (let ((x 13) (y (+ x y)) (z x))
    (- (+ x z) y)))

(let ((x 5) (y 6) (z 7))
  (+ (let ((z (+ x z))) (* z (+ z x)))
     (let ((z (* x y))) (+ z (* z (- z y))))))
```

☐

○ *Exercise 3.1.2*

Write `let->application`, which takes a `let` expression (represented as a list) and returns the equivalent expression, also represented as a list: an application of a procedure created by a `lambda` expression. Your solution should not change the body of the `let` expression.

```
> (let->application '(let ((x 4) (y 3))
                       (let ((z 5))
                         (+ x (+ y z)))))
((lambda (x y)
   (let ((z 5))
     (+ x (+ y z))))
  4 3)
```

☐

3.1.2 `letrec`

Frequently it is desirable to bind procedures locally. For example, in section 2.2 we defined the procedure *partial-vector-sum* for use by *vector-sum*. If a procedure is not likely to be of use in other contexts, it is good practice to restrict the scope of its binding to the section of code where it is needed. Thus within the definition of *vector-sum* we would like to use something like

```
(let ((partial-vector-sum
        (lambda (von n)
          (if (zero? n)
              0
              (+ (vector-ref von (- n 1))
                 (partial-vector-sum von (- n 1)))))))
  (partial-vector-sum von (vector-length von)))
```

but this does not work. Recall that the region of a `let` binding is restricted to the body of the `let`. The difficulty is that in *partial-vector-sum* the recursive call (partial-vector-sum von (- n 1)) is not within the scope of the binding for *partial-vector-sum*. The same difficulty arises whenever there is a need to bind a recursive procedure locally.

Scheme provides the special form `letrec` to make local recursive definitions. The general form follows:

$$(\texttt{letrec}\ ((var_1\ exp_1)$$
$$\ldots$$
$$(var_n\ exp_n))$$
$$body)$$

This is similar to `let`, except that the region of the declarations $var_1, \ldots, var_n$ is the entire `letrec` expression, including the expressions $exp_1, \ldots, exp_n$. Thus $exp_1, \ldots, exp_n$ may define mutually recursive procedures. In most uses of `letrec`, $exp_1, \ldots, exp_n$ are lambda expressions, but this is not required. It is required, however, that no reference be made to $var_1, \ldots, var_n$ during the evaluation of $exp_1, \ldots, exp_n$. For example,

```
(letrec ((x 3)
         (y (+ x 1)))
   y)
```

is illegal. This restriction is necessary because the bindings of $var_1, \ldots, var_n$ cannot have values until $exp_1, \ldots, exp_n$ have been evaluated. The requirement is easily met if these are lambda expressions, because references to variables within the body of a lambda expression are evaluated only when the resulting procedure is invoked, not when the lambda expression is evaluated. Thus

```
(letrec ((x 3)
         (y (lambda () (+ x 1))))
  (y))
```

is legal and evaluates to 4.

Using `letrec`, *vector-sum* may be defined as in figure 3.1.1. We no longer need to pass *von* to *partial-vector-sum*, since *von* does not change and the reference to *von* in the *vector-ref* call is within the scope of *vector-sum*. A simple example of mutual recursion using `letrec` is shown in the program of figure 3.1.2, where the procedures *even?* and *odd?* are defined for nonnegative integers.

There are several advantages to using `letrec`, or `let` for procedures, rather than using `define`:

Figure 3.1.1 The procedure `vector-sum` using `letrec`

```
(define vector-sum
  (lambda (von)
    (letrec ((partial-vector-sum
               (lambda (n)
                 (if (zero? n)
                     0
                     (+ (vector-ref von (- n 1))
                        (partial-vector-sum (- n 1))))))))
      (partial-vector-sum (vector-length von)))))
```

Figure 3.1.2 Example of mutual recursion

```
(letrec ((even? (lambda (n)
                  (if (zero? n)
                      #t
                      (odd? (- n 1)))))
         (odd? (lambda (n)
                 (if (zero? n)
                     #f
                     (even? (- n 1))))))
  (even? 3))
```

1. When studying a procedure call, finding a local definition is easier than finding a global one.

2. The code that could be affected by a modification to a procedure is limited to the scope of a local declaration.

3. Frequently the number of arguments required is reduced when a local declaration is used, because some bindings are provided by the context (as with von in the `vector-sum` example above).

4. By reducing the number of global definitions, the chance of a conflict occurring because the same name is used for more than one global definition is reduced. In large programs to which many people contribute code, this last point is very important. We shall have more to say about this in chapter 7.

We have seen that Scheme allows any expression to contain local definitions. Some languages allow local procedure declarations only in certain contexts, such as at the head of procedure declarations or even larger units such as files.

- *Exercise 3.1.3*

  Rewrite *subst* using `letrec`. □

○ *Exercise 3.1.4*

  The special forms `let` and `letrec` are both binding forms. Extend the definitions of *occurs free* and *occurs bound* to accommodate `let` and `letrec` expressions. Augment your programs *free-vars* and *bound-vars* to take your new rules into account. □

○ *Exercise 3.1.5*

  Extend the language of exercise 2.3.10 to include `let` and `letrec` expressions. Adapt your program *lexical-address* so that it recognizes `letrec` expressions. □

3.2 Logical Connectives

Most programming languages provide a means for expressing the *conjunction* of expressions with the connective *and*, which forms a logical expression that is true if and only if *all* its subexpressions are true. Similarly, logical *disjunction* may be expressed with the connective *or*, which forms an expression that is true if *any* of its subexpressions are true.

In some languages, *and* and *or* are provided as procedures. In this case, all the subexpressions of a conjunction or disjunction are always evaluated, since operands are evaluated prior to a procedure call. This may be unnecessary. As soon as a false subexpression of a conjunction is found, it is known that the entire expression is false, and when a true subexpression of a disjunction is found, true may be returned immediately. Evaluation of all the subexpressions of a conjunction or disjunction not only may result in wasted computation, but also restricts the way in which they may be used. For example, consider this conjunction:

```
(and (pair? x) (number? (car x)))
```

Since `car` may only be passed a pair, the second subexpression may be evaluated only if it is known that the first is true. Thus it would be an error to write such an expression if `and` were a procedure.

Therefore in many languages, including Scheme, logical conjunction and disjunction are implemented as special forms that evaluate their subexpressions from left to right and do not evaluate subexpressions unnecessarily. There is one more factor that complicates the special forms and and or in Scheme. Any value other than #f is treated as true, so when a value has been computed and found to be true, it may still be useful to return it as the result of an and or or expression. Thus and returns the value of its *last* subexpression if all its subexpressions are true, and or returns the value of its *first* true subexpression (or #f if none are true).

```
> (and 3 (number? #t))
#f
> (and #t (number? 3) 4)
4
> (or (number? #t) 3 4)
3
```

The special form and may be specified inductively. Defining (and *test*) to be equivalent to *test* provides the basis of the induction. The induction step specifies that

$$(\text{and } test_1 \ test_2 \ \ldots \ test_n)$$

is equivalent to

```
(if test₁
    (and test₂ ... testₙ)
    #f)
```

The special form or may also be specified inductively. Defining (or *test*) to be equivalent to *test* provides the basis. In the induction step, we are careful to record the value of the first subexpression so it may be returned without reevaluation if it is true. We specify that

$$(\text{or } test_1 \ test_2 \ \ldots \ test_n)$$

is equivalent to

```
(let ((*value* test₁))
  (if *value*
      *value*
      (or test₂ ... testₙ)))
```

where it is assumed that *value* does not occur free in $test_2, \ldots, test_n$.

∘ *Exercise 3.2.1*

Write conjunction procedures `and-proc` and `or-proc` as variable arity procedures. Can you think of any uses for these procedures where `and` and `or` could not be used? □

3.3 Branching

So far we have used only one built-in branching mechanism, `if`, which performs a two-way branch based on a single test. In this section we introduce the special forms `cond` and `case`, which perform multi-way branching based on multiple tests.

3.3.1 cond

The special form `cond` performs a multi-way branch based on a series of test expressions. Its syntax follows:

$$
\begin{aligned}
&\texttt{(cond}\\
&\quad (test_1 \;\; consequent_1)\\
&\quad \ldots\\
&\quad (test_n \;\; consequent_n)\\
&\quad (\texttt{else} \;\; alternative))
\end{aligned}
$$

Here `else` is a keyword that is part of the syntax of `cond`. The test expressions are evaluated in the order in which they occur until one returns true. The associated consequent expression is then evaluated, and its value is the value of the `cond` expression. If none of the test expressions are true, the alternative expression is evaluated and its value returned. Such `cond` expressions are thus equivalent to a nested series of `if` expressions of this form:

$$
\begin{aligned}
&\texttt{(if } test_1\\
&\quad consequent_1\\
&\quad \ldots\\
&\qquad \texttt{(if } test_n\\
&\qquad\quad consequent_n\\
&\qquad\quad alternative) \;\ldots)
\end{aligned}
$$

A `cond` expression with a single consequent is equivalent to a single `if` expression, in which case the `if` expression is generally preferred.

The (`else` *alternative*) clause is optional. If none of the test expressions are true and there is no `else` clause, the value of a `cond` expression is unspecified.

Using `cond`, we can rewrite our original version of `subst` as follows

```
(define subst
  (lambda (new old slst)
    (cond
      ((null? slst) '())
      ((symbol? (car slst))
       (if (eq? (car slst) old)
           (cons new (subst new old (cdr slst)))
           (cons (car slst) (subst new old (cdr slst)))))
      (else (cons (subst new old (car slst))
                  (subst new old (cdr slst)))))))
```

An if is still used in this example because both the consequent and alternative
of the if expression are to be evaluated only if (symbol? (car slst)) is true.
If we started with this version of subst and then wished to use let as in
the last section, we would first need to convert the cond expression into its
corresponding nested if expression.

○ *Exercise 3.3.1*
Write a procedure *if->cond* that takes an if expression and returns the corresponding cond expression (but does not expand consequent expressions).
What does this procedure do with (if else 1 2)? In addition, write a procedure *cond->if* that takes a cond expression as its argument and returns the
corresponding if expression.

```
> (if->cond '(if a b c))
(cond (a b) (else c))

> (if->cond '(if a b (if c d (if e f g))))
(cond (a b) (c d) (e f) (else g))

> (if->cond '(if a (if b c) (if d e f)))
(cond (a (if b c)) (d e) (else f))

> (cond->if '(cond (a b) (c d) (else e)))
(if a b (if c d e))
```
□

○ *Exercise 3.3.2*
Extend the language of exercise 2.3.10 to include cond expressions. Adapt
your lexical-address program so that it recognizes cond expressions. □

3.3.2 `case`

A common form of multi-way branch involves comparison of a value with a fixed set of symbols or numbers. In Scheme this is facilitated by the special form `case` with the following syntax:

```
(case key
      (key-list₁  consequent₁)
      . . .
      (key-listₙ  consequentₙ)
      (else alternative))
```

where each *key-list* is a list of symbols, numbers, booleans, or characters, and the else clause is optional. The expression *key* is evaluated, and its value is compared with the key list elements. The *consequent* corresponding to the first matching key list element is then evaluated and its value returned. If no match is found, *alternative* is evaluated and its value returned, unless the else clause is omitted, in which case the value of the `case` expression is unspecified.

A `case` expression can always be transformed into an equivalent expression using `let` and `cond` as follows

```
(let ((*key* key))
  (cond
    ((memv *key* 'key-list₁) consequent₁)
    . . .
    ((memv *key* 'key-listₙ) consequentₙ)
    (else alternative)))
```

where the variable `*key*` does not occur free within the consequent or alternative expressions and the standard procedure `memv` takes a key and a list and returns true if the key is equal to an element of the list (using `eq?`, `=`, or `char=?`, as appropriate for the type of the key). Here, `let` is used so that *key* is only evaluated once. If *key* is simply a variable, the `let` could be omitted and the references to `*key*` replaced by this variable.

○ *Exercise 3.3.3*
Transcribe the following `case` expression into a `let` and `cond` expression.

```
(case (get-position-of item)
  ((one first 1) (car lst))
  ((two second 2) (cadr lst))
  (else (error "Invalid position")))
```
☐

Transcribe the following `cond` expression into a `case` expression

```
(cond
  ((memv color '(red pink mauve)) 'reddish)
  ((memv color '(white off-white cream)) 'whiteish)
  ((memv color '(blue azure navy)) 'blueish)
  (else (error "Invalid color" color)))
```

☐

In the next section we introduce a third form for multi-way dispatch, called `variant-case`.

3.4 Records

So far we have seen two methods of creating compound data in Scheme: pairs (with which lists are made) and vectors. Elements of these structures are accessed by their position in the structure. Most programming languages support data structures, called *records* (or *structures*), whose elements are accessed by name. This section presents a record facility for Scheme that we use extensively in this book. (Though records are not a standard feature of Scheme, this facility may be implemented without difficulty in any Scheme system with a syntactic extension facility. See appendix A for details.)

3.4.1 `define-record`

Each type of record has a type name and a set of field names. Our record facility only supports the definition of new record types at top level using the special form `define-record`. Definitions have this general form:

$$\texttt{(define-record } name \texttt{ (} field_1 \; \dots \; field_n \texttt{))}$$

This defines a procedure for creating records of type *name*, a predicate for identifying records of this type, and an accessing procedure for each field. The creation procedure, called `make-`*name*, takes n arguments and returns a new record of the given type with $field_i$ containing the ith argument value. The type predicate, called *name*`?`, returns true only when passed records of the new type. The accessing procedures, called *name*`->`$field_i$, for $1 \leq i \leq n$, take a record of the new type and return the value of the indicated field.

For example, consider the representation of binary trees used in section 2.1:

⟨tree⟩ ::= ⟨number⟩ | (⟨symbol⟩ ⟨tree⟩ ⟨tree⟩)

Here a record type, call it `interior`, could be used with advantage to represent interior nodes. This allows us to assign names, say `symbol`, `left-tree`, and `right-tree`, to the three components of an interior node.

```
> (define-record interior (symbol left-tree right-tree))
> (define tree-1 (make-interior 'foo (make-interior 'bar 1 2) 3))
> (interior? tree-1)
#t
> (interior->symbol tree-1)
foo
> (interior->right-tree (interior->left-tree tree-1))
2
```

We now define *leaf-sum*, which sums the leaves of a tree.

```
(define leaf-sum
  (lambda (tree)
    (cond
      ((number? tree) tree)
      ((interior? tree) (+ (leaf-sum (interior->left-tree tree))
                           (leaf-sum (interior->right-tree tree))))
      (else (error "leaf-sum: Invalid tree" tree)))))
```

In general, a distinct record type may be used to represent each alternative of a BNF specification. Each nonterminal within an alternative is recorded in a field of the associated type of record. Using this approach, we require an additional record type to represent trees. We provide it with

```
(define-record leaf (number))
```

This makes it possible to distinguish a tree that consists of a single leaf from a number.

• *Exercise 3.4.1*
Redefine *leaf-sum* for trees with `leaf` records. ☐

3.4.2 Variant Records and `variant-case`

A type that combines two or more other types as alternatives is called a *union* type. The tree type is a union of records of type `leaf` or `interior`. A union type all of whose alternatives are records is called a *variant record* type. Many languages provide support for unions or variant records. Though Scheme does not provide explicit means for declaring type unions, they may be used implicitly, as in the tree example above. The alternatives of the union can be distinguished using the predicates provided for each type.

In this book we shall make frequent use of variant records, so it is convenient to have a special facility for branching on the type of the record. Furthermore, when the type has been identified, it is helpful to bind some or all of its field values to variables named after the fields. The special form `variant-case` performs both of these services. Its syntax is

$$
\begin{array}{l}
(\texttt{variant-case}\ \textit{record-expression} \\
\quad (\textit{name}_1\ \textit{field-list}_1\ \textit{consequent}_1) \\
\quad \cdots \\
\quad (\textit{name}_n\ \textit{field-list}_n\ \textit{consequent}_n) \\
\quad (\texttt{else}\ \textit{alternative}))
\end{array}
$$

where for $1 \leq i \leq n$, *field-list*$_i$ is a list of fields for records of type *name*$_i$. (Each record type should be distinct, as should the field names within a given field name list.) First, *record-expression* is evaluated, resulting in some value v. If v is not a record of one of the indicated types, *alternative* is evaluated and its value returned. If v is a record of type *name*$_i$, each of the names in *field-list*$_i$ is bound to the value of the field of v with the same name. Then *consequent*$_i$ is evaluated within the region of these bindings and its value returned.

For example, using `variant-case`, it is easy to define *leaf-sum* for a tree built from records of the type defined above.

```
(define leaf-sum
  (lambda (tree)
    (variant-case tree
      (leaf (number) number)
      (interior (left-tree right-tree)
        (+ (leaf-sum left-tree) (leaf-sum right-tree)))
      (else (error "leaf-sum: Invalid tree" tree)))))
```

The `symbol` field of the record type `interior` is not used, so it need not be mentioned. This is equivalent to

```
(define leaf-sum
  (lambda (tree)
    (let ((*record* tree))
      (cond
        ((leaf? *record*)
         (let ((number (leaf->number *record*)))
           number))
        ((interior? *record*)
         (let ((left-tree (interior->left-tree *record*))
               (right-tree (interior->right-tree *record*)))
           (+ (leaf-sum left-tree) (leaf-sum right-tree))))
        (else (error "leaf-sum: Invalid tree" tree))))))
```

In this case the outer let expression is clearly unnecessary because the *record expression* is simply the variable tree. As in the expansion of case, however, the outer let expression is in general necessary since *record-expression* should only be evaluated once. Care must also be taken, as in the case expansion, that the variable introduced by this let expression does not appear free in any of the expansions of the *alternative* or *consequent* expressions.

- *Exercise 3.4.2*

Use variant-case to write *max-interior*, which takes a binary tree of numbers with at least one interior node and returns the symbol associated with an interior node with a maximal leaf sum.

```
> (define tree-a (make-interior 'a (make-leaf 2) (make-leaf 3)))
> (define tree-b (make-interior 'b (make-leaf -1) tree-a))
> (define tree-c (make-interior 'c tree-b (make-leaf 1)))
> (max-interior tree-b)
a
> (max-interior tree-c)
c
```

The last invocation of *max-interior* might also have returned a, since both the a and c nodes have a leaf sum of 5. Your program should not perform more additions than necessary, which means that *leaf-sum* cannot be used. Instead, use an auxiliary procedure that is similar to *max-interior* but returns both the symbol of a maximal sum node and the value of the maximal sum. Use a new type of record to contain both the symbol and the sum. Returning multiple values in this way is another important use of records. □

3.4.3 Abstract Syntax and its Representation Using Records

Programs that process other programs, such as interpreters or compilers, are usually *syntax directed*. What is done with each part of a program is guided by knowledge of the grammar rules associated with the part, and any subparts corresponding to nonterminals in the grammar rules should also be readily accessible. For example, when processing the lambda calculus expression (lambda (x) (f (f x))), we must first recognize it as a lambda expression, corresponding to the BNF rule

---

⟨exp⟩ ::= (lambda (⟨var⟩) ⟨exp⟩)

Then the formal parameter is x and the body is (f (f x)). The body must in turn be recognized as an application, and so on.

An *abstract syntax* is a representation that identifies the syntactic rule associated with each syntactic component and provides ready access to subcomponents. Syntax that is designed for human consumption is *concrete syntax*.

In designing an abstract syntax for a given concrete syntax, we must name each production of the concrete syntax and each occurrence of a nonterminal in each production. The same nonterminal occurrence name may not be used twice in the same production. For the lambda calculus syntax introduced in the last chapter we might choose the names given on the right below, where the nonterminal occurrence names in parentheses are listed in the order of their appearance in the production. This grammar also differs from the previous one, since we include numbers.

⟨exp⟩ ::= ⟨number⟩	lit (datum)
| ⟨varref⟩	varref (var)
| (lambda (⟨var⟩) ⟨exp⟩)	lambda (formal body)
| (⟨exp⟩ ⟨exp⟩)	app (rator rand)

The symbols lit, varref, app, rator, and rand abbreviate *literal, variable reference, application, operator,* and *operand,* respectively.

The abstract syntax representation of an expression is most readily viewed as an *abstract syntax tree*. For example, see figure 3.4.1 for the abstract syntax tree of the lambda calculus expression (lambda (x) (f (f x))). Each node of the tree corresponds to a step in a syntactic derivation of the expression, with internal nodes labeled with their associated production name. Edges are labeled with the name of the corresponding nonterminal occurrence. Leaves

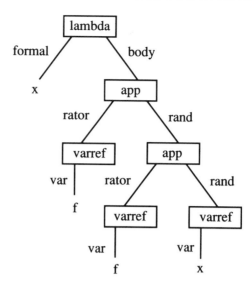

Figure 3.4.1 Abstract syntax tree for `(lambda (x) (f (f x)))`

correspond to terminal strings. (Leaves associated with terminals such as parentheses, which convey no information, are usually omitted from abstract syntax.)

○ *Exercise 3.4.3*

Generate a syntactic derivation and associated abstract syntax tree for the lambda calculus expression `((lambda (a) (a b)) c)`. □

In programs, abstract syntax is best represented by variant records. A record type is associated with each production name, and the fields are named after the corresponding nonterminal occurrences. Thus for the lambda calculus with numbers we use the following record definitions:

```
(define-record lit (datum))
(define-record varref (var))
(define-record lambda (formal body))
(define-record app (rator rand))
```

If a program is represented as a string of characters, it may be a complex business to derive the corresponding abstract syntax tree. This task, which is called *parsing,* is unrelated to whatever we may wish to do with the abstract syntax tree. Thus the job of parsing is best performed by a separate program, called a *parser.* Since abstract syntax trees are produced by parsers, they are also known as *parse trees.* Chapter 11 provides a general introduction to parsers.

If the concrete syntax of a language happens also to be list structures (including symbols and numbers), the parsing process is greatly simplified. For example, every expression specified by the previous lambda calculus grammar is also a list structure. Thus the Scheme `read` routine automatically parses these expressions into lists and symbols. It is still of value to parse these list structures into abstract syntax trees based on the record types previously defined. This is easily accomplished as follows:

```
(define parse
  (lambda (datum)
    (cond
      ((number? datum) (make-lit datum))
      ((symbol? datum) (make-varref datum))
      ((pair? datum)
       (if (eq? (car datum) 'lambda)
           (make-lambda (caadr datum) (parse (caddr datum)))
           (make-app (parse (car datum)) (parse (cadr datum)))))
      (else (error "parse: Invalid concrete syntax" datum)))))
```

If we would like to view an expression represented in abstract syntax, it is useful to be able to "unparse" it. We need only convert it back to the list and symbol representation, and the Scheme print routines will then display it in its concrete syntax. This is performed by the following procedure.

```
(define unparse
  (lambda (exp)
    (variant-case exp
      (lit (datum) datum)
      (varref (var) var)
      (lambda (formal body)
        (list 'lambda (list formal) (unparse body)))
      (app (rator rand) (list (unparse rator) (unparse rand)))
      (else (error "unparse: Invalid abstract syntax" exp)))))
```

A version of *free-vars* (exercise 2.3.1) that takes a parsed expression may be defined as follows.

```
(define free-vars
  (lambda (exp)
    (variant-case exp
      (lit (datum) '())
      (varref (var) (list var))
      (lambda (formal body) (remove formal (free-vars body)))
      (app (rator rand)
        (union (free-vars rator) (free-vars rand))))))
```

where `union` appends two lists of symbols and removes duplicates. A comparison of this definition with your solution to exercise 2.3.1 illustrates the utility of abstract syntax and `variant-case`.

○ *Exercise 3.4.4*

The procedure *parse* above does not detect several possible syntactic errors, such as (a b c), and aborts with inappropriate error messages for other expressions, such as (lambda). Modify *parse* so that it will accept any list structure and issue an appropriate error message if it does not represent a lambda calculus expression. □

● *Exercise 3.4.5*

Write a predicate *free?* that takes a variable, *v*, and a lambda calculus expression in abstract syntax and indicates whether *v* occurs free in it. Also rewrite the procedure *bound-vars* of exercise 2.3.1 using *parse*.

```
> (free? 'x (parse '(lambda (y) (x (x y)))))
#t
> (free? 'y (parse '(lambda (y) (x (x y)))))
#f
```
□

Where a Kleene star or plus is used in concrete syntax, it is most convenient to use a *list* of associated subtrees when constructing an abstract syntax tree. For example, consider a variant of the exercise 2.3.10 syntax:

⟨exp⟩ ::= ⟨number⟩	lit (datum)
| ⟨varref⟩	varref (var)
| (if ⟨exp⟩ ⟨exp⟩ ⟨exp⟩)	if (test-exp then-exp else-exp)
| (lambda ({⟨var⟩}*) ⟨exp⟩)	lambda (formals body)
| (⟨exp⟩ {⟨exp⟩}*)	app (rator rands)

Here `formals` and `rands` are associated with lists of formal parameters and operand expressions, respectively.

Define the record types and parse procedure for the above grammar. Then implement *lexical-address* of exercise 2.3.10 using abstract syntax. It will be helpful to extend the abstract syntax with this definition:

```
(define-record lex-info (var distance position))
```

These records represent the lexical distance and position information of a given variable reference. The value returned by *lexical-address* may then be generated using an unparse procedure that takes an abstract syntax tree of the form indicated by the above grammar, but with lex-info records in place of varref records. □

3.4.4 An Implementation of Records

As we have presented them so far, records are *abstract* in the sense that we have not committed to a specific representation of records. They could be represented as vectors, or lists, or even binary trees built with pairs, or they might be provided by a Scheme implementation in a form distinct from all other types. We shall have more to say shortly about the importance of such data abstraction.

To conclude this section, we present one possible implementation of records, in which they are represented as vectors. In many cases this is the most efficient representation in terms of both storage space and field access time. The first element of the vector that represents a record is a symbol identifying the record type. The remaining elements contain the field values in the order in which the fields appeared in the type's define-record statement. For example,

```
> (parse '(lambda (x) (y x)))
#(lambda x #(app #(varref y) #(varref x)))
```

From now on we assume this representation of records when record values are printed. Given this representation, the tree leaf record definition

```
(define-record leaf (number))
```

would produce definitions equivalent to

```
(define make-leaf
  (lambda (number)
    (vector 'leaf number)))

(define leaf?
  (lambda (obj)
    (and (vector? obj)
         (= (vector-length obj) 2)
         (eq? (vector-ref obj 0) 'leaf))))

(define leaf->number
  (lambda (obj)
    (if (leaf? obj)
        (vector-ref obj 1)
        (error "leaf->number: Invalid record" obj))))
```

○ *Exercise 3.4.7*
Assuming this vector representation of records, directly define the five procedures that result from this record definition:

```
(define-record interior (symbol left-tree right-tree))
```
☐

3.5 Data Abstraction

Data representations are often complex, so we do not want to be concerned with their details when we can avoid them. For example, a table might be stored as a balanced binary search tree, but we need not be concerned with the details of maintaining and searching a balanced tree when invoking procedures that update or access the table. We may also decide to change the representation of the data. The most efficient representation is often a lot more difficult to implement, so we may wish to develop a simple implementation first and only change to a more efficient representation if it proves critical to the overall performance of a system. For example, unbalanced binary trees, or even a simple list, may provide adequate performance as representations of tables, and they are much easier to implement than balanced trees. It is also frequently not known which representation will be most efficient until considerable experience has been obtained with a system, perhaps including experimentation with alternative representations. If we decide to change the representation of some data for any reason, we must be able to locate all parts of a program that are dependent on the representation.

Details of the representation of data should be isolated, both so details of the representation do not complicate our understanding of a program and so the representation can be readily changed. This is accomplished using *data abstraction* techniques. The approach is to define a small set of procedures that create and operate on a given type of data and allow only these procedures direct access to the data. This set of procedures and the chosen data representation constitute an *abstract data type,* or *ADT*. Since access to data of an ADT is only possible through the procedures of the ADT, the rest of a program is independent of the representation chosen for the data. This property is *representation independence*. It ensures that if the representation is changed, only the procedures of the ADT are affected.

The properties of an ADT may be specified in ways that are independent of the representation, and only these properties are of concern when using the procedures of the ADT. Such specifications provide an *interface* between the ADT and the rest of the program. ADT specifications may take the form of equations relating the procedures of the type. The study of formal equational specification techniques is beyond the scope of this book, but whether the specification technique is formal or informal, the data abstraction principle on which the specification is based is of primary importance.

The record mechanism introduced in the last section is an example of data abstraction. The procedures defined by `define-record` are in effect an ADT for a new record type, however, this abstraction mechanism is flawed. There is nothing to prevent procedures other than those created by `define-record` from being applied to records in ways that expose, or even corrupt, the representation we have chosen. We have already seen one example of this: the representation is exposed when records are printed. The following transcript reveals other difficulties.

```
> (interior? tree-1)
#t
> (vector? tree-1)
#t
> (vector-ref tree-1 0)
interior
```

In some systems, types are *disjoint,* that is, each value is of one and only one type. The predicate calls in this transcript demonstrate that *tree-1* has both type *interior* and type *vector,* however, so vector and record types are not disjoint. Furthermore, the *vector-ref* call above reveals that records are represented as vectors with the record name in the first element.

If the representation of a type is hidden, so it cannot be exposed by any operation (including printing), the type is said to be *opaque*. Otherwise, it is said to be *transparent*. The *primitive* (built-in) types in Scheme are procedure, number, pair, vector, character, symbol, string, boolean, and empty list. These types are mutually disjoint and opaque. Lists are a *derived* type consisting of pairs and the empty list. No attempt at abstraction is made with the list type, since it shares the construction and selection procedures `cons`, `car`, and `cdr` with the pair type. The empty list is a *singleton* type with only one element, which is tested for with the type predicate `null?`.

We would like records to be opaque types, but there is no standard mechanism in Scheme for creating new opaque types. (The ability to define new opaque types is problematic. Opaque types are hard to debug, since you cannot see inside them.) Thus we settle for the intermediate level of abstraction provided by our record facility. As long as no procedures other than those created by `define-record` are used to create, identify, and access records, our programs will be independent of the representation chosen for records. Though we do not use a formal mechanism for defining new abstract types, we informally define a number of types in this book. Representation independence is maintained provided that only the procedures associated with the type are used to create and access elements of the type.

In section 7.1 we consider language mechanisms that encapsulate the data and operations of an ADT in an opaque object.

- *Exercise 3.5.1*
  Define the procedures of the `interior` and `leaf` record types in the last section such that records are represented as lists rather than vectors. Verify that `leaf-sum` works without modification using the new procedures. □

3.6 From Procedural to Data Structure Representations

In the last section we saw that when data abstraction is used, programs have the property of representation independence: programs are independent of the particular representation used to implement an abstract data type. It is then possible to change the representation by redefining the small number of procedures belonging to the ADT. In later chapters we shall frequently exploit representation independence. Initially we represent data as procedures. This

Syntactic Abstraction and Data Abstraction

"high-level" representation concisely conveys the intended semantics of the data type. (Another advantage of using procedures to represent a new type is that the representation is in a way opaque, since procedures are themselves usually opaque. For instance, when printing them, we can see that they are procedures, but no more.) We then convert to the record representation, which is usually more efficient and can be implemented in a straightforward manner in low-level languages (including assembly language) that do not support first-class procedures.

3.6.1 Procedural Representation

In this section we illustrate the transformation from procedural to record representation using a data type for *finite functions*. A finite function associates a value with each element of a finite set of symbols. There are many uses for finite functions. One example is an *environment*, which associates variables with their values in a programming language implementation. A *symbol table*, which among other things may associate variables with lexical address information at compile time, is another example (see exercise 12.4.12).

The simplest way of creating finite functions is to have a representation of the empty finite function, which makes no associations, and a way of adding a new symbol/value association to an existing finite function. This motivates the interface of our finite-function ADT, which consists of three procedures:

1. *create-empty-ff* is a procedure of no arguments that returns the empty finite function, which makes no associations.

2. *extend-ff* takes a symbol, *sym*, a value, *val*, and a finite function, *ff*, and returns a new finite function that preserves the associations of *ff* and also associates *sym* with *val*. Any association with *sym* that might already exist in *ff* is ignored by the new finite function.

3. *apply-ff* takes a finite function and a symbol and returns the value associated with the symbol.

In mathematics a finite function is generally represented as a set of pairs, such as $\{(d, 6), (x, 7), (y, 8)\}$, which may be constructed and accessed as follows.

```
> (define dxy-ff
    (extend-ff 'd 6
      (extend-ff 'x 7
        (extend-ff 'y 8
          (create-empty-ff)))))
> (apply-ff dxy-ff 'x)
7
```

A finite function may be represented as a Scheme procedure that takes a symbol and returns the associated value. With this representation, the finite-function interface may be defined as follows:

```
(define create-empty-ff
  (lambda ()
    (lambda (symbol)
      (error "empty-ff: no association for symbol" symbol))))

(define extend-ff
  (lambda (sym val ff)
    (lambda (symbol)
      (if (eq? symbol sym)
          val
          (apply-ff ff symbol)))))

(define apply-ff
  (lambda (ff symbol)
    (ff symbol)))
```

The empty finite function, created by invoking *create-empty-ff*, indicates with an error message that the given symbol is not in its domain. The procedure *extend-ff* returns a new procedure that represents the extended finite function. Finally, the procedure *apply-ff* simply performs procedure application.

3.6.2 Record Representation

This procedural representation is easy to understand, but it requires that procedures be first-class objects. We can systematically transform this representation into one using records by noting the information that is contained in each of the finite-function procedures. There are only two kinds of finite-function procedures: the ones returned by creating an empty finite function and those returned by *extend-ff*. The specification of what is to be done when one of these procedures is invoked is given by the bodies of their respective (lambda (symbol) ...) expressions. Since these bodies do not change, the finite functions themselves need only contain an indication of which kind of procedure they represent so that the appropriate actions may be taken when *apply-ff* is invoked. But in the (lambda (symbol) ...) lambda expression of *extend-ff*, the variables sym, val, and ff occur free. A procedure created by evaluating a lambda expression must record the values of all variables that occur free in the body of the lambda expression. The values recorded must be the bindings that are in effect *at the time the procedure is created*.

We conclude that we can capture the information that is unique to each finite-function procedure with two record types:

```
(define-record empty-ff ())
(define-record extended-ff (sym val ff))
```

We can implement the finite-function abstraction by redefining *create-empty-ff* and *extend-ff* to build the appropriate records and by redefining *apply-ff* to interpret the information in these records and perform the actions specified by the body of the appropriate (lambda (symbol) ...) expression. The definition of the finite-function ADT using this new representation follows:

```
(define create-empty-ff
  (lambda ()
    (make-empty-ff)))

(define extend-ff
  (lambda (sym val ff)
    (make-extended-ff sym val ff)))

(define apply-ff
  (lambda (ff symbol)
    (variant-case ff
      (empty-ff ()
        (error "empty-ff: no association for symbol" symbol))
      (extended-ff (sym val ff)
        (if (eq? symbol sym)
            val
            (apply-ff ff symbol)))
      (else (error "apply-ff: Invalid finite function" ff)))))
```

Observe that the consequent expressions of the variant-case expression are *exactly* the same as the bodies of the respective (lambda (symbol) ...) expressions in the procedural representation. Also, the definitions above could be replaced by these two:

```
(define create-empty-ff make-empty-ff)
(define extend-ff make-extended-ff)
```

With this representation, the last transcript might continue as follows.

```
> dxy-ff
#(extended-ff d 6 #(extended-ff x 7 #(extended-ff y 8 #(empty-ff))))
```

The importance of the technique illustrated above for transforming a procedural representation into a record representation is its generality. It may be applied to *any* set of procedures that represents an ADT, provided that these procedures are always invoked by an apply procedure that is specific to the data type. The key steps in the transformation follow:

1. Identify the lambda expressions whose evaluation yields values of the type, and create a distinct record type for each of these expressions.

2. Identify the free variables in these lambda expressions whose values are distinct for each element, and allocate a field of the corresponding record type for each of these variables.

3. Define the apply procedure for the type using a `variant-case` expression with one case per record type, where the variable list of each case lists the free variables identified in (2) and the consequent expression of each case is the body of the corresponding lambda expression.

Suppose we wish to define a procedure *extend-ff** that takes a list of symbols, *sym-list*, a list of values, *val-list*, and a finite function, *ff*, and returns a new finite function that associates each symbol of *sym-list* with the value in the corresponding position in *val-list*, as well as maintaining the associations of *ff* for symbols other than those in *sym-list*. It happens that *extend-ff** can be defined entirely in terms of existing elements of the finite-function interface.

```
(define extend-ff*
  (lambda (sym-list val-list ff)
    (if (null? sym-list)
        ff
        (extend-ff (car sym-list) (car val-list)
          (extend-ff* (cdr sym-list) (cdr val-list) ff)))))
```

Sometimes, however, new procedures on a data type can be defined only in terms of the underlying representation of the type, so the procedure must be added to the interface of the type. In other cases it may be desirable to extend the interface for reasons of efficiency. To illustrate how such situations may be handled, we employ the technique introduced above to add *extend-ff** to the finite-function interface. We always begin extensions of an ADT by returning to the original procedural representation and then repeating the transformation to other representations with whatever modifications are necessary to accommodate the new addition.

Thus we first define *extend-ff** to directly return a new procedure representing a finite function. This is simplified by making use of the procedure *ribassoc* of exercise 2.2.7.

```
(define extend-ff*
  (lambda (sym-list val-list ff)
    (lambda (symbol)
      (let ((val (ribassoc symbol
                   sym-list (list->vector val-list) '*fail*)))
        (if (eq? val '*fail*)
            (apply-ff ff symbol)
            val)))))
```

(We assume the symbol **fail** is not in the domain of the finite function.) Since the value returned by (list->vector val-list) is always the same for a given finite-function procedure, a let expression may be used to compute this vector only once and bind its value in the newly created finite-function procedure. We have

```
(define extend-ff*
  (lambda (sym-list val-list ff)
    (let ((val-vector (list->vector val-list)))
      (lambda (symbol)
        (let ((val (ribassoc symbol sym-list val-vector '*fail*)))
          (if (eq? val '*fail*)
              (apply-ff ff symbol)
              val))))))
```

The free variables in the (lambda (symbol) ...) expression above that vary from one evaluation to the next are sym-list, val-vector, and ff. This motivates two new definitions and an extension of our earlier definition of *apply-ff*.

```
(define-record extended-ff* (sym-list val-vector ff))

(define extend-ff*
  (lambda (sym-list val-list ff)
    (make-extended-ff* sym-list (list->vector val-list) ff)))
```

```
(define apply-ff
  (lambda (ff symbol)
    (variant-case ff
      (empty-ff ()
        (error "empty-ff: no association for symbol" symbol))
      (extended-ff (sym val ff)
        (if (eq? symbol sym)
            val
            (apply-ff ff symbol)))
      (extended-ff* (sym-list val-vector ff)
        (let ((val (ribassoc symbol sym-list val-vector '*fail*)))
          (if (eq? val '*fail*)
              (apply-ff ff symbol)
              val)))
      (else (error "apply-ff: Invalid finite function" ff)))))
```

```
> (define ff1 (extend-ff* '(d x y) '(6 7 8) (create-empty-ff)))
> (define ff2 (extend-ff* '(a b c) '(1 2 3) ff1))
> (apply-ff ff2 'd)
6
> ff2
#(extended-ff* (a b c) #(1 2 3)
   #(extended-ff* (d x y) (6 7 8) #(empty-ff)))
> (define ff3 (extend-ff* '(d e) '(4 5) ff2))
> (apply-ff ff3 'd)
4
> (apply-ff ff3 'a)
1
> ff3
#(extended-ff* (d e) #(4 5)
   #(extended-ff* (a b c) #(1 2 3)
      #(extended-ff* (d x y) #(6 7 8) #(empty-ff))))
```

3.6.3 Alternative Data Structure Representations

As mentioned above, the transformation from procedure to record representation is completely general, so we can always use it as a first step in deriving
data structure representations. In many cases we can exploit patterns in the

Syntactic Abstraction and Data Abstraction

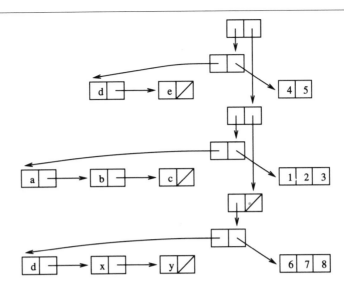

Figure 3.6.1 Ribcage environment structure

record representations to obtain further simplifications. Assume for example that `extend-ff` is no longer part of the finite-function interface.

In this case all finite functions are built by starting with the empty finite function and applying `extend-ff*` n times, for some $n \geq 0$. Thus the resulting representations are always of the form

$$\#(\texttt{extended-ff*} \; \textit{sym-list}_n \; \textit{val-vector}_n$$
$$\dots$$
$$\#(\texttt{extended-ff*} \; \textit{sym-list}_1 \; \textit{val-vector}_1$$
$$\#(\texttt{empty-ff})) \dots)$$

where $\textit{sym-list}_i$ and $\textit{val-vector}_i$ were contributed by the ith application of `extend-ff*`. The information in this record structure can be represented in other ways, which may be more convenient or efficient. One natural representation would be as a list of pairs, where the ith pair joins $\textit{sym-list}_i$ and $\textit{val-vector}_i$. The resulting general form would be

$$((\textit{sym-list}_n \;\; . \;\; \textit{val-vector}_n)$$
$$\dots$$
$$(\textit{sym-list}_1 \;\; . \;\; \textit{val-vector}_1))$$

This list may be pictured as a ribcage, where each *sym-list/val-vector* pair is a pair of ribs joined by a cons cell (see figure 3.6.1). The procedure `ribassoc` was named with this picture in mind.

- *Exercise 3.6.1*
  Define the finite-function ADT using the ribcage representation. □

- *Exercise 3.6.2*
  Write `extend-ff` in terms of `extend-ff*`. □

- *Exercise 3.6.3*
  Another way for `ribassoc` to handle its error condition is to return a *list* containing the associated value as its only element, or `#f` if there is no associated value. Thus if the associated value is `#f`, then `(#f)` is returned, and `#f ≠ (#f)`. Of course the `errvalue` argument to `ribassoc` is no longer needed. Implement `ribassoc` and `apply-ff` using this technique. □

3.7 Summary

Some important patterns of usage are not expressible as procedures. Some of these are encapsulated as syntactic abstractions. These include the local binding forms `let` and `letrec`, the logical connectives `and` and `or`, and the multi-way branching forms `cond` and `case`. The syntactic abstractions `define-record` and `variant-case` provide an interface for manipulating variant records. Abstract syntax represents the syntactic structure of an expression as a tree.

An abstract data type, or ADT, establishes an interface to a class of data. It is then possible to change the representation of this data by changing only the procedures that implement the interface. Programs that use the interface need not be modified. This is the principle of data abstraction.

Frequently it is convenient to initially represent data as procedures. Such a representation can then be transformed systematically into one based on records, in which each record contains the same dynamic information in the corresponding procedure, with the static information collected in a single procedure that interprets the records.

4 Reduction Rules and Imperative Programming

In this chapter we first introduce transformation rules for reasoning about procedures. These rules are studied, for simplicity, in the context of the lambda calculus. We next show how an evaluation mechanism for the lambda calculus may be obtained from these transformation rules and survey the main features of this mechanism.

In the second part of this chapter we introduce assignment and evaluation sequencing, along with a few facilities for input/output. A simple approach to object-oriented programming is presented as an example of the interaction between environment sharing and assignment. Finally, we use these techniques to provide several implementations of an abstract data type for streams. These are useful for representing input sequences when experimenting with programming language implementations developed in later chapters.

4.1 Reasoning about Procedures

In chapter 1 we informally introduced procedures as they are created and used in Scheme. In this section we consider procedures in a more formal light to isolate some simple rules for reasoning about programs.

To determine the result of a procedure call, we must look at the body of the procedure being called. When a reference to one of the procedure's formal parameters is encountered in the body, we can imagine the corresponding argument from the call as appearing in place of the variable. For example, given the definition

```
(define foo
  (lambda (x y)
    (+ (* x 3) y)))
```

and the procedure call

```
(foo (+ 4 1) 7)
```

we might obtain the result by evaluating (+ (* (+ 4 1) 3) 7), yielding 22.

The rule we have used here may be stated informally as follows:

> The result of a procedure call may be obtained by substituting the call's operands for the corresponding variables in the procedure's body.

As we shall see, we shall need some restrictions (to be spelled out in section 4.3.1) to make this rule an accurate description of what happens in most languages (including Scheme), but in cases where it applies, it is a valuable tool for reasoning about programs.

We can express this kind of reasoning by writing a derivation in which at each step some subexpression is replaced by an equivalent subexpression. For example, we can record the reasoning above with this derivation:

```
    (foo (+ 4 1) 7)

⇒ ((lambda (x y) (+ (* x 3) y))
    (+ 4 1)
    7)

⇒ (+ (* (+ 4 1) 3) 7)

⇒ 22
```

For brevity, we sometimes omit steps of the first kind, in which a reference to a defined procedure is replaced by the definition of the procedure.

Alternatively, we might first find the arguments of the call by evaluating the operands, and then substitute literal representations of these arguments for occurrences of the corresponding formal parameters in the body of the procedure. The following derivation applies this kind of reasoning to the same example:

```
    (foo (+ 4 1) 7)

⇒ (foo 5 7)

⇒ (+ (* 5 3) 7)

⇒ (+ 15 7)

⇒ 22
```

We obtained the final answer by replacing calls to standard procedures with literal operands by a literal representing the value of the call.

As another example, the result of the call ((c+ 5) 3) using the curried procedure

```
(define c+
  (lambda (n)
    (lambda (m)
      (+ n m))))
```

can be obtained by the following derivation:

```
((c+ 5) 3)
```

$\Rightarrow$ `((lambda (m) (+ 5 m)) 3)`

$\Rightarrow$ `(+ 5 3)`

$\Rightarrow$ `8`

We saw in the last chapter that some special forms, such as `let`, are just syntactic sugar for other forms. Sugaring rules can also be expressed as transformations. For example,

```
(let ((var₁ exp₁) ... (varₙ expₙ))
  body)
```

$\Rightarrow$ `((lambda (var₁ ... varₙ) body)`
   `exp₁ ... expₙ)`

Such rules may be used in conjunction with procedure call substitutions of the type introduced in this section to derive the value of this complex expression:

```
(let ((x 3)
      (add5 (c+ 5)))
  (add5 x))
```

$\Rightarrow$ `(let ((x 3)`
        `(add5 (lambda (m) (+ 5 m))))`
     `(add5 x))`
$\Rightarrow$ `((lambda (x add5) (add5 x))`
      `3`
      `(lambda (m) (+ 5 m)))`

```
⇒ ((lambda (m) (+ 5 m)) 3)

⇒ (+ 5 3)

⇒ 8
```

In the preceding discussion, we have used the phrase "literal representation of a value" several times. We cannot put values themselves in expressions. The examples above have used only numeric literals, so it may be difficult to see the difference. The difference becomes clear when the values include lists. We mark the literal representation of a list with `quote`.

```
(let ((second (lambda (x) (car (cdr x)))))
    (second (list 1 2 3)))

⇒ ((lambda (second) (second (list 1 2 3)))
    (lambda (x) (car (cdr x))))

⇒ ((lambda (x) (car (cdr x)))
    (list 1 2 3))

⇒ ((lambda (x) (car (cdr x)))
    '(1 2 3))

⇒ (car (cdr '(1 2 3)))

⇒ (car '(2 3))

⇒ 2
```

In this example, if we had used the list (1 2 3) itself in the expression (car (cdr (1 2 3))), we would have had an application of the number 1 to some arguments, which is not what was intended. The use of `quote` marks the occurrence of the literal representation of the list in the expression.

4.2 The Lambda Calculus and β-Conversion

In order to study these transformation rules with a minimum of distraction, we initially study it in the most abstract context possible. This is the language of the *lambda calculus*, which was introduced in section 2.3.1. This language has only variable references, `lambda` expressions with a single formal parameter, and procedure calls. It is given by the following grammar:

⟨exp⟩ ::= ⟨varref⟩
   | `(lambda (`⟨var⟩`) `⟨exp⟩`)`
   | `(`⟨exp⟩ ⟨exp⟩`)`

Constants are frequently added to the lambda calculus. They make it more convenient to express intuitive examples. We use numbers as constants.

⟨exp⟩ ::= ⟨number⟩

This does not affect the theoretical properties of the lambda calculus.

In this language, the transformation rule applies to calls of the form

$$((\text{lambda } (var) \; exp) \; rand)$$

The basic idea is that such an expression is equivalent to the expression obtained by replacing references to *var* in *exp* by *rand*. Using the notation introduced to define variable renaming in chapter 2, this replacement can be expressed concisely as *exp*[*rand*/*var*]. As with variable renaming, however, care must be taken to avoid conflicts due to different uses of the same variable name. In this case the difficulty is that free variables in *rand* may be captured by bindings of *var* in the lambda expression, or by other lambda expressions in *exp*. For example, it would be incorrect to transform

```
((lambda (x)
   (lambda (y) (x y)))
 (y w))
```

into

```
(lambda (y) ((y w) y))
```

The reference to `y` in `(y w)` should remain free, but it has been captured by the inner lambda expression. This is wrong, because the `y` in `(y w)` refers to the current value of `y` in the original expression (perhaps `c+` defined above), but in the transformed expression it refers to the value of the `y` to which the resulting procedure will be applied. Admittedly this example is contrived, but this sort of thing can easily happen in much more complicated expressions, where it might go undetected unless care is taken.

The solution is to change the name of the inner variable `y` to some name, say `z`, that does not occur free in the argument `(y w)`:

```
((lambda (x)
   (lambda (z) (x z)))
 (y w))
```

This expression is equivalent, by the α-conversion rule, to our original example. Now we can perform the substitution without capturing the reference to y, obtaining

```
(lambda (z) ((y w) z))
```

So, in order to make our procedure-application rule precise, we need to formalize the substitution process in a way that avoids variable capture.

We inductively define the substitution of M for x in E, written $E[M/x]$. The induction is based on the form of E, with separate rules for each form of expression in the lambda calculus. If E is the variable x, the result is M.

$$x[M/x] = M.$$

If E is any other variable, y, or a constant, c, the result is simply that variable or constant

$$y[M/x] = y,$$
where y is distinct from x.
$$c[M/x] = c$$

If E is an application of the form $(F\ G)$, we simply perform the substitution on F and G.
$$(F\ G)[M/x] = (F[M/x]\ G[M/x]).$$

The interesting case is when E is of the form (lambda (y) E'). If y is the same as x (the variable we are replacing), no further replacements should be done, since there are no free occurrences of x in (lambda (x) E'). The lambda creates a hole in the scope of the outer x.

$$(\text{lambda } (x)\ E')[M/x] = (\text{lambda } (x)\ E').$$

Also, no further replacement is required if x does not occur free in E'.

$$(\text{lambda } (y)\ E')[M/x] = (\text{lambda } (y)\ E'),$$
where x does not occur free in E'.

If $y \neq x$ and y does not occur free in M, then we can perform the substitution on E'.

$$\texttt{(lambda (}y\texttt{) }E'\texttt{)}[M/x] = \texttt{(lambda (}y\texttt{) }E'[M/x]\texttt{)},$$

where y does not occur free in M.

The only case left is the most interesting one: $y \neq x$, x occurs free in E', and y occurs free in M. This is the situation in which accidental capture will occur. The solution is to rename y (using α-conversion) to some other name, say z, that does not occur free in E' or M

$$\texttt{(lambda (}y\texttt{) }E'\texttt{)}[M/x] = \texttt{(lambda (}z\texttt{) }(E'[z/y])[M/x]\texttt{)},$$

where z does not occur free in E' or M.

Given this rigorous definition of substitution, the rule we have been seeking for procedure calls is simply

$$\texttt{((lambda (}x\texttt{) }E\texttt{) }M\texttt{)} = E[M/x].$$

This is called β-*conversion* (β is pronounced "beta".) An expression of the form

$$\texttt{((lambda (}x\texttt{) }E\texttt{) }M\texttt{)}$$

to which this rule may be applied is called a β-*redex*.

When the β-conversion rule is used in the left-to-right direction to transform a β-redex, it is called β-*reduction*. As we shall see, the term "reduction" is appropriate because β-reduction may be used to reduce expressions to their "simplest" form.

The β-conversion rule may also be used in the right-to-left direction. This is what is done when `let` is introduced into a program to avoid repetition of some expression. For example,

```
  ((f (a (b c))) (a (b c)))

⇒ ((lambda (x) ((f x) x))
    (a (b c)))

⇒ (let ((x (a (b c))))
      ((f x) x))
```

- *Exercise 4.2.1*

  Use β-reductions to simplify the following expressions as much as possible.

  1.   `((lambda (x) (x (y x)))`
          `z)`

  2.   `((lambda (x) (x y))`
          `(lambda (y) (x y)))`

  3.   `((lambda (x)`
           `(lambda (y) ((x y) z)))`
          `(lambda (a) y))`

  4.   `((lambda (x)`
           `(lambda (y)`
            `((lambda (x) (z x))`
             `(lambda (y) (z y)))))`
          `(lambda (y) y))`

  ☐

- *Exercise 4.2.2*

  Write a predicate `beta-redex?` that takes a parsed lambda calculus expression and indicates whether it is a β-redex. Use a parser like the one in section 3.4.3 to test `beta-redex?`.

  ```
  > (beta-redex? (parse '(lambda (x) (y z))))
  #f
  > (beta-redex? (parse '((lambda (x) (y x)) z)))
  #t
  > (beta-redex? (parse '(lambda (x) ((lambda (x) (y x)) z))))
  #f
  ```
  ☐

- *Exercise 4.2.3*

  Write a procedure `substitute`, that takes two expressions, `e` and `m`, and a variable `x`, and returns $e[m/x]$. The definition of this procedure should closely follow the inductive definition of substitution given above. When α-conversion is required, it is necessary to obtain a variable that does not occur free either in the body of the lambda expression or in the operand that is being substituted. Most systems include the procedure *gensym*, which generates a new symbol guaranteed to be distinct from all other symbols. If *gensym* is not available, see exercise 4.6.3 for a simplified one, which we call *next-symbol*.

```
> (unparse (substitute (parse '(a b)) (parse 'c) 'b))
(a c)
> (unparse (substitute (parse '(lambda (a) (a b))) (parse 'a) 'b))
(lambda (g01234) (g01234 a))
```

The symbol g01234 is typical of those produced by *gensym*. □

- *Exercise 4.2.4*
  Write a procedure `beta-reduce` that takes a parsed β-redex and returns the result of applying the β-reduction rule.

  ```
  > (unparse (beta-reduce (parse '((lambda (x) (y x)) z))))
  (y z)
  > (unparse (beta-reduce (parse '((lambda (x) (lambda (y) (x y)))
                                     (y w)))))
  (lambda (g01235) ((y w) g01235))
  ```

  What would happen if `beta-reduce` were called with

  ```
  (parse '((lambda (x) (x x)) (lambda (x) (x x))))
  ```

  and why? □

  We noted earlier in section 3.6 that

  ```
  (define extend-ff
    (lambda (sym val ff)
      (make-extended-ff sym val ff)))
  ```

was equivalent to

  ```
  (define extend-ff make-extended-ff)
  ```

Since the first version simply passes its arguments along unchanged to `make-extended-ff`, it behaves in exactly the same way as `make-extended-ff`, so it might as well be `make-extended-ff`.

This is an application of a general rule, which when simplified (so it applies only to procedures with a single operand) may be stated as

$$(\text{lambda } (x) \ (E \ x)) = E$$

where E denotes a function of one variable and x does not occur free in E.

In the lambda calculus this is known as η-*conversion* (η is pronounced "eta"), or when applied only from left to right, η-*reduction*. An expression on the left-hand side of this equation is an η-*redex* if x does not occur free in E. Though not as fundamental as β-conversion, this is at times a useful optimization.

○ *Exercise 4.2.5*

Write a predicate `eta-redex?` that takes a parsed lambda calculus expression and indicates whether it is an η-redex.

```
> (eta-redex? (parse '(lambda (x) (y x))))
#t
> (eta-redex? (parse '(lambda (x) ((lambda (y) y) x))))
#t
> (eta-redex? (parse '((lambda (x) (y x)) z)))
#f
> (eta-redex? (parse '(lambda (x) ((lambda (y) x) x))))
#f
```
☐

○ *Exercise 4.2.6*

Write a procedure `eta-reduce` that takes a parsed η-redex and returns the result of applying the η-reduction rule.

```
> (unparse (eta-reduce (parse '(lambda (x) ((lambda (y) y) x)))))
(lambda (y) y)
```
☐

○ *Exercise 4.2.7*

Write a procedure `eta-expand` that takes a parsed expression `exp` (that may be presumed to denote a function of one argument) and returns a parsed expression of the form (for some x not free in `exp`)

$$(\text{lambda } (x) \ (\text{exp } x))$$

```
> (unparse (eta-expand (parse '(lambda (y) y))))
(lambda (g01236) ((lambda (y) y) g01236))
> (unparse (eta-expand (parse '((lambda (v) (lambda (y) (v y)))
                                (lambda (x) x)))))
(lambda (g01238)
  (((lambda (v) (lambda (y) (v y)))
    (lambda (x) x))
   g01238))
```
☐

4.3 Reduction Strategies

We have seen how β-reduction can be used to model the effect of evaluating an application. We need more information, however, before we can use this model to transform expressions to their answers. The problem is that a lambda expression may have more than one redex, so there may be more than one way to reduce the expression. We saw that in the very first example in this chapter, where in

```
((lambda (x y) (+ (* x 3) y))
 (+ 4 1)
 7)
```

we could reduce either the β-redex or the (+ 4 1). In that example, we were lucky: both reduction sequences gave the same answer, 22.

This leads to an important question: *Can an expression be reduced to more than one constant?* Fortunately, no. This is not at all obvious, since an expression may have many redexes and nothing has been said about the order in which reductions are performed. There is an important theorem, however, called the *Church-Rosser theorem,* which says that if an expression E can be reduced to either $E1$ or $E2$, using different reduction sequences, then there is some expression N that can be reached from both $E1$ and $E2$. This is called the *Church-Rosser, confluence,* or *diamond* property. The latter term refers to the figure below, in which arrows represent reduction sequences.

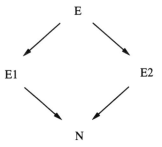

Figure 4.3.1 Diamond Property

How does this theorem answer our question? If an expression reduced to two different constants, then the Church-Rosser theorem says that there would have to be some other term N to which both constants reduced. But constants cannot be reduced! So there could not have been two different constants to which our expression is reducible.

This is helpful, but does the Church-Rosser theorem tell us that we can apply β-reduction blindly and be guaranteed to find an answer? No, because not every expression is reducible to a constant. Consider

```
((lambda (x) (x x))
 (lambda (x) (x x)))
```

This expression is a β-redex, but β-reduction results in the same expression. (Try it.)

Perhaps a weaker result holds: does the Church-Rosser theorem tell us that if an answer exists, we can find it by blindly applying β-reduction? Again, the answer is no. Some expressions reduce to a constant, but still have infinite reduction sequences in which the computation could get lost. Consider this example:

```
((lambda (y) 3)
 ((lambda (x) (x x))
  (lambda (x) (x x))))
```

The whole expression is a β-redex, which reduces immediately to 3, since y does not occur free in the body of the first lambda expression. However, the operand of this application is just the expression we used above as an example of an expression that does not reduce to a constant. Therefore a reduction sequence that repeatedly reduced the operand expression would never find the answer for the whole expression. So different strategies for reducing an expression may differ in whether or not they find an answer, but they will always agree on the constant they find.

4.3.1 Applicative-Order Reduction

We began studying the lambda calculus because we wanted to reason about procedures in Scheme. Therefore the next question is: *What reduction strategy best models the behavior of Scheme?* It is a strategy called *applicative-order reduction*. For applicative-order reduction, an *answer* is either a constant, a variable, or an abstraction (a lambda expression): anything but an application. In applicative-order reduction, β-reduction may be applied only if both the operator and operand are already answers. If they are not, then either the operator or the operand can be reduced. A redex in the body of an abstraction is never reduced, and η-reduction is never applied. This variation is sometimes called the *lambda-value calculus*.

We can now rephrase a version of the β rule to be accurate for Scheme:

$$((\texttt{lambda}\ (x)\ E)\ M) = E[M/x]$$

where M is an answer.

Let us develop a procedure *reduce-once-appl* that takes a (parsed) lambda calculus expression and reduces the first redex it finds according to applicative-order reduction, if there is such a redex, and returns the entire reduced expression. If the expression is a constant, a variable, or a lambda-expression, it cannot be reduced. If the expression is an applicative β-redex, we simply perform the reduction (using *beta-reduce* from exercise 4.2.4) and return the result. If it is an application but not a β-redex, we first try to reduce the operator. If this fails (the operator is already an answer), then we try to reduce the operand. Whenever we succeed in reducing a subexpression, we must construct a new expression that contains the reduced form of the subexpression.

Somehow we must indicate whether a call to *reduce-once-appl* succeeds in performing a reduction or fails. One way to do this would be to return a special value indicating failure, as was done with *ribassoc* in exercise 2.2.7. This is somewhat awkward, for every time *reduce-once-appl* is called, the value it returns must be recorded using let, and then this value must be tested, since the way the computation continues depends on whether a reduction was performed. Here we use another approach. We pass *reduce-once-appl* two additional arguments: a procedure *succeed* that is passed the reduced expression in the event of success, and a procedure *fail* of no arguments that is invoked if the reduction fails.

Thus the specification for *reduce-once-appl* is

(reduce-once-appl exp succeed fail) =
   (*succeed exp′*) if *exp* contains an applicative β-redex, in which case *exp′*
      is the result of performing one applicative-order reduction on *exp*, or
   (*fail*) if *exp* has no applicative β-redex.

The procedures *succeed* and *fail* are called *continuations,* because they indicate how the computation is to continue in the event of success or failure. The technique of passing one or more continuations to a procedure is of use in a number of contexts. Chapter 8 is devoted to a study of continuations, and they are used extensively in chapters 8–11. For another example, see exercise 4.3.3.

Figure 4.3.2 *reduce-once-appl* for the lambda calculus

```
(define answer?
  (lambda (exp)
    (not (app? exp))))

(define reduce-once-appl
  (lambda (exp succeed fail)
    (variant-case exp
      (lit (datum) (fail))
      (varref (var) (fail))
      (lambda (formal body) (fail))
      (app (rator rand)
        (if (and
              (beta-redex? exp)
              (answer? rator)
              (answer? rand))
            (succeed (beta-reduce exp))
            (reduce-once-appl rator
              (lambda (reduced-rator)
                (succeed (make-app reduced-rator rand)))
              (lambda ()
                (reduce-once-appl rand
                  (lambda (reduced-rand)
                    (succeed (make-app rator reduced-rand)))
                  fail)))))))))
```

Using this approach, the *reduce-once-appl* procedure may now be defined as in figure 4.3.2. Note that if reduction of an application's `rator` fails, `fail` tries to reduce the `rand`. When *reduce-once-appl* is called with the `rand` there is nothing else to try if the reduction fails, so `fail` is passed as the failure continuation. The next two exercises are easily solved by invoking *reduce-once-appl* with the appropriate success and failure continuations.

- *Exercise 4.3.1*
  Write a procedure *reduce-history* that takes an unparsed lambda calculus expression, *exp*, and a positive integer, *n*, and returns a list of unparsed expressions indicating a (perhaps incomplete) reduction history of *exp*. The last element in the list is the answer, or the result of the *n*th reduction if the answer cannot be obtained in *n* reductions. For example,

```
> (reduce-history '((lambda (x) (x ((lambda (x) y) z))) w) 5)
((w ((lambda (x) y) z))
 (w y))
> (reduce-history '((lambda (x) (x x)) (lambda (x) (x x))) 3)
(((lambda (x) (x x)) (lambda (x) (x x)))
 ((lambda (x) (x x)) (lambda (x) (x x)))
 ((lambda (x) (x x)) (lambda (x) (x x))))
```
☐

- *Exercise 4.3.2*

  Write a procedure *reduce** that takes an unparsed lambda calculus expression, *exp*, and a positive integer, *n*, and returns the answer for *exp* if it can be obtained by *n* or fewer applicative-order reductions, and #f otherwise.

  ```
  > (reduce* '((lambda (x) (x ((lambda (x) y) z))) w) 5)
  (w y)
  > (reduce* '((lambda (x) (x x)) (lambda (x) (x x))) 100)
  #f
  ```
  ☐

- *Exercise 4.3.3*

  Write *ribassoc* using success and failure continuations and use it to rewrite *apply-ff* with the ribcage representation. ☐

- *Exercise 4.3.4*

  Modify *reduce-once-appl* so it can deal with standard procedures like +. ☐

4.3.2 Leftmost Reduction

Applicative-order reduction is a good model of Scheme's behavior on procedures, but we have seen that it may fail to find an answer, even if one exists. For example, applicative order fails on

```
((lambda (y) 3)
 ((lambda (x) (x x)) (lambda (x) (x x))))
```

because it will be caught in an infinite loop trying to reduce the operand to an answer. The next question is: *Is there a reduction strategy which is guaranteed to find the answer if it exists?* Yes, it is called *leftmost* reduction, and it is the strategy of reducing the β-redex whose left parenthesis comes first.

In fact, leftmost reduction does better than just finding constants. Let us say that a lambda expression is in *normal form* if it contains no β-redexes. If an expression is in normal form, then no further reduction is possible. For example, (lambda (x) x) is in normal form, but is not a constant. By the same argument we used above, the Church-Rosser theorem leads us to the conclusion that an expression can have at most one normal form. It can be shown that leftmost reduction will always find the normal form of an expression, if one exists. For this reason, leftmost reduction is sometimes called *normal order* reduction.

Leftmost reduction obtains this generality, however, at the expense of efficiency. For example, consider the following leftmost reduction sequence, in which the operand ((lambda (w) w) z) is reduced twice:

```
    ((lambda (x) (x (x y)))
     ((lambda (w) w) z))

 ⇒ (((lambda (w) w) z)
     (((lambda (w) w) z)
      y))

 ⇒ (z (((lambda (w) w) z) y))

 ⇒ (z (z y))
```

If the operand ((lambda (w) w) z) is reduced before calling the procedure (lambda (x) (x (x y))), one less reduction is required to obtain the normal form.

```
    ((lambda (x) (x (x y)))
     ((lambda (w) w) z))

 ⇒ ((lambda (x) (x (x y)))
     z)

 ⇒ (z (z y))
```

In general, applicative-order reduction is more efficient than leftmost reduction. Therefore, most modern programming languages use some variation on applicative-order reduction. There are a few languages that use leftmost reduction to guarantee that a normal form will be found whenever one exists. Compilers for these languages typically do an extensive analysis (called strictness analysis) to find those places where it is safe to use applicative-order reduction. (See section 6.5 for related strategies.)

We can easily modify the procedure of figure 4.3.2 to do leftmost reduction. If the expression is a variable or a constant, it cannot be reduced. If the expression is a `lambda` expression, then the leftmost redex, if it exists, must be in the expression's body, so we can call the reduction procedure recursively to perform the reduction. If the expression is a β-redex, we simply perform the reduction (using `beta-reduce` from exercise 4.2.4) and return the result. If it is an application but not a β-redex, we first try to reduce the leftmost redex in the operator. If this fails, then we try to reduce the operand. Whenever we succeed in reducing a subexpression, we must construct a new expression that contains the reduced form of the subexpression.

- *Exercise 4.3.5*
  Modify `reduce-once-appl` to obtain a procedure `reduce-once-leftmost` that implements one step of leftmost reduction. □

○ *Exercise 4.3.6*
  Modify `reduce-once-leftmost` to use η-reduction as well as β-reduction. □

4.4 Defining Recursive Procedures in the Lambda Calculus

We conclude our discussion of the lambda calculus by considering the problem of expressing recursive procedures. The lambda-calculus, unlike Scheme, does not have a `letrec` or `define` mechanism. So how are we to define a recursive procedure in the lambda calculus?

Assume *exp* is a lambda expression defining a recursive procedure, where recursion is performed by reference to a variable, say *g*, that occurs free in *exp*. That is, *g* is supposed to be a name for the same procedure as *exp*. The variable *g* must itself be introduced by a lambda expression, such as

$$\text{(lambda (g) } exp)$$

For example, to define a procedure that computes the factorial function, we might write something like

```
(lambda (g)
  (lambda (n)
    (if (zero? n) 1 (* n (g (- n 1)))))))
```

where we are assuming the lambda calculus is extended with `if`, *zero?*, `*`, `-` and `1`, and where *g* is intended to be bound to the factorial function. Call this expression *f*. How can it be turned into the recursive factorial function?

We need to write a procedure, called Y, such that (`Y` `f`) is the desired recursive procedure. The assumption that recursion may be obtained by reference to *g* may be satisfied by binding *g* to (`Y` `f`) with the application (`f` (`Y` `f`)). But since *f* also returns the recursive procedure, we conclude that Y should satisfy this equation:

$$(\text{Y } f) \ = \ (f \ (\text{Y } f))$$

Can Y be written as a lambda expression, or must it be added to the lambda calculus as a special feature? Remarkably, Y can be defined as

```
(lambda (f)
  ((lambda (x) (f (x x)))
   (lambda (x) (f (x x)))))
```

This is called the *Y combinator,* since it has no free variables. Notice that the Y combinator has no normal form.

- *Exercise 4.4.1*
Verify, by β-conversion, that the Y combinator satisfies the equation (`Y` `f`) = (`f` (`Y` `f`)). ☐

This version of Y does not work when applicative order reduction is used. Reduction of the subexpression (`x` `x`) results in divergence. This may be prevented by η-expanding the (`x` `x`) subexpressions to obtain the *applicative order Y combinator*.

```
(lambda (f)
  ((lambda (x) (f (lambda (y) ((x x) y))))
   (lambda (x) (f (lambda (y) ((x x) y))))))
```

This also demonstrates that η-conversion can affect termination under applicative order reduction. In the most common cases in which it is used, however, where the simpler form is merely a variable reference, termination is not a problem.

- *Exercise 4.4.2*
Use the applicative order Y combinator to define the factorial function in Scheme. ☐

Reduction Rules and Imperative Programming

Here we have considered the definition of only a single recursive procedure. Mutual recursion is also possible using the Y combinator, but it presents added technical difficulties. The general approach is to pass Y a procedure that represents a record structure containing all the mutually recursive procedures, which refer to each other by selecting the appropriate fields of the record. (All manner of data structures can be represented as lambda expressions using appropriate tricks.)

○ *Exercise 4.4.3*
Implement mutual recursion using the Y combinator and test it using `even?` and `odd?` of section 3.1.2. ▢

We are able to touch on only the highlights of the lambda calculus. Though the syntax and evaluation rules of the lambda calculus are very simple, the calculus provides an extraordinarily rich framework for the study of programming languages (as well as issues in mathematical logic, for which it was invented). For example, it is possible to translate numbers and other data objects into lambda calculus expressions and implement customary operators such as addition in terms of other expressions in the lambda calculus. In fact, *any* algorithm can be translated into the lambda calculus. Of particular interest to the study of programming languages, many programming language features, and sometimes entire languages, are conveniently defined by specifying methods for translating them into the lambda calculus. The simplicity of the lambda calculus then makes it easier to prove theoretical results. Fascinated readers are urged to explore the references suggested at the end of the book.

4.5 Sequencing and Imperative Programming

The subset of Scheme introduced so far is purely *functional*—every expression is evaluated just for its value. No other effects of evaluation need be considered. We have seen that many problems can be solved in a straightforward manner using only functional programming. This is especially true when procedures are first class. We have also seen that we can reason about functional programs using simple, yet powerful, rules.

Yet in some situations the purely functional style is awkward or inefficient. Therefore most programming languages, including Scheme, support *imperative* operations that are performed not to obtain a value but rather for some *side effect* on the computation. These may be broadly characterized as assignment and input/output operations. When operations perform side effects, the order of their evaluation is critical. This introduces the need for *sequencing* mechanisms.

Though imperative programming sometimes allows problems to be solved in a more efficient and straightforward way than is possible using functional programming, imperative programs are often more complicated and more difficult to reason about than equivalent functional programs. In particular, the β-conversion and η-conversion rules presented in the last section are *not* applicable when imperative operations are involved. For example, consider a case in which an operand is not fully reduced before multiple copies of it are made in a β-reduction step. If further reduction of these copies involves side effects, they will occur multiple times—once for each copy. On the other hand, with applicative order reduction the side effects would occur only once. But the result of a computation should be the same regardless of the reduction order (providing the reduction sequence terminates).

In this section we introduce those imperative operations and sequencing mechanisms that will be required later. A few applications of these operations are introduced by way of example. Special attention is given to one application: the development of several implementations of a *stream* ADT. Streams provide a convenient way of connecting and interacting with the program analysis and evaluation procedures developed in chapter 5. We do not attempt a careful study of when the functional or imperative styles of programming are most appropriate. For this, the interested reader is urged to consult the suggested readings mentioned at the end of this book.

4.5.1 Sequencing

Sequencing refers to the order in which side effects are performed. In statement-oriented languages, sequencing is indicated simply by the ordering of statements. In an expression-oriented language, sequencing is required only for expressions that result in side effects. For these, Scheme provides this special form:

$$(\texttt{begin } exp_1 \ exp_2 \ \ldots \ exp_n)$$

The expressions $exp_1, exp_2, \ldots, exp_n$ are evaluated in order, and the value of exp_n is the value of the entire $\texttt{begin}$ expression. The values of the other expressions are discarded. (We shall sometimes informally use the term *statement* when referring to expressions that are evaluated entirely for their side effects. With this usage, $exp_1, exp_2, \ldots, exp_{n-1}$ are statements.)

For our examples, we use two output procedures: *display*, which prints its argument (omitting the quotes when printing strings), and *newline*, which has no arguments and simply forces further output to begin on a new line. As with most standard procedures that produce side effects, the values returned by these procedures are not specified. Implementations may return anything, so programs should never rely on the value returned.

The following example illustrates the use of begin and some peculiarities of output programming.

```
> (begin (display "Two plus two = ") (display (+ 2 2)))
Two plus two = 44
>
```

Where did the extra 4 come from? It is the unspecified value that happened to be returned by the second call to *display*, which was printed as the value of the begin expression by the read-eval-print loop. It is on the same line as the displayed output because we forgot to print a newline at the end of the line. A different value might be returned by *display* in another system or even in the same system at another time.

```
> (begin (display "Two plus two = ") (display (+ 2 2)) (newline))
Two plus two = 4
()
>
```

Here the empty list was returned by *newline*. Henceforth when top-level expressions return unspecified values, our transcripts will not display the value.

Recall that *map* generally takes a procedure, *proc*, and a list, *lst*, and returns a new list with values obtained by applying *proc* to each element of *lst*. Though the order of elements in the new list is determined, the order in which *proc* is invoked on elements of *lst* is not specified. (For example, the new list might be built from left to right or right to left or any other sequential order) A related procedure, *for-each*, is useful for procedures that perform side effects. It takes the same arguments as *map*, but it always invokes *proc* on elements of *lst* in left-to-right order. It is not specified what *for-each* returns. It could be defined by

```
(define for-each
  (lambda (proc lst)
    (if (null? lst)
        'done
        (begin
          (proc (car lst))
          (for-each proc (cdr lst))))))
```

The procedure *for-each* may be used to define a procedure that displays its arguments in order, followed by a newline.

```
> (define displayln
    (lambda lst
      (begin
        (for-each display lst)
        (newline))))
> (displayln 2 "+" 2 "=" (+ 2 2))
2+2=4
>
```

Sequences of expressions may also appear in several places other than `begin` expressions, including the bodies of `lambda`, `let`, and `letrec` expressions and the consequents of `cond`, `case`, and `variant-case` expressions. All of these are treated as if the sequence of expressions were contained in a `begin` expression. For example,

```
(lambda lst
  (begin
    (for-each display lst)
    (newline)))
```

may be simplified to

```
(lambda lst
  (for-each display lst)
  (newline))
```

and

```
(case skip-amount
  ((1 one) (newline))
  ((2 two) (begin (newline) (newline)))
  (else (begin (newline) (newline) (newline))))
```

is equivalent to

```
(case skip-amount
  ((1 one) (newline))
  ((2 two) (newline) (newline))
  (else (newline) (newline) (newline)))
```

Reduction Rules and Imperative Programming

One advantage of *implicit* `begin` is that it becomes easier to add output statements to expressions for debugging purposes.

```
> (define fact
    (lambda (n)
      (displayln "Entering fact with n = " n)
      (let ((ans (if (zero? n)
                     1
                     (* n (fact (- n 1))))))
        (displayln "Returning from fact with " ans)
        ans)))
> (fact 3)
Entering fact with n = 3
Entering fact with n = 2
Entering fact with n = 1
Entering fact with n = 0
Returning from fact with 1
Returning from fact with 1
Returning from fact with 2
Returning from fact with 6
6
```

Most Scheme implementations have a debugging facility that provides this sort of procedure tracing. Even in such systems, however, debugging statements are often useful for other purposes.

4.5.2 More Input-Output

We have seen that sequencing becomes important when input and output are considered. The output procedures *display* and *newline* have already been introduced. We shall also use the output procedure *write*. It is similar to *display*, but it prints objects in their standard literal representation. Thus *write* prints strings with quotation marks and characters with the #\ prefix.

```
> (begin
    (write "written string")
    (display " displayed string ")
    (write #\x)
    (display #\space)
    (display #\x)
    (display #\newline))
"written string" displayed string #\x x
>
```

Input may be done either a character at a time, using *read-char*, or an entire datum at a time, using *read*. Both of these standard procedures take no arguments and return the character or other value read. If an end of file condition is encountered when either input procedure is called, an object is returned for which the standard predicate *eof-object?* returns #t. It returns #f for any value that can be read by *read* or *read-char*. An error is signaled if an end of file is encountered while *read* has read an incomplete datum.

By default, input is typically from the keyboard or terminal and output is typically to the screen or terminal. The standard input and output procedures may optionally take a port argument to allow input and output to files.

Most Scheme implementations provide the procedure *eval*. It takes a value, whose printed representation should be a Scheme expression, and returns the value of this expression. This procedure has a long tradition, dating from early versions of Lisp, and has been much overused. Implementing a read-eval-print loop is one application for which it is appropriate.

```
> (define read-eval-print
    (lambda ()
      (display "--> ")
      (write (eval (read)))
      (newline)
      (read-eval-print)))
> (read-eval-print)
--> (+ 1 2)
3
--> (car (cons "foo" 'foo))
"foo"
--> (cdr 3)
Error: Invalid argument to cdr: 3
>
```

The use of *write* rather than *display* allows us to distinguish between the values of "foo" and 'foo. For variety, we used a different prompt, -->. Errors typically cause all user procedures to be aborted, with control returning to the system read-eval-print loop. By using alternative *eval* procedures, read-eval-print loops for other languages may easily be obtained. These are convenient when testing language evaluation procedures, such as those developed in later chapters.

○ *Exercise 4.5.1*
Write a read-eval-print loop for the lambda calculus using *reduce** of exercise 4.3.2 instead of *eval*. ▢

4.5.3 Data Structure Mutation

Another kind of side-effect that requires the use of sequencing is data structure *mutation*. For example, the car and cdr fields of pairs and the elements of vectors are locations whose contents may be changed.

Mutation of pairs is performed by the standard procedures *set-car!* and *set-cdr!*, respectively. Each takes two arguments, the pair to be mutated and the new value to be assigned. As with all assignments, the value returned is not specified.

```
> (define lst (list 1 2))
> (set-car! lst 3)
> lst
(3 2)
> (set-cdr! lst (list 4 5))
> lst
(3 4 5)
> (set-cdr! lst 6)
> lst
(3 . 6)
```

Using *set-cdr!* it is possible to define the procedure *reverse!*, which reverses a list "in place" by destroying the original list. The first pair of the original list becomes the last pair of the new list, and the last pair of the original list is returned as the first pair of the new list.

```
> (define reverse!
    (letrec ((loop
               (lambda (last ls)
                 (let ((next (cdr ls)))
                   (set-cdr! ls last)
                   (if (null? next)
                       ls
                       (loop ls next))))))
      (lambda (ls)
        (if (null? ls)
            ls
            (loop '() ls)))))
> (define ls (list 1 2 3))
> (reverse! ls)
(3 2 1)
> ls
(1)
```

After (`reverse!` `a`) below, what value is printed for a, b, c, x, y, and z?

```
> (define c (cons 3 '()))
> (define b (cons 2 c))
> (define a (cons 1 b))
> (define x (cons 4 a))
> (define y (cons 5 b))
> (define z (cons 6 c))
> (reverse! a)
```

☐

Mutation of vectors is accomplished with the standard procedure *vector-set!*, which takes a vector, a valid index for that vector, and an arbitrary value, and assigns the given value to the location of the indicated element of the vector.

```
> (define v (vector 1 2 3))
> (vector-set! v 1 4)
> v
#(1 4 3)
```

Data elements that may be changed are said to be *mutable,* as are data objects that contain mutable elements. Pairs created by *cons* and *list*, vectors created by *make-cell* (see exercise 4.5.5) and *vector*, and strings created by *string* are mutable, but symbols and numbers are *immutable.* Pairs and vectors that result from evaluating `quote` expressions may be immutable, so an attempt to mutate them is an error.

o *Exercise 4.5.3*

Consider the following:

```
> (define p (cons 1 '()))
> (begin (set-cdr! p p) 'done)
done
```

Describe *p* after its mutation. Why did we avoid returning the result of the *set-cdr!* expression to the read-eval-print loop? Hint: In some systems *set-cdr!* returns the mutated pair. ☐

Figure 4.5.1   Cell ADT

```
(define cell-tag "cell")

(define make-cell
  (lambda (x)
    (vector cell-tag x)))

(define cell?
  (lambda (x)
    (and (vector? x)
         (= (vector-length x) 2)
         (eq? (vector-ref x 0) cell-tag))))

(define cell-ref
  (lambda (x)
    (if (cell? x)
        (vector-ref x 1)
        (error "Invalid argument to cell-ref:" x))))

(define cell-set!
  (lambda (x value)
    (if (cell? x)
        (vector-set! x 1 value)
        (error "Illegal argument to cell-set!:" x))))

(define cell-swap!
  (lambda (cell-1 cell-2)
    (let ((temp (cell-ref cell-1)))
      (cell-set! cell-1 (cell-ref cell-2))
      (cell-set! cell-2 temp))))
```

○ *Exercise 4.5.4*

Implement the procedures of figure 4.5.1 using cons cells instead of vectors. □

○ *Exercise 4.5.5*

Using the definitions of figure 4.5.1, fill in the following transcript:

```
> (define c (make-cell 3))
> c

> (define c1 (make-cell 100))
> (cell-set! c 8)
> (cell-ref c)

> (cell-swap! c c1)
> (cell-ref c)
```

□

4.6 Variable Assignment and Sharing

So far, we have thought of variables as being bound directly to values. To introduce variable assignment, we instead think of variables as being bound to *locations*. Variable references now refer to the values contained in these locations. Variable assignment is performed with the special form

$$(\text{set!} \ var \ exp)$$

which evaluates expression *exp*, places its value in the location that is the binding of variable *var*, and returns an unspecified value. In Scheme, operations that involve assignment generally have names that end with an exclamation mark, read "bang." The bang signals danger, since it is hard to reason about programs that use assignments. A few examples follow.

```
> (define x 1)
> (set! x 2)
> x
2
> (let ((y 3))
    (set! y 4)
    (+ y 1))
5
```

If a global binding for a variable does not exist, one must be created using
`define` before assigning to it using `set!`. The first meaningful value for a
binding may be an assignment that is not at top level. In such cases we
initially bind the variable to some arbitrary value. For example,

```
> (define a '*)
> (let ((b 'not-three))
    (displayln "b is " b)
    (set! a 3)
    (if (= a 3) (set! b 'three))
    b)
b is not-three
three
> a
3
```

Variables appearing on the left-hand side of assignment statements (*var* in
the above syntax for `set!`) denote locations, not the values of locations. The
denoted values in Scheme, which are locations, are distinct from the expressed
values, which can never be locations.

In order to understand the effect of `set!`, we must understand how bindings
are shared. For example, the following implements a simple stack.

```
> (define push! '*)
> (define pop! '*)
> (define top '*)
> (let ((stk '()))
    (set! empty?
      (lambda ()
        (null? stk)))
    (set! push!
      (lambda (x)
        (set! stk (cons x stk))))
    (set! pop!
      (lambda ()
        (if (empty?)
            (error "Stack empty")
            (set! stk (cdr stk)))))
    (set! top
      (lambda ()
        (if (empty?)
            (error "Stack empty")
            (car stk)))))
```

```
> (push! 1)
> (push! 2)
> (top)
2
> (pop!)
> (top)
1
> (pop!)
```

The procedures *empty?*, *push!*, *pop!*, and *top* share the same *stk* binding.
Because this binding is not accessible elsewhere, the stack is a data abstraction. For instance, the definitions could be changed to represent the stack as
a vector rather than as a list. The limited scope of the *stk* binding prevents
this change from being detected elsewhere. Actually, this abstraction is flawed
because the value returned by the set! operation in *push!* is unspecified and
might be the stack itself. The *stk* binding itself would still be secure, but
the nature of its value would be exposed and could even be modified using
the mutation operations introduced in section 4.5.3. This flaw could be fixed
by modifying *push!* to return some meaningless value or perhaps the value
pushed.

A related use of set! is to modify a binding that is local to a single procedure. For example, consider an implementation of a stack as a procedure that
takes a symbolic argument, where the argument is interpreted as a message
requesting some service based on its local binding. Using this technique, the
stack example becomes the program of figure 4.6.1. The transcript shows an
interactive session with *stack*.

```
> ((stack 'push!) 1)
> ((stack 'push!) 2)
> ((stack 'top))
2
> ((stack 'pop!))
> ((stack 'top))
1
> ((stack 'pop!))
```

Note that the let, which introduces the *stk* binding, contains the lambda
expression that evaluates to the stack procedure. If the let expression were
inside this lambda expression, a new stack would be created each time the
procedure was invoked, which would be inconsistent with our intentions.

Only one stack is provided above. We can easily define a procedure for
generating many stacks as in figure 4.6.2. A transcript follows.

Figure 4.6.1 A simple stack

```
(define stack
  (let ((stk '()))
    (lambda (message)
      (case message
        ((empty?) (lambda ()
                    (null? stk)))
        ((push!) (lambda (x)
                    (set! stk (cons x stk))))
        ((pop!) (lambda ()
                  (if (null? stk)
                      (error "Stack empty")
                      (set! stk (cdr stk)))))
        ((top) (lambda ()
                  (if (null? stk)
                      (error "Stack empty")
                      (car stk))))
        (else (error "stack: Invalid message" message))))))
```

```
> (define s1 (make-stack))
> (define s2 (make-stack))
> ((s1 'push!) 1)
> ((s2 'push!) 2)
> ((s1 'top))
1
> ((s2 'top))
2
```

Each time `make-stack` is invoked, a new stack procedure, with its own `stk` binding, is returned. Thus, `make-stack` implements an abstract data type, with the push!, pop!, and top messages corresponding to the operations of the ADT.

If a procedure has bindings that have been modified by assignment or whose values have been mutated, it is said to have *state*. When message passing is used to access this state, these procedures are often called *objects*. We have sketched here one approach to a style of programming in which many or all values used in a computation may be objects. When this is combined with the concept of *inheritance,* the resulting style is known as as *object-oriented programming,* In section 7.2 we discuss inheritance and develop a non-procedural representation for objects.

Figure 4.6.2 A simple stack maker

```
(define make-stack
  (lambda ()
    (let ((stk '()))
      (lambda (message)
        (case message
          ((empty?) (lambda ()
                      (null? stk)))
          ((push!) (lambda (x)
                     (set! stk (cons x stk))))
          ((pop!) (lambda ()
                    (if (null? stk)
                        (error "Stack empty")
                        (set! stk (cdr stk)))))
          ((top) (lambda ()
                   (if (null? stk)
                       (error "Stack empty")
                       (car stk))))
          (else (error "stack: Invalid message" message)))))))
```

○ *Exercise 4.6.1*

Modify `make-stack` to take a positive integer `n`, indicating the maximum size of the stack, and return an object that represents the stack as a vector of length `n`. □

○ *Exercise 4.6.2*

Implement the finite function ADT of section 3.6 with a procedure `make-ff` that returns a new object that responds to the messages `empty?`, `extend`, and `apply`. New procedures must be returned in response to the `extend` and `apply` messages to receive additional arguments. □

● *Exercise 4.6.3*

Below is a definition of `next-symbol`. When invoked, it generates the next symbol in the sequence g1, g2, etc.

```
(define next-symbol
  (let ((c 0))
    (lambda ()
      (set! c (+ c 1))
      (string->symbol (string-append "g" (number->string c))))))
```

What is displayed in the following transcript, and why?

```
> (eq? (next-symbol) 'g1)

> (eq? (next-symbol) 'g1)

> (eq? (next-symbol) (next-symbol))
```

☐

Variable assignment makes it possible to implement `letrec` via the following syntactic transformation.

$$(\texttt{letrec} \ ((var_1 \ exp_1) \ \ldots \ (var_n \ exp_n))$$
$$\qquad body)$$

$$\Rightarrow \ (\texttt{let} \ ((var_1 \ \texttt{'*}) \ \ldots \ (var_n \ \texttt{'*}))$$
$$\qquad (\texttt{set!} \ var_1 \ exp_1)$$
$$\qquad \ldots$$
$$\qquad (\texttt{set!} \ var_n \ exp_n)$$
$$\qquad body)$$

The `let` expression first introduces variable bindings that initially contain some irrelevant value. The expressions $exp_1, \ldots, exp_n$ are then evaluated in the scope of these bindings, and their values assigned to the bindings. Finally, *body* is evaluated in the scope of the bindings. This implementation fixes a specific order for the evaluation of $exp_1, \ldots, exp_n$, though in general this order is unspecified. In section 5.6 we present another version of `letrec` that solves the order of evaluation problem. In some implementations, `letrec` may be implemented directly (not as a syntactic transformation) using techniques similar to those introduced later.

4.7 Streams

A *stream* is a possibly infinite sequence of values that allows access, if need be, to initial values while later ones are still being generated. For example, the characters typed in an interactive session may be represented as a stream. The number of characters is potentially infinite (no bound can be given on the length of a session), and it is often necessary to process initial input while later characters have yet to be typed.

We present several implementations of an ADT for streams that may be used with programs developed in later chapters. The stream interface consists of the following procedures:

1. *stream-car* takes a nonempty stream and returns the first element in the stream.

2. *stream-cdr* takes a nonempty stream and returns a stream that contains the same values as the given stream, in the same order, less the first value.

3. *make-stream* takes a value, v, and a procedure of no arguments, p, and returns a new stream s such that (stream-car s) is v and (stream-cdr s) is the stream obtained by invoking p.

4. *the-null-stream* is the empty stream.

5. *stream-null?* is the predicate for recognizing empty streams.

The key difference between the stream interface and the list interface is that the second argument to *make-stream* is not the rest of the stream but rather a procedure of no arguments that returns the rest of the stream. This delays the formation of the rest of the stream until it is required by *stream-cdr*. Procedures of no arguments that are used in this way to delay evaluation are called *thunks*.

The following is a version of *for-each* for streams.

```
(define stream-for-each
  (lambda (proc stream)
    (letrec ((loop (lambda (stream)
                     (if (not (stream-null? stream))
                         (begin
                           (proc (stream-car stream))
                           (loop (stream-cdr stream)))))))
      (loop stream))))
```

A simple use of *stream-for-each* follows.

```
(define display-stream
  (lambda (stream)
    (stream-for-each display stream)
    (newline)))
```

The next procedure takes a string and returns a stream containing its characters.

Reduction Rules and Imperative Programming

```
(define string->stream
  (lambda (string)
    (let ((string-len (string-length string)))
      (letrec
        ((loop (lambda (cursor)
                 (if (= cursor string-len)
                     the-null-stream
                     (make-stream
                       (string-ref string cursor)
                       (lambda ()
                         (loop (+ cursor 1)))))))))
        (loop 0)))))
```

For finite streams, we can define a procedure *stream->list* that takes a stream and returns the corresponding list.

```
(define stream->list
  (lambda (stream)
    (if (stream-null? stream)
        '()
        (cons (stream-car stream)
          (stream->list (stream-cdr stream))))))
```

Another useful procedure is *stream-filter*, which takes a predicate *pred* and a stream *stream*, and produces a stream consisting of those values from *stream* that satisfy *pred*. Using it, we can easily produce a stream of even positive integers from a stream of positive integers.

```
(define stream-filter
  (lambda (pred stream)
    (cond
      ((stream-null? stream) the-null-stream)
      ((pred (stream-car stream))
       (make-stream (stream-car stream)
         (lambda ()
           (stream-filter pred (stream-cdr stream)))))
      (else (stream-filter pred (stream-cdr stream))))))

(define even-positive-integers
  (stream-filter even? positive-integers))
```

Another useful procedure returns a (possibly infinite) stream of characters read from the terminal.

```
(define make-input-stream
  (lambda ()
    (let ((char (read-char)))
      (if (eof-object? char)
          the-null-stream
          (make-stream char make-input-stream)))))
```

This may be used to construct a read-print loop.

```
(define read-print
  (lambda ()
    (display "--> ")
    (display-stream (make-input-stream))
    (read-print)))
```

In the following *read-print* transcript, <eof> indicates entry of an end-of-file.

```
> (read-print)
--> A line of input<eof>
a line of input
--> This input is
three lines
long.<eof>
This input is
three lines
long.
-->
```

In chapter 5 and appendix F we present several approaches to read-eval-print loops.

○ *Exercise 4.7.1*
Your Scheme system may not allow an end-of-file to be generated from the keyboard, or you may prefer a different input terminator, such as two carriage returns in a row. Modify *make-input-stream* to use another input terminator and test it with *read-print*. □

Because streams and lists are so similar, an obvious implementation strategy is to represent a stream as the list of its elements. This only works for finite streams.

```
(define stream-car car)

(define stream-cdr cdr)

(define make-stream
  (lambda (value thunk)
    (cons value (thunk))))

(define the-null-stream '())

(define stream-null?
  (lambda (stream)
    (eq? stream the-null-stream)))
```

If we do not know whether the stream is finite or infinite, then we cannot represent the stream as a list. In this case, the stream can be represented as a pair with the car containing the first element and the cdr containing a thunk that returns the rest of the stream. Unlike the case of a list or pair, in which the car and cdr are both computed before the pair is built, this representation defers computation of the rest of the stream until *stream-cdr* is invoked. The thunk is a finite representation of the possibly infinite stream. Streams based on thunks may be obtained by changing the definitions of *stream-cdr*, *make-stream*, and *the-null-stream* above to

```
(define stream-cdr
  (lambda (stream)
    ((cdr stream))))

(define make-stream
  (lambda (value thunk)
    (cons value thunk)))

(define the-null-stream
  (make-stream "end-of-stream" (lambda () the-null-stream)))
```

Streams of this kind are sometimes called *lazy lists*. They are lazy because they delay generating their cdr as long as possible.

This definition works when the rest of the same stream is never taken twice. If evaluation of the thunk involves a side-effect, however, then taking *stream-cdr* of a stream twice will perform the side-effect twice. This is unpleasant, especially if the side-effect is an input/output operation.

We can solve this problem by using mutation to build streams. When asked for the rest of a stream, we check if the cdr contains a procedure. If so, we invoke the procedure (a thunk) and then install the value returned in the cdr of the stream. Henceforth if we are asked for the rest of the same stream, we notice that the cdr contains a pair, not a procedure, and we simply return the pair. (The procedure `make-stream` is unchanged.)

```
(define stream-cdr
  (lambda (stream)
    (if (pair? (cdr stream))
        (cdr stream)
        (let ((s ((cdr stream))))
          (set-cdr! stream s)
          s)))))
```

This illustrates a general technique that is an important use of assignment. The first time a value is computed, it is recorded using some form of assignment. If it is required again, it can then be returned without recomputation. This is known as *memoizing* or *caching*. In general usage, the term *stream* often refers to streams in which the `stream-cdr` operation is memoized. Variations are possible in the implementation technique. For example, rather than testing the type of the cdr field, the stream data structure may include a boolean flag indicating whether a suspension is present.

○ *Exercise 4.7.2*
Sometimes it may not be possible or desirable to generate the head of a stream before the stream is created. In that situation the stream mechanism presented here cannot be used. This problem may be overcome by memoizing the car, as well as the cdr, of the stream. Implement two versions of such *fully lazy* streams, one that memoizes `stream-car`, and one that does not. Your implementations may memoize `stream-cdr` or not, as you choose. □

4.8 Summary

The β-conversion rule of the lambda calculus is a powerful rule for reasoning about functional programs. By repeatedly applying this rewrite rule in one direction only, expressions in the lambda calculus may be reduced to answers. The Church-Rosser theorem implies that each expression may be reduced to at most one constant. The order in which the reductions are performed may affect the termination of the reduction process, but not the answer obtained if the process terminates. Leftmost reduction terminates whenever possible, while applicative order reduction is usually more efficient and is used in most programming languages. Recursive procedures may be defined directly in the lambda calculus.

Imperative programming techniques, which involve side effects, are sometimes useful. If they are used, however, it becomes more difficult to reason about programs. Sequencing mechanisms control the order in which side effects are performed. Data structure mutation involves assignment to locations in data. Variable assignment involves mutation of locations that are bindings of variables. Assignment in combination with lexical scope gives a simple model of object-oriented programming.

Streams allow potentially infinite sequences of data to be represented. Infinite streams must be lazy, that is, they must be generated on demand. Procedures of no arguments, called thunks, may be used to construct lazy streams. Memoization uses assignment to store results so they need not be recomputed.

5   Interpreters

We now have the necessary background to study the semantics of programming languages via *interpreters*. These are procedures that take the abstract syntax tree of a program and perform the indicated computation.

An interpreter is a program that looks at a data structure and performs some actions that depend on its structure. We have already developed several such data- or table-driven procedures. These include the parser and unparser of section 3.4.3 and `apply-` procedures that interpret data structures derived from procedures in section 3.6, as well as the lambda calculus reducer of section 4.3.1. Each of these procedures took data in the form of variant records and performed some action determined by the type of record.

The interpreters developed in this chapter reveal the semantics of a language with sufficient clarity that they are often suitable for specifying the semantics of programming languages. Indeed, they will be our major tool for understanding the semantics of the programming language features we wish to study.

5.1   A Simple Interpreter

In this section we develop a simple interpreter. It reflects the fundamental semantics of many modern programming languages and is the basis for most of the material in the rest of this book. We build this interpreter in stages, starting with the simplest forms: literals, variables, and applications. Then we add other forms one at a time.

An important part of the specification of any programming language is the set of values that the language manipulates. In chapter 1, we introduced two sets of values that are associated with a programming language: the *expressed values* and the *denoted values*. The expressed values are the possible values of expressions, and the denoted values are the values bound to variables. In Scheme, for example, there are many kinds of expressed values, such as numbers, pairs, characters, and strings, but there is only one kind of denoted value: cells containing expressed values.

For simplicity, our language has only two types of expressed values: integers and procedures. For the moment, the denoted values will be the same as the expressed values. We write this as follows:

$$\text{Expressed Value} = \text{Number} + \text{Procedure}$$

$$\text{Denoted Value} = \text{Number} + \text{Procedure}$$

We use equations like this as informal reminders of the expressed and denoted values for each of our interpreters.

We also need to distinguish two languages: the *defined language,* which is the language we are specifying with our interpreter, and the *defining language,* which is the language in which we write the interpreter. In our case the defining language is Scheme. The equations above describe the expressed and denoted values of the defined language.

We start with the following concrete and abstract syntax

⟨exp⟩ ::= ⟨integer-literal⟩	lit (datum)
| ⟨varref⟩	
| ⟨operator⟩ ⟨operands⟩	app (rator rands)
⟨operator⟩ ::= ⟨varref⟩ | (⟨exp⟩)	
⟨operands⟩ ::= ( ) | (⟨operand⟩ {,⟨operand⟩}*)	
⟨operand⟩ ::= ⟨exp⟩	
⟨varref⟩ ::= ⟨var⟩	varref (var)

Typical expressions in our language follow:

```
3
n
+(3, n)
add1(+(3, n))
(add1)(+(3, n))
```

The abstract syntax trees are built, as before, of records with type definitions based on the abstract syntax names given with the grammar.

```
(define-record lit (datum))
(define-record varref (var))
(define-record app (rator rands))
```

Figure 5.1.1   A simple interpreter using `variant-case`

```
(define eval-exp
  (lambda (exp)
    (variant-case exp
      (lit (datum) datum)
      (varref (var) (apply-env init-env var))
      (app (rator rands)
        (let ((proc (eval-exp rator))
              (args (eval-rands rands)))
          (apply-proc proc args)))
      (else (error "Invalid abstract syntax: " exp)))))

(define eval-rands
  (lambda (rands)
    (map eval-exp rands)))
```

The `rands` field of an app record contains a list of abstract syntax trees for the application's operands. The abstract syntax tree for the third or fourth example above is

```
#(app
  #(varref add1)
  (#(app
     #(varref +)
     (#(lit 3) #(varref n)))))
```

Our first interpreter is shown in figure 5.1.1. The main procedure, *eval-exp*, is passed the abstract syntax tree of an expression and returns the value of the expression. It follows a familiar pattern, dispatching on the type of record at the root of the tree. The first case is easy: If *exp* is a literal, the datum is returned.

If *exp* is a node that represents a variable, the value of the expression should be the value bound to that variable. Now we need to decide from where we should retrieve this value. We need to supply an *environment*: a finite function that takes a symbol and returns the associated denoted value. This environment is consulted to find the value of any variable in the language. In this language, there is (at least for the moment) only one environment, the initial environment *init-env*.

We define an ADT for environments by borrowing the finite function ADT.

```
(define the-empty-env (create-empty-ff))
(define extend-env extend-ff*)
(define apply-env apply-ff)
```

Since we follow the principle of data abstraction, we may use any implementation of finite functions that supports *extend-ff**, which simultaneously adds multiple bindings to the environment. The ribcage implementation of section 3.6.3 is a good choice.

When evaluating a variable, the interpreter need only look up its binding in *init-env*. Thus we have the following variant-case clause in *eval-exp*:

```
(varref (var) (apply-env init-env var))
```

This leaves the case of an application. Since the operator may be any expression, we must evaluate it to obtain the procedure to be called. This is easily done with the recursive call (eval-exp rator) in figure 5.1.1. As with most languages, including Scheme, the language we are interpreting uses applicative-order evaluation: the operands of an application are evaluated before calling the procedure. The auxiliary procedure *eval-rands* is called to evaluate the list of operands and returns a list of arguments (operand values). It uses *map* to recursively invoke *eval-exp* on each operand.

How application is performed depends on the representation of procedures. We isolate dependence on this representation within the procedure *apply-proc*, allowing *eval-exp* to be completed as in figure 5.1.1.

We now turn to the representation of procedures. Initially we shall have only one kind of procedure: *primitive procedures* that are supported directly by the underlying implementation. To be precise, we use a BNF grammar to specify the data that *apply-proc* must manipulate:

⟨procedure⟩ ::= ⟨prim-op⟩	prim-proc (prim-op)
⟨prim-op⟩ ::= ⟨addition⟩	+
| ⟨subtraction⟩	–
| ⟨multiplication⟩	*
| ⟨increment⟩	add1
| ⟨decrement⟩	sub1

This specification says that there is only one kind of procedure, a primitive procedure, and that there are five of these: addition, subtraction, multiplication, increment (adding 1), and decrement (subtracting 1). Furthermore, such procedures are represented by records specified by

```
(define-record prim-proc (prim-op))
```

Later this will allow us to easily distinguish them from other types of procedures. The only item stored in a `prim-proc` record is the symbol naming the operator. The procedures *make-prim-proc* and *apply-proc* define an ADT for procedures.

All that *apply-proc* does at this point is verify that its first argument is a primitive procedure and then invoke *apply-prim-op*.

```
(define apply-proc
  (lambda (proc args)
    (variant-case proc
      (prim-proc (prim-op) (apply-prim-op prim-op args))
      (else (error "Invalid procedure:" proc)))))

(define apply-prim-op
  (lambda (prim-op args)
    (case prim-op
      ((+) (+ (car args) (cadr args)))
      ((-) (- (car args) (cadr args)))
      ((*) (* (car args) (cadr args)))
      ((add1) (+ (car args) 1))
      ((sub1) (- (car args) 1))
      (else (error "Invalid prim-op name:" prim-op)))))
```

We could have represented primitive operators in any convenient way that would allow *apply-prim-op* to do its work. We have chosen to represent each primitive operator by a symbol: the same symbol that the initial environment will use as a name for that primitive operator. Hence we can build the initial environment as follows:

```
(define prim-op-names '(+ - * add1 sub1))

(define init-env
  (extend-env
    prim-op-names
    (map make-prim-proc prim-op-names)
    the-empty-env))
```

This completes our first interpreter. Before we can conveniently test our interpreter, however, we need a front end that parses expressions and invokes *eval-exp*. There are several approaches to building such a front end.

One approach is to ignore, for the moment, the details of the concrete syntax at the beginning of this section, and to write our expressions as list structures, as we did in section 4.1. Thus, instead of writing add1(+(3, n)), we might write (add1 (+ 3 n)). For this approach, all we need is a procedure *parse*, which takes a Scheme list, symbol. or number and returns the corresponding abstract syntax tree. Our interpreter can then be tested easily; see appendix G and appendix H.

```
> (define run
    (lambda (x)
      (eval-exp (parse x))))
> (run '5)
5
> (run '(add1 2))
3
```

○ *Exercise 5.1.1*

Write *parse*. See section 3.4.3. □

A read-eval-print loop may also be defined for our interpreter.

```
(define read-eval-print
  (lambda ()
    (display "-->")
    (write (eval-exp (parse (read))))
    (newline)
    (read-eval-print)))
```

This provides a more convenient interface if a number of tests are to be made.

```
> (read-eval-print)
--> 5
5
--> (add1 2)
3
--> (* (add1 2) (- 6 4))
6
```

From now on, if the prompt --> appears in a transcript, it indicates that the current version of *eval-exp* is performing the evaluation.

This approach is simple, but may lead to confusion between the defined language and the defining language. Alternatively, by using the code of appendix D and appendix E, we can write a character string parser.

```
> (define parse character-string-parser)
> (run "5")
5
> (run "add1(2)")
3
```

By using appendix F, we can have a read-eval-print loop for ⟨exp⟩. In this case, we need to terminate each top-level expression to be evaluated with a semicolon, so we can distinguish between add1 and add1(2). For example,

```
> (read-eval-print)
--> 5;
5
--> add1(2);
3
--> *(add1(2),-(6,4));
6
```

• *Exercise 5.1.2*
Implement *eval-exp* and test it using both *run* and a read-eval-print loop. You may use either a list structure or a character string parser. ☐

• *Exercise 5.1.3*
Extend the initial environment with the operator minus, which takes one argument, n, and returns $-n$.

```
--> minus(+(minus(5), 9));
-4
```
☐

• *Exercise 5.1.4*
Add list processing features to *init-env*, including *cons*, *car*, *cdr*, *list*, and a new variable, *emptylist*, which is bound to the empty list. (Since there is no support for symbols, lists can contain only numbers and other lists.)

```
--> list(1, 2, 3);
(1 2 3)
--> car(cons(4, emptylist));
4
```
☐

Another way to represent procedures in our interpreter is to represent them as procedures of the defining language. For example, + would be bound in *init-env* to the Scheme addition procedure. We could then say

```
(define apply-proc apply)
```

Rewrite the interpreter of this section to use this procedure representation. □

5.2 Conditional Evaluation

To study the semantics and implementation of a wide range of programming language features, we now begin adding these features to our defined language. For each feature, we add a production to the grammar of ⟨exp⟩, specify an abstract syntax for that production, and then include an appropriate variant-case line in *eval-exp* to handle the new type of abstract syntax tree node.

First we add a conditional expression with the concrete and abstract syntax,

---

⟨exp⟩ ::= if ⟨exp⟩ then ⟨exp⟩ else ⟨exp⟩   if (test-exp then-exp else-exp)

---

and then we define the record type that supports its abstract syntax.

```
(define-record if (test-exp then-exp else-exp))
```

To avoid adding booleans as a new type of expressed value, we let zero represent false and any other value represent true and use the procedure *true-value?*, which abstracts this decision:

```
(define true-value?
  (lambda (x)
    (not (zero? x))))
```

If the value of the test-exp subexpression is a true value, the value of the entire if expression should be the value of the then-exp subexpression; otherwise it should be the value of the else-exp subexpression. For example,

```
--> if 1 then 2 else 3;
2
--> if -(3, +(1, 2)) then 2 else 3;
3
```

This behavior is obtained by adding the following clause in *eval-exp*

```
(if (test-exp then-exp else-exp)
   (if (true-value? (eval-exp test-exp))
       (eval-exp then-exp)
       (eval-exp else-exp)))
```

This code uses the `if` special form of the defining language to define the `if` form of the defined language. This illustrates how we are dependent on our understanding of the defining language: if we did not know what Scheme's `if` did, this code would not help us understand the new language. In this case, of course, we do understand Scheme's `if`, and our code provides some additional information on the defined language's conditional expression as it considers any nonzero value to be true.

• *Exercise 5.2.1*
Test `if` forms by extending the interpreter of figure 5.1.1. Use either the string syntax given above or this list syntax:

⟨exp⟩ ::= (if ⟨exp⟩ ⟨exp⟩ ⟨exp⟩)

▯

• *Exercise 5.2.2*
Add the numeric equality, zero-testing, and order predicates `equal`, `zero`, `greater` and `less` to the initial environment. These predicates should use 1 to represent true.

```
--> equal(3, 3);
1
--> zero(sub1(5));
0
--> if greater(2, 3) then 5 else 6;
6
```
▯

• *Exercise 5.2.3*
Extend exercise 5.1.4 by adding the predicate `null`. ▯

Next we address the problem of creating new variable bindings in the context of a `let` form. We add to the interpreted language a syntax in which the keyword `let` is followed by a series of declarations, the keyword `in`, and the body. For example,

```
let x = 5;
    y = 6
in +(x, y)
```

The entire `let` form is an expression, as is its body, so `let` expressions may be nested. The usual lexical scope rules for block structure apply: the binding region of a `let` declaration is the body of the `let` expression, and inner bindings create holes in the scope of outer bindings. Thus in

```
let x = 3
in let x = *(x, x)
   in +(x, x)
```

the references to `x` in the first application refer to the outer declaration, whereas the references to `x` in the second application refer to the inner declaration, and hence the value of the entire expression is 18.

The concrete syntax of the `let` form is

⟨exp⟩ ::= let ⟨decls⟩ in ⟨exp⟩   `let (decls body)`
⟨decls⟩ ::= ⟨decl⟩ {;⟨decl⟩}*
⟨decl⟩ ::= ⟨var⟩ = ⟨exp⟩   `decl (var exp)`

The abstract syntax uses the following record types:

```
(define-record let (decls body))
(define-record decl (var exp))
```

The `decls` field of a `let` record is associated with a ⟨decl⟩ nonterminal that may be repeated zero or more times (indicated by the Kleene star). Thus it contains a list of `decl` records.

The body of a `let` expression should be evaluated in an environment in which the declared variables are bound to the values of the expressions on

Figure 5.3.1   Interpreter with explicit environment-passing

```
(define eval-exp
  (lambda (exp env)
    (variant-case exp
      (lit (datum) datum)
      (varref (var) (apply-env env var))
      (app (rator rands)
        (let ((proc (eval-exp rator env))
              (args (eval-rands rands env)))
          (apply-proc proc args)))
      (if (test-exp then-exp else-exp)
        (if (true-value? (eval-exp test-exp env))
            (eval-exp then-exp env)
            (eval-exp else-exp env)))
      (else (error "Invalid abstract syntax:" exp)))))

(define eval-rands
  (lambda (rands env)
    (map (lambda (rand) (eval-exp rand env))
         rands)))
```

the right-hand sides of the declarations, whereas other bindings should be obtained from the environment in which the entire let expression is evaluated.

With the introduction of let, different expressions may be evaluated using different environments. This is a significant change, because so far our interpreter evaluated all expressions with respect to a single environment, *init-env*. Therefore, we first rewrite *eval-exp* to take two arguments: an expression and an environment. The new *eval-exp* evaluates the given expression with respect to the given environment. The resulting interpreter is shown in figure 5.3.1. It looks up variables using the environment *env*, rather than *init-env*, and we are careful to pass the environment on each call to *eval-exp*. This requires that the environment be passed to *eval-rands*.

When a let expression is evaluated, the subexpressions on the right-hand side of its declarations are evaluated first. Since the scope of these declarations is restricted to the let expression's body, the right-hand side subexpressions are evaluated in *env*, the environment of the entire let expression. The body is then evaluated in an environment obtained by extending *env* to bind the declared variables to the values of their right-hand subexpressions. We obtain this behavior by adding the let clause in figure 5.3.2. First the variable names

Figure 5.3.2   Interpreter with `let`

```
(define eval-exp
  (lambda (exp env)
    (variant-case exp
      (lit (datum) datum)
      (varref (var) (apply-env env var))
      (app (rator rands)
        (let ((proc (eval-exp rator env))
              (args (eval-rands rands env)))
          (apply-proc proc args)))
      (if (test-exp then-exp else-exp)
        (if (true-value? (eval-exp test-exp env))
            (eval-exp then-exp env)
            (eval-exp else-exp env)))
      (let (decls body)
        (let ((vars (map decl->var decls))
              (exps (map decl->exp decls)))
          (let ((new-env (extend-env vars
                            (eval-rands exps env)
                            env)))
            (eval-exp body new-env))))
      (else (error "Invalid abstract syntax:" exp)))))
```

and expressions are extracted from the declaration records. Then `eval-rands` is used to evaluate the declaration expressions in the environment `env`. Finally, the body is evaluated in a new environment obtained by extending the current environment with bindings that associate the declared variables with the values of their right-hand side expressions.

In accordance with our expectation for a lexically-scoped language, a fixed region of text, *body*, is associated with the new environment bindings. Also, if `extend-env` creates a binding for an already bound variable, the new binding takes precedence over the old. Inner declarations thus shadow, or create holes in the scope of, outer declarations. For example, in

```
let x = 1
in let x = +(x, 2)
   in add1(x)
```

the subexpression `add1(x)` is evaluated in a new environment obtained by extending an environment binding x to 1 with a binding of x to 3. Since the binding of x to 3 takes precedence, the reference to x in add1(x) yields 3 and the final value is 4. This satisfies the lexical scope rule associated with block-structured languages: a variable reference is associated with the nearest lexically enclosing binding of the variable.

- *Exercise 5.3.1*
  Test the let form of the interpreter of figure 5.3.2. The parser may accept either the syntax of let used in this section or the syntax of Scheme's let. The procedure *run* must also be modified to pass *init-env* to *eval-exp*. ▯

o *Exercise 5.3.2*
  Extend exercise 5.1.4 by adding the primitive procedure eq, which should correspond to the Scheme procedure *eq?*. Why could this predicate not be adequately tested until now? ▯

5.4 Procedures

So far our language has only the procedures that were included in the initial environment. For our interpreted language to be at all useful, we must allow new procedures to be created. We use the following syntax:

$\langle exp \rangle ::= $ proc $\langle varlist \rangle \langle exp \rangle$ proc (formals body)
$\langle varlist \rangle ::= ( ) \mid (\langle vars \rangle)$
$\langle vars \rangle ::= \langle var \rangle \{ , \langle var \rangle \}^*$

Thus we can write programs like

```
let f = proc (y, z) *(y, -(z, 5))
in f(2, 8)
```

Since the proc form may be used anywhere an expression is allowed, we can also write

```
(proc (y, z) *(y, -(z, 5)))(2, 8)
```

This is the application of the procedure proc (y, z) *(y, -(z, 5)) to the literals 2 and 8.

When a procedure is applied, its body is evaluated in an environment that binds the formal parameters of the procedure to the arguments of the application. Variables occurring free in the procedure should also obey the lexical scope rule. This requires that they retain the bindings that were in force *at the time the procedure was created*. Consider the following example:

```
let x = 5
in let f = proc (y, z) *(y, -(z, x));
       x = 28
   in f(2, 8)
```

When *f* is called, its body should be evaluated in an environment that binds y to 2, z to 8, and x to 5. Recall that the scope of the inner declaration of x does not include the procedure declaration. Thus from the position of the reference to x in the procedure's body, the nearest lexically enclosing declaration of x is the outer declaration, which associates x with 5.

A first-class procedure may be passed to and returned from other procedures and stored in data structures. As a result, it may be invoked at a place in the program that is distant from the place at which the procedure was created. This is also true of the "second-class" procedures found in many languages, which may be passed as arguments to procedures but not returned as values or stored in data structures. We shall have more to say about this in chapter 10.

In order for a procedure to retain the bindings that its free variables had at the time it was created, it must be a *closed* package, independent of the environment in which it is used. Such a package is called a *closure*. In order to be self-contained, a closure must contain the procedure body, the list of formal parameters, and the bindings of its free variables. It is convenient to store the entire creation environment, rather than just the bindings of the free variables. We sometimes say the procedure is *closed over* or *closed in* its creation environment. We represent closures as records.

```
(define-record closure (formals body env))
```

In a compiled implementation, where lexical address calculations have been performed (as in section 2.3), only the number of formal parameters need be recorded in a closure, along with free variable bindings and a reference to the compiled code of its body.

We now modify `apply-proc` to recognize closures. We may write down the data that `apply-proc` needs to recognize with this equation:

$$\text{Procedure} = \text{Primitive Procedure} + \text{Closure}$$

The procedure `apply-proc` first checks to see what kind of procedure it was passed. If it was a closure, it simply invokes the body of the closure in an appropriately extended environment.

```
(define apply-proc
  (lambda (proc args)
    (variant-case proc
      (prim-proc (prim-op) (apply-prim-op prim-op args))
      (closure (formals body env)
        (eval-exp body (extend-env formals args env)))
      (else (error "Invalid procedure:" proc)))))
```

When a `proc` expression is evaluated, all that is done is to build a closure and return it immediately.

```
(define eval-exp
  (lambda (exp env)
    (variant-case exp
      (proc (formals body)
        (make-closure formals body env))
      ...)))
```

The body of the procedure is not evaluated here: it cannot be evaluated until the values of the formal parameters are known, when the closure is applied to some arguments. The interpreter is shown in figure 5.4.1.

- *Exercise 5.4.1*
Test user-defined procedures with the interpreter of figure 5.4.1. The parser may accept either the character string or the list structure syntax. □

- *Exercise 5.4.2*
In exercise 5.1.5, primitive operators are represented as procedures of the defining language, allowing *apply-proc* to be *apply*. To pursue this approach, closures must also be represented as procedures of the defining language. Define *make-closure* for this representation of closures. Hint: Use an expression of the form (`lambda args` ...). □

o *Exercise 5.4.3*
As a variation on the previous exercise, we can define *apply-proc* to be (`lambda (f args) (f args)`). Redefine *make-closure* and primitive operations using this variation. Hint: Use the form (`lambda (args)` ...). For example, bind the symbol + to (`lambda (args) (+ (car args) (cadr args))`).
□

Figure 5.4.1   Interpreter with user-defined procedures

```
(define eval-exp
  (lambda (exp env)
    (variant-case exp
      (lit (datum) datum)
      (varref (var) (apply-env env var))
      (app (rator rands)
        (let ((proc (eval-exp rator env))
              (args (eval-rands rands env)))
          (apply-proc proc args)))
      (if (test-exp then-exp else-exp)
        (if (true-value? (eval-exp test-exp env))
            (eval-exp then-exp env)
            (eval-exp else-exp env)))
      (let (decls body)
        (let ((vars (map decl->var decls))
              (exps (map decl->exp decls)))
          (let ((new-env (extend-env vars
                                     (eval-rands exps env)
                                     env)))
            (eval-exp body new-env))))
      (proc (formals body)
        (make-closure formals body env))
      (else (error "Invalid abstract syntax:" exp)))))

(define apply-proc
  (lambda (proc args)
    (variant-case proc
      (prim-proc (prim-op) (apply-prim-op prim-op args))
      (closure (formals body env)
        (eval-exp body (extend-env formals args env)))
      (else (error "Invalid procedure:" proc)))))
```

We saw in section 3.1 that a `let` expression is equivalent to an application in which the operator is a `proc` (or `lambda`) expression. This equivalence can be verified in our interpreter by observing that in either case the result is obtained by evaluating the `let` or `proc` body in the same environment. The only difference is that the application creates a closure, whereas the `let` does not. Since `let` can be treated as an abbreviation for the equivalent application, we omit it from subsequent interpreters.

- *Exercise 5.4.4*

Write a procedure `syntax-expand` that takes a syntax tree for the language of this section and returns a syntax tree with every `let` record replaced by a semantically equivalent `app` record with a `proc` record in its `rator` field. Use this procedure to process the output of the parser before it is passed to `eval-exp`. The `let` clause may now be removed from `eval-exp`, while retaining `let` in the language. □

5.5 Variable Assignment

Next we wish to add variable assignment (`:=`) to our interpreter. First we must change our environment abstraction, since it currently does not provide a means for modifying the value bound to a variable. At present, environments bind each variable directly to its associated expressed value (the value of some expression). Thus denoted values (the values of variable bindings) and expressed values are the same.

Our approach is to introduce a level of indirection between variable bindings and expressed values. In the new arrangement, variables will be bound to locations in memory, and it is the contents of these locations that are modified by variable assignment. Thus denoted values are locations or cells whose contents are expressed values:

$$\text{Denoted Value} = \text{Cell (Expressed Value)}.$$

Scheme does not allow the programmer to mutate (modify, or assign to) arbitrary memory locations. Instead it provides procedures, such as `set-cdr!`, that allow changes to mutable data structure elements. We use cells as developed in exercise 4.5.5 for modeling abstract memory locations. The collection of all locations, including mutable data structure fields, is called the *store*.

We next modify the interpreter to use the cells as denoted values. This requires two changes. First, when a closure is invoked (in `apply-proc`), the new bindings must be cells that contain the arguments. This is accomplished by writing

```
(extend-env formals
  (map make-cell args)
  env)
```

instead of (`extend-env formals args env`). Second, when variables are referenced, it is necessary to dereference their bindings, since the bindings are now cells. Thus in *eval-exp* we have the `variant-case` clause

```
(varref (var) (cell-ref (apply-env env var)))
```

instead of

```
(varref (var) (apply-env env var))
```

This design, in which formal parameters are bound to fresh cells containing the values of the operands, is known as call-by-value. Call-by-value is the most commonly used form of parameter passing, and is the standard against which other parameter passing mechanisms are usually compared.

- *Exercise 5.5.1*
  Add cells to the interpreter of figure 5.3.2. In addition to the changes mentioned above, you will have to alter the `let` clause and add cells to the initial environment. □

To add assignment to the interpreter, we choose the concrete syntax

---

⟨exp⟩ ::= ⟨var⟩ := ⟨exp⟩   varassign (var exp)

---

and an abstract syntax based on records defined by

```
(define-record varassign (var exp))
```

To implement assignment, we add the following `variant-case` clause to *eval-exp*:

```
(varassign (var exp)
  (cell-set! (apply-env env var) (eval-exp exp env)))
```

Cells or locations, such as the cells passed to *cell-set!*, are sometimes called *L-values*. This reflects their association with variables appearing on the left-hand side of assignment statements. Analogously, expressed values, such as the values of the right-hand side expressions of assignment statements, are known as *R-values*. See figure 5.5.1 for the complete interpreter with variable assignment.

Figure 5.5.1   eval-exp with variable assignment call-by-value

```
(define eval-exp
  (lambda (exp env)
    (variant-case exp
      (lit (datum) datum)
      (varref (var) (cell-ref (apply-env env var)))
      (app (rator rands)
        (let ((proc (eval-exp rator env))
              (args (eval-rands rands env)))
          (apply-proc proc args)))
      (if (test-exp then-exp else-exp)
        (if (true-value? (eval-exp test-exp env))
            (eval-exp then-exp env)
            (eval-exp else-exp env)))
      (proc (formals body)
        (make-closure formals body env))
      (varassign (var exp)
        (cell-set! (apply-env env var) (eval-exp exp env)))
      (else (error "Invalid abstract syntax: " exp)))))

(define apply-proc
  (lambda (proc args)
    (variant-case proc
      (prim-proc (prim-op) (apply-prim-op prim-op args))
      (closure (formals body env)
        (eval-exp body
          (extend-env
            formals
            (map make-cell args)
            env)))
      (else (error "Invalid procedure:" proc)))))
```

○ *Exercise 5.5.2*

In the ribcage representation of environments (figure 3.6.1), the values are stored in vectors. We can use the fact that vector elements are mutable in Scheme to avoid introducing cells. To do this, let the binding associated with the nth variable be the nth location of the vector. Thus, using *vector-set!*, we can directly mutate the binding of a variable. Implement this idea. □

- *Exercise 5.5.3*

  The following definition of `apply-proc` no longer assumes that `args` will be bound to a list of expressed values but will be bound to a list of denoted values. This means that `args` will be bound to a list of cells. Redefine `eval-rands` of figure 5.3.1 to use this version of `apply-proc`.

  ```
  (define denoted->expressed cell-ref)

  (define apply-proc
    (lambda (proc args)
      (variant-case proc
        (prim-proc (prim-op)
          (apply-prim-op prim-op (map denoted->expressed args)))
        (closure (formals body env)
          (eval-exp body
            (extend-env formals args env)))
        (else (error "Invalid procedure:" proc)))))
  ```

  □

- *Exercise 5.5.4*

  Now that we have introduced side effects into the language, it is natural to introduce a form for sequencing expressions.

$\langle\text{exp}\rangle ::= \texttt{begin } \langle\text{exp}\rangle \ \langle\text{compound}\rangle$	`begin (exp1 exp2)`
$\langle\text{compound}\rangle ::= \{ \, ; \langle\text{exp}\rangle \}^* \ \texttt{end}$	

  A `begin` expression may contain an arbitrary number of subexpressions separated by semicolons. These are evaluated in order and the value of the last is returned. For example,

  ```
  --> let x = 3
      in begin
            x := add1(x);
            x := +(x, x);
            +(x, 2)
         end;
  10
  ```

  The abstract syntax of `begin` contains only two subexpressions. A `begin` expression containing more than two subexpressions generates a nested `begin` internally. A `begin` expression containing only one subexpression generates the abstract syntax of that expression. Thus, the above example parses to

```
#(let (#(decl x #(lit 3)))
   #(begin
      #(varassign x #(app #(varref add1) (#(varref x))))
      #(begin
         #(varassign x #(app #(varref +) (#(varref x) #(varref x))))
         #(app #(varref +) (#(varref x) #(lit 2)))))))
```

Extend the interpreter to implement the `begin` form. □

- *Exercise 5.5.5*

Define a *form* to be a *definition* or expression. Modify the parser for the following abstract and concrete syntax

---

⟨form⟩ ::= define ⟨var⟩ = ⟨exp⟩	define (var exp)
| ⟨exp⟩	

This syntax intentionally prevents definitions (as opposed to local declarations) from appearing inside expressions.

Modify the read-eval-print loop so that it reads a sequence of forms, with definitions performed and expressions evaluated as they are encountered. A definition is performed by first evaluating the given expression in the initial environment. If the given variable is not bound in the initial environment, the initial environment should be extended to bind the variable to a cell containing the expression's value. If the initial environment already contains a binding for the given variable, the expression's value is assigned to this binding as if by a top-level assignment. After performing a definition, the next prompt is printed without printing any value. After evaluation of an expression, the value of the expression should be printed, as usual, before prompting for the next definition or expression.

```
--> define x = 3;
--> +(x, 1);
4
--> define x = 5;
--> x;
5
--> begin
      x := 6;
      x
    end;
6
```

```
--> let x = 3
    in begin
          define y = 4;
          +(x, y)
       end;
   Error: Invalid parse-exp token: #3(token define *)
[]
```

○ *Exercise 5.5.6*

Typically the value of an expression such as assignment, whose purpose is
to perform a side effect, is unspecified. In our interpreter this value will be
whatever value the procedure *cell-set!* returns (which is, of course, unspecified in Scheme, since it is defined with *vector-set!*). Extend the parser to
include assignment expressions and modify the interpreter in figure 5.5.1 so
that the symbol *unspecified* is returned when the assignment expression is
evaluated.

```
--> let x = 3
    in x := 4;
   *unspecified*
[]
```

○ *Exercise 5.5.7*

In the interpreter of figure 5.5.1, all variable bindings are mutable (as in
Scheme). Another alternative is to allow both mutable and immutable variable bindings:

$$\text{Denoted Value} = \text{Cell (Expressed Value)} + \text{Expressed Value}$$

Then variable assignment works only when the variable to be assigned to has
a mutable binding.

One approach to supporting both mutable and immutable variable bindings
is to add a letmutable form for introducing mutable bindings. For example,
we could use a syntax similar to the let form.

⟨exp⟩ ::= letmutable ⟨decls⟩ in ⟨exp⟩   letmutable (decls body)

Modify the parser and interpreter so that the letmutable form is just the
same as the let form, except that it introduces mutable bindings to the environment, whereas let bindings remain immutable. []

○ *Exercise 5.5.8*

Local variable binding need be mutable only if there is an assignment expression to the variable somewhere within its scope. Process the output of the parser and modify the interpreter so that only bindings for variables that might change their values are mutable, while all other bindings remain immutable. ☐

○ *Exercise 5.5.9*

Our understanding of assignment, as expressed in this interpreter, depends on the semantics of side effects in Scheme. In particular, it depends on *when* these effects take place. If we could model assignment without using Scheme's side-effecting operations, our understanding would not be dependent on Scheme in this way. We can do this by modeling the store not as a collection of cells but as a finite function. The domain of the store function is some arbitrary set of addresses (say the nonnegative integers) that represents locations or cells, and its range is the set of expressed values. Mutation of a location in the store is then modeled by extending this finite function to associate the location with the new value. This new association supersedes any earlier associations for the same cell.

In order for the new store to be used in subsequent evaluation, it is passed as an additional argument to all interpreter procedures that might need it (`eval-exp`, `eval-rands`, `apply-proc`, etc.). For example,

```
(define eval-exp
  (lambda (exp env store)
    (variant-case exp
      (varref (var) (apply-store store (apply-env env var)))
      ...)))
```

Every procedure that might modify the store will return not just its usual value but a pair consisting of the value and a new store. The trickiest interpreter procedure to modify is *eval-rands*. It can no longer just use `map`. Instead, it must evaluate the operands in some specific order, with the store resulting from each evaluation being used in the next evaluation. We can evaluate the operands from left to right and accumulate the partial answers in reverse order.

```
(define-record interp-result (value store))

(define eval-rands
  (lambda (rands env store)
    (letrec
      ((loop
         (lambda (rands ans store)
           (if (null? rands)
               (make-interp-result (reverse ans) store)
               (let ((first-result
                       (eval-exp (car rands) env store)))
                 (loop
                   (cdr rands)
                   (cons (interp-result->value first-result) ans)
                   (interp-result->store first-result)))))))
      (loop rands '() store))))
```

Modify the rest of the interpreter according to this design. Be sure to define your store ADT explicitly. Then rewrite *eval-rands* so it does not use the accumulator variable ans. □

5.6 Recursion

The last issue that must be addressed to complete our simple interpreter is recursion. We have already seen two approaches to implementing recursion in section 4.4. The first approach, the Y combinator, is of theoretical importance because it requires only the ability to create and apply first-class procedures. We could write the applicative-order Y combinator directly in our defined language and use it to define recursive procedures. In most implementations, however, an approach like this is too inefficient for routine use.

The second approach is frequently used to implement letrec in Scheme. A letrec expression is syntactically transformed into an expression that first uses let to create an environment with dummy variable bindings. Recursive procedures are closed in this environment, after which variable assignment is used to store the closures in the cells bound to the associated variables. The transformation that accomplishes this is similar to the equation for letrec, which was presented in section 4.6. This equation, however, maintains the property that the order of evaluation of the exp_i is left undetermined.

```
(letrec ((var₁ exp₁) ... (varₙ expₙ))
  body)
```

$\Rightarrow$
```
(let ((var₁ '*) ... (varₙ '*))
  (let ((v₁ exp₁) ... (vₙ expₙ))
    (set! var₁ v₁)
    ...
    (set! varₙ vₙ)
    'unspecified)
  body)
```

Here $v_1, \ldots, v_n$ are fresh variables that appear nowhere else in the letrec expression. The inclusion of 'unspecified is to guarantee that the inner let always has a body, even when there are no definitions.

In this way recursive procedures are created by closing them in an environment that includes the variables to which they will be bound. Note that an attempt to dereference one of the variables var_i in any of the exp_j may lead to strange results, but after the set!'s are done all the cells will contain the right values. If each exp_i is a lambda, then we are guaranteed that none of the letrec variables will be prematurely dereferenced, and that the order of evaluation of the exp_i is not important.

In Scheme, letrec can be used even when the exp_i are not lambda expressions. This generality is rarely needed but is important in some applications such as streams.

Top-level definitions may also be used to create recursive procedures in a similar way. This works because procedures defined at the top level of the read-eval-print loop (see exercise 5.5.5) will be closed in the initial environment, and the initial environment will include the new definition. This is the way top-level recursive procedures are defined in Scheme.

This approach implements recursion by introducing cycles in the data structure representing the run-time environment. For example, the local environment created by

```
(letrec ((fact (lambda (n)
                 (if (zero? n)
                     1
                     (* n (fact (- n 1)))))))
  ...)
```

contains a circularity. The environment contains a binding that points to a closure that in turn contains a reference to the environment (see figure 5.6.1).

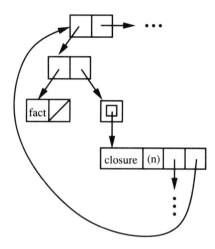

Figure 5.6.1   Circular environment for `fact`

In most languages only procedures may be defined recursively, and circular environments are created by the same mechanism that creates recursive procedures. We look now at how recursion may be added directly to an interpreter *without* circularity.

We use a variation on the `letrec` syntax that restricts the right-hand side of recursive declarations to `proc` expressions. The concrete and abstract syntax is described by this grammar:

⟨exp⟩ ::= `letrecproc` ⟨procdecls⟩   `letrecproc (procdecls`
               `in` ⟨exp⟩   `body)`
⟨procdecls⟩ ::= ⟨procdecl⟩ {`;`⟨procdecl⟩}*
⟨procdecl⟩ ::= ⟨var⟩ ⟨varlist⟩ `=` ⟨exp⟩   `procdecl (var formals body)`

The left-hand side of a recursive declaration is the name of the recursive procedure and a list of formal parameters. To the right of the `=` is the procedure body. For example,

```
letrecproc
  fact(x) = if zero(x) then 1 else *(x, fact(sub1(x)))
in fact(6)
```

Figure 5.6.2 Environment ADT without circular closures

```
(define-record extended-rec-env (vars vals old-env))

(define extend-rec-env
  (lambda (procdecls env)
    (make-extended-rec-env
      (map procdecl->var procdecls)
      (map (lambda (procdecl)
             (make-proc
               (procdecl->formals procdecl)
               (procdecl->body procdecl)))
           procdecls)
      env)))

(define apply-env
  (lambda (env var)
    (variant-case env
      (extended-rec-env (vars vals old-env)
        (if (memq var vars)
            (variant-case (ribassoc var vars vals)
              (proc (formals body)
                (make-closure formals body env)))
            (apply-env old-env var)))
      ...)))
```

or

```
letrecproc
  even(x) = if zero(x) then 1 else odd(sub1(x));
  odd(x)  = if zero(x) then 0 else even(sub1(x))
in odd(13)
```

In some languages, variables that are referenced before they are defined must first be declared using a *forward* declaration. For example, in the body of even, it would be necessary to declare odd to be forward. This is not necessary in Scheme or our interpreter, since all the variables in a mutually recursive declaration are identified before analyzing the procedure bodies.

To add letrecproc to the interpreter, we first introduce a new operator to the environment ADT. This operator, called *extend-rec-env*, extends the environment with a set of mutually recursive procedures. The letrecproc variant-case clause in *eval-exp* is similar to the `let` clause, except that *extend-rec-env* is used instead of *extend-env* to create the environment in which the body is evaluated.

```
(letrecproc (procdecls body)
  (eval-exp body (extend-rec-env procdecls env)))
```

We assume for the time being that this clause is being added to figure 5.4.1, and not figure 5.5.1, so that environment bindings are not cells.

An environment ADT with *extend-rec-env* may be implemented in many ways. We do so in a manner that does not involve the use of side effects. We cannot build a recursive closure directly, since the only way to build a cyclic structure is to use side effects. Instead, we store all the information contained in the recursive closure, *except* the environment, in a `proc` record. Before a value is returned from the environment, we build a complete closure by adding the environment. This is possible because the environment is available at the time we *build* the closure. Using this approach, the environment ADT is defined as in figure 5.6.2

- *Exercise 5.6.1*
  Add `letrecproc` to the interpreter of figure 5.4.1 using the environment ADT given above. ☐

○ *Exercise 5.6.2*
  The use of *make-proc* in the definition of *extend-rec-env* may seem a bit odd. We can avoid this by introducing a new form `letrec`, whose abstract syntax is much like that of `let`.

⟨exp⟩ ::= letrec ⟨decls⟩ in ⟨exp⟩   letrec (decls body)

The `decls` is a list of `decl`s and each `decl` is composed of a `var` and an `exp`. The `exp` of the `decl`, however, must be a `proc` record. Replace `letrecproc` by `letrec` and redefine *extend-rec-env* to utilize `letrec`'s abstract syntax. ☐

○ *Exercise 5.6.3*
  The environment ADT of figure 5.6.2 can be made compatible with the interpreter of figure 5.5.1, in which bindings are cells, by wrapping recursive closures in cells before *apply-env* returns them. If this were done, what would happen if `:=` were used to assign a variable bound by a `letrecproc` expression? ☐

○ *Exercise 5.6.4*

It is somewhat inefficient to build a new closure each time a variable bound to a recursive procedure is referenced. Modify the environment ADT of figure 5.6.2 to build a single recursive closure for each recursive procedure. As in implementations of `letrec` via syntactic extension, begin by building an environment with bindings that are cells containing dummy values. Then build the closures and use *cell-set!* to install them in the environment. Use this new ADT to add `letrecproc` to the interpreter of figure 5.5.1. Then write a program in the defined language that behaves differently with this environment ADT than it does with the environment ADT of figure 5.6.2. Hint: Extend the predicate `eq` of exercise 5.3.2 to test equality of procedures as well as of lists. □

We have seen that `letrec` (or `letrecproc`), like `let`, can be implemented as a syntactic extension into expressions using only forms that are already supported by the interpreter. Thus, as with `let`, we shall not include `letrec` (or `letrecproc`) in subsequent interpreters.

○ *Exercise 5.6.5*

Extend *syntax-expand* of exercise 5.4.4 to replace all `letrecproc` records with syntactically equivalent `let` records, as indicated by the syntactic transformation for `letrec` given above. Be sure that *syntax-expand* also expands these `let` records. Then `letrecproc` may be used with the interpreter of figure 5.5.1. □

5.7 Dynamic Scope and Dynamic Assignment

In this section we present two different approaches to dynamically rearranging information in an environment. The first approach, dynamic scope, is a kind of binding mechanism that adds additional expressiveness at the cost of making programs far more difficult to understand. The second approach, dynamic assignment, provides most of the expressiveness of dynamic scope without abandoning the clarity of lexical scope.

5.7.1 Dynamic Scope

We have emphasized that when a procedure is applied, it is the environment in which the procedure was *created* that is used to evaluate the procedure's body. This is necessary for variables to be lexically scoped, but it requires that a new closure be formed each time a proc expression is evaluated. It would seem simpler to evaluate the body in the environment of application. We now explore this alternative.

Consider this program:

```
let a = 3
in let p = proc (x) +(x, a);
       a = 5
    in *(a, p(2))
```

By the lexical scope rule, the reference to a in the body of *p* refers to the first binding of a, yielding 3, and the entire expression yields 25. This is achieved by closing *p* in the environment established by the outer let. If instead the body of *p* were evaluated in the environment of its application, this reference to a would refer to the call-time binding of a, yielding 5, and the entire expression would yield 35. The scope of the inner binding of a changed with the application to *p* so that the body of *p* was included in the scope. The scope of variables is now dynamic, not lexical: it changes with each application. This is referred to as *dynamic binding* and obeys the following rule:

> A dynamic binding is *extant* during the evaluation of the body associated with the binding form. References to a dynamically-bound variable refer to the *most recent* extant binding of that variable.

As we shall see later in this section, dynamic scoping is more difficult to reason about than lexical scoping, but it is often easier to implement. Since procedures are not closed over their creation environment, the only information that needs to be recorded in a procedure is the formal parameter list and body. This is exactly the information in a proc abstract syntax record. Thus when evaluating a proc expression, rather than building a new data structure to represent the dynamic procedure, we can simply return the proc record. The proc clause of the variant-case in *eval-exp* is simply

```
(proc (formals body) exp)
```

Dynamic scope makes the evaluation of proc expressions particularly simple and efficient, which was at least in part responsible for its early popularity in some programming languages, including Lisp.

When apply-proc receives a proc record, it must extend the *current* environment to obtain the environment in which to evaluate the body. This

Figure 5.7.1   Interpreter with dynamic scope

```
(define eval-exp
  (lambda (exp env)
    (variant-case exp
      (lit (datum) datum)
      (varref (var) (cell-ref (apply-env env var)))
      (app (rator rands)
        (let ((proc (eval-exp rator env))
              (args (eval-rands rands env)))
          (apply-proc proc args env)))
      (if (test-exp then-exp else-exp)
        (if (true-value? (eval-exp test-exp env))
            (eval-exp then-exp env)
            (eval-exp else-exp env)))
      (proc (formals body) exp)
      (varassign (var exp)
        (cell-set! (apply-env env var) (eval-exp exp env)))
      (else (error "Invalid abstract syntax:" exp)))))

(define apply-proc
  (lambda (proc args current-env)
    (variant-case proc
      (prim-proc (prim-op) (apply-prim-op prim-op args))
      (proc (formals body)
        (eval-exp body
          (extend-env formals (map make-cell args) current-env)))
      (else (error "Invalid procedure:" proc)))))
```

requires that the current environment be passed as an additional argument to *apply-proc*. The resulting interpreter is shown in figure 5.7.1.

With dynamic scope, when a binding is added to the environment, it remains in effect (is extant) until all subsequent bindings are removed. In other words, the environment obeys a last-in-first-out, or stack, discipline. We take advantage of this by modifying the interpreter of figure 5.7.1 to use a single global environment stack, rather than passing the environment between the procedures of the interpreter. See figure 5.7.2, where a new environment ADT is used. This ADT has procedures *push-env!*, *pop-env!*, *lookup-in-env*, and *initialize-env!* that perform the expected stack operations on the global environment stack. Here *eval-exp* uses the global environment stack instead of an environment argument. When *eval-exp* returns, it must leave the global environment stack in the same state that it found it. Therefore, *apply-proc* calls *push-env!* to add a new set of bindings to the environment, evaluates the procedure body, and then calls *pop-env!* to restore the environment stack.

- *Exercise 5.7.1*
  Implement the interpreter of figure 5.7.1. □

- *Exercise 5.7.2*
  With dynamic scope, recursive procedures may be bound by let; no special mechanism is necessary for recursion. This is of historical interest, because in the early years of programming language design other approaches to recursion, such as letrec and the Y combinator, were not widely understood. To demonstrate recursion via dynamic scope, define and test the factorial procedure for your interpreter. Do this by expanding a let expression that binds fact into its equivalent application with a proc expression as the operator. □

- *Exercise 5.7.3*
  Implement the interpreter of figure 5.7.2. □

- *Exercise 5.7.4*
  Modify the results of exercise 5.4.3, in which procedures are represented as procedures in the defining language, so that variables are dynamically scoped. Hint: Use an expression of the form (lambda (args env) ...). □

The structure of the stack environment cannot be determined statically. There is no way of knowing in advance how "deep" the binding of a variable may be in the environment. Since a linear search of the stack is required for each variable reference, this approach to storing dynamic bindings, called *deep binding,* is characterized by inefficient variable reference. Another approach, called *shallow binding,* maintains a separate stack for each variable name. The environment maps variable names to their associated stacks. When a variable is bound, the binding is pushed onto the stack associated with its name, and when it is *unbound* (no longer extant), its stack is popped. There is exactly one stack per variable, so a compiler can make the association between variable references and stacks at compile time. Since the current binding is always at the top of the stack, variable reference is more efficient. If the procedure has several formal parameters, however, entry and exit is less efficient than with deep binding, because a separate stack must be pushed and popped for each formal parameter.

Figure 5.7.2   Interpreter with dynamic scope and environment stack

```
(define eval-exp
  (lambda (exp)
    (variant-case exp
      (lit (datum) datum)
      (varref (var) (cell-ref (lookup-in-env var)))
      (app (rator rands)
        (let ((proc (eval-exp rator))
              (args (eval-rands rands)))
          (apply-proc proc args)))
      (if (test-exp then-exp else-exp)
        (if (true-value? (eval-exp test-exp))
            (eval-exp then-exp)
            (eval-exp else-exp)))
      (proc (formals body) exp)
      (assign (var exp)
        (cell-set! (lookup-in-env var) (eval-exp exp)))
      (else (error "Invalid abstract syntax:" exp)))))

(define eval-rands
  (lambda (rands)
    (map (lambda (exp) (eval-exp exp))
         rands)))

(define apply-proc
  (lambda (proc args)
    (variant-case proc
      (prim-proc (prim-op) (apply-prim-op prim-op args))
      (proc (formals body)
        (push-env! formals (map make-cell args))
        (let ((value (eval-exp body)))
          (pop-env!)
          value))
      (else (error "Invalid procedure:" proc)))))
```

```
let a = 3
in let p = proc () +(x, a);
       f = proc (x, y) *(p(), y);
       a = 5
   in *(a, f(let a = 2 in a, 1))
```

(a)

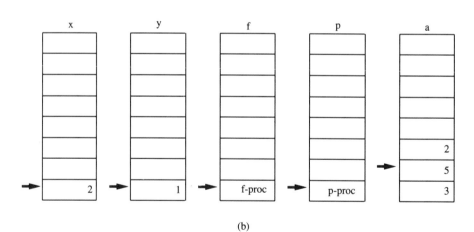

(b)

Figure 5.7.3 Example of dynamic scope and environments when *p* is called

Interpreters

To get a better feeling for dynamic scope and binding techniques, consider the program in figure 5.7.3. The deep and shallow binding environments at the time the reference to a in the body of p is evaluated are given in figure 5.7.3 (a) and (b), respectively. Here stacks grow in an upward direction. At this time a will have been most recently bound to 2 in the innermost let. however, this binding is no longer extant, since evaluation of the body of the innermost let is completed before p (or f) is called. The most recent extant binding is that of the second let. The evaluation of its body is not complete until the entire expression has been evaluated. Therefore the reference to a in the body of p yields 5. The binding of the first let is extant at the time p is called, but it is not the most recent binding. The reference to x in the body of p yields 2, since the binding of x created when f was called is still extant, and hence the entire expression yields 35.

o *Exercise 5.7.5*
Modify the interpreter of figure 5.7.1 to use a shallow-bound environment. Create a stack ADT with *push!*, *pop!*, *top*, and *make-stack* operations. See figure 4.6.2. The procedure *make-stack* takes no arguments and returns a newly created empty stack. For convenience, you may use a globally bound finite function to associate variable names with stacks. ☐

A number of program transformation techniques that are supported by lexical scope rules, such as α-, β-, and η-conversion, are not valid when dynamic scope is used. For example, consider the effect of α-converting y to a in the program of figure 5.7.3, so that the declaration of f becomes

```
f = proc (x, a) *(p(), a)
```

The reference to a in the body of p then refers to the binding established by f, with value 1, instead of to the inner binding established by the inner let, with value 5. Thus parameter names must be chosen in such a way as to avoid possible conflicts with other parameters declared at very distant points in a program. Binding variables with dynamic scope may have *global* effect, whereas binding variables with lexical scope has *local* effect.

If all of this gives you the impression that it is difficult to reason about programs that use dynamic scope, you are right. Imagine the problem of locating the most recent extant binding in a program of, say, 100,000 lines. It is natural to ask, "Are there any good uses for dynamic scope?" There are a few. We shall review them briefly after considering another form of dynamic binding.

What is the value of the following expression if variables are dynamically scoped?

```
let x = 1;
    f = proc (x) +(x, y);
    g = proc (y) f(+(z, x));
    z = 2
in g(+(x, z))
```
☐

5.7.2 Dynamic Assignment

The interpreters we have been examining have introduced bindings with lexical scope. These bindings also have *indefinite extent*: they are retained as long as they are needed. Bindings recorded in a closure are maintained as long as the closure is accessible. We then saw how bindings were created with dynamic scope, and we saw that these bindings had dynamic extent. Now we explore yet another alternative: assignments with dynamic extent to bindings that have lexical scope. This is also called "fluid binding."

In the defined language we express dynamic assignment using a form with concrete and abstract syntax given by

---

$\langle$exp$\rangle$ ::= $\langle$var$\rangle$:= $\langle$exp$\rangle$ during $\langle$exp$\rangle$ dynassign (var exp body)

The effect of

$$var \; := \; exp \; \textbf{during} \; body$$

is to temporarily assign the value of *exp* to *var*, evaluate *body*, reassign *var* to its original value, and return the value of *body*. For example, in

```
let x = 4
in let p = proc (y) +(x, y)
   in +(x := 7 during p(1),
        p(2))
```

the value of x, which is free in procedure *p*, is 7 in the call p(1), but is reset to 4 in the call p(2), so the value of the expression is $8 + 6 = 14$.

This may be implemented by adding the following variant-case clause to figure 5.5.1.

```
(dynassign (var exp body)
  (let ((a-cell (apply-env env var))
        (b-cell (make-cell (eval-exp exp env))))
    (cell-swap! a-cell b-cell)
    (let ((value (eval-exp body env)))
      (cell-swap! a-cell b-cell)
      value)))
```

- *Exercise 5.7.7*

  If the dynamic assignment x := 7 during p(1) of the preceding example were replaced by let x = 7 in p(1), what would be the value of this new expression? ☐

o *Exercise 5.7.8*

  Dynamic assignment may change the values of several variables at one time. Use the following syntax, which allows multiple variables to be dynamically set, and modify figure 5.5.1 to include letdynamic.

⟨exp⟩ ::= letdynamic ⟨decls⟩ in ⟨exp⟩   letdynamic (decls body)

For example,

```
--> define x = 1;
--> define y = 2;
--> define p = proc (x, a) +(a, *(x, y));
--> letdynamic
        x = +(x, y);
        y = +(x, 3)
    in p(x, y);
16
--> p(x, y);
4
```

☐

o *Exercise 5.7.9*

  Include dynassign in the procedure *syntax-expand* of exercise 5.4.4. Replace instances of dynassign in the syntax tree by instances of varassign and let. State any assumptions you make about variables not occurring free in the *exp* or *body* parts. ☐

One of the most common uses of dynamic binding or assignment is the redirection of input and output. I/O operations usually use "standard" input and output ports (connected, say, to a keyboard and the display), unless a specific port is indicated. But we may want all the output generated as a result of invoking a particular procedure call, such as p(1, 2), to be directed to a port associated with a new file, say port (instead of the standard output port). If the variable standardoutput were bound to the default standard output port, this could be accomplished by

```
standardoutput := port
during p(1, 2)
```

Or in a language with dynamic scope, we could use

```
let standardoutput = port
in p(1, 2)
```

which is equivalent to

```
(proc (standardoutput) p(1, 2))(port)
```

In the absence of dynamic binding or assignment, it would be necessary to pass the new port as an argument to *p*. This might not be a problem, but *p* would also have to pass the port unaltered to all the procedures it calls that do output, and these procedures would have to do the same. Some of these procedures may not do any output directly, but they must still receive and pass on the output port if any procedure they call does output, either directly or by calling other procedures.

In any situation in which a change must be made dynamically, that is, from the beginning to the end of the time required to evaluate an expression, dynamic binding or assignment may eliminate the need for much parameter passing. For example, in addition to the output port, there are often a number of formatting parameters that affect the generation of output, such as line length. It is frequently convenient to set these dynamically. For this reason, all binding is dynamic in some text formatting languages (such as TeX, with which this book was typeset).

Another common use of dynamic assignment or binding is in dealing with *exceptions,* that is, situations, such as errors, that must be handled outside of the program's normal flow of control. In some programming languages, it is possible to build *exception handlers:* procedures that are invoked by the system in the event that an exception is detected while the program executes.

It is frequently desirable to dynamically assign or bind exception handlers. For example, it may be that during the call to a particular procedure, it is desired that all divide-by-zero exceptions result in the largest possible number being returned as the result of the division, whereas at most times the response to this exception is to abort the program. This is easily accomplished with dynamic assignment.

The ability to use dynamic assignment or binding may also, in a sense, make procedures more abstract. For example, in the situation above it may be that not only does p not do any direct output, the programmer may not know whether any of the procedures it calls produce output. Furthermore, the writer of procedure p and its users may not even care whether output occurs while p executes. It is counter to the notion of abstraction for p to take an output port as a parameter and pass it to the procedures it calls just in case they might need it.

Dynamic assignment avoids most of all the difficulties of dynamic scope. For example, α-conversion is valid. Dynamic assignment does, however, share the problems of other forms of assignment. For example, procedures do not behave functionally: the value they return may be dependent on more than the values of their parameters. The advantage of dynamic assignment is that it can be used in a lexically-scoped language. The difficulties associated with dynamic behavior are then restricted to the few cases where dynamic assignment or scope is advantageous. For more discussion on dynamic assignment, see section 9.3.

5.8 Summary

An interpreter takes an abstract syntax tree representing a program and performs the computation directed by that program. Interpreters give a high-level, comprehensible specification of the action of a phrase in a programming language.

The expressed values of a language are the possible values of expressions. The denoted values are the possible values of variables.

Local bindings and user-defined procedures require that new environments be created and passed around within the interpreter. Variable assignment requires that denoted values be mutable cells containing expressed values, rather than the values themselves.

Recursive procedures can be defined either by building a circular environment or by building a specialized contour that closes the procedures at the time they are retrieved.

Dynamically-scoped binding is useful for applications such as changing output routine parameters and exception handlers during the evaluation of an expression. Pure dynamic scoping allows a simplified implementation, since procedures do not have to close over their creation environment. This simplicity is deceptive, however, since dynamic scope makes understanding programs much more difficult. Dynamic assignment to lexical variables is of use in the same contexts as dynamic scope, but retains the advantages of lexical scope.

6 Parameter Passing

In the last chapter we explored the semantics of language features that are to be found in most programming languages, though sometimes in restricted forms. In this chapter we explore a number of semantic variations that are commonly found in programming languages. Once more, we find interpreters to be valuable tools in the study of programming language semantics. By modifying these interpreters to express each semantic alternative, we obtain precise specifications of each alternative and highlight their essential differences.

In this chapter, we explore several areas of language design. In section 6.1, we look at two models of arrays and similar data structures. In sections 6.2–6.5, we study different mechanisms for the transmission of parameters to procedures. Along the way, in section 6.4, we look at some of the implications of our choice of expressed and denoted values. Finally, in section 6.6 we explore optional parameters and keyword arguments.

6.1 Adding Arrays

Most programming languages include data structures composed of multiple elements, such as arrays and records. Such structures are called *aggregates*. The introduction of aggregates brings with it new choices in language design.

The primitive aggregate data types of Scheme are vectors, pairs, and strings. Values of these types are typically represented by consecutive memory locations that contain their elements. When an aggregate value is passed to a procedure, what is passed is a pointer to the first memory location of the structure. We call this an *indirect* representation, since the values of aggregate elements are obtained indirectly, by reference to the aggregate's pointer. Later, we shall see what a direct representation of aggregates might mean.

A characteristic feature of this design is that when an aggregate value is passed to a procedure, the procedure and its caller both see the same memory locations. This sharing is visible when the procedure assigns a new value to one of the aggregate elements. Then the caller sees the change in the aggregate value. For example,

```
> (let ((p (lambda (b) (set-car! b 3)))
        (a (cons 1 2)))
    (p a)
    (car a))
3
```

To illustrate these ideas, we add arrays to the defined language. Other types of aggregate values may be treated the same as arrays for parameter-passing purposes.

To support arrays, we extend the language with special forms for creating array bindings, accessing array elements, and assigning to array elements. We use the following concrete and abstract syntax:

⟨form⟩ ::= definearray ⟨var⟩ [⟨exp⟩]	definearray (var dim-exp)
⟨exp⟩ ::= letarray ⟨arraydecls⟩ in ⟨exp⟩	letarray (arraydecls body)
| ⟨array-exp⟩ [⟨exp⟩]	arrayref (array index)
| ⟨array-exp⟩ [⟨exp⟩] :=	arrayassign (array index
⟨exp⟩	exp)
⟨array-exp⟩ ::= ⟨exp⟩	
⟨arraydecls⟩ ::= ⟨arraydecl⟩ {;⟨arraydecl⟩}*	
⟨arraydecl⟩ ::= ⟨var⟩ [⟨exp⟩]	decl (var exp)

An array is a sequence of cells containing expressed values. We write this as

$$\text{Array} = \text{Cell*(Expressed Value)}$$

The asterisk is meant to suggest the Kleene star (section 2.1). For our Scheme implementation, arrays are built from vectors, which provide a sequence of mutable elements; see figure 6.1.1.

The defined language's expressed values include arrays, and its denoted values are still simply cells containing expressed values as in section 5.5.

$$\text{Expressed Value} = \text{Number} + \text{Procedure} + \text{Array}$$

$$\text{Denoted Value} = \text{Cell (Expressed Value)}$$

Array indexing is zero based, so a[0] refers to the first element of array a. For example, with indirect arrays we obtain

Figure 6.1.1　Array ADT

```
(define-record aggregate (vector))

(define make-array
  (lambda (dimension)
    (make-aggregate (make-vector dimension))))

(define array? aggregate?)

(define array-ref
  (lambda (array index)
    (vector-ref (aggregate->vector array) index)))

(define array-set!
  (lambda (array index value)
    (vector-set! (aggregate->vector array) index value)))

(define array-copy
  (lambda (array)
    (make-aggregate (list->vector (vector->list (aggregate->vector array))))))
```

```
--> define p = proc (b) b[0] := 3;
--> letarray a[2]
      in begin
           a[0] := 1; a[1] := 2;
           p(a);
           a[0]
         end;
3
```

much as we did with the Scheme example above.

Figure 6.1.2 shows the core of an interpreter for handling arrays. In *eval-exp*, the letarray, arrayref, and arrayassign cases are, of course, new. The procedure *apply-proc* now expects *args* to be a list of denoted values, so it is the responsibility of *eval-rands*, not *apply-proc*, to call *make-cell* (as in exercise 5.5.3.) The procedure *eval-rands* now maps *eval-rand* across the operands. We introduce *eval-rator*, whose definition starts out as *eval-exp*. The lit, if, proc, and begin cases in *eval-exp* are omitted in figure 6.1.2, for they are the same as those we have seen in chapter 5, as are auxiliary procedures such as *apply-env*.

Figure 6.1.2   Interpreter for illustrating parameter-passing variations

```
(define eval-exp
  (lambda (exp env)
    (variant-case exp
      (varref (var) (denoted->expressed (apply-env env var)))
      (app (rator rands)
        (apply-proc (eval-rator rator env) (eval-rands rands env)))
      (varassign (var exp)
        (denoted-value-assign! (apply-env env var) (eval-exp exp env)))
      (letarray (arraydecls body)
        (eval-exp body
          (extend-env (map decl->var arraydecls)
            (map (lambda (decl)
                   (do-letarray (eval-exp (decl->exp decl) env)))
              arraydecls)
            env)))
      (arrayref (array index)
        (array-ref (eval-array-exp array env)
          (eval-exp index env)))
      (arrayassign (array index exp)
        (array-set! (eval-array-exp array env)
          (eval-exp index env)
          (eval-exp exp env)))
      ...)))

(define eval-rator
  (lambda (rator env)
    (eval-exp rator env)))

(define eval-rands
  (lambda (rands env)
    (map (lambda (rand) (eval-rand rand env)) rands)))

(define eval-rand
  (lambda (exp env)
    (expressed->denoted (eval-exp exp env))))

(define apply-proc
  (lambda (proc args)
    (variant-case proc
      (prim-proc (prim-op) (apply-prim-op prim-op (map denoted->expressed args)))
      (closure (formals body env) (eval-exp body (extend-env formals args env)))
      (else (error "Invalid procedure:" proc)))))
```

Figure 6.1.3   Auxiliaries for call-by-value with indirect arrays

```
(define denoted->expressed cell-ref)

(define denoted-value-assign! cell-set!)

(define do-letarray (compose make-cell make-array))

(define eval-array-exp eval-exp)

(define expressed->denoted make-cell)
```

Figure 6.1.2 introduces five new procedures that are not defined there. These are *denoted->expressed*, *denoted-value-assign!*, *do-letarray*, *eval-array-exp*, and *expressed->denoted*. By varying the definitions of these procedures, we can model a variety of parameter-passing mechanisms.

For the indirect representation of arrays, the code for these auxiliary procedures is shown in figure 6.1.3. A denoted value is a cell, so to convert a denoted value to an expressed value we simply take the contents of the cell, and to assign to a denoted value, we use *cell-set!*. The procedure *do-letarray* first makes an array and then places it in a new cell. This cell can then be bound to a variable. Since arrays are expressed values, *eval-array-exp* can simply be *eval-exp*. Last, *expressed->denoted* just creates a cell containing the expressed value.

- *Exercise 6.1.1*

  Implement this interpreter and run some examples. ☐

○ *Exercise 6.1.2*

  Replace the `letarray` construct by a new primitive procedure `makearray` that takes one argument, the dimension of the array, and returns an array of the specified size. ☐

Scheme and C both use the indirect model of arrays. Some other languages, like Pascal and ML, use a different model of arrays, in which an array is a sequence of expressed values, not a sequence of cells:

$$\text{Array} = (\text{Expressed Value})^*$$

Figure 6.1.4   Auxiliaries for call-by-value with direct arrays

```
(define denoted->expressed
  (lambda (den-val)
    (let ((exp-val (cell-ref den-val)))
      (if (array? exp-val) (array-copy exp-val) exp-val))))

(define eval-array-exp
  (lambda (exp env)
    (variant-case exp
      (varref (var) (let ((exp-val (cell-ref (apply-env env var))))
                      (if (array? exp-val)
                          exp-val
                          (error "Expecting an array:" exp-val))))
      (else (eval-exp exp env)))))
```

In this model, when an array is passed by value, the formal parameter is bound to a cell containing a *copy* of the sequence of values in the original array. Then, if the procedure performs array assignment, we know that only the local copy of the array is modified, just as in ordinary parameter passing. We call this the *direct* model of arrays.

Modeling direct arrays in Scheme is somewhat tricky because Scheme uses the indirect model. The simplest way to do this is to model an array with a vector, as in the indirect case, but to copy it when it is returned as a value. We can do this by redefining *denoted->expressed* as in figure 6.1.4. Values other than arrays do not need to be copied because Scheme already copies them. In an array reference or array assignment, however, we don't want to copy the array, so we modify *eval-array-exp* so that the array is returned without copying whenever possible. See figure 6.1.4.

The difference between indirect and direct models of arrays is illustrated by figure 6.1.5. For the indirect version, x and u are both bound to cells that point at the first location of an array containing 5, 6, and 4 and v is bound to a cell that points to the first location of an array containing 3 and 8. Executing the assignment x[1] := 7 changes the 6 to a 7. Then executing x := v changes the x cell to point at the same array as v does. Finally, executing x[1] := 9 then changes the 8 to a 9. See figure 6.1.6 (a). For the direct version, x is bound to a cell that contains an array just like u's. Executing x[1] := 7 changes the 6 in x's array to a 7. The assignment x := v replaces the contents of x's cell by a copy of v's array. See figure 6.1.6 (b).

Figure 6.1.5　Example illustrating direct and indirect array models

```
letarray u[3]; v[2]
in begin
    u[0] := 5; u[1] := 6; u[2] := 4; v[0] := 3; v[1] := 8;
    let p = proc (x)
              begin
                x[1] := 7;
                x := v;
                x[1] := 9
              end
    in p(u)
  end
```

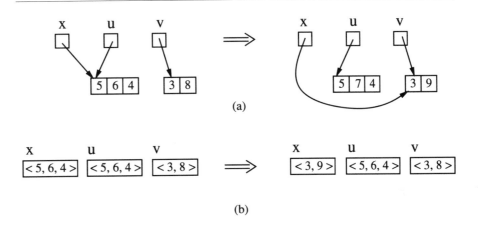

(a)

(b)

Figure 6.1.6　Effect of figure 6.1.5 using call-by-value

○ *Exercise 6.1.3*
Is it true that using direct arrays, call-by-value parameter passing in a procedure really prevents side-effects from being visible to the caller? □

○ *Exercise 6.1.4*
Do the interpreters presented in this section do the right thing when an array element contains another array? Modify the direct array interpreter to behave correctly in this case. □

When an operand is a variable and the called procedure assigns to the corresponding formal parameter, is this visible to the caller as a change in the binding of its variable? The indirect model of arrays provides such visibility for arrays modified by array assignment, but for ordinary variables, with modification by variable assignment, the answer to this question has been no. If an assignment is made to a procedure's call-by-value parameter, it affects only the binding made when the procedure was called. For example, in

```
let p = proc (x) x := 5
in let a = 3;
       b = 4
   in begin
        p(a);
        p(b);
        +(a, b)
      end
```

on each call to procedure p, the variable x is bound to a fresh cell. Therefore the assignment to x does not affect a or b, and so the expression yields 7. The effect of an assignment is always restricted to the scope of the assigned variable. This is generally desirable, especially given the difficulties inherent in understanding assignment. It is clear what code needs to be examined to understand the effect of an assignment.

There are times, however, when it is necessary or convenient for a procedure to be capable of assigning a binding passed by its caller, even though the procedure may not be defined within the scope of the associated variable. For example, it may be intended above that a and b both be set to 5, in which case the expression should yield 10.

This may be accomplished by a different parameter-passing technique in which the arguments passed to p are the bindings of a and b, not their corresponding expressed values. This form of parameter passing is known as *call-by-reference*.

Call-by-reference allows us to write some procedures that cannot be written using call-by-value. The classic example is a procedure that swaps the contents of its arguments. For example, using call-by-reference we can write

```
--> define swap =
      proc (x, y)
         let temp = 0
         in begin temp := x; x := y; y := temp end;
--> define c = 3;
--> let b = 4
      in begin
            swap(c, b);
            b
         end;
3
--> c;
4
```

○ *Exercise 6.2.1*
Why doesn't this work under call-by-value? □

In most languages with call-by-reference, references can be array elements as well as variable bindings. If an array element is passed by reference to a procedure and the procedure assigns to its corresponding formal parameter, the effect is to assign a new value to the array element. Thus *swap* may be used to exchange the values of array elements.

```
--> define b = 2;
--> letarray a[3]
      in begin
            a[1] := 5;
            swap(a[1], b);
            a[1]
         end;
2
--> b;
5
```

In some languages, call-by-reference operands may be expressions other than variable or data structure references (such as applications). In these languages the value of the operand is placed in a new location, and assignments to this location by the called procedure have no effect that is visible to the caller. For example, consider

```
--> define c = 3;
--> define p = proc (x) x := 5;
--> begin
      p(add1(c));
      c
    end;
3
```

Here c refers to a location that initially contains 3. The assignment changes the value of the binding of x from 4 to 5 but does not affect the binding of c. In such cases call-by-value and call-by-reference behave the same way.

More than one call-by-reference parameter may refer to the same location:

```
--> let b = 3;
       p = proc (x, y)
             begin
               x := 4;
               y
             end
    in p(b, b);
4
```

The reason this yields 4 is that x and y both refer to the cell that is the binding of b. This phenomenon is known as *aliasing*. Here x and y are aliases (names) for the same location. Aliasing makes it very difficult to understand programs. Generally, we do not expect an assignment to one variable to change the value of another. Virtually all rules for reasoning formally about programs are invalid in the presence of aliasing.

If references to array elements are passed as arguments, then in general it is impossible to detect aliasing without costly run-time checks. For example, swap(a[1], a[f(b)]) results in aliasing if and only if f(b) yields 1, which may be impossible to predict.

The preceding definition of *swap* happens to work even if its parameters are aliased, but aliasing can provide unpleasant surprises. The following version of swap cleverly avoids the use of a temporary variable by assuming that its arguments are integers.

```
--> define swap2 =
      proc (x, y)
        begin
          x := +(x, y); y := -(x, y); x := -(x, y)
        end;
```

```
--> define b = 1;
--> define c = 2;
--> swap2(b, c);
--> b;
2
--> c;
1
--> swap2(b, b);
--> b;
0
```

The first call to *swap2* works correctly. In the second call, however, x and
y are aliases for b, so b is assigned $2 + 2 = 4$, and then $4 - 4 = 0$. Clearly
swap2 works only if its arguments are not aliased.

How is call-by-reference to be modeled? The clue is that the denoted values
of the caller are the same as the denoted values of the procedure. Thus, if the
operand is a variable, we can pass its binding directly to the procedure, rather
than copying its contents to a new cell, as we did in call-by-value. So we can
obtain a simple version of call-by-reference by changing the production

$$\langle \text{operand} \rangle ::= \langle \text{exp} \rangle$$

to

$$\langle \text{operand} \rangle ::= \langle \text{varref} \rangle$$

and changing `eval-rand` to

```
(define eval-rand
  (lambda (rand env)
    (variant-case rand
      (varref (var) (apply-env env var))
      (else (error "Invalid operand:" rand)))))
```

What other forms can operands take? We have seen that when an array
reference appears as an operand in call-by-reference, we must pass a reference to the array element, not the value of the array element. In a typical
implementation, a reference to an array element is simply a pointer to the
element. Since it is not possible in Scheme to obtain a pointer directly to
a vector element, we represent array elements by the `ae` record type, which
records the array and the index of an element within the array's vector.

```
(define-record ae (array index))
```

So in general, an L-value in the language is either a cell or an array element; in either case the contents of the L-value is an expressed value. We write this as

L-value = Cell (Expressed Value) + Array Element (Expressed Value)

Denoted Value = L-value

Later we introduce denoted values that are not L-values.

We have explored two possibilities for call-by-reference operands: variables and array references. We could restrict call-by-reference operands to these two forms, but instead we adopt the more common design alternative, suggested earlier in this section, that arbitrary expressions be allowed as call-by-reference operands, with their values passed to the procedure in fresh cells as in call-by-value. Hence we write the grammar for operands as

---

⟨operand⟩ ::= ⟨varref⟩
    | ⟨array-exp⟩ [⟨exp⟩]   `arrayref (array index)`
    | ⟨exp⟩

To obtain an interpreter for call-by-reference, we start off with the interpreter for call-by-value and modify the auxiliary procedures that deal with operands and denoted values, since those are the ones that change.

If we start with an interpreter for call-by-value with indirect arrays, we get the auxiliary procedures shown in figure 6.2.1. Corresponding to the grammar for operands, `eval-rand` has three cases. If the operand is a variable or an array reference, the corresponding L-value should be passed directly to the procedure; otherwise the expression should be evaluated and copied into a new cell, as for call-by-value.

Since we have changed the set of denoted values (or at least the set of representations of denoted values), we need to change the procedures that deal with denoted values. There are only two of these: `denoted->expressed` and `denoted-value-assign!`. We modify each of them to check what kind of denoted value they are given and to do the right thing in each case. In this interpreter, the error lines in each of these two procedures should never be executed, but they allow for extension later.

The distinction between direct and indirect parameter passing is orthogonal to the distinction between call-by-value and call-by-reference. The former concerns allocation and sharing of aggregate values, which are mutated through array assignment, whereas the latter concerns allocation and sharing of variable bindings, which are mutated through variable assignment.

Figure 6.2.1   Auxiliaries for call-by-reference with indirect arrays

```
(define eval-rand
  (lambda (rand env)
    (variant-case rand
      (varref (var) (apply-env env var))
      (arrayref (array index)
        (make-ae (eval-array-exp array env) (eval-exp index env)))
      (else (make-cell (eval-exp rand env)))))))

(define denoted->expressed
  (lambda (den-val)
    (cond
      ((cell? den-val) (cell-ref den-val))
      ((ae? den-val) (array-ref (ae->array den-val) (ae->index den-val)))
      (else (error "Can't dereference denoted value:" den-val)))))

(define denoted-value-assign!
  (lambda (den-val val)
    (cond
      ((cell? den-val) (cell-set! den-val val))
      ((ae? den-val) (array-set! (ae->array den-val) (ae->index den-val) val))
      (else (error "Can't assign to denoted value:" den-val)))))
```

The combination of direct parameter passing and call-by-reference is used, for example, when arrays are bound to var parameters in Pascal. Though the combination of indirect parameter passing and call-by-reference is less common, it is occasionally used, as in Modula-2, when passing an aggregate value whose type is "hidden."

Figure 6.2.2 shows the effect of executing the program in figure 6.1.5 under both the indirect and direct models. In the indirect model, both x and u are bound to a cell containing a pointer to the first location in the array containing the sequence 5, 6, and 4. The assignment x := v mutates that cell, so that now u and x both point to the other array. (See figure 6.2.2 (a).) In the direct model, x and u are both bound to the same cell, which contains the sequence $<5, 6, 4>$. The assignment x := v mutates that cell, so it contains the same contents as the other array. Since we are using the direct model, this means the sequence of numbers $<3, 8>$, rather than a sequence of cells containing them, so we are forced to copy the array. The final assignment x[1] := 9 mutates the copied array, so at the end of the procedure x and u

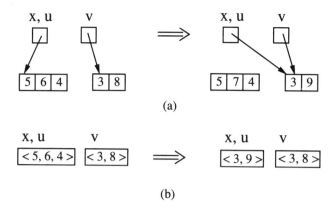

(a)

(b)

Figure 6.2.2 Effect of figure 6.1.5 using call-by-reference

are both bound to a cell containing the sequence <3, 9>, and v is bound to a cell containing the sequence <3, 8>. (See figure 6.2.2 (b).)

One advantage of call-by-reference is that it allows a procedure to "return" more than one value by side-effecting some of its parameters. For example, a procedure may take a call-by-reference parameter to which it assigns a status code indicating what sort of exception, if any, it may have encountered. This allows the procedure to return normal results in the usual way without danger of confusion with error codes. There are other ways of returning multiple results using call-by-value (for example, continuation-passing style as in exercise 11.4.4 or variant records as used in exercise 5.5.8).

As we saw in section 6.1, passing structured objects such as arrays by value requires copying the object. For reasons of efficiency structured objects may be passed by reference, even when other arguments are passed by value. Another alternative when call-by-value is used by default is to provide specific declarations that force certain parameters to be passed by reference. If such a declaration is forgotten when passing an array, an inefficient copy may be performed without the programmer's knowledge. Of course, assignments to elements of an array are visible to the caller if the array has been passed by reference, but not if it has been copied. Heap-allocated objects, including Scheme's cons cells and vectors, are always accessed via references. They are not copied when these references to them are passed by value.

Figure 6.2.3   Program for exercise 6.2.5

```
letarray u[3]; v[2]
in begin
    u[0] := 5; u[1] := 6; u[2] := 4; v[0] := 3; v[1] := 8;
    let p = proc (x, y)
               begin
                 write(y);
                 x[1] := 7;
                 write(y);
                 x := v;
                 x[1] := 9;
                 write(y)
               end
    in begin
         p(u, u[1]);
         write(u[1])
       end
    end
```

- *Exercise 6.2.2*

  Modify this interpreter to use the direct model of arrays rather than the indirect model. What does it mean to pass an array element by reference in the direct model? ☐

- *Exercise 6.2.3*

  Implement the call-by-reference interpreters for both direct and indirect arrays. Test them using *swap* and *swap2*. Also verify that only with indirect arrays can the caller of a procedure notice assignments made by the procedure to array elements. ☐

- *Exercise 6.2.4*

  Draw appropriate diagrams and describe how the program in figure 6.2.3, whose parameter passing protocol uses call-by-reference with indirect arrays, prints 6779. ☐

It is often possible for compilers to allocate memory (cells) for call-by-value parameters of a procedure in locations that the procedure's code can access directly. This contrasts with call-by-reference parameters, the locations of which are not known until the procedure is called. This usually makes variable references less efficient when call-by-reference is used. The *call-by-value-result* parameter-passing technique combines the variable reference efficiency of call-by-value with the ability, provided by call-by-reference, to return information to the caller through parameters. The trick is to pass a pointer to the caller's cell, as in call-by-reference, and then to copy the contents of the cell in a location local to the called procedure. The called procedure then uses the local cell just as it would with call-by-value. Then, just before the procedure returns, the contents of the local cell is copied back into the caller's cell.

Call-by-value-result achieves more efficient variable reference than call-by-reference at the expense of less efficient procedure call and return. In this respect it is superior only if variables are referenced many times in a typical call, as in a loop. Even in such cases, a compiler may be able to eliminate the indirection of call-by-reference using optimization techniques that are beyond the scope of this book.

There may, however, be other reasons to prefer call-by-value-result over call-by-reference. One is that call-by-value-result does not suffer from the aliasing problems of call-by-reference. For example, swap2 is correct if parameters are passed by value-result. Given the difficulties that aliasing poses for formal proof and other approaches to reasoning carefully about programs, call-by-value-result may be preferred when attempting to write highly reliable programs.

In the absence of aliasing, call-by-value-result has the same effect as call-by-reference. Therefore, some language specifications allow the use of either call-by-reference or call-by-value-result. The compiler is then free to choose for each parameter the passing technique that is optimum under the circumstances of the call. The danger is that if aliasing does occur, the results are unpredictable. This may have serious consequences. For example, though a program may at times alias two arguments, it might still work correctly because the compiler happens to choose call-by-value-result for one or both of the arguments. If the program is then compiled using a different compiler, or even using the same compiler after the program has been changed in ways that affect optimization of the call, call-by-reference may be used for both arguments. This exposes an error in a program that may have performed correctly for some time. To make matters worse, the error may not actually cause damage for a long time, since the arguments may be array elements that are aliased only under run time conditions that rarely occur.

Call-by-reference and call-by-value-result allow information to be passed both to and from a called procedure. The *call-by-result* parameter-passing technique is appropriate when a parameter is used only to pass information from a procedure to its caller. It is simply a variation on call-by-value-result in which the local L-value of a parameter is uninitialized. It may be used, for example, to return an error code to the caller.

Call-by-value, call-by-value-result, and call-by-result are sometimes known collectively as *call-by-copy,* since they all involve making a copy of a variable binding when the operand is a variable reference.

- *Exercise 6.3.1*
  Modify the parameter-passing of the call-by-reference with indirect arrays interpreter so that parameters are passed by value-result. ⬜

- *Exercise 6.3.2*
  Write a program (without using `swap2`) in which call-by-value, call-by-reference, and call-by-value-result all yield different results. ⬜

6.4 Expressed or Denoted Values?

The languages we have developed follow the tradition of Scheme and similar languages in that they have a rich set of expressed values, but the denoted values are comparatively simple: they are always cells containing expressed values. Having a rich set of expressed values is important, because the primary way in which computed information is returned is as the value of a procedure: an expressed value.

In traditional imperative languages, however, expressions occur primarily inside assignment statements, so the set of expressed values corresponds roughly to the set of values that are *storable* in a memory location. In such languages, the set of expressed values is generally simple, but the set of denoted values is quite rich. In Pascal, for example, the expressed values are scalars, such as integers and characters, but the denoted values include arrays and procedures. We shall now see how this change in perspective is reflected in our interpreters.

The next language has the simplest possible set of expressed values:

$$\text{Expressed Value} = \text{Number}$$

but we make the set of denoted values much richer:

$$\text{Denoted Value} = \text{L-value} + \text{Array} + \text{Procedure}$$

So arrays and procedures are denoted values but not expressed values. This does not cause much problem for arrays, since arrays are already introduced with `letarray`, but procedures are more complicated. The fact that procedures are expressed values is built into our syntax and interpreters. Procedures are created as expressed values by `proc`, and retrieved as expressed values when *eval-exp* evaluates the operator portion of an application.

So our first task is to change the language's syntax. Since a procedure (or array) can exist only as the binding of a variable, we make ⟨operator⟩ (or ⟨array-exp⟩) be a variable. In addition, we need to introduce a form, like `let`, that allows us to introduce variables, without using procedure application. To do this, we delete the productions

⟨exp⟩ ::= `proc` ⟨varlist⟩ ⟨exp⟩	`proc (formals body)`
⟨operator⟩ ::= ⟨exp⟩	
⟨array-exp⟩ ::= ⟨exp⟩	

and replace them by the productions

⟨exp⟩ ::= `letproc` ⟨procdecls⟩ `in`	`letproc (procdecls`
⟨exp⟩	`body)`
¦ `local` ⟨decls⟩ `in` ⟨exp⟩	`local (decls body)`
⟨operator⟩ ::= ⟨varref⟩	
⟨array-exp⟩ ::= ⟨varref⟩	

In order to have something interesting to pass to these procedures, we use call-by-reference. Our starting point is the call-by-reference interpreter of section 6.2, shown in figure 6.1.2 and figure 6.2.1. Figure 6.4.1 shows the resulting interpreter. There are only two changes in the code of figure 6.4.1. First, we replace *eval-rator*, which was *eval-exp*, with code that uses *apply-env*, since the `rator` is known to be a variable reference.

Figure 6.4.1   Interpreter with denoted procedures and arrays

```
(define eval-exp
  (lambda (exp env)
    (variant-case exp
      (letproc (procdecls body)
        (let ((vars (map procdecl->var procdecls))
              (closures (map (lambda (decl)
                               (make-closure
                                 (procdecl->formals decl)
                                 (procdecl->body decl)
                                 env))
                             procdecls)))
          (let ((new-env (extend-env vars closures env)))
            (eval-exp body new-env))))
      (local (decls body)
        (let ((vars (map decl->var decls))
              (exps (map decl->exp decls)))
          (let ((new-env (extend-env vars
                           (map (lambda (exp)
                                  (make-cell (eval-exp exp env)))
                                exps)
                           env)))
            (eval-exp body new-env))))
      ...)))

(define eval-rator
  (lambda (rator env)
    (let ((den-val (apply-env env (varref->var rator))))
      (if (closure? den-val)
          den-val
          (denoted->expressed den-val)))))
```

The second change is the new construction `letproc`. The code for `letproc` builds a list of closures, and then evaluates the body in a new environment in which each of the names is bound to the corresponding closure. See figure 6.4.1.

Since the set of denoted values has changed, we also need to review the auxiliary procedures introduced in section 6.1, which manipulate denoted values. The results are shown in figure 6.4.2. The procedures *denoted->expressed* and *denoted-value-assign!* can be the same as for the call-by-reference

Figure 6.4.2   Procedures for call-by-reference with denoted indirect arrays

```
(define denoted->expressed
  (lambda (den-val)
    (cond
      ((cell? den-val) (cell-ref den-val))
      ((ae? den-val) (array-ref (ae->array den-val) (ae->index den-val)))
      (else (error "Can't dereference denoted value:" den-val)))))

(define denoted-value-assign!
  (lambda (den-val val)
    (cond
      ((cell? den-val) (cell-set! den-val val))
      ((ae? den-val) (array-set! (ae->array den-val) (ae->index den-val) val))
      (else (error "Can't assign to denoted value:" den-val)))))

(define do-letarray make-array)

(define eval-array-exp
  (lambda (array-exp env)
    (apply-env env (varref->var array-exp))))
```

case, since they already contain checks to make sure that only legal L-values
are dereferenced or mutated. Similarly, *expressed->denoted* and *eval-rand*
remain unchanged. In `letarray`, the variables are bound directly to the arrays, rather than to cells pointing to the arrays, so *do-letarray* need not
call *make-cell*. Since array expressions must be variables, *eval-array-exp*
can be simplified to use *apply-env*. This completes the interpreter.

Typically, languages that use a stack as their basic run-time structure (see
section 10.4) allocate their environments on the stack, so denoted values are
restricted to values that are storable on the stack. These typically include
single-word quantities, such as small integers and pointers, but may also include quantities that take up several words on the stack. In Pascal, for example, even arrays are allocated on the stack, and are copied when they are
passed by value, an expensive operation. Denoted values typically include
cells, since these are represented by pointers, which are easily stored on the
stack. In section 10.4, we study the issue of stack allocation and the representation of various values on the stack in much more detail.

Imperative languages typically equate expressed values with those values that are storable in a memory cell. Therefore the set of expressed values is restricted to those that fit into a single machine word, such as small integers and pointers. Languages vary in the specification of what values are storable, and particularly when those values are pointers. In Pascal, for example, the pointers refer to heap-allocated data structures, similar to cons cells in Scheme. C, on the other hand, allows pointers to almost any type of value, including procedures.

Even functional and almost-functional languages differ in this respect. Scheme has a rich set of expressed values, using an indirect model of aggregates, so that most values are represented as pointers, but cells are not expressed values. This is reflected in our need to define a `cell` ADT, and in our simulation of array element pointers. Scheme's denoted values are just cells or L-values. By contrast, the language ML, which shares many design goals with Scheme, is quite different in its value structure. It uses a direct model of aggregate structures, but still has a rich set of expressed values. These are mostly represented by pointers, but this is hidden from the programmer. Expressed values include cells, but not array references, because of the use of the direct model. Denoted values are the same as expressed values. There is no variable assignment, which would normally require denoted values to differ from expressed values. Instead, assignment is accomplished by explicit operations on cells. This is very similar to the style we have adopted in the interpreters.

We have only touched upon the study of the value structures of programming languages. Studying the denoted and expressed values of a language provides deep insight into its structure. Choosing a value structure is quite difficult. The choice, however, determines a great deal of the language's expressive power and, as we have seen, greatly affects its efficiency.

- *Exercise 6.4.1*
Implement this interpreter and run some examples. []

o *Exercise 6.4.2*
This interpreter, like our earlier ones, assumes that the initial environment consists of cells containing primitive procedures. In this design, these cells can be modified by variable assignment. Modify the interpreter to prevent this by having the initial environment contain procedures rather than cells. []

- *Exercise 6.4.3*

  Modify this interpreter to use call-by-value instead of call-by-reference. □

○ *Exercise 6.4.4*

  Modify this interpreter to pass structures directly, rather than indirectly. □

○ *Exercise 6.4.5*

  Modify this interpreter so that `letproc` defines its procedures recursively, as `letrecproc` does. □

○ *Exercise 6.4.6*

  Several times during the course of this chapter we have presented a grammar rule that weakens the expressiveness of the language. For example, ⟨array-exp⟩ was any expression and now it can be only a variable. Modify the parser or the interpreter to support these restrictions. □

6.5 Call-by-Name and Call-by-Need

In section 4.3, we saw that lambda calculus expressions may be evaluated using β-reduction. In this model, procedures are called by performing the body of the procedure after the operands are substituted for each reference to the corresponding variable. This substitution may require (α-conversion) to avoid capturing of variable references that occur free in the operands. Such rewriting techniques, which require manipulation of program text during evaluation, are heavily used in the theoretical study of programming languages. In general, however, they are too inefficient for practical use.

β-reduction does have one characteristic that is sometimes of practical importance and is not shared by the parameter-passing techniques discussed so far: the possibility of delaying (through normal order reduction) the evaluation of operands until their values are needed. This may avoid unnecessary, or even nonterminating computation.

The price paid for avoiding non-termination is that if there are repeated references to the same parameter, then the associated operand is reevaluated with each reference. Another subtlety of this evaluation scheme is that the index subexpression of an array reference is not evaluated until the time of assignment. In the following example, the delay of array index evaluation is critical.

```
--> define p = proc (x)
                 begin
                   i := 1;
                   x := 2
                 end;
--> define i = 0;
--> letarray a[2]
    in begin
         a[0] := 1;
         p(a[i]);
         writeln(a[0], a[1])
       end;
  1 2
```

Delayed evaluation and assignment do not combine well, since it is hard
to understand the effect of assignment if it is unclear when the assignment
will happen. Nevertheless, this combination is supported by some languages,
notably Algol 60, and there are times when it is useful. A classic example is
Jensen's device (exercise 6.5.4). Nevertheless, parameter-passing mechanisms
that use delayed evaluation are used in some programming languages, so they
are worth studying.

To delay operand evaluation without program rewriting, it is tempting simply to pass a reference to some representation such as an abstract syntax tree
(or compiled code) of the operand. However, it is necessary to prevent free
variables in the operand from being captured by declarations in the called
procedure. We have already encountered the variable capture problem when
creating procedures, and the solution is the same: close the operand in the
calling environment. We do this by forming a data structure that includes
both some representation of the text of the operand and also the bindings of
all variables that occur free in the operand. Closures created to delay evaluation are called *thunks*. For example, in section 4.5.2, we saw how thunks
(created as procedures of no arguments) may be used to delay evaluating a
stream's tail.

Parameter passing in which argument evaluation is delayed using thunks
that are reevaluated with every variable reference is called *call-by-name*. To
develop an implementation for a call-by-name interpreter employing indirect
parameter passing, we first identify the expressed and denoted values. We
begin with the language of section 6.1. For this language we had

$$\text{Expressed Value} = \text{Number} + \text{Procedure} + \text{Array}$$

What should the denoted values be? As suggested above, these values should include thunks that encapsulate an operand and its environment. But what kind of value should invocation of such a thunk return? Since a formal parameter may appear on the left-hand side of a variable assignment, the only safe answer is that invocation of a thunk must return an L-value. We write this as

$$\text{Thunk} = () \rightarrow \text{L-value}$$

meaning that a thunk is a procedure of no arguments, which returns an L-value when called. We represent a thunk, containing an operand and an environment, using the following record type:

```
(define-record thunk (exp env))
```

As in the case of call-by-reference, the possible L-values include array elements:

L-value = Cell (Expressed Value) + Array Element (Expressed Value)

Since these L-values are the same as in section 6.2, we can use most of the same auxiliary procedures.

We would also like to have local variables, either scalars or arrays, in procedure bodies. It is unnecessary and inefficient to use the thunk mechanism for these variables, so we can represent them in the usual way. Thus, the denoted values are either L-values or thunks:

$$\text{Denoted Value} = \text{L-value} + \text{Thunk}$$

We can continue to use *eval-exp* from figure 6.1.2, which we extend with local in figure 6.5.1. The call-by-name interpreter contains one big difference: *eval-rands* does not evaluate the operands. Instead, it merely packages them in thunks.

A thunk is evaluated when the variable to which it is bound is evaluated. Since the body of a thunk is an operand, *eval-rand* is used to evaluate the thunk body. Since invocation of a thunk returns an L-value, we cannot use *eval-exp* here. Instead, we use a grammar for operands that recognizes the special case of an operand that is a variable or array reference. In this case we can pass the corresponding L-value directly. This is the same situation as in call-by-reference.

Figure 6.5.1   Call-by-name interpreter

```
(define eval-exp
  (lambda (exp env)
    (variant-case exp
      (local (decls body)
        (let ((vars (map decl->var decls))
              (exps (map decl->exp decls)))
          (let ((new-env (extend-env vars
                           (map (lambda (exp)
                                  (make-cell (eval-exp exp env)))
                                exps)
                           env)))
            (eval-exp body new-env))))
      (app (rator rands)
        (apply-proc (eval-rator rator env) (eval-rands rands env)))
      (varref (var) (denoted->expressed (apply-env env var)))
      (varassign (var exp)
        (denoted-value-assign! (apply-env env var) (eval-exp exp env)))
      (letarray (arraydecls body)
        (eval-exp body
          (extend-env (map decl->var arraydecls)
            (map (lambda (decl)
                   (do-letarray (eval-exp (decl->exp decl) env)))
                 arraydecls)
            env)))
      (arrayref (array index)
        (array-ref (eval-array-exp array env) (eval-exp index env)))
      (arrayassign (array index exp)
        (array-set!
          (eval-array-exp array env)
          (eval-exp index env)
          (eval-exp exp env)))
      ...)))

(define eval-rands
  (lambda (rands env)
    (map (lambda (rand) (make-thunk rand env)) rands)))
```

Figure 6.5.2   Auxiliaries for call-by-name interpreter

```
(define eval-rand
  (lambda (rand env)
    (variant-case rand
      (varref (var) (denoted->L-value (apply-env env var)))
      (arrayref (array index)
        (make-ae (eval-array-exp array env) (eval-exp index env)))
      (else (make-cell (eval-exp rand env))))))

(define denoted->L-value
  (lambda (den-val)
    (if (thunk? den-val)
        (eval-rand (thunk->exp den-val) (thunk->env den-val))
        den-val)))

(define denoted->expressed
  (lambda (den-val)
    (let ((l-val (denoted->L-value den-val)))
      (cond
        ((cell? l-val) (cell-ref l-val))
        ((ae? l-val)
         (array-ref (ae->array l-val) (ae->index l-val)))
        (else (error "Can't dereference denoted value:" l-val))))))

(define denoted-value-assign!
  (lambda (den-val exp-val)
    (let ((l-val (denoted->L-value den-val)))
      (cond
        ((cell? l-val) (cell-set! l-val exp-val))
        ((ae? l-val) (array-set! (ae->array l-val) (ae->index l-val) exp-val))
        (else (error "Can't assign to denoted value:" l-val))))))

(define expressed->denoted make-cell)

(define do-letarray (compose make-cell make-array))

(define eval-array-exp eval-exp)

(define eval-rator eval-exp)
```

We write the grammar for operands as

$$\langle\text{operand}\rangle ::= \langle\text{varref}\rangle$$
$$| \;\; \langle\text{array-exp}\rangle \; [\langle\text{exp}\rangle] \qquad\qquad \texttt{arrayref (array index)}$$
$$| \;\; \langle\text{exp}\rangle$$

and we invoke thunks with a slightly modified version of the call-by-reference `eval-rand`, shown in figure 6.5.2. If the thunk contains a variable or an array reference, the corresponding L-value is returned. The invocation (`apply-env env var`) may return another thunk rather than an L-value, so `denoted->L-value` is called, which in turn invokes that thunk. If the thunk contains a more complex expression, the best we can do is to evaluate it and put it in a new cell. Because this mechanism tries to return an L-value rather than copying its contents, call-by-name often coincides with call-by-reference.

All that remains is to define the auxiliary procedures used in figure 6.5.1. Since these L-values are the same as in the call-by-reference case, we can do this by adapting them to invoke thunks when necessary; see figure 6.5.2.

The procedure `denoted->expressed` first coerces its denoted value to an L-value by using `denoted->L-value` to invoke the thunk if necessary. It then dereferences the L-value, just as it did in the call-by-reference case. The procedure `denoted-value-assign!` works similarly. Since arrays are expressed but not denoted, we use the version of `do-letarray` that calls `make-cell`. Furthermore, since arrays are expressed values, array expressions may be arbitrary expressions, and `eval-array-exp` must be `eval-exp`. Similarly, `eval-rator` must be `eval-exp`. This completes the procedures that need to be defined for the interpreter.

- *Exercise 6.5.1*
Since call-by-name is so much like call-by-reference, you might expect *swap* to work under call-by-name. One example of an unpleasant surprise provided by the interaction between delayed array index evaluation and assignment is that *swap* may fail. What values are printed by the following expression?

```
letarray a[2]
in local i = 0
   in begin
        a[0] := 1; a[1] := 0;
        swap(i, a[i]);
        writeln(a[0], a[1])
      end
```

☐

- *Exercise 6.5.2*

What values are returned when these two program terminate?

```
let p = proc (x)
        begin
          x := 3; x := +(x, 5); x := +(x, 5)
        end
in local a = 10
   in begin p(a); a end
```

```
local a = 10
in let p = proc (x)
          begin
            a := 3; a := +(x, 5); a := +(x, 5)
          end
   in begin p(+(a, a)); a end
```

What values are returned if the `local` is replaced by `let`? Remember that `let` is syntactic sugar for procedure application. ☐

○ *Exercise 6.5.3*

Write an interpreter that implements procedure calling by substituting the operands for the formal parameters of the procedures. What difficulties do you encounter? ☐

○ *Exercise 6.5.4*

Although the combination of assignment and delayed evaluation is problematic, there are times when it is useful. The classic example is a procedure that computes integral approximations. Write a procedure `int` that takes an integrand expression E, an integration parameter x (a variable occurring free in the integrand expression E), lower and upper bounds a and b, and an increment δ, and returns an approximation to the integral using the rectangular rule. That is,

$$\mathtt{int}(E \ x \ a \ b \ \delta) = \left(\sum_{\substack{x=a,a+\delta,\ldots, \\ a+\lceil (b-a)/\delta \rceil \delta}} E \right) \approx \int_a^b E \, dx$$

For example, assuming arithmetic operations are defined on floating point numbers (written with decimal points) as well as integers, and a primitive division procedure has been added to the initial environment, we could obtain a rough approximation of $\int_1^5 2x \, dx$ as follows.

```
--> define x = 0;
--> int(*(x, 2), x, 1, 5, quotient(1, 2))
35.0
--> x;
5.0
```

(Here we have assumed that the numbers in the defined language include real numbers under suitable arithmetic operations, but for this example we can avoid real-number literals). The variable x could have been initialized to any value. Assignments to x performed by int leave it with the value of the upper bound (or a bit more). The trick of assigning to an argument that is the binding of a variable occurring free in another argument is called *Jensen's device*. How should int be written using first-class procedures? □

When side effects are not involved, a delayed argument yields the same value each time it is referenced. Repeated evaluation of such arguments is a waste of effort. By saving the value obtained the first time such an argument is needed, it is possible to avoid redundant computation. This is *call-by-need*. A similar technique, memoization, was used in section 4.5.2 to avoid repeated evaluation of a stream's tail.

We can turn the call-by-name interpreter into a call-by-need interpreter by memoizing the result of invoking a thunk, so that later evaluations of the same variable will see the result instead of the thunk. To do this, we must change the set of denoted values slightly:

$$\text{Denoted Value} = \text{L-value} + \text{Memo}$$

$$\text{Memo} = \text{Cell} \, (\text{Thunk} + \text{L-value})$$

so that a denoted value is either an L-value or a memo, which is a cell containing either a thunk or its resulting L-value. We represent a memo as a record type:

```
(define-record memo (cell))
```

To incorporate this into the interpreter, we need change only *eval-rands*, to produce memos, and *denoted->L-value*, to actually do the memoization. The procedure *denoted->L-value* looks to see if its denoted value is a memo. If not, it must be an L-value, so it is returned directly. Otherwise, it looks at the contents of the cell. If the cell contains an L-value, it returns that L-value. If not, the cell contains a thunk, so the thunk is invoked with *eval-rand*, returning an L-value. This L-value is put in the cell, and then returned; see figure 6.5.3.

Figure 6.5.3   Auxiliaries for call-by-need interpreter

```
(define eval-rands
  (lambda (rands env)
    (map (lambda (rand)
           (make-memo (make-cell (make-thunk rand env))))
         rands)))

(define denoted->L-value
  (lambda (den-val)
    (if (memo? den-val)
        (let ((cell (memo->cell den-val)))
          (let ((contents (cell-ref cell)))
            (if (thunk? contents)
                (let ((l-val (eval-rand
                               (thunk->exp contents)
                               (thunk->env contents))))
                  (cell-set! cell l-val)
                  l-val)
                contents)))
        den-val)))
```

○ *Exercise 6.5.5*

What do call-by-name and call-by-need print for this program?

```
local a = 10
in let p = proc (x) +(x, x)
   in p(+(begin write(a); a end, a))
```
▯

6.6 Optional and Keyword Arguments

In most languages, procedures usually require a fixed number of arguments, and an exception is raised if they are called with the wrong number. If a given argument is the same in most calls to a procedure, it is convenient to omit this argument from these calls. This is possible if there is provision for *optional* arguments. If an optional argument is omitted from a call, the corresponding formal parameter is associated with a *default* value that is specified by the called procedure. For example, it is usually possible to supply a port to an output procedure so that output may be directed to a chosen file. In most cases, however, there is a "standard output port" to which most output is directed, such as the terminal in an interactive system. Thus the port argument of an output procedure is often optional and defaults to the standard output port.

Procedures may have several optional arguments. Usually optional parameters must follow required parameters in formal parameter lists. If there are n required parameters and m optional parameters, the procedure may be called with i arguments, where $n \leq i \leq n + m$, and the last $n + m - i$ parameters assume their default values. Arguments that it would most often be convenient to omit should be placed last, since omission of an argument requires omission of all the following arguments. Scheme input and output procedures take optional port arguments in this way.

Scheme procedures with optional arguments may be created using a syntax in which an improper list is used to specify the formal parameters.

$$(\texttt{lambda}\ (var_1\ \ldots\ var_n\ .\ opt)\ body)$$

When a procedure created with this syntax is invoked with $m \geq n$ arguments, opt is bound to a (possibly empty) list of arguments $n + 1$ through m. This generalizes the Scheme expression of the form ($\texttt{lambda}\ var\ body$) discussed in section 1.3, which may be used to create procedures in which all arguments are optional.

The Scheme optional-argument form does not allow the specification of default values for optional arguments. We can characterize this feature by a translation into Scheme as follows:

```
(lambda-opt (var₁ ... varₙ (opt₁ exp₁) ... (optₖ expₖ))
    body)

⇒ (lambda (var₁ ... varₙ . opts)
      (let ((len-opts (length opts)))
        (let ((opt₁ (if (< len-opts 1) exp₁ (list-ref opts 1)))
              ...
              (optₖ (if (< len-opts k) expₖ (list-ref opts k)))))
          body)))
```

This translation highlights some design decisions about the default values. The expressions exp_i appear inside the scope of the var_j, but they could have been placed outside that scope. Furthermore, the exp_i are evaluated each time the procedure is called. Even if the exp_i were not in the scope of the var_j, we might get different values because of side-effects.

- *Exercise 6.6.1*

Modify the parser to accept the following extended syntax for ⟨varlist⟩.

⟨varlist⟩ ::= ( )
       | (⟨vars⟩ {,⟨keydecl⟩}*)
       | (⟨keydecls⟩)
⟨keydecls⟩ ::= ⟨keydecl⟩ {,⟨keydecl⟩}*
⟨keydecl⟩ ::= :⟨var⟩ = ⟨exp⟩   `decl (var exp)`

Then modify the interpreter of figure 5.5.1 to support optional arguments. When a procedure with optional formals is called, the expressions associated with optional arguments are evaluated in the scope outside the procedure to obtain their default values before evaluating the procedure body. It is a run-time error to omit an argument that has not been given a default value.

```
--> (proc (x, :a = 1) +(x, a))(100);
101
--> let y = 3
    in (proc (x, :a = 1, :b = +(2, y))
           +(x, +(a, b)))
       (100, 10);
115
```
☐

o *Exercise 6.6.2*

The default values may appear inside or outside the scope of the non-optional formals var_j, and they may be evaluated at procedure creation time or at procedure call time. This gives two design decisions, for a total of four possible designs. Are all of them sensible? Give examples to show how the same program would give different answers in each possible design. Modify the equation for `lambda-opt` to express each design. ☐

In most languages, formal parameters are associated with arguments by *position*: the value of the nth operand of an application is associated with the nth variable in the procedure's formal parameter list. It is also possible to make this association by pairing operands with *keywords* that name the corresponding formal parameter. It then does not matter in what order these operands appear. In Lisp dialects that support keyword parameters, these keywords are typically indicated with a colon followed by the associated variable name. For example, a procedure `make-window` with keyword parameters named `height` and `width` might be called with

```
make-window(:height = 1, :width = +(2, 3)),
```

which is the same as

```
make-window(:width = +(2, 3), :height = 1).
```

Some languages use only keyword operands. In others, both positional and keyword operands may be used in the same call, with the positional operands occurring first. With keyword operands, the programmer must remember the name but not the operand's position, whereas for positional operands it is the position, not the name, that matters.

Keyword operands add significantly to the visual complexity of applications, unless they allow the number of operands to be significantly reduced. This is the case when they are used in combination with optional operands. Then any collection of optional operands may be used in a call. An optional operand identified by a keyword is especially useful when the behavior of a procedure is determined by a large number of parameters whose default values are suitable most of the time. There may be many optional parameters that a programmer does not even know exist, but a rarely needed parameter may be specified using the appropriate keyword. Operating system commands often use some form of keyword parameter mechanism.

○ *Exercise 6.6.3*
Modify the parser and interpreter of exercise 6.6.1 to support keyword parameters by extending the grammar of ⟨operands⟩.

⟨operands⟩ ::= ( )
          | (⟨exps⟩ {,⟨keydecls⟩}*)
          | (⟨keydecls⟩)
    ⟨exps⟩ ::= ⟨exp⟩ {,⟨exp⟩}*

For example,

```
--> (proc (x, y) -(x, y)) (:y = 3, :x = 2);
-1
--> (proc (x, :a = 1, :b = +(2, 3))
        +(x, +(a, b)))
    (100, :b = 2);
103
```
☐

In the indirect model of arrays, an array is a sequence of cells, so when an array is passed by value, the procedure and its caller both see the same cells. In the direct model, an array is a sequence of values, so the procedure and its caller see different copies of the same sequence.

Call-by-reference allows a procedure to return information to its caller by assigning new values to its parameters. This is made possible by parameters that are references to variable bindings or data structure elements belonging to the caller. With call-by-reference it is possible for two parameters to refer to the same location. This phenomenon, known as aliasing, makes it difficult to understand programs. Call-by-value-result also allows information to be returned to the caller through variables but avoids the aliasing problem.

Analysis of the expressed and denoted values of our languages play an important role in the design of all these alternatives. Some languages are rich in expressed values but poor in denoted values, and others have the opposite mix.

Call-by-name delays evaluation of arguments until their values are needed, as with leftmost evaluation in the lambda calculus. This is achieved by passing thunks that close arguments over the calling environment. Call-by-name in combination with assignment is dangerous, since it may be difficult to predict just when assignments will take place. Call-by-need is a memoized variation on call-by-name. It avoids the inefficiency of repeatedly evaluating the same argument, but in combination with assignment it may not yield the same results as call-by-name.

Optional arguments and keyword operands are useful when a procedure has many parameters. With keyword operands the programmer need not remember the order of the arguments, and optional arguments may be omitted when a default value supplied by the procedure is appropriate.

7

Object-Oriented Languages

In this chapter we review the essential principles of object-oriented languages. This chapter is divided into three sections. The first discusses simple classes and objects, the second extends classes to include inheritance, and the last presents meta-classes. The interpreters of this section build from the interpreters of chapter 5.

7.1 Objects and Classes

In chapter 3 we introduced the notion of an abstract data type, or ADT. A data type is *abstract* when information about its representation is restricted to a designated set of procedures associated with the type. The techniques we use for implementing ADTs in Scheme are simple and adequate for our purposes. These techniques rely on our programming style, rather than on a language mechanism, to enforce data abstraction. We must be careful not to violate the abstraction of a data type by making any assumptions about a chosen representation except in the procedures that implement the ADT.

Data abstraction is aided by *modularity* mechanisms that group all the procedures that operate on elements of an ADT. Modularity facilities usually enforce *information hiding,* which ensures that only the procedures of an ADT operate on its values. When dynamic (or *latent*) type checking is used (as with Scheme's opaque primitive types) representation information is hidden by attaching to each value a tag indicating its type, and by requiring that all procedures check these tags before operating on values. Type tags are not needed if analysis prior to evaluation can prove that values are accessed only by appropriate operations. (Type checkers perform this job in statically-typed languages.) In either case, a fixed set of operations is associated with each type and adding support for user-defined data types may be difficult.

A more flexible approach to information hiding is to represent values as *objects*. An object is a set of operations that share a *state*. The state consists of one or more values that may be viewed and modified only by operations belonging to the object. These operations are often called *methods*. The operations supply the interface of the ADT to which the object belongs. Associating operations directly with the representation of a value makes it easy to create new data types. It also allows two objects of the same ADT to be represented differently, as long as their operations implement that same abstract interface. Extensive use of objects, particularly in conjunction with inheritance (discussed in the next section), characterizes a programming style called *object-oriented programming*.

Objects that share the same methods are said to be of the same *class*. In object-oriented programming, a typical style is to specify a set of methods (a class), and then to create objects that use those methods. The objects are then said to be *instances* of the class. A class is not the same as an ADT: one might have several different classes that give different implementations of the same ADT. Since the operations are associated directly with the object, it is possible to invoke the operation, which is in the interface, directly on the object without knowing which implementation it uses.

We shall see that it is useful for classes to be objects themselves, in which case creation of an instance is just another operation of the object that represents the class.

In languages with first class procedures, it is possible to represent objects as procedures. The simplest approach is to use a *message passing* protocol: a procedure representing an object is passed a message that selects the operation to be performed on the object. We have already seen one example of this approach in the `stack` and `make-stack` procedures of section 4.6. In this section we review this approach briefly and then present an interpreter that represents classes and instances as records. This interpreter gives a better understanding of techniques that may be employed to implement objects, and is extended further in the next section to reflect additional principles of object-oriented programming.

The `make-stack` procedure of figure 7.1.1 extends that of section 4.6. This procedure represents a class; each time it is invoked it returns a new instance of a stack object. These instances take a symbol representing a message and return a procedure that takes any additional arguments required by the operation and then performs the operation.

Each instance and class may have its own state, which is maintained as the bindings of one or more *instance variables* and *class variables,* respectively. In figure 7.1.1 there are two instance variables, `stk` and `local-pushed`, and one

Figure 7.1.1   Procedural stack class

```
(define make-stack
  (let ((pushed 0))
    (lambda ()
      (let ((stk '()) (local-pushed 0))
        (lambda (message)
          (case message
            ((empty?) (lambda () (null? stk)))
            ((push!) (lambda (x)
                       (set! pushed (+ pushed 1))
                       (set! local-pushed (+ local-pushed 1))
                       (set! stk (cons x stk))))
            ((pop!) (lambda ()
                      (if (null? stk)
                          (error "Stack: Underflow")
                          (begin
                            (set! pushed (- pushed 1))
                            (set! local-pushed (- local-pushed 1))
                            (set! stk (cdr stk))))))
            ((top) (lambda ()
                     (if (null? stk)
                         (error "Stack: Underflow")
                         (car stk))))
            ((local-pushed) (lambda () local-pushed))
            ((pushed) (lambda () pushed))
            (else (error "Stack: Invalid message" message))))))))
```

class variable, *pushed*. Class variables maintain information that is common
to *all* instances of a class, whereas each instance of a class has its own value
for every instance variable. The following transcript illustrates the use of
local-pushed and *pushed*.

```
> (define s1 (make-stack))
> (define s2 (make-stack))
> ((s1 'push!) 13)
> ((s2 'push!) 14)
> ((s2 'push!) 15)
> ((s1 'local-pushed))
1
> ((s2 'local-pushed))
2
```

```
> ((s1 'pushed))
3
> ((s2 'pushed))
3
```

We now turn to modeling objects with an interpreter. The interpreted language includes the following concrete and abstract syntax.

⟨exp⟩ ::= ⟨instance-var⟩
     | ⟨class-var⟩
     | ⟨instance-var⟩ := ⟨exp⟩   i-varassign (var exp)
     | ⟨class-var⟩ := ⟨exp⟩   c-varassign (var exp)
     | method ⟨varlist⟩ ⟨exp⟩   method (formals body)
     | $⟨var⟩ ((⟨exps⟩))   meth-app (name rands)
     | simpleinstance ⟨exp⟩   new-simpleinst (class-exp)
     | simpleclass ⟨varlist⟩   new-simpleclass (c-vars
       ⟨varlist⟩ ⟨methdecls⟩ ⟨exp⟩   i-vars methdecls init-exp)
⟨instance-var⟩ ::= &⟨var⟩   i-varref (var)
⟨class-var⟩ ::= &&⟨var⟩   c-varref (var)
⟨methdecls⟩ ::= ( )
       | (⟨decls⟩)

References to instance and class variables are distinguished by the prefixes & and &&, respectively. Method declarations are composed of two parts: the method name and an expression that evaluates to an *open method*. When open methods are supplied in a class declaration as the values of method declaration expressions, they are incorporated into the class and become *closed* methods. (Though open methods usually appear in method declarations, they do not have to; open methods are first-class values, like procedures.) The components of a simple class definition are lists of class and instance variables (without prefix), a series of method declarations, and an expression that is evaluated when the class is created. This expression is typically used to initialize class variables.

The transcript in figure 7.1.2 illustrates how a stack class, similar to that of figure 7.1.1, may be defined and used in the concrete syntax of our language of objects. We assume the initial environment supports the usual list operations. The simpleinstance form is used to create instances. We reserve the keywords class and instance for use in the next sections. Method calls have the syntax of procedure calls, preceded by a dollar sign. The name of the method to be invoked appears in the operator position (as if it were a variable reference),

Figure 7.1.2   Stack class definition transcript

```
--> define stackclass =
    simpleclass (pushed) (stk, localpushed)
     (initialize = method ()
                     begin
                       &localpushed := 0;
                       &stk := emptylist
                     end;
     empty = method () null(&stk);
     push = method (x)
              begin
                &&pushed := +(&&pushed, 1);
                &localpushed := +(&localpushed, 1);
                &stk := cons(x, &stk)
              end;
     pop = method ()
             if null(&stk)
             then error()
             else begin
                    &&pushed := -(&&pushed, 1);
                    &localpushed := -(&localpushed, 1);
                    &stk := cdr(&stk)
                  end;
     top = method ()
             if null(&stk)
             then error()
             else car(&stk);
     pushed = method () &&pushed;
     localpushed = method () &localpushed)
    &&pushed := 0;
--> define stack = simpleinstance(stackclass);
--> $push(stack, 7);
--> $top(stack);
7
```

the first operand of the application is evaluated to obtain the current object of the call, and any remaining operands supply arguments to the selected method.

We are now ready to describe the interpreter, which will reveal additional elements of the interpreted language's semantics. First we consider its environments. Class and instance variable environments associate class and instance variable names with their values. Since all instances of a particular class have the same instance variable names, we split the instance variable environment, storing an instance variable list in the class record and an instance value vector in the instance record. The only other information in an instance record is a pointer to its class, which will include all the other information needed to process a message sent to the instance.

```
(define-record instance (class i-vals))
```

All instances of a particular class share the same set of methods, which are recorded in the class's method environment. Given an instance, the appropriate method environment can be found using the `class` field of the instance record and the `m-env` field of the class record. Thus a class record contains four fields: one for each half of the class variable environment, one for the variable list of the instance variable environment, and one for the method environment.

```
(define-record class (c-vars c-vals i-vars m-env))
```

The interpreter also employs the usual lexical variable environment.

The interpreter for this language is shown in figure 7.1.3. The current class and instance are now passed to *eval-exp* for use in variable lookup. Although the current class may be easily obtained from the current instance, we pass both in anticipation of developments in the next section.

Instance and class variable lookup and assignment is performed by the procedure *cell-lookup* (see figure 7.1.4), which takes the variable being looked up, the variable list, and its value vector, and returns the associated cell. See the i-varref, c-varref, i-varassign, and c-varassign clauses of *eval-exp* in figure 7.1.3.

Since instance and class variables are assignable, their environments bind variables to cells that contain the binding values. Each instance and class variable environment is represented as a single rib consisting of a list of symbols and a vector of value cells. These cells are stored in an order that is the *reverse* of the corresponding symbols list. This anticipates developments in the next section.

Figure 7.1.3   Interpreter for language of objects

```
(define eval-exp
  (lambda (exp env class inst)
    (variant-case exp
      (i-varref (var) (lookup var (class->i-vars class) (instance->i-vals inst)))
      (c-varref (var) (lookup var (class->c-vars class) (class->c-vals class)))
      (i-varassign (var exp)
        (let ((value (eval-exp exp env class inst)))
          (assign var value (class->i-vars class) (instance->i-vals inst))))
      (c-varassign (var exp)
        (let ((value (eval-exp exp env class inst)))
          (assign var value (class->c-vars class) (class->c-vals class))))
      (method (formals body)
        (let ((new-formals (cons 'self formals)))
          (lambda (class-thunk)
            (lambda (args)
              (eval-exp body (extend-env new-formals (map make-cell args) env)
                (class-thunk)
                (car args))))))
      (meth-app (name rands)
        (let ((args (map (lambda (rand) (eval-exp rand env class inst)) rands)))
          (meth-call name (instance->class (car args)) args)))
      (new-simpleinst (class-exp)
        (let ((inst-class (eval-exp class-exp env class inst)))
          (let ((new-inst (make-instance inst-class
                            (make-vals (class->i-vars inst-class)))))
            (meth-call 'initialize (instance->class new-inst) (list new-inst))
            new-inst)))
      (new-simpleclass (c-vars i-vars methdecls init-exp)
        (let ((open-methods
                (map (lambda (decl)
                       (eval-exp (decl->exp decl) env class inst))
                     methdecls)))
          (letrec ((new-class
                     (make-class c-vars (make-vals c-vars) i-vars
                       (extend-env (map decl->var methdecls)
                         (map (lambda (open-method)
                                (open-method (lambda () new-class)))
                              open-methods)
                         init-meth-env))))
            (eval-exp init-exp env new-class inst)
            new-class)))
      ...)))
```

Figure 7.1.4   Auxiliary definitions for the language of objects interpreter

```
(define lookup
  (lambda (var vars vals)
    (cell-ref (cell-lookup var vars vals))))

(define assign
  (lambda (var value vars vals)
    (cell-set! (cell-lookup var vars vals) value)))

(define cell-lookup
  (lambda (var vars vals)
    (letrec ((loop (lambda (vars c)
                     (cond
                       ((null? vars) (error "Unassigned variable:" var))
                       ((eq? (car vars) var) (vector-ref vals c))
                       (else (loop (cdr vars) (- c 1)))))))
      (loop vars (- (length vars) 1)))))

(define meth-call
  (lambda (name class args)
    (let ((method (meth-lookup name class)))
      (method args))))

(define meth-lookup
  (lambda (name class)
    (apply-env (class->m-env class) name)))

(define make-vals
  (lambda (vars)
    (list->vector (map make-empty-cell vars))))

(define init-meth-env
  (lambda (var)
    (if (eq? var 'initialize)
        (lambda (args) "Not initialized")
        (error "Unbound method name:" var))))

(define init-env
  (extend-env '(classof)
    (list (make-cell (make-prim-proc 'instance->class)))
    base-env))
```

In the first line of the method clause, the variable `self` is added to the front of the list of formals that are used to extend the lexical environment of the method at the time of method call. This is appropriate, since the first argument to a method is always the current instance of the call. By referring to the object bound to `self`, the methods of an instance may call each other as if they were mutually recursive. For example, the expression `null(&stk)` in the `pop` and `top` methods of figure 7.1.2 could be replaced by `$empty(self)`.

Evaluation of method expressions simply involves returning an open method procedure that is closed over the current lexical environment (*env*). When an open method is incorporated into a class, it is supplied with a *class thunk*. When the method is called, this class thunk is invoked to obtain the identity of the class to which it belongs. It might be preferable to put a reference to the class directly in the method when it is incorporated into the class. Unfortunately, this is impossible because at that time the class has not yet been fully formed. The best we can do at method-incorporation time is to put in the method a thunk that will evaluate at method-application time to the right class. This is similar to the technique we used in section 5.6 to implement `letrecproc` without circular environments. In that case we needed to construct procedures whose bodies were evaluated in an environment in which the procedures themselves were contained. In this case we construct methods that must refer to the class in which they are contained.

Method application uses the auxiliary procedure *meth-call*. It is straightforward, based on the calling convention for methods.

When a `simpleinstance` expression is evaluated its subexpression is first evaluated to obtain the class of the new instance. A new instance record is then formed that contains a reference to the class and an instance value vector that associates instance variables with cells that initially contain unspecified values. The `initialize` method of the new class is then called, and finally the new instance is returned.

When creating a new class, a new method environment must be formed (see figure 7.1.3). The expressions of the method declarations are evaluated to obtain open methods. These open methods are then closed in the class by being passed a class thunk. Note the circularity introduced by the `letrec` in the code. Method environments have only one rib, so the environment that is extended is always a trivial environment. After the method environment is created it is included in a new class record, along with class and instance variable lists and a vector of class value bindings. These bindings are cells whose values are initially unspecified. The initialization expression of the class expression is then evaluated with the newly created class as the current class. Thus references to class variables in the initialization expression refer to the variables of the new class, allowing them to be assigned meaningful values. The `inst` argument that is passed to `eval-exp` is useless, since there are no instances of the newly created class.

The remaining clauses of `eval-exp` are the same as those in earlier interpreters, except that the new class and instance arguments must be passed to `eval-exp`. The programmer is given access to the class of any instance via the primitive procedure `classof` supplied in the initial environment. See `init-env` in figure 7.1.4. It is assumed that `base-env` provides bindings for primitive procedures and values.

○ *Exercise 7.1.1*
We have said that object-oriented programming allows an ADT to have multiple implementations that coexist in a single program. Extend the example of figure 7.1.2 by defining a second implementation of the stack ADT. Write a procedure in the defined language to count the number of elements on a stack. Show that it behaves correctly with either kind of stack object as an argument. □

• *Exercise 7.1.2*
Some object-based languages do not syntactically distinguish applications and method calls (as we do using a dollar sign). In such a language, if the first argument of an application is an object and the operator names one of the object's methods, the application is actually a method call. Modify the interpreter of figure 7.2.4 to support this calling convention by removing the `meth-app` clause and redefining the `app` clause. □

○ *Exercise 7.1.3*
In section 5.6 we saw that another approach to the implementation of `letrec` is to use assignment, which effectively forms a circular data structure. Modify the interpreter of figure 7.1.3 to avoid the use of class thunks by the introduction of side-effects. □

○ *Exercise 7.1.4*
Since in the interpreter of figure 7.1.3 the current class is always the class of the current instance, the `class-thunk` variable is not necessary. Rewrite `eval-exp` of figure 7.1.3 without using the `class-thunk` variable. □

• *Exercise 7.1.5*

The syntax of our defined language requires that all the methods associated with a class be specified at the time the class is created. Modify the defined language and the interpreter of figure 7.1.3 to allow methods to be added to or deleted from a class at any time. ☐

○ *Exercise 7.1.6*

Redefine the Scheme procedure `make-stack` of figure 7.1.1 so that the lexical variable `self` is bound to the current instance in the scope of the class operations. For example, in the `pop!` and `top` operations this would allow the expression (`null? stk`) to be replaced by (`self 'empty?`). ☐

○ *Exercise 7.1.7*

We have chosen to make `self` a lexical variable. It could be an instance variable instead. In that case it could be installed permanently in the instance variable environment when the instance is made. Of course, this requires a side-effect. Modify the interpreter so that `self` is an instance variable and not a variable of the method's lexical environment. ☐

○ *Exercise 7.1.8*

At the time open methods are included in a class, instance variable addresses (locations in the corresponding instance value vector) can be statically determined. Write a procedure that takes a method expression and a list of instance variables and replaces each instance variable reference and assignment record by a new record that contains an address rather than a variable symbol. Then rewrite instance variable lookup to support these variable references. Remember that the instance value vector is treated as if it were reversed, so for example, the address of b in (a b c d e) is 3. ☐

• *Exercise 7.1.9*

The decision to require an `&` to precede an instance variable is arbitrary. We could instead allow instance variables to appear like lexical variables within method bodies. We would then have to decide which would have precedence. We arbitrarily decide that instance variables within method bodies shadow free lexical variables of the same name. Modify the interpreter to support this behavior. ☐

Large object-oriented programs typically use many classes. Frequently a class is similar to another class in the same program in that it requires some of the same variables and methods, but it supports some additional or modified methods, and perhaps requires additional class or instance variables.

For example, a program might require a class of bounded stacks, as well as a class of simple stacks. The bounded-stack class supports all the methods of the simple-stack class, plus an additional method for setting a limit on the size of the stack and a modified method for pushing elements on the stack, which checks that the limit is not exceeded. Of course the bounded-stack class also requires an additional instance variable to record the limit.

The techniques of inheritance and delegation allow similar objects to share common methods and variables. This sharing has advantages at many points in the software development process. It simplifies program specification, speeds coding, and eases program maintenance, as well as encouraging the development of libraries of general purpose classes that may easily be extended to meet specific needs.

The range of opportunities for code sharing, and the scope of its benefits, are striking. An adequate appreciation of the utility of inheritance and delegation can be obtained only by studying a number of examples drawn from a variety of programming contexts. It is not our purpose to provide such examples, which may be found in a number of object-oriented programming books. We are concerned rather with understanding the programming language mechanisms that support this style of programming.

Delegation refers to code sharing that is determined by the organization of objects. In delegation, if an object receives a message that it does not know how to handle, it simply passes the message on to another object, thereby delegating authority for handling the message. *Inheritance,* on the other hand, refers to code sharing that is determined by the organization of classes. Each class may have one or more *parent* classes from which methods and variables are inherited.

In the procedural model of objects, it is easy to implement delegation. Consider the bounded-stack class mentioned above, which extends the previous stack class with a new `set-bound!` method and modifies the `push!` method (see figure 7.2.1). The class *make-bounded-stack* has two instance variables, `bound` and `stack`. The latter is an instance of the simple stack class of figure 7.1.1, to which `empty?`, `pop!`, `top`, `pushed`, and `local-pushed` messages are delegated. The `push!` message is also delegated to the simple stack if the number of elements in the stack is less than the bound. The bound is 10

Figure 7.2.1   Bounded stack with delegation

```
(define make-bounded-stack
  (lambda ()
    (let ((bound 10) (stack (make-stack)))
      (lambda (message)
        (case message
          ((push!) (if (< ((stack 'local-pushed)) bound)
                       (stack 'push!)
                       (error "Bounded stack: bound exceeded")))
          ((set-bound!) (lambda (x) (set! bound x)))
          (else (stack message)))))))
```

by default. Alternatively, we could have made the bound an argument to *make-bounded-stack*.

Delegation is more dynamic than inheritance, and hence more flexible. It is possible, for example, for an object to determine when and how to delegate responsibility for a given message based on the state of the system at the time of method call. Patterns of inheritance, on the other hand, are the same for all instances of a class and are determined at the time of class creation. Inheritance is the more common method of code sharing, since the flexibility of delegation often comes at the expense of efficiency, and the added flexibility is seldom required. Also, unnecessary flexibility may be a liability, since flexible program behavior is often harder to understand. If necessary, delegation may even be simulated with inheritance by creating classes dynamically.

Inheritance may be either *single,* if each class has just one parent, or *multiple,* when classes are permitted to have more than one parent. With single inheritance, the class structure of a program may be represented as a tree. Such hierarchical organizations are natural in a great many contexts. A method inherited by a class is supplied by the nearest ancestor of the class that supplies the method..

Multiple inheritance results in a less structured class organization that may be represented as a directed acyclic graph. Locating an inherited method with multiple inheritance is more complicated than the linear search through ancestor classes that suffices for single inheritance. Since two parent classes may in turn inherit (directly or indirectly) from a common ancestor, we must be careful that the method search does not visit some classes more than once. Some languages impose the restriction that methods of the same name may not belong (either directly or by inheritance) to multiple parents of a

Figure 7.2.2   Bounded-stack class

```
define boundedstackclass =
  class stackclass, () (bound)
   (initialize = method ()
                    begin
                       &bound := 10;
                       $initialize(super)
                    end;
    push = method (x)
            if less(&localpushed, &bound)
            then $push(super, x)
            else error();
    setbound = method (x) &bound := x)
   noop
```

class. This makes multiple inheritance relatively simple to understand and implement. If a class is allowed to have two parents that each supply a method with the same name, which method is to be called, or should both methods be somehow called? One approach is to use the first method of a given name that is encountered in a depth-first search of the ancestors of a class. A variety of other approaches are possible, but they are beyond the scope of this text.

We now extend the interpreted language of the last section to model single inheritance. There are two changes to the syntax of our interpreted language. First, we replace the `simpleclass` form with the `class` form that is similar but includes an expression that is evaluated to obtain the parent of the new class. Second, we provide a special form for *super* method application. This provides access to inherited methods that would otherwise be inaccessible by virtue of being "shadowed" by other methods of the same name. Its syntax is the same as that of ordinary method application but with the variable name super as the first operand.

⟨exp⟩ ::= class ⟨exp⟩, ⟨c-vars⟩   new-class (parent-exp c-vars
            ⟨i-vars⟩ ⟨methdecls⟩ ⟨exp⟩   i-vars methdecls init-exp)
          | $⟨var⟩ ⟨super-rands⟩   super-meth-app (name rands)
⟨super-rands⟩ ::= (super)
              | (super, ⟨exps⟩)

Figure 7.2.3   Count class

```
define countclass =
 class baseobject, (classinstcount) ()
  (initialize = method () &&classinstcount := +(&&classinstcount, 1);
   howmany = method () &&classinstcount)
  &&classinstcount := 0
```

For example, figure 7.2.2 shows the definition of a bounded-stack class that inherits from a stack class. The stack class may be defined as in figure 7.1.2 but with simpleclass ... replaced by class baseobject ... , where baseobject is a primitive object used as the parent of a class that does not need to inherit from another class. Instances of boundedstackclass support not only the methods setbound and push, but also (by inheritance) those of stackclass other than push. The instance variable localpushed is also inherited from stackclass. In general, a class inherits all the instance and class variables of its ancestors. Since there are no class variables, the class initialization expression does nothing (indicated by a variable noop that may be bound to any value). In this example two uses of super method application are required to invoke the initialization and push methods of the stack class, since both of these methods are also defined by the bounded-stack class.

Most often a new class inherits from an existing class, as in the bounded-stack example. It is also possible to create a new class that is to be inherited by several classes in order to support some behavior that they all have in common. For example, countclass of figure 7.2.3 keeps track of the total number of instances of its inheriting classes. Thus if stackclass inherited from countclass instead of baseobject, and i were an instance of stackclass or boundedstackclass, then $howmany(i) would return the total number of instances of stackclass and boundedstackclass. For this example, we assume that every initialization method invokes $initialize(super), so that the initialization method of the count class will be run whenever an instance of an inheriting class is created.

We obtain an interpreter for modeling inheritance by extending the interpreter of the last section. Each class record is extended with a field that records its parent.

```
(define-record class (parent c-vars c-vals i-vars m-env))
```

Instance records are unchanged.

Figure 7.2.4   Interpreter and initial environment for inheritance language

```
(define eval-exp
  (lambda (exp env class inst)
    (variant-case exp
      (new-class (parent-exp c-vars i-vars methdecls init-exp)
        (let ((parent-class (eval-exp parent-exp env class inst))
              (open-methods (map (lambda (decl)
                                    (eval-exp (decl->exp decl) env class inst))
                                 methdecls)))
          (let ((new-c-vars (append c-vars (class->c-vars parent-class)))
                (new-i-vars (append i-vars (class->i-vars parent-class))))
            (letrec ((new-class
                        (make-class parent-class new-c-vars (make-vals new-c-vars)
                          new-i-vars
                          (extend-env (map decl->var methdecls)
                            (map (lambda (open-method)
                                    (open-method (lambda () new-class)))
                                 open-methods)
                            (class->m-env parent-class)))))
              (eval-exp init-exp env new-class inst)
              new-class))))
      (super-meth-app (name rands)
        (let ((args (map (lambda (x) (eval-exp x env class inst)) rands)))
          (meth-call name (class->parent class) (cons inst args))))
      ...)))

(define init-env
  (extend-env '(parentof classof baseobject)
    (map make-cell
         (list (make-prim-proc 'class->parent arg)
               (make-prim-proc 'instance->class)
               (make-class '* '() '#() '() init-meth-env)))
    base-env))
```

Evaluation of a `class` form begins by evaluating the subexpression that provides the identity of its parent. See figure 7.2.4. Lists of class and instance variables are then obtained by *appending* the variables introduced by the class to those of its parent. If the list of instance variables of the class overlap with those of its parent, the ones in the class shadow those of the parent. The reason we count backward from the end of the value vector while we search forward in the variable list is to facilitate static instance variable lookup (see exercise 7.1.8). The method environment of the new class is formed by extending the method environment of the parent class with the newly declared methods.

Super method application is similar to a standard method application, except that the class used for method lookup is the parent of the current class and the current instance is passed as the first argument of the method. Thus method lookup will be in the environment of the current class, and the current instance will be bound to `self` in the body of the method.

The rest of the interpreter is the same as in the first object interpreter except that the initial environment *init-env* now contains bindings for two class-related primitive procedures and a special object. The `parentof` procedure returns the parent of a class, and the old `classof` procedure returns the class of an instance. The variable `baseobject` is bound to an object that has no parent, no variables, and no methods. It is used as the parent of classes that do not inherit from other classes.

We now have at least four categories of variables: instance variables, class variables, method names, and ordinary lexical variables. Why do we need such complex mechanisms? The procedural model, for example, uses lexical variables to simulate instance and class variables. However, this may not suffice in general, especially when inheritance is used. We often want to create a class that inherits from another class whose instance and class variables are not in the current scope. See figure 7.2.5. Under lexical scoping, there would be no way for the methods of `bclass` to see the class or instance variables of `aclass`. Indeed, whenever we inherit from a class, the new methods get to see the instance variables of the parent class, which are not lexically apparent, as in the use of `&iv` in the `getiv` method in figure 7.2.5.

We ended chapter 5 knowing that variables could be scoped in two ways: statically (i.e., lexically) and dynamically. The same can be said about instance and class variables. (Keep in mind, though that in this context, static is not the same as lexical. It is called static because for each variable an address can be determined, but it is not the lexical address.) Consider the program in figure 7.2.6. Is c 6 or 7? Is i 8 or 9? References to class and instance variables within a method are resolved in the environment of the

Figure 7.2.5   Example showing lexical scope vs. instance variables

```
define aclass = class baseobject, (cv) (iv) () noop;

let x = 3; cv = 4
in let bclass = class aclass, () ()
                  (initialize = method () +(x, &&cv);
                   getiv = method () &iv)
                  noop
    in ...
```

Figure 7.2.6   Static vs. dynamic inheritance of class and instance variables

```
define aclass =
 class baseobject, (cv) (iv)
  (initialize = method () &iv := 8;
   getcv = method () &&cv;
   getiv = method () &iv)
  &&cv := 6;

define bclass =
 class aclass, (cv) (iv)
  (inititialize = method ()
                     begin
                       $initialize(super);
                       &iv := 9
                     end)
  &&cv := 7;

define x = simpleinstance bclass;
define c = $getcv(x);
define i = $getiv(x)
```

class to which the method belongs. (See the variable reference and assignment clauses of figure 7.1.3 and the method clause of figure 7.2.4.) Thus in this example &&cv and &iv refer to the bindings introduced by aclass, so that c is 6 and i is 8. In this case the relationship between class and instance variable references and their bindings is static, and the interpreted language is said to employ *static inheritance* of class and instance variables.

In the interpreter of figure 7.1.3, except for when `init-exp` was evaluated, the *current class* (bound to the `class` argument of `eval-exp`) was always the class of the current instance (bound to `inst`). As the example of figure 7.2.6 demonstrates, this is not always the case once inheritance has been introduced. When a method is called, its body is evaluated with `inst` bound to the current instance and `class` bound to the class containing the method. This class will not be the same as the current class if the method is found in an ancestor of the current class. Inheritance mechanisms in which the current instance supplies the environment, even for methods associated with ancestors of the current class, are said to be *dynamic*. With dynamic inheritance of class and instance variables, c will be 7 and i will be 9. It is possible for class and instance variables to inherit differently. For example, by replacing the `class` by `(instance->class inst)` in the subexpression `(class->i-vars class)` in both the `i-varref` and `i-varassign` clauses of figure 7.2.4, we would support dynamic inheritance of instance variables, but retain static inheritance of class variables. Among some of the widely used object-oriented languages are C++ and Smalltalk. C++ statically inherits, whereas Smalltalk dynamically inherits.

● *Exercise 7.2.1*
Modify the program in figure 7.1.2 to keep a count of the number of instances of `stackclass` and all other classes (such as `boundedstackclass`) that inherit directly or indirectly from `stackclass`. ◻

○ *Exercise 7.2.2*
In Samlltalk, a reference to the variable `super` in a position other than the first argument of a method call is treated exactly like a reference to `self`. Modify the interpreter of figure 7.2.4 to provide this feature. ◻

○ *Exercise 7.2.3*
Another representation of the method environment is to store all the closed methods accessible from a particular class in a single vector and use an index, instead of a symbol, to reference into the method environment. This may be the basis for further optimizations, such as hashing and caching. Modify the interpreter of figure 7.2.4 and its associated parser to preprocess method expressions so that the abstract syntax of method applications and super method applications includes an index that is used for method lookup. This exercise, along with that of exercise 7.1.8, gives a large part of the object mechanism of C++. ◻

- *Exercise 7.2.4*

  Modify the interpreter of figure 7.2.4 to support dynamic inheritance of class and instance variables. ☐

o *Exercise 7.2.5*

  In our discussion of figure 7.2.3, we relied on the assumption that each `initialize` method called `$initialize(super)`. How might this be guaranteed? Design and implement a mechanism to do so. ☐

o *Exercise 7.2.6*

  Modify the interpreter to support multiple inheritance, with the provision that no two ancestors of any class supply methods of the same name. ☐

7.3 Meta-Classes

Suppose we wanted to keep track of the total number of classes that inherit from a given class. This is similar in character to the problems of keeping a count of all the instances of a class (as in figure 7.2.3) and keeping a count of the number of pushes in all stacks (as in figure 7.1.2). We have seen these problems are solved naturally using class variables. Due to the inheritance of class variables and methods, the instance and class counts need be kept in only one class. It would be desirable if a count of the number of stack classes could be maintained with similar ease.

In the interpreted language this is not possible, since the only expression that is evaluated when a class is created is the initialization expression of the new class. We wish the class count to be incremented automatically when we create a class, without our having to program this in each class definition. To achieve this, we move class initialization code into a method body, so that we have class creation as well as class initialization methods. If classes may be created under varying circumstances, it might even be desirable to support multiple class-creation methods. To what class should class-creation methods belong? They cannot belong to a parent of the class, for it would not then be able to access the class variables of the new class (unless the system uses dynamic class variable inheritance).

Class-creation methods are stored in a new class, called a *meta-class*. Just as instances have an associated class, it is natural to associate a meta-class with each class. The class variables of a class are then the instance variables of its meta-class. Thus it is only necessary to declare instance variables. We still maintain the notion of class variable references and assignments, but they are understood to be operating on variables declared in the meta-class of the current class. The values of the instance variables of a class are, of course, still stored in the instances of the class. Similarly, a class contains the values of its class variables, which are declared as instance variables in its meta-class. For example, the stack class could declare instance variables named `stk` and `localpushed` (whose values would be contained in instances of the class), and contain values for the instance variables `pushed` and `instcount` declared by its meta-class.

Consider a class-creation method belonging to a meta-class. To count the number of classes created, it must increment a class variable. Since we declare only instance variables, this class variable must be declared as an instance variable of a meta-meta-class of which the meta-class is an instance.

We provide for an unlimited number of meta-levels by eliminating the distinction between instances and classes. All objects are then instances, and each instance has an associated parent and class. This is supported by the syntactic form `instance`, which replaces the `simpleinstance` and `class` forms. It is similar to the `class` form but has a subexpression for indicating a class as well as a parent.

⟨exp⟩ ::= instance ⟨exp⟩, ⟨exp⟩,   new-instance (class-exp parent-exp
          ⟨varlist⟩ ⟨methdecls⟩   i-vars methdecls)

Adding support for meta-classes would seem to complicate the defined language, but since we are eliminating the class/instance distinction, the interpreter is simplified. Instance records now have a parent field.

```
(define-record instance (class parent i-vars m-env i-vals))
```

Class records are now replaced by instance records, but for continuity we continue to use class record field selection procedures when an instance is being used as a class.

```
(define class->m-env instance->m-env)
(define class->i-vars instance->i-vars)
(define class->parent instance->parent)
```

The class variable reference and assignment clauses of *eval-exp* are modified to obtain the class variable lists from the meta-class of the current class. See figure 7.3.1. The new-instance clause is similar to the new-class clause of

Figure 7.3.1   Meta-class interpreter

```
(define eval-exp
  (lambda (exp env class inst)
    (variant-case exp
      (c-varref (var)
        (lookup var (instance->i-vars (instance->class class))
          (instance->i-vals (instance->class inst))))
      (c-varassign (var exp)
        (let ((value (eval-exp exp env class inst)))
          (assign var value (instance->i-vars (instance->class class))
            (instance->i-vals (instance->class inst)))))
      (new-instance (class-exp parent-exp i-vars methdecls)
        (let ((inst-class (eval-exp class-exp env class inst))
              (parent-class (eval-exp parent-exp env class inst))
              (open-methods
                (map (lambda (decl)
                       (eval-exp (decl->exp decl) env class inst))
                     methdecls)))
          (let ((new-i-vars (append i-vars (instance->i-vars parent-class))))
            (letrec ((new-inst
                       (make-instance inst-class parent-class
                         new-i-vars
                         (extend-env (map decl->var methdecls)
                           (map (lambda (open-method)
                                  (open-method (lambda () new-inst)))
                                open-methods)
                           (class->m-env parent-class))
                         (make-vals (class->i-vars inst-class)))))
              (meth-call 'initialize (instance->class new-inst) (list new-inst))
              new-inst))))
      ...)))

(define init-env
  (extend-env '(parentof classof baseobject)
    (map make-cell
         (list (make-prim-proc 'class->parent)
               (make-prim-proc 'instance->class)
               (make-instance '* '* '() init-meth-env '#())))
    base-env))
```

figure 7.2.4, but it now evaluates the class subexpression and stores its value in the record representing the new instance. The initial environment is the same except for the representation of the base object.

The program of figure 7.3.2 illustrates the use of meta-classes. The program creates eight instances. It first defines `metametacountclass`, which simply declares that any instance of `metametacountclass` will have a binding for the variable `classcount`. Then it defines `metacountclass` as an instance of `metametacountclass`. The initialization method of its class is invoked to set its binding of `classcount` to zero. This variable is incremented as a class variable by the initialization method of `metacountclass`. It also provides a `new` method for creating simple (methodless) instances of a given class and a `howmany` method for returning the current value of `classcount`. The class, `metacountclass`, is inherited by `metastackclass`, which declares the `pushed` variable used as a class variable by the stack class. Finally, `countclass`, `stackclass`, and `boundedstackclass` are defined based on the earlier examples, and instances of the stack and bounded stack classes are created using `new`.

Figure 7.3.3 illustrates the instance structure created by the program of figure 7.3.2. We have chosen short names to label each instance that correspond to the longer names used in the program below. For example, `BO` is `baseobject` and `MCC` is `metacountclass`. There are nine instances in figure 7.3.3. Each instance represents the five fields of an instance record as follows. A pointer emanating from the left of an instance is a class pointer and one emanating from its top is a parent pointer. The remaining three fields are its `i-vars`, which are stored in the top section; the first rib of its `m-env`, which is stored in the middle section; and the `i-vals`, which are stored in the bottom section. Blank sections denote the obvious default values: the empty list, the `init-meth-env`, or an empty vector. The ellipses indicate omitted methods. When looking at such figures, it is important to keep in mind that the `i-vars` and `i-vals` of the same instance are not related: The `i-vals` of any object correspond to the `i-vars` of its class. For example, in `BSI` there are three i-vals and zero `i-vars`. There are, however, three `i-vars` in its class `BSC`. Also this figure does not show all the details of the data structures used by our implementation. For example, the order of the `i-vals` is not reversed as they are in our implementation, nor is the presence of updatable cells shown.

Figure 7.3.4 is a trace, using the abbreviated names, of assignments to instance variables that occur when the program in figure 7.3.2 is run.

Figure 7.3.2   Meta-class example

```
define metametacountclass =
  instance baseobject, baseobject, (classcount)
    (initialize = method () &classcount := 0);

define metacountclass =
  instance metametacountclass, baseobject, (instcount)
    (initialize = method () begin
                            &instcount := 0;
                            &&classcount := +(&&classcount, 1)
                          end;
      new = method () instance self, baseobject, () ();
      howmany = method () &&classcount);

define countclass =
  instance metacountclass, baseobject, ()
    (initialize = method () &&instcount := +(&&instcount, 1);
      howmany = method () &&instcount);

define metastackclass =
  instance classof(metacountclass), metacountclass, (pushed)
    (initialize = method () begin &pushed := 0; $initialize(super) end);

define stackclass =
  instance metastackclass, countclass, (stk, localpushed)
    (initialize = method () begin
                            &localpushed := 0;
                            &stk := emptylist;
                            $initialize(super)
                          end;
      ...);

define boundedstackclass =
  instance classof(stackclass), stackclass, (bound)
    (initialize = method () begin
                            &bound := 10;
                            $initialize(super)
                          end;
      ...);

define stackinstance = $new(stackclass);

define boundedstackinstance = $new(boundedstackclass);
```

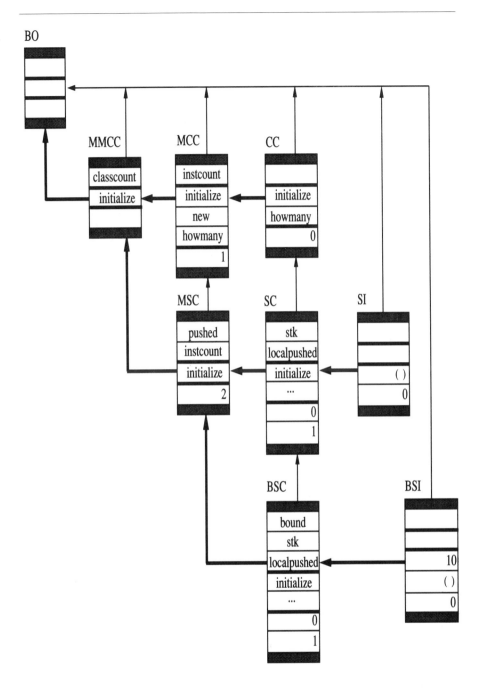

Figure 7.3.3 Structure of meta-class example

| Instance | Instance value assigned | | |
created	Value in	Name	Value
MMCC			
MCC	MCC	classcount	0
CC	CC	instcount	0
	MCC	classcount	1
MSC	MSC	classcount	0
SC	SC	pushed	0
	SC	instcount	0
	MSC	classcount	1
BSC	BSC	pushed	0
	BSC	instcount	0
	MSC	classcount	2
SI	SI	stk	()
	SI	localpushed	0
	SC	instcount	1
BSI	BSI	bound	10
	BSI	stk	()
	BSI	localpushed	0
	BSC	instcount	1

Figure 7.3.4 Trace of figure 7.3.2

- *Exercise 7.3.1*

Extend figure 7.3.3 if the program continues as follows:

```
define stackinstance2 = $new(stackclass);
define boundedstackinstance2 = $new(boundedstackclass);
define boundedstackinstance3 = $new(boundedstackclass);
define boundedstackinstance4 = $new(boundedstackclass);
$push(boundedstackinstance, 13);
$push(boundedstackinstance2, 14);
$push(boundedstackinstance2, 15)
```

⬜

○ *Exercise 7.3.2*

In figure 7.3.2 the `new` method is provided by `metacountclass`. It may be desirable for the `new` method to be inherited by all classes in a system, while `metacountclass` is inherited by some, but not all, classes. To allow for this possibility, modify the program of figure 7.3.2 so that the `new` method is provided by a class named `metabaseclass`, rather than by `metacountclass`. ☐

○ *Exercise 7.3.3*

This system of meta-classes is extremely general. Take your favorite object system and formulate it in this scheme. What regularities or restrictions does your system obey? ☐

7.4 Summary

An object is a set of operations that share a state. Objects are a way for a language to enforce data abstraction. Objects may be modeled using lexical scoping and message passing. The `self` variable allows the operations of an object to send messages to each other recursively.

A class is a set of objects, called instances, that share the same operations, called methods. A class may have state through the mechanism of class variables, which are accessible to all its instances.

Classes may be defined incrementally by the use of inheritance. The `super` variable allows access to methods of the parent class that would otherwise be shadowed. Class and instance variables may be scoped statically or dynamically, but static scoping for these variables is distinct from ordinary lexical scoping.

A class can be considered to be an ordinary object, among whose methods is an operation for making an instance of the class. The operation for making a new class must therefore be a method of a meta-class. This leads to a design in which each class is an instance of its meta-class but inherits its operations from a parent class.

Continuation-Passing Style

We have seen how interpreters can be used to model and explain the behavior of programming languages. The explicit treatment of environments serves to explain scope and identifier-lookup rules, and the modeling of procedures as closures explains how procedures use lexical scope to make their behavior independent of the environment in which they are invoked. Our interpreters are written in Scheme but are suitable for implementation in many other languages because they use ordinary data structures and procedure calls.

The interpreters we have written so far require, however, that the implementation language supports recursive procedures. Thus recursion in the defined language has used recursion in the defining language. If we do not understand recursion, or we wish to use an implementation language that does not directly support recursion, this situation would be unsatisfactory.

The difficulty in implementing recursive procedures is that when a procedure call is made, it is necessary to record the operations that remain to be performed when the call returns. For example, when an interpreter is invoked recursively to evaluate the test part of a conditional expression, it must be noted that the result is to be used to determine whether the next subexpression to evaluate is the `then` part or the `else` part. This information, which is used to control the future course of the computation, is called *control* information. So far our interpreters have relied on Scheme to transparently keep track of control information for the defined language. We now wish to handle recursion by making the control information explicit.

We have already seen an example of how the future course of a computation may be represented explicitly. The *reduce-once-appl* procedure of section 4.3 is passed procedures that express how the computation is to be continued. The procedure is written so that it never returns values directly but instead passes them to one of these procedural arguments. These arguments are called *continuations*.

This technique is called *continuation-passing style*, or *CPS*. There are several reasons why CPS may be useful. In the `reduce-once-appl` procedure it is used because there are two possible continuations, one to be followed in the event of success and the other in the event of failure. It is more convenient to let the procedure choose between its continuations than to force its caller always to perform a test based on some returned result, particularly since the nature of the information that must be returned depends on how the computation is to continue. Another use of CPS is to return multiple results by passing them to a multiple-argument continuation. This is often better than returning some data structure out of which the caller of the procedure would have to extract the values. Examples of this style are found in the use of the procedure `find-all-argcont` in chapter 10 and in exercise 11.4.4 on recursive descent parsing in chapter 11. The concept of continuation passing has broad applicability, but the details of CPS are determined by the context of its use. For example, in chapter 12 we shall see how compilers may be viewed as translating expressions into a different form of CPS with a finer "granularity" than the CPS of this chapter.

In this chapter we explore the use of the simplest version of this style, in which procedures are passed a single continuation of one argument. We show how any expression may be translated into CPS. This is the first (and most challenging) step in a systematic process that may be used to transform any program into a form that may be translated directly into assembly language. Thus the CPS algorithm is a fundamental program development tool and can play a critical role in compiler generation.

In section 8.1 we illustrate the distinction between iterative and recursive control behavior and introduce an important implementation property called proper tail recursion. In section 8.2 we give some examples of how a procedure may be transformed into an equivalent procedure in continuation-passing style; the new procedure is guaranteed to have iterative control behavior. In section 8.3 we define a static property of programs called tail form, which is enjoyed by programs that have been transformed into CPS, and in section 8.4 we develop the CPS conversion algorithm itself. Section 8.5 presents examples of the transformation algorithm in action. In section 8.6 we present an implementation of our CPS algorithm. Last, in section 8.7 we refine the characterization of proper tail-recursive implementation.

The subject of conversion to continuation-passing style is deep and subtle. Most CPS algorithms are simpler than ours, but the results generated by those algorithms are primarily to be interpreted by a computer, not a programmer. Much of the complication in this chapter is caused by our desire to present a CPS transformation algorithm that incorporates knowledge about the special forms and primitive operations of Scheme, and gives results as readable as those done by hand.

A good introduction to the subject can be obtained by reading sections 8.1 and 8.2, and going through the examples in section 8.5. This knowledge will generally be adequate for the rest of the material in the book and will also lay the ground for a more fruitful reading of the rest of the chapter.

8.1 Iterative Control Behavior and Proper Tail Recursion

Consider the following definition of the factorial function.

```
(define fact
  (lambda (n)
    (if (zero? n) 1 (* n (fact (- n 1))))))
```

We can use a derivation to model a calculation with `fact`:

```
  (fact 4)
⇒ (* 4 (fact 3))
⇒ (* 4 (* 3 (fact 2)))
⇒ (* 4 (* 3 (* 2 (fact 1))))
⇒ (* 4 (* 3 (* 2 (* 1 (fact 0)))))
⇒ (* 4 (* 3 (* 2 (* 1 1))))
⇒ (* 4 (* 3 (* 2 1)))
⇒ (* 4 (* 3 2))
⇒ (* 4 6)
⇒ 24
```

This is the natural recursive definition of factorial. Each call of `fact` is made with a promise that the value returned will be multiplied by the value of n at the time of the call. Thus `fact` is invoked in larger and larger control contexts as the calculation proceeds.

Compare this behavior with that of the following procedures.

```
(define fact-iter
  (lambda (n)
    (fact-iter-acc n 1)))

(define fact-iter-acc
  (lambda (n a)
    (if (zero? n) a (fact-iter-acc (- n 1) (* n a)))))
```

With these definitions, we calculate:

```
   (fact-iter 4)
⇒ (fact-iter-acc 4 1)
⇒ (fact-iter-acc 3 4)
⇒ (fact-iter-acc 2 12)
⇒ (fact-iter-acc 1 24)
⇒ (fact-iter-acc 0 24)
⇒ 24
```

Here, `fact-iter-acc` is always invoked in the same context (in this case, no context at all). When `fact-iter-acc` calls itself, it does so at the "tail end" of a call to `fact-iter-acc`. That is, no promise is made to do anything with the returned value other than return it as the result of the call to `fact-iter-acc`. Thus each step in the derivation above has the form (`fact-iter-acc` n a).

When a procedure such as `fact` executes, additional control information must be recorded with each recursive call, and this information must be retained until the call returns. This reflects growth of the control context in the first derivation above. Such a process is said to exhibit *recursive control behavior*. This control behavior places a potentially serious limit on the utility of such procedures, since in practice execution is limited to a finite amount of memory. For example, if `fact` is called with a sufficiently large value of n, an exception will be signalled indicating that the system ran out of memory.

By contrast, no additional control information need be recorded when `fact-iter-acc` calls itself. This is reflected in the derivation by recursive calls occurring at the same level within the expression (on the outside in the above derivation). In such cases the system does not need an ever-increasing amount of memory as the depth of recursion (the number of recursive calls without corresponding returns) increases. A process that uses a bounded amount of memory for control information is said to exhibit *iterative control behavior*.

The concept of *tail position* is used to determine whether additional control information need be recorded when a call is made. When certain subexpressions are evaluated, their value is immediately taken as the value of the enclosing expression. The primary example is the then and else subexpressions of an if expression. These subexpressions are said to be in tail positions of the enclosing expression. Thus when evaluating a subexpression in a tail position of the body of a procedure, no control information need be stored. This was the case, for example, in the recursive call of `fact-iter-acc`.

While evaluating an expression, if the value of a subexpression is returned, but some action must be performed after the subexpression's value is obtained,

Continuation-Passing Style

but before the expression's value is returned, the subexpression is not in a tail position of the expression. For example, even if a Scheme `set!` expression returned the value of its subexpression, the subexpression would not be in tail position because the assignment must be performed after it is evaluated, but before evaluation of the `set!` expression is complete.

The concept of tail position generalizes naturally to deeply nested subexpressions. A subexpression E' of E is said to be in a *tail position with respect to E* if every subexpression of E containing E' is in a tail position of the expression within which it is immediately contained. For example, the subexpressions (f (g x)), 1, and (f x) are in tail position with respect to the expression

```
(if (zero? x)
    (f (g x))
    (if (positive? x)
        1
        (f x)))
```

but all other subexpressions are not in tail position with respect to the entire expression. We say that an expression is in *tail position* if it is in tail position with respect to the nearest lexically enclosing lambda expression. (Though we discuss lambda expressions in this chapter, the concepts apply to procedural expressions in general.)

Evaluation of an application is said to *initiate* a call of the procedure obtained by evaluation of its operator. For example, evaluation of (f (g x)) initiates a call of f, but not g. The call of g is initiated by the subexpression (g x). The term *tail call* refers to a call initiated by an application in tail position.

The significance of tail calls is that no additional control information need be recorded when a tail call occurs. An implementation in which tail calls result in no net growth of control space is said to be a *properly tail-recursive implementation,* or simply a *tail-recursive implementation.* (Though this definition suffices now, we refine it in section 8.7.) Scheme implementations are required to be properly tail recursive, but this is unusual. Most language specifications do not require that implementations be properly tail recursive, and most implementations are not.

In a tail-recursive implementation, procedures such as *fact-iter-acc* are guaranteed to exhibit iterative control behavior. There are many forms of iterative control behavior, each of which is subsumed by recursion in a language that is properly tail recursive. In the absence of proper tail recursion, language designers must provide other means of expressing iteration. Typically a variety of iteration mechanisms are provided, such as `while` loops, `until` loops, and `for` loops, and often mechanisms for breaking out of iterative loops at various points in their bodies. The life of programmers (and compilers) is complicated by the need to deal with this variety of iteration mechanisms, and yet, in practice, the need invariably arises for iteration mechanisms that the language designer did not anticipate—all for the lack of proper tail recursion.

This section introduces the concept of iterative control behavior by example but is deliberately vague about just when iterative control behavior is possible and how programs may be analyzed for this behavior. These issues are addressed more formally in section 8.3.

In chapter 10 we shall see that procedures such as `fact-iter-acc` may be systematically transformed into equivalent procedures in which no arguments are passed in calls to recursive procedures. As an example of a procedure in such a "flowchart" form, consider the following version of `fact-iter`.

```
(define fact-iter
  (lambda (n)
    (let ((a 1))
      (letrec ((loop (lambda ()
                       (if (zero? n)
                           a
                           (begin
                             (set! a (* n a))
                             (set! n (- n 1))
                             (loop))))))
        (loop))))))
```

Since a zero-argument tail call is equivalent to a "goto" statement, such a procedure may be expressed in a language that does not support recursion. In fact, such a transformation goes a long way toward compiling the procedure into assembly language.

In the case of `fact-iter`, the amount of memory required to store argument values does not increase either (as long as the result is less than the maximum value for the standard number representation). A process whose total memory requirements are bounded is said to exhibit *iterative behavior*. The following procedure is an example of one that executes (in Scheme) with iterative control behavior, but not iterative behavior, since the maximum size of its accumulator argument is a function of the length of its first argument (and hence is not bounded by a constant).

```
(define revappend
  (lambda (ls1 ls2)
    (if (null? ls1)
        ls2
        (revappend (cdr ls1) (cons (car ls1) ls2)))))
```

- *Exercise 8.1.1*
  Trace the behavior of the flowchart version of *fact-iter* when called with
  the argument 4. Compare this trace with a trace of *fact-iter-acc*. ▢

- *Exercise 8.1.2*
  Construct a derivation for the call (revappend '(a b c d) '(1 2)). Note that
  the size of *ls2* increases (and hence *revappend* does not exhibit iterative
  behavior), but recursive calls occur on the outside (and hence it exhibits
  iterative control behavior). ▢

- *Exercise 8.1.3*
  Use a derivation to compute the value of (even-length? '(a b c)) for each of
  the definitions below. Then write a version in flowchart form using the one
  that exhibits iterative control behavior.

```
(define even-length?
  (lambda (ls)
    (if (null? ls) #t (odd-length? (cdr ls)))))

(define odd-length?
  (lambda (ls)
    (if (null? ls) #f (even-length? (cdr ls)))))


(define even-length?
  (lambda (ls)
    (even? (length ls))))

(define length
  (lambda (ls)
    (if (null? ls) 0 (+ 1 (length (cdr ls)))))))
```
▢

In the last section we saw that the `fact` procedure

```
(define fact
  (lambda (n)
    (if (zero? n) 1 (* n (fact (- n 1))))))
```

does not have iterative control behavior, but it can be replaced by one, `fact-iter`, that does. This transformation introduces another procedure, `fact-iter-acc`, taking an extra argument, a, that serves as a register into which the answer is accumulated. This technique is useful, but not every procedure can be converted so simply. In this section, we demonstrate some techniques that will work on any procedure. Our presentation in this section is informal; in section 8.4 we formally specify a conversion algorithm.

The problem with `fact` is that the call (* n (fact (- n 1))) requires us to store information about what is to be done *after* the call to `fact`. Looking at the derivation, we see that a step in the calculation looks something like this:

$$(* \ 4 \ (* \ 3 \ (* \ 2 \ (\text{fact } 1))))$$

Here the procedure call is being computed in the *context*

$$(* \ 4 \ (* \ 3 \ (* \ 2 \ \square)))$$

where $\square$ represents (fact 1). We may represent a context—an expression with a hole in it—by a one-argument lambda expression that fills the hole. For example, the above context may be represented by the following:

```
(lambda (v) (* 4 (* 3 (* 2 v))))
```

If we named this lambda expression k, we would have this:

$$(\text{k } (\text{fact } 1)) \ \Rightarrow \ (* \ 4 \ (* \ 3 \ (* \ 2 \ (\text{fact } 1))))$$

In a derivation of a call of `fact`, each line will be of the form $(k \ (\text{fact } n))$ for some integer n and some lambda expression k.

This prompts us to write another version of `fact`, which we call `fact-cps`, such that (fact-cps n k) computes $(k \ (\text{fact } n))$.

```
(define fact-cps
  (lambda (n k)
    (if (zero? n)
        (k 1)
        (fact-cps (- n 1)
          (lambda (v) (k (* n v)))))))
```

We argue, by induction on n, that (k (fact n)) $\Rightarrow$ (fact-cps n k) for any
k. If $n = 0$, (k (fact 0)) $\Rightarrow$ (k 1) $\Rightarrow$ (fact-cps 0 k). If $n > 0$, we reason as
follows:

$$
\begin{array}{lll}
& \text{(k (fact n))} & \\
\Rightarrow & \text{(k (* n (fact (- n 1))))} & \text{by the definition of \textbf{fact}} \\
\Rightarrow & \text{((lambda (v) (k (* n v)))} & \text{by } \beta\text{-conversion} \\
& \text{(fact (- n 1)))} & \\
\Rightarrow & \text{(fact-cps (- n 1)} & \text{by the induction hypothesis} \\
& \text{(lambda (v) (k (* n v))))} & \\
\Rightarrow & \text{(fact-cps n k)} & \text{by the definition of \textbf{fact-cps}}
\end{array}
$$

Another way to see what is happening here is to calculate the result of a
call to *fact-cps*.

$$
\begin{array}{lll}
& \text{(fact-cps 4 k)} & \\
\Rightarrow & \text{(fact-cps 3 (lambda (v) (k (* 4 v))))} & \\
\Rightarrow & \text{(fact-cps 2 (lambda (v)} & \\
& \qquad\qquad \text{((lambda (v) (k (* 4 v)))} & \text{by definition of \textit{fact-cps}} \\
& \qquad\qquad \text{(* 3 v))))} & \\
\Rightarrow & \text{(fact-cps 2 (lambda (v) (k (* 4 (* 3 v)))))} & \text{by } \beta\text{-reduction} \\
\Rightarrow & \text{(fact-cps 1 (lambda (v)} & \\
& \qquad\qquad \text{((lambda (v)} & \\
& \qquad\qquad\quad \text{(k (* 4 (* 3 v))))} & \text{by definition of \textit{fact-cps}} \\
& \qquad\qquad \text{(* 2 v))))} & \\
\Rightarrow & \text{(fact-cps 1 (lambda (v) (k (* 4 (* 3 (* 2 v))))))} & \text{by } \beta\text{-reduction} \\
\Rightarrow & \text{(fact-cps 0 (lambda (v)} & \text{by definition of \textit{fact-cps}} \\
& \qquad\qquad \text{(k (* 4 (* 3 (* 2 (* 1 v)))))))} & \\
\Rightarrow & \text{((lambda (v) (k (* 4 (* 3 (* 2 (* 1 v))))))} & \\
& \text{1)} & \text{by definition of \textit{fact-cps}} \\
\Rightarrow & \text{(k (* 4 (* 3 (* 2 (* 1 1)))))} & \text{by } \beta\text{-reduction} \\
\Rightarrow & \text{(k 24)} &
\end{array}
$$

Here we have shown most of the intermediate steps in the calculation. The
pattern becomes clearer if we show only the result of each application of
fact-cps followed by a β-reduction.

```
     (fact-cps 4 k)
⇒ (fact-cps 3 (lambda (v) (k (* 4 v))))
⇒ (fact-cps 2 (lambda (v) (k (* 4 (* 3 v)))))
⇒ (fact-cps 1 (lambda (v) (k (* 4 (* 3 (* 2 v))))))
⇒ (fact-cps 0 (lambda (v) (k (* 4 (* 3 (* 2 (* 1 v)))))))
⇒ (k (* 4 (* 3 (* 2 (* 1 1)))))
⇒ (k 24)
```

These derivations show that *fact-cps* has iterative control behavior, since the calls of *fact-cps* always occur in the same context, though its arguments may grow. The procedure uses its second argument k to represent the context in which the calculation of *fact* was to take place. We can think of k as representing a *promise* of the calculation to be done after computing the factorial of n. We recognize that k, which fulfills such a promise and represents a context such as (* n □), is being used as a *continuation*. Hence we say that *fact-cps* is written in *continuation-passing style*.

For a second example, consider `length`:

```
(define length
  (lambda (ls)
    (if (null? ls)
        0
        (+ (length (cdr ls)) 1))))
```

This can be expressed in continuation-passing style as

```
(define length-cps
  (lambda (ls k)
    (if (null? ls)
        (k 0)
        (length-cps (cdr ls)
          (lambda (v) (k (+ v 1)))))))
```

By convention, we use the variable k for continuations and pass the continuation as the last argument. The application (length-cps ls k) simulates the calculation of (length ls) in the context k. When *ls* is empty, it returns 0 to the context k. If *ls* is nonempty, then we need to determine the value of (+ (length (cdr ls)) 1) in the context k. This is the same as calculating (length (cdr ls)) in the context (k (+ □ 1)), which may be represented as (lambda (v) (k (+ v 1))).

- *Exercise 8.2.1*

  Prove that (length-cps ls k) = (k (length ls)). □

8.3 Tail Form

We would like to develop a systematic method for transforming any procedure into an equivalent procedure that has iterative control behavior. (When we say a procedure has iterative control behavior, we mean that a call to the procedure executes with iterative control behavior in a properly tail-recursive implementation.)

There is no completely general way of determining whether the control behavior of a procedure is iterative or not. Consider

```
(lambda (n)
  (if (strange-predicate? n)
      (fact n)
      (fact-iter n)))
```

This procedure is iterative only if *strange-predicate?* always returns false. However, it may not always be possible to determine the truth or falsity of this condition, even if it were possible to examine the code of *strange-predicate?*.

Therefore the best we can hope for is to define a static criterion that guarantees iterative control behavior. Because it is impossible to tell whether an arbitrary program has iterative control behavior, our criterion will reject some programs that actually have iterative control behavior, but that is unavoidable.

The static criterion is called *tail form*. Our intention is that in a tail-form expression, procedure calls always occur at the outermost level of a derivation of the result of a call. Thus the result of any procedure call is the result of the whole expression. For example, in *fact-iter-acc*, the result of the procedure call is the result of the whole call. In calculating (fact-iter 4), this means that when we do a procedure call, we do not build any context. This is in contrast to *fact*, in which the procedure call is "wrapped" in the code (* n □), where □ represents the procedure call. A promise must be made to execute this code when the procedure call returns.

Before we can define tail form, we need to describe the sort of language that we shall be analyzing. We assume we are using a language in which programs consist of expressions of the following five types.

- Variables and literals, as usual.
- Procedural expressions.

- Primitive applications. We assume that we have identified a class of *primitive operations* that have the following properties:

  a. they are not implemented using procedure calls,

  b. they never invoke any procedures that may be passed to them as arguments, and

  c. they are not first class (they may not be passed as arguments to other procedures).

Our intention is that primitive operations can be implemented in a few lines of machine code, without involving procedure calls.

In our previous interpreters, we put such primitive operations in the initial environment. In this chapter, however, we treat invocations of primitive operations as special forms, recognizable by the parser, that are distinct from ordinary applications. We call such invocations *primitive applications* and provide them with their own type of abstract syntax record.

```
(define-record prim-app (primitive rands))
```

This organization is used in most programming languages, in which applications of primitive operations often have syntactic forms that are distinct from procedure calls: compare x+y to p(x,y).

The assumption that primitive procedures are not first class is only a minor restriction. For example, if we want to pass the primitive + as an argument, we could pass (lambda (x y) (+ x y)) instead. In the examples of this chapter, we assume all the Scheme procedures introduced prior to section 1.3 are primitive. This precludes, among others, apply and map.

- Special forms in which all subexpressions are evaluated in an arbitrary order. In all cases some operation (e.g., an application or assignment) is performed after the subexpressions are evaluated, and this operation determines the value of the whole expression. In this chapter we treat application as the prototype for special forms of this type. Other forms of this type, such as assignment (set!) forms, are treated similarly.

For the purposes of this chapter, we distinguish primitive applications and (general) applications. For example,

$$(+\ (p\ 3)\ ((lambda\ (x)\ (+\ x\ 1))\ 4))$$

is a primitive application whose operands are both applications.

- Special forms that are evaluated as follows:

    a. First those subexpressions in certain positions are evaluated, in arbitrary order.

    b. Then exactly one of the remaining subexpressions is evaluated, and its value is immediately returned. (Hence these subexpressions are in tail position.)

There are two common forms in Scheme that do not fit any of the five types above: `begin` and `cond`. Fortunately, these forms may be expanded into equivalent forms that are of the required types. Although we develop the concepts of this chapter using Scheme, it must be emphasized that these concepts apply to a broad class of languages—not just Scheme.

Those subexpressions that may be evaluated first are said to be in *head* position. Expressions in tail position may be evaluated within the scope of certain variables, called the *binding positions* of the form. With one exception, all subexpressions of forms belonging to one of the five types must be in either head or tail position. The exception is the body of a lambda expression. The body is not evaluated at the time the lambda expression is evaluated; it is evaluated only when the resulting closure is applied.

In the Scheme forms of figure 8.3.1, the head positions are indicated by H, the tail positions by T, the binding positions by b, and those in neither head nor tail position by E. Note that in a primitive application (with primitive operation *prim-op*), the operand positions are all head positions, since they all are evaluated prior to invocation of the primitive operation. Similarly, the operator and operand positions of an application are all head positions. The formal parameters of a lambda are not considered binding positions, since their scope does not include any tail positions.

○ *Exercise 8.3.1*
Write an interpreter for the language of figure 8.3.1, plus variables and literals. For each production in the language, consider the action specified for that type of expression. Observe that the head positions are those for which evaluation of the subexpression is in head position in the action, and that the tail positions are those for which evaluation of the corresponding subexpression is in tail position in the action. □

We wish to identify those procedures in a program that may be responsible for recursive (noniterative) control behavior. To do so, we assign "responsibility" for the use of control space to procedures and to subexpressions of procedure bodies. We hold a given procedure responsible for control space

```
(lambda (v ... v) E)
(prim-op H ... H)
(H H ... H)
(set! v H)
(if H T T)
(let ((b H) ... (b H)) T)
(letrec ((b H) ... (b H)) T)
(variant-case H (x (b ... b) T) ... (x (b ... b) T))
(case H ((x ... x) T) ... ((x . . x) T))
```

Figure 8.3.1   Some forms, with their head, tail, and binding positions

that is required by calls initiated directly by it, but not for calls initiated by other procedures, including other procedures defined within its body.

To identify those subexpressions of a procedure's body for which it is responsible, we require a new term: we say a subexpression E' of E is *available* in E if it is not contained within a lambda subexpression of E. For example, in the expression

```
(if (f a) (lambda () (g 2)) (h x y))
```

the applications (f a) and (h x y) are available, while the application (g 2) is not. Thus a procedure is responsible only for the control space required for calls initiated by applications that are available in its body.

Next we define a class of expressions whose evaluation cannot possibly be responsible for recursive control behavior. We call these *simple* expressions. The easiest way to identify simple expressions is to assume that any procedure call may result in recursive control behavior. Thus we say an expression is simple if it does not contain an available application. (Though this characterization of simple expressions suffices for our present purpose, less restrictive characterizations are possible. This is discussed in section 8.7.)

Thus (car x) and (if p x (car (cdr x))) are simple, but (f (car x)) and (car (f x)) are not. On the other hand, (lambda (x) (car (f x))) is simple, since the procedure application (f x) is not available. Simple expressions may be evaluated without executing procedure calls (without the interpreter calling *apply-proc*).

The program of figure 8.3.2 determines whether an expression is simple. If the expression is an application, it is not simple. Otherwise, *simple?* checks the subexpressions in head and tail position to see if they are simple. This recursion terminates when the expression has no head or tail expressions, that is, when it is a variable, a literal, or a lambda expression. This program depends on the fact that all subexpressions in figure 8.3.1 (except for the body of a lambda expression) are either in head or tail position. Note that *head-exps*, *tail-exps*, and *binding-vars* of figure 8.3.2 are *not* recursive. In addition, letrec variables can be bound to arbitrary values, not just procedures. This necessitates using a syntax more like let, which we assume for the remainder of this chapter; see exercise 5.6.2.

We are now prepared to define our static criterion. A *tail-form expression* is one in which every subexpression in nontail position is simple.

Expressions may be in tail form but not simple, or simple but not in tail form. For example,

(car x)	simple	tail-form
(if p x (car (cdr x)))	simple	tail form
(f (car x))	not simple	tail form
(car (f x))	not simple	not tail form
(if p x (f (cdr x)))	not simple	tail form
(if (f x) x (f (cdr x)))	not simple	not tail form
(lambda (x) (f x))	simple	tail form
(lambda (x) (car (f x)))	simple	not tail form

Because we know that when an application in tail position is evaluated, no control information need be stored, and because in a tail-form expression all procedure applications are in tail position, we conclude:

> If an expression is in tail form, and any procedures accessible through variable bindings are also in tail form, then the expression will execute with iterative control behavior in a properly tail-recursive implementation.

Thus our criterion guarantees iterative control behavior, as desired.

One more definition will be useful. We say a procedure is in *first-order form* if it contains no lambda subexpressions and if all operator expressions are variables referring to top-level bindings. For example, fact, fact-iter and fact-iter-acc are all in first-order form, but the following procedures are not:

```
(lambda (x) (x 3))
(lambda () (lambda (x) x))
```

Figure 8.3.2   *simple? head-exps tail-exps binding-vars*

```
(define simple?
  (lambda (exp)
    (and (not (app? exp))
         (andmap simple? (head-exps exp))
         (andmap simple? (tail-exps exp)))))

(define head-exps
  (lambda (exp)
    (variant-case exp
      (lit (datum) '())
      (varref (var) '())
      (if (test-exp then-exp else-exp) (list test-exp))
      (proc (formals body) '())
      (let (decls body) (map decl->exp decls))
      (letrec (decls body) (map decl->exp decls))
      (prim-app (primitive rands) rands)
      (app (rator rands) (cons rator rands)))))

(define tail-exps
  (lambda (exp)
    (variant-case exp
      (lit (datum) '())
      (varref (var) '())
      (if (test-exp then-exp else-exp) (list then-exp else-exp))
      (proc (formals body) '())
      (let (decls body) (list body))
      (letrec (decls body) (list body))
      (prim-app (primitive rands) '())
      (app (rator rands) '()))))

(define binding-vars
  (lambda (exp)
    (variant-case exp
      (let (decls body) (map decl->var decls))
      (letrec (decls body) (map decl->var decls))
      (else '()))))
```

A set of procedure definitions whose bodies are in first-order tail form can be translated to flowchart form as we did for *fact-iter*.

Our goal is to develop a systematic process by which any program may be translated into a set of first-order tail-form procedures. In this chapter we see how to perform the first step in this process: the transformation of a procedure into an equivalent tail-form procedure in continuation-passing style. We shall consider the conversion to first-order form in chapter 9.

• *Exercise 8.3.2*

Write a program that takes an abstract syntax tree for a language that includes literals, variables, if, lambda, let, letrec, and application expressions and translates it to a syntax tree in which applications whose operators are known to be primitives (that is, found in the initial environment) are represented using prim-app nodes (defined above). Write an unparser to convert your abstract syntax trees back into Scheme syntax. Be careful to consider procedures like

```
proc (+) +(x, y)
```

You will need this program in order to use the Scheme-based CPS algorithm presented in this chapter. ☐

• *Exercise 8.3.3*

Determine whether each of the following expressions is simple and whether it is in tail form. Assume car, cdr, cons, and zero? are primitive.

a. (car (f (cdr x)))

b. (f (car (cdr x)))

c. (if (zero? x) (car y) (car (cdr y)))

d. (letrec ((x (lambda (y) (y x)))) (cons x '()))

e. (let ((f (lambda (x) x))) (f 3))

f. (case (f x) ((a) (g x)) (else y)) ☐

○ *Exercise 8.3.4*

Using BNF grammar, define two mutually recursive syntactic categories, one of tail-form expressions and one of simple expressions, for a subset of Scheme consisting of the following forms: variable, literal, primitive application, application, if, cond, lambda, let, and letrec. ☐

• *Exercise 8.3.5*
Define a predicate `tail-form?` for the language of exercise 8.3.2 that takes an expression and returns a boolean value indicating whether the expression is in tail form. □

8.4 Converting to Continuation-Passing Style

In this section we develop a set of rules for transforming any procedure into an equivalent procedure in tail form. We do this by transforming the procedure into continuation-passing style, as we did for *fact-cps* and *length-cps*; CPS procedures are always in tail form.

Automation of the CPS transformation may be useful, for example in the early phase of compilation, but it is also a valuable technique for transforming code "by hand." Though our algorithm for CPS transformation may be automated, as in section 8.6, it is also designed to reflect the way an experienced programmer would transform code into CPS and clearly expose the code's control component.

The *fact* and *length* examples suggest how a CPS transformation might be accomplished. The CPS transformation changes the procedure-calling convention so that every procedure takes an extra argument: the continuation to which the answer should be passed. It is then possible to transform every expression so that only simple expressions occur in nontail positions.

We do this in two stages. In the first stage, we rewrite *every* lambda expression so that it takes an extra argument (the continuation) to which the procedure returns its answer. By convention, we append the variable k to the end of each formal parameter list. (We assume the variable k is not used for other purposes. A new name could always be used to avoid a name conflict.)

The new body of each procedure is an application of k to the value of the old body. This transformation may be expressed as follows.

$$\begin{array}{l} \text{(lambda } (x_1 \ \ldots \ x_n) \ E) \\ \Rightarrow \text{(lambda } (x_1 \ \ldots \ x_n \ \text{k}) \ (\text{k } E)) \end{array}$$

For example,

```
   (lambda (x) (f x 1))
⇒ (lambda (x k) (k (f x 1)))
```

The subexpression (k (f x 1)) is underscored to indicate that it must be transformed further. Since all procedures are transformed at once, the procedure f must now be passed a continuation. Thus after this first step we shall not have a working program until the CPS transformation has been completed.

The second stage of our CPS algorithm involves repeatedly finding an unprocessed (underscored) application of the form (k E) and applying one of four rules given below. These rules either "drive the k inward" (this phrase will mean something shortly) or determine that it has been driven inward as far as it can be. In general, we may have several k's to work on, but it makes no difference which one we choose at any step. (Of course, any implementation of this algorithm must include a strategy for making this choice.) We use a darker underscore to distinguish an unprocessed subexpression of an already underscored expression. Furthermore, we never underscore a lambda (and its formal parameters) that is generated by the first step of the algorithm.

The four transformation rules for unprocessed expressions of the form (k E), handle four cases, depending on the structure of E. The first two are relatively straightforward:

C_{simple}: If E is simple, k cannot be driven further through E, so we are done processing this k.

For example, both (k (cons v w)) and (k 0) are already in tail form. After applying this rule, there may still be lambda expressions inside E that need to be processed. Thus in (k (lambda (x y k) (k (g (- n 1))))), we cannot do anything more with the outside k, but we must still transform the inner one.

C_η: If E is a procedure application of the form $(E_1 \ldots E_n)$, where $E_1,\ldots,$ E_n are simple, the procedure call is converted to the new protocol by replacing (k E) by $(E_1 \ldots E_n$ k).

For example, (k (g (- n 1))) becomes (g (- n 1) k). As before, there may still be lambda expressions inside $E_1, \ldots, E_n$ that need to be processed.

The remaining two cases are more complicated. In each case, we must find an "innermost" expression to be evaluated first. This is usually an application, in which case we create a call with a new continuation that abstracts the context in which the innermost application appears. For example, if we had

```
(k (* n (fact (- n 1))))
```

then the innermost call is (fact (- n 1)), so we perform the following transformation.

```
     (k (* n (fact (- n 1)))) 
  ⇒ (fact (- n 1) (lambda (v) (k (* n v))))
```

Observe that k has been "driven inward," and the application needs no further
processing except for the body of the new continuation.

In this example, the body of the continuation is already in tail form, so
there is nothing else to do. If it were not, then we would continue processing
the expression. For example, in `(k (+ (f x) (g y)))`, there are two innermost
applications: `(f x)` and `(g y)`. Choosing to evaluate `(f x)` first, we obtain

```
     (k (+ (f x) (g y))) 
  ⇒ (f̃ x (lambda (v) (k (+ v (g y))))) 
  ⇒ (f̃ x (lambda (v) (g̃ y (lambda (w) (k (+ v w)))))) 
  ⇒ (f̃ x (lambda (v) (g̃ y (lambda (w) (k (+ v w))))))
```

We use a tilde above the name to denote the transformed procedure, which
takes an additional argument. More precisely, we need to locate an *innermost
nonsimple subexpression that can be evaluated first*. We call this an *initial
expression* of E. By an *innermost subexpression* we mean one whose immediate subexpressions in head position are all simple. Thus the following are all
innermost expressions:

```
(f x y) 
(f (+ x y) z) 
(if (> x y) (f (g x)) (h (j x)))
```

The last expression is innermost because it has only one immediate subexpression in head position, `(> x y)`, and it is simple.

Of all the subexpressions, how do we determine which ones may be evaluated first? To do this, we look once again at the forms of figure 8.3.1. Recall
that the first step in evaluating each of these forms is to evaluate (in any
order) the subexpressions in head position, indicated by H. Thus, if E is not
itself innermost, then the candidates for the initial expression must be found
in the head-position subexpressions of E.

Therefore, we search for an initial expression as follows. If the expression
E is nonsimple, but all its immediate subexpressions in head position are
simple, then the expression is its own initial expression. Otherwise, we move
our search to any one of the nonsimple immediate subexpressions of E that
are in head position. Figure 8.4.1 gives a program for finding the leftmost
initial expression.

For example, the initial expression of `(p x y)` is the application itself, since
all of its subexpressions are simple. The initial expression of

Figure 8.4.1 Finding an initial expression

```
(define initial-exp
  (lambda (exp)
    (letrec
      ((loop (lambda (ls)
               (cond
                 ((null? ls) exp)
                 ((simple? (car ls)) (loop (cdr ls)))
                 (else (initial-exp (car ls)))))))
      (loop (head-exps exp)))))
```

```
(if (null? x) (f x y) z)
```

is also the entire expression, since `(null? x)`, the only expression in head position, is a simple primitive application. The expression

```
(g (f a b)
   (h (p x y))
   (if (null? x) (f x y) z))
```

has three initial expressions. The first, `(f a b)`, is in head position and all of its immediate subexpressions are simple, so it is an initial expression. The subexpression `(h (p x y))` is also in head position, but it contains a nonsimple subexpression `(p x y)` in head position, so `(h (p x y))` is not an innermost nonsimple expression that can be evaluated first. Moving the search for an initial expression inward, we find `(p x y)`, which is nonsimple *and* contains no nonsimple subexpressions, so it is an initial expression. Finally, the expression `(if (null? x) (f x y) z)` is an initial expression, since it is nonsimple, it is in head position with respect to the entire expression, and it contains only the simple subexpression `(null? x)` in immediate head position.

As further examples, in the expressions that follow, the initial expressions are enclosed within a rectangle. (Verify!)

```
┌───────────┐
│(f (* a b) 3)│
└───────────┘
```

```
(+ │(fact 3)│ (* (fact │(fib 2)│) 5))
```

```
(if │(f 3)│ (g 4) (g 5))
```

```
┌───────────────┐
│(let ((y 4)) (f 4))│
└───────────────┘
```

```
(let ((x [(let ((y 4)) (f 3))])
      (y (+ a b))
      (z [(f 3)]))
  (g 5))
```

- *Exercise 8.4.1*

  Place a rectangle around the initial expressions of each of the following expressions. Remember that a single expression may have more than one initial expression.

  a. (k (a (+ 1 b)))

  b. (k (+ (f (g (h 3))) (a (+ 1 b))))

  c. (k (f (if (zero? x) (g 3) (g 4)) (g 5)))

  d. (k (f (if (zero? x) 3 4) (if (p x) 3 4)))

  e. (k (let ((x 3) (y (fact 4))) (p x b))) □

- *Exercise 8.4.2*

  Modify *initial-exp* in figure 8.4.1 to produce a list of all the initial expressions in its argument. □

Once we find an initial expression, the next step in the algorithm depends on whether or not the initial expression is an application. If it is, the CPS version must perform that application first, using a suitable continuation. Therefore we make the application the outermost form of the CPS transformation. Thus if an application $(E_1 \ldots E_n)$ is an initial expression of $(k\ E)$, then the transformed expression will be of the form

$$(E_1 \ \ldots \ E_n \ K)$$

for some suitable continuation K.

This continuation K must take a value v and complete the computation of $(k\ E)$ using v as the result of the initial expression. Such a continuation may be created by constructing a lambda expression whose body is formed by replacing the initial expression with the formal parameter of the lambda expression. To avoid name clashes, we choose as the formal parameter a variable that does not occur free in the expression.

This is not as complicated as it sounds. Let us look at some examples. Consider first (k (h (p x y))). The only initial expression is (p x y), so we transform:

$$\frac{\texttt{(k (h (p x y)))}}{\Rightarrow \texttt{(p̃ x y (lambda (v) } \underline{\texttt{(k (h v)))}} \texttt{)}}$$

Since (h v) is its own initial expression, we continue the transformation using the rule C_η.

$$\Rightarrow \texttt{(p̃ x y (lambda (v) (h̃ v k)))}$$

Next consider the expression (k (+ (f x) (g y))), which has two initial expressions, (f x) and (g y). If we choose to evaluate (f x) first, we obtain the following derivation:

$$\frac{\texttt{(k (+ (f x) (g y)))}}{\begin{array}{l}\Rightarrow \texttt{(f̃ x (lambda (v) } \underline{\texttt{(k (+ v (g y))))}}\texttt{)}\\ \Rightarrow \texttt{(f̃ x (lambda (v) (g̃ y (lambda (w) } \underline{\texttt{(k (+ v w)))))}}\texttt{)}\end{array}}$$

Since (k (+ v w)) is in tail form, the whole expression is in tail form, and we are done. We could just as correctly and easily have chosen to evaluate (g y) first.

A somewhat more complicated expression is

(k (+ ⌈(f a b)⌉
      ⌊(g (lambda (a k) (k (f a b))))⌋))

Here we have already performed the algorithm's first stage, adding an extra continuation argument k to every lambda expression and passing its body to k. There are two occurrences of (f a b) in this expression: the first is an initial expression, and the second is not. We choose the first occurrence of the expression (f a b) as the initial expression and obtain

```
  (k (+ (f a b)
        (g (lambda (a k)
             (k (f a b)))))))
⇒ (f̃ a b
     (lambda (v)
       (k (+ v
             (g (lambda (a k)
                  (k (f a b))))))))))
```

Here we performed the substitution of v for the chosen occurrence of (f a b), *not for all* occurrences: the second, noninitial occurrence should not be changed. Continuing the derivation, we see that the application of g is an initial expression of the body of the first procedural expression. This gives us

```
⇒ (f̃ a b
      (lambda (v)
        (g̃ (lambda (a k) (k (f a b)))
           (lambda (w) (k (+ v w))))))
```

We still have two occurrences of k to deal with. The second is already in tail form, but the first can still be pushed farther inward. The result of one more push is

```
⇒ (f̃ a b
      (lambda (v)
        (g̃ (lambda (a k) (f̃ a b k))
           (lambda (w) (k (+ v w))))))
```

and we are done. (At this point we drop the tilde notation. Although, confusion can arise between the original procedure and its transformed counterpart, the transformed program only contains transformed procedures. Furthermore, it is simpler to think about the original and transformed procedures having the same name, since they accomplish equivalent tasks.)

To formalize these operations, we introduce the notion of *positional substitution*. We write $E\{M/X\}$ to denote the positional substitution of M at the position of X in E. This means we substitute M for a particular occurrence of the subexpression X, not for every occurrence. Positional substitution is rather different from the notion of substitution considered in section 4.2. There, when we wrote $E[M/x]$, x had to be a variable, whereas here the analogous quantity refers to an expression. Furthermore, the substitution renamed formal parameters to avoid capture of bound variables. Here capture of bound variables does not occur, due to the nature of our algorithm. We are now ready to state formally our third CPS transformation rule, which is illustrated in figure 8.4.2.

C_{app}: If (k E) has an initial expression I that is an application (E_1 ... E_n), replace (k E) by

$$(E_1 \ ... \ E_n \ \texttt{(lambda} \ (v) \ \texttt{(k} \ E\{v/I\})))$$

where v is a previously unused variable.

See figure 8.4.3 for a program to compute a *simultaneous* positional substitution. In this program the use of the procedure *eq?* (by assq) is essential, since we are substituting at specific positions regardless of their content.

Continuation-Passing Style

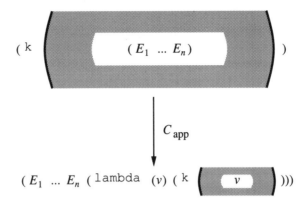

Figure 8.4.2   The CPS rule for application in a context: C_{app}

- *Exercise 8.4.3*

  Our transformation of (k (+ (f x) (g y))) evaluated the immediate subexpressions left-to-right by evaluating the left initial expression first. CPS-transform (k (+ (f x) (g (h y)))) to correspond to right-to-left evaluation. □

- *Exercise 8.4.4*

  CPS-transform (k (p (+ 8 x) (q y))). □

∘ *Exercise 8.4.5*

  Find the CPS transformation for

  ```
  (k (+ (f a b)
        (g (lambda (a k)
            (k (f a b)))))))
  ```

  in which the application of *g* is chosen as the initial expression. □

∘ *Exercise 8.4.6*

  C_η corresponds to the case of C_{app} in which the initial expression of (k *E*) is *E* itself. Compare the result of applying C_{app} and C_η to (k (f x y)). □

Figure 8.4.3   Simultaneous positional substitution

```
(define positional-substitution
  (lambda (exp pairs)
    (letrec
      ((loop
        (lambda (exp)
          (let ((found-pair (assq exp pairs)))
            (if (pair? found-pair)
                (cdr found-pair)
                (variant-case exp
                  (lit (datum) exp)
                  (varref (var) exp)
                  (if (test-exp then-exp else-exp)
                    (make-if
                      (loop test-exp)
                      (loop then-exp)
                      (loop else-exp)))
                  (proc (formals body)
                    (make-proc formals (loop body)))
                  (let (decls body)
                    (make-let
                      (map (lambda (decl)
                             (make-decl
                               (decl->var decl)
                               (loop (decl->exp decl))))
                           decls)
                      (loop body)))
                  (letrec (decls body)
                    (make-letrec
                      (map (lambda (decl)
                             (make-decl
                               (decl->var decl)
                               (loop (decl->exp decl))))
                           decls)
                      (loop body)))
                  (prim-app (primitive rands)
                    (make-prim-app primitive (map loop rands)))
                  (app (rator rands)
                    (make-app (loop rator) (map loop rands)))))))))
      (loop exp))))
```

If all we had to deal with were applications (as in the lambda calculus), we could have escaped with a much simpler description of the conversion process. Transforming special forms, however, requires more care. Thus we have one more case, in which the initial expression is not an application but is instead a special form.

If a special form is initial, then its head subexpressions are all simple. Furthermore, its value is the value of *one* of its tail subexpressions. For example, consider

```
(k (if (null? ls) 0 (+ (length (cdr ls)) 1)))
```

The conditional expression is initial, because its only head subexpression, (null? ls), is simple. The value of the conditional is either 0 or (+ (length (cdr ls)) 1), so the value of the whole expression is the same as

```
(if (null? ls)
    (k 0)
    (k (+ (length (cdr ls)) 1)))
```

Once more k is pushed inward, and in this example it splits into two. From here, the other rules can be used.

Let us consider a slightly more complicated case.

```
(k (* (if (null? ls) x (+ (length (cdr ls)) 1))
      3))
```
```
⇒ (if (null? ls)
       (k (* x 3))
       (k (* (+ (length (cdr ls)) 1) 3)))
```

From such examples we surmise that *each* tail expression of the special form must be wrapped in the entire context in which the special form appears within the application of k.

There is one further complication. Because the special form may bind variables, such as let or letrec, we must be careful to avoid variable capture. For example, consider

```
(k (g (let ((g 3))
        (+ g x))))
```

Here the `let` expression is initial, and its body is its only tail expression. If we wrap the body in the context (`k` (`g` □)), then the context's outer `g` will be brought inside the scope of the inner `g` and be captured:

```
(let ((g 3))
  (k (g (+ g x))))
```

This is clearly wrong, since the outer `g` is a procedure and the inner one is a number.

This problem may be avoided by α-converting the offending binding variables. Substituting `g:` for the inner `g` in our example, the transformation proceeds as follows.

```
(k (g (let ((g 3))
        (+ g x))))
```

$\Rightarrow$
```
(k (g (let ((g: 3))
        (+ g: x))))
```
by α-conversion

$\Rightarrow$
```
(let ((g: 3))
  (k (g (+ g: x))))
```

$\Rightarrow$
```
(let ((g: 3))
  (g (+ g: x) k))
```

Figure 8.3.1 shows the positions of the variables bound by each special form. To formalize the notion of α-conversion here, we need some notation. We write $E\langle x_1, \ldots, x_p \rangle$ for the expression obtained by α-converting E to rename the bound variables $x_1, \ldots, x_p$ (see figure 8.4.5). To maintain readable programs, it is helpful when renaming a variable if the new name is obtained in a systematic fashion from the old name. Our convention is to add a colon to the end of the old name. (We presume that user variable names do not end with a colon.)

Combining these observations, we obtain the final CPS transformation rule (illustrated with `if` in figure 8.4.4).

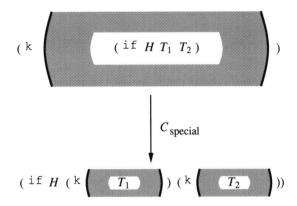

$$(\text{k} \quad (\text{if } H \ T_1 \ T_2) \quad)$$

$$C_{\text{special}}$$

$$(\text{if } H \ (\text{k} \quad T_1 \quad) \ (\text{k} \quad T_2 \quad))$$

Figure 8.4.4 Typical CPS rule for special form in a context: C_{special}

C_{special}: If (k E) has an initial expression I with $n > 0$ expressions in tail position, and $b_1, \ldots, b_p$ are the binding variables of I that occur free in E, transform E as follows:

1. First let $I' = I\langle b_1, \ldots, b_p \rangle$ and $E' = E\{I'/I\}$.

2. Then replace E' by I', with each tail position expression T_i of I' replaced by (k $E'\{T_i/I'\}$), that is,

$$I'\{(\text{k } E'\{T_1/I'\})/T_1, \ldots, (\text{k } E'\{T_n/I'\})/T_n\}$$

- *Exercise 8.4.7*
  Apply rule C_{special} to the following expressions.

  a. (k (zero? (if a (p x) (p y))))

  b. (k (zero? (let ((x 3)) (p x))))

  c. (k (let ((x (let ((y 8)) (p y)))) x))

  d. (k (let ((x (if a (p x) (p y)))) x))

  e. (k (variant-case x (a () (p a)) (b () (q a)) (c (x) (f x)))) □

Figure 8.4.5   An alpha converter

```
(define alpha-convert
  (lambda (exp bvs)
    (let ((table
            (let ((pairs (map (lambda (bv)
                                (cons bv (next-symbol-right bv)))
                              bvs)))
              (lambda (sym)
                (let ((found-pair (assq sym pairs)))
                  (if (pair? found-pair)
                      (cdr found-pair)
                      sym))))))
      (variant-case exp
        (let (decls body)
          (make-let
            (map (lambda (decl)
                   (make-decl
                     (table (decl->var decl))
                     (decl->exp decl)))
                 decls)
            (beta body table)))
        (letrec (decls body)
          (make-letrec
            (map
              (lambda (decl)
                (make-decl
                  (table (decl->var decl))
                  (beta (decl->exp decl) table)))
              decls)
            (beta body table)))
        (else exp)))))
```

Figure 8.4.5   An alpha converter (continued)

```
(define beta
  (lambda (exp table)
    (variant-case exp
      (lit (datum) exp)
      (varref (var) (make-varref (table var)))
      (if (test-exp then-exp else-exp)
        (make-if
          (beta test-exp table)
          (beta then-exp table)
          (beta else-exp table)))
      (proc (formals body)
        (make-proc formals
          (beta body (lambda (var)
                       (if (memq var formals) var (table var))))))
      (let (decls body)
        (make-let
          (map (lambda (decl)
                 (make-decl (decl->var decl)
                   (beta (decl->exp decl) table)))
               decls)
          (beta body (let ((vars (map decl->var decls)))
                       (lambda (var)
                         (if (memq var vars) var (table var)))))))
      (letrec (decls body)
        (let ((new-table
                (let ((vars (map decl->var decls)))
                  (lambda (var)
                    (if (memq var vars) var (table var))))))
          (make-letrec
            (map (lambda (decl)
                   (make-decl (decl->var decl)
                     (beta (decl->exp decl) new-table)))
                 decls)
            (beta body new-table))))
      (prim-app (primitive rands)
        (make-prim-app primitive
          (map (lambda (rand) (beta rand table)) rands)))
      (app (rator rands)
        (make-app (beta rator table)
          (map (lambda (rand) (beta rand table)) rands))))))
```

○ *Exercise 8.4.8*

If an `if` expression such as

```
(if (null? ls) 0 (+ (length (cdr ls)) 1))
```

appears as an initial subexpression of a large expression, then the CPS transform will look like

```
(if (null? ls) (K 0) (length (cdr ls) (lambda (v) (K (+ v 1)))))
```

where K represents the continuation that abstracts the context of the large expression. This reveals a shortcoming of the CPS transformation, since the program text of K appears in two places. If we wrap a `let` expression binding `k` to K around the entire expression, we would obtain

```
(let ((k K))
  (if (null? ls) (k 0) (length (cdr ls) (lambda (v) (k (+ v 1))))))
```

This technique keeps the expression from growing exponentially. Discuss the advantages and disadvantages of such an approach. This shortcoming is addressed more completely in chapter 12, where the output of a CPS transformation corresponds to the output of a compiler. □

● *Exercise 8.4.9*

Modify rule C_{app} to obtain a transformation rule for `set!`. □

8.5 Examples of the CPS Transformation

To obtain a feel for the CPS transformation rules, it is necessary to work through a number of examples. Let us try *remove* from section 2.2.2 first.

```
(define remove
  (lambda (s los)
    (if (null? los)
        '()
        (if (eq? s (car los))
            (remove s (cdr los))
            (cons (car los) (remove s (cdr los)))))))
```

Our first step is to add the extra continuation argument to each procedural expression; in this case there is only one:

```
(lambda (s los k)
  (k (if (null? los)
         '()
         (if (eq? s (car los))
             (remove s (cdr los))
             (cons (car los) (remove s (cdr los)))))))
```

We now begin pushing the k through the expression. In this example the only subexpression in head position is (null? los), and it is simple. Thus we apply C_{special} and obtain

```
(lambda (s los k)
  (if (null? los)
      (k '())
      (k (if (eq? s (car los))
             (remove s (cdr los))
             (cons (car los) (remove s (cdr los)))))))
```

The first application of k is in tail form, so after observing this we remove the underscoring. (We do this without comment from now on.) The if subexpression of the second application of k is its initial expression, since (eq? s (car los)) (its only head expression) is simple. Hence we apply rule C_{special} and obtain

```
(lambda (s los k)
  (if (null? los)
      (k '())
      (if (eq? s (car los))
          (k (remove s (cdr los)))
          (k (cons (car los) (remove s (cdr los)))))))
```

Now we can apply the simple-application rule C_η to the first unprocessed k to obtain

```
(lambda (s los k)
  (if (null? los)
      (k '())
      (if (eq? s (car los))
          (remove s (cdr los) k)
          (k (cons (car los) (remove s (cdr los)))))))
```

The subexpression `(remove s (cdr los))` is an initial expression of the last application of k, so by C_{app} we obtain

```
(lambda (s los k)
  (if (null? los)
      (k '())
      (if (eq? s (car los))
          (remove s (cdr los) k)
          (remove s (cdr los)
            (lambda (v)
              (k (cons (car los) v)))))))
```

and we are done.

To create a tail-form version of the original *remove* procedure, we rename the CPS version of remove to remove-cps throughout the program and redefine *remove* as follows:

```
(define remove
  (lambda (s los)
    (remove-cps s los (lambda (v) v))))
```

For another example, consider *subst* from section 2.2.2.

```
(define subst
  (lambda (new old slst)
    (if (null? slst)
        '()
        (if (symbol? (car slst))
            (if (eq? (car slst) old)
                (cons new (subst new old (cdr slst)))
                (cons (car slst) (subst new old (cdr slst))))
            (cons (subst new old (car slst))
                  (subst new old (cdr slst)))))))
```

This is an interesting example, since it contains four applications, two of which are initial expressions of the same primitive application. Also, here we see the importance of positional substitution since there are three different instances of `(subst new old (cdr slst))`.

Again, we start by transforming the lambda expression.

```
(lambda (new old slst k)
  (k (if (null? slst)
         '()
         (if (symbol? (car slst))
             (if (eq? (car slst) old)
                 (cons new (subst new old (cdr slst)))
                 (cons (car slst) (subst new old (cdr slst))))
             (cons (subst new old (car slst))
                   (subst new old (cdr slst)))))))

⇒ (lambda (new old slst k)
     (if (null? slst)
         (k '())
         (k (if (symbol? (car slst))
                (if (eq? (car slst) old)
                    (cons new (subst new old (cdr slst)))
                    (cons (car slst) (subst new old (cdr slst))))
                (cons (subst new old (car slst))
                      (subst new old (cdr slst)))))))

⇒ (lambda (new old slst k)
     (if (null? slst)
         (k '())
         (if (symbol? (car slst))
             (k (if (eq? (car slst) old)
                    (cons new (subst new old (cdr slst)))
                    (cons (car slst) (subst new old (cdr slst)))))
             (k (cons (subst new old (car slst))
                      (subst new old (cdr slst)))))))

⇒ (lambda (new old slst k)
     (if (null? slst)
         (k '())
         (if (symbol? (car slst))
             (if (eq? (car slst) old)
                 (k (cons new (subst new old (cdr slst))))
                 (k (cons (car slst) (subst new old (cdr slst)))))
             (subst new old (car slst)
               (lambda (v)
                 (k (cons v (subst new old (cdr slst)))))))))
```

In the last step, we chose the first application in the last *cons* primitive application as the initial expression to evaluate, effectively guaranteeing a left-to-right evaluation order of the cons operands. The second application could just as well have been chosen, since the order of operand evaluation is unspecified in Scheme. In continuing our trace, we use v as the parameter for newly created continuations when it does not shadow another binding of v.

```
⇒ (lambda (new old slst k)
    (if (null? slst)
        (k '())
        (if (symbol? (car slst))
            (if (eq? (car slst) old)
                (subst new old (cdr slst)
                  (lambda (v) (k (cons new v))))
                (subst new old (cdr slst)
                  (lambda (v) (k (cons (car slst) v)))))
            (subst new old (car slst)
              (lambda (v)
                (k (cons v (subst new old (cdr slst)))))))))

⇒ (lambda (new old slst k)
    (if (null? slst)
        (k '())
        (if (symbol? (car slst))
            (if (eq? (car slst) old)
                (subst new old (cdr slst)
                  (lambda (v) (k (cons new v))))
                (subst new old (cdr slst)
                  (lambda (v) (k (cons (car slst) v)))))
            (subst new old (car slst)
              (lambda (v)
                (subst new old (cdr slst)
                  (lambda (v1) (k (cons v v1)))))))))
```

Following our convention of using names ending in -cps for procedures in CPS, we would define *subst-cps* using the expression above with each occurrence of subst replaced by subst-cps.

Our rules are designed to work on expressions with embedded lambda expressions. Let us consider another version of *remove* that uses letrec:

```
(define remove
  (lambda (s los)
    (letrec
      ((loop
        (lambda (los)
          (if (null? los)
              '()
              (if (eq? s (car los))
                  (loop (cdr los))
                  (cons (car los) (loop (cdr los)))))))))
      (loop los))))
```

Our first step is to add a continuation argument to each lambda expression. Here, there are two such expressions. We obtain

```
(lambda (s los k)
  (k (letrec
       ((loop
         (lambda (los k)
           (k (if (null? los)
                  '()
                  (if (eq? s (car los))
                      (loop (cdr los))
                      (cons (car los) (loop (cdr los)))))))))
      (loop los))))
```

Consulting figure 8.3.1, we see that the only head expression of the letrec is the declaration of loop, which is a lambda expression and therefore simple. Hence the letrec is the initial expression, and we can apply C_{special} to get

```
(lambda (s los k)
  (letrec
    ((loop
      (lambda (los k)
        (k (if (null? los)
               '()
               (if (eq? s (car los))
                   (loop (cdr los))
                   (cons (car los) (loop (cdr los)))))))))
    (k (loop los))))
```

Applying the rule C_η for simple applications, we obtain

```
(lambda (s los k)
  (letrec
    ((loop
       (lambda (los k)
         (k (if (null? los)
               '()
               (if (eq? s (car los))
                   (loop (cdr los))
                   (cons (car los) (loop (cdr los)))))))))
    (loop los k))))
```

Now we can continue transforming the body of the inner lambda expression.

∘ *Exercise 8.5.1*
Finish this transformation. □

To transform a `cond` expression, we can always convert it into an `if` expression and transform that. But, often the test expressions of a `cond` form are all simple. When such `cond` forms are expanded into `if` expressions, the nesting structure of the `if` expressions is retained after CPS transformation. This allows the transformed `if` expressions in the resulting CPS code to be converted back into a `cond` expression. From these observations we conclude that when all of the test expressions of a `cond` expression are simple, rule C_{special} may be applied directly to the expression, treating each test expression as if it were in head position. For example, if *remove* were expressed using `cond`, its CPS transformation would include the following step:

```
(k (cond
     ((null? los) '())
     ((eq? s (car los)) (remove s (cdr los)))
     (else (cons (car los) (remove s (cdr los))))))
⇒ (cond
     ((null? los) (k '()))
     ((eq? s (car los)) (k (remove s (cdr los))))
     (else (k (cons (car los) (remove s (cdr los))))))
```

and so on. If one of the tests is nonsimple, the best we can do is to convert that part of the `cond` expression into an `if` expression and transform that into CPS.

Verify the statements made in the last paragraph. ☐

Consider the definition and use of *final-valcont* below.

```
> (define final-valcont
    (lambda (v)
      (display "The answer is: ")
      (write v)
      (newline)))
> (remove-cps 'b '(a b c b a) final-valcont)
The answer is: (a c a)
```

Here we have used something other than (lambda (v) v) as the continuation that receives the final value. When testing CPS procedures, it is better to use this *final-valcont* rather than the identity procedure. since correct solutions will print The answer is: just one time for each test of a CPS procedure. This avoids confusion between values received by the final value continuation and those printed by the read-eval-print loop.

● *Exercise 8.5.3*
Transform these procedures to CPS and then test them using *final-valcont*.

a. remove*

```
(define remove*
  (lambda (a alst)
    (cond
      ((null? alst) '())
      ((pair? (car alst))
       (cons (remove* a (car alst)) (remove* a (cdr alst))))
      ((eq? (car alst) a) (remove* a (cdr alst)))
      (else (cons (car alst) (remove* a (cdr alst)))))))
```

b. member*

```
(define member*
  (lambda (a alst)
    (cond
      ((null? alst) #f)
      ((pair? (car alst))
       (or (member* a (car alst)) (member* a (cdr alst))))
      ((eq? (car alst) a) alst)
      (else (member* a (cdr alst))))))
```

c. remfirst*

```
(define remfirst*
  (lambda (a alst)
    (letrec ((loop (lambda (alst)
                     (cond
                       ((null? alst) '())
                       ((not (pair? (car alst)))
                        (if (eq? (car alst) a)
                            (cdr alst)
                            (cons (car alst) (loop (cdr alst)))))
                       ((equal? (loop (car alst)) (car alst))
                        (cons (car alst) (loop (cdr alst))))
                       (else (cons (loop (car alst)) (cdr alst)))))))
      (loop alst))))
```

d. depth

```
(define depth
  (lambda (alst)
    (cond
      ((null? alst) 1)
      ((not (pair? (car alst))) (depth (cdr alst)))
      ((< (+ (depth (car alst)) 1) (depth (cdr alst)))
       (depth (cdr alst)))
      (else (+ (depth (car alst)) 1)))))
```

e. depth-with-let

```
(define depth-with-let
  (lambda (alst)
    (if (null? alst)
        1
        (let ((drest (depth-with-let (cdr alst))))
          (if (pair? (car alst))
              (let ((dfirst (+ (depth-with-let (car alst)) 1)))
                (if (< dfirst drest) drest dfirst))
              drest)))))
```

□

- *Exercise 8.5.4*

Transform the following procedures into CPS.

a. *map-cps*—the procedure `map` in continuation-passing style. Its first argument must also be a procedure that is written in continuation-passing style. For example, we could map `car` over a list as follows:

```
> (map-cps
    (lambda (v k) (k (car v)))
    '((1 2 3) (a b c) (x y z))
    final-valcont)
The answer is: (1 a x)
```

b. *fnlr>n*—takes any list of numbers and a number *n* and returns the first number in the list (in left-to-right order) that is greater than *n*. Once the result is found, no further elements in the list are examined. For example

```
> (fnlr>n '(1 (3 (2) 7 (9))) 6 final-valcont)
The answer is: 7
```

c. *add>n*—takes any list of numbers and a number *n* as arguments. It returns the sum of all numbers in the list that are greater than *n*.

d. *andmap-cps*—takes a predicate and a list and returns true if the predicate returns true for each list element. Use this definition:

```
(define andmap
  (lambda (f ls)
    (if (null? ls)
        #t
        (and (f (car ls)) (andmap f (cdr ls))))))
```

☐

8.6 Implementing the CPS Transformation

The CPS transformation in section 8.4 changes the procedure-calling protocol to a continuation-passing style in which every procedure takes an additional continuation argument and every call supplies that argument. We described the transformation in terms of two passes: one to change all the lambda expressions and one to change all the applications. The second pass was described in terms of pushing a continuation argument k through the expression until its argument was simple.

Figure 8.6.1 *cps-simple*

```
(define cps-simple
  (lambda (exp)
    (if (proc? exp)
        (make-proc (append (proc->formals exp) '(k))
          (cps-exp (proc->body exp)))
        (positional-substitution exp
          (map (lambda (head-or-tail-exp)
                 (cons head-or-tail-exp
                   (cps-simple head-or-tail-exp)))
            (append (head-exps exp) (tail-exps exp)))))))))
```

Our description specified the individual transformation rules, but it was vague about the control structure of the algorithm. To implement this algorithm, we must be more specific about the control structure. Observe that no expression ever gets transformed twice: once we have pushed k through a piece of code, we are through transforming that code. This allows us to combine the two stages of the transformation into a single traversal of an expression's parse tree. We use two procedures, *cps-simple* and *cps-exp*, one for each stage of the transformation, which call each other recursively.

The procedure cps-simple is shown in figure 8.6.1. Rather than code the algorithm directly in terms of the abstract syntax tree, we use a set of auxiliary procedures, such as *head-exps* and *positional-substitution*, which deal with the syntax tree. Therefore, to modify the language being transformed, we need only modify these auxiliary procedures, not the main procedures of the algorithm.

If *exp* is a lambda expression, *cps-simple* adds an additional argument to its formal parameter list and then initiates the second phase on the body of the procedure. Otherwise, it continues to search through the parse tree, using *positional-substitution* to rebuild the transformed tree.

The procedure *cps-exp* is shown in figure 8.6.2. It simulates pushing the continuation variable k through its argument by calling an auxiliary procedure to perform the appropriate rule. If its argument is simple, it calls the procedure *c-simple* to perform rule C_{simple}. Otherwise, it finds an initial expression. If the initial expression is an application, it performs rule C_η if the initial expression is E and rule C_{app} otherwise. If the initial expression is not an application, then it performs rule C_{special}.

Figure 8.6.2 `cps-exp`

```
(define cps-exp
  (lambda (exp)
    (if (simple? exp)
        (c-simple exp)
        (let ((init-exp (initial-exp exp)))
          (if (app? init-exp)
              (if (eq? init-exp exp)
                  (c-eta init-exp)
                  (c-app init-exp exp))
              (c-special init-exp exp))))))
```

Figure 8.6.3   Procedures for generating new symbols

```
(define next-symbol-right
  (lambda (sym)
    (string->symbol
      (string-append (symbol->string sym) ":"))))

(define next-symbol-left
  (lambda (rator)
    (variant-case rator
      (varref (var)
        (string->symbol
          (string-append ":" (symbol->string var))))
      (else (next-symbol)))))
```

The procedures for applying the rules are shown in figure 8.6.4. Most of this code is just what is in the rules, using *positional-substitution* to reassemble the parse trees. In *c-simple*, note that we apply *cps-simple* to *exp* in order to continue the first-stage search for embedded procedural expressions. Similarly, *cps-simple* is applied to the operator and operands in each procedure application and to the head positions of each special form. In *c-special*, we perform alpha conversion on some of the binding variables of let and letrec expressions. If the operator is a variable, we place a colon on the left of the variable's symbol; see figure 8.6.3. When the operator is a lambda expression, we use *next-symbol* from exercise 4.6.3.

Figure 8.6.4   Procedures for the C-rules

```
(define c-simple
  (lambda (exp)
    (make-app (make-varref 'k) (list (cps-simple exp)))))

(define c-app
  (lambda (init-exp exp)
    (make-app (cps-simple (app->rator init-exp))
      (append (map cps-simple (app->rands init-exp))
        (list (let ((g (next-symbol-left (cps-simple (app->rator init-exp)))))
                (make-proc (list g)
                  (cps-exp
                    (positional-substitution exp
                      (list (cons init-exp (make-varref g)))))))))))))

(define c-eta
  (lambda (init-exp)
    (make-app (cps-simple (app->rator init-exp))
      (append
        (map cps-simple (app->rands init-exp))
        (list (make-varref 'k))))))

(define c-special
  (lambda (init-exp exp)
    (let ((new-exp (positional-substitution exp
                     (list (cons init-exp
                             (alpha-convert init-exp
                               (intersect
                                 (binding-vars init-exp)
                                 (free-vars exp)))))))))
      (let ((new-init-exp (initial-exp new-exp)))
        (positional-substitution new-init-exp
          (append
            (map (lambda (h)
                   (cons h (cps-simple h)))
                 (head-exps new-init-exp))
            (map (lambda (t)
                   (cons t (cps-exp
                             (positional-substitution new-exp
                               (list (cons new-init-exp t))))))
                 (tail-exps new-init-exp))))))))
```

- *Exercise 8.6.1*

  Since the parser expands `begin` expressions into two subexpressions, modifying the CPS algorithm to include `begin` expressions is now quite easy. Add `begin` expressions to the implementation of the CPS algorithm. □

- *Exercise 8.6.2*

  Modify the implementation of the CPS algorithm to include `set!`. □

○ *Exercise 8.6.3*

  Rewrite the algorithm to work directly in terms of the parse tree, rather than working through the various intermediary procedures. The resulting code should have only two occurrences of *positional-substitution*, one in `c-app` and the other in `c-special`. □

○ *Exercise 8.6.4*

  The algorithm as stated does not work if the symbol `k` is used as a parameter in the input code. Modify the algorithm to work correctly in this case. □

○ *Exercise 8.6.5*

  Extend the implementation to handle `cond` expressions, by expanding them into `if` expressions. Then modify the unparser to replace nested `if` expressions by `cond` expressions. □

○ *Exercise 8.6.6*

  While our algorithm is organized to take only a single pass over the syntax tree, it actually makes several subpasses as it works, because each call to *initial-exp* or *positional-substitution* initiates a traversal of at least part of the tree. Rewrite the algorithm so that initial expressions and continuation arguments are computed "on-the-fly." Your final code should not use *positional-substitution* at all. Hint: Give *cps-exp* a second argument representing the continuation context. □

8.7 Call Chains

In this section we define the concept of a "call chain" in a manner appropriate for analysis of iterative control behavior. This allows us to formulate a more general definition of proper tail recursion, to clarify the connection between proper tail recursion and iterative control behavior, and to develop a less restrictive characterization of simple expressions. This in turn makes the definition of tail form less restrictive and improves the CPS algorithm.

Consider (+ (fact-iter n) m). When *fact-iter* is called, the context of the outer primitive application must be recorded, so some control space is required. This space is certainly bounded, and since *fact-iter* just calls the tail-form procedure *fact-iter-acc*, the entire expression evaluates with iterative control behavior. Thus *fact-iter* need not be expressed in CPS.

According to the characterization of simple expressions in section 8.3, however, the expression (+ (fact-iter n) m) is not simple, and hence the CPS algorithm will transform it into

```
(fact-iter n (lambda (v) (k (+ v m))))
```

If *fact-iter* is not in CPS, the appropriate result is

```
(k (+ (fact-iter n) m))
```

which can be obtained only if (+ (fact-iter n) m) is simple.

The solution is to introduce a less restrictive characterization of simple expressions. Recall that simple expressions were introduced as a way of identifying a class of expressions whose evaluation would not be responsible for recursive control behavior. Our characterization of simple expressions as those expressions that contained no available applications certainly has this property. Many other expressions, however, such as (+ (fact-iter n) m), also enjoy this property. No static analysis will be able to identify precisely those expressions that are responsible for recursive control behavior, but by using call chains, we can obtain a less restrictive characterization of simple expressions.

A *call chain* is associated with every call to a procedure. When a procedure initiates a call to another, the call chain of the current call to the first procedure is extended to include the initiating application. For example, consider the following definitions.

```
(define f (lambda (x) (g x)))
(define g (lambda (y) (f (h y))))
(define h (lambda (z) z))
```

The application (f 3) creates an infinite call chain that alternatively contains the applications (f (h y)) and (g x). Though call chains including (h y) are created, these applications are not in the call chain created by (f 3), since *h* returns to *g* before *g* calls *f*.

It is tempting to think of a call chain as a stack onto which an application is pushed when a procedure is called and from which an application is popped when a procedure "returns." The problem with this view is that procedures with iterative control behavior do not perform a return for every time they are called—they return just once when they are done. The call (`fact-iter-acc` 100 0) results in *fact-iter-acc* being called 100 times, but it is misleading to think that it then "returns" 100 times; in a properly tail-recursive implementation the answer is returned in a single operation.

In section 8.1 we said a properly tail-recursive implementation was one in which tail calls resulted in no net growth of control space. Using call chains, we can give it a more precise and general definition.

> A properly tail-recursive implementation, or simply a tail-recursive implementation, is one in which any chain of tail calls results in bounded growth of control space.

Thus a properly tail-recursive implementation might use additional control space for some tail calls, as long as it is guaranteed that *any* chain (even an infinite one) composed entirely of tail calls will not require an unbounded amount of control space. In the discussion that follows, a tail-recursive implementation is assumed.

We are ultimately concerned with call chains that are unbounded. A call chain is unbounded if it is infinite (no limit can be placed on its length) or if a bound on its length can only be obtained with knowledge of run-time data. It is these call chains that may require unbounded control storage space (if they contain nontail calls) and hence result in recursive control behavior.

There are only a finite number of applications in the text of a given program. Thus in an unbounded call chain there must be an unbounded number of occurrences of at least one application. We say an application is *repeating* if it *may* occur an unbounded number of times in a call chain. Thus, the only time that a procedure can exhibit recursive control behavior is when it contains a repeating application in nontail position.

Now we can present a more general characterization of simple expressions.

> An expression is simple if it is known that none of its available applications are repeating.

For example, it is easy to verify that (+ (`fact-iter` n) m) is simple, because although (`fact-iter` n) is not in tail position, it appears only once (hence a bounded number of times) in its call chain.

By introducing a less restrictive characterization of simple expressions, we have also made the definition of tail form considerably less restrictive. For example, (+ (fact-iter n) m) is now in tail form, provided we know that the application (fact-iter n) is not repeating. It is still the case that if an expression is in tail form, and any procedures accessible through variable bindings are also in tail form, the expression executes with iterative control behavior (in a properly tail-recursive implementation). This is the property that any characterization of simple expressions must preserve.

Though we cannot always know if an application is repeating, it is often possible to determine that applications are not repeating by using a *call graph*. A call graph contains a node for every procedure in a program. A link from one node to another in the graph indicates that the procedure at the tail of the link *may* call the procedure at the head of the link. For example, the graph for the *fact-iter* program will have a link from *fact-iter* to *fact-iter-acc* and another link from *fact-iter-acc* to itself.

If an available application in a procedure A initiates a call to a procedure B, the application can be repeating only if there is a cycle in the call graph that includes the link from A to B. The presence of a call graph cycle including this link does not mean that the application will necessarily occur an unbounded number of times in a call chain, but there is at least that possibility. If there is no call graph cycle including the link from A to B, however, then the application cannot occur an unbounded number of times in a call chain, so the application cannot be repeating.

- *Exercise 8.7.1*
Write a CPS version of the following program, using call graph analysis to avoid unnecessary CPS conversion. The resulting program should exhibit iterative-control behavior using a minimum number of continuations.

```
(letrec ((p1 (lambda (n)
               (list (p3 n))))
         (p2 (lambda (n)
               (- n 1)))
         (p3 (lambda (n)
               (if (p4 n) 1 (* n (p5 n)))))
         (p4 (lambda (n)
               (zero? n)))
         (p5 (lambda (n)
               (p3 (p2 n)))))
  (p1 5))
```

In a language with first-class procedures, such as Scheme, it is not always possible to construct call graphs by static analysis of a program. In the most common situation, however, in which procedures are bound directly to variables and these variables appear only in operator positions, it is possible to construct a call graph by program analysis.

Assume that `lambda` expressions can occur only on the right-hand side of `letrec` bindings and that `letrec`-bound variables may appear only in operator position. Write a procedure that takes a program represented as a `letrec` expression and constructs a list of pairs representing its call graph. Redefine *simple?* to make use of this list. Use *cps-exp* to test *simple?* on examples that demonstrate the advantages of this approach. ☐

8.8 Summary

Continuations make the control behavior of a program explicit by representing the portion of the computation to which the result of a subcomputation should be sent.

A subexpression of an expression is in tail position if the value of the subexpression is guaranteed to be returned immediately as the value of the expression. Procedure calls in tail position require no additional control information to be stored. Programs in which every non-trivial procedure call is in tail position are said to be in tail form, and a proper implementation will execute them like a flowchart, without requiring extra space for control information.

Any program can be transformed to an equivalent program in tail form by translating it into continuation-passing style. In continuation-passing style, every procedure takes an extra argument which is the continuation to which the result of the procedure should be sent. Procedure calls that are not in tail position are transformed into tail calls with a continuation argument that represents the context of the original call.

The exact definitions of tail form and of the CPS transformation algorithm are complicated by the need to account for the special forms and primitive operations of Scheme. The key step in the algorithm is the identification of an innermost non-simple subexpression that can be evaluated first, called an initial subexpression.

9 Continuation-Passing Interpreters

In the previous chapter we showed how to convert an arbitrary program in a Scheme-like language into tail form. In this chapter, we continue this transformation. First, in section 9.1 we show how to convert procedural continuations into data structures. The result is a program in first-order tail form that can be directly transformed into flowchart form. We shall consider the details of the transformation to flowcharts in chapter 10. Then, in section 9.2, we apply this transformation to an interpreter. The resulting interpreter achieves our goal of explaining recursive procedures without using recursion. Next, in section 9.3 we turn to the use of continuations as values in programming languages, and show how continuations as denoted values can be used to escape from procedures. In section 9.4, we show how continuations as expressed values can be used to build complex control structures such as coroutines. Last, in sections 9.5 and 9.6, we consider some of the complexities that first-class continuations add to a language.

9.1 Data Structure Representations of Continuations

We now have a method for transforming any program into tail form. However, this method introduces new procedures in the form of continuations. In this section we show how these continuations can be represented as data structures, rather than as procedures. This allows us, among other things, to take a procedure that was in first-order form before CPS transformation and return it to first-order form.

We want the ability to use alternative representations for continuations. The first step is to make continuations *abstract* by constructing an abstract data type (ADT) for them, as we did for finite functions in section 3.6. For an example, consider a version of *remove* using cond.

```
(define remove
  (lambda (s los)
    (remove-cps s los (lambda (v) v))))

(define remove-cps
  (lambda (s los k)
    (cond
      ((null? los) (k '()))
      ((eq? s (car los)) (remove-cps s (cdr los) k))
      (else (remove-cps s (cdr los)
              (lambda (v)
                (k (cons (car los) v))))))))
```

There are only four points in this program at which continuations are created or invoked. The expressions `(lambda (v) (k (cons (car los) v)))` and `(lambda (v) v)` indicate points at which continuations are created. The two points at which a continuation is invoked are the `(k (cons (car los) v))` and `(k '())`.

By defining a procedure for invoking continuations and a set of procedures for creating continuations, one for each kind of continuation, we obtain an ADT for continuations. By using such an ADT, a CPS procedure can be factored into two parts: the implementation of the ADT, which is of course dependent on the representation of continuations, and the remainder of the procedure, which is independent of this representation.

When a lambda expression representing a continuation is evaluated, a closure is formed that captures the current bindings of variables that occur free in the lambda expression. These bindings contain information that must be passed to procedures that create continuations. (For the purposes of this analysis, variables such as `cons` and `car` that refer to top-level bindings are not considered free, since their bindings always contain the same information and this information is available anywhere in the program.) These considerations lead us to the following code for the representation-independent portion of *remove*, where *apply-continuation*, *make-final-valcont*, and *make-rem1* are the procedures of the continuation ADT.

```
(define remove
  (lambda (s los)
    (remove-cps s los (make-final-valcont))))
```

```
(define remove-cps
  (lambda (s los k)
    (cond
      ((null? los) (apply-continuation k '()))
      ((eq? s (car los)) (remove-cps s (cdr los) k))
      (else (remove-cps s (cdr los) (make-rem1 los k))))))
```

To implement the continuation ADT, we must choose a representation for continuations. Initially, we represent them as procedures, using lambda expressions that are identical to those used in our initial version of *remove-cps*. For each expression (lambda (v) M) that builds a continuation, the corresponding constructor is (lambda $(x_1 \ldots x_n)$ (lambda (v) M')), where $x_1, \ldots, x_n$ are the free variables of M, and M' is M with suitable instances of apply-continuation inserted.

```
(define make-final-valcont
  (lambda ()
    (lambda (v) v)))

(define make-rem1
  (lambda (los k)
    (lambda (v)
      (apply-continuation k (cons (car los) v)))))

(define apply-continuation
  (lambda (k v)
    (k v)))
```

It is now straightforward to replace the procedural representation of continuations by data structure representations, as we did for finite functions in section 3.6.2. We define a different type of record for each type of continuation and a procedure apply-continuation that determines what type of continuation it has been passed and simulates an application of the appropriate procedure.

```
(define-record final-valcont ())
(define-record rem1 (los k))

(define apply-continuation
  (lambda (k v)
    (variant-case k
      (final-valcont () v)
      (rem1 (los k) (apply-continuation k (cons (car los) v))))))
```

These three definitions complete a new implementation of the continuation ADT. The code for `remove` and `remove-cps` remains unchanged.

Next consider a more complex example.

```
(define subst
  (lambda (new old slst)
    (subst-cps new old slst (lambda (v) v))))

(define subst-cps
  (lambda (new old slst k)
    (if (null? slst)
        (k '())
        (if (not (pair? (car slst)))
            (if (eq? (car slst) old)
                (subst-cps new old (cdr slst)
                  (lambda (v) (k (cons new v))))
                (subst-cps new old (cdr slst)
                  (lambda (v) (k (cons (car slst) v)))))
            (subst-cps new old (car slst)
              (lambda (v)
                (subst-cps new old (cdr slst)
                  (lambda (v1) (k (cons v v1)))))))))))
```

Here we have five different continuations, corresponding to the four procedure calls to *subst-cps* and the final value continuation. We note, however, that the continuations

```
(lambda (v) (k (cons new v)))
```

and

```
(lambda (v1) (k (cons v v1)))
```

are the same except for variable names. Thus we need only make four different types of continuations. As before, the procedures of the ADT for continuations take as arguments those free variables of the corresponding `lambda` expressions that contain variable information. This gives us the following ADT for *subst-cps* continuations.

```
(define make-final-valcont
  (lambda ()
    (lambda (v) v)))

(define make-subst1
  (lambda (new k)
    (lambda (v)
      (apply-continuation k (cons new v)))))

(define make-subst2
  (lambda (slst k)
    (lambda (v)
      (apply-continuation k (cons (car slst) v)))))

(define make-subst3
  (lambda (new old slst k)
    (lambda (v)
      (subst-cps new old (cdr slst)
        (make-subst1 v k)))))

(define apply-continuation
  (lambda (k v)
    (k v)))
```

Using this ADT, the definition of *subst* becomes

```
(define subst
  (lambda (new old s)
    (subst-cps new old s (make-final-valcont))))

(define subst-cps
  (lambda (new old slst k)
    (if (null? slst)
        (apply-continuation k '())
        (if (not (pair? (car slst)))
            (if (eq? (car slst) old)
                (subst-cps new old (cdr slst)
                  (make-subst1 new k))
                (subst-cps new old (cdr slst)
                  (make-subst2 slst k)))
            (subst-cps new old (car slst)
              (make-subst3 new old slst k))))))
```

To represent continuations as data structures rather than as procedures, the following record types are used.

```
(define-record final-valcont ())
(define-record subst1 (new k))
(define-record subst2 (slst k))
(define-record subst3 (new old slst k))
```

The fields of these records correspond exactly to the formal parameters of the *make-* procedures in the continuation ADT. The knowledge of what actions to perform for each type of continuation must now be contained in apply-continuation, which dispatches on the record type. How do we find the action performed for each record type? That action is exactly the action performed by the body of the lambda expression associated with the corresponding continuation (when continuations were represented as procedures).

```
(define apply-continuation
  (lambda (k v)
    (variant-case k
      (final-valcont () v)
      (subst1 (new k)
        (apply-continuation k (cons new v)))
      (subst2 (slst k)
        (apply-continuation k (cons (car slst) v)))
      (subst3 (new old slst)
        (subst-cps new old (cdr slst)
          (make-subst1 v k)))
      (else (error "Invalid continuation:" k)))))
```

In this case, the expression on the right-hand side of each variant-case clause is exactly the same as the body of the corresponding lambda expression. This is possible whenever the formal parameters of each procedural continuation are the same (in this case v). When this is not the case, α-conversion can be used to make the formal parameters of all the continuation procedures the same as the second argument of *apply-continuation*.

These examples complete the second step in our transformation: from continuation-passing style to first-order tail form. Therefore we can now take an arbitrary recursive procedure and convert it into such a form. We show in chapter 10 how we can transcribe the resulting program into virtually any programming language.

So far, we have used a very simple representation of continuations as record structures. In chapter 10 we also explore several other representations for continuations, and in chapter 12 we demonstrate how a suitable choice of representation leads to the development of a simple compiler.

- *Exercise 9.1.1*
  First write recursive definitions for the procedures listed below. Then transform these definitions to continuation-passing style. Next, transform them into a form using a continuation ADT in which continuations are represented as procedures. Finally, modify the ADT implementation so that continuations are represented as records.

  a. `reverse`

  b. `append`

  c. `fact`
  ☐

- *Exercise 9.1.2*
  Transform the CPS procedures developed in the solution of exercise 8.5.3 into a form that uses a record-based representation of continuations. ☐

9.2 The Continuation Interpreter

We have now learned how to take a recursive program and transform it into first-order tail form. This allows us to implement a recursive program in a language that does not support recursion. In this section we perform this transformation on an interpreter. The resulting interpreter defines the semantics of recursion in the defined language in a way that is independent of recursion in the defining language.

The interpreter that we shall transform is given in figure 9.2.1. This is the same as the interpreter of figure 5.4.1, except that the abstract syntax of expressions does not include `let` expressions, which can be handled by the parser, and we have expanded the definition of *eval-rands* so that it does not use *map*, thus avoiding the use of *map-cps*.

As with our previous examples, we first translate the interpreter into CPS form using procedural continuations. Since *eval-exp*, *eval-rands*, and *apply-proc* are mutually recursive procedures, they must be transformed into CPS simultaneously. The result is shown in figure 9.2.2. The transformation

Figure 9.2.1   Interpreter for transformation to CPS

```
(define eval-exp
  (lambda (exp env)
    (variant-case exp
      (lit (datum) datum)
      (varref (var) (apply-env env var))
      (app (rator rands)
        (let ((proc (eval-exp rator env))
              (args (eval-rands rands env)))
          (apply-proc proc args)))
      (if (test-exp then-exp else-exp)
        (if (true-value? (eval-exp test-exp env))
            (eval-exp then-exp env)
            (eval-exp else-exp env)))
      (proc (formals body) (make-closure formals body env))
      (else (error "Invalid abstract syntax:" exp)))))

(define eval-rands
  (lambda (rands env)
    (if (null? rands)
        '()
        (cons (eval-exp (car rands) env)
              (eval-rands (cdr rands) env)))))

(define apply-proc
  (lambda (proc args)
    (variant-case proc
      (prim-proc (prim-op) (apply-prim-op prim-op args))
      (closure (formals body env)
        (eval-exp body (extend-env formals args env)))
      (else (error "Invalid procedure:" proc)))))
```

treats *apply-env* and *apply-prim-op* as primitive operations, because they are guaranteed to return a value in a few steps; a more detailed transformation might regard these as nonprimitive as well. Of course when invoking the new *eval-exp*, it is necessary to pass a suitable continuation to receive the final value.

This code could have been obtained using the CPS transformation exactly as presented in chapter 8, except that we have chosen meaningful names for the continuation arguments and have not passed a continuation to the procedure *error*, since, for simplicity, we have chosen not to continue the computation after an error is reported. Passing the continuation to *error* procedure would allow the building of sophisticated exception handlers; see section 9.5 for some ideas on how this might be done.

Our CPS interpreter evaluates the operator of an application first, then evaluates the operands in left-to-right order. This contrasts with the interpreter of figure 9.2.1, in which the order of operator and operand evaluation in the defined language is determined by the order of evaluation in the defining language.

Because CPS makes control behavior explicit, a CPS interpreter will always specify the order of subexpression evaluation. The order in which the operator and operands of an application are evaluated is left unspecified in many languages (including Scheme), leaving implementors to chose an order that is most convenient or efficient. In such languages, programs that rely on a fixed order of evaluation are incorrect. If an interpreter is used to specify the semantics of such a language, the use of CPS in the interpreter will *overspecify* the order of operator and operand evaluation. If CPS is not used, however, the control semantics will usually be *underspecified*. For example, if the interpreter of figure 9.2.1 were evaluated by a defining language in which all procedures, including *cons*, were call-by-name, the defined language would also have call-by-name semantics, which might not have been intended.

- *Exercise 9.2.1*
If a Scheme implementation in which the subexpressions of an application are evaluated from right to left were used to execute the interpreter of figure 9.2.1, in what order will subexpressions of an application be evaluated in the defined language? □

- *Exercise 9.2.2*
Modify the CPS interpreter of figure 9.2.2 to evaluate the subexpressions of an application in right-to-left order. The order in which subexpressions are evaluated can be detected by using operations with side effects, as in `+(write(1), write(2))`. □

o *Exercise 9.2.3*
Modify the CPS interpreter of figure 9.2.2 to evaluate the operator of an application first, and then evaluate its operands in right-to-left order. □

o *Exercise 9.2.4*
Add `begin` to the interpreter of figure 9.2.2; see exercise 5.5.4. □

Figure 9.2.2   CPS interpreter

```
(define eval-exp
  (lambda (exp env k)
    (variant-case exp
      (lit (datum) (k datum))
      (varref (var) (k (apply-env env var)))
      (app (rator rands)
        (eval-exp rator env
          (lambda (proc)
            (eval-rands rands env
              (lambda (all)
                (apply-proc proc all k))))))
      (if (test-exp then-exp else-exp)
        (eval-exp test-exp env
          (lambda (test)
            (if (true-value? test)
                (eval-exp then-exp env k)
                (eval-exp else-exp env k)))))
      (proc (formals body) (k (make-closure formals body env)))
      (else (error "Invalid abstract syntax:" exp)))))

(define eval-rands
  (lambda (rands env k)
    (if (null? rands)
        (k '())
        (eval-exp (car rands) env
          (lambda (first)
            (eval-rands (cdr rands) env
              (lambda (rest)
                (k (cons first rest)))))))))

(define apply-proc
  (lambda (proc args k)
    (variant-case proc
      (prim-proc (prim-op) (k (apply-prim-op prim-op args)))
      (closure (formals body env)
        (eval-exp body (extend-env formals args env) k))
      (else (error "Invalid procedure:" proc)))))
```

Figure 9.2.3   A representation-independent CPS interpreter

```
(define eval-exp
  (lambda (exp env k)
    (variant-case exp
      (lit (datum)
        (apply-continuation k datum))
      (varref (var)
        (apply-continuation k (apply-env env var)))
      (app (rator rands)
        (eval-exp rator env
          (make-proc-valcont rands env k)))
      (if (test-exp then-exp else-exp)
        (eval-exp test-exp env
          (make-test-valcont then-exp else-exp env k)))
      (proc (formals body)
        (apply-continuation k
          (make-closure formals body env)))
      (else (error "Invalid abstract syntax:" exp)))))

(define eval-rands
  (lambda (rands env k)
    (if (null? rands)
        (apply-continuation k '())
        (eval-exp (car rands) env
          (make-first-valcont rands env k)))))

(define apply-proc
  (lambda (proc args k)
    (variant-case proc
      (prim-proc (prim-op)
        (apply-continuation k
          (apply-prim-op prim-op args)))
      (closure (formals body env)
        (eval-exp body (extend-env formals args env) k))
      (else (error "Invalid procedure:" proc)))))
```

The next step is to transform our interpreter into a form that is independent of the representation chosen for continuations. As before, we replace each invocation of a continuation with an invocation of the procedure `apply-continuation`, and we replace each lambda expression that constructs a continuation by a call to a procedure. These procedures are passed the information contained in the free variables of the corresponding lambda expressions. The result is shown in figure 9.2.3.

To complete the representation-independent CPS interpreter, we implement the continuation ADT. We name the constructors after the values their continuations are intended to receive. For example, `make-final-valcont` builds the continuation that will receive the final value of the computation, and `make-test-valcont` builds a continuation that will receive the value of the test in a conditional expression. Initially, we represent continuations as procedures, as in figure 9.2.4. The procedure `make-final-valcont` is invoked when `eval-exp` is first called. In the continuations created by `make-proc-valcont` and `make-first-valcont` other types of continuations are formed. This requires that we introduce two additional procedures, `make-all-argcont` and `make-rest-argcont`.

Finally, we convert the continuation ADT implementation to use a record-based data structure representation. See figure 9.2.5. As before, the right-hand sides of the `variant-case` clauses in `apply-continuation` are obtained directly from the bodies of the corresponding lambda expressions in figure 9.2.4, however, this time instead of using α-conversion and arbitrarily renaming the variable, we use a `let` expression to bind `val`.

Figure 9.2.3 and figure 9.2.5 define an interpreter in first-order tail form. This was our goal: an interpreter for recursive procedures that does not rely on recursion to explain its behavior. All the control information in the interpreter has been made explicit in the continuation records. All procedure calls in the interpreter are in tail position, so no other control information need be stored; this intuition will be made precise by a translation to imperative form in the following chapter. Furthermore, since the interpreter does not use the power of recursion or first-class procedures in the defining language, it can be translated into a variety of other languages. All that remains is to implement the parser and the data structures in the desired implementation language.

● *Exercise 9.2.5*

Add variable assignment, `let`, `letrecproc`, `begin`, and dynamic assignment to the interpreter of figure 9.2.1 and repeat the series of transformations to first-order tail form for this extended interpreter. ☐

Figure 9.2.4   Operations in procedural representation of continuations

```
(define make-final-valcont
  (lambda ()
    (lambda (final) final)))

(define make-proc-valcont
  (lambda (rands env k)
    (lambda (proc)
      (eval-rands rands env (make-all-argcont proc k)))))

(define make-all-argcont
  (lambda (proc k)
    (lambda (all)
      (apply-proc proc all k))))

(define make-test-valcont
  (lambda (then-exp else-exp env k)
    (lambda (test)
      (if (true-value? test)
          (eval-exp then-exp env k)
          (eval-exp else-exp env k)))))

(define make-first-valcont
  (lambda (rands k)
    (lambda (first)
      (eval-rands (cdr rands) env
        (make-rest-argcont first k)))))

(define make-rest-argcont
  (lambda (first k)
    (lambda (rest)
      (apply-continuation k (cons first rest)))))

(define apply-continuation
  (lambda (k val)
    (k val)))
```

Figure 9.2.5   Data structure representation of continuations

```
(define-record final-valcont ())
(define-record proc-valcont (rands env k))
(define-record all-argcont (proc k))
(define-record test-valcont (then-exp else-exp env k))
(define-record first-valcont (rands env k))
(define-record rest-argcont (first k))

(define apply-continuation
  (lambda (k val)
    (variant-case k
      (final-valcont ()
        (let ((final val))
          final))
      (proc-valcont (rands env k)
        (let ((proc val))
          (eval-rands rands env
            (make-all-argcont proc k))))
      (all-argcont (proc k)
        (let ((all val))
          (apply-proc proc all k)))
      (test-valcont (then-exp else-exp env k)
        (let ((test val))
          (if (true-value? test)
              (eval-exp then-exp env k)
              (eval-exp else-exp env k))))
      (first-valcont (rands env k)
        (let ((first val))
          (eval-rands (cdr rands) env
            (make-rest-argcont first k))))
      (rest-argcont (first k)
        (let ((rest val))
          (apply-continuation k (cons first rest)))))))
```

We have implemented a recursive language using an interpreter that exhibits iterative control behavior. We have done this by applying the CPS transformation to the interpreter itself. Another strategy is to apply the CPS transformation to the source program and then use the original interpreter. Do this for the interpreter of figure 9.2.1. The process involves two steps. First, write a CPS transformation program that takes as input programs in the language of the interpreter in figure 9.2.1 and produces abstract syntax trees of programs in the same language but in continuation-passing style. Next, confirm that the interpreter of figure 9.2.1 actually has iterative control behavior when it is given a tail-form program to interpret. □

9.3 Making Continuations Available to the Programmer

We have seen that "standard" control operations, such as procedure call and the sequencing of argument evaluation, can be made explicit in an interpreter through the use of continuations. In this section we shall first see how continuations can express nonstandard control operations in an interpreter. Then we shall see how continuations can be made available to the programmer as objects of computation, thereby allowing the programmer to obtain a variety of nonstandard control behaviors.

Every continuation of our CPS interpreter, except for the one that receives a final value, concludes its business by invoking the immediately prior continuation—the one that was current at its creation. This is characteristic of standard control operations but need not always be the case. Consider, for example, adding an "abort" procedure to our defined language. When invoked, the procedure `abort` should terminate the computation immediately, returning the value of its argument as the value of the entire computation. Thus the value of

```
+(1, *(abort(2), +(3, 5)))
```

should be 2.

The procedure `abort` can be implemented as a new kind of procedure object, represented by the record type `abort`, that is interpreted by extending `apply-proc`.

```
(define final-valcont (make-final-valcont))

(define apply-proc
  (lambda (proc args k)
    (variant-case proc
      (prim-proc (prim-op)
        (apply-continuation k (apply-prim-op prim-op args)))
      (closure (formals body env)
        (eval-exp body (extend-env formals args env) k))
      (abort () (apply-continuation final-valcont (car args)))
      (else (error "Invalid procedure:" proc)))))
```

When applied to the list *args* of arguments, *abort* returns the first argument to the final value continuation. The continuation *k*, to which the result would normally be passed, is ignored. In this way the first argument is effectively returned as the value of the entire computation.

- *Exercise 9.3.1*
  Modify the CPS interpreter of figure 9.2.2 so that *apply-prim-op* is passed the current continuation, *k*. Then implement *abort* as a primitive operation, rather than as a new type of procedure. □

- *Exercise 9.3.2*
  Modify the CPS interpreter of figure 9.2.2 so that *apply-env* is written in CPS. Then modify *apply-env* so that when reference is made to an unbound variable, the procedure *error* is not invoked. Instead, a message is printed (using *display* and *newline*) and then the final value continuation is invoked with the symbol *error*. □

- *Exercise 9.3.3*
  The capability to abort a computation can be added to a language with the concrete and abstract syntax

  ---

  ⟨exp⟩ ::= abort ⟨exp⟩   abort (exp)

  ---

  instead of as a procedure. Modify the CPS interpreter of figure 9.2.2 so that it handles this form by evaluating the argument to abort in the context of the final value continuation. □

So far we have seen that values can be returned by passing them to the current continuation or to a continuation that receives a final value. We can allow control to be passed to an arbitrary continuation by creating a new kind of procedure. We represent one of these procedures with a record of type continuation that contains a continuation, *cont*. When this procedure is invoked with one argument, the argument is simply passed to *cont*, ignoring the continuation that is current at the time.

```
(define-record continuation (cont))

(define apply-proc
  (lambda (proc args k)
    (variant-case proc
      (prim-proc (prim-op)
        (apply-continuation k (apply-prim-op prim-op args)))
      (closure (formals body env)
        (eval-exp body (extend-env formals args env) k))
      (abort ()
        (apply-continuation final-valcont (car args)))
      (continuation (cont)
        (apply-continuation cont (car args)))
      (else (error "Invalid procedure:" proc)))))
```

How might continuation procedures be created, and how might they be used? Suppose we have added some list-processing primitives to our defined language. We wish to write the procedure *listindex*, which takes a symbol and a list, and returns the zero-based index of the symbol in the list, or -1, denoted by the variable minus1 in the initial environment, if the symbol does not occur in the list. We might try to implement *listindex* as follows:

```
define listindex =
  proc (a, alst)
    letrecproc
      loop(alst) =
        if null(alst)
        then minus1
        else if equal(a, car(alst))
              then 0
              else add1(loop(cdr(alst)))
      in loop(alst)
```

Unfortunately, this does not work. Let us assume that k is the length of the list. If a is not in $alst$, then the value returned is $k - 1$, not -1, because the -1 is sent to a continuation that invokes $add1$ k times. What we want is to return -1 immediately to the caller of $listindex$. If it were possible to obtain the continuation of the call to $listindex$ as a procedural object and bind it to some variable, say f, then -1 could be returned by evaluating f(minus1). We can express this by introducing a new expression type, letcont.

```
define listindex =
  proc (a, alst)
    letcont f
    in letrecproc
        loop(alst) =
          if null(alst)
          then f(minus1)
          else if equal(a, car(alst))
              then 0
              else add1(loop(cdr(alst)))
      in loop(alst)
```

When f is invoked with -1, the current continuation is ignored and -1 is returned to the continuation that was current at the time the letcont expression was entered, which is the continuation of the call to $listindex$. The procedure f is like abort in that it never returns to its caller but rather transfers control to another point in the program.

We use the following concrete and abstract syntax of letcont:

⟨exp⟩ ::= letcont ⟨var⟩ in ⟨exp⟩   letcont (var body)

Given this abstract syntax we define the record type that contains the symbol and the expression, and then modify eval-exp.

```
(define-record letcont (var body))

(define eval-exp
  (lambda (exp env k)
    (variant-case exp
      (letcont (var body)
        (eval-exp body
          (extend-env (list var) (list (make-continuation k)) env)
          k))
      ...)))
```

Thus body will be evaluated in an environment in which the given variable is bound to a continuation procedure. This makes continuations denoted values.

- *Exercise 9.3.4*
  Another approach to implementing listindex is to write it in continuation-passing style. Compare this to the solution using letcont. □

This is not the only way to make continuations available to the programmer. In Scheme, continuation procedures are obtained via the procedure *call-with-current-continuation*, which we abbreviate as *call/cc*. The single argument to *call/cc* must be a procedure of one argument. This procedure is called with the current continuation (the continuation of the call to *call/cc*), represented as a one-argument continuation procedure, *k*. Informally, *k* represents the remainder of the computation from the *call/cc* application point. At any time, *k* can be invoked with any value, with the effect that this value is taken as the value of the *call/cc* application.

If our defined language had a similar procedure *callcc*, we could replace expressions of the form letcont *var* in *body* by callcc(proc (*var*) *body*). (We use the variable callcc rather than call/cc because of the lexical structure of our language; see chapter 11.) Our *listindex* example would then be

```
define listindex =
  proc (a, alst)
    callcc(proc (f)
             letrecproc
               loop(alst) =
                 if null(alst)
                 then f(minus1)
                 else if equal(a, car(alst))
                      then 0
                      else add1(loop(cdr(alst)))
             in loop(alst))
```

This approach has two advantages. First, it separates the creation and use of continuation procedures from variable binding. Second, it does not require adding new syntax, such as letcont, to the language. All that is required is to add callcc to the initial environment and bind to it a new type of procedure that must be recognized by *apply-proc*.

```
(define-record callcc-proc ())

(define apply-proc
  (lambda (proc args k)
    (variant-case proc
      (prim-proc (prim-op)
        (apply-continuation k (apply-prim-op prim-op args)))
      (closure (formals body env)
        (eval-exp body (extend-env formals args env) k))
      (continuation (cont)
        (apply-continuation cont (car args)))
      (callcc-proc ()
        (apply-proc
          (car args)
          (list (make-continuation k))
          k))
      (else (error "Invalid Procedure:" proc)))))
```

The new line in *apply-proc* does just what the description of *call/cc* said: the first (and only) argument to *callcc* is applied as a procedure to the current continuation. More precisely, it is applied to a continuation procedure containing the current continuation. Furthermore (and this was not specified in the description!), this is done using the current continuation as the continuation of the call that passes the current continuation. Thus

$$\text{callcc}(\text{proc (k) } body)$$

is equivalent to

$$\text{callcc}(\text{proc (k) } k(body))$$

Though *callcc* is a procedure, it is unlike all other procedures. Many primitive operations can be added to or deleted from a language with little effect on the language's expressive power or on the techniques that can be used to implement it. But *callcc* provides an expressive power that is difficult or impossible to achieve without an equivalent facility, and its presence has a profound impact on the way in which control information must be maintained by an implementation.

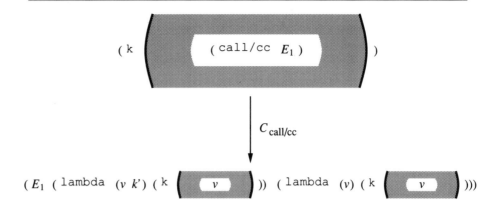

Figure 9.3.1   The CPS rule for `call/cc` expression in a context: $C_{\text{call/cc}}$

• *Exercise 9.3.5*
Using `letcont`, define `callcc` as a procedure in the defined language. □

○ *Exercise 9.3.6*
Add `callcc` to the defined language with syntax

⟨exp⟩ ::= `callcc` ⟨exp⟩   `callcc (exp)`

---

instead of as a procedure. □

○ *Exercise 9.3.7*
The interpreter we have sketched in this section actually treats continuations as expressed values. Modify it to enforce the restriction that continuations be denoted but not expressed. □

○ *Exercise 9.3.8*
Add `call/cc` to a CPS interpreter in which procedures and continuations are represented as procedures, as in exercise 5.4.3. □

○ *Exercise 9.3.9*
If expressions in the defining language are transformed to CPS before being interpreted or compiled and `call/cc` is treated as a special form, rather than as a procedure, it can be implemented with the addition (see figure 9.3.1) of the following CPS transformation rule.

9.3 Making Continuations Available to the Programmer   *311*

$C_{\text{call/cc}}$: If (k E) has an initial expression I of the form (call/cc E_1), then replace (k E) by

$$(E_1 \ (\texttt{lambda} \ (v \ k') \ (\texttt{k} \ E\{v/I\})) \ (\texttt{lambda} \ (v) \ (\texttt{k} \ E\{v/I\})))$$

where v and k' do not occur free in E_1.

This rule makes call/cc disappear. The two procedures constructed by this rule have identical bodies. The first procedure is the continuation procedure passed to E_1 (which never refers to k'), and the second procedure is the continuation required by the CPS transformation. Add this case to the interpreter of exercise 9.2.6. □

9.4 Upward Continuations and Coroutines

In the last section we introduced continuations as denoted values and saw that they could be used to exit prematurely from a computation. Since they are denoted, continuations can be passed "down" as arguments to procedures or otherwise bound to lexical variables. Such continuations are sometimes called *escape procedures,* since they are used to escape from computations.

If continuations are allowed as expressed values, they become first-class values, and can also be returned "upward" from procedures, assigned to variables, and stored in data structures. These operations allow continuations to be invoked after control has left the dynamic context in which the continuation was created. Some languages provide escape procedures, or equivalent control mechanisms, but do not provide first-class continuations.

In this section we illustrate the use of upward continuations. In the remaining two sections, we consider the problem of maintaining the proper notion of dynamic context in the presence of continuations.

Perhaps the simplest use of upward continuations is to provide a breakpoint facility. When a breakpoint is reached, control is transferred to a designated point in a program or programming system, usually for programmer interaction, with the possibility of continuing the computation as if the breakpoint had not occurred. To allow a breakpoint to return control to the read-eval-print loop of the computation, we first obtain the top-level read-eval-print loop continuation and save it in a global variable.

```
--> define toplevel = ignored;
--> letcont cont
    in toplevel := cont;
```

We next define a procedure `break` that captures the continuation of its call, stores it in the variable `resume`, and then invokes the top-level continuation. Initially `resume` is bound to a procedure that raises an error, since no computation can be resumed unless a break has occurred. This break procedure passes on its argument, which can be used to identify the breakpoint, to the top-level continuation.

```
--> define resume = proc (x) error();
--> define break =
      proc (x)
        letcont cont
        in begin
             resume := cont;
             write(breakmsg);
             toplevel(x)
           end;
```

(Here we assume that we have a primitive *write*, and that *breakmsg* is some suitable string) To return from a breakpoint, the *resume* continuation is invoked. Whatever value is passed to the resume continuation is the value with which the most recent application of a break procedure will continue.

```
--> +(break(1), break(2));
break:
1
--> resume(5);
break:
2
--> resume(3);
8
```

o *Exercise 9.4.1*

Consider the following transcript:

```
--> +(10000, break(2));
break:
2
--> *(100, break(4));
break:
4
--> resume(10);
1000
```

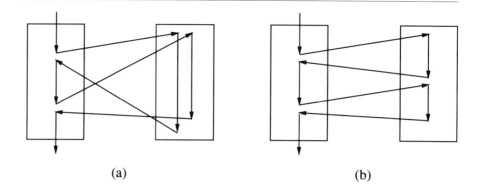

(a)   (b)

Figure 9.4.1   Procedures and coroutines

```
--> resume(20);
2000
```

What happened to the waiting addition? Redefine **break** using a stack of **resume** continuations so that we don't lose the addition operation. □

First-class continuations can also be used to implement a *coroutine* mechanism. Coroutines contain code, like procedures, but their control behavior is different. The control relationship between a procedure and its caller is asymmetric: a procedure can call another from any expression in its body, with the result that control transfers to the beginning of the called procedure's body. Control always leaves a procedure when it reaches the end of the body (assuming that no first-class continuation is invoked) and returns to the point at which the procedure was called. See figure 9.4.1 (a).

The control relationship between coroutines is symmetric. When control first enters a coroutine, it starts at the beginning of its body. Control can leave a coroutine at any point and when it returns, the computation continues from the point where it last left the coroutine. This behavior is illustrated in figure 9.4.1 (b). Coroutines are said to *resume*, rather than call, each other. Although in some systems it is meaningful for coroutines to return, a coroutine does not normally "fall off the end" of its body.

Whereas the interpreter must maintain control information for procedure calls, no record need be kept of coroutine resumptions. The essence of any coroutine mechanism is that each coroutine maintains its own *local control state:* the point from which it will continue its computation when it is next resumed. Thus a coroutine is like an object: it encapsulates some local state, except that its local state is a control state rather than a data stack. Indeed, we shall implement coroutines as procedures with local state, like the simple objects in section 4.6, except that the local state will contain a continuation.

We invoke our coroutines using a global procedure *resume*, which takes a procedure representing a coroutine and a value to be passed to the coroutine. The procedure *makecoroutine* takes a procedure of one argument and returns a coroutine that invokes the procedure with an argument, which is the first value passed to the new coroutine. When *resume* is called inside a coroutine, the coroutine suspends its activities. When the coroutine is resumed, the value passed to it appears as the value of the call to *resume* that suspended the coroutine. It is an error if a coroutine procedure ever returns, but it can exit by invoking another continuation.

Let us consider the simple example shown in figure 9.4.2. Here we create two coroutines, *co1* and *co2*, and start *co1* with the value 33 as initval1. The first coroutine prints 1 33 and then resumes *co2* with the value 34, which becomes *initval2*. The second coroutine prints 2 34 and then restarts *co1* with 35, which appears as the value of the *resume* in *co1*. Then *initval1* is assigned 35, and *co1* prints 1 35. It then resumes *co2* with 36, so *co2* prints 2 36 and resumes *co1* with 37. Finally, *co1* exits by escaping to *returncont* with 37. So the entire program prints 1 33 2 34 1 35 2 36 37. Note that the two coroutines refer to each other through a shared binding, as in the implementation of recursion through side effects in section 5.6. We cannot use letrecproc because the right-hand side of a letrecproc declaration must be a procedure expression and not an application.

A classic illustration of coroutine behavior is provided by the *samefringe* problem. The "fringe" of a tree can be represented by a list containing the tree's leaf node values in the order in which they are encountered by a depth-first traversal of the tree. (The *flatten* procedure of exercise 2.2.7 returns the fringe of a tree that is represented as a nested list structure.) Two trees may have very different shapes but still have the same fringe. The easy way to determine if two trees have the same fringe is to construct the fringe of each one as a list and then test the lists for equality. This solution requires that storage be allocated to construct the fringe lists. The samefringe problem is to determine if two tree have the same fringe *without* constructing fringe lists.

The solution is to create two coroutines, one for traversing each tree. Each time one of these traversal coroutines is resumed, it finds the next leaf, if there is one. It then resumes a third coroutine that drives the computation, passing it the leaf value, or zero (representing false) if there are no more leaves. See figure 9.4.3 for the definition of the *makesfcoroutine* procedure, which

Figure 9.4.2   Two interacting coroutines

```
define example =
  proc ()
    letcont returncont
    in let co1 = ignored;
           co2 = ignored
       in begin
            co1 := makecoroutine(proc (initval1)
                                     begin
                                       write(1);
                                       write(initval1);
                                       initval1 := resume(co2, add1(initval1));
                                       write(1);
                                       write(initval1);
                                       initval1 := resume(co2, add1(initval1));
                                       returncont(initval1)
                                     end);
            co2 := makecoroutine(proc (initval2)
                                     begin
                                       write(2);
                                       write(initval2);
                                       initval2 := resume(co1, add1(initval2));
                                       write(2);
                                       write(initval2);
                                       resume(co1, add1(initval2))
                                     end);
            co1(33)
          end
```

returns a traversal coroutine for a given tree and driver.

The procedure *samefringe* of figure 9.4.3 introduces let bindings for the
three coroutines and then installs the coroutines using assignment. After the
coroutines have been installed so they can refer to each other, the driver
is invoked with an initial value that is ignored. The driver resumes each
of the traversal coroutines and checks that they have passed back the same
value. This is repeated until both traversal coroutines indicate simultaneously
that they have no more leaves, at which point the driver exits by sending
a 1 to the escape continuation *returncont*, indicating that the fringes are
the same. If one of the traversal coroutines runs out of leaves before the

Figure 9.4.3   Samefringe coroutine program

```
define makesfcoroutine =
  proc (driver, tree)
    makecoroutine(proc (initvalue)
                    letrecproc
                      traverse(tree) =
                        if pair(tree)
                        then begin
                               traverse(car(tree));
                               if pair(cdr(tree))
                               then traverse(cdr(tree))
                               else noop
                             end
                        else resume(driver, tree)
                    in begin
                         traverse(tree);
                         resume(driver, 0)
                       end);

define samefringe =
  proc (tree1, tree2)
    letcont returncont
    in let co1 = ignored;
           co2 = ignored;
           driver = ignored
        in begin
             driver :=
               makecoroutine(proc (initvalue)
                               letrecproc
                                 loop() =
                                   let leaf1 = resume(co1, ignored);
                                       leaf2 = resume(co2, ignored)
                                   in if equal(leaf1, leaf2)
                                      then if zero(leaf1)
                                           then returncont(1)
                                           else loop()
                                      else returncont(0)
                               in loop());
             co1 := makesfcoroutine(driver, tree1);
             co2 := makesfcoroutine(driver, tree2);
             driver(ignored)
           end
```

other, or they do not find the same leaves, the driver exits by sending a 0 to *returncont*, indicating that the fringes differ. No extra storage is used, and the program returns as soon as it finds that fringes are different. Unlike our first example, where data was passed back and forth between the coroutines, the only place where data flows from one coroutine to another is from *co1* and *co2* to *driver*, so this example does not use the full power of bidirectional data transmission in *resume*.

Now we can show the implementation of coroutines; see figure 9.4.4. The key to this bit of code is the procedure *localresume*. Assume that *localresume* is called from within the coroutine with a continuation argument *cont* and a value *value*. The procedure *localresume* gets a continuation *localcont* and stores it in *lcs*. This saves the control state of the coroutine at the time *localresume* was called. It then jumps to the continuation argument *cont* (passing it *value*) and continues from there.

What happens when the continuation stored in `lcs` is invoked? This is the continuation waiting for the result of the `letcont` expression, so when it is invoked, the value that it is passed is bound to the variable `value` in the `let`, the expression `resume := localresume` is evaluated, and the value is returned. So when this continuation is invoked it is (except for the assignment statement) as if the call to *localresume* had just returned with this new value. This is just the behavior we expect from a *resume* procedure.

Now we have two more mysteries to solve. How do we call *localresume* from the body of the coroutine even though it is not lexically visible there? And how do we get the coroutine initialized?

To answer the first question, assume that a coroutine will always be resumed by invoking its `lcs` continuation. The first thing the `lcs` continuation does is to copy the *localresume* of its coroutine into the global variable *resume*. So when *body* calls *resume*, it will always get the right version, which refers to this coroutine.

How is the coroutine initialized? When the procedure *makecoroutine* is called, a binding for the local control state `lcs` of the new coroutine is created, along with the procedures that will represent the new coroutine and the new coroutine's local resume procedure. The `letcont exit` expression is then evaluated. What does the call `localresume(exit, newcoroutine)` do? It doesn't return immediately. It stores its continuation (extended by the `resume := localresume` statement) in `lcs` and applies *exit* to *newcoroutine*. If this continuation is ever applied to a value, the assignment statement will be executed, and the value will be passed to *body*. Therefore the first time this continuation is invoked, the coroutine body will be started, with *resume* set to the right value. This is enough to get the coroutine started.

Figure 9.4.4   Coroutines via first-class continuations

```
define makecoroutine =
  proc (body)
    let lcs = ignored
    in letrecproc
         newcoroutine(value) = lcs(value);
         localresume(cont, value) =
           let value = letcont localcont
                       in begin
                            lcs := localcont;
                            cont(value)
                          end
           in begin
                resume := localresume;
                value
              end
       in letcont exit
          in begin
               body(localresume(exit, newcoroutine));
               error()
             end
```

But `localresume(exit, newcoroutine)` invokes *exit* on *newcoroutine*. Since *exit* is an escape continuation, this means that the value of the call to *makecoroutine* is the procedure *newcoroutine*. So executing

$$co1 := makecoroutine(body)$$

assigns *newcoroutine* to *co1*. What does *newcoroutine* do? When *newcoroutine* is called, it dereferences *lcs* to find the saved control state of the coroutine and invokes it, resetting *resume* and continuing from the last point at which the coroutine called *resume*. So if any other coroutine calls `resume(co1, value)`, that coroutine's state will be saved and this coroutine's control state will be restarted. Thus the value in *co1*, a procedure that is closed over the coroutine's control state, represents the coroutine.

○ *Exercise 9.4.2*
In our implementation of coroutines, what happens if *body* ever returns? ☐

○ *Exercise 9.4.3*
Draw a diagram that explains the behavior of *makecoroutine*. ☐

- *Exercise 9.4.4*

A common programming need is to copy characters between buffers of different lengths. There are two operations called get and put that use the buffer. Initially, get attempts to take items from the buffer, but if none are available, it resumes put. The put operation processes until it can install a value in the buffer at which time it resumes the get operation. This is a cumbersome program using traditional techniques, but it has a natural solution using coroutines. This problem can be simulated in our defined language as the problem of converting a list of lists of length n to a list of lists of length m, such that the result of flattening the two lists is the same. Write a procedure using coroutines to solve this problem. □

- *Exercise 9.4.5*

Translate the procedure makecoroutine into Scheme. □

- *Exercise 9.4.6*

Add a coroutine facility to the defined language by adding a new special form coroutine to the CPS interpreter of section 9.2, with grammar given by

---

$\langle exp \rangle ::= $ coroutine $\langle exp \rangle$ coroutine (exp)

This should behave like *makecoroutine*. □

9.5 Leaving and Entering Control Contexts

Previously, we understood the concept of the dynamic extent: it was the period from the time a procedure was called until it exited. But in the presence of first-class continuations, this concept is no longer so clear. What happens if the procedure invokes a continuation instead of returning normally? What happens if a continuation jumps back into the middle of the procedure? This is not merely an academic question. Certain operations must sometimes be performed whenever control enters or leaves a dynamic context. We must assure that these operations are performed whether control enters or leaves normally, or "flies" in or out via invocation of a continuation. For example, a file might need to be closed on exit from a procedure, whether the exit is normal or via an escape procedure or exception.

The simplest example is the dynamic assignment, which has the form *var := exp* during *body*. In the context of the assignment—the evaluation of *body*—the value of *var* is to be the value of *exp* (unless reassigned). When control leaves the context, the value of *var* must be restored to the value it had on entry to the context. The implementation of dynamic assignment that was presented in section 5.7.2 (or exercise 9.2.5) is incorrect in the presence of first-class continuations, because the original value of *var* is restored only if control leaves the procedure via its original continuation. If control leaves the procedure via some other continuation, then the original value will not be restored.

A simpler but related problem arises in many programming languages, whether they support first-class continuations or not. When an exception occurs, such as a divide by zero or a problem with file I/O, some exception handling mechanism is usually invoked. In most cases, exception handlers are effectively escape procedures. Many errors in large computer systems are the result of failure to recover properly from exceptions, because it is difficult to write a program in such a way that sufficient information about the state of the computation is available to the exception handler. A common example is failure to close a file when an exception forces the computation to exit prematurely from the dynamic context in which the file is used.

These problems can all be solved with a mechanism that explicitly manages dynamic contexts. This mechanism is called *dynamic wind* because it winds and unwinds a computation when control enters and leaves a dynamic context. (The term *unwind protect* is used instead in systems that support only downward escape procedures.) We use the following syntax.

⟨exp⟩ ::= wind ⟨exp⟩ within ⟨exp⟩ unwind ⟨exp⟩   wind (pre body post)

A wind expression consists of a body surrounded by prelude and postlude expressions, which are to be evaluated before and after body, respectively. This causes the dynamic context within which the body is evaluated to ensure that the prelude (respectively, postlude) expression is evaluated whenever control enters (respectively, leaves) it. It is assumed that the prelude and postlude are executed for effect only; their values are ignored, and the value of the wind expression is the value of the body.

Our coroutine implementation suffers from the same problem; if control leaves a coroutine via a continuation and then re-enters it, there is no guarantee that the resume variable will be reset to the proper value. We want to guarantee that *resume* is set to *localresume* on each entry into the dynamic context of the coroutine's body. This can be accomplished by wrapping the body of the coroutine in a wind expression whose prelude expression assigns the coroutine's local resume procedure to the global resume variable every time

Figure 9.5.1   Coroutines using `wind`

```
define makecoroutine =
  proc (body)
    let lcs = ignored
    in let newcoroutine = proc (value) lcs(value);
           localresume = proc (cont, value)
                             letcont localcont
                             in begin
                                   lcs := localcont;
                                   cont(value)
                                 end
       in letcont exit
          in wind resume := localresume
             within begin
                       body(resume(exit, newcoroutine));
                       error()
                     end
             unwind noop
```

control enters the dynamic context within which the coroutine body executes; see figure 9.5.1. In this example the postlude does not need to do anything, provided only coroutines use the global `resume` variable.

In other cases there may be a need for a postlude expression but no prelude. For example, it may be required that a file be closed when control leaves a dynamic context, even in the event of an exception that causes control to leave the context prematurely. Dynamic assignment is a simple example requiring both a prelude and a postlude.

• *Exercise 9.5.1*

Using `wind`, but not dynamic assignment, write an expression in our defined language that achieves the effect of an expression of the form $x := exp$ during *body*. □

We now extend our previous CPS interpreter (extended with assignment as in exercise 9.2.5) to support dynamic wind and first-class continuations. Dynamic wind is implemented by building a graph representing the active dynamic contexts. A node is created each time a `wind` expression is executed. Each node contains the prelude and postlude expressions of the associated `wind` expression, plus *creator* and *context* links that refer to other nodes. Since the

Figure 9.5.2 Adding a node to the context graph

context-link is modified during the course of a computation, it is stored in a cell.

```
(define-record context-node (prelude postlude creator context-cell))
```

When a context node is created, its creator field points to the node representing the existing dynamic context. When the computation exits from the new context, the node becomes inaccessible and can be reclaimed. In the absence of first-class continuations, this gives us a stack of contexts. If we have first-class continuations, however, a computation might exit from a context but save a continuation that allows the context to be re-entered, as in the breakpoint example of section 9.4. That is, we might exit from a context and yet have it still accessible. If we then enter a new context, this creates a tree of contexts.

At any given time, a single node represents the current dynamic context. The global variable **current** is always bound to this node. In order to help the interpreter navigate through the tree, the context link of every node points along the unique path from that node to the current node. The context link of **current** is always the empty list. See figure 9.5.2. There the thin arrows represent the creator links and the thick arrows the context-links. Initially the context graph consists of a single node with prelude and postlude fields that are ignored, a context cell that contains the empty list, and a creator link that is anything *but* the empty list. See figure 9.5.3.

A new context node is created each time a wind expression is evaluated. The wind clause of *eval-exp* creates prelude, postlude, and body thunks and passes them to the auxiliary procedure *create-context*, which adds a new context node to the graph, sets the context cell of the current node to point to the new node, and makes the new node the current node. Fig-

Figure 9.5.3 Context graph manipulation procedures

```
(define make-initial-context-graph
  (lambda ()
    (make-context-node '* '* #t (make-cell '()))))

(define **current** (make-initial-context-graph))
```

ure 9.5.2 (a) and (b) shows the context graph before and after the addition of the new node. It then executes the prelude and body thunks. The postlude thunk will be executed when control leaves the body.

The prelude, body, and postlude of a context node are represented as thunks. Since we are using a CPS interpreter, these procedures take one argument—a continuation. See figure 9.5.5 for an implementation of a thunk ADT that represents thunks as procedures. The *make-thunk* procedure creates a new thunk given an expression and an environment, and the procedure *apply-thunk* executes the thunk by supplying it with a continuation. The procedure *wrap-thunk* will be discussed below.

The central operation on a context graph is changing ***current*** when a continuation is invoked. First-class continuations created by letcont retain the node that represents the dynamic context at the time the continuation was created. See the letcont line of *eval-exp* in figure 9.5.4. When the continuation is invoked, this saved dynamic context must be restored. This job is performed by the procedure *throw* (figure 9.5.7).

When a previously saved node is to be restored as the current context, all the links in the context-link chain from the saved node to the current node must be reversed, since all the context-links must point toward the current node. Furthermore, these are the only links that need to be reversed. For example, Figure 9.5.6 (a) shows a context graph. Figure 9.5.6 (b) shows the same graph, but with the ***current*** moved to another node. The only difference between (a) and (b) is that the direction of the context-link on the path between the two nodes has been reversed to maintain the property that every context-link points in the direction of ***current***.

The *throw* procedure first calls *reverse-context-links!*, which performs this link reversal and returns the last node in the chain. If this node is not the current node, an error is signalled; we shall see later how this might occur. After the links have been reversed, the current node is the head of a context-link chain that ends with the saved node.

Figure 9.5.4   CPS interpreter with context graph

```
(define eval-exp
  (lambda (exp env k)
    (variant-case exp
      (wind (pre body post)
        (create-context
          (wrap-thunk (make-thunk pre env))
          (make-thunk body env)
          (wrap-thunk (make-thunk post env))
          k))
      (letcont (var body)
        (eval-exp body
          (extend-env
            (list var)
            (list (make-cell
                    (make-continuation k **current**)))
            env)
          k))
      ...)))

(define create-context
  (lambda (prelude body postlude k)
    (let ((saved-context **current**))
      (set! **current**
        (make-context-node prelude postlude saved-context (make-cell'())))
      (cell-set! (context-node->context-cell saved-context) **current**)
      (apply-thunk prelude
        (lambda (ignored)
          (apply-thunk body
            (lambda (val) (throw k val saved-context)))))))))

(define apply-proc
  (lambda (proc args k)
    (variant-case proc
      (prim-proc (prim-op) ...)
      (closure (formals body env) ...)
      (continuation (cont saved-context-node)
        (throw cont (car args) saved-context-node)))))

(define-record continuation (cont saved-context-node))
```

Figure 9.5.5   A CPS thunk ADT

```
(define make-thunk
  (lambda (exp env)
    (lambda (k)
      (eval-exp exp env k))))

(define apply-thunk
  (lambda (thunk k)
    (thunk k)))

(define wrap-thunk
  (lambda (thunk)
    (lambda (k)
      (let ((saved-context **current**))
        (set! **current** (make-initial-context-graph))
        (apply-thunk thunk
          (lambda (ignored)
            (set! **current** saved-context)
            (k '*)))))))
```

The next step is to walk along this chain, unwinding and then winding its contexts. This walk has two stages, the *postlude walk* and the *prelude walk*. The postlude walk visits nodes associated with dynamic contexts being exited. The postlude thunks of these nodes are invoked as they are visited. This part of the walk travels "upward" in the creator tree. Then the prelude walk visits nodes associated with dynamic contexts being entered. The prelude thunks of these nodes are invoked as they are visited. This part of the walk travels "downward" toward the saved node (soon to be restored as the current node) in the creator tree. The postlude walk occurs before the prelude walk because we must leave all the contexts that we are in before re-entering the contexts associated with the continuation.

How do we know where the postlude walk ends and the prelude walk begins? We can get an answer by examining figure 9.5.6. So long as the creator- and context-links are the same, we are traveling upward, on the postlude walk. The first node on the walk for which the creator- and context-links differ will be the node at the "top" of the walk. Since control is neither leaving nor entering this context, it is passed by without invoking a postlude or prelude. The remaining nodes of the chain are those of the prelude walk. See the

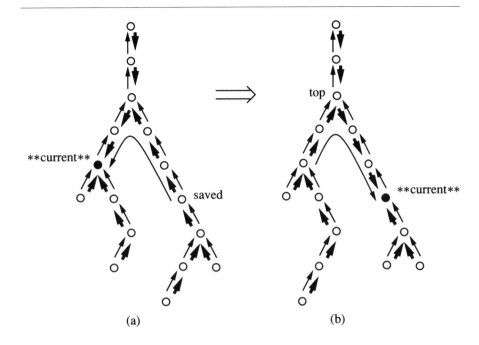

Figure 9.5.6 Changing the current node in the context graph

procedures *postlude-walk* and *prelude-walk* of figure 9.5.7. The continuation of the prelude walk is to assign the new root to the global **current** variable and, finally, invoke the continuation to which control is actually being thrown.

Either the postlude walk or the prelude walk may be trivial (involve no nodes). Commonly continuations are created and invoked within the same dynamic context, with no **wind** operations performed while evaluating this body. In this case both the postlude walk and prelude walk will be trivial.

To maintain the integrity of the context graph, we do not allow control to enter or leave a prelude or postlude via invocation of a first-class continuation. This constraint is enforced by "wrapping" prelude and postlude thunks in their own context graphs. The procedure *wrap-thunk* saves **current**, creates an entirely new context graph for the evaluation of the thunk, and then restores the old one when the thunk returns. An attempt to invoke a continuation that does not belong to the current context graph can now be detected by *throw*, because the context-link chain terminates in the "current" node of the wrong graph, and an error is signalled.

Figure 9.5.7   Procedures for switching the current context

```
(define throw
  (lambda (k value saved-context)
    (if (not (eq? (reverse-context-links! saved-context) **current**))
        (error "Context violation")
        (postlude-walk **current**
          (lambda (top-node)
            (prelude-walk (cell-ref (context-node->context-cell top-node))
              (lambda (ignored)
                (set! **current** saved-context)
                (apply-continuation k value)))))))))

(define reverse-context-links!
  (letrec
    ((loop
       (lambda (node last)
         (let ((cell (context-node->context-cell node)))
           (let ((next (cell-ref cell)))
             (cell-set! cell last)
             (if (null? next) node (loop next node)))))))
    (lambda (node)
      (if (null? node) node (loop node '())))))

(define postlude-walk
  (lambda (node k)
    (if (top-node? node)
        (k node)
        (apply-thunk (context-node->postlude node)
          (lambda (ignored)
            (postlude-walk (cell-ref (context-node->context-cell node)) k))))))

(define prelude-walk
  (lambda (node k)
    (if (null? node)
        (k '*)
        (let ((next (cell-ref (context-node->context-cell node))))
          (apply-thunk (context-node->prelude node)
            (lambda (ignored) (prelude-walk next k)))))))

(define top-node?
  (lambda (node)
    (not (eq? (cell-ref (context-node->context-cell node))
              (context-node->creator node)))))
```

• *Exercise 9.5.2*

Write a Scheme procedure `dynamic-wind` that takes prelude, body, and postlude thunks (procedures of no arguments), and performs the same context graph operations used in our interpreter. This procedure may be of great value when programming with continuations in Scheme. For example, the code of figure 9.5.1 where `wind` is used would become

```
(dynamic-wind
  (lambda () (set! resume localresume))
  (lambda () (begin
                (body (resume exit newcoroutine))
                (error)))
  (lambda () noop))
```
☐

○ *Exercise 9.5.3*

If a prelude is executing for the first time, or a postlude is executing after the body has returned normally, it would be acceptable for control to enter or leave the prelude or postlude via invocation of a continuation. The effect in these cases would be that obtained if the dynamic wind expression were replaced by

```
begin
    prelude
    let ans = body
    in begin
            postlude
            ans
        end
end
```

where ans does not occur free in *postlude*. Modify the wrapping operation of the context-graph algorithm to allow this behavior. ☐

○ *Exercise 9.5.4*

There are two places in the programs of figure 9.5.4 that do a `throw`. In one of them, the distance from `**current**` to the node to be restored as the current node is one. Determine which of the throws is simpler, and rename it `little-throw`. Then implement `little-throw` to take advantage of this observation. ☐

• *Exercise 9.5.5*

What is written in the evaluation of the following expression?

```
letcont return
in wind write(0)
   within wind write(1)
          within wind write(2)
                  within cons(return(3), 4)
                  unwind write(200)
          unwind write(300)
   unwind write(400)
```

☐

9.6 Dynamic Assignment Revisited

In the previous section we claimed that our implementation of dynamic assignment was flawed when used with first-class continuations. We now have the tools to fix dynamic assignment. Each time control moves out of the body of a dynamic assignment, the original value of the variable must be reset. Furthermore, the current value of the variable must be saved for a subsequent re-entrance, in the event that a continuation was captured within the body. The top portion of figure 9.6.1 is a program that shows how that might happen. The result of executing this program should be 114, not 100.

The lower portion of Figure 9.6.1 shows a program that uses wind to model the behavior of dynamic assignment. The difference is that this program has a prelude and a postlude that manage the resetting of the variable x, using two additional variables, fluidx and lexicalx. The lexicalx variable always contains the lexical value of x while control is *in* the body of the dynamic assignment and the fluidx variable always contains the fluid value of x while control is *out* of the body of the dynamic assignment. When control re-enters the body of the dynamic assignment, the lexical value is saved again (because assignments to it may have occurred).

• *Exercise 9.6.1*

The program in figure 9.6.1 uses two additional variables, fluidx and lexicalx. Rewrite it with just one additional variable tempx. ☐

The solution to adding dynamic assignment to the defined language in the presence of first-class continuations is now straightforward. First, we add a new make- procedure, *make-swap-thunk*, to the thunk ADT.

Figure 9.6.1   Two programs that do dynamic assignment

```
let x = 3;
    a = 12
in let ans = letcont out
             in let ret = letcont k
                          in x := +(a, 20) during begin
                                                     x := +(x, x);
                                                     letcont k1 in k(k1);
                                                     out(x)
                                                   end
                in begin
                     x := 50;
                     a := 100;
                     ret(5)
                   end
   in +(ans, x)

let x = 3;
    a = 12
in let ans = letcont out
             in let ret = letcont k
                          in let fluidx = +(a, 20);
                                 lexicalx = ignored
                             in wind begin
                                       lexicalx := x;
                                       x := fluidx
                                     end
                                within begin
                                        x := +(x, x);
                                        letcont k1 in k(k1);
                                        out(x)
                                      end
                                unwind begin
                                         fluidx := x;
                                         x := lexicalx
                                       end
                in begin
                     x := 50;
                     a := 100;
                     ret(5)
                   end
   in +(ans, x)
```

```
(define make-swap-thunk
  (lambda (cell-1 cell-2)
    (lambda (k)
      (cell-swap! cell-1 cell-2)
      (k '*))))
```

This procedure returns a thunk that simply swaps the contents of two cells; see figure 4.5.1. One of the cells corresponds to the binding of the dynamic assignment variable, and the other acts like a temporary (see exercise 9.6.1). Here is the `dynassign` clause to be added to the interpreter of figure 9.5.4.

```
(dynassign (var exp body)
  (eval-exp exp env
    (lambda (value)
      (let ((swap (wrap-thunk
                    (make-swap-thunk
                      (apply-env env var)
                      (make-cell value)))))
        (create-context swap (make-thunk body env) swap k)))))
```

The first step in this clause is to evaluate *exp*. Then a wrapped thunk is created that swaps the contents of the cell of the environment representing the L-value of `var` and its associated temporary cell; see exercise 9.6.1 to see why we need only one swapping routine. Finally, as in the execution of the program in the lower portion of figure 9.6.1, *create-context* is invoked.

● *Exercise 9.6.2*
In the top portion of figure 9.6.1 the program uses dynamic assignment. In chapter 5 we showed that the operation of dynamic assignment was just manipulating the values stored in lexical variables. Rewrite that program without using dynamic assignment, but with using `fluidx` and `lexicalx` to behave as the dynamic assignment did in the earlier chapter. The result should be 114, the wrong answer. □

9.7 Summary

The CPS transformation converts programs to tail form, but at the expense of relying on the existence of first-class procedures in the defining language. This reliance can be eliminated by representing continuations as data structures.

Applying these transformations to an interpreter yields an interpreter in first-order tail form. This provides an interpreter that does not rely on first-class procedures or recursion in the defining language.

If the interpreter for the defined language is in continuation-passing style, these continuations can be made available in the defined language. Such continuations can be used to escape from inside nested procedures. If the defined language includes continuations as expressed values, then complex control structures such as coroutines can be defined without further extending the defined language.

First-class continuations complicate the definition of dynamic extent. Sometimes it is necessary to guarantee that certain actions, such as opening or closing a file, are taken on entrance to or exit from a dynamic extent, whether by normal control flow or invocation of a continuation. This can be accomplished by a mechanism, called dynamic wind, that manipulates a graph of managed contexts.

10   Imperative Form and Stack Architecture

In chapter 8 we saw that by using continuation-passing style, any procedure can be transformed into an equivalent tail-form procedure, in which all recursive procedures are called in tail position. In this chapter we show that any tail-form procedure may be transformed into an equivalent set of procedures in *imperative form*, in which all procedures have no arguments. Procedures in imperative form receive information from their callers in variable bindings that are assigned by the caller prior to procedure invocation, rather than via arguments.

A tail call of no arguments simply transfers control to the beginning of the called procedure's body: it is equivalent to a *go to* (unconditional jump) statement. Thus, through continuation-passing and imperative form transformations it is possible to reduce procedure calls to the most rudimentary form of control transfer.

In section 10.1 we introduce the imperative form transformation with simple examples and show how it may be applied to procedures to which the CPS transformation of chapter 8 and the first-order transformation of chapter 9 have first been applied. In section 10.2 we then show how these procedures may be further transformed so that control information is recorded on a stack, rather than in heap-allocated continuations. In section 10.3 we apply these transformations to an interpreter that heap-allocates its argument lists, closures, continuations and environments. In this section, we successfully move all but the environments to the control stack. Finally, in section 10.4 we show how the interpreter's environment bindings may also be recorded on the control stack if restrictions on the extent of procedures are imposed. The resulting stack architecture is typical of those used to implement block structured imperative-style programming languages. Then a heap is required only if heap-allocated run-time structures are supported.

We have seen that, in general, execution of a procedure call requires the following steps:

1. saving the current control context,

2. extending the environment with new variable bindings for the arguments of the call, and

3. transferring control to the beginning of the called procedure's body.

In chapter 8 we saw that a tail call requires no additional control information be recorded, so in such cases step 1 may be omitted. If step 1 is omitted whenever possible, tail-form procedures exhibit iterative control behavior. Such an implementation is properly tail recursive. Next we introduce a technique by which any tail-form procedure may be transformed into one in which all tail calls have no operands. This eliminates step 2, leaving only step 3, which is equivalent to a *go to* statement.

When a procedure calls itself from a tail position, the bindings of its formal parameters will never be used again, since control does not return to the procedure following the call. Therefore, the new values required by the call could be assigned to the bindings prior to the call. For example, consider *member?*.

```
(define member?
  (lambda (s los)
    (cond
      ((null? los) #f)
      ((equal? (car los) s) #t)
      (else (member? s (cdr los))))))
```

This is equivalent to

```
(define member?
  (lambda (s los)
    (cond
      ((null? los) #f)
      ((equal? (car los) s) #t)
      (else (set! los (cdr los))
            (member? s los)))))
```

Since *s* and `los` are not changed by the tail call, they could both be global variables, provided they were properly initialized by assignments. We use the term *register* when referring to variables that are assigned in this manner and name these variables with the suffix -reg. An *imperative,* or register, version of *member?* is obtained as follows using global registers.

```
(define s-reg '*)
(define los-reg '*)

(define member?
  (lambda (s los)
    (set! s-reg s)
    (set! los-reg los)
    (member?/reg)))

(define member?/reg
  (lambda ()
    (cond
      ((null? los-reg) #f)
      ((equal? (car los-reg) s-reg) #t)
      (else (set! los-reg (cdr los-reg))
            (member?/reg)))))
```

Such a program, in which all first-order tail-form procedures have no arguments, is said to be in *imperative form.* We use the suffix /reg (read "with registers") in naming imperative form procedures.

As a second example, here is a version of the *fact-iter* example of chapter 8, in which we have converted the inner loop *fact-iter-acc* to imperative form:

```
(define n-reg '*)
(define a-reg '*)

(define fact-iter
  (lambda (n)
    (set! n-reg n)
    (set! a-reg 1)
    (fact-iter-acc/reg)))
```

```
(define fact-iter-acc/reg
  (lambda ()
    (if (zero? n-reg)
        a-reg
        (begin
          (set! a-reg (* n-reg a-reg))
          (set! n-reg (- n-reg 1))
          (fact-iter-acc/reg)))))
```

Since the subexpression of the first set! expression refers to *n-reg*, the transformation would be incorrect if the order of the set! statements were reversed. Since it is essential that there be no references to a variable from the point at which it is assigned to the point of the tail call, the order of assignments may be critical. In some cases, no order is correct unless one or more of the old variable bindings is temporarily recorded using a let expression or some other means. For example, in the following version of fact the order of the set! statements has been reversed.

```
(define fact-iter-acc/reg
  (lambda ()
    (if (zero? n-reg)
        a-reg
        (let ((temp-n-reg n-reg))
          (set! n-reg (- n-reg 1))
          (set! a-reg (* temp-n-reg a-reg))
          (fact-iter-acc/reg)))))
```

• *Exercise 10.1.1*
Transform the following tail-form procedures *reverse-acc* and *fib-acc* to imperative form and make the appropriate changes to *reverse* and *fib*.

```
(define reverse
  (lambda (ls)
    (reverse-acc ls '())))

(define reverse-acc
  (lambda (ls a)
    (if (null? ls)
        a
        (reverse-acc (cdr ls) (cons (car ls) a)))))
```

Imperative Form and Stack Architecture

```
(define fib
  (lambda (n)
    (fib-acc n 0 1)))

(define fib-acc
  (lambda (n a1 a2)
    (if (= n 0)
        a2
        (fib-acc (- n 1) a2 (+ a1 a2)))))
```
☐

In general, the imperative-form transformation only works on programs that are first-order tail form. In some cases accumulators will suffice for translation into tail form, but the CPS transformation always does the job.

We next demonstrate the imperative-form transformation on a procedure that is similar to the one we derived in chapter 8.

```
(define subst
  (lambda (new old s)
    (subst-cps new old s (lambda (x) x))))

(define subst-cps
  (lambda (new old s k)
    (if (pair? s)
        (subst-cps new old (car s)
          (lambda (v)
            (subst-cps new old (cdr s)
              (lambda (w)
                (k (cons v w))))))
        (if (eq? s old) (k new) (k s)))))
```

Before we can apply the imperative-form transformation, we must first convert *subst-cps* to first-order form. Applying our imperative-form transformation to the first-order form, we obtain the program of figure 10.1.1. It is not necessary for the continuation data structures to close over *new-reg* and *old-reg*, because these values remain the same throughout a call to *subst-cps*.

One final note: if the continuation was created by the CPS transformation, it is always safe to perform the continuation assignment before other assignments. (The other operands never refer to the continuation because they existed before the CPS transformation created the continuation.) Often the continuation *must* be first, because it contains the values of other variables.

Figure 10.1.1   First-order imperative-form transformation example

```
(define-record final-valcont ())
(define-record subst1-cont (s k))
(define-record subst2-cont (v k))

(define new-reg '*)      (define s-reg '*)
(define old-reg '*)      (define k-reg '*)
(define v-reg '*)

(define subst
  (lambda (new old s)
    (set! k-reg (make-final-valcont))
    (set! new-reg new)
    (set! old-reg old)
    (set! s-reg s)
    (subst-cps/reg)))

(define subst-cps/reg
  (lambda ()
    (if (pair? s-reg)
        (begin (set! k-reg (make-subst1-cont s-reg k-reg))
               (set! s-reg (car s-reg))
               (subst-cps/reg))
        (if (eq? s-reg old-reg)
            (begin (set! v-reg new-reg)
                   (apply-continuation/reg))
            (begin (set! v-reg s-reg)
                   (apply-continuation/reg))))))

(define apply-continuation/reg
  (lambda ()
    (variant-case k-reg
      (final-valcont () v-reg)
      (subst1-cont (s k)
        (set! k-reg (make-subst2-cont v-reg k))
        (set! s-reg (cdr s))
        (subst-cps/reg))
      (subst2-cont (v k)
        (set! k-reg k)
        (set! v-reg (cons v v-reg))
        (apply-continuation/reg)))))
```

- *Exercise 10.1.2*

  Apply the imperative form transformation to the procedures developed in exercise 8.5.4. ☐

- *Exercise 10.1.3*

  Apply the imperative form transformation to the interpreter of figure 9.2.3 and figure 9.2.5. ☐

○ *Exercise 10.1.4*

  The imperative-form transformation does not work correctly if the program is not in first-order form. Demonstrate this by converting the CPS version of *subst*. What goes wrong? ☐

10.2 Control Stacks

In the *subst-cps/reg* program, the subst1-cont and subst2-cont continuations both contain a single continuation, in addition to other information, and the final value continuation contains no continuations. A similar pattern arises in all CPS programs. Thus every continuation may be thought of as being the head of a chain of continuations, the tail of which is the continuation that it contains and the end of which is the final value continuation. See figure 10.2.1 (a). For uniformity, we consider the final value continuation to contain an empty chain.

This observation prompts us to transform the representation of continuations so that they are not structures containing other continuations but lists of structures, called *frames*, which contain the information other than the continuation that was recorded in the corresponding continuation structures. We refer to this as a *list of frames* representation. See figure 10.2.1 (b).

To transform the *subst-cps/reg* program to use a list of frames representation, we first define the frame structures.

```
(define-record final-valframe ())
(define-record subst1-frame (s))
(define-record subst2-frame (v))
```

Since the *subst-cps/reg* procedure is independent of the representation of continuations, it does not need to be redefined. We need only redefine the procedures in its continuation ADT. Each of the procedures that create a continuation now returns a list, rather than a record.

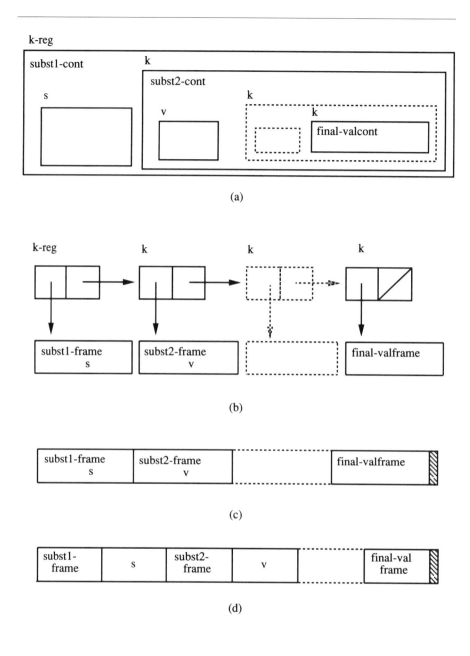

Figure 10.2.1   Representations of continuations

```
(define make-final-valcont
  (lambda ()
    (cons (make-final-valframe) '())))

(define make-subst1-cont
  (lambda (s k)
    (cons (make-subst1-frame s) k)))

(define make-subst2-cont
  (lambda (v k)
    (cons (make-subst2-frame v) k)))

(define apply-continuation/reg
  (lambda ()
    (let ((frame (car k-reg)) (k (cdr k-reg)))
      (variant-case frame
        (final-valframe () v-reg)
        (subst1-frame (s)
          (set! k-reg (make-subst2-cont v-reg k))
          (set! s-reg (cdr s))
          (subst-cps/reg))
        (subst2-frame (v)
          (set! k-reg k)
          (set! v-reg (cons v v-reg))
          (apply-continuation/reg))))))
```

Examining the assignments to k-reg, we next observe that in every case the new continuation is obtained either by consing a new frame onto the current continuation or by taking the cdr of the current continuation. Thus frames are accessed in a last-in-first-out order; in other words, the continuation data structure (in this case a list) is being used as a stack. To express this, we modify our list of frames program to use a stack ADT with the procedure *push!*, which pushes its argument onto a stack, and two procedures of no arguments, *top* and *pop!*, which return the top value on the stack and pop the stack, respectively. See figure 10.2.2.

In implementing the stack ADT, we can store all continuation frames in a single vector, rather than requiring a cons cell for each new continuation. Of course we must assume that it is possible to place a reasonable limit, say *stack-size*, on the maximum number of stack elements.

• *Exercise 10.2.1*
Implement the stack ADT, representing the stack as a vector, and use it to test the code of figure 10.2.2. ☐

Figure 10.2.2   Using stack of frames representation of continuations

```
(define subst
  (lambda (new old s)
    (push! (make-final-valframe))
    (set! new-reg new)
    (set! old-reg old)
    (set! s-reg s)
    (subst-cps/reg)))

(define subst-cps/reg
  (lambda ()
    (if (pair? s-reg)
        (begin
          (push! (make-subst1-frame s-reg))
          (set! s-reg (car s-reg))
          (subst-cps/reg))
        (if (eq? s-reg old-reg)
            (begin
              (set! v-reg new-reg)
              (apply-continuation/reg))
            (begin
              (set! v-reg s-reg)
              (apply-continuation/reg))))))

(define apply-continuation/reg
  (lambda ()
    (let ((frame (top)))
      (pop!)
      (variant-case frame
        (final-valframe () v-reg)
        (subst1-frame (s)
          (push! (make-subst2-frame v-reg))
          (set! s-reg (cdr s))
          (subst-cps/reg))
        (subst2-frame (v)
          (set! v-reg (cons v v-reg))
          (apply-continuation/reg))))))
```

Figure 10.2.3   An example using an unframed-stack representation

```
(define subst
  (lambda (new old s)
    (push! 'final-valframe)
    (set! new-reg new)
    (set! old-reg old)
    (set! s-reg s)
    (subst-cps/reg)))

(define subst-cps/reg
  (lambda ()
    (if (pair? s-reg)
        (begin (push! s-reg)
               (push! 'subst1-frame)
               (set! s-reg (car s-reg))
               (subst-cps/reg))
        (if (eq? s-reg old-reg)
            (begin (set! v-reg new-reg)
                   (apply-continuation/reg))
            (begin (set! v-reg s-reg)
                   (apply-continuation/reg))))))

(define apply-continuation/reg
  (lambda ()
    (let ((frame-tag (top)))
      (pop!)
      (case frame-tag
        ((final-valframe) v-reg)
        ((subst1-frame)
         (let ((s (top)))
           (pop!)
           (push! v-reg)
           (push! 'subst2-frame)
           (set! s-reg (cdr s))
           (subst-cps/reg)))
        ((subst2-frame)
         (let ((v (top)))
           (pop!)
           (set! v-reg (cons v v-reg))
           (apply-continuation/reg)))))))
```

To complete our derivation of a stack architecture for `subst`, we eliminate the frame records. Instead of pushing a frame onto the stack, we push onto the stack any values that were contained in the stack frame and then we push a tag (a symbol) representing the type of frame. The `variant-case` expression in `apply-continuation/reg` must then be replaced with a `case` expression that dispatches on the tag that was on the top of the stack, and the `case` expression consequent clauses must remove any associated values from the stack. We refer to this as an *unframed-stack* representation. See figure 10.2.1 (b), (c), and (d) for a graphic comparison of the list of frames, stack of frames, and unframed-stack control representations, and see figure 10.2.3 for an implementation of `subst` using an unframed stack.

This completes our series of transformations of `subst`. We started by transforming a procedure into CPS. This introduced new procedures: the continuations. The next transformation made the program independent of the representation of continuations, which allowed us to then change the representation of continuations from procedures to records. The resulting program is said to be in first-order tail form. This enabled us to transform our program to an imperative form. By observing a pattern in the structure of continuations, we next transformed the continuations into a list of frames representation. Then we noticed that the frames were being added to and taken from the list in a last-in-first-out manner, like a stack, resulting in a stack of frames representation. In our final transformation we eliminated the frame records by placing their contents directly on the stack, resulting in an unframed-stack representation.

These transformations are of great value because they reduce the mechanics of procedures to the level of assembly language: register assignments, jumps, and stack operations. Furthermore, the transformations may be applied to *any* program, and each transformation is well defined and preserves the correctness of the program.

- *Exercise 10.2.2*
Transform the programs of exercise 9.1.2 so that the continuations are represented successively as a list of frames, a stack of frames, and an unframed stack. ☐

- *Exercise 10.2.3*
Transform the interpreter of exercise 9.2.5 so that the continuations are represented successively as a list of frames, a stack of frames, and an unframed stack. ☐

10.3 Interpreter Stack Architecture

Though programs may use heap-allocated objects (such as Scheme's pairs, records, and closures) for a variety of purposes, it is sometimes possible to transform programs so that no dynamic heap allocation is required. In such cases the run-time system necessary to support the program may be greatly simplified, since dynamic heap management (such as garbage collection) is no longer required. This typically results in implementations that are simpler and more efficient.

For example in *subst-cps/reg*, dynamic heap allocation was required when new continuation closures or records were created. In section 10.1 we saw that the continuations could be recorded on a stack, rather than in a heap. Our interpreters have used heap allocation for continuations, argument lists, environments, and closures. In this and the next section we derive an interpreter that records all this information using a single stack.

We know that the transformations in the previous sections allow us to represent continuations using an unframed stack. Our goal, therefore, is to transform the interpreter of figure 9.2.2 to avoid heap allocation of argument lists, environments, and closures. We instead incorporate this information in the continuation. Since the continuation is a stack, the entire interpreter will then obey stack discipline.

The stack architecture of our final interpreter is of special interest because it is typical of stack architectures used by implementations of most block-structured programming languages. This architecture is familiar and efficient, but it comes at two costs. First, it will not allow procedures or continuations to be returned as values from other procedures or to be stored in heap-allocated data structures. Second, it does not implement proper tail recursion (though, using other techniques, a properly tail-recursive implementation may employ a control stack). We shall discuss these limitations at the end of section 10.4.

10.3.1 Value and Argument Continuations

We assume the interpreted language has only literals, variables, procedures, and applications. Adding other forms is straightforward. We assume that all primitive procedures are unary or binary. We distinguish these based on their arity and represent them by Scheme procedures of one and two arguments, respectively. The interpreter is easily extended to accommodate primitive operators of other arities. Also, we change the functionality of `apply-env` to take a continuation argument, as in exercise 9.3.2. See figure 10.3.1.

Figure 10.3.1 Interpreter with abstract data representations

```
(define eval-exp
  (lambda (exp env k)
    (variant-case exp
      (lit (datum) (k datum))
      (varref (var) (apply-env env var k))
      (proc (formals body) (k (make-closure formals body env)))
      (app (rator rands)
        (eval-exp rator env
          (lambda (proc)
            (eval-rands rands env
              (lambda (all)
                (apply-proc proc all k))))))
      (else (error "Invalid abstract syntax:" exp)))))

(define eval-rands
  (lambda (rands env k)
    (if (null? rands)
        (k '())
        (eval-exp (car rands) env
          (lambda (first)
            (eval-rands (cdr rands) env
              (lambda (rest)
                (k (cons first rest)))))))))

(define apply-proc
  (lambda (proc args k)
    (variant-case proc
      (prim-1 (unary-op)
        (k (unary-op (unary-arg args))))
      (prim-2 (binary-op)
        (k (binary-op (binary-arg-1 args) (binary-arg-2 args))))
      (closure (formals body env)
        (eval-exp body (extend-env formals args env) k))
      (else (error "Invalid primitive operation:" proc)))))
```

Our first step is to introduce abstract data types for the continuations. We provide separate abstractions (ADTs) for *argument continuations*, which expect to receive argument lists, and for *value continuations*, which expect values. The argument continuations are exactly the continuations that are passed to `eval-rands`; all the remaining continuations are value continuations.

This is a good opportunity to eliminate one instance of heap allocation: the one in `make-closure`. We can do this by adding an additional argument to value continuations. Let us explore this idea in more detail.

The formals list and body components of a closure are static, but the environment is dynamic. Our approach is to represent the static and dynamic components of a closure separately, but in such a manner that they are available together when they are both needed (that is, when a procedure is invoked). We represent the static component of a nonprimitive procedure as the abstract syntax tree for the expression that defines it; this contains the formals list and the body, as desired. One way of associating the static and dynamic components would be to join them using a pair in the heap.

We can avoid this heap allocation by having value continuations take two arguments: one for the ordinary values, including the static parts of closures, and one for closure environments. Closures no longer exist as physical data values, but we shall still use this term to refer to a procedure expression and an environment that are linked in this way. If the value being passed is not a closure, the second argument will be a dummy value.

For now, we still represent continuations of both kinds as procedures. See figure 10.3.2 for the basic interpretation procedures, along with new versions of the procedures that interpret environments and primitive procedures. We assume that the primitive procedures take and return only ordinary (nonclosure) values; we leave it as an exercise to rewrite `unary-arg`, etc., to extract only the ordinary value.

See figure 10.3.3 and figure 10.3.4 for the value and argument continuation ADTs, respectively. The extra argument to value continuations propagates through these procedures, resulting in extra arguments in all of the continuation builders. The extra argument is finally used in `apply-proc`. For the final value continuation, we add a test to see whether the value being returned is a closure or not; if it is a closure, we return a distinguished symbol `<Procedure>`, since we presume it should be impossible for the user of the language to see the internals of a closure.

The environment ADT, using a procedural representation, is shown in figure 10.3.5. The procedure `extend-env` takes a list of value-environment pairs, as built by the `rest` continuation of figure 10.3.4; when the right pair is found, its pieces are reported as the two arguments of the continuation `vk`.

Figure 10.3.2   Interpreter with abstract continuations

```
(define eval-exp
  (lambda (exp env vk)
    (variant-case exp
      (lit (datum) (apply-valcont vk datum dummy))
      (varref (var) (apply-env env var vk))
      (proc (formals body) (apply-valcont vk exp env))
      (app (rator rands)
        (eval-exp rator env (make-proc-valcont rands env vk)))
      (else (error "Invalid abstract syntax:" exp)))))

(define eval-rands
  (lambda (rands env ak)
    (if (null? rands)
        (apply-argcont ak '())
        (eval-exp (car rands) env
          (make-first-valcont rands env ak)))))

(define apply-proc
  (lambda (proc proc-env args vk)
    (variant-case proc
      (prim-1 (unary-op)
        (apply-valcont vk
          (unary-op (unary-arg args))
          dummy))
      (prim-2 (binary-op)
        (apply-valcont vk
          (binary-op (binary-arg-1 args) (binary-arg-2 args))
          dummy))
      (proc (formals body)
        (eval-exp body (extend-env formals args proc-env) vk))
      (else (error "Invalid primitive operation:" proc)))))

(define dummy '*)
```

Figure 10.3.3   Value continuation ADT

```
(define make-final-valcont
  (lambda ()
    (lambda (final final-env)
      (if (eq? final-env dummy)
          final
          '<Procedure>)))))

(define make-first-valcont
  (lambda (rands env ak)
    (lambda (first first-env)
      (eval-rands (cdr rands) env
        (make-rest-argcont first first-env ak)))))

(define make-proc-valcont
  (lambda (rands env vk)
    (lambda (proc proc-env)
      (eval-rands rands env
        (make-all-argcont proc proc-env vk)))))

(define apply-valcont
  (lambda (vk val val-env)
    (vk val val-env)))
```

10.3.2 Transforming Continuations

Our next step is to convert the value and argument continuations to a data structure representation. We shall then be able to convert the resulting first-order program to imperative form.

First we introduce two record types for argument continuations:

```
(define-record rest-argcont (val env-or-dummy ak))
(define-record all-argcont (proc proc-env vk))
```

and three record types for value continuations:

```
(define-record final-valcont ())
(define-record first-valcont (rands env ak))
(define-record proc-valcont (rands env vk))
```

To go with this record representation of argument continuations, we define apply-argcont as in figure 10.3.6.

Figure 10.3.4   Argument continuation ADT

```
(define make-rest-argcont
  (lambda (first first-env ak)
    (lambda (rest)
      (apply-argcont ak
        (cons (cons first first-env) rest)))))

(define make-all-argcont
  (lambda (proc proc-env vk)
    (lambda (all)
      (apply-proc proc proc-env all vk))))

(define apply-argcont
  (lambda (ak args)
    (ak args)))
```

Figure 10.3.5   Environment ADT

```
(define apply-env
  (lambda (env var vk)
    (env var vk)))

(define extend-env
  (lambda (formals args env)
    (lambda (var vk)
      (if (memq var formals)
          (letrec
            ((loop (lambda (formals rib)
                     (if (eq? var (car formals))
                         (apply-valcont vk
                           (car (car rib))
                           (cdr (car rib)))
                         (loop (cdr formals) (cdr rib))))))
            (loop formals args))
          (apply-env env var vk)))))
```

- *Exercise 10.3.1*

  Define `apply-valcont` to interpret the value continuations constructed from the `final-valcont`, `first-valcont`, and `proc-valcont` record types. ☐

Figure 10.3.6 `apply-argcont` using record representation

```
(define apply-argcont
  (lambda (ak args)
    (variant-case ak
      (rest-argcont (val env-or-dummy ak)
        (let ((rest args))
          (apply-argcont ak
            (cons (cons val env-or-dummy) rest))))
      (all-argcont (proc proc-env vk)
        (let ((all args))
          (apply-proc proc proc-env all vk)))))))
```

The argument continuation record type declarations reveal that every argument continuation has the form

```
#(rest-argcont val-n env-or-dummy-n
   ...
     #(rest-argcont val-1 env-or-dummy-1
        #(all-argcont proc proc-env vk)))
```

where the values of the operand expressions, *val-1*, *val-2*, ... with their associated environment slots, *env-or-dummy-1*, *env-or-dummy-2*, ... appear in reverse order. The value of the first operand is innermost, just outside the `all-argcont`, and the most recently evaluated operand (*val-n*) is outermost.

When `apply-argcont` is invoked by *eval-rands*, each of the `rest-argcont` continuations causes its argument to be added to the argument list. When the `all-argcont` continuation is reached, `apply-proc` is invoked to apply a primitive procedure or closure with the newly constructed argument list and the continuation `vk`. This effectively pops the control stack to the point representing `vk`.

Thus the only purpose of `apply-argcont` is to collect information for the benefit of `apply-proc`. By making `apply-proc` smarter, we can avoid `apply-argcont` altogether and simply pass the argument continuation to `apply-proc`, since it has all the information needed.

What information does `apply-proc` need to extract from the argument continuation? It needs to find the procedure value and environment to be applied, which are located inside `all-argcont`. The value continuation to be used is in the same continuation. We use a procedure, *find-all-argcont*, with a 3-argument receiver continuation to avoid doing the same search three

Figure 10.3.7   Procedures that avoid the creation of argument lists

```
(define eval-rands
  (lambda (rands env ak)
    (if (null? rands)
        (apply-proc ak)
        (eval-exp (car rands) env
          (make-first-valcont rands env ak)))))

(define apply-proc
  (lambda (ak)
    (find-all-argcont ak
      (lambda (proc proc-env vk)
        (variant-case proc
          (prim-1 (unary-op)
            (apply-valcont vk
              (unary-op (unary-arg ak))
              dummy))
          (prim-2 (binary-op)
            (apply-valcont vk
              (binary-op (binary-arg-1 ak) (binary-arg-2 ak))
              dummy))
          (proc (formals body)
            (eval-exp body
              (extend-env formals ak proc-env)
              vk))
          (else (error "Invalid primitive operation:" proc)))))))

(define find-all-argcont
  (lambda (ak receiver)
    (variant-case ak
      (all-argcont (proc proc-env vk)
        (receiver proc proc-env vk))
      (rest-argcont (val env-or-dummy ak)
        (find-all-argcont ak receiver)))))
```

Figure 10.3.8   Environments using argument continuations

```
(define extend-env make-extended-env)

(define apply-env
  (lambda (env var vk)
    (variant-case env
      (init-env () (init-env var vk))
      (extended-env (formals ak env)
        (if (memq var formals)
            (letrec
              ((loop (lambda (formals ak)
                       (variant-case ak
                         (rest-argcont (val env-or-dummy ak)
                           (if (eq? var (car formals))
                               (apply-valcont vk val env-or-dummy)
                               (loop (cdr formals) ak)))
                         (else (error "Invalid environment"))))))
              (loop (reverse formals) ak))
            (apply-env env var vk))))))
```

times. We also need to recode the procedures that extract the arguments for primitive operations. See figure 10.3.7.

The representation of environments must also be changed to account for the location of values in the argument continuation, rather than in heap-allocated lists. To do this, we change the record types for environments to

```
(define-record init-env ())
(define-record extended-env (formals ak env))
```

The procedure *apply-env* must search for values in the argument continuation. Since the arguments appear in reverse order in the continuation, the search loop in *apply-env* begins with a reversed formals list. See figure 10.3.8.

We now have an interpreter in which storage is allocated only for continuations and environments, and this allocation is in the form of records.

○ *Exercise 10.3.2*

The preceding statement is not quite accurate: there is still heap allocation taking place in the expression (reverse formals) in *apply-env*. This reversal could have been done at a number of points. Modify your parser so that it reverses the formals lists in `proc` records, thus avoiding the need to perform this operation at run time. □

• *Exercise 10.3.3*
Implement the interpreter described in this section. □

10.4 Stack Allocation of Continuations and Environments

We have now laid the groundwork for putting continuations and environments on a stack. This is done in two steps. First, we put continuations on a stack, leaving environments alone. Then we finish the job by putting environments on the stack as well.

First we define a suitable stack ADT. This ADT provides access to a single stack that is initialized by calling `init-stack!`. The procedure *push!* puts its argument on the top of the stack. Though of course values may only be added to or removed from this stack at its top, this stack ADT allows pointers to be maintained that refer to locations within the stack. The contents of the stack location referred to by a stack pointer may be obtained by passing the pointer to the procedure *stack-ref*. The variable *top-ptr* is always a pointer to the top of the stack. The procedure *pop-to-ptr!* takes a stack pointer and pops the stack until the pointer refers to the top of the stack, and *decrement-ptr* takes a stack pointer p and a number n and returns a pointer to the location n elements below the location referred to by p. Our implementation of this ADT represents the stack as a vector (allowing random access to its elements), with stack pointers represented as vector indices. See figure 10.4.1.

We now rewrite our interpreter in imperative style. The current continuation is represented by the global stack, as in section 10.2, rather than by a `k-reg` variable. The environment is communicated through a global register, `env-reg`. All other variables remain as they originally appeared in figure 10.3.2. It is left as an exercise to pass these in registers. We begin by defining *eval-exp* and *eval-rands*, which we rename *eval-exp/stack* and *eval-rands/stack*.

Continuations are represented as stack pointers into an unframed stack. The current continuation is obtained using `top-ptr`. Other continuations are also represented as stack pointers. Each procedure that constructs continuations simply pushes data on the stack, along with an appropriate tag, as in figure 10.2.3. See figure 10.4.3.

Figure 10.4.1   Control stack ADT

```scheme
(define top-ptr '*)
(define the-stack '*)
(define stack-ptr-limit 100)

(define init-stack!
  (lambda ()
    (set! top-ptr -1)
    (set! the-stack (make-vector (+ stack-ptr-limit 1)))))

(define push!
  (lambda (val)
    (if (= top-ptr stack-ptr-limit)
        (error "Stack overflow")
        (begin
          (set! top-ptr (+ 1 top-ptr))
          (vector-set! the-stack top-ptr val)))))

(define pop-to-ptr!
  (lambda (ptr)
    (set! top-ptr ptr)))

(define stack-ref
  (lambda (ptr)
    (vector-ref the-stack ptr)))

(define decrement-ptr
  (lambda (ptr n)
    (- ptr n)))

(define extract
  (lambda (ptr n receiver)
    (letrec
      ((loop (lambda (k)
               (let ((next (decrement-ptr ptr k)))
                 (if (> k n)
                     (list next)
                     (cons (stack-ref next) (loop (+ 1 k))))))))
      (apply receiver (loop 1)))))
```

Figure 10.4.2   Top-level interpretation procedures

```
(define eval-exp/stack
  (lambda (exp)
    (variant-case exp
      (lit (datum) (apply-valcont/stack datum dummy))
      (varref (var) (apply-env/stack env-reg var))
      (proc (formals body) (apply-valcont/stack exp env-reg))
      (app (rator rands)
        (make-proc-valcont! rands env-reg)
        (eval-exp/stack rator))
      (else (error "Invalid abstract syntax:" exp)))))

(define eval-rands/stack
  (lambda (rands)
    (if (null? rands)
        (apply-proc/stack)
        (begin
          (make-first-valcont! rands env-reg)
          (eval-exp/stack (car rands))))))
```

A typical stack segment, pushed by calling *make-tag-cont!* with components *val-1 ... val-n,* has the form

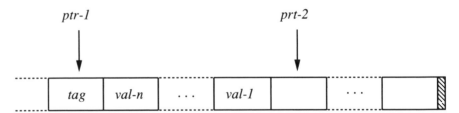

where *ptr-1* and *ptr-2* are pointers delimiting the segment. (The top of the stack is to the left.)

It will be useful to have a procedure, *extract*, that retrieves the values in a stack segment and also returns a pointer to the stack location immediately past the segment; see figure 10.4.1. In the above example, the call (*extract ptr-1 n receiver*) will result in the procedure *receiver* being called with arguments *val-n ... val-1* and *ptr-2.* Using *extract*, it is easy to code *apply-valcont/stack.* See figure 10.4.4.

Figure 10.4.3   Constructors for stack interpreter continuations

```
(define make-rest-argcont!
  (lambda (first first-env)
    (push! first-env)
    (push! first)
    (push! '*rest)))

(define make-all-argcont!
  (lambda (proc proc-env)
    (push! proc-env)
    (push! proc)
    (push! '*all)))

(define make-final-valcont!
  (lambda ()
    (init-stack!)
    (push! '*final)))

(define make-first-valcont!
  (lambda (rands env)
    (push! env)
    (push! rands)
    (push! '*first)))

(define make-proc-valcont!
  (lambda (rands env)
    (push! env)
    (push! rands)
    (push! '*proc)))
```

○ *Exercise 10.4.1*
The procedure *extract* is called with *n* being 1, 2, or 3. Rewrite *extract* so that it does not use *cons* or *apply*, and thus avoid the use of heap space. □

We also have to modify *apply-env* because it deals with the internal representation of argument continuations. The argument continuation *ak* is now a stack pointer. We modify the procedure *apply-env* of figure 10.3.8 to search in the stack and rename it *apply-env/stack*. See figure 10.4.5.

We next modify the procedure *apply-proc* to obtain *apply-proc/stack*. Before doing that, however, we first consider the structure of the stack at the time this procedure is called. The stack is pictured below, where it is assumed

Figure 10.4.4   `apply-valcont/stack` (first version)

```
(define apply-valcont/stack
  (lambda (val env-or-dummy)
    (case (stack-ref top-ptr)
      ((*final)
       (if (eq? env-or-dummy dummy)
           val
           '<Procedure>))
      ((*first)
       (extract top-ptr 2
         (lambda (rands env ak)
           (pop-to-ptr! ak)
           (make-rest-argcont! val env-or-dummy)
           (set! env-reg env)
           (eval-rands/stack (cdr rands)))))
      ((*proc)
       (extract top-ptr 2
         (lambda (rands env vk)
           (pop-to-ptr! vk)
           (make-all-argcont! val env-or-dummy)
           (set! env-reg env)
           (eval-rands/stack rands)))))))
```

the called procedure is being passed n arguments, $v_1, \ldots, v_n$ and $e_1, \ldots, e_n$ represent the argument values and argument environment-or-dummy elements, respectively, *proc* is the procedure being called, and *env* is the associated environment if the procedure is a closure, or a dummy value if it is a primitive.

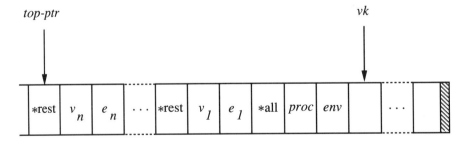

First we naively transform `apply-proc` of figure 10.3.7 to imperative form. If a primitive procedure is being called, `apply-proc/stack` extracts the argument values from the stack and calls the procedure with these values. The

Figure 10.4.5   *apply-env/stack*

```
(define apply-env/stack
  (lambda (env var)
    (variant-case env
      (initial-env ()
        (apply-valcont/stack (init-env var) dummy))
      (extended-env (formals ak env)
        (if (memq var formals)
            (letrec
              ((loop (lambda (formals ak)
                       (case (stack-ref ak)
                         ((*rest)
                          (extract ak 2
                            (lambda (val env-or-dummy ak)
                              (if (eq? var (car formals))
                                  (apply-valcont/stack val
                                    env-or-dummy)
                                  (loop (cdr formals) ak)))))
                         (else (error "Invalid tag:" ak))))))
              (loop (reverse formals) ak))
            (apply-env/stack env var))))))
```

answer that is returned must be passed to the value continuation, *vk*, that is just below the *all continuation. This requires that the stack be popped until *vk* becomes the top of the stack before *apply-valcont/stack* is called. See figure 10.4.4 for our initial version of *apply-valcont/stack* and figure 10.4.7 for a new version of *find-all-argcont* that searches for *all down the stack and passes its receiver the values immediately to its right indicated by *proc, env,* and *vk* in the diagram above.

If the procedure being called is a closure, an extended environment is created that contains a reference to the argument continuation, which is the current top of the stack. The body of the called procedure is then evaluated in this environment by a call to *eval-exp/stack*; however, this procedure is expecting a value continuation, not an argument continuation, to be on the top of the stack. The value continuation *vk* that is just below the *all continuation is waiting to receive the value of the procedure call, so we are tempted to pass *vk* to *pop-to-ptr!* before calling *eval-exp/stack*, as in figure 10.4.6, but this does not work. The environment used when evaluating the body refers to the procedure's arguments via a pointer to the *rest con-

Figure 10.4.6 *apply-proc/stack* (first version)

```
(define apply-proc/stack
  (lambda ()
    (find-all-argcont top-ptr
      (lambda (proc proc-env vk)
        (variant-case proc
          (prim-1 (unary-op)
            (let ((ans (unary-op (unary-arg top-ptr))))
              (pop-to-ptr! vk)
              (apply-valcont/stack ans dummy)))
          (prim-2 (binary-op)
            (let ((ans (binary-op
                         (binary-arg-1 top-ptr)
                         (binary-arg-2 top-ptr))))
              (pop-to-ptr! vk)
              (apply-valcont/stack ans dummy)))
          (proc (formals body)
            (let ((ak top-ptr))
              (pop-to-ptr! vk)
              (set! env-reg (extend-env formals ak proc-env))
              (eval-exp/stack body)))
          (else (error "Invalid primitive operation:" proc)))))))
```

Figure 10.4.7 *find-all-argcont*

```
(define find-all-argcont
  (lambda (ptr receiver)
    (case (stack-ref ptr)
      ((*all) (extract ptr 2 receiver))
      ((*rest)
       (extract ptr 2
         (lambda (ignored ignored-env-or-dummy ak)
           (find-all-argcont ak receiver)))))))
```

tinuation that was on the top of the stack at the time that `apply-proc/stack` was called. When that evaluation of the body begins, however, the top of the stack is below the `*all` continuation. We may picture the environment and continuation at the time evaluation of the body begins as follows.

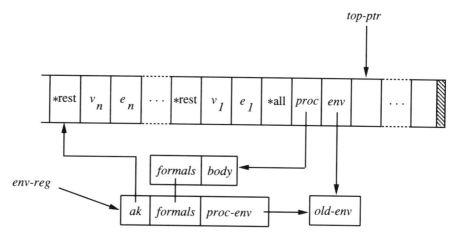

In the course of the body's evaluation, other values will likely be pushed on the stack, overwriting the procedure's arguments. The environment is said to contain a *dangling pointer*: a pointer into an invalid region of the stack (above the top of the stack or below its bottom).

This problem may be solved by pushing a new value continuation on the top, rather than popping the stack to an existing value continuation. We call this a *return value* continuation, since it is applied when a closure returns. See figure 10.4.8. When applied, a return value continuation pops the stack to the value continuation just below the `*all` continuation that referred to the returning procedure.

How else could dangling pointers arise? The only time that dangling pointers can be created is when we pop the stack. The problem with our first version of `apply-proc/stack` was that we popped the stack on procedure entry, thus losing the arguments. Now we have arranged things so that the stack is not popped on procedure entry but only on procedure exit. So to avoid dangling pointers, we must ensure that after a procedure returns, there will be no further references to its arguments. This can most easily be arranged by not allowing procedures to return closures or store closures in data structures. Such a returned (or stored) closure is called an *upward funarg* ("funarg" abbreviates "functional argument"). To enforce our "no upward funarg" rule, we insert a run-time check in `apply-valcont/stack` to ensure that closures are never returned. See figure 10.4.9.

- *Exercise 10.4.2*

Checking to see if a closure is being returned as in figure 10.4.9 is more restrictive than is necessary. A less restrictive test to avoid a dangling pointer

Figure 10.4.8   `apply-proc/stack` with return value continuations

```
(define apply-proc/stack
  (lambda ()
    (find-all-argcont top-ptr
      (lambda (proc proc-env vk)
        (variant-case proc
          (prim-1 (unary-op)
            (let ((ans (unary-op (unary-arg top-ptr))))
              (pop-to-ptr! vk)
              (apply-valcont/stack ans dummy)))
          (prim-2 (binary-op)
            (let ((ans (binary-op
                          (binary-arg-1 top-ptr)
                          (binary-arg-2 top-ptr))))
              (pop-to-ptr! vk)
              (apply-valcont/stack ans dummy)))
          (proc (formals body)
            (let ((ak top-ptr))
              (make-return-valcont! vk)
              (set! env-reg (extend-env formals ak proc-env))
              (eval-exp/stack body)))
          (else (error "Invalid primitive operation:" proc)))))))

(define make-return-valcont!
  (lambda (vk)
    (push! vk)
    (push! '*return)))
```

is to compare the environment pointer of the procedure with the appropriate value continuation pointer. Although this is less restrictive, language designers have avoided this test because it is more difficult to enforce using grammar rules and leads to costly run-time checks. Implement `apply-valcont/stack` using this less restrictive check and test it by passing `map` a higher-order procedure. □

Our interpreter now uses the heap only for allocating environments. We conclude by putting the environment on the stack as well. Environments are formed when closures are called. We have just seen that return value continuations are placed on the stack at this time. Thus if environments are to be put on the stack, it is natural to include them in *return continuations.

Figure 10.4.9 `apply-valcont/stack` (second version)

```
(define apply-valcont/stack
  (lambda (val env-or-dummy)
    (case (stack-ref top-ptr)
      ((*final)
       (if (eq? env-or-dummy dummy)
           val
           '<Procedure>))
      ((*first)
       (extract top-ptr 2
         (lambda (rands env ak)
           (pop-to-ptr! ak)
           (make-rest-argcont! val env-or-dummy)
           (set! env-reg env)
           (eval-rands/stack (cdr rands)))))
      ((*proc)
       (extract top-ptr 2
         (lambda (rands env vk)
           (pop-to-ptr! vk)
           (make-all-argcont! val env-or-dummy)
           (set! env-reg env)
           (eval-rands/stack rands))))
      ((*return)
       (if (eq? env-or-dummy dummy)
           (extract top-ptr 1
             (lambda (vk ak)
               (pop-to-ptr! vk)
               (apply-valcont/stack val env-or-dummy)))
           (error "Can't return procedures"))))))
```

To include an environment in a *return continuation, it is only necessary to record the formals list and old environment. It is not necessary to include the argument list, since it is already represented in the continuation.

```
(define make-return-valcont!
  (lambda (vk env formals)
    (push! formals)
    (push! env)
    (push! vk)
    (push! '*return)))
```

The corresponding *return case in `apply-valcont/stack` follows.

```
((*return)
 (if (eq? env-or-dummy dummy)
     (extract top-ptr 3
       (lambda (vk proc-env-ignored formals-ignored ak)
         (pop-to-ptr! vk)
         (apply-valcont/stack val env-or-dummy)))
     (error "Can't return procedures:" val)))
```

In this representation, environments, like continuations, are represented by stack pointers. When we build the return value continuation, we just push the formals and the saved environment on the stack. The extended environment is now represented by a pointer to the top of the stack. The initial environment may be represented by an illegal stack pointer; we use the integer -1. The code for `apply-env/stack` is similar to that of figure 10.4.5, except that we now test for the initial environment in a different way, and we extract the pieces of an extended environment differently. The code that searches a given contour remains the same. See figure 10.4.10.

The stack architecture we have derived is representative of the techniques that are often used in the implementation of typical block-structured programming languages. The portion of the stack containing the argument and return value continuations of a given call is called the *stack frame* or *activation record* of the call. A stack frame typically includes (1) arguments of the call, (2) a pointer to the next stack frame below on the stack, termed the *dynamic link*, and represented by the `vk` element of our return value continuations, and (3) a link to the environment at the surrounding lexical level, termed the *static link*, and represented by the `env` element of our return value continuations.

We now show a trace of a small program that utilizes all the concepts we have been discussing. The program is

```
let x = 89
in let f = proc (g) g(72)
   in f(proc (y) +(x, y))
```

which is equivalent to

```
(proc (x)
  (proc (f) f(proc (y) +(x, y)))
  (proc (g) g(72)))
(89)
```

Figure 10.4.10   Procedures for stack-allocated environments

```
(define apply-proc/stack
  (lambda ()
    (find-all-argcont top-ptr
      (lambda (proc proc-env vk)
        (variant-case proc
          (prim-1 (unary-op)
            (let ((ans (unary-op (unary-arg top-ptr))))
              (pop-to-ptr! vk)
              (apply-valcont/stack ans dummy)))
          (prim-2 (binary-op)
            (let ((ans (binary-op (binary-arg-1 top-ptr) (binary-arg-2 top-ptr))))
              (pop-to-ptr! vk)
              (apply-valcont/stack ans dummy)))
          (proc (formals body)
            (make-return-valcont! vk proc-env formals)
            (set! env-reg top-ptr)
            (eval-exp/stack body))
          (else (error "Invalid primitive operation:" proc)))))))

(define apply-env/stack
  (lambda (env var)
    (if (= env -1)
        (apply-valcont/stack (init-env var) dummy)
        (case (stack-ref env)
          ((*return)
           (extract env 3
             (lambda (ignored-vk env formals ak)
               (if (memq var formals)
                   (letrec
                     ((loop (lambda (formals ak)
                              (case (stack-ref ak)
                                ((*rest)
                                 (extract ak 2
                                   (lambda (val env-or-dummy ak)
                                     (if (eq? var (car formals))
                                         (apply-valcont/stack val env-or-dummy)
                                         (loop (cdr formals) ak)))))
                                (else (error "Invalid continuation"))))))
                     (loop (reverse formals) ak))
                   (apply-env/stack env var)))))
          (else (error "Invalid environment:" env))))))
```

and its trace is found in figure 10.4.11. In the trace, the numbers on the left are stack references. Each snapshot is concerned with what positions on the stack have changed. Stack pointers are preceded by an indicator of its type: E for environment, S for static link, D for dynamic link, and A for argument list. With the exception of the final value continuation, each tag is formed by concatenating * to the first letter of each part of the hyphenated continuation name. So, rest-argcont becomes *ra, etc. Since each procedure uses a different formal parameter list, the procedure can be identified by just referring to #(proc formals ..). Primitives are expressed by naming the primitive with a tag that indicates its arity. Operands and formal parameters are enclosed in parentheses. Lines beginning with ==> contain the four important locations that are used in apply-proc/stack.

In figure 10.4.12 we present the state of the stack at line 30-21 of figure 10.4.11. This demonstrates that static links from two activation records can reference the same location, whereas dynamic links always reference different locations. The boldface boxes that contain three items of information can be conceptually thought of as one box, so that pointers to 20, 19, and 18 can be treated as a pointer to location 20. When this is done, we can say that the static links are a subset of the dynamic links. For example, there is a dynamic link, but not a static link, that references location 20.

We have succeeded in freeing our interpreter from reliance on the heap by using stack allocation, but this has come at substantial cost. We have given up two desirable features: upwards funargs (but see exercise 10.4.2) and tail recursion.

In order to deallocate the stack safely on procedure exit, we introduced a restriction on the interpreted language: it no longer allows procedures to be returned as values from other procedures or to be stored in heap-allocated data structures. This restriction explains why most programming languages do not allow upward funargs: language designers typically assume implementors will insist on using stack-allocated environments. Of course, Scheme allows upward funargs, so environments cannot always be stack allocated in Scheme. Procedures that are passed to other procedures as arguments, termed *downward funargs*, do not pose this problem. Downward funargs must be represented as closures, but their environments may be stack allocated.

We have derived an interpreter for a language with the no-upward-funarg rule, for this rule is the norm in contemporary languages. This restriction is often unfortunate, however. We have shown many examples of the power of upward funargs, but their uses extend well beyond these. Of course, heap allocation of environments is one way of avoiding restrictions on upward funargs. We explore others in the exercises.

Figure 10.4.11   Stack trace

```
0-0: *final-v
3-1: *pv (89) E-1
3-1: *aa #(proc (x) ..) E-1
6-4: *fv (89) E-1
6-4: *ra 89 dummy
==> #(proc (x) ..) E-1 A6 D0
8-7: S-1 (x)
10-9: *rv D0
13-11: *pv (#(proc (g) ..)) E8
13-11: *aa #(proc (f) ..) E8
16-14: *fv (#(proc (g) ..)) E8
16-14: *ra #(proc (g) ..) E8
==> #(proc (f) ..) E8 A16 D10
18-17: S8 (f)
20-19: *rv D10
23-21: *pv (#(proc (y) ..)) E18
23-21: *aa #(proc (g) ..) E8
26-24: *fv (#(proc (y) ..)) E18
26-24: *ra #(proc (y) ..) E18
==> #(proc (g) ..) E8 A26 D20
28-27: S8 (g)
30-29: *rv D20
33-31: *pv (72) E28
33-31: *aa #(proc (y) ..) E18
36-34: *fv (72) E28
36-34: *ra 72 dummy
==> #(proc (y) ..) E18 A36 D30
38-37: S18 (y)
40-39: *rv D30
43-41: *pv (x y) E38
43-41: *aa #(prim-2 -) dummy
46-44: *fv (x y) E38
46-44: *ra 89 dummy
49-47: *fv (y) E38
49-47: *ra 72 dummy
==> #(prim-2 +) dummy A49 D40
40-31: *rv D30 S18 (y) *ra 72 dummy *aa #(proc (y) ..) E18
30-21: *rv D20 S8 (g) *ra #(proc (y) ..) E18 *aa #(proc (g) ..) E8
20-11: *rv D10 S8 (f) *ra #(proc (g) ..) E8 *aa #(proc (f) ..) E8
10-1: *rv D0 S-1 (x) *ra 89 dummy *aa #(proc (x) ..) E-1
0-0: *final-v
161
```

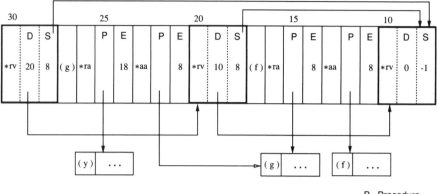

Figure 10.4.12   Static and dynamic links

Besides the exclusion of upward funargs, we have paid another price for the allocation of argument lists on the control stack: our interpreter is no longer properly tail recursive. Each time a procedure is called, even when the call is in tail position, the control stack is extended by pushing a return value continuation. Thus tail-form programs no longer exhibit iterative control behavior. We saw in chapter 8 that this is a major disadvantage. As in the case of upward funargs, there are strategies for recovering proper tail recursion when argument lists are stack allocated, though at present they are not widely used. See, for example, exercise 10.4.11.

- *Exercise 10.4.3*
  Add if, let, begin, and := to this interpreter. ☐

- *Exercise 10.4.4*
  Add letrecproc to the language using environments, as developed in section 5.6. ☐

- *Exercise 10.4.5*

Using the results of the previous two exercises, solidify your understanding of how dynamic and static links work by drawing the stack diagrams for the evaluation of the following expression.

```
letrecproc p(f, g, n) =
  if zero(n)
     then f(0)
     else let t = if even(n)
                    then proc (x) f(+(x, n))
                    else proc (x) g(+(x, n))
             in p(t, g, -(n, 1))
  in p(proc (x) x, proc (x) x, 4)
▯
```

- *Exercise 10.4.6*

Finish the imperative transformation on the last interpreter of this section, so that all procedures communicate via registers, including `find-all-argcont`. ▯

○ *Exercise 10.4.7*

The argument continuation tags now serve only to allow the interpreter to search through and locate the end of an argument list. Eliminate this search in the definition of `apply-argcont` by including additional information about the total number of stack locations occupied by the arguments. Also eliminate the argument continuation tags. ▯

○ *Exercise 10.4.8*

Avoid the linear search for the `*all` continuation by maintaining a register (sometimes called the *base pointer*) containing a pointer to its location in the stack. ▯

○ *Exercise 10.4.9*

Is it possible to move the argument continuations to the stack without moving the value continuations to the stack at the same time, or to move the value continuations without moving the argument continuations? ▯

○ *Exercise 10.4.10*

Avoid reversing the formals list by searching upward in the stack, starting with the `*all` continuation. ▯

○ *Exercise 10.4.11*

It can be determined statically, that is, by analysis of program text, whether a call is in tail position. When evaluation of such a tail call begins, there will be a return value continuation for the currently executing procedure on top of the control stack. The argument continuations for the tail call will be placed on top of this return value continuation. Since control need not return to the procedure making the call, its arguments are no longer necessary. This allows the control stack to be collapsed prior to the call by copying its argument list and *return continuation down over the locations previously occupied by the argument list and *return continuation of the procedure making the call. Thus as the result of a tail call one argument list and return value continuation is created and one is destroyed, so there is no net growth in the number of return value continuations. This technique is called *tail call optimization.* (Compilers may refine this technique so that in specific instances the number of stack elements that need to be copied is reduced, or it may even be possible to eliminate copying altogether.)

Modify our interpreter to perform tail call optimization. □

○ *Exercise 10.4.12*

When accessing a nonlocal variable binding (one with a lexical depth greater than zero), one static link is traversed for every level of lexical depth. An alternate representation of closures allows variable references to be performed in constant time and also allows upward funargs to be supported while argument lists are stack allocated. With this representation, a closure is a vector containing, in addition to the procedure, the bindings of all its free variables. Bindings that are assignable (with varassign) must be represented by cells that are shared by any closures that close over them. In this way static links are avoided. Compiled code can access a nonlocal (free) variable binding by indexing into the closure's vector using an offset computed at compile time. This makes access to nonlocal variables more efficient, at the expense of less efficient closure creation.

Modify our interpreter to use this closure representation. You will first need to write a procedure to compute the free variables of a procedure. You may also need to store variable binding names as well as their values. □

○ *Exercise 10.4.13*

Another approach to achieving constant time variable access is to use a *display*. The idea is to collect all of the static links associated with the current environment and store them in a vector. If the lexical depth of variable references is precomputed, it is then possible to access the appropriate environment contour in constant time. Since there is only one global display, it is in general necessary to update the display when a procedure is called and to restore its previous state when the procedure returns. Thus increased efficiency of nonlocal variable access is obtained at the expense of decreased procedure call efficiency. Since most program variables typically have a low lexical depth, this tradeoff is seldom favorable, but it is still useful at times. (Also, displays do not solve the upward funarg problem as closure-vectors do, since the environment contours remain stack allocated.)

Modify our interpreter to use a display. □

○ *Exercise 10.4.14*

Another way to solve the no-upward-funarg problem is to convert the source program to continuation-passing style. Then the only procedure that ever "returns" is the final value continuation. What is wrong with this solution? □

○ *Exercise 10.4.15*

Just as stack allocation of environments makes it more difficult to implement upward funargs, so stack allocation of continuations makes it more difficult to implement first-class continuations, such as those provided by `callcc` of section 9.3. When control information has been captured in a first-class continuation, it is essential that it not be lost due to popping of the control stack (at least as long as the first-class continuation is accessible). A brute-force solution is to copy the entire control stack into a heap-allocated structure whenever a first-class continuation is created. This approach is acceptable only when first-class continuations are infrequently created, however, refinements of this technique allow first-class continuations to be supported along with stack allocation of control information with only a very small performance penalty.

Modify an interpreter with stack allocated continuations to support `callcc`. □

10.5 Summary

A program in first-order tail form can be converted easily to iterative form, in which binding is replaced by variable assignment and a procedure call is a tail call of no arguments, which is effectively a jump. Therefore a program in first-order tail form is effectively a flowchart.

If the transformation to iterative form is applied to a program obtained by converting to continuation-passing style, the continuations can be stack-allocated, rather than heap-allocated.

If this transformation is applied to an interpreter that does not support first-class continuations, then continuations can be represented using a stack, but environments are still allocated from the heap. By further transformations, the environment can also be allocated on the stack. This greatly simplifies storage management for the interpreter, at the expense of losing procedures as first-class values and of losing the proper implementation of tail-recursion. Common imperative languages have traditionally used this design strategy.

11   Scanners and Parsers

Humans generate programs as strings of characters, using rules of concrete syntax. Interpreters and compilers cannot attach meaning to programs until their characters are grouped into meaningful units. For clarity and efficiency this analysis is divided into two parts: scanning and parsing.

Scanning is the process of analyzing a sequence of characters into larger units, called *lexical items, lexemes,* or *tokens*. This process is sometimes called *lexical* scanning. Typical tokens are variables, keywords, numbers, punctuation, whitespace, and comments. The output of a scanner is a sequence of tokens. These are represented using a convenient data structure, so that later processing stages do not have to deal with the details of character codes and the like. Thus, scanning creates a token sequence that abstracts a character sequence by removing unnecessary details.

Parsing organizes a sequence of tokens into syntactic elements such as expressions, statements, and blocks. These are generally specified using BNF or some equivalent formalism. The syntactic elements are typically nested, so the output of a parser is usually called a *parse tree* or *abstract syntax tree,* and they provide convenient access to the syntactic components of a program.

11.1 Lexical Scanning Using Finite Automata

In every language, part of the design is the specification of the lexical structure of the language. Typical pieces of such a specification might be:

- Any sequence of spaces and newlines is equivalent to a single space.

- A comment begins with % and continues until the end of the line.

- An identifier is a sequence of letters and digits starting with a letter, and a variable is an identifier that is not a keyword.

These specifications serve to define the lexical items or tokens of the language. A scanner analyzes a sequence of characters and returns a sequence of corresponding tokens. One could take a specification of the tokens, such as that given above, and write from scratch a program to do scanning. Such an approach is error prone, however, and it is difficult to modify the scanner if the specification changes.

A better approach is to introduce a formal model for the specification of tokens. We can then implement this model in various ways. In this section we introduce finite automata as a model for scanning. We then show how to implement this model using a few higher-order procedures that abstract the basic actions of a scanner.

We can specify tokens in a formal way using *finite automata*, also known as *finite state machines*. A finite automaton is a machine that takes a sequence of characters and produces a result in the following way: At any given moment, a finite automaton is in one of a finite number of *states*. At each step of operation, the automaton takes a character from the sequence. Based on this character and the current state, it may do one of two things: *halt*, producing a result, or *move to a new state*, becoming ready to consume more of the sequence. These actions are sometimes called *transitions*.

A finite automaton is specified by giving a *start state,* in which it begins to process the character sequence, and a *transition function* that specifies the next state or halts with a result for various possible combinations of character and current state. As an illustration, the table in figure 11.1.1 indicates the transition function of a finite automaton with start state `start-state`. It formally specifies the identifier, comment, and whitespace tokens previously defined.

Another method of representing a transition function is to draw a graph. The nodes of the graph represent the various states and the edges the possible transitions between states. The edges are directed so that they connect each state with the possible next states. Each edge is labeled with the characters that affect the transition. See figure 11.1.2 for a graph corresponding to the above table.

Initially the automaton is in state `start-state`. Based on the first character, it enters `identifier-state`, `whitespace-state`, or `comment-state`, depending on whether the character is the beginning of an identifier, whitespace, or comment. The automaton continues in that state, collecting the characters in the token until it sees the first character that is *not* in the token at which point it halts. This signifies completion of the token.

State	Character	Next State	Result
start-state	any letter	identifier-state	
start-state	space or newline	whitespace-state	
start-state	%	comment-state	
start-state	anything else		error
identifier-state	any letter or digit	identifier-state	
identifier-state	anything else		identifier
whitespace-state	space or newline	whitespace-state	
whitespace-state	anything else		whitespace
comment-state	any except newline	comment-state	
comment-state	newline		comment

Figure 11.1.1   Finite automaton table for a scanner

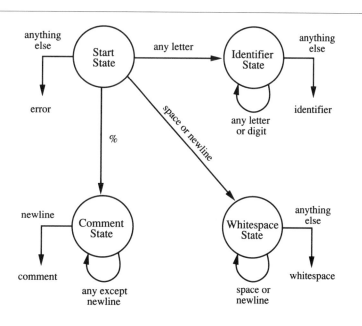

Figure 11.1.2   Finite automaton diagram for a scanner

For example, consider the action of the automaton on `foo3(bar)`.

State:	`start-state`
Character:	`f`
State:	`identifier-state`
Character:	`o`
State:	`identifier-state`
Character:	`o`
State:	`identifier-state`
Character:	`3`
State:	`identifier-state`
Character:	`(`
Result:	`identifier`

When the automaton sees the left parenthesis, it concludes that the current token is finished and returns `identifier`, signifying that an identifier has been found.

Of course, to make this into a useful language-processing tool, we need to add some additional features to our automaton. Not only should it return the symbol `identifier`, but it should report which identifier was found. To do this, we equip our automaton with a buffer in which it can collect the characters as they are seen. Furthermore, we also need to make sure that the terminating character (the left parenthesis in our example) is not lost, since it is part of the next token. We shall see how to accomplish these tasks in the next section.

11.2 Simulating a Scanning Automaton

We would like to write programs that model the behavior of such automata. Since an automaton finds only the first token, if we wish to find all the tokens, the automaton can be called repeatedly. We shall see how to do this later. Our goal, of course, is not to build a program corresponding only to the automaton we sketched but to be able to build any program of this sort. We therefore create a general design and some standard components from which such programs can be built. Using the power of functional abstraction, we represent the components of our automata as procedures.

At each state, the automaton looks at the next character and decides what action to perform. Thus we define *scanner states* to be procedures that take a character as an argument and return a scanner action. These actions correspond to the transitions, or edges, in a finite automaton.

A common scanner action is to shift a character from the sequence to the buffer of characters that have been scanned as part of a token. This suggests that scanner actions be procedures that take two arguments: a buffer and a character sequence. When the scanner detects the end of a token, it returns the token and the character sequence. Thus we define *scanner actions* to be procedures that take a buffer and a character sequence and return a token and character sequence.

When a shift action is performed, it is not known whether the current token is complete. Thus the next action is passed a new buffer, formed by adding the character at the head of the character sequence to the old buffer, and the tail of the character sequence. We express this with the `shift` procedure of figure 11.2.1, which is passed an action and returns another action. For example, (`shift` *action*) returns an action that takes the first character from a sequence, places it in a buffer, and then runs *action* on the remaining character sequence and extended buffer.

Assuming sequences are represented as lists, the behavior of the `shift` procedure may be illustrated by this equation:

```
      ((shift action) buffer           '(a b ...))
⇒  (action           (cons 'a buffer)  '(b ...))
```

Here is a slightly longer example:

```
      ((shift (shift (shift action))) '() '(a b c d ...))
⇒  ((shift (shift action))            '(a)   '(b c d ...))
⇒  ((shift action)                    '(b a) '(c d ...))
⇒  (action                            '(c b a) '(d ...))
```

In this example we see how elementary actions can be strung together to make complex actions, and how the behavior of the program mimics that of a machine with two registers. We also note that the characters are accumulated in the buffer in reverse order.

We have used `char-seq-head` and `char-seq-tail` instead of `car` and `cdr` so that we may represent a sequence of characters in some way other than as a list. We shall see later how this might be useful.

A second type of scanner action is to drop the first character of the sequence. This is useful, for example, when the first character is a whitespace or comment character. We express this with the procedure *drop* of figure 11.2.1. Like *shift*, *drop* is really an action maker, since it takes an action and returns an action.

Figure 11.2.1   Scanner actions

```
(define shift
  (lambda (next-action)
    (lambda (buffer char-seq)
      (next-action
        (cons (char-seq-head char-seq) buffer)
        (char-seq-tail char-seq)))))

(define drop
  (lambda (next-action)
    (lambda (buffer char-seq)
      (next-action buffer (char-seq-tail char-seq)))))

(define goto-scanner-state
  (lambda (state)
    (lambda (buffer char-seq)
      (let ((next-action (state (char-seq-head char-seq))))
        (next-action buffer char-seq)))))

(define-record scanner-answer (token unscanned))

(define emit
  (lambda (cooker)
    (lambda (buffer char-seq)
      (make-scanner-answer
        (cooker (reverse buffer))
        char-seq))))
```

The equational picture for *drop* is

$$((\text{drop } action) \; buffer \; '(\text{a b } \ldots))$$
$$\Rightarrow (action \qquad buffer \qquad '(\text{b } \ldots))$$

Thus we might compute as follows:

$$((\text{drop (drop (shift } action))) \; '() \; '(\text{a b c d } \ldots))$$
$$\Rightarrow ((\text{drop (shift } action)) \qquad '() \qquad '(\text{b c d } \ldots))$$
$$\Rightarrow ((\text{shift } action) \qquad '() \qquad '(\text{c d } \ldots))$$
$$\Rightarrow (action \qquad '(\text{c}) \qquad '(\text{d } \ldots))$$

Next we address the control behavior of our machine. To do this, let us reconsider the notion of a *state* of a finite state machine. We described the behavior of our machine as a transition function that took as inputs a state and a character and produced as output the action to be performed. If we curry this function, we get for each state a function from characters to actions. Therefore, in our simulation we model a state as a procedure that takes an input character and returns an action.

To invoke a state, we introduce the procedure *goto-scanner-state* (see figure 11.2.1), which takes a state and returns an action. Executing (goto-scanner-state *state*) applies *state* to the first character to find the next action to execute and then invokes this action on the current buffer and character sequence. The effect is to go to the given state. A typical action might be expressed by

```
(drop (drop (shift (goto-scanner-state state))))
```

Our machine finishes when the next character is not part of the current token. The current buffer is then passed to a procedure that builds a convenient data structure representing the token. We call such a procedure a *cooker* because it "cooks" the raw characters into a token. The buffer is reversed before being passed to the cooker, so that it sees the characters in their original order. The new token is then returned along with the sequence of unprocessed characters. We use a record type to return these two values. See the definition of *emit* in figure 11.2.1. Note that *char-seq* is returned as is, so that the first character in the sequence can become the first character of the next token.

Before writing cookers, we must be specific about the representation of tokens. We often need only a small amount of information about a token, such as "this token is an identifier," "this token is an assignment symbol," or "this token is a left parenthesis." We call this information the *class* of the token. For some classes of tokens we are also interested in additional information. For a variable we need to know which symbol represents the variable, and for a number we need to know what number is represented by the digits in the token. We call this additional information the *data* of the token. We therefore represent a token by a record containing its class (represented as a symbol) and its data.

The procedure *cook-punctuation* takes a symbol identifying a class and returns a cooker that ignores the buffer and produces a token of the indicated class. This is useful for parentheses, assignment symbols (:=), etc. See figure 11.2.2. The procedure *cook-number* converts the buffer to a number using the Scheme procedure *string->number*.

The procedure *cook-identifier* cooks potential program variables. We might simply record the list of characters already in the buffer as the data of

Figure 11.2.2   Cooking procedures for a scanner

```
(define-record token (class data))

(define cook-punctuation
  (lambda (class)
    (lambda (buffer)
      (make-token class '*))))

(define cook-number
  (lambda (buffer)
    (make-token 'number
      (string->number (list->string buffer)))))

(define cook-identifier
  (lambda (buffer)
    (let ((symbol (string->symbol (list->string buffer))))
      (if (memq symbol keywords-list)
          (make-token symbol '*)
          (make-token 'variable symbol)))))
```

identifier tokens, but then determining whether two identifiers were the same would be time consuming. Instead, we convert each buffer into a unique value that the rest of the language processor can easily handle.

In most language processors, this is done by building a *symbol table*: a database of all the identifiers appearing in a program. An identifier is represented by a reference to a record in this database (for example, a pointer to an entry in a hash table). Whenever an identifier appears, the scanner consults the database to see if the identifier is already there. If it is, a reference to its entry is returned. If not, a new entry is created, and a reference to the new entry is returned. Then it is easy for the rest of the language processor to determine if two identifiers are the same: it just compares the references. This is easier than comparing the strings. Also, the database allows a more sophisticated language processor to keep track of other attributes of an identifier, such as its type, internal representation, etc. For our interpreters, however, all we need is a quick way of testing identifiers for equality.

Scheme maintains its own symbol table, with one entry per symbol. Scheme represents these symbols internally as pointers into this table. The Scheme reader and the procedure *string->symbol* make or find entries in this table. Thus our scanner uses *string->symbol* instead of maintaining its own table.

When `cook-identifier` has obtained the symbol corresponding to the characters in the buffer, it checks whether this symbol is in a global list of keywords. If the symbol is a keyword, it produces a token using the keyword as its class (as `cook-punctuation` does); otherwise, it produces a `variable` token. Of course, this precludes using `number` or `variable` as a keyword.

Now we have enough machinery to write a sample automaton. See figure 11.2.3 and exercise 11.2.1. Each scanner state is a procedure that takes a character and returns an action. We have four states: one for the starting state, in which we have seen no characters, and one for each of the three major classes of tokens. In `scanner-identifier-state`, for example, the machine is accumulating an identifier token. So long as the next character is alphabetic or numeric, it shifts that character into the buffer. If it is any other character (either whitespace or a delimiter), it is not part of the current token, so the machine performs an (emit cook-identifier) action. The offending character remains at the head of the sequence to be processed later. We choose the character #\nul arbitrarily to represent some character, not in the character set of the language being scanned, to act as a character sequence terminator. Similarly, we use a token of class `end-marker` to act as a token sequence terminator. Since our automaton is built as a scanner state, we start it by using `goto-scanner-state`. See the procedure `scan-once` of figure 11.2.4. Here is a simple test:

```
> (define char-seq-head car)
> (define char-seq-tail cdr)
> (define keywords-list '())
> (define raw-data
    (append (string->list "abc is 652") (list #\nul)))
> (set! x (scan-once scanner-start-state raw-data))
> x
#(scanner-answer
  #(token variable abc)
  (#\space #\i #\s #\space #\6 #\5 #\2 #\nul))
> (set! x (scan-once scanner-start-state
               (scanner-answer->unscanned x)))
> x
#(scanner-answer
  #(token variable is)
  (#\space #\6 #\5 #\2 #\nul))
> (set! x (scan-once scanner-start-state
               (scanner-answer->unscanned x)))
> x
```

Figure 11.2.3   A scanner written in functional style

```scheme
(define scanner-start-state
  (lambda (c)
    (cond
      ((char-whitespace? c)
       (drop (goto-scanner-state scanner-start-state)))
      ((char-alphabetic? c)
       (shift (goto-scanner-state scanner-identifier-state)))
      ((char-numeric? c)
       (shift (goto-scanner-state scanner-number-state)))
      ((char=? c #\%)
       (drop (goto-scanner-state scanner-comment-state)))
      ((char=? c #\()
       (drop (emit (cook-punctuation 'lparen))))
      ((char=? c #\))
       (drop (emit (cook-punctuation 'rparen))))
      ((char=? c #\nul)
       (emit (cook-punctuation 'end-marker)))
      (else (scan-error c)))))

(define scanner-identifier-state
  (lambda (c)
    (cond
      ((char-alphabetic? c)
       (shift (goto-scanner-state scanner-identifier-state)))
      ((char-numeric? c)
       (shift (goto-scanner-state scanner-identifier-state)))
      (else (emit cook-identifier)))))

(define scanner-number-state
  (lambda (c)
    (cond
      ((char-numeric? c)
       (shift (goto-scanner-state scanner-number-state)))
      (else (emit cook-number)))))

(define scanner-comment-state
  (lambda (c)
    (cond
      ((char=? c #\newline)
       (drop (goto-scanner-state scanner-start-state)))
      (else (drop (goto-scanner-state scanner-comment-state)))))))
```

Figure 11.2.4   Procedures to drive a scanner

```
(define scan-once
  (lambda (start-state char-seq)
    ((goto-scanner-state start-state) '() char-seq)))

(define scan-char-seq
  (lambda (start-state char-seq)
    (let ((next-answer (scan-once start-state char-seq)))
      (variant-case next-answer
        (scanner-answer (token unscanned)
          (make-token-seq
            token
            (lambda ()
              (if (eq? (token->class token) 'end-marker)
                  '()
                  (scan-char-seq start-state unscanned)))))))))
```

```
#(scanner-answer
 #(token number 652)
 (#\nul))
> (set! x (scan-once scanner-start-state
            (scanner-answer->unscanned x)))
> x
#(scanner-answer
 #(token end-marker *)
 (#\nul))
```

Each call of *scan-once* returns the next token and the unscanned sequence
of characters. To obtain a sequence of all the tokens corresponding to a
sequence of characters, we use a loop that recognizes the end-marker token. See the procedure *scan-char-seq* of figure 11.2.4. Here we have used
make-token-seq to build the answer. The procedure *make-token-seq* takes
a thunk as its second argument. This allows for the possibility that the token
sequence may be represented as a stream rather than as an ordinary list. For
an ordinary list, we would simply use

```
(define make-token-seq
  (lambda (token thunk)
    (cons token (thunk))))
```

as we did in section 4.5.2. In this case we could repeat our test.

```
> (scan-char-seq scanner-start-state
    (append (string->list "abc is 652") (list #\nul)))
(#(token variable abc)
 #(token variable is)
 #(token number 652)
 #(token end-marker *))
```

This completes our scanner, but we have done more than write a single scanner. We have developed a set of components that may be used to assemble any scanner.

- *Exercise 11.2.1*
  Provide a suitable definition for the procedure *scan-error* used in figure 11.2.3. The procedure *scan-error* should return an action. ☐

- *Exercise 11.2.2*
  When building large programs, it is not good programming style to clutter up the global name space with names like `scanner-identifier-state` that do not need to be known globally. Rewrite the procedures in figure 11.2.3 using `letrec` to hide all the state names except for `scanner-start-state`. ☐

- *Exercise 11.2.3*
  Extend our grammar and scanner to allow numbers to have an optional sign and decimal point (with at least one digit required before the decimal point), such as 142, 12.3, -5., and +0.9876. ☐

- *Exercise 11.2.4*
  A string begins with a double quote and ends with the next double quote that is not immediately preceded by a backslash character (\). A double quote character preceded by a backslash is interpreted as a single double quote character in the string, and a sequence of two backslash characters is interpreted as a single backslash character. (The backslash is used here as an *escape* character. Other escape characters or sequences of escape characters are frequently used to indicate nonprinting characters, such as newline and tab.) Extend our grammar and scanner with the lexical class `string`, such as "ab cd" and

  ```
  "!? % ( \\
  )\"(
  % )"
  ```

  ☐

- *Exercise 11.2.5*

  Modify *scanner-start-state* so that it produces comments as tokens rather
  than dropping them. Represent the datum associated with a comment token
  as a string. □

○ *Exercise 11.2.6*

  In most programming languages, a number or identifier must be followed by a
  delimiter, such as whitespace, (,), or ". Thus the character sequence 108ifcar
  would produce a lexical error. (In most programming languages a number of
  other special characters, such as +, =, and :, are also delimiters.) This rule
  also clarifies why ab is a single identifier, ab, and not two identifiers, a and
  b. Modify *scanner-start-state* so that numbers and identifiers must be
  followed by a delimiter. □

We have used *char-seq-head* and *char-seq-tail* to manipulate character
sequences so that we have the option of representing them as something other
than lists. For example, we could store the characters of the initial character sequence in a globally bound string, called chars-to-scan, and represent
character sequences via a number that indexes a character of the string. The
characters that have yet to be scanned will be the indexed character and all
those that follow it in the string. For this representation we define

```
(define chars-to-scan '*)

(define char-seq-head
  (lambda (n)
    (string-ref chars-to-scan n)))

(define char-seq-tail
  (lambda (n)
    (+ n 1)))
```

We also must define *scan-string* so that the string it is passed is communicated to *char-seq-head* via *chars-to-scan*. This is one of the rare cases
where an assignment is appropriate in our programs.

```
(define scan-string
  (lambda (start-state char-string)
    (set! chars-to-scan
      (string-append char-string (string #\nul)))
    (scan-char-seq start-state 0)))
```

• *Exercise 11.2.7*

Modify the scanner so that its character and token sequences are represented as streams (cf. section 4.5.2). □

• *Exercise 11.2.8*

Using the techniques of this section, produce a scanner for the concrete syntax of the interpreted language as specified in appendix C. For the list of keywords, use

```
(if then else let in proc begin end letmutable letrecproc letrec
   during letdynamic letarray letproc method define definearray
   simpleclass simpleinstance class instance abort letcont callcc
   coroutine wind unwind within sum)
```

An answer to this exercise may be found in appendix E. □

○ *Exercise 11.2.9*

We have represented automaton states as procedures, with an entire automaton being represented by its start state. Another approach would be to

1. represent states as symbols, called *labels,*

2. define automata to be procedures that map labels to scanner actions,

3. define actions to be procedures whose arguments include an automaton, as well as a buffer and a character sequence, and

4. replace `goto-scanner-state` by `goto-label`, which takes an automaton and a label and applies the automaton to the label.

Implement a scanner corresponding to the automaton of figure 11.1.1 and figure 11.1.2 using this approach. □

○ *Exercise 11.2.10*

Make the buffer representation independent by adding the procedures `make-empty-buffer`, `buffer-extend`, and `buffer-contents` to the procedures in figure 11.2.1. Define these procedures using a global vector of bounded size. Also test the scanner with the procedures that follow. What are the advantages and disadvantages of the two representations? Why is it okay to use side-effecting procedures with the following representation?

```
(define make-empty-buffer
  (lambda ()
    (let ((c (cons '() '*)))
      (set-cdr! c c)
      c)))

(define buffer-contents car)

(define buffer-extend
  (lambda (value buffer)
    (let ((end-cell (cdr buffer))
          (new-cell (cons value '())))
      (set-cdr! end-cell new-cell)
      (if (eq? end-cell buffer)
          (set-car! buffer new-cell)
          (set-cdr! buffer new-cell))
      buffer)))
```

☐

11.3 Constructing a Predictive Parser

We now address the problem of parsing the sequence of tokens returned by a
scanner to obtain a parse tree. For each scanner or scanner/parser combination there is an associated set of character sequences that is accepted without
error. Sets that can be defined in this way by finite state automata are said
to be *regular*. Typically the set of character sequences that makes up a token
is regular, however, the set of token sequences that correspond to the programs in a language is seldom a regular set. Programs are typically members
of *context-free* sets defined by context-free grammars. Regular sets are also
context free, but many context-free sets are not regular.

The property that distinguishes context-free and regular sets, and hence
distinguishes parsing from scanning, is that context-free elements may be
nested to arbitrary depth. For example, expressions may typically contain
subexpressions, with no limit on the depth of nesting. It is possible, though
awkward, for scanners (finite state automata) to recognize nested structures if
there is a limit on the depth of nesting, but they cannot recognize structures
with arbitrarily deep nesting.

Although the BNF grammar of exercise 11.2.8 defines a regular set, in general, BNF grammars define context-free sets. A simple programming language might be described in BNF as follows:

⟨command⟩ ::= `begin` ⟨command⟩ ; ⟨command⟩ `end`
     | `while` ⟨expression⟩ `do` ⟨command⟩
     | `if` ⟨expression⟩ `then` ⟨command⟩ `else` ⟨command⟩
     | ⟨variable⟩ := ⟨expression⟩

⟨expression⟩ ::= ⟨variable⟩
     | ⟨constant⟩
     | (⟨expression⟩ + ⟨expression⟩)

The job of a parser is to take a sequence of tokens and analyze it to see if it fits the form specified by a grammar. Before implementing a parser for the grammar above, we specify its input and output. The input to the parser is a sequence of tokens, so the grammar we are really working with is

⟨command⟩ ::= `begin` ⟨command⟩ `semicolon` ⟨command⟩ `end`
     | `while` ⟨expression⟩ `do` ⟨command⟩
     | `if` ⟨expression⟩ `then` ⟨command⟩ `else` ⟨command⟩
     | ⟨variable⟩ `assign-sym` ⟨expression⟩

⟨expression⟩ ::= ⟨variable⟩
     | ⟨constant⟩
     | `lparen` ⟨expression⟩ `plus-sym` ⟨expression⟩ `rparen`

where `begin`, `end`, etc., are the token classes corresponding to the keywords and `semicolon`, `assign-sym`, `plus-sym`, `lparen`, and `rparen` are the token classes corresponding to the various special characters or character sequences appearing in the token sequence. We assume the scanner has removed comments and whitespace.

The result from the parser must do more than indicate whether the token sequence meets the specifications of the grammar. An interpreter or compiler needs to know which portions of the token sequence are associated with which elements of the grammar. This indicates *why* the string belongs to the language defined by the grammar. As we saw in chapter 3, this knowledge is conveyed by a *parse tree* or *abstract syntax tree*. We form parse trees using records, with a distinct record type associated with each production alternative of a grammar. For our sample grammar, we use the following record types.

```
(define-record compound-command (cmd1 cmd2))
(define-record while-command (exp cmd))
(define-record if-command (exp cmd1 cmd2))
(define-record assignment-command (variable-symbol exp))

(define-record var-expression (variable-symbol))
(define-record constant-expression (number))
(define-record sum-expression (exp1 exp2))
```

There is one type of parse tree for each kind of command and expression. As an example, the program

```
begin x := foo; while x do x := (x + bar) end
```

is represented by this tree

```
#(compound-command
  #(assignment-command x #(var-expression foo))
  #(while-command
    #(var-expression x)
    #(assignment-command x
      #(sum-expression #(var-expression x) #(var-expression bar)))))
```

Abstract syntax trees do not contain entries for tokens, such as keywords and semicolons, that carry no information. The interior nodes of the syntax tree correspond to productions, whereas its leaves correspond to information-carrying tokens, such as variables and numbers.

• *Exercise 11.3.1*
In the second assignment statement of the above syntax tree, why is the first occurrence of x represented by x, but the second by #(var-expression x)? □

In this section we illustrate one way of writing parsers by hand. We do this by extending the approach used in our scanner. Our scanner took a character sequence and returned a token and a sequence of those characters remaining after scanning the characters of the token. Our parser will take a token sequence and return a parse tree displaying the structure represented by an initial series of tokens and a sequence of the remaining tokens.

We use a strategy called *predictive parsing*: the action to be performed at each step is determined by a nonterminal to be matched and the first token of the sequence. We therefore introduce the notion of a *parser state*, analogous to a scanner state, that takes a token and returns a parser action. Each state looks at the first element of the token sequence, decides which production to use, and then tries to match some leading portion of the sequence against that production.

The main difference between a parser and a scanner is that when a parser goes from one state to the next, it is always possible to retain a record of the previous state, which a scanner (a finite state automaton) cannot do. This effectively allows parsers to enter states *recursively,* since a return to the previous state is possible when the work of the new state is finished. Thus there is no limit to the depth to which structures recognized by parsers may be nested.

At a given time a parser may have matched some initial elements, say B, C, and D, of some production, say A, with other elements of the production remaining to be matched. We picture this example as follows:

$$A \longrightarrow B \ C \ D \ \ ? \ \ldots$$

Parsing activity will be done by *parser actions* whose functionality is similar to that of scanner actions: they take a buffer and a token sequence and return a parse tree and a token sequence. The buffer contains information corresponding to the parts of the production that have already been matched (B, C, and D in our example). The two values returned by parser actions are represented using a new record type, `parser-answer`.

The action taken by a parser at a given point in matching a production depends on the next element of the production (? in our example). There are four possibilities, each of which corresponds to an action procedure defined in figure 11.3.1.

1. The next element in the production is a token without data, like a semi-colon. We need to check that the next item in the token sequence is indeed a semicolon, but we do not put the semicolon in the parse tree, because it carries no useful information. In general, we check that the next token is of the right class and then drop it. This job is performed by actions returned by the procedure *check/drop*. Once again we use a sequence ADT, including the procedures `token-seq-head` and `token-seq-tail`, to avoid committing to a particular representation of token sequences.

2. The next element in the production is a token with data, such as a variable. Again, we need to check that the next item in the token sequence is of the right class, but in this case, we need to shift its data into the buffer. This is done by actions that `check/shift` returns.

3. There are no more items in the production. In this case, we need to return a syntax tree for the production, along with the remainder of the token

Figure 11.3.1   Parser procedures

```
(define check/drop
  (lambda (class next-action)
    (lambda (buffer token-seq)
      (let ((token (token-seq-head token-seq)))
        (if (eq? (token->class token) class)
            (next-action buffer (token-seq-tail token-seq))
            (error "Syntax error: expecting a" class "not a" token))))))

(define check/shift
  (lambda (class next-action)
    (lambda (buffer token-seq)
      (let ((token (token-seq-head token-seq)))
        (if (eq? (token->class token) class)
            (next-action (cons (token->data token) buffer) (token-seq-tail token-seq))
            (error "Syntax error: expecting a" class "not a" token))))))

(define-record parser-answer (tree unparsed))

(define reduce
  (lambda (prod-name)
    (lambda (buffer token-seq)
      (make-parser-answer
        (apply (get-constructor-from-name prod-name) (reverse buffer))
        token-seq))))

(define goto-parser-state
  (lambda (state)
    (lambda (buffer token-seq)
      (let ((next-action (state (token-seq-head token-seq))))
        (next-action buffer token-seq)))))

(define process-nt
  (lambda (state next-action)
    (lambda (buffer token-seq)
      (let ((next-answer ((goto-parser-state state) '() token-seq)))
        (next-action (cons (parser-answer->tree next-answer) buffer)
          (parser-answer->unparsed next-answer))))))

(define emit-list
  (lambda ()
    (lambda (buffer token-seq)
      (make-parser-answer (reverse buffer) token-seq))))
```

sequence. For historical reasons this is called a *reduce* action, though it is similar to the `emit` action of our scanners. The syntax tree returned by a reduce action is a record whose type is associated with the production that has just been completed. This record will have a field associated with each element of information collected while parsing the production. The buffer contains precisely this information when the reduce action is performed, so all that is required is to apply the record construction procedure associated with the production to the buffer. The procedure *reduce* takes a production name and returns a parser answer record with a parse tree constructed in this way. It reverses the buffer, since the first value in the buffer contains the last piece of information provided by an element of the production. The procedure `get-constructor-from-name` is used to obtain the appropriate record-building procedure when given the production name. Although the procedures of figure 11.3.1 may be used in any parser constructed in this way, the procedure `get-constructor-from-name` is specific to each grammar, just as `keywords-list` is specific to each scanner. For our sample grammar we use

```
(define get-constructor-from-name
  (lambda (prod-name)
    (case prod-name
      ((compound-command) make-compound-command)
      ((while-command) make-while-command)
      ((if-command) make-if-command)
      ((assignment-command) make-assignment-command)
      ((var-expression) make-var-expression)
      ((constant-expression) make-constant-expression)
      ((sum-expression) make-sum-expression)
      (else (error "Invalid production name:" prod-name)))))
```

4. The last, and most interesting, case arises when the next item in the production is a nonterminal. In this case we want to parse the portion of the token sequence that matches the nonterminal. For this we need something like the `goto-scanner-state` action in the scanner. See the procedure `goto-parser-state` in figure 11.3.1, which invokes a parser state on the first token in the sequence, yielding an action that is then applied to the *entire* token sequence.

This is useful for getting states started, but it is not quite what we want because it continues to collect parse trees in the *current* buffer. What we want instead is to generate a fresh parse tree by invoking the parser *recursively,* starting with an empty buffer.

This action is performed by procedures returned by the procedure *process-nt* of figure 11.3.1. The given state is started with the current token sequence and an empty buffer. The state returns with `parser-answer` containing the parse tree for the given nonterminal and the unparsed part of the token sequence. The tree is added to the buffer, and parsing continues by performing the next action with the new buffer and unparsed token sequence.

To illustrate this, imagine that we are working on the production

$$A \longrightarrow B\ C\ D\ X\ \ldots$$

where X is a nonterminal and is the next element in the production. Assuming sequences are represented by lists, at this point the state of our parser looks like this:

```
((process-nt X next-action)
 '(D-tree  C-tree  B-tree)
 '(x ... y ... ))
```

The parser action returned by (`process-nt` X *next-action*) is applied to the buffer and the sequence. The buffer contains parse trees for the parts of the token sequence corresponding to the B, C, and D. The token sequence now consists of $(x \ldots y \ldots)$, where $x \ldots$ denotes the tokens corresponding to an X production and $y \ldots$ denotes the remaining tokens. Of course, the parser doesn't know the location of the boundary between the xs and the ys; that is what it has to determine. The procedure *process-nt* starts a parser to match an initial segment of the token sequence against X:

```
((goto-parser-state X) '() '(x ... y ... ))
```

This returns an answer consisting of the parse tree for the $x \ldots$ and the part of the token sequence that follows them:

```
#(parser-answer X-tree '(y ... ))
```

Next, *process-nt* pushes *X-tree* on the buffer and continues parsing the remaining sequence.

```
(next-action
 '(X-tree  D-tree  C-tree  B-tree)
 '(y ... ))
```

Figure 11.3.2   A parser written in functional style

```
(define parse-command
  (lambda (token)
    (case (token->class token)
      ((begin)
       (check/drop 'begin
         (process-nt parse-command
           (check/drop 'semicolon
             (process-nt parse-command
               (check/drop 'end
                 (reduce 'compound-command)))))))
      ((variable)
       (check/shift 'variable
         (check/drop 'assign-sym
           (process-nt parse-expression
             (reduce 'assignment-command)))))
      (else (parse-error token)))))

(define parse-expression
  (lambda (token)
    (case (token->class token)
      ((variable)
       (check/shift 'variable
         (reduce 'var-expression)))
      ((number)
       (check/shift 'number
         (reduce 'constant-expression)))
      ((lparen)
       (check/drop 'lparen
         (process-nt parse-expression
           (check/drop 'plus-sym
             (process-nt parse-expression
               (check/drop 'rparen
                 (reduce 'sum-expression)))))))
      (else (parse-error token)))))
```

Figure 11.3.3   Procedures to drive a parser

```
(define parse-once
  (lambda (start-state token-seq)
    ((goto-parser-state start-state) '() token-seq)))

(define parse-token-seq
  (lambda (start-state token-seq)
    (let ((answer (parse-once start-state token-seq)))
      (variant-case answer
        (parser-answer (tree unparsed)
          (if (eq? (token->class (token-seq-head unparsed))
                   'end-marker)
              tree
              (error "Tokens left over:" unparsed)))))))
```

This accomplishes our goal of finding the parse tree, explaining an initial segment of the token sequence as an instance of production X. (We shall discuss *emit-list* later.)

Now we have enough parsing technology to write a parser for our simple grammar. We do this by writing a set of mutually recursive states. Each state is a procedure that takes a token and dispatches on its class, returning an action. See figure 11.3.2.

A scanner requires a driver loop, but a parser does not, because it only produces a single tree. It is only necessary to invoke the start state of the parser and check that there are no tokens left over when it returns. See the definition of *parse-token-seq* in figure 11.3.3.

- *Exercise 11.3.2*

  Finish the parser and scanner for this language. You will have to include ;, +, and := in *scanner-start-state*; while and if commands in *parse-command*; and definitions for *token-seq-head* and *token-seq-tail*. ☐

In an interactive system, we do not want to produce just a single parse tree. Instead, we must take a stream of tokens and produce a stream of parse trees. A read-eval-print loop may be constructed by modifying the scanning and parsing routines so that the scanner takes a stream of characters (generated by calls to *read-char*) and produces a stream of tokens and the parser takes a stream of tokens and returns a stream of parse trees.

- *Exercise 11.3.3*

Modify the parser driver to create an interactive read-eval-print loop. This loop should call the procedure *top-level-eval*, passing it the parse tree for evaluation. Use the prompt -->. The loop should exit when the special token end is encountered prior to parsing a command. If *eval-print* is defined only to write, *read-eval-print* becomes a convenient device for testing the parser. For example,

```
> (read-eval-print)
--> x:=y
#(assignment-command x #(var-expression y))
--> begin x:=y ; u := (v + u) end
#(compound-command
 #(assignment-command x #(var-expression y))
  #(assignment-command u
   #(sum-expression #(var-expression v) #(var-expression u))))
--> begin x:=y ;
         uu := ((x + v) + u) end
#(compound-command
 #(assignment-command x #(var-expression y))
 #(assignment-command uu
  #(sum-expression
   #(sum-expression #(var-expression x) #(var-expression v))
   #(var-expression u))))
--> end
>
```

An answer to this exercise may be found in appendix F. □

Our approach to parsing can handle only grammars of a rather restricted form: those with the property that if we know what nonterminal we are looking for and what item is at the head of the token sequence, we can easily determine which production to use. Thus parsing procedures always know what to match next, and matching never fails unless there is a syntactic error in the sequence. This class of grammars is called LL(1). In general, the process of choosing the lexical classes that predict the use of a given production is far more subtle than our examples might suggest. For more details, see the references on compiler theory at the end of the book.

All the programs in this book can be obtained by anonymous FTP.

To obtain these programs by Internet FTP,
* Connect to iuvax.cs.indiana.edu (129.79.254.192)
* Login as "anonymous" with your name as password
* go to directory pub/eopl ("cd pub/eopl")
* put ftp in binary mode ("binary")
* transfer the relevant files in that directory ("get sources.ss.Z")
* uncompress the files, if necessary ("uncompress sources.ss.Z")

A typical FTP session might look as follows:

```
>ftp 129.79.254.192
Connected to iuvax.cs.indiana.edu
220 iuvax FTP server (. . .) ready.
Name (. . .): anonymous
331 Guest login ok, send ident as password
Password: <Your last name is entered here.>
230 Guest login ok, access restrictions apply.
ftp>cd pub/eopl
250 CWD command successful.
ftp> binary
200 Type set to I.
ftp> get sources.ss.Z
200 PORT command successful.
    . . .
226 Transfer complete.
ftp>quit
221 Goodbye.
>uncompress sources.ss.Z
><The file sources.ss is now ready to be accessed.>
```

For questions contact any of the authors:

dfried@iuvax.cs.indiana.edu
wand@corwin.ccs.northeastern.edu
chaynes@iuvax.cs.indiana.edu

The grammar we used was a simple example of a grammar in this class. We can write more complicated grammars that are still in this class. For example, we often use the Kleene star in grammar rules to indicate sequences of entries, as in

⟨command⟩ ::= `begin` ⟨command⟩ {`semicolon` ⟨command⟩}* `end`

This defines a compound command as a nonempty sequence of commands separated by semicolons and surrounded by a `begin-end` pair. For such constructs, we want to build a parse tree that contains a list of parse trees.

```
(define-record compound-command (cmd-list))
```

For example, parsing the command

```
begin C1; C2; C3 end
```

should produce this parse tree:

```
#(compound-command (C1-tree  C2-tree  C3-tree))
```

To do this, we can add a new action, defined by the procedure *emit-list* of figure 11.3.1. This procedure returns the *list* of parse trees in the buffer, without making them into a tree. With this action, we can define compound commands as shown in figure 11.3.4. When the state *parse-command* sees a `begin`, it calls the state *parse-command-list*. The procedure *parse-command-list* parses a command and then goes to state *command-list-loop*, which continues accumulating command trees in its buffer.

For example, assume that *C1*, *C2*, and *C3* abbreviate sequences of tokens that form commands and that token sequences are represented as lists. Then we may expand the code for *goto-parser-state*, *parse-command*, and *check-drop* to deduce that

```
((goto-parser-state parse-command)
 '()
 '(begin C1 semicolon C2 semicolon C3 end ...))
```
⇒ ```((process-nt parse-command-list next-action)
     '()
     '(C1 semicolon C2 semicolon C3 end ...))```

Figure 11.3.4   Parsing lists of commands using `emit-list`

```
(define parse-command
  (lambda (token)
    (case (token->class token)
      ((begin)
       (check/drop 'begin
         (process-nt parse-command-list
           (check/drop 'end
             (reduce 'compound-command)))))
      ...)))

(define parse-command-list
  (lambda (token)
    (process-nt parse-command
      (goto-parser-state command-list-loop))))

(define command-list-loop
  (lambda (token)
    (case (token->class token)
      ((semicolon)
       (check/drop 'semicolon
         (process-nt parse-command
           (goto-parser-state command-list-loop))))
      ((end) (emit-list)))))
```

where *next-action* is (check/drop 'end (reduce 'compound-command)),

$\Rightarrow$ (let ((next-answer *recursive-call*))
        (*next-action*
          (cons (parser-answer->tree next-answer) '())
          (parser-answer->unparsed next-answer)))

Via a subderivation, we compute

   recursive-call

$\Rightarrow$ ((goto-parser-state parse-command-list)
      '()
      '($C1$ semicolon $C2$ semicolon $C3$ end ...))

      ...

```
⇒ ((emit-list)
   '(C3-tree  C2-tree  C1-tree)
   '(end ...))

⇒ #(parser-answer
     (C1-tree  C2-tree  C3-tree)
     (end ...))
```

Continuing the main derivation,

```
(let ((next-answer recursive-call))
  (next-action
    (cons (parser-answer->tree next-answer) '())
    (parser-answer->unparsed next-answer)))

⇒ (let ((next-answer '#(parser-answer
                          (C1-tree  C2-tree  C3-tree)
                          (end ...)))))
    (next-action
      (cons (parser-answer->tree next-answer) '())
      (parser-answer->unparsed next-answer)))

⇒ (next-action
    '((C1-tree  C2-tree  C3-tree))
    '(end ...))
```

By expanding *next-action*, we continue:

```
⇒ ((check/drop 'end (reduce 'compound-command))
   '((C1-tree  C2-tree  C3-tree))
   '(end ...))

⇒ ((reduce 'compound-command)
   '((C1-tree  C2-tree  C3-tree))
   '(...))

⇒ #(parser-answer
     #(compound-command
       (C1-tree  C2-tree  C3-tree))
     (...))
```

Thus the call to the parser returns a compound-command with a single *list* of parse trees for *C1*, *C2*, and *C3*, as desired.

The emit-list action, in conjunction with *goto-parser-state*, is flexible enough to handle most of the repetitive lists that arise in practice.

∘ *Exercise 11.3.4*
Modify `parse-command` to accept semicolon-*terminated* compound statements, given by

⟨command⟩ ::= begin ⟨command⟩ ; ... ; ⟨command⟩ ; end

instead of the semicolon-separated commands used above. ▯

• *Exercise 11.3.5*
Using the scanner of exercise 11.2.8, prepare a parser for the interpreted language as specified in appendix C. Here is a sample program for testing your parser: (see figure 11.3.5)

```
letrecproc
   add(x, y) = if x
                  then y
                  else add(sub1(x), add1(y));
   mult(x, y) = if x
                  then 0
                  else if sub1(x)
                        then y
                        else add(y, mult(sub1(x), y))
in let x = 1;
       y = 2;
       z = proc (x, y) mult(add(3, x), y);
       w = proc () add := proc (x, y) x
    in letarray a[8];
                 b[add(x, mult(y, x))]
       in begin
           b[add(x, 1)]  := 17;
           y := mult(x, b[y]);
           y := add(x, y);
           w();
           z(x, y)
          end
```

▯

∘ *Exercise 11.3.6*
Extend the parser of exercise 11.3.5 and modify the interpreter in figure 6.1.2 so that some arguments may be passed by reference (use the abstract syntax brvar (var)), and others by value. Call-by-value should be the default and call-by-reference variables should be preceded by an ⊚. For example, in

Figure 11.3.5   Sample parser output

```
#(letrecproc
   (#(procdecl add (x y)
       #(if #(varref x)
            #(varref y)
            #(app #(varref add)
                  (#(app #(varref sub1) (#(varref x)))
                   #(app #(varref add1) (#(varref y)))))))
    #(procdecl mult (x y)
       #(if #(varref x)
            #(lit 0)
            #(if #(app #(varref sub1) (#(varref x)))
                 #(varref y)
                 #(app #(varref add)
                       (#(varref y)
                        #(app #(varref mult)
                              (#(app #(varref sub1) (#(varref x)))
                               #(varref y)))))))))
   #(let (#(decl x #(lit 1))
          #(decl y #(lit 2))
          #(decl z #(proc (x y)
                        #(app #(varref mult)
                              (#(app #(varref add) (#(lit 3) #(varref x)))
                               #(varref y)))))
          #(decl w #(proc () #(varassign add #(proc (x y) #(varref x))))))
      #(letarray (#(decl a #(lit 8))
                  #(decl b #(app #(varref add)
                                 (#(varref x)
                                  #(app #(varref mult) (#(varref y) #(varref x)))))))
         #(begin
            #(arrayassign #(varref b)
                          #(app #(varref add) (#(varref x) #(lit 1))) #(lit 17))
            #(begin
               #(varassign y
                 #(app #(varref mult)
                       (#(varref x) #(arrayref #(varref b) #(varref y)))))
               #(begin
                  #(varassign y #(app #(varref add) (#(varref x) #(varref y))))
                  #(begin
                     #(app #(varref w) ())
                     #(app #(varref z) (#(varref x) #(varref y)))))))))))
```

```
--> let p = proc (@x, y)
            begin
              y := +(y, 1);
              x := +(x, 1)
            end;
        z = 5
    in begin
         p(z, z);
         z
       end;
  6
```

a new cell is created for y but not for x, so z is incremented once. □

11.4 Recursive Descent Parsers

If we are using an implementation language that does not have first-class procedures, the techniques we have described so far are not directly applicable. We can avoid using first-class procedures by expanding the definitions of parsing actions. The result is a self-contained parsing program. Parsers of this form are called *recursive descent parsers*.

Let us start with the parser of figure 11.3.2. Consider a typical parsing action

```
((check/shift 'variable (check/drop 'assign-sym ...))
 buffer token-seq)
```

Expanding the definition of *check/shift*, this is equal to

```
((lambda (buffer token-seq)
   (if (eq? (token->class (token-seq-head token-seq)) 'variable)
       ((check/drop 'assign-sym ...)
        (cons (token->data (token-seq-head token-seq)) buffer)
        (token-seq-tail token-seq))
       (parse-error (token-seq-head token-seq))))
 buffer token-seq)
```

Using the fact that ((lambda (*x* *y*) ...) *e1* *e2*) is the same as (let ((x *e1*) (*y* *e2*)) ...), we can rewrite this as

```
(let ((buffer buffer)
      (token-seq token-seq))
  (if (eq? (token->class (token-seq-head token-seq)) 'variable)
      ((check/drop 'assign-sym ...)
       (cons (token->data (token-seq-head token-seq)) buffer)
       (token-seq-tail token-seq))
      (parse-error (token-seq-head token-seq))))
```

Since *check/drop* is also defined by a lambda expression whose bound
variables are `token-seq` and `buffer`, we can expand the application of
(check/drop 'assign-sym ...) into another `let`:

```
(let ((buffer buffer)
      (token-seq token-seq))
  (if (eq? (token->class (token-seq-head token-seq)) 'variable)
      (let ((buffer (cons (token->data (token-seq-head token-seq))
                          buffer))
            (token-seq (token-seq-tail token-seq)))
        (if (eq? (token->class (token-seq-head token-seq))
                 'assign-sym)
            (let ((buffer buffer)
                  (token-seq (token-seq-tail token-seq)))
              next-action-body)
            (parse-error (token-seq-head token-seq))))
      (parse-error (token-seq-head token-seq))))
```

We continue expanding *next-action-body* until it is a **reduce** action. The
procedure **reduce** was defined by

```
(define reduce
  (lambda (prod-name)
    (lambda (buffer token-seq)
      (make-parser-answer
        (apply (get-constructor-from-name prod-name)
               (reverse buffer))
        token-seq))))
```

We can then replace

```
((reduce prod-name) buffer token-seq)
```

by

```
(make-parser-answer
 (apply constructor (reverse buffer))
 token-seq)
```

where *constructor* is the procedure associated with `prod-name` by `get-constructor-from-name`.

This takes care of actions, but what about states? In our functional parser of figure 11.3.2, states were of this form:

```
(lambda (token)
  (case (token->class token)
    ((class) action)                                            (*)
    ...
    (else (parse-error ...)))))
```

States are only invoked at one point, which is in `goto-parser-state`:

```
(define goto-parser-state
  (lambda (state)
    (lambda (buffer token-seq)
      (let ((next-action (state (token-seq-head token-seq))))
        (next-action buffer token-seq)))))
```

Thus

```
    (goto-parser-state state)
```

$\Rightarrow$ (lambda (buffer token-seq)
    (let ((next-action (*state* (token-seq-head token-seq))))
      (next-action buffer token-seq)))

which by β-reduction

$\Rightarrow$ (lambda (buffer token-seq)
    (case (token->class (token-seq-head token-seq))
      ((*class*) (*action* buffer token-seq))
      ...
      (else (parse-error ...)))))

by substituting (*) for *state* and β-reducing again.

Similarly, recalling the definition of `process-nt`

```
(define process-nt
  (lambda (state next-action)
    (lambda (buffer token-seq)
      (let ((next-answer ((goto-parser-state state) '() token-seq)))
        (variant-case next-answer
          (parser-answer (tree unparsed)
            (next-action (cons tree buffer) unparsed)))))))
```

we can derive the equivalence

```
((process-nt state next-action) buffer token-seq)
```

⇒ (let ((buffer *buffer*)
        (token-seq *token-seq*))
      (let ((next-answer ((goto-parser-state *state*) '() token-seq)))
        (variant-case next-answer
          (parser-answer (tree unparsed)
            (let ((buffer (cons tree buffer))
                  (token-seq unparsed))
              next-action-body)))))

When we are done, the parser consists of a set of mutually recursive procedures of the following form:

```
(define parse-some-nonterminal
  (lambda (buffer token-seq)
    (case (token->class (token-seq-head token-seq))
      ((class) (action buffer token-seq))
      ...
      (else (parse-error ...)))))
```

Whenever a nonterminal appears in the right-hand side of a production, the corresponding procedure is called recursively. See figure 11.4.1 for the recursive descent translation of parse-command of figure 11.3.2. In this parser, we have mechanically expanded the code using the above techniques, except that we have not included any of the (else (parse-error ...)) lines. An optimized version would not contain redundant let and if expressions.

Recursive descent parsers are commonly used in situations where more sophisticated parser generation techniques, such as table-driven parsers, are unnecessary or impractical. They can be coded in almost any language that allows recursion.

Figure 11.4.1   A recursive descent version of `parse-command`

```
(define parse-command
  (lambda (buffer token-seq)
    (case (token->class (token-seq-head token-seq))
      ((begin)
       (if (eq? (token->class (token-seq-head token-seq)) 'begin)
           (let ((buffer buffer)
                 (token-seq (token-seq-tail token-seq)))
             (let ((next-answer (parse-command '() token-seq)))
               (variant-case next-answer
                 (parser-answer (tree unparsed)
                   (let ((buffer (cons tree buffer))
                         (token-seq unparsed))
                     (if (eq? (token->class (token-seq-head token-seq)) 'semicolon)
                         (let ((buffer buffer)
                               (token-seq (token-seq-tail token-seq)))
                           (let ((next-answer (parse-command '() token-seq)))
                             (variant-case next-answer
                               (parser-answer (tree unparsed)
                                 (let ((buffer (cons tree buffer))
                                       (token-seq unparsed))
                                   (if (eq? (token->class (token-seq-head token-seq))
                                            'end)
                                       (let ((buffer buffer)
                                             (token-seq (token-seq-tail token-seq)))
                                         (make-parser-answer
                                           (apply make-compound-command
                                             (reverse buffer))
                                           token-seq)))))))))))))))
      ((variable)
       (if (eq? (token->class (token-seq-head token-seq)) 'variable)
           (let ((buffer (cons (token->data (token-seq-head token-seq)) buffer))
                 (token-seq (token-seq-tail token-seq)))
             (if (eq? (token->class (token-seq-head token-seq)) 'assign-sym)
                 (let ((buffer buffer)
                       (token-seq (token-seq-tail token-seq)))
                   (let ((next-answer (parse-expression '() token-seq)))
                     (variant-case next-answer
                       (parser-answer (tree unparsed)
                         (let ((buffer (cons tree buffer)) (token-seq unparsed))
                           (make-parser-answer
                             (apply make-assignment-command (reverse buffer))
                             token-seq)))))))))))
```

Figure 11.4.2   A two-argument continuation version of `parse-command`

```
(define parse-command
  (lambda (token-seq future-action)
    (case (token->class (token-seq-head token-seq))
      ((begin)
       (parse-command (token-seq-tail token-seq)
         (lambda (tree1 unparsed1)
           (if (eq? (token->class (token-seq-head unparsed1)) 'semicolon)
               (parse-command (token-seq-tail unparsed1)
                 (lambda (tree2 unparsed2)
                   (if (eq? (token->class (token-seq-head unparsed2)) 'end)
                       (future-action
                         (make-compound-command tree1 tree2)
                         (token-seq-tail unparsed2))
                       (parse-error ...))))
               (parse-error ...)))))
      ((variable)
       (let ((unparsed1 (token-seq-tail token-seq)))
         (if (eq? (token->class (token-seq-head unparsed1)) 'assign-sym)
             (parse-expression (token-seq-tail unparsed1)
               (lambda (tree2 unparsed2)
                 (future-action
                   (make-assignment-command
                     (token->data (token-seq-head token-seq))
                     tree2)
                   unparsed2)))
             (parse-error ...))))
      (else (parse-error ...)))))
```

- *Exercise 11.4.1*
  Rewrite `parse-expression` as a recursive descent parser. □

- *Exercise 11.4.2*
  The code in figure 11.4.1 is unnatural, since it was generated mechanically from the definitions given in the text. Rewrite it to be optimized in some of the ways that humans typically write programs. □

○ *Exercise 11.4.3*
  The parser in figure 11.4.1 is not quite free of higher-order procedures, since it still contains instances of `apply`. Rewrite it to eliminate these instances. □

- *Exercise 11.4.4*
  The parser developed in this section can be written in a continuation-passing style. For example, the buffer can be replaced by a two-argument continuation `future-action` as in figure 11.4.2. The final value continuation might be `make-parser-answer`. Write `parse-expression` using this approach. ☐

11.5 Table-Driven Parsers

In section 11.3, we derived a general strategy and a set of useful components for building parsers. In section 11.4, we showed how to eliminate the use of higher-order procedures in these parsers by expanding the definitions of the components; the result was a strategy for building recursive descent parsers by hand.

In this section, we shall use the techniques of section 3.6 to derive a different representation of these components that will not require first-class procedures. As in our representation of finite functions in section 3.6, we create a grammar showing the ways in which each class of procedures can be put together and then write special-purpose `apply-` procedures for each class. The result will be a single parsing program that can be customized by simply changing a table: such procedures are said to be *table driven*.

The transformation of our procedural parsers into a data structure representation is useful for several reasons. We shall have a single driver program that scans the token sequence, basing its decision on a table: a data structure that describes a specific parser. To change the lexical specification of the language we are processing, we need only change the table. The resulting representation is declarative: it looks very much like a grammar. This eliminates an important source of coding errors. Finally, the table-driven parser avoids the use of first-class procedures, so it can be implemented in a language that does not support first-class procedures. We do this, however, at the cost of restricting ourselves to parsers built using only our six actions.

The parsers we built in section 11.3 had a very stylized form. We write a grammar that describes this form, choose an alternate representation that is more convenient, and then write special-purpose `apply-` procedures that interpret this form. The form we choose is a *parsing table*. These tables are similar to a BNF grammar, so they are easy to write.

We begin by modifying the procedures of figure 11.3.1. First we make them independent of the representation of parser actions by introducing the procedure `apply-parser-action`. Then we make the modification, as sug-

Figure 11.5.1   Parser actions in procedural representation

```
(define check/drop
  (lambda (class next-action)
    (lambda (buffer token-seq grammar)
      (let ((token (token-seq-head token-seq)))
        (if (eq? (token->class token) class)
            (apply-parser-action next-action
              buffer
              (token-seq-tail token-seq)
              grammar)
            (error "Syntax error: expecting a" class "not a" token))))))

(define check/shift
  (lambda (class next-action)
    (lambda (buffer token-seq grammar)
      (let ((token (token-seq-head token-seq)))
        (if (eq? (token->class token) class)
            (apply-parser-action next-action
              (cons (token->data token) buffer)
              (token-seq-tail token-seq)
              grammar)
            (error "Syntax error: expecting a" class "not a" token))))))

(define reduce
  (lambda (prod-name)
    (lambda (buffer token-seq grammar)
      (make-parser-answer
        (apply (get-constructor-from-name prod-name)
               (reverse buffer))
        token-seq))))

(define goto-label
  (lambda (label)
    (lambda (token-seq buffer grammar)
      (let ((next-action
              (apply-parser-state
                (apply-parser-grammar grammar label)
                (token-seq-head token-seq))))
        (apply-parser-action next-action
          buffer
          token-seq
          grammar)))))
```

```
(define process-nt
  (lambda (label next-action)
    (lambda (buffer token-seq grammar)
      (let ((next-answer
              (apply-parser-action
                (goto-label label) '() token-seq grammar)))
        (variant-case next-answer
          (parser-answer (tree unparsed)
            (apply-parser-action next-action
              (cons tree buffer)
              unparsed
              grammar)))))))

(define emit-list
  (lambda ()
    (lambda (buffer token-seq grammar)
      (make-parser-answer (reverse buffer) token-seq))))
```

gested in exercise 11.2.9, of adding a grammar as a third register and replacing goto-parser-state by goto-label. The resulting definitions are shown in figure 11.5.1. The only substantial change is in *goto-label*. It uses *apply-parser-grammar* to find a state, applies that state to the head of the sequence to find an action, and applies that action to the current sequence, buffer, and grammar.

Proceeding along the lines suggested in section 3.6.2, our next step is a transformation to a data structure representation of parser actions. This is obtained by creating a record type for each action and moving the code for interpreting actions from the action procedures into *apply-parser-action*. Since three of our six actions take a *next-action* argument, we adopt a list of frames representation.

Each frame contains one of the following record types.

```
(define-record check/shift (class))
(define-record check/drop (class))
(define-record process-nt (label))
(define-record reduce (prod-name))
(define-record goto-label (label))
(define-record emit-list ())
```

Assuming the use of our customary representation of records as vectors, the form of our action data structures may be represented by the following grammar.

$action$ ::= (#(check/shift $class$) . $action$)
    | (#(check/drop $class$) . $action$)
    | (#(process-nt $label$) . $action$)
    | (#(reduce $prod$-$name$))
    | (#(goto-label $label$))
    | (#(emit-list))

Dot notation is used in the first three productions. Thus an action is a list of frames of the form (check/shift $class$), (check/drop $class$), or (process/nt $label$), terminated by a (reduce $prod$-$name$), (goto-label $label$), or (emit-list) frame. For example:

```
(#(check/drop begin)
 #(process-nt command)
 #(check/drop semicolon)
 #(process-nt command)
 #(check/drop end)
 #(reduce compound))
```

The procedure `apply-parser-action` takes an action represented as a list of frames, a buffer, a token sequence, and a grammar. It dispatches on the type of action record and then does the same thing the action did when actions were represented as procedures. See figure 11.5.2.

This completes the representation for actions. What about states? In the original parser, states were of this form:

```
(lambda (token)
  (case (token->class token)
    ((class) action)
    ...
    (else (parse-error ...)))))
```

Figure 11.5.2   List of frames version of parser actions

```
(define apply-parser-action
  (lambda (action buffer token-seq grammar)
    (let ((first-frame (car action))
          (next-action (cdr action)))
      (variant-case first-frame
        (check/drop (class)
          (let ((token (token-seq-head token-seq)))
            (if (eq? (token->class token) class)
                (apply-parser-action next-action
                  buffer (token-seq-tail token-seq) grammar)
                (error "Syntax error: expecting a" class "not a" token))))
        (check/shift (class)
          (let ((token (token-seq-head token-seq)))
            (if (eq? (token->class token) class)
                (apply-parser-action next-action
                  (cons (token->data token) buffer)
                  (token-seq-tail token-seq)
                  grammar)
                (error "Invalid token class" class token))))
        (process-nt (label)
          (let ((next-answer (apply-parser-action
                               (apply-parser-state (apply-grammar grammar label)
                                 (token-seq-head token-seq))
                               '() token-seq grammar)))
            (variant-case next-answer
              (parser-answer (tree unparsed)
                (apply-parser-action next-action
                  (cons tree buffer) unparsed grammar)))))
        (reduce (prod-name)
          (make-parser-answer
            (apply (get-constructor-from-name prod-name) (reverse buffer))
            token-seq))
        (goto-label (label)
          (let ((next-action (apply-parser-state (apply-grammar grammar label)
                               (token-seq-head token-seq))))
            (apply-parser-action next-action buffer token-seq grammar)))
        (emit-list () (make-parser-answer (reverse buffer) token-seq))
        (else (error "Invalid frame:" first-frame))))))
```

Figure 11.5.3 List of frames version of `apply-parser-state`

```
(define apply-parser-state
  (lambda (state token)
    (letrec
      ((loop
        (lambda (alternatives)
          (if (null? alternatives)
              (error "Invalid token:" token)
              (let ((this-alternative (car alternatives)))
                (cond
                  ((eq? (car this-alternative) 'else)
                   (cdr this-alternative))
                  ((memq (token->class token)
                         (car this-alternative))
                   (cdr this-alternative))
                  (else (loop (cdr alternatives)))))))))
      (loop state))))
```

Alternately, the information in a state may be represented by a data structure of a form indicated by the syntax

---

$state$ ::= (*alternative* ...)

$alternative$ ::= ((*class*) . *action*)
              | (else . *action*)

A state is a list of alternatives. Each alternative is a list whose first element is the list of applicable token classes (or the keyword else), followed by an action. Here are two typical alternatives

```
((variable) (check/drop variable) (reduce var-expression))
(else (goto-label command))
```

The procedure `apply-parser-state` interprets these data structures by checking each alternative in turn. See figure 11.5.3.

Figure 11.5.4   Redefinition of *parse-once*

```
(define parse-once
  (lambda (grammar token-seq)
    (let ((start-state (car (car grammar))))
      (let ((start-action (list (make-goto-label start-state))))
        (apply-parser-action start-action '() token-seq grammar)))))
```

Finally, we represent a grammar as an association list of label-state pairs:

grammar ::= ((*label . state*) ...)

or equivalently, by expanding *state*,

grammar ::= ((*label alternative* ...) ...)

The procedure *apply-grammar* is simply this:

```
(define apply-grammar
  (lambda (grammar label)
    (cond
      ((null? grammar) (error "Invalid label:" label))
      ((eq? (caar grammar) label) (cdar grammar))
      (else (apply-grammar (cdr grammar) label)))))
```

(This is essentially the same as the composition of the Scheme procedures *cdr* and *assq*.)

We now rewrite *parse-once* as in figure 11.5.4 to use the data structure representation. By convention, we assume that the first state in our grammars is the start state.

Now we can define our sample grammar in the data structure representation. Assuming the representation of records as vectors, we may use the data structure defined in figure 11.5.5. The entire grammar is a quoted list structure that can be read and interpreted by *apply-parser-state*. The table looks very much like the underlying grammar.

This completes the transformation of our procedural parsers into a data structure representation. We now have a single driver program (parse-token-seq) that scans the token sequence, basing its decision on a table that describes a specific parser. The table representation is declarative: it looks very much like a grammar. To change the lexical specification, we need only change the

Figure 11.5.5   The parsing table for figure 11.3.2

```
(define command-grammar
  '((command
      ((begin)
        #(check/drop begin)
        #(process-nt command)
        #(check/drop semicolon)
        #(process-nt command)
        #(check/drop end)
        #(reduce compound-command))
      ((variable)
        #(check/shift variable)
        #(check/drop assign-sym)
        #(process-nt expression)
        #(reduce assignment-command)))
    (expression
      ((variable)
        #(check/shift variable)
        #(reduce var-expression))
      ((number)
        #(check/shift number)
        #(reduce constant-expression))
      ((lparen)
        #(check/drop lparen)
        #(process-nt expression)
        #(check/drop plus-sym)
        #(process-nt expression)
        #(check/drop rparen)
        #(reduce sum-expression)))))
```

table. Abstracting the control structure in the states eliminates an important source of coding errors. Finally, the table-driven parser avoids the use of first-class procedures, so it can be implemented in a language that does not support first-class procedures. We do this, however, at the cost of restricting ourselves to parsers built using only our six actions.

• *Exercise 11.5.1*
Rewrite the parser of exercise 11.3.5 using a parsing table. ☐

Figure 11.5.6 A scanner table

```
(define scanner-table
  '((start-state
      (((whitespace) #(drop) #(goto-label start-state))
       ((alphabetic) #(shift) #(goto-label identifier-state))
       ((numeric) #(shift) #(goto-label number-state))
       ((#\%) #(drop) #(goto-label comment-state))
       ((#\() #(drop) #(emit lparen))
       ((#\)) #(drop) #(emit rparen))
       ((#\nul) #(emit end-marker))
       (else #(scan-error))))
    (identifier-state
      (((alphabetic) #(shift) #(goto-label identifier-state))
       ((numeric) #(shift) #(goto-label identifier-state))
       (else #(emit identifier))))
    (number-state
      (((numeric) #(shift) #(goto-label number-state))
       (else #(emit number))))
    (comment-state
      (((#\newline) #(drop) #(goto-label start-state))
       (else #(shift) #(goto-label comment-state))))))
```

• *Exercise 11.5.2*
Transform the scanner components of section 11.2 into a table representation.
A typical scanning table might look something like figure 11.5.6. □

○ *Exercise 11.5.3*
Some people do not like using many parentheses in their programs. Choose
a representation for parsing tables that uses keywords instead of parentheses.
Write a lexical specification and a grammar for your representation. □

○ *Exercise 11.5.4*
Repeat the previous exercise for scanning tables. The concrete syntax should
look something like figure 11.1.1. □

○ *Exercise 11.5.5*
Write a program that takes a parsing table and generates the corresponding
recursive descent parser. □

Before actual processing, programs must be translated from human-readable syntax into an abstract syntax more suitable for machine manipulation. This translation is divided into two phases: scanning and parsing.

A scanner groups the characters used to express the concrete syntax and processes these groups to form tokens, such as variables, keywords, and numbers. Finite automata are used to model the scanning process. These automata may be simulated using highly stylized higher-order procedures. The resulting scanning procedure accepts a sequence of characters and returns a sequence of tokens. This includes processing tokens into forms that are more easily used in later processing; for example, forming numbers from digit strings and maintaining a symbol table.

A parser takes a sequence of tokens and returns a parse tree reflecting the syntactic structure of the program. A predictive parser can be built by extending the approach of the scanning automata to recursively start a new automaton when a non-terminal must be parsed. A parser built in this way may be transformed into a recursive descent parser, which does not rely on the existence of first-class procedures in the defining language, by expanding the definitions of the higher-order functions in the automata.

Because these programs are highly stylized, the portions that vary can be represented compactly in a table. The set of such tables is a new special-purpose programming language, which can be interpreted by a single program.

The approach to parsers illustrated in this chapter is restricted to grammars with certain properties. Although many grammars satisfy these properties, more advanced techniques are sometimes required.

Besides illustrating basic scanning and parsing techniques, the programs developed in this chapter illustrate important programming techniques that will be used again in chapter 12.

12 Compiler Derivation

We have seen that an interpreter may be viewed as a machine implemented in software that "executes" a parse tree. The process of compilation is the translation of an expression into a data representation (object code) that can be executed on a machine implemented efficiently in hardware.

In this chapter we start with a standard CPS interpreter for a small language. Through systematic transformation of this interpreter we then simultaneously derive a compiler and an idealized machine architecture for the compiler's object code. This is done in several steps. First, in section 12.1, we abstract the elementary actions performed by the interpreter and the formation of continuations. We then modify the interpreter so that instead of performing each action it generates a bit of code representing the action. The resulting code corresponds to a CPS version of the source program, where each action has an explicit continuation. We next define a procedure that takes this code and executes it. This procedure, which defines an abstract machine for the object code, is derived systematically from the actions performed by the original interpreter.

Next, in section 12.2, we transform our compiler and machine so that the object code more closely resembles typical machine language. Once more, this is accomplished by simultaneously transforming the compiler and machine to take advantage of certain patterns in the object code. In the third section we show how to make the output of the compiler look more realistic.

The source language of the compilers in the first two sections includes several forms that together present most of the object code patterns that compilers typically generate, with one important exception: procedures. Thus we conclude, in section 12.4, by adding procedure expressions to the source language and deriving a compiler and machine that support closures.

By following a methodical discipline of program development, we are assured of the correctness of the resulting programs. Each step in the development is verifiable. In effect, the original interpreter provides a semantic specification for our language, and we are proving the correctness of the compiler and machine implementation with respect to this specification.

12.1 Deriving a Compiler and Machine from an Interpreter

We begin with a simple language with literal, variable, and conditional forms, plus a form that sums the values of multiple subexpressions. As in our earlier interpreters, zero denotes false and other values denote true. We assume the literal, variable, and conditional (`if`) forms have the concrete syntax of the corresponding forms and the abstract syntax introduced in chapter 5. For the addition operator, we use the following concrete and abstract syntax.

$\langle exp \rangle ::= \mathsf{sum}(\langle operands \rangle)$ sum (rands)

See figure 12.1.1 for a CPS interpreter for this language. As usual, `apply-env` is borrowed from an environment ADT. The procedure `add-list` sums the values in a list. To test the interpreter, we define the procedure *run*.

```
(define run
  (lambda (exp)
    (eval-exp (parse exp) init-env (lambda (val) val))))
```

An identity procedure serves as the final value continuation. We assume in our sample transcripts that *init-env* is an initial environment that binds the variables `five` and `six` to the respective integers. (Since our language does not have procedures, the initial environment is the only environment. Though the environment argument is always the same, we include it to aid the later treatment of procedures.)

```
> (run "if sum(1, five) then 3 else six")
3
```

Interpreters perform several sorts of operations. For example, the operations performed by our present interpreter may be categorized as follows:

1. dispatching on the type of an expression (by `variant-case`),

2. calling itself and *eval-rands* to evaluate subexpressions,

3. forming continuations,

Figure 12.1.1 An interpreter

```
(define eval-exp
  (lambda (exp env k)
    (variant-case exp
      (lit (datum) (k datum))
      (varref (var) (k (apply-env env var)))
      (if (test-exp then-exp else-exp)
        (eval-exp test-exp env
          (lambda (test)
            (if (true-value? test)
                (eval-exp then-exp env k)
                (eval-exp else-exp env k)))))
      (sum (rands)
        (eval-rands rands env
          (lambda (sum-args)
            (k (add-list sum-args)))))
      (else (error "Invalid abstract syntax:" exp)))))

(define eval-rands
  (lambda (rands env k)
    (if (null? rands)
        (k '())
        (eval-exp (car rands) env
          (lambda (first)
            (eval-rands (cdr rands) env
              (lambda (rest)
                (k (cons first rest)))))))))
```

4. invoking continuations with the results of elementary operations,

5. making if tests, and

6. returning results when done (in the final value continuation).

Operations of type 4, 5, and 6 correspond to machine operations that must be performed at run time. We refer to them as *actions*. On the other hand, we would like operations of type 1 and 2 to be performed at compile time. The forming of continuations (type 3) corresponds to maintaining a sequential ordering of instructions in the object code.

Our goal is to modify this interpreter so that it still does dispatching on the form of expressions and recursion on subexpressions but does not perform actions at compile time. Instead, it should return object code that will perform actions at run time. The first step toward this goal is to abstract the actions by creating a procedure for each one. In general, the body of such a procedure is a subexpression of the interpreter definition that performs an action, whereas the formal parameters of the procedure are the free variables of the body that vary with program execution. Except for `halt-action` (called by the final value continuation), the free variables always include a continuation, k, that is invoked after the action has been performed.

For example, variable lookup may be abstracted as follows:

```
(define eval-exp
  (lambda (exp env k)
    (variant-case exp
      ...
      (varref (var) (varref-action var env k))
      ...)))

(define varref-action
  (lambda (var env k)
    (k (apply-env env var))))
```

For our language, this technique works in all but one case: the test action. If this transformation were applied directly to the test action in the `if` clause of the interpreter, we would obtain the following definition.

```
(define test-action
  (lambda (var then-exp else-exp env k)
    (if (true-value? var)
        (eval-exp then-exp env k)
        (eval-exp else-exp env k))))
```

The difficulty is that evaluation of a subexpression is not an elementary action. The solution is to simplify the test action by using procedures that package evaluation of the then and else expressions. Thus the test action need only invoke the appropriate procedure.

We have already seen instances in which procedures of no arguments, called thunks, have been used to delay evaluation. When CPS is used (as in our interpreter), however, a thunk must take one argument: a continuation. In the context of our interpreter, we refer to these procedures as *action thunks*. An action thunk for evaluation of an expression, *exp*, in an environment, *env*, may be created by an expression of this form:

```
(lambda (k) (eval-exp exp env k))
```

Figure 12.1.2   An interpreter that abstracts actions

```
(define eval-exp
  (lambda (exp env k)
    (variant-case exp
      (lit (datum) (lit-action datum k))
      (varref (var) (varref-action var env k))
      (if (test-exp then-exp else-exp)
        (eval-exp test-exp env
          (build-cont
            (lambda (test)
              (test-action test
                (lambda (k)
                  (eval-exp then-exp env k))
                (lambda (k)
                  (eval-exp else-exp env k))
                k)))))
      (sum (rands)
        (eval-rands rands env
          (build-cont
            (lambda (arg-list)
              (sum-action arg-list k)))))
      (else (error "Invalid abstract syntax:" exp)))))

(define eval-rands
  (lambda (rands env k)
    (if (null? rands)
        (emptyargs-action k)
        (eval-exp (car rands) env
          (build-cont
            (lambda (first)
              (eval-rands (cdr rands) env
                (build-cont
                  (lambda (rest)
                    (rest-action first rest k)))))))))))
```

See figure 12.1.2 and figure 12.1.3 for the resulting interpreter, which abstracts actions. Each action is called at only one point. Figure 12.1.3 also includes a new version of the *run* procedure that invokes the procedure *halt-action* to return a result. The procedure *build-cont* is introduced in anticipation of a subsequent code transformation. At this point, it is trivial.

An interpreter executes actions in some appropriate sequence, and a compiler generates code that reflects the same sequence. Before we can modify our interpreter to perform compilation, we must abstract this sequencing behavior. Since continuations control the sequencing of execution, our next step is to abstract the creation of continuations.

We are now prepared to transform our interpreter into a compiler. Since we have abstracted actions, the core of the interpreter, in figure 12.1.2, is unchanged by this transformation. The transformation is performed by redefining the actions and continuation-building procedures of figure 12.1.3. For the procedures' names to make sense, *eval* now means "compile," rather than "execute," and *action* means "generate code," rather than "perform an action."

Thus *eval-exp* no longer returns a final result. Instead it returns code that may be viewed as a symbolic (data structure) representation of the result. The environment and continuation passed to *eval-exp* must also be represented symbolically. After we complete the transformation of *eval-exp* into a compiler, we then derive an abstract machine that interprets compiled code to obtain final values.

First, we create a record type for each action. Each action procedure, with one exception, is then redefined to be the record creation procedure of its record type. Thus the work to be performed by each action is postponed by creating a data structure with all the necessary information. See figure 12.1.4. The exception is *test-action*, which invokes the then and else thunks before invoking its record creation procedure. This allows the then and else expressions to be compiled. It is possible to invoke these thunks at compile time because they call *eval-exp*, which returns actions that delay final evaluation.

The remaining step is to create continuations that are represented symbolically, rather than as procedures. We use a single record type named cont.

```
(define-record cont (reg code))
```

The first field corresponds to the formal parameter of a continuation procedure. The symbol in this field denotes a *register,* since the locations in which continuations receive values will correspond to registers in our target machine.

Figure 12.1.3   Action procedures, with *build-cont* and *run*

```
(define halt-action
  (lambda (val)
    val))

(define lit-action
  (lambda (datum k)
    (k datum)))

(define varref-action
  (lambda (var env k)
    (k (apply-env env var))))

(define test-action
  (lambda (test then-action-thunk else-action-thunk k)
    (if (true-value? test)
        (then-action-thunk k)
        (else-action-thunk k))))

(define sum-action
  (lambda (sum-args k)
    (k (add-list sum-args))))

(define emptyargs-action
  (lambda (k)
    (k '())))

(define rest-action
  (lambda (first rest k)
    (k (cons first rest))))

(define build-cont
  (lambda (k)
    (lambda (v)
      (k v))))

(define run
  (lambda (exp)
    (eval-exp (parse exp) init-env
      (build-cont
        (lambda (val)
          (halt-action val))))))
```

Figure 12.1.4   Action construction procedures

```
(define-record halt-instruc (val-reg))
(define halt-action make-halt-instruc)

(define-record lit-instruc (datum k))
(define lit-action make-lit-instruc)

(define-record varref-instruc (var env-reg k))
(define varref-action make-varref-instruc)

(define-record sum-instruc (arg-list-reg k))
(define sum-action make-sum-instruc)

(define-record emptyargs-instruc (k))
(define emptyargs-action make-emptyargs-instruc)

(define-record rest-instruc (first-reg rest-reg k))
(define rest-action make-rest-instruc)

(define-record test-instruc (test-reg then-code else-code))
(define test-action
  (lambda (test then-action-thunk else-action-thunk k)
    (make-test-instruc test
      (then-action-thunk k)
      (else-action-thunk k))))
```

We call this the *formal register* of the continuation, by analogy with the formal parameter of a lambda expression. It is important not to confuse these registers with variables in the source program or variables in the interpreter itself. The second field of a cont record contains code representing the body of the corresponding continuation procedure.

Since a register is simply a machine location, we must be sure that the register we choose will not be in use (contain needed information) at the time its continuation is invoked. Thus when forming a continuation, we must allocate a suitable register to receive its argument. For simplicity, we initially assume the existence of an unlimited number of registers named r1, r2, ... A new register is allocated for each continuation by the procedure allocate-reg. In section 12.2 we introduce a more practical register allocator that reuses registers.

Thus continuations are represented by records generated by calling `make-cont` with a newly generated register and an action that refers to that register. To create these continuation records, we redefine `build-cont`.

```
(define build-cont
  (lambda (action-generator)
    (let ((reg (allocate-reg)))
      (make-cont reg
        (action-generator reg)))))
```

Here `action-generator` refers to a procedure that takes a register and returns an action that may use this register. Thus the lambda expressions of figure 12.1.2 that once defined continuations now define action generators, and their formal parameters are now bound to register names, rather than values.

When invoking `eval-exp`, we use the *symbol* env-reg to represent the register that will contain the initial environment. Here is a simple test.

```
> (define compile
    (lambda (exp)
      (eval-exp (parse exp) 'env-reg
        (build-cont
          (lambda (reg)
            (halt-action reg))))))
> (compile "six")
#(varref-instruc six env-reg
 #(cont r0
  #(halt-instruc r0)))
```

To better understand the code returned by `eval-exp`, it may be translated into a corresponding Scheme expression. Each -instruc record is replaced by an application to the corresponding -action procedure, and each cont record is replaced by a corresponding lambda expression. Thus (compile "six") returns the code

```
(varref-action 'six init-env
  (lambda (r0)
    (halt-action r0)))
```

Some of the language's literals and all of its variables, such as six, must be quoted, since operands are evaluated, and references to env-reg must be replaced by init-env.

Next we try a more complicated example.

```
> (compile "sum(five, 9)")
#(varref-instruc five env-reg
 #(cont r2
  #(lit-instruc 9
   #(cont r4
    #(emptyargs-instruc
     #(cont r5
      #(rest-instruc r4 r5
       #(cont r3
        #(rest-instruc r2 r3
         #(cont r1
          #(sum-instruc r1
           #(cont r0
            #(halt-instruc r0)))))))))))))
```

When executed, this code does the following:

1. loads the value of the variable five in the initial environment into r2,

2. loads the literal 9 into r4,

3. loads the empty list into r5,

4. starts forming a list of arguments by making a pair from the contents of registers r4 and r5 and places the result in r3,

5. completes the argument list by consing the contents of r2 onto the list in r3 and places the result in r1,

6. sums the elements of the list in r1 and places the result in r0, and

7. halts, returning the result in r0.

The Scheme expression corresponding to this code follows:

```
(varref-action 'five init-env
 (lambda (r2)
  (lit-action 9
   (lambda (r4)
    (emptyargs-action
     (lambda (r5)
      (rest-action r4 r5
       (lambda (r3)
        (rest-action r2 r3
         (lambda (r1)
          (sum-action r1
           (lambda (r0)
            (halt-action r0)))))))))))))
```

Observe that these Scheme expressions corresponding to code are in continuation-passing style. This CPS differs from the CPS of chapter 8 in the granularity of the actions for which continuations are created. Here each action is very small, corresponding to a single machine instruction. In chapter 8, on the other hand, continuations were only created for procedure calls.

There is another important relationship between our code and lambda expressions. We say that a register r *occurs free* in code C if C contains a use of r that is not contained within a cont record in which r is the formal register. Thus register r occurs free in C if and only if the variable r occurs free in the Scheme expression corresponding to C.

The next example illustrates the compilation of conditional code.

```
> (compile "if 0 then sum(3, 4) else sum(five, six)")
#(lit-instruc 0
 #(cont r1
  #(test-instruc r1
   #(lit-instruc 3
    #(cont r3
     #(lit-instruc 4
      #(cont r5
       #(emptyargs-instruc
        #(cont r6
         #(rest-instruc r5 r6
          #(cont r4
           #(rest-instruc r3 r4
            #(cont r2
             #(sum-instruc r2
              #(cont r0
               #(halt-instruc r0)))))))))))))))
    #(varref-instruc five env-reg
     #(cont r8
      #(varref-instruc six env-reg
       #(cont r10
        #(emptyargs-instruc
         #(cont r11
          #(rest-instruc r10 r11
           #(cont r9
            #(rest-instruc r8 r9
             #(cont r7
              #(sum-instruc r7
               #(cont r0
                #(halt-instruc r0)))))))))))))))))))
```

Figure 12.1.5   A machine

```
(define eval-code
  (lambda (code)
    (variant-case code
      (halt-instruc (val-reg) (get-reg val-reg))
      (lit-instruc (datum k) (apply-cont k datum))
      (varref-instruc (var env-reg k)
        (apply-cont k (apply-env (get-reg env-reg) var)))
      (sum-instruc (arg-list-reg k)
        (apply-cont k (add-list (get-reg arg-list-reg))))
      (emptyargs-instruc (k) (apply-cont k '()))
      (rest-instruc (first-reg rest-reg k)
        (apply-cont k
          (cons (get-reg first-reg) (get-reg rest-reg))))
      (test-instruc (test-reg then-code else-code)
        (if (true-value? (get-reg test-reg))
            (eval-code then-code)
            (eval-code else-code)))
      (else (error "Invalid code:" code)))))

(define apply-cont
  (lambda (k v)
    (variant-case k
      (cont (reg code) (set-reg! reg v) (eval-code code))
      (else (error "Invalid continuation:" k)))))

(define goto-cont
  (lambda (k)
    (variant-case k
      (cont (reg code) (eval-code code))
      (else (error "Invalid continuation:" k)))))

(define build-cont
  (lambda (action-generator)
    (let ((reg (allocate-reg)))
      (make-cont reg
        (action-generator reg)))))

(define run
  (lambda (exp)
    (eval-code (compile exp))))
```

The notion of "simple" expressions was introduced to assure that continuations were not created for simple actions.

- *Exercise 12.1.1*
Translate the preceding code into a corresponding Scheme expression and trace its evaluation by hand. Use care in translating `test-instruc`. ☐

o *Exercise 12.1.2*
Define a procedure *code->scheme* that takes code generated by *eval-exp* and returns a corresponding Scheme expression. For example,

```
> (code->scheme (compile "sum(five, 9)"))
(varref-action 'five init-env
 (lambda (r2) ...))
> (eval (code->scheme (compile "sum(five, 9)")))
14
```
☐

Finally, we create a procedure, *eval-code*, for executing code produced by *eval-exp*. This procedure is in effect a machine for executing the object code produced by our compiler.

Since each type of code record represents a different action, it is only necessary for *eval-code* to dispatch on the code record type and perform the corresponding action. We systematically derive *eval-code* from the definitions of the action procedures in figure 12.1.2. (This is analogous to the transformation from procedural to data structure representation introduced in section 3.6.) It is necessary to allow for the representation of continuations as data structures by introducing the procedure *apply-cont*. To account for the use of registers, we also use the procedure *get-reg* to obtain the values of registers associated with continuations. We also assume that the current environment is recorded in a register that is always named env-reg. Register values are assigned using the procedure *set-reg!* in *apply-cont*. When no register should be set, we use *goto-cont*. Although *goto-cont* will not be used until we discuss the interpretation of compiled procedures, we include it here to show just how similar it is to *apply-cont*. See figure 12.1.5, which also includes the latest definition of *build-cont* and a *run* procedure that performs parsing, compilation, and execution. Before testing, we must define the register ADT. This is simplified by using the finite function ADT from chapter 3 and the cell ADT from chapter 4. See figure 12.1.6.

Figure 12.1.6   Implementation of a register allocation ADT

```
(define reg-file
  (extend-ff 'env-reg (make-cell init-env) (create-empty-ff)))

(define get-reg
  (lambda (sym)
    (cell-ref (apply-ff reg-file sym))))

(define set-reg!
  (lambda (sym val)
    (cell-set! (apply-ff reg-file sym) val)))

(define reg-counter 0)

(define allocate-reg
  (lambda ()
    (let ((reg (string->symbol
                 (string-append
                   (symbol->string 'r)
                   (number->string reg-counter)))))
      (set! reg-file (extend-ff reg (make-cell '*) reg-file))
      (set! reg-counter (+ reg-counter 1))
      reg)))
```

12.2 Register Allocation

In this section we modify the compiler of the last section to employ a more realistic register allocation algorithm. This algorithm reuses registers when they no longer contain useful information.

To better understand the register allocation problem, suppose the same register, r0, were used for every continuation returned by

```
(build-cont
  (lambda (first) ...))
```

We might then observe the following.

```
> (compile "sum(five, 9)")
#(varref-instruc five env-reg
 #(cont r0
  #(lit-instruc 9
   #(cont r0
    #(emptyargs-instruc
     #(cont r3
      #(rest-instruc r0 r3
       #(cont r2
        #(rest-instruc r0 r2
         #(cont r1
          #(sum-instruc r1
           #(cont r0
            #(halt-instruc r0)))))))))))))))
```

This code is (up to renaming) the same as that of the sum(five, 9) example in the last section, except that r2 and r4 have both been replaced by r0. In the two rest-instruc lines reference is made to the same register, r0. At the time these lines are executed, r0 will contain 9 (the value of the second argument), while the reference to r0 in the second rest-instruc line should have referred to 5 (the value of the first argument).

In the last section we avoided this problem by allocating a new register for each continuation. This is impractical because the registers that are referred to by most instructions are those in the CPU, and their number is strictly limited. The register allocation performed by compilers should make the best possible use of the available CPU registers, while assuring that a register is not reused as long as it still contains needed information.

When allocating a register for a new continuation, we may select any register that does not occur free in any of the pieces of code from which the body of the new continuation is being constructed. It is precisely these free registers that contain needed information. Thus the register allocation problem is analogous to the lexical variable capture problem of chapter 4 in that we can choose any register that does not occur free in the code representing the continuation's body.

To allocate a new register, we use a modified version of allocate-reg. This procedure now takes a list of registers that are in use and returns a register that is not in use, selected from a list of general registers. We define reg-names to contain the list of registers named r0 through r5 and redefine reg-file to include these new registers.

```
(define reg-names '(r0 r1 r2 r3 r4 r5))
```

```
(define reg-file
  (extend-ff*
    reg-names
    (map (lambda (x) (make-cell '*)) reg-names)
    (extend-ff 'env-reg (make-cell init-env) (create-empty-ff)))))

(define allocate-reg
  (lambda (used-regs)
    (letrec
      ((loop
         (lambda (avail)
           (cond
             ((null? avail) (error "No more registers"))
             ((memq (car avail) used-regs) (loop (cdr avail)))
             (else (car avail))))))
      (loop reg-names))))
```

All the continuation construction procedures (except the final value continuation created by *compile*) take a continuation as an argument and use this continuation to create the body of the new continuation. Since registers that occur free in the argument continuation will appear free in the body, we must have a way of determining which registers occur free in a continuation. This is easiest if we determine the free variables in a new continuation at the time we build it and record this information in the record representing the continuation. Thus we extend the cont record type.

```
(define-record cont (reg free-regs code))
```

Given a list of free registers, it is now easy to build a new continuation.

```
(define build-cont
  (lambda (free-regs action-generator)
    (let ((reg (allocate-reg free-regs)))
      (make-cont reg free-regs (action-generator reg)))))
```

The evaluation (compilation) procedures of figure 12.2.1 are the same as those of figure 12.1.2 except that *build-cont* now receives a list of free registers as well as an action generator. In the final value continuation built by *compile* this list is empty, whereas in other cases it is obtained using *cont->free-regs*. In the continuation of the call of *eval-rands* on the cdr of the operand list, the register *first* occurs free as well as the free registers

Figure 12.2.1   A compiler with register allocation

```
(define compile
  (lambda (exp)
    (eval-exp (parse exp) 'env-reg
      (build-cont '()
        (lambda (final) (halt-action final))))))

(define eval-exp
  (lambda (exp env k)
    (variant-case exp
      (lit (datum) (lit-action datum k))
      (varref (var) (varref-action var env k))
      (if (test-exp then-exp else-exp)
        (eval-exp test-exp env
          (build-cont (cont->free-regs k)
            (lambda (test)
              (test-action test
                (lambda (k)
                  (eval-exp then-exp env k))
                (lambda (k)
                  (eval-exp else-exp env k))
                k)))))
      (sum (rands)
        (eval-rands rands env
          (build-cont (cont->free-regs k)
            (lambda (arg-list)
              (sum-action arg-list k)))))
      (else (error "Invalid abstract syntax:" exp)))))

(define eval-rands
  (lambda (rands env k)
    (if (null? rands)
        (emptyargs-action k)
        (eval-exp (car rands) env
          (build-cont (cont->free-regs k)
            (lambda (first)
              (eval-rands (cdr rands) env
                (build-cont (cons first (cont->free-regs k))
                  (lambda (rest)
                    (rest-action first rest k)))))))))))
```

in *k*. This is accounted for by adding *first* to the free register list when building this continuation.

The list of registers that is maintained in each continuation should, of course, be removed from the output of our compiler, but we take care of that later. Here is the code produced for "sum(five, 9)".

```
#(varref-instruc five env-reg
 #(cont r0 ()
  #(lit-instruc 9
   #(cont r1 (r0)
    #(emptyargs-instruc
     #(cont r2 (r1 r0)
      #(rest-instruc r1 r2
       #(cont r1 (r0)
        #(rest-instruc r0 r1
         #(cont r0 ()
          #(sum-instruc r0
           #(cont r0 ()
            #(halt-instruc r0)))))))))))))))
```

• *Exercise 12.2.1*

Modify the interpreter for the language of this section to use the following version of eval-rands:

```
(define eval-rands
  (lambda (rands args env k)
    (if (null? rands)
        (k args)
        (eval-exp (car rands) env
          (lambda (first)
            (eval-rands (cdr rands) (cons first args) env k))))))
```

Next use the resulting interpreter to derive a compiler similar to the one in figure 12.2.1. Now observe that for this compiler, register allocation may be simplified by assigning a distinct register to each continuation construction procedure that uses a register. For example, *first* could always be r3, provided r3 was not used for other purposes. Modify the procedures that construct continuations accordingly. □

In some cases it may be necessary to maintain more intermediate results than will fit the available CPU registers. Our `allocate-reg` procedure issues an error message in such cases. A practical compiler would arrange for the excess results to be stored in main memory. This is called *register spilling* and occurs rarely if there are a reasonable number of general-purpose CPU registers (say a dozen or more).

○ *Exercise 12.2.2*
Modify the compiler of this section to perform register spilling. Use a register file with only four registers, a vector of 100 elements to simulate the portion of memory used for spilled registers, and a new action, called `move`, that copies a spill-vector element indicated by an index to a given register. □

12.3 Obtaining More Realistic Object Code

Traditional object code consists of a sequence of machine instructions. Although actions are analogous to typical machine instructions in the functions they perform, the nesting of a continuation within each action is not typical. The next step in the evolution of our compiler is to simply "flatten" the code representation so that it becomes a list of actions, without nesting of continuations.

To derive this change in code representation, it helps to view the present code structure (without free register lists) using a BNF grammar.

⟨code⟩ ::= #(halt-instruc ⟨reg⟩)
     | #(lit-instruc ⟨datum⟩ ⟨cont⟩)
     | #(varref-instruc ⟨var⟩ ⟨reg⟩ ⟨cont⟩)
     | #(sum-instruc ⟨reg⟩ ⟨cont⟩)
     | #(emptyargs-instruc ⟨cont⟩)
     | #(rest-instruc ⟨reg⟩ ⟨reg⟩ ⟨cont⟩)
     | #(test-instruc ⟨reg⟩ ⟨code⟩ ⟨code⟩)

⟨cont⟩ ::= #(cont ⟨reg⟩ ⟨code⟩)

Since there is only one production for ⟨cont⟩, we can substitute its right-hand side for each appearance of ⟨cont⟩, obtaining the following grammar.

$\langle$code$\rangle$ ::= #(halt-instruc $\langle$reg$\rangle$)
     | #(lit-instruc $\langle$datum$\rangle$ #(cont $\langle$reg$\rangle$ $\langle$code$\rangle$)))
     | #(varref-instruc $\langle$var$\rangle$ $\langle$reg$\rangle$ #(cont $\langle$reg$\rangle$ $\langle$code$\rangle$)))
     | #(sum-instruc $\langle$reg$\rangle$ #(cont $\langle$reg$\rangle$ $\langle$code$\rangle$)))
     | #(emptyargs-instruc #(cont $\langle$reg$\rangle$ $\langle$code$\rangle$)))
     | #(rest-instruc $\langle$reg$\rangle$ $\langle$reg$\rangle$ #(cont $\langle$reg$\rangle$ $\langle$code$\rangle$)))
     | #(test-instruc $\langle$reg$\rangle$ $\langle$code$\rangle$ $\langle$code$\rangle$)

Now each form of code, except for test-instruc and halt-instruc, contains a single embedded code (the "normal" continuation). This suggests a list of frames representation, which avoids unnecessary nesting (See section 10.2.).

$\langle$code$\rangle$ ::= (#(halt-instruc $\langle$reg$\rangle$)))
     | (#(lit-instruc $\langle$datum$\rangle$ $\langle$reg$\rangle$) . $\langle$code$\rangle$)
     | (#(varref-instruc $\langle$var$\rangle$ $\langle$reg$\rangle$ $\langle$reg$\rangle$) . $\langle$code$\rangle$)
     | (#(sum-instruc $\langle$reg$\rangle$ $\langle$reg$\rangle$) . $\langle$code$\rangle$)
     | (#(emptyargs-instruc $\langle$reg$\rangle$) . $\langle$code$\rangle$)
     | (#(rest-instruc $\langle$reg$\rangle$ $\langle$reg$\rangle$ $\langle$reg$\rangle$) . $\langle$code$\rangle$)
     | (#(test-instruc $\langle$reg$\rangle$ $\langle$code$\rangle$) . $\langle$code$\rangle$)

Except for test code, the code now has the form of a list of simple instructions terminated by a halt instruction.

It is easy to modify our previous code to use this new representation: we simply redefine the code construction procedures of figure 12.1.4. The new procedures add a record representing the new action to a list that represents its continuation. Since these records closely resemble standard machine instructions, we give them names that would be familiar to assembly language programmers: stop, fetch, sum-list, move-imm (move immediate), and brz (branch on zero). There are also instructions, cons-3 (cons with three arguments, one being a destination register) and cons-1 (corresponding to placing the empty list into a destination register) that would be unfamiliar to most assembly language programmers, since machines typically do not maintain lists. It is possible to eliminate list operations from the machine by representing the argument list on a stack, rather than in a heap.

See figure 12.3.1 for the new code construction procedures. While we are defining these procedures, we have the opportunity to remove the list of free registers from the object code (though of course not from the internal representation of continuations).

Figure 12.3.1   Action construction procedures for flat code

```
(define-record stop (reg))
(define halt-action
  (lambda (val)
    (cons (make-stop val) '())))


(define-record move-imm (datum reg))
(define lit-action
  (lambda (datum k)
    (cons (make-move-imm datum (cont->reg k))
          (cont->code k))))


(define-record fetch (var env reg))
(define varref-action
  (lambda (var env k)
    (cons (make-fetch var env (cont->reg k))
          (cont->code k))))


(define-record sum-list (sum-args reg))
(define sum-action
  (lambda (sum-args k)
    (cons (make-sum-list sum-args (cont->reg k))
          (cont->code k))))


(define-record cons-1 (reg))
(define emptyargs-action
  (lambda (k)
    (cons (make-cons-1 (cont->reg k))
          (cont->code k))))


(define-record cons-3 (first rest reg))
(define rest-action
  (lambda (first rest k)
    (cons (make-cons-3 first rest (cont->reg k))
          (cont->code k))))


(define-record brz (test else-instruc))
(define test-action
  (lambda (test then-action-thunk else-action-thunk k)
    (cons (make-brz test (else-action-thunk k))
          (then-action-thunk k))))
```

Figure 12.3.2   Machine for flat object code

```
(define eval-code
  (lambda (code)
    (let ((ir (car code)) (pc (cdr code)))
      (variant-case ir
        (stop (reg) (get-reg reg))
        (move-imm (datum reg)
          (set-reg! reg datum)
          (eval-code pc))
        (fetch (var env reg)
          (set-reg! reg (apply-env (get-reg env) var))
          (eval-code pc))
        (sum-list (sum-args reg)
          (set-reg! reg (add-list (get-reg sum-args)))
          (eval-code pc))
        (cons-1 (reg)
          (set-reg! reg '())
          (eval-code pc))
        (cons-3 (first rest reg)
          (set-reg! reg (cons (get-reg first) (get-reg rest)))
          (eval-code pc))
        (brz (test else-instruc)
          (if (zero? (get-reg test))
              (eval-code else-instruc)
              (eval-code pc)))
        (else (error "Invalid code:" code))))))
```

A simple test demonstrates that (in the absence of `brz` instructions) our object code now has the usual form of a sequence of simple instructions.

```
> (compile "sum(five, 9)")
(#(fetch five env-reg r0)
 #(move-imm 9 r1)
 #(cons-1 r2)
 #(cons-3 r1 r2 r1)
 #(cons-3 r0 r1 r0)
 #(sum-list r0 r0)
 #(stop r0))
```

The continuation of each instruction is the sequence of instructions that follows it.

Since we have changed the object code representation, a new machine (`eval-code` procedure) is required to execute our code. This machine begins by binding the first instruction of its code to the variable ir and binding the code representing the continuation of the first instruction to the variable pc. These variables correspond to the instruction register and program counter of typical hardware machines. Our machine then dispatches on the record type of *ir*, which corresponds to instruction decoding in hardware. Execution of each instruction (except stop and possibly brz) concludes with the recursive call (eval-code pc), which corresponds to repetition of the fetch-execute cycle in hardware. See figure 12.3.2.

The procedure *eval-code* can be made to resemble hardware more closely by transforming it to imperative form in the style chapter 10. The result is displayed in figure 12.3.3. We have introduced two more variables, done and result, which model additional machine states and allow us to use a single recursive call to *eval-code/reg*.

It would be even more realistic if we represented object code as a *vector* of instructions, rather than as a *list* of instructions. The machine procedure would then use (set! pc (+ pc 1)), instead of (set! pc (cdr pc)), to update the program counter. This more closely resembles the program counter increment operation of a traditional fetch-execute cycle. The code vector is also more realistic in that it embodies the random access character of a typical machine's main memory. This allows absolute code addresses to be represented by vector indices.

Our list-of-instructions object code is not entirely flat, since the else branch code of a brz instruction is contained within the instruction itself. See the top portion of figure 12.3.4.

Using the vector-of-instructions code representation, we can place the else code at the end of the code vector. A brz instruction then includes a vector index (absolute address) referring to the else code, instead of the code itself. The code is now completely flat. See the lower portion of figure 12.3.4.

Many compilers output *relocatable code* in which structure such as that introduced by conditional statements is represented by *symbolic addresses*. A system software utility called a *linker* is then used to read this code file and write a code file in which these symbolic addresses are replaced by numeric memory addresses.

o *Exercise 12.3.1*

Write a procedure `link` that takes list-of-instructions code and returns flat vector-of-instructions code. Modify *eval-code/reg* to execute vector-of-instructions code. □

Figure 12.3.3   Register machine for flat object code

```
(define ir '*)
(define pc '*)
(define done '*)
(define result '*)

(define eval-code
  (lambda (code)
    (set! pc code)
    (set! done #f)
    (eval-code/reg)))

(define eval-code/reg
  (lambda ()
    (set! ir (car pc))
    (set! pc (cdr pc))
    (variant-case ir
      (stop (reg)
        (set! done #t)
        (set! result (get-reg reg)))
      (move-imm (datum reg)
        (set-reg! reg datum))
      (fetch (var env reg)
        (set-reg! reg (apply-env (get-reg env) var)))
      (sum-list (sum-args reg)
        (set-reg! reg (add-list (get-reg sum-args))))
      (cons-1 (reg)
        (set-reg! reg '()))
      (cons-3 (first rest reg)
        (set-reg! reg (cons (get-reg first) (get-reg rest))))
      (brz (test else-instruc)
        (if (zero? (get-reg test)) (set! pc else-instruc)))
      (else (error "Invalid instruction:" ir)))
    (if done result (eval-code/reg))))
```

Figure 12.3.4   Comparison of compiled code

```
> (compile "if 0 then sum(3, 4) else sum(five, six)")
(#(move-imm 0 r0)
 #(brz r0 (#(fetch five env-reg r0)
          #(fetch six env-reg r1)
          #(cons-1 r2)
          #(cons-3 r1 r2 r1)
          #(cons-3 r0 r1 r0)
          #(sum-list r0 r0)
          #(stop r0)))
 #(move-imm 3 r0)
 #(move-imm 4 r1)
 #(cons-1 r2)
 #(cons-3 r1 r2 r1)
 #(cons-3 r0 r1 r0)
 #(sum-list r0 r0)
 #(stop r0))

> (compile "if 0 then sum(3, 4) else sum(five, six)")
#(#(move-imm 0 r0)
  #(brz r0 9)
  #(move-imm 3 r0)
  #(move-imm 4 r1)
  #(cons-1 r2)
  #(cons-3 r1 r2 r1)
  #(cons-3 r0 r1 r0)
  #(sum-list r0 r0)
  #(stop r0)
  #(fetch five env-reg r0)
  #(fetch six env-reg r1)
  #(cons-1 r2)
  #(cons-3 r1 r2 r1)
  #(cons-3 r0 r1 r0)
  #(sum-list r0 r0)
  #(stop r0))
```

○ *Exercise 12.3.2*

A shortcoming of our compiler is that conditional expressions can lead to multiple copies of code. For example, the code for

```
"sum(f(x), if z then x else y)"
```

will contain two copies of the addition. Modify the compiler so that conditional expressions never duplicate code. □

● *Exercise 12.3.3*

Add the form `greater`(exp_1, exp_2), which is nonzero if the value of exp_1 is greater than the value of exp_2, to the source language, and derive an associated compiler and machine. □

● *Exercise 12.3.4*

Add `begin` and `:=` forms to the source language, and derive an associated compiler and machine. □

12.4 Compiling Procedures

The techniques introduced so far may be used with minor variations to enrich the source language of our compiler with a great many language features, such as additional primitive operators and control structures. However, there is one especially important extension that requires new techniques: the addition of procedures. In this section we introduce these techniques.

We begin by extending the CPS interpreter of figure 12.1.1 to interpret forms for creation and application of procedures. See figure 12.4.1. All procedural values are closures, since in our small language there are no first-class primitives. (Primitives, such as `sum`, are special forms.)

The next step in the transformation of our interpreter is to define procedures that abstract actions and use *build-cont* to abstract continuations, as in section 12.1. We also use the register allocation technique of section 12.2. A naive approach to this transformation would result in the following definitions.

Figure 12.4.1   Interpreter for a language with procedures

```
(define-record closure (formals body env))

(define eval-exp
  (lambda (exp env k)
    (variant-case exp
      (proc (formals body)
        (k (make-closure formals body env)))
      (app (rator rands)
        (eval-exp rator env
          (lambda (closure)
            (eval-rands rands env
              (lambda (args)
                (apply-closure closure args k))))))
      ...)))

(define apply-closure
  (lambda (closure args k)
    (variant-case closure
      (closure (formals body env)
        (eval-exp body (extend-env formals args env) k)))))
```

```
(define eval-exp
  (lambda (exp env k)
    (variant-case exp
      (proc (formals body)
        (close-action formals body env k))
      (app (rator rands)
        (eval-exp rator env
          (build-cont
            (lambda (closure)
              (eval-rands rands env
                (build-cont
                  (lambda (args)
                    (apply-closure closure args k)))))))
      ...)))

(define close-action
  (lambda (formals body env k)
    (k (make-closure formals body env))))
```

If we try to write `apply-closure` with this approach, however, we run into two difficulties. First, the body of a closure is not passed to `eval-exp` until the closure is invoked (at run time). This defeats the purpose of compilation. Second, even if the body were represented in some form such that `apply-closure` did not have to call `eval-exp`, it would still be necessary to (1) extend the environment, (2) evaluate the body with the argument list, environment, and current continuation, and then (3) return a result to the caller. Since in most machines environment extension, procedure call (code invocation), and procedure return are performed by separate instructions, we would like to break the work of `apply-closure` down into more primitive actions.

To avoid these difficulties, we first introduce a new type of object, called an *exec*, that executes a procedure's body given an environment, argument list, and continuation and returns the result. A closure then contains only an exec and an environment:

```
(define-record closure (exec env)).
```

Initially we represent execs as procedures. When an exec is invoked with an environment, argument list, and continuation, it extends the environment. The extended environment is then passed to a continuation that executes the body of the associated procedure with a continuation that returns the result. We abstract these actions and continuations with the following procedures.

```
(define build-exec
  (lambda (formals body)
    (lambda (env args k)
      (extend-env-action formals args env
        (lambda (extended-env)
          (eval-exp body extended-env
            (lambda (val)
              (return-action val k)))))))))

(define extend-env-action
  (lambda (formals args env k)
    (k (extend-env formals args env))))

(define return-action
  (lambda (v k)
    (k v)))
```

We begin evaluation of an application by evaluating its operator with a continuation that accepts the value of the operator, which must be a closure. This continuation then evaluates the operands by calling *eval-rands* with a continuation that applies the closure's exec to the closure's environment, the argument list, and the continuation of the application. This may be expressed by extending the interpreter of figure 12.2.1 as follows.

```
(define eval-exp
  (lambda (exp env k)
    (variant-case exp
      (proc (formals body)
        (close-action (build-exec formals body) env k))
      (app (rator rands)
        (eval-exp rator env
          (build-cont (cont->free-regs k)
            (lambda (closure)
              (eval-rands rands env
                (build-cont (cons closure (cont->free-regs k))
                  (lambda (args)
                    (apply-closure-action closure args k))))))))
      ...)))

(define close-action
  (lambda (exec env k)
    (k (make-closure exec env))))

(define apply-closure-action
  (lambda (closure args k)
    (variant-case closure
      (closure (exec env) (exec env args k)))))
```

The full interpreter employs the action procedures of figure 12.1.3 in addition to those above.

We are now ready to transform the interpreter into a compiler and derive a machine that interprets the compiler's object code. This object code is composed of data structures that symbolically represent actions, continuations, and execs.

Once more, the transformation from an interpreter to a compiler is accomplished by redefining the action procedures, without further modification of *eval-exp*. We add the record type and action procedure definitions of figure 12.4.2 to those of figure 12.1.4.

Figure 12.4.2 Actions to support procedures

```
(define-record extend-env-instruc (formals args-reg env-reg k))
(define extend-env-action make-extend-env-instruc)

(define-record return-instruc (return-reg k))
(define return-action make-return-instruc)

(define-record close-instruc (exec env-reg k))
(define close-action make-close-instruc)

(define-record save-instruc (reg-list k))
(define save-action make-save-instruc)

(define-record restore-instruc (k))
(define restore-action make-restore-instruc)

(define-record apply-closure-instruc (closure-reg args-reg k))
(define apply-closure-action
  (lambda (closure-reg args-reg k)
    (variant-case k
      (cont (reg free-regs code)
        (save-action
          (append '(save-regs k-reg env-reg) free-regs)
          (make-cont 'ignore-reg '()
            (make-apply-closure-instruc closure-reg args-reg
              (make-cont reg '()
                (restore-action
                  (make-cont 'ignore-reg '() code)))))))
      (else (error "Invalid continuation:" k)))))
```

These transformations have been entirely straightforward. The interesting transformation is that of *build-exec*. The naive approach would be to define an exec record type as follows.

```
(define-record exec (formals body))
(define build-exec make-exec)
```

The difficulty with this approach is that the body will not be compiled (passed to *eval-exp*) until the exec record is interpreted at run time. Since *eval-exp* now accepts environments and continuations symbolically, it should be possible to compile the body of a closure prior to run time. At compile time we do not know what the environment, argument list, or continuation will be when an exec is invoked, but it is enough to know what registers they will be in. It is common practice for the environment, argument list, and continuation to be recorded in standard locations prior to a procedure call. Thus, by convention, we assume that these values are conveyed to a called procedure in registers named `env-reg`, `args-reg`, and `k-reg`, respectively. It follows that execs may be represented simply as the code generated by an `extend-env-action`. This code creates an extended environment for a procedure call with a continuation that invokes a procedure in the new environment. We use *make-cont* instead of *build-cont* because we want to name the register ourselves.

```
(define build-exec
  (lambda (formals body)
    (extend-env-action formals 'args-reg 'env-reg
      (make-cont 'env-reg '()
        (eval-exp body 'env-reg
          (build-cont '()
            (lambda (val)
              (return-action val 'k-reg)))))))))
```

A simple example illustrates that an application compiles to a `close-instruc` command that forms a closure containing an `extend-env-instruc` command and the current environment. This closure is then passed to a continuation that evaluates the operands of the application and then applies the closure to the argument list, with the continuation of the application (in this case the final value continuation). We leave the free register lists in the following code.

```
> (compile "(proc (x) x)(17)")
#(close-instruc
  #(extend-env-instruc (x) args-reg env-reg
    #(cont env-reg ()
      #(varref-instruc x env-reg
        #(cont r0 ()
          #(return-instruc r0 k-reg)))))
  env-reg
  #(cont r0 ()
    #(lit-instruc 17
      #(cont r1 (r0)
        #(emptyargs-instruc
          #(cont r2 (r1 r0)
            #(rest-instruc r1 r2
```

```
                    #(cont r1 (r0)
                      #(save-instruc (save-regs k-reg env-reg)
                        #(cont ignore-reg ()
                          #(apply-closure-instruc r0 r1
                            #(cont r0 ()
                              #(restore-instruc
                                #(cont ignore-reg ()
                                  #(halt-instruc r0)))))))))))))))))
```

This corresponds to the following Scheme CPS code.

```
(close-action
 (lambda (env-reg)
  (lambda (args-reg k-reg)
   (extend-env-action '(x) args-reg env-reg
    (lambda (env-reg)
     (varref-action 'x env-reg
      (lambda (r0)
       (return-action r0 k-reg)))))))
 init-env
 (lambda (r0)
  (lit-action 17
   (lambda (r1)
    (emptyargs-action
     (lambda (r2)
      (rest-action r1 r2
       (lambda (r1)
        (save-action '(save-regs k-reg env-reg)
         (lambda ()
          (apply-closure-action r0 r1
           (lambda (r0)
            (restore-action
             (lambda ()
              (halt-action r0)))))))))))))))

(define save-action
  (lambda (lst goto)
    (goto)))

(define restore-action
  (lambda (goto)
    (goto)))
```

Figure 12.4.3   Interpreter for procedure code

```
(define eval-code
  (lambda (code)
    (variant-case code
      (close-instruc (exec env-reg k)
        (apply-cont k
          (make-closure exec
            (get-reg env-reg))))
      (extend-env-instruc (formals args-reg env-reg k)
        (apply-cont k
          (extend-env formals (get-reg args-reg) (get-reg env-reg))))
      (save-instruc (reg-list k)
        (set-reg! 'save-regs
          (map (lambda (reg)
                 (cons reg (get-reg reg)))
               reg-list))
        (goto-cont k))
      (apply-closure-instruc (closure-reg args-reg k)
        (set-reg! 'k-reg k)
        (set-reg! 'args-reg (get-reg args-reg))
        (set-reg! 'env-reg (closure->env (get-reg closure-reg)))
        (eval-code (closure->exec (get-reg closure-reg))))
      (restore-instruc (k)
        (for-each (lambda (file-entry)
                    (set-reg! (car file-entry) (cdr file-entry)))
                  (get-reg 'save-regs))
        (goto-cont k))
      (return-instruc (return-reg k)
        (apply-cont (get-reg k) (get-reg return-reg)))
      ...)))
```

In converting code to such Scheme expressions, it is necessary to create thunks for continuations when the corresponding machine instruction invokes *goto-cont* instead of *apply-cont*. These machine instructions are save-instruc and restore-instruc. The associated actions, *save-action* and *restore-action*, are included for completeness.

Next, we extend the *eval-code* procedure in figure 12.1.5 to support the new action codes. See figure 12.4.3. In the apply-closure-instruc clause, the continuation register, k-reg, is set to the continuation of the procedure call. This corresponds to saving the program counter before jumping to a procedure in conventional architectures. The first argument of `set-reg!` is the *name* of a register, so it must be quoted. The argument list must also be moved from the register in which it is currently stored to the standard register, named `args-reg`, in which the exec expects to find it. Finally, the environment stored in the closure is moved to `env-reg` and the exec is executed. Derivation of the other clauses of `eval-code` from the corresponding action procedures is straightforward.

Before running code, we create a register file not only to contain r0, r1, r2, r3, r4, r5, and `env-reg`, but also to include `args-reg`, `k-reg`, and `save-regs`.

```
(define reg-file
  (extend-ff*
    reg-names
    (map (lambda (x) (make-cell '*))
         (append '(args-reg k-reg save-regs) reg-names))
    (extend-ff 'env-reg (make-cell init-env) (create-empty-ff))))
```

- *Exercise 12.4.1*
  Modify the definitions of *eval-exp* and *eval-code* in this section for list-of-instruction code representation. ☐

- *Exercise 12.4.2*
  Modify the definitions of *eval-exp* and *eval-code* in this section for vector-of-instruction code representation. ☐

- *Exercise 12.4.3*
  Modify the definitions of *eval-exp*, *eval-code*, and *init-env* to support primitive procedures, such as +, -, and *. ☐

- *Exercise 12.4.4*
  Extend the compiler and machine to handle `letrecproc`. ☐

- *Exercise 12.4.5*
  Modify the compiler so that it uses labels and `goto` instructions in place of procedure call instructions whenever possible. ☐

- *Exercise 12.4.6*
  One way of verifying the correctness of our compiler is to show that for any source expression *exp*

$$(\text{eval-code (compile } \textit{exp})) \Rightarrow (\text{eval-exp } \textit{exp env-reg k-reg})$$

where *eval-exp* is an evaluator, not the compiler. Verify, by induction on the structure of *exp*, that this relation holds. Note that *env-reg* and *k-reg* do not appear explicitly on the left-hand side of this equation, but they appear in the code generated by (compile *exp*). Be careful about this in your proof. ▯

○ *Exercise 12.4.7*
Modify the compiler and machine to use lexical addresses as in exercise 2.3.10. To do this, give the compiler a second argument, symbol-table, a map from variables to lexical addresses (pairs of integers). In the machine, env-reg will hold a *lexical environment*: a map from lexical addresses to values. Then varref-instruc is replaced by an instruction of the form (lex-varref-instruc ⟨integer⟩ ⟨integer⟩ ⟨register⟩ ⟨code⟩), so that program variables no longer appear in compiled code. ▯

○ *Exercise 12.4.8*
To relate the lexical scope compiler of the preceding exercise to the interpreter, we must relate the symbol table and lexical environment used in this compiler and machine to the ordinary environments used in the interpreter. This can be done by reconstructing the interpreter environment as the composition of these two maps. The compiler must obey the specification below. Verify, by induction on *exp*, that this relation holds.

$$\begin{aligned}
&(\text{eval-code (compile } \textit{exp symbol-table}))\\
\Rightarrow \ &(\text{eval-exp } \textit{exp} \ (\text{compose } \textit{env-reg symbol-table}) \ \textit{k-reg})
\end{aligned}$$
▯

○ *Exercise 12.4.9*
The compiler and machine of this section do not properly handle tail recursion, because the implementation of *build-exec* specifies that a new continuation is built every time a procedure is entered. Figure 12.4.4 contains an implementation of a compiler that generates code that runs tail recursively. It does this by using a special-case compiler, *tr-eval-exp*, to compile code in tail position. Notice how *tr-eval-exp* calls *eval-exp* on the subexpressions (in nontail position) of an application.

First, implement this compiler. Then verify that it produces code that executes tail-recursive procedures iteratively. To do this, modify the machine to keep track of the length of the continuation (the contents of k-reg). Then write a tail-recursive program in the source language and confirm that when

Figure 12.4.4   Properly tail-recursive compiler

```
(define tr-eval-exp
  (lambda (exp env free-regs k)
    (variant-case exp
      (lit (datum) (tr-lit-action datum free-regs k))
      (varref (var) (tr-varref-action var env free-regs k))
      (proc (formals body)
        (tr-close-action (build-exec formals body) env free-regs k))
      (app (rator rands)
        (eval-exp rator env
          (build-cont free-regs
            (lambda (closure)
              (eval-rands rands env
                (build-cont (cons closure free-regs)
                  (lambda (args)
                    (tr-apply-closure-action closure args free-regs k))))))))
      (if (test-exp then-exp else-exp)
        (eval-exp test-exp env
          (build-cont free-regs
            (lambda (test)
              (tr-test-action test
                (lambda (free-regs k)
                  (tr-eval-exp then-exp env free-regs k))
                (lambda (free-regs k)
                  (tr-eval-exp else-exp env free-regs k))
                free-regs
                k)))))
      (sum (rands)
        (eval-rands rands env
          (build-cont free-regs
            (lambda (arg-list)
              (tr-sum-action arg-list free-regs k)))))
      (else (error "Invalid abstract syntax: " exp)))))

(define tr-return-to
  (lambda (free-regs k-reg)
    (build-cont (cons k-reg free-regs)
      (lambda (new-var)
        (return-action k-reg new-var)))))
```

Figure 12.4.4   Properly tail-recursive compiler (continued)

```
(define tr-lit-action
  (lambda (datum free-regs k-reg)
    (make-lit-instruc datum (tr-return-to free-regs k-reg))))

(define tr-varref-action
  (lambda (var env-reg free-regs k-reg)
    (make-varref-instruc var env-reg
      (tr-return-to free-regs k-reg))))

(define tr-sum-action
  (lambda (arg-list-reg free-regs k-reg)
    (make-sum-instruc arg-list-reg (tr-return-to free-regs k-reg))))

(define tr-close-action
  (lambda (exec env-reg free-regs k-reg)
    (make-close-instruc exec env-reg
      (tr-return-to free-regs k-reg))))

(define-record tr-apply-closure-instruc (closure-reg args-reg k-reg))
(define tr-apply-closure-action
  (lambda (closure-reg args-reg free-regs k-reg)
    (make-tr-apply-closure-instruc closure-reg args-reg k-reg)))

(define build-exec
  (lambda (formals body)
    (extend-env-action formals 'args-reg 'env-reg
      (make-cont 'env-reg '()
        (tr-eval-exp body 'env-reg '() 'k-reg)))))

(define eval-code
  (lambda (code)
    (variant-case code
      (tr-apply-closure-instruc (closure-reg args-reg k-reg)
        (set-reg! 'k-reg (get-reg k-reg))
        (set-reg! 'args-reg (get-reg args-reg))
        (set-reg! 'env-reg (closure->env (get-reg closure-reg)))
        (eval-code (closure->exec (get-reg closure-reg))))
      ...)))
```

it runs, the size of the continuation is independent of the number of iterations of the program. □

○ *Exercise 12.4.10*

Extend the compiler of exercise 12.4.9 to handle :=, `begin`, and `letrecproc`. □

• *Exercise 12.4.11*

Here is a somewhat different approach to compiling. In this approach, the compiled code is regarded as acting on a machine with four registers: an accumulator, a buffer, a lexical environment, and a continuation. Such a machine can be modeled as we did in chapter 11, by writing the actions as procedures that take the values of the registers as their arguments. See figure 12.4.5 for the definition of such a machine, in a procedural representation.

The compiler takes four arguments: a boolean flag (true if the source expression is in tail position), a source expression, a symbol table, and machine code, and produces another code. See figure 12.4.6. A suitable top-level procedure might be

```
(define run
  (lambda (exp)
    ((compile-exp #t (parse exp)
       initial-symbol-table restore-code)
     '*
     '()
     initial-lex-env
     (lambda (x) x))))
```

a. Write the rest of the auxiliary functions to implement the compiler of figure 12.4.6 and the machine of figure 12.4.5.

b. Confirm that it executes tail-form programs iteratively, as you did for the `tr-eval-exp` compiler of exercise 12.4.9.

c. Add :=, `begin`, and `letrecproc` to this compiler.

d. Modify the compiler and machine so that it emits useful trace information on every procedure call.

e. Add `callcc` to the initial lexical environment.

f. Add dynamically-scoped globals to the language; these should behave like Scheme procedures defined using `define`. □

Figure 12.4.5 Actions of the four-register machine

```
(define lit-action
  (lambda (datum code)
    (lambda (acc val* lex-env k)
      (code datum val* lex-env k))))

(define varref-action
  (lambda (lex-addr code)
    (lambda (acc val* lex-env k)
      (code (lookup-lex-env lex-env lex-addr) val* lex-env k))))

(define if-action
  (lambda (then-code else-code)
    (lambda (acc val* lex-env k)
      (if acc
          (then-code acc val* lex-env k)
          (else-code acc val* lex-env k)))))

(define proc-action
  (lambda (code-of-body code)
    (lambda (acc val* lex-env k)
      (code
        (lambda (args new-k)
          (code-of-body '* '() (extend-lex-env args lex-env) new-k))
        val*
        lex-env k))))

(define restore-code (lambda (acc val* lex-env k) (k acc)))

(define invoke-code (lambda (acc val* lex-env k) (acc val* k)))

(define save-action
  (lambda (code1 code2)
    (lambda (acc val* lex-env k)
      (code1 '* '() lex-env
        (lambda (v) (code2 v val* lex-env k))))))

(define push-action
  (lambda (code)
    (lambda (acc val* lex-env k)
      (code acc (cons acc val*) lex-env k))))
```

Figure 12.4.6   Compiler for the four-register machine

```
(define compile-exp
  (lambda (tail-pos? exp symbol-table next-code)
    (variant-case exp
      (lit (datum) (lit-action datum next-code))
      (varref (var)
        (varref-action
          (lexical-addr symbol-table var)
           next-code))
      (if (test-exp then-exp else-exp)
        (compile-exp #f test-exp symbol-table
          (if-action
            (compile-exp tail-pos? then-exp
              symbol-table
              next-code)
            (compile-exp tail-pos? else-exp
              symbol-table
              next-code))))
      (proc (formals body)
        (proc-action
          (compile-exp #t body
            (extend-symbol-table formals symbol-table)
            restore-code)
          next-code))
      (app (rator rands)
        (let ((app-code (compile-rands rands
                          symbol-table
                          (compile-exp #f rator symbol-table invoke-code))))
          (if tail-pos?
              app-code
              (save-action app-code next-code)))))))

(define compile-rands
  (lambda (rands symbol-table next-code)
    (if (null? rands)
        next-code
        (compile-exp #f (car rands) symbol-table
          (push-action
            (compile-rands (cdr rands) symbol-table next-code))))))
```

- *Exercise 12.4.12*

In this exercise we shall prove the correctness of the compiler of figure 12.4.6. Because the compiler and machine are functional, the correctness criterion is simpler than that of exercise 12.4.6, although the proof is somewhat more complicated because it is necessary to account for tail recursion. The correctness criterion requires three statements:

```
      ((compile-exp #f exp symbol-table next-code) acc val* lex-env k)
   ⇒ (eval-exp exp (compose lex-env symbol-table)
         (lambda (z) (next-code (cons z val*) lex-env k)))


      ((compile-exp #t exp symbol-table next-code) acc '() lex-env k)
   ⇒ (eval-exp exp (compose lex-env symbol-table) k)


      ((compile-rands rands symbol-table next-code) acc val* lex-env k)
   ⇒ (eval-rands rands (compose lex-env symbol-table)
         (lambda (w)
            (next-code (append (reverse w) val*) lex-env k)))
```

We can explain each of these statements as follows:

1. The goal of the code for *exp* in nontail position is to evaluate *exp* in a continuation that pushes the value of *exp* onto the buffer and then performs the next action.

2. The goal of the code for *exp* in tail position is to evaluate *exp* and pass the value to the continuation *k*. Note that in this case, *val** will always be empty, and *next-code* is ignored. This accounts for the '* in run above.

3. The goal of the code for a list of operands is to accumulate the values in reverse order on the top of the stack *val** and then to perform the next action.

Prove, using induction on the structure of *exp*, that each of these three relations is true. ☐

- *Exercise 12.4.13*

The compiler uses a four-register machine in much the same way as the scanner of chapter 11 uses a two-register machine. Careful attention to the use of acc and val* makes it clear that it is acting in the same way as the buffer, if we think about acc being consed onto val*. Rewrite the compiler so that it combines the uses of acc and val* and hence uses just three registers. ☐

12.5 Summary

An interpreter can be modified to become a translator from the defined language to the defining language by introducing an ADT of interpreter actions, and then redefining the action-building procedures to emit code rather than perform actions.

If the interpreter is a CPS interpreter, the output from the translator is CPS code that strongly resembles ordinary assembly language. Variables in the CPS code correspond to machine registers, and the binding patterns in the CPS code correspond to the setting of those registers.

Because the CPS output code is stylized, it is possible to build an interpreter that is specialized for this code. The resulting interpreter is analogous to the microprogram of a conventional machine.

The CPS output code can be transformed into a sequence of machine instructions by a simple regrouping of its components, or by changing the action procedures to emit this syntax initially.

Appendix A Record Implementation

Standard Scheme does not support records, though most implementations provide some such mechanism (sometimes called structures). Here we provide an implementation of the record facility used in this book.

In order to introduce the new special forms `define-record` and `variant-case`, some syntactic extension (or "macro") facility is required. See figure A.1 and figure A.2 for an implementation of `define-record` and `variant-case` using `extend-syntax`. See Dybvig [1987] for details of this `extend-syntax` mechanism.

Figure A.1   Auxiliaries for `define-record` and `variant-case`

```
(define record-proc-names
  (lambda (name fields)
    (let ((name-str (symbol->string name)))
      (cons (string->symbol (string-append (symbol->string 'make-) name-str))
            (cons (string->symbol (string-append name-str "?"))
                  (map (lambda (field)
                         (string->symbol (string-append name-str
                                                        "->"
                                                        (symbol->string field))))
                       fields))))))

(define record-indices
  (lambda (vec-len)
    (letrec ((loop (lambda (i)
                     (if (= i vec-len) '() (cons i (loop (+ i 1)))))))
      (loop 1))))

(define make-unique-name
  (lambda (names)
    (string->symbol (apply string-append (map symbol->string names)))))
```

Figure A.2   Implementation of `variant-case` and `define-record`

```
(extend-syntax (variant-case else)
  ((variant-case var) (error "variant-case: no clause matches" var))
  ((variant-case var (else exp1 exp2 ...)) (begin exp1 exp2 ...))
  ((variant-case exp clause ...)
   (not (symbol? 'exp))
   (with ((var (gensym)))
     (let ((var exp)) (variant-case var clause ...))))
  ((variant-case var (name (field ...) exp1 exp2 ...) clause ...)
   (with (((make-name name? name->field ...)
            (record-proc-names 'name '(field ...))))
     (if (name? var)
         (let ((field (name->field var)) ...) exp1 exp2 ...)
         (variant-case var clause ...)))))

(extend-syntax (define-record)
  ((define-record name (field ...))
   (with (((make-name name? name->field ...) (record-proc-names 'name '(field ...)))
           (unique-name (make-unique-name '(name field ...)))
           (vec-len (+ 1 (length '(field ...)))))
     (with (((i ...) (record-indices 'vec-len)))
       (begin
         (define make-name
           (let ((unique-name vector))
             (lambda (field ...)
               (unique-name 'name field ...))))
         (define name?
           (lambda (obj)
             (and (vector? obj)
                  (= (vector-length obj) vec-len)
                  (eq? (vector-ref obj 0) 'name))))
         (define name->field
           (lambda (obj)
             (if (name? obj)
                 (vector-ref obj i)
                 (error "name->field: bad record" obj))))
         ...)))))
```

Appendix B   Abstract Syntax

In this book, although we present syntax for a character string language, we also support a list structure language. Both of the languages parse to identical parse trees, using the record declarations given here. This way the program processing programs all have the same abstract view, regardless of the choice of language.

Figure B.1   Abstract syntax record declarations for chapter 5

```
(define-record define (var exp))
(define-record varref (var))
(define-record lit (datum))
(define-record app (rator rands))
(define-record if (test-exp then-exp else-exp))
(define-record let (decls body))
(define-record decl (var exp))
(define-record proc (formals body))
(define-record varassign (var exp))
(define-record letmutable (decls body))
(define-record begin (exp1 exp2))
(define-record letrecproc (procdecls body))
(define-record procdecl (var formals body))
(define-record letrec (decls body))
(define-record dynassign (var exp body))
(define-record letdynamic (decls body))
```

```
(define-record definearray (var dim-exp))
(define-record letarray (arraydecls body))
(define-record arrayref (array index))
(define-record arrayassign (array index exp))
(define-record letproc (procdecls body))
(define-record local (decls))
(define-record keydecl (var exp))
```

Figure B.3   Abstract syntax record declarations for chapter 7

```
(define-record super-meth-app (name rands))
(define-record meth-app (name rands))
(define-record i-varref (var))
(define-record c-varref (var))
(define-record i-varassign (var exp))
(define-record c-varassign (var exp))
(define-record method (formals body))
(define-record new-simpleinstance (class-exp))
(define-record new-simpleclass (c-vars i-vars methdecls init-exp))
(define-record new-class (parent-exp c-vars i-vars methdecls init-exp))
(define-record new-instance (class-exp parent-exp i-vars methdecls))
```

Figure B.4   Abstract syntax record declarations for chapter 9

```
(define-record abort (exp))
(define-record letcont (var body))
(define-record callcc (exp))
(define-record coroutine (exp))
(define-record wind (pre body post))
```

Figure B.5   Abstract syntax record declaration for chapter 12

```
(define-record sum (rands))
```

Appendix C Character String Syntax

The tokens of the language are defined by the following grammar.

$$\langle\text{identifier}\rangle ::= \langle\text{nondigit-id-char}\rangle \{ \langle\text{nondigit-id-char}\rangle \mid \langle\text{digit}\rangle \}^*$$
$$\mid \texttt{+} \mid \texttt{-} \mid \texttt{*}$$
$$\langle\text{integer-literal}\rangle ::= \langle\text{digit}\rangle \{\langle\text{digit}\rangle\}^*$$
$$\langle\text{whitespace}\rangle ::= \{ \langle\text{space}\rangle \mid \langle\text{newline}\rangle \}^+$$
$$\langle\text{comment}\rangle ::= \texttt{\%} \{\langle\text{any-char-but-newline}\rangle\}^*$$
$$\langle\text{assign-sym}\rangle ::= \texttt{:=}$$
$$\langle\text{ampersand}\rangle ::= \texttt{\&}$$
$$\langle\text{double-ampersand}\rangle ::= \texttt{\&\&}$$
$$\langle\text{lparen}\rangle ::= \texttt{(}$$
$$\langle\text{rparen}\rangle ::= \texttt{)}$$
$$\langle\text{lbracket}\rangle ::= \texttt{[}$$
$$\langle\text{rbracket}\rangle ::= \texttt{]}$$
$$\langle\text{comma}\rangle ::= \texttt{,}$$
$$\langle\text{eqsign}\rangle ::= \texttt{=}$$
$$\langle\text{semicolon}\rangle ::= \texttt{;}$$
$$\langle\text{colon}\rangle ::= \texttt{:}$$
$$\langle\text{dollar-sign}\rangle ::= \texttt{\$}$$

The letters are the 52 upper and lower case letters; the digits are the ten decimal digits; a "nondigit-id-char" is any letter.

The language is defined by the following concrete and abstract syntax.

⟨form⟩ ::= define ⟨var⟩ = ⟨exp⟩   define (var exp)

    | definearray ⟨var⟩ [⟨exp⟩]   definearray (var dim-exp)

    | ⟨exp⟩

⟨exp⟩ ::= ⟨integer-literal⟩   lit (datum)

    | ⟨varref⟩

    | ⟨operator⟩ ⟨operands⟩   app (rator rands)

    | if ⟨exp⟩ then ⟨exp⟩ else ⟨exp⟩   if (test-exp then-exp else-exp)

    | let ⟨decls⟩ in ⟨exp⟩   let (decls body)

    | proc ⟨varlist⟩ ⟨exp⟩   proc (formals body)

    | ⟨var⟩ := ⟨exp⟩   varassign (var exp)

    | letmutable ⟨decls⟩ in ⟨exp⟩   letmutable (decls body)

    | begin ⟨exp⟩ ⟨compound⟩   begin (exp1 exp2)

    | letrecproc ⟨procdecls⟩   letrecproc (procdecls

      in ⟨exp⟩   body)

    | letrec ⟨decls⟩ in ⟨exp⟩   letrec (decls body)

    | ⟨var⟩ := ⟨exp⟩ during ⟨exp⟩   dynassign (var exp body)

    | letdynamic ⟨decls⟩ in ⟨exp⟩   letdynamic (decls body)

    | letarray ⟨arraydecls⟩ in ⟨exp⟩   letarray (arraydecls body)

    | ⟨array-exp⟩ [⟨exp⟩]   arrayref (array index)

    | ⟨array-exp⟩ [⟨exp⟩] := ⟨exp⟩   arrayassign (array index exp)

    | letproc ⟨procdecls⟩ in ⟨exp⟩   letproc (procdecls body)

    | local ⟨decls⟩ in ⟨exp⟩   local (decls body)

    | ⟨instance-var⟩

    | ⟨class-var⟩

    | ⟨instance-var⟩ := ⟨exp⟩   i-varassign (var exp)

    | ⟨class-var⟩ := ⟨exp⟩   c-varassign (var exp)

    | method ⟨varlist⟩ ⟨exp⟩   method (formals body)

    | $⟨var⟩ (⟨exps⟩)   meth-app (name rands)

    | simpleinstance ⟨exp⟩   new-simpleinst (class-exp)

    | simpleclass ⟨varlist⟩   new-simpleclass (c-vars

      ⟨varlist⟩ ⟨methdecls⟩ ⟨exp⟩   i-vars methdecls init-exp)

    | class ⟨exp⟩, ⟨c-vars⟩   new-class (parent-exp c-vars

      ⟨i-vars⟩ ⟨methdecls⟩ ⟨exp⟩   i-vars methdecls init-exp)

    | $⟨var⟩ ⟨super-rands⟩   super-meth-app (name rands)

    | instance ⟨exp⟩, ⟨exp⟩,   new-instance (class-exp

      ⟨varlist⟩ ⟨methdecls⟩   parent-exp i-vars methdecls)

    | abort ⟨exp⟩   abort (exp)

```
|  letcont ⟨var⟩ in ⟨exp⟩              letcont (var body)
|  callcc ⟨exp⟩                        callcc (exp)
|  coroutine ⟨exp⟩                     coroutine (exp)
|  wind ⟨exp⟩ within ⟨exp⟩             wind (pre body
     unwind ⟨exp⟩                           post)
|  sum ⟨operands⟩                      sum (rands)
```

```
           ⟨var⟩ ::= ⟨identifier⟩
      ⟨operator⟩ ::= ⟨varref⟩
                 |  (⟨exp⟩)
       ⟨operand⟩ ::= ⟨exp⟩
        ⟨varref⟩ ::= ⟨var⟩                      varref (var)
         ⟨decls⟩ ::= ⟨decl⟩ {;⟨decl⟩}*
          ⟨decl⟩ ::= ⟨var⟩ = ⟨exp⟩              decl (var exp)
       ⟨varlist⟩ ::= ( )
                 |  (⟨vars⟩ {,⟨keydecl⟩}*)
                 |  (⟨keydecls⟩)
          ⟨vars⟩ ::= ⟨var⟩ {,⟨var⟩}*
      ⟨compound⟩ ::= {;⟨exp⟩}* end
      ⟨procdecls⟩ ::= ⟨procdecl⟩ {;⟨procdecl⟩}*
      ⟨procdecl⟩ ::= ⟨var⟩ ⟨varlist⟩ = ⟨exp⟩    procdecl (var formals body)
     ⟨array-exp⟩ ::= ⟨exp⟩
     ⟨arraydecls⟩ ::= ⟨arraydecl⟩ {;⟨arraydecl⟩}*
      ⟨arraydecl⟩ ::= ⟨var⟩ [⟨exp⟩]             decl (var exp)
       ⟨keydecls⟩ ::= ⟨keydecl⟩ {,⟨keydecl⟩}*
        ⟨keydecl⟩ ::= :⟨var⟩ = ⟨exp⟩            decl (var exp)
       ⟨operands⟩ ::= ( )
                 |  (⟨exps⟩ {,⟨keydecls⟩}*)
                 |  (⟨keydecls⟩)
           ⟨exps⟩ ::= ⟨exp⟩ {,⟨exp⟩}*
   ⟨instance-var⟩ ::= &⟨var⟩                     i-varref (var)
      ⟨class-var⟩ ::= &&⟨var⟩                    c-varref (var)
      ⟨methdecls⟩ ::= ( )
                 |  ( ⟨decls⟩ )
    ⟨super-rands⟩ ::= (super)
                 |  (super, ⟨exps⟩)
```

Appendix D Character String Parser

This appendix is composed of nine figures. In order to run programs from chapter 5, you must include the record declarations from appendix B, the scanner from appendix E, and all of figures D.1 through D.4. Once chapter 5 works, it is very easy to add either chapter 6, section 6.6, chapter 7, chapter 9, or chapter 12. To run chapter 6, section 6.6, chapter 7, chapter 9, or chapter 12, include figure D.5, figure D.6, figure D.7, figure D.8, or figure D.9, respectively. These are modular, so for example, to run chapter 9, include everything necessary to run chapter 5, plus figure D.8. The definitions of figure D.6 redefine *parse-rands* and *parse-varlist* and they are needed only when the defined language supports section 6.6.

If you choose to use the interactive capabilities of appendix F, you will want to add those definitions and thus override some of these. This design is intentional. Often it is better to get the character string parser working smoothly before making it run interactively with unbounded character streams.

The code of this appendix is explained in chapter 11. The procedures *parse-loop** and *parse-loop+* are not presented in that chapter. Once that chapter is understood, their use will become clear. The * and the + correspond to Kleene star and Kleene plus, respectively. They are useful when parsing expressions that have an arbitrary number of items, such as argument and parameter lists.

The procedure *error* is not part of Scheme, but virtually every Scheme system supports it. Here is the definition we used throughout the book:

```
(define error
  (lambda args
    (for-each (lambda (x) (display x) (display " ")) args)
    (newline)
    (reset)))
```

Figure D.1   Parser procedures

```scheme
(define check/drop
  (lambda (class next-action)
    (lambda (buffer token-seq)
      (let ((token (token-seq-head token-seq)))
        (if (eq? (token->class token) class)
            (next-action buffer (token-seq-tail token-seq))
            (error "Syntax error: expecting a" class "not a" token))))))

(define check/shift
  (lambda (class next-action)
    (lambda (buffer token-seq)
      (let ((token (token-seq-head token-seq)))
        (if (eq? (token->class token) class)
            (next-action (cons (token->data token) buffer)
                         (token-seq-tail token-seq))
            (error "Syntax error: expecting a" class "not a" token))))))

(define goto-parser-state
  (lambda (state)
    (lambda (buffer token-seq)
      (let ((next-action (state (token-seq-head token-seq))))
        (next-action buffer token-seq)))))

(define reduce
  (lambda (prod-name)
    (lambda (buffer token-seq)
      (make-parser-answer
        (apply (get-constructor-from-name prod-name) (reverse buffer))
        token-seq))))

(define process-nt
  (lambda (state next-action)
    (lambda (buffer token-seq)
      (let ((next-answer ((goto-parser-state state) '() token-seq)))
        (next-action
          (cons (parser-answer->tree next-answer) buffer)
          (parser-answer->unparsed next-answer))))))

(define emit-list
  (lambda ()
    (lambda (buffer token-seq)
      (make-parser-answer (reverse buffer) token-seq))))
```

```
(define-record parser-answer (tree unparsed))
(define token-seq-head car)
(define token-seq-tail cdr)

(define character-string-parser
  (lambda (a-string)
    (parse-token-seq parse-form
      (character-string-scanner a-string))))

(define parse-token-seq
  (lambda (start-state token-seq)
    (let ((answer (parse-once start-state token-seq)))
      (variant-case answer
        (parser-answer (tree unparsed)
          (if (eq? (token->class (token-seq-head unparsed)) 'end-marker)
              tree
              (error "Tokens left over:" unparsed)))))))

(define parse-once
  (lambda (start-state token-seq)
    ((goto-parser-state start-state) '() token-seq)))

(define parse-loop*
  (lambda (terminator separator action)
    (letrec
      ((more (lambda (token)
               (let ((class (token->class token)))
                 (cond
                   ((eq? class terminator) (emit-list))
                   ((eq? separator class)
                    (check/drop separator
                      (action (goto-parser-state more))))
                   (else "Invalid separator token:" token)))))
       (lambda (token)
         (let ((class (token->class token)))
           (if (eq? class terminator)
               (emit-list)
               (action (goto-parser-state more))))))))))
```

Figure D.1   Parser procedures (continued)

```
(define parse-loop+
  (lambda (terminator separator action)
    (letrec
      ((more (lambda (token)
               (let ((class (token->class token)))
                 (cond
                   ((eq? class terminator) (emit-list))
                   ((eq? separator class)
                    (check/drop separator
                      (action (goto-parser-state more))))
                   (else "Invalid separator token:" token)))))))
      (lambda (token)
        (action (goto-parser-state more))))))
```

Figure D.2   Parser globals needed for all chapters

```
(define parse-form
  (lambda (token)
    ((case (token->class token)
       ((define) seen-define)
       ((definearray) seen-define)
       (else parse-exp))
     token)))

(define parse-exp
  (lambda (token)
    ((case (token->class token)
       ((number) seen-number)
       ((variable) seen-variable)
       ((lparen) seen-lparen)
       ((if) seen-if)
       ((let) seen-let)
       ((proc) seen-proc)
       ((begin) seen-begin)
       ((letmutable) seen-letmutable)
       ((letrecproc) seen-letrecproc)
       ((letrec) seen-letrec)
```

```
        ((letdynamic) seen-letdynamic)
        ((letarray) seen-letarray)
        ((letproc) seen-letproc)
        ((local) seen-local)
        ((dollar-sign) seen-dollar-sign)
        ((ampersand) seen-ampersand)
        ((double-ampersand) seen-double-ampersand)
        ((method) seen-method)
        ((simpleclass) seen-simpleclass)
        ((simpleinstance) seen-simpleinstance)
        ((class) seen-class)
        ((instance) seen-instance)
        ((abort) seen-abort)
        ((letcont) seen-letcont)
        ((callcc) seen-callcc)
        ((coroutine) seen-coroutine)
        ((wind) seen-wind)
        ((sum) seen-sum)
        (else (error "Invalid parse-exp token:" token)))
      token)))

(define parse/var
  (lambda (token)
    (case (token->class token)
      ((lparen) (seen-var&lparen token))
      ((assign-sym) (seen-var&assign-sym token))
      ((lbracket) (seen-var&lbracket token))
      (else (reduce 'varref)))))
```

Figure D.3 Constructors

```
(define get-constructor-from-name
  (lambda (prod-name)
    (case prod-name
      ((chain) (lambda (x) x))
      ((lit) make-lit)
      ((app) make-app)
      ((app/var) (lambda (var rands) (make-app (make-varref var) rands)))
      ((begin) (letrec ((loop (lambda (exps)
                                (if (null? (cdr exps))
                                    (car exps)
                                    (make-begin (car exps) (loop (cdr exps)))))))
                 loop))
      ((define) make-define)
      ((varref) make-varref)
      ((if) make-if)
      ((proc) make-proc)
      ((let) make-let)
      ((letmutable) make-letmutable)
      ((letrecproc) make-letrecproc)
      ((letrec) make-letrec)
      ((decl) make-decl)
      ((procdecl) make-procdecl)
      ((varassign) make-varassign)
      ((dynassign) make-dynassign)
      ((letdynamic) make-letdynamic)
      ((definearray) make-definearray)
      ((arrayref) make-arrayref)
      ((arrayref/var) (lambda (var index)
                        (make-arrayref (make-varref var) index)))
      ((arrayassign) make-arrayassign)
      ((arrayassign/var) (lambda (var index val)
                           (make-arrayassign (make-varref var) index val)))
      ((letarray) make-letarray)
      ((letproc) make-letproc)
      ((local) make-local)
```

```
((stuff-and-keydecls) append)
((keydecl) make-keydecl)
((i-var) make-i-varref)
((c-var) make-c-varref)
((method) make-method)
((letcont) make-letcont)
((i-varassign) make-i-varassign)
((c-varassign) make-c-varassign)
((new-simpleinst) make-new-simpleinst)
((new-simpleclass) make-new-simpleclass)
((new-class) make-new-class)
((instance) make-new-instance)
((meth-app) (lambda (var rands)
              (if (null? rands)
                  (error "Invalid method rands:" rands)
                  (let ((rand (car rands)))
                    (if (and (varref? rand)
                             (eq? (varref->var rand) 'super))
                        (make-super-meth-app var (cdr rands))
                        (make-meth-app var rands))))))
((abort) make-abort)
((letcont) make-letcont)
((callcc) make-callcc)
((coroutine) make-coroutine)
((wind) make-wind)
((sum) make-sum)
(else (error "Bad production name:" prod-name)))))
```

Figure D.4   Chapter 5 parsing procedures

```
(define seen-define
  (lambda (token)
    (check/drop 'define
      (check/shift 'variable
        (check/drop 'eqsign
          (process-nt parse-exp (reduce 'define)))))))

(define seen-number
  (lambda (token)
    (check/shift 'number (reduce 'lit))))

(define seen-variable
  (lambda (token)
    (check/shift 'variable (goto-parser-state parse/var))))

(define seen-lparen
  (lambda (token)
    (check/drop 'lparen
      (process-nt parse-exp
        (check/drop 'rparen
          (goto-parser-state parse-proc))))))

(define seen-if
  (lambda (token)
    (check/drop 'if
      (process-nt parse-exp
        (check/drop 'then
          (process-nt parse-exp
            (check/drop 'else
              (process-nt parse-exp (reduce 'if)))))))))

(define seen-proc
  (lambda (token)
    (check/drop 'proc
      (check/drop 'lparen
        (process-nt parse-varlist
          (check/drop 'rparen
            (process-nt parse-exp (reduce 'proc))))))))
```

```
(define seen-begin
  (lambda (token)
    (check/drop 'begin
      (process-nt parse-compound
        (check/drop 'end (reduce 'begin))))))

(define seen-let
  (lambda (token)
    (check/drop 'let
      (process-nt parse-decls
        (check/drop 'in (process-nt parse-exp (reduce 'let)))))))

(define seen-letmutable
  (lambda (token)
    (check/drop 'letmutable
      (process-nt parse-decls
        (check/drop 'in
          (process-nt parse-exp (reduce 'letmutable)))))))

(define seen-letrec
  (lambda (token)
    (check/drop 'letrec
      (process-nt parse-decls
        (check/drop 'in (process-nt parse-exp (reduce 'letrec)))))))

(define seen-letrecproc
  (lambda (token)
    (check/drop 'letrecproc
      (process-nt parse-procdecls
        (check/drop 'in (process-nt parse-exp (reduce 'letrecproc)))))))

(define seen-letdynamic
  (lambda (token)
    (check/drop 'letdynamic
      (process-nt parse-decls
        (check/drop 'in (process-nt parse-exp (reduce 'letdynamic)))))))
```

Figure D.4   Chapter 5 parsing procedures (continued)

```
(define seen-var&lparen
  (lambda (token)
    (check/drop 'lparen
      (process-nt parse-rands
        (check/drop 'rparen (reduce 'app/var))))))

(define seen-var&assign-sym
  (lambda (token)
    (check/drop 'assign-sym
      (process-nt parse-exp
        (goto-parser-state parse-assign-or-dynassign)))))

(define parse-proc
  (lambda (token)
    (case (token->class token)
      ((lparen)
       (check/drop 'lparen
         (process-nt parse-rands (check/drop 'rparen (reduce 'app)))))
      (else (reduce 'chain)))))

(define parse-assign-or-dynassign
  (lambda (token)
    (case (token->class token)
      ((during)
       (check/drop 'during (process-nt parse-exp (reduce 'dynassign))))
      (else (reduce 'varassign)))))

(define parse-varlist
  (parse-loop* 'rparen 'comma
    (lambda (action) (check/shift 'variable action))))

(define parse-compound
  (parse-loop* 'end 'semicolon
    (lambda (action) (process-nt parse-form action))))

(define parse-rands
  (parse-loop* 'rparen 'comma
    (lambda (action)
      (process-nt parse-exp action))))
```

Figure D.4   Chapter 5 parsing procedures (continued)

```scheme
(define parse-decls
  (parse-loop+ 'in 'semicolon
    (lambda (action) (process-nt parse-decl action))))

(define parse-procdecls
  (parse-loop+ 'in 'semicolon
    (lambda (action) (process-nt parse-procdecl action))))

(define parse-decl
  (lambda (token)
    (case (token->class token)
      ((variable)
       (check/shift 'variable
         (check/drop 'eqsign
           (process-nt parse-exp (reduce 'decl)))))
      (else (error "Invalid parse-letdecl token:" token)))))

(define parse-procdecl
  (lambda (token)
    (case (token->class token)
      ((variable)
       (check/shift 'variable
         (check/drop 'lparen
           (process-nt parse-varlist
             (check/drop 'rparen
               (check/drop 'eqsign
                 (process-nt parse-exp (reduce 'procdecl))))))))
      (else (error "Invalid parse-procdecl token:" token)))))
```

Figure D.5   Chapter 6 parsing procedures

```
(define seen-var&lbracket
  (lambda (token)
    (check/drop 'lbracket
      (process-nt parse-exp
        (check/drop 'rbracket
          (goto-parser-state
            parse-arrayassign-or-arrayref/var))))))

(define seen-definearray
  (lambda (token)
    (check/drop 'definearray
      (check/shift 'variable
        (check/drop 'lbracket
          (process-nt parse-exp
            (check/drop 'rbracket (reduce 'definearray))))))))

(define seen-letarray
  (lambda (token)
    (check/drop 'letarray
      (process-nt parse-arraydecls
        (check/drop 'in (process-nt parse-exp (reduce 'letarray)))))))

(define seen-letproc
  (lambda (token)
    (check/drop 'letproc
      (process-nt parse-procdecls
        (check/drop 'in (process-nt parse-exp (reduce 'letproc)))))))

(define seen-local
  (lambda (token)
    (check/drop 'local
      (process-nt parse-decls
        (check/drop 'in (process-nt parse-exp (reduce 'local)))))))

(define parse-arrayassign-or-arrayref
  (lambda (token)
    (case (token->class token)
      ((assign-sym)
       (check/drop 'assign-sym
         (process-nt parse-exp (reduce 'arrayassign))))
      (else (reduce 'arrayref)))))
```

Figure D.5   Chapter 6 parsing procedures (continued)

```
(define parse-arrayassign-or-arrayref/var
  (lambda (token)
    (case (token->class token)
      ((assign-sym)
       (check/drop 'assign-sym
         (process-nt parse-exp (reduce 'arrayassign/var))))
      (else (reduce 'arrayref/var)))))

(define parse-arraydecls
  (parse-loop+ 'in 'semicolon
    (lambda (action) (process-nt parse-arraydecl action))))

(define parse-arraydecl
  (lambda (token)
    (case (token->class token)
      ((variable)
       (check/shift 'variable
         (check/drop 'lbracket
           (process-nt parse-exp
             (check/drop 'rbracket (reduce 'decl))))))
      (else (error "Invalid parse-arraydecl token:" token)))))
```

Figure D.6   Section 6.6 parsing procedures

```
(define parse-vars-until-optdecls
  (parse-loop* 'rparen 'comma
    (lambda (action)
      (goto-parser-state
        (lambda (token)
          (case (token->class token)
            ((colon) (emit-list))
            ((variable) (check/shift 'variable action))
            (else (error "Invalid parse-vars-until-optdecls:" token))))))))

(define parse-optdecls
  (parse-loop* 'rparen 'comma
    (lambda (action) (process-nt parse-optdecl action))))
```

```
(define parse-optdecl-var
  (lambda (token)
    (case (token->class token)
      ((variable)
       (check/shift 'variable
         (check/drop 'eqsign
           (process-nt parse-exp (reduce 'keydecl)))))
      (else (error "Invalid parse-optdecl-var token:" token)))))

(define parse-optdecl
  (lambda (token)
    (case (token->class token)
      ((colon) (check/drop 'colon
                 (goto-parser-state parse-optdecl-var)))
      (else (error "Invalid parse-optdecl token:" token)))))

(define parse-exps-until-keydecls
  (parse-loop* 'rparen 'comma
    (lambda (action)
      (goto-parser-state
        (lambda (token)
          (case (token->class token)
            ((colon) (emit-list))
            (else (process-nt parse-exp action))))))))

(define parse-keydecls
  (parse-loop* 'rparen 'comma
    (lambda (action) (process-nt parse-keydecl action))))

(define parse-keydecl
  (lambda (token)
    (case (token->class token)
      ((colon)
       (check/drop 'colon
         (check/shift 'variable
           (check/drop 'eqsign
             (process-nt parse-exp (reduce 'keydecl))))))
      (else (error "Invalid parse-opts token:" token)))))
```

Figure D.6   Section 6.6 parsing procedures (continued)

```
(define parse-varlist
  (lambda (token)
    (process-nt parse-vars-until-optdecls
      (process-nt parse-optdecls (reduce 'stuff-and-keydecls)))))

(define parse-rands
  (lambda (token)
    (process-nt parse-exps-until-keydecls
      (process-nt parse-keydecls (reduce 'stuff-and-keydecls)))))
```

Figure D.7   Chapter 7 parsing procedures

```
(define seen-dollar-sign
  (lambda (token)
    (check/drop 'dollar-sign
      (check/shift 'variable
        (check/drop 'lparen
          (process-nt parse-rands
            (check/drop 'rparen (reduce 'meth-app)))))))))

(define seen-ampersand
  (lambda (token)
    (check/drop 'ampersand
      (check/shift 'variable (goto-parser-state parse/ivar)))))

(define seen-double-ampersand
  (lambda (token)
    (check/drop 'double-ampersand
      (check/shift 'variable (goto-parser-state parse/cvar)))))

(define seen-method
  (lambda (token)
    (check/drop 'method
      (check/drop 'lparen
        (process-nt parse-varlist
          (check/drop 'rparen
            (process-nt parse-exp (reduce 'method))))))))
```

```
(define seen-simpleinstance
  (lambda (token)
    (check/drop 'simpleinstance
      (process-nt parse-exp (reduce 'new-simpleinst)))))

(define seen-simpleclass
  (lambda (token)
    (check/drop 'simpleclass
      (check/drop 'lparen
        (process-nt parse-varlist
          (check/drop 'rparen
            (check/drop 'lparen
              (process-nt parse-varlist
                (check/drop 'rparen
                  (check/drop 'lparen
                    (process-nt parse-methdecls
                      (check/drop 'rparen
                        (process-nt parse-exp
                          (reduce 'new-simpleclass)))))))))))))

(define seen-class
  (lambda (token)
    (check/drop 'class
      (process-nt parse-exp
        (check/drop 'comma
          (check/drop 'lparen
            (process-nt parse-varlist
              (check/drop 'rparen
                (check/drop 'lparen
                  (process-nt parse-varlist
                    (check/drop 'rparen
                      (check/drop 'lparen
                        (process-nt parse-methdecls
                          (check/drop 'rparen
                            (process-nt parse-exp
                              (reduce 'new-class)))))))))))))))
```

Figure D.7   Chapter 7 parsing procedures (continued)

```
(define seen-instance
  (lambda (token)
    (check/drop 'instance
      (process-nt parse-exp
        (check/drop 'comma
          (process-nt parse-exp
            (check/drop 'comma
              (check/drop 'lparen
                (process-nt parse-varlist
                  (check/drop 'rparen
                    (check/drop 'lparen
                      (process-nt parse-methdecls
                        (check/drop 'rparen (reduce 'instance)))))))))))))))

(define parse/ivar
  (lambda (token)
    (case (token->class token)
      ((assign-sym)
       (check/drop 'assign-sym
         (process-nt parse-exp (reduce 'i-varassign))))
      (else (reduce 'i-var)))))

(define parse/cvar
  (lambda (token)
    (case (token->class token)
      ((assign-sym)
       (check/drop 'assign-sym
         (process-nt parse-exp (reduce 'c-varassign))))
      (else (reduce 'c-var)))))

(define parse-methdecls
  (parse-loop* 'rparen 'semicolon
    (lambda (action) (process-nt parse-decl action))))
```

Figure D.8   Chapters 9 parsing procedures

```
(define seen-abort
  (lambda (token)
    (check/drop 'abort
      (process-nt parse-exp (reduce 'abort)))))

(define seen-letcont
  (lambda (token)
    (check/drop 'letcont
      (check/shift 'variable
        (check/drop 'in (process-nt parse-exp (reduce 'letcont)))))))

(define seen-callcc
  (lambda (token)
    (check/drop 'callcc
      (process-nt parse-exp (reduce 'callcc)))))

(define seen-coroutine
  (lambda (token)
    (check/drop 'coroutine
      (process-nt parse-exp (reduce 'coroutine)))))

(define seen-wind
  (lambda (token)
    (check/drop 'wind
      (process-nt parse-exp
        (check/drop 'within
          (process-nt parse-exp
            (check/drop 'unwind
              (process-nt parse-exp (reduce 'wind)))))))))
```

Figure D.9   Chapter 12 parsing procedure

```
(define seen-sum
  (lambda (token)
    (check/drop 'sum
      (check/drop 'lparen
        (process-nt parse-rands (check/drop 'rparen (reduce 'sum)))))))
```

Appendix E Character String Scanner

This appendix gives a complete implementation of a scanner that supports the character string syntax of the defined language. The character #\nul represents some character, not in the language being scanned.

Figure E.1   Character string scanner

```
(define shift
  (lambda (next-action)
    (lambda (buffer char-seq)
      (next-action (cons (char-seq-head char-seq) buffer) (char-seq-tail char-seq)))))

(define drop
  (lambda (next-action)
    (lambda (buffer char-seq)
      (next-action buffer (char-seq-tail char-seq)))))

(define goto-scanner-state
  (lambda (state)
    (lambda (buffer char-seq)
      ((state (char-seq-head char-seq)) buffer char-seq))))

(define emit
  (lambda (cooker)
    (lambda (buffer char-seq)
      (make-scanner-answer (cooker (reverse buffer)) char-seq))))

(define-record token (class data))

(define-record scanner-answer (token unscanned))
```

Figure E.1   Character string scanner (continued)

```
(define char-seq-head car)

(define char-seq-tail cdr)

(define cook-punctuation
  (lambda (class)
    (lambda (buffer) (make-token class '*))))

(define cook-number
  (lambda (buffer)
    (make-token 'number (string->number (list->string buffer)))))

(define cook-identifier
  (lambda (buffer)
    (let ((symbol (string->symbol (list->string buffer))))
      (if (memq symbol keywords-list)
          (make-token symbol '*)
          (make-token 'variable symbol)))))

(define scan-once
  (lambda (start-state char-seq)
    ((goto-scanner-state start-state) '() char-seq)))

(define scan-char-seq
  (lambda (start-state char-seq)
    (let ((next-answer (scan-once start-state char-seq)))
      (variant-case next-answer
        (scanner-answer (token unscanned)
          (make-token-seq token
            (lambda ()
              (if (eq? (token->class token) 'end-marker)
                  '()
                  (scan-char-seq start-state unscanned)))))))))

(define character-string-scanner
  (lambda (a-string)
    (scan-char-seq scanner-start-state
      (string->list (string-append a-string (string #\nul))))))

(define make-token-seq
  (lambda (token thunk)
    (cons token (thunk))))
```

Figure E.2   Finite state automaton

```
(define scanner-start-state
  (lambda (c)
    (cond
      ((char-whitespace? c)
       (drop (goto-scanner-state scanner-start-state)))
      ((char-alphabetic? c)
       (shift (goto-scanner-state scanner-identifier-state)))
      ((char-numeric? c)
       (shift (goto-scanner-state scanner-number-state)))
      ((char=? c #\%)
       (drop (goto-scanner-state scanner-comment-state)))
      ((char=? c #\()
       (drop (emit (cook-punctuation 'lparen))))
      ((char=? c #\))
       (drop (emit (cook-punctuation 'rparen))))
      ((char=? c #\[)
       (drop (emit (cook-punctuation 'lbracket))))
      ((char=? c #\])
       (drop (emit (cook-punctuation 'rbracket))))
      ((char=? c #\,)
       (drop (emit (cook-punctuation 'comma))))
      ((char=? c #\=)
       (drop (emit (cook-punctuation 'eqsign))))
      ((char=? c #\;)
       (drop (emit (cook-punctuation 'semicolon))))
      ((char=? c #\&)
       (drop (goto-scanner-state scanner-ampersand-state)))
      ((char=? c #\$)
       (drop (emit (cook-punctuation 'dollar-sign))))
      ((char=? c #\:)
       (drop (goto-scanner-state scanner-assign-state)))
      ((or (char=? c #\+) (char=? c #\-) (char=? c #\*))
       (shift (emit cook-identifier)))
      ((char=? c #\nul)
       (emit (cook-punctuation 'end-marker)))
      (else (error "Invalid character to scan:" c)))))
```

```
(define scanner-identifier-state
  (lambda (c)
    (cond
      ((char-alphabetic? c)
       (shift (goto-scanner-state scanner-identifier-state)))
      ((char-numeric? c)
       (shift (goto-scanner-state scanner-identifier-state)))
      (else (emit cook-identifier)))))

(define scanner-number-state
  (lambda (c)
    (cond
      ((char-numeric? c)
       (shift (goto-scanner-state scanner-number-state)))
      (else (emit cook-number)))))

(define scanner-comment-state
  (lambda (c)
    (cond
      ((char=? c #\newline)
       (drop (goto-scanner-state scanner-start-state)))
      (else (drop (goto-scanner-state scanner-comment-state))))))

(define scanner-assign-state
  (lambda (c)
    (cond
      ((char=? c #\=)
       (drop (emit (cook-punctuation 'assign-sym))))
      (else (emit (cook-punctuation 'colon))))))

(define scanner-ampersand-state
  (lambda (c)
    (cond
      ((char=? c #\&)
       (drop (emit (cook-punctuation 'double-ampersand))))
      (else (emit (cook-punctuation 'ampersand))))))

(define keywords-list
  '(if then else let in proc begin end letmutable letrecproc letrec
     during letdynamic letarray letproc method define definearray
     simpleclass simpleinstance class instance abort letcont callcc
     coroutine wind unwind within sum))
```

Appendix F A Read-Eval-Print Loop

Here is an implementation of the read-eval-print loop for the character string syntax of the interpreted language. The interactive nature of the read-eval-print loop and the side effect of reading a character require us to introduce a somewhat unorthodox stream ADT.

Figure F.1   A stream ADT for interactive computing

```
(define stream-car
  (lambda (s)
    (car (s))))

(define stream-cdr
  (lambda (s)
    (cdr (s))))

(define make-stream
  (lambda (car-val th)
    (lambda ()
      (cons car-val (let ((cdr-val #f))
                      (lambda ()
                        (if (pair? cdr-val)
                            cdr-val
                            (begin (set! cdr-val ((th))) cdr-val)))))))))

(define the-null-stream
  (make-stream 'end-of-stream (lambda () the-null-stream)))

(define stream-null?
  (lambda (s)
    (eq? (stream-car s) 'end-of-stream)))
```

Figure F.2　Auxiliaries using stream ADT

```
(define stream-for-each
  (lambda (proc stream)
    (letrec
      ((loop
         (lambda (stream)
           (if (not (stream-null? stream))
               (begin
                 (proc (stream-car stream))
                 (loop (stream-cdr stream)))))))
      (loop stream))))

(define make-input-stream
  (lambda ()
    (let ((char (read-char)))
      (if (eof-object? char)
          the-null-stream
          (make-stream char make-input-stream)))))
```

Figure F.3　Interface to the parser

```
(define make-char-seq make-stream)

(define char-seq-head stream-car)

(define char-seq-tail stream-cdr)

(define make-token-seq make-stream)

(define token-seq-head stream-car)

(define token-seq-tail stream-cdr)
```

Each expression is thought of as if it were placed in a begin expression, and hence each must be followed by a ;. When the last expression is entered, it must be followed by end to match the implied begin. As the sequence of parse trees is consumed, each tree is evaluated and the result of the evaluation is usually written, followed by a new prompt. The procedure *eval-print* reflects the desired form of evaluation and whether or not printing should occur. Below are two versions: one for testing the parser, which just writes the tree, and the other for making calls to *eval-exp* using an initial environment. Other versions are possible as the arguments to *eval-exp* vary.

Figure F.4 An eval loop for interactive computing

```
(define eval-print
  (lambda (tree)
    (write tree)))

(define eval-print
  (lambda (tree)
    (let ((result (eval-exp tree init-env)))
      (if (not (or (define? tree)
                   (definearray? tree)
                   (varassign? tree)
                   (arrayassign? tree)))
          (write result)))))

(define read-eval-print
  (lambda ()
    (display "--> ")
    (stream-for-each
      (lambda (tree)
        (eval-print tree)
        (newline)
        (display "--> "))
      (parse-token-seq parse-semicolon-terminated-form
        (scan-char-seq scanner-start-state (make-input-stream))))))
```

If **end** is entered after the last expression to be evaluated, the read-eval-print loop terminates.

Figure F.5   Token sequence parser

```
(define parse-semicolon-terminated-form
  (lambda (token)
    (process-nt parse-form
      (goto-parser-state parse-terminated-by))))

(define parse-terminated-by
  (lambda (token)
    (case (token->class token)
      ((semicolon)
       (check/drop 'semicolon (reduce 'chain)))
      ((end)
       (reduce 'chain))
      (error "Invalid terminator:" token))))

(define parse-token-seq
  (lambda (start-state token-seq)
    (let ((token (token-seq-head token-seq)))
      (if (or (eq? (token->class token) 'end)
              (eq? (token->class token) 'end-marker))
          the-null-stream
          (variant-case (parse-once start-state token-seq)
            (parser-answer (tree unparsed)
              (make-stream tree
                (lambda ()
                  (parse-token-seq start-state unparsed)))))))))
```

Appendix G List Structure Syntax

The list structure language is defined by the following concrete and abstract syntax.

⟨form⟩ ::=	(`define` ⟨var⟩ ⟨exp⟩)	`define (var exp)`
|	(`definearray` ⟨var⟩ ⟨exp⟩)	`definearray (var dim-exp)`
|	⟨exp⟩	
⟨exp⟩ ::=	⟨integer-literal⟩	`lit (datum)`
|	⟨varref⟩	
|	(⟨operator⟩ ⟨operands⟩)	`app (rator rands)`
|	(`if` ⟨exp⟩ ⟨exp⟩ ⟨exp⟩)	`if (test-exp then-exp else-exp)`
|	(`let` ⟨decls⟩ ⟨exp⟩)	`let (decls body)`
|	(`proc` ⟨varlist⟩ ⟨exp⟩)	`proc (formals body)`
|	(`varassign` ⟨var⟩ ⟨exp⟩)	`varassign (var exp)`
|	(`letmutable` ⟨decls⟩ ⟨exp⟩)	`letmutable (decls body)`
|	(`begin` ⟨exp⟩ ⟨compound⟩)	`begin (exp1 exp2)`
|	(`letrecproc` ⟨procdecls⟩ ⟨exp⟩)	`letrecproc (procdecls body)`
|	(`letrec` ⟨decls⟩ ⟨exp⟩)	`letrec (decls body)`
|	(`dynassign` ⟨var⟩ ⟨exp⟩ ⟨exp⟩)	`dynassign (var exp body)`
|	(`letdynamic` ⟨decls⟩ ⟨exp⟩)	`letdynamic (decls body)`
|	(`letarray` ⟨arraydecls⟩ ⟨exp⟩)	`letarray (arraydecls body)`
|	(`arrayref` ⟨array-exp⟩ ⟨exp⟩)	`arrayref (array index)`
|	(`arrayassign` ⟨array-exp⟩ ⟨exp⟩ ⟨exp⟩)	`arrayassign (array index exp)`
|	(`letproc` ⟨procdecls⟩ ⟨exp⟩)	`letproc (procdecls body)`
|	(`local` ⟨decls⟩ ⟨exp⟩)	`local (decls body)`

| (i-varref ⟨var⟩)	i-varref (var)
| (c-varref ⟨var⟩)	c-varref (var)
| (i-varassign ⟨var⟩ ⟨exp⟩)	i-varassign (var exp)
| (c-varassign ⟨var⟩ ⟨exp⟩)	c-varassign (var exp)
| (method ⟨varlist⟩ ⟨exp⟩)	method (formals body)
| (meth-app ⟨var⟩ ⟨operands⟩)	meth-app (name rands)
| (simpleinstance ⟨exp⟩)	new-simpleinst (class-exp)
| (simpleclass ⟨varlist⟩ ⟨varlist⟩ ⟨methdecls⟩ ⟨exp⟩)	new-simpleclass (c-vars i-vars methdecls init-exp)
| (class ⟨exp⟩ ⟨c-vars⟩ ⟨i-vars⟩ ⟨methdecls⟩ ⟨exp⟩)	new-class (parent-exp c-vars i-vars methdecls init-exp)
| (meth-app ⟨var⟩ super ⟨operands⟩)	super-meth-app (name rands)
| (instance ⟨exp⟩ ⟨exp⟩ ⟨varlist⟩ ⟨methdecls⟩)	new-instance (class-exp parent-exp i-vars methdecls)
| (abort ⟨exp⟩)	abort (exp)
| (letcont ⟨var⟩ ⟨exp⟩)	letcont (var body)
| (callcc ⟨exp⟩)	callcc (exp)
| (coroutine ⟨exp⟩)	coroutine (exp)
| (wind ⟨exp⟩ ⟨exp⟩ ⟨exp⟩)	wind (pre body post)
| (sum ⟨operands⟩)	sum (rands)

⟨varref⟩ ::= ⟨var⟩	varref (var)
⟨var⟩ ::= ⟨symbol⟩	
⟨decls⟩ ::= (⟨decl⟩ {⟨decl⟩}*)	
⟨decl⟩ ::= (⟨var⟩ ⟨exp⟩)	decl (var exp)
⟨varlist⟩ ::= ({⟨var⟩}* {⟨keydecl⟩}*)	
⟨compound⟩ ::= { ⟨exp⟩}*	
⟨procdecls⟩ ::= (⟨procdecl⟩ {⟨procdecl⟩}*)	
⟨procdecl⟩ ::= (⟨var⟩ ⟨varlist⟩ ⟨exp⟩)	procdecl (var formals body)
⟨arraydecls⟩ ::= (⟨arraydecl⟩ {⟨arraydecl⟩}*)	
⟨arraydecl⟩ ::= (⟨var⟩ ⟨exp⟩)	decl (var exp)
⟨array-exp⟩ ::= ⟨exp⟩	
⟨keydecls⟩ ::= ⟨keydecl⟩ {⟨keydecl⟩}*	

$\langle \text{keydecl} \rangle ::= (: \langle \text{var} \rangle \ \langle \text{exp} \rangle)$ `decl (var exp)`

$\langle \text{methdecls} \rangle ::= (\ ) \ | \ \langle \text{decls} \rangle$

$\langle \text{operands} \rangle ::= \{ \langle \text{exp} \rangle \}^* \ \{ \langle \text{keydecl} \rangle \}^*$

$\langle \text{operator} \rangle ::= \langle \text{exp} \rangle$

Appendix H List Structure Parser

This appendix contains a list structure parser for the language of appendix G. The assumption here is that the argument to *parse* has been read by Scheme's *read* procedure. With this, we have given up some of the flexibility that comes with a character string parser, since we are basically letting Scheme do the scanning for us. This allows us to ignore the character structure of a program and focus in on its tree structure. Use the record declarations of appendix B for building the actual abstract syntax. The form table for chapter 5 is stored in `form-table`. When you wish to extend the form table to include chapter 6, 7, 9, or 12, just append one table to another and redefine `form-table`. For example, to add the special forms of chapter 7, simply

```
(define form-table (append form-table form-table-for-chapter-7))
```

There is an additional test in the procedure *parse-with-keys* that is only of use when running section 6.6.

We have defined the predicate *approve?* to always return true. This means that the parser is quite willing to accept illegal programs, such as `if` expressions with too many parts. It is a worthwhile exercise to implement your own version of *approve?* Use an `approve-table` like the `form-table` that associates each symbol with a procedure of the form `(lambda (exp) ...)`. For example, the `approve-table` entry for `if` is `(lambda (exp) (= (length exp) 4))`.

Figure H.1   List structure parser

```
(define parse
  (lambda (exp)
    (if (form? exp)
        (parse-form exp)
        (parse-exp exp))))

(define form?
  (lambda (x)
    (and (pair? x) (memq (car x) '(define definearray)))))

(define parse-form
  (lambda (form)
    (let ((form-pair (assq (car form) form-table)))
      (if (and (pair? form-pair) (approve form))
          (apply (cdr form-pair) (cdr form))
          (error "Invalid top-level form:" form)))))

(define parse-exp
  (lambda (exp)
    (cond
      ((symbol? exp) (make-varref exp))
      ((number? exp) (make-lit exp))
      ((and (pair? exp) (not (form? exp))) (parse-pair exp))
      (else (error "Invalid expression:" exp)))))

(define parse-pair
  (lambda (exp)
    (let ((x (car exp)))
      (if (symbol? x)
          (let ((form-pair (assq x form-table)))
            (if (and (pair? form-pair) (approve exp))
                (apply (cdr form-pair) (cdr exp))
                (make-app (parse-exp (car exp)) (parse-rands (cdr exp)))))
          (make-app (parse-exp (car exp)) (parse-rands (cdr exp)))))))
```

```
(define approve
  (lambda (x) #t))

(define parse-decl
  (lambda (decl)
    (make-decl (car decl) (parse-exp (cadr decl)))))

(define parse-procdecl
  (lambda (triple)
    (make-procdecl (car triple) (cadr triple) (parse-exp (caddr triple)))))

(define parse-with-keys
  (lambda (proc)
    (letrec ((loop (lambda (exps)
                     (cond
                       ((null? exps) '())
                       ((and (pair? (car exps)) (eq? (car (car exps)) ':))
                        (map (lambda (decl)
                               (make-keydecl (cadr decl) (parse-exp (caddr decl))))
                             exps))
                       (else (cons (proc (car exps)) (loop (cdr exps))))))))
      loop)))

(define parse-rands (parse-with-keys parse))
(define parse-formals (parse-with-keys (lambda (x) x)))
```

Figure H.2 Form tables for language of appendix G

```
(define form-table
  (list
    (cons 'define
      (lambda (var exp)
        (make-define var (parse-exp exp))))
    (cons 'definearray
      (lambda (var exp)
        (make-definearray var (parse-exp exp))))
    (cons 'if
      (lambda (test-exp then-exp else-exp)
        (make-if (parse-exp test-exp) (parse-exp then-exp) (parse-exp else-exp))))
    (cons 'let
      (lambda (decls body)
        (make-let (map parse-decl decls) (parse-exp body))))
    (cons 'proc
      (lambda (formals body)
        (make-proc (parse-formals formals) (parse-exp body))))
    (cons 'varassign
      (lambda (var body)
        (make-varassign var (parse-exp body))))
    (cons 'letmutable
      (lambda (decls body)
        (make-letmutable (map parse-decl decls) (parse-exp body))))
    (cons 'begin
      (letrec ((loop (lambda (exps)
                       (if (null? (cdr exps))
                           (parse-exp (car exps))
                           (make-begin (parse-exp (car exps)) (loop (cdr exps)))))))
        (lambda exps
          (loop exps))))
    (cons 'letrecproc
      (lambda (procdecls body)
        (make-letrecproc (map parse-procdecl procdecls) (parse-exp body))))
    (cons 'letrec
      (lambda (decls body) (make-letrec (map parse-decl decls) (parse-exp body))))
    (cons 'dynassign
      (lambda (var exp body)
        (make-dynassign var (parse-exp exp) (parse-exp body))))
    (cons 'letdynamic
      (lambda (decls body)
        (make-letdynamic (map parse-decl decls) (parse-exp body))))))
```

```
(define form-table-for-chapter-6
  (list
    (cons 'letarray
      (lambda (arraydecls body)
        (make-letarray (map parse-decl arraydecls) (parse-exp body))))
    (cons 'arrayref
      (lambda (array index)
        (make-arrayref (parse-exp array) (parse-exp index))))
    (cons 'arrayassign
      (lambda (array index exp)
        (make-arrayassign (parse-exp array) (parse-exp index) (parse-exp exp))))
    (cons 'letproc
      (lambda (procdecls body)
        (make-letproc (map parse-procdecl procdecls)
          (parse-exp body))))
    (cons 'local
      (lambda (decls body)
        (make-local (map parse-decl decls) (parse-exp body)))))))

(define form-table-for-chapter-7
  (list
    (cons 'i-varref
      (lambda (var) (make-i-varref var)))
    (cons 'c-varref
      (lambda (var) (make-c-varref var)))
    (cons 'i-varassign
      (lambda (var exp) (make-i-varassign var (parse-exp exp))))
    (cons 'c-varassign
      (lambda (var exp) (make-c-varassign var (parse-exp exp))))
    (cons 'method
      (lambda (formals body)
        (make-method (parse-formals formals) (parse-exp body))))
    (cons 'meth-app
      (lambda args
        (let ((name (car args)) (rands (cdr args)))
          (if (and (pair? rands) (symbol? (car rands)) (eq? (car rands) 'super))
              (make-super-meth-app name (parse-rands (cdr rands)))
              (make-meth-app name (parse-rands rands))))))))
```

```
      (cons 'simpleinstance
        (lambda (class-exp)
          (make-new-simpleinst (parse-exp class-exp))))
      (cons 'simpleclass
        (lambda (c-vars i-vars methdecls init-exp)
          (make-new-simpleclass c-vars i-vars
            (map parse-decl methdecls)
            (parse-exp init-exp))))
      (cons 'class
        (lambda (parent-exp c-vars i-vars methdecls init-exp)
          (make-new-class (parse-exp parent-exp) c-vars i-vars
            (map parse-decl methdecls)
            (parse-exp init-exp))))
      (cons 'instance
        (lambda (class-exp parent-exp i-vars methdecls)
          (make-new-instance (parse-exp class-exp) (parse-exp parent-exp)
            i-vars
            (map parse-decl methdecls))))))

  (define form-table-for-chapter-9
    (list
      (cons 'abort
        (lambda (exp) (make-abort (parse-exp exp))))
      (cons 'letcont
        (lambda (var body) (make-letcont var (parse-exp body))))
      (cons 'callcc
        (lambda (exp) (make-callcc (parse-exp exp))))
      (cons 'coroutine
        (lambda (exp) (make-coroutine (parse-exp exp))))
      (cons 'wind
        (lambda (pre body post)
          (make-wind (parse-exp pre) (parse-exp body) (parse-exp post))))))

  (define form-table-for-chapter-12
    (list
      (cons 'sum
        (lambda rands
          (make-sum (parse-rands rands))))))
```

Appendix I Scheme Procedures Used

Figure I.1 is a list of the Scheme procedures used in the book. This list does not include arithmetic operations or combinations of car and cdr, such as cadr. Those procedures that are not in the IEEE Scheme standard are marked with a dagger (†). Of these, eval and gensym are discussed in the text; the others should be self-explanatory.

append	eval†	number?	string-length
apply	for-each	pair?	string-ref
assq	gensym†	positive?	string?
boolean?	length	procedure?	symbol->string
car	list	read	symbol?
cdr	list->string†	read-char	vector
char-alphabetic?	list->vector	remainder	vector->list†
char-numeric?	list-ref	reverse	vector-length
char-whitespace?	make-vector	reverse!	vector-ref
char=?	map	set-car!	vector-set!
char?	member	set-cdr!	vector?
cons	memq	string	write
display	memv	string->list†	zero?
eof-object?	newline	string->number	
eq?	not	string->symbol	
equal?	null?	string-append	

Figure I.1   Scheme procedures used in the book

For Further Reading

This book is an analytic study of programming language concepts, not a survey or a history. Therefore, we do not list all the relevant references. To find such a list, start with any good survey book (say Sethi [1989]) and chase a few pointers, and you will have enough references to last a lifetime.

What we have decided to do instead is share with you a list of papers and books that have given us the most hours of enjoyment. In some instances the hours of enjoyment came because we were the authors, and in other instances it came because the excitement of learning a new idea gave us such exhilaration.

The most important books are those that change the way you look at the world. So we will begin our reading list with two books in this category. The first is *Structure and Interpretation of Computer Programs,* by Hal Abelson and Gerry Sussman with Julie Sussman [1985]. This is a challenging introduction to programming that emphasizes general problem-solving techniques and uses Scheme throughout. We often list this book as a required text in our courses, just because every computer scientist and programmer should read it. A second mind-expanding book is *Godel, Escher, Bach: an Eternal Golden Braid* by Douglas R. Hofstadter [1979]. If you have not read this, take some time off and get acquainted with it. It is a joy to read and will open your mind to new and exciting ways to think about recursion, especially as it occurs in the real world, and the meaning of symbols. We hope our book will have as deep an effect on you as these books did on us.

If you are new to recursive programming and symbolic computation, then we suggest you look at *The Little Lisper* by Friedman and Felleisen [1989]. Another good choice is Springer and Friedman's *Scheme and the Art of Programming* [1989]. This introduction to programming using Scheme is less ambitious than *Structure and Interpretation of Computer Programs*.

Scheme was introduced in Sussman and Steele [1975]. Its development is recorded in Steele and Sussman [1978] and Rees and Clinger [1986]. The specification of Scheme is the IEEE standard [1991]. Dybvig [1987] provides a short introduction to Scheme along with a complete reference manual that includes some features specific to the Chez Scheme implementation. It also includes a number of insightful examples.

We learned a great deal about the use of higher-order procedures for programming from Burge [1975]. A more recent text on functional programming is Reade [1989]. The technical reports by Steele and Sussman, listed in the references, are extremely instructive on many topics.

Almost any text on discrete mathematics for computer science contains additional material on induction and Backus-Naur Form.

Most implementations of languages that are dialects of Lisp provide a syntactic abstraction mechanism, traditionally called *macros,* for extending the language with new special forms. Kohlbecker [1986] reviews traditional approaches to macros and proposes mechanisms for conveniently specifying syntactic transformations and avoiding the unintended capture of variables through such transformations.

The idea of data abstraction was a prime innovation of the 1970's, and has a large literature, from which we mention only Parnas [1972] on the importance of interfaces as boundaries for information-hiding.

We learned about the representation of sets of procedures as data structures from Reynolds [1972]. This technique was formalized under the name of *supercombinators* by Hughes [1982]. For more detail, see Peyton Jones [1987].

The lambda calculus was introduced by Alonzo Church [1941] to study mathematical logic. More introductory treatments of the lambda calculus may be found in Peyton Jones [1987] or Stoy [1977]. Barendregt [1981] provides an encyclopedic reference.

Refinements of the lambda calculus that give sound rules for reasoning about programs using call-by-value were studied by Plotkin [1975]. Felleisen and Friedman *et al.* [1987,1989] extend this to include assignment and control operations. Techniques for reasoning about imperative programs were pioneered in Floyd [1967] and Hoare [1969], which started a large literature in the 1970's.

Streams are discussed at length in Springer and Friedman [1989] and Abelson and Sussman [1985].

Chapters 5–7

When we wrote the first interpreter that used if in the defining language to explain if in the defined language, we wrote a *meta-circular interpreter.* Metacircular interpreters were used in McCarthy [1960] to show the power of Lisp. See also McCarthy [1965]. Smith [1982] took that concept to its limit by imagining an infinite tower of interpreters.

Denotational semantics allows the definition of languages in terms of the lambda calculus, rather than depending on another programming language. See Stoy [1977], Gordon [1979], Schmidt [1986], or the encyclopedic Milne and Strachey [1976]. Our use of Scheme allows most of the formal precision of denotational semantics in an executable form. The idea that the expressed and denoted values of a language determined a great deal of its structure was stressed by Strachey [1973].

Object-oriented languages first appeared with Simula 67 (Birtwistle et al. [1979]). The object-oriented metaphor was extended by Smalltalk (Goldberg and Robson [1980]) and Carl Hewitt's Actors (Hewitt [1977]). Both used human interaction and sending and receiving messages as the metaphor for explaining their ideas. Scheme grew out of Sussman and Steele's attempts to understand Hewitt's work. Springer and Friedman [1989] and Abelson and Sussman [1985] both provide further examples of object-oriented programming in Scheme and discuss when functional and imperative programming styles are most appropriate. Steele [1990] and Keene [1989] describe CLOS, the powerful object-oriented programming facility of Common Lisp. A later arrival, gaining rapid popularity at the time of this writing, is C++ (Stroustrup [1986], Ellis and Stroustrup [1990]), which trades some of the generality of Smalltalk or Actors for run-time efficiency.

Chapters 8–10

The current interest in continuation-passing style is commonly dated from Strachey and Wadsworth [1974]. Reynolds [1972] shows how transforming an interpreter into CPS eliminates some of the difficulties of metacircular interpreters. Plotkin [1975] gives a very clean version of the CPS transformation and studies its theoretical properties. The translation of programs in tail form to imperative form dates back to McCarthy [1962].

Steele's RABBIT compiler (Steele [1978]) uses CPS conversion as the basis for a compiler. In this compiler, the source program is converted into CPS and then into iterative form; it can then be compiled easily. This line of development led to the ORBIT compiler (Kranz *et al.* [1986]), and to the Standard ML of New Jersey compiler (Appel and Jim [1989]).

Our treatment of coroutines is based on Haynes, Friedman, and Wand [1986]. An introduction to using first-class continuations can be found in Springer and Friedman [1989]. The discussion of dynamic wind is based on Baker [1978].

Continuations may be used for a variety of purposes beyond those discussed in the text. The use of continuations as a model of lightweight processes and as program transformations are explored in Wand [1980a,b]. The efficient implementation of continuations is treated in Hieb, Dybvig, and Bruggeman [1990].

Chapters 11–12

The theory of scanner and parser design is well developed. It provides systematic techniques for dealing with a wide range of programming language grammars that do not satisfy the properties required by the techniques of chapter 11. Parsing theory relies in turn on the extensive theory of formal grammars, which studies general classes of grammars and the types of automata that are required for parsing their languages. A compiler textbook, such as Aho, Sethi, and Ullman [1986] or Fisher and LeBlanc [1988], should be consulted for details.

Our treatment of compiler derivation is motivated by Appel and Jim [1989] and Hudak and Kelsey [1989], who treat CPS code as an assembly language. Exercise 12.4.12 is based on Clinger [1984].

General Readings

A rich source of material on the early history of programming languages is Wexelblat [1981]. Braffort and Hirschberg [1963] and Steel [1966] contain several seminal papers. Horowitz [1983] anthologizes many classic papers on programming language design.

The major professional organizations in computing, the Association for Computing Machinery (ACM) and the IEEE Computer Society, are rich sources for learning more about programming languages. They sponsor major conferences and publish several journals that cover this field. Some of the major conferences are the ACM Symposium on Principles of Programming Languages, ACM Symposium on Programming Language Design and Implementation. ACM Symposium on Lisp and Functional Programming, and ACM Symposium on Functional Programming Languages, and Computer Architecture. For details, see the listings that are published regularly in the *Communications of the ACM* and IEEE Computer.

Some of the journals that publish important papers in programming languages are *ACM Transactions on Programming Languages and Systems*, *IEEE Software*, *Journal of Computer Languages*, *Software: Practice and Experience*, *Lisp and Symbolic Computation*, and the *Journal of Functional Programming*.

We hope we have given you some useful directions. Enjoy!

References

Aho, A.V., Sethi, R., and Ullman, J.D. [1986] *Compilers: Principles, Techniques, and Tools*, Reading, MA: Addison-Wesley.

Appel, A.W., and Jim, T. [1989] "Continuation-Passing, Closure-Passing Style," *Conf. Rec. 16th ACM Symp. on Principles of Programming Languages*, 293–302.

Backus, J. [1973] "Programming Language Semantics and Closed Applicative Languages," *Proc. 1st ACM Symp. on Principles of Programming Languages*, Boston, 71–86.

Baker, H. [1978] "Shallow Binding in Lisp 1.5" *Comm. ACM 21*, 565–569.

Barendregt, H.P. [1981] *The Lambda Calculus: Its Syntax and Semantics*, North-Holland, Amsterdam.

Birtwistle, G.M., Dahl, O.J., Myhrhaug, B., and Nygaard, K. [1979] *Simula Begin*, Studentlitteratur, Box 1717, S-221 01 Lund, Sweden.

Braffort P., and Hirschberg D. (eds.) [1963] *Computer Programming and Formal Systems*, Amsterdam: North-Holland.

Burge, W.H. [1975] *Recursive Programming Techniques*, Reading, MA: Addison-Wesley.

Church, A. [1941] *The Calculi of Lambda Conversion*, Princeton University Press; reprinted 1963 by University Microfilms, Ann Arbor, MI.

Clinger, W. [1984] "The Scheme 311 Compiler: An Exercise in Denotational Semantics," *Conf. Rec. 1984 ACM Symposium on Lisp and Functional Programming*, 356–364.

Dybvig, K. [1987] *The Scheme Programming Language*, Prentice-Hall, Englewood Cliffs, NJ.

Ellis, M.A. and Stroustrup, B., [1990] *The Annotated C++ Reference Manual*, Reading, MA: Addison-Wesley.

Felleisen, M., Friedman, D.P., Kohlbecker, E., and Duba, B. [1987] "A Syntactic Theory of Sequential Control," *Theoret. Comp. Sci. 52*, 205–237.

Felleisen, M., and Friedman, D.P. [1989] "A Syntactic Theory of Sequential State," *Theoret. Comp. Sci. 69*, 243–287.

Fischer, C.N., and LeBlanc, R.J. [1988] *Crafting a Compiler*, Menlo Park, CA: Benjamin/Cummings.

Friedman, D.P., and Felleisen, M. [1989] *The Little LISPer* (third edition), New York, NY: Macmillan.

Goldberg, A., and Robson, D. [1983] *Smalltalk-80: The Language and its Implementation*, Reading MA: Addison-Wesley.

Gordon, M.J.C. [1979] *The Denotational Description of Programming Languages*, Springer, Berlin.

Haynes, C.T., Friedman D.P., and Wand, M. [1986] "Obtaining Coroutines with Continuations," *Computer Languages 11*, 143–153.

Hewitt, Carl [1977] "Viewing Control Structures as Patterns of Passing Messages," *Artificial Intelligence 8*, 323–364.

Hieb, R., Dybvig, K., and Bruggeman, C. [1990] "Representing Control in the Presence of First-Class Continuations" *Proc. ACM SIGPLAN 1990 Conference on Programming Language Design and Implementation*, 66–77.

Hoare, C.A.R. [1969] "An Axiomatic Basis for Computer Programming," *Comm. ACM 12*, 576–580, 583.

Hofstadter, D.R. [1979] *Gödel, Escher, Bach: An Eternal Golden Braid*, New York: Basic Books.

Horowitz, E. [1983] *Programming Languages: A Grand Tour*, Rockville, MD: Computer Science Press.

Hughes, R.J.M., [1982] "Super Combinators: A New Implementation Method for Applicative Languages," *Proc. 1982 ACM Symp. on Lisp and Functional Programming*, 1–10.

IEEE Computer Society [1991] *IEEE Standard for the Scheme Programming Language*, IEEE Std 1178-1990, New York: IEEE.

Keene, S.E. [1989] *Object-Oriented Programming in Common Lisp*, Reading, MA: Addison-Wesley.

Kelsey, R., and Hudak, P. [1989] "Realistic Compilation by Program Transformation," *Conf. Rec. 16th Ann. ACM Symp. on Principles of Programming Languages*, 281–292.

Kohlbecker, E.M. [1986] *Syntactic Extensions in the Programming Language Lisp*, PhD thesis, Indiana University. Portions published as: Kohlbecker, E., Friedman, D.P., Felleisen, M., and Duba, B. "Hygienic Macro Expansion," *Proc. 1986 ACM Conference on Lisp and Functional Programming*, 151–161, and Kohlbecker, E.M., and Wand, M., "Macro-by-Example: Deriving Syntactic Transformations from their Specifications" *Conf. Rec. 14th ACM Symp. on Principles of Prog. Lang.* (1987), 77–84.

Kranz, D.A., Kelsey, R., Rees, J.A., Hudak, P., Philbin, J., and Adams, N.I. [1986] "Orbit: An Optimizing Compiler for Scheme," *Proc. SIGPLAN '86 Symp. on Compiler Construction, SIGPLAN Notices 21*, 7, 219–223.

McCarthy, J. [1960] "Recursive Functions of Symbolic Expressions and their Computation by Machine, Part I," *Comm. ACM 3*, 184–195. Also reprinted in Horowitz [1983].

McCarthy, J. [1962] "Towards a Mathematical Science of Computation," *Information Processing 62* (Popplewell, ed.) Amsterdam: North-Holland, 21–28.

McCarthy, J. *et al.* [1965] *LISP 1.5 Programmer's Manual*, Cambridge, Mass: MIT Press. Portions reprinted in Horowitz [1983].

Milne, R. and Strachey C. [1976] *A Theory of Programming Language Semantics*, Chapman & Hall, London, and Wiley, New York.

Parnas, D.L. [1972] "A Technique for Module Specification with Examples," *Comm. ACM 15*, 330–336.

Peyton Jones, S.L. [1987] *The Implementation of Functional Programming Languages*, Englewood Cliffs, NJ: Prentice-Hall International.

Plotkin, G.D. [1975] "Call-by-Name, Call-by-Value and the λ-Calculus," *Theoret. Comp. Sci. 1*, 125–159.

Reade, C. [1989] *Elements of Functional Programming*, Reading, MA: Addison-Wesley.

Rees, J., and Clinger, W., eds. [1986] "Revised[3] Report on the Algorithmic Language Scheme," *SIGPLAN Notices 21*, 12, 37–79.

Reynolds, J.C. [1972] "Definitional Interpreters for Higher-Order Programming Languages," *Proc. ACM Nat'l. Conf.*, 717–740.

Schmidt, D.A. [1986] *Denotational Semantics: A Methodology for Language Development*, Boston: Allyn and Bacon.

Sethi, R. [1989] *Programming Languages: Concepts and Constructs*, Reading, MA: Addison-Wesley.

Smith, B.C. [1982] *Reflection and Semantics in a Procedural Language*, MIT/LCS/TR-272, Mass. Inst. of Tech., Cambridge, MA. Portions published as "Reflection and Semantics in Lisp," *Conf. Rec. 11th ACM Symp. on Principles of Programming Languages* (1984), 23–35.

Springer, G., and Friedman, D.P. [1989] *Scheme and the Art of Programming*, Cambridge MA: MIT Press, and New York: McGraw-Hill.

Steel, T.B. (ed.) [1966] *Formal Language Description Languages for Computer Programming*, Amsterdam: North-Holland.

Steele, G.L. [1976] "LAMBDA: The Ultimate Declarative," MIT AI Memo #379, Cambridge, MA.

Steele, G.L. [1978] "Rabbit: A Compiler for Scheme," MIT AI Lab TR 474, Cambridge, MA.

Steele, G.L. [1990] *Common Lisp: the Language* (2nd edition), Burlington MA: Digital Press.

Steele, G.L. Jr. and Sussman, G.J. [1976] "LAMBDA: The Ultimate Imperative," MIT AI Memo #353, Cambridge, MA.

Steele, G.L. and Sussman, G.J. [1978] "The Revised Report on SCHEME," MIT AI Memo #452, Cambridge, MA.

Steele, G.L. Jr. and Sussman, G.J. [1978a] "The Art of the Interpreter or, the Modularity Complex (Parts Zero, One and Two)," MIT AI Memo #453, Cambridge, MA.

Steele, G.L. and Sussman, G.J. [1980] "Design of a LISP-Based Microprocessor," *Comm. ACM 23*, 628–645.

Stoy, J.E. [1977] *Denotational Semantics: The Scott-Strachey Approach to Programming Language Theory*, MIT Press, Cambridge, MA.

Strachey, C. [1973] "The Varieties of Programming Language," Oxford University Computing Laboratory, Technical Monograph PRG-10.

Strachey, C. and Wadsworth, C.P. [1974] "Continuations: A Mathematical Semantics for Handling Full Jumps," Oxford University Computing Laboratory Technical Monograph PRG-11.

Sussman, G.J. and Steele, G.L., Jr. [1975] "SCHEME: An Interpreter for Extended Lambda Calculus," MIT AI Memo #349, Cambridge, MA.

Wand, M. [1980a] "Continuation-Based Multiprocessing" *Proc. 1980 LISP Conference* (J. Allen, ed.), Palo Alto, CA: The Lisp Company, pp. 19–28.

Wand, M. [1980b] "Continuation-Based Program Transformation Strategies," *J. ACM 27*, 164–180.

Wexelblat, R.L. [1981] *History of Programming Languages*, New York: Acadmic Press.

Index

MOUNTAINEERING
The Freedom of the Hills

Fifth Edition

Mountaineering
The Freedom of the Hills

Fifth Edition

Editor: Don Graydon

Revision Committee Chairpersons:
Paul Gauthier
Myrna Plum

The Mountaineers/Seattle

No part of this book may be reproduced in any form, or by any electronic, mechanical, or other means, without permission in writing from the publisher.

Published by The Mountaineers
1011 SW Klickitat Way, Seattle, Washington 98134

Published simultaneously in Canada by Douglas & Mc-Intyre, Ltd., 1615 Venables Street, Vancouver, B.C. V5L 2H1

Published simultaneously in Great Britain by Cordee, 3a DeMontfort Street, Leicester, England, LE1 7HD

Manufactured in the United States of America
Edited by Maureen O'Neal
Illustrations by Bob Cram, Nick Gregoric, Ross Prather, Ramona Hammerly
Cover design by Elizabeth Watson
Book layout by Barbara Bash

8 7 6 5 4
Pbk: 10 9 8 7
Cloth: 8 7 6 5 4

Cover photograph: Midnight on the summit of Mount McKinley, Alaska. Photo by Patrick Morrow
Frontispiece: Climbers on Vowell Pinnacle, Howser Spire in the distance, Bugaboos, Purcell Range, British Columbia. Photo by Baiba Morrow

The following trademarks appear in this book: Ball Nuts, Band-Aids, Camalots, Chevron Blazo, Clog, Coleman, Diamox, Friends, Gibbs, Gore-Tex, Hexentrics, Jumar, Kevlar, Masonite, Mylar, Polypro, Quickies, RURP, Rock 'n Rollers, RPs, Spectra, Stoddard, Stokes, Stones, Stopper, Styrofoam, Teflon, Therm-a-Rest, TCUs, Tri Cams, Velcro, and Vibram.

Library of Congress Cataloging in Publication Data

Mountaineering : the freedom of the hills / editor, Don Graydon. — 5th ed.
p.   cm.
Includes bibliographical references (p.   ) and index.
ISBN 0-89886-201-9 — ISBN 0-89886-309-0 (pbk.)
1. Mountaineering. 2. Rock climbing. 3. Snow and ice climbing.
I. Graydon, Don. II. Mountaineers (Society)
GV200.M688 1991
796.5'22—dc20   91-26342
                                                       CIP

A NOTE ABOUT SAFETY

Safety is an important concern in all outdoor activities. No book can alert you to every hazard or anticipate the limitations of every reader. Therefore, the descriptions of equipment and techniques in this book are not representations that a particular tool or technique will be safe for you or your party. When you participate in the activities described in this book, you assume responsibility for your own safety. Keeping informed on current conditions and exercising common sense are the keys to a safe, enjoyable outing.

The Mountaineers

CONTENTS

PREFACE

Mountaineering, the Freedom of the Hills is intended to present both introductory and advanced information on the sport of mountaineering. This fifth edition is an extensive revision of the fourth edition, the longtime, leading English-language text on mountaineering.

Each of the chapters from the fourth edition has been revised, rewritten, and, where necessary, expanded. These revisions reflect the rapid changes occurring in various areas of mountaineering and are due to increased popularity, the development of new techniques, and the introduction of new and improved equipment. Chapters considerably enhanced by these changes include: First Steps, Leading and Placing Protection, Rock Climbing Technique, Aid Climbing and Pitoncraft, and Belaying. This edition presents a completely new chapter on Winter and Expedition Climbing.

Many improvements make this edition more interesting to read, easier to use, and more accessible. A professional writer rewrote the material from all contributors, bringing the various parts and chapters together to form a comprehensive text. Additional headings clarify the topics and direct the reader to pertinent information. Completely new illustrations of techniques and equipment clearly and accurately illustrate the text. Line figure drawings were created from photographs of climbers demonstrating the precise technique.

SCOPE OF THE BOOK

As in previous editions, *Freedom* provides sound, clear, and current coverage of the concepts, techniques, and problems involved in the pursuit of mountain climbing. Individual topics, such as rock climbing technique or aid climbing, are detailed enough to be useful to readers with specific interests in those topics. The book provides a fundamental understanding of each topic. It is not intended, however, to be exhaustive or encyclopedic. In addition to presenting information for the novice, much of the material in this book can help experienced climbers review and improve their skills.

Mountaineering cannot be learned just by studying a book. *Freedom* was originally written as a textbook for students and instructors participating in organized climbing courses. The context of learning that is provided in a course of instruction, given either individually or in groups, and by competent instructors, is essential for beginning climbers.

Traditionally, climbing has been a thinking person's sport. The individual climber and climbing team bring their knowledge, skills, and experience to the problem at hand and apply their own solutions. In this fifth edition, *Freedom* presents widely used techniques and practices outlining both their advantages and limitations. It is presented not as dogma or the final word but as the basis for making sound judgments. This problem-solving approach is especially important in mountaineering because of the potential dangers that exist. Such dangers are inherently magnified by harsh conditions, insufficient skill, inexperience, and poor judgment.

Freedom characteristically describes not just simple climbing but wilderness mountaineering. Any person who becomes a wilderness mountaineer has a deep and abiding responsibility to help preserve the wilderness environment for present and future generations. Walking softly is a fair start. The mountain regions throughout the world constitute the domain of mountaineering. This dwindling and finite resource depends on the wilderness traveler for its future preservation.

ORIGINS OF THE BOOK

Freedom's direction and emphasis originated from the development of climbing in the Pacific Northwest. The wild and complex character of the mountains in this region, with their abundance of snow and glaciers throughout the year, furthered the mountaineering challenge. Access was inherently difficult. There were few roads, and the initial explorations were themselves expeditions, often with native guides.

When The Mountaineers was organized in 1906, one of its major purposes was to explore and study the mountains, forests, and watercourses of the Northwest. The journey to the mountain summit was a long and difficult one, and it required a variety of skills. With the knowledge of these skills, the competence that comes from their practice, and the experience gained through climbing mountains, more than a few had the exhilarating experience of the freedom of the hills.

As interest in mountaineering in the region grew, so did a tradition of tutelage. Increasingly, experienced climbers took novices under their wings to pass on their knowledge and skills. The Mountaineers formalized that exchange by developing a series of climbing courses. This book grew out of six decades' worth of teaching mountaineering and conducting numerous climbs in the Northwest and throughout the world.

LEGACY OF THE FIFTH EDITION

Issac Newton said, "If I see farther than others, it is because I stood on the shoulder of giants." The various editions of *Freedom* represent a tradition of bringing together and sorting through the knowledge, techniques, opinions, and advice of a large number of practicing climbers. Students, both in training and on actual climbs, have been an especially pivotal source of information.

Prior to the publication of the first edition of *Freedom* in 1960, The Mountaineers climbing courses had used European works, particularly Young's classic *Mountaincraft,* as required reading. These works did not cover various subjects unique and important to American and Pacific Northwest mountaineering. To fill in the gaps, course lecturers prepared outlines, which they distributed to students. Eventually these outlines were fleshed out and gathered together as the *Climber's Notebook,* subsequently published, in 1948, as the *Mountaineers Handbook.* By 1955, tools and techniques had changed so drastically, and the courses had become so much more complex, that the new and more comprehensive textbook was needed.

Members of the first edition editorial committee were: Harvey Manning, chairman; John R. Hazle; Carl Henrikson; Nancy Bickford Miller; Thomas Miller; Franz Mohling; Rowland Tabor; and Lesley Stark Tabor. A substantial portion of the then relatively small Puget Sound climbing community participated—some seventy-five as writers of preliminary, revised, advanced, semifinal, and final chapter drafts, and another one or two hundred as reviewers, planners, illustrators, typists, proofreaders, financiers, promoters, retailers, warehousemen, and shipping clerks. At the time, there were few Mountaineer climbers who did not have a hand in making or selling the book.

Efforts leading to the publication of the second edition (in 1967) began in 1964. Members of the second edition editorial committee were: John M. Davis, chairman; Tom Hallstaff; Max Hollenbeck;

Jim Mitchell; Roger Neubauer; and Howard Stansbury. Even though much of the first edition was retained, the task force was, again, of impressive proportions, numbering several dozen writers, uncounted reviewers, and helpers. Survivors of the previous committee, notably John R. Hazle, Tom Miller, and Harvey Manning, provided continuity to the effort. As he had with the first edition, Harvey Manning once more edited the entire text and supervised production.

The third edition editorial committee was formed in 1971 and headed by Sam Fry. Initially, a planning committee analyzed the previous edition and set guidelines for its revision. A steering committee, consisting of Jim Sanford, Fred Hart, Sean Rice, Howard Stansbury, and Sam Fry, directed the revision and had overall responsibility for the text. A large number of climbers contributed to individual chapters; the reviewing, revising, editing, and collation of chapters and sections was a true community effort. Peggy Ferber edited the entire book, which was published in 1974.

The fourth edition of Freedom involved a major revision and included the complete rewrites of many chapters, most notably the entire Ice and Snow section. A cast of hundreds was guided by a team of technical editors: Ed Peters, chairman; Roger Andersen; Dave Enfield; Lee Helser; John Young; Dave Anthony; and Robert Swanson. A large number of climbers submitted comments to the committee. Small teams of "writers" prepared a series of drafts for review by the technical editors. In addition to the substantial contribution of such writers, many others provided valuable help through critiques of subsequent and final drafts not only for technical accuracy and consistency, but also for readability and comprehension.

THE FIFTH EDITION

In late 1987, climbing committee chairman Ken Small responded to concerns of The Mountaineers Books staff and initiated an effort to assess the need for a new edition. A *Freedom* Ad Hoc Study Committee was formed to make specific recommendations to the club's board of trustees. The committee reported the need for a revision of many technique sections, overall improvement in the writing quality, and an upgraded visual format. It also recommended that this revision be carried out in the tradition of a volunteer committee. Chaired by Paul Gauthier, the committee's members were Ben Arp, Steve Costie, Nancy Jackson, Tom Merritt, and Susan Price. In order to assess the current strengths and the specific needs for improvements to the fifth edition, the committee solicited the opinions of Mountaineer members and well-known climbers and writers from outside the Club. The committee is grateful for the well-thought-out responses received from Greg Child, Randall Green, Michael Loughman, Eric Perlman, Doug Robinson, and Gary Speer. Many of their suggestions were incorporated into this latest edition of the book.

The board of trustees selected Paul Gauthier to spearhead a substantial revision of the fourth edition. The committee was organized into a coordinators' group, which took on the responsibility for overall guidance, and into subcommittees for subject areas. The individual subcommittees used various methods to produce detailed narrative "outlines." These were reviewed and modified by the coordinators' group to incorporate a wide range of critique by the whole committee. Professional writer Don Graydon wrote "drafts" from these narratives, which were reviewed and revised by the committee. Graydon showed extraordinary skill in working both with a diverse committee and the Books staff and in enhancing the overall style.

The coordinator group consisted of Paul Gauthier, chairman; Ben Arp, editorial coordinator; Marty Lentz, Safety and Rescue section coordinator; Margaret Miller, Rock section coordinator; Judy Ramberg, Approaching the Peaks section coordinator; and Craig Rowley, Snow and Ice section coordinator. In 1990, Paul Gauthier moved to England, and the committee was subsequently chaired by Myrna Plum.

The Approaching the Peaks Subcommittee jointly developed five chapters with major contributors as follows: "First Steps," Bill Deter and Judi Maxwell; "Clothing and Equipment," Judy Ramberg; "Camping and Food," Judy Ramberg and Judi Maxwell; "Routefinding and Navigation," Bob Burns with consultation on maps section by Stewart M. Wright; and "Wilderness Travel," Judi Maxwell, Bill Deters, and Judy Ramberg.

The Fundamentals and Rock Climbing Subcommittee jointly reviewed the revisions developed by the following lead individuals: "Ropes, Knots, and Carabiners," Jack E. Bennett and Larry Longley; "Belaying," Allen Frees; "Rappelling," Ken Small; "Rock Climbing Technique," Susan Price; "Leading and Placing Protection," Dan Bean; "Aid Climbing and Pitoncraft," Jeff Johnson; and Rating Systems appendix, Jan Green. Cal Magnusson of REI consulted on the "Belaying" chapter.

The Snow and Ice Climbing Subcommittee jointly revised each of their chapters with the major contributors as follows: "Snow Travel and Climb-ing," Kurt Hanson, Jim Cade, and Don Heck; "Ice Climbing," Don Heck; "Glacier Travel and Crevasse Rescue," Craig Rowley and Nancy Jackson; and "Winter and Expedition Climbing," Kurt Hanson, Nancy Jackson, and Jim Cade.

The Safety and Rescue Subcommittee, with contributions by Paul Gauthier and Ben Arp, condensed and revised materials into "Safety and Leadership," revision led by Marty Lentz, and the "Alpine Rescue" chapter, led by Pete A. Bustanoby.

As the text was reaching a final form, Books staff organized efforts to revise figures and illustrations and provide artwork and photography. The committee end of this large effort was coordinated by Marilyn O'Callaghan. Concurrently, the professional design and layout was directed by Books production and design manager Marge Mueller.

THE MOUNTAINEERS, founded in 1906, is a non-profit outdoor activity and conservation club, whose mission is "to explore, study, preserve and enjoy the natural beauty of the outdoors...." Based in Seattle, Washington, the club is now the third largest such organization in the United States, with 12,000 members and four branches throughout Washington State.

The Mountaineers sponsors both classes and year-round outdoor activities in the Pacific Northwest, which include hiking, mountain climbing, ski-touring, snowshoeing, bicycling, camping, kayaking and canoeing, nature study, sailing, and adventure travel. The club's conservation division supports environmental causes through educational activities, sponsoring legislation, and presenting informational programs. All club activities are led by skilled, experienced volunteers, who are dedicated to promoting safe and responsible enjoyment and preservation of the outdoors.

The Mountaineers Books, an active, non-profit publishing program of the club, produces guidebooks, instructional texts, historical works, natural history guides, and works on environmental conservation. All books produced by The Mountaineers are aimed at fulfilling the club's mission.

If you would like to participate in these organized outdoor activities or the club's programs, consider a membership in The Mountaineers. For information and an application, write or call The Mountaineers, Club Headquarters, 300 Third Avenue West, Seattle, Washington 98119; (206) 284-6310.

PART ONE

APPROACHING THE PEAKS

Stratocumulus front over the High Sierra, Mount Whitney region, California. Photo by Galen Rowell/Mountain Light

◆ 1 ◆
FIRST STEPS

Mountaineering is more than climbing, panoramic views, and wilderness experience. It is also challenge, risk, and hardship. And it is not for everyone. Those drawn to the mountains can find them exhilarating and irresistible, as well as frustrating and sometimes even deadly. There are qualities to mountaineering that inspire us and bring us to revel in a pursuit that is more than a pastime, more than a sport; a passion, certainly, and sometimes a compulsion.

"What was the force that impelled me?" asks American mountaineer Fred Beckey. "Something complex and undefinable, the attraction of uncertainty." British climber George Leigh Mallory, many years earlier, offered another version of mountaineering's attraction: "What we get from this adventure," he said, "is just sheer joy."

Distant views of mountains may speak of adventure, but they seldom more than hint at the joys and hardships that await. If you want to climb mountains, be prepared for the totality of nature—storms as well as soft breezes, tangled brush as well as alpine flowers, biting insects as well as singing birds. Climbing mountains is a tough way to spend your spare time, and anyone who does it knows what Polish climber Voytek Kurtyka meant when he said that "alpinism is the art of suffering." Mountaineering takes place in an environment indifferent to human needs, and not everyone is willing to pay the price in hardship for its rich physical and spiritual rewards.

FREEDOM OF THE HILLS

"Freedom of the hills" is a concept that combines the simple joy of being in the mountains with the skill, gear, and strength to travel where we will without harm to ourselves, others, or the environment.

This book, with its roots in the mountains of the Pacific Northwest, champions this freedom by providing information for climbers of all levels, from novice to advanced. It represents the combined experiences of many climbers, who have traveled most of the major mountain ranges on earth. This does not make it gospel. Although learning from the experiences of others is valuable, time and again the student returns to instruct the teacher.

As you read, remember that new techniques and technical advances occur so frequently that any attempt to document the "state of the art" is quickly dated. With this caution in mind, this book can serve as your general passport to the freedom of the hills.

CARING FOR THE WILDERNESS

The beauty of wild places could be their undoing as they attract us to them—leaving them touched by human hands and eventually less than wild. We are consuming wilderness at an alarming rate, using it and changing it as we do so.

Though we sometimes act otherwise, the mountains don't exist for our amusement. They owe us nothing and they require nothing from us. Hudson Stuck wrote that he and the other members of the first party to climb Mount McKinley felt they had been granted ''a privileged communion with the high places of the earth.'' As mountaineers traveling in the wilderness, our minimum charge for this privilege is to leave the hills as we found them, with no sign of our passing. We must study the places we visit and become sensitive to their vulnerability, then camp and climb in ways that minimize our impact.

The privileges we enjoy in the mountains bring responsibilities. Therefore, the facts of mountaineering life today include permit systems that limit access to the backcountry, road and trail closures, environmental restoration projects, legislative alerts, and the clash of competing interest groups. While we tread softly in the mountains, it's also time to speak loudly back in town for support of wilderness preservation and sensitive use of our wild lands. As mountaineers, we need to be activists as well as climbers if we want our children to be able to enjoy what we take for granted.

KNOWLEDGE AND SKILLS

As part of our passport to travel the mountains, we need the skills for safe, enjoyable passage. For our sake and the sake of everyone we climb with, we learn the tools and techniques of camping, navigation, belaying, rappelling, glacier travel, safety, rescue, and climbing on rock, snow, and ice. This book is a guide to this learning.

PHYSICAL PREPARATION

Mountaineering is a demanding activity, both physically and mentally. Rock climbing, in particular, has become increasingly athletic, especially at the higher levels of difficulty. Climbers today accomplish what was considered impossible only a few years ago. Many serious rock climbers work out at specialized gymnasiums, and the sport features international climbing competitions. In the world of alpine climbing, the highest peaks are commonly climbed without supplementary oxygen, in record times, and by more and more difficult routes. Most of us, however, appreciate such world-class performance from the sidelines. It's not necessary to devote your life to mountaineering in order to enjoy the activity at a level that provides personal satisfaction.

Levels of performance are rising even among recreational climbers and mountaineers. Good physical conditioning is one of the keys and can make the difference between enjoying an outing and merely enduring it. More important, the safety of the whole party may hinge on the strength—or weakness—of one member.

Most mountaineers train regularly. Aerobic activities such as running, cycling, swimming, cross-country skiing, snowshoeing, hiking uphill with a heavy pack, and climbing stairs are popular exercises. Many climbers lift weights to build strength and perform stretching exercises for flexibility. Specific exercises, those closest to climbing itself, are probably the best preparation. Physical fitness is the foundation for all the strenuous activities of mountaineering.

MENTAL PREPARATION

Just as important as physical conditioning, our mental attitude often determines success or failure. Once physical fitness is adequate, the ''mind games'' we play with ourselves are what really get us past a difficult move or help us decide to back off.

We need to be positive, realistic, and honest with ourselves. There is a personal balance required here. A ''can do'' attitude may turn into dangerous overconfidence if it isn't tempered with a realistic appraisal of ourselves and the situation.

Many a veteran mountaineer says the greatest challenges are mental. Perhaps this is one of mountaineering's greatest appeals: while seeking the freedom of the hills, we come face to face with ourselves.

JUDGMENT AND EXPERIENCE

This book outlines the basics of equipment and techniques and suggests how to learn from practice. But judgment, the most important of all mental qualities in climbing, develops from how we integrate our knowledge and experience.

Much of what we need are coping skills—the ability to deal with adverse weather, long hikes, thick brush, high exposure, and the like. As we endure these situations, we become better decision-makers, and the experiences we gain are useful for comparison the next time the going gets tough.

New situations, however, will still arise for which we have no trustworthy precedent. We won't be able to make an automatic, confident response, so we will have to exercise careful judgment. In this uncertainty lies much of the charm and challenge of mountaineering—as well as the potential for tragedy.

Many years ago, The Mountaineers club of Washington State devised a set of guidelines to help people conduct themselves safely in the mountains. Based on careful observation of the habits of skilled climbers and a thoughtful analysis of accidents, it has served well for not only climbers but, with slight adaptation, for all wilderness travelers. It is not inflexible doctrine, but it has proven to be a sound guide to practices that minimize risk.

A CLIMBING CODE

• A climbing party of three is the minimum, unless adequate prearranged support is available. On glaciers, a minimum of two rope teams is recommended.
• Rope up on all exposed places and for all glacier travel. Anchor all belays.
• Keep the party together, and obey the leader or majority rule.
• Never climb beyond your ability and knowledge.
• Never let judgment be overruled by desire when choosing the route or deciding whether to turn back.

• Carry the necessary clothing, food, and equipment at all times.
• Leave the trip schedule with a responsible person.
• Follow the precepts of sound mountaineering as set forth in textbooks of recognized merit.
• Behave at all times in a manner that reflects favorably upon mountaineering.

This code is by no means a step-by-step formula for reaching summits, but rather a guideline to safe and sane mountaineering. Climbers sometimes question the need for such standards for a sport in which much of the appeal lies in the absence of formal rules. But many serious accidents could have been avoided or their effects minimized if these simple principles had been followed. This climbing code is built on the premise that mountaineers want strong chances of safety and success, even in risk-filled or doubtful situations, and that they want safeguards in case they have misjudged those chances.

Experienced mountaineers often modify the code in practice, taking an independent course that combines an understanding of risk with the skill to help control it. The code is recommended especially for beginners, who have not yet developed the judgment that comes from years of experience.

If we learn to climb safely and skillfully, body and spirit in tune with the wilderness, we will be able to accept the lifetime invitation that John Muir extended to us so many years ago.

"Climb the mountains," he told us, "and get their good tidings. Nature's peace will flow into you as sunshine flows into trees. The winds will blow their own freshness into you and the storms their energy, while cares will drop off like autumn leaves."

◆ 2 ◆

CLOTHING AND EQUIPMENT

In packing for a wilderness trip, it's a simple matter of take it or leave it. The idea is to take what you need and to leave the rest at home. With thousands of choices widely available in outdoor clothing and equipment, it's no longer a question of how to find what you need, but rather of limiting your load to just the items that will keep you safe, dry, and comfortable.

To strike a balance between too much and too little, monitor what you take with you. After each trip determine what was used, what was really needed for a margin of safety, and what was not needed. As you buy equipment, go for lightweight alternatives if the weight reduction does not jeopardize the item's performance and durability. Whenever possible, look for versatile equipment you can use for several purposes.

If you're new to mountaineering, you don't

have the experience yet to know what works best for you. So don't buy all your basic gear right away. Take it one trip at a time, one purchase at a time. Whether it's boots, packs, or sleeping bags, wait until you have enough experience to make intelligent decisions before spending your money. Rent, borrow, or improvise during your early outings until you learn what you need and what you don't need. Get advice by talking to seasoned hikers and climbers, by window-shopping at outdoors stores, and by reading mountaineering magazines.

This chapter is one useful source of information on basic wilderness gear, including guidelines on what constitutes good equipment. It won't tell you what brands to purchase, but it will help you find high-quality items among those thousands of choices.

FOOTGEAR

BOOTS

Not many years ago almost all boots were made of leather, but some modern materials have certain performance advantages. Plastic boots and lightweight hiking boots have now joined the classic leather boot as common footgear for wilderness travelers, although leather is still the first choice for general-purpose mountaineering.

Leather boots

A general mountaineering boot is a compromise between conflicting requirements. It should be

tough enough to withstand the scraping of rocks, stiff and solid enough for kicking steps in hard snow, yet comfortable enough for the approach hike. In a single day of climbing, the boots may have to contend with streams, mud, logs, brush, scree, hard snow, and steep rock.

The classic leather mountaineering boot (fig. 2-1) has the following features: high uppers ($5^1/2$ to $7^1/2$ inches) to protect the ankles in rough terrain; Vibram-type soles for traction on slippery vegetation, mud, and snow; midsoles for insulation and shock absorption; and a semi-rigid shank.

The length and rigidity of a boot's shank (fig.

length shank impairs walking but greatly reduces
leg fatigue when front-pointing with crampons or
standing on small rock nubbins.

The sole of the boot should be attached to the
uppers by means of a durable method of stitching,
with the Norwegian welt (fig. 2-3) considered the
longest lasting. The welt should be narrw (fig.

Fig. 2–1. A classic leather mountaineering boot

2-2) is a much-debated topic. The ideal length depends on how the boot will be used. For hiking,
easy snow climbs, and rock routes, choose a boot
with a half-length nylon or fiberglass shank, which
keeps the sole reasonably flexible. Boots used primarily for technical ice climbing or difficult mountain routes benefit from being made of plastic or
having a full-length shank. The rigid plastic or full-

*Fig. 2–2. The shank
length determines the
flexibility of the boot
sole: a, full-length
shank boot; b,
half-length shank boot.*

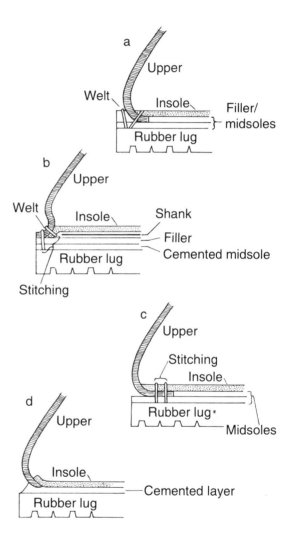

*Fig. 2–3. Four common methods of boot
construction: a, Goodyear welt; b, Norwegian
welt; c, Littleway; d, cemented.*

Fig. 2–4. A narrow-welt boot works well on small footholds.

Inside of foot

2-4) to prevent it from bending on small holds.

Other desirable boot features include the following:

• Tops that open wide so that even when the boots are frozen or wet, they can be put on easily.
• A minimum number of seams, to decrease the places water can leak through.
• A gusseted tongue, or a bellows tongue, to keep water from easily entering the boot.
• Double- or triple-layered leather or fabric at areas of high wear (toes and heels).
• Hard toe counters (stiffeners) built in to protect the feet, reduce compression caused by crampon straps, and facilitate kicking of steps in hard snow.
• Hard heel counters (stiffeners) built in to increase foot stability and facilitate plunge-stepping down steep snow slopes.

Lightweight hiking boots

Improvements in boot technology have led to evolution of the medium- and lightweight hiking boot (fig. 2-5). Made of leather and nylon, these boots weigh one-third to one-half as much as traditional boots, yet are sturdy enough for three-season trekking on moderate terrain. The uppers of these boots typically are glued to the sole, eliminating the need for a welt. Check that the boots are high enough for ankle protection, that a stiff counter wraps the heel and toe, and that abrasion areas are reinforced.

Advantages of lightweight boots include reduced cost, increased breathability, improved comfort, shorter break-in time, and faster drying. However, they are not as durable and cannot be made as waterproof as leather boots, and they lack the weight and stiffness for kicking steps in firm snow. On difficult off-trail terrain and on snow, leather boots are still preferred.

Fig. 2–5. Lightweight trail boots: a, leather; b, synthetic.

Plastic boots

Plastic boots (fig. 2-6), originally designed for technical ice climbing, have found a much wider market among general mountaineers interested in snow routes or winter climbing. The plastic shell of the boot is waterproof, so the inner insulating boot remains dry and keeps your feet warm. This inner boot can be removed, which helps in drying out perspiration.

Plastic boots need to fit well from the start because their rigid shape will not mold around your feet over time. The boot's relative rigidity and its

Fig. 2–6. Plastic boot: a, waterproof shell; b, insulating inner boot.

high degree of warmth makes it a poor choice for general trail use. When fitting plastic boots, make sure that they do not constrict the feet. Feet swell at high altitude, and plastic boots are frequently used for high-altitude expeditions.

The proper fit

Whether you're looking at leather, plastic, or lightweight boots, the fit is critical. Try on several makes and styles, with socks similar to the ones you will wear on a climb. Be sure to bring along any orthotic devices, insoles, or other inserts you plan to use. Wear the boots in the store for several minutes to give your socks time to compress around your feet. Then note whether the boots have any uncomfortable seams or creases and whether they pinch against your foot or Achilles' tendon. In properly fitting boots, your heels will feel firmly anchored in place while your toes will have plenty of room to wiggle and will not jam against the toe box when you press forward. Boots that are too tight constrict circulation, causing cold feet and increased susceptibility to frostbite. Loose boots, on the other hand, cause blisters.

Most people's feet swell during the course of the day, so consider buying boots in the evening for the best fit. Given the choice between boots that are a hair too big and ones that are a bit too small, go with the larger boots. You can fill the space with a thicker sock, and most boots can shrink as much as a half size over time (because the toe of a boot has a tendency to curl).

Boot care

With proper care, good boots can last several years. Keep mildew at bay by washing the boots frequently. After washing, stuff them with a boot tree or newspaper, and dry them in a warm (not hot), ventilated area. Heat can damage the welt and the adhesive used on boot soles. Avoid drying or storing boots at high temperatures: the boots dried over a campfire are likely to be the ones that fall apart on a future trip. Boot soles usually wear out long before the uppers. High-quality boots can be resoled, although this may change the original fit because new soles tighten the size somewhat.

During an outing, water can get into boots over the top and through the leather and seams. Wearing gaiters keeps water from running into boots from the top. Waterproofing agents applied to the leather and seams stop water from going through the boots.

With new boots, treat the welt first with one of the waterproofing products designed for this purpose. It's a process that needs to be repeated periodically. Boots must be clean and dry, with any wax removed. Apply the material directly to the threads and stitching holes, and let it dry before applying waterproofing to the rest of the boot. Some boot makers use waterproof rubber rands to seal the welt, a desirable feature that simplifies boot maintenance and keeps your feet drier.

Apply waterproofing to the boots a day or two before a trip to give the agents time to penetrate the leather. The makeup of the waterproofing used on leather uppers depends on how the leather was tanned, so follow the manufacturer's recommendations. The nylon in many lightweight boots is difficult to seal completely, but you can make it more water resistant by applying silicone-based sprays. Whatever you use on your boots, apply it frequently if you expect your feet to stay dry.

After using plastic boots, remove the inner boots and clean them with mild soap and water. Remove any debris from inside the plastic shells to prevent abrasion and excessive wear between the outer and inner boots.

Specialized footwear

Depending on the trip, a climber may wear one kind of boot for the approach hike, another type of footwear in camp, and yet another on the climb. If you can afford additional footgear and are willing to carry the extra weight, consider these options:

• Lightweight, flexible trail shoes for long trails, easy approaches, stream crossings, and for wearing in camp. They are less likely to cause blisters and are less fatiguing to wear. (The rule of thumb is that 1 pound of weight strapped to the foot is comparable to 5 on the back.) However, these lightweight shoes may not provide the support you

need when carrying a heavy pack.
• Camp footwear (booties for comfort and warmer sleeping; running or tennis shoes, or sandals, for comfort and to give boots a chance to dry).
• Lightweight nylon-mesh socks for camp use and stream crossings. They are very light, have waffled soles for traction, and dry fast, but give no support.
• Special rock-climbing shoes for technical rock (see Chapter 9 for details).
• Full-shank boots that you can use with rigid crampons for ice climbing.

SOCKS

Socks cushion and insulate your feet, absorb perspiration, and reduce friction between the boot and the foot. Socks made of wool or synthetic materials can perform all these functions, while those made of cotton cannot. Cotton absorbs too much water, which destroys its insulating qualities and increases friction between the boot and the foot.

Most climbers wear two pairs of socks. Next to the skin, a smooth polyester or polypropylene sock transports perspiration from the foot to the outer sock. Over this goes a heavier, rougher sock made of wool or synthetics.

Of course there are many exceptions. A rock climber wants flexible rock shoes to fit like a glove, and so usually wears only one thin pair of socks. A hiker using trail shoes on a warm day keeps feet cooler by wearing just a single pair of socks, while a winter climber may wear three pairs of socks inside oversized boots. Always keep your toes free enough to wiggle. Three pairs of socks give less protection from the cold than two if the last pair constricts circulation.

Before donning socks, consider putting protective moleskin or tape on your feet at places prone to blisters, such as the back of the heel. Moleskin is especially valuable when breaking in new boots or early in the climbing season before your feet have toughened up. Another blister fighter is foot powder sprinkled on your socks and in your boots.

On expeditions or in cold weather, a vapor-barrier sock may be worn between the two main sock layers. Vapor-barrier liners keep moisture next to your foot and prevent perspiration from wetting your thick socks. They also keep your feet warmer by inhibiting the evaporation of sweat. In subfreezing temperatures, these socks reduce the danger of frostbite, but over time the moisture that is kept inside can result in trench foot—a serious problem. If you use vapor-barrier socks, dry your feet thoroughly at least once each day.

Insoles added to the inside of your boots provide extra insulation and cushioning. Synthetic insoles are non-absorbent, do not become matted when damp, and have a loose structure that helps ventilate your foot. Insoles made of felt, leather, and lambskin all absorb moisture and must be removed when drying boots. When trying on new boots, be sure to insert the insoles you intend to wear.

CLOTHING

Humans maintain body comfort by creating a microenvironment of warm air next to the skin. Combinations of cold temperatures, rain, and wind remove this warm air and can initiate a dangerous reduction in body temperature. If left unchecked, this condition, known as hypothermia, leads to uncontrolled shivering, loss of judgment, and eventually death.

Clothing protects you from the cold, wind, and wet and maintains a compatible environment next to your skin. Clothing also must help cool you when conditions become too hot. Over-exertion or excessive temperatures can cause the improperly clothed body to suffer heat exhaustion—an affliction that can be just as deadly as hypothermia.

LAYERING

Clothing maintains the body's microenvironment best when it is worn in multiple layers, letting you adapt easily to the fluctuating temperatures in the mountains. To keep pace with changing conditions, add or subtract layers of clothing one by one.

Three levels form the basis of this clothing system: a layer next to the skin, insulating layers, and an outer protective layer.

The layer next to the skin (long underwear) allows for ventilation so the body can cool itself. During the warmer parts of a day, many climbers wear just their long underwear and a pair of shorts. When it's cold, long underwear, covered by additional clothing, increases your insulation. This layer also transports perspiration away from your skin without absorbing the moisture. (Wet garments in contact with your skin draw away twenty-five times more heat than dry ones.)

The insulating layers (shirts, sweaters, pile coats) trap warm air next to the body. The thicker the layer of trapped or "dead" air, the warmer

you'll be. However, several light, loosely fitting layers are usually warmer than one thick garment. They are also more versatile because the various pieces can be worn in different combinations depending on the temperature and your level of exertion.

The outer protective layer is essential for minimizing heat loss from wind and rain. Wind stirs up the warm air next to the body and blows it away, a process known as convection. The stronger the wind, the faster heat is blown away, producing a wind-chill effect that makes it feel much colder. When the air temperature is 10 degrees Fahrenheit, a 20-mile-per-hour wind produces a wind-chill effect (fig. 2-7) that is equivalent to −25 degrees. Rain dampens clothing and reduces its insulating

Fig. 2–7. Wind-chill chart

Wind Speed MPH	Temperature (°F)										
	50	40	30	20	10	0	−10	−20	−30	−40	−50
	Equivalent Chill Temperature										
Calm	50	40	30	20	10	0	−10	−20	−30	−40	−50
5	48	37	27	16	6	−5	−15	−26	−36	−47	−57
10	40	28	16	4	−9	−21	−33	−46	−58	−70	−83
15	36	22	9	−5	−18	−36	−45	−58	−72	−85	−99
20	32	18	4	−10	−25	−39	−53	−67	−82	−96	−110
25	30	16	0	−15	−29	−44	−59	−74	−88	−104	−118
30	28	13	−2	−18	−33	−48	−63	−79	−94	−109	−125
35	27	11	−4	−20	−35	−49	−67	−83	−98	−113	−129
40	26	10	−6	−21	−37	−53	−69	−85	−100	−116	−132
above 40	little additional effect										

Danger of Freezing Exposed Flesh if Dry and Properly Clothed:	Little Danger	Great	Extreme

To use this table, which illustrates the intensely chilling effect of wind, find wind speed (in miles per hour) in left-hand column and temperature (in degrees F) in top row; the intersection of these is the equivalent temperature. For example, at a temperature of 0°F a breeze 15 mph has the cooling effect of a temperature of −36° on a calm day and precautions should be taken to protect exposed flesh from frostbite. The zones shown on the table indicate the danger of frostbite to any exposed flesh of an average person in good condition whose body is properly clothed for the conditions. When the effective temperature is −25°F or less, care should be taken to minimize exposure of bare skin to wind.

value, and wet clothing conducts heat from the body at an alarming rate. A waterproof shell over your insulating layers eliminates heat loss from conduction and convection. Wind cannot penetrate the shell, so warm air next to your body stays put. The shell also keeps the insulating layers drier so that body heat is not conducted away.

FABRICS

Clothing for the outdoors is made from a variety of fabrics, each with advantages and disadvantages.

Cotton is comfortable to wear when dry but absorbs many times its weight in water and loses its insulating qualities when wet. Because it absorbs so much water, it takes a long time to dry. In hot weather, however, cotton ventilates well and helps cool the body. Wet it down on a hot day, and the water evaporating from the cotton will cool you off.

Silk readily absorbs water, but not as much as cotton, so it dries faster. Silk is also useful in hot weather. Wetted down, it helps cool the body through evaporation.

Wool is far less absorbent than cotton, so it holds less water when wet. Consequently, it does not conduct away as much body heat and requires far less heat to dry. Wool is also warmer when wet because it does not collapse and therefore retains much of its dead-air space.

Synthetic pile does not absorb any water. Some moisture is held in suspension between the filaments of the fabric when it is wet, but most of the water can be wrung out. Garments made from synthetic pile are comparatively warm when wet, and they dry fast. Pile is also very light and fluffy so that, ounce for ounce, it traps more dead air than natural fibers like wool. All these features contribute to make pile a versatile and effective insulating material.

Polyester, acrylic, and polypropylene fabrics are used for a variety of long underwear and insulating garments. The synthetic filaments in these fabrics are also lightweight, non-absorbent, and quick drying. The filaments of some are also very good at transporting perspiration away from the body, making them well suited for use next to the skin. More and more fabrics are being designed to do this, and these fabrics have largely replaced wool, cotton, and silk for use in long underwear. When selecting items of clothing, consult the tags on individual garments or get help from a salesperson.

Down is still, ounce for ounce, the warmest insulation available. It is also the most compressible, so it packs away small yet quickly regains its loft—and therefore its warmth—when unpacked. These qualities make down an excellent insulator for cold-weather use. Unfortunately, down loses all its insulating value when wet and is almost impossible to dry in the mountains, making it a poor insulator in wet climates.

Spun synthetic filaments do not collapse when wet, as down does. Therefore they make excellent insulation for coats and sleeping bags used in moist climates. Although cheaper and more easily cleaned than down, they are not as warm, weigh more, and are less compressible. The useful life of synthetics is much shorter than down.

Nylon shells, which go over the insulating layers, give protection from the wind but are not waterproof unless the nylon is coated. Typically, polyurethane coatings are used to waterproof nylon. The thickness of the coating is measured by its weight per square yard, and a 1-ounce coating is the minimum weight you should consider. Polyurethane coatings are lightweight and effective when cared for but are not very resistant to abrasion or mildew, so some climbers prefer shells coated with synthetic rubber. These shells are more durable, but most rubber-coated raingear is too heavy for mountaineering.

Although most coatings keep rain out, they also seal sweat in. If you're working hard, the sweat generated can dampen your insulation from within. Microporous coatings were designed to attack this problem. These coatings have billions of microscopic holes per square inch. Moisture vapor from your skin has a much smaller molecular size than liquid water. The holes in the coating are large enough to let vapor escape but too small for liquid water to get in, so the coating breathes but is still waterproof. Gore-Tex, the first waterproof/breathable fabric on the market, works on the same theory but, rather than using a honeycombed coating, a Teflon film with microscopic holes is laminated to the inside of the nylon shell.

Many climbers see the waterproof/breathables as an improvement over the old-style coated nylons, but the new-generation materials are not perfect. If you work hard, you will exceed the garment's ability to blow off steam, and sweat will condense inside the shell. Once in liquid form, the sweat can no longer escape through the garment. Ventilating the garment helps keep you from overheating and building up perspiration. Most waterproof/breathables need maintenance. When water stops beading and rolling off the surface, the material should be washed, rinsed, dried, and treated with silicone or another waterproofing spray. Apply the spray generously three times over the course of three days.

HEADGEAR

When the rest of the body is covered in clothing, an unprotected head is like a radiator that accounts for more than half of the body's heat loss. The head is the first part of the body to uncover when you're overheated, and the first part to cover when you're cold. The old adage says "If your feet are cold, put on a hat." There's some truth to this because as the head and trunk get cold, the body reduces blood flow to the arms and legs in an attempt to warm vital areas. To increase blood flow back to the arms and legs, you need to warm the vital head and torso areas.

Climbers usually carry several different types of hats. Cotton glacier hats and baseball caps are popular for sun protection. A bandanna can be draped from a hat to help shade your neck, ears, and face, or it can be dipped in water and tied around your head to cool you on a hot day. A lightweight rain hat is useful for warm-weather trips because it keeps your head dry while allowing ventilation at the neck of your rain parka.

Warm insulating caps of wool, polypropylene, or pile are standard for cold weather. Consider carrying two hats, because an extra hat affords almost as much warmth as an extra sweater but weighs much less. Warm hats should also be part of your summer wardrobe in case of a forced bivouac. Balaclavas are versatile insulating hats. Rolled down, they protect the face and neck from the cold; rolled up, they warm the head but allow ventilation of the upper body through the neck area.

THE UPPER BODY

Long underwear

Protection of the torso begins with appropriate underwear. Synthetics like polypropylene and polyester are currently the best fabrics for this purpose. They are soft, stretchy, ventilate well, and wick moisture away from the skin. The underwear comes in a variety of weights, and you can choose which suits your climate and metabolism.

It's smart to buy light-colored long underwear. Light colors absorb *and* radiate heat more slowly. If it is warm enough to strip down to your underwear, you will appreciate having a white rather than black or dark blue shirt exposed to the sun.

Insulating layers

In hot weather a thin cotton shirt will keep you comfortable and serve as a first line of defense against sunburn. Stick to light colors. In cold weather you'll carry several insulating layers for your torso. Shirts and sweaters should be made of wool or synthetics, such as pile, so they still provide warmth if they get wet. Cotton sweatshirts are useless once wet, so don't bring them.

Shirts and sweaters should be long in the torso so they tuck into or pull over the waist of the pants. Gaps between the pants and upper body let valuable heat escape. Similarly, turtleneck sweaters can keep much of the torso's heat from escaping. Tests show that the addition of a turtleneck alone can increase a garment's comfort level by 5 to 10 degrees Fahrenheit.

Jackets insulated with down or synthetic fills are not usually needed on summer trips but are valuable in cold climates and for winter travel. These jackets, weighing between 2 and 3 pounds, are seldom worn while climbing but are needed for emergencies, bivouacs, and the cold hours in camp.

Rain and wind protection

On top of everything comes a shell of nylon or other synthetic material as an outer layer to provide protection from rain and wind. The ideal shell is uninsulated, windproof, waterproof, and breathable. Another option is to carry both a lightweight, unlined nylon windshirt and a coated rain parka. The breathable wind shirt (which won't be completely windproof) will reduce heat lost to the wind yet let sweat pass out of your clothing. The raincoat goes on when the dampness caused by precipitation exceeds the dampness caused by perspiration.

Many of the qualities you should look for in a good rain parka (fig. 2-8) are the same whether or not the fabric breathes.

• A size large enough to allow for additional layers of clothing underneath without compressing your insulation or restricting your movement.
• A hood with a brim, neck flap, and good drawstring to keep water from dribbling down your face and neck. The hood should be large enough to accommodate a hat (or climbing helmet) and should not impair vision when you glance to the side.
• Seams sealed at the factory with tape. Check that the tape has bonded well to the coat. All seams need to be sealed to prevent moisture from entering along the stitching, and it's preferable to have factory-sealed seams rather than trying to seal them later yourself.
• Zippers with large, durable teeth and good flaps that keep the zipper dry.
• Pockets that are easily accessible with gloved hands and with a pack on. Pockets also need good rain flaps that keep water out.
• A coat length that extends below the hips, and a drawstring at the waist that allows you to seal off the bottom of the coat.
• Sleeves that cover the wrists. Snaps, elastic, or Velcro should keep the sleeve in place at the wrist.
• Ventilation: controllable openings at the front,

waist, underarms, sides, and cuffs that allow you to open up for ventilation or shut tight for trapping warm air next to your body.

Some climbers prefer anoraks, a pullover jacket with no front zipper, to standard rain parkas. The front zipper of a standard parka helps ventilation but can also leak, jam, or break. Cagoules (knee-length anoraks) are an option preferred by a few climbers. Ponchos, used by many hikers, are nearly useless in the wind and are not viable rain protection in the high mountains.

Fig. 2–8. Rain parkas: a, anorak (pullover parka); b, standard (zip-front parka).

THE LOWER BODY

Long underwear

Winter travel and cold alpine conditions call for long underwear, made of polypropylene, other synthetic material, or wool. Under these conditions, long underwear is not optional clothing, but an integral part of the layering system. The convenience and versatility of layering is compromised if a climber faced with a sudden storm has to strip to the skin to put on long underwear. Like your long underwear top, the bottoms should go on first and come off last. It is your heavier insulating pants that should be taken on or off as necessary. Down or synthetic pile underwear can also be carried and worn as outer wear during a bivouac. Synthetic briefs are an alternative to cotton.

Pants

Your insulating pants should be loose fitting for freedom of movement and made of a closely woven fabric with a hard finish so that it's resistant to wind and abrasion. Wool and wool/polyester blends work well. In cool, wet climates, synthetic pile is another good choice because it retains most of its insulating qualities when wet. Pile is not wind resistant, but a nylon shell, integral to the pants or separate, will remedy the problem.

To help layer your lower-body clothing, look for pants with full-length zippers that allow you to put the pants on while wearing boots. The life of your pants can be extended by reinforcing the seat and knees with patches of nylon or other durable fabrics.

Some climbers prefer knickers to long pants because knickers give better freedom of movement. By opening the leg straps and rolling down the socks, you can ventilate the knickers better than standard pants. Shorts are handy for hiking in the rain and for stream crossings, letting you keep your long pants dry inside the pack. Nylon shorts or gym pants worn over long underwear bottoms make a good summertime combination when shorts alone give inadequate protection against wind or cooler temperatures.

Wind and rain protection

Wind and rain pants should parallel your solution for protecting the upper half of your body. A pair of waterproof/breathable pants is one solution. Here again, full-length zippers are convenient. The zippers also help you ventilate the pants. An alternative to the waterproof/breathable fabrics is to carry both lightweight nylon wind pants and a pair of coated, non-breathable rain pants. Don the wind pants in blustery conditions, and the rain pants when it is raining hard.

Waterproof rain chaps are another outer covering for the legs, though they are now seen less and less frequently. Chaps protect the pant legs from rain, while the uncovered seat is protected by a long parka or cagoule. The system saves weight and improves ventilation but is more likely to fail in severe conditions, such as bushwhacking through wet brush or walking in blowing snow.

Some climbers use bibs made from waterproof/breathable fabrics and held up with suspenders. Bibs are best suited to winter snow and ice climbs, ski mountaineering, and cold-weather expeditions. They are considerably warmer than rain pants because they cover much of the torso and keep snow from melting around the waistline, but they are too warm for most summer uses.

Gaiters

The boundary between your trousers and boots is protected by gaiters (fig. 2-9). Climbers often carry gaiters both summer and winter to prevent wet brush, mud, or snow from saturating pant cuffs, socks, and boots. Gaiters are usually made from nylon packcloth and close with snaps, zippers, and/or Velcro. A cord running under the foot from one side of the gaiter to the other helps the gaiter hug your boot, while a drawstring at the top keeps the gaiter from sliding down. A tight fit around the boot is essential to prevent snow from entering underneath the gaiter. A tight fit also helps prevent catching your crampon points on the gaiters.

Short gaiters, those extending 5 or 6 inches over the top of the boot, are adequate for keeping corn

Fig. 2–9. Gaiters: a, short length; b, full length; c, supergaiter.

snow and gravel out of your boots in summer. The deep snows of winter, however, usually call for long gaiters that extend up over the calf.

The portion of the gaiter covering the boot should be made of coated nylon. The upper portion of long gaiters should be made of a waterproof/breathable fabric or an uncoated nylon so that the legs can breathe. Zippers are the usual failure point of a gaiter. Make sure yours are heavy-duty with large teeth. A flap that closes with snaps or Velcro protects the zipper from damage and can keep the gaiter closed and make it functional even if the zipper breaks.

The strap under the foot will wear out during the life of the gaiter. Neoprene straps work well in snow but wear quickly on rock, while heavy cord survives rock better but sometimes balls up with snow. Whatever you use, be sure the gaiter strap is designed for easy replacement.

Supergaiters completely cover the boot from the welt up but leave the lug soles exposed for good traction. Insulation built into these gaiters covers the boots and reduces the chance of frostbite during cold-weather climbs.

HANDS

Mittens are warmer than gloves because they allow your fingers to snuggle together and share warmth. A pair of synthetic pile or heavy wool mittens worn inside waterproof overmitts is fine for most non-technical climbs. Pile mitts can be wrung out when soaking wet and retain most of their insulating loft. Wool is not quite as effective once wet, so carry an extra pair of inner mitts (in a pinch, socks will work). Get inner mitts that cover the wrist.

Outer mitts can be made of a waterproof or waterproof/breathable nylon on the palm side. An increasing number of manufacturers use a non-slip coating on the palm to improve the climber's ability to grip ice tools. The backhand side of the overmitt should breathe, so choose a style that uses waterproof/breathable fabric. The overmitt should overlap the parka sleeve some 4 to 6 inches, and elastic or Velcro closures can cinch the overmitt around the forearm.

To prevent losing your mittens and overmitts, it's a good idea to sew on security cords (unless yours came so equipped). You'll find it's well worth the effort, especially when you need bare hands for snow or rock climbing, or if you take the mittens off in a high wind.

Many climbers wear polypropylene glove liners or a thin pair of fingerless gloves inside their mitts. Both give excellent dexterity for delicate chores. In very cold temperatures (around 0 degrees Fahrenheit, or −18 degrees Celsius), the polypropylene liners are better at keeping exposed flesh from freezing to metal. Fingerless gloves give slightly better dexterity and are preferred for cold-weather rock climbing when you don't want a layer of fabric between your fingers and the rock. You can buy fingerless gloves or make your own by cutting the fingers off a pair of army-surplus wool gloves.

Thin leather gloves are important for safety when rappelling or managing a hip belay because they prevent rope burns that could cause you to release the rope. These gloves are difficult to waterproof and they soak up water, so don't rely on them for warmth.

PACKS

Climbers usually own at least two packs: a rucksack to hold enough paraphernalia for a day climb and a large-capacity pack to carry the necessities for multiday trips. All packs should allow you to carry weight close to your body and center the load over your hips and legs.

INTERNAL AND EXTERNAL FRAMES

Soft packs with internal frames (fig. 2-10) that help maintain the pack's shape and transfer weight to the hips are by far the most popular packs among climbers and ski mountaineers. These packs allow the weight to be carried lower, and they do a better job of hugging the back. Internal frame packs are designed to move with you, while external frame packs tend to shift suddenly as you climb or ski. The sudden movement of 40 pounds or so can easily make you lose your balance.

The volume of most internal frame packs is easy to adjust. Most have compression straps so that the large-capacity pack used to approach a peak can be transformed into a compact, closely fitting summit pack. The clean, narrow profile of internal frame packs allows them to be hauled up rock pitches or taken through heavy brush with far fewer snags than external frame packs.

External frame packs (fig. 2-10) use a long rigid frame that is held away from the back by taut nylon

Fig. 2–10. Packs: a, small internal frame summit pack; b, large internal frame pack with padded hip band; c, external frame pack with padded hip band.

back bands. These packs provide excellent weight distribution by allowing the load to be carried high over the hips. This design lets the hips—not just the shoulders and back—share in the heavy work. Because the frame is held away from the back, these packs keep you cooler. External frame packs were designed for trail use and do a better job here than most internal frame packs. Some climbers use them for long, easy approaches and carry a small day pack for the summit day.

BUYING AN INTERNAL FRAME PACK

First and foremost, buy a pack that fits. The pack's adjustment range must be compatible with your back size, extending from the top of your sacrum to the top of your shoulders. Some packs adjust to a wide range of sizes, others don't.

Before buying a pack, loosen all the adjustments and load it up. Without a typical load, you can't tell how the pack rides or if the adjustments provide a good fit. Now put it on. The frame should follow the curve of your back. If it doesn't, can the stays or frame be bent so it does? The shoulder straps should attach to the pack about 2 or 3 inches below the crest of your shoulders and leave little or no gap behind your back. Check that the load-lifter straps work. These straps transfer weight between the shoulders and hips, allowing different muscle groups to share in the work.

Once the pack is adjusted to your liking, check the head clearance. Can you look up without hitting your head on the frame or top pocket? Can you look up if you're wearing a helmet? Next check for adequate padding wherever the pack touches your body. Pay particular attention to the thickness and quality of padding used in the shoulder straps and hip belt. Padding in the hip belt should extend beyond the hip bone. See that the hip belt goes around the top of the hip and not around the waist, because you want the bone structure of the hips to carry the weight of the pack.

Decide what capacity is right for your intended uses. A rucksack for day climbs and lightweight overnight trips usually has a capacity between 1,800 and 2,200 cubic inches. Longer trips and winter climbs require a pack with a capacity between 3,500 and 5,000 cubic inches.

Here are some additional questions to ask when shopping for a pack:

• Does it have a double bottom? This feature will greatly extend its life.
• Does the pack have haul loops and ice axe loops?
• Is there a means of increasing the pack's capacity for extended trips, such as an expandable snow skirt and an adjustable top pocket that will slide higher?
• Are there compression straps to reduce the pack's volume or to prevent the load from shifting while climbing or skiing?
• Does the pack offer a convenient way to carry crampons, skis, snowshoes, and other items?
• Are removable side pockets available? This feature can help convert a day pack into a weekender.
• Does the pack have a sternum strap, which will help keep the pack from shifting on difficult terrain?
• If you will be using the pack for technical climbs or in thick brush, does it have a smooth profile so it will not get hung up?
• Is the pack cloth durable enough for the activities you have in mind?
• How waterproof is the pack?
• Does the pack have load-restraining zippers? If the zippers fail, can you still use the pack?

TIPS ON PACKING

Packs constructed from waterproof materials are not necessarily waterproof. They can leak through seams, zippers, pockets, the top opening, and places where the coating has worn off. Individual plastic bags or good stuff sacks can protect the contents. You can use a large plastic bag as a liner, storing dry items inside the liner and wet clothing between the liner and the sides of the pack.

A climbing pack should allow you to carry the load closer to the pelvic area, the body's center of rotation. This prevents the pack's weight from shifting on the shoulders. On trails, however, the load should be carried high and close to the back.

ESSENTIAL EQUIPMENT

There is a selection of small but critical items that deserve a place in almost every pack. You won't use every one of these items on every trip, but they can be lifesavers in an emergency, insurance against the unexpected.

Exactly how much "insurance" you should carry is a matter of debate. Some respected minimalists argue that weighing down your pack with insurance items causes you to climb slower, making it more likely you'll get caught by a storm or nightfall and be forced to bivouac. "Don't carry bivy gear unless you plan to bivy," they argue.

The majority of climbers, however, take along carefully selected safety items to survive the unexpected. They sacrifice some speed but argue they will always be around tomorrow to attempt again what they failed to climb today.

The special items most climbers believe should always be with you have become known as the Ten Essentials. They are:

1. Map
2. Compass
3. Flashlight/headlamp, with spare bulbs and batteries
4. Extra food
5. Extra clothing
6. Sunglasses
7. First-aid supplies
8. Pocket knife
9. Matches, in waterproof container
10. Fire starter

Other critical items often join the list of essential equipment, depending on the trip. We will take a look at the Ten Essentials and at a number of these additional items in the sections that follow.

THE TEN ESSENTIALS

1. Map

Always carry a detailed map of the area you are visiting, in a protective case or plastic covering. (Chapter 4 gives details about maps, including how to interpret those all-important topographic maps.)

2. Compass

A compass is an essential tool of navigation and routefinding. (Chapter 4 explains the workings of a compass and describes how to use another navigation instrument, the altimeter.)

3. Flashlight/headlamp

Headlamps (fig. 2-11) and hand-held flashlights are important enough and temperamental enough to make it worthwhile to invest in only quality equipment. Waterproof flashlights are worth the added expense. They function reliably in all weather, and the contacts or batteries won't corrode even if stored in a moist garage for months.

Fig. 2–11. Examples of headlamps

Few headlamps are waterproof, but some are more water-resistant than others. If you decide that a truly waterproof headlamp is important, start by buying a small waterproof flashlight. Sew a wide length of elastic into a headband, then sew several small retaining loops of thinner elastic onto the headband to hold the flashlight in place. The flashlight will be held on the side of your head, much like a pencil resting on top of your ear.

All lights need durable switches that cannot turn on accidentally in the pack, a common and potentially serious problem. Switches tucked away in a recessed cavity are excellent. So are rotating switches in which the body of the flashlight must be twisted a half turn. If it looks like your light switch could be tripped accidentally, guard against this danger by taping the switch closed or removing the bulb or reversing the batteries.

Adjustable focus is an excellent feature available on some lights. The reflector rotates so that the lamp gives flood lighting for chores close at hand or spot lighting for viewing objects far away. Adjustable focus permits maximum use of your light, often letting you see farther and accomplish more than a brighter light lacking this feature.

Flashlight bulbs don't last long, so carry spare bulbs in addition to spare batteries. You don't have to stick with the bulb that comes with your light. If it's a vacuum bulb, you can get a brighter beam with a replacement bulb filled with a gas, such as halogen, krypton, or xenon. These gases allow filaments to burn hotter and brighter than in vacuum bulbs, though they also draw more current (amperage) and shorten battery life.

Most bulbs have their amperage requirement marked on the base. You can get a rough idea of battery life by dividing the bulb's amperage figure into the amp/hours assigned to the batteries. For example, batteries rated at 4 amp/hours will burn about 8 hours with a .5-amp bulb.

It's a good idea to carry bulbs drawing different amperages. Conserve batteries by using low-amperage bulbs for tasks around camp. Switch over to high-amperage bulbs when you need a brighter beam.

Alkaline batteries are the best general-purpose batteries commonly available at mass merchandisers. They pack more energy than cheaper lead-zinc batteries. The major problems with alkalines are that voltage (hence brightness) drops significantly as they discharge, they can't be recharged, and their life is drastically shortened by cold temperatures (they operate at only 10 to 20 percent efficiency at 0 degrees Fahrenheit).

Nickel-cadmium batteries (nicads) can be recharged up to a thousand times, maintain their voltage and brightness throughout most of their discharge, and function well in the cold (about 70 percent efficient at 0 degrees Fahrenheit). However, they don't store as much energy as alkalines.

For climbing, look for high-capacity nicads, which pack two to three times the charge of standard nicads and are worth the added expense.

Lithium batteries have twice the voltage of regular batteries, so you'll need to rewire your light to run off half as many batteries. But one lithium cell packs more than twice the amp/hours of two alkalines. The voltage remains almost constant over the life of a lithium battery, and its efficiency at 0 degrees Fahrenheit is nearly the same as at room temperature. They are expensive.

4. Extra food

A one-day supply of extra food is a reasonable emergency stockpile in case you are delayed by foul weather, faulty navigation, injury, or other reasons. The food should require no cooking, be lightweight and easily digestible, and store well for long periods. A combination of jerky, nuts, candy, granola, and dried fruit works well. Some climbers also bring extra cocoa, dried soup, and tea if a heat source is available.

5. Extra clothing

How much extra insulation is necessary for an emergency? The garments used during the active portion of a climb and considered to be your basic climbing outfit are the inner and outer socks, boots, underwear, trousers, shirt, sweater or pile coat, hat, mitts or gloves, and raingear. These garments suffice over a wide range of temperatures and weather if the climber is active. Extra clothes for an unplanned bivouac are added to these basics according to the season. Ask yourself this question: what do I need to survive the worst conditions I could realistically encounter?

Extra underwear is a valuable addition that weighs little. During a strenuous climb, perspiration can soak the next-to-skin layer and conduct heat away from the core. It is important to get rid of wet garments in contact with the skin before donning thicker insulation, such as down or synthetic coats and an outer shell. Protection for the neck and head can be gained by using long underwear with a zippered turtleneck, and a balaclava. An additional thick hat will retain almost as much warmth as an additional sweater. For the feet, bring an extra pair of heavy socks; for the hands, an extra pair of polyester or pile mitts.

For winter and expedition climbing in severe conditions, you'll need more insulation for the torso as well as insulated overpants for the legs. In addition to your rain shell, carry some sort of extra shelter from the rain, such as a plastic tube tent, a Mylar "space blanket" taped into the shape of a bivy sack, or plastic trash-can liners. Carry an ensolite seat pad to reduce heat loss to the snow (some packs can double for this purpose).

Some climbers carry a bivouac sack, weighing about a pound, as part of their survival gear and go a little lighter on their insulating layers. It's a good strategy. (Chapter 3 has details on bivouacs and bivy sacks.) The sack protects your insulation from foul weather, minimizes the effects of convection by quieting the air surrounding you, and traps much of the heat escaping from your body so that the temperature of your cocoon rises.

6. Sunglasses

Eyes are particularly vulnerable to the brilliance of mountain skies, visible light reflecting off snow, and ultraviolet rays—which at 10,000 feet are 50 percent greater than at sea level. The retinas of unprotected eyes can be easily burned, causing the excruciatingly painful condition known as snow-blindness.

Because damage occurs to the eyes before discomfort is felt, it is essential to wear sunglasses to reduce the visible light and invisible ultraviolet rays. Don't let cloudy conditions fool you into leaving your eyes unprotected. Ultraviolet rays penetrate clouds, and the glare of reflected light can cause headaches. Sunglasses should filter 95 to 100 percent of the ultraviolet light. They should also be tinted so that only a fraction of the ambient light is transmitted through the lens to your eyes. For glacier glasses you want a lens with a 5 to 10 percent transmission rate. For more general outdoor use, the lenses should have about a 20 percent transmission rate. Look in a mirror when trying on sunglasses: if you can easily see your eyes, the lenses are too light. Lens tints should be gray or green if you want the truest color, and yellow if you want visibility in overcast or foggy conditions.

There is little proof that infrared rays (heat-carrying rays) harm the eyes unless you look directly at the sun, but any product that filters out a high percentage of infrared, as most sunglasses do, is added eye insurance.

The frames of sunglasses should have side shields that reduce the light reaching your eyes, yet allow adequate ventilation to prevent fogging. Problems with fogging can be reduced by using one of the many anti-fog lens cleaning products that are available.

Groups should carry at least one pair of spare sunglasses in case a pair is lost or forgotten. You can also improvise eye protection by cutting small slits in an eye cover made of cardboard or cloth.

A climber who depends on corrective lenses should carry a spare pair of glasses. Normal glasses with clip-on sunglasses can function as one pair, and good prescription sunglasses with extra-dark coatings can be the second pair. Alternatively, this climber can carry two normal pairs of prescription glasses plus a well-ventilated pair of ski goggles outfitted with a very dark lens.

Many climbers who need corrective lenses prefer using contact lenses instead of glasses. Contacts improve visual acuity, don't slide down your nose, don't get water spots, and allow the use of non-prescription sunglasses. Contacts do have some problems, however. Sun and blowing dust and dirt can dry out or irritate your eyes, though good side shields reduce the ill effects. Backcountry conditions make it difficult to clean and maintain the lenses.

7. First-aid supplies

Don't let a first-aid kit give you a false sense of security. It cures very few ills. Doctors say that in the field there is often little they can do for a serious injury or affliction except initiate basic stabilizing procedures and evacuate the patient. The best course of action is to take the steps necessary to avoid injury or sickness in the first place. Still, you want to be prepared for the unexpected.

Your first-aid kit should be small, compact, and

sturdy, with the contents wrapped in waterproof packaging. Commercial first-aid kits are widely available, though many are inadequate. (Two of the best sources of information on items to include in a first-aid kit are *Medicine for Mountaineering*, by James A. Wilkerson, M.D., and *Mountaineering First Aid*, by Marty Lentz, Steven C. MacDonald, and Jan D. Carline, both published by The Mountaineers.)

The contents of your kit will be items you carry on all trips: Band-Aids or other small adhesive bandages, moleskin, adhesive tape, cleansers, soap, butterfly bandages, scissors, triangular bandages, a carlisle bandage, roller gauze, and gauze pads in various sizes. Carry enough bandages and gauzes to absorb a significant quantity of blood. Severe bleeding wounds are a common backcountry injury, and sterile absorbent material cannot be readily improvised.

In addition to the basics, consider the length and nature of your trip. If you are traveling on a glacier, for example, tree branches won't be available for improvised splints, so a wire ladder splint would be extremely valuable in the event of a fracture. For a climbing expedition, you may need to consider appropriate prescription medicines.

8. Pocket knife

Knives are so essential for food preparation, fire building, first aid, and even rock climbing that every climber needs to carry one. The knife should have two folding blades, a can opener, a combination screwdriver and bottle opener, scissors, and an awl. The tools and the inside of the casing should be made of stainless steel. Although you may carry a few additional tools on certain trips, the knife is your basic tool kit. A cord attached to the knife and secured to your belt lets you keep the knife in your pocket for ready access without danger of losing it.

9. Matches

An emergency supply of matches, stored in a watertight container, should be carried on every trip in addition to the matches or butane lighter used routinely. Storing waterproof or wooden matches and a strip of sandpaper in a film canister makes a good emergency system.

10. Fire starter

Fire starters are indispensable for igniting wet wood or starting a fire quickly in an emergency. They can even be used to warm a cup of water or soup, if you have a metal cup to heat it in. Common fire starters are candles or solid chemical fuel (such as heat tabs or canned heat).

OTHER IMPORTANT ITEMS

Water and water bottles

High peaks are often bone dry or frozen solid, so you usually carry the water that is needed to prevent dehydration and maintain energy. A single 1-quart bottle usually suffices, but if it's hot and you sweat a lot, you may need to carry two. Widemouthed polyethylene bottles are the most popular because they can be easily refilled with snow or water, and they impart no flavor to the water, unlike aluminum. If you do use an aluminum bottle, be careful not to mix up the water bottle with the bottle that carries fuel for the stove.

Giardiasis, a waterborne bacterial infection, is a major health concern for alpine travelers. The cyst of the bacteria has tainted many water sources in the wilds, and it takes only one swallow of contaminated water to get sick. The illness takes six to twenty days to manifest itself, with symptoms that include nausea, flatulence, diarrhea, cramps, belching, fever, and dehydration.

Several methods of water purification make water safe to drink by killing or filtering out *Giardia lamblia* and other contaminants. Chemical treatment with tablets of iodine or halazone is effective, and tetraglycine hydroperidide (TGHP) tablets are better yet. Follow directions closely. The required amount of chemical and soaking time increases dramatically with colder water. If you fill your bottle from a glacial stream, you may need to place the bottle in the sun or inside your shirt to raise the water's temperature.

Bringing water to a rolling boil will kill *Giardia*

cysts but may not kill other disease-causing bacteria and viruses unless the water boils for nearly 20 minutes. A combination of chemical treatment and a short boil makes water safe.

Water filters are another option. Filters with a pump can strain a quart of water in minutes and do not impart any unpleasant taste to the water. A good water-filtering device provides a method to clean and extend the life of the filter, which is replaceable. Buy only filters with pore sizes smaller than $4/10$ micron (.4 micron) to ensure you will filter out *Giardia* cysts, flukes, tapeworms, and protozoa.

Sunburn prevention

Sunlight at high altitudes has a burning capacity many times greater than at sea level, so much so that it is a threat to both comfort and health. Climbers cannot avoid long exposure to the sun so they must reduce the burning ultraviolet rays reaching their bodies by covering their skin with clothing or burn-preventing creams (sunscreens).

Individuals vary widely in natural pigmentation and the amount of protection their exposed skin needs. There is only one rule here: the penalty for underestimating the degree of protection needed is so severe, including the possibility of skin cancer, that you should always protect your skin.

Clothing is by far the best sun protection and is worth the discomfort it causes on a hot day. Skin not covered by clothing should be covered with sunscreen. Most sunscreens use *p*-amino benzoic acid (PABA), but if your skin is sensitive to PABA there are other chemicals that yield the same sun protection factor (SPF) as PABA creams.

For glacier travel or a snowy environment, get a sunscreen with an SPF of 15 or more. Cover all exposed skin, even if it's shaded, because reflected light can burn the underside of your chin and nose and the insides of your ears. Some sunscreens are advertised as waterproof and will protect you longer than regular products when you are sweating heavily. Regardless of the sunscreen used, reapply it occasionally if you are perspiring.

Actor's grease paint (clown white) or zinc-oxide pastes ensure complete protection, and the grease bases keep them from washing off. One application lasts the entire climb, except where fingers or equipment rub the skin bare. The disadvantages of these creams is that they are messy and so difficult to remove that you may need help from a cold-cream cleanser.

The area around the mouth is particularly susceptible to fever blisters caused by sun exposure. The lips should be covered with a total-blocking cream that resists washing, sweating, and licking. Zinc oxide and lip balms containing PABA are both good. Reapply lip protection frequently.

Insect repellent

The wilderness is an occasional home for people but the permanent habitat of insects. Some of them—mosquitoes, biting flies, "no-see-um" gnats, ticks, chiggers—want to feast on your body. You can protect your body and blood with heavy clothing, including gloves and head nets in really buggy areas.

In hot weather, covering your body with heavy clothing may be unbearable, and insect repellents become a good alternative. Repellents with *N,N*-diethyl-metatoluamide (DEET) claim to be effective against all these insects, but are really best for keeping mosquitoes at bay. One application of a repellent with a high concentration of DEET will keep mosquitoes from biting for several hours, though they will still hover about. Mosquito repellents are marketed under many names, have differing potencies, and come in liquid, cream, spray, and stick form. Be aware that DEET can discolor or dissolve plastics, paints, and synthetic fabrics.

Despite claims by manufacturers, DEET is not very effective at repelling biting flies. Products with ethyl-hexanediol and dimethyl phthalate are much more effective against black flies, deer flies, and gnats. Unfortunately fly repellents don't do much to ward off mosquitoes.

Ticks are a potential health hazard due to the diseases they can carry, such as Lyme disease and Rocky Mountain spotted fever. In tick country, check clothing and hair frequently during the day.

At night, give your clothes and body a thorough inspection to locate ticks before they embed themselves. If you find a tick on your body, cover it with heavy oil (mineral, salad, etc.) to close its breathing pores. The tick may disengage at once. If not, allow the oil to remain in place for half an hour, then carefully remove the tick with tweezers, taking care to remove all body parts. Once a tick is deeply embedded, you may need a physician to remove its buried head.

REPAIR KIT

It's helpful to carry an emergency repair kit for your equipment. It could include wire, tape, safety pins, thread, needles, yarn, string, patches, and small pliers. This kit will probably grow over time as you add items you wished were along on a previous trip.

ICE AXE

An ice axe is indispensable on snowfields and glaciers and on snow-covered alpine trails in spring and early summer. It also has great value when you are traveling in steep heather, scree, or brush, crossing streams, and digging sanitation holes. However, an axe is more dangerous than helpful in unpracticed hands. (Chapters 5 and 12 give the details on using an ice axe.)

EQUIPMENT CHECK LIST

Experienced climber or not, it's easy to forget an important item in the rush to get ready for the next trip. Seasoned climbers have learned that using a check list is the only sure way to avoid an oversight. The following list is a good foundation for formulating your own personal check list. Add to or subtract from this list as you see fit, then get in the habit of checking your own list before each trip.

Items in parentheses are optional, depending on your own preference and the nature of the trip.

Items marked with an asterisk can be shared by the group.

ALL TRIPS

The Ten Essentials

1. Map
2. Compass
3. Flashlight/headlamp, with spare bulbs and batteries
4. Extra food
5. Extra clothing
6. Sunglasses
7. First-aid supplies
8. Pocket knife
9. Matches, in waterproof container
10. Fire starter

Clothing

Boots
Socks: inner and outer
Long underwear
Pants: wool or pile
Sweater or shirt: wool or pile
Parka: wind and rain
Hats: wool, rain, sun
Mittens, gloves
Down or synthetic garments
Wind/rain pants
(Gaiters)
(Shorts)
(Hot-weather shirt)

Other

Rucksack
Ice axe
Emergency shelter or bivy sack
Water bottle/purification tablets
Lunch

Sunscreen and lip protection
Bandanna
Toilet paper
Whistle
(Cup)
(Insect repellent)
(Moleskin)
(Nylon cord)
(Altimeter)
(Watch)
(Camera and film)
(Binoculars)
(Insulated seat pad)

ADDITIONAL ITEMS
FOR OVERNIGHT TRIPS

Internal- or external-frame pack
Sleeping bag and stuff sack
Sleeping pad
Spoon
*Shelter: tent or tarp
*Food
*Water container
*Repair kit
*Stove, fuel, and accessories
*Pots and cleaning pad
(Fork)
(Toiletries)
(Spare clothing)
(Camp footwear)
(Pack cover)

ADDITIONAL GEAR
FOR GLACIER OR WINTER CLIMBS

Crampons
Carabiners

Slings: chest and prusik
Seat harness
Additional warm clothing: mittens, mitten shells, socks, balaclava, down or synthetic clothing, long underwear
Extra goggles
(Helmet)
(Supergaiters)
(Snowshoes or skis)
(Candles)
(Avalanche beacon)
*Climbing rope
*Rescue pulley
*Snow shovel
*Group first aid
*Alarm clock or alarm watch
*(Flukes, pickets, ice screws)
*(Wands)
*(Snow saw)

ADDITIONAL GEAR
FOR ROCK CLIMBS

Helmet
Carabiners
Belay gloves
Runners
Seat harness
Prusik sling
*Climbing rope
*Rack: chocks, stoppers, etc.
*Chock pick
(Belay/rappel device)

---

* = equipment shared by the group
( ) = optional items

• 3 •

CAMPING AND FOOD

Camping, like mountaineering in general, is part ecstacy, part drudgery. You can make life easier on yourself by learning the art of camping and alpine cookery. Setting up a temporary home in the wilds ought to be quick work and provide cozy shelter, a warm bag, and good food.

Camping has another critical component: respect for the wilderness. In fact, that's number one. Let's face it: our comfort is secondary to preserving the mountain environment. The peaks aren't there for us, they're just there, and it's really not hard to do the things that show our respect for the places that bring us such happiness. That's why this chapter includes a lot of tips on camping clean in addition to camping easy.

LOW-IMPACT CAMPING

THE CAMPSITE

Mountain climbers don't always set up camp in the most comfortable places. They may walk right past an idyllic spot in the forest in favor of a windy mountain ledge because that puts them closer to the summit. What other reasons might there be for picking a particular campsite? Because it's comfortable? Scenic? Environmentally sound? Sometimes you can have it all, but at other times you need to give a little to help preserve the wilderness.

Let's look at camps from the standpoint of the wilderness to see which sites are least damaging to the environment. From best to worst, they are:

Snow: The snow will melt and show no sign of your tenancy.

Rock slab: Solid rock resists most damaging effects of a campsite.

Sandy, dirt, or gravelly flat: This is the next-best choice.

Open, plant-sparse area in deep forest: This is less ideal than the first three choices.

Grass-covered meadow above timberline: Meadows above timberline have a brief growing season and are the most fragile of mountain ecosystems. A tent left on a grass-covered meadow for a week can wipe out an entire growing season for the covered patch. Moving a long-term camp every few days reduces the harm to any one spot.

Plant-covered meadow above timberline: Alpine plants grow very slowly. Heathers, for example, have only a couple of months to bloom, seed, and add a fraction of an inch of growth. They could take years to recover from the damage of a brief encampment.

Waterfront: Waterside plant life is especially delicate and water pollution is a growing problem as more people head into the backcountry. A large proportion of long-established campsites in American mountains are on the banks of lakes and streams, but many areas now ban camping within 200 feet of the water.

In general, you want to honestly visualize the impact of any campsite. Camp away from water, meadows, trails, and other campers. Look for a resilient, naturally bare site. Try to find a spot that has just the right natural slope so you won't have to level it or dig channels for drainage. If there happens to be an established campsite far enough back from a water source, use it rather than setting up a new one.

From the standpoint of comfort, wind is a big consideration in choosing a campsite. You will find that alpine breezes are capricious. An up-slope afternoon breeze may reverse at night to an icy down-slope draft from snowfields. Cold air, heavier than warm air, flows downward during settled weather, following valleys and collecting in depressions. Thus there is often a chill breeze down a creek or dry wash and a pool of cold air in a basin. Night air is often several degrees cooler near a river or lake than on the knolls above.

Consider wind direction in pitching your tent. It can be a good idea to face an opening into the wind so that wind blowing in will distend the tent, equalizing interior and exterior pressure and minimizing tent flapping. But alpine winds are reversible without warning. One consolation of foul weather is that storm winds are fairly consistent.

CAMPFIRES

The old romantic days of cooking over an open fire and lounging around a big campfire are just about over. The price is too high in old scarce trees, especially at higher elevations. And no matter where, campfire scars are a blemish. Mountaineers now cook almost exclusively on lightweight stoves they carry with them, a big step toward low-impact, no-trace camping.

Some simple rules apply in case you do build a campfire. Keep it small, within an existing fire ring, and only where it's safe and legal. Stay there until the fire is dead and the ashes cold. For firewood, use only dead or downed wood from outside the camp area; never cut a standing tree or snag. You might consider using a stove, even if campfires are permitted, because the stove fire doesn't mar the landscape and because it's more dependable than counting on finding firewood.

WASHING

You can keep dishes reasonably clean without soap. By taking moderate care in cleaning pots with hot water after each meal, parties commonly remain healthy on week-long trips without so much as a pinch of soap or biodegradable detergent. Fill pots with water as soon as they are empty and clean them right away or leave them to soak. Be sure to get rid of the cleaning water a long way from water sources, and if you do use soap, use a biodegradable product and keep it off the plant life. On weekend trips it can be easiest to carry dishes and pots home dirty.

Woven plastic or metal scouring pads are handy and weigh next to nothing. Teflon-coated pots are easy to clean, but of course they can be easily damaged with metal or abrasive cleaners. Using sand, gravel, or grass to clean pots can leave unsightly bits of food to attract flies and rodents. Carry leftovers out with you, and try to do better meal planning next time. Also as part of the cooking routine, it helps to have a large water container along to save yourself and the terrain from a lot of trips to the water source.

If you need to wash yourself or your clothing, stay at least 200 feet from water. Go without soap, or use only biodegradable soap in very small quantities.

SANITATION

Plastic bags can be indispensable. Mountaineers use them to package food, as emergency mini-tents, and sometimes to keep the water away from their feet. Keep a heavy-duty plastic bag on hand to carry the garbage. The old rule about food containers is that if you can carry it into the wilderness full, you can carry it out empty. Mountaineers clean up every bit of their garbage (yes, even aluminum-foil flecks from a campfire) and often pack out anything they find in camp or on the trail, no matter who left it. Never bury garbage or dump it in latrines. The golden rule of camping: Leave the campsite cleaner than you found it.

Heavily used campsites usually have a pit toilet,

set away from any source of water. Otherwise, go at least 200 feet from any open water (allowing for maximum level around lakes), dig a hole 8 to 10 inches in diameter and no deeper than 8 inches. Fill it after use with loose soil and tamp the sod back in place. Pack out used non-biodegradable items of personal hygiene, such as sanitary napkins, in airtight containers. In snow, find an unobtrusive toilet area, such as a clump of trees well away from camp, and wherever possible burn the used toilet paper. Pick up any trash before it gets covered with new-fallen snow, where it will lie hidden until the spring thaw.

ANIMALS AND FOOD

Bears and rodents will gnaw through plastic bags, packs, and even tents for food. A food sack or pack hung from a tree or suspended from a pole must be farther from the tree trunk and higher from the ground than a bear can reach. Watch out for mice that can walk a tight line and drop down to the food. Hanging food 4 feet from the tree trunk and 8 feet from the ground gives you a fighting chance against animals.

Some other tips: Keep the cooking area and food storage well away from where you sleep. Package food in containers with tight lids or in sealed plastic bags to conceal the smell. Don't encourage the wildlife by feeding them.

Hiding a food cache for your party in the wilderness is generally not acceptable. Animals can get into an improperly protected food cache and leave a big mess, which will only draw more animals.

SHELTER

When you settle in for a night in the mountains, your home away from home will be a tent, bivy sack, tarp, snow shelter, or hut. We will take a close look here at the kinds of shelters you can carry on your back or build from the snow. (Chapter 15 discusses tents, snow shelters, stoves, and sleeping bags as they are used in winter and expedition climbing.)

Tents are the most common shelter because of their many virtues. They are relatively quick and easy to put up, rainproof, private, usable almost anywhere, a refuge from wind or sun, and often roomy enough for you *and* your gear. They also are heavy and expensive. Tents are usually the best shelter above timberline and for glacier camps, winter camping, in strong winds, and in mosquito country. Alpine climbers in a hurry can get nighttime protection from a lightweight bivy sack, though the sack is not much help in heavy rain and has limited room inside for gear. A tarp in combination with a bivy sack increases protection from the elements. A snow shelter is a haven from wind and storm, but building it is hard work and time consuming.

Curiously enough, shelter is often more necessary on a clear night than on a cloudy one. When two opposing surfaces differ in temperature, the warmer radiates heat to the colder. Since the human body is usually warmer than the night sky, exposed portions of the body or sleeping bag radiate heat and grow cold. Any shelter at all serves as a baffle. Clouds often reflect heat back to earth, and thus have the effect of a huge tarp between sleeper and sky. The clear nights are the cold ones.

TENTS

The choice of a tent depends on what you like and what you plan to use it for. Will it be used only in the summer, or for three or four seasons of the year? Above or below timberline? For you alone, or for two people, or three, or four? Are you after luxurious space, or just the bare minimum? How much weight are you willing to carry? How much money are you able to spend? Manufacturers offer almost any combination of size, weight, and design. The choice is yours, after consulting catalogs, stores, your friends, and neighboring campers.

Water resistance

Tents are built with either single or double walls, of either waterproof or breathable materials. A completely enclosed unit must be well ventilated and preferably should "breathe." If the tent is waterproof, the moisture you exhale condenses on the cold walls and runs down to collect in puddles on the floor. In a single night, you and your tentmate can expel enough water vapor to drench the sleeping bags. Watch out for the cheap tents built of a single layer of unbreathable waterproof material. They are only good for the mildest of conditions below timberline where the door and windows can be left open for ventilation; even then, you can expect some condensation. Some single-walled nylon tents have a design that uses gravity to spread and remove condensation, but to be effective, the tents must be well ventilated.

The dilemma of a waterproof yet breathable tent is solved by using double walls. The inner wall is breathable: it is not waterproof, so it allows your breath and perspiration to pass through to the outside. The outer layer is a waterproof rain fly, usually separate, that keeps the rain off the tent and also collects and disposes of the body moisture from inside the tent. The rain fly must not touch the inner walls, because where it touches, water will condense inside. The fly should come fairly close to the ground to cover the tent and entrance, discouraging wind-driven rain. Even in a double-walled tent, sleeping bags can get wet from condensation that forms on the waterproof side panels that extend a foot or so up from the floor in some models.

An important step in keeping a tent dry is to close up the needle holes from stitching by painting all seams with waterproof seam sealer. Do this before the tent is ever used. Some tents come with factory-sealed seams; on others, it's up to you, but it's got to be done. In camp, put a plastic or nylon ground cloth under the tent to stop ground moisture from entering the floor of the tent and to keep the bottom clean and protected from abrasion.

Strength

Many tents are rated by a "relative strength factor," the speed of wind a tent can withstand before the frame deforms. If you expect to run into wind and snow, this is an important consideration. The tent should stand up to high winds and snow loads without structural failure.

Fig. 3–1. Two types of mountain tents: a, dome; b, tunnel (hoop).

Weight

It's usually a tradeoff: light weight, or more comfort and durability. Lightweight tents are available, but the question is whether they are big enough or tough enough for your particular uses. Simply look for the lightest tent that meets your requirements for number of occupants, head room, floor space, gear storage, strength, climate, and weather conditions. A two-person tent for summer camping might be light, while a three-person, four-season expedition tent could weigh twice as much, and be two to three times as expensive.

Shape

The trend in tent shapes has been to tunnels and domes (fig. 3-1). These designs make maximum use of space and minimize the number of stakes and guy lines. The free-standing dome needs no guy lines at all and can be picked up and moved as a unit, but it still must be staked down so it won't blow away. The two- or three-hoop tunnel tent, usually not free standing, offers efficient use of space and has wind-shedding characteristics. The traditional A-frame doesn't give as much usable space, but it's a simple, proven design.

Size

The two-person tent is probably the most popular size and offers the greatest flexibility in weight and choice of campsite. For versatility in a group, it's generally better to bring, for example, two two-person tents rather than one four-person tent. Many two-person tents handle three in a pinch, yet are light enough to be used by one person occasionally. Some three- and four-person tents are light enough to be carried by two people who crave luxurious living. Larger tents, especially those high enough to stand in, are big morale boosters during an expedition or long storm. For carrying, you can distribute the weight among a group by dividing the tent into parts.

Color

Warm tent colors such as yellow, orange, and red are cheerier if you're stuck inside, and they make it easier to spot camp on the way back. On the other hand, more subdued hues blend into the landscape. One's an eyesore; the other may be camouflaged only too well if you're having a little trouble finding camp.

Other features

Entrance designs offer zip doors, tunnels, alcoves, vestibules, and hoods. Compare designs to find the one that looks like it will keep out the most rain and snow as you're coming and going. Vestibules can be nice as a way to shelter the entrance and provide more room for gear, cooking, and dressing. There are a lot of options in the arrangement and type of ventilation holes and windows. Mosquito netting can help keep out rodents as well as flies and mosquitoes.

Cooking inside a tent

Avoid cooking inside a tent, especially with stoves that use white gas. Fumes, spilled fuel, and stove flare-ups are fire hazards. Asphyxiation is a danger in a closed tent, particularly from the combination of a watertight coated-nylon tent and cooking fumes. Cooking also adds greatly to inside condensation.

If you must cook inside the tent, do it in an alcove or vestibule. Well-placed ventilation holes can lessen the danger. Always start the stove outside the tent and use an insulating pad under the stove once it's inside.

Care and cleaning

Your tent will give more years of good service if you are careful to air-dry it thoroughly before storing it away after each trip.

To clean a tent, hose it off with water, or wash with mild soap and water. Scrub stains with a sponge or brush. Don't put the tent in a washer or dryer. High temperatures or prolonged exposure to sun are damaging to tent material.

TARPS

A tarp is light in weight and low in cost, and may offer adequate shelter (fig. 3-2) from all but extreme weather in lowland forests and among subalpine trees. It gives less protection than a tent from heat loss and wind, none at all from insects or rodents, and demands ingenuity on your part and some cooperation from the landscape to set up.

Plastic tarps don't hold up very well, but are cheap enough that you can replace them often. Coated-nylon tarps come with reinforced grommets on the sides and corners for easy rigging. If your tarp doesn't have grommets, sew on permanent loops of fabric, such as nylon or twill tape, before leaving home. Alternatively, you can just tie off each corner (fig. 3-3) around a small cone or pebble from the campsite. Take along some lightweight cord to string the tarp and perhaps a few light stakes.

Fig. 3–3. Securing a tarp without grommets

The most versatile tarp size is about 9 by 12 feet—luxurious space for two people and their gear, and adequate for three, or even four. An 11-by 14-foot size will handle four campers comfortably. Since the outer margins of tarp-covered ground are usually only barely protected, usable space quickly approaches the vanishing point if your tarp is smaller than 9 by 12 feet. Put down a waterproof ground sheet, but if rain results in a surprise flood, be ready to move camp. A tarp is not meant to be used as a blanket, because perspiration will condense inside the waterproof material and leave you damp.

BIVOUAC SACK

For super-lightweight alpine traveling, the bivy sack takes the place of a tent in providing shelter

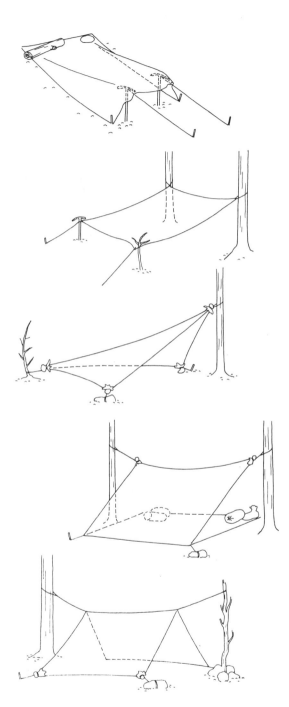

Fig. 3–2. Improvising a shelter with the basic tarp

from wind and rain. The sack is a large envelope of tightly woven fabric with a zipper entrance at one end. The bottom, usually of waterproof coated nylon, goes against an insulating ground pad. The upper side, of a breathable, waterproof material such as Gore-Tex, allows moisture to escape into the atmosphere. The bivy sack is designed for one person, two in an emergency. It needs no poles or stakes, but usually has strong loops for anchoring and can be used by itself or to add extra warmth to a sleeping bag.

SNOW SHELTERS

Newcomers to snow camping are sometimes surprised at what a warm, comfortable, and beautiful experience it can be. To make it work, a good shelter and insulation are essential. At the very least, every snow traveler needs the skills and equipment to survive overnight in the snow.

Tents in the snow

The most convenient snow shelter is a tent installed on a stamped-out platform slightly larger than the tent floor. It's easy to put up and gets you quickly out of the elements. When conditions are serious, a tent can shelter double to triple the usual number of occupants.

There are a few tricks to anchoring a tent in snow, where metal or plastic stakes can melt out during the day. Stakes can be replaced by ''deadman'' anchors (fig. 3-4), such as a rock, a bag filled with rocks, or a nylon stuff sack filled with snow. Attach a cord or sling to the deadman, bury the deadman in the snow, stamp down the snow above it, and then connect a tent guy line to the cord or sling. Stakes themselves can be used as deadman anchors by burying them horizontally in a snow trench, perpendicular to the guy line. Even better, prepare the deadman in advance by drilling holes in a stake or metal plate and attaching a bridle, to which the guy line can be tied. Snowshoes and ice axes also make solid anchors, but of course you can't use them for anything else while they're holding down the tent.

Snow campers have to watch out that heavy, wet snow does not pile up on the tent or fly, because too much force can break rigging or tent poles and bring the whole structure down. A heavy snow load can even bury a tent and its occupants, asphyxiating them. Shake the walls and shovel out around the tent as often as necessary to keep a big load of snow off. A snow wall built around the tent helps give protection from blowing snow and heavy wind.

Snow caves

A snow cave (fig. 3-5) provides more protection, comfort, and insulation from a storm than a flapping, gale-swept tent, and it's an emergency shelter when you have no tent. Knowing how to build snow caves is an essential mountaineering skill. Be prepared for the fact that it's a time-consuming job.

You can dig an emergency cave with a cooking pot, a hard hat, or whatever gear might be handy, but a lightweight snow shovel is the best tool. (A

Fig. 3–4. Deadman anchors: a, metal plate; b, tent stake; c, nylon stuff sack.

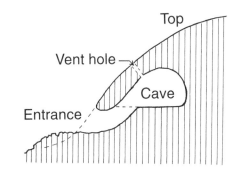

Fig. 3–5. Cross-section of snow cave

grain scoop—a lightweight shovel with a very broad blade—can move a lot of snow, but it's difficult to use in tight quarters.) Holes can be drilled in the shovel base to make it lighter, without sacrificing its scooping power. Even with two shovels in the party, it can take 2 or 3 hours to dig a shelter for four people.

Here's how to go about building a snow cave:

Find a location. Look for obvious hazards. Are you on a potential avalanche slope? Could wind blow snow over the opening and seal you in? Look for fairly firm snow at least 6 feet deep. A short steep slope, such as along a riverbank or on the side of a snowdrift, makes for a better cave than trying to dig one on the flat.

Get to work. Keep your clothing dry. Work slowly to avoid excessive sweating.

Dig an entryway into the slope, far enough to start a tunnel. Continue to dig inward about 3 feet to form the entrance to the cave, then angle upward to excavate a living area. There should be at least 1 foot of snow on the slope above the cave ceiling to provide enough strength to keep it from collapsing.

Put the cave floor above the top of the entry tunnel, in order to trap warm air inside. Make the ceiling smooth, with no bumps or protrusions, so melting snow will run down the walls rather than drip on the climbers. Put down a ground sheet to keep things dry and prevent loss of equipment in the snow. A small tarp over the entrance will help keep the weather out.

Punch a ventilation hole through the ceiling.

Enlarge the hole if it gets too warm inside.

There is even a way to build an emergency snow cave in shallow powder snow (fig. 3-6). You need at least 6 inches of snow, and it takes about 3 hours. Step by step, this is the way to do it. Drive a 6-foot stick vertically into the snow. Take another and draw a circle 12 feet in diameter around the stake. Lay the second stick on the snow, one end touching the vertical stick. (The second stick becomes a ''guide'' to point you toward the vertical stick after you've buried it within the cave.) Shovel snow into a big pile within the circle, packing it down until its center is about 1 foot above the top of the vertical stick. Let the pile sit for an hour or so, then tunnel into the pile following the guide stick. Excavate enough snow to make a small room, large enough for two or three people, with 2-foot-thick walls. Remove the vertical stake.

Fig. 3–6. Snow cave built in less than 6 inches of snow

Tree-pit shelter

With a little improvisation, natural shelters can be converted into snow hideaways in an emergency. Such shelters occur under logs, along riverbanks, or in the pits formed when snow melts and settles away from large trees. For a tree-pit shelter, enlarge the natural hole around the trunk and roof it with any available covering, such as ice blocks, tree limbs, or canvas. Boughs and bark can provide insulation (but don't cut live boughs unless it is a life-or-death emergency).

Snow trenches

When it is getting dark or the weather is especially bad, a snow-block shelter might be your answer. The trench igloo (fig. 3-7), built on either a slope or on the flat, is a quick emergency shelter for one or two people. Dig a narrow trench and then roof the trench, A-frame style, with snow blocks. (The blocks can be created as part of the process of removing snow for the trench, or they can be quarried nearby.) Then enlarge the interior and provide a vent hole. Smooth out any irregularities in the ceiling so that condensation will run down the blocks and not drip on the occupants. This shelter is not as easy to build as it looks, so practice first in good weather.

A more basic emergency snow shelter can be built by digging a trench some 4 to 6 feet deep and large enough for the party, then stretching a tarp over the top, perhaps gaining a slight angle by anchoring one side to a ridge of snow. This works well in wind or rain, but a heavy snowfall can collapse a roof that is so nearly flat. The smaller the trench, the easier it is to keep warm. Again, be sure to provide for ventilation.

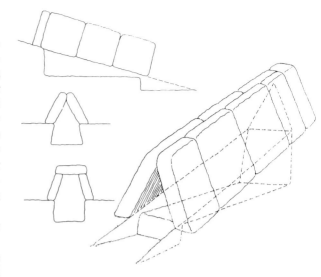

Fig. 3–7. Trench igloo

Igloos

Igloos are equal in protection to snow caves, but the traditional dome-shaped igloo (fig. 3-8) built of snow blocks that spiral upward to the top requires

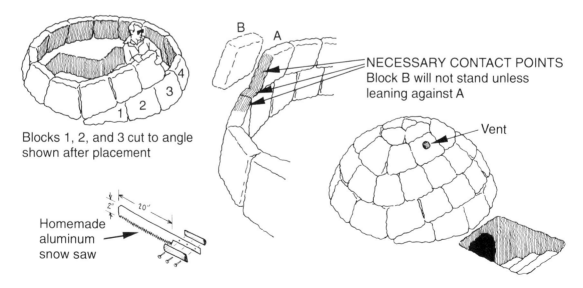

Blocks 1, 2, and 3 cut to angle shown after placement

Homemade aluminum snow saw

2" 20"

B A

NECESSARY CONTACT POINTS
Block B will not stand unless leaning against A

Vent

Fig. 3–8. Construction of a traditional igloo

proper snow consistency or preparation, plus a builder with a good bit of expertise. Wet, packed snow provides blocks that stick together and stay in place, but makes them heavy and difficult to handle. Wind-packed snow is the easiest to work with. If the snow is soft, stomp it down and let it consolidate for a few minutes before starting to saw blocks with a snow saw or shovel. Each snow block should measure about $2^1/2$ feet by $1^1/2$ feet by $1/2$ foot. Bevel the bottom of each block so the wall will tilt inward at the proper angle. Hold each block in place as it is installed while the cracks are chinked with snow. The igloo entrance should be below floor level so that warm air is trapped inside.

SLEEPING BAGS

Your sleeping bag should be lightweight, warm, comfortable, easily compressible, have a hood or other way to keep your head covered, and generally suit the climate where you do your camping.

WARMTH

The warmth of a sleeping bag is provided by insulating material that traps dead air. How warm a particular bag is depends on the type and amount of this insulating fill, the thickness (loft) of the fill, and the bags's size, style, and method of construction.

Sleeping bags are generally categorized as recommended for summer, three-season, or winter expedition use. (See Chapter 15 for tips on sleeping bags for winter climbs.) Manufacturers give their bags comfort ratings, meant to indicate the lowest temperature at which the bag will be comfortably warm. Methods of rating the bags vary from manufacturer to manufacturer, so they can give only a general idea of how the bag will perform. Bags are usually rated to a minimum temperature of somewhere between 40 degrees and –20 degrees Fahrenheit (between about 5 degrees and –30 degrees Celsius).

How closely a rating matches you personally depends on whether or not you are in a tent, the clothing you are wearing, the ground insulation, and your body size, metabolic rate, and caloric intake. Look for a rating that matches your use. If you're mainly a summer backpacker, a bag rated to –20 degrees Fahrenheit will be too warm.

The warmest, lightest sleeping-bag design is the mummy bag—tapered toward the feet, hooded to fit over the head, and with a small face opening secured with drawstrings. Whatever the design, your bag should have a form-fitting hood or a semicircular piece with drawstrings to keep your head warm and prevent heat loss. Some bags incorporate an insulated collar to provide extra warmth around the shoulders, and some include extra insulation at critical areas, such as chest or feet. You can buy a thin over-bag to put around the sleeping bag during colder weather to improve the bag's performance. Also available are vapor-barrier liners (for inside the sleeping bag) that can increase your bag's comfort range by 10 or 15 degrees Fahrenheit. However, figure that whatever clothing you have on in the bag is going to get damp from body vapor that has nowhere else to go. These liners are best used at below freezing temperatures.

There are some basic procedures for sleeping warmer, regardless of the bag you are in. Undress inside the bag. Wear a wool hat and dry socks to bed. Secure the bag closely around your face. Breathe through a sweater to reduce heat loss from exhalation. You can put your head inside the bag to help warm them both, though the water vapor from your breath will likely make it damper inside.

The comfort of the bag offers a chance to warm up not only you, but some of your things. Small items, like mittens and socks, can come into the bag to dry. Don't try to dry larger items of clothing by wearing them to bed, because they will just keep you cold and make the bag wet. In very cold weather, you may want to bring boots inside, wrapped in plastic. You may also need to make room for a water bottle, to keep it from freezing.

TYPES OF INSULATION

The warmth, weight, and cost of a sleeping bag depend chiefly on the kind and quantity of insulation, which is either goose down or a synthetic material.

Goose down is still the most efficient insulation per unit weight. Down bags are warm, very compressible, retain their loft well, and are long-lasting. Disadvantages? High cost and water absorbency. A wet down bag loses most of its loft and insulating value, making it almost worthless until it can be dried out. A down bag takes so long to dry—more than a day in good conditions—that it can't be dried during wet periods in the mountains. This characteristic makes down a questionable choice in a wet climate, unless you take extra care to keep it dry.

Synthetic insulation is resistant to moisture, retains most of its loft when wet, and dries relatively quickly. Bags with synthetic insulation are less expensive than down-filled designs. These bags are still slightly heavier than comparable down styles and do not compress quite as easily, thus making a weightier, bulkier load. Synthetic insulation does not last as long as down, and loses much of its loft with use.

CONSTRUCTION

Down bags are made with one of three basic construction methods (fig. 3-9) to keep the fill uniformly distributed: sewn-through, slant-tube, or overlapping tube. In sewn-through construction, the inner cover is stitched directly to the outer, a simple and inexpensive method but one with substantial heat loss at the seams. Most down bags are of slant-tube construction, which eliminates cold spots at the seams. The most efficient design, overlapping tubes, is used only in the most expensive bags. In addition, many designs incorporate channel blocks, baffles that prevent down from shifting.

Synthetic bags are built using a variety of methods. There are two basic types of synthetic fills. The first is a long, stable polyester fiber, manufactured in batts that stand up well to use and laundering. A widely used construction method is the shingle style, in which sections of batting are sewn in the bag, overlapping like roof shingles to cover cold spots. The second type of fill is a short, stable polyester fiber that is quilted or sewn into fine scrims to keep it from wadding up or moving around. To avoid cold spots, these must be shingled, or quilted in double or triple layers with quilted lines offset (fig. 3-10).

Fig. 3–10. Synthetic sleeping bag construction: a, triple-offset quilting; b, shingle.

Zippers are the almost universal means of closure even though they sometimes snag the fabric or go off the trolley. They are backed up with a tube of insulating material to reduce heat loss through the zipper. Long zippers make it easy to get in and out of the bag and are a big help in ventilating the lower portion. If you want to zip two bags together, be sure one zipper is right-sided and the other is left-sided.

EFFECTS OF WETNESS

Do yourself a big favor and keep your sleeping bag dry, especially if it is filled with down. Compared with down bags, polyester-filled bags retain much of their warmth when wet and are easier to dry, but a wet polyester bag is still a wet bag and colder than a dry one. You can buy a Gore-Tex sleeping-bag shell that lets body vapor escape

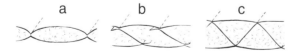

Fig. 3–9. Down sleeping bag construction: a, sewn through; b, slant tubes; c, overlapping tubes.

while helping to protect the bag from condensation inside a tent or dripping water in a snow cave. Consider putting the sleeping bag inside a plastic sack before putting it on your pack, because most stuff sacks don't keep water out.

CARE AND CLEANING

Dirt decreases insulating efficiency. You should spot-clean soiled areas, especially around the head of the bag. A removable, washable liner or an outer cover of breathable material can provide protection from dirt and abrasion.

Both down and polyester bags can be hand-washed with any mild soap or with one of the excellent down soaps that are available. Rinse thoroughly to remove all soap. Squeeze water out gently by hand, or put the bag carefully through the spin cycle of a front-loading washing machine (with no agitator).

Down or polyester bags also can be washed in a front-loading washing machine on the gentle cycle because it doesn't have an agitator. The agitator will blow out the baffles in a down bag, which must be babied when wet to prevent damage to the inner structure.

Hang bags to air dry; do not dry either polyester or down bags in a dryer. Allow more drying time for a down bag (several days), and shake and turn the bag frequently to break up lumps of wet down. Both polyester and down bags can be put in a dryer after they have been line dried; use the fluff setting (air only—no heat), to fluff up the bag. A clean tennis shoe put in with the down bag may help break up any clumps of down.

A polyester or down bag can be dry-cleaned, but only by a professional who knows how to handle the material and only if it is thoroughly aired afterward to remove all traces of toxic fumes, which can cause illness or death. For best results, do what the manufacturer says.

GROUND INSULATION

The foundation for a comfortable night in the out-of-doors is a good piece of insulation under your sleeping bag. Summer or winter, in a tent or outside, that pad makes for a softer, warmer bed. On wet ground or snow, it's essential.

A thin pad of closed-cell foam, such as ensolite (more durable) or polyethylene (lighter weight), provides good insulation. Improved designs in closed-cell pads feature softer sleeping surfaces, lower weight, and an increased ability to trap air, resulting in greater thermal efficiency. Other pads use open-cell foam that offers $1^1/_2$ inches of padding, but it makes for a bulky roll and must be protected from absorbing water.

An air mattress by itself is soft but provides no insulation. In fact, the air in the mattress carries heat away from the body. A pad, such as the Therm-a-Rest, that combines the insulation of open-cell foam with the softness of an air mattress is very popular and effective. Insulation pads come in a variety of lengths, but one that's only 4 feet long is usually adequate because you can use items of gear to support or insulate feet and legs. If you're stuck without a pad, use extra clothing, the pack, rope, or boots for padding and insulation.

BIVOUACS

A bivouac is a lightweight, no-frills overnight stay—sometimes planned, sometimes not. Climbers plan spartan bivouacs so they can travel fast and light and start high on the mountain. An unplanned bivouac comes as a not-so-pleasant surprise due to injury, bad weather, or getting off route.

Climbers at a planned bivouac camp make sure they have the essentials for a tolerable if not comfortable night, such as a bivy sack or cagoule, perhaps a tarp, some special food, and plenty of clothing.

Climbers at an emergency bivouac also carry everything necessary for survival—all the Ten Essentials and usually a good bit more. You can prepare for your own eventual unplanned bivouac by carrying an emergency shelter in your day pack, in the form of a very light bivy bag or plastic tube tent or even a couple of very large plastic trash bags. Another alternative for shelter from wind and rain is your pack. When it's time to settle down for a bivouac night, put your feet inside the empty pack, and pull the pack's load extension collar (the ''bivouac sleeve'') up over your legs and hips. Wear a waterproof parka or poncho to take care of the rest of your body.

A low-altitude bivouac might be a fairly comfortable affair, where you can get by comfortably by donning some extra clothing and sitting on a small insulating pad in front of a fire while you enjoy a hot drink. Most bivouacs aren't so pleasant. For a climbing bivouac, you may have to anchor yourselves and your gear to the mountain for safety during the night. Always conserve body heat by taking off wet boots, putting on dry socks and other dry clothes, keeping snow off your clothes, loosening belts and other items that can impede circulation, and putting on all the warm clothing you need or have. Huddle together with your bivouac-mates for as much warmth as possible.

How much clothing and gear should you carry to ensure that you survive a bivouac? The answer depends on a lot of other factors, including your experience, physical condition, and mental attitude. A mountaineer in top shape, who climbs 150,000 feet a year and has a positive outlook, might handle several planned bivouacs and perhaps a couple of emergency overnighters each year with no difficulty. Experience has shown this climber what we all can eventually figure out: how to distinguish that fine line between carrying too much and carrying too little.

FOOD

The art of camping includes the ability to set up a safe and comfortable camp and to provide food that's tasty and nutritious. Because mountaineering is such a strenuous and demanding activity, your body will need water and a variety of foods to provide sufficient carbohydrates, protein, and fats. With planning, it's not hard to choose foods that keep well, are lightweight, and meet your nutritional needs. But don't forget the other requirement of camping food: it must taste good, or you simply won't eat it. If fueling your body quickly and simply is the first aim of alpine cuisine, the enjoyment of doing so is a worthy secondary goal.

COMPOSITION OF FOODS

Each of the three major food components—carbohydrates, protein, and fats—provides energy, and each must be supplied in approximately the right amount to maintain a healthy mind and body. Food intake for mountaineers can go as high as 6,000 calories per day, possibly even more for larger folks. You will have to determine what is best for you depending on how demanding a trip you are planning and your own size, weight, metabolic rate, and level of conditioning.

Carbohydrates are easiest for the body to convert into energy, so they should constitute most of the total calories in your diet. Foods high in carbohydrates provide vitamins, minerals, protein, fiber, water, and essential fats. Good sources of carbohydrates include whole grains, rice, potatoes, cereals, pasta, bread, crackers, and granola bars. Eat small amounts but eat them often for sustained vigor and endurance.

Protein is important to include in your basic diet; the daily requirement is nearly constant regardless of activity. Your body cannot store protein, so once the requirement is met, the excess is either converted to energy or stored as fat. High-protein foods include cheese, peanut butter, nuts, beef jerky, canned meats and fish, powdered milk and eggs, and foil-packaged meals with meat or cheese.

Fats are also an important energy source, especially long-term. During moderate muscular exercise, energy is derived in approximately equal amounts from the body's stores of fats and carbohydrates. Fats occur naturally in small amounts in vegetables, grains, and beans, and when these are combined with fish, red meat, or poultry, your requirements for fat are easily met. High-fat foods include butter, margarine, peanut butter, nuts, canned bacon, salami, beef jerky, sardines, oils, meat, eggs, seeds, and cheese. Fats in the diet serve other functions in addition to providing energy. Stored body fats protect vital organs from shock and act as insulation to protect your body against the thermal stresses of a cold environment.

Eating for endurance

How efficient your body is in using its energy fuels is closely related to physical condition, rest, and nutrition. The better your condition, the greater the efficiency with which food and water will provide energy during heavy exercise. A well-rested, well-fed climber is less likely to experience difficulties from exertion, heat, cold, and illness.

WATER

Water is as vital to life as oxygen. You need it for energy metabolism, controlling your core and body temperature, and for eliminating metabolic wastes. During strenuous activity, particularly at high altitude, the amount of fluids lost through perspiration and evaporation of moisture from the lungs can be as much as 5 quarts or more per day.

If a substantial amount of fluid is lost and not replaced, the body's chemical equilibrium is upset and illness is more likely. The body can survive for a long time without food, but not without water. After hard exercise, replace fluids and carbohydrates as soon as possible. Then continue rehydration throughout the evening in preparation for the next day's activity.

Fluid intake for a 12-hour day of moderate activity in temperate climates should be at least 2 quarts (about 2 liters). For a longer climb or for more severe activity, you will need from 2 to 5 quarts.

The loss of salt through heavy sweating is normally not a problem, as most salts are replaced naturally in a well-balanced diet. If you're concerned about salt intake, you can use "sports drinks" that help replenish fluids and supply extra salt, sugar, calories, and minerals. Drinking additional water will also help.

Water sources

Water is sometimes at a premium in the wilderness. On a day trip, you can carry it from home. On longer trips, your sources will be lakes, streams, and snow.

You can often melt some snow for drinking by carrying it packed inside a water bottle. Start with a bit of water already in the bottle in order to hasten the melting time. When there is both sun and enough time, you can set out pots of snow to melt. Or, find a tongue of snow that is slowly melting into a trickle, dredge a depression below, let the water clear, and channel the resulting puddle into a container. You can also try catching the drips from melting overhanging eaves of snow. The most convenient and reliable way to get water on a snow-camping trip is to simply melt snow in a pot on the stove, though this obviously takes time and uses up cooking fuel.

Water purification

Clear, cold water looks pure, but may well be contaminated with harmful bacteria, *Giardia*, or other parasites that inhabit backcountry lakes and streams. For personal protection, it's best to purify all water. Common methods of purification are to put iodine in the water, to boil it (1 minute at sea level, or 5 minutes at 10,000 feet, will kill most bacterial or parasitic contaminants), or to use one of the filtration devices available at outdoors stores.

FOOD PLANNING

Put a reasonable amount of thought and effort into planning, and you should have no trouble ensuring the right combination of foods for optimum performance and enjoyment, whether your trip is for a day or for a week. As a rough general guideline, provide 2 pounds of food per person per day.

On very short trips, you can carry homemade sandwiches, fresh fruits and vegetables, and just about anything else you wish. For trips of two or three days—or longer if base camp is close to the road—any food from the grocery store is fair game. You can concoct a grocery-store stew from items selected almost at random, or by intuition. Canned or packaged items can be cooked together in one pot, then eaten with bread, a hot drink, and a dessert.

Cup-cooking works well for one-person meals. From one pot of hot water, eat each course in sequence from your cup, using instant foods such as soup, potatoes, rice, applesauce, or pudding.

For longer or more complicated trips, weight and packaging become more critical. Then freeze-dried foods are an easy, compact, lightweight option. Outdoors stores carry a large array of these prepackaged meals and snacks, and their variety and quality is constantly improving. They're expensive, but wonderfully convenient. Some require little or no cooking; you just add hot water, soak for a while, and eat from the package. Others are less easily hydrated, and require cooking in a pot. Freeze-dried meals include just about everything: main courses, potatoes, vegetables, soups, breakfasts, and desserts. Persons with access to a food dehydrator can make simple and nutritious foods from fruits, vegetables, and meat at a substantial savings.

Planning for a group

Because meals are social events, small groups often plan all food together. A common, carefully planned menu also reduces the overall weight carried by each person. Another typical arrangement is to leave breakfast and lunch to each individual, with only dinner, the most complicated meal of the day, as a group effort.

The number of people in a cooking group should rarely exceed four. Beyond that, group efficiency is outweighed by the complexities of large pots, small stoves, and longer cooking times. The ideal number is two to three people per stove. For longer trips, an extra stove is a good idea in case one breaks down.

Selecting the menu

A group can pack along just about whatever its members want on a short outing, but longer trips require precise food planning. It takes careful figuring to meet the conflicting goals of moderate-weight packs and plenty of good, nutritious food. You want to avoid unnecessary weight, but at the same time you need to ensure that right down to the last meal, there is enough food for all.

Meals can be planned by the group or by a chosen individual. In either case, the usual procedure is to write down a menu, discuss it with the group, compile an ingredients list, and then go shopping.

Packaging

The elaborate packages of commercial foods are too bulky and heavy for most trips, so repack the food in plastic bags. Place a label or cooking instructions inside each bag, or write on the outside with a felt pen. Smaller packages can be placed in larger ones that are labeled in broad categories, such as "breakfast," "dinner," or "drinks." For precise planning and packaging, a small kitchen scale comes in handy. Items such as jam, peanut butter, and honey pack best in squeeze tubes or in small plastic containers with airtight lids.

MENU SUGGESTIONS

Breakfast

When you're in a hurry to get under way, breakfast is merely the first installment of lunch. For a fast start, prepackage a standard meal before the trip, measuring a prepared cold cereal (such as granola), raisins or other fruit, and powdered milk into a breakfast bag. Stir in water—cold for a cold meal, hot for a hot one—and breakfast is ready.

A hot drink is a pleasant addition to a cold breakfast and a standard element of a hot one. Common choices are instant cocoa, coffee, malted milk, coffee-cocoa (mocha), tea, eggnog, and instant breakfast drinks. Fruit-flavored drinks include hot cider and flavored gelatin.

Other possibilities for breakfast are cooked grains such as oatmeal or rice, toaster pastries, bakery items, dried fruits, nuts, meat or fruit bars, and applesauce. If there's time, you can prepare a full-scale breakfast, with such items as potato slices, hash browns, omelets, scrambled eggs, bacon (canned or bars), and pancakes with syrup (made with brown sugar or syrup crystals).

Lunch and snacks

As soon as breakfast is over, lunch begins and is eaten throughout the day. Eat small amounts and eat often. You should have plenty of food, as half of your daily allotment is for lunch and snacks.

A good munching staple is gorp, a mixture of nuts, candy, raisins, and other dehydrated fruits. One handful makes a snack, several make a meal. Also good for munching is granola, with its mixture of grains, honey or sugar, and perhaps some bits of fruit and nuts. Gorp and granola are available premixed at many food stores or you can make your own. Other snack items are fruit leather and fruit pemmican.

Your basic lunch can include any of the following:

Protein: Canned meats and fish, beef jerky, precooked sausage, meat spreads, cheese, nuts, and seeds (sunflower and others).

Starches: Whole grain breads, bagels, granola and other cereals, crackers, brown-rice cakes, chips or pretzels, and granola bars.

Sugars: Cookies, chocolate, candy bars, hard candy, muffins, pastries, and honey.

Fruit: Fresh fruit, fruit bars, jam, and dried fruit such as raisins, peaches, and apples.

Vegetables: Fresh carrot or celery sticks, cucumbers, etc.

Dinner

The evening meal should have it all. It should be both nourishing and delicious, yet easily and quickly prepared. To supplement your liquid intake, include some items that take a lot of water, such as soup. A cup of soup makes a quick and satisfying first course while the main course is being prepared.

One-pot meals with a carbohydrate base of noodles, macaroni, rice, beans, potatoes, or grains are easy and nutritious. To ensure adequate protein, fat, and flavor, you can add other ingredients such as canned or dried chicken, beef or fish, sausage, freeze-dried vegetables or fruits, butter or margarine, and a dehydrated soup or sauce mix.

Meals from the grocery store are relatively easy to fix and many are quick cooking, such as spaghetti, macaroni, rice mixes, ramen noodles, and instant salads. There are also meals prepackaged in Styrofoam cups: just add boiling water, cover, and let sit for a few minutes, and your dinner is ready.

Freeze-dried meals offer a lot of dinner choices: almond chicken, chili, shrimp newberg, turkey, beef stroganoff, and many more.

A hearty soup can serve as the main course for dinner. Good choices include minestrone, multibean, beef barley, or chicken. Add instant potatoes, rice, crackers, cheese, or bread and the meal is complete. Bouillon is an old favorite that has minimal food value but weighs little and is helpful in replacing water and salt.

Side dishes of freeze-dried vegetables or beans add variety and substance. They can also be added to soup, along with instant rice or potatoes. Precooked beans or processed soy products (in powdered or textured forms) are excellent low-cost protein additions. For those more interested in nutrition and health foods, there are packaged supplements and organic items at stores that specialize in natural foods.

Staples and seasonings

Sugar is a matter of preference. Brown is one-third heavier than white because of moisture, but it's preferred by many for flavor. Instant powdered milk is a good protein supplement that can be added to many dishes. Margarine, which keeps better than butter on long trips, improves the flavor of many foods and is available in liquid or canned form. Dried butter substitutes are available, but they don't have the fat content of the original. For seasonings, try salt, pepper, herbs, garlic, chili powder, bacon bits, dehydrated onions, Parmesan cheese, or a dash of soy sauce.

Drinks and desserts

Cold drinks after a hot day on the mountain are necessary and can be especially satisfying. Lemonade, orange juice, grape juice, and sugar-free drinks are all available in powdered mixes. Just add water. Hot drinks such as cocoa, tea, or mocha taste good after the evening meal.

Occasional full-scale desserts are possible if you've planned the menus carefully. They can include cookies, candy, no-bake cheesecake, applesauce, cooked dried fruit, and that old standard, instant pudding. Freeze-dried desserts include pies, ice cream, and berry cobblers.

HIGH ALTITUDE

High-camp cooking is often difficult because cooking times are longer and conditions can be challenging, at best. Cooking that requires boiling becomes a problem. As you gain altitude and the atmospheric pressure decreases, water boils at lower and lower temperatures. Therefore, it takes longer to cook things. For every drop of about 10 degrees Fahrenheit (or 5 degrees Celsius) in boiling temperature, cooking time is approximately doubled (fig. 3-11). The most suitable foods are those that require only warming, such as canned chicken and instant rice. The weight of the fuel you have to pack is another argument for simple

Fig. 3–11. Boiling point of water

| Elevation | | Temperature | | Cooking Time |
ft	m	°C	°F	(sea level = 1)
sea level		100°	212°	1.0
5,000	1525	95°	203°	1.9
10,000	3050	90°	194°	3.8
15,000	4575	85°	185°	7.2
20,000	7000	80°	176°	13.0

menus.

The rigors of quick visits to higher altitudes require special attention to food. A typical quick gain to a relatively high elevation is the weekend ascent of Mount Rainier in Washington State, where climbers normally spend Friday night near sea level, Saturday night at 10,000 feet (about 3,000 meters), and perhaps only 20 hours after leaving tidewater, reach the 14,411-foot (4,392-meter) summit. Many climbers fall victim to symptoms of mountain sickness, ranging from a slight malaise to vomiting and severe headaches. The abrupt ascent doesn't allow time for acclimatization. Under these conditions it is more difficult to digest large meals because the stomach and lungs are competing for the same blood supply.

To repeat, eat light and eat often, stressing carbohydrates, which are easiest to digest. Bring foods that have proven themselves appealing at high altitude, because climbers often lose their appetite. Trial and error will teach you what foods your body can tolerate at altitude. You must continue to eat and drink, whatever the effort, for the loss of energy from a lack of food or water will only reinforce the debilitating effects of reduced oxygen.

UTENSILS FOR COOKING AND EATING

The simplest eating utensils are a spoon and a single large cup (or small pot). Some people like to add a bowl; bowls are available in plastic, stainless steel, metal, and lexan polycarbonate. Cook sets (fig. 3-12) should be durable and lightweight and nest for convenient carrying. You can get the cook sets in aluminum, stainless steel, and coated cookware for easy cleaning. The size of the set you pack along will vary depending on the needs of a particular trip, but generally you need at least two pots: one for food and one for water. You can even get it down to one if you use only freeze-dried dinners that are rehydrated in their own packaging. Be sure your pots have bails or handles for carrying and tight-fitting lids to conserve heat (and serve as makeshift fry pans).

Fig. 3–12. Cooking accessories: pots and lids; windscreen; utensils and cup.

STOVES

Stoves are now a necessity for backcountry travelers because many camping areas no longer have enough firewood, and others have banned natural-fuel fires. Stoves have a minimal impact on the wilderness and can be used in a variety of conditions.

In choosing a stove, consider a number of factors, including its weight, the altitude and temperature where it will be used, fuel availability, and its reputation for reliability. Whichever stove you select should be easy to start, operate, and maintain, even in cold, wet, or windy conditions.

Practice starting a new stove at home before a trip to be sure it's working and to be sure you know how to operate it. A stove kept in good working order will last for years. Check the stove frequently for dirt and carbon build-up. Stoves with pumps periodically need replacements for deteriorated pump leathers and gaskets. Mountaineering stoves typically weigh 1 to 1¹/₂ pounds and burn about an hour on approximately ¹/₂ pint (¹/₄ liter or so) of fuel.

You'll be rewarded with a more productive stove if you make sure it has a wind shield to screen the flame and prevent heat from being blown away. If you don't have a shield for your stove, improvise a way to block the wind. Most mountaineering stoves will boil about 1 quart (ap-

proximately 1 liter) of water at sea level in 4 to 8 minutes. Wind can increase the time to as much as 25 minutes, or even prevent boiling.

Some preventive maintenance will help guard against dumping a pot of stew on the ground. Check the stability of the metal framework that supports the pot on the stove. Also see that the stove is solidly supported on the ground. In snow, a small square of Masonite or ensolite serves well as both a smooth base and insulation under the stove.

A direct flame under the pot is desirable for boiling water or melting snow. For heating food, you might consider some means to diffuse the direct heat of the flame, such as a large metal lid. Just place the lid on the burner, then sit the cooking pot on the lid. Some stoves have an adjustment valve that permits you to further control the stove's heat output and prevent scorched food and wasted fuel.

Mountaineers have a range of choices in stove designs (fig. 3-13) and in fuels (with white gas, kerosene, and butane being the most common). All stoves require a means of pressurization to force the fuel to flow to the burner. This is usually provided by a hand pump for white gas and kerosene stoves and by a pressurized cartridge for butane units. All stoves also need a way to vaporize the liquid fuel before it is burned. With white gas and kerosene stoves, a common method is to prime (preheat) the stove by burning a small amount of fuel in a priming cup to start the fuel vaporizing in the main supply line. With butane stoves, the fuel vaporizes inside the pressurized cartridge.

A pump on a stove lets you increase the pressure in the fuel tank; this causes the fuel to burn faster and hotter and brings water to a boil more quickly. Stoves that boil water fastest often do not simmer well, while those with a lower heat output give you more control at lower cooking temperatures.

Stove fuels

White gas is probably the most popular fuel in the United States for mountaineering stoves. It tends to burn hotter than butane and is excellent for melting large amounts of snow, boiling water, or heating food quickly. Unlike kerosene, white gas

Fig. 3–13. Types of outdoor stoves

Kerosene stove: high heat output; requires white gas, alchohol, or lighter fluid for priming.

White gas stove with enclosure: compact carrier for safe, convenient packing.

Butane/propane cartridge stove: uses 80 percent butane/20 percent propane for better cold-weather performance.

White gas stove: white gas only; burns hotter and boils water more quickly than other fuels.

Multi-fuel stove: burns most fuels--white gas, leaded or unleaded automobile gas, aviation gas, deodorized or regular kerosene, Stoddard Solvent No. 1, diesel fuel or No. 1 stove oil; easy to clean; ideal when clean fuel not available.

White gas/kerosene stove: burns either fuel; ideal stove for international use.

Isobutane stove: uses isobutane for best performance in cold weather.

can be used as its own priming agent. Use only refined or white gasoline prepared for pressurized stoves; don't use automotive gasoline, including unleaded gas. The correct fuel is less likely to clog jets, build up excess pressure, or emit toxic fumes. However, spilled white gas evaporates readily, with little odor, and is very flammable.

Kerosene is not as volatile as white gasoline and therefore is safer to transport and store. Kerosene stoves need to be pressurized in addition to being primed with either white gas, alcohol, or lighter fluid. (Liquid kerosene does not burn hot enough to preheat its own burner.) If the burner has not been heated sufficiently, the stove will burn with a sooty yellow flame, producing lots of smoke and carbon. But when it burns efficiently, a kerosene stove has a high heat output, equal to or greater than white gas.

Butane cartridge stoves are popular because of their convenience: easy to light, good flame control, immediate maximum heat output, and no chance of fuel spills. The pressure forces the fuel out as soon as the valve is opened, eliminating both pumping and priming. Most butane stoves are not recommended for temperatures below freezing unless the fuel is warmed. An exception is a stove that uses isobutane fuel, which has performed well at high altitude and in cold, wet conditions. With its windscreen/heat reflector, this stove has proven superior in the wind as well.

The disposable butane cartridges cannot be refilled. Therefore, you may end up leaving home with a cartridge that is only half full because it was already used on an earlier trip. The cartridges are bulky, and all too frequently the spent canisters are found discarded in the wilderness. Pack them out. Another drawback is that the maximum intensity of the flame declines as the fuel is used up (and the pressure in the cartridge drops correspondingly). This problem is partly compensated for at higher elevations, where lower atmospheric pressure means the interior cartridge pressure is relatively higher. Some cartridges cannot be changed until they are empty. Always change cartridges outside your tent because residual fuel in spent canisters can be a fire hazard.

Solid fuels such as candles and canned heat serve primarily as fire starters. They are lightweight and cheap, but provide only limited heat. Most are carried for emergency use only, along with a metal cup for heating small amounts of water.

Foreign travel

On foreign trips, fuel filters may be necessary because a high grade of fuel is often hard to find. Find out beforehand what fuels are available and take an appropriate stove. Kerosene is generally available worldwide, while white gas is not. Check airline restrictions about carrying fuel on planes. Most do not allow it.

Fuel storage

Carry extra fuel in a tightly closed metal container that has a screw top backed up by a rubber gasket. Plastic containers aren't good because fuel gradually diffuses out through the material. Plainly mark the fuel container and stow it in a place where it can't possibly contaminate any food. Some stoves have their fuel bottles directly attached to them, while others require a pouring spout or funnel to transfer the fuel from a storage container to a stove fuel tank.

How much fuel should you take along? It will depend on the conditions of the trip and the food you plan to cook. Will you have to melt snow for water? Will you cook your dinners on the stove or simply heat water for pouring into a food package? Practice and experience will eventually tell you how much fuel you need, but a good beginning would be to bring between $1\frac{1}{2}$ and 2 quarts for two people for one week.

Fuel safety

Tents have been blown up, equipment burned, and people injured by careless stove use. Apply rules of safety and common sense. Don't use a stove inside a tent unless it is absolutely necessary. If you must cook in a tent, provide plenty of ventilation to minimize the danger of fuel escaping and igniting. Always change pressurized fuel cartridges, and fill and start liquid-fueled stoves, outside the tent and away from other open flames.

◆ 4 ◆

ROUTEFINDING
AND NAVIGATION

Where am I? How can I find my way from here to there? Are we almost there? These are three of the most popular questions in mountaineering, and this chapter shows how to find the answers by using routefinding, orientation, and navigation.

By the time you finish this chapter, you will have a good handle on the tools of navigation and the proven, painfully acquired techniques of top-notch routefinders. You will have the basic knowledge to eventually head into the wilds, work out the way to the mountain, and find the way home.

These tools and techniques are simple and straightforward, but exacting. Study them carefully to help make your mountain adventures successful and keep you safe within the ranks of surviving routefinders. Before you immerse yourself in this chapter, remember two things: Navigation is easy. Navigation is fun. A positive attitude will get you through the learning phase in a hurry and out into the field to use these indispensable skills of mountaineering.

First, a few definitions:

Orientation is the science of determining your exact position on the earth. It requires mastery of map and compass. People who spend a reasonable amount of time and effort usually gain this mastery, even when they have little background or interest in math or science.

Navigation is the science of determining the location of your objective and of keeping yourself pointed in the right direction all the way from your starting point to the destination. Like orientation, this takes map and compass and is a required skill for all wilderness travelers.

Routefinding is the art of locating and following a route that is appropriate to the abilities and equipment of the climbing party. It takes a lot to be a good routefinder: an integrated sense of terrain, distance, and direction; a combination of good judgment, experience, and instinct; and a solid grounding in the technical aspects of orientation and navigation. As with other arts, routefinding skills can be sharpened through practice, regardless of your basic aptitude.

A related activity is *orienteering*, a sport in which participants compete with each other and the clock in finding the way with map and compass to destinations along a structured course. Orienteering is not a part of mountaineering, but mountaineers can learn from those who compete. It is no accident that many of the best routefinders are people who have engaged in orienteering.

TRIP PREPARATION

Routefinding begins at home. Before heading out the door, you need to know not only the name of your wilderness destination, but a great deal about how to get there. The information is accessible to anyone who takes the trouble to seek it out, from guidebooks and maps and from people who have already been there.

Prepare for each trip as if you were going to lead it, even if you aren't. Each person in a climbing group needs to know wilderness navigation and must keep track of where the party has been, where it is, and where it's going. In case of emergency, each climber must be able to get back alone.

Guidebooks provide critical information such as a description of the route, the estimated time necessary to complete it, elevation gain, mileage, and so forth. Climbers who have made the trip will tell you about landmarks, hazards, and routefinding hassles. Useful details are packed into maps of all sorts: Forest Service maps, road maps, aerial maps, sketch maps, and topographic maps. For a trip into an area that's especially unfamiliar, more preparation is needed. This might include scouting into the area, observations from vantage points, or study of aerial photos.

If the route comes from a guidebook or from a description provided by another climber, plot it out on the topographic map you'll be carrying along, noting junctions and other important points. It can help to highlight the route with a yellow felt-tip marking pen, which doesn't obliterate map features. Other maps or route descriptions should be taken along, marked with notes on any more up-to-date information. In selecting the route, consider a host of factors, including the season, weather conditions, the abilities of the party members, and the equipment available.

Before you've even shouldered your pack, you should have a mental image of the route. From experience, and from all the sources of information about the climb, you'll know how to make the terrain work in your favor. To avoid brush, try not to follow watercourses or drainages; select ridges over hillsides and gullies. Clearcuts are often full of slash or brushy second-growth trees, so stick to old-growth forest if possible.

A rock-slide area can be a feasible route—providing you watch carefully for new rockfall. One problem in planning the route, however, is that a rock-slide area may look the same on a map as an avalanche gully, which can have avalanche hazard in winter and spring and be choked with brush in summer and fall. If your sources aren't helpful, only a firsthand look will clear up this question.

The most straightforward return route is often the same as the route going in. If you plan to come back a different way, that route also needs careful advance preparation.

Don't let outdated information ruin your trip. Check beforehand with the appropriate agencies about roads and trails, especially closures, and about climbing routes and regulations, permits, and camping requirements.

THE MAP

A map is a symbolic picture of a place. In convenient shorthand, it conveys a phenomenal amount of information in a form that is easy to understand and easy to carry. No mountaineer should travel without a map or the skill to translate its shorthand into details on the route. Note the publication date of the map because roads, trails, and other features may have changed since that time. Try to use the latest information. A number of different types of maps are available.

Relief maps are the maps that attempt to show terrain in three dimensions by the use of shadings of green, gray, and brown tones, terrain sketching, or raised surfaces. They help in visualizing the ups and downs of the landscape and have some value in trip planning.

Land management and recreation maps are updated frequently and thus are very useful for current details on roads, trails, ranger stations, and other marks of the human hand. They usually show only the horizontal relationship of natural features, without the contour lines that indicate the shape of the land. These maps, published by the U.S. Forest Service and other government agencies and by timber companies, are suitable for trip planning.

Climbers' sketch maps are generally crudely

drawn but often make up in specialized route detail what they lack in draftsmanship. These rough and ready drawings can be effective supplements to other map and guidebook information.

Guidebook maps vary greatly in quality— some are merely sketches, while others are accurate modifications of topographic maps. They generally contain useful details on roads, trails, and climbing routes.

Topographic maps are the best of all for climbers. They depict topography, the shape of the earth's surface, by showing contour lines that represent constant elevations above sea level. These maps, essential to off-trail travel, are produced in many countries. As an example of this type of map, we will look in detail at the maps produced by the U.S. Geological Survey (USGS).

USGS TOPOGRAPHIC MAPS

It might be interesting to start this discussion of USGS maps with a refresher on how cartographers divide up the earth. The distance around our planet is divided into 360 units called degrees. A measurement east or west is called *longitude*; a measurement north or south is *latitude*. Longitude is measured 180 degrees, both east and west, starting at the Greenwich meridian in England. Latitude is measured 90 degrees, both north and south, from the equator.

By determining the intersection of longitude and latitude lines, any point on the earth's surface can be pinpointed. New York City, for instance, is situated at 74 degrees west longitude and 41 degrees north latitude. Each degree is divided into 60 units called minutes, and each minute is further subdivided into 60 seconds. On a map, a latitude of 47 degrees, 52 minutes, and 30 seconds north would probably be written like this: 47°52′30″N.

One type of USGS map used by mountaineers covers an area of 15 minutes (that is, $1/4$ degree) of longitude by 15 minutes of latitude. These maps are part of what is called the *15-minute series*. Another type covers an area of 7.5 minutes (that is, $1/8$ degree) of latitude by 7.5 minutes of longitude. These maps are part of the *7.5-minute series*.

The *scale* of a map is a ratio between measure-

ments on the map and measurements in the real world. A common way to state the scale is to compare a map measurement with a ground measurement (as in 1 inch equals 1 mile), or to give a specific mathematical ratio (as in 1:24,000, where any one unit of measure on the map equals 24,000 units of the same measure on the earth). The scale is usually shown graphically at the bottom of a map.

In the USGS 7.5-minute series, the scale is 1:24,000, or roughly $2^1/2$ inches to the mile, and each map covers an area of approximately 6 by 9 miles. It is the standard topographic map for all of the United States except Alaska.

In the 15-minute series, the scale is 1:62,500, or about 1 inch to the mile, and each map covers an area of four times that of the 7.5-minute series (about 12 by 18 miles). The 15-minute maps are no longer in production and are being replaced by the 7.5-minute series for all states except Alaska. (Most 15-minute maps will be permanently out of print by the mid-1990s.) For Alaska only, the 15-minute maps are still the standard, and the scale is somewhat different: 1:63,360, or exactly 1 inch to the mile. The east–west extent of each Alaska map is actually greater than 15 minutes because the lines of longitude are converging toward the North Pole.

The 15-minute and 7.5-minute maps are the ones that mountaineers use for cross-country routefinding and navigation. The USGS also produces maps that cover larger areas (with such scales as 1:100,000 and 1:250,000), and these are suitable for some trip planning and trail navigation. In some areas, private companies produce maps based on USGS topographic maps, but they are updated with more recent trail and road details and sometimes combine sections of USGS maps. These maps are often useful supplements to standard topographic maps.

How to read a topographic map

Consider this a language lesson, but in a language quite easy to learn and one that pays immediate rewards to any wilderness traveler. Some of this language is in words, but most of it is in the form of symbols drawn on a map. The best way to follow the lesson is to study it along with an actual USGS topographic map. Any one will do.

Each map is referred to as a quadrangle (or quad) and covers an area bounded on the north and south by latitude lines that differ by an amount equal to the map series (7.5 minutes or 15 minutes) and on the east and west by longitude lines that differ by the same amount. Each quadrangle is given the name of a prominent topographic or human feature of the area.

What the colors mean

Colors on a USGS topographic map have very specific meanings. This is what the different colors stand for:

Red: Major roads and survey information.

Blue: Rivers, lakes, springs, waterfalls, and other water-related features. The contour lines of glaciers and permanent snowfields are in solid blue, with their edges indicated by dashed blue lines.

Black: Roads, trails, railroads, buildings, and other features not part of the natural environment.

Green: Areas of substantial vegetation. Solid green marks a forested area while mottled green indicates scrub vegetation. The lack of green doesn't mean there's no vegetation in the area, simply that it is too small or scattered to show on the maps. Don't be surprised if a small, narrow gully with no green color on the map turns out to be choked with slide alder or vine maple.

Brown: Contour lines and elevations.

Purple: Partial revision of an existing map.

Translating contour lines

The heart of a topographic map is its overlay of contour lines, each line indicating a constant elevation as it follows the shape of the landscape. A map's *contour interval* is the difference in elevation between two adjacent contour lines (usually 40 feet on 7.5-minute maps and 80 feet on 15-minute maps). Every fifth contour line is printed darker than other lines and is labeled periodically with elevation.

One of the most important bits of information a topographic map reveals is whether you will be hiking uphill or downhill. If the route crosses lines of increasingly higher elevation, you will be going uphill. If it crosses lines of decreasing elevation, the route is downhill. Flat side-hill travel is indicated by a route that crosses no lines, remaining within a single contour interval.

This is only the start of the picture that contour lines paint of your actual wilderness route. They also show cliffs, passes, summits and other features (fig. 4-1). You will get better and better at interpreting these lines by comparing actual terrain with its representation on the map (fig. 4-2). The goal is to someday glance at a topographic map and realize you have a rather sharp mental image of just what the place will look like. The following listing shows the main features sketched by contour lines.

Flat areas: No contour lines at all.

Gentle slopes: Widely spaced contour lines.

Steep slopes: Closely spaced contour lines.

Cliffs: Contour lines extremely close together or touching.

Valleys, ravines, gullies, couloirs: Contour lines in a pattern of "U's" pointing in the direction of higher elevation, if the valley or gully is gentle and rounded; a pattern of "V's," if the valley or gully is sharp and narrow.

Ridge or spur: Contour lines in a pattern of "U's" pointing in the direction of lower elevation, if the ridge is gentle and rounded; a pattern of "V's," if the ridge is sharp.

Saddle, pass, col: A low point on a ridge, with higher contour lines on each side and often with a characteristic hourglass shape.

Cirques, bowls: Patterns of contour lines forming a semicircle (or as much as three-quarters of a circle), rising from a low spot in the center of the partial circle to form a natural amphitheater at the head of a valley.

Peak: A concentric pattern of contour lines with the summit being the innermost and highest ring. Peaks often are also indicated by X's, elevations, benchmarks (BM), or a triangle symbol.

The margin of a USGS map holds important information, such as date of publication and revision, names of maps of adjacent areas, contour

Fig. 4–1. Basic topographic features

interval, and map scale. The margin also provides a diagram showing the area's magnetic declination, which is the difference between true north and magnetic north.

Keep a couple of cautionary thoughts in mind as you study a topographic map, because they do have certain limitations. The map won't show all the terrain features you actually see on the climb because there's a limit to what can be jammed onto the map without reducing it to an unreadable clutter. If a feature is not at least as high as the contour interval, it may not be shown, so a 30-foot cliff may come as a surprise in an area mapped with a 40-foot contour interval. Check the date of the map

Fig. 4–2. Photograph of a mountainous area; keyed features are represented on topographic map.

KEY

1. Basin: moderate slope, camp spots
2. Snow or ice line: dashed line ends on cliffs, rock
3. Buttress: change in features of wall may provide approach to ridge
4. Twin summits: which is higher?
5. Gendarmes, aiguilles, or pinnacles
6. Gully or couloir
7. Saddle, pass, or col
8. Rock face
9. Summit: highest point on map
10. Ridge or arete
11. East slope: note shadows and ice accumulation
12. Cirque wall: glacier occupies this cirque
13. Moat
14. Crevasses: indicated by irregular contours, not smooth as near buttress, 3, above
15. Bergschrund: not seen on map but inferred possibility when rock and snow are steep

Mount Torment

Forbidden Peak

Boston Basin

(CASCADE PASS)
1780 I NE
SCALE 1:24 000

CONTOUR INTERVAL 40 FEET
DOTTED LINES REPRESENT 20-FOOT CONTO
DATUM IS MEAN SEA LEVEL

because topographic maps are not revised very often and information on forests and on roads and other manufactured features could be out of date. A forest may have been logged or a road either extended or closed since the last updating. Although topographic maps are essential to wilderness travel, they must be supplemented with information from visitors to the area, guidebooks, and other maps. As you learn about changes, note them on your map.

Sometimes a trip runs through portions of two or more maps. Adjoining maps can be folded at the edges and brought together, or you can create your own customized map by cutting out the pertinent areas and splicing them with tape. Include plenty of territory so that you have a good overview of the entire trip, including surrounding area. Photocopies, good for marking on, don't show colors and may distort, meaning they should be used only in addition to the real thing.

As the precious objects they are, maps deserve tender care in the wilds. A map can be kept in a plastic bag or map case. You can also laminate the map with plastic film or coat it with waterproofing, though these coatings are difficult to mark on. Some maps come already waterproofed. On the trip, carry the map in a jacket pocket or some other easily accessible place so you don't have to take off your pack to get at it.

ORIENTING A MAP

During a trip it sometimes helps to hold the map open so that north on the map is pointed in the actual direction of true north. This is known as orienting the map, a good way to gain a better feel of the relationship between the map and the countryside.

It's a simple process (fig. 4-3). Place your compass on the map, near its declination diagram. Turn the map and compass together until the north-seeking end of the compass needle is aligned with, or parallel to, the magnetic-north arrow on the diagram. The map is now oriented to the scene before you. (This orientation can give a general feel for the area but can't replace the precise methods of

Fig. 4–3. Using the compass to orient a map

orientation and navigation that we will cover later in this chapter.)

ROUTEFINDING WITH THE MAP

Before the trip

Most wilderness orientation, navigation, and routefinding is done by simply looking at your surroundings and comparing them with the map.

One useful technique is to identify a navigational "handrail," a linear feature on the map that lies in the same direction you are traveling. The handrail should be within frequent sight of the route, so it can serve as an aid to navigation. Features that can be used from time to time as handrails during a trip include roads, trails, power lines, railroad tracks, fences, borders of fields and meadows, valleys, streams, ridges, lake shores, and the edges of marshes.

A handrail helps in staying on route. Another map technique can help in finding the way home if you've gone off track. This is the "base line," a long unmistakable line that always lies in the same direction from you, no matter where you are during the trip. Pick out the base line on the map during trip planning. It does not have to be something you can see during the trip. You just have to know that it is there, in a consistent direction from you. A base line (sometimes called a catch line) can be a road, the shore of a large lake, a river, trail, power line, or any other feature that's at least as long as your climbing area. If the shore of a distant lake always lies west of your climbing area, you can be sure that heading west at any time will get you to this identifiable landmark. It's not the fastest way to travel, but it saves you from being truly lost.

Also before the trip, anticipate specific route-finding problems. For example, if the route traverses a glacier, you may consider carrying route-marking wands, especially if the weather outlook is marginal. Make a note of any escape routes that can be used in case of sudden bad weather or other setbacks.

During the trip

Get off on the right foot by making sure that everyone understands the route. Gather the crew around a map and take time to discuss the route and make contingency plans in case the party gets separated. Point out on the map where you are and associate the surroundings with the piece of paper in front of you, orienting the map to true north if you wish. This is a good time for everyone to make a mental note of the main features the party will see during the trip, such as forest, streams, or trails.

Along the way, everyone needs to keep associating the terrain with the map. Ignorance of the territory is definitely not bliss for any daydreaming climber who gets separated from the party. Whenever a new landmark appears, connect it with the map. At every chance—at a pass, at a clearing, or through a break in the clouds—update your fix on the group's exact position. Keeping track of progress this way makes it easy to plan each succeeding leg of the trip. It also may turn you into an expert map interpreter because you'll know what a specific valley or ridge looks like compared with its representation on the map.

Look ahead to the return trip

The route always looks amazingly different on the way back. Avoid surprises and confusion by glancing back over your shoulder from time to time on the way in to see what the route should look like on the return. Fix in your mind this over-the-shoulder shape of the route. If you can't keep track of it all, jot down times, elevations, landmarks, and so on in a notebook. A cryptic few words—''7,600, hit ridge''—can save a lot of grief on the descent as a reminder that when the party has dropped to 7,600 feet, it's time to leave the ridge and start down the snow slope.

Think

Your brain is your most valuable navigational tool. As the party heads upward, keep asking yourself questions. How will we recognize this important spot on our return? What will we do if the climb leader is injured? Would we be able to find our way out in a white-out or if snow covered our tracks? Should we be using wands or other route-marking methods right now? Ask the questions as you go and act on the answers. It's a matter of think now or pay later.

Mark the route if necessary

There are times it may be best to mark the route going in so you can find it again going out. This situation can come up when the route is over snow-fields or glaciers during changeable weather, in heavy forest, or when fog or nightfall threaten to hide landmarks. On snow, climbers use thin bamboo wands with tiny flags on top to mark the path. (Chapter 12 explains the construction and use of wands.) In the forest, the recommended marker is brightly colored crepe paper in thin rolls. Plastic surveyors' tape is also used.

One commandment here: REMOVE YOUR MARKERS. Markers are litter, and mountaineers never, ever litter. If there's any chance you will not come back the same way and will not be able to remove the markers, be especially sure to use the crepe paper, which will disintegrate over the winter. The plastic tape, on the other hand, might outlive the careless climbers who put it there.

Rock cairns appear here and there as markers, sometimes dotting an entire route and at other times signaling the point where a route changes direction. These heaps of rock are another imposition on the landscape, and they can create confusion for any traveler but the one who put them together—so don't build them. If there comes a time you decide you must, then tear them down on the way out. The rule is different for existing cairns. Let them be, on the assumption someone may be depending on them.

Keep track

As the trip goes on, it may be helpful to mark your progress on the map. Some climbers even note on the map the time that streams, ridges, and other landmarks are reached. Keep yourself oriented so that at any time you can point out your actual position to within 1/2 mile on the map.

Part of navigation is having a sense of your speed. Given all the variables, will it take your party 1 hour to travel 2 miles or will it take 2 hours to travel 1 mile? The answer is rather important if it's noon and base camp is still 5 miles away. After enough trips into the wilds, you'll be good at estimating wilderness speeds. With a watch and a notebook (or good memory), you can monitor the rate of progress on any single outing. Here are some typical speeds for an average party, though there will be much variation:

• On a gentle trail, with a day pack: 2–3 miles per hour.
• Up a steep trail, with full overnight pack: 1–2 miles per hour.
• Traveling cross-country on gentle terrain, with a day pack: 1,000 feet of elevation gain per hour.
• Traveling cross-country up a moderate slope, with full overnight pack: 500 feet of elevation gain per hour.

In heavy brush, the rate of travel can drop to a third or even a quarter of what it would be on a good trail.

On technical portions of the climb

When the going gets tough, the tough forget about navigation and start worrying about the next handhold. But keep your map and other route information handy for the occasional rests. On rock climbs, don't let the mechanics of technical climbing overwhelm the need to stay on a particular route.

On the summit

Here is your golden opportunity to rest, relax, and enjoy—and to learn more about the area and about map reading by comparing the actual view with the way it looks on the map.

On the summit is the place to lay final plans for the descent, a journey often responsible for many more routefinding errors than the ascent. Repeat the trailhead get-together by discussing the route and emergency strategies with everyone. Stress the importance of keeping the party together on the descent, when some climbers will always want to race ahead while others lag behind.

During the descent

The descent is a time for extra caution as you fight to keep fatigue and inattention at bay. As on the ascent, everyone needs to maintain a good sense of the route and how it relates to the map. Stay together, don't rush, and be even more careful if you're taking a different descent route.

Now imagine your team is almost back to the car after a tough 12-hour climb. You follow a compass bearing right back to the logging road—but is the car to the left or the right? It's a bad ending to a good day if the car is a half-mile to the right and the climbers go left. It will be even worse if the car is parked at the end of the road and a routefinding error takes the party beyond that point and on and on through the woods (fig. 4-4a). The intentional offset (also called "aiming off") was invented for this situation (fig. 4-4b). Just travel in a direction that is intentionally offset some amount to the right or the left of where you really want to be. When you hit the road (or the river or the ridge), there will be no doubt about which way to turn.

After the climb

Back home, write a description of the route and of any problems, mistakes, or unusual features, and do it while the details are fresh in your mind. Imagine what you would like to know if you were

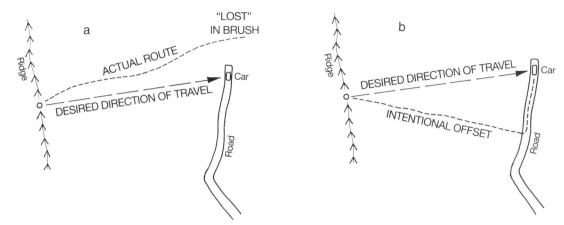

Fig. 4–4. Navigating to a specific point on a line: a, inevitable minor errors can sometimes have disastrous consequences; b, to avoid such problems, follow a course with an intentional offset.

about to make the climb for the first time, so you'll be ready with the right answers when another climber asks about it. If the guidebook was confusing or wrong, take time to write to the publisher.

THE COMPASS

The compass is a very simple device that can do a wondrous thing. It can reveal at any time and any place exactly what direction you are heading. On a simple climb in good weather, the compass may never leave your pocket. But as the route becomes more complex or the weather worsens, it comes into its own as a critical tool of mountaineering.

A compass is nothing more than a magnetized needle that responds to the earth's magnetic field. Compass-makers have added a few things to this basic unit in order to make it easy to read accurately. But stripped to the core, there's just that needle, aligned with the earth's magnetism, and from that we can figure out any direction.

These are the basic features (fig. 4-5a) of a mountaineering compass:

• A freely rotating magnetic needle. One end is a different color from the other so you can remember which end is pointing north.
• A circular rotating housing for the needle. This is filled with a fluid that dampens (reduces) the vibrations of the needle, making readings more accurate.
• A dial around the circumference of the housing. The dial is graduated clockwise in degrees from 0 to 360.
• An orienting arrow and a set of parallel meridian lines. These are located beneath the needle.
• An index line. Read bearings here.
• A transparent, rectangular base plate for the entire unit. This includes a direction-of-travel line (sometimes with an arrow at one end) to point toward your objective. The longer the base plate, the easier it is to get an accurate reading.

The following are optional features (fig. 4-5b) available on some mountaineering compasses:

• Adjustable declination arrow. It's well worth the added cost because it's such an easy, dependable way to correct for magnetic declination.
• Sighting mirror. This provides another way to improve accuracy.
• Ruler. This is calibrated in inches or millimeters.

Fig. 4–5. Features of mountaineering compasses: a, essential features; b, useful optional features.

Use it for measuring distances on a map.
• Clinometer. Use it to measure the angle of a slope. It can help resolve arguments over the steepness of slopes, and it can determine if you are on the higher of two summits. If there is an upward angle between you and the top of another mountain, then the other summit is higher.
• Magnifying glass. Use it to help read closely spaced contour lines.

The small, round, cheap compasses without base plates are not precise enough for mountaineering, nor can they be used for precise work with a map. For routefinding, the compass must be accurate to within 1 or 2 degrees. A larger margin of error, say 5 degrees, would land a moun-

taineering party 1/2 mile off target at the end of a 6-mile hike.

BEARINGS

A bearing is the direction from one place to another, measured in degrees of angle with respect to an accepted reference line. This reference is the line to true north.

The round dial of a compass is divided just as cartographers divide the earth, into 360 degrees. The direction in degrees to each of the cardinal directions, going clockwise around the dial starting from the top, is: north, 0 degrees (the same as 360 degrees); east, 90 degrees; south, 180 degrees; and west, 270 degrees.

The compass is used for two basic tasks regarding bearings:

1. The compass is used to *take* bearings. (You can also say that the compass is used to *measure* bearings.) To take a bearing means to measure the direction from one point to another, either on a map or on the ground.
2. The compass is used to *plot* bearings. (You can also say that the compass is used to *follow* a bearing.) To plot a bearing means to set a specified bearing on the compass and then to plot out, or to follow, where that bearing points, either on a map or on the ground.

Bearings on the map

The compass is used as a protractor to both measure and plot bearings on a map. Magnetic north and magnetic declination have nothing to do with these calculations. Therefore, ignore the magnetic needle. Never make any use of the magnetic needle when taking or plotting bearings on a map. (The only time the magnetic needle is used on the map is whenever you choose to orient the map to true north, which was explained earlier in this chapter. But there's no need to orient the map simply in order to measure or plot bearings.)

To take (measure) a bearing on the map: Place the compass on the map with one long edge of the base plate running directly between two points of interest. As you measure the bearing from

Point A to Point B, see that the direction-of-travel line is pointing in the same direction as from A to B. Then turn the rotating housing until its set of meridian lines is parallel to the north–south lines on the map. (Be sure the orienting arrow that turns with the meridian lines is pointing to the top of the map, to north. If you point it toward the bottom, your reading will be 180 degrees off.)

Now read the number that is at the index line. This is the bearing from Point A to Point B.

In the example shown in figure 4-6, the bearing from Point A, Panic Peak, to Point B, Deception Dome, is 40 degrees.

If your map doesn't happen to have north–south lines, just draw some in, parallel to the edge of the map and at intervals of an inch or two.

Fig. 4–6. Measuring a bearing on a map with the compass as a protractor

To plot (follow) a bearing on the map: In this case you are starting with a known bearing. And where does that bearing come from? From an actual landscape compass reading. Let's take a hypothetical example (fig. 4-7): A friend returns from a trip, disgusted at himself for leaving his camera somewhere along the trail. During a rest stop, he had taken some pictures of Mount Magnificent. At the same time, he had taken a bearing on Mount Magnificent and found it to be 135 degrees. That's all you need to know. You're heading into that same area next week, so get out the Magnificent

Fig. 4–7. Plotting a bearing on a map with the compass as a protractor

quadrangle, and here is what you do:

First set the bearing of 135 degrees at the compass index line. Place the compass on the map, one long edge of the base plate touching the summit of Mount Magnificent, with the direction-of-travel line pointing toward Mount Magnificent. Rotate the entire compass (not just the housing) until the meridian lines are parallel with the map's north–south lines, and make sure the edge of the base plate is still touching the summit. Again, be sure the orienting arrow points to the top of the map, toward north. Follow the line made by the edge of the base plate, heading in the opposite direction from the direction-of-travel line because the original bearing was measured toward the mountain. Where the line crosses the trail is exactly where your friend's camera is (or was).

Bearings in the field

Now the magnetic needle gets to do its job. All bearings in the field are based on where the needle points. For the sake of simplicity in these first two examples, we will ignore the effects of magnetic declination, a subject that will be taken up in the next section. Let's imagine we are taking the bearings in Ohio, which happens to be along the line of zero declination.

Fig. 4–8. Taking a compass bearing in the field in an area with zero declination

To take (measure) a bearing in the field: Hold the compass in front of you and point the direction-of-travel line at the object whose bearing you want to find. Rotate the compass housing until the pointed end of the orienting arrow is aligned with the north-seeking end of the needle. Read the bearing at the index line (fig. 4-8). And that's all there is to it.

If the compass has no sighting mirror, hold it at or near arm's length and at or near waist level. With a sighting mirror, hold the compass at eye level with the sight pointing at the object. Observe the magnetic needle and the orienting arrow in the mirror as you rotate the housing to align the needle and the arrow. In either case, hold the compass level. Keep it away from ferrous metal objects, which can easily deflect the magnetic needle.

To plot (follow) a bearing in the field: Simply reverse the process used to take a bearing. Start by rotating the compass housing until you have set a desired bearing at the index line, say 270 degrees (due west). Hold the compass level in front of you and then turn your entire body until the north-seeking end of the magnetic needle is aligned with the pointed end of the orienting arrow. The direction-of-travel line is now pointing due west. And that's all there is to that.

MAGNETIC DECLINATION

A compass needle is attracted to *magnetic* north, while most maps are oriented to a different point on the earth, the *geographic* north pole ("true north"). This difference between the direction to true north and the direction to magnetic north, measured in degrees, is called *magnetic*

declination. A simple compass adjustment or modification is necessary to correct for magnetic declination.

In areas west of the line of zero declination, the magnetic needle points somewhere to the east (to the right) of true north (fig. 4-9), so these areas are said to have *east declination*. It works just the opposite on the other side of the line of zero declination. Here, the magnetic needle points somewhere to the west (left) of true north, so these areas have *west declination*.

Consider a mountain traveler in Colorado, where the declination is 14 degrees east. The true bearing is a measurement of the angle between the line to true north and the direction-of-travel line. The magnetic needle, however, is pulled toward magnetic north, not true north. So instead it measures the angle between the line to magnetic north and the direction-of-travel line. This "magnetic bearing" is 14 degrees less than the true bearing. To get the true bearing, you must add 14 degrees to the magnetic bearing.

Like those in Colorado, climbers in all areas west of zero declination must add the declination to the magnetic bearing. In central California, for example, about 18 degrees must be added. In Washington State, it is about 20 degrees.

East of the zero-declination line, the declination is subtracted from the magnetic bearing. In Maine, for example, the magnetic bearing is 20 degrees greater than the true bearing. Subtracting the declination of 20 degrees gives a wilderness traveler in Maine the true bearing.

This is all very simple in theory but can be confusing in practice, and the wilderness is no place to practice mental arithmetic that can have life-and-death consequences. A more practical way to handle the minor complication of declination is to pay somewhat more for your compass and get one with an adjustable declination arrow instead of a fixed orienting arrow. The declination arrow can be easily set for any declination. Then the bearing you read at the index line will automatically be the true bearing, and concern about a declination error is one worry you can leave at home.

On compasses without adjustable declination ar-

Fig. 4–9. Relationship between true and magnetic north in the United States

rows, you can get the same effect by sticking a thin strip of tape to the top or bottom of the rotating housing to serve as a customized declination arrow. Trim the tape to a point, with the point aimed directly at the specific declination for the area where you will be climbing.

In Colorado, your taped declination arrow must point at 14 degrees east (clockwise) from the 0 point (marked N for north) on the rotating compass dial (fig. 4-10a). In Maine, the declination arrow must point at 20 degrees west (counterclockwise) from the 0 point on the dial (fig. 4-10b). In Wash-

Fig. 4–10. Compass declination corrections: a, for the area west of the zero-declination line; b, for the area east of the zero-declination line.

ington State, the declination arrow must point at 20 degrees east (clockwise) from the 0 point.

To take or to follow a bearing in the field, follow exactly the same procedure used in the earlier examples from Ohio, where the declination is zero. The only difference is that from now on, you will align the magnetic needle with the declination arrow instead of with the orienting arrow.

From here on in this chapter, it is assumed you are using a compass with a declination arrow—either an adjustable arrow or a taped arrow that you have added. For all bearings in the field, you will align the needle with this declination arrow. Unless otherwise stated, all bearings referred to are true bearings, not magnetic.

PRACTICING WITH THE COMPASS

Before you count on your compass skills in the wilderness, test them in the city. The best place to practice is a place where you already know all the answers, like a street intersection where the roads run north–south and east–west.

Take a bearing in a direction you know to be east. When you have lined up the declination arrow with the magnetic needle, the number at the index line should be 90 degrees, or within a few degrees of 90. Repeat for the other cardinal directions, south, west, and north. Then do the reverse. Pretend you don't know which way is west. Set 270 degrees (west) at the index line and hold the compass in front of you as you turn your entire body until the needle is again aligned with the declination arrow. The direction-of-travel line should now point west. Does it? Repeat for the other cardinal directions. This set of exercises will help develop precision and self-confidence at compass reading and also is a way to check the accuracy of the compass. And if you make a mistake or two, well, no harm done.

Look for chances to practice in the mountains. A good place is any known location—such as a summit or a lake shore—from which you can see identifiable landmarks. Take bearings as time permits, plot them on the map, and see how close the result is to your actual location.

CAUTIONS ABOUT COMPASS USE

As you've gathered by now, there's a big difference between using a compass for working with a map and using a compass for field work. When measuring and plotting bearings on a map, the compass needle is ignored. Just align the meridian lines on the compass housing with the north–south lines on the map. In the field, you *must* use the magnetic needle.

You may have heard that metal can mess up a compass reading. It's true. Ferrous objects—iron, steel, and other materials with magnetic properties—will deflect the magnetic needle and produce false readings, as will a battery-powered watch that is within 6 inches of a compass. Keep the compass away from belt buckles, ice axes, and other metal objects. If a compass reading doesn't seem to make sense, see if it's being sabotaged by nearby metal.

Keep your wits about you when pointing the declination arrow and the direction-of-travel line. If either is pointed backward—an easy thing to do—the reading will be 180 degrees off. If the bearing is north, the compass will say it's south. Remember that the north-seeking end of the magnetic needle must be aligned with the pointed end of the declination arrow. And that the direction-of-travel line must point from you to the objective, not the reverse.

There's yet another way to introduce a 180-degree error in a compass reading. The way to do it is to align the compass meridian lines with the north–south lines on a map, but have the declination arrow pointing backward. The way to avoid this is to check that your declination arrow is pointing more or less to north (rather than more or less to south). This check has nothing to do with declination. It just happens that the arrow is placed in a convenient spot to serve as a reminder of which way to direct the meridian lines.

If in doubt, trust your compass. The compass, correctly used, is almost always right, while your contrary judgment may be clouded by fatigue, confusion, or hurry. If you get a nonsensical reading, check to see you aren't making one of those 180-

degree errors. If not, and if there is no metal in sight, verify the reading with other members of the party. If they get the same answer, trust the compass over hunches, blind guesses, and intuition.

THE MAP AND COMPASS: A CHECK LIST

Do you have the hang of it? Let's run through the whole procedure. Check off each step as you do it.

To take (measure) a bearing on a map:

1. Place compass on map, with edge of base plate joining two points of interest.
2. Rotate housing to align compass meridian lines with north–south lines on map.
3. Read bearing at index line.

To plot (follow) a bearing on a map:

1. Set desired bearing at index line.
2. Place compass on map, with edge of base plate on feature from which you wish to plot bearing.
3. Turn entire compass to align meridian lines with map's north–south lines. The edge of the base plate is the bearing line.

To take (measure) a bearing in the field:

1. Hold compass level, in front of you, and point direction-of-travel line at desired object.
2. Rotate housing to align declination arrow with magnetic needle.
3. Read bearing at index line.

To plot (follow) a bearing in the field:

1. Set desired bearing at index line.
2. Hold compass level, in front of you, and turn your entire body until magnetic needle is aligned with declination arrow.
3. Travel in direction shown by the direction-of-travel line.

And for the last time:

• Never use the magnetic needle or the declination arrow when measuring or plotting bearings on the map (except to check that the declination arrow is pointing more or less north on the map, not south, as a check that the compass meridian lines are not upside-down).
• When taking or following a bearing in the field, always align the pointed end of the declination arrow with the north-seeking end of the magnetic needle.

THE ALTIMETER

An altimeter (fig. 4-11), like a compass, provides one simple piece of information that forms the basis for a tremendous amount of vital detail. The compass merely points the direction to magnetic north. The altimeter merely gives the elevation. But by monitoring the elevation and checking it against the topographic map, mountaineers keep track of their progress, pinpoint their location, and find the way to critical junctions in the route. Every climbing party should have an altimeter.

An altimeter is basically a modified barometer.

A barometer measures air pressure (the weight of air) and displays it on a scale calibrated in inches or millimeters of mercury, or in millibars. Because air pressure decreases at a uniform rate with increasing altitude, a barometer can measure elevation if it is fitted with a scale calibrated in feet or meters instead of units of pressure.

To read a mountaineering altimeter, begin by holding it level in the palm of one hand. Look directly down on the needle, your eyes at least a foot above it, to reduce errors due to viewing

Fig. 4–11. Typical altimeters

angle. Tap it lightly several times to overcome slight friction in the mechanism, and then take an average of several readings. The elevations determined by an altimeter are only approximate because the instrument is strongly affected by variations in temperature and weather. Check the reading whenever you reach a point of known elevation so you can reset it if necessary.

HOW ALTIMETERS AID MOUNTAINEERS

The altimeter helps in deciding whether to continue a climb or to turn back, by letting you calculate your rate of ascent. Let's say you have been keeping an hourly check on time and elevation during a climb. It has taken the party 4 hours to climb 3,000 feet, an average of 750 feet per hour. But you know that the actual rate of ascent has been declining with each hour. In fact, the party gained only 500 feet in the past hour, compared with 1,000 feet the first hour. You know that the summit is at an elevation of 8,400 feet, and an altimeter reading shows you're now at 6,400. So you can predict that it will take roughly 4 more hours to reach the summit. Take that information, courtesy of the altimeter, combine it with a look at the weather, the time of day, and the condition of the climbers, and you have the data on which to base a sound decision.

An altimeter also can help determine exactly where you are. If you are climbing a ridge shown on the map, but don't know exactly where you are along the ridge, check the altimeter for the elevation. Where the ridge reaches that contour line on the map is your likely location.

Another way to ask the altimeter where you are is to start with a compass bearing to a summit or some other known feature. Find that peak on the map, and plot the bearing line from the mountain back toward the climbing party. You now know you must be somewhere along that line. But where? Take an altimeter reading and find out the elevation. Where the compass bearing line crosses a contour line at that elevation is your likely location. This could lead to an ambiguous answer, of course, because the line might cross that contour at several points. That's when you turn to further observations, common sense, and intuition.

Navigation gets easier with the aid of an altimeter. If you top a convenient couloir at 9,400 feet and gain the summit ridge, make a note of that elevation. On the way back, descend the ridge to that elevation and you will easily find the couloir again.

Guidebook descriptions sometimes specify a change in direction at a particular elevation. If it's on an open snowfield or a forested hillside, good luck in making the turn at the right place without an altimeter. The route you have worked out on a topographic map also may depend on course changes at certain elevations, and again the altimeter will keep the party on target. An altimeter obviously helps in mapping, providing elevations of key points along routes included on the map.

Last but not least, an altimeter will reveal if you're on the real summit when the visibility is too poor to be able to tell by looking around.

HOW TO GET THE MOST FROM YOUR ALTIMETER

Knowing all the facts about an altimeter—the pluses and minuses—will make it as valuable as possible in the wilderness. First of all, keep in mind that temperature and weather are always working their will on an altimeter's accuracy. A high-pressure weather area will tend to cause a lower elevation reading than a low-pressure area. Warmer, lighter air will tend to result in a higher elevation reading than colder, heavier air.

There's no need to be surprised if an elevation reading of 5,200 as you go to sleep turns into 5,300 when you wake up the next morning, even though the tent appears to be in the same spot. The elevation hasn't changed, but the weather has, and with it, the air pressure that is the basis for an altimeter's determination of elevation. That's just the way altimeters are, and as with any good friend, you've got to accept them despite their bad habits. The best way to keep them relatively honest is to check the reading at every known elevation point and reset the altimeter accordingly. Topographic maps give the correct elevations of many of the features you encounter on a trip, such as trailheads, lakes, and summits.

Try to keep the temperature of the altimeter relatively constant, perhaps by carrying it in your pocket. The altimeter expands and contracts due to variations in its temperature, causing changes in the indicated elevation. A bimetallic element in temperature-compensated altimeters adjusts for this effect of temperature when there is no actual change in elevation. The element counterbalances the effect on other parts of the instrument. When you are gaining or losing elevation, however, this adjustment sometimes is not enough, resulting in errors even in altimeters that are temperature-compensated.

The altimeter can help in predicting weather. The altimeter and barometer scales operate in opposition to each other. When one goes up, the other goes down. An altimeter reading showing an increase in elevation when no actual elevation change has taken place (such as at camp overnight) means a falling barometer, which generally indicates deteriorating weather. A decreasing altimeter reading, on the other hand, means increasing barometric pressure, generally associated with improving weather. This is an oversimplification, of course, as weather forecasting is complicated by the wind, local weather peculiarities, and the rate of barometric pressure change. Stay observant on climbing trips if you want to figure out the relationship between weather and altimeter readings in your area.

Because even the most accurate and costly altimeters bow to the weather, don't be misled into trusting them to accuracies greater than are possible. A typical high-quality altimeter may have a scale of resolution (smallest marked division) of 20 feet and a stated accuracy of plus-or-minus 30 feet. This doesn't mean the altimeter will always be that close to the truth. Get to know your own altimeter, use it often, check it at every opportunity, and note differences of opinion between it and the map. You'll soon know just what accuracy to expect, and it will then be a dependable aid to roving the wilds.

ORIENTATION BY INSTRUMENT

Figuring out exactly where you are is usually a relatively simple affair, just looking around and comparing what you see with what is on the map.

Sometimes this is not accurate enough, or there is just nothing much nearby to identify on the map. The usual solution then is to get out the compass and try for bearings to some faraway landscape features. This is orientation by instrument.

The goal of orientation is to determine that precise point on the earth where you now stand. Your position can then be represented by a mere dot on the map which is known as your *point position*. There are two lower levels of orientation. One is called *line position*: the travelers know they are along a certain line on a map—such as a river, a trail, or a bearing line—but they do not know where they are along the line. The lowest level is *area position*: they know the general area they are in, but that's about it. The primary objective of orientation is to find out your exact point position.

POINT POSITION

With point position known, there is no question about where you are, and you can use that knowledge in identifying on the map any major feature visible on the landscape. You can also identify on the landscape any visible feature shown on the map.

For example, climbers on the summit of Forbidden Peak know their point position. It's at the top of Forbidden Peak. (You can refer back to the Forbidden topographic map, fig. 4-2.) They see an unknown mountain and want to know what it is. They take a bearing and get 275 degrees. They plot 275 degrees from Forbidden Peak on their topographic map, and it passes through Mount Torment. They conclude that the unknown peak is Mount Torment.

However, if you start by wanting to find Mount Torment, do the map work first. The climbers measure the bearing on the map from where they are, Forbidden, to Mount Torment, and come up with 275 degrees. Keeping 275 at the index line on the compass, one climber holds the compass out and turns until the magnetic needle is aligned with the declination arrow. The direction-of-travel line then points to Mount Torment.

LINE POSITION

With line position known, the goal is to determine point position. Knowing they are on a trail, ridge, or some other identifiable line, the climbers

Fig. 4–12. Orientation with line position known

need only one more piece of information. For example, they are on Unsavory Ridge (fig. 4-12)—but exactly where? Off in the distance is Mount Majestic. A bearing on Majestic indicates 220 degrees. Plot 220 degrees from Mount Majestic on the map. Run this line back toward Unsavory Ridge, and where it intersects the ridge is exactly where the climbers are.

AREA POSITION

The climbers know their area position: they are in the general area of Fantastic Crags (fig. 4-13). They want to determine line position and then, from that, point position. To move from knowing area position to knowing point position, two trustworthy pieces of information are needed.

The climbers may be able to use bearings on two visible features. They take a bearing on Mount Majestic and get a reading of 40 degrees. They plot a line on the map, through Mount Majestic, at 40 degrees. They know they must be somewhere on that bearing line, so they now have line position. They can also see Unsavory Spire. A bearing on the spire shows 130 degrees. They plot a line on the map, through Unsavory Spire, at 130 degrees. The two bearing lines intersect, and that's where they are.

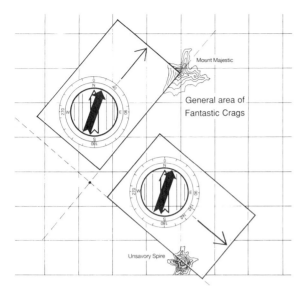

Fig. 4–13. Orientation with area position known

When you know the area position and there is just one visible feature to take a bearing on, the compass can't provide anything more than line

position. That can be a big help, though. Climbers in the general vicinity of Fantastic River then know they are near where the bearing line plotted from the one feature intersects the river. Perhaps from a study of the map they can then figure out just where they are. They can also read the altimeter and see on the map where the bearing line intersects the contour line for that elevation. The closer an angle of intersection is to 90 degrees, the more accurate the point position will be.

Use every scrap of information at your disposal, but be sure your conclusions agree with common sense. If the climbers who took bearings on Mount Majestic and Unsavory Spire find that the two lines on the map intersect in the river, but the climbers are on a high point of land, something is wrong. Try again. Try to take a bearing on another landmark, and plot it. If lines intersect at a map location with no similarity to the terrain, there might be some magnetic anomaly in the rocks, or you may have an inaccurate map. And who knows? Maybe those peaks weren't really Majestic and Unsavory in the first place.

NAVIGATION BY INSTRUMENT

Getting from here to there is usually just a matter of keeping an eye on the landscape and watching were you're going, helped by an occasional glance at the map. However, if the current objective is out of sight, you can take compass in hand, set a bearing, and follow the direction-of-travel line as it guides you to the goal. This is navigation by instrument. Sometimes this is the only practical method for finding the pass or base camp or whatever. It also serves as a supplement to other methods and a way of verifying that you're on the right track. Again, use common sense and challenge a compass bearing that defies reason. (Is your declination arrow pointing the wrong way, sending you 180 degrees off course?)

MAP AND COMPASS

The most common situation requiring instrument navigation comes when the route is unclear

because the topography is featureless or because landmarks are obscured by forest or fog. You do know exactly where you are and where you want to go, and can identify both the current position and the destination on the map. Simply measure the bearing from your position to your objective on the map, then follow that bearing. Let's say you get a bearing of 285 degrees (fig. 4-14a). Read this bearing at the index line and leave it set there as is (fig. 4-14b). Hold the compass out in front of you as you rotate your body until the north-seeking end of the magnetic needle is aligned with the pointed end of the declination arrow. The direction-of-travel line now points to the objective (fig. 4-14c). Start walking.

COMPASS ALONE

Navigators of air and ocean often travel by instrument alone; so can climbers. For example, if

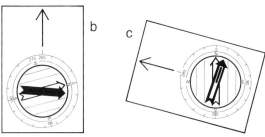

Fig. 4–14. Navigation using the map and compass: a, measuring the bearing from point A to point B on the map; b, bearing at index line; c, following the bearing.

you are scrambling toward a pass and clouds begin to obscure it, take a quick compass bearing. Then follow the bearing, compass in hand if you wish. You don't even have to note the numerical bearing; just align the magnetic needle with the declination arrow and keep it aligned. Likewise, if you are heading into a valley where fog or forest will hide the mountain that is your goal, take the bearing to the peak before you drop into the valley (fig. 4-15). Then navigate by compass through the valley. This method becomes more reliable if several people travel together with compass in hand, checking each other's work.

USING INTERMEDIATE OBJECTIVES

A handy technique is available for those frustrating times you try to stay exactly on a compass bearing, but keep getting diverted by obstructions such as cliffs, dense brush, or crevasses. Try the technique of intermediate objectives. Sight past the obstruction to a tree or rock or other object that is exactly on the bearing line to the principal objective (fig. 4-16a). Then you're free to scramble over to the tree or rock by whatever route is easiest. When you get there, you can be confident that you

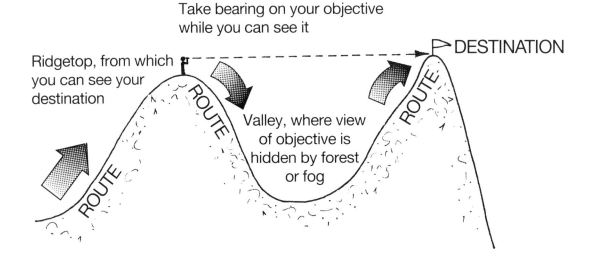

Fig. 4–15. Following a compass bearing when the view of the objective is obscured by forest or fog

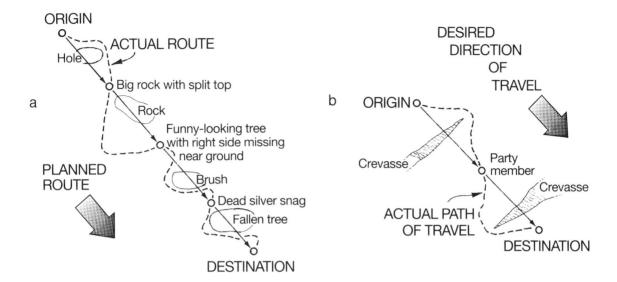

Fig. 4–16. Use of intermediate objectives: a, in a forest; b, on a glacier.

are still on the correct route. The technique is useful even when there is no obstruction. Moving from intermediate objective to intermediate objective means you can put the compass away for those short stretches rather having to check it every few steps.

Sometimes on snow or in fog, there *are* no natural intermediate objectives, just a white, undifferentiated landscape. Then another member of the party can serve as the target (fig. 4-16b). Send that person out to near the limit of visibility. Wave this new intermediate objective left or right, directly onto the bearing line. That person can then improve the accuracy of the route by taking a "back bearing" to you. (For a back bearing, keep the same bearing set at the index line, but for this purpose, align the *south-seeking* end of the magnetic needle with the pointed end of the declination arrow.) The combination of a bearing and a back bearing tends to counteract any compass error.

LOST

Why do people get lost? Lots of reasons. Some travel without a map because the route seems obvious. Others fail to check on recent changes in roads and trails. Some folks trust their own instincts over the compass. Others do not bother with the map homework that can start them off with a good mental picture of the area. Some don't pay enough attention to the route on the way in to be able to find it on the way out. Some rely on the skill of their climbing partner, who is just now in the process of getting them lost.

Why *do* people get lost? They don't take the time to think about where they are going, because they are in a hurry. They miss junctions or wander off on game trails. They charge mindlessly ahead despite deteriorating weather and visibility, fatigue, or flagging spirits.

Good navigators are never truly lost—but having learned humility through years of experience, they always carry enough food, clothing, and bivouac gear to get them through hours or even days of temporary confusion.

WHAT IF YOUR PARTY IS LOST?

The first rule is to STOP. Avoid the temptation to plunge hopefully on. Try to determine where you are. If that doesn't work, figure out the last time the group *did* know its exact location. If that spot is fairly close, within an hour or so, retrace your steps and get back on route. But if that spot is hours back and you can at least make an intelligent guess about the current position, continue forward, but cautiously and with a sharp eye out for landmarks. If the party tires or darkness falls before you find the route, bivouac for the night.

Groups of two or more rarely become dangerously lost, even if they have no wilderness experience. The real danger comes to an individual who is separated from the rest of the party. For this reason, always try to keep everyone together, and assign a rear guard to keep track of the stragglers.

WHAT IF YOU ARE LOST ALONE?

Again, the first rule is to STOP. Look around for other members of the party, shout, and listen for answering shouts. If the only answer is silence, sit down, try to regain your calm, and combat terror with reason.

Once you've calmed down, start doing the right things. Look at your map in an attempt to determine your location, and plan a route home in case you don't connect with the other climbers. Mark your location with a cairn or other objects, and then scout in all directions, each time returning to the marked position. Well before dark, prepare for the night by finding water, firewood, and shelter. Staying busy will raise your spirits. Keep a fire going to give searchers something to see, and try singing so you will have something to do and they will have something to hear.

The odds are that you will be reunited with your group by morning. If not, fight panic. After a night alone, you may decide to hike out to a base-line feature you picked out before the trip—a ridge or stream or highway. If the terrain is too difficult to travel alone, it might be better to concentrate on letting yourself be found. It's easier for rescuers to find a lost climber who stays in one place in the open, builds a fire, and shouts periodically, than one who thrashes on in hysterical hope, one step ahead of the rescue party.

FREEDOM OF THE HILLS

The wilderness awaits those who have learned the skills of routefinding and navigation. In large part, routefinding is the subject of this entire book because it is so essential to all off-trail adventure.

In medieval times the greatest honor a visitor could receive was the rights of a citizen and the freedom of the city, sometimes even today symbol-ized by presenting a guest with the "keys to the city." For the modern alpine traveler, routefinding is the key to wandering at will through valleys and meadows, up cliffs and over glaciers, earning the rights of a citizen in a magical land, a mountaineer with the freedom of the hills.

• 5 •

WILDERNESS TRAVEL

Climbing the mountain is one thing. Getting from the car to the mountain is another. Wilderness travel is the art of getting there—across streams, around brush, along trails, and over snow.

When climbers leave the trailhead deep in a valley of Washington State's Cascade range or head inland from the beach of a British Columbia fiord, tough wilderness travel may lie ahead. The techniques of muddling through brush are not as glamorous as fifth-class rock climbing, but many a peak has been lost in thickets of slide alder. The biggest barriers on the way to a mountaintop often appear below snow line. Learn the skills of wilderness travel and you open the gateway to the summit.

WILDERNESS ROUTEFINDING

Routefinding is the art of working out an efficient route that is within the abilities of the climbing party. Navigation, on the other hand, is the science of using map and compass, and often an altimeter, to determine the location of the objective and to keep moving in the right direction toward it. Navigation points the way from where you are to where you want to be, but it takes skill in routefinding to surmount the hazards and hurdles between here and there. Intuition and luck play a role in routefinding, but there also are principles that can be learned. And there is no substitute for firsthand experience. Climb with experienced mountaineers, watch their techniques, and ask questions. Routefinding is one of the most satisfying of mountain crafts to master.

Each mountain range has its own peculiarities of geology and climate that affect routefinding.

Mountaineers familiar with the Canadian Rockies, accustomed to broad valleys and open forests, will need to learn new rules to contend with the heavily vegetated, narrow canyons of British Columbia's Coast Range. The Pacific Northwest mountaineer used to deep snow at 4,000 feet in June will discover drastically different June conditions in the Sierra. Prolonged mountaineering in a single range teaches the lore of routefinding in that area, but a climber entering a new range has to be ready to learn again.

Some of the most detailed advice on routes will come out of conversations with local experts. Talk to geologists, rangers, and fellow mountaineers. Ask about climbers' trails that don't show on the map and about the best place to ford a stream. Stop at the ranger station on the way to the mountains and get word on current weather and route conditions. Spend a few minutes chatting with the other climbers who have stopped at the ranger station on the way to their own mountain adventure. Doing your homework makes for easier trips with fewer routefinding frustrations.

APPROACH OBSERVATIONS

Keep an eye on the mountain during the approach hike, studying it for climbing routes. The distant view reveals gross patterns of ridges, cliffs, snowfields, and glaciers, as well as the average angle of inclination.

As you get closer, details of fault lines, bands of cliffs, and crevasse fields show up. Gross patterns seen from far away usually are repeated in finer detail when viewed closer. Ledges revealed by snow or shrubs from a distance often turn out to be "sidewalks" with smaller ledges between. The major fault lines, or weaknesses, visible at a distance are usually accompanied by finer, less obvious repetitions.

If the approach skirts the base of the mountain, it can be viewed from various perspectives. A system of ledges indistinguishable against background cliffs may show clearly from another angle with the sky behind. The change of light as the sun traverses the sky often creates revealing shadows. A study of these lengthening or shortening shadows may disclose that apparently sheer cliffs are only moderately angled slopes.

The presence of snow often promises a modest angle and easy climbing, because it doesn't last long on slopes greater than 50 degrees. But beware of nature's illusions. Rime ice adhering to vertical or overhanging cliffs can at first appear to be snow. Deep high-angle couloirs (gullies) often retain snow or ice year-round, especially when shaded. And what look like brilliantly shining snowfields high on the mountain may actually be ice.

As you near the peak, look for climbing clues: ridges with lower average inclination than the faces they divide; cracks, ledges, and chimneys leading up or across the faces; snowfields or glaciers offering easier or predictable pitches.

Spot climbing hazards. Study snowfields and icefalls for avalanche danger, and cliffs for signs of possible rockfall. Snowfields reveal recent rockfall by the appearance of dirty snow or the presence of rock-filled "shell-craters." If the route goes through avalanche and rockfall territory, travel in the cold hours of night, or very early morning before the sun melts the ice mortar bonding precariously perched boulders and ice towers.

Throughout the approach, follow the old mountaineering dictum to "climb with your eyes." Keep evaluating hazards and looking for continuous routes. When the route information gets too complex to remember, begin making quick sketches during rest stops. These memory aids can prove invaluable during a climb when a critical exit gully, for example, becomes lost from view.

While you're at it, keep an eye out for emergency campsites, water supplies, firewood, and anything else that might make your return trip easier and safer.

WALKING

The basic skill for mountaineering is a simple act we all do every day: walking. But just as the ability to write doesn't mean you're a writer, the ability to walk doesn't mean you're a wilderness-ready walker. To walk efficiently in the mountains, you've got to take into account the varied terrain, the weight of your pack, and your physical condition.

PACE

Beginners often make one of two mistakes: they walk faster than they should, or they walk slower than they could.

The most common mistake is walking too fast, perhaps out of concern for the long miles ahead or from a desire to perform well in front of companions. But why wear yourself out on the first mile of a 10-mile hike if the whole day happens to be available for the walk? Take your time and enjoy it.

A simple test will reveal if your pace is too fast. If you cannot sustain it hour after hour, you're going too fast.

The other mistake is hiking too slowly. Your body complains long before it is hurt. Your muscles may ache but still have 10 miles left in them; your lungs may gasp but be able to go on gasping another 3 hours. A degree of suffering is inevitable on the way to becoming a good walker.

The most desirable hiking speed varies during a day. Get ready for a hike by stretching your legs, hips, back, and shoulders. Walk slowly at the start, letting the body become aware of the demands to come. Then start striding out, using will power to get through this period of increasing work until the body experiences its "second wind."

Physiologically, this means the heart has stepped up its beat, the blood is circulating more rapidly, the muscles have loosened. Psychologically, the hiker feels happy and strong.

Vary your pace depending on the trail. Plod slowly and methodically up steep hills; as the grade lessens, pick up the tempo. Your pace will slow late in the day as fatigue sets in. Adrenaline may fuel short bursts of exertion, but there is no "third wind."

THE REST STEP

The most valuable technique in wilderness hiking is setting the right pace. A very important way of controlling your pace is the rest step (fig. 5-1), used whenever legs or lungs need a little time to recuperate between steps on steep slopes. Once you learn it, you'll use it often.

The pace is slow, because for every step there is a pause. The rest takes place after one foot is swung forward for the next step. Support the entire weight of your body on the rear leg while relaxing the muscles of the forward leg. Important: keep your rear leg straight and locked at the knee so that bone, not muscle, supports the weight.

Synchronize breathing with the sequence. In a

Fig. 5–1. The rest step

typical sequence, you may take a new breath with each step—but the number of breaths per step will be less or more depending on how hard the work is. With one breath per step, inhale as you bring your back foot up to the front; exhale as your front leg rests and your rear leg supports the body's weight. Keep repeating this sequence. Where the air is thin, the lungs need an extra pause—sometimes three or four breaths per step. Make a conscious effort to breathe deeply.

Mental composure is important with the rest step. The monotony of the pace, especially on glaciers and snowfields, can undermine morale. You must trust the technique to slowly but steadily chew up the miles, even when the summit seems to be getting no closer.

RESTS

Even the strongest and most experienced hikers need occasional full rests.

During the first half-hour of a hike, stop for a shakedown rest. This lets hikers loosen or tighten boot laces, adjust pack straps, add or take off layers of clothing.

In groups that include both men and women, remember to declare regular party separations (toilet stops), especially out of courtesy to the hiker who may be too shy to express the need. With large groups, the day's first party separation should come before the hike begins, at a service station or outhouse near the trailhead.

During the early part of the day, while your body is fresh, take short, infrequent breathers. Rest in a standing or semi-reclining position, leaning against a tree or hillside to remove pack weight from the shoulders, take deep breaths, and have a bite to eat.

Later, with the body demanding more complete relaxation, the party can take a sackout rest every hour or two. When it's about time for a stop, look for a place with special advantages, such as water, view, flowers, and convenient slopes for unslinging packs. Don't prolong such lovely rests. It's agonizing to resume a march once muscles become cold and stiff. But do remember to eat small amounts of food and drink water during rest stops.

A climbing party sprawled along the trail is not getting any closer to its objective. Take rests when necessary. Otherwise keep moving, unless there's so much extra time in the day that you can afford a luxury rest.

DOWNHILL AND SIDE-HILL

Walking downhill is less tiring than walking uphill, but it's a mixed blessing. Going down a trail, body weight drops roughly and abruptly on legs and feet. Toes are jammed forward. Jolts travel up the spine to jar the entire body. The result can be blisters and knee cartilage damage, sore toes and blackened nails, headaches, and back pain.

Hikers use a few tricks to ease their way downhill. Tighten laces to reduce movement inside the boot (and keep your toenails trimmed). Maintain a measured pace that is slower than the one urged by gravity. Bend your knees to cushion the shock with each step, and place your feet lightly,

as if they were already sore. This restraint will tire your upper leg muscles, and you'll learn that rests going down a trail are just as essential as on the way up.

The ups and downs of hiking are far preferable to the torments of side-hilling (traversing). Walking across a side hill twists the ankles, contorts the hips, and destroys balance. If you can abandon a side hill in order to drop down into a brush-free valley or go up onto a rounded ridge, do it. It's worth going the extra distance. If you're stuck with side-hilling, switchback now and then to shift the strain. Work into your route any flat spots of relief provided by rocks, animal trails, and clumps of grass or heather.

ETIQUETTE

Walking with others requires certain courtesies that are nothing more than common-sense thoughtfulness.

• Avoid following too close. Instead of shadowing your companion, give the hiker ahead of you some space by staying perhaps seven or eight paces back.
• Avoid following too far back, so you don't lose contact with the other hikers or make them continually wait for you.
• Take a look back before you release the branches you've pushed aside along the route. If the hiker behind you has violated the first rule, that person is in danger of getting swatted.
• Step aside when you stop to tie a shoe lace, adjust your pack, or admire the view. (Step above those passing by, if possible.)
• Ask permission to pass, instead of elbowing your way forward.
• Step aside on the way downhill to let a party of uphill hikers continue forward without breaking their pace.
• Set a pace that everyone in the party can maintain. If someone can't keep up, slow the party's pace. Give the last person time to catch up with the party at rest stops—and time to rest after getting there.

TRAILS

The simplest way into the wilderness will always be a trail. They come in many shapes and sizes. One trail will be wide and well marked, while another will have a quality of magic about it: now you see it, now you don't. One big job of the wilderness traveler is to find trails and use them.

TRAIL FINDING

Very few trails were created for the use of climbers. Miners built trails to ore, fishermen to the high lakes, trappers along valleys, pioneers over passes, and animals to food and shelter. But the mine or the lake or the pass might make a good base camp, and any track is worth following as long as it heads the right way.

Even in popular areas with heavy foot traffic and lots of signs, keep alert to find the trail and stay on it. It's easy to stagnate mentally on a long, monotonous walk and miss a turnoff where a sign is missing or where logging has obliterated part of the trail.

Old blazes cut in tree trunks or ribbon tied to branches often mark the trail through a forest, and rock cairns may show the way above timberline. But these pointers don't last forever, and they aren't always reliable. A tiny cairn or a wisp of ribbon may reflect nothing more than the passage of a climber who was lost or was laying out a route to another destination.

As a trail-seeker, you become a detective who combines the clues (a bit of beaten path here, a tree blaze there) with the use of map, compass, and altimeter and with tips from guidebooks and the experts. You'll soon delight in rediscovering the trail just as your companions pronounce it lost forever. And you'll shock the lowland Sunday-afternoon hiker with your definition of the word "trail": any visible route, no matter how ragged, that efficiently gets you where you want to go without battling through brush.

The trick is to stay on the trail until the inevitable moment it disappears or until it becomes necessary to head off-trail in order to keep going in the right direction. Then create your own trail, choosing a course that a trail would follow if there were one. Trail builders look for the easiest way to go. Do as they do.

SOUND TRAIL PRACTICES

Finding the trail is only one half of trailcraft. Using it in a sensitive, caring way is the other. Here are some guidelines:

• Walk in single file to protect trail-side vegetation.
• Stay on the trail even if it's muddy, snow-covered, or rutted.
• Help save vegetation and prevent erosion by not cutting switchbacks.
• Select resilient areas instead of fragile vegetation for rest breaks.
• Look and photograph instead of picking or collecting.
• Guard against damage to stream banks.
• Do light trail maintenance and remove litter.
• Leave trailless areas free of cairns and flagging unless they're already there. Let others have the same adventure of routefinding that you experienced. If you need to mark your route, remove the markers on your way down.
• Choose talus instead of fragile meadows for cross-country travel.

BRUSH

Brush can be a backcountry horror, but there are ways to avoid it.

Wherever there is running water or sliding snow, brush thrives. The classic example is a low-altitude gully swept by avalanches in winter and a torrent in summer. Conditions are perfect for shrubs that flourish during the short summer season, bend undamaged under the snow, and quickly sprout again.

Along riverbanks, brush keeps a window on the sun and builds a narrow, dense thicket. A river that frequently changes course prevents large trees from growing but permits a wide belt of entangling brush. At subalpine elevations, avalanche snow that lasts late into summer prevents the growth of forests and leaves the valley floor crowded with brush.

Mountaineers prefer mature forests. The forests help by blocking sunlight, stifling growth of the deciduous brush that makes for rough going. Young forests, however, only add to the brush problem. The second-growth timber that springs up densely after a fire or windstorm or logging is at its worst when about 20 feet high. The branches fill the space between trees, and deciduous brush continues to thrive.

Blowdowns, avalanche fans, and logging trash are even tougher to get through. The chaotic jumble can slow progress to a crawl and justify a major change of route. Tough and twisted scrub cedar that clings to cliffs and bands of rock presents another hurdle.

When a skirmish with brush is inevitable, there are ways to minimize the hassle. Choose the shortest route across the brushy area. Use fallen trees with long straight trunks as elevated walkways. Push and pull the bushes apart—sometimes by stepping on lower limbs and lifting higher ones to make a passageway. On steep terrain, use hardy shrubs as handholds.

Brush can be dangerous: down-slanting vine maple or alder is slippery; brush obscures the peril of cliffs, boulders, and ravines; and brush snares ropes.

The best policy is to avoid brush. Here are some tips:
- Use trails as much as possible. Five miles of trail may be less work than 1 mile through brush.
- Consider traveling when snow covers brush. Some valleys are easy going in May when you can walk on snow but almost impossible in July when you must burrow through brush.
- Avoid avalanche tracks. The best route up a long valley may be on southern or western slopes, where avalanches hit less frequently than on northern and eastern slopes. When climbing a valley wall, stay in the trees between avalanche tracks.
- Aim for the heaviest timber. Brush is thinnest under the big trees.
- Travel on talus or scree and remnants of snow, rather than in adjacent thickets.
- Consider traveling on ridges and ridge spurs. They may be dry and brushless, while creek bottoms and valley floors are choked with vegetation.
- Consider climbing directly to timberline to take a high route above the brush. This may be worthwhile if the valley bottom seems impassable, and the valley sides are scarred by avalanche tracks.
- Consider going right into the stream channel. The stream bed could be a tunnel through the brush, though you may have to do some wading. Dry stream beds are sometimes ideal. In deep canyons, however, streams usually are choked with fallen trees or interrupted by waterfalls.
- Look for game trails. Animals generally follow the path of least resistance.

TALUS

Talus slopes can either help or hinder the climber. Most offer handy brush-free pathways to the mountains, but some are loose and dangerous.

The peaks constantly crumble, dropping fragments that pile up below as talus and scree. Most of the rubble pours from gullies and spreads out in fan-shaped cones that often merge into one another, forming a broad band of talus between valley greenery and the peaks. Talus fans also often alternate with forest.

Talus slopes build gradually over the ages. On the oldest slopes, soil fills the gap between rocks, making smooth pathways. But talus can be dangerous on volcanos and younger mountains, where rocks are only loosely consolidated because vegetation hasn't filled in the spaces. Move nimbly here, ready to leap away if a rock shifts underfoot. Disturbing one key stone on a glacial moraine or a talus slope can even set off a serious rock avalanche.

Climbers on talus slopes need to keep alert because almost everyone will knock loose a rock or two. Try to travel outside the fall line of climbers above and below. If you're in a narrow gully and this isn't possible, tread gently and be ready to shout ''Rock!'' if a stone is dislodged. Keep close together so a rock set off by one climber can't gain dangerous momentum by the time it reaches other team members. Or permit only one climber to move at a time, while the rest stay in a protected spot.

Slopes with the smallest fragments, called scree, are sometimes as loose as sand. This makes the uphill going a slow-motion torment, but on the way down it might permit some careful ''screeing.'' This involves shuffling your feet to start a minor slide of pebbles and riding it down, in a standing glissade. If there is any vegetation on the slope, skip the screeing out of regard for the plants.

SNOW

Snow can be a blessing in wilderness travel. Many peaks are best climbed early in the season because talus, brush, and logging slash are covered by consolidated snow, and snow bridges provide an easy way over streams.

There are hazards, however. Streams will melt the underside of a snow bridge until it can no longer support your weight. You may break through, the result being wet feet or, much worse, being carried under the snow by a swift stream. To guard against a dunking, watch for depressions in the snow and variations in color or texture, and listen for sounds of running water. Water emerging at the foot of a snowfield gives a clue to the existence and perhaps the size of a cavity beneath the snow. Probe thin spots with your ice axe.

The snow next to logs and boulders often covers holes and soft spots, caused when the snow melts partially away from the wood and the rock. Probe or avoid likely trouble spots, and step wide off logs and rocks. As spring merges into summer, the best route along a valley floor may be somewhat erratic, taking advantage of each remaining snow patch for the few steps of easy walking it provides.

The techniques of snow travel are the same whether the snow lies high in the mountains or deep in the woods. On steep slopes, you may need safeguards such as an ice axe, a rope, or crampons. With experience, you'll recognize both the dangers and the advantages of snow and learn to use the medium to make wilderness travel easier and more enjoyable.

STREAMS

In a wilderness without trails or bridges, streams can become a major impediment. In Alaska or the Canadian Coast Range, climbers may spend more time and energy crossing a perilous river than on their ultimate objective, the mountain.

FINDING THE CROSSING

When the peak lies on the far side of a sizable river, the crossing is a major factor in route selection. Try to get a distant overall view of the river, perhaps from a ridge before dropping into the valley. This view can be more useful than a hundred close looks from the riverbank. When a distant view isn't possible or isn't helpful, you're stuck with either thrashing through the river-bottom brush looking for a way across or sticking to the slopes high above the river in hopes of spotting a sure crossing.

In deep forest there's a good chance of finding

easy passage on a log jam over even the widest river. Higher in the mountains, foot logs are harder to come by, especially if the river changes course periodically and prevents growth of large trees near its channel.

A particular river may be impassable. If it's fed by snow, early morning is the time of minimum flow, and a party may camp overnight to wait for lower water. Sometimes it's necessary to hike for hours or days seeking a crossing. For the widest and deepest rivers, rafts are the only alternative short of hiking to the headwaters.

MAKING THE CROSSING

Unfasten the waist and chest straps of your pack before trying any stream crossing that would require swimming if you fell. You must be able to shed the pack in a hurry.

A foot log is a great way across, with an ice axe, stick, or tightly stretched handline to help with balance and support if the log is thin, slippery, or steeply inclined. Sit down and scoot across if that helps.

Boulders offer another way. Move from boulder to boulder—but only after mentally rehearsing the entire sequence of leaps. Safety lies in smooth and steady progress over stones that may be too slippery and unsteady for you to stop for more than an instant. Use an ice axe or pole for added balance.

If you must wade across, use the widest part of the river. The narrows may be appealing as the shortest way, but they're also the deepest, swiftest, and most dangerous.

If the water is placid and the stones rounded, put your boots in the pack and keep them dry as you wade across. In tougher conditions, wear your boots, but put socks and insoles in the pack. You can drain the boots on the far side, replace the insoles, and put the dry socks back on. You may decide to remove your pants or other clothing in deeper crossings. Loose clothing increases the drag from the water, but it also reduces chilling and may permit a longer crossing before your legs go numb.

The force of moving water is easy to underestimate. A swift stream flowing only shin-deep boils up against the knees. Knee-deep water may boil above the waist and give a disconcerting sensation of buoyancy. Whenever water boils above the knee, it is dangerous, and one false step could have you bouncing in white water from boulder to boulder. Frothy water, containing a great deal of air, is wet enough to drown in but may not be dense enough to float the human body. Streams fed by glaciers present an added difficulty because the bottom is hidden by milky water from glacier-milled rock flour.

If the stream is deep but not swift, you can cross by angling downstream at about the same speed as the current. But it's usually best to face upstream, lean into the current, and stab an ice axe or stout pole upstream for a third point of support. The leading foot probes for solid placement on the shifting bottom, the following foot advances, and the axe or pole is thrust into a new position.

Two travelers can cross together, taking turns securing the other as that person moves to a solid new stance. Team-crossing with a pole is another method. Team members enter the water, each grasping the pole, which is held parallel to the flow of the stream. The upstream member breaks the force of the current. Anyone who slips hangs on to the pole while the others keep the pole steady.

Using ropes for stream crossings is hazardous and not generally recommended. A taut handline can be helpful, but belaying someone across a river holds the danger that the person could be held by the belay and trapped under water.

THE ICE AXE

The tool is called an ice axe, but it's really an invaluable all-purpose item that often goes to work long before snow or ice is reached.

The axe has a lot of unsuspected uses. It pro-vides a "third leg" during stream fording. It gives a brief touch-and-go balance point while you hop across talus. It also helps with balance on steep trails, serving as a heavy-duty cane going uphill and a brake going down. The axe held diagonally across the body, spike touching the slope, will help you hold a stable, vertical stance on steep hillsides. The ice-axe self-arrest is taught as a technique for snow, but many climbers have been happy to use their ''dirt axe'' to stop themselves in steep meadows, forest, and heather.

On open trails many climbers strap the axe on the pack. It comes off the pack and into the hands as the route gets rougher (and as the axe on the pack begins snagging on brush and tree limbs). The ice axe is truly the mountaineer's friend, but it's also probably the most dangerous implement of mountaineering. Its pick (the pointed end of the head), adze (broad end of the head), and spike are always ready to poke, gouge, and impale a climber or nearby companions. Leather or rubber guards are available to cover sharp points and edges when the axe is not needed. Be aware that these guards often get knocked off by brush. Remove the guards when on steep, slippery terrain, whether it's mud, needles, grass, or snow.

Carrying an axe without the skill to use it provides a false sense of security. All too often, climbers slip on hard snow and discover they don't know enough about self-arrest to stop their fall. This indispensable skill comes from practicing on slopes with safe run-outs. (See Chapter 12 for details on this technique and much more information on ice axes.)

The safe way to carry an axe while walking

Fig. 5–2. Carrying an ice axe: a, in your hand on easy terrain; b, as a cane.

along a trail (fig. 5-2a) is to grasp the shaft at the balance point (shaft parallel to the ground), with the spike forward, and the head to the rear with the pick down. This way, the hiker behind is safeguarded against running into the spike and the pick is less likely to jab you in case you stumble. To use the axe as a cane while hiking (fig. 5-2b), grasp the head, with the spike toward the ground. It's usually easiest to have the pick pointing forward, permitting the palm of your hand to rest comfortably on top of the adze.

READY FOR THE WILDERNESS

Wilderness travel can be a complicated business because of all the variables of terrain, weather, snow, water, and vegetation. By putting the information in this chapter into practice, you can learn to travel safely and efficiently through some of the most awe-inspiring landscapes on earth. Combine this information with the advice in earlier chapters on navigation, camping, food, clothing, and equipment, and you should be ready for the wilderness.

PART TWO

CLIMBING FUNDAMENTALS

Climbing at dawn on the Park Glacier, Mount Baker, Washington. Photo by Alan Kearney

• 6 •

ROPES, KNOTS, AND CARABINERS

The rope, more than any other piece of equipment, symbolizes climbing and the climber's dependence on another person. Most climbers remember that very first tie-in—and their sudden dependence on the rope and on their partner or partners who joined them on that length of lifesaving line.

The rope is a "safety net" to catch you when the difficulty of a pitch exceeds your abilities or when the unexpected happens—a foothold crumbles, a snow bridge collapses, or a falling rock knocks you off an exposed stance. It is also fundamental to climbing because, when anchored, it can be climbed or descended.

The rope does not work alone in protecting you, but is one link in your chain of safety. Other links in that chain include the knots that allow you to use the rope for specialized tasks, the seat harness the rope is tied to, the loops of webbing known as runners that help connect the rope to rock or snow, and the carabiners that join parts of the climbing system. These links are the topics of this chapter.

ROPES

During climbing's infancy, ropes made of natural fibers (manila and sisal) were used to protect climbers, but these ropes were not reliable for holding severe falls. The development of nylon ropes during World War II forever changed the sport. Suddenly, climbers were offered lightweight lines capable of bearing more than 2 tons. The nylon ropes also had the remarkable quality of elasticity. Rather than bringing a falling climber to an abrupt, jolting stop, the nylon ropes stretched to dissipate much of the force of a fall.

The first nylon ropes were of "laid" or "twisted" construction. Like braided hair, these ropes were composed of many thin nylon filaments bunched into three or four major strands which were then woven together to form the rope.

The early nylon ropes were light-years ahead of natural fiber ropes, but they were stiff to handle and created substantial friction when run through the points of protection used by climbers. Also, they were so elastic that direct-aid climbing with them was inconvenient; they stretched too much when climbers ascended the rope.

Gradually, twisted nylon ropes were replaced by kernmantle ropes, synthetic ropes designed specifically for climbing. Today's kernmantle ropes (fig. 6-1) are composed of a core of braided or parallel nylon filaments encased in a smooth, woven sheath of nylon. Kernmantle rope maintains the advantages of nylon but improves upon the problems associated with twisted ropes—stiffness, friction, and excessive elasticity. Kernmantle

90

Fig. 6–1. Construction of a kernmantle rope

ropes are now the only climbing ropes approved by the Union Internationale des Associations d'Alpinisme (UIAA), the internationally recognized authority in setting standards for climbing equipment.

PERFORMANCE TESTS

The UIAA tests equipment to determine which gear meets its standards. In a sport where equipment failure can be fatal, it's wise to purchase equipment that has earned UIAA approval.

A principal UIAA test checks the strength of single ropes, the basic ropes used in most climbing. These ropes generally measure between 9.8 and 12 millimeters in diameter. For the test, the UIAA attaches an 80-kilogram (176-pound) weight to one end of a 2.8-meter (9-foot) length of rope. The other end is attached to a fixed point after passing through a carabiner-type ring about 1 foot above the point of attachment. The weight is raised as high as it can go, which puts it 2.5 meters above the ring, and dropped for a free fall of 5 meters (fig. 6-2).

The test mimics a severe real-life climbing fall. To receive UIAA approval, a rope must survive at least five of these falls. The test also measures the impact force of the rope, which determines the stress of the fall on the climber's body and on the pieces of protection. UIAA standards require that the impact force not exceed 1,200 kilograms (about 2,700 pounds) on the first fall.

The UIAA also tests double ropes, those used in climbing techniques that utilize two ropes at a time. (Double-rope technique and twin-rope technique are explained in Chapter 10.) These ropes generally measure between 8 and 9 millimeters in

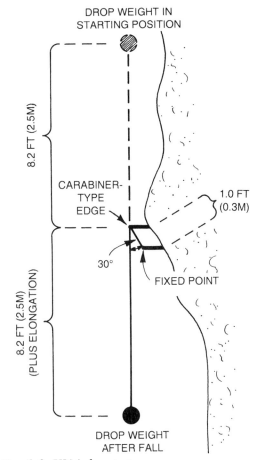

Fig. 6–2. UIAA drop test

diameter. The test for any individual rope used with two-rope technique is identical to the test for single ropes, except that a weight of only 55 kilograms (121 pounds) is used. Each rope must survive at least five falls, and the maximum permitted impact force on the first fall is 800 kilograms (about 1,800 pounds).

The UIAA also applies static tension tests to the ropes it approves, to keep rope stretch below a certain maximum. A load of 80 kilograms is applied to a 1-meter section of rope. A larger rope (between 9.8 and 12 millimeters in diameter) cannot elongate by more than 8 percent. A lighter rope used in two-rope climbing cannot elongate by more than 10 percent.

WATER-REPELLENT ROPES

Wet ropes are more than unpleasant to handle and heavy to carry. They can freeze and become difficult to manage. Equally important, studies show that ropes hold fewer falls and have about 30 percent less strength when they are wet.

Rope manufacturers treat some of their ropes to make them more water repellent and therefore stronger in wet conditions. The sheaths and cores of these ''dry'' ropes are treated with either a silicone-based or Teflon-based coating. The treatment improves the abrasion resistance of some ropes and also reduces friction of the rope as it runs through carabiners. The dry ropes cost about 15 percent more than untreated ropes.

ROPE CARE

When you consider what a climbing rope protects—your life—it's easy to understand why it deserves pampering. A new rope is extremely strong, but abusive treatment can soon destroy it.

Stepping on a rope is a common form of abuse that grinds sharp particles into and through the sheath. Over time, the particles act like tiny knives that slice the rope's nylon filaments. Stepping on the rope creates even more damage if it happens to be trapped between a sharp edge and your boot. Be doubly careful about keeping off the rope when you're wearing crampons. The havoc these metallic points can wreak is obvious, though not always visible. Crampons can damage the core of a rope without leaving any visible gash on the sheath.

Nonetheless, the sheath gives the best picture of the rope's overall condition. If a crampon wound, excessive abrasion, rockfall, or a sharp edge leaves the sheath looking tattered, the rope's integrity should be seriously questioned. Often the damaged portion of the sheath is near an end and cutting off a small segment of the rope solves the problem. But if the damaged section is closer to the center, retire the rope.

If no obvious blemishes scar the sheath, it's harder to decide when to retire the rope. Its actual condition depends on many factors including frequency of use, the care it has received, the number of falls it has endured, and how old it is. Following are some general guidelines to help you decide when to retire your rope:

• A rope used daily should be retired within a year.
• A rope used during most weekends should give about two years of service.
• An occasionally used rope should be retired after four years (nylon deteriorates over time).
• After one very severe fall, it may be wise to replace your rope. A *new* rope may be certified to take five falls, but if your rope is not new, consider all the other factors affecting its condition.

These guidelines assume proper cleaning and storage. A rope should be washed frequently with tepid water and a gentle detergent. Wash it by hand or in a side-loading machine (ropes can get caught under the agitator in top-loading machines). Rinse the rope several times in fresh water, and then hang it to dry in a shady area.

Before storing any rope, be sure it is completely dry. Remove all knots, coil the rope loosely, and store it in a cool, dry area away from sunlight, battery acid, and other strong chemicals.

Get in the habit of inspecting your rope frequently. Is the sheath clean? If not, wash the rope. Are the ends of the rope fraying or unraveling? If so, fuse them with a small flame. Are the ends and middle of the rope well-marked for easy detection? If not, mark them according to the manufacturer's guidelines.

COILING THE ROPE

For carrying or storing, the rope is normally coiled, most commonly in the mountaineeer's coil (fig. 6-3) or the butterfly coil (fig. 6-4). Most climbers prefer one or the other, but knowing both is useful. The mountaineer's coil is advantageous when the rope is carried over a pack. But the butterfly coil is faster, doesn't kink the rope, and ties snugly to your body if you are not wearing a pack.

Whatever your method, uncoil the rope carefully before use. Untie the cinch knot and then uncoil the rope, one loop at a time, into a pile. If you just drop the coils and start pulling on one end,

Fig. 6–3. Mountaineer's coil

you'll probably create a tangled mess.

Rope throw bags offer an alternative to coiling. These bags protect the rope, keep it cleaner and drier, and reduce chances of tangling. Throw bags have a loop of webbing sewn into the bottom of the inside. One end of the rope is tied into the loop before the rest of the rope is threaded and stuffed into the bag uncoiled. Do not connect the rope with a carabiner, because the carabiner could be damaged if the bag is thrown. Before tossing the bag—in preparation for a rappel, for example—don't forget to anchor the free end of the rope.

Fig. 6–4. Butterfly coil

KNOTS

Knots allow you to use the rope for many special purposes. They let you tie into the rope, anchor yourself to the mountain, tie two ropes together for long rappels, use slings to climb the rope itself, and much more.

Climbers rely most heavily on a dozen or so different knots (figs. 6-6 through 6-26). Practice these knots until tying them is second nature. If you really want a test, try tying them in a cold, dark shower to give you an idea of the conditions you may someday encounter on a climb.

In some cases, more than one knot can perform a particular task, and the knot chosen is a matter of personal preference. Some knots may be preferred because they have a higher breaking strength (fig. 6-5). Others may be chosen because they are easier to tie or are less likely to come apart in use.

Regardless of the knot, tie it neatly, keeping the separate strands of the knot parallel and free of twists. Cinch every knot tight, and tie off loose ends with the insurance of overhand knots.

	%		%
Without knot	100	Double fisherman's	65-70
Bowline	70-75	Water knot (ring bend)	60-70
Figure 8	75-80	Clove hitch	60-65
Fisherman's	60-65	Overhand	60-65

Fig. 6–5. Relative strengths of knots for single kernmantle rope (courtesy the American Alpine Journal*)*

Overhand knot

The overhand knot (fig. 6-6a) is most often used to secure loose rope ends after another knot has been tied. For instance, it can be used to secure rope ends after tying a square knot (fig. 6-6b) or a rewoven figure-8 (fig. 6-6c).

Overhand loop

The overhand loop (fig. 6-7) is often used for leg loops in prusik slings or to make a loop in a doubled rope or a length of webbing.

Fig. 6–7. Overhand loop

Water knot

The water knot (fig. 6-8), also known as the ring bend or tape knot, is used most often to tie a length of tubular webbing into a runner. This knot can work loose over time, so be sure the knot is

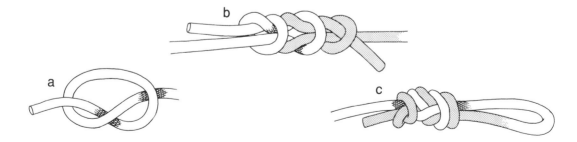

Fig. 6–6. Overhand knot: a and b, tying an overhand knot; c, overhand knot with a rewoven figure-8.

Fig. 6–8. Water knot

cinched very tight, and the tails of the knot are at least 2 inches long. Check the knot often in runners and retie any that have short tails.

Square knot

The general-purpose square knot (fig. 6-9) has many applications around camp. It is often used to finish off a coiled rope.

Fig. 6–9. Square knot

Fig. 6–10. Fisherman's knot

Fisherman's knot

The fisherman's knot (fig. 6-10) can be used to join two ropes together. It has been replaced to a large degree by the double fisherman's knot and is shown here primarily to provide a clearer understanding of the double fisherman's knot.

Fig. 6–11. Double fisherman's knot

Double fisherman's knot

The double fisherman's knot (fig. 6-11), also known as the grapevine knot, is the most secure and preferred knot for tying the ends of two ropes together for a rappel.

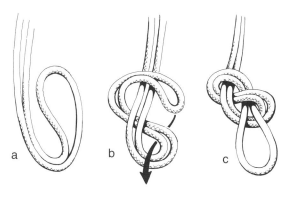

Fig. 6–12. Figure-8 loop

Figure-8 loop

The figure-8 loop (fig. 6-12) is a strong knot that can be readily untied after being under a load.

Rewoven figure-8

The rewoven figure-8 (fig. 6-13) is an excellent knot for tying into a seat harness at the end of the rope. Finish it off by tying one or two overhand knots in the loose end. This knot also can be used to connect a rope to an anchor.

Fig. 6–13. Rewoven figure-8

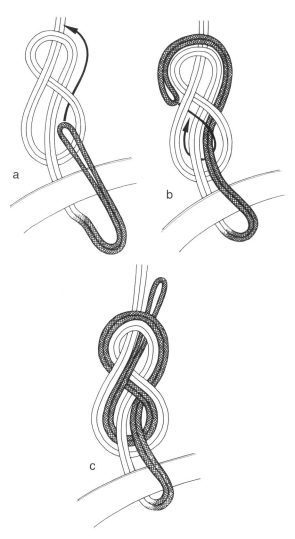

Fig. 6–14. Double rewoven figure-8

Double rewoven figure-8

The double rewoven figure-8 (fig. 6-14) is used by the middle person in a three-person rope team to tie the rope to the seat harness. Secure the resulting end loop with an overhand knot or a carabiner.

Single bowline

The single bowline (fig. 6-15) makes a loop at the end of the climbing rope that will not slip, and

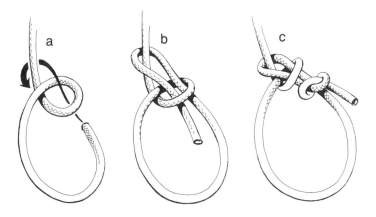

Fig. 6–15. Single bowline

it can secure the rope around a tree or other anchor. Tie off the loose end with an overhand knot. The free end of the rope should come out on the inside of the loop, because the knot is much weaker if this end finishes on the outside.

Rewoven bowline

The rewoven bowline (fig. 6-16) is another excellent knot for tying into a seat harness at the end of the rope. It can be used in place of the rewoven figure-8. If the rewoven portion of the bowline comes untied, you are still tied in with a single bowline.

Fig. 6–16. Rewoven bowline

Fig. 6–17. Double bowline

Double bowline

The middle person on a three-person rope can tie the double bowline (fig. 6-17) to a seat harness. The resulting end loop should be secured with an overhand knot or a carabiner.

Fig. 6–18. Clove hitch

Clove hitch

The clove hitch (figs. 6-18 and 6-22) is a quick knot for clipping into a carabiner attached to an anchor. With the clove hitch, it is easy to adjust the length of the rope between the belayer and the anchor without unclipping.

Fig. 6–19. Double sheet bend

Double sheet bend

The double sheet bend (fig. 6-19) is sometimes used instead of a water knot as the tie-off knot on homemade seat harnesses because it is easier to adjust. This knot has a tendency to work loose. Tie off the loose ends with backup overhand knots.

Girth hitch, overhand slip knot, and clove hitch

The girth hitch (fig. 6-20), the overhand slip knot (fig. 6-21), and the clove hitch (fig. 6-22) are simple knots that can be used to tie off partially driven pitons or ice screws.

Fig. 6–20. Girth hitch

Fig. 6–21. Overhand slip knot

Fig. 6–22. Clove hitch

FRICTION KNOTS

Friction knots provide a quick and simple way to set up a system for ascending or descending a climbing rope. The knots grip the climbing rope when weight is on them, but are free to move when the weight is released. The best known friction knot is the prusik, but others such as the Bachmann and the Klemheist are also useful.

Prusik knot

The prusik (fig. 6-23) requires a few wraps of a light accessory cord around the climbing rope, and it's ready to go to work. The cord is usually a loop (sling) of 5-millimeter to 7-millimeter perlon, wrapped two or three times around the rope. Icy ropes or heavy loads require more wraps than dry ropes or light loads. The accessory cord must be smaller in diameter than the climbing rope, and the greater the difference in diameter, the better it grips. Webbing isn't used for prusik knots because it may not hold.

By attaching two slings to a climbing rope with prusik knots, you can "walk" up the rope. To do this, stand in one sling and take all your weight off the other; now you can slide that knot 1 foot or so up the rope. Then transfer your weight to the second sling, and slide the first sling another foot up the rope. Keep repeating the process and you'll slowly but steadily ascend the rope. (Chapter 13

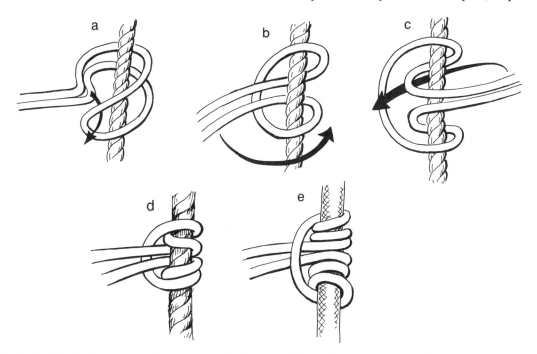

Fig. 6–23. Prusik knot: a–c, tying sequence for the prusik knot; d, a two-wrap prusik knot; e, a three-wrap prusik knot.

describes this process in detail as it is used in getting out of a crevasse.) The knot is also used to help in raising and lowering people and equipment during rescues.

Bachmann knot

The Bachmann knot is used for the same purposes as a prusik knot. The Bachmann (fig. 6-24) is tied around a carabiner, making it much easier to loosen and slide than a prusik. It has the virtue of sometimes being ''self-tending'' when it's being used to help hoist an injured climber.

Klemheist knot

The Klemheist (fig. 6-25) is another alternative to the prusik, with the advantage that it allows you to use a sling made from either accessory cord or webbing. This can be a big help to a climber caught with an ample supply of webbing but little cord.

The cord or webbing is wound around the main rope in a spiral and then threaded through the loop of the top wrap. The Klemheist tied off with a sheet bend is an improved version that is less likely to jam and easier to loosen and slide. The knot also can be tied around a carabiner, providing a good handhold.

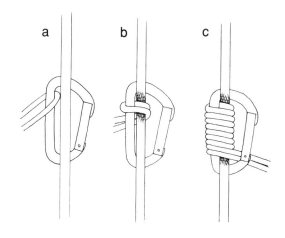

Fig. 6–24. Bachmann knot

The Münter hitch

The Münter is a simple hitch in the rope that is clipped into a carabiner to put friction on the line. It provides an excellent method of belaying a leader or lowering a climber because the hitch is

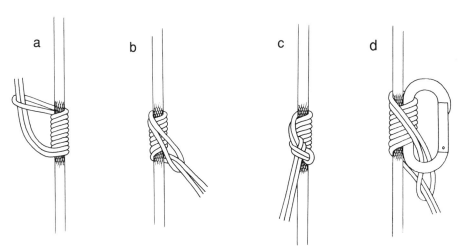

Fig. 6–25. Klemheist knot: a–b, winding and threading Klemheist knot; c, Klemheist tied off with a sheet bend; d, Klemheist tied around a carabiner.

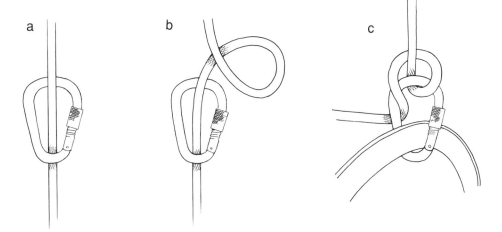

Fig. 6–26. The Münter hitch

reversible (you can feed rope out of the carabiner or pull rope back in) and because the hitch slides (yet is easy to stop if you hold the braking end of the rope). It can also provide the necessary rope friction for rappelling, though it puts more twist in the rope than other rappel methods.

The Münter hitch (fig. 6-26) is very easy to set up and use, and the only equipment needed is a large pear-shaped locking carabiner. Even if you prefer to use a specialized belay device, this hitch is worth knowing as a backup for the time you lose or forget the gear.

HARNESSES

In the old days, climbers looped the climbing rope around the waist several times and tied in with a bowline-on-a-coil (fig. 6-27). That practice is no longer encouraged because long falls onto waist loops can injure your back and ribs. Falls that leave you hanging, such as a fall into a crevasse or over the lip of an overhang, will constrict your diaphragm and suffocate you.

Nowadays, climbers who value their health tie the rope into a harness designed to distribute the force of a fall over a larger percentage of the body. (The bowline-on-a-coil is an option for emergency use if no harness or harness material is available.) The rope is tied into the harness with knots such as the rewoven figure-8 or rewoven bowline (for climbers at the ends of the rope) or with the double rewoven figure-8 or double bowline (for middle climbers).

COMMERCIAL SEAT HARNESSES

With properly fitted leg loops, a seat harness rides comfortably on the hips, yet transfers the force of a fall over the entire pelvis. It also provides a comfortable seat while rappelling.

Several features are particularly desirable in a mountaineering seat harness (fig. 6-28a). Adjustable leg loops allow you to maintain a snug fit no matter how few or how many layers of clothing you wear. The loops also can be unbuckled to permit toilet calls without having to remove the harness, or even untie from the rope. Having the waist buckle located toward one side helps avoid conflict with the locking carabiner clipped to the front of the harness, and lets you move the carabiner left or right of center. Hardware loops are desirable for carrying carabiners and other pieces of climbing

Loop must be rotated in the direction shown to be tied properly

Fig. 6–27. Bowline-on-a-coil: a–f, for climber at the end of a rope; g–h, for middleman. It is not recommended that this knot be used around the body except in emergencies.

Fig. 6–28. Commercial seat harnesses showing principal features mentioned in text

gear, while padded waist and leg loops give added comfort.

Follow the manufacturer's instructions for buckling into these harnesses. For most harnesses, you will need to pass the waist strap back over and through the main buckle a second time for safety. Be sure that at least 2 inches of the strap extends beyond the buckle after reweaving it.

HOMEMADE SEAT HARNESSES

Homemade seat harnesses are an option for linking yourself to the rope, and you can make a simple one from 22 feet of 1-inch tubular webbing. Starting about $4\frac{1}{2}$ feet from one end of the webbing, tie two leg loops in the webbing using overhand loops. Make the loops just large enough to fit

Fig. 6–29. Homemade seat harness

over your clothing, and leave about a 6-inch bridge between the loops. Once tied, leave the loops in place. That completes construction of the harness. To wear it, step into the leg loops and wrap the webbing as shown in the accompanying illustration (fig. 6-29). Use a square knot, water knot, or double sheet bend to tie off the harness, then secure the ends with overhand knots.

SWAMI BELTS

Swami belts (fig. 6-30), another method of tying into the rope, are usually commercially made and are secured to the waist with a buckle or a water knot. The climbing rope is tied through the belt with a rewoven figure-8 or a rewoven bowline.

The belts are wide enough to provide support around the middle of the waist and lower back and to help distribute the force of a fall. Still, if you are left hanging, the belt can creep up and restrict your breathing. Adding leg loops keeps a swami belt from creeping up and distributes the force of a fall to an even larger area, much like a seat harness. In fact, with leg loops attached, the swami belt becomes a seat harness.

Fig. 6–30. Swami belt

BODY HARNESSES

The only commercial harnesses approved by the UIAA are full body harnesses (fig. 6-31). Body harnesses, which incorporate both a chest and a seat harness, have a higher tie-in point. This greatly reduces the chance of flipping over backward during a fall, especially if a pack makes you top heavy. Because a body harness distributes the force of a fall throughout the trunk of your body, there is less danger of lower-back injury.

Although they are unquestionably safer, body harnesses are resisted by many climbers. They are more expensive and restrictive, and make it hard to add or remove clothing. Instead, many climbers prefer a seat harness for most climbs, and improvise a chest harness when one is warranted, such as when climbing with a heavy pack, crossing glaciers, or aid-climbing under large overhangs.

CHEST HARNESSES

A chest harness can be readily improvised with a long loop of webbing (a long runner). One popular design depends on a carabiner to bring the ends of the harness together at your chest. Another uses a knot instead to attach the ends.

The carabiner chest harness: Start with a double-length runner. Give the runner a half twist to create two temporary loops, and push one arm all the way through each loop. Lift the runner over your head and let it drop against your back, then pull the two sides together and clip with a carabiner at your chest. Connect the chest and seat harnesses with a short piece of webbing or cord to keep the chest harness from riding up around your neck in a fall (fig. 6-32).

The final step is to link the chest harness to the climbing rope to prevent you from being flipped upside down during a fall. There are two ways to do this. You can simply run the climbing rope from your seat harness up through the chest carabiner. Or, you can tie a short prusik sling onto the rope in front of you and clip this into the chest harness. If you use the prusik, be sure it is carefully adjusted to help keep you upright, but still permit your weight to be borne by the seat harness (not by the prusik).

Fig. 6–31. Full body harness

The baudrier chest harness: The harness known as the baudrier also is made from a runner, though it will take a somewhat longer runner than the carabiner harness. Put your arm through the runner and hang it over one shoulder. Pull the other end around your back, under the opposite arm, and across your torso. Wind it around a short loop from the other side of the runner, push it through the loop, and cinch the knot tight. Clip the tail of this chest harness directly into the locking carabiner on your seat harness (fig. 6-33).

This harness is linked to the climbing rope in the same way as the carabiner chest harness: either by running the climbing rope up through a carabiner clipped to the chest harness or by attaching a short prusik sling from the rope to the chest harness.

Regardless of the system used, remember that harnesses also deteriorate with use, abuse, and disuse. Replace them about as often as your climbing rope.

Fig. 6–32. The carabiner chest harness

Fig. 6–33. The baudrier chest harness

RUNNERS

Loops of tubular webbing or cord, called runners, are among the simplest pieces of climbing equipment and among the most useful. You'll use them in endless ways as a critical link in climbing systems that involve you, your rope, safety anchors and carabiners.

Fig. 6–34. Runners made of webbing: a, tied runner; b, sewn runner.

Runners are most commonly made by tying a loop with $9/16$-inch to 1-inch webbing or with 8-millimeter to 9-millimeter perlon accessory cord. With webbing, a water knot is typically used to make the loop; with cord, a double fisherman's knot does the job. Melt the ends of your runners with a match or candle to keep the nylon from unraveling.

Most standard runners are made from about $5^1/2$ feet of webbing. You will also need several double-length runners, which take $9^1/2$ feet of material. To help you quickly identify the different lengths, make standard runners from one color of webbing and double-length runners from another color. You should also write your initials and the "manufacturing" date on the tails of all your runners so that you know which are yours and when to retire them.

Tied runners (fig. 6-34a) have several advantages over commercially made sewn runners. They are inexpensive to make, can be untied and threaded around trees and natural chockstones, or can be untied and tied to another length of webbing to create extra-long runners. However, sewn runners (fig. 6-34b) also have some advantages. Sewn runners, always made of webbing, are stronger, lighter, and less bulky than knotted runners. They also eliminate the possibility of the knot untying, a continual concern with homemade runners.

Sewn runners come in four normal lengths: 2-inch and 4-inch "quick draws," 12-inch "half-lengths," and 24-inch "full-lengths." They also come in a variety of widths, with $9/16$-inch, $11/16$-inch, and 1-inch being most common. Runners made from Spectra—a high-performance fiber that is stronger, more durable, and less susceptible to ultraviolet deterioration—are usually made from $9/16$-inch webbing.

CARABINERS

Carabiners are another versatile and indispensable tool of climbing. These ingenious metal snap-links are used for belaying, rappelling, prusiking, clipping into safety anchors, securing the rope to points of protection, and a hundred and one other jobs.

Carabiners for climbing are made of aluminum alloy and require a UIAA minimum breaking strength of 2,000 kilograms (about 4,400 pounds) along the long axis and 400 kilograms (about 900 pounds) along the minor axis. The UIAA minimum breaking strength with the gate open is 600 kilograms (about 1,300 pounds) along the long axis.

Carabiners come in many sizes and shapes (fig. 6-35). Ovals (fig. 6-35a) are very popular because their symmetry makes them a good all-purpose shape. "D" carabiners (fig. 6-35b) also offer a good general-purpose shape and are stronger than ovals because more of the load is transferred to the long axis and away from the gate, the typical point of failure. Offset Ds (fig. 6-35c) have the strength advantage of standard Ds, but the gate on an offset D opens wider, making them easier to clip in awkward situations. Bent-gate carabiners (fig. 6-35d) are a specialty design most commonly used

Fig. 6–35. Carabiners: a, oval carabiner, with inset showing safe (notched) and unsafe (unnotched) carabiner gates; b, standard D carabiner; c, offset D carabiner; d, bent-gate carabiner; e, standard locking carabiner; f, locking pear-shaped carabiner.

on difficult routes where it's important to quickly clip and unclip the carabiners from the feel of the gates alone. These carabiners should always be used with a runner so that they are free to rotate.

Locking carabiners (fig. 6-35e), with a sleeve that screws over one end of the gate to prevent accidental opening, give a wider margin of safety for rappelling, belaying, or clipping into anchors. Some locking carabiners even have a spring that automatically positions the sleeve whenever the gate is closed. You can't forget to lock these carabiners, but you must always unlock them as well, which can be a nuisance. Pear-shaped locking carabiners (fig. 6-35f) are much larger at the gate-opening end than at the hinge end and are ideal for belaying with the Münter hitch.

A few basics apply to the use and care of all carabiners. First, always make sure the force on a carabiner falls on the long axis, and be especially careful that the gate does not receive the load. Check the carabiner gates occasionally. A gate should open easily, even when the carabiner is loaded, and the gate should have good side-to-side rigidity when open. A dirty gate can be cleaned by applying a solvent or lubricant to the hinge (oil, kerosene, white gas), working the hinge until it operates smoothly again, and then dipping the carabiner in boiling water for about 20 seconds to remove the cleaning agent. Finally, remember that a carabiner that has fallen off a cliff onto a hard surface has probably suffered hairline fractures and should be retired. Resist using such a "treasure" found at the base of a cliff.

In fact, you should resist using any equipment discussed in this chapter if you don't know its history. Ropes, harnesses, runners, and carabiners are all vital links in your chain of protection. Second-hand equipment, whether found or passed along without an account of its use, increases the possibility of a weak link in the chain you depend upon for safe climbing.

• 7 •

BELAYING

Belaying is a bedrock technique of climbing safety, a system of setting up the rope to hold a climber in the event of a fall. Belaying works like magic, but like any good magic trick, it takes a lot of practice to do well and requires a basic understanding of underlying principles.

In its simplest form, a belay consists of nothing more than a rope that runs from a climber to another person, the belayer, who is ready to put immediate friction on the rope to stop a fall. Three things make the magic work: a skilled belayer to apply friction to the rope, a stance or anchor to take the forward pull of the fall, and a method of amplifying the friction of the belayer's hand. There are many ways to amplify this friction, a variety of stances, and any number of methods for tying into the anchor. This chapter introduces the principal techniques and major options of belaying, so you can choose the methods that work best in your own climbing. The last section introduces the physics of belaying; you can skip this until you are thoroughly familiar with the procedures.

HOW BELAYS ARE USED IN CLIMBING

Before we move into the details of belay setups and procedures, it might be helpful to get a general feel of how belays are used on a climb (fig. 7-1). For the moment, picture just the essentials of a belay. There are two climbers, each tied into an end of a 150-foot rope. As one climbs, the other belays. The belay is connected to an anchor, a point of secure attachment to the rock or snow. The belayer pays out or takes in rope as the climber ascends, ready to use one of the methods of applying friction in case the climber falls.

Belay setups are usually established on the ground or on a ledge that is reasonably comfortable. One climber takes the lead, belayed from below, and moves up the route to the next desirable spot and sets up a new belay. The climber at the bottom then takes apart the belay and climbs up, belayed from above. The distance between belays is known as a pitch, or a lead. The climbers typically leapfrog their way up so that the one who goes first leads all of the odd-numbered pitches, and follows second on all of the even-numbered pitches. Each climber belays at the top of every pitch he leads, which allows a rest before following the next pitch.

The climber belayed from above—known as the follower, or the second—can climb aggressively, confident that any fall will be held easily by the belayer and will be very short, typically involving only a slight stretching of the rope.

It's a different matter for the leader of a pitch, who is belayed from below and will drop some distance before the rope begins to stop the fall. To reduce the distance of a potential fall, the leader attaches pieces of climbers' hardware—called protection—to the rock on the way up. The leader

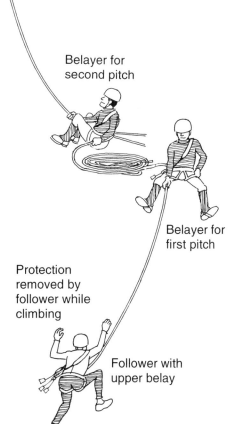

Fig. 7–1. The belay system for two pitches of a climb

tage to pushing the first lead as far as possible, and you can just pick the most convenient intermediate belay spot.

The minimum belay location should have two attributes: good placement for anchors and reasonable comfort. Belayers also try to find a position where they can see the partner they are belaying. And they keep an eye out for rockfall if the climber is above. If there is significant rockfall danger, you might belay from the shelter of an overhang or bulge, or perhaps have your pack ready to hold above you, and wear a hard hat.

attaches a carabiner to each piece of protection and clips the rope inside the carabiner so the rope is free to be pulled through as the ascent continues. Now, a fall can be no more than double whatever the distance the leader is above the highest piece of protection (plus some rope stretch and sometimes belayer movement or a bit of rope slippage at the belay).

The length of each pitch is usually determined by the location of a comfortable, convenient spot to establish the next belay. Being the belayer can be tough work—long, awkward and boring, but requiring nearly constant vigilance—making it essential to find a secure belay spot that is as comfortable as possible. Longer leads are more efficient, so if there are several nice belay ledges within reach of the rope, go for the highest one. The conditions of the moment can change this general rule. You may decide to set up the next belay somewhat early because the drag of the rope through pieces of protection and over rock is becoming too annoying. Or if a huge, enticing ledge is only $1^1/_2$ rope lengths away, there is no advan-

BASIC TECHNIQUES

A climber who is just learning to belay should select and stick to one method, perfecting it to the point that setup is largely automatic. At that stage, some climbers become very opinionated about the choice they've made. But the most experienced climbers often learn other methods and use them whenever they offer an advantage.

As you learn belaying, you will discover your own favorite tools and techniques. However you belay, the methods all boil down to a means of stopping a fall by applying friction to the rope and by resisting the forward pull of the fall.

PREPARING FOR THE PULL OF A FALL

There are two general approaches to belaying, depending upon whether the forward pull of the fall goes first to your body, or directly to the anchor.

Belaying from the anchor: Belaying directly from the anchor (fig. 7-2a) requires, at a minimum, complete confidence that the anchor is bombproof; in short, it will not fail under any conceivable force. If you are using one of the many available belay devices for applying friction to the rope, you must be able to assume a specific brak-

Fig. 7–2. Belaying: a, directly from an anchor; b, from the harness, with support from the anchor.

ing position for a fall. You need to be near the anchor, and of course you should be comfortable for the entire time or your attention will be divided and a poor belay will result. (In belaying from the anchor, there are unique advantages to the Münter hitch as a way to apply friction. The Münter hitch will be covered later in this chapter.)

Belaying from your body: In the other approach, the pull of the fall goes directly to your body (fig. 7-2b). You assume a belay stance by bracing against solid features of the mountain, and back this up with a snug attachment from you to the anchor. Friction on the rope comes from a belay device or Münter hitch attached to the front of the seat harness, or from a wrap of the rope around your hips. Your body, supported by the stance, takes the initial pull of the fall and keeps the anchor—the ultimate line of defense—from being fully tested. The inevitable movement of the belayer a few inches under the force of the fall also helps reduce the forces. If the consequences of a fall have been correctly visualized ahead of time, the impact on the belayer is small. You may be surprised to discover how readily a small belayer can catch a big climber. Belaying from a stance, with the climbing rope running directly to your body, helps prevent ''sleeping at the wheel'' during the sometimes dreary duty of belaying.

Which method is most popular depends in part on both local tradition and geology. In some mountain ranges or on certain routes, you will find belay spots where every available anchor is suspect; here a stance is essential. In other situations there will be a bombproof anchor but poor stances. The belayer may still set up a stance to simplify rope handling, knowing full well that the pull of the fall goes directly to the anchor. The stance can be used almost anytime, even when the stance itself plays a minor role in controlling forces. Belaying directly from the anchor, however, is done *only* when the anchor is believed to be bombproof.

Parts of the setup, and the constant task of rope handling, are the same for every belay, whether it's from your body in a stance or directly from an anchor. All belays depend on applying friction to the rope, and all belays (with occasional exceptions) require an anchor, either to take the pull directly or as backup for a stance.

The belay anchor

As the ultimate security for any belay, the anchor should be able to hold the longest possible fall and the full weight of both climbers. Anchors are essential on rock, snow, and ice for belaying and rappelling. You'll get a few tips here on selecting good anchors for belays, but for full details on finding and using natural features, and on using artificial protection on rock, snow, and ice, study Chapters 10, 12, and 14. This chapter will concentrate on ways to tie in to one or more anchors for belaying.

A large natural feature, such as a tree or pillar of sound rock, is an ideal anchor. However, it's easy to overestimate the stability of large boulders, which may be more lethal than stable. More important than size is the shape of the boulder's bottom, the shape of the socket it is sitting in or the angle of the slope it is on, and the ratio of height to width. Imagine the hidden undersurface and the block's center of gravity: will it pull over under a big load? Test it, but don't send it over the edge.

The beginner should not necessarily accept the first anchors that look good enough, but search widely for simple and obviously solid placements. When placing hardware, bend down, feel deep in cracks, and include everything within arm's length above or to the sides of your ledge. To save time, don't immediately pull out earlier hardware placements that seem less than optimal, as you may find nothing better. If a single bombproof anchor can't be set up, try to establish two or three that in combination will be capable of holding a pull. If you find an old bolt or piton already in place at the belay site, back it up with a second anchor because of the danger that the old placement is weak.

When the belay depends upon a single carabiner, use one locking carabiner or two regular carabiners with the two gates forming an X when held open and the carabiners are aligned (fig. 7-3). In free climbing, avoid chaining carabiners in suc-

Fig. 7–3. How to use two ordinary carabiners instead of a locking carabiner

cession, as a twisting motion relative to each other weakens them and can open a gate.

Tying into the anchor

The belayer ties in to the anchor with the climbing rope itself, using the first few feet of rope as it comes from its tie-in at the belayer's harness. The rest of the rope is available for use by the climber. The belayer faces quite an array of choices when it comes to knots and methods for tying in to the anchor. Let's take a look at them to identify some of the more useful.

One method of dealing with a large natural anchor is the simple technique of looping rope around it and clipping the loop back on itself with a carabiner (in a quasi–girth hitch). Tie an overhand knot in the end of the loop and clip the carabiner through that (fig. 7-4).

When a knot is needed to tie to an anchor carabiner, the figure-8 knot or the clove hitch is usually preferred. The figure-8 is strong, stable, and easy to untie. The clove hitch has the advantage of being adjustable after it is tied, and is the easiest way to back up a stance with a taut line from you to the anchor.

An anchor is often backed up with one or two other anchors. Because of its adjustability, a clove hitch on the carabiner at each anchor is the most convenient way to minimize slack between the anchors (fig. 7-5a). (Make sure the clove hitch is tight, or normal rope play will make it expand and possibly open the carabiner's gate. Beware of any

Fig. 7–4. Anchoring to a large object with a quasi–girth hitch

pull on a clove hitch that makes it slide away from the end of the carabiner, which could also make it expand and open the gate.)

There is quite a disadvantage, however, in tying separate knots in a series of anchor carabiners, as in the series of clove hitches. If the anchor takes the force of a fall, all the impact first goes to a single anchor. The other anchors come into play only if the first one fails.

There are a couple of ways to overcome this disadvantage and spread the load so that more than one anchor takes the initial impact.

One way is to tie a clove hitch to each anchor carabiner, as before—but to run the rope back to a

Fig. 7–5. Tying into several anchors: a, with a series of knots—only one anchor holds weight at any given time; b, so that they all hold weight simultaneously.

locking carabiner at the harness and tie in (with a clove hitch) after every other clove hitch at an anchor (fig. 7-5b). This results in a section of rope tied between your seat harness and each anchor carabiner. You can then adjust the clove hitches to snug up the strand to each carabiner. Then if the anchor takes the force of a fall, the impact will be shared by the multiple placements, and if one fails, no drop results before the others come into play.

Another way to spread the load is the technique of self-equalization, which automatically distributes any force among all the anchors.

Two-point equalizing, using two anchors, is the simplest method of self-equalization (fig. 7-6a). Put a half twist in a high-strength runner (such as one made of Spectra), which divides the runner into two parts, and clip each end into an anchor with a carabiner. Then clip a locking carabiner over the X formed in the middle, from one half of the runner to the other, and tie into that carabiner.

Multipoint equalizing, using any number of anchors, is another technique in setting up a secure belay (fig. 7-6b). Take one high-strength runner, and clip it into the carabiners on each of the three anchors. Grasp the runner between each anchor, twist it 180 degrees, and clip each resulting loop into the main carabiner. Such twists guarantee that the main carabiner is clipped into, and not around, the runner, so that it will stay attached to the runner even if two of the three anchors fail. The smaller the runner, the smaller the drop if one anchor fails. Therefore, if the anchors are widely

Fig. 7–6. Equalization: a, two-point; b, multi-point.

ANGLE	V	TRIANGLE
0°	50%	70%
60°	60%	100%
90°	70%	130%
120°	100%	190%
140°	150%	290%
150°	190%	380%
160°	290%	570%
170°	580%	1100%

Fig. 7–7. The force on two anchors depends upon the method of sharing the force and the angle at the bottom of the sling.

separated, bring them together with other slings before equalizing.

How well an equalization setup reduces the pull on each individual anchor depends on the angle at the bottom where the parts of the runner come together. The smaller the angle, the less force each anchor will have to absorb. As the angle increases, each anchor is subject to an increasing force. Be sure that the angle is always less than 120 degrees. Above that, each anchor will actually be subject to a greater force than if equalization wasn't even used. This is true whether it's two-point or multi-point equalization.

Climbers also use the "triangle" method, instead of equalization, to spread the weight between two separate anchors. In a triangle, the runner simply goes through each carabiner in turn, without returning to the main carabiner between each anchor. Just as in equalization, the angle at the bottom where the two sides of the runner come together is critical. But with triangles, a significantly greater force hits each anchor for any given angle, compared with equalization (fig. 7-7). With

triangles, the maximum angle can only be 60 degrees; beyond that, each anchor faces a greater force than if the method wasn't used at all. And for any given length of runner, the triangle puts more force on the anchors than equalization.

The triangle performs better when it comes to another aspect of hooking into two anchors. If one of the anchors fails in either the equalization or triangle methods, the belay will drop as far as needed to throw the weight onto the remaining anchor. This drop, though usually quite short, hits the remaining anchor with additional force. The drop will be less in a triangle setup, for any given length of runner used, than with equalization. This difference in the length of the drop increases with the length of the sling and with the distance between the two anchors.

Sometimes the length of the tie-in from you to the anchor is critical to the stability of your stance. Until now we have mainly discussed the situation in which the knots are located at the anchor. But if the anchor is out of reach, you can't adjust the knots while in your stance, so precise adjustment is tedious or impossible. The solution is to tie in with a knot only on your harness. Take the rope—after it has run from the harness and simply been clipped through the anchor carabiner—and tie it again at the seat harness. Make the new tie-in with a clove hitch, so you can easily adjust the tension on the rope between you and the anchor. In this option, the rope runs freely around a natural anchor or through a main anchor carabiner (fig. 7-8).

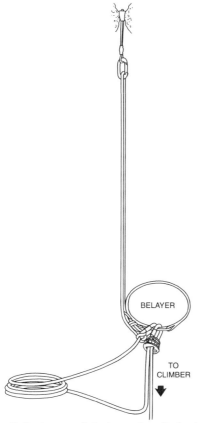

BELAYER

TO
CLIMBER

Fig. 7–8. A second tie-in on the climber's harness to allow convenient adjustment of tension on the anchor rope

The belay stance

If you belay from your harness or body rather than directly from the anchor, you usually will brace against the forward pull of a fall with a solid stance. The stance can help keep the anchor from being fully tested. You will usually support the stance with a short, tight rope to a strong anchor to greatly increase your stability. But for the moment we will consider the strength of the stance alone, based in part upon studies by the Sierra Club. Although the club's experiments used the hip wrap, the results apply to stances with modern belay devices (though perhaps a little on the conservative side). They give a good picture of the comparative value of different stances (fig. 7-9).

Located behind a solid object: In unusually fortunate situations, you can assume the strongest stance of all, directly behind an immovable object, such as a rock protrusion. Don't count on this luck often.

Sitting stances: The most common and versatile is the sitting stance, in which your feet and seat make three solid contacts with the mountain. It is most stable if the rope passes between your feet or legs, for it then resembles a tripod. The tripod's apex is the attachment of the belay to the front of your harness; one leg is your pelvic bones and seat, the other two your own legs. In that configuration, the average person can hold 350 pounds of tension on the rope for several seconds, or an impact about twice as great. Knees are strongest when the angle at the joint is nearly straight (180 to 140 degrees). The stance is only about half as strong if the knees are bent at an angle below 100 degrees, or if the rope runs over the foot support (directed slightly outside the tripod). The stance is suitable for rock, snow, or brush.

Standing stances: In the standing position there are only two points of contact with the rock. With one foot well forward, the average belayer can hold 200 pounds from below, but less than half as much with a pull to the side or with the feet together. Belaying a leader from a standing position (''slingshot'' belay) is extremely weak if the pull is forward. It should be done only with a short tight

Behind solid
object: very strong

Standing: weak

"Sling shot:"
very weak

Three-point,
sitting: strong

Three-point,
leaning: strong

Fig. 7–9. The strength of various types of stance, before adding support from the anchor rope to the anchor, which will take most of the force, or when standing just below the first protection, so that you cannot be pulled over.

Even if your stance fails and you are pulled out of position, you *must* keep control of the rope. If you don't, it means loss of the belay and a disastrous plunge for the climber. Before tying in, visualize the consequences if you are pulled out of what you thought was a solid stance. Ask yourself if you will be able to keep charge of the rope and maintain the belay. The force on you will come from a new direction, pulling you into the straight line between the anchor and where the rope goes over the edge, or between the anchor and the first protection. The momentum of your body will carry you even farther; look to see whether you would strike something.

Imagine the results of being pulled in various directions, sideways or up or down, particularly if you are standing. There is less chance you will be jerked about, and you will be moved less, if you have a short tie-in from you to the anchor. This short tie-in is necessary if the direction of pull will change as the climber ascends. The longer the anchor tie-in, the more powerful and dangerous the pull. You must not be dragged, lifted into the air, or strike anything. It's OK to risk some movement in order to take advantage of a strong rock feature for a stance. But think it through. Visualize the possible consequences if you are pulled from the stance. If a loss of control of the rope is possible, find another solution.

Preparing to belay the follower

Because there are so many things to remember and balance, setting up the belay is one of the slower tasks for beginners. The more aggressively you search for anchors and stances, the more likely you will discover a simple solution. Don't rush the visualization stage. Here are factors to consider as you complete leading a pitch and have just reached a spot to set up a belay for the follower:

Establish an anchor for yourself and clip into it, and then call out ''off belay'' so the follower can stop belaying and start preparing to climb. Then attend to yourself. Take off your pack and the rack of climbing hardware. Put on extra clothes, if necessary, for the long period of staying stationary while you belay.

Search out available options for belay anchors and for a stance.

Visualize the consequences if your stance collapses.

Consider other factors. Assess the rockfall danger. Make the belay comfortable enough so you can belay without distraction. Try to be in position to watch the climber and route as you belay. An experienced climber can establish a belay that is also useful for belaying the next pitch, when the follower moves past and up into the lead.

Pick the best combination of anchor and stance, after weighing all the choices.

Check to be sure that knots are complete, that coils of rope won't snarl or catch on projections, and that your pack is conveniently nearby. For your very first belay, verify with your partner that you know the correct braking position—and that you are belaying the end of the rope that goes to the climber, not the end to the coils. (Partners should check each other's harness buckle and rope tie-in whenever roping up.)

Prepare to belay the next lead as soon as you have belayed the follower up to your position.

Preparing to belay the leader

Belaying the leader is a big change from belaying the follower because the pull is from a new direction, usually above. A new stance is often necessary.

The anchor for belaying the leader must hold a pull toward the first piece of protection, possibly straight up, so your existing anchor may have to be revised or augmented. Fortunately the follower has brought up all the hardware from the pitch below, so you should have plenty of gear to work with. Before setting up your belay, pull in all the slack rope, and pile it neatly to avoid snarls later.

The difference between a strong and weak stance is the direction of the expected pull in comparison with how your legs are placed. By putting in a piece of protection near you that the climber's rope will travel through, you can aim this pull to provide a stronger stance.

Aiming the pull is particularly useful with standing stances. If you are facing the anchor, a simple method is to add another carabiner to the anchor and clip the climbing rope through that. Later, after the climber has put in other protection higher up, this link becomes unnecessary, and you can remove it to reduce rope friction and increase your "feel" of the climber.

The belayer needs to be extra alert when the climbing is difficult right off a ledge because the leader may not be able to get in enough protection to prevent hitting the ledge in case of a fall. In fact, broken ankles are among the most common rock-climbing injuries. Of course, the climber should land with knees bent. Head injuries can be reduced by the belayer "spotting" the climber, preferably while tied in and otherwise ready to belay. Spotting does not mean cushioning the climber's weight with your body, but simply helping the falling climber land upright or preventing his head from hitting the ground.

The "zipper effect" is a concern for both belayer and climber. Whenever possible, the climber should position the lowest piece of protection to prevent this phenomenon, in which the bottom protection pulls out under the forces of a fall, and succeeding pieces up the route are yanked out one by one like the opening of a zippered jacket. To avoid it, the lowest protection should be multidirectional; that is, able to hold a pull from any direction, including outward or upward. If a zipper starts opening, you can only hope that a multidirectional piece of protection has been placed higher up that can put a stop to it. (Chapter 10 includes an illustration of the zipper effect.)

ROPE HANDLING
AND COMMUNICATING

Ideally, when you are belaying the leader, the rope is never taut, which would impede the climber's next move. An alert belayer keeps just a hint of slack and responds immediately to the leader's advance by paying out more rope. When the climbing is easy, more slack is permissible.

As the leader climbs, it is inevitable that some friction will develop along the rope. This rope drag can greatly increase the difficulty of the climb or make the leader stop, creating time-consuming extra belays, often in uncomfortable spots. The problem can be caused by the terrain the climber passed, such as blocks of rock or rope-sized notches, or by poorly placed protection that forces the rope over convexities or into acute angles. Any friction applied by the belayer is multiplied by these, so if the leader tells you that rope drag is a problem, keep a few feet of slack in the rope and do everything possible to eliminate any pull. If the climber falls when there is a lot of friction in the system, the belayer may actually be unsure whether a fall took place. If it is impossible to communicate with the climber, you can find out by letting out a few inches of rope. If the same tension remains, then you are probably holding the climber's weight.

Ideally, when you are belaying a follower, there is no slack in the rope. At the same time, the rope should not be taut, which would hamper the climber's movement and balance.

When belaying a follower up to you, pile the rope where it won't be disturbed later. Don't let loops hang down if there are projections that could snag a loop. If the entire pile must be moved, picking it up is tempting but will produce snarls later. It is best to re-pile the entire rope twice, so the leader's end is on top. If the follower is climbing rapidly, you can take in more rope with each pull by leaning forward or bending over.

Your braking hand must never leave the rope. This is easier when belaying the leader because the leader is pulling up the slack. But when belaying a follower, you pull the slack in against gravity, and when you reset your braking hand, the natural tendency is to lift it off the rope. The correct procedure must be consciously learned (fig. 7-10).

To minimize falling distance, leaders preparing to make difficult moves often place protection well above their harness tie-in and clip in before moving up. This means the direction of rope movement will reverse twice. As you are belaying the leader and letting out rope, you will suddenly find yourself taking in slack as the climber moves up to the

Fig. 7–10. How to take slack in from a follower so the braking hand is always on the rope: a, pull in the rope with both hands; b, extend whichever hand is near your body, and grab both ropes with it, so that; c, the braking hand can slide back toward your body while remaining closed and ready to brake. Although a through c is commonly used with belay devices, another method offers extra security, as when the climber is at a crux. Keep the ropes in steps b and c apart and grab only the braking rope, as shown in the lower row of illustrations (d, e, and f).

protection, then letting it out again as the climber moves past the protection and puts renewed pull on the rope. These switches call for extra attention, especially as this tends to happen at the most difficult spots.

As climber and belayer get farther apart and hearing begins to be difficult, stick exclusively to the set of short commands that have been developed to express essential climbing communications. Prefacing them with explanations or justifications makes them harder to recognize and defeats their purpose. Use the commands alone. They have been chosen so that the sounds and number of syllables produce a distinctive pattern. Toward the end of the rope, shout as loudly as possible and space out each syllable, using very big spaces if there are echoes. In a crowded area, preface commands with your partner's name. Don't expect an audible response; just do your best the first time.

Three problems are common at the end of each pitch, when hearing is most difficult. First, when calling out to your leader the length of rope remaining in the coils, the first syllable is often lost, and if normal word order is used, the leader hears only ''—ty feet.'' Instead, invert the word order and pronounce each digit separately: ''Feet: . . . three . . . zero,'' for 30 feet. The climber will pause upon the first word and have a better chance of understanding the remainder. Second, when the leader completes a pitch and calls ''Off belay,'' do not respond with ''Belay off'' to indicate you heard him, as is the natural reaction of a beginner. ''Belay off'' means you have taken apart your belay and the rope coils are ready to be pulled up, and you won't be ready to shout that command truthfully for a while yet. Third, avoid the impatient question ''On belay?'' unless a truly inordinate amount of time has passed. Usually the leader, at work on setting up anchors, is out of earshot anyway.

Commands are sometimes transmitted by rope pulls, but there is no universal system. Because of rope stretch at the end of long leads, it's necessary to greatly exaggerate the pulls. A simple tug will seldom be felt at the other end. Take in all slack and for each signal, yank 1 foot or more, holding it tight for awhile before releasing the tension. If there is much friction, pulls may not be distinguishable from normal rope movements. The most common commands correspond to the number of syllables in these verbal equivalents: one pull means ''Slack,'' two means ''Up rope,'' and three means ''Belay on.''

In reality the follower often decides when the belay is ready, based upon a partner's known rope-handling habits. Regular partners familiar with each other's habits can dispense with all normal commands, which is more aesthetic.

APPLYING FRICTION TO THE ROPE

In any belay method, the rope from the climber goes to a belay device or Münter hitch or around the belayer's hips, and then to the belayer's braking hand. This braking hand produces the belay, the controllable friction that is multiplied by a factor of as high as fourteen by the belay method and stops a falling climber.

Belay devices

Belay devices amplify the friction of the braking hand by passing the rope through an opening and wrapping it around a post. The opening guarantees a minimum of wrap, or bend, in the rope to produce enough friction on the post. The post is a locking carabiner or part of the device itself. The opening must be large enough to allow the device to touch the carabiner.

To stop a fall, the belayer pulls back on the free end of the rope to create a separation of at least 90 degrees between the rope entering the device and the rope leaving it. Nothing must be in the way of your braking hand or elbow carrying out this critical task, and it must not require an unnatural body twist or motion. The simplest way to learn to do this conveniently in all situations is to clip the device into a locking carabiner on your harness (currently the most popular belay method in the United States) rather than directly to the anchor. In this section on belay devices, we will stick to a description of their use when attached to the climber's harness.

Basic voice commands used by climbers:

Follower:	"That's me"	You have pulled up all the slack in the rope and are now tugging on my body; don't pull any more.
Belayer:	"Belay on"	I am belaying you.
Climber:	"Climbing"	I am, or will resume, moving up.
Belayer:	"Climb"	Response to "Climbing."
Climber:	"Slack"	Give me some slack in the rope and leave it out until I call "Climbing." (If you want to indicate how much slack you need, the command would be "Slack X feet," with X being the amount of slack.)
Climber:	"Up rope"	(Usually to upper belayer.) There is slack in the rope; pull it in.
Climber:	"Tension"	(Usually to upper belayer.) Take up all slack and hold my weight. (Should be used sparingly by beginners, to avoid overdependence on rope. Say "Watch me" instead.)
Climber:	"Falling!"	Assume your braking position and brace for a pull on the rope.
Belayer:	"Halfway"	About half of the rope remains.
Leader:	"How much rope?"	What length of rope remains?
Belayer:	"Feet … four … zero"	Forty feet of rope remains; find a belay soon (best used when 50 to 20 feet remain).
Leader:	"Off belay"	I am secure and no longer need your belay. Take it apart and prepare to follow the pitch.
Anyone:	"OK"	I heard you.
Follower:	"Belay off"	(After taking apart the belay.) You may pull in all the slack and remaining coils when you are ready.
Anyone:	"Rock!" "Ice!"	(Very loudly, immediately, and repeatedly until falling object stops; mandatory.) Falling objects. Look up or take cover.
Anyone:	"Rope"	A rappel rope is about to be thrown down by another party. Look up or take cover.

Climbers also use some discretionary voice commands, depending on local custom or prior agreement with a climbing partner. These are examples, and many idiosyncratic variations are also used.

Leader:	"Pro in"	I have just clipped into the first protection. Or I have clipped into protection located above my harness tie-in, so the direction of rope movement will reverse twice as I move up through a difficult spot.
Climber:	"Protection" or "Cleaning"	I am placing or cleaning protection and will not move up for awhile.
Climber:	"Good belay" or "Watch me"	I anticipate a fall or difficult move.
Climber:	"On top"	I have passed the difficulty.

Contrary to a popular misconception, there is no automatic clamping effect with a properly designed belay device. Your hand is the ultimate source of friction, and without your braking hand on the rope, there is no belay. The total friction is determined by the strength of your grip, the total number of degrees in the bends or turns the rope makes, and the rope's internal resistance to bending and deforming against the sides of the device and carabiner.

There are a number of popular belay devices (fig. 7-11). One general type may be referred to as an aperture device: It simply provides an aperture through which a bight (loop) of rope is pushed and then clipped to the locking carabiner on your harness or at the anchor. In one widely used version of this type, the aperture consists of a slot, or slots, in a metal plate. (The original and best known of these is the Sticht plate [fig. 7-11a].) In another version, the aperture is a cone-shaped tube (fig. 7-11b).

The figure-8 device (not to be confused with the figure-8 knot) was originally designed only for rap-pelling, not belaying. Some figure-8s now serve double-duty, for both rappelling and belaying. Figure-8s are seen in three different configurations as belay devices. One is the standard rappel configuration (fig. 7-11f). Another is set up like the Bachli (fig. 7-11e), described below. If the hole in the small end of the figure-8 is the size of a typical aperture device hole, it can also be used similarly to a slot or tube (fig. 7-11c). Make certain that your figure-8 was intended for belaying use by the manufacturer; most are not.

The Bachli device (fig. 7-11d) is, in appearance, a sort of streamlined figure-8. The bight of rope goes up through the large hole and is then clipped into a locking carabiner attached both to your harness and to the small hole in the device.

Your tie-in to the anchor should be on the braking-hand side when using a belay device. This way, your body rotation under the force of a fall will assist, rather than hinder, you in separating the ropes.

In belaying a lead climber, try to prepare for the possibility that before placing the first piece of pro-

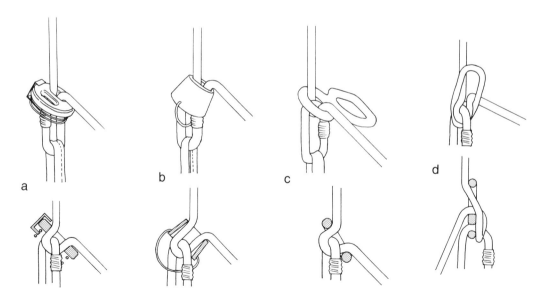

Fig. 7–11. Major categories of belay device: a, slot; b, tube; c, figure-8 in aperture configuration; d, Bachli; e, figure-8 in Bachli configuration; f, figure-8 in rappel configuration.

tection, the leader could fall, plunging below your position. The braking hand should be on the opposite side of this possible fall, or you won't be able to separate the ropes entering and leaving the device.

Belayers rarely wear gloves when using a belay device, in part because the device itself provides a greater proportion of the total friction. However, rope burns are a possibility, although they seem to be rare.

When taking in or letting out slack with an aperture device (slot or tube), keep the ropes strictly parallel. Otherwise, the rope will pull the device up against the carabiner, and braking begins. Eventually the practice becomes automatic.

Among devices, slots and tubes produce the least friction in routine rope handling, which allows you to take in rope faster when the climber is on easy ground, and a slightly improved feel for small movements of the climber and elimination of slack. The Bachli configuration, however, generates less friction than slots and tubes when it holds a fall. This characteristic lends the Bachli to use on

e

f

ice and snow, where stances and anchors are usually weaker and would benefit from a lower force, and where the consequences of a longer fall are often less important.

A belayer is called upon not just to stop falls, but to hold the climber stationary under tension, or lower him to a ledge. Devices vary significantly in how easily they perform these tasks. Slot devices require the least force to hold the climber's weight, but are the least smooth in lowering the climber.

Slots and tubes can be attached to a tether to keep them from sliding out of reach. Some of these devices include a hole for attaching the tether. A tether to your harness must be long enough so it doesn't interfere with belaying in any direction.

Like any piece of critical equipment made of metal, a belay device that is dropped a significant distance should be retired because internal stresses could cause it to break when holding a big fall.

Hard-anodized devices tend to glaze the outermost surface of the rope when stopping a fall, but this effect is purely cosmetic and not harmful. (The metallurgic process of hard-anodizing produces a thin layer of aluminum oxide whose surface is hard and microscopically pitted, and appears dull gray, black, or brown.)

Belay devices are also used for rappelling. Slot devices produce a jerky ride that puts unnecessarily high loads on the anchor. However, the slot design that has a spring may be OK, and tube devices may be acceptably smooth. The Bachli device and figure-8s are the smoothest for rappelling. However, figure-8s put one twist in the rope for every 10 feet of descent, producing snarls in the coils later.

The Münter hitch

The Münter hitch is a very effective method of using only the rope and a carabiner to provide the friction necessary to stop a fall. This method requires a large pear-shaped locking carabiner in order to allow the knot to pass through the interior. It amplifies the effect of your braking hand with the friction both of rope on rope and of rope on carabiner. When attached to the front of your harness it works much like a belay device. Although no belay method is foolproof, the Münter hitch requires the least skill and attention.

The Münter hitch is the only traditional belay method that provides sufficient friction regardless of the angle between the ropes entering and leaving it (fig. 7-12). This offers a number of advantages:

• No special braking position is required. Consider the situation of a belayer who cannot see the climber and is distracted at the moment of a fall. The belayer, caught by surprise, might merely squeeze the rope at the start, rather than immediately yanking it into the angle required by all other methods. This situation is unusual, but could occur at any time. The Münter hitch would hold. The other methods may not.
• If all of the slack rope is hanging down a wall, you may be unable to raise your braking hand high enough, as required by a standard belay device, to arrest a follower fall. The problem is caused by the weight of the rope, the extra force exerted by the falling climber, and the difficult arm position. But with a Münter hitch, it doesn't matter (fig. 7-13).

The friction of the Münter hitch is also unique in being less with the ropes 180 degrees apart than when 0 degrees apart. This usually means its friction is relatively less for leader falls than follower falls. But in absolute terms it often provides more friction than any other belay method, regardless of the angle between the ropes. This high friction means a quicker stop to a fall.

75% Friction

100 % Friction

Fig. 7–12. The friction provided by the Münter hitch does not depend greatly upon the angle between the ropes.

Fig. 7–13. The Münter hitch works when the ropes must be hanging down a wall.

The Münter hitch has some drawbacks. Its friction, often higher than other methods, means more impact on a leader's protection and more danger that poor placements will pull out. It kinks the rope more than any other method, producing snarls in the last few feet of rope after several pitches, especially if the same person always leads. To unsnarl the rope, shake it out while it is hanging free. After a big fall, the outermost layer of the sheath is glazed (which, like the effect of hard-anodized devices, is probably only cosmetic). The Münter hitch isn't good for rappelling because it twists the rope once for every 5 feet of descent, and makes ropes very fuzzy if used regularly.

Every time the direction of pull on the hitch reverses, the entire knot first flip-flops through the carabiner oval. This can get a bit awkward when the leader clips into protection above, moves up toward it, and then passes it, because it requires the belayer to pay out, take in, and pay out rope in rapid succession, reversing the direction of pull on the Münter hitch each time. For a fall of a follower, or of a leader below a piece of protection, the Münter hitch produces an additional drop of 6 inches, as the knot pulls through the carabiner, before braking begins.

You may run across the Münter hitch under a variety of names, such as the friction hitch, Italian hitch, half ring bend, carabiner hitch, running R, half-mast belay, and UIAA method. It was introduced in Europe in 1973 as the *halbmastwurf sicherung* (half clove-hitch belay), now abbreviated as HMS. (Chapter 6 gives details on tying the Münter hitch.)

The hip wrap

The hip wrap (fig. 7-14) amplifies friction by passing the rope around your back—just below the top of your hips—and around your sides. Its main advantage is the speed with which you can belay a follower who is moving rapidly over easy ground. It can be set up quickly and requires no hardware.

The use of the hip wrap in climbing on upper fifth-class rock is rapidly declining. Because your back and sides provide most of the friction on the rope, you must wear a lot of clothes, preferably several thick layers—highly undesirable in hot climates. Even a short leader fall can cut through a polypropylene jacket. Although the belayer will feel the pain from the burn as it is produced, the fall will be completely arrested before he or she has time to react to the pain.

Because your hands provide a greater proportion of friction than in other methods, gloves are essential. Contrary to the usual expectation, burns

are reduced with a tighter grip and less rope slippage (because slower rope velocity and less rope slippage generates less heat), another reason for wearing gloves. However, gloves can make your hands damp and soft, the opposite of what is necessary for difficult rock climbing.

There are additional problems with the hip wrap: if the climbing rope runs over the anchor attachment, it may be burned. In a big fall, the outermost layer of the rope sheath may be glazed and covered with melted fabric from your clothes. Because more time is required to attain the braking position and because it has the least braking friction of any method, the hip wrap more often results in rope slippage, and the climber usually falls

Fig. 7–14. The hip wrap is often used for the impromptu belaying of a fast-moving follower.

farther. If your stance fails, you will probably also lose control of the rope, which is less likely with other methods.

To catch a fall with the hip wrap, your elbow must be straight before you begin to grip hard (fig. 7-15), so that bone and not muscle resists the pull of the rope. (Your natural reaction will be to grip the rope first, but this may pull your arm into a helpless position, requiring you to let go and grasp the rope again.) Then bring your braking arm across in front of your body, to increase the amount of wrap for maximum friction. An optimal braking position can only be learned with practice, for which schools and climbing clubs have constructed belay towers.

Several precautions must be observed to prevent the hip wrap from unwrapping in a fall. With frequent practice, they should become automatic.

1. Run your anchor attachment from the side opposite the braking hand (fig. 7-16). If you put the line to the anchor on the same side as the braking hand, the rotation of your body under the impact of a climber's fall can unwrap the hip wrap, decreasing friction and stability.

2. If you are facing toward the rock, belaying the leader, have the braking hand on the same side as any fall that could happen before the leader puts in the first piece of protection. If the fall is on the opposite side and the leader drops below you, the rope could be unwrapped from your hip.

3. Clip a control carabiner on your harness anytime the climbing rope goes straight up or down from your hips (fig. 7-17). The carabiner goes well forward of the hip bone, on the same side as the rope coming from the climber. Clipping the rope into this carabiner keeps the rope where you want it, at your hip, and also counteracts body rotation.

Fig. 7–15. The correct braking arm position for the hip wrap must be achieved before braking begins, left; *or the arm will be pulled into a helpless position,* right.

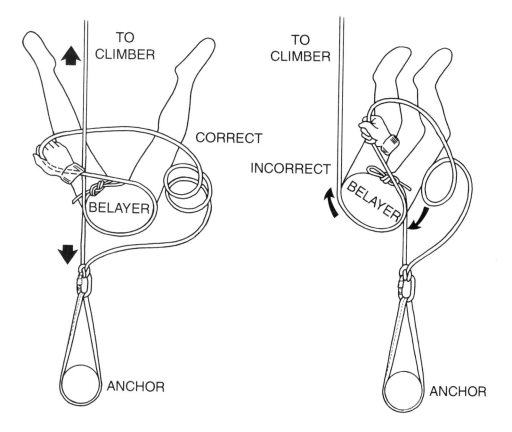

Fig. 7–16. *The anchor attachment on the side opposite the braking hand,* left, *keeps the hip belay from unwrapping.*

4. If you don't use a control carabiner, take advantage of your anchor attachment to keep the climbing rope from being pulled over your head or under your seat. If the pull will come from below, put the rope above the anchor attachment. If the pull will come from above, put the rope below the anchor line.

Of all braking methods, the hip wrap exerts the smallest force for a given grip of the braking hand. In a fall, this lower force might preserve questionable protection when any other method would pull it out. This would be extremely important if both your stance and anchor were weak. On the other hand, the climber will fall farther, increasing the danger of hitting something.

Fig. 7–17. *A control carabiner on the harness keeps the hip belay from unwrapping.*

Fig. 7–18. A variant of the hip wrap, in which the forward pull of a fall goes directly to the anchor

As with belay devices, it is possible to arrange the hip wrap so that the forward pull of the fall goes directly to the anchor (fig. 7-18). This provides the same advantages as belaying directly from the anchor with a device. The friction of rope running against your back is replaced by the climbing rope's wrap of at least 90 degrees around the carabiner, a few inches to 1 foot or more behind your back. (If you are far from the anchor, a big fall could pull you toward it, especially on snow or wet rock.)

Fig. 7–19. Major belay options

METHOD	REQUIRES	FEATURES, ADVANTAGES	DISADVANTAGES
Resisting the pull of the fall			
Belay attached to harness	Ledge permitting a stance	Force is absorbed before reaching anchor	Relationship between stance and anchor must be carefully visualized
Belay attached directly to anchor	Bombproof anchor	Simple set-up (except hip wrap); easy to tie off	Anchor not always available, or conveniently placed for rope-handling
Applying friction to the rope			
Belay device	Device, locking carabiner	Some devices useful for rappelling	Figure-8s kink rope to some extent
Münter hitch	Large pear-shaped locking carabiner	Braking possible with ropes parallel	Slightly slower passing knot through carabiner; kinks rope; follower fall of at least 6 inches
Hip wrap	Protective clothes, gloves	Least braking friction; fast taking in rope	Burns possible unless much clothing worn; complex precautions required; greater chance of loss of control of rope if stance collapses

Fig. 7–20. Common beginner problems

PROBLEM	CORRECTION
Removes braking hand from braking rope (especially with hip belay)	Use the rope-handling procedure shown in fig.10,forcing yourself to be conscious of your braking hand at all times, until the technique becomes automatic.
Produces rope tension on leader	Watch leader or free-hanging sections of rope (if any) near your belay; keep hand on rope to feel movements; react quickly.
When belaying follower, unable to pull in rope fast enough	Bend over and extend your full reach for each cycle.
Great difficulty communicating when separated by a rope length	Stick to standard or agreed-upon commands; omit explanations; space out words more

OTHER TECHNIQUES

DECIDING WHEN TO ROPE UP

Climbers don't rope up and belay for every exposed place. There are occasions when it may be safer not to, even though you might wish you could. Rubble-strewn slopes are much more hazardous when dragging a rope. Some terrain has no suitable points for anchors. If you must pass through an area subject to rockfall or avalanche, roping is usually secondary to speed. Very experienced climbers may climb on solid rock well below their limit, "third-classing" what may nominally be a fifth-class route.

Anyone in the party may ask for a belay at any time, and must receive it immediately and without complaint from other members of the party. The primary exception is when roping up would significantly decrease the safety of the entire party. As difficulty and exposure increase on an alpine climb, natural differences in ability tend to spread the party out. It is just then, as the anticipated limit of the weakest member is approached, that the party must concentrate on keeping together, to enable roping up easily.

TYING OFF THE BELAY

There's at least one aspect of belaying you hope you'll never have to use: tying off the belay in order to help an injured partner. If your climbing partner is seriously injured and other climbers are nearby, it is usually best to let them help while you continue to belay. By staying there you could also help in raising or lowering the victim, if necessary. But if the two of you are alone, it is rare but conceivable that you may want to tie off the climbing rope to remove yourself from the belay system, so you can investigate, help your partner, or go for help.

If you are using a belay device or Münter hitch attached directly to the anchor, you need only to prevent rope from sliding through the belay. Simply form a knot such as the clove hitch in the braking rope and clip it to another carabiner on the anchor. You can now take your hand off the braking rope and it will be held by the knot.

If you are using a stance, with a belay device or Münter hitch attached to your harness, it is possible to tie off using one hand. However, it is easier and safer to put a clove hitch in the braking rope and clip it temporarily to your harness. Then while the clove hitch is doing the job of holding the belay rope, attach a normal sling to the climbing rope with a friction knot (prusik or Klemheist). Clip the sling into the anchor, chaining slings if necessary to make the connection long enough. If you can't reach the anchor, attach another sling with a friction knot to the rope that is holding you to the anchor, and join the slings with a carabiner. Transfer tension from the belay to the anchor by letting rope slip through the belay. But first tell the climber to expect being lowered a few inches, and not to worry.

With the hip wrap it may be impossible to tie off with one hand while in the braking position, so the first step may be to free yourself from holding the weight. Wrap the rope coming from your braking hand around the foot opposite the braking hand, keeping your knee locked (fig. 7-22). You can then proceed with both hands, attaching a sling to the climbing rope with a friction knot and clipping the sling to the anchor.

In any case, you should eventually back up the arrangement by tying the climbing rope itself directly to the anchor, with a figure-8 knot on a separate carabiner (fig. 7-21).

SELF-BELAYED SOLO CLIMBING

Self-belay devices, which allow roped solo climbing, have begun to appear. It is worn by the climber, and works like a ratchet, sliding up the rope during the climb, but not down it in a fall. To lead a pitch, the rope is first anchored at the bottom, and the climber protects as he ascends. Then

Fig. 7–21. Tying off a fallen climber

Fig. 7–22. Freeing the hands before tying off the climber when using the hip wrap

the rope is anchored at the top, and the climber rappels. Finally, the climber removes the bottom anchor and climbs the pitch a second time, retrieving the protection as he goes.

This is not just another belaying alternative to be chosen on occasion. It is a different form of climbing, requiring a commitment to relearn many fundamentals. Shortcomings compared to a belay by a live partner are almost inevitable. Read the manufacturer's literature critically, and practice in a safe situation. Is the belay static? Does it work if you fall in a horizontal or head-down position? When climbing, does the rope feed automatically, without producing extra slack or drag, especially at the top of a pitch, or on a traverse? Can you clip into protection above your waist without trouble? To fully evaluate the device, you should understand the basic physics of belaying, as described in the next section.

THE PHYSICS OF BELAYING:
WHAT HAPPENS WHEN THE CLIMBER FALLS

Many years ago, the leader's main fear in a fall was the very real possibility that the rope would break. Ropes were made of the natural fiber hemp, and if a belayer held on too strongly, the rope would snap, even in a fall that by today's standard is not long. To prevent this, early editions of this book said that beginners had to study the theory of something called dynamic belay technique and practice it every year by holding simulated falls with heavy weights. Today, this is no longer necessary. Everyone takes for granted that a belay, correctly set up and executed, will eventually hold any fall. Modern ropes seldom, if ever, break (although they can be cut by a sharp edge of rock).

Today, the leader's main fear in a fall is the failure of his *protection*. Protection is explained fully in Chapter 10, but its general purpose is shown in figure 7-23. The topmost piece of protection stops a leader fall. If it is pulled out of the mountain, then the climber falls much farther, until the next protection gets a chance to hold the fall. Unfortunately, the protection is the weakest link in the belay system. This is partly because the force on the protection is greater than anywhere else, 50 percent greater than in the rope between the top protection and the climber. But the major factor is the uncertainty of the protection itself. Usually the limiting factor is not the breaking strength of the hardware, but the firmness of its fit in the rock and the quality of the rock (or ice) itself. Climbing lore is replete with true horror stories of supposedly "bombproof" protection that pulled out of the mountain in a fall, or even after a firm test tug. Therefore, the older belay techniques for reducing forces, described below, are still relevant. They are not necessary to save the rope and the climber's life, but many experienced climbers know them and occasionally use them to protect the protection. Be forewarned: there are few simple rules. Many decisions involve some trade-off between benefit and risk. The best choice is seldom clear. However, if you understand how a belay works,

Fig. 7-23. If the topmost protection fails, the climber will fall an additional distance, which is twice the distance to the next protection down.

you can, at least, decide what would be a bad choice in certain situations.

We will progress from simple concepts of belay physics to complex ones. A little history can illustrate the principles.

WHAT DETERMINES THE FORCES IN A FALL

Static belay

The simplest belay is the one the word originally meant. The sailor wraps rope around a cleat so that it cannot be pulled; the earliest climbers wrapped rope around or over a boulder or rock horn or the like, hoping for the same result. The only difference between this and tying the rope directly to an anchor was that the rope could be fed out or taken in without untying and retying a knot. Today, a firm grip on the rope, coupled with a sufficiently small protected fall, produces the same functional result—no rope is pulled through the belay. By definition, this is a *static* belay. In fact, most falls today are held by static belays.

In a static belay we encounter the strangest truth in all of belay theory. The forces are determined only by the distance of the fall, divided by the length of the rope between climber and belayer (see fig 7-24). This number is so important it has a name: the *fall factor*. It is a pure number, independent of the scale, such as feet, used to calculate it. Thus, for example, a 20-foot fall on 100 feet of rope has the same fall factor as a 2-foot fall on 10 feet of rope: 0.2. Both falls produce the same force in a static belay, if the climber's weight and the rope's characteristics are identical. If a climber falls before placing any protection, the fall factor is 2, the maximum possible. No matter whether the climber was just above the belayer, or if he was at the top of a 150-foot pitch on an ice face, the resultant forces are the same (neglecting friction on the rock and in the system, air resistance, etc.). The energy of the longer fall is absorbed by the proportionally longer rope.

The rope's characteristics are crucial, because in a static belay, the rope absorbs nearly all of the energy of the fall. The more the rope stretches, the

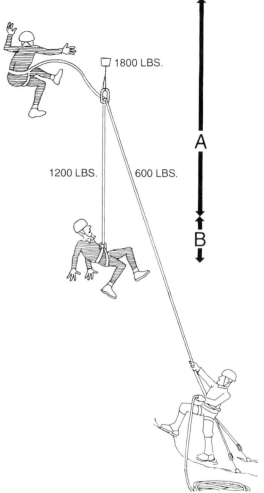

Fig. 7–24. Fall factor is defined as the fall length A, divided by the length of rope between the climber and belayer. (Slack rope contributes to A. B is due to rope stretch and/or slippage at the belay.)

lower the forces become. The effect is dramatic. An old hemp rope stretches little, producing forces so high that it will break if the fall factor is greater than about 0.25 and the belay is static! A modern climbing rope stretches so much that no fall should exceed its strength if the rope is new and undamaged. Therefore, manufacturers no longer specify rope strength by the force required to break it, but by the number of standard static falls it will hold before breaking. The standard is administered by the Union Internationale des Associations d'Alpinisme (UIAA). In order to pass this test, a rope must hold at least five such falls, spaced five minutes apart. The maximum force on the protection must not exceed 2,700 pounds (1,800 pounds for a half rope) on the first fall. However, this is still basically a rope-strength test. Because it uses a static belay and the extremely high fall factor of 1.7, it does not show the forces produced by real belays of typical falls. The only fall length tested is 16 feet long.

If all belays were static, fall factor alone would determine the forces of a fall, and forces could be controlled quite simply. The rule would be: it is more important to place protection at the beginning of a pitch, than at the end. This is because a given fall produces the highest force early in the pitch, the lowest force at the top. Although it is still good to keep that rule in mind, the forces in a real fall are reduced by two other factors. They constitute the difference between the static belay of the sailor and the actual belay given by the climber. These are: movement of the belayer, and friction on the rope at the belay. We will introduce them in their historical context.

The early climber's equivalent of a "cleat," a rock feature around which to belay a rope, was not always conveniently located near a place to stand or sit. The belayer, therefore, often substituted his own body for the cleat. It was quickly realized that if the belayer moved under the force of the fall, the force was significantly reduced. Sometimes called the *resilient belay*, this had one problem: the greater the movement, the greater the chance of collapse and total failure. Some authorities encouraged belayer movement, others warned against it. It is not surprising that up to the middle of the twentieth century, the situation was summed up in the golden rule of climbing, "the leader must not fall."

But world-famous climbers did in fact survive leader falls, which the theory of the day said should have broken their ropes. Some suspected that rope slip in the hands of their belayer played a role in saving their lives. But this was considered

to be a partial loss of control of the rope, embarrassingly close to total failure of the belay. Its implications were seldom even discussed.

Dynamic belay

The first real breakthrough in belaying was the full realization of the value of substituting a frictional grip on the rope for a static belay. When the rope was pulled through a belayer's gloved hand, the climber decelerated slowly. The energy of the fall, instead of being absorbed in a small fraction of a second, was spread out and thereby reduced. The Sierra Club, in the 1930s and 1940s, demonstrated the value of the new *dynamic belay* theoretically, experimentally, and by putting it into actual practice. It was so successful that it allowed modern rock climbing to begin in Yosemite. The new golden rule became, "the rope must run."

There is a fundamental trade-off in a dynamic belay. It decreases the forces on the top protection at the expense of a longer fall and a greater risk of hitting something before being stopped by the belay. However, the benefit can be surprisingly great, as you can see from figure 7-25, which shows the effect with modern ropes. For example, if the climber is 8 feet directly above the protection

Fig. 7–25. The trade-off in a dynamic belay

and 32 feet from the belayer, the fall factor is 0.5. If rope slippage at the belay increases the fall 33 percent (5 feet), the force on the protection will be reduced by almost half. The benefit is greatest at high fall factors, which is also when rope slippage is most likely to occur. (This graph is based upon the current standard theory of belaying developed forty years ago by Wexler, which includes several simplifying assumptions, including simplifying the rope's characteristics and neglecting friction in the system and between the climber and the rock).

Modern kernmantle ropes stretch so well that they removed the necessity for the beginner to learn dynamic belay theory and technique. The golden rule ''the rope must run'' passed into history. Indeed, kernmantle ropes are frequently called ''dynamic ropes.'' But that does not mean a dynamic belay—rope slippage—never occurs; it means only that it is now very uncommon. Rope slippage is still possible if the fall factor is high, or the belay friction is low. In either case, the pull on the rope exceeds the friction in the belay, so the rope slides.

We have just considered separately the three factors that determine the forces of a fall: fall factor, belayer movement, and belay friction. To see how they work together, we will use the graph in figure 7-26. A given fall held by a given belay

method produces a certain tension in the rope between the climber and the protection, which can be calculated using the current standard theory. The result is a point in this graph. A series of falls at different fall factors produces a line in the graph. In other words, each line shows the force produced by a given type of belay, at different fall factors. The solid lines represent static belays wherein all of the energy is absorbed only by rope stretch. There are two lines, showing the great difference between modern kernmantle and early hemp ropes. The dashed lines show the effect of 1 foot of belayer movement, holding an 8-foot fall, with each rope. The two horizontal lines show the effect of dynamic belays with two different levels of friction. These levels are the highest and lowest friction that have been suggested by various authorities in the past twenty years.

To illustrate, consider the previous example, whose fall factor was 0.5. If the belay is static, the peak tension is 1,200 pounds. If the belayer moves one foot during the fall, the tension is reduced by only 75 pounds. The ''strong dynamic belay'' in the graph reduces the force to 900 pounds, and the ''weak'' one reduces the force to 400 pounds. (The fall would be 2 and 12 feet longer, respectively). The same dynamic belays would, be definition, result in the same tensions in a hemp rope, regardless of fall factor. Of course, a static belay would break the hemp rope.

In summary, the friction applied to the rope at the belay places the real practical upper limit on the forces that a fall can produce. In other words, rope slippage at the belay dissipates excessive force, just like a safety valve on a boiler dissipates excessive pressure. How the belay is chosen and applied determines the force at which the rope slips, just as how the valve is designed determines the pressure at which it opens. Let's look more closely at how the belayer's ''safety valve'' works.

WHAT THE BELAYER CAN CONTROL

Three factors, which are at least theoretically under your control, determine the amount of friction that your belay will produce. The strength of your hand grip is one factor. Since the belay ampli-

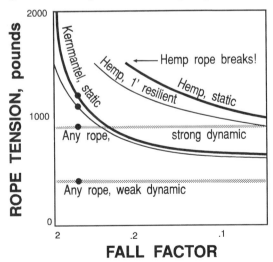

Fig. 7–26. Comparison of the major belay types

Fig. 7–27. Comparison of some dynamic belay methods

fies this grip, your choice of belay method is a second factor. Both of these factors are shown in figure 7-27. For example, virtually anyone can grip a rope hard enough to hold a 50-pound pull. A standard slot device or the Münter hitch will amplify this grip so that your belay can hold a 350-pound steady pull before the rope begins to slide. (But as you grip harder, the Münter hitch grips harder than slot devices do, as shown by the diverging lines.) Figure-8 devices come in a wide variety of sizes and surface finishes, so their belay varies from 250 to 430 pounds, with a 50-pound grip. A standard slot device with two carabiners holds 700 pounds. (Different ropes can produce somewhat different numbers. For example, using a half rope, forces are reduced by an average of 20 percent.)

The third factor determining belay friction is the angle between the ropes entering and leaving the belay device or the Münter hitch, or the total number of degrees in all the wraps of the rope in the hip belay. Varying this factor produces a continuous change in the total grip, with no angle at which a sudden change occurs, for any belay method.

The belay method is the most important of the three factors, because it operates for every fall. Hand strength and rope angle can usually be varied only when a fall is expected by the belayer. Taken by surprise, a belayer will react as he has trained himself to do, with full braking efforts.

Although you can predetermine the level of friction to some extent, it would be an overstatement to say that you can precisely control it. Probably the most you can do is to seek to avoid the extremes. High friction is justified whenever protection is known to be bombproof. Low friction might be called for when protection and anchors are poor, or rope drag (acting just like the belay itself) is very high, or for a very long fall on uncertain protection, provided the extra fall length is not itself a hazard.

Most belays are chosen and executed by a given belayer in that belayer's customary way, to allow concentration on other aspects of climbing, as it should be. But armed with a knowledge of how belays work, informed climbers can recognize extreme conditions and may decide to vary their belay accordingly.

◆ 8 ◆

RAPPELLING

Rappelling can be so easy and exhilarating that you forget what a serious undertaking it really is. It's an indispensable activity in climbing, but it's also one of the more dangerous. If you learn it carefully from the start, you should have no trouble using this technique for sliding down a rope, controlling your speed with friction on the line. You will be able to descend almost any climbing pitch on rappel and, in fact, rappelling will be the only way to get down some faces of rock or ice.

You can get a sense of the danger by considering that as you rappel down a high cliff, full body weight on the rope, your life depends all the way on the anchor to hold the rope and on you to use the correct technique. If you fail or the anchor fails, you fall. Unlike belaying, where a large force comes on the system only if you fall, the force on the rappel system is always there. Despite the danger, it's easy to become cocky and careless after you learn how simple rappelling can be, and the exhilaration can encourage hazardous technique.

Coming down from a climb, there's often a choice between rappelling and downclimbing. Sometimes rappelling is the fastest and safest way to descend a particular pitch, but many times it is not. Think it through, considering the terrain, the weather, how much time is available, and the strength and experience of the party. If you decide to rappel, do it safely and efficiently. One of the hidden dangers of rappelling is that it can waste an awful lot of time in the hands of inexperienced rappellers.

RAPPEL SYSTEMS

A rappel system has four basic requirements: a rope, an anchor, someone to rappel, and a means of applying friction to the rope. The midpoint of the rope is looped through the anchor (a point of attachment to the rock or snow), with the two ends hanging down the descent route. The rappeller slides down this doubled rope and retrieves it from below by pulling on one end.

In mechanical rappel systems, the doubled rope passes through a friction device attached to your seat harness. In non-mechanical systems, friction is provided by wrapping the rope around your body. In either case, your braking hand grasps the rope to control the amount of friction. Gloves are usually worn to prevent rope burns.

Short rappels can be handled with just one rope, but longer rappels need the extra length of two ropes tied together, usually with a double fisherman's knot. The ropes are joined next to the anchor, with the two loose ends hanging down the cliff. With a two-rope rappel, you can even join ropes of different diameters, mating, for example, an 11-millimeter line with a 9-millimeter.

On rare occasions, climbers use a single-strand rappel, in which the rope is simply tied at one end to the anchor.

136

MECHANICAL SYSTEMS

Most climbers use a mechanical system (fig. 8-1) as their principal rappelling method, and all operate essentially the same. The two strands of rope are run through a rappel device attached to your harness. As you begin the rappel and gravity pulls you downward, the rope slides through the device. Your braking hand controls this natural pull by adjusting the amount of friction on the rope as it runs through the device. It does this through a combination of variations in grip and hand position. With some setups, you get additional friction by wrapping the rope partly around your back. You control the speed of descent, and you can come to a stop anytime you wish.

It takes less effort to produce friction at the top of a rappel than at the bottom, because the weight of the rope hanging below you puts added friction on the rappel device. This is especially so on very steep or overhanging rappels where most of the rope hangs free. But no matter how little grip strength may be required to control your descent, your braking hand must never leave the rope. Your other hand—the guiding, or uphill, hand—slides freely along the rope to help maintain balance.

To rappel with a mechanical system, you need to wear a seat harness, or an improvised diaper sling or figure-8 rappel seat. Never rappel with a simple loop of webbing tied around your waist, because it can constrict your diaphragm enough to make you lose consciousness.

Fig. 8–1. Mechanical rappel system

Fig. 8–2. Diaper sling

The diaper sling (fig. 8-2) takes about 10 feet of webbing tied into a large loop. With the loop behind your back, pull an end around to your stomach from each side. Bring a piece of the webbing from behind your back, between your legs, and up to your stomach to meet the other two parts. Clip them together in front with doubled carabiners or a locking carabiner. The diaper may also be clipped to a waist loop.

The figure-8 seat (fig. 8-3) is improvised from a standard-length runner. It must be clipped to a waist loop for stability.

Carabiner brake method

A very widely used mechanical system, the carabiner brake is somewhat complex to set up, but has the virtue of not requiring any special equip-

ment—just carabiners. All climbers should know how to use the carabiner brake method, even if they normally use a specialized rappel device. It's a great backup if the device is lost or forgotten, and it's the safest method of rappelling without a special device.

To create the carabiner brake setup, start by attaching one locking or two regular carabiners to your seat harness. Any time a regular carabiner could be subjected to a twisting or side load, two carabiners or a locking carabiner are needed, and this is one of those cases. If you use two regular carabiners, position the gates to keep them from being forced open and accidentally unclipping (fig. 8-4). The correct position is with the gates on opposing sides, forming an X when they are opened at the same time.

Fig. 8–3. Figure-8 sling

CORRECT   POOR   POOR   DANGEROUS

Fig. 8–4. Proper and improper positioning of gates on double carabiners

After attaching the harness carabiners (or locking carabiner), clip another pair of carabiners to that, in the same correct position. Then face the anchor, if you can. Lift a loop of the rappel ropes through the outer carabiner pair. Take yet another carabiner and clip it across the outer carabiner pair, beneath the rope loop. The rope then runs across an outer edge of this final carabiner, known as the braking carabiner.

One braking carabiner (fig. 8-5a) provides enough friction for most rappels on ropes that are 10 or 11 millimeters in diameter. You might need a second or even a third braking carabiner (fig. 8-5b) for thinner ropes, heavy climbers or heavy packs, or steep or overhanging rappels. The ropes must always run over the solid side of the braking carabiners, never across the gate.

There are a couple of things to watch for as you're setting up the carabiner brake system. First, it's sometimes not possible to face the anchor as you pull the loop of rappel rope into the carabiner brake, and this can get confusing. A common beginner's mistake is to pull the rope into the system backward, as if preparing to rappel uphill toward the anchor.

Second, the weight of the rope hanging down the cliff may make it very difficult to pull the loop of rope up through the outer pair of carabiners and hold it while you clip in the braking carabiner. It helps to get that weight off the system. You can do that before pulling the loop of rope through by yanking up some slack rope and throwing a couple of wraps around a leg to take the weight. Or you can do it by pulling the loop through first, but making it extra large so you can lay it over your shoulder while you clip in the braking carabiner. Then drop the downhill strands back through the system so the brake remains close to the anchor.

Fig. 8–5. Carabiner brake system: a, with one carabiner clipped across the outer carabiner pair; b, with two carabiners clipped across the outer carabiner pair in order to give greater friction.

If you are near the edge while setting up the carabiner brake or any other rappel method, you should be attached to an anchor for safety.

Figure-8 rappel device

The figure-8 is probably the most popular special device for rappelling (fig. 8-6). It is simpler to set up and requires less force to control than the carabiner brake method.

Keep in mind the disadvantages. It means carrying an extra piece of equipment, and most figure-8s are relatively heavy. If you lose or forget it, you must be prepared to use another rappel method. Most figure-8s require use of a locking carabiner and don't give you the option of using doubled carabiners. And the figure-8 puts some twists in the rope. The figure-8 was designed for rappelling, though some climbers use the device in one of several possible configurations for belaying.

Other rappel devices

Many other devices are used for rappelling. Most are primarily belay devices that can also be used for rappelling, such as belay plates (slots) and tubes. Some have disadvantages, such as being difficult to feed rope through or heating up easily. Before buying any new device, check climbing literature for evaluation and test data, and read the manufacturer's instructions closely.

Other mechanical systems

Several mechanical rappel systems require no special device, just a locking carabiner. It can be worthwhile insurance to learn at least one of them.

To set up the carabiner wrap system (fig. 8-7), clip a locking carabiner into the locking carabiner or doubled carabiners that are clipped to your seat harness. Run the rappel rope through the outer end of the outside carabiner, and wrap it around the carabiner's solid back, giving it more turns if you want more friction. Two turns are usually just about right. Position the outer carabiner so that the locked gate opening is at the far end. A hazard of the carabiner wrap system is that the carabiner could flip around, and the movement of the wrapped rope might then unlock it.

The Münter hitch used for belaying can also be used for rappelling (see Chapter 7 for details on

Fig. 8–6. Attaching a figure-8 device for use in rappelling: a, figure-8 rappel device; b, attaching rope to the figure-8 device; c, figure-8 rappel device in use.

Fig. 8–7. The carabiner wrap system

using the Münter hitch while belaying). It's very easy to set up, but is the worst method for twisting the rope.

A method common in Europe merely runs the rappel rope through a locking carabiner at the harness, up over the climber's shoulder, and then down across the back to the opposite hand for braking. A danger is that, like non-mechanical systems, it is easy to fall out of.

NON-MECHANICAL SYSTEMS

Two traditional rappel methods use no hardware whatsoever to create friction on the rope. It's just the rope and your body.

The arm rappel (fig. 8-8) isn't used much, but it's occasionally helpful for quick descent of a low-angle slope. Lay the rappel rope behind your back, under your armpits, then wrap it once around each arm. Control your rate of descent by hand grip. For an arm rappel with a pack, be sure the rope goes behind the pack rather than on top or underneath.

Fig. 8–8. The arm rappel

The dulfersitz (fig. 8-9) is a simple all-purpose method that should be mastered by every climber for emergency use if you have no carabiners or seat harness. Face the anchor and step into the dulfersitz by straddling the rope. Bring it from behind around one hip, up across your chest, over the opposite shoulder, then down your back to be held by the braking hand on the same side as the wrapped hip. The other hand is your guiding hand to hold the rope above you to help stay upright.

The dulfersitz has a number of drawbacks compared with mechanical rappel systems. It can unwrap from your leg, especially on high-angle rappels, though it helps to keep the wrapped leg slightly lower than the other. Stay under careful control and try to pad your body, because rope friction around your hip and across the shoulder will be painful, especially on steep rappels. Turn your collar up to protect your neck. If you're wearing a pack, the dulfersitz is even more awkward. The dulfersitz is used in modern climbing only when there is no reasonable alternative or for short, easy rappels to save the trouble of putting a seat harness back on.

RAPPEL ANCHORS

You will often be hanging your full weight on the rappel anchor, which is simply some point of attachment to the rock, snow, or ice. Set up the anchor as close as possible to the edge of the rappel route (providing you can get a solid anchor). This provides the longest possible rappel. It also makes it easier to pull the rope down from below after the rappel, and often reduces the danger of rockfall as

Fig. 8–9. The dulfersitz

you do so.

Think about possible effects on the rope as you are looking for an anchor. Locate the anchor so as to minimize chances of the rope being pulled into a constricting slot or otherwise hanging up when you try to pull it down from below. Check the position of the rope over the edge of the rappel route as the person before you finishes rappelling. If the rope moves near or into a slot in the surface that could restrict its movement, consider relocating the anchor.

You can use natural anchors or artificial (manufactured) anchors, just as you do for belaying or for placing points of protection during a climb.

NATURAL ANCHORS

The best natural anchor is a living good-sized, well-rooted tree. The rappel rope usually goes through a runner that is attached to the anchor. If you can attach this runner to a tree branch rather

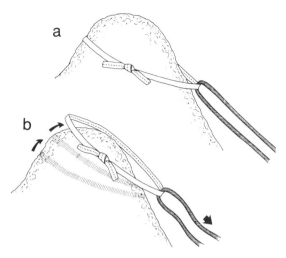

Fig. 8–10. Runner looped around a rock horn: a, a dangerous rappel anchor; b, runner rides up and off rock horn.

than low on the trunk, it helps limit the rope's contact with the ground, making it easier to retrieve the rope and reducing rope abrasion and the risk of rockfall. But note that connecting to a branch rather than the trunk puts more leverage on the tree, increasing the danger that it could be pulled out. Be cautious in using bushes as an anchor, and if you do use one you'll probably want an additional anchor or two for safety. Also be careful using trees and bushes in very cold weather, when they can become brittle. Rock features—horns, columns, chockstones, large boulders—are commonly used as anchors. On snow or ice, you can make bollards (see Chapter 12 for illustrations of snow bollards).

Test a natural anchor if there's any question about whether it can support the weight of the heaviest climber, plus a large safety margin in case a rappeller puts extra force on the anchor by stopping quickly. You can test rock horns and smaller trees by pushing against them with your foot. Test the anchor before rappel gear is attached, and never after the rope or the rappeller is hooked in.

If you run the rappel rope through a runner looped around a rock horn (fig. 8-10a), be rigorous in determining the angle of force on the horn. You must eliminate the deadly possibility the runner could ride up and off the horn during a rappel (fig. 8-10b). Most climbers use only a single anchor if it's a solid, dependable natural anchor—but add another anchor or two if there are any doubts.

ARTIFICIAL ANCHORS

As a rule of thumb, if you are using artificial (manufactured) anchors, use at least two and try to equalize the load between them.

In unknown alpine terrain, some climbers carry pitons and a hammer to set anchors. The most common artificial rappel anchors are bolts or pitons that have been left in place by previous climb-ers, and which must be evaluated for safety just as if you were using them for belaying or for protection while climbing.

The climbers' hardware known as chocks—nuts, hexes, and so forth—are usually used only if no good alternative is available, but better a couple of good chocks than a shaky rock horn. It's not a good idea to trust chocks that you find already in place, left behind by climbers who weren't able to work them loose from their crack in the rock. However, sometimes you can take advantage of an abandoned chock by using it like a natural chock-stone—looping a runner directly around it and making no use whatsoever of the sling attached to the old chock.

SETTING UP THE ROPE

To get the rope ready for rappelling, you attach it to an anchor. In the simplest case, you would untie a runner and retie it around a tree as a rappel sling. Then the midpoint of the rope is suspended from the sling (fig. 8-11a).

If you're using just one rope, put one end of the rope through the sling and pull it until you reach the midpoint. Or you can put the sling around the midpoint before you retie it around the tree. If

Fig. 8–11. Rappel rope attached to tree: a, rappel rope through a sling around a tree; b, poor—rappel rope directly around tree.

you're joining two ropes together for the rappel, put one end of a rope through the sling and tie it to the other rope with a double fisherman's knot, backed up with overhand knots.

You could put the rope directly around the tree (fig. 8-11b), without use of a rappel sling—but this causes rope abrasion, makes it harder to retrieve the rope and, if done enough times, can kill the tree.

If your anchor is a rock feature or bolts or pitons, always attach a sling to the anchor, then run the rappel rope through the sling. Never put the rope directly around the rock or through the eye of the bolt hanger or piton, because the friction may make it impossible to pull the rope back down from below. Some climbers prefer to use two slings instead of one for added security. If you normally carry only sewn runners (which cannot be untied), you may want to bring along some $9/16$-inch web-bing to cut and tie as needed for rappel slings.

On popular climbs, you will find established rappel anchors encircled with the slings that must be left behind when a rappel rope is retrieved. Some of the older slings will feel dry and less supple. It's a good idea to cut out a couple of the oldest slings and add a new one before running your rappel rope around them. If you are using

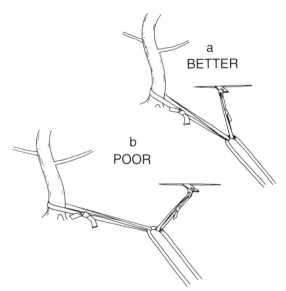

Fig. 8–12. The most common method of attaching the rappel rope to multiple anchors, with a separate sling attached to each of two anchors and meeting at the rappel rope: a, a narrow angle between slings is best; b, the angle between slings is too wide.

more than one sling, try to use the same length to help distribute the load.

When using two anchors to support the rappel, the most common method is to run a separate sling from each anchor, with the slings meeting at the rappel rope. Generally try to adjust the slings so the force is the same on each anchor. For the strongest setup, keep a narrow angle between the two slings (fig. 8-12). (You can also use just a single sling run through the two anchors, employing either self-equalization or the triangle method. Both are described in Chapter 7.)

You can help to avoid binding and abrasion of the rappel rope by making sure the point of connection between the rappel sling and the rope is away from the rock (fig. 8-13).

You can use a tiny piece of rappel hardware known as a descending ring to help reduce rope wear and make retrieval easier. It's simply a metal ring, $1^1/2$ inches or so in diameter. Thread the rappel sling through the ring before tying the sling.

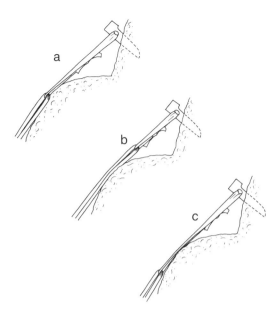

Fig. 8–13. The point of connection between the rappel sling and the rappel rope: a, poor—rope binds and abrades against rock; b, better; c, best.

Then thread the rappel rope through the ring until you reach the rope's midpoint (fig. 8-14). When you pull the rope down later, it slides more easily through the descending ring than it would directly over the sling, which also can be weakened by rope friction.

The descending ring, however, does add another possible point of failure. Newer rings are continuous non-welded designs, much better than the welded type, which cannot be trusted. Some

Fig. 8–14. Rappel rope through descending ring

climbers insist on two rings, even if both are non-welded. An alternative is a single ring, backed up by a non-weight-bearing sling from the anchor through the rope, ready to hold the rope in case the ring fails.

Throwing down the rope

After the rappel rope is looped at its midpoint through an anchor, it's time to get the rope ready to toss down the rappel route.

Beginning from the rappel sling, coil each half of the rope separately into two butterfly coils. You'll end up with four butterfly coils, two on each side of the anchor. Throw the coils out and down the route, one at a time. Start on one side of the anchor by tossing the coil nearest the anchor, then the rope-end coil. Repeat for the other half of the rope (fig. 8-15). This sequence reduces rope snags and tangling. Before tossing, have another climber hold onto the rope near the anchor to make sure your tosses won't cause the rope to pull through the anchor. (Commercial rope bags are available which make it easier to carry ropes and to keep them clean and tangle-free, and rope-tossing is usually easier if you are using a rope bag.)

You won't always end up with a perfect toss, with the rope hanging straight down the rappel route. If you end up with tangles, hangups, or bunching, it's usually best to pull it back up, re-coil, and toss again. But sometimes it's just as well to work with what you've got. For instance, in a high wind, you're not likely to get a perfect toss. So just rappel down to the first problem, recoil the strands below that point, toss again, and continue the rappel.

Shout "Rope!" before you throw the rope down a rappel route. Some climbers shout the word two times, to give anyone below a little time to respond or to watch out for the rope. Others shout just once, but wait for a moment for any response. Be sure you're attached to an anchor as you stand at the edge of the route to toss the rope.

Fig. 8–15. Throwing down the rope

RAPPEL TECHNIQUE

In preparing to rappel, you will go through a sequence of establishing the anchor, attaching the rope to the anchor, throwing the rope down, and hooking yourself into the rappel system. At this point, you are facing the anchor, your back to the descent route, ready to head down the rope. Here's how to do it.

Start with a final check of the entire system: seat harness, rappel hardware, attachment to the rope, and anchor. Then, unless you're the last to rappel, wait while a partner checks your entire system. Pay special attention to the brake system: it's not set up backward, is it, as if you were rappelling uphill? Are the gates of carabiner pairs opposed correctly? Are locking carabiners securely closed? If another climber rappels before you, don't let the rappel begin until you've thoroughly checked out the setup.

GETTING STARTED

Now comes the most nerve-wracking part of most rappels. To gain stability, your legs must be nearly perpendicular to the slope. Therefore, at the very brink of a precipice, you're required to lean outward (fig. 8-16). In some cases you may be able to ease the transition by climbing down several feet before leaning out and putting your full weight on the rope to start the rappel (fig. 8-17).

With the carabiner brake or other mechanical systems, you may be able to sit on the edge of the

Fig. 8–16. Starting rappel from a high anchor

Fig. 8–17. Climbing below a low anchor before starting rappel

are keeping the feet together and failing to lean back far enough. (Some go to the other extreme and lean too far back, bringing the chance of tipping over.)

Move slowly and steadily, with no bounces or leaps. Higher speeds put more heat and stress on the rappel system, and it's especially important to

rappel ledge and wiggle gently off, simultaneously turning inward to face the slope. This technique is particularly useful when starting the rappel above an overhang (fig. 8-18).

POSITION, SPEED, AND MOVEMENT

As you move downward, your position should be something like this: feet apart, knees flexed, body at a comfortable angle to the slope, and facing a little toward the braking hand for a view of the route. The most common beginners' mistakes

Fig. 8–18. Sitting down on ledge and squirming off to get started

go slowly on any questionable anchor. If you have to stop quickly while moving fast down the rope, the anchor comes under a great deal of additional force. Use extreme caution rappelling a face with loose or rotten rock. The danger here is that rock can be knocked loose and hit you or chop the rope.

Overhangs on the route can be a problem. It's easy to end up swinging into the face below the overhang and banging your hands and feet. There also is the danger of getting the brake system jammed on the lip of the overhang. One way to help get past that difficult transition from moving down against the rock wall to hanging below the overhang is to bend your knees sharply while your

feet are at the edge of the overhang, then quickly drop three or four feet. This stresses the rappel system, of course, but it helps reduce both the chance of swinging into the face below and of jamming the brake on the lip.

Below an overhang, you will be dangling free on the rope. Assume a sitting position, hold yourself upright with the guiding hand on the rope above and continue steadily downward. Don't be surprised if you spin as twists in the rope unwind.

Sometimes, in order to reach the next rappel spot, you'll have to move at an angle to the fall line, walking yourself to one side instead of moving straight down. Be careful you don't lose your footing here. If you do, you will swing on the rappel rope back toward the fall line in what could be a nasty pendulum fall. And it could leave you in a position you can't recover from without climbing back up the rope with prusik slings or ascender devices.

POTENTIAL PROBLEMS

Shirttails, hair, chinstraps from a hard hat, and just about anything else have the potential to get pulled into the braking system. Keep a knife handy in case you have to cut foreign material out of the system.

If you run across a tangled or jammed rope on the way down, fix it while you're still above the problem. Stop at the last convenient ledge above the area, or stop with a leg wrap (explained in the next section). Pull the rope up, correct the problem, then throw it down again. Sometimes there's a simple solution. For instance, rappelling down blank slabs, you can often just shake out tangles as they are encountered.

STOPPING IN MID-RAPPEL

If it's ever necessary to stop partway down a rappel, wrap the rope two or three times around one leg (fig. 8-19a). The friction around your leg, increased by the weight of the hanging rope, is usually enough to hold you and to free your hands. Keep a braking hand on the rope until the wraps are completed and tested with your weight. Make the wraps tight, or you could end up a foot or two

Fig. 8–19. Stopping in mid-rappel: a, with rope wrapped around leg; b, with a carabiner brake or other mechanical rappel system.

lower than you intended as you put weight on the wraps and they tighten.

With the carabiner brake or other mechanical rappel system, an alternative method is to pass the rope around your waist, and tie two or three half-hitches around the rappel rope above the brake system (fig. 8-19b). This can be released easily when you're ready to continue the rappel.

MULTIPLE RAPPELS

A descent route often involves a series of rappels. These multiple rappels, especially in alpine terrain, present special problems and require maximum efficiency to keep the party on the move.

The trickiest is a rappel into the unknown, down a route you're not familiar with. Avoid this kind of multiple rappel. If you cannot, take the time to check out the possible rappel lines as carefully as time and the terrain permit. Sometimes you can find a photo of the route before you leave on the climb and bring it with you. Keep in mind that the first couple of rappels down an unfamiliar route may commit you to it all the way, for better or for worse.

If you can't see to the bottom of an unfamiliar rappel pitch, the first person down has got to be prepared to climb back up in case the rappel leads nowhere. This rappeller should carry prusik slings or mechanical ascenders for going up the rope. As additional preparation, the rappeller can tie both strands of the rappel rope to the anchor with figure-8 knots before starting the rappel. This secures the strands so the rappeller can climb up either strand if necessary. The next rappeller unties the knots before heading down.

Rappelling down unfamiliar terrain brings an increased risk of getting the ropes hung up. You can minimize the problem by downclimbing as much of the route as possible, instead of rappelling. You might also consider doing rappels using just one rope, even if two ropes are available, because one rope is easier to retrieve and less likely to hang up than two.

Even though it's nice to gain the maximum distance from each rappel, don't bypass a good rappel spot even 40 feet or so from the end of the rope if there are doubts about finding a good place farther down.

As a party moves through a series of rappels, the first person down each pitch usually carries gear to use in setting up the next rappel (after tying into an anchor at the bottom and trying to find shelter from rockfall). Climbers can take turns being first and last, though it's best for beginners to be somewhere in the middle.

SAFETY BACKUPS

Climbers have several options to increase the safety of a rappel. The options are occasionally useful in specific situations or for helping a beginner gain confidence in rappelling.

Knots in the end of the rope: It's possible to rappel off the end of the rope if you're not paying attention. Some climbers put a knot in the end of each rope, or tie the ends together, to eliminate this danger. If you add knots, don't rely blindly on them to tell when you've reached the end of the rope. The knots might come untied, of course, and in any case you want to keep an eye on the end of the rope so you can plan where to stop. The knots themselves can cause a problem by jamming in the rock if you ever find it necessary to pull the rope back up to work on it.

Pulling on the rappel ropes: A person standing below a rappeller can easily control the rappeller's movement, or stop it altogether, by pulling down on the rappel ropes, putting friction on the brake system. To safeguard the rappeller with this method, the person at the bottom simply holds the rope strands loosely, ready to pull them tight the instant the rappeller has difficulty (fig. 8-20).

Top belay: The rappeller can also be protected by a belay from above with a separate rope. If the belayer uses a separate anchor, the rappeller is safe

Fig. 8–20. Rappel halted by climber below, who is pulling down on the ends of the rope.

from even a total failure of the rappel anchor. A top belay is recommended for all beginners, for climbers with minor injuries, and for the first person down on a suspect anchor. The belays are too time-consuming for routine use because they drastically increase a party's descent time.

Prusik backup: Some climbers like the security of a prusik or Bachmann knot while rappelling, sliding the knot along the rappel ropes as they descend. The knot is in place above the brake system, and the prusik loop is clipped to a carabiner linked to your seat harness. If the brake system fails and you start to drop, the pull causes the prusik knot to automatically grip the ropes and stop the fall (fig. 8-21).

Backing up your rappel with a prusik knot has its dangers. Be careful it doesn't lock up unexpectedly—once it's under tension it can be tough to get loose—and keep the loop short so you can reach it if it locks. There's also the opposite danger: that the prusik knot will fail to lock when it should, particularly if you forget to release your

HARNESS

ROPE DOES NOT RUN THROUGH CARABINER

TO BRAKE HAND

Fig. 8–21. Prusik backup for a carabiner brake rappel system

hold on the knot. The prusik also has the unfortunate potential to burn through during a sudden stop from a high-speed rappel. Remember that controlling the prusik requires the full-time use of your guiding hand, which then isn't available for balance or protection.

RETRIEVING THE RAPPEL ROPE

Successful rope retrieval after a rappel depends on some important steps even before the last rappeller starts down the rope. It takes just one frightening experience with a stuck rappel rope to guarantee that you'll always take these precautions.

If you're using two ropes for the rappel, they will be tied together near the anchor. It's critical that you know which rope to pull on from below. Pull the wrong one, and you'll be attempting the impossible task of pulling the knot through the rappel sling. In some parties, the last two rappellers say out loud which rope is to be pulled, as an aid to remembering which is which.

The last rappeller should take a good final look at the rope and the rappel sling to see that everything is in order and that the rope isn't about to catch on the rock or the sling. Before the last person starts down, a climber at the bottom can test the rope by pulling to check that it can be moved and to see that the connecting knot in a two-rope

rappel can be pulled free of the edge.

With such a two-rope rappel, the last person who starts down may want to stop at the first convenient ledge and pull enough of the rope down so that the connecting knot is clear of the edge. This helps take some of the uncertainty out of the difficult business of recovering a long rappel rope. However, it also shortens one rope end, so be sure the rappeller still has enough rope to reach the bottom.

The last rappeller has the main responsibility for spotting any retrieval problems. This last person can get twists out of the rope by keeping one finger of the braking hand between the ropes throughout the descent. (The same purpose is served by splitting the two ropes through a carabiner on your harness, just uphill of the braking hand.)

With the last rappeller down, it's time to retrieve the rope. First take out any visible twists. Then give the rope a slow, steady pull. Other climbers should take shelter to stay out of the way of falling rope or rockfall. If you've taken all the right steps and luck is on your side, the rope will pull free.

A jammed rappel rope is among a climber's worst nightmares. If it hangs up, either before or after the end clears the anchor, try flipping the rope with whipping motions before trying to get it down with extreme pulling. If you can, move both left and right and try more flipping or pulling. If all else fails, it may be necessary to climb up and free the rope. Belay the climber if enough rope is avail-

able. As a final resort if the party can't proceed without the rope, a climber might decide to attempt the desperate and very dangerous tactic of ascending the stuck rope with prusik slings or mechanical ascenders.

After you've studied rappelling and tried it a few times, it will be easy to see why climbers approach the technique with a fair degree of caution. But it's one of the activities central to climbing, and if you know what you're doing, it works well.

◆ **PART THREE** ◆

ROCK CLIMBING

Sherpa climber rappelling on a crag with Ama Dablam in the background, Khumbu region, Nepal. Photo by Gordon Wiltsie

◆ 9 ◆

ROCK CLIMBING TECHNIQUE

Climbing is a joyous, instinctive activity. As children, we scurry up trees, garden walls, building facades, and anything else steep and enticing. Then we grow up. For some of us, however, the adult urge to climb finds a beautiful outlet in rock climbing.

It's an exciting activity you can go at in many different styles and many different settings. For many, the ultimate pleasure is scaling steep solid granite in an isolated alpine setting far from the city. For them, the crags close to home are only a practice ground to hone skills in preparation for an escape to the mountains. For others, the primary pleasure is the kinesthetic joy of moving on rock, executing the most difficult and gymnastic moves. Mastering the challenge of the rock may be more important than the setting, and a long alpine approach a nuisance rather than a pleasure. And there are those who treasure the whole range of rock-climbing experiences, from working out a single move in a difficult bouldering problem or training on an artificial climbing wall, to completing sustained challenging pitches on a towering rock wall or climbing short sections of rock during an alpine climb on a glaciated peak.

The joys of rock climbing are found in all these ways, and despite their differences, the skills and techniques are essentially the same.

PREPARATION

PHYSICAL CONDITIONING

Climbing is physically demanding, and if you don't have the needed strength, some climbs will be too difficult. However, many climbs are possible without an abundance of strength. To some extent, technique can compensate for a lack of strength, while extra strength can sometimes compensate for a deficiency of technique. Some climbs, especially at the higher end of the rating scale, demand a high degree of both strength and technique.

ATTITUDE

To climb rock well, you must have the desire. Rock climbing calls for a commitment of both mind and body, and making the necessary moves requires total concentration and complete confidence. This confidence can come by practicing with a top rope (belayed from above), which minimizes possible injury in case of a fall and allows you to safely attempt harder and harder moves, eventually finding the limits of your ability.

Confidence goes hand in hand with physical conditioning. If hand, arm, or leg strength is not sufficient, it doesn't matter that the mind is willing. Conversely, physical ability alone won't move you if your mind says no.

An equally important component of attitude is an awareness of safety. This includes knowing your limits, and knowing when and how to back off when you don't have the strength or technique for a given route on a given day.

GEAR

Footwear

Mountaineering boots are commonly used on alpine climbs of modest technical difficulty or where weather or conditions (such as presence of snow or ice) favor their use. Boots generally hold on larger edges quite well, but are less useful on tiny edges or for "smearing" on holds.

For more difficult rock climbs, there are shoes made specifically for rock climbing (fig. 9-1). For many routes, rock shoes are essential. They are generally superior for smearing, and often will edge quite well also.

Most rock shoes consist of a flexible upper, often made of soft leather or cordura and leather, and a smooth flexible rubber sole. In recent years, new rubber compounds have been developed to create "stickier" soles that provide greater friction between rock and sole, and have aided in success on increasingly difficult routes. Rock shoes should fit very snugly to allow maximum control and feel of the rock. Specialized rock shoes are now available that are especially well suited for certain types of climbing, such as edges, pockets, and friction.

Clothing

Clothing for rock climbing should be chosen for appropriateness to weather conditions and for freedom of movement. Some climbers prefer loosely fitting pants; others prefer body-hugging tights made of stretchy material such as Lycra. Some climbers find that knickers provide a desirable combination of freedom of movement and utility in an alpine environment. Remove jewelry and watches that can get caught in equipment or abraded on holds or in cracks.

Tape

Athletic tape can protect hands from abrasion against rock, especially when climbing difficult jam cracks. There are a number of different taping methods, but no matter what the method, the tape must stay securely in place and not begin to peel off part way up a pitch. The tape also must protect

Fig. 9–1. Rock shoes: a, all-around shoe; b, more specialized edging shoe; c, slipper.

vulnerable areas, especially knuckles and the back of the hand, while allowing maximum freedom of hand movement (fig. 9-2). A common mistake is to wrap the tape too tightly.

Some taping methods leave most of the palm untaped to increase sensitivity to the rock. Tape can also be used to provide support and/or protection for finger joints that are easily overstressed by difficult rock climbing or vigorous training.

Fig. 9–2. Hand taped for climbing: back of hand and knuckles are protected; palm is mostly left open.

Chalk

Many climbers use gymnastic chalk to improve their grip, especially in hot sweaty weather. The chalk is usually carried in a chalk bag worn on the back of the harness or attached to a separate runner tied around the waist, so you can dip a hand in the chalk whenever you need it.

Some climbers feel that chalk detracts from the rock by leaving white smudges. They also argue that the chalk identifies the holds, robbing other climbers of the experience of finding the holds and figuring out the climbing sequence for themselves. A compromise solution used by some is colored chalk that blends in with the rock. Several colors are commercially available.

On frequently climbed pitches, sweat and chalk can leave holds slimy and difficult to use. Some climbers carry a small brush, such as a toothbrush, to clean the holds.

Other gear

Additional gear is covered in other chapters. This includes equipment that is less specific to rock climbing, such as ropes and harnesses, and the varieties of hardware specific to the skills of leading and placing protection.

BASIC CLIMBING TECHNIQUES

PRINCIPLES OF MOVEMENT

Climbing with the feet

Pay attention to footwork and balance and you'll reduce the need to rely on arm and hand strength.

Stand erect over your feet and fight the tendency to lean in and hug the rock. On very steep rock, however, pressing the hips close to the rock can help push body weight directly down onto small footholds.

When possible, keep arms outstretched to avoid hanging on bent arms, which is very tiring. As you raise your feet to the next foothold, try to keep your arms straight, avoiding the tendency to use them to haul yourself from one hold to the next. Legs are much stronger than arms. Let the legs lift the body.

Three-point suspension

In this elementary approach, you move one hand or foot at a time while the other three limbs remain stationary (fig. 9-3). Be sure you're in balance over your feet before releasing a handhold to reach for the next one. This is an especially useful approach when the rock may be unsound, because it allows you to balance securely on three

Fig. 9–3. Three-point suspension: hands and right foot provide secure stance; left foot is moved to a higher hold.

holds while testing the next one.

Know where your center of gravity is. The optimal position will vary, but it's often useful to keep a low center of gravity, with weight directly over the feet. Move your center of gravity over a new foothold before committing weight to it. Only when your body is in balance over the new hold should you transfer weight onto it.

As you try more difficult climbs, you'll learn moves that don't adhere to the principle of three-point suspension. There may be only one or two sound holds and body position will be used to maintain a delicate balance over those holds. For example, a hand or foot may be positioned over a non-existent hold, or hips may be thrust in one direction, to counterbalance other parts of the body.

Fig. 9–4. "Resting" on an outstretched arm

CONSERVING ENERGY

Plan a move before trying to execute it. Move smoothly and deliberately, without wasted motion. Strive for fluidity, as if dancing a ballet with the rock, to conserve both time and energy.

Once you begin to step up on a foothold, transfer all your weight and complete the move. Avoid hanging with bent arms and bent knees in an awkward and tiring position while deciding what to do next.

Look for natural resting places such as ledges or secure footholds. If a no-hands rest isn't possible, try for a stance that uses as natural a body position as possible, and that requires the least amount of upper body strength.

If you must hang on handholds, the least tiring way is to hang on straight arms rather than bent arms (fig. 9-4). Do this either by lowering your center of gravity (bend knees, even squat) or by leaning out, away from the rock. Always maximize the proportion of weight being supported by the feet rather than the arms. It also helps to hang your arms down and shake them out, allowing a brief rest and return of circulation to stressed muscles.

USE OF HOLDS

Selection

In general, select holds based on solidness, convenience, and size. A visual inspection will often tell all you need to know. But if you doubt the soundness of a hold, test it with a kick, or with a blow from the heel of the hand. You can also push or pull on it. Keep alert to the consequences if the hold fails during testing: be sure it won't fall on people below, and be sure your stance is secure so you yourself won't fall. Remember that the hold must be useful in the context of the route. A large firm hold is useless if it leads away from the planned route and puts you into a position where you can't move to the next hold. A smaller but more conveniently placed hold may be a better choice.

Footholds should be comfortably spaced whenever possible. High steps are strenuous and make balance awkward, while steps close together waste energy without providing much upward progress.

Handholds at about head height provide a good stance and often are not as fatiguing as handholds above the head. They also let you lean away from the rock to view other potential hand- and footholds. Often, however, you won't have much choice in the matter, because the nature and difficulty of the rock may dictate where the holds are.

Footholds

Climbers use most footholds by employing one of two techniques, edging or smearing. On many holds, either technique will work, and the one to use depends on your own preference and type of footwear. We'll take up a third technique, called the foot jam, in a later section.

In edging, the edge of the boot or rock shoe is placed over the hold (fig. 9-5a). You can use either the inside or outside edge, but the inside is usually preferred for greater ease and security. The ideal point of contact may vary, but generally it's between the ball of the foot and the end of the big toe. Keeping the heel higher than the toes provides greater precision, but lowering the heel is a more restful position. Using the actual toe of the boot or rock shoe ("toeing in") may be very tiring. With practice, you will become proficient using progressively smaller footholds.

In smearing, the foot points more uphill, with the sole "smeared" over the hold (fig. 9-5b). The technique of smearing works best with rock shoes or flexible boots. On lower-angle rock, you may not need an actual hold, but will only have to achieve enough friction between sole and rock. On steeper terrain, smear the front of the foot over a hold, and see how even tiny irregularities in the rock can provide significant friction and security.

Fatigue, often aggravated by anxiety, can lead to troublesome vibrations in the muscles of the leg, known as "sewing-machine leg." The best way to stop it is to try to relax your mind and to change leg position, either by moving on, lowering the heel, or straightening the leg.

In using footholds, optimize the direction of

Fig. 9–5. Footholds: a, edging; b, smearing.

force on the hold. Flexing the ankle may increase the surface area of contact between sole and rock, giving maximum friction. Leaning away from the rock can create inward as well as downward force on the hold, increasing security.

Decide the best way to use a hold before you put your foot on it. Then maintain your position on the hold. Although it's sometimes necessary to reposition the foot into a better relationship to the hold, avoid thrashing and repeated repositioning to try to find something better. This wastes time and energy and may cause you to slip off altogether. On marginal footholds it may be mandatory to maintain the position exactly, as any movement or rotation could cause the foot to slip off. Keeping your foot in position can take a lot of concentration and skill as you move up on the hold and step above with the other foot.

With the large footholds called buckets, place only as much of your foot as necessary on the hold (fig. 9-6). Putting your foot too far into the bucket can sometimes force the lower leg outward, making for an out-of-balance stance.

Generally avoid using your knees, which are susceptible to injury and offer little stability. Nevertheless, even experienced climbers occasionally use a knee to avoid an especially high or awkward step. The main considerations are to avoid injury from pebbles and sharp crystals, and to avoid becoming trapped on your knees, unable to rise to your feet. This can be a big problem if you find yourself beneath an overhanging bulge with insufficient space to easily stand up.

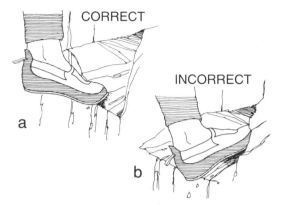

Fig. 9–6. Bucket hold: a, correct; b, incorrect.

Handholds

You can use handholds for balance, to help raise yourself by pulling up on the hold, or to provide various forms of counterpressure.

Handholds (fig. 9-7) offer maximum security when all fingers are used. Ways to use fingers aren't always obvious on small holds. For example, with fingers holding onto a tiny ledge, you may be able to use the thumb in opposition on a minor rugosity (fig. 9-7a). On a very narrow hold or a small pocket in the rock, you can stack fingers on top of each other to increase pressure on the hold (fig. 9-7b).

The most common handhold is the cling hold (fig. 9-7c). Large cling holds allow the entire hand to be cupped over the hold, while smaller variations (fig. 9-7e) may allow room for only the fingertips. Keeping fingers close together provides a stronger grip on the hold. If the hold is not large enough for all fingers to be placed on it, at least curl the other ones, which permits the fingers in use to get the most force from the muscle/tendon system (fig. 9-7f). When using cling holds, be aware that certain hand configurations put extreme stress on the fingers and may lead to injury (fig. 9-7e). (Other types of handholds will be discussed later in this chapter.)

DOWNPRESSURE

For this technique, place the finger tips, palm, side or heel of your hand on the hold and press down (fig. 9-8a). Pressing down with a thumb can

Fig. 9–7. Handholds: a, thumb used in opposition to other fingers; b, stacking fingers to apply greater pressure on a small hold; c, large cling hold; d, open grip. Keeping distal finger joints flexed puts less stress on joints and tendons. e, Cling grip on small hold. Extension of distal finger joints is more stressful and is more likely to cause injury than the open grip. f, Pocket grip: useful for small pockets only large enough to admit a single digit. Keeping other fingers curled helps get the most force out of the muscle-tendon system, but stresses the finger and may cause injury.

Fig. 9–8. Downpressure: a, using heel and palm of hand; b, used in combination with other holds.

be useful on very small holds.

Holds are often used as cling holds from below, then as downpressure holds as you move above them. Downpressure holds may be used by themselves or in combination with other holds (fig. 9-8b), such as in counterforce with a lieback hold, or as part of a stemming move. With your arm extended and elbow locked, you can balance one-handed on a downpressure hold as you move the other hand to the next hold.

MANTEL

The mantel is a very specific use of the downpressure technique. It lets you use hand downpressure to permit your feet to get up onto the same hold as your hands when no useful handholds are available higher.

For the classic mantel (fig. 9-9), place both hands flat on a ledge at about chest height, palms down, with the fingers of each hand pointing toward the other hand. Then raise your body up onto stiffened arms. This will be easier if you can first walk your feet a ways up the rock, or if you can spring up from a foothold. Then lift one foot up onto the ledge and stand up.

This basic mantel, however, isn't always

Fig. 9–9. Mantel: the climber turns his hand with the fingers pointed down to make use of the natural shape of the ledge, then reaches up to use a face hold.

possible, because a ledge will often be higher or smaller or steeper than you might wish. If the ledge is narrow, you may be able to use the heel of your hand, with the fingers pointed down. If the ledge is over your head, you'll use it first as a cling hold, and then convert to a downpressure hold as you move upward. If the ledge isn't big enough for both hands, you'll mantel on just one arm while the other hand makes use of any available hold, or perhaps just balances against the rock (fig. 9-10). Don't forget to leave room for your foot.

Avoid using knees on a mantel because it may be difficult to get off your knees and back on your feet, especially if the rock above is steep or overhanging. Sometimes in mid-mantel you'll be able to reach up to a handhold to help as you begin standing up.

Fig. 9–10. Manteling with one hand while using a face hold with the other

COUNTERFORCE

Counterforce is the use of pressure in opposing directions to help keep you in place. For instance, with both hands in a vertical crack, you can create outward pressure by pulling in opposite directions on the sides of the crack—a pulling-apart action (fig. 9-11a). Or you can create inward pressure by pulling in on widely spaced holds—a pulling-together action—or by pressing in on both sides of a sharp ridge. You can also use the hands in counter-

Fig. 9–12. Undercling: converting from a pinch grip (a) to an undercling (b).

force to the feet (fig. 9-11b). Counterforce plays a part in many of the climbing maneuvers described in this chapter.

UNDERCLING

In the undercling, the hands (palms up) push up beneath a lip of rock while the body leans out and the feet push against rock (fig. 9-12). The arms pull while the feet push, creating a counterforce. Try to keep your arms extended. Both hands can undercling at the same time, or one hand can undercling while the other uses a different type of hold.

An undercling hold may have multiple uses. For example, you can hold the bottom edge of a rock flake in a pinch grip from below, then convert to an undercling as you move up to the flake.

Fig. 9–11. Counterforce: a, outward pressure; b, hands in counterforce to feet.

STEMMING

Stemming is a valuable counterforce technique that lets you support yourself between two spots on the rock that might be of little or no use alone. It often provides a method of climbing steep rock where no hold is apparent, simply by pressing in opposing directions with the feet or with a hand and a foot.

The classic use of stemming (also called bridging) is in climbing a rock chimney. It also comes into play in climbing dihedrals, where two walls meet in approximately a right-angled inside corner. One foot presses against one wall of the chimney or dihedral, while the other foot or an opposing hand pushes against the other wall (fig. 9-13a).

Stemming may also open an avenue of ascent on a steep face, where you can press one foot against a slight protrusion, while the other foot or a hand gives opposing pressure against another wrinkle in the rock (fig. 9-13b). When stemming between widely spaced holds on a steep face, be careful that your body doesn't rotate away from the

Fig. 9–13. Stemming: a, across a chimney; b, on a steep face.

a

b

INCORRECT

Fig. 9–14. The barn door effect: a, the climber is balanced over two footholds with the left hand on a hold up and to the side. When the right hand is removed from the hold, the climber can no longer hold herself into the rock, creating the "barn door" effect, b, with the climber swinging away from the rock.

CORRECT

Two methods of avoiding the barn door effect: c, the climber moves the right foot to the hold where the left was to keep her weight more centered under the secure left handhold; d, the climber flags the left foot behind the right. Both techniques allow the climber to release the right hand to reach up to a new hold.

c

d

rock the second you release a hand to reach for a new hold (fig. 9-14b). Several methods can be used to avoid the barn-door effect. Sometimes a strong stem against the foot below the hand being moved is effective. Other times centering your weight over the foot below the stationary hand is more helpful (fig. 9-14c). One method is to try rearranging the body position using a counterbalance technique such as flagging one leg behind the other (fig. 9-14d).

LIEBACK

The classic lieback technique, another form of counterforce, uses hands pulling and feet pushing in opposition as the climber moves upward in shuffling movements (fig. 9-15a). It's used to climb a crack in a corner, or a crack with one edge offset beyond the other, or along the edge of a flake.

Grasp one edge of the crack with both hands and lean back and to the side on straightened arms. Push your feet against the opposite wall of the crack. Then get a move on. It's a strenuous technique, and it's best to move as quickly and efficiently as possible.

Keep arms extended to minimize stress on tensed muscles. The right relationship of hands and feet will vary, but it becomes easier to determine with practice. In general, keep your feet high enough to maintain friction on the rock, unless a foothold is available. But the higher you bring your feet, the more strenuous the lieback becomes.

The lieback has variations. You can lieback on a single handhold in combination with other holds, or use one hand and foot in a lieback while utilizing face holds for the opposite hand and foot (fig. 9-15b).

Fig. 9–15. Lieback: a, a classic lieback; b, combining a lieback (right hand and foot) with face holds (left hand and foot).

JAMMING

The technique of jamming consists of wedging parts of the body, such as hands or feet, securely enough into a crack to bear weight. Jamming isn't as instinctive or natural-feeling as many other climbing techniques, but it works. It's the principal technique for working your way up the cracks that constitute a big part of rock climbing.

The basic procedure is to insert part of a hand or foot, usually just above a narrower part of the crack. Jams are usually locked by twisting (torquing) so the hand or foot is wedged against both sides of the crack.

Jamming can be used by itself, with both feet and hands utilizing jams, or in combination with other types of holds. As you move up on a jam handhold, you can maintain the jammed position but use it almost like a downpressure hold.

Cracks vary a great deal in size and configuration. The descriptions of jams that follow are just some basic techniques, with a lot of room remaining for creativity and ingenuity.

Finger jams

Finger jams make it possible to climb some of the narrowest cracks, where you may only be able to insert one or more fingers, or perhaps just the finger tips. Finger jams are commonly done with the thumbs down. Slip fingers into the crack and twist the hand to lock the fingers in place (fig. 9-16a). You get added strength by stacking fingers and also by pressing the thumb against the index finger in a ring jam (fig. 9-16b).

In slightly wider cracks, you can try a thumb lock. Place the up-pointing thumb in the crack, the

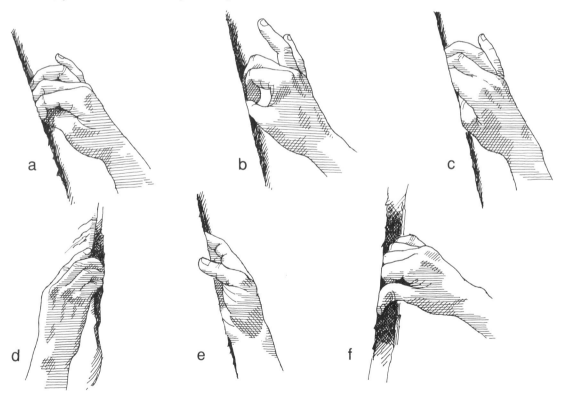

Fig. 9–16. Finger jams: a, thumb-down jam; b, ring jam; c, thumb lock; d, pinkie jam; e, jamming heel of hand as well as finger; f, using counterpressure with thumb.

pad against one side of the crack and the knuckle against the other. Slide the tip of the index finger tightly down over the first joint of the thumb to create the lock (fig. 9-16c).

Here are two other variations on the finger jam, done with the thumbs up (fig. 9-16d,e). You can put the little finger in a crack and stack the other fingers on top (finger tips down, nails up) for a ''pinkie jam.'' In slightly larger cracks, you may be able to wedge the heel of the hand and the smaller fingers into a crack that isn't quite wide enough for a full hand jam. The weight here is borne by the heel of the hand.

For another variation, you can use counterpressure of thumb pushing against one side of the crack, fingers pushing against the other (fig. 9-16f).

Hand jams

With a wider crack, you'll gain the luxury of inserting your entire hand, cupping it as needed to provide adequate expansion against the walls of the crack (fig. 9-17a). To increase pressure against the walls, you'll sometimes tuck your thumb across the palm, especially in wider cracks (fig. 9-17b).

You can often improve the hold by bending your wrist so the hand points into the crack rather than straight up and down.

The hand jam is done either thumbs up or thumbs down. Thumbs up often is easiest and most comfortable for a vertical crack, and it works especially well when the hand is relatively low. The thumbs-up configuration is most secure when the body leans to the same side as the hand that is jammed.

The thumbs-down technique may allow a more secure reach to a jam high above your head, because the hand can be twisted for better adhesion, and you can lean in any direction off this jam (fig. 9-17c). Climbers use a combination of thumbs up and thumbs down, especially in diagonal cracks where it's often useful to jam the upper hand thumb down and the lower hand thumb up (fig. 9-17d).

With both finger and hand jams, keep alert to the effect of your elbow and body position on the security of the hold. As you move up, you may have to rotate your shoulder or trunk to keep sufficient torque and downward pressure to maintain the jam. Direction of force should be pulling

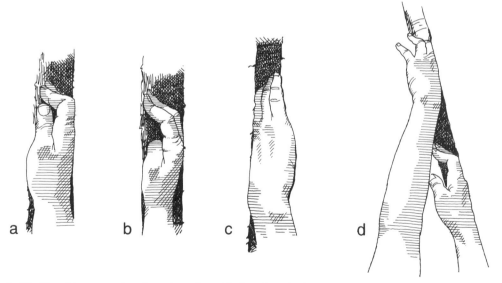

a   b   c   d

Fig. 9–17. Hand jams: a, thumb-up jam; b, with thumb tucked across palm; c, thumb-down jam; d, combining thumb-down and thumb-up jams in a diagonal crack.

down, and not out of the crack.

In dealing with hand jams, you'll run across variants at both ends of the size scale: thinner cracks that won't admit the entire hand but are larger than finger cracks, and wider cracks that aren't quite large enough for a fist jam but require extra hand-twisting to create enough expansion for a secure jam. The size of your hand is a major factor in determining the appropriate technique and the degree of difficulty for any particular crack.

Fist jams

In a crack that's too wide for a hand jam, you can insert your fist (fig. 9-18). The thumb may be inside or outside the fist, depending on which provides the best fit. Your palm may face the back of the crack, the front, or either side. Flexing the muscles in the fist can expand the fist slightly to help fit the crack. Fist jams are often painful, but

Fig. 9–19. Toe jams: a, jamming in a crack; b, smearing in a corner.

can be very useful. For the most secure hold, try to find a constriction in the crack that you can jam your fist above.

Toe jams

You can wedge your toe into a crack by turning your foot sideways—usually with the inside ankle up—and inserting the toe in the crack, then twisting the foot to jam it (fig. 9-19a). You can also wedge the toe into a steep inside corner with a smearing technique, keeping the heel lower than the toe and putting pressure down and in to keep the toe in place (fig. 9-19b).

Foot jams

If the crack is wide enough, jam more of the toe or even the entire foot into the crack. As with the toe jam, insert the foot sideways with the sole facing the side of the crack, then twist to jam (fig. 9-20a). Avoid twisting the foot so securely that it gets stuck, leaving you open to serious injury in case of a fall.

In even wider cracks, you can jam the foot diagonally or heel-to-toe (fig. 9-20b).

Fig. 9–18. Fist jam: three different positions

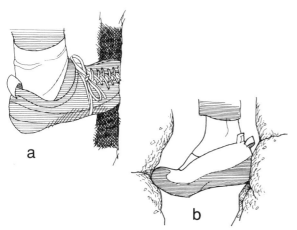

Fig. 9–20. Foot jams: a, foot jam in a crack; b, heel and toe jam.

Body jams

Climbers have figured out ways to jam arms, shoulders, hips, knees, and just about anything else into cracks that are too large for fist jams but too small to accommodate the entire body. These are the awkward off-width cracks, so called because they aren't the right width for any of the more standard jamming techniques. Details of off-width climbing are outlined later in this chapter.

COUNTERBALANCE

Counterbalance is not a specific type of move, but rather a principle that can be used in all kinds of climbing. It's the principle of distributing your body weight in a way that maintains your balance.

This means selecting holds that do the best job of keeping your body in balance. But it also sometimes means putting a hand or foot in a particular location, even if no hold is available, in order to provide counterbalance to the rest of the body. The hips and shoulders also come into play as you move them to provide counterbalance (fig. 9-21).

Fig. 9–21. Two examples of counterbalance: a, the left foot is extended to the side to provide counterbalance; b, the left foot is flagged behind the right for counterbalance.

LONG REACHES

What do you do when the next available hand-hold is a long reach away—or even out of reach?

The climber has several techniques available.

First, make the most of available holds, by using one or more of these tips: stand up on your toes; pull your body into the rock to achieve maximum extension of the body; use a foot for counterbalance to help in standing up completely on the other foot; move your foot higher on a sloped hold; move your foot more to the side that the next handhold is on. Additional tips: move your foot to the edge of a foothold for a traversing move; lean your body and hips out or to the side to allow a longer sideways reach; use a handhold for downpressure to allow maximum upward reach with the opposite hand. Sometimes a longer reach is possible by standing on the outside edge of your boot, which tends to turn your body somewhat sideways to the rock. And remember that the longest reach is possible with the hand that is opposite of the foot you're standing on.

Another option is to consider quick intermediate moves, using holds that are marginal but will be used just long enough to scamper up to the next good hold.

The last resort may be a dynamic move that could involve a lunge or simply a quick move before you lose your balance or grip. The time to grab the next higher handhold while making a dynamic move is at the "dead point"—at the apex of your arc of movement when the body is weightless for a fraction of a second before it begins to fall. Movement is most efficient at that point.

There's a built-in danger if a dynamic move fails: you're no longer in complete control and a fall is likely. Make a dynamic move only after calculating and accepting the consequences of failure. You should know beforehand that the protection is secure and that a fall onto the protection won't result in hitting a ledge or the ground or otherwise risking injury. Keep in mind that dynamic moves are for accomplished climbers, not for desperate novices.

EXCHANGING PLACEMENTS ON A SMALL HOLD

Sometimes you need to move one foot onto a small hold already occupied by the other foot, or one hand onto a hold being used by the other hand. Either move can be made several different ways.

To exchange a foot placement, you can make an intermediate move, using a poorer, even marginal hold to get the one foot off the good hold long enough for the other one to take it over. And there's the hop, in which you hop off the hold as you replace one foot with the other.

You can also try sharing the hold by matching feet, moving one foot to the very edge of the hold to make enough room for the other. Another technique is the crossover, in which you cross one foot in back of the other to occupy the far side of the hold (fig. 9-22).

Fig. 9–22. Foot crossing to change feet on a small hold

To trade hands, you can make an intermediate move, much as you might in exchanging feet. You have the option to match hands, placing both hands on the same hold. If space is limited, you can also try picking up the fingers of one hand, one finger at a time, and replacing them with the fingers of the other hand. The crossover technique also is occasionally useful.

PUTTING IT ALL TOGETHER

Once you've learned the basic climbing techniques, you are ready to begin combining them in ways that make different types of climbs possible.

You'll soon discover the value of planning before you start up a new pitch. Always plan several moves ahead to help you conserve energy and stay on route. Identify and examine difficult sections before you get to them, make a plan, then move through them quickly. Look ahead for good rest spots.

Many climbs require a variety of techniques, rather than pure jamming, or pure stemming, or pure anything. You'll often use one technique with one hand, or one side of the body, and another technique with the other. You can be jamming with one side of the body as you use face holds with the other. A single pitch may require different techniques in sequence: a jam followed by a lieback, then face climbing followed by a mantel onto what had been a cling hold.

Basic techniques are combined in various ways for climbing faces, slabs, cracks, dihedrals, chimneys, and overhangs.

FACE CLIMBING

In some ways, face climbing is the most natural type of climbing (fig. 9-23). You move up a series of handholds and footholds, somewhat like climbing a ladder.

Remember that a single hold may be used in a variety of ways, by feet and hands. What initially appears to be a good cling hold may allow a lieback, a mantel, or a stemming move. Be creative.

SLAB CLIMBING

Also referred to as friction climbing, slab climbing (fig. 9-24) requires liberal use of smearing moves. Balance and footwork are the keys to success, and smearing with the feet is the primary technique.

Remember to flex the ankle (lowering the heel) and keep weight directly over the ball of the foot for maximum friction between rock and sole. Avoid leaning into the slope with your body, which pushes your feet away from the rock. Instead, keep weight over the feet, bending at the waist to allow your hands to touch the rock, and pushing hips and buttocks away.

Fig. 9–23. Face climbing

Fig. 9–24. Slab climbing

Take short steps to maintain balance with weight over the feet. Look for the small edges, rough spots, or changes in angle that provide the best foot placements. On the toughest slabs, footholds may be so subtle you'll have to feel with your hand or foot to find the roughest surface.

Don't forget that other techniques can be useful on slabs. Face holds may be intermittently available, as well as cracks. You can use downpressure on small edges or irregularities, with the finger tips, thumb, or heel of your hand. A lieback with one hand might be possible using tiny edges. Look for an opportunity for stemming, which could mean a chance to rest.

CLIMBING CRACKS AND DIHEDRALS

Cracks may be climbed with a pure jamming technique or by a combination of techniques. A very potent combination is to jam with one side of the body and use face holds with the other (fig. 9-25).

Cracks also may be climbed with a pure lieback technique or by liebacking with one arm in combination with face holds for the other hand (fig. 9-26). This may result in a kind of stemming action.

Dihedrals (inside corners) may be climbed by pure stemming. You can also use various combinations, such as hands jammed in a crack splitting the dihedral combined with feet stemming on opposite sides of the dihedral (fig. 9-27). You may even use

Fig. 9–25. Combining jamming with face climbing

classic chimney technique, described later in this chapter.

Useful edges or other holds may be found hidden within cracks—on the sides or even at the back of wide cracks. Remember that horizontal cracks can also be used as cling holds.

Off-width cracks

Cracks that are too wide for standard jamming, but too narrow to admit the entire body for chimneying, call for specialized off-width technique. You stand sideways to the crack, and one full side of your body goes into the off-width.

When confronted by an off-width, first decide which side of your body to put inside the crack.

Fig. 9–27. Climbing a dihedral using stemming and jamming

Fig. 9–26. Liebacking combined with face holds

This depends on several things, such as holds in the crack or on the face, and the lean, flare, and offset of the crack.

After you've settled on which side to use, the inside leg goes inside the crack and forms a leg bar, usually with counterpressure between foot and knee or foot and hip. This foot is often placed in a heel-toe jam.

The outside foot also is inside the crack in a heel-toe jam. Try to keep the heel above the toe (for better friction) and turned into the crack (to allow the knee to turn out).

Fig. 9–28. Off-width technique: a, arm bar; b, arm lock.

As for the arms, a primary body-jam technique is the arm bar (fig. 9-28a). With the body sideways to the crack, insert the arm fully into the crack, with the elbow and the back of the upper arm on one side of the crack giving counterpressure to the heel of the hand on the other side. Get the shoulder in as far as possible, and have the arm lock extend diagonally down from the shoulder.

In a variation, the arm lock, fold the arm back at the elbow and press the palm against the opposite side in counterforce to the shoulder (fig. 9-28b).

The outside arm is used to give downpressure to help hold you in the crack, or is brought across the front of the chest and pushed against the opposite side of the crack, elbow out.

You're now wedged securely in the crack. To climb, move the outside leg upward to establish a higher heel-toe jam. When this jam is set, stand up on it. Then re-establish the inside leg bar and arm bar (or arm lock), and reposition the outside arm. This again wedges the body in the crack. You're now ready to move the outside leg upward again to establish a yet higher heel-toe jam. Continue repeating this procedure (fig. 9-29).

You may use your outside foot occasionally on face holds, but watch out for the tendency for these outside footholds to pull you out of the crack.

CHIMNEY TECHNIQUE

A chimney is any crack big enough to climb inside, ranging in size from those that will barely admit the body (squeeze chimneys) to those the climber's body can barely span.

The basic principle is to span the chimney somehow with the body, using counterforce to keep from falling. Depending on the width of the crack, you will either face one side of the chimney, or face directly into or out of the chimney. The best body position and technique to use depends on the situation and on the size of the climber. Which direction you face may depend on what holds are available outide the chimney and on how you plan to climb out of it.

Fig. 9–29. Climbing an off-width crack

In squeeze chimneys, wedge your body in whatever way works best and squirm upward. Look for handholds on the outside edge or inside the chimney. Arm bars and arm locks may be useful. It's helpful, sometimes, to press the left foot and knee, for example, against opposite sides of the chimney. You might try stacking your feet in a T configuration, with one foot placed parallel to one side of the rock, while the other is placed perpendicular to it, jammed between the first foot and the opposite wall. Squeeze chimneys can be very strenuous, and the best approach here may be to look for an alternative way to climb that section.

In a crack that's somewhat wider than a squeeze chimney, you begin to have some room to maneuver (fig. 9-30a). You can then press your back and feet against one side of the chimney as your knees and hands push against the other side. You can move upward by squirming your way. Or try a sequence of wedging the upper body while raising the feet and knees, then wedging them and raising the upper body.

A wide chimney calls for stemming technique, with the climber facing directly into or out of the chimney (fig. 9-30b). Counterforce is between the right hand and foot on one side and the left hand and foot on the other. Press down as well as against the sides, especially if there are holds on the sides of the chimney. Ascend by alternately moving arms and legs, or by moving each leg, then each arm.

In a standard moderate-width chimney, perhaps 3 feet wide, you'll again face one wall of the chimney, your back to the other. For the upper body, your hands may push against one wall in counterforce to your back pressed against the other. Or the

a

b

Fig. 9–30. Chimney techniques: a, in a narrow chimney; b, in a wide chimney.

counterforce may be between hands on opposing walls. For the lower body, your feet may push against one wall in counterforce to your buttocks against the other. Or the counterforce may be between your two feet.

To climb this moderate-width chimney, use the following sequence (fig. 9-31): Start with your back toward one wall. Press one foot against each wall and one hand against each wall. Move upward by straightening your legs and then re-establishing hand positions. Immediately bring your back leg across to the same side as the forward leg. Then swing the forward leg across to the back position. You're now again in position to move upward by straightening your legs.

Beware of getting too far inside a chimney. Although psychologically it may feel more secure, you can get lodged deep inside and find it difficult to move back out. You have a better chance of finding useful hand- and footholds if you stay near the outside of the chimney.

Climbing deep inside the chimney also can make it harder to exit at the top. The transition from the top of the chimney to other types of climbing is often challenging and may require extra thought and creativity.

Chimney technique may be useful in places that don't look like classic chimneys. It can be used to climb dihedrals (fig. 9-32), or short wide sections of otherwise narrower cracks.

NEGOTIATING OVERHANGS AND ROOFS

Depending on the situation, overhangs and roofs require a variety of techniques such as manteling, face climbing, or crack climbing.

There are two important points to remember: maintain balance and conserve strength.

Fig. 9–31. Chimney techniques in a moderate-width chimney

To maintain balance, look for good footholds and make the most of them. This often means keeping feet high and hips low to help press weight against footholds (fig. 9-33). In some situations, it means pressing your hips into the rock, with back arched, to keep weight over the feet while poised under an overhang. While balanced over your feet beneath the overhang, locate the handholds you will use to move up and over the bulge. A cling hold, a jam, a lieback, or a combination of these may be the key.

Fig. 9–32. Chimney techniques in a dihedral

To conserve strength, weight your feet as much as possible. Keep arms straight while raising the feet. When the feet are as high as possible, lift the body with your legs rather than pulling up on your arms. Avoid hanging on bent arms, as this will quickly exhaust arm strength. Move quickly through crux sections of the pitch to minimize the time spent in strenuous positions (fig. 9-34).

Occasionally you may need to raise up on your feet while making a dynamic reach (a lunge) to a handhold. Another trick is to throw one foot up

Fig. 9–33. Climbing an overhanging route

Fig. 9–34. *Climbing over a roof: a, the climber is poised under the roof with hips close to the rock; b, she leans out on an outstretched arm to locate a hold above the roof; c, she has both hands above the roof and feet are high, pushing against the rock; d, finally, she brings one foot up and begins to pull over the roof.*

onto a ledge, perhaps hooking the heel on it while pushing with your other foot and pulling with your arms to swing up onto the top foot.

TRAVERSING

Traversing—going sideways across a section of rock instead of up or down—again calls for a catalog of climbing techniques (fig. 9-35). The main ones are side clings, liebacks, and stemming. And counterbalance is important when making a long sideways reach.

The climber usually faces into the rock, toes pointed away from each other. Hands and feet are commonly shuffled sideways, although exchanging one hand for the other, or one foot for the other, on a single hold can be very useful. You may occasionally cross one foot behind the other to reach the next hold, or cross one hand over the other.

On a steep pitch it's very tiring to hold yourself into the rock on bent arms. When possible, lean out from the rock on straight arms. This conserves arm strength, and it gives a better view of where you're going.

A specialized type of traverse is the hand traverse, used when footholds are marginal or nonexistent (fig. 9-36). The hands grip a series of holds or shuffle along an edge, while the feet provide a counterforce by pushing against the rock, as in a lieback or undercling. Keep the feet high and the center of gravity low so the feet are pushed into the rock. And once again, keep the arms straight to

Fig. 9–36. Hand traverse

Fig. 9–35. Traversing a steep face: a, lieback with one hand, leaning out to reach another hold with the other hand; b, climber twists body to take long sideways reach—an advanced technique.

conserve arm strength and to let the legs do as much of the work as possible.

EXITING ONTO LEDGES

As you approach a ledge, avoid the temptation to reach forward and pull yourself onto it. This may throw you off balance and also make it impossible to keep an eye on your footholds (fig. 9-37a).

Instead, continue to walk your feet up the rock, and then use downpressure with the hands near the edge of the ledge. You might do a classic mantel. Be careful not to exit onto the ledge on your knees and then find yourself beneath an overhang, unable to stand (fig. 9-37b).

DOWNCLIMBING

While you're learning lots of ways to climb upward, also allow some time to learn the valuable technique of downclimbing (fig. 9-38). Downclimbing at times is faster, safer, or easier than rappelling, such as when rappel anchors aren't readily available. Downclimbing provides a way to retreat when you find yourself off route or on a pitch where the rock above is more difficult than you care to attempt.

Downclimbing has its special difficulties, however, which helps explain why some climbers resist learning the skill. Holds are harder to see than when you're climbing upward—and holds on the steepest, most difficult sections are the most difficult to see, especially if the rock is undercut below a bulge or small roof. It's hard to test holds without committing to them, an unpleasant fact if you doubt the soundness of the rock. And unless you climbed up the same way, the terrain below is unknown, and you may not be able to anticipate the consequences of a fall.

For downclimbing on low-angle rock, face outward for the best visibility. Keep hands low and use downpressure holds whenever possible. Going down friction slabs, keep weight over your feet to maximize friction. It may help to keep your center

INCORRECT
a

CORRECT
b

Fig. 9–37. Exiting onto a ledge: a, incorrect; b, correct.

Fig. 9–38. Downclimbing: a, facing out; b, facing sideways; c, facing in.

of gravity low, with knees well bent.

As the rock steepens, turn sideways, leaning away from the rock for better visibility. If the cliff gets even steeper, face into the rock. Keep hands low, and lean away from the rock to look for holds below.

SPECIAL DEMANDS OF ALPINE ROCK CLIMBING

GENERAL CONSIDERATIONS

When you take the rock-climbing skills you've learned during pleasant days on small nearby crags out into the mountains proper, some of the conditions of the game change. There are new things to keep in mind when it comes to alpine climbing which involves a mix of hiking, scrambling, routefinding, snow and ice climbing, and rock climbing.

First of all, you'll probably be climbing with a pack, a significant impediment to speed and performance. With a pack, it can be a challenge to climb rock several levels easier than what you lead comfortably on the crags. For a real test, try climbing a chimney or an off-width crack. Sometimes it's necessary to haul the pack up separately with a rope, and this again slows the climb.

Decisions about how much gear to take become extremely important as each extra pound cuts into speed and performance and, ironically, adds to the possibility that the extra gear may be needed to survive an unplanned bivouac or accident.

On the crags, you use light, flexible shoes specially designed for rock climbing. But on alpine climbs, heavy mountaineering boots are the usual footwear for approaches, for snow travel, and often for much or all of the climbing. As with carrying a pack, climbing in mountaineering boots adds to the challenge of otherwise moderate rock. If you decide to change to rock shoes for the more technical portions of a climb, you're stuck with packing the mountaineering boots. If you're wearing boots and crampons for hard snow or ice and encounter a short section of rock, you may have to ascend the rock in crampons, adding yet another dimension to the climb.

Use special care in testing holds on alpine climbs, where loose rocks may not have been discovered and discarded by previous climbers the way they are at popular crags. Unsound rock is common on alpine climbs because of the many different types and the constant weathering it receives. You may want to place protection even on rock that appears easy to climb. However, occasionally on low-angle loose rock, using the rope may be more hazardous than climbing unroped, because the rope can dislodge rocks onto climbers below.

Unpredictable weather, arduous approaches, high altitude, and routefinding problems all add to the commitment and challenge of alpine rock climbing.

SPEED AND SAFETY

A speedy ascent is sometimes an important part of safety on an alpine climb. On long routes, speed minimizes the risk of being caught by darkness. It provides extra time to deal with equipment breakdown, routefinding problems, injury, or illness. It lessens the length of exposure to rockfall, storms, or lightning.

Speed doesn't mean careless rushing. It means developing efficiency in such activities as testing holds, belaying, exchanging gear, and rope management. It means looking ahead at the route, formulating a plan, and moving smoothly ahead without thrashing over routefinding dilemmas.

As a team, climbing efficiently requires planning and practice, as well as development of a systematic approach to all basic activities. Moving efficiently over the rock saves a lot of time, promotes safety, and conserves energy for each member of a climbing team.

A light pack helps in completing a route quickly. Safety lies in having enough gear to do the climb and survive unexpected situations—not in carrying every piece of gear and shelter that might possibly come in handy.

The size of the climbing party and of the rope teams has an important bearing on speed. The more rope teams there are, the slower the party generally will move. However, rope teams of two are considerably more efficient than teams of three on an alpine route. Other things being equal, two rope teams of two can move much more quickly than a single team of three.

TRAINING FOR ROCK CLIMBING

Rock climbers need a fitness program tailored to their needs. Overall fitness is helpful, but general conditioning programs don't usually promote the forearm and finger strength needed by climbers.

TRAINING GOALS AND REGIMENS

A training program should be designed to develop and maintain strength, endurance, balance, and flexibility. Added benefits will be greater confidence and fluidity on the rock.

The energy required for muscular contraction is derived from three energy-producing systems (each of which produces adenosine triphosphate [ATP], the final common source of chemical energy for muscle).

The primary source of energy for sustained or repeated muscular contraction requires oxygen and is referred to as the aerobic system.

The other two systems do not utilize oxygen and are referred to as anaerobic. They are important when the demand for energy temporarily exceeds the capacity of the aerobic system, or during sudden muscular contractions demanding energy before the aerobic system can supply it.

Training should include use of all three of these energy-producing systems.

Be careful you don't hurt yourself while you

train. Common causes of injury are overtraining, trying to increase strength too quickly, and failing to pay attention to early signs of overuse or acute injury, especially to tendons of the elbows and of the fingers.

Strength

Strength refers to the maximum force that can be exerted against a resistance. A practical example might be the heaviest weight you could lift a single time.

Developing strength is useful for individual moves or short sequences when maximum strength is required for a brief time. Maximum muscular effort requires use of the anaerobic energy systems. These can be trained using routines that alternate periods of intense muscular work, from seconds to less than 2 minutes, with periods of rest.

The best approach is progressive muscular overload exercises. This includes weight training with heavy loads and few repetitions, or other short-duration, near-maximal efforts, such as hanging from small holds for brief periods. A description of training regimens is beyond the scope of this chapter, but climbers can consult books and magazine articles devoted to strength training.

Endurance

Endurance is the ability to sustain muscular effort over time. Although crux sections of a pitch may require considerable absolute strength, climbing a full pitch, or more particularly a multipitch route, requires muscular endurance.

The primary energy system involved is aerobic, and the best training approach is lower-resistance, higher-repetition exercises than the ones used for strength training. You can adapt this approach to weight training, finger-board routines, or sustained bouldering.

Aerobic activities—such as jogging, bicycling, swimming, or rowing—help develop cardiovascular fitness, which aids in any sustained rock climbing effort. This is particularly true for alpine climbs, where the approach may be strenuous and where rapid progress up a long route can be essential.

Balance

Perhaps the best way to improve your balance is simply to climb. Try climbing exercises, such as moving up a slab without the use of hands, or working on difficult boulder problems that require balance. You can also devise other exercises, such as walking across a tightly stretched rope suspended above the ground. Many dancers take readily to climbing; dance lessons might improve both balance and flexibility.

Flexibility

Flexibility is essential for all rock climbing beyond an elementary level. Many books are available that describe stretching exercises to improve flexibility. They should be done regularly, like any training exercise. Take care to avoid injury.

Weight loss

You can increase your relative strength and endurance by losing excess weight, thereby decreasing the number of extra pounds you have to lift with your arms and legs. A lower body weight may enhance balance and flexibility as well.

USING AVAILABLE RESOURCES

Climbers can take advantage of natural resources to train specifically for the strength, endurance, and technique required in climbing.

Look for opportunities to climb on boulders at local crags or at developed climbing areas. Bouldering lets you practice close to the ground without needing a belay. Work on low-level traverses and on short but difficult problems.

Buildering is the same idea as bouldering, but using the sides of buildings instead of the sides of rocks. Beware of conflicts with authority.

Top-roped climbing is another training tool. In top roping, you are belayed so that any fall will result in only a short drop—just the distance the rope stretches when it takes your weight. Because you're safe, you can practice techniques and push the limits of your ability, increasing strength and confidence. You can try moves you wouldn't be willing to go for if you were leading a climb, belayed only from below and risking a leader fall.

SPECIALIZED EQUIPMENT

Climbers now have access to a growing catalog of manufactured climbing aids. They let you train whenever you want and tailor a fitness program to your own needs.

Artificial climbing walls are appearing both indoors and out, where you can boulder in the absence of readily available natural areas. The walls help develop both strength and technique, and they allow creation of specific problems to work on. These problems can even simulate a difficult sequence on an established natural route. Of course, indoor walls are especially welcome during bad weather.

Manufactured finger boards (fig. 9-39) have a selection of hand and finger holds to hang from or pull up on. Using a finger board improves upper

Fig. 9–39. Finger board

body strength and also lets you concentrate on developing the finger strength needed to take advantage of small holds.

Other training tools have been developed and more are on the way. There are rope ladders and peg boards for improving upper body strength. There also are artificial cracks designed to improve strength and endurance with hands in specific configurations.

STYLE AND ETHICS

Climbing generates endless debate over which styles are fair and which are less than sporting, over which practices are harmful, and which are "none of your damn business." The terms "style" and "ethics" are sometimes used interchangably by climbers, but style usually refers to a person's mode of climbing, which is principally a personal decision. Ethics usually refers to issues where preservation of the rock itself, and thus the experience of other climbers, is at stake.

Climbers soon discover that getting to the end of the pitch or the top of the peak isn't the only goal—that it's also getting there in a way that feels right, that respects the rock, and that tests a person's skill and resolve as a climber. These are questions of style and ethics.

DIVERSITY OF STYLES

Styles change and attitudes evolve, but the core of the debate on climbing styles is about how to maintain the challenge of climber against rock and how to play the game in a way that fairly tests the climber.

Climbers adhering to traditional style prefer to climb each route strictly from the ground up, with no help from such aids as top ropes or preplaced protection. New routes are explored and protected only on the lead. After a fall, the climber returns to the start of the climb or at least to a no-hands resting place.

Climbers following the European-influenced sport-climbing style are more likely to find other techniques acceptable as well. This can include inspecting the route on rappel before trying to lead it from below. It can also mean cleaning the route and perhaps placing protection on rappel. Routes may be climbed with multiple falls, by resting on the rope while checking out the next move ("hang-dogging"), or by rehearsing moves with the help of a top rope.

These sport-climbing techniques have made it possible to climb harder and harder routes. A particular climbing area may lend itself more to one style than another because of the type of rock, the difficulty of the routes, or the conventional style of the local climbers. In the world of climbing, there's room for a diversity of styles, and most climbers will experience a variety of them.

No matter what the style, a climber will work to eventually climb the route by putting no weight on the rope or on any piece of protection. The goal is to "redpoint" the route; that is, to eventually lead a complete no-falls ascent. Better yet is to "flash" the route, leading it all the way with no falls on the very first try. Best of all is to flash it "on sight"; that is, without prior inspection or knowledge.

ETHICS AND THE ROCK

The subject of ethics has to do with respecting the rock and every person's chance to use it. Unlike climbing style, ethics involves personal decisions that do affect the experience and the enjoyment of others. This includes the sticky question of the manner in which bolts are placed on a route. Are bolts placed on rappel different—less "ethical"—than bolts placed on the lead? Traditional climbers may argue that bolts placed while on rappel rob others of the chance to try the route from the ground up. But other climbers may say that placing the bolts gives a chance at a route that otherwise would be unclimbable.

Each area has its own tradition of what styles and ethics are acceptable, and visiting climbers should observe the local standards. It's not hard to find out what they are. The guidebook will say, the locals can tell you, and you can always just look around at what the other climbers are doing.

This book won't try to resolve issues of style and ethics. But there is general agreement on a couple of principles.

First of all, preservation of the rock is paramount. Chipping the rock to create new holds is almost universally condemned. And while bolt-protected routes are common in many areas, bolting should not be indiscriminate. In the mountains or other wilderness areas, away from concentrated centers of rock climbing, it's particularly important to preserve the environment for those who follow.

If possible, stick to clean climbing, using only removable chocks for protection.

Secondly, it's almost never justified to add a bolt to an existing route. If you feel you can't safely climb the route as it is, don't try it. Exceptions may occur when a consensus of local climbers, usually including the person who first climbed the route, agree that another bolt should be placed to promote safety and enjoyment. There's rarely any objection if you replace an old bolt with a newer, stronger one or add a bolt at an established belay or rappel point.

COURTESY

Keep other climbers in mind when you're out climbing. If your party is moving up a multipitch route much slower than the people behind you, let them pass at a safe spot, such as a belay ledge.

Beware of tackling climbs that are beyond your abilities. You may prevent more capable climbers from enjoying the route. And if your inexperience gets you in trouble, you may end up dragging the other climbers into your rescue.

CLIMBING ACCESS

Access to many climbing areas is threatened and two issues are usually at stake. The people who own or manage the land are worried about liability for accidents and are concerned that climbers are defiling the environment.

As climbers, we can help by taking responsibility for our own actions. It's up to us to put in dependable anchors and otherwise promote safety—and to provide rescue services when they're needed, rather than expecting others to do it for us.

It's also up to us to leave areas in as natural a state as possible. Chalk, rappel runners, fixed protection, and litter can be eyesores. We can help by establishing rappel anchors that don't require leaving slings, using colored chalk that blends in with the rock, keeping bolt placements to a minimum, and removing all litter. These efforts can promote public acceptance of the sport and help maintain access to climbing areas.

◆ 10 ◆

LEADING AND PLACING PROTECTION

Climbers who have learned the basic techniques of rock climbing and who know how to belay and rappel are ready to take up the study of leading and of placing protection.

Leading is the skill of climbing first up a pitch, utilizing a belayer, rope, and intermediate protection for added safety. To many climbers, leading is one of the most satisfying activities in all of climbing. As leader, you're not just following; you've taken on the challenge and responsibility of determining the direction of the climb.

Placing protection is the skill of establishing points of protection along the route by using natural features such as trees and rock horns or by lodging safety devices in the rock. It's the technique that makes safe leading possible. The leader clips the rope through each piece of protection, while the belayer at the bottom of the pitch waits in position to hold the leader with the rope after any fall.

The skills of belaying, leading, and placing protection are combined in a two-person team for safe rock climbing. One climber, belayed by the second, leads up a pitch, placing protection along the way, and establishes a belay station at the top. The leader belays the second climber up. The leader then starts the next pitch, or alternates the lead (swings leads) with the second. The process is repeated until the end of the climb.

It's easy to picture how placing protection can save your life by limiting the severity of a fall.

Unless there's an obstruction to stop the fall, you as the lead climber will fall just a bit more than twice the distance between you and your belayer. If you are climbing 20 feet above your belayer and have placed no protection, you could fall 40 feet: 20 feet back down to the level of the belayer, and another 20 feet to straighten the rope out again—plus a bit more due to rope stretch (fig. 10-1b). But add an intermediate point of protection, and the length of the fall is dramatically reduced. The fall now will be shortened to just twice the length of the rope between you and the last point of protection (fig. 10-1a).

The leader accepts more risk than the second, who has the luxury of a belay from above. The second doesn't have to place protection, and doesn't have to worry about dropping more than a short distance before the belayer stops a fall. The leader, on the other hand, has to place protection at intervals along the route and has to face the possibility of a longer fall.

Unless the leader falls, a piece of protection usually gets no use whatsoever. This is free climbing, in which the leader climbs free of the protection, never holding onto a piece of protection and never putting weight on the rope. In another type of climbing—aid climbing—the climber purposely hangs from the protection. (Aid climbing is covered in Chapter 11.)

Climbers distinguish between two main types of protection: natural protection and artificial protec-

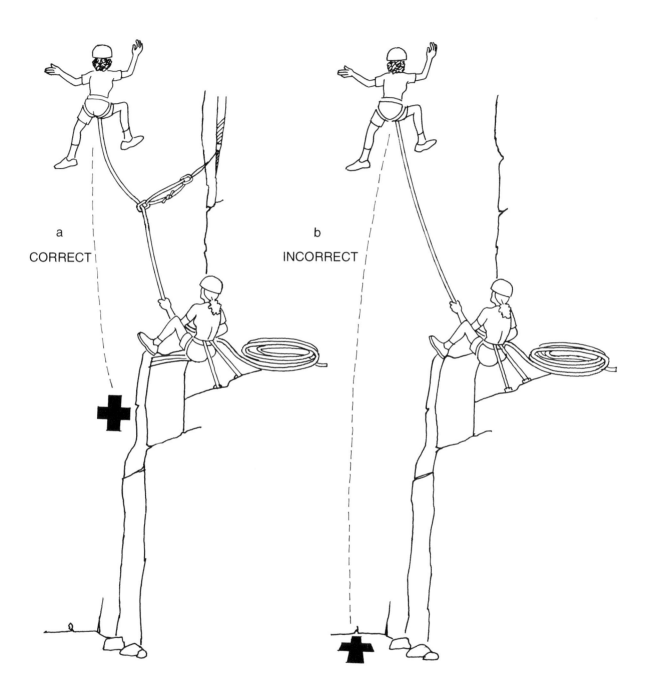

a
CORRECT

b
INCORRECT

Fig. 10–1. Leader fall: a, with protection in place; b, no protection in place.

tion. With natural protection, you're relying on nature to provide something to connect the rope to. When natural protection is not available, you rely on metal wedges and cams (known as artificial chockstones, or chocks), and bolts and pitons, to establish artificial protection.

NATURAL PROTECTION

Some of the very best protection is already in place, just waiting for you. It's natural protection: trees and bushes, horns and flakes, chockstones, boulders, and other natural features. The leader can save the fancy hardware for later in the climb. Only the simplest tools—runners and carabiners— are needed to take advantage of these gifts from Mother Nature.

The basic technique for using all natural protection is identical: position a runner around the natural feature, clip a carabiner to the runner, clip the rope into the carabiner. And that's it.

Some things to pay attention to in using natural protection:

• **Test** every potential piece of natural protection before you trust your life to it. Take a close look at every tree and every rock. Does the tree look healthy? Does the rock appear unfractured, without cracks or other weaknesses? Carefully push them and pull them, tap and prod, kick and shake. Is everything solid?

• **Remember** the climbers down below as you're kicking and prodding. Be careful not to dislodge anything.

• **Try** to identify the type and composition of a rock feature as clues to its strength.

• **Check** to see if the protection will hold a pull in only one direction, or if it can take a tug from multiple directions. That is, is the protection one-directional or multidirectional? Multidirectional protection, such as a tree, is best because it can withstand an outward and upward pull.

• **Choose** an appropriate method of attaching the runner (fig. 10-2). You'll usually start by looping the runner around or over the natural feature. A runner that is looped around is secured by using a

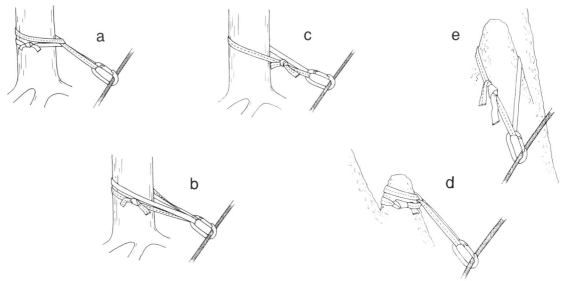

Fig. 10–2. Methods of attaching a runner to natural protection: a, secured around a tree using a girth hitch; b, looped around a tree with the ends clipped together with a carabiner; c, retied around a tree trunk; d, attached to a rock horn using a clove hitch; e, looped over a flake.

girth hitch (fig. 10-2a) or by connecting the two ends with a carabiner (fig. 10-2b). If you clip the ends together with a carabiner, be sure the runner is long enough to permit the carabiner to extend out from the natural feature; this reduces the chance that the weight of a fall will be taken directly on the carabiner gate. Another method of attachment is to untie a runner and then retie it around the protection (fig. 10-2c). With rock horns, you also have the option of attaching the runner with a clove hitch (fig. 10-2d).

• **Position** carabiners with the gates down and facing out to lessen the chance that the rock will force the gate open during a fall. If there's danger of a carabiner being forced open, use a locking carabiner or two carabiners with opposing gates.

• **Pad** all sharp edges that the runner may touch.

TREES AND BUSHES

Trees and large bushes offer the most common and obvious natural protection. To judge their trustworthiness, look for vigorous growth and a well-developed root system. Avoid trees or bushes rooted in shallow soil, gravel, talus, or cracks. If you can identify the tree or bush, you may then know if it's one that tends to be shallow-rooted or especially brittle. Shake it. If the dirt or roots move, avoid it.

Select the largest tree or clump of bushes possible. Be wary of bushes, in general, and back them up with another point of protection if there's any doubt.

To reduce the leverage on a tree or clump of bushes—leverage that could bend or break them—it's best to position the runner as low as possible. However, sometimes it's desirable on a large tree to place the attachment point higher on the trunk, or even on a large branch, to avoid putting a sharp bend in the rope. If the runner is placed on a branch, keep it close to the trunk to reduce the leverage.

HORNS AND FLAKES

Horns are the most common type of natural rock protection. They also are called spikes, knobs, bosses, chicken heads, and rock bollards. They're small protrusions in the rock, and they come in handy.

Flakes are narrow pieces of rock partially detached from the main rock, and they also provide natural protection (fig. 10-2e).

Be aware that a horn or flake that was solid when you climbed the same pitch a year ago might have been weakened by frost action over the winter. Test the rock by pushing or pulling, gently at first, then with more force. Finally, hit it with your hand or foot and listen for a hollow sound. If it moves or creates a hollow sound, avoid it. If you use a girth hitch to secure the runner to a horn or flake, be sure it's placed so it can cinch up tight (fig. 10-3).

Horns and flakes frequently offer protection in only one direction. The runner may stay in place if there is a downward tug, but come loose if the pull is upward or sideways.

There are several ways to help overcome this problem. Attach some extra climbing gear to the runner in order to weight it and help keep it in place. Use a longer runner (or extend a short run-

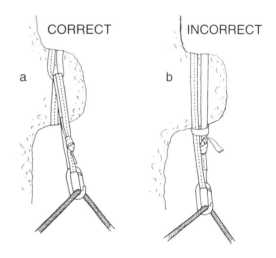

Fig. 10–3. Runner attached to a horn: a, correct, attached by a correctly placed girth hitch. Girth hitch will cinch properly; b, incorrect, attached by an incorrectly placed girth hitch. Girth hitch will not cinch.

ner), a trick that will minimize the chance that rope movement will pull the runner off the rock. Place opposing protection that can take an upward pull. (We'll get into the theory and practice of opposing protection later in this chapter.)

CHOCKSTONES

A chockstone is a rock wedged in a crack. It can make a great protection point—if it passes a few tests. Does it have substantial contact with the sides of the crack? Is the chockstone, and the walls of the crack, of a non-friable type of rock (that won't tend to crumble and let the chockstone fall)? Does the crack narrow below the chockstone, causing it to be well-wedged? Will it jam even tighter if it must withstand the force of a fall?

Arrange a runner around the chockstone so the runner can't be pinched or jammed in case the chockstone comes under such a load. Be sure it can't be pulled sideways through a point of contact between the chockstone and rock. If you choose to simply clip the ends of the runner together with a carabiner, twist one end before clipping in. This ensures that if the runner does pull through one side of the chockstone, the carabiner won't drop off (fig. 10-4a). You also can attach the runner by a girth hitch around the point of contact between chockstone and rock, which can help hold the chockstone in place (fig. 10-4b).

You may be able to use an artificial chock to help thread the runner behind the chockstone.

Sometimes you can move a chockstone to a spot in the crack where it's more secure. Be careful you don't knock it loose and send it hurtling down the climbing route.

BOULDERS

A boulder, or a block detached from the main body of rock, can be used as a protection point if it's well-embedded or too heavy to move. Steer clear of boulders that look chancy—ones that lean, are perched precariously, or rest (temporarily) on a slope.

A runner is usually looped around the boulder to create the protection placement. Keep the runner low to reduce leverage and to keep it from being

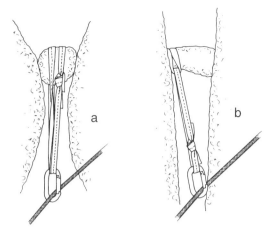

Fig. 10–4. Attaching a runner to a chockstone: a, looped around a chockstone; b, using a girth hitch on one side of a chockstone.

pulled off the top of the boulder. Use extreme care in using a boulder as a protection point because of the danger it poses to others if it comes loose.

THREADED PLACEMENTS

Threaded protection can be created from natural tunnels (fig. 10-5), arches, or the contact point between two blocks of rocks. If the rock feature is strong, the protection is usually a good choice because it is multidirectional; it can take a pull in any direction.

If you decide to use the contact point between two rocks, be sure the rocks can't move under the force of a fall. However, it's often difficult to test threaded protection, and you will usually have to rely on visual inspection and good judgment.

Fig. 10–5. Creating a threaded placement using a rock tunnel

ARTIFICIAL PROTECTION

In the absence of natural protection, climbers use artificial protection devices. These devices include chocks (artificial chockstones), bolts, and pitons. In most cases, the leader will use a chock or bolt, although pitons still have their uses. On a climb, the leader secures the piece of protection in the rock, providing a point of attachment for a runner, which is then connected to the climbing rope using carabiners.

CHOCKS

Chockcraft—the art of placing and removing chocks—is the preferred technique for protecting climbs. This supports the ethic of clean climbing, which is climbing that does not permanently alter the environment. Chocks are relatively easy to place and to remove and, unlike bolts and pitons, leave no scars on the rock.

Chocks are either wedges or cams (fig. 10-6). Wedges hold a fall by wedging against a constriction in a crack or against another wedge. Cams hold a fall by rotating slightly within a crack, creating a camming action that jams the chock against the rock.

Wedges and cams are either passive or spring-loaded. Passive wedges and cams are single pieces of metal, without moving parts, that are simply placed firmly in an appropriate location in the rock. Spring-loaded wedges and cams are chocks with moving parts that are retracted in order to fit them into a spot, then allowed to open fully again to hold them in that place.

To become proficient at chockcraft, a climber learns the strengths and weaknesses of different types of chocks and learns to place them correctly.

The lead climber should know the breaking strength of each chock, information published by manufacturers or independent testers. Larger chocks are usually heavier and stronger than smaller chocks, and therefore have a higher breaking strength. Some smaller chocks aren't even meant to hold a fall, but are strong enough to support a climber's weight in aid climbing.

All chocks are designed to use in a rock feature—usually a crack, sometimes a pocket. Before placing a chock, the climber inspects the rock, both to judge its soundness and to decide what chock to use.

Fig. 10–6. Examples of artificial protection: a, passive wedge; b, passive cam; c, spring-loaded wedge; d, spring-loaded cam.

The type of rock and its condition help indicate whether the chock will hold a fall. Specifically, chocks tend to hold well in solid rock. Crumbling or deteriorating rock is unreliable, and should be avoided.

If you're thinking of putting a piece of protection behind a rock flake, remember the hollow-sound test. Hit it with the palm of one hand, and if you hear a hollow sound, don't use the flake. Under load, it takes only a slight movement of the rock for the chock to lose its grip and fail.

The size, shape, and orientation of the crack or pocket determines what chock to use. Does the crack or pocket flare outward, flare inward, or have parallel sides? Is it shallow or deep? Is it vertical or horizontal? Some types of chocks work well in one situation, not so well in another.

Some other general considerations in placing chocks:

• **Learn** to estimate the right chock size for a particular placement. The better the estimate, the faster the placement—and the less chance the climber will tire and fall.
• **Choose** the best chock, not necessarily the largest one possible. A larger chock usually will hold a harder fall, but first decide if it actually provides the soundest protection or if a smaller piece would be more secure.
• **Decide** whether a particular chock is likely to be adequate, based on the characteristics of the rock and the magnitude of a possible fall. If not, reinforce it with another chock or find a better placement.
• **Check** out every chock after it's in place. Look to see that it's placed correctly. Tug on it to help determine the strength and security of the placement, especially in the likely direction of pull.
• **Guard** against the chock being dislodged by rope movement. A runner is usually attached, with carabiners, between the chock and the rope. This helps reduce the effect of rope movement. Wired chocks are more affected by rope movement and have a greater tendency to rotate out of place.
• **Guard** against the chock being dislodged by an outward or upward pull. Many chock placements are one-directional; they will take a load in only one direction. If a one-directional placement could come under a load from multiple directions, make it multidirectional by placing opposing chocks. (This procedure gets a full explanation later in this chapter.)
• **Remember** the climber who will be following behind you and removing the protection. Make your placements secure, but also try to make them reasonably easy to remove.

Chock slings

A climber's high-priced pieces of protection won't do any good until they're connected to the rope. So every chock must include some type of sling as a part of the attachment system from the chock to the rope. The sling is usually made from accessory cord, tubular webbing, or wire cable.

Smaller chocks usually come with a wire cable sling, which is much stronger than cord or webbing of the same size. The ends of the cable are swaged together. Larger chocks come pre-drilled with holes for accessory cord, which is usually added by the climber. Some chocks come pre-slung with tubular webbing.

There is a bonus advantage to using wire cable with passive wedges, such as Black Diamond (formerly Chouinard) Stopper nuts or Wild Country Stones. The wire's relative stiffness makes the wedges easier to handle and to place.

However, with passive camming chocks, such as Black Diamond Hexentric nuts, it's better to have accessory cord, providing it's strong enough. The cord permits the chock to rotate and cam freely as it's meant to do. Most modern hexes are drilled to accept 5.5-millimeter accessory cord.

For many years, climbers used 6- to 9-millimeter nylon cord and 1-inch nylon webbing to make chock slings. Nylon is durable and inexpensive but requires relatively larger diameters for strength, creating bulky and heavy chock slings.

An alternative fiber called Kevlar came into use for accessory cord. Kevlar cord at 5.5 millimeters in diameter is smaller, lighter, and stronger than nylon. However, Kevlar cord is weakened by repeated bending. Consequently, the manufacturer recommends it only for tying chock slings, because these slings are knotted just once and are not subjected to repeated bending.

A new fiber, Spectra, is even lighter, stronger, and more abrasion resistant than Kevlar. For use as chock slings, the Spectra fiber is used in 5.5-millimeter cord or $^9/_{16}$-inch webbing.

Here are some things to keep in mind when attaching accessory cord as a sling to a chock:

• **Inspect** the holes that are drilled in the chock for the cord. They should have rounded edges to reduce the chance the sling could be cut under stress.
• **Tie** the ends of the cord together with a double fisherman's knot. Check it frequently in use to be sure it stays tight.
• **Determine** the right length for the sling. A sling is usually between 8 and 14 inches long, and some manufacturers provide information on how much sling material is needed for chocks of different sizes. One caution: If you make a chock sling too long, it could hang down far enough to interfere with footwork during climbing.

Passive wedging chocks

Out on a climb, no one will mention anything called a "passive wedging chock." Out there, passive wedging chocks go by a lot of catchier names: brands such as Stoppers, Stones, and RPs, and terms such as nuts, steel nuts, micronuts, tapers, and just plain chocks.

Wedging chocks are tapered down from top to bottom so they will fit into a constriction in a crack. They have a wide side and a narrow side, and are strongest when the wide surface area is touching the rock (fig. 10-7). The object is to get the greatest possible contact between chock and rock. Many wedging chocks, especially the smaller sizes, are not designed to be placed with the narrow side in contact with the rock.

A passive wedging chock has no moving parts to hold it in place. It sits passively in a constricting crack until it takes a load—such as a leader fall.

Fig. 10–7. Wide-side and narrow-side placement of passive wedging chocks: a, wide sides are in contact with the rock, a stronger placement; b, narrow sides are in contact with the rock, a weaker placement.

Then the chock wedges into the crack, generating expansion forces and increased friction. It holds tight.

Though they all taper, there are variations in the shapes of wedging chocks (fig. 10-8). Manufacturers try subtle changes in design to improve performance, and new designs continue to appear.

Some wedging chocks are straight-sided, some

Fig. 10–8. Design variations in passive wedging chocks: a, wide side, straight sides; b, narrow side, straight sides; c, wide side, curved sides; d, narrow side, curved sides; e, top view, rectangular; f, top view, trapezoidal.

have slightly curved sides. They can also have a combination of straight and curved sides. Smaller wedging chocks are usually straight-sided, while larger chocks may have pronounced curvature. Viewed from the top, wedging chocks can be rectangular or trapezoidal.

The goal in using any wedging chock, regardless of shape, is to create a stable and secure point of protection—something you can stake your life on. A straight-sided chock may not place well in a crack with an uneven surface, whereas a curved chock may fit nicely. In another spot, the straight-sided chock could be just the thing.

A curved-sided chock creates three points of contact, which adds to stability (fig. 10-9). However, it may seat so securely that it can be tough to remove. If the edges on a wedging chock are slightly rounded, it tends to be easier to remove.

Fig. 10–9. Curved-sided chock, with three points of contact with the rock

The Hexentric passive camming chock can also be used as a passive wedge. Even though it doesn't look like a wedge, the ends of the Hexentric are tapered, allowing it to wedge in a constricting crack (fig. 10-10).

In an emergency, the knot of a runner can be jammed into a constricting crack and serve as a wedging chock.

Vertical cracks

Here's where wedging chocks work the best. Put the chock above a constriction in a vertical crack. A downward pull wedges the chock more tightly into the crack.

If the sides of the crack are generally smooth, a

Fig. 10–10. Hexentric used sideways in a crack as a passive wedging chock

straight-sided chock works well. If the sides are rougher or slightly curved, a curved-sided chock works better.

For the most secure placement, slot the wedge completely into the crack (fig. 10-11).

Passive wedging chocks usually are able to hold a load only in one direction. However, if the chock is slotted deeply into a crack and seated correctly, it can handle pulls from multiple directions.

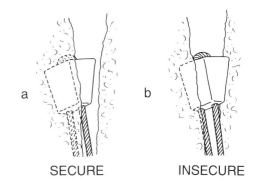

SECURE   INSECURE

Fig. 10–11. Passive wedge slotted in a vertical crack: a, secure, slotted completely into a vertical crack; b, insecure, slotted partially into a vertical crack.

Passive wedging chocks do not work in parallel-sided vertical cracks (fig. 10-12). If the sides of the crack are straight and parallel, the chock has very little contact with the rock, and a severe downward pull can cause the contact points on the chock to shear.

Fig. 10–12. Incorrect, a passive wedge placed in a parallel-sided vertical crack with little contact to the rock

There's a way around this problem: use two wedges in a method called stacking. Stacked chocks can be created from two independent chocks or from a specially made chock stack.

The theory is the same in either case. The chocks are placed in opposition in a parallel crack. A downward pull on the larger chock causes it to wedge between one side of the crack and one side of the opposing chock. All stacked chocks should be seated with a firm tug before use.

If two independent chocks are used (fig. 10-13a), they should be connected with a carabiner so that if the placement fails, a chock will not be lost.

A chock stack (fig. 10-13b) is constructed by putting two passive wedging chocks on the same sling. The chocks are different sizes, with the smaller chock at the end so that either can be used in a non-stacking chock placement.

Stacked wedges aren't used so much any more because climbers now have the option of spring-loaded wedges or spring-loaded cams, which work better and are easier to place.

Horizontal cracks

Although wedging chocks work best in vertical or near-vertical cracks, horizontal cracks sometimes can be used. The horizontal crack should constrict at the lip of the crack. The chock can be slotted in a wider section and then slid behind the constriction (fig. 10-14). A well-placed wedging chock in a horizontal crack can be very secure because it tends to be multidirectional.

The chock should be well recessed, and the sling should not be able to contact a sharp upper or lower lip on the crack. A chock set at the lip of a

Fig. 10–13. Stacking chocks: a, two independent chocks stacked together; b, chock stack.

Fig. 10–14. Passive wedge slotted behind a constriction in a horizontal crack

crack is more likely to fail. The edge of the chock can cause the sling to shear, and the chock itself will create a camming action at the lip of the crack that could cause it to crumble (fig. 10-15).

Fig. 10–15. Passive wedge placed in a horizontal crack, side view: a, correct, slotted deep within the crack; b, incorrect, slotted at the lip of the crack.

Flaring cracks

A wedge that's trapezoidal in shape from a top view may work well in a crack that flares outward. Used with the narrow sides of the chock against the rock, this shape can provide a stronger and more stable placement in this particular situation because it increases surface contact with the rock (fig. 10-16a).

A crack that flares inward can cause a seemingly strong placement to be insecure (fig. 10-16b). If you keep alert you should be able to see this situation before making a bad placement.

Fig. 10–16. Using passive wedges in flaring cracks: a, a secure placement in an outwardly flaring crack; b, an insecure placement in an inwardly flaring crack.

Pockets and threaded placements

Passive wedging chocks don't work well in pockets.

For a threaded placement, where a crack constricts to form a tunnel, a wedging chock can sometimes be threaded through to form a protection point (fig. 10-17). The chock can be threaded upward or downward. A wired chock will thread more easily than a chock that has accessory cord for a sling.

Be sure the crack does not widen too much behind the constriction, possibly permitting the chock to pull through. Good threaded placements, however, can be very secure because they are often multidirectional.

Fig. 10–17. A passive wedge threaded through a tunnel in a crack

Passive camming chocks

Climbers also have a batch of popular names and brand names to use in referring to passive camming chocks: hexes, hex nuts, Hexentrics, Tri Cams.

A passive camming chock is placed in a crack in such a way that when it takes a load—from, for example, a 160-pound climber at the end of a 30-foot leader fall—it tries to rotate. The rotation causes the chock to cam and lock in place.

The shapes of camming chocks vary. One manufacturer will use a design completely different from that of another, and designs continue to evolve.

Traditional camming chocks had a balanced hexagonal shape. Both pairs of opposing sides used for camming were the same distance apart. These hex nuts could cam and lock in place, but had limited versatility because each nut could fit only a small range of crack sizes.

Chouinard Equipment (now Black Diamond Equipment) modified the basic hex nut in creating its Hexentric nut, in which each pair of opposing sides is a different distance apart. The Hexentric can be used in a greater range of crack sizes because it can be placed for narrow camming or wide camming and provides different camming angles (fig. 10-18). It can also be used endwise as a passive wedge.

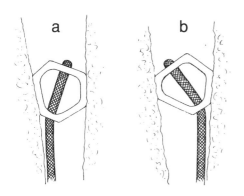

Fig. 10–18. Camming modes of a Hexentric chock: a, narrow camming; b, wide camming.

The Lowe Tri Cam is another design, using a completely different shape to generate the camming action. Because of its shape, the Tri Cam can be used in a range of crack sizes (fig. 10-19).

Any single camming chock works only within a

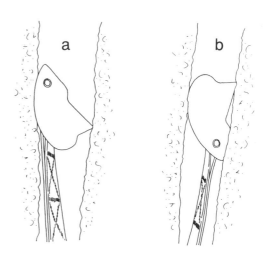

Fig. 10–19. Camming modes of a Lowe Tri Cam chock: a, major cam mode; b, minor cam and wedging mode.

specific range of crack sizes. If a crack is too wide, the chock can fall out. An excessively tight fit, on the other hand, can prevent the camming action from occurring. Then the camming chock would simply act like a passive wedging chock.

After you've placed a passive camming chock, give a sharp tug on the sling. This will initiate some camming action and seat the chock in place.

Vertical cracks

Passive camming chocks work well in vertical cracks that are parallel or that do not expand too much. Place a chock that is tight enough to have maximum contact with the rock, but that has enough room for proper camming action to take place under load.

If the chock is too small, only its edges may be in contact with the rock and, under load, these edges can shear off. A loose chock also can be dislodged by rope movement. The fit should be snug, which will help hold the chock in place when it's not under load (fig. 10-20).

One trick that can create a stable placement is to build a combination stack using a passive wedging chock with a passive camming chock—a Stopper with a Hexentric (fig. 10-21).

Fig. 10–20. Placement of a Hexentric in a vertical crack: a, correct, Hexentric in proper camming mode with sides fully contacting the rock; b, incorrect, Hexentric is too small for the vertical crack. No camming will occur.

Fig. 10–21. A combination stack using a passive wedge and a passive camming chock

Horizontal cracks

Passive camming chocks also like parallel cracks that are horizontal. Place the chock so the sling leaves the crack closer to the roof than to the floor of the crack (fig. 10-22a). Otherwise, it won't cam (fig. 10-22b). Be careful that the chock isn't rotated out of position by sideways forces.

The crack shouldn't widen inward too much or proper camming action won't take place (fig. 10-22c).

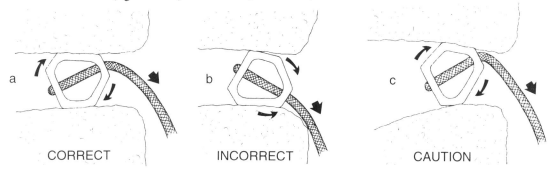

Fig. 10–22. Placement of a Hexentric in a horizontal crack: a, correct, chock sling exits near roof of crack, proper camming will occur; b, incorrect, chock sling exits near bottom of crack, little or no camming will occur; c, caution, if the Hexentric moves back in the inwardly flaring crack, proper camming will not occur.

Flaring cracks

Passive camming chocks don't work well in flaring cracks, where they tend to be unstable and don't make maximum surface contact. Tri Cams work in some flaring cracks. However, all points must still be able to contact the rock and that may not be possible.

Pockets and threaded placements

If the pocket is deep enough, a Tri Cam will work, but it must be recessed completely into a pocket for maximum surface contact and stability (fig. 10-23). Rope movement can easily dislodge this placement.

Fig. 10–23. Tri Cam placed in a pocket

Like passive wedging chocks, some passive camming chocks can be threaded through a small rock tunnel to create a protection point. In this case, the chock is relying on wedging and not camming action to hold a load.

Spring-loaded wedging devices

This is another of those technical terms you won't usually hear while moving up a rock face: spring-loaded wedging devices (fig. 10-24). That's what they're called here, because it's a good technical description. In action, you'll hear them referred to under such names as Quickies, Rock 'n Rollers, and Ball Nuts.

These gadgets use variations on the chock stacking theme to create protection in tiny finger

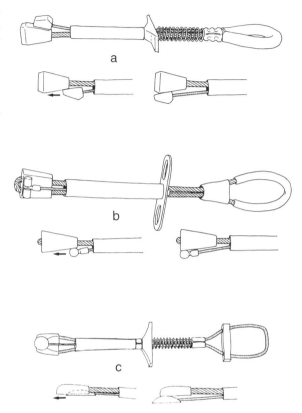

Fig. 10–24. Examples of spring-loaded wedging devices: a, D. Best Quickie, contracted and expanded; b, Go-Pro Rock 'n Roller, contracted and expanded; c, Lowe Ball Nut, contracted and expanded.

cracks. A spring-loaded wedging device features two sliding pieces in opposition. A trigger mechanism held by a spring controls the position of the smaller sliding piece.

Pull the trigger, and the smaller piece slides lower against the larger piece—narrowing the profile of the device so it can fit into the thin crack. Release the trigger, and the smaller piece springs back higher against the larger piece—expanding the profile and wedging the pieces against each other and against the walls of the crack. The force of a fall wedges the pieces even tighter.

You can place a spring-loaded wedge in a vertical crack using only one hand, a big improvement in efficiency over passive chock stacks. After placing a spring-loaded wedge, give it a tug to seat it securely.

Spring-loaded wedges also can be used in horizontal cracks. Try to place them so the stem of the device won't be bent sharply around a rock edge in case of a fall. The stems are flexible, but may not be designed to hold a fall if they are bent too much.

Some spring-loaded wedges are designed to be separated and used as individual wedges if you wish. This makes the device more versatile, but be sure that's what the manufacturer had in mind before you try it.

The orientation of the smaller piece on some spring-loaded wedges, such as the Quickie, is fixed in relation to the larger piece, limiting these devices to parallel-sided cracks. But the smaller piece on designs such as the Rock 'n Roller and the Ball Nut rotates relative to the larger piece. This allows the smaller piece to conform better to un-

even or flaring cracks and reduces the possibility it will be dislodged by rope movement.

Spring-loaded wedges don't work in pockets and threaded placements.

Spring-loaded camming devices

First came Friends. The original spring-loaded camming device was developed in the mid-1970s and dramatically expanded the limits of free climbing by providing protection that could be placed with one hand and that could adapt to a variety of cracks. Climbers now could take on tough routes that would be very difficult to protect with conventional chocks.

Since the development of Friends, variations on the basic design have been created. Newer designs tend to use cable stems, more flexible than the solid stems of the original Friends. Some include three cams instead of the four used in each Friend. Among today's most popular spring-loaded camming devices (fig. 10-25) are Friends and Flexible Friends (manufactured by Wild Country), Camalots (made by Black Diamond Equipment), and TCUs (Three-Cam Units, by Metolius).

The three or four cams in a spring-loaded camming device are connected to a trigger mechanism.

Fig. 10–25. Examples of spring-loaded camming devices: a, Wild Country Friend, expanded and b, contracted; c, Wild Country Flexible Friend; d, Black Diamond Camalot; e, Metolius TCU (tri-cam unit).

Pull the trigger and the cams retract—narrowing the profile of the device so it can fit into a particular crack. Release the trigger and the cams again rotate outward—expanding the profile until the cams grip the sides of the crack (fig. 10-25a). In a fall, the cams try to rotate and expand again, gripping the crack even more securely.

The three or four cams rotate independently of each other, permitting each to expand to the maximum, wherever it may sit in a particular crack.

All is well if you've placed a spring-loaded camming device and all the cams, expanded to their midpoint, are in contact with the rock and the stem of the device is pointing in the likely direction of pull (fig. 10-26a).

But beware of these potential problems:

1. All the cams don't touch the rock. The placement will be unstable. Find a better spot.
2. The cams are over-retracted in the crack (fig. 10-26b). The device may be jammed in so tightly that it can't cam, and it may be very hard to get the thing out. Use a smaller spring-loaded cam.

3. The cams are over-expanded, with only the tips of the cams touching the rock (fig. 10-26c). No camming action can take place, and the device will serve only as a passive wedging chock. Under load, most devices will structurally fail. Use a larger spring-loaded camming device. (An exception is the Camalot, which is strong enough in the "umbrella" position to be used as a passive chock.)
4. The stem does not point in the likely direction of pull (fig. 10-26d). A fall can force the device to rotate, perhaps causing the cams to lose their grip.

In an uneven crack, the independent cams can expand to different widths. This is good. It means the device will adjust to variations in the crack. But if the cams are too unbalanced, proper camming action won't occur and the placement could fail. This is bad. So always try to make sure that each pair of cams is symmetrically oriented and that all cams contact the rock.

The spring-loaded camming devices that use

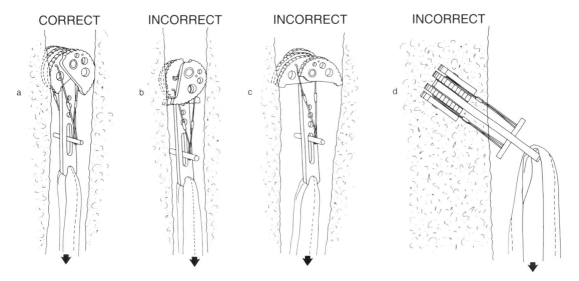

CORRECT   INCORRECT   INCORRECT   INCORRECT

Fig. 10–26. Correct and incorrect placement of spring-loaded camming devices: a, correct, cams expanded to midpoint, stem in likely direction of pull; b, incorrect, cams are over-retracted, proper camming may not occur; c, incorrect, cams are over-expanded, no camming will occur; d, incorrect, stem is not pointed in likely direction of pull.

only three cams, instead of four, are smaller and narrower. They're designed for shallower placements, though they can also be used more conventionally. The four-cam devices have a bad habit of "walking" into cracks as a result of rope movement, making them sometimes difficult to retrieve. The three-cam units will rotate more and are less likely to walk.

Vertical cracks

Spring-loaded camming devices really come into their own in parallel-sided vertical cracks. They're easier, faster, and safer than stacked wedges or passive cams. When correctly placed, the stem of the device will point in the anticipated direction of pull, allowing the load to be transmitted along the axis of the stem and maximizing strength of the placement.

Horizontal cracks

You can also use spring-loaded cams in horizontal and diagonal cracks, but watch out for stem breakage.

The original Friends design uses a solid stem. This is fine as long as the direction of pull is along the axis of the stem, which is usually the case in a vertical crack. The picture changes with horizontal cracks.

Newer designs from the makers of Friends and from other manufacturers use flexible cable stems, which can bend and adjust if the direction of pull is not along the axis (fig. 10-27a). However, the original Friends are still being made and are in wide use, so it's important to know how to minimize the danger of having a solid stem break in a horizontal placement.

If the solid stem doesn't extend beyond the edge of the horizontal crack, the stem won't come under any dangerous forces. However, if the crack is shallow and the stem extends beyond the edge of the crack, the stem would be forced against an edge during a fall and could shear at the lip of the crack.

You can reduce the danger of breakage by adding a tie-off loop, of accessory cord or webbing, to the largest hole in the stem. Make it slightly shorter than the regular chock sling. Clip into the tie-off loop so the force of any load will be taken closer to the cams (and farther from the end of the stem). As a backup, also clip in the regular sling in case the tie-off loop fails (fig. 10-27b).

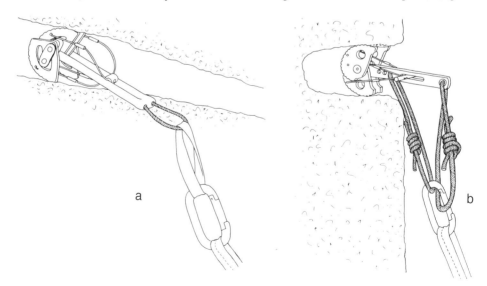

Fig. 10–27. Spring-loaded camming device placement in a horizontal crack: a, flexible cable stem can bend and adjust to the direction of pull; b, a tie-off loop can reduce the danger of solid-stem breakage.

Flaring cracks

Because each cam works independently, they can individually expand to fit a flaring crack. Problems occur if the crack flares too much. Some of the cams could over-expand, making for an unstable placement. The device may then be more susceptible to rotation or rope movement and less able to cam properly under load.

Pockets and threaded placements

Spring-loaded camming devices don't work for threaded placements.

They are usable in some pockets, but only if the pocket is deep enough to allow all cams to touch the rock.

Spring-loaded tube chocks

It's difficult to place protection in wide cracks because most chocks aren't big enough.

Sometimes the answer is a large spring-loaded camming device, but these can get awfully heavy. An alternative spring-loaded device for protecting wide cracks is the telescoping tube chock.

The tube chock has a spring-loaded inner sleeve. Release the spring and the sleeve pops out

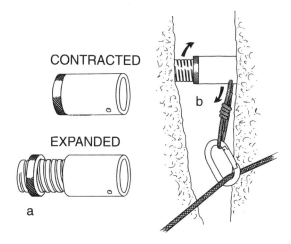

Fig. 10–28. *Spring-loaded tube chock: a,
Mountain Hardwear Big Bro, contracted and
expanded; b, Big Bro correctly placed in a
vertical crack.*

far enough for the tube to bridge the crack (fig. 10-28a). A locking collar keeps the tube extended. After setting the chock, the climber clips in to a sling attached to one end. With a load on that end resulting in an upward force on the other end, the device acts like a passive camming chock (fig. 10-28b).

The wedging factor

Under load, a chock creates expansion forces. The relative amount of expansion force created by a chock—whether it's a wedge or a cam—is known as the wedging factor.

Splitting firewood with a wedge is an illustration of wedging action. A chock is a wedge in the rock. Put a load on the chock, and it tries to expand the rock—just as hitting a wedge with a hammer causes it to split firewood.

The relative amount of expansion force depends on the angle of a chock face (fig. 10-29a). If the taper angle is smaller, the wedging factor will be higher and it will put more force on the rock (fig. 10-29b). Conversely, if the taper angle is larger, the wedging factor will be lower (fig. 10-29c).

Friction between the rock and the chock affects the wedging factor. Rougher rock increases friction, which decreases the wedging factor. Dirt or vegetation can lubricate the chock, reducing friction and increasing the wedging factor.

The applied load and the wedging factor combine to determine the actual amount of expansion force generated. A high applied load, such as a falling climber, taken on a chock with a high wedging factor results in a very large expansion force.

A couple of examples can give an idea of how the wedging factor affects expansion forces. A chock with a taper angle of 14.4 degrees will cause it to push against the walls of a crack with a force equal to four times the load. Therefore, a 170-pound climber who puts full weight on this chock would generate 680 pounds of expansion force (and a little hop could easily double the force). Now take a smaller chock, with a taper angle of 4.5 degrees. The wedging factor goes much higher, now equal to 12 times the load. The 170-

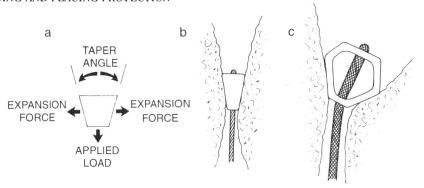

Fig. 10–29. The wedging factor: a, illustration of taper angle and expansion forces; b, narrow chocks have small taper angles and generate greater expansion force under load; c, wide chocks have large taper angles and generate less expansion force under load.

pound climber who puts full weight on the chock now generates 2,040 pounds of expansion force.

The wedging factor becomes particularly important when placing a chock behind a flake. Expansion force could push the flake outward, loosening the protection. It could even knock the flake off, destroying the protection point. Chocks with higher wedging factors are more likely to generate this magnitude of expansion force.

A flake best resists expansion force near its point of attachment. Consequently, it may be better to use a smaller chock (with greater wedging factor) near the attachment point, than a larger chock (with lower wedging factor) higher up. The tradeoff in using a smaller chock is that it is a weaker piece of protection.

The camming action of a spring-loaded camming device generates very concentrated expansion force. Be cautious in using them behind flakes.

BOLTS AND PITONS

Bolts and pitons are protection devices that are drilled into the rock or pounded into cracks. They sometimes provide protection where there's no place to lodge a chock.

A bolt is a permanent piece of protection driven into a hole drilled in the rock (fig. 10-30a). A bolt hanger provides attachment for a carabiner, and a threaded nut is sometimes needed to attach the hanger to the bolt.

A piton is a metal spike that is pounded into a crack to provide a point of protection (fig. 10-30b). The blade of the piton is the part driven into the rock; the eye is the point of attachment for the carabiner.

Placing pitons is called pitoncraft, a skill that will be studied in Chapter 11. Pitons and bolts are being introduced here because it's necessary to know how to deal with ones you will encounter on climbs, put in place by previous climbers. You need to know how to check these placements to determine if they can be trusted as protection for your climb.

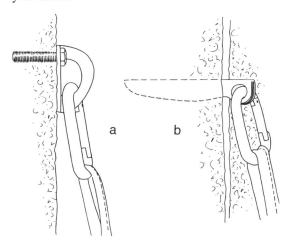

Fig. 10–30. Bolts and pitons: a, bolt with a bolt hanger; b, piton driven into a vertical crack.

Pitons are seldom used in modern free climbing. They still get some use on climbs in remote areas or on routes requiring mixed free and aid climbing.

Bolts are now widely used to protect some of today's severe free rock climbs. The bolts create artificial protection where there are no rock features to accept either chocks or pitons. However, climbing ethics encourage the use of clean-climbing techniques when possible, to prevent the permanent scarring caused by pitons and bolts.

Bolts

Look at fixed bolts with a skeptical eye.

How safe a particular bolt may be is going to depend on the quality of the hardware, the type of rock, the skill of the climber who placed the bolt, and so forth. It's to your advantage, to say the least, to carefully check out every bolt you encounter before clipping into it.

Check to see that the bolt is placed in rock that is solid, not crumbling or deteriorating. Be sure the hanger is flush to the rock. Look for corrosion or cracks on the bolt or hanger. Beware of aluminum hangers because they can become brittle with use. Steel hangers tend to be stronger.

Do not tap on a bolt to test its strength or security as repeated hammering only loosens the bolt. The bolt can be partially tested by hand or by clipping a runner onto it and tugging. If it moves, or if for any reason the placement doesn't seem solid, forget it except possibly for backup protection.

If you like the bolt, use a carabiner to clip a runner to the bolt hanger. In some climbing areas, bolt hangers are customarily removed by climbers after use, so it may be necessary to carry along a few hangers and nuts in $1/4$-inch and $3/8$-inch sizes.

If a hanger is not available, a hangerless bolt can be used by sliding a wired chock down its cable sling so the resulting wire loop can be placed over the bolt. Slide the chock back up the sling to create a snug noose, then clip into the sling (fig. 10-31). Rope movement easily dislodges this type of placement, so don't use it for protection unless it's an emergency. Nevertheless, it can be used in

Fig. 10–31. Placing a wired chock on a hangerless bolt: a, create a loop by sliding the chock down the chock sling; b, slide the chock up the sling to form a noose around the hangerless bolt.

aid climbing or in constructing opposing chock placements.

Pitons

Can you trust an old piton? Well, it depends ...

A fixed piton that you run across during a climb may be a quick and easy way to get some good protection. It may also be old and in bad condition. Over the years, pitons rust, weaken, and become loose.

Take a close look at the piton. Is the eye broken or badly rusted? Is the piton rusting in the crack or perhaps even loose enough to pull out by hand? Is the piton bent?

Ideally, the fixed piton is perpendicular to the likely direction of pull, and it's driven in all the way, with the eye up close to the rock. Examine the condition of the rock, looking for deterioration. Test the piton first by hand. Then tap on it with a piton hammer or a large chock. If it moves, it's unreliable. Beware of older pitons that use iron rings as an attachment point because the rings tend to be very weak. If there is any doubt about a piton's strength or security, try to find other protection.

If the piton seems to be strong, secure, and in good condition, use it. Attach a runner with a carabiner clipped to the piton eye. Be sure the carabiner will not bind against the rock under load, which could cause carabiner failure.

If a piton is only partially driven, tie it off next to the rock with a runner, using a girth hitch or clove hitch (fig. 10-32). The tie-off reduces the leverage on the piton under the impact of a fall. It's also possible to get a marginal attachment by using a cabled chock in the same manner as in connecting to a hangerless bolt. (Slide a wired chock down its cable sling, place the resulting wire loop over the piton, and slide the chock back up the sling to make a snug noose.)

Fig. 10–32. Partially driven piton, with a tie-off next to the rock to reduce leverage

If a piton eye is bent so much that the carabiner won't fit through, it may be possible to thread a cabled chock through the eye. Don't count on it to hold a hard fall, however, and avoid this placement if you have an alternative.

The best judge of fixed pitons is the climber who knows how to place them correctly in the first place. (See Chapter 11 for information on placing pitons.)

DOUBLE PLACEMENTS

Two pieces of protection are sometimes linked in order to do a better job than a one-piece placement. This technique is commonly used in two different ways: to set up opposing chocks so the placement gives multidirectional protection, or to equalize the load over two pieces of protection.

Multidirectional protection

Most chock placements will hold only a downward pull. They are one-directional, providing protection for a load from only a single direction.

No problem, you might say. If I fall, I'll only fall downward. True. But there are times a chock must be able to hold an upward or sideways pull. When the route changes direction at or above a placement, the resulting bend in the rope may simply pull a passive chock up and out of the crack. In some cases a fall taken on a higher chock will put upward and outward forces on lower chocks.

What's needed in these situations is multidirectional protection—placements that will hold fast whether the pull is down, up, or out. The most obvious multidirectional protection is provided by trees, natural tunnels, pitons, and bolts. Otherwise, the standard method of providing multidirectional protection is to place a pair of opposed chocks—chocks that are linked so that they pull toward each other. This method also is used to hold passive wedging chocks in horizontal cracks that won't take a simple placement.

Vertical opposition

An "iffy" chock in a vertical crack needs help from an opposed "keeper" chock.

The basic procedure is simple. Place one chock in the crack so it can take a downward pull. Below that, place a chock that can take an upward pull. Clip a carabiner to each chock sling. Using a clove hitch or half hitches, tie the two carabiners together with a runner so there is tension between the two chocks, which helps hold them in place (especially the bottom chock—the keeper—which otherwise might drop out). Then clip the rope into this arrangement. Three methods are shown here in figure 10-33.

Another setup, recommended in some climbing

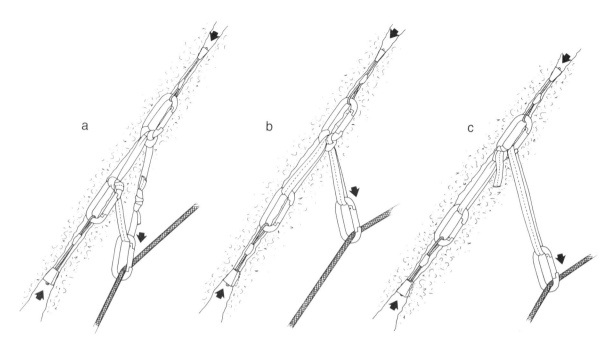

Fig. 10–33. Three methods for creating vertical opposition: a, using one runner, chocks are held by tension on one side of the runner using clove hitches; b, using one long runner, a clove hitch or two half hitches holds the tension between the chocks; c, using two short runners, one runner creates the tension between the chocks using a clove hitch or two half hitches, the other runner clips to the rope.

texts, should be avoided (fig. 10-34). This setup has two principal disadvantages compared with the preferred methods.

First of all, it places a dangerous multiplication of forces on the upper chock. Because the runner is not tied off to the upper chock, the runner moves freely through the carabiner, which acts like a pulley. This will double the usual force on the upper chock, perhaps causing it to fail.

Secondly, the bottom chock has nothing to hold it in place. This chock may stay put if it's set securely or if there is some tension on the rope. Otherwise, it could simply drop out.

The preferred methods (illustrated in figure 10-33) avoid the dangers of load multiplication. Each preferred method creates tension between the chocks to hold them in place and includes a tie-off at the upper chock to prevent the carabiner from acting like a pulley and multiplying the load.

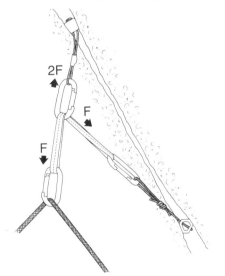

Fig. 10–34. Incorrect method of creating vertical opposition

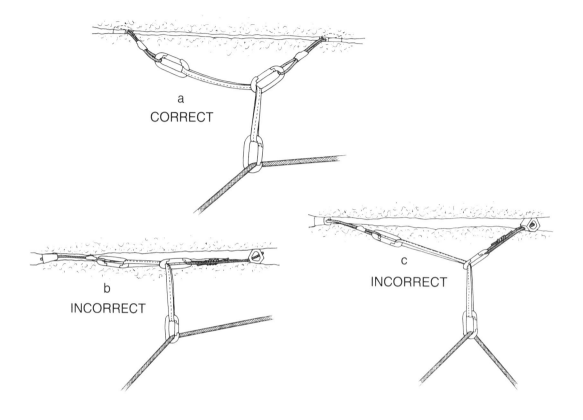

Fig. 10–35. Creating horizontal opposition in a crack: a, correct, chocks are slotted back into the crack and angled to resist rotation and outward pull under load; b, incorrect, chocks are slotted at the lip of the crack and face directly at each other; c, incorrectly placed chocks in vertical opposition can be rotated out of the crack under load.

Horizontal opposition

If a horizontal crack doesn't have a nice constriction to slot a passive wedging chock behind, you can try to set up opposing chocks. Under load, the opposition pulls the chocks toward each other, creating tension that keeps them in the crack.

Here's the basic procedure: slot two chocks back in the crack. They should face in the general direction of each other, yet be set at enough of an angle to withstand some outward and downward loading. If at least one chock cannot withstand some downward loading, the horizontal opposition is likely to fail.

There are a couple of ways to link the chocks to each other and to the rope. In one method, a runner clipped to the carabiner at one chock sling simply runs through the carabiner at the other sling and then is clipped to the rope (fig. 10-35a). Be *sure* the chocks are slotted back into the crack and are partially angled outward. If not, the chocks could rotate out of the crack and fail under load (fig. 10-35b and c). Also, be aware that the usual force felt by the right-hand chock in figure 10-35a will be increased because its carabiner will act like a pulley. Choose a strong chock for this placement.

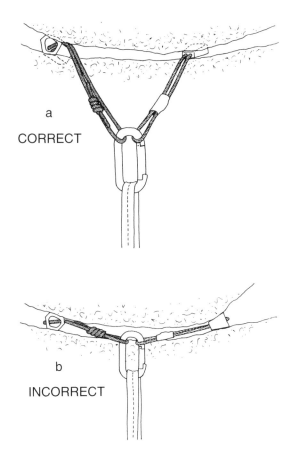

Fig. 10–36. Clipping two chocks together to create horizontal opposition: a, correct, chocks are slotted back into the crack and angled to resist rotation and outward pull under load; b, incorrect, chocks are slotted at the lip of the crack and face directly at each other. The chocks are susceptible to rotation and outward pull under load.

Another method is to clip the two chocks together with a carabiner (fig. 10-36). The carabiner can either be clipped into both chock slings or into runners that extend from the slings.

In either case, there are two important things to remember:

First, slot the chocks back in the crack, facing in the general direction of each other but angled partially outward. At least one must be able to withstand outward and downward loading.

Second, keep the angle between the chock slings as small as possible. When two chocks are connected and subjected to a load, the angle between the slings determines how much force they will experience. The larger the angle, the greater the force on the chocks (fig. 10-37). Too large an

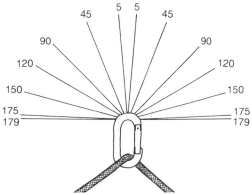

If the load on the carabiner is 100 lbs., then each anchor will be subjected to X pounds of force depending on the angle:

ANGLE BETWEEN PROTECTION (DEGREES)	LOAD ON PROTECTION (LBS.)
179	5727
175	1147
150	200
120	100
90	71
45	54
5	51

Fig. 10–37. How the angle between protection affects the force exerted on the protection under load

angle and the protection could fail. The angle should be kept below 90 degrees, and ideally around 45. Using runners to extend out from the slings will reduce the angle, helping minimize the force felt by the chocks during a fall.

Equalizing protection

Faced with a hard move and questionable protection, a leader may decide to place two pieces of protection close together. If the upper chock fails, the lower chock is there as a backup (fig. 10-38).

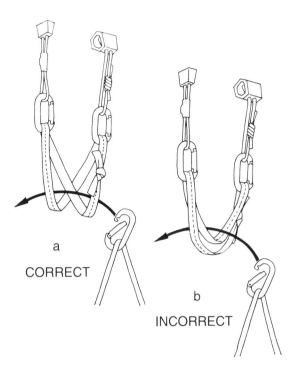

Fig. 10–39. Constructing the two-point equalizing protection: a, correct, the carabiner is clipped from one loop of the twisted runner to the other; b, incorrect, the carabiner is clipped across the twisted runner.

a
CORRECT

b
INCORRECT

Fig. 10–38. Placing a backup chock to help protect a questionable placement

Another option is to equalize the load over two protection points, subjecting each to only a portion of the total force. (A more complicated version of equalizing protection, with three or more protection points, can be used at belay points to establish an anchor. See Chapter 7.)

Two-point equalizing protection can be placed

with one hand and requires the use of only one runner. Twist the runner into two halves, then clip each end into a protection point. Clip a carabiner between the two halves, providing an attachment point for the rope (fig. 10-39a). A load on the rope causes this carabiner to slide between the questionable protection points, adjusting the runner to equalize the force exerted on each point.

Important: clip the carabiner from one loop of the twisted runner to the other loop, not crosswise (fig. 10-39b). You'll find out why if you fall and one of the protection points fails. If you've done it right, the carabiner will stay connected to the runner, which stays connected to the remaining protection. Do it wrong, and the carabiner, with you attached, will plummet.

TECHNIQUES OF PROTECTION: LEADING A PITCH

A SAFE LEADING STRATEGY

After you get to know the tools for protection and how to place them, it's time for the next move—literally.

It's one thing to recognize a Stopper and a hex and a Friend and to be able to use them in individual placements. You can learn all this at home or while standing safely at the base of a cliff.

It's another thing to get up on the cliff and take the lead. You now need to learn the protection techniques that let you use these tools safely in mapping strategy for an entire pitch.

You'll learn to think of the entire pitch as you make each placement. How will this placement affect the total climbing system—and vice versa? Learn these techniques and you shouldn't have any nasty surprises in a fall. That beautifully placed chock won't pop out, because you used the right tricks to make it do its job in the context of protection for the entire pitch.

Leading is a complex business. Beginners usually need an apprenticeship, moving behind seasoned climbers, before they can safely take the sharp end of the rope. Don't ever take a lead if you don't feel ready, and don't pressure others into leading. Keep the art of leading what it ought to be: exciting, challenging, satisfying, and safe.

DECIDING FREQUENCY OF PROTECTION

The universal fear of falling leads many climbers to place protection before almost every move. They deplete their hardware and waste valuable time. They also miss one of the great attractions of rock climbing, the exhilaration of moving smoothly and continuously up the rock.

Other climbers under-protect, sometimes to show off their strength and daring. They get a psychological lift that doesn't do a thing to counteract the law of gravity.

But the sensible climbers—you and I—base our decisions about protection on a careful assessment of our personal abilities, the character of the rock, and the time and equipment available.

The closest thing to a general rule is to place protection where you feel uncomfortable without it. Of course, comfort level isn't always determined by a rational assessment of danger. A climber who feels comfortable making a difficult move a mere 6 feet above the last piece of protection may risk a nasty fall onto a sharp rock horn, while a climber on a low-angle friction slab with no projections to hit if he falls may be terrified at running out 20 feet beyond the protection.

In coming to your own decision on when to place another piece of protection, keep in mind the quality of the placements on a pitch. If they're tending to be poor or questionable, you'll probably put in more to increase the likelihood that at least one will hold. Knowing the fall factor, discussed next, also helps in deciding the next placement.

DETERMINING THE FALL FACTOR

The relative forces generated by a leader fall are measured by the fall factor, determined by dividing the length of a fall by the length of rope run out from the belay. The higher the fall factor, the greater the force.

The fall factor is lower when the length of rope run out from the belay is relatively great, because a long length of rope stretches more and absorbs more energy than a short length. The practical effect of this fact is that when the length of rope between belayer and climber is great, a fall will usually result in a smaller force than the same fall on a short length. Therefore, it's possible to place protection less frequently toward the end of a pitch without increasing the fall factor.

The fall factor is an important concept for the lead climber to understand because it provides an estimate of the relative forces that will be generated in a fall. The lead climber—not the belayer—determines the fall factor by deciding when to place protection. Therefore, the leader should keep the fall factor in mind and take steps to minimize it. Place protection as soon as possible after leaving the belay stance, in order to eliminate chances of a fall with the maximum fall factor of two. Then place intermediate protection as the opportunity arises while you climb. You can roughly estimate the potential fall factor at different points during the lead, to help in deciding when to place more protection. Just remember that a fall near the start of a pitch puts relatively more force on you and the protection, so it generally promotes safety to place more protection near the beginning.

Your belayer has the capability to adjust the belay technique to help accommodate the fall factor and minimize the effects of the fall on you and the climbing system. However, if you allow too much friction to develop in the climbing system or lead out the full length of the rope, the belayer will not be able to dynamically feed out rope to reduce the fall forces. This can create a static belay and cause the actual fall forces experienced by the leader to be higher.

SELECTING A PLACEMENT

As you lead a pitch, moving up from the belay station or from the last piece of protection, you'll reach a point where you would like to put in another piece—either because you want the extra protection at that point, or because a good opportunity for a placement presents itself. Find a stance for yourself that is secure and comfortable as possible. It can take some time to put in a good placement, so you need a stance where you won't slip off or become dangerously tired.

If there's no good stance, you're stuck with some unpleasant options: downclimb and ask the belayer to lead the pitch; hang on desperately and hope to get in a placement before arms or legs give out; or charge on to the next available placement point. This unhappy situation usually can be avoided by planning ahead and placing protection before it's urgently needed. When such a situation does develop, however, don't panic. Make a decision and stick with it. Surprisingly often, the correct decision is to continue without protection to the next possible placement.

When you find a good stance, however, go ahead with the protection placement. Sometimes you'll be faced with a choice between two or more

usable cracks for placing chocks. It's tempting to always place the largest possible chock, but which one you use should depend on considering several factors. Which placement would be the strongest? What size chocks should be conserved for use higher on the pitch? Which placement will be easiest for the second climber to remove? Choose your placement after thinking through all the consequences of your choice.

ATTACHING THE ROPE TO THE PROTECTION

The normal method of attaching the rope to any piece of artificial protection is very simple and very important. A runner clipped by a carabiner to the artificial protection is also clipped by another carabiner to the rope. The finished chain of protection is this: a piece of protection, a carabiner, a runner, another carabiner, the rope (fig. 10-40a).

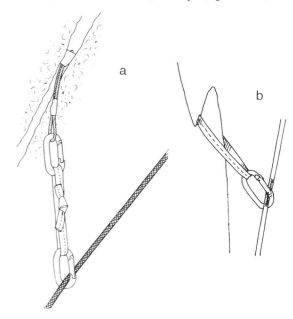

Fig. 10–40. Attaching the rope to the protection: a, attaching the rope to a piece of artificial protection (artificial protection, carabiner, runner, carabiner, rope); b, attaching the rope to natural protection (natural protection, runner, carabiner, rope).

With natural protection, the usual method of attaching the rope is to clip it to a carabiner that is clipped to a runner around the point of natural protection—whether it's a tree, flake, rock horn, or whatever. The finished chain of protection is: the point of natural protection, a runner, a carabiner, the rope (fig. 10-40b).

These standard methods of extending the protection point with a runner have two critical virtues: they reduce the effect of rope movement on the protection, and they reduce the drag on the rope as it moves through the climbing system.

Carabiners

The carabiner is a basic tool for connecting parts of the climbing system. A carabiner's reliability in the event of a climber's fall is largely determined by how it is placed and used.

Clip each carabiner so the solid side is against the rock and the gate is down and facing out. This helps ensure that contact with the rock won't force the gate open—resulting in a much weaker carabiner—and makes it easier to clip a runner or rope into the carabiner.

The carabiner should allow the rope to run smoothly without twists or kinks. Avoid chaining carabiners, which can become unclipped if severely twisted. Use locking carabiners, or two carabiners with gates opposed, if there's danger of a carabiner being forced open as the result of a fall.

It's always best to use a carabiner to attach the runner to a chock sling, rather than tying the runner directly to the sling (fig. 10-41a). This is particularly important with wired chocks because the wire cable under load could cut the runner. In an emergency, you can loop a runner through a wire sling (fig. 10-41c). But never attach the runner to a wire sling with a girth hitch (fig. 10-41b).

When a carabiner is clipped directly into protection (usually a bolt or piton), see that the carabiner

Fig. 10–41. Attaching a chock to a runner: a, correct, a carabiner is used to connect the chock to the runner; b, emergency only, the runner is looped through the chock sling; c, incorrect, the runner is girth-hitched to the chock. A cable chock sling could cut the runner under load.

will not bind against the rock. A fall could subject the carabiner to loads from several directions and cause carabiner failure.

Runners

Single runners and the shorter runners known as quick draws are usually used with artificial protection. Double runners are often used to loop around natural protection such as trees and boulders.

You can create a large runner by connecting one runner to another with a girth hitch. Two single runners connected together like this will be about the length of a double runner.

For single runners or quick draws, there's a choice of using sewn or tied runners. Each has certain advantages and disadvantages. Sewn runners are stronger, lighter, less bulky, and have no knot that needs rechecking or retying. However, they cannot be untied and retied around a protection placement. Tied runners are cheaper and have a knot for use as a passive wedging chock in emergencies. They also can be untied and then retied around a tree or other point of protection. But tied runners are bulkier, and the knot (the weakest part of a tied runner) must be checked regularly for looseness.

Energy-absorbing runners can be used to reduce the load on marginal protection. This type of runner has a series of bar tacks designed to rip out as they absorb some of the load in a fall (fig. 10-42).

A safety consideration in using energy-absorbing runners: as each bar tack breaks, it can cause vibration that opens the gate of the attached carabiner. If all the bar tacks break, the final load could be on an open carabiner. (A locking carabiner would be insurance against this problem.) With these special runners, it's important to study the manufacturer's instructions.

KEEPING THE ROPE IN A STRAIGHT LINE

Keeping the rope in roughly a straight line from the belayer to the climber is the best way to reduce rope drag and to guard against unanticipated fall forces. Rope drag is at best an annoyance and at

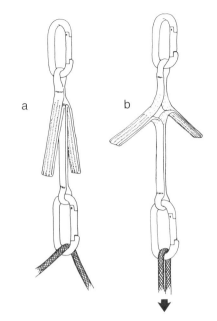

Fig. 10–42. Energy-absorbing runner: a, Yates Screamer energy-absorbing runner in use; b, during a fall, the bar tacks will break to absorb energy and help reduce the load on marginal protection.

worst can cause a leader fall. Fall forces, if they're not anticipated and planned for, can yank your protection right out of the rock.

Reducing rope drag

Rope drag causes all sorts of problems. It can hold a climber back. It can throw a climber off balance. It makes it hard for the leader to pull up enough rope to clip into the next protection. It adds friction to the climbing system, which can increase the force on the top piece of protection in a fall. Also, rope drag can affect how well a belayer responds to a fall, by reducing the ability to provide a dynamic belay.

If the protection placements do not follow a straight line up the pitch and if the rope is clipped directly in to these placements, it will zig-zag up the cliff, causing severe rope drag (fig. 10-43b). That's one main reason to extend runners from protection to rope, allowing the rope to hang straighter and run more freely through the protection system (fig. 10-43a).

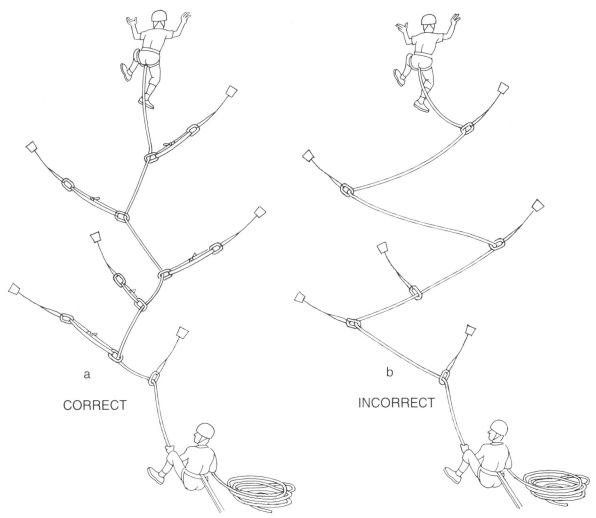

Fig. 10–43. Reducing rope drag: a, correct, the protection placements are extended using runners to straighten the rope and reduce rope drag; b, incorrect, the rope was allowed to excessively zig-zag, causing severe rope drag.

There's another problem that can occur here: the increased fall distance when using an extra-long runner. The extension may help keep the rope in a straight line. But it may also add dangerous extra feet to the length of a fall. In such a case, it's sometimes better to accept some rope drag in order to get better security in case of a fall.

If the protection placements happen to be in a straight line, the rope will, of course, be straight and experience less rope drag, even if it's clipped directly to the protection. And by clipping the rope directly to the protection, the distance of any fall is minimized. However, be aware that rope movement might jiggle a chock out of position in this situation. When a rope is clipped directly to bolts or pitons, a short runner (known as a quick draw) or two linked carabiners are normally used to separate the rope from the protection.

Judging the direction of fall forces

The mechanics of placing protection is only one skill a leader must acquire. The leader must also anticipate the direction of forces that will be created by a fall and how they affect the protection placements.

Climbers can be so wrapped up in placing the next piece of protection that they fail to analyze the effect it will have on the entire climbing system. This can create a false sense of security. A protection point may seem solid and secure—but it may not withstand a fall that generates forces in directions not anticipated. It's the responsibility of the lead climber to anticipate and protect against these fall forces.

The dangers of a zig-zagging rope again command our attention. The zig-zag not only puts a dangerous amount of drag on the rope, but also can bring unanticipated forces to bear on the protection. The pieces of protection may have been placed only with the thought of holding a downward pull. Now they are in danger of taking sharp pulls from a number of directions during a fall.

Consider this: when a climber falls, the rope becomes taut in an attempt to form a straight line from the belayer up to the highest protection and then back down to the falling climber. The zig-zag rope tries to go straight—tugging sideways or up or outward on every piece of protection as it does so (fig. 10-44). If the placements are designed to take a pull in only one direction, they may come loose. If the highest piece of protection fails, the whole system could collapse.

During a fall, the top piece of protection is

Fig. 10–44. Judging the direction of fall forces: a, a zig-zagging rope can bring unanticipated fall forces to bear on the protection; b, as the rope tries to straighten, it can pull up or outward on the protection, causing it to fail, especially if it was placed only for a downward pull.

Fig. 10–45. The combined force on the top protection placement during a fall

loaded with the sum of two forces: the impact of the falling climber and the force exerted by the belay in arresting the fall (fig. 10-45). If a fall is taken by a weak piece of protection, it could fail. In this situation, it would be nice to know the protection below could be counted on to stay in place. But with the rope zig-zagging all over the hill, this might not be the case.

As in the problem of rope drag, keeping the rope in a straight line will prevent most of the problems caused by fall forces. Try to make all the protection placements form a straight line back to the belayer, or extend the protection with runners to permit the rope to run straight.

Work for placements that will take some upward or outward pull. Try to ensure that all awkward placements are multidirectional by using natural protection, such as a tree or a tunnel, or by setting up opposing chocks.

Consider ending the pitch early, before the normal belay point, to avoid awkward placements. Two smaller pitches may be better than one long meandering pitch.

GUARDING AGAINST THE ZIPPER EFFECT

The full-scale zipper effect is a dramatic demonstration of the importance of anticipating force directions. It happens most readily where the belay is established away from the base of the climb. The rope runs at a low angle from the belayer to the

Fig. 10–46. The zipper effect in action: force on the bottom chock is up and out.

first piece of protection on the cliff. There, the rope changes direction and goes abruptly upward. In a leader fall, the rope goes taut and tries to run in a straight line from the belayer to the top piece of protection—putting great outward pressure on that bottom chock. If it pulls out, the line of chocks could be yanked out one by one from the bottom up—the zipper effect in action (fig. 10-46).

The zipper effect can also occur at placements higher on the pitch. Danger points are found on overhanging and traversing routes.

The zipper effect can be prevented by making the suspect placement multidirectional, using natural protection or opposing vertical chocks. At the bottom of the pitch, another method of prevention is to move the belay to the base of the climb. (This may not be possible, however, because of the danger of falling rock.)

PROTECTING SPECIAL SITUATIONS

Overhangs

That overhang looks intimidating, doesn't it? But for purposes of placing protection, simply pay close attention to the consequences of every placement, just as you've been doing on the rest of the pitch. Keep the rope running as free of the overhang as possible. Extend the rope with runners in order to reduce rope drag, prevent dangerous fall forces (the zipper effect), and keep the rope from being cut by the edge of the overhang (fig. 10-47). On small overhangs, it may be possible to lean out and place protection above it.

Traverses

A lead climber often places protection both before and after a hard move, which guards not only the leader but the climber who follows (fig. 10-48). This is particularly important on traverses, where the second climber could otherwise face a long pendulum fall. In addition to the danger of injury, that kind of fall could leave the second in a tough spot, off route and with no easy way back.

As you lead a diagonal or traversing section, keep in mind the effect each placement could have on a second. Put yourself in the second's shoes and ask, Would I like some extra protection here? If so, place it.

It's possible to belay the second with an extra rope, which may help protect against a pendulum

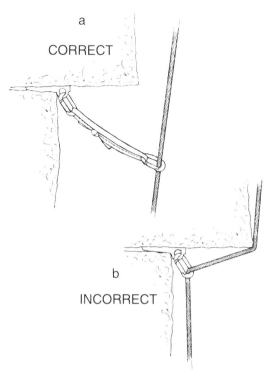

Fig. 10–47. Placements under overhangs: a, correct, rope runs free of the overhang; b, incorrect, bends cause rope drag and rope could be cut by rock edge during a fall.

fall and provide better protection than the leader's rope. If you happen to be using the double-rope technique (described later in this chapter), do not clip in both ropes during the traverse so that the follower can receive a belay from above on the free rope.

PLANNING A FULL CLIMB

WHAT GEAR TO BRING

You're planning a climb. And the question before you is: what should we carry along for protection?

If you're in an established climbing area, no problem. A guidebook will often tell what you need to know before deciding what to carry: type of rock, width of cracks, amount of fixed or natural protection, length and direction of each pitch, difficulty rating—even the precise sizes of chocks needed.

It's a different matter on first ascents or in remote climbing areas. The leader then has much

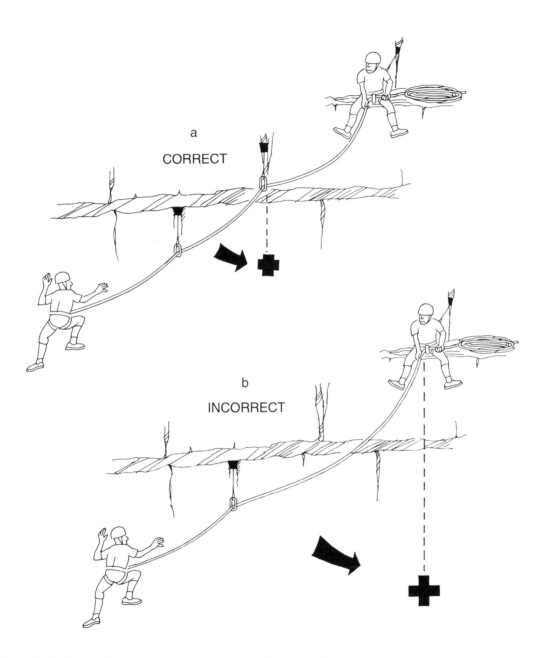

Fig. 10–48. Protecting a traverse: a, correct, placing protection after a hard move on a traverse can reduce the potential pendulum fall for the second climber; b, incorrect, if the second climber falls on a traverse with inadequate protection, he faces a long pendulum fall.

less information to use in estimating what to take along. Take too much, and the extra weight and equipment make the climbing awkward and harder than necessary. Take too little, and you may be forced to "run it out"—to climb higher above the protection than is safe.

For protection, a leader always packs a selection of chocks, carabiners, and runners. But how many and what kind? These questions can't be answered without knowing some specifics of the climb at hand. However, there are some general considerations in choosing what to bring.

First of all, there's an endless variety of protection available—in the climbing shops. Because of the cost, most climbers own only a moderate number of protection devices. So the two climbers in a typical rock climbing team can really choose only from the protection they own (or borrow). The climbers usually combine their equipment to increase the choices of protection.

Chocks: It's very difficult to know just what size you'll need. Pick sizes and types that fit a wide range and offer more options.

Carabiners: In most cases, each protection placement requires at least two carabiners. Nonlocking carabiners are the norm, though locking carabiners can be used in cases where the gate might be forced open during a fall. Many climbers carry extra carabiners (free carabiners) for contingencies.

Runners: These will be in three lengths: short (quick draws), medium (single runners), and long (double runners). Each point of protection commonly requires one runner. The proper runner at any point is the one that helps the rope stay in as straight a line as possible. Additional runners are needed for belay anchors and unanticipated protection placements.

Chock picks: Sometimes chocks are harder to get out than to put in. That's why each climbing team needs a chock pick—a thin metal tool that helps the second climber remove pieces of protection from a pitch (fig. 10-49). The second climber uses the tool to pry and poke and tap and tug at chocks that are too tightly lodged to come out by hand. Even with the pick, it often takes persistence

Fig. 10–49. Chock picks, left to right: shelf bracket, piton type, Leeper, skewer type or tent stake, Friend of a Friend.

to remove a chock. Give up if it refuses to budge. Wasting time trying to remove a badly stuck chock only tires you out and delays the climb.

In addition to chocks, carabiners, runners, and a chock pick, a rock climber often carries a belay device, a chalk bag, and tie-off loops (for such uses as emergency prusiking and for tying off a climber after a fall).

HOW TO CARRY THE GEAR

Once you've decided what gear to take, it must be organized for carrying. The technique of organizing the gear is called racking. The collection of gear is the rack.

Typically, pieces of protection are carried on a gear sling which is slung over the head and under one arm. (Climbing shops sell gear slings, or you can make your own by sewing 2-inch flat webbing into a loop and then rolling and sewing about half of it into a rope-like shape.) Single runners are grouped together and slung over the head—on top of the gear sling and under the opposite arm (fig. 10-50a).

Double runners are too long to handle without a little extra work. A double runner can just be doubled before it goes over your head. An alternative method, which makes it easier to get it when you need it, is to drape the double runner over one shoulder and then clip the two ends together under the opposite arm with a carabiner. Make one twist in the runner before attaching the carabiner, which will eliminate the possibility of the carabiner falling off when the runner is removed. When you need the runner, simply unclip the carabiner from one end and yank; the double runner will pull free.

Typical ways to rack gear

The ideal racking method would permit the leader to place protection efficiently and to climb without awkwardness despite carrying the gear. No such ideal method exists, but a variety of compromises are in use.

One carabiner per chock

In one common method, each chock and each runner gets its own carabiner (fig. 10-50b). In this setup, the gate of each carabiner that carries a chock should be up and toward your body, making it easier to unclip the carabiner from the gear sling.

This method can be very efficient for placing protection. The leader simply places the chock in the rock, clips the chock's carabiner to a runner, and clips the runner's carabiner to the rope. Easy.

Disadvantages of this method are bulkiness and poor weight distribution. The rack tends to be wider and more cumbersome, and there are fewer free carabiners. With a carabiner on each runner, the runners are more weighted and tend to shift, making climbing awkward.

Several chocks on one carabiner

In a second method, pieces of protection are grouped together, each group held by a single carabiner (fig. 10-50c). In this setup, the gate of each carabiner that carries a set of chocks is down and facing away from your body. In this method, single runners don't have carabiners, and extra

Fig. 10–50. Example racking methods: a, a climber carrying runners and a typical rack; b, a racking method where most pieces of protection get their own carabiner; c, a racking method where most pieces of protection are grouped together, each group held by a single carabiner.

carabiners are clipped to the gear sling in chains of two or three.

This second method can make climbing easier because it results in a less bulky rack with better weight distribution. But it also can make it more difficult to place protection. First of all, you have to decide whether to remove a single piece from the group of chocks on a carabiner, or to unclip the carabiner and hold the whole batch of chocks up to the placement.

If you've got a good eye and know what you'll want, you can remove a single chock and place it. But a wrong guess means you've got to put the chock back and try again.

On the other hand, if you unclip the carabiner with its batch of chocks, you can easily try out each chock and place the one that fits. You can then clip the carabiner to the rope for safekeeping while you finish constructing the placement. Finally, unclip the carabiner from the chock and return the carabiner and the unused chocks to the gear sling.

This method of racking gear with several chocks per carabiner usually means slower placements and more equipment handling. Even after placing a chock, the leader must handle two free carabiners and a runner to create the extension to the rope. All this increases the danger that the leader will drop gear or become exhausted. But some climbers feel the increased ease of climbing is worth the extra work.

Other methods

There are other ways to rack gear. Some climbers clip a separate carabiner to each larger chock, but group the smaller chocks so that several will be attached to one carabiner.

Some climbers carry part of the equipment on the gear loops of their harnesses. This helps distribute the weight of the rack, but be sure the gear doesn't hang down far enough to interfere with footwork.

Whatever the method, rack the protection in a systematic order that never varies, so you can find a particular piece in a hurry. The usual order is to start at the front with the smallest wired wedges and to work back with larger-size chocks.

A final point on runners

It's a good idea to carry a couple of runners readily accessible on the harness gear loops in case you can't get to the ones slung under one arm. (If that arm is being used in a jam crack, you won't be able to remove the runners.) You can carry quick draws on the gear loops. To shorten a longer runner so it won't trip you up, you can double it or "chain" (fig. 10-51) the runner and attach it to the

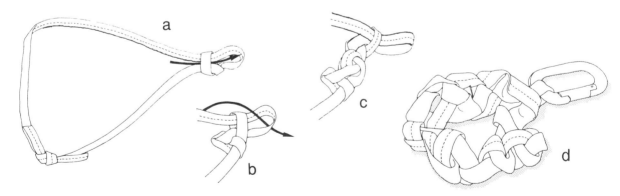

Fig. 10–51. "Chaining" a long runner: a, form a slip knot; b, pull runner through the loop formed by the slip knot; c, repeat this process until the runner is "chained"; d, the final loop can be attached to a carabiner for carrying and to ensure it does not unravel.

harness. When needed, just shake out the chained runner to remove the knots.

PLANNING THE ROUTE

The question of finding your way to the top depends on where you're climbing. If you're sport climbing in a popular spot, just follow the line of fixed pins and bolts, or look up the climb in the guidebook.

There's more involved in finding the route in alpine rock climbing. Even with a guidebook, the description may be sketchy: "Ascend NE Buttress for several hundred feet of moderate climbing." Figure on some planning and routefinding.

Start working out the route as soon as you can see the buttress, face, ridge, or whatever you plan to climb. Look for major features that the line of ascent might follow: crack systems, dihedrals, chimneys, areas of broken rock. Note areas of small trees or bushes that could indicate belay ledges.

Keep an eye out for deceptively tempting lines that lead to broad roofs or blank walls. These may not be visible from near the start of the ascent and if the climbers don't pay attention on the approach, they could climb four or five pitches only to hit a dead end.

Develop a flexible plan for the line of ascent, keeping in mind likely alternatives. Continue planning and routefinding as the actual climb begins, looking for more local features. The general principles are the same: look for natural lines to follow, such as cracks, chimneys and ledges; form a tentative plan for the pitch, perhaps including a place for the first piece of protection and a spot for the next belay station; and note alternative moves in case the planned line leads to a blank wall. Be prepared to look around the corner for easier alternatives not visible from below.

Faced with a choice between pitches of differing difficulty, look at the next pitch before deciding. It's better to climb two moderate pitches than to go for an easy pitch and then be faced with one that exceeds the party's ability.

On the way up, keep track of retreat possibilities in case the climb is aborted, as well as good descent routes from the summit if you don't know of any established route.

PLANNING THE BELAY

It's simple enough: if it's a one-pitch climb, the second belay setup only needs to be directed against a downward pull from the second climber. If it's a multipitch climb, the belay station will also be used to belay the next lead. The climber who sets up this dual-purpose station should try to arrange anchors that will handle the downward pull from the second climber and then, with minimal change, the upward pull of the leader. An efficient belay setup is faster, safer, and leaves more time for climbing.

CLEANING A PITCH

The climber who follows and cleans a pitch should be neat and efficient. A second who is slow and sloppy can drop chocks, allow dangling protection to dangerously interfere with the next move, and hold up the climb while the hardware is untangled at the belay station.

Here are some suggestions for the second:

Start preparing to climb as soon as the leader is off belay. Get out of the belay setup and break down the anchor system (staying clipped into one anchor until you are on belay).

Put on the pack before anything else, except perhaps a hardware sling. Rack all chocks and carabiners on a hardware sling or runner worn over one shoulder and under the opposite arm; then put your runners over the other shoulder and under the other arm. Give the area a last look to make sure nothing is left. Then, once you are on a belay, start climbing.

Remove a chock in reverse order of the way it was placed. If it was slotted down and behind a constriction, remove it by pushing back and up.

Be persistent. Although vigorous pulling or tugging may only set the chock more solidly, it may be necessary to tap or wiggle the chock to free it. Sometimes it takes a lot of work.

Carry a chock pick. You'll need it to tug and

push on stubborn placements. Some chock picks also can be used to pull the retraction trigger on a spring-loaded camming device that has ''walked'' back into a crack. Wired chocks can also sometimes be used for that purpose.

Consider leaving the chock behind if it won't budge. Sure, they're expensive. But you can waste too much time and energy on a chock that won't come out.

The second can minimize the risk of dropping gear by using a careful cleaning procedure, which may depend on how you prefer to rack the hardware. In general, cleaning from the rock to the rope is best.

Consider a typical placement consisting of chock-carabiner-runner-carabiner-rope. If your rack features one carabiner on each chock and on each runner, the following cleaning procedure is very efficient. First, remove the chock from the crack. Hold the carabiner that is clipped to the chock, unclip it from the runner, and clip the carabiner-chock combination directly to your gear sling. Then loop the runner over your head, unclip the carabiner from the rope, slip the carabiner-runner combination under one arm and continue climbing.

If your rack features several chocks per carabiner, the following cleaning procedure works well with that method. First, remove the chock from the crack, unclip it, and rack it. Then remove the carabiner from the runner and rack it, then the runner, and finally the carabiner on the rope.

TRANSFERRING EQUIPMENT AT THE TOP OF A PITCH

If the second was neat and efficient in cleaning the pitch, organizing gear as it was removed, the transfer at the belay station will probably go quickly and the fun can resume.

First reconstruct the original leader's rack. The second clips the removed pieces to the leader's rack or hands them to the leader, who can rack them. Caution: don't drop any gear. The second then passes over the removed runners. If the original leader plans to lead the next pitch, the climbers

then carefully switch places in the belay setup. This is one way to do it, but if the second is also a competent leader, it's a lot more efficient to swing leads, with the second now taking the lead.

To swing leads, the second usually takes over the leader's rack and runners. The original leader hands the runners to the second (an arm makes a good ''post'' to place the runners on). The rack is next, passed to the second, who places it over the head and under one arm. The runners then go over the head and under the other arm. The new leader checks and adjusts the rack to ensure that everything is ready for the new lead. During this whole procedure, the new leader stays clipped into a separate anchor and, as a backup, can remain on belay.

RUNNING BELAYS

The running belay is an old technique that is still occasionally used for the time it saves. Both climbers tie in and move simultaneously. There is no belayer. The leader places occasional protection and clips the rope through it. The leader also can weave between blocks and spires to take advantage of natural protection. The climbers can reduce rope friction and also stay closer together for communication by carrying some of the rope coiled. In any case, the follower usually carries a few coils in hand to avoid unpleasant jerks when the leader moves fast.

In a fall, the rope—running through the protection—will be held at some point by the weight of the other climber, because the rope is tied to both climbers' harnesses and neither is anchored. The friction of rope running over rock or snow also helps slow the fall. This technique probably only makes the difference between serious injury and total disaster. If either climber falls, both may fall—and a big fall is arrested only by dragging one's partner.

A running belay is not to be confused with moving in coils, which is simply carrying the rope over truly easy ground without using intermediate protection and when any type of belay is unnecessary.

HAULING PACKS

You may decide to shed your pack sometime because you can't fit inside a chimney with it or because the weight would make a pitch too difficult. Then you'll have to haul the pack up after you.

One way to handle this chore is to trail a rope behind you as you climb, tied to the pack down below. This can be either the unneeded end of the climbing rope, if the pitch is short enough, or a separate rope. At the end of the pitch, put in an anchor, haul the pack up hand-over-hand, untie it, and throw the end of the rope down to haul up your partner's pack. If you lack extra rope, have your partner untie from the climbing rope so you can pull it up through the protection and toss the end down for pack hauling.

Ice axes are often hauled separately so there is less danger the pack will snag as it is being pulled up. Tie the ice axe, and any other gear, securely to the rope.

Be sure you have a compelling reason for shedding your pack. If you're doing it only because climbing without it is more fun, think twice. Hauling packs takes valuable time, especially when they get stuck, and they do. It's also hard work that can rob you of precious arm strength. And remember, packs launch rocks.

CLIMBING WITH A PARTY OF THREE

Most rock climbing is done in teams of two, but occasionally a party will end up with three climbers. This works, though it's usually more awkward than climbing with just two.

A three-person team climbing on one rope is limited to pitches of only 70 to 80 feet, just half the rope length. Because many climbs have pitches much longer than this, a three-person team may need to carry two ropes.

With three climbers, the leader climbs while the second belays and the third remains anchored at the belay station. At the top of the pitch, the leader sets up a belay and brings up the second (who can also be belayed from below by the third).

If the pitch follows a straight line up, the second can clean the pitch. But if the line includes some traversing, the protection should stay in for the third climber, to help prevent a pendulum fall. In this situation, the second climber unclips each piece of protection from the first rope and clips it to the second rope. At the top of the pitch, the belay is reset to bring up the third climber. The climbers then may decide to swing leads, with the third climber leading the next pitch. The second generally doesn't do any leading in a party of three.

With all the anchors, ropes, and climbers involved, it can get messy and confusing at the belay station. A lot of time can be taken up setting and resetting belays. Throughout the commotion, it's critical that each of the three climbers be securely anchored. (The belay stations on some tough climbs are so small they couldn't accommodate a three-person team in the first place.)

There are occasional advantages to a three-person team, such as the added help in hauling packs and the availability of an extra rope if a full-length rappel is required. But the disadvantages usually outweigh the advantages.

SPECIAL ROPE TECHNIQUES

Much of this book describes climbing situations in which only a single rope, with a diameter between 10 and 11 millimeters, is used. However, climbers can opt for a system that uses two separate ropes (double-rope technique) instead of a single rope, or another in which two smaller-diameter ropes are used as one to replace the single rope (twin-rope technique).

Double-rope technique

Double-rope technique uses two ropes that serve as independent belay lines. The leader clips each rope into its own protection points on the way up, and a single belayer manages the ropes separately.

Yes, it's complicated, but the system offers some important rewards, such as reduced rope drag and safer traverses. The technique is widely used by British climbers and by an increasing number of climbers everywhere to protect highly technical routes. Double-rope technique usually employs color-coded 9-millimeter ropes.

The leader clips one rope into one series of protection placements and the other rope into another series, the goal being to keep each rope in as straight a line as possible so rope drag is at a minimum (fig. 10-52). The drag is usually less than what it would be on a single rope on the same pitch because the single rope would have to follow a more meandering route. The double ropes typically run in roughly parallel routes, and do not cross. However, if both ropes must be attached to one protection placement, each rope should be attached using a separate carabiner.

The system also helps reduce the worries of the leader who is straining to clip in to the next piece of protection. In single-rope climbing, the rope is slack as the climber pulls up a big hunk of it to clip the next placement. But on a double rope, only the one rope is slack if the belayer is holding the other snug. If the climber falls at this point, the fall will be taken on the nearest placement used by the snug rope, usually making for a shorter fall.

The system has the advantage that both ropes are unlikely to be cut by sharp rock edges or

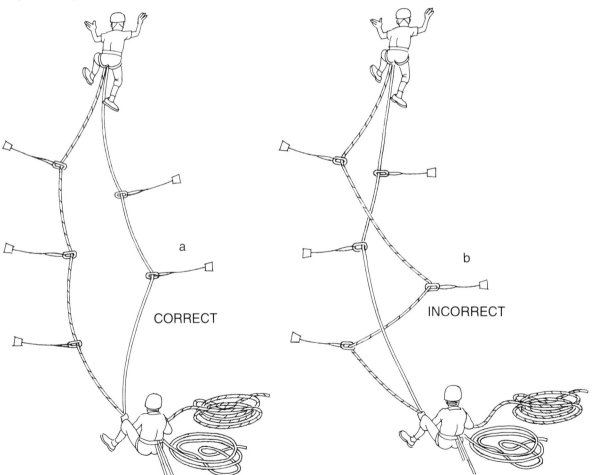

Fig. 10–52. Double-rope technique: a, correct, the two ropes do not cross but run straight to reduce rope drag; b, incorrect, the two ropes cross and run in a zig-zag, increasing rope drag.

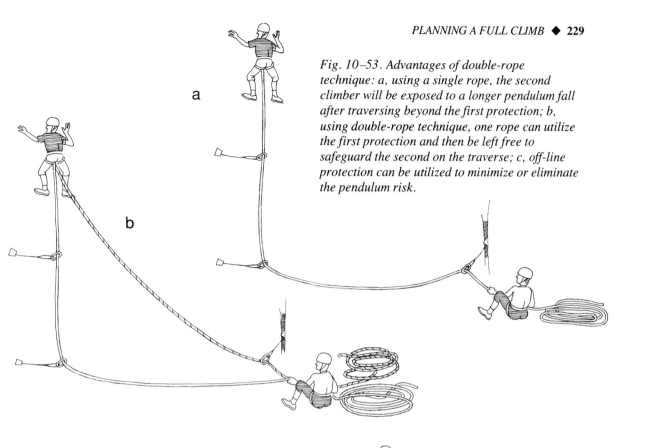

Fig. 10–53. Advantages of double-rope technique: a, using a single rope, the second climber will be exposed to a longer pendulum fall after traversing beyond the first protection; b, using double-rope technique, one rope can utilize the first protection and then be left free to safeguard the second on the traverse; c, off-line protection can be utilized to minimize or eliminate the pendulum risk.

rockfall, or to otherwise fail, at the same time. And it provides two ropes for rappels.

The double ropes can also be used to protect a traverse, particularly one at the start or the middle of a pitch which then goes straight up. In the event of a fall, without a second rope the second climber risks a long pendulum (see Fig. 10-53a). With double ropes, the pendulum can be minimized or avoided. The leader can use one of the ropes for protection on the traverse and leave the other free to protect the second from above (see Fig. 10-53b, 10-53c).

Disadvantages of the double-rope technique? The two ropes weigh more and cost more than the single rope (though often each climber will contribute one rope). The principal problem is that the belayer's job is more complex as he must handle the movements of two ropes, often letting out slack on one rope while taking it in on the other. For this type of climbing a double slot Sticht belay plate is particularly useful, though other belay techniques can be used. Moreover, the rope has to be constantly monitored to avoid tangling or kinking. With practice these difficulties are soon mastered, and on long and complex rock pitches the advantages vastly outweigh the disadvantages.

Twin-rope technique

Twin-rope technique—with two ropes used as one—features ropes that are 8 to 8.8 millimeters in diameter. Both ropes are clipped into each piece of protection, just as in single rope technique (fig. 10-54).

The twin ropes absorb more energy and thus can withstand more falls than a single rope. Two ropes also are safer running over an edge, as it's unlikely that both ropes would be cut through at the same time. The smaller-diameter ropes are individually easier for the lead climber to handle than a standard single rope.

However, the technique means the belayer has to handle and belay with two ropes, so rope management is tricky. As with the double-rope method, both belayer and leader need a good bit of practice before taking this technique out on the cliffs. And again, twin ropes cost more than a standard single rope.

Fig. 10–54. Twin-rope technique: two small-diameter ropes are used as one, with both attached to each protection placement.

PERSONAL RESPONSIBILITY

ETHICS AND STYLE OF PLACING PROTECTION

Local climbers at each area have usually settled on some basic rules to play by, including standards for placing protection. Some climbing areas are more traditional, encouraging leading and placing protection "from the ground up." Other areas have embraced newer techniques, such as inspecting a route on rappel before climbing it, or placing bolts on rappel. You'll have your own opinions regarding protection, of course, but be sensitive to the climbing ethics and styles developed and demonstrated by local climbers.

ENVIRONMENTAL IMPACT

Everything about mountaineering, including rock climbing, is linked to affection and respect for the environment and consideration for the travelers who come after you. The general rule is the same whether you're hiking, backpacking, alpine mountaineering, or rock climbing: leave the world the way you found it. Specifically on a rock pitch, this means avoiding permanent scarring of trees, rock, and vegetation. If possible, stick to clean climbing, using only chocks for protection.

SAFETY

You know by now that climbing is a balancing act in more ways than one. There's not always one "correct" technique for doing something, and you often need to balance different factors in deciding on a course of action.

Likewise there's no simple set of commandments to memorize and mechanically follow to ensure safety. You may be called on to make life-and-death decisions despite incomplete knowledge, with no clear rule to follow, and without the luxury of being able to consult your favorite expert, even if that expert is on the other end of the rope.

Controlling the risks of climbing is a matter of understanding the reasons that underlie the techniques you've learned, being aware of everything that affects a safe choice, and being able to gauge all the consequences of your actions. And then making a decision as thoughtfully as time allows.

The important thing is that you'll be acting on knowledge, not ignorance; on deep understanding, not superficial rules. A climber who uses techniques without understanding them or who mechanically follows a set of safety rules is not thinking and is a danger to himself and fellow climbers. But learn the principles, make them yours, and you'll be free to do what we all want to do: climb hard, climb high, climb safe.

• 11 •

AID CLIMBING AND PITONCRAFT

Aid climbing is the technique of using gear to support your weight as you climb. It can be as simple as using a bolt as a single handhold, or as complex as climbing an entire route with your full weight on pieces of specialized gear you have placed.

Aid climbing is clearly a sharp departure from free climbing, where weighting the rope or the protective hardware is poor style. Free ascents are one of the goals of the sport of climbing, while aid climbing is a valuable skill for ascending currently ''unfreeable'' routes and for use in emergencies.

As standards of difficulty continue to rise, top climbers are freeing many of the routes originally climbed with aid. But despite the rise in free-climbing standards, there will always be tempting routes that are more difficult still—and so devoid of natural features that a climber will need some artificial assistance.

Skills in aid climbing and pitoncraft can also help overcome unexpected difficulties during normal free climbing. They can provide a way to move safely up or down when weather or accident puts your party in jeopardy. Knowing how to use pitons for aid also helps you in evaluating the soundness of fixed pitons you encounter while free climbing. In winter mountaineering, pitons may be the only protection that will hold in ice-filled cracks.

Any advice to use pitons always comes with a stern caveat: pitons permanently damage the rock. Don't use them unless you must. And don't use them at all on established free routes.

Aid climbing and pitoncraft require skill, judgment, and a lot of practice. To learn both the basics and the many ''tricks'' of the techniques, try to work with an experienced partner, and climb often.

CLEAN AID CLIMBING

Aid climbing takes a lot of gear, but it needn't be damaging to the rock. With all the chocks and camming devices on the market, you now have a better chance to climb routes clean, without putting in a single piton or bolt. The chocks and other devices can be removed without defacing the rock, and the next climber won't even be able to tell you were there.

Aid climbing may still require bolts and pitons, but keep them to a minimum. Pitons (also called pins) chip the rock, especially when you remove them. On popular routes, tiny cracks sometimes evolve into finger or hand cracks after generations of climbers force them to accept pitons.

When climbers make the first ascent of a major wall, they often carry bolts and pins to make it go. Once placed, the best approach is to leave them so future parties can use them without marring the rock further. In general, make clean climbing your goal.

TYPES OF AID CLIMBING

We can roughly categorize aid climbing based on the extent of its use on a particular climb.

Mountaineering alpine aid climbing uses a minimal amount of aid techniques and equipment to overcome short, blank (or extremely difficult) sections of a route that otherwise goes free. This type of climbing requires little or no specialized aid equipment. Usually you'll just use the free-climbing gear you have along.

General aid climbing often uses aid for extended distances, although artificial and free-climbing techniques may be interspersed. Long one-day climbs may involve "fixing" the initial pitches—putting up ropes and leaving them in place so they can be climbed quickly with mechanical ascenders the following morning to reach the previous high point.

Big-wall aid climbing involves ascents that take longer than one day to complete, even if the initial pitches are fixed. These climbs include either a hanging bivouac or ledge bivouac and require sack-hauling techniques.

Take a look at Appendix 2, Rating Systems, for a discussion of the various grades of difficulty in aid climbing.

AID CLIMBING EQUIPMENT

Probably more so than in any other type of climbing, you're now in for the true "nuts and bolts" of the sport. This section details the range of equipment used in aid climbing, and builds on all the gear and techniques described in Chapter 10. If you're not interested in aid climbing, this section may hold all the drama of a hardware catalog. But if you've become intrigued with the subject, you'll find this material both thorough and fascinating.

BASIC EQUIPMENT FOR CLEAN AID CLIMBING

Clean aid relies heavily on standard free-climbing equipment. You'll simply need more of it.

Chocks and camming devices: Because you'll be setting placements every several feet, a long pitch can require more than 50 assorted chocks and camming devices. The sling attached to each piece should be as short as possible to help you get the maximum elevation gain out of each placement.

Carabiners: While a minimum of 40 free carabiners are needed on an aid rack, it's not unusual to use 80 on a long pitch and more than 100 on a particularly difficult pitch. Many aid climbers prefer oval carabiners rather than D carabiners because ovals minimize the unnerving shifting that occurs when a D takes your weight. Regardless of the shape, you should be able to open the carabiner gate whenever you wish, even while it is holding your weight.

Small nuts: Aid racks include specialty small nuts, beyond those on free-climbing racks. These tapered nuts are often used instead of thin pitons, but they are not as strong. They are designed to support body weight, and may fail if fallen upon.

Two general styles of nuts are available. The first is a smaller version of a normal tapered Stopper. The second style has both horizontal and vertical taper and is more secure in flaring cracks and old pin scars (piton scars).

The heads of small nuts are made from aluminum, brass, or stainless steel. Aluminum and brass bite into the rock and hold better in marginal placements, but steel nuts are less likely to deform and fail if you take a fall on one of them.

Ropes: The tough duty of aid climbing usually requires 11-millimeter or 12-millimeter kernmantle ropes, 165 feet long. The haul line is typically an 11-millimeter or 9-millimeter line which doubles as a backup rope and a second rope for long rappels. If your route entails pendulums or other unusual problems, you may need a third rope.

Hero loops: Very short slings are useful for aid climbing. These tie-off (hero) loops—4 to 6 inches long—are threaded through fixed protection in place of a carabiner. Climbers usually tie their own out of 1/2-inch webbing. You'll use many of them if the route has a lot of fixed bolts or pitons. They are also used to prevent the loss of stacked pieces (described later), and to tie off partially driven pins. Also carry at least six regular-length slings for establishing anchors, extending placements to reduce rope drag, and other normal rock-climbing uses.

Chock picks: Picks used for aid climbing should be sturdy, because you'll often hammer on the pick to tap out lodged nuts.

Gloves: Over and above their value for belaying and rappelling, gloves protect your hands while "jugging" (ascending the climbing rope with mechanical ascenders) and removing protection placements.

Rock shoes: If the route involves only a small amount of aid, normal free-climbing rock shoes perform best. If sustained aid is anticipated, boots with greater sole rigidity provide a better working platform and more comfort. Some new boots on the market provide a rigid arch support and good torsional rigidity for aid climbing, yet have a flexible toe and a sole of soft friction rubber for good free-climbing capabilities.

Energy-absorbing slings: These slings increase security when climbing above placements of questionable strength. In a fall, the slings limit the shock delivered to the protection. Their use, however, limits the amount of elevation gained from the placements to which they are attached.

UNIVERSAL AID-CLIMBING EQUIPMENT

In addition to equipment normally used in free climbing, you will need a selection of gear that is used for both clean aid climbing and for aid that involves placing pins.

Etriers: These ladder-like slings (fig. 11-1) allow climbers to step up from one placement to the next when they are clipped to a chock, piton, or other aid piece. Consider the intended use when

Fig. 11–1. Types of etriers: a, sewn; b, tied; c, the frost knot. Tied etriers require twice their finished length plus 10 inches for each step (overhand knot) and the frost knot. A 60-inch etrier with five steps (four overhand knots) takes 170 inches of runner.

Fig. 11–2. Tied daisy chain

making or buying etriers. For alpine climbs, minimize weight by using a single pair of etriers made
of $9/16$-inch or $11/16$-inch webbing. For most aid
climbing, four- or five-step etriers made of 1-inch
webbing are standard. Etriers should be long
enough to let you step smoothly from the top step
of one to the bottom step of another that has been
clipped into a piece at arm's reach above.

Tying your own etriers lets you tailor their size
to your own. However, commercially made or
home-sewn etriers are preferred for routes with extensive aid because they remain open for foot
placement when weighted. Metal-rung etriers have
the same advantage and are less prone to blow in
the wind, but they can cause more pain if they do
hit you or your partner.

Some climbers use two pairs of etriers while aid
climbing; others use a single pair—it depends on
the nature of the route and on personal preference.
Likewise, some climbers prefer to attach a short
grab sling to the carabiner loop of their etriers.

Daisy chains are tied or sewn slings with a
loop—formed by a knot or stitching—every 3 to 6
inches (fig. 11-2). The proper length for you is a
daisy chain that, when attached to your harness,
reaches as far as your raised hand. Attach a carabiner to every loop (or every other loop) in the
chain so you can quickly clip into an aid placement
and rest on your harness.

Carry a second daisy chain, without carabiners
in each loop, for other purposes, such as attaching
yourself to your ascenders while jugging or for
preventing loss of etriers if a hook placement fails.

Fifi hooks function somewhat like daisy chains
but are attached to your harness with a sling only 2
to 6 inches long (fig. 11-3). You can quickly clip
the hook into an aid piece, allowing you to rest on
your harness. Be careful. If you release the tension
or change the angle, it could come unhooked. Aid

Fig. 11–3. Fifi hook with sling

climbers usually carry one fifi hook for use on bolt
ladders and fixed pitches.

A double rack, with equipment slings on both
sides of the body, distributes the weight of the
hardware (fig. 11-4). It improves your balance and

Fig. 11–4. Double rack

comfort and reduces the neck strain caused by a single rack. If it's built right, a double rack can also serve as a chest harness as you jug up a rope with mechanical ascenders. Some climbers carry a single rack in addition, for their free carabiners or as a supplemental free-climbing rack.

A belay seat with two- or three-point attachment is a great creature-comfort during hanging belays (fig. 11-5). One urgent warning: never let the belay seat be your sole means of attaching to an anchor. Clip in from your harness to the anchor with the climbing rope as usual—and then set up the belay seat for comfort.

Mechanical ascenders (fig. 11-6) serve the same function as prusik knots but are stronger, safer, faster, and less tiring. The devices are a requirement for sack hauling on big walls.

All ascenders employ a cam, allowing the ascender to slide freely in one direction on a rope but to grip tight when pulled in the opposite direction. They also have a trigger or locking mechanism to keep them from accidentally coming off the rope. Some triggers are difficult to release, decreasing the chance of accidental removal but making it harder to get them off when you want to. If your ascenders are made of cast aluminum, back up their frames with webbing to reduce the danger created should they break.

If you plan to use ascenders for cold-weather climbing, look for a pair with openings large enough to accommodate heavily gloved hands. Carabiner holes at the top and the bottom of the ascender come in handy for a number of purposes, such as sack hauling. If the ascender doesn't have

Fig. 11–5. Two-point belay seat; note the anchored climbing rope.

Fig. 11–6. Mechanical ascender with backup sling; ascender is attached in preparation for diagonal ascent.

these holes, you'll have to attach slings for clip-in points.

Piton hammers have a flat striking surface for cleaning and driving pitons, and a blunt pick for prying out protection, cleaning dirty cracks, and placing malleable pieces (fig. 11-7). Hammer shafts should be long enough to forcefully drive pins, and short enough to fit comfortably in a belt holster. The shafts should also be sturdy and taped for protection. A carabiner hole in the head is useful for cleaning pins and malleable pieces.

Attach a sling to your hammer that allows full arm extension when the hammer is in use (fig. 11-8). If you happen to drop the hammer, it will just hang below your feet on the sling. Be sure to check the sling regularly for wear.

Hooks come in many shapes and forms, and are most commonly used to grip ledges or small holes

Fig. 11–8. Hammer sling properly used

(fig. 11-9). With etriers attached to the hook, you have a rather delicate placement for moving upward. Hooks should be made of chrome-moly steel (for strength), and the non-hook end should be wider and curved (for stability). Attach slings to the bottom of your hooks with a girth hitch, positioned so that when the sling is weighted, the "legs" (lower end) of the hook are pulled into the

Fig. 11–7. Piton hammer styles: a, Mjollnir; b, Chouinard; c, less adequate.

Fig. 11–9. Hook types: a, sky hook; b, Logan hook; c, bat hook.

Fig. 11–10. Hangers: a, wire; b, wire hanger on a bolt; c, keyhole; d, regular hanger on a bolt.

rock. To accomplish this, the sling should hang from the rock side of the hook.

Sky hooks look almost like giant fish hooks and are useful for small flakes and ledges. Greater stability is achieved on some routes if the tip of the hook is filed to a point, which can be set into small holes drilled at the back of tiny ledges. Fish hooks, or ring claws, are like large sky hooks and are used to grip larger flakes and ledges. Logan hooks are L-shaped: the wide style is stable on tiny ledges and flakes, and the narrow style can be used in shallow pockets. Bat hooks are basically a narrow-style Logan hook with a pointed blade, allowing their use in shallow 1/4-inch holes drilled for their use.

Wire hangers (fig. 11-10a and b) are loops of wire 1/8 inch or 3/32 inch in diameter, with a slider to cinch the wire tight over bolt studs and rivets (basically, bolts with a wide head). Small tapered chocks (Stoppers) with wire slings can also be used for this purpose, with the chock itself acting as the slider to tighten the wire against the bolt stud. However, because the chocks have a longer wire loop than the wire hangers, you won't get as much elevation gain from them.

Regular hangers and keyhole hangers serve a similar function to the wire hangers, but are shaped pieces of metal rather than wire loops (fig. 11-10c and d). They are useful, especially at belay anchors

and for fixed bolts that have no hangers. Keyhole hangers have the metal between the bolt hole and carabiner hole filed out to allow placement over rivets and buttonhead bolts.

IRONMONGERY FOR FULL AID CLIMBING

To master the full range of aid-climbing techniques, climbers must have a knowledge of pitons and bolts.

Pitons

Modern pitons—or pins—are made of chrome-moly (hard) steel. Rather than molding to cracks like the malleable pitons of old, they mold the crack to their form. Because of the damage that pitons cause and because of improvements in clean-climbing hardware, piton use has declined greatly. They are still important, however, on overhanging rock and very thin cracks. For winter mountaineering, when cracks are filled with ice, they may offer the only viable means of protection. To fit the diverse cracks encountered on rock walls, pitons vary tremendously in size and shape (fig. 11-11).

The Realized Ultimate Reality Piton (RURP) is the smallest piton, a postage-stamp-sized, hatchet-shaped pin used in incipient cracks. It will usually support only body weight and derives what little strength it has by minimizing the leverage between the piton and carabiner supporting your etriers. Some styles come with offset sides for use in corners.

Birdbeaks are similar to RURPs but have a longer arm for attaching a carabiner or sling. Generally they are easier to place and remove.

Knifeblades are long thin pitons that have two eyes—one at the end of the blade and a second in the offset portion of the pin. They come in different lengths and in thicknesses between $1/8$ inch and $3/16$ inch, and they are commonly used to fit many cracks that are too thin for tiny nuts.

Lost arrows are similar to knifeblades but have a single eye which is centered and set perpendicular to the end of the blade. These too are commonly used pitons that come in several lengths and thicknesses ($5/32$ to $3/8$ inch). They are very good in horizontal cracks.

Angles are pitons formed into a "V." The V varies in height from $1/4$ inch to $1^1/2$ inches (smaller ones are most popular). Their strength is derived from the metal's resistance to bending and spreading. Angles and other large pitons have largely been replaced by modern free-climbing hardware.

Leeper Z pitons obtain their thickness through their Z profile as opposed to the V profile of an angle. These pitons are very solid and work well for stacking because of their short length, useful in bottoming cracks.

Bongs are large angle pitons that vary from 2 to 6 inches in width. In addition to their use as pitons, they can double as large chocks. Camming devices like Friends have largely replaced bongs.

Sawed-off pins are handy on routes that have been heavily climbed using pitons, leaving shallow pin scars. Several $3/4$-inch and 1-inch angles with a few inches cut off the end are useful for shallow placements.

Malleable hardware (bashies)

Malleable hardware (fig. 11-12) is designed to hold weight by melding the soft head of the placement to the irregularities of the rock. The security

Fig. 11–11. Piton (pin) types: a, lost arrow; b, knifeblade; c, shallow angle; d, Leeper Z; e, angle; f, large angle; g, bong; h, birdbeak; i, RURP.

Fig. 11–12. Malleable head types: a, copperhead; b, aluma-head; c, circlehead.

of these bashies varies greatly, and it is difficult to gauge their strength, making them last-resort equipment.

Copperheads (fig. 11-12a) have a swage of copper attached to one end of a short cable that has a loop at the other end. They are placed by pounding the copper head into an irregularity in the rock. They tend to form well and are more durable than similar pieces with aluminum heads (aluma-heads).

Aluma-heads (fig. 11-12b) are not as tough as copperheads but are more malleable, so they tend to be used for the larger sizes, while the smaller heads are usually copper.

Circleheads (fig. 11-12c) consist of a wire loop with an extra copper swage on the loop, which is pounded into the rock like a copperhead. They are used in horizontal cracks.

Bolts

Chapter 10 includes a section on the use of existing bolts found on climbing routes. Bolts permanently scar the rock and alter the style of a climb, and very serious consideration should be given before placing one. Proper bolt placement is a special skill, beyond the scope of this book. Bolt placement is best left to the skill and judgment of very experienced climbers.

BIG-WALL EQUIPMENT

Climbers undertaking a big wall have other specialized equipment to consider.

Pulleys will be required to ease the chore of sack hauling. They receive much abuse, so they must be durable. Pulleys with bearings and larger wheels operate more smoothly.

Haul bags carry your clothing, water, food, sleeping bag, and other non-climbing paraphernalia. A good haul bag should have adequate cargo capacity, a solid haul suspension, durable fabric, an absence of snag points, and a removable backpacking harness system. Duffels can be converted into haul sacks by reinforcing the wear areas. A top cap to the haul bag is a good idea to protect the knot connecting the sack to the haul line and help reduce snagging problems while hauling.

Cheater sticks allow you to clip a carabiner into a piece of hardware beyond your reach. Although rarely needed, they are often used to avoid "top stepping" in etriers. Cheater sticks should have a means of holding a carabiner solidly while you clip in with your arm fully extended.

Knee pads protect your knees, which are regularly in contact with the rock during aid climbing. Pads should be comfortable and allow good circulation.

Portaledges or hammocks: Portaledges, which are lightweight cots, offer greater comfort from a single point of suspension than hammocks. Unfortunately, they are much heavier and bulkier. As with belay seats, climbers must *always* be anchored to the rock when using this equipment.

If you take on a big wall, safeguard important equipment with tie-in loops to attach anything you might drop. Bring gear that will get you through the worst possible weather, because there's not likely to be any easy way to retreat. Be sure your equipment is durable and beef up any item that could fail, such as water containers. Select only the sturdiest, and reinforce them with duct tape.

AID PLACEMENTS

The main rule for aid climbing is to place each aid piece as high as possible. If you make placements at 5-foot rather than 4-foot intervals, over the course of a 160-foot pitch you'll save eight placements, many more carabiners, and much time.

Most of the techniques for placing free-climbing protection apply to aid climbing. For aid climbing, if possible, you'll shorten the slings to your pieces and often use hero loops on fixed protection rather than clipping in directly with a carabiner.

Placing small nuts during an aid climb is similar to placing larger ones on a free climb. But because aid nuts take the weight of the lead climber and because they may be smaller than the chock pick, they can be difficult to remove. If you place small nuts near the outside of the crack, they will be easier to remove and there will be less danger of damaging them in the process. Test small nuts gently before committing your weight to them.

Fixed pins, bolts, or rivets must be evaluated before use (see Chapter 10). If you decide to use a fixed piece, thread a hero loop through its eye and clip a single carabiner into the two ends of the loop. This saves a carabiner. Note: use a direct carabiner clip-in every three or four pieces as a backup. The hero-looped pieces are not as safe for stopping a fall because of the danger the loop could be cut by the edge of the metal eye. It's also wise to carry a few bolt hangers and nuts (in both $1/4$-inch and $3/8$-inch sizes) for bolts with missing or damaged hangers.

PITON PLACEMENT

Here are some basic guidelines for the sound placement of pitons (pins) (fig. 11-13):

• Horizontal placement of pins is generally more secure than vertical placement because rotation is reduced or eliminated.
• Ideally, the eye should point downward.

Fig. 11–13. Piton placements and problems

• As with chocks, place pins in locally wider portions of a crack. If the crack is thinner below and above the pin, the pin will be supported when it has to take a climber's weight.

• A properly sized pin can be placed one-half to two-thirds of the way by hand. The remainder of the pin is hammered in place. Select the correct pin to fit the crack. Don't try to make the crack fit the pin; this practice causes needless destruction of the rock.

• A sound piton rings with a higher-pitched "ping" with each strike of the hammer. After the pin is driven, tap it to test for rotation. Rotation indicates the pin is not biting the rock. Replace such pins with a larger size.

• Knowing just how much to hammer a piton is a matter of touch and experience. Excessive hammering wastes energy, makes it harder for the second to remove the piton, and needlessly damages the rock. Under-driving a piton, however, increases the risk of it pulling out. If several pins are under-driven, the failure of one could result in a long fall as the series of pins zippers out.

• When possible, avoid placing a pin in a three-way corner. Such placements are often impossible to clean because the pin cannot be tapped back and forth for removal. Just leave it as a fixed pin.

• If the position of the piton causes the connecting carabiner to extend over an edge, add a hero loop to the piece (fig. 11-14). This prevents loading the carabiner across its sides.

• On overhangs, place pins with some horizontal orientation when possible (fig. 11-15). This reduces the odds of total failure should the pin shift when weighted.

• Place knifeblades in vertical cracks with the offset eye down.

• When placing angles, keep the three points of the V in contact with the rock (fig. 11-16). The back (point of the V) *always* must contact one wall, while the edges (two tips of the V) contact the opposing wall. In a horizontal crack, put the back of the angle up and the edges down.

• Bongs (fig. 11-17), being made of aluminum, are quite fragile, so pound them as little as possible. Bongs are often placed as chockstones,

Fig. 11–14. Safely extending a piton; right figure eliminates side loading the carabiner.

and you can add a sling to a bong before using it that way.

• Expanding cracks present problems for pins because as subsequent pins are placed, lower ones loosen. When possible, use chocks in such situations, because they minimize flake expansion. If pins must be used, try to work with long minimum-taper pins placed lightly in natural slots, to minimize expansion of the rock flake.

• In shallow cracks and flutings, a piton may be driven over a chock. The chock creates a second "wall" against which the pin wedges. Because the chock would fall and be lost if the pin failed, attach a "keeper" sling to the chock and clip it into the

Fig. 11–15. Overhang piton placement

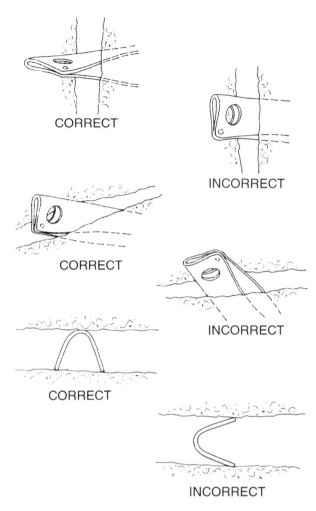

CORRECT

INCORRECT

CORRECT

INCORRECT

CORRECT

INCORRECT

Fig. 11–16. Proper placements for angle pitons

Fig. 11–18. Sawed-off piton driven over a Stopper; note the non–load-bearing keeper sling on the Stopper.

sling or carabiner of the load-bearing pin. The keeper sling must not bear any weight (fig. 11-18).
• When a pin "bottoms out" in a crack (that is, cannot be driven in all the way), stop hammering, to avoid loosening it. The piton must be tied off around the shaft at the point where it emerges from the rock. A hero loop tied to the piton with a girth hitch or clove hitch supports your weight and re-

a   b   c

Fig. 11–17. Bong placements: a, driven and tied off through lightening holes; b and c, girth-hitched for use as a large chock.

duces the levering action on the pin (fig. 11-19). Bongs can be tied off through their lightening holes. Loop a longer keeper sling (or a second carabiner) through the eye of the pin and clip it into the hero loop or hero-loop carabiner. The keeper sling doesn't bear weight, but will catch your pin if it pops.

Fig. 11–19. Tied-off piton; note the use of a keeper sling through the piton eye.

STACKING AND NESTING

When no single pin or chock fits the crack at hand, aid climbing gets very creative. Whether you've run out of the proper-sized pieces or are facing a shallow flaring crack, it's time to improvise by stacking or nesting your hardware in whatever combination works (fig. 11-20).

Blades are nested back to back and are usually driven together. If a third blade is necessary, the first two are inserted by hand, and then the third is driven in between.

Some disagreement exists about the best way to stack angles. Most climbers stack them by keeping the backs of both angles against the rock, but any combination will work. Try to avoid stacking angles by simply placing one over the other, as these may be very hard to separate once removed. Leeper Z pitons are especially useful in stacking.

It may be possible to use a camming combination of a pin and a chock—or a pin and a wire hanger—in very difficult situations (fig. 11-21). The concept relies on the camming force exerted by the chock or wire on the back of the pin. The chock or wire loop is partially inserted into the

Fig. 11–20. Examples of pitons stacked and nested (some keeper slings omitted for clarity); inset, angles stacked over each other.

crack. Then, the pin is inserted to anchor the chock or wire and to create an artificial wall against which the chock or wire can cam. You can often achieve a solid aid placement this way with minimal use of the hammer. Note, however, that wires used this way wear quickly.

These special combinations present another situation that requires non-load-bearing keeper slings to catch any pitons should the placement fail.

HOOK PLACEMENT AND USE

Before placing a hook, clip an etrier to it. Also make sure to connect a sling (or daisy chain) between the etrier's carabiner and your harness. The

Fig. 11–21. Camming combinations: a, piton and chock; b, piton and wire hanger (keeper sling omitted for clarity).

sling will prevent the loss of your gear if the hook pops off its purchase.

Now set the hook on the ledge, flake, or hole where it will be used. Test it gently before applying full body weight (or gently ''ooze'' onto the hook). Avoid standing with your face directly in front of the hook because it could pop out with a good deal of force.

If the hook is used in a shallow bolt hole, a very slight tap to set the point is sometimes useful. However, this practice increases the possibility the hook will pop out. It also erodes the existing hole, and eventually a bolt will need to be placed.

MALLEABLE PLACEMENTS

Because you often can't tell how secure they are, do not use malleable heads unless you're dealing with a pocket or flare where other protection just won't work.

Copperheads, aluma-heads, and circleheads take more practice to place than other types of aid and require some specialized tools. The hammer pick works for setting large heads, but small heads require a striking tool like a blunt chisel or, in a pinch, a lost arrow.

Figure 11-22 illustrates the following procedure for placing a head:

1. Place it. Insert a head as you would a chock—in a narrowing portion of a flare or seam.
2. ''X'' it. Pound it in using angled strokes that form an X pattern on the head.
3. Paste it. Now pound the right and left sides to ''pin'' the head.
4. Rotate it. Hit the bottom and top to see if the head rotates. If so, X it and paste it again.
5. Sniff it. If the head emits a metallic odor, it is under-driven or over-driven; do not use it. The smell arises from the cutting or cracking of the head rather than its molding to the rock.
6. Use it. Heads are used like any other aid piece—but remember their inescapable weakness. Inspection cannot guarantee the molding of the head to the rock. Some heads may hold a short fall, others will just support body weight, and others might fail. All malleable-head placements are suspect, and an acceptance of this fact is inherent in their use.

Fig. 11–22. Placing a malleable piece: a, place it; b, ''X'' it; c, paste it; d, rotate test it.

BASIC AID TECHNIQUES

Before starting up any aid pitch, study the terrain and make a plan. Determine the best rest spots, figure how to minimize rope drag, plan what gear you'll need and what you can leave for the second to carry, spot any obstructions that might plague sack hauling, and decide whether to save certain sizes of aid pieces for the end of the pitch.

Then gear up for the pitch. Place pitons (between three and six to a carabiner) on one side with the larger pieces to the rear. Place chocks and other gear for clean aid climbing on the other side, again with the larger pieces to the rear. Balance the

a   b

Haul line

Fig. 11–23. The basic sequence (some equipment omitted for clarity): a, climb high; b, place piece; c, clip etrier to carabiner on higher piece; d, test, move onto new placement, remove lower etriers; e, clip rope into lower carabiner on new piece and clip in daisy chain if desired.

weight with free carabiners racked in groups of four (two pairs). Short slings are best racked (several to a carabiner) and clipped to an easily accessible part of your harness. Finally, check that the hammer is accessible, with its sling untangled.

THE BASIC SEQUENCE

The basic aid sequence (fig. 11-23) is the same whether you are starting from the ground, a comfortable free stance, or the top step of your etriers:

1. Look and feel the terrain above and select an aid piece to place at the highest spot within reach (fig. 11-23a).
2. Place the piece (fig. 11-23b).
3. Clip in a free carabiner. Some climbers prefer to clip in a two-carabiner chain (fig. 11-23c);

c   d   e

the second carabiner will later take the climbing rope. Other climbers feel two carabiners get in the way at this point. If you are moving onto a pin, first attach a hero loop to the pin, and then clip a carabiner to the loop.

4. If the aid piece you are currently weighting is questionable, you may want to clip the rope to the second carabiner of the higher piece if you are positive the higher placement is solid. Otherwise, the rope is not clipped into the higher piece yet.

5. Clip your free etrier(s) to the carabiner on the higher piece (the higher of the two carabiners if you used two) (fig. 11-23c). If moving onto a pin, clip the etrier(s) directly into the hero loop.

6. Test the new piece with a gentle, one-footed hop (the other foot is kept in an etrier on the lower piece). If the new piece is questionable, you may decide to avoid the test and simply "ooze" onto the new placement, applying your weight as gradually and smoothly as possible. Warn your belayer when you are about to test or move onto a dubious placement.

7. Move onto the higher etrier(s) (fig.11-23d). Clip the daisy chain into the new piece while in the lower step, if you wish.

8. Remove the lower etrier(s) (fig. 11-23d). For extended aid climbing, you will normally carry two pairs of etriers, so now you will remove the lower pair and clip it to your harness. (If you are climbing with just a single pair of etriers, remove the lower etrier and clip it to the highest aid piece.) Climb up the etriers until the daisy chain (or fifi hook) can be clipped in close to the new piece, if you wish.

9. Add a second carabiner (in chain fashion) to the new piece and clip in the rope. If you initially clipped two carabiners to the piece, clip the rope into the lower carabiner (fig. 11-23d).

10. Study the area immediately above to determine likely spots for the next placement. Then climb as high as possible, reclip the daisy if desired, and begin the process anew. Note: how high you climb in your etriers depends on

the terrain, but ideally you want to place the new piece from the top step.

Top stepping

Moving onto the top step of your etriers can be unnerving, but the ability to do so greatly improves the efficiency of aid climbing. The process is simple on low-angle rock where the top steps are used like any other foothold, and the hands provide balance.

Vertical and overhanging rock makes top stepping difficult because your center of gravity moves away from the rock *and* above the point where the etriers are clipped to the aid placement. If the rock offers any features, your hands may provide the balance. If the rock is blank, keep your weight on your feet while leaning back and applying tension to the daisy chain between your harness and your aid placement. That tension provides the means of balancing yourself (fig. 11-24).

Special considerations

Problems encountered while aid climbing may cause you to add variations to the basic sequence. As in free climbing, rope drag can become a problem. Use long slings to keep the rope running straight. Add the slings after you have moved to the next higher piece so that you obtain the maximum gain out of each placement.

You may also realize you're short of certain-sized pieces and that you will need to reuse these sizes. As you move onto a higher placement, you may opt to pull the piece you were just using and save it for future use. As a general rule, however, leave at least every other piece as your protection against a fall.

RESTING

Don't wear yourself out. Climb in a relaxed fashion and take rests as often as necessary to conserve your strength or plot the next series of moves.

Here's a quick and easy rest: with each foot in separate etriers and one foot one step below the other, bend the knee of the higher leg and bring that foot under you. Most of your weight rests over the bent leg. The outstretched leg takes minimal weight but maintains balance (fig. 11-25).

You can also clip your daisy chain or fifi hook into the piece supporting you and rest in your harness.

Once the climbing rope is clipped into the supporting piece, you can also ask the belayer for tension and rest on the climbing rope. This is not an efficient method, however, due to stretch in the

Fig. 11–24. Top stepping; note the use of daisy-chain tension.

Fig. 11–25. Resting on a foot

rope. It also places unnecessary strain on the belay system.

Finally, you can often find relaxing stances in your etriers. Generally, the greatest stability is obtained with the heels together and the toes spread apart against the rock.

SWITCHING BETWEEN AID AND FREE CLIMBING

Timing is the key problem in switching between the techniques of aid and free climbing.

From free to aid: Free climbers must remember that the switch to aid requires some preparation. Begin the aid sequence before stretching yourself to the limit of your ability. This is easy if you know you will be changing to aid, but problems arise if you are not expecting to use aid but suddenly need it. Finding yourself in this bind, you can improvise etriers by interconnecting several slings and aid your way over the blank area. Such creativity is particularly important when climbing in a remote alpine environment. The climb's style may be damaged, but your body will be spared.

From aid to free: To free-climb a few moves during an aid pitch, simply clip the etriers to the back of your harness, and then make the moves. It is best to continue climbing on aid until you can comfortably switch to free techniques. If the change is made too early, you may have trouble retrieving your etriers from the last aid placement.

When beginning a longer section of free climbing, clip etriers, daisies, and so forth to your harness and be sure they will not hinder your movement. This may entail removing most of your aid implements and hanging them behind you.

TENSION TRAVERSES AND PENDULUMS

These techniques allow you to move horizontally across blank sections of a wall that would normally require placement of bolts.

Tension traverses are the simpler technique, useful for short traverses. The leader takes tension from the belayer, then leans to the side and uses friction on small holds to work sideways.

Pendulums let you cross wider blank sections without bolts but often require more ropes and pose special problems for the second climber. Start by placing a bombproof anchor at the top of the planned pendulum. The equipment used for this anchor cannot be retrieved unless it is possible to come back to it from above.

Next, you'll be lowered by the belayer (or rappel while on belay) until you have enough rope to run back and forth across the rock and swing into a new crack system. If a rappel is used for the pendulum, an extra rope will be required. When being lowered by the belayer, it is best to be lowered too little than too much, because if you're too low it may be very difficult to correct the error.

Once in the new crack system, climb as high as safety allows before clipping your belayed climbing rope into aid pieces for protection. The higher you get, the easier and safer it will be for your belayer, who will second the pendulum.

See the section later in this chapter on seconding pendulums for more details and an illustration of pendulum technique.

OVERHANGS

Before leading an overhang, check that you have enough equipment for the job. It may be impossible to obtain more gear later from the second climber. Keep your ascenders handy, because if a piece pulls and you end up hanging, you'll need ascenders to climb back up to your last secure piece. Also, check that your belayer is securely anchored, or you could both end up hanging free in the event of a fall.

Balance will be difficult as you scale an overhang because you can't effectively place your feet against the rock. Use of a daisy chain or fifi hook, however, allows you to hang from the harness and achieve a stable position. As an overhang approaches the horizontal, you can achieve greater balance still by clipping a sling from a chest harness to the supporting aid piece (fig. 11-26).

Despite the difference in balance, the basic sequence for aiding over a roof is the same as described earlier, but you may find it more comfortable to sit with your legs through the middle

Fig. 11–26. Aiding under a roof; note the use of a chest harness for support, and the availability of ascenders.

step of the etriers rather than standing in the bottom steps. Expect to experience some swinging. Finally, because your belayer will probably aid over the overhang rather than use ascenders, consider the length of your partner's reach when making your placements.

Rope drag is a common side effect of overhangs, but liberal use of longer slings will help. You may also want to pull along a second belay rope and start climbing on it after clearing the lip of the overhang.

Finally, try to relax when working out over a big roof. Have confidence in your pieces. Clutching at them won't keep them in place but will drain your strength.

HANGING BELAYS

Upon reaching the end of the pitch, the leader establishes an anchor as a new belay station (fig. 11-27). Place this anchor, when possible, to the side of the route (especially if you are sack hauling) so that your second can easily climb through. Also try to place at least one aid piece at the start of the next pitch to give the second a stance while changing leads.

When establishing your anchor, make sure *all* anchor points (including the haul anchor) are connected to *all* other anchor points. If an existing anchor system is in place do not simply place a sling over the system. This is an easy mistake to make and experienced climbers have paid for this error with their lives. Clip in, instead, in such a way that should any portion of the anchor fail, your attachment won't slide off the failed end.

Similarly, complete anchor systems have failed when a separate haul anchor, which was not interconnected with the main anchor, failed. In these cases the force generated by the falling haul sack overloaded the main anchor.

Once you are clipped in, anchor the climbing

Fig. 11–27. Hanging-belay sequence: a, leader establishes anchor; b, with climbing rope anchored and the haul system set, the second frees the haul sack (note that the first piece of the next pitch is set); c, while the second ''jugs,'' the leader hauls the sack; d, the haul sack is anchored, and the second moves onto the first piece of the next pitch; e, after re-racking, the new leader begins to lead.

d

e

rope so that the second can ascend it as a fixed line. Now prepare the hauling system, if you are hauling. Remove the aid rack and use it as the counterweight for the hauling system. Inform the second to free the haul sack so that you can hoist it while the second ascends the fixed climbing rope.

After the hauling is completed (or after the climbing rope was fixed if you are not hauling), establish your belay seat, get comfortable, and prepare for the exchange of leads. Sort the rack, organize the ropes, prepare your belay system, and so forth.

TYROLEAN TRAVERSES

Tyrolean traverses are most often used to return to a main wall after ascending a detached pillar. Ropes are strung between the main wall and the top of the pillar, allowing you to traverse through the air, attached to the rope.

You can establish a Tyrolean traverse like this:

1. After setting up a bombproof anchor on the main wall—one that can take both a horizontal and vertical pull—rappel on two ropes to the saddle between the main wall and the pinnacle. (You can use just one rope for the rappel if the traverse will be short enough.) Do not pull down the rappel ropes. If it takes more than one rappel to reach the saddle, you'll have to tie a light line to the two ends of the main rappel rope to give you a way to retrieve the ends once you're on top of the pinnacle.

2. Climb the pinnacle using an additional climbing rope. The second climber brings up the free ends of the rappel ropes.

3. Once atop the pinnacle, the free ends of the rappel ropes (now the traverse ropes) are stretched tight and anchored to the pinnacle.

After the traverse, you will not be able to recover the equipment used for the pinnacle anchor.

4. While belayed, one climbers now "jugs" across the open area on *one* of the ropes, using the Texas prusik (which is explained in Chapter 13, in the section on crevasse rescue). The forward ascender is attached to the harness with a daisy chain. To the rear ascender is attached an etrier, and a second daisy chain attached to the climber's harness. Finally, the climber connects an additional safety sling between the traverse rope and the harness. This sling rides on a carabiner between the two ascenders. What would normally be the lower ends of the ascenders must be clipped to the rope with a safety carabiner (as shown in figure 11-6, earlier in this chapter).

5. After the first climber has jugged across, the second climber unties the ropes at the pinnacle anchor, threads the end of one rope through the anchor, and ties the ropes together as if preparing a rappel. This climber notes which rope will be pulled when it comes time to retrieve the ropes. (If it's a short traverse and you are using just a single rope, the climbers on each side of the traverse need to pull the rope around so that its center moves to the pinnacle anchor and the two ends are back on the main wall. Otherwise you will have problems retrieving the rope later.)

6. The first climber then tightens and anchors the rope ends on the main wall and belays the second, who will traverse in the same manner as the first.

7. Once both climbers are reunited, the ropes are untied at the main wall and retrieved by pulling on the appropriate rope.

SECONDING

As the second climber on short sections of aid, you will usually follow the same sequence as the leader, while belayed from above. You will, however, unclip the rope from a placement before clipping on the etriers, and clean the placement below

you after stepping up higher. If you cannot reach a lower piece after moving up, lengthen your etriers with another sling, and then step down to clean the piece.

When climbing long sections of aid, a different

strategy is called for. You will use mechanical ascenders to jug the fixed climbing rope and clean
the route as you go. Before heading up, free the
haul bag so the leader can start hauling it up the
route. If it hangs up along the way, you will be the
one to free it.

USING ASCENDERS

Although you could ascend fixed climbing
ropes on slings attached with prusik knots, mechanical ascenders are both safer and more efficient (fig. 11-28). Attach an etrier and a daisy
chain to each ascender. The etriers give you a platform to stand on, and the daisy chains positively
connect the ascenders to your harness. Use a carabiner—not a fifi hook—to clip each daisy chain to
an ascender. To expedite the process of preparing
your ascenders, mark the loops in both the daisies
and etriers where the gear is properly adjusted for
length while jugging.

You do *not* untie from the end of the climbing
rope while ascending. Remaining tied in serves as
a backup in case both ascenders fail. To further
decrease the likelihood of a long fall, you should
periodically ''tie in short.''

Tying in short is an easy precaution that has
saved lives. As the second ascends, an ever-length-
ening loop of climbing rope forms below him,
making for a long fall if the ascenders fail. To
avoid this danger, stop periodically and, using the
climbing rope just below the ascenders, tie a fig-
ure-8 loop and clip the loop into your harness with
a locking carabiner. This guarantees a much
shorter fall. Repeat this procedure about every 20
feet. Each time, unclip and untie the last figure-8
loop *after* the new figure-8 loop is clipped into
your harness. Even when tying in short, *do not
untie from the end of the rope.*

Often while jugging, it is necessary to remove
the upper ascender from the rope and place it above
a piece from which the rope cannot be unclipped
while weighted from below. This same situation
arises when the rope runs over an edge. Before
removing the ascender, tie in short; this is a convenient time to do so.

After reattaching the upper ascender above the

*Fig. 11–28. Use of
ascenders; note daisy
chains from each
ascender to harness,
and climber tied in
short.*

piece, check that the cam trigger is fully locked or the ascender could pop off the rope. This is especially true if you are jugging on a diagonal rope because the ascender has a tendency to twist to a vertical position once weighted. This twisting can be minimized by clipping a carabiner between the ascender and the rope as well (fig.11-6). Once the upper ascender is reattached and your weight is on it, you will be able to unclip the rope from the problem piece of aid.

Other precautions should also be taken while ascending. First, carry a spare prusik sling just in case an ascender fails. And, as in all climbing, beware of sharp edges. Jugging places the rope under tension and sharp edges can damage it. Ascend as smoothly as possible to minimize the sawing motion of the rope running over an edge.

CLEANING

Efficiency in aid climbing is very much related to organization. While ascending and cleaning a pitch, rack the equipment as it will be placed on the lead rack. This greatly facilitates the lead changes.

Clean protection and aid placements that are lightly set often pop out if you jug right through them. Lift up on the placement as you slide your ascender up the rope. If clean aid has been used, you can often ascend from one tying-off-short spot to the next without stopping. After tying in short again, rack the pieces that have accumulated on the rope above your ascender.

This general system works even if a placement does not pop out as you move the ascenders upward. Keep the piece clipped into the climbing rope and use a chock pick and hammer to dislodge it. Once it pops free, continue ascending without reracking until you tie in short again. If, however, you must remove the upper ascender frequently, you should rack the pieces as they are removed.

Fixed pins found on the route should be left in place unless they are obviously unsafe or interfere with a chock placement. Take care not to break the eyes off these old pins, leaving a useless pin.

When cleaning one of your own pins, pound it back and forth along the axis of the crack, as far as it will go in each direction. Once the pin is loose enough to move easily back and forth, you can remove it by any of several means (fig. 11-29):

Fig. 11–29. Piton removal: a, use of "cleaner biner"; b, hammer used to pry; c, hammer swing.

1. Attach a "cleaner biner"—a carabiner no longer used for climbing—and a sling to the pin. Pull out on the sling while tapping the pin back and forth until it pops out (fig. 11-29a).
2. Pry out on the loose pin with the pick of the hammer, taking care not to break the hammer (fig. 11-29b).
3. Attach a "cleaner biner" and sling to the loose pin, then attach the sling to the hammer with another carabiner. Starting with slack in the sling, swing the hammer in the direction the pin should come out (fig. 11-29c).

Because the heads of malleable placements can only be reused a limited number of times, it is often best to leave them fixed. This is especially true if you think the wire will pull off the head as you remove the piece. If you decide to remove a malleable piece, attach a cleaner biner and sling between the head and your hammer. Then, as with pins, give the hammer a quick swing outward. It may take several swings before the head pops out. Inspect the head closely before reusing it because they deteriorate quickly. But if your attempt to remove the head merely strips the wire away, take the time to clean the head out of the rock. It is easier for you to do so on a fixed rope than for another climber on lead.

SECONDING TRAVERSES AND OVERHANGS

When traversing a long distance, it is generally more efficient if you aid across the traverse as if leading. Aiding in this fashion, you can receive a belay from above or self-belay by attaching ascenders to your harness with slings and sliding the ascenders along the climbing rope as you aid. When using the latter method, tie in short from time to time.

Short traverses, and those that are more diagonal than horizontal, can be crossed using normal jugging (mechanical ascender) techniques. The nearer the traverse is to horizontal, the less efficient this technique becomes, for at each piece you are faced with a small pendulum.

When jugging, remove the upper ascender at each placement and move it as far as possible above the currently weighted piece. This practice minimizes the pendulum that will result when you transfer your weight onto the upper ascender. Before doing this, however, allow some distance between the lower ascender and the placement so that the lower ascender does not jam into the piece as you transfer your weight to the upper ascender. Also, be sure to still tie in short at regular intervals.

The same basic methods just described for traverses also apply to seconding overhangs.

SECONDING PENDULUMS

The best method to second a pendulum depends on the length of the pendulum and the ropes available. The placements, slinging, and carabiner for the pendulum anchor usually will all need to be left behind, unless they can be reached from above after completing the pendulum.

Seconding long pendulums

All long pendulums require at least one rope in addition to the climbing and haul ropes. There are a number of ways to second a long pendulum, but the method shown in figure 11-30 will handle all such cases.

Figure 11-30a: All pendulums begin with a leader, of course, who rappels off a bombproof pendulum point using either one rope or two ropes tied together, depending on the width of the pendulum. The rappel rope should be clipped into the anchor so there's no danger of losing it. While on the pendulum, the leader is belayed on the climbing rope, which is not clipped into the pendulum anchor. At the bottom of the rappel, the leader runs back and forth across the rock to gain enough momentum to swing into the new crack system. On a very long pendulum, the leader may haul along an extra belay rope. The belayer keeps one end of this rope as the leader drags the other end.

Figure 11-30b: The leader ascends the new crack system and sets up an anchor. The leader attaches the climbing rope and the extra belay rope to the new anchor, the latter to serve as a belay

Fig. 11–30. Long pendulum sequence: a, leader rappels on two ropes while belayed on two; b, leader begins climbing, clipping in one of the belay ropes; c, with anchor set, leader belays with rope not clipped to aid pieces (the second rappels across the pendulum—note that the end of one rappel rope is attached to the second climber to prevent its loss); d, the second pulls the rappel ropes, ties in short, and "jugs" anchored climbing rope.

rope for the second climber. With the first climber now set to belay, the second climber frees or lowers the haul bag. The follower also unclips the rappel rope tie-in from the pendulum anchor so the rope can be retrieved later. (The follower can clip one end of the rappel rope to an out-of-the-way place on the seat harness to again ensure the rope can't be dropped.)

Figure 11-30c: The follower rappels the pendulum, with the first climber belaying and helping to pull the follower toward the new crack system at the end of the pendulum. (There's an alternative if the leader didn't drag an extra pendulum rope across. The second can pull across the pendulum on the lead climbing rope by hand, or with the help of mechanical ascenders.)

Figure 11-30d: Safely across, the second attaches ascenders to the climbing rope, ties off short, retrieves the rappel rope, and is ready to climb up the new crack system.

Seconding short pendulums

Climbers also have a variety of ways to handle the challenge of seconding a short pendulum. One clever and useful method is shown in figure 11-31. For this method to work, the slack rope from the pendulum anchor to the follower's harness must be at least double the arc of the pendulum. The follower stays tied in to the climbing rope during the sequence.

As shown in figure 11-31, here's how you as the follower could second a short pendulum:

Figure 11-31a: Connect the upper ascender with its attached etrier to the climbing rope beyond the pendulum anchor, facing across the pendulum. Clip a daisy chain from your harness to the ascender. Connect the lower ascender and etrier to the section of rope between the pendulum anchor and yourself. Clip it in with another daisy chain. Place your weight on the upper ascender. Next, attach a rappel device to the rope, below the lower ascender, and grasp the rope where it exits the device. Then, while keeping the safety trigger locked, release the cam of the lower ascender by pulling on the rope below it (this will take some effort). You're now ready to move.

Figure 11-31b: With one hand grasping the climbing rope as it leaves the rappel device and the other hand sliding the lower ascender, lower yourself across the pendulum. To put the brakes on at any time, simply let go of the lower ascender and the cam will again lock. (In fact, if a rappel device is not used, this ascender will often lock onto the rope by itself, requiring you to repeat the previous tactic of pulling hard on the rope below it.)

Figure 11-31c: Once across the pendulum, tie in short and move the lower ascender above that point. Now untie yourself from the end of the rope so you can pull it through the pendulum anchor. Once you've re-tied into the end of the climbing rope, you're set to ascend the climbing rope again.

The rappel device makes it easier to hold the rope while lowering yourself across the pendulum. However, you can also second a short pendulum this way without the device.

CHANGING LEADS

Unorganized belay stations can become a rat's nest of tangled ropes, twisted slings, and assorted hardware. Basic organization keeps the belay station manageable and the team functioning efficiently. Following are several methods to improve organization:

- All ropes should be different colors.
- After hauling the sack, the leader stacks the haul line and organizes the other ropes and hardware at the anchor.
- Once the second arrives at the anchor and begins consolidating the lead rack, the old leader (now the belayer) makes butterfly coils in the climbing rope and stacks these coils at the anchor with a sling. This prevents the climbing rope from getting snagged below and from tangling, and helps it pay out smoothly.
- If the second was carrying a rucksack, it can be packed with gear that won't be utilized on the next pitch and clipped into the anchor.
- Fina'y, the second (now the new leader) clips the free end of the haul rope to his or her harness, is placed on belay, and starts climbing.

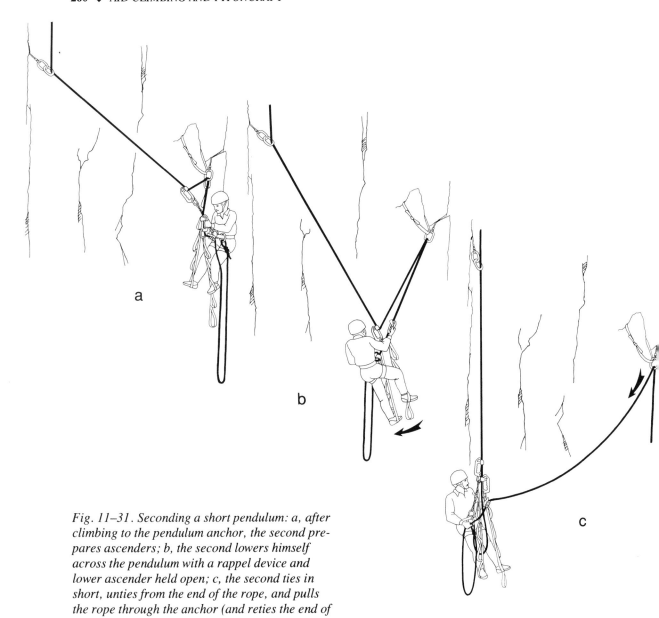

Fig. 11–31. Seconding a short pendulum: a, after climbing to the pendulum anchor, the second prepares ascenders; b, the second lowers himself across the pendulum with a rappel device and lower ascender held open; c, the second ties in short, unties from the end of the rope, and pulls the rope through the anchor (and reties the end of the rope).

BIG-WALL MULTIDAY TECHNIQUES

"Big walls," the saying goes, "are 90 percent work and 10 percent fun." Not everyone agrees with those percentages, but few climbers will say big walls are easy. There's no question that proper conditioning is essential for the hauling of heavy loads and the scaling of multiple aid pitches.

Big walls also call for a high degree of mental composure. Inexperienced wall climbers easily find themselves the victim of heightened fears brought on by prolonged and severe exposure. If you're new to the game, perhaps you can soothe your fears by realizing that techniques for dealing with major walls are much the same as those needed for smaller climbs. Concentrate on the problem at hand and work away at the objective one move at a time.

In preparing for a big wall, guidebooks and other climbers are often helpful sources of information. Beware, however, of overdependence on climbers' topographic maps and equipment lists. Routes do change over time, especially if pins are used regularly.

Solid, efficient aid technique is a prerequisite if a major wall is to be completed within the time constraints dictated by reasonable food and water supplies. For success on the big walls, you must develop competency in hoisting heavy sacks up the route, and you should be able to live comfortably in a vertical world for days at a time.

HAULING

After anchoring yourself and fixing the climbing rope for the second, it's your job as the leader to begin hauling (fig. 11-32):

1. Attach a pulley, through which the haul line passes, to the anchor.
2. Attach an upside-down ascender to the haul line on the haul-sack side of the pulley. The end of the ascender closest to the pulley (normally the bottom) is clipped into the anchor, while the end pointing toward the haul sack is counterweighted with the remains of the rack (or another weight).
3. Attach a second ascender, in the normal direction, to the haul line on the opposite side of the pulley (between yourself and the pulley). Use a daisy chain to connect this ascender to your harness.
4. Push back from the wall using your legs and palms; your body weight will raise the haul sack. When you stop pushing, the upside-

Top end
of haul line

Fixed
climbing
rope

Fig. 11–32. Sack-hauling system; hauler is preparing to move ascender up haul line and ascend etriers for next power haul.

down ascender acts as a brake to prevent backward slippage of the haul bag. You'll need a little slack in the climbing rope between yourself and the anchor to allow your hauling movement.

You can also haul by allowing slack of 6 to 8 feet between you and the anchor. Then, with the daisy chain connected between your harness and the haul line ascender, walk down the wall 6 to 8 feet until the anchor rope tightens. Climb back to your original position by stepping upward in etriers attached to the anchor, pulling the ascender with you. Repeat the process.

This method is also used if two people are needed to lift a very heavy bag. Both of you clip to the ascender on the haul rope, give yourself 6 to 8 feet of slack, and walk down the wall together. Regardless of the method used, *always* connect yourself to the anchor with the climbing rope.

FIXING PITCHES

On multiday climbs, you will often fix two or three pitches beyond the bivouac site and leave gear not needed for the bivouac at the high point. The lower end of each fixed rope is attached to the anchor of the previous pitch.

The next morning the pitches are jugged—one climber on a rope at a time. This gives a head start on the day and lets you warm up before new climbing begins.

RETREATING

Before a major climb, plan retreat lines in case of bad weather, accident, or other emergency. Locate other routes that are easy to reach to speed the ascent or that have fixed retreat lines.

If no retreat route exists, consider carrying a bolt kit for emergencies, allowing you to place

rappel anchors. Also, as you climb each pitch, consider how you would descend it. On major walls rescues may be slow and difficult, if possible at all. It may be up to you to get back down in an emergency.

LIVING IN THE VERTICAL WORLD

Living for days on a vertical wall of rock brings some intriguing problems.

Dropped gear, for instance. Once dropped, it's gone. All vital items must have clip-in loops. Learn your gear so you can work it confidently. Get acquainted with unfamiliar items, such as Portaledges or hammocks, beforehand.

It's usually necessary to carry all your water with you. Each climber generally needs 2 quarts per day. For hot weather, especially if the route gets a lot of sun, you will need to carry even more.

Waste disposal poses another challenge. Tossing garbage down the wall is not acceptable, so you'll have to haul it up and off the climb. On popular routes, use paper bags for your excrement and toss these off the wall—warning climbers below when you are about to launch a bag. On seldom-climbed routes (or when no portion of a popular route is in your fall line), you can let your excrement fall out into space because this waste will decay far more quickly when not bagged. Keep all bivouac sites clean and sanitary, with no sign of your passing.

After completing a major wall, you need to get your gear back down. In the past, common practice was to toss the haul bag loaded with gear off the wall. Today, sack tossing is illegal at popular climbing areas like Yosemite; it endangers climbers below. Furthermore, many climbers have had their gear stolen by the time they got down to it. Carry down what you hauled up.

THE FUTURE OF AID CLIMBING

Free-climbers may feel that aid climbing isolates the climber from the rock. But anyone who has struggled to place a piece of aid while standing above a series of marginal placements understands

that aid is not only climbing but a test of technical abilities and nerves.

To ensure that these routes will continue to be a test of skill and nerves, aid climbers are asked to respect certain ethics. If you are climbing an established route, adhere to the ethics of the first-ascent climbers. If they did not need a piton or bolt, *don't place one*. Use creativity and boldness to overcome the difficulty. A party following you on a route should find it in the condition you found it.

If you're putting up a new route, you are establishing the style for those who follow. Remember that routes once considered difficult using pitons are now free-climbed and that old bolt ladders are often viewed with disdain. Make it your goal to climb cleanly and in a style that climbers can respect. As time goes on, more of today's aid routes will be free-climbed, while aid climbers will push their limits on ever thinner and more remote climbs.

◆ **PART FOUR** ◆

SNOW AND
ICE
CLIMBING

Ice climbing on Habegger Falls, Bishop Creek in California's Sierra Nevada. Photo by Gordon Wiltsie

· 12 ·

SNOW TRAVEL AND CLIMBING

Climbing in snow is a fundamental part of moun-taineering. Snow adds beauty and challenge—but even if you wanted to avoid snow, it wouldn't be easy. Climbers work in a world in which their medium, the mountains, is sculpted by the action of snow, ice, and water. To avoid snow would mean climbing in only a select few mountain ranges or for only a few months each year.

Climbers like snow for at least a couple of rea-sons. First of all, it makes many climbs a lot easier by providing a pathway over brush and other ob-stacles on the approach hike and reducing the danger of loose rock on the ascent. It also brings new beauty to the mountains at the same time that it conceals the impact of people.

Snow is a complex medium that shows up in many forms that continually change, making snow travel trickier than trail hiking or rock climbing. Snow falls in a form that varies from tiny crystals to coarse pellets, depending on temperature and wind. Once fallen, snow begins to change as it is acted upon by sun, wind, temperature variations, and precipitation.

A rock face stays basically the same, while snow goes through many changes. It may start as a dusting of snow over a brush slope, progress to an unconsolidated powder bowl waiting to avalanche, then to a solid surface offering rapid ascent to a ridge top, and finally back to a brush slope with only scattered snow patches. Even in the course of a day, the snow can change from rock hard in the morning to thigh-sucking slush in the afternoon.

The changeable nature of snow means moun-taineers have to be flexible in their mode of travel, ready to use snowshoes, skis, or crampons instead of boots alone. Snow conditions also affect deci-sions on route and climbing technique. Should you hike up the comfortable, snow-covered valley bot-tom or on the ridge top away from avalanche hazard? Should you go for the easy step-kicking of the sunny slope or the firmer, more stable snow of the shaded hill? Do the conditions mean it is safer to travel roped or unroped?

In this chapter we'll take a look at the equip-ment you need to travel in snow and techniques for traveling quickly and safely—with special empha-sis on avalanche recognition and rescue.

EQUIPMENT

At the top of the list of basic snow-climbing equipment are ice axes and crampons. Snowshoes, skis, and ski poles are other important snow-travel aids. Climbers also use equipment for snow an-chors, which will be taken up later in this chapter in the section on roped climbing.

ICE AXE

The ice axe (fig. 12-1) is one of the most ver-satile and important pieces of mountaineering equipment a climber owns. Without it, safe alpine travel is restricted to easy scrambles. With an axe,

Fig. 12–1. Parts of the ice axe

and the skill to use it, you can can venture onto all forms of snow and ice, enjoying a greater variety of mountain landscapes during more seasons of the year.

The modern ice axe is an inherently simple tool with many uses. Below the snow line, it's used for balance, as a walking cane, and to help brake going downhill. But its main role is in snow and ice travel, where it provides balance or a point of security to prevent a fall and serves to stop any fall that takes place.

The design of an ice axe often is a trade-off between features that make the tool better for particular uses. A longer axe may be OK for cross-country travel and scrambling, where it's used as a cane and to provide security in low-angle climbing. You'll probably want a shorter axe for the steeper slopes in alpine climbing. For ice climbing, the axes get shorter still and other design aspects become more specialized, such as the droop of the pick, placement of the teeth, and shape of the adze. These specialized axes are covered in Chapter 14.

Parts of the ice axe

The head of an ice axe—which includes the pick and the adze—is usually made of steel, a material strong enough for snow and ice climbing. Although the hole in the head of the axe is commonly called a carabiner hole, most climbers attach their wrist leash through it.

The pick on most ice axes (fig. 12-2) is curved or drooped, a design that provides better hooking action in snow or ice, causing the axe to dig in faster when you're trying to stop yourself (self-arrest) after a fall. A moderate hooking angle of 65 to 70 degrees from the shaft is right for general moun-

Fig. 12–2. Ice-axe picks: shapes and teeth patterns

taineering uses. A sharper angle of 55 to 60 degrees is better for technical ice climbing as it coincides with the arc followed by the axe head when it is planted in steep ice. Teeth on the pick provide grip for ice and hard snow.

The pick's hold for self-arrest is affected to some degree by its clearance (fig. 12-3). If the end edge of the pick is parallel to the shaft, the pick has neutral clearance. If the angle of the pick end tends toward the shaft, it has negative clearance. If the angle tends away from the shaft, it has positive clearance. Picks with neutral or negative clearance can skate or drag on an icy surface and not penetrate reliably during self-arrest. Picks with positive clearance tend to pull into the surface when pressure is applied—so much so that they can bite into hard snow with such suddenness that the axe may be yanked out of the climber's hands. To beat this

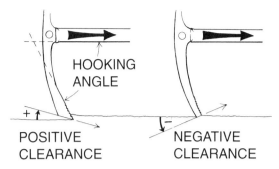

Fig. 12–3. Ice-axe clearance

problem, some climbers prefer a negative clearance to help with a more gradual stop in hard snow. But in most cases, the clearance probably makes little difference because self-arrest on ice is almost impossible regardless of the clearance, and in softer snow the pick will dig in whether the clearance is positive or negative.

The adze of the axe is used mainly for step-chopping on hard snow or ice. The flat top of the adze is also a firm, comfortable platform for the palm of your hand while holding the axe in the self-belay grasp during snow climbing. Adzes for general mountaineering may be flat or curved, straight-edged or scalloped, straight-out or drooped. A flat, straight-edged, non-drooped adze with sharp corners is probably the best all-around tool for step-chopping.

The shaft of your axe will most likely be made of metal (aluminum or titanium) or a composite (fiberglass, Kevlar, or carbon filament), or a combination of both. The wooden shafts of yesterday—often dense, straight-grained hickory—have been replaced by these stronger materials. Even the historical advantages of wood in dampening vibrations and offering a warmer grip have been minimized by the new composites.

Some shafts are covered at least partly by a rubber-type material for a better grip. The material helps give surer command of the axe during self-arrest and also dampens vibrations and increases control in placing the pick in ice. You can improve your hold on a shaft that doesn't have a rubber grip by adding athletic grip tape or using gloves with rubberized palms. However, the gripping material

on the shaft can keep the axe from slipping as easily into the snow when you're using it for a boot-axe belay, probing, or self-belay. For this reason, it is recommended that ice axes for basic mountaineering not have this grip.

The spike, the metal tip of the axe, must be kept sharp so that it pokes readily into snow and ice. The axe does come in handy on rocky trails and talus slopes by helping with balance, but beware of dulling the spike.

Ice-axe length

Ice axes range in length from 40 centimeters (about 16 inches) to 90 centimeters (about 3 feet)—still much shorter than the 5-foot alpenstocks of the alpine pioneers. The shortest axes are for technical ice climbing; the longest ones are for tall mountaineers using the axe as a cane on easy terrain.

The optimal length for an ice axe may depend more on what you plan to do with it than on how tall you are. Axes less than 60 centimeters long are ice-climbing tools, excellent for placements on steep slopes but not so good for self-arrest. An axe of 70 centimeters is the longest that is generally useful for ice climbing. A length of 60 to 70 centimeters works well in most alpine situations, where you are climbing moderately steep snow slopes and using the axe for self-belay and self-arrest. Longer axes are better for cross-country travel and scrambling, and also are good as snow anchors and for probing for cornices and crevasses.

Ice-axe leash

The leash provides a way to attach the ice axe to your wrist or your harness when you want to ensure it won't be dropped. The leash also has other uses that we'll get to. Although the length of a leash can vary, it usually consists of a piece of accessory cord or webbing attached through the hole in the head of the ice axe (fig. 12-4).

The leash is valuable insurance on crevassed glaciers or long steep slopes where losing an axe would leave you without a principal tool for safety and put climbers below in danger from the runaway axe. The leash also lets the ice axe hang freely

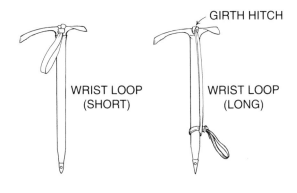

Fig. 12–4. Ice-axe leashes (wrist loops), attached through carabiner hole in head of axe

while you make a move or two on occasional rock during a snow climb.

Short wrist leashes are favored by those who find them adequate for basic snow and glacier travel—easy to use and an aid to quicker control of the ice axe during a fall. During an uncontrolled fall in which you lose your grip on the axe, the short leash prevents the axe from flailing around as dangerously as it would on a longer leash. Ice axes sometimes come with a short wrist loop attached by the manufacturer.

A longer leash is now preferred, however, for all but the most basic of snow travel. With a long leash, you no longer have to switch the leash from wrist to wrist as you move the axe to the other hand for a change in direction up a snow slope. The long leash also makes the axe more versatile for climbing steep snow or ice.

A long wrist leash is usually about as long as the axe itself, and if it's just the right length, it can help reduce arm fatigue during step-chopping and ice climbing. It should be long enough to let you grasp the shaft near the spike through the wrist loop as you hold the leash taut from the head of the axe. This way, the wrist can share the work of the arm, and the head of the axe will be more stable. You can shorten the leash when you don't need it by wrapping it around the shaft.

With the long leash attached to your seat harness, the axe can serve as a personal anchor.

If you buy an ice axe without a leash, one can easily be made from a length of 5- or 6-millimeter accessory cord or $1/2$-inch to 1-inch flat webbing, tied into a sling, and then girth-hitched through the hole in the axe head. Tie a slip knot at the end of the sling to form the wrist loop. Ready-made leashes are also available at climbing stores.

Ice-axe maintenance

Modern metal-shaft ice axes require very little special care. Inspect the shaft before each use for deep dents that might weaken it to the point of failure under load (but don't worry about minor nicks and scratches). Clean mud and dirt off the axe after each climb and remove any rust.

Check the pick, adze, and spike regularly. To sharpen, use a small hand file instead of a grinding wheel, which could change the temper and strength of the metal.

CRAMPONS

Mountaineering is unthinkable without crampons, but when the first 10-point crampons came on the scene in Europe in the early 1900s, many alpinists thought the gadgets took unsporting advantage of the peaks. However, crampons proved to be the one aid that could relieve climbers of the tremendous burden of step-cutting and open up a vast array of new snow and ice faces. They have since evolved into the 12-point crampons of today, with 10 bottom points and 2 front points.

As with ice axes, the different crampon designs involve a trade-off between what's good for general alpine use and what's good for technical ice climbing. Most crampons are made from chrome-molybdenum steel, an extremely strong, lightweight alloy.

Climbers face a number of questions in shopping for crampons. What type of crampons should I buy? How will I know when the crampons fit my boots? Which attachment system should I use? This section provides information to help answer these questions and offers tips on crampon maintenance.

Crampon points

The early 10-point crampon has long-since been eclipsed by the addition of two forward-slanting points in the 1930s to create the 12-point crampon. The 12-point models eliminated even more step-chopping and permitted "front-pointing" up steep snow and ice. Because 10-point crampons usually don't have front points, they're no good for very steep ice and are no longer available except as used equipment.

The angles of the first two rows of points determine the best use for a set of crampons. When the first row (front points) is drooped and the second row is angled toward the toe of the boot (fig. 12-5), the crampons are better suited for front-pointing than for general mountaineering. This configuration allows the boot heel to be lower without additional calf strain. Straight points are better for flat-footing and general use.

Tiny instep crampons with four or six points are sold for use by backpackers who need to cross an occasional short snowfield. Because there are no points at the heel or toe, they're unsuitable for

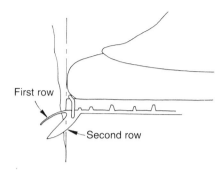

First row

Second row

Fig. 12–5. Angle of first two rows of points, best suited for front-pointing

mountaineering and can be dangerous on steep snow or ice.

Hinged vs. rigid crampons

Mountaineers have a choice of either hinged or rigid crampons (fig. 12-6). Rigid crampons are for technical ice climbing. For most mountaineering, hinged crampons are preferable.

A hinged crampon flexes at the instep and is

a

b

Fig. 12–6. Types of crampons: a, rigid; b, hinged.

meant to bend with the natural rocking action of walking. It can be attached to any mountaineering boot, full shank or not, and to plastic boots. Attached to a full-shank or plastic boot, hinged crampons perform nearly as well for ice climbing as rigid crampons, because the boot provides the stable climbing platform that's required. If you buy only one set of crampons, buy hinged. If your goal is steep technical ice, then you can consider a rigid crampon. Some hinged crampons can be made rigid simply by adding a screw to each side of the crampon.

A rigid crampon is inflexible and not meant to bend at the instep. In most cases, it must be used with full-shank or plastic boots because it could break from the natural flex of another boot. Rigid crampons don't perform well in mixed terrain, where some flexibility is desired, and they can be heavier than hinged crampons. Rigid crampons come into their own when you're front-pointing up technical ice. They vibrate less than hinged crampons when you swing them into the ice, and their stiffness makes for less tiring front-pointing by allowing you to keep your heel lower.

Crampon attachment

Anyone who has had a crampon come loose in the middle of a steep slope of hard snow on a dark, cold morning knows the urgency of keeping crampons attached until you really want them off. To keep the crampons on the boots, climbers can choose from a variety of traditional strapping methods or the newer step-in/clamp-on bindings. The various systems are available on either hinged or rigid crampons.

Straps

Buckled straps do a good job of attaching crampons to boots. Neoprene-coated nylon is the best strap material because it is strong, doesn't absorb water, won't stretch, and can be easily transferred from one pair of crampons to another. Leather straps are less expensive but stretch when wet and will eventually rot or break. Nylon or fabric webbing is least desirable, since it readily accumulates snow and may freeze to the buckle.

Three strap-on designs are in general use:

Four independent straps per crampon are used in one design: two short straps, with buckles, attached to one side of the crampon and two longer straps attached to the other side. One long strap then connects the front four attachment posts over the instep of the boot, while the other wraps around the ankle and connects the two rear posts (fig. 12-7a).

Two independent straps per crampon are used

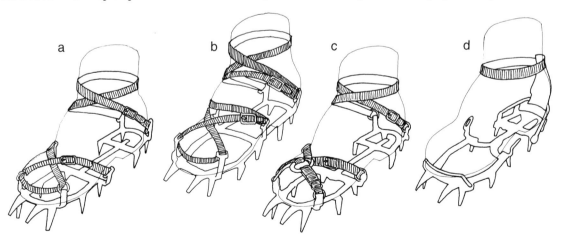

Fig. 12–7. Systems for attaching crampons to boots: a, four-strap; b, two-strap; c, Scottish; d, step-in/clamp on.

in an alternative strapping system: one connecting the front four attachment posts over the instep and the other wrapping around the ankle from the two rear posts (fig. 12-7b).

The Scottish system is a third strap-on method that is quicker than the other two and is gaining widespread use. A strap with a ring in the middle is permanently connected to the two front posts. A strap then runs from one side post through this ring to the other side post. The rear strap is the same as in the two-strap system (fig. 12-7c).

When strapping on crampons, position the buckles on the outward side of the boots to minimize the chance of catching a buckle with your foot as you walk. To reduce the danger of the front straps loosening on the two-strap and four-strap systems, thread the strap through the hole at each front attachment post *from the outside in*, and then give the strap an extra twist.

A word to beginning mountaineers: whatever you do, don't head out on a climb until you practice strapping on your crampons in the comfort of home. You'll have plenty of chances later to put the crampons on in the dark by feel, or by flashlight, with cold, numbed fingers. Lay the crampons on the floor with all straps started through the hole at an attachment post, put on your boots, place each boot in turn on its crampon, and attach the straps. Do the crampons fit? Do the straps have holes punched in them at the right places for attaching to the buckles? Do the straps need to be longer to accommodate insulated gaiters or overboots? Are they tight enough to keep the crampons on through thick and thin, but not so tight that they restrict blood flow? As best you can, work out all the wrinkles before you get out on that steep slope of hard snow in the cold, dark morning.

Step-in/clamp-on bindings

The old agony of fumbling with crampon straps and buckles is largely eliminated by the newer step-in/clamp-on bindings (fig. 12-7d). The crampons attach to the boot with a wire toe bale and a snap-up bale on the rear. They're fast and easy to put on, and each crampon has a safety strap so you won't lose it if it ever comes off. However, there

are a couple of considerations in addition to higher cost to keep in mind before you decide to use step-in/clamp-on bindings.

The fit to the boot is more critical than with crampons that are strapped on. The boot must have a pronounced welt at both the heel and toe and, therefore, the step-in/clamp-ons fit especially well on plastic boots. Crampons with straps often work better on leather boots, particularly those without a decided heel welt. And some climbers, nervous about the possibility of the clamp-ons releasing, continue to use straps for technical ice.

Crampon fit

To ensure that crampons stay attached and perform well, it's essential they fit just right. Here are some tips to help in fitting crampons, either the kind that attach with straps or the step-in/clamp-on type.

• When buying crampons, try them on with the boots you'll be wearing. If you plan to use them on more than one pair of boots, check the fit on all pairs.
• If you'll be wearing gaiters with a rubber band that fits around the welt and instep of the boot, be sure to wear the gaiters when you fit the crampons.
• The front crampon points should protrude about $3/4$ inch to 1 inch beyond the toe of the boot.
• Many crampons are adjustable to one degree or another. This can include adjustments for length and for the width of instep, heel, and toe. Being able to adjust the heel and toe widths can be especially important if you're using telemark boots (for a climbing/skiing trip) or overboots.
• The attachment posts at the sides and rear of strap-on crampons should hug the boot snugly without significant bending to fit. Test the fit by lifting the boot upside down by the crampon. The posts should hold to the boot without the use of straps.
• The heel wire found on some strap-on crampons helps keep the boot heel in place by preventing it from slipping through the rear post, especially when using plastic boots.
• The welt on a boot is especially important with

step-in/clamp-on bindings, which grip the welt at toe and heel. Most desirable are Norwegian-style double-stitched welts on heavy leather boots and the indented toe and heel on plastic boots.

• Some climbers place a flat piece of foam, shaped like the bottom of the boot, between the boot and crampon to help insulate the foot from the snow. If you want to do this, take it into account when you fit your crampons.

Crampon maintenance and safety

Regular simple maintenance is required for safe, dependable crampons. Keep the points sharp, clean the crampons after every climb, and inspect them before the next outing.

Snow and ice routes often include short sections of rock that you'll climb with crampons on. The crampons should be able to take the punishment, but too much of this will dull the points. As with ice axes, sharpen crampon points with a hand file, not a grinding wheel (fig. 12-8).

After you return home from each climb, wipe dirt and water from crampons to prevent rust. Check the points before each climb. They should be clean and reasonably sharp, though very sharp points are needed only for technical ice climbing. Also check alignment of the points, because splayed points make the crampons less efficient at gripping the snow and more effective as a weapon that can slash pants and legs. It's probably best to retire a pair of crampons with badly misaligned points. Check the tightness of nuts and bolts on adjustable crampons. And while you're looking over the crampons, don't forget to inspect the straps if you have the strap-on type. Look for rotting, abrasion, cracks, or cuts.

In the mountains, following a few easy rules can protect you, your gear, and your companions from sharp crampon points. Walk carefully to avoid snagging your pants, gashing your leg, or stepping on the rope. When you're carrying the crampons, use a set of rubber protectors to cover the points, or keep the crampons in a special pouch. Both the 12-point protectors and the crampon pouch are available commercially.

One little trick makes crampons safer and more effective in soft, sticky snow. Just wrap the bottom of the crampon with duct tape to minimize the amount of snow that balls up under the crampon. This balling of snow can be dangerous, particularly where slushy snow overlays an icy base. Or you might be able to just take the crampons off.

WANDS

To find their way back over snow and glacier routes, mountaineers often mark the path with tiny flags atop thin bamboo wands. Climbers usually make their own, using the green-stained bamboo sticks sold at garden supply stores for plant supports. Convert them to wands by attaching a piece of bright, durable, water-repellent material to one end; plastic route-marking tape or coated nylon is best (fig. 12-9). A common method is to slit the first couple of inches at one end of a wand, slip the flag in the slit, tie it, then tape the slit closed. Be sure the flag is secure enough to withstand the high winds of open snow slopes and glaciers.

Wands usually vary in length from 30 inches to 4 feet. Less than 30 inches and the flag may not be high enough to be easily seen; longer than 4 feet and the wands are awkward to carry. Use your longest wands in winter when they have to be

FILE EDGES OF POINTS

Fig. 12–8. How to sharpen crampons

FILE TOP OF POINTS

Fig. 12–9. Wand construction

pushed in farther because of soft snow and when new snowfall can bury them even deeper.

SKI POLES

Ski poles aren't only for use with skis. They beat an ice axe for balance when you're trudging with a heavy pack over level or low-angle snow, slippery ground or scree, or when you're trying to cross a stream or boulder field. They also can take some of the weight off your lower body. And the basket at the bottom keeps the poles from slipping deep into soft snow, a favorite trick of ice axes unless they're fitted with a special snow collar.

A variety of ski poles have features helpful to the trekker or mountaineer. Some poles telescope for adjustability on slopes and ease of strapping on a pack. With removable baskets, they can serve as a probe for crevasses or avalanche victims. Some poles fasten together to form an extra-long probe (fig. 12-10). Some poles both telescope out and fasten together. You can also buy a special self-arrest grip that has a pick protruding forward from the top, but this definitely is not a substitute for an ice axe on technical terrain. Most of these poles can be used whether you're traveling by foot, snowshoes, or skis.

SKIS

Mountaineering has become a popular four-season pursuit with the widespread use of Nordic and mountaineering skis fitted with climbing skins.

The Nordic ski, light and skinny, is worn with a special boot held in a toe binding that leaves the heel free (fig. 12-11a). Depending on the design

Fig. 12–10. Adjustable-length ski poles that can be fastened together to create an avalanche probe

and purpose of the ski, it may be referred to as a cross-country, touring, or telemark ski. Because the heel is not attached, Nordic skiers need the special skill of telemark turning for going downhill.

Ski mountaineering employs a wider, heavier ski (sometimes called a randonée ski) that is closer to a traditional alpine (downhill) ski (fig. 12-11b). It has a binding that leaves the heel free for uphill travel but can secure the heel for standard downhill technique. Special boots are sold for use with mountaineering skis, though plastic mountaineering boots are often adequate.

Both kinds of skis will get you into the backcountry in winter for touring or mountain approaches. To provide uphill traction, both are used with removable climbing skins, in a textured material known as nylon plush, that adhere to the bottom of the skis (fig. 12-11c).

If you're accustomed to using only boots or snowshoes for backcountry snow travel, you may find certain disadvantages to skis. During the times you have to pack them, there's extra weight. It's difficult to self-arrest on steep slopes, though self-arrest grips on your ski poles can help. The skis are awkward on rocky or forested snow slopes; skiing can be difficult if you have a heavy pack; and

Fig. 12–11. Ski equipment for mountaineering: a, Nordic skis; b, mountaineering skis, boots, and bindings; c, climbing skins for skis.

you'll need a well-matched party in terms of skiing ability in order to keep a steady pace, especially for roped glacier travel.

But after all is said and done, skis are undeniably easier and faster for basic snow travel. They are giving more and more mountaineers a way to get to areas they couldn't readily reach before and to travel at more times of the year. Skis also can offer a safety bonus for crevasse crossings because with your weight distributed over a wider area, there is less danger of breaking through. They can also come in handy for rescue work, converting into a makeshift stretcher or sled.

Backcountry ski travel is a complex activity, with special techniques and equipment. For detailed information, take a look at articles or books devoted to the subject.

SNOWSHOES

Snowshoes (fig. 12-12) are a traditional aid to snow travel that have been updated into the small lightweight designs of today. Bindings hold your

boots on the snowshoes, and metal claws or crampon-like devices improve traction on hard snow and ice.

Snowshoes are better than boots alone for traveling across fields of soft snow, where snowshoers float over the surface while hikers laboriously post-hole. But snowshoes are cumbersome for step-kicking uphill, even though modern snowshoes have an opening that lets you get the toe of your boot into the snow. Of course, when you're not wearing the snowshoes, they add extra weight to your pack.

Fig. 12–12. Snowshoes

Although snowshoes are a lot slower than skis, they can be used on mixed terrain where skis would be awkward, and they're often more practical than skis if you have a heavy pack. If your climbing party includes some people who aren't very good on skis, it's probably more efficient for everyone to travel on snowshoes, which are easy to learn. You wear normal mountaineering boots with snowshoes, unlike Nordic skis and some mountaineering skis that call for special footwear.

SHOVEL

A broad-bladed shovel is a utility and safety tool for snow travel (fig. 12-13). It's the only practical tool for uncovering an avalanche victim. Shovels are also used for digging snow shelters and leveling off tent platforms and have even been used as a climbing tool to shovel a pathway up a particularly snowy route.

A good snow shovel has a blade large enough to move snow efficiently and a handle long enough for good leverage but short enough for use in a confined area. It should strap easily to the pack for quick access in an emergency. Some shovels come with a detachable handle or with a blade that locks perpendicular to the handle so it can be used as a

Fig. 12–13. Snow shovel

trenching tool. For projects such as building snow caves, mountaineers sometimes carry a grain scoop, a broad-bladed shovel that can move a lot of snow.

SNOW-CLIMBING TECHNIQUES

USING THE ICE AXE

How to carry an ice axe

The first rule is to carry your ice axe carefully. Keep in mind what its sharp points and edges could do to you or your partners. Whenever the axe is not in your hands, be sure it's secure against slipping down a snow slope or cliff.

When you're on the move and don't need the axe, the best bet is to slip it through the ice-axe loop on your pack and strap it down (fig. 12-14a). It's a good idea to keep rubber or leather guards on the pick, adze, and spike, particularly on an axe that's sharp as an axe should be. If you're simply carrying the axe in one hand, grasp the shaft at the balance point (shaft parallel to the ground), the spike forward and the pick down (fig. 12-14b).

During travel on snow that alternates with rocks or steep brush where you need both hands free, you can get the axe out of the way by sliding it diagonally between your back and the pack (fig. 12-14c). The spike is down and the pick, between the two shoulder straps, is well seated, clear of your neck, and pointing in the same general direction as the angle of the shaft. The axe can be stowed and retrieved quickly, and this works fine for short stretches. To avoid chances of a runaway axe, retrieve it before taking off the pack.

How to grasp an ice axe

How you hold the head of the axe when climbing in snow depends on your preference and on the climbing situation.

There are two principal ways to grasp the axe:

Self-arrest grasp: The thumb goes under the adze and the palm and fingers go over the pick, near the shaft (fig. 12-15a). As you climb, the adze points forward.

Self-belay grasp: The palm sits on top of the adze and the thumb and index finger drop under the pick (fig. 12-15b). As you climb, the pick points forward.

The self-arrest grasp puts you in perfect position to use the axe instantly to brake a fall down a steep

Fig. 12–14. Carrying an ice axe: a, attached to a pack by an ice-axe loop, with guards on the pick, adze, and spike; b, in the hand while walking; c, temporarily between back and pack.

slope. However, you're not going to fall very often, and in the meantime all the pressure of planting the axe as you climb is concentrated where the narrow top edge of the pick meets your palm. That hurts after awhile, and therefore you may not plant the axe as securely as you might otherwise. This compromises the safety of your critical self-belays (which are explained in the next section).

The self-belay grasp is much more comfortable because the pressure of placing the axe is spread over the wide, flat top of the adze, where your palm now rests. If you fall, you'll have to immediately flip to a self-arrest grip to put the brakes on. (This is something to practice during self-arrest drills.)

How to self-belay

The technique of planting the ice-axe shaft to help guard yourself against falls while snow climbing is called self-belay. We'll learn later in this chapter about what to do in the event you or a ropemate start sliding down a steep snow slope. Then self-arrest and other techniques come into

their own. But knowing how to avoid the slide in the first place with a self-belay is as important as knowing what to do if it occurs.

Self-belay (fig. 12-16) is a way to lessen the likelihood that a simple slip or misstep on a snow slope will turn into a long fall. It is used repeatedly to help safeguard the way up or down a steep snow

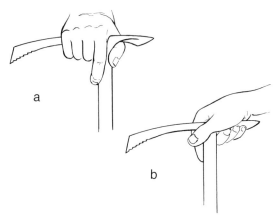

Fig. 12–15. Grasping an ice axe: a, self-arrest grip; b, self-belay grip.

Fig. 12–16. The self-belay: a, climbing; b, falling; c, recovering.

slope when the potential for a fall is the highest: when you are moving or when you are in an out-of-balance position. You can create the belay with either a self-belay grasp or a self-arrest grasp on the axe, though you'll probably find more power and ease in the self-belay grasp.

Here's how to do the self-belay: be sure both feet are secure (in the position of balance described in the next section). Then jam the spike and shaft of the axe into the snow and continue to grip the head of the axe with one hand as you move a step forward with each foot. When both feet are again secure, pull the axe out and replant it farther along (fig. 12-16a). Continue this procedure until you feel it's safe to proceed without it.

Used like this, the ice axe is ready as a safety post as you are moving your feet. To be reliable,

the shaft must be placed deep enough, in snow that's firm enough, to hold your full weight. If you slip, keep one hand on the head of the axe as you grab hold of the shaft at the surface of the snow and trust your weight to it (fig. 12-16b). The key to a successful self-belay recovery is the grabbing of the shaft right where it emerges from the snow, so that your pull is against the buried shaft while the hand on the head of the axe minimizes the risk of it levering out.

Practice this technique on a slope of hard snow with a safe runout to develop the confidence to know when a self-belay will hold while you replant your feet after a slip. If you're on a climb and begin to doubt your self-belays, it's time to make a critical decision: whether to back off, to rope up, or to climb on, recognizing the risk you're taking.

ASCENDING SNOW

Climbing up—and down—snow slopes takes a set of special skills. Different techniques come into play depending on how hard or steep the slope is. (The related skills of cramponing and step-cutting are covered in Chapter 14.)

Climbing in balance

As with rock climbing, staying in balance while moving on snow is less tiring, more efficient, and safer than struggling to keep from falling only by clinging to something—in this case, the ice axe or the snow. Snow climbers move from one balanced position to another, avoiding any prolonged stance in an unbalanced position.

On a diagonal uphill route, the most balanced position is with the inside (uphill) foot in front of and above the trailing outside (downhill) leg, which is fully extended to make use of the skeleton and minimize muscular effort. In that position, let the trailing leg bear most of your weight. Always grip the ice axe with your uphill hand.

The diagonal ascent is a two-step sequence: from a position of balance through an out-of-balance position and back to a position of balance (fig. 12-17). From the in-balance position, place the axe above and ahead into the snow. Move up two steps before repositioning the ice axe. The first step brings the outside (downhill) foot in front of the inside (uphill foot), putting the climber out of balance. The second step brings the inside foot up from behind and places it beyond the outside foot, putting the climber back in the balance position. Keep your weight over your feet and avoid leaning into the slope.

If you're heading straight up the fall line instead of moving diagonally, there's no longer an uphill or downhill leg, or an uphill or downhill hand. So carry the axe in the hand that feels most comfortable and climb in a steady, controlled manner. Regardless of the direction of travel, placing the axe firmly before each move will provide self-belay protection.

Fig. 12–17. Ascending a snow slope, diagonally, in balance

The rest step

Climbing a long featureless snow slope can give you the frustrating sensation that you're getting nowhere. Few landmarks help measure your progress, so distances are deceiving. Novice climbers try a dash-and-gasp pace in an attempt to rush the objective. But the only way to the top of the slope is to find a pace you can maintain, and then maintain it.

The solution is the rest step, a technique that conserves energy as it moves you methodically forward. (The rest step is illustrated in Chapter 5.) Use the rest step whenever legs or lungs need a bit of recuperation between steps. At lower elevations it's usually the leg muscles that require a break. At higher elevations, the lungs need the pause.

Here's a review of the rest step: the rest takes place after one foot is swung forward for the next step. Support all body weight on the rear leg while the unweighted forward leg muscles relax. During each mini-rest, the weighted rear leg must be kept straight and locked at the knee so that bone, not muscle, carries the load. The climbing pace is slow, because for every step there is a pause. Synchronize breathing with the sequence. At higher elevations you'll need to make a conscious effort to breath deeply and often.

Step-kicking

The technique of step-kicking is basic to snow climbing. It's a way to create a path of upward steps that provide the best possible footing with the least expenditure of energy. It is all that's needed for footing when the snow is yielding enough to permit security without the help of crampons or chopped steps.

The most efficient kick to create snow steps is a swing of the leg that lets its own weight and momentum provide the needed impact, with little muscular effort. This works fine in soft snow. On harder snow, you'll end up putting in more effort, and the steps will usually be smaller and less secure.

The definition of a secure step varies with the climber's skill and strength and with the effects of such factors as wind, altitude, and the weight of the pack. An average climber probably needs steps deep enough to take the ball of the foot when going straight up and at least half of the boot on a diagonal ascent. Steps that are kicked level or tilted slightly into the slope are more secure. The less space there is on a step, the more important it is that the step slope inward.

When you're kicking steps, keep the other climbers in mind. They can follow up your staircase in good balance if your steps are spaced evenly and somewhat close together. Make allowance for climbers whose legs aren't as long as yours.

Followers use the same leg swing as the leader, improving the steps as they climb. The follower must kick into the step, because simply walking onto the existing platform will not set the boot securely in position. In compact snow the kick should be somewhat low, the toe driving in and deepening the step. However, in very soft snow it is usually easier to bring the boot down from above, shearing off an edge of snow, which helps build a stronger step.

A basic principle of snow travel is that parties move in single file when ascending. If you're in the lead, you will be doing by far the hardest work. You also have to think harder in order to avoid potential hazards to the group and to choose the best route. Take turns leading so that no climber is worked to exhaustion.

Direction of ascent

You can either go directly up a snow slope or ascend it diagonally. If you're in a hurry, a direct ascent is usually the way to go. Speed is a primary consideration on a long snow climb, and a fast, direct ascent is the order of the day if you face bad weather, avalanche or rockfall danger, poor bivouac conditions, or a difficult descent.

When time permits, most climbers prefer a diagonal ascent, switchbacking up moderately angled slopes. They reason that the lower angle of ascent requires less energy for each step while it ends up gaining the same elevation as the fewer— but steeper—steps of a direct ascent. The strength of this argument probably depends on snow conditions. In good step-kicking snow, the energy you save at each step on a diagonal ascent can be used to kick the additional steps required by that angle. But in marginal step-kicking conditions, many climbers figure that a diagonal route is more difficult because of the work of kicking edged, traversing steps in hard snow.

Ice-axe technique: direct ascent

In a straight shot up a snowfield, step-kicking is the basic technique for your feet. Ice-axe technique, however, will vary depending on snow conditions and steepness.

Cane position: On a slope that is at a low or moderate angle (roughly up to 30 or 35 degrees), climb with the axe in the cane position, holding it in one hand by the head and using it for balance (fig. 12-18). You can continue in the cane position as the snow gets even steeper, as long as you feel

Fig. 12–19. Direct ascent, ice axe in stake position

secure with it. Setting the axe firmly before each move will provide a self-belay.

Stake position: At some point as the snow steepens, a climber may choose to switch to the two-handed stake position, a more secure stance often used for angles over 45 degrees (fig. 12-19). Before moving upward, plant the axe, with both hands, as far as it will go into the snow. Then continue to grasp it with both hands on the head, or with one hand on the head and one on the shaft. This position is particularly useful on steeper soft snow.

Horizontal position: This is a technique effective on steeper, harder snow that is covered with a soft layer. Hold the axe with both hands, one in the self-arrest grasp on the head and the other near the end of the shaft. Jab the axe horizontally into the

Fig. 12–18. Direct ascent, ice axe in cane position

Fig. 12–20. Direct ascent, ice axe in horizontal position

Fig. 12–21. Diagonal ascent, ice axe in cross-body position

snow above you, the pick down and the shaft at right angles to your body (fig. 12-20). This jabs the pick into the harder base while the shaft gets some purchase in the softer surface snow. (Don't forget to take advantage of the rest step as you head up the hill, regardless of the ice-axe technique being used.)

Ice-axe technique: diagonal ascent

On a diagonal route, remember to climb in balance as you kick steps up the slope. (Figure 12-17 shows the sequence of moves in a diagonal ascent.) For slopes angled less than about 40 or 45 degrees, the axe usually works fine in the cane position. As the slope steepens, the cane position becomes awkward and it's time to switch to the cross-body position.

Cross-body position: For this position, hold the axe perpendicular to the angle of the slope, one hand grasping the head and the other holding the shaft, which is jabbed into the snow (fig. 12-21). The axe will cross diagonally in front of you. (Be sure the pick does not point toward your body.) Most of the weight placed on the axe should bear on the shaft, while the hand on the head merely stabilizes the axe. Move your feet upward in the same manner as with the cane position.

Diagonal ascents often mean switchbacks, which mean changes in direction. There's a specific sequence of steps for a safe change in direction on a diagonal route, whether you have the axe in the cane position or the cross-body position (fig. 12-22).

Start from a position of balance, the inside (uphill) foot in front of and above the outside (downhill) foot. Jab the axe shaft straight down into the snow at a spot as directly above your location as possible. Grasp the head of the axe with both hands as you move your outside foot forward, bringing you into the out-of-balance position. Continue holding onto the head with both hands as you move into a stance facing uphill, moving your inside foot toward the new direction of travel, and ending with splayed feet. Finally, a turn in the new direction of travel returns you to a position of balance, with the new uphill foot now in front and above. With the cane position, the new uphill hand now grasps the axe head. With the cross-body position, the hands holding the head and the shaft are now reversed. If splayed feet feel unstable as you change direction at a steep angle, kick the steps more directly into the slope.

Traversing

Long horizontal traverses, which neither gain nor lose elevation, are rarely any fun. This "sidehill gouging" works OK on soft snow at low and moderate angles, though it's still not as comfortable or efficient as a diagonal route. On horizontal traverses over harder or steeper snow, you can face into the slope and kick straight forward for more secure steps. But try to avoid horizontal traverses in the first place.

DESCENDING SNOW

One mark of a skillful snow climber is the ability to go downhill efficiently and confidently. Many otherwise competent and aggressive climbers blanch at the prospect of going forward down a steep snow gully. Why? Because there's a superb view—perhaps too superb—of the exposure. And because on steep snow the axe must be placed very low to move down, leaving the climber without the comforting stance and handhold that was there on the way up. You can minimize those downhill jitters by mastering a few descent techniques.

Fig. 12–22. Changing direction on a diagonal ascent: a, jab axe shaft straight down; b, face uphill with feet splayed; c, turn in new direction of travel.

Plunge-stepping

In going down, just like going up, technique is determined mainly by the hardness and angle of the snow. In soft snow on a moderate slope, simply face outward and walk down. With harder snow or a steeper angle, use the plunge step (fig. 12-23).

The plunge step is a confident, aggressive move. Face outward, step assertively away from the slope and land solidly on your heel with your leg vertical, transferring weight solidly to the new position. No timid steps allowed. Avoid leaning back into the slope, which could result in a glancing blow, less secure steps, and perhaps an unplanned glissade. Plunge-stepping can be secure with steps that hold only the heel of the boot, but most climbers do not trust steps more shallow than that.

When plunge-stepping, keep the knees bent a bit, not locked, to maintain control of balance. The degree of bending depends on the angle of the slope (the steeper the slope, the greater the bend) and the firmness of the surface (the harder the snow, the greater the bend). With bent knees, a forward lean is also needed to help with balance. An aggressive stride creates a deep step, so be careful in very soft snow that a plunging leg isn't injured by being buried so deep it can't be yanked back out as you take the next step.

The plunge-stepping climber holds the ice axe in one hand in either the self-arrest or self-belay grasp, with the spike close to the surface, well forward and ready to plant in the snow. You can spread and move the other arm for balance. Some climbers hold the axe in both hands in the full self-arrest position—one hand on the head, the other near the end of the shaft—but this allows less movement of the arms to maintain balance.

At some point, on harder or steeper snow, this style of plunge-stepping will not feel secure. Then it's necessary to plant the axe as low as possible in a self-belay before each move and advance the feet in a sort of crouched, modified plunge step (fig. 12-24).

Glissading

Glissading is one of the joyous bonuses of mountain climbing, offering the fastest, easiest, and most exhilarating way down many snow slopes for a climber on foot. It's an alternative to walking or plunge-stepping, for use on slopes where you can keep your speed under control. There are three principal methods of glissading. Which one you use will depend on how hard and steep the slope is, how safe the runout is at the bottom of the hill, and how good you are at glissading.

The sitting glissade (fig. 12-25a) is the easiest to learn and works on soft snow where you would bog down if you tried a standing glissade. You'll get the slickest and driest ride by wearing coated-nylon rain pants. For the sitting glissade, simply sit in the snow and let 'er rip, holding the axe in self-arrest position as you slide downhill. The standard posture is to sit fairly erect, knees bent and boot soles planing along the surface. However, to get started and maintain momentum in snow that

Fig. 12–23. Plunge-stepping, moderate slope

Fig. 12–24. Plunge-stepping with self-belay

is quite soft, it helps to stretch out your legs, spreading body weight over a greater area.

Run the spike of the axe, like a rudder, along the snow on one side of you. Putting pressure on the spike helps reduce speed and thwarts any tendency of your body to pivot head-downward. The standard posture, with knees bent and feet flat, also reduces speed. This posture is the most helpful in uncomfortable conditions: when the snow is crusted or firmly consolidated, pitted with icy ruts or small suncups, or dotted with rocks or shrubs. It provides more stability and control than with your legs straight out in front, and it helps minimize wear and tear on your bottom.

To stop, use the spike to slow down, then dig in your heels—but not at high speed or a somersault may be the result. For an emergency stop, simply self-arrest by rolling into position toward the side opposite the spike. (The indispensable technique of self-arrest will be explained in the next section of this chapter).

Turns are almost impossible in a sitting glissade. The spike, dragged as a rudder and assisted by body contortions, can exert a change in direction of a few degrees at most. The best way to get around an obstruction is to stop, walk sideways to a point that is not directly above the obstacle, and take off again.

The standing glissade (fig. 12-25b) is the best one, if you know how to do it and conditions are right. This position offers the earliest look at hazards of the route, is the most maneuverable, and saves your clothes from wetness and abrasion. The standing glissade is most effective on a firm base with a softer layer on top. The softer the snow, the steeper the slope needed to maintain speed. You can do a standing glissade down slopes of harder snow, but these will usually be at lower angles and with a safe runout. Slopes at very low angles can be skated, if the snow is firm.

Correct standing glissade technique is very similar to downhill skiing. The position is a semi-crouch over the feet with bent knees and outspread arms. The feet can be together or spread, as needed for stability, with one foot advanced slightly to further improve stability and prevent nose dives. Increase speed by bringing the feet closer together and leaning farther forward over the feet. Slow down and stop any number of ways: stand up and dig in the heels; turn the feet sideways and edge; crouch and drag the ice-axe spike as in the crouching glissade (described next); or perform a turn similar to skiing in which you rotate the shoulders, upper body, and knees in the direction of the turn and roll the knees and ankles in the same direction to rock the feet onto boot edges.

Transition areas, where the snow texture changes, are tricky. If you hit softer, slower snow, your head and torso will suddenly be outpacing your legs, so move one boot forward for stability. If you hit harder, faster snow or ice below the surface, lean well forward to prevent a slip. Keep speed under control by regular braking and traversing.

The crouching glissade (fig. 12-25c) is done

Fig. 12–25. Glissades: a, sitting; b, standing; c, crouching.

much like the standing glissade, except the climber holds the axe in the self-arrest position to one side of the body, sits back, and drags the spike in the snow. It's slower than a standing glissade and easier to learn. With three points of contact, it is also more stable. However, turning is more difficult, as is controlling speed with edging.

As in much of mountaineering, efficiency in glissading takes a smooth blend of several techniques. In particular, climbers who lack finesse in the standing glissade often use a combination: breaking into a plunge step to control speed, stepping off in a new direction rather than making a

ski-style turn, and skating to maintain momentum as the slope angle lessens.

Glissading can be hazardous. Glissade only when there is a safe runout, close enough that if you slide out of control, you won't be injured before reaching it. Unless there is a view of the entire run, the first person down must use extreme caution and stop frequently to look ahead. The biggest risk is losing control at such high speed that self-arrest is not possible. This is most likely to happen on the best glissading slope, one with firm snow. Maintain control of speed.

Adjust equipment before beginning the descent,

and stow crampons and other hardware in the pack. Don't try a sitting glissade while wearing crampons, because it's too easy to catch a point in the snow. Wear mittens, even on a warm day; snow is so cold and abrasive it can chill and flay the hands until they lose control of the axe.

Sometimes in soft snow, a glissader accidentally sets off a mass of surface snow, which slides down the slope with the glissader aboard. These are really small avalanches, known as avalanche cushions. The trick is to decide if it's a cushion safe to ride or if it is about to become a serious avalanche. If the moving snow is more than a few inches deep, self-arrest won't work because the ice-axe pick can't penetrate to the layer below. Sometimes the spike can be driven deep enough to slow, though probably not stop, the glissader. Unless you're sure the cushion is safe and your speed is under control, get off. Just roll sideways a few feet out of the path of the moving snow, then self-arrest.

Downclimbing

On steep snow where you may not feel secure glissading or plunge-stepping, you can face into the slope and downclimb backward by kicking steps straight into the slope. Use the axe in the stake position as a self-belay.

SELF-ARREST

Self-arrest is the lifesaving technique of using the ice axe to stop your own uncontrolled slide down a snow slope. It's used when you slip on the snow without a self-belay or when your self-belay fails. If you are unroped, it offers your only chance to stop the slide. It's the single most important snow-climbing skill, one you should continue to practice as long as you climb so that it remains an automatic response to a fall.

The technique also serves to brace you solidly in the snow if you have to hold the fall of a ropemate. Therefore a climber's own life and those of fellow climbers could hinge on self-arrest skills. Every climber must be proficient and reliable at self-arrest, learned through practice on increasingly steep and hard snow with a safe runout.

Strength obviously helps in self-arrest, but knowing the correct methods is more important than simple muscle power.

The first rule of self-arrest is: act fast. Good self-arrest form may be aesthetically satisfying, but fast is better than pretty when instantaneous action is critical. From the self-arrest position, get the ice-axe pick in as hard and as quickly as possible, before you've accelerated to an unstoppable speed.

Here's what you should look like as you complete a successful self-arrest, lying face down in the snow, head uphill, with the ice axe beneath you (fig. 12-26, last panel):

The hands hold the axe in a solid grip, one hand in the self-arrest grasp with thumb under the adze and fingers over the pick, the other hand on the shaft just above the spike.

The pick is pressed into the snow just above your shoulder so that the adze is near the angle formed by neck and shoulder.

The shaft crosses your chest diagonally and is held close to the opposite hip. Gripping the shaft near the end prevents that hand from acting as a pivot around which the spike can swing to jab the thigh. (A short axe is held the same way, although the spike will not reach the opposite hip.)

The chest and shoulder are pressed strongly down on the ice-axe shaft.

The spine is arched slightly away from the snow. This arch is critical; it places the bulk of your weight on the axe head and on your toes or knees, the points that dig into the snow to force a stop. Pull up on the end of the shaft, which starts the arch and rolls weight toward the shoulder by the axe head. (Note: the arch can be carried to excess by those unwilling to get their chest and face down into the snow.)

The knees are against the surface, helping slow the fall in soft snow. On harder surfaces, where they have little stopping power, they help stabilize your body position.

The legs are stiff and spread apart, toes digging in. But if you have crampons on, keep them above the snow until you've nearly come to a halt. A crampon point could catch on hard snow or ice and flip you over backward.

CORRECT

Fig. 12–26. Correct self-arrest technique, head uphill, on your back

Self-arrest from different positions

The position you find yourself thrown into when you fall determines how you self-arrest. You'll likely be sliding in one of four positions: head uphill or head downhill and, in either case, face down or on your back. The immediate goal is to get your body into the only usable self-arrest position: with your head uphill and your face down. And the first move toward that goal is to grasp the axe in both hands, one hand on the axe head in the self-arrest grasp and the other at the base of the shaft. From that point, here is how to handle each of the four situations:

Head uphill, face down: You're already in the desired self-arrest position. All you have to do is get your body over the axe shaft, as described above.

Head uphill, on your back: This isn't much more difficult than the first version. Roll toward the head of the axe and jab the pick into the snow at your side as you roll over onto your stomach (fig. 12-26). If the axe head is on the right, roll to the right. If it's on the left, roll to the left. Beware of rolling the other way, toward the spike, which could jam the spike in the snow before the pick and wrench the axe from your hands (fig. 12-27).

Head downhill, face down: self-arrest from

INCORRECT

Fig. 12–27. Incorrect self-arrest technique; do not roll toward spike

head-first falls is more difficult because the feet have to first be swung downhill. In this face-down predicament, reach downhill and off to the axe-head side and get the pick into the snow to serve as a pivot to swing the body around. Work to help swing the legs around so they are pointing downhill (fig. 12-28). Never jab the spike into the snow and pivot on that end of the axe. That would bring the pick and adze of the axe across your slide path and on a collision course with your chest and face.

Head downhill, on your back: Hold the axe across your torso and slide the pick into the snow, then twist and roll toward it (fig. 12-29). Once again, the pick placed to the side serves as a pivot point. But merely planting the pick won't bring you around to the final self-arrest position. You must work at rolling your chest toward the axe head at the same time as you help your legs to swing around and point downhill. A sitting-up motion helps the roll.

Variations: In the loose snow of winter and early spring, the pick may not be able to reach compact snow, making the usual self-arrest useless. The best brakes in this case are feet and knees and elbows, widely spaced and deeply pressed into the snow. In this case the greatest drag potential of

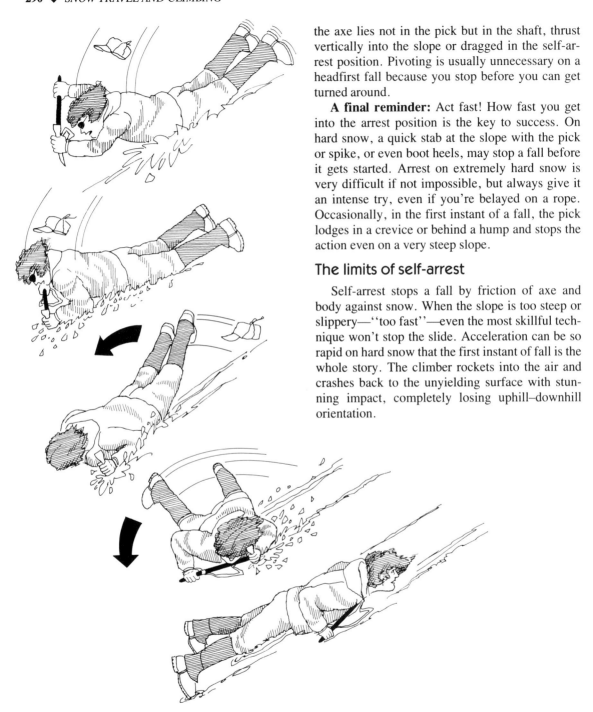

the axe lies not in the pick but in the shaft, thrust vertically into the slope or dragged in the self-arrest position. Pivoting is usually unnecessary on a headfirst fall because you stop before you can get turned around.

A final reminder: Act fast! How fast you get into the arrest position is the key to success. On hard snow, a quick stab at the slope with the pick or spike, or even boot heels, may stop a fall before it gets started. Arrest on extremely hard snow is very difficult if not impossible, but always give it an intense try, even if you're belayed on a rope. Occasionally, in the first instant of a fall, the pick lodges in a crevice or behind a hump and stops the action even on a very steep slope.

The limits of self-arrest

Self-arrest stops a fall by friction of axe and body against snow. When the slope is too steep or slippery—"too fast"—even the most skillful technique won't stop the slide. Acceleration can be so rapid on hard snow that the first instant of fall is the whole story. The climber rockets into the air and crashes back to the unyielding surface with stunning impact, completely losing uphill–downhill orientation.

Fig. 12–28. Self-arrest technique, head downhill, face down

Fig. 12–29. Self-arrest technique, head downhill on your back

Even successful arrests require at least a little time, during which the climber slides some distance. Therefore the effectiveness of the self-arrest is limited by the climber's speed of reaction and the steepness and length of the slope.

If all initial efforts at self-arrest are unsuccessful, don't give up. Keep fighting. Self-arrest might work in softer snow or at a lower angle farther down the slope. Even if you don't stop, the attempt may slow you down and help prevent rolling, tumbling, and bouncing. It may also help keep you sliding feet first, the best position if you end up hitting rocks or trees. And if you are roped to other climbers, anything you can do to slow your fall increases the chance that their self-arrests or belays will hold.

Keep alert at all times to the limits of self-arrest. If a slope seems too fast or too short, or members of a climbing party doubt their strength or skill, use one of the techniques of roped protection outlined later in this chapter.

The uses of self-belay and self-arrest

Self-belay is preventive; self-arrest is a recovery measure. Some climbers who learned self-arrest as the primary security technique on snow fear too much emphasis on self-belay. But the purposes of the two techniques are different and you need them both. Where the axe can be planted securely, self-belay is usually all that is needed, so any fall is prevented in the first place. If self-belay fails, you can then self-arrest.

While self-belaying on a climb, keep alert to changes in snow conditions that make the belays insecure. If the snow on a steep slope is so hard that axe placement might not hold a slip, it may be best to change to the self-arrest grasp, ready to instantly self-arrest. Of course, under these conditions, a self-arrest will also be very difficult. Even with the self-arrest grasp, you can continue to make self-belay placements, though they will be a little more difficult because your palm will no longer be on the flat, comfortable top of the adze.

On important skill comes into play if you are using the self-belay grasp and slip into a fall. You must be able to instantly flip the ice axe from the self-belay grasp to a self-arrest grasp. Grab the shaft of the axe just above the spike, then change the hand to the self-arrest grasp—and arrest. This takes practice. If you don't have the skill or confi-

dence to do it, then it will be safer to do your self-belays holding the axe head in the self-arrest grasp.

ROPED CLIMBING TECHNIQUES

When is it time to rope up on a snow climb? In general, when the overall risks to the climbing party of continuing unroped are higher than those of roping up. It's often an issue of trade-offs, weighing the pros and cons of both choices.

On a glacier, the risks to unroped climbers of falling into a crevasse clearly exceed the risks to the team of roping up. So teams rope up.

As slopes steepen and snow hardens, the easy decisions disappear. It becomes a matter of deciding whether the risks to unroped climbers of being unable to stop their own individual falls exceed the risks to the team of roping up. These team risks are not trivial. They include the possibility of one person's fall pulling the entire rope team off the mountain and the danger that roped climbing will slow the climb, adding to avalanche and rockfall exposure and the likelihood of an unplanned bivouac. It becomes a delicate decision involving an evaluation of each climber's skills and the variety of alternatives for roped team protection.

OPTIONS FOR ROPED TEAM PROTECTION

If your party decides it would be safer overall to rope up, there are several different ways to match the type of rope protection to the conditions of the climb and the strengths of the climbers.

Team arrest (roped but unbelayed)

Team arrest depends on each climber to stop a personal fall and on the rest of the rope team to provide backup in case the attempt fails. Everyone involved uses self-belay or self-arrest.

Relying on team arrest as the ultimate team security makes sense only in selected situations, such as on a low- or moderate-angle glacier or on a moderate snow slope where a less skilled climber

could be saved from a dangerous slide by the more proficient members of the rope team. On steeper, harder slopes you face that appraisal of risks, trying to decide which is safer: continuing to rely on team arrest, unroping and letting each climber go it alone, or switching to a more secure mode of roped travel.

You may be able to increase the odds that team arrest will work on a snow slope by trying the following procedures:

• Carry a few feet of rope coiled in your hand if there are any climbers below you. If a climber falls, drop the loose rope and it will give you an extra instant to get the axe into self-belay position and to brace yourself. (Note: do not carry coils on a glacier, because the extra rope simply increases the distance the victim will fall into the crevasse.)

• Put the weakest climber on the downhill end of the rope. As a rule, the least skilled climber should be last on the rope while ascending and the first on the rope while descending. This puts the climber most likely to fall in position where a fall will be of the least serious kind: below the other climbers and coming quickly onto the rope. Unfortunately, it also means the weakest climber will be the team's last hope if the climbers above fall.

• Climb on a shortened rope. This is most applicable to a two-person rope team. If a climbing pair uses only a portion of the rope—say 60 to 75 feet instead of the full length—they will reduce the sliding distance and the tug from the fall if one partner falls while above the other.

• Climb in separate parallel tracks. This is also most applicable to a two-person rope team. The climbers will be abreast of each other, separated by the rope. A falling climber will pendulum down, putting force on the rope to the side of and below the partner. The tug on the rope will be less than if the climber fell from high above. Also, the friction of the rope as it pendulums across the snow will absorb some of the force. Traveling in separate tracks may be impractical on ascents where kicking two sets of steps would be a waste of time and energy. However, it might be used on ascents of harder snow and should be considered for any descent.

Running belays

The use of running belays (fig. 12-30) offers a middle level of protection, somewhere between team arrest and fixed belays. It can help in situations where a successful team arrest is improbable but where fixed belays aren't practical because they would take too much time. For example, running protection may do the job on long snow faces and couloirs.

To place running belays, the leader puts in pieces of snow protection as needed and uses a carabiner to clip the rope into each one. (Types of snow protection are discussed in the next section of this chapter, on snow anchors.) The climbers continue to make good progress because all members of the rope team climb at the same time, just as in unbelayed travel. Except that now there's protection in the snow that, if it is securely placed, will put an end to any fall. Traveling this way, the last

Fig. 12–30. A running belay setup

climber on the rope removes each piece. Of course the use of running protection means the team must pack the extra weight of the gear and must take the time to place it.

Fixed belays

The ultimate in safety comes from having climbers belay each other up snow pitches, in the same manner as in rock climbing. The catch is that this procedure may be so time-consuming it becomes impractical on the snow faces of major alpine routes. However, there is a wide variety of snow belays, varying in security and in the amount of time they take to set up. They are described later in this chapter.

Combination protection techniques

The reality of most serious snow climbs is that success calls for a combination of protection techniques. It's not likely a party will take on an entire climb unroped. It's just as unlikely that the party will use fixed belays all the way.

In deciding when to rope up, a climbing team is actually asking itself a series of questions. The team always ropes up on glaciers. But on snow or mixed terrain, the team asks:

1. Is each member of the party able to use self-belay or self-arrest to save himself or herself in case of a fall? If the answer is yes, the party can continue unroped. If the answer is no, the team asks:
2. Can we stop all falls by roping up and depending on team arrest? If so, rope up and continue climbing, unbelayed. If not, then ask:
3. Is it feasible to use some form of belay (a running belay or a fixed belay) and will this belay provide adequate protection? If so, begin belaying. If it's not feasible, because of poor terrain or lack of time, then the party must ask itself:
4. Shall we turn around, or shall we proceed unroped and assume the risks?

In practice, long snow routes are climbed roped and mostly unbelayed, with belays of some kind on steeper, harder snow or when climbers are tired or

hurt. Most of the reliance is on team arrest or running protection, though some sections may lend themselves to unroped travel.

The option of turning around is always worth considering. If things aren't going well, select a new route, another destination, or just head home.

SNOW ANCHORS

Anchors are needed in snow for the same reasons they are needed on rock. The equipment is different but the purposes are the same: to anchor belays and rappels. But rock anchors are usually easy to inspect and predictable in performance. Snow anchors are not. They vary widely in strength depending on snow conditions and placement, and their strength changes during the day with changes in the snow. This uncertainty makes it even more imperative than on rock to check and recheck any belay or rappel anchor. Snow anchors can also require a lot of time to put in place. They include deadman anchors (such as snow flukes), pickets, and bollards.

A deadman anchor is any object you bury in the snow as a point of attachment for the rope. The most common is the snow fluke, a specially shaped aluminum plate with a metal cable attached (fig. 12-31a). Snow flukes are available in various sizes, their holding ability generally increasing with size. For maximum strength and reliability, a buried fluke should be angled back about 45 degrees from the direction of pull (fig. 12-31b). Dig a slot in the snow to permit the cable to be pulled in as direct a line as possible.

In theory, the fluke serves as a dynamic anchor, burrowing deeper into the snow when it takes a load, such as the weight of a climber on rappel. In practice, it may behave in more complicated ways, even coming out if it is tipped too far forward or back, or if the load is to the side rather than straight out. If the plate or the cable travels down into the snow and hits a harder layer, the fluke could be deflected and pull out. Flukes are available with bent faces, flanged sides, or fixed cables—features intended to make them maintain the correct orientation and to make them self-correct if deflected.

Flukes are most reliable—but also more diffi-

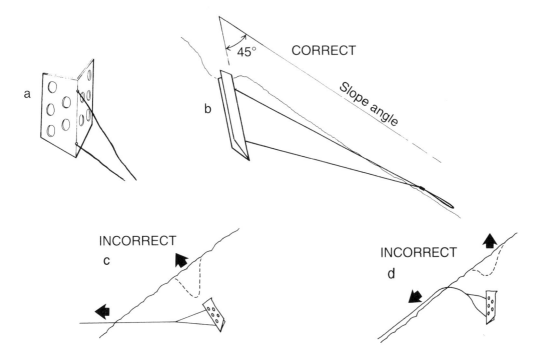

Fig. 12–31. Placing snow flukes: a, typical snow fluke; b, correct angle for fluke placement; c, incorrect, not angled back sufficiently; d, incorrect, no slot for cable.

cult to place—in the hard homogeneous snow of summer. They are generally used in a softer but dense pack, snow that is moist and heavy. They are least reliable under typical winter conditions, with snow layers of varying density where they may deflect off harder layers. Neither do they do well in dry, unconsolidated snow.

Ice axes, ice tools, and snow pickets can serve as deadman anchors (fig. 12-32). Bury the implement horizontally in the snow, with a runner attached at the midpoint. Cut a slot in the snow to let the runner lie in the direction of pull, and then clip into the runner.

A picket is a stake driven into the snow as an anchor (fig. 12-33). Aluminum pickets are available in lengths from 18 to 36 inches and are found in different styles, including round or oval tubes and angled or T-section stakes.

Pickets work well in snow too firm for flukes but too soft for ice screws. As with flukes, angle

Fig. 12–32. Ice axe buried as deadman anchor

Fig. 12–33. Picket placement

them back about 45 degrees from the direction of pull. Attach a carabiner or runner to the picket at the snowline—not higher on the picket, or a pull may lever it out. You can drive a picket into the snow with a rock or the side of an ice axe, but a North Wall hammer or other ice hammer works best and reduces the chance of equipment damage. An ice axe or ice tool can serve as a makeshift picket.

A bollard is a mound of snow that serves as an anchor when rope or webbing is positioned around it (fig. 12-34). Snow bollards provide highly reliable anchors for belaying or rappelling in soft snow and are possibly the most reliable in all snow conditions. There's a significant trade-off here, however. It takes a long time to build one.

Create the mound by making a trench around an oval area of snow. In hard snow, chop out the trench; in soft snow, just stamp it out. The bollard should end up as an oval-shaped island of snow. The softer the snow, the broader and deeper the bollard must be: up to 10 feet wide and $1^{1}/_{2}$ feet deep.

Try to use webbing around the bollard instead of rope because it's less likely to saw into the mound. For the same reason, avoid pulling on the rope or webbing after placing it. For more security, pad the rope or webbing with packs and clothing and whatever, especially in soft snow. For safety, inspect the bollard after each use to see it hasn't been damaged. You can also back up the bollard with a picket or fluke (which the last person on a rappel removes before rappelling).

Fig. 12–34. Snow bollard

Multiple anchors are the best insurance because of the inherent weakness and unpredictability of snow anchors. As with questionable anchors in rock, multiple anchors are safest. Two anchors can be chained sequentially so that the first takes the hit, but has a backup to absorb any remaining force. Or they can be connected in a way that will permit them to share any load (fig. 12-35). (More details and illustrations on joining multiple anchors are in Chapters 7, 8, and 10.) In general, place multiple snow anchors one behind the other to reduce the angle of pull and the potential load on the surviving anchor if the other one fails. Keep the anchors several feet apart so they don't end up sharing any localized weakness in the snow.

BELAYING ON SNOW

Snow climbers choose from a catalog of techniques that provide belay protection to their ropemates. They sometimes give belays using established snow anchors, and sometimes they give quicker and less formal belays using the ice axe. The changeable nature of snow and the difficulty of inspecting snow protection usually result in anchors that can't be considered bombproof like a good anchor in rock. But they are still effective because most mishaps on snow do not generate the high loads of rock-climbing falls. Snow falls are usually slides on relatively moderate (30- to 60-degree) slopes, with help from the friction of rope against snow and with no direct vertical pull.

No matter what the belaying technique, every snow belay should be as dynamic as possible to help limit the force on the anchor. The dynamic, shock-absorbing quality of climbing rope helps minimize chances of an abrupt, static stop to a fall. As a belayer, plan your stance so the force is taken on your body and dissipated as much as possible by the belay and the dynamic quality of the rope. The standard hip belay provides a more gradual, dynamic belay than mechanical belay devices. Think of the consequences if a heavy hit on a question-

Fig. 12–35. Two methods of connecting snow anchors: a, two pickets linked serially, top anchor supports lower anchor; b, two independent anchors with equalized connecting runner.

Fig. 12–36. Boot-axe belay

able snow belay yanks you and any anchor off your perch.

Set up a belay close to the climbing difficulties. If you're belaying the lead climber, get out of the line of fire by setting up the belay stance to one side of the fall line—not within it. If the leader is heading up on a diagonal, get outside any point where the climber's route could cross directly above you. On a ridge crest, it is not always possible to predict a fall line and plan a belay in advance. If a ropemate slips off one side of the ridge, the best reaction may actually be to jump off the opposite side, with the rope running over the ridge saving you both.

Quick belays

Snow climbers have a couple of quick belays for times the consequences of a fall would not be great, as in a sliding pendulum across a snow face. They are useful for belaying a climber who is probing a cornice or crevasse edge, or for providing a top belay to a weaker climber.

The boot-axe belay is a fast and easy way to provide protection as a rope team moves up together (fig. 12-36). Despite some naysayers, it has proven to be useful, provided its principal limitation is understood: it can't be expected to hold a high fall force. With thorough practice, you should be able to set up this belay in a couple of seconds with a jab of the ice axe and a quick sweep of the rope.

Step by step, here is how to do it (and after trying it a few times, you'll realize it is not as complicated as it sounds):

1. Stamp a firm platform in the snow, big enough for the axe and uphill boot.
2. Jam the ice-axe shaft as deeply as possible into the snow at the rear of the platform, the shaft tilted slightly uphill against a possible fall. Have the pick perpendicular to the fall line, thus applying the broadest side of the shaft against the force of a fall.
3. Stand below the axe, at approximately a right angle to the fall line and facing the side on which the climber's route lies.
4. Plant your uphill boot into the snow against the downhill side of the shaft, bracing it against a downward pull.
5. Plant the downhill boot in a firmly compacted step far enough below the other boot so that the downhill leg is straight, providing a stiff brace.
6. Flip the rope around the axe. The final configuration will have the rope running from the direction of potential load, across the toe of the uphill boot, around the uphill side of the axe, then back across the boot above the instep.
7. Hold the rope with the downhill (braking) hand, applying extra friction by bringing the rope uphill behind the heel, forming an S-

bend. The braking hand must never leave the rope.

8. Use the uphill hand for two jobs: to grasp the head of the axe to further brace the shaft and then, as the belayed climber moves upward, to take in rope.

Climbers must be equally adept at setting up the boot-axe belay with either foot uphill, because it is essential that the belayer face the climber's fall line. If a lead climber falls behind the belay, the rope unwraps from the axe and there is no belay.

The carabiner/ice-axe belay provides the same level of security as a boot-axe belay, with easier rope handling (fig. 12-37). To set it up, plant the axe as deeply as possible, the pick perpendicular to the fall line. Attach a very short sling with a girth hitch to the axe shaft at snowline and clip on a carabiner. Stand at right angles to the fall line, facing the same side as the climber's route. Brace the axe with your uphill boot, standing atop the sling but leaving the carabiner exposed. (Keep crampons off the sling.) The rope runs from the

Fig. 12–38. Sitting hip belay

potential direction of pull up through the carabiner, then around the back of your waist and into your uphill (braking) hand. One nice thing about the carabiner/ice-axe belay: the force of a fall pulls the belayer more firmly into the stance.

Anchored belays

Other snow belays usually are used with formal anchors, such as flukes, pickets, or bollards.

The sitting hip belay, with an anchor, is inherently dynamic and very secure on hard snow or deep, heavy, wet snow (fig. 12-38). The sitting belayer may face the prospect of a cold, wet assignment, and the belay can be difficult to work if the rope is frozen.

To set up the belay, stamp or chop a seat in the snow plus a platform to brace each boot against. Put down a pack, ensolite pad, or other material as insulation from the snow, then settle into a standard hip belay, with outstretched, stiffened legs.

The standing hip belay is easier to set up than a sitting hip belay, as it needs only deep, secure slots for each boot. However, it is far less secure because the belayer tends to be toppled under the force of a fall. Standing hip belays must be backed up with an anchor.

These belays can be arranged so the climber

Fig. 12–37. Carabiner/ice-axe belay

faces into the slope, out from the slope, or sideways. Facing into the slope is the poorest choice because the belayer will be completely wrapped by the rope if the climber falls below the belay stance. And it is difficult to pay out rope for a smooth belay. Facing out is an improvement because it gives a less complete wrap around the belayer and also permits a view of a fall below, important in timing a dynamic belay. But it shares a major weakness with the face-in stance: no way to brace the legs against toppling downhill. In both stances, the belayer should lean into the slope, against a downhill pull.

For the most reliable standing hip belay, stand sideways, facing the same side as the climber's route (fig. 12-39). The downhill leg is straight, locked at the knee, and braced in a snow slot. The uphill leg is on a line with the downhill leg and the direction of a potential fall. The downhill hand should be the braking hand to allow best control for a gradual dynamic belay.

Mechanical belay devices can be used in snow belaying. They are easy to set up and operate even with wet or icy ropes. With a device, you can belay

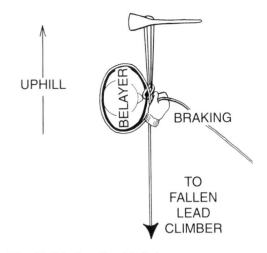

Fig. 12–39. Standing hip belay

directly from the anchor rather than from your seat harness, permitting you to get into a drier, more comfortable position. Be aware that belay devices provide a less dynamic belay than a hip belay, increasing the peak force of a fall on questionable snow anchors.

ROUTEFINDING ON SNOW

Snow gives us passage over some frustrating obstacles, such as tundra, talus, brush, streams, and logging debris. At its best, it provides a smooth, uniform surface and a straight shot up the mountain. But because its very nature means it constantly changes, we always have to study typical seasonal weather patterns as well as current reports for an idea of what conditions to expect on any climb.

Snow can be too soft to support our weight, or it can be hard and slick. It covers obstacles in our path, but it also obscures trails, cairns, and other guideposts to the route, especially above tree line. Dangers often lie beneath the surface: crevasses, moats, or creeks hidden by a thin snow cover. Unstable slopes avalanche.

You can minimize the frustrations and dangers

of snow by studying the medium. (The appendix in this book on ''The Cycle of Snow'' provides information on snow formation, types of snow, and the creation of glaciers.) Mountaineers let the snow work for them. They read the snow surface and terrain features to determine a safe, efficient route.

SURFACE CONSIDERATIONS

Evaluating the snow surface begins before you even leave home, by considering the effects of both the current weather and of conditions over the last several months.

If you are climbing during a cold, snowy spring following a prolonged late-winter thaw, the thaw's thick crust could hold a heavy load of spring snow ready to avalanche. If spring is cold but sunny, and follows a winter with little snow, a gully that usually offers good step-kicking in May could be filled with rock-hard consolidated snow. However, much of the change in the snow surface takes place rather quickly, so the weather just before and during a climb is the most important.

The best snow, from a mountaineer's point of view, is snow that is safe from avalanche and that will comfortably support a climber's weight for easy step-kicking. Such snow exists, but you have to seek it out. Location of the best snow varies from day to day, even from hour to hour. If the snow is slushy in one spot, or too hard or too crusty or too something, look around: there may be better snow a few feet away.

Here are some tips for making best use of the snow surface:

• Find patches of firmer snow on a slushy slope by walking in shade or using suncups as stairs.
• Try to find patches of softer snow on a slope that is too firm for good step-kicking.
• When the going is difficult, detour toward any surface with a different appearance and possibly more comfortable support.
• Use a different descent route if necessary to find the best snow.
• If you want a firmer surface, look for dirty snow, which absorbs more heat and therefore consolidates more quickly than clean snow.
• Remember that south and west slopes in the Northern Hemisphere, bearing the heat of afternoon sun, consolidate earlier in the season and quicker after storms. They offer hard surfaces when east and north slopes are still soft and unstable.
• Get an early start after a clear, cold night that follows a hot day, in order to take advantage of strong crusts on open slopes before they melt.
• Beware of the hidden holes next to logs, trees, and rocks, where the snow has melted away from these warmer surfaces.
• If you don't like the snow conditions on one side of a ridge, gully, clump of trees, or large boulder, try the other side. The difference may be just what you need.

TERRAIN CONSIDERATIONS

Major terrain features present both obstacles and opportunities (fig. 12-40). Some you use, some you avoid, but they all have to be reckoned with.

Couloirs

A main avenue for all mountain climbing is provided by angled gullies (couloirs). They can hold the key to upward progress because their overall angle is often less than that of the cliffs they breach, offering less technical climbing.

Deeply shaded couloirs are more often lined with ice than snow, especially in late season. Even in spring, however, when open slopes are deep in slush, the couloirs are likely to hold hard snow or ice caused by freezing or avalanche scouring.

Safe passage through a couloir usually depends on the time of day. They can be safe in early morning when the snow is solid and rocks and ice are frozen in place. It's often a different story later in the day, when they can turn deadly. Gullies are the garbage chutes of mountains and with the arrival of the sun they begin to carry down such rubbish as avalanching snow, rocks loosened by frost-wedging, and ice blocks weakened by melting. Most of the debris comes down the center. But even if you keep to the sides, listen for suspicious sounds from above and keep an eye out for quiet slides and silent falling rock.

Avalanches erode deep ruts in many steep couloirs. Climbers usually avoid these ruts or cross them rapidly. However, early in the year the floors of the ruts offer the soundest snow available, and in cold weather they may be quite safe, particularly for a fast descent. Try to be out of a couloir before the sun hits. This means an early start for a round trip, or else a bivouac or an alternative descent route.

Couloirs can become increasingly nasty the higher they are ascended, presenting extreme steepness, verglas, moats, rubble strewn loosely over smooth rock slabs, and cornices. Many lead to difficulties, as when the gentle angle at the bot-

Fig. 12–40. Alpine terrain features

1. Horn or aiguille
2. Ridge
3. Rock arete
4. Cornice
5. Glacier basin
6. Seracs
7. Fallen seracs
8. Erratic blocks
9. Icefall
10. Glacier
11. Crevasses
12. Lateral moraine
13. Snout
14. Moraine lake
15. Terminal moraine
16. Glacial runoff
17. Rock band
18. Shoulder
19. Col
20. Coulior or gully
21. Bergschrund
22. Hanging glacier
23. Buttress
24. Cirque or bowl
25. Headwall
26. Flutings
27. Ice wall
28. Summit
29. Ice arete
30. Towers or gendarmes
31. Avalanche chute
32. Avalanche debris
33. Snowfield

tom is more than balanced by a frosty vertical chimney at the top. However, when the couloir ends at a col (small, high pass), it can offer a lower average angle than the face.

If the bed of the couloir is too steep, try the moat along the sides, formed when the snow melts and settles away from the rock. Moats can be rather deep and will vary in width. Portions of a moat can require bridging between the snow and the rock wall, while other parts present either a tight squeeze or a gap too wide to bridge. You might crampon or step-cut up the couloir, and then drop into the moat on the way down to avoid a nerve-wracking descent on steep ice and exposure to rockfall.

Despite the problems, many snow and ice routes follow couloirs. The techniques are usually simple cramponing and step-kicking, but the frequent presence of moats, crevasses, suncups, and blocks of fallen rock and ice make rock-climbing techniques useful. Some of these irregularities are welcome as a good place to set up a belay.

Ridges

Routes along a ridge crest are free of rockfall and avalanche hazard, so they can be the best choice for a long ascent in a region of moderate to heavy snowfall. Routefinding on a ridge top is generally easier than other places on the mountain, and you can usually find a safe way to retreat. Ridge routes take the full brunt of wind and bad weather, but the most significant hazard of ridge routes is presented by cornices.

Cornices

The shape of a ridge crest helps determine the extent of cornice-building (fig. 12-41). A ridge that slopes on one side and breaks into an abrupt cliff on the other is a good candidate for a gigantic cornice. A knife-edge ridge or one gentle on both sides will have only a tiny cornice, if any at all.

When the physical features are right for building cornices, wind direction decides their exact location. Because storm winds have definite patterns in each mountain range, most cornices in the same area face the same way. In the Pacific Northwest

Fig. 12–41. Cornice building

region of the United States, for example, most storms blow from the southwest so the wind-drifted snow of the cornices mostly overhangs on the north and east. These same northern and eastern exposures were steepened by past glaciation, making the ridges ideally shaped for cornice formation.

Temporary or local wind deflection can contradict the general pattern. In rare instances cornices are even built one atop the other, facing in opposite directions, the lower one partially destroyed and hidden by later formations.

Approaching from windward: A cornice gives little sign of its presence as you approach from windward. It simply appears to be a smooth snow slope that runs out to meet the sky. Look at nearby ridges for an idea of the frequency, size, and location of cornices in the area.

Not every snowy ridge conceals a cornice—but be sure to find out whether the ridge you are on does. Try to view the lee side of the ridge from a safe vantage point, such as a rock or tree jutting through the crest. If you can't, have a belayed climber approach the ridge at right angles while probing with an ice axe or reversed ski pole to see if the snow is solid. Look for a crack or indentation in the snow, which could indicate a cornice that has partially collapsed.

It's hard to judge the extent of a cornice overhang and the danger it presents. Don't be misled by appearances. For a mature cornice, the probable line of fracture could be 30 feet or more back from the lip—no doubt farther back than an examination would lead you to expect. And although rocks and trees projecting from the snow suggest safety, they could be on the tops of buttresses with a connecting ridge that curves far back into bays supporting wide cornices. Lots of climbers have had the enlightening experience of looking back along a ridge and discovering their tracks on snow poised above a chasm. The safe course along a corniced crest is well behind the probable fracture line.

Approaching from leeward: You can't miss a cornice from the leeward side. Resembling a wave frozen in the act of breaking, a large cornice close above you is an awesome sight. If you doubt the stability of the cornice, stay among trees or on spur crests as you travel below it. At times, it's quite safe to climb under a cornice. The colder the weather, the more secure the cornice. A late-season cornice, almost completely broken down, is not a problem.

Climbers sometimes even push directly through a cornice to force their way to a ridge crest or pass. It's easiest to penetrate an overhang at a rock spur or where the cornice already has partially collapsed. The leader cuts straight uphill at the point of least overhang, undermining as little of the mass as possible. Generally though, the safest bet with cornices is to avoid traveling on them, under them, or through them.

Bergschrunds

A bergschrund is the giant crevasse found at the upper limit of glacier movement, formed where the moving glacier breaks away from the ice cap. The downhill lip of the bergschrund can be considerably lower than the uphill edge, which may be overhanging. Sometimes the bergschrund is the final problem of the ascent.

Moats

The gap that separates a snowfield from its rock borders is a moat, formed when the snow melts and settles away from the warmer rock. Crossing a moat at the top of a snowfield can be as tough as getting past a bergschrund, with the main difference being that the far wall of a moat is rock instead of snow.

Rockfall hazard

Snowfields and glaciers are prime targets for rockfall from bordering walls and ridges—espe-cially on volcanic peaks, where the rock is often rotten and unstable. Climbers can reduce rockfall danger by wearing hard hats in hazardous areas and by timing climbs for less dangerous periods.

Early-season outings usually face less rockfall than summer climbs because snow still helps cement loose rock in place. Whatever the season, the general rule for glacier climbs is "early on and early off." Nighttime cold often freezes rock in place and prevents most rockfall, but direct sun melts the bonds. The greatest hazard comes in the morning when sun melts the ice, and in evening when meltwater expands as it refreezes, breaking rocks loose.

In the Northern Hemisphere, southern and eastern slopes get the sun first, and therefore should be climbed very early. The shadier northern exposures usually offer less rockfall danger.

ROUTEFINDING AIDS

Crossing a snowfield or glacier, especially at night or in a white-out, can feel like being at sea, without landmarks. However, mountaineers have a couple of navigational opportunities denied to mariners. Mountaineers have a solid surface for planting their own landmarks (wands), and they experience changes in elevation that can be measured by an altimeter as a way to show progress.

The thin bamboo wands topped with tiny flags are left to mark the return route. Try to place wands so that on the return, the next one is visible when the last member of the party is at the previous wand. Coordinate communication so the last person doesn't leave that wand until the next one is sighted. The wands can also be used to mark points of danger (such as moats and crevasses), changes in direction, the boundaries of safe areas for unroped walking in camp, and the location of buried supplies (caches).

An altimeter helps determine your progress and location when you use it along with a topographic map and compass, especially above timberline on a large snowfield with few natural features. You may know that an established camp is located at 11,000 feet, 5 miles due east of the trailhead. By determining the elevation periodically with an altimeter and then finding that elevation on the map along the route, you can find just where you are and how far you have to go. Also relate the altimeter's findings to natural features whenever possible. If you know you are supposed to cross a ridge at an elevation of 9,500 feet in order to keep on the right track to the camp, check the altimeter when you hit the crest. You'll get a good indication of whether you have topped the ridge at the right spot.

A good routefinder uses a variety of tools to stay on route or reach a destination, including compass, map, altimeter, wands, cairns, sun, and visual landmarks. The creative use of several methods becomes especially important when visibility is poor.

AVALANCHES

Avalanches are the number-one hazard facing snow travelers. Avalanche hazard and the conditions that create it are fairly easy to recognize, though there's no way to predict an individual avalanche. Whenever the strength and cohesion of snow on a slope are no longer enough to support the accumulated weight of the snow, an avalanche is due.

Evaluating the stability of a specific snow pack is highly technical work, beyond the scope of this book. A little knowledge about digging snow pits or studying snow crystals sometimes does nothing but give climbers a false sense of security as they rely on an evaluation that may be little more than guesswork. However, climbers do need to learn to recognize generally hazardous terrain and weather.

Four out of five avalanches strike during and just after a storm. Danger increases rapidly with snowfall of an inch or more per hour, or accumulations of a foot or more. Storms starting with low temperature and dry snow, followed by rising temperatures, are even more likely to set up avalanche conditions. The dry snow forms a poor bond, without strength to support the heavier snow that falls later in the storm. Rainstorms, or spring weather with warm winds and cloudy nights, can result in water percolating into the snow and causing wet-snow avalanches. Rapid changes in temperature and wind increase avalanche danger.

Be prepared for two types of avalanches.

A slab avalanche has an obvious fracture line at the top (fig. 12-42). The avalanche is a large area of snow that begins to move suddenly at the same time, sliding on a weak layer within the snowpack or on the ground. The snow in a slab

Fig. 12–42. Slab avalanche

avalanche can be from soft to hard, from wet to dry.

A loose-snow avalanche, on the other hand, starts at one point and grows in size as it slips

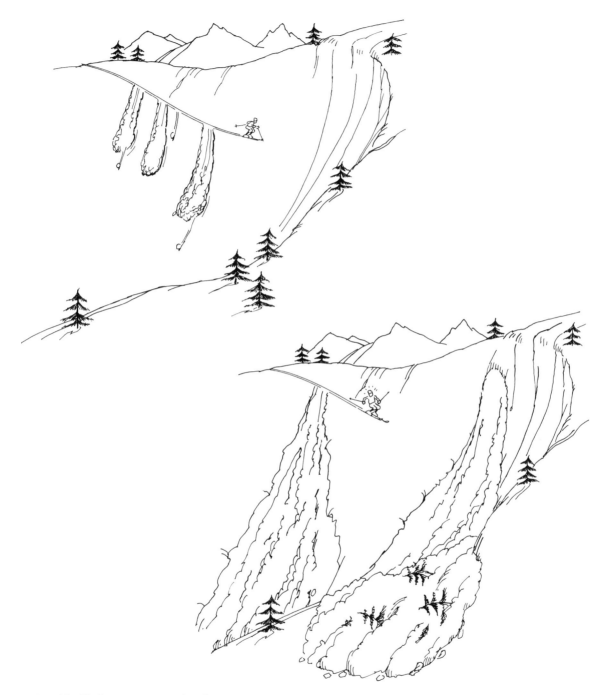

Fig. 12–43. Loose-snow avalanche

Hazard Evaluation Summary

Note: **Bold type** indicates the most critical factors in the evaluation.

1. COULD THE SLOPE PRODUCE AVALANCHES?

   Is the slope steep enough to slide?
   - [ ] **Slopes greater than 25°**
   - [ ] Variations in incline — cliff bands

   What's the orientation of the slope to wind?
   - [ ] **Lee slopes**

   What's the orientation of the slope to sun?
   - [ ] **S and SW slopes exposed to strong radiation.**
   - [ ] First major thaw of spring

   What's the nature of the slope?
   - [ ] **Open slopes**
   - [ ] Thin forest
   - [ ] Confined slide path — gully or bowl
   - [ ] Weak areas that might initiate failure

2. IS THE SNOW STABLE? COULD IT FAIL?

   How deep is the snowpack?

   Are there any signs of avalanche activity?

   What layers are there in the snowpack?
   - [ ] **Very hard or soft layers**
   - [ ] Weak bond between layers
   - [ ] 30 cm or more of snow above a weak layer
   - [ ] Loose, cold snow
   - [ ] Wet snow

   How much snow has fallen?
   - [ ] **Snowfall greater than 2 cm (3/4 in.) per hour**
   - [ ] New snow depth greater than 30 cm (12 in.)
   - [ ] Slow settlement of new snow
   - [ ] Very light or very heavy snow
   - [ ] Heavily rimed crystals, graupel

   - [ ] Heavy stiff layer above a light weak layer
   - [ ] Heavy rain
   - [ ] Very easy or easy shovel test on new snow layer

   Wind
   - [ ] **Moderate or strong wind**
   - [ ] Cracking and settling of snow

   Air temperature
   - [ ] **Rapid rise in temperature**
   - [ ] Above freezing temperatures
   - [ ] Sun on slope under consideration
   - [ ] Sun with hazy sky
   - [ ] Temperature inversions

   Humidity
   - [ ] **High relative humidity during snowfall or during periods of moderate and strong wind.**

3. WHAT WILL HAPPEN TO ME IF THE SLOPE AVALANCHES?

   Depth of avalanche
   - [ ] **Deep weak layers in snowpack**
   - [ ] Foot penetration greater than 60 cm

   Type of avalanche
   - [ ] **Stiff slab above weak layers**
   - [ ] Slope has not yet avalanched recently

   Terrain
   - [ ] **Long open slope above**
   - [ ] Restricted deposition zone
   - [ ] Drop-off below
   - [ ] Trees to wrap around

4. WILL CONDITIONS GET WORSE?
   - [ ] **Continuing snowfall**
   - [ ] Increasing temperature
   - [ ] Strong wind

Fig. 12–44. Hazard evaluation summary (reproduced by permission of the author from Avalanche Safety for Skiers & Climbers *by Tony Daffern, Rocky Mountain Books, 1983)* downhill (fig. 12-43). The snow has little internal cohesion. There is no obvious fracture line and no clear layer where the sliding snow separates from snow beneath. A loose-snow avalanche can be wet and loose or soft and dry.

RECOGNIZING HAZARDOUS TERRAIN

It's easy to spot large slopes and wide swaths of avalanche activity. You'll get a lot of additional information on hazardous terrain by taking into account the time of year, previous weather, prevailing winds, snow characteristics, and the lay of the land (fig. 12-44). The classic law of avalanches says mountaineers face the least danger on ridges, more on the valley floor, and most on the slopes. Let's look first at the biggest danger zone.

The slopes

On slopes, danger comes in many shapes, angles, and sizes.

Slope angles between 30 and 45 degrees are the main originators of avalanches, although slides can start on inclines from 25 to 55 degrees (fig. 12-45). Angles above 55 degrees are generally too steep to collect a lot of snow, which tends to sluff off immediately after falling. Angles lower than 25 degrees are usually safe except for danger from

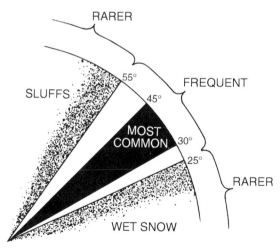

Fig. 12–45. The frequency of avalanches on slopes of various angles

very wet, and usually slow, avalanches. Climbers commonly overestimate the angle of a slope. Get a clinometer, built into a compass or as a separate instrument, if you want to end the guesswork.

Slope shapes also affect the hazard (fig. 12-46). Snow on a slope that is straight, open, and moderately steep presents the most obvious danger. Snow on a convex slope, under tension as it stretches tightly over the curve of the hill, is more prone to avalanche than snow on a concave slope. Coming down a convex slope, you may not know how steep it will get until you're past the curve obstructing your view and are down on the face. Regardless of the shape of the slope, look at them all, large and small, for avalanche hazard. They all can slide.

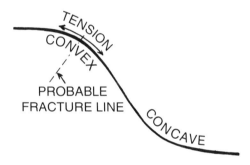

Fig. 12–46. Convex and concave slopes

Bowls and cirques have a shape that invites wind-deposited snow. Once an avalanche starts, it often spreads to an entire face and dumps a great depth of snow into the constricted area below.

Couloirs are enticing, because they offer a direct route up a mountainside, and intimidating, because they are natural avalanche chutes. Always weigh the merits of these gullies against the dangers, and trust them only at certain times under certain conditions. Take into acccount the snow conditions and the amount of snow both in the couloir and adjoining slopes. A slide on a slope within the drainage system of a couloir can sweep the main channel. This slide, by undercutting every tributary on its descent, may pick up bigger loads or leave the tributaries poised and ready to dump their loads at the slightest provocation. Beware of lower-angled couloirs and canyons that are obvious collection areas for avalanche debris.

Forested slopes offer some protection but don't put too much trust in trees. Slides aren't likely to originate in a dense forest, but they can smash through from above. Look around as you climb. Do you spot shattered trees in avalanche fans, and wide swaths cut through old timber? This is evidence of large avalanches penetrating even thick forest. Does a slope grow only brush and small trees, all downslanting? This is probably a slope that avalanches so often that timber has no chance to grow. Are tree limbs missing from the uphill side in open timber? It might be the result of avalanches. There's little or no avalanche protection in open timber, such as you can easily ski through. Another type of vegetation—grass—can increase avalanche danger by providing a slick surface for a slide.

Valleys and flat terrain

In a valley, the question to ask is whether an avalanche on the slopes above could reach you. The danger is obvious in a narrow-floored canyon, but large avalanches have swept for more than a mile across a valley, even climbing the opposite wall. As you trek through a valley, keep an eye out for damaged trees and other signs of avalanching. Remember to pitch tents outside the potential reach of an avalanche.

A route beneath a cliff is a gamble unless you're convinced that conditions are in your favor. Cliffs above flat terrain may harbor cornices, icicles, or ledges piled high with snow—temporarily. All this stuff is ready to drop, and if it doesn't get your party, it could start an avalanche that will.

Ridges

Safe at last! Well, perhaps not quite. A ridge, especially a forested ridge, is usually the safest route when the avalanche hazard is high. However, a ridge presents its own problems of cornices and of crests that can be too jagged to serve as a practical route.

The elements

Climbers pay attention to how sun and wind hit a slope for invaluable clues to avalanche danger.

The sun

The direction a slope faces determines how much sun it gets—and this tells a great deal about its avalanche potential. Here's how it works in the Northern Hemisphere, and of course it's just the opposite on mountains south of the equator.

South-facing slopes receive more sun, and therefore snow settles and stabilizes faster than on northern slopes. In general (with plenty of local exceptions), this makes south-facing slopes safer in winter. They also release avalanches sooner after a storm, so if they are avalanching it's an indication that slopes facing in other directions may soon follow their lead. As warmer spring and summer days arrive, south slopes become prone to wet-snow avalanches and north-facing slopes may be safer.

North-facing slopes receive little or no sun in the winter, so consolidation of the snowpack takes longer. Colder temperatures cause depth hoar within the snowpack, creating weak layers. Therefore, in general (again with local exceptions), north slopes are more likely to slide in midwinter. In spring and summer, as south slopes become dangerously soft, look to the north side for firmer, safer snow.

The wind

Windward slopes—those that face into the wind—tend to be safer. They retain less snow because the wind blows some of it away, and what snow remains is compacted by the blast of the wind.

Lee slopes—those that face the same way the wind is blowing—collect snow rapidly during storms and on windy days as snow blows over from the windward slopes. The result is cornices on the lee side of ridges, snow that is deeper and less consolidated, and formation of wind slabs ready to avalanche.

The snow is full of clues to the prevailing wind

direction. Cornices face the same way the wind is blowing. Deposits of rime, on the other hand, face into the wind: the larger the deposits, the stronger the wind. The steep faces of sastrugi and the rounded ends of snow drifts around trees and rocks also head into the wind (fig. 12-47).

Snow characteristics

Take a close at the nearby snow for more information on avalanche hazard. Are there new avalanches in the area? Do you see cracks close by, indicating you are on an unstable slab? Does an area of snow settle as you walk across it, again warning of a slab that could slide? Does the snow settle with a loud thump, indicating a hard slab ready to release?

The stability of the snow can be tested by probing with an ice axe or ski pole to feel for layers of varying solidity or by digging a pit to examine the layers for weakness. Specialized publications give details of these tests, which are mainly used during winter travel.

MINIMIZING THE RISK

Climbers have many ways to minimize the risk of avalanches and increase their chances of survival if one hits. These efforts begin before they leave home and continue throughout the climb. It's obvious advice, but check the weather report before starting the trip. Heed the detailed avalanche hazard reports prepared by agencies in many mountain areas. Talk to people with local knowledge.

Plan the route before getting under way, but be ready to adjust it depending on conditions. Lots of factors influence avalanche safety, and a problem with any one of them should be grounds to rethink your well-laid plans. During periods of general danger, are you willing to travel only in the morning and evening, when avalanche danger is lowest? Do you have a retreat route in mind? Are you prepared for an emergency bivouac? And don't let summit lust outweigh safety. The safest course might be to go home, or not to leave in the first place.

How to cross a questionable slope

Nobody likes it, but sometimes there's no way to avoid questionable avalanche terrain. The problem then is to make the passage with the least danger of disturbing the slope, and to minimize the consequences if the climbers set off an avalanche or one sweeps down from above.

Before heading out onto a questionable slope, check that your electronic avalanche rescue beacon is switched to the transmit position. Everyone in

Fig. 12–47. Wind-blown snow: a, sastrugi; b, rime-coated trees

the party should carry one of the small battery-powered devices. If one climber is carried away by an avalanche, the others switch their devices to receive and then use the signal from the buried beacon to find the victim.

After you've checked your avalanche beacon, put on mittens and warm clothing. Get set to jettison your gear so it can't drag you down in the event of an avalanche. Loosen the shoulder straps and undo the waist and chest bands on your pack.

When the route lies up a slope, head straight up the fall line instead of switchbacking, which undercuts the snow. Only one person moves at a time, and everyone else watches from safe places, ready to shout if a slide starts. If the climber is on belay, don't tie the rope directly to the belayer, who would risk being pulled in if it proved impossible to stop a climber hit by a wet, heavy avalanche.

On a traverse, it's usually best to take it as high up the slope as possible, above most of the dangerous snow. Again, only one person moves at a time. Cross gingerly, with long, smooth strides, being careful not to cut a trench across the slope. Each climber follows in turn, stepping in the leader's footprints. Everyone listens and watches for an avalanche.

How to survive an avalanche

If you're caught, don't give up. Yell to your partners. Throw off equipment, pack, skis, anything and everything you can get rid of. At the start, grab a rock or tree, or stab your axe or ski pole into the underlying snow, and hold on. Try to stop before you're swept away. If that doesn't work, swim. Stay on the surface by using swimming motions, flailing arms and legs, or by rolling.

Close your mouth if your head goes below the surface. As the snow slows, try to stand up if your feet are below you. If you are buried, try to make a breathing space by putting your elbow or hand in front of your face. Inhale deeply before the snow stops, in order to expand your ribs. As the snow closes around you, it will become impossible to move. Don't shout or struggle. Conserve oxygen and energy. Your partners know what to do, and they have begun rescue efforts.

RESCUE

The rescue effort starts even before the avalanche has stopped. The first step in a successful rescue is a tough one in the shock of the moment: someone must pay attention to where a victim is first caught, where the person disappears beneath the snow, and where the point of disappearance on the moving surface of the avalanche finally stops—and be able to relate these three points to fixed objects, such as trees or rocks. With this information, the search area is immediately reduced in size.

Then mark these three points and search. Do NOT go for help. This is a critical principle of avalanche rescue. Do not go for help. The chance of a person surviving depends almost certainly on everyone staying put, searching efficiently, and digging the victim from the snow. You can go for help after the victim is unburied or all search efforts turn out to be futile.

Select a search leader so the operation will be thorough and methodical. Approach the scene carefully, posting an avalanche lookout in case of another slide. Start with a quick scuff search of the snow surface, looking for someone partially buried, any castoff equipment, or any logical spot the victim might have come to a stop against a tree or rock. The missing climber could turn up in this quick and immediate search. If not, the next step is a thorough search with avalanche beacons, if the climbers are carrying them, or with snow probes if they are not.

Probing

A probe is anything you can use to poke into the snow in hopes of feeling the victim's body, such as wands, ski poles, ice axes, or commercial snow probe poles. Probing is a slow and uncertain mechanical process, but it's all there is in lieu of avalanche beacons. Probe first at likely areas—near pieces of the victim's equipment, at the marked points of disappearance, and around trees and rocks. Then set up a probe line.

The probe line must be highly organized and methodical. Searchers stand elbow to elbow in a line and insert their probes once between their feet. They take one step forward, uphill along the most likely search route, and probe again. Another step, another probe, each movement in unison at the spoken command of the leader. If a searcher hits something, they dig in that spot. After one run up the slope, the probe line moves to one side of the original course and probes some more, again starting at the bottom and probing uphill.

Searching with avalanche rescue beacons

The small electronic device known as an avalanche rescue beacon is the principal tool for finding buried victims.

A rescue beacon can be switched to either transmit or receive signals at a set radio frequency. Rescue depends on each member of a climbing party carrying a beacon, which during the climb is left switched on to the transmit mode. Searchers switch their beacons to the receive mode to zero in on the automatic transmission from a victim. A rescuer who has taken the time to practice with the battery-powered beacon, also called an avalanche transceiver, should locate a victim in short order.

Climbers will encounter beacons that use a frequency of 2275 hertz (most common in North America) or 457 kilohertz. The United States is switching to the world-standard 457 kilohertz frequency, with the change to be completed at the end of 1995. In the meantime, to avoid incompatibility, the American Association of Avalanche Professionals recommends the use of only 2275 hertz or dual frequency beacons through the end of 1995, and 457 kilohertz or dual frequency beacons only after 1995. Some models transmit both frequencies at the same time.

The main thing is that all the beacons in a climbing party transmit and receive a frequency in common. The workings are packaged in a crushproof case inside a pouch that a climber typically straps around the neck and carries under the shirt. The device comes out for rescue work, and the searcher listens for transmissions through a tiny earphone carried with the beacon.

Initial beacon search

If the original quick scuff search for an avalanche victim turns up nothing, start an organized beacon search. The leader checks every beacon to be sure they are switched from transmit to receive. A line of searchers spaced no more than 60 feet apart across the slope starts where the victim was last seen and works its way downhill.

Put the volume control all the way up on every beacon. Move in unison, stay in a straight line, and keep talk to a minimum. Searchers stop every 10 paces and slowly rotate their beacons left and right, then front and back, listening closely for a signal. When a signal is picked up, one or two persons start to track down the sound with a final beacon search. (If there is more than one victim, the rest of the line continues its work. As each victim is found, turn off his or her beacon so searchers won't continue to pick up those signals.)

Final beacon search

Using a single rescue beacon, the final searchers follow a very critical series of steps to zero in on the signal from the buried victim (fig. 12-48). This is what they do:

First of all, orient the beacon for maximum signal strength, moving the unit back and forth, front and back, to find the best position. Then reduce volume as low as possible while still hearing the signal. Keep the beacon in the same orientation as you walk in any straight line. As soon as the signal reaches a peak and begins to drop, again reorient the beacon for maximum signal, and then reduce the volume as low as possible. Holding this orientation, continue on the same path. When the signal fades out, mark the spot.

Without changing orientation of the beacon, turn yourself around and retrace the same pathway. When the signal fades out again, mark that spot. You now have a straight line bracketed at the end by points where the signal disappears. Run to the center of this bracketed line and make a 90-degree turn. Repeat the process. Reorient the beacon for maximum signal, reduce volume to the minimum, and walk in a straight line until the signal fades out. Mark the spot, turn around without disturbing

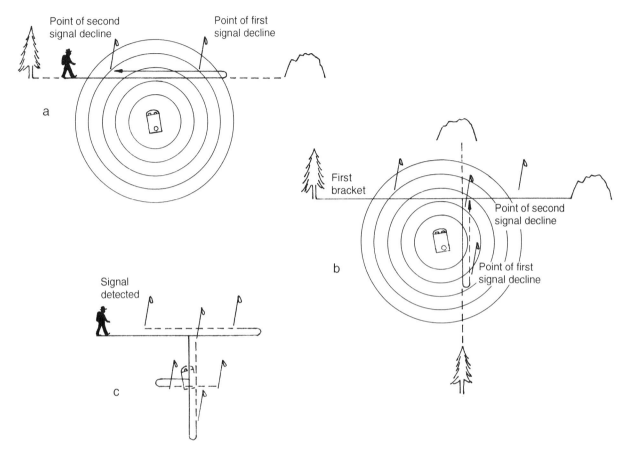

Fig. 12–48. Beacon search bracketing: a, first bracket; b, second bracket; c, summary of beacon search bracketing. (Illustrations by Ray Smutek, reprinted by permission, from "Avalanche Beacons." Summit *[March–April] 1984.)*

orientation of the beacon, and retrace your steps until the signal again disappears. You now have another straight line bracketed by two fade-out points. Run to the center of this new line and again make a 90-degree turn.

Work fast and efficiently, without worrying too much about precision. Continue this process of making bracketed lines until the distance between fade-out points on a line is less than 6 feet. You are now very close to the victim.

Finally, on hands and knees pinpoint your missing partner by moving the beacon from side to side and front to back in a small criss-cross. A loud signal when the volume control is down means you are close. Then dig. Use the beacon to recheck the victim's location with each 2 feet that you dig down. You have successfully found your stricken partner as quickly as possible.

· 13 ·

GLACIER TRAVEL AND CREVASSE RESCUE

Traveling on a glacier is just like crossing any other field of snow, except for the crevasses. They say there's nothing worse than fear of the unknown, and perhaps that's what makes crevasses special. Many of them are hidden, they are deep and cold and scary, and they will kill you if you don't know what you're doing. The purpose of this chapter is to show you how to spot crevasses and stay clear of them, and how to get out if you fall in.

HOW CREVASSES FORM

Think of a glacier as a frozen river flowing slowly down the mountain (figs. 13-1 and 13-2). When the slope steepens, the glacier flows faster.

Just as rivers form rapids, glaciers form crescentic crevasses when ice on steeper pitches flows faster and breaks away from slower moving ice above.

Fig. 13–1. Cross-section of a glacier showing principal features

315

Ice features
1. Moat
2. Bergschrund
3. Crescentic crevasses
4. Firn line
5. Nunatak
6. Marginal crevasses
7. En echelon crevasses
8. Terminus or snout
9. Braided outwash stream

Moraine features
10. Outwash plain (and ground moraine)
11. Erratic
12. Old lateral moraine
13. Moraine lake

14. Terminal moraine
15. Old terminal moraine
16. Medial moraine
17. Lateral moraine

Fig. 13–2. Aerial view of a glacier showing principal features

The crevasses form at a right angle to the direction of flow.

In a river, a steep drop brings a waterfall; the glacial counterpart is an icefall. Crevasses shoot out in all directions from the base of an icefall, and large ice towers (seracs) hang above. Gradually, gravity combined with the forward movement of the glacier will bring these seracs crashing down.

Below steep sections, the glacier slows again, and there may be no crevasses at this point. But if the decrease in slope is too sudden, the glacier may buckle, creating broken, uplifted waves (pressure ridges) as fast-moving ice rams slower ice.

The glacier moves faster in the center than along the sides, where friction along the walls of its route slows it down. This difference in speed often creates lateral (marginal) crevasses, which trend up-valley, near the sides of the glacier. Both lateral and crescentic crevasses tend to angle upstream toward the glacier center, a good clue in guessing the hidden extension of a crevasse from a single hole on the surface. (Any series of crevasses that are parallel to each other are known as *en echelon* crevasses.)

Unfortunately, minor irregularities underneath a glacier can produce random fractures with no pattern. For example, protuberances of rock under the ice, called nunataks, usually form a halo of crevasses. If the rock doesn't actually reach the surface so you can see it, you may be at a loss to explain the odd crevassing. Because of bottom irregularities like this, the only absolute rule about crevasses is that they can form just about anywhere, anytime.

Crevasses are most dangerous in the accumulation zone, that portion of a glacier high enough to receive more snow every year than it loses to melting. Here, crevasses are frequently covered with snow, either filling the hole or forming bridges over the void. Some of the bridges are too weak to support a climber. Others are strong enough for the moment, but will weaken as the bridge melts or the crevasse widens.

Below the accumulation zone is the area of the glacier called the ablation zone, where annual melting matches or exceeds the yearly snowfall. Between the two zones is the firn line (also known as the névé line), named for the words that designate old snow.

Often a giant crevasse known as a bergschrund forms at the glacier's upper limit, where it pulls away from a stationary ice cap. Sometimes a bergschrund presents the final problem in a climb, with the summit a short stroll beyond. Other times, a snowfield above a bergschrund is separated from a higher rock face by a moat, formed by melting and the downhill creep of the snow. A moat can be every bit as hard to cross as a bergschrund.

EQUIPMENT FOR GLACIER TRAVEL

Take a look at your gear with glaciers and crevasses in mind. Here are some considerations in getting ready for glacier travel.

THE ROPE

The rope you need depends on the glacier. If steep technical climbing is expected, with the possibility of severe leader falls, use a standard 10- to 11-millimeter climbing rope or two 9-millimeter ropes. But for "easy" glaciers, a single 9-millimeter rope will handle crevasse falls. For the snow, use one of the "dry" ropes treated by the manufacturer to reduce moisture absorption. This keeps the rope lighter, drier, stronger, and easier to handle.

Some parties carry an additional 100-foot rope, 8 or 9 millimeters in diameter, as an emergency rescue line.

HARNESS

For glacier travel, tie your climbing rope into a seat harness combined with a separate chest harness, or into a full body harness. You don't want to simply tie into a rope around your waist because it would dangerously constrict breathing if you fell into a crevasse and dangled from the rope. The chest harness keeps you from being flipped backward by the weight of your pack during a fall. (Chapter 6 gives details on this equipment.)

ICE AXE AND CRAMPONS

An ice axe and crampons are as important for safe glacier travel as a rope and harness. Crampons help you keep your footing if the snow is icy or the glacier slope gets steep. The ice axe does its usual job of aiding with balance and providing a tool for self-belay and self-arrest. It's also what you use to stop a ropemate's tumble into a crevasse, by falling into self-arrest position with the axe.

In order to keep the axe with you in case *you're* the one who falls in, attach a leash of accessory cord or webbing through the hole in the head of the axe. You can attach the other end of the leash around your wrist with a snug loop or to your waist harness with a locking carabiner. A short wrist leash can be somewhat inconvenient because you need to shift it from one wrist to the other when you change hands on the axe, while a long leash attached to one wrist or to your harness lets you switch hands freely. With the leash clipped to your harness, the axe can provide a quick personal anchor. (Chapter 12 includes a more complete discussion of ice-axe leashes.)

PRUSIK SLINGS AND ASCENDERS

Among the most important gear to help a climber out of a crevasse are slings, tied with prusik knots or other friction knots, and mechanical ascenders.

A prusik sling can be as simple as a mere loop of 5- to 7-millimeter accessory cord. One of these slings tied to a climbing rope with a prusik knot will slide up or down the rope when loosened but grip the rope firmly when tightened. The Bachmann knot does the same thing, but is tied around both a carabiner and the climbing rope. The Klemheist knot works best if the sling is made of webbing instead of cord. (Check back to Chapter 6 for refreshers on any of these knots.)

The simplest prusik slings are used as the link between a snow anchor and the rope that holds a fallen climber. More complicated prusik slings, with foot and safety loops, will be described later in this chapter in the section on crevasse self-rescue.

Mechanical ascenders (such as Jumars and Clogs) attached to slings can be used to replace friction knots such as the prusik for self-rescue and for anchoring an accident rope. Ascenders attach to the rope more easily than the knots. They work better on icy ropes and they can be operated more readily with gloved hands.

On the debit side, ascenders are heavy and expensive. As mechanical devices, they are more prone to failure than knots are and have popped off the rope under unusual circumstances.

On an expedition that fixes some of its ropes in place, most climbers will carry one or two ascenders for self-belay on the fixed lines. These climbers usually use the ascenders for glacier travel as well.

Other rescue gear: At a *minimum,* every glacier climber should carry a single-length runner and a double-length runner of 1-inch tubular webbing to attach to buried anchors; enough carabiners for rappelling (or two carabiners plus a belay device); and one rescue pulley (a carabiner will work in a pinch, but it adds considerable friction). Each rope team should carry at least one snow picket or ice screw (depending on snow conditions) for setting up a solid anchor. Anchors that use two placements are preferred for security, so a rope team may want to pack more anchoring hardware along, or they may have to borrow some from another team in an emergency.

CLOTHING

Dress for the crevasse, not for the glacier. It's frigid in the crevasses even when it's sunny and windless topside, and you want to be ready in case of a fall.

Even on a hot day, wear long trousers and a long-sleeve shirt (they can be wool or synthetic). Try to wear garments that can be ventilated, such as pants with side zippers or a parka with underarm zippers. You can zip these closed if you end up in a crevasse.

As further insurance against hypothermia, keep a jacket on the outside of your pack, where you can reach it easily. Stash a cap and gloves in your pockets. And wear light-colored garments that reflect the heat of the sun while you are on the glacier but will still provide insulation inside a crevasse.

SKIS AND SNOWSHOES

Skis or snowshoes are usually essential for winter or arctic mountaineering because they keep you from sinking too deeply into the snow by distributing your weight over a larger area. This same feature makes them helpful on some glacier climbs by reducing your danger of breaking through the snow bridging a hidden crevasse.

WANDS

Bamboo wands are valuable aids in marking the location of crevasses, identifying turns, and showing the climbing route for the return. Even on climbs where you intend to descend a different route, consider marking the ascent with these flag-topped sticks in case you're forced to retreat.

(Chapter 12 explains how to make your own wands.)

If the visibility is poor, the safest spacing for the wands is a distance equal to the total length of your party (when roped and moving in single file). On the way down, the party can "feel" its way if necessary. The last person in the line stops at each wand and doesn't continue until it is confirmed that the next wand has been found. If visibility is fairly good, space the wands farther apart.

A few other tips on wands: if you tilt each wand as you place it so that it points toward the one below, the search will be narrowed on the way down. Remember that you'll be looking from above for the wands on the return trip, so avoid placing them in hollows or on the down side of ridges where they'll be hard to see. Mark critical spots with some kind of code, such as two wands pointing in the new direction for a turn, or two wands crossing each other for a snow bridge or hidden crevasse.

FUNDAMENTALS OF GLACIER TRAVEL

On a cold, clear morning in late spring, 2 hours before dawn, the glacier is a place of peace and beauty. Above this great silent sweep of ice and snow, the mountain stands silhouetted against a star-filled sky. Climbers fiddling with their headlamps or adjusting their gaiters or squirming into their seat harnesses are too busy and too sleepy to think much about the adventure that lies ahead. But from training and experience, they know just what to do to get ready for a long day on a big glacier. It's one of those days when all the training and preparation for staying out of trouble around crevasses will pay off.

USING THE ROPE

The first rule of glacier travel is very simple: rope up. This holds whether or not you're familiar with the glacier and whether or not you can see any crevasses.

It's tempting to walk unroped onto a glacier that looks like a benign snowfield, especially if you've gone up similar routes time after time without mishap. Avoid the temptation. The extra time and trouble of dealing with the rope, like wearing a seat belt in a car, greatly increases your chances of surviving the most likely accident on a glacier, falling into a crevasse.

Rope teams

Rope teams of three climbers each are a good size for moderate glaciers because they provide two people, not just one, to arrest a ropemate's fall into a crevasse. Glacier rope teams usually keep 40 or 50 feet between climbers, putting three people on a 120-foot rope and three or four on a 150-foot or 165-foot rope. Putting the climbers much closer together increases the danger that more than one will be dragged into a crevasse before a fall can be arrested.

On severely crevassed or very steep glaciers where frequent belaying is required, rope teams of only two climbers (as in rock climbing) are the most practical.

A minimum of two rope teams is recommended for glacier travel so that a rope team involved in an accident will have backup help. While the team with the fallen climber concentrates on holding the rope fast, the second team can set up a snow anchor and then help with the rescue, including providing a second rope.

Tying in

Every climber ties into a seat harness. For glacier travel, each person also needs to wear a chest harness. (Review the details in Chapter 6 about making and tying in to chest harnesses). Here are some general glacier tie-in procedures, depending on the size of the rope team:

Three-person rope: This is the standard size for a rope team on a moderate glacier. The middle climber ties into the very center of the rope, most commonly with a double bowline through the tie-in loops of the seat harness. The small loop that remains at the end of the double bowline should be clipped with a locking carabiner to the harness to ensure the knot can't come loose. The two other climbers tie in at the very ends of the rope, usually with a rewoven figure-8.

Four-person rope: Divide the rope into thirds. Two climbers tie in at the ends, the other two tie in at the one-third points.

Two-person rope: Although a three-person rope is preferred for moderate glacier travel, ropes will sometimes have only two climbers. The most convenient procedure is to use only a part of the rope so you don't have to drag the whole thing through the snow. Each climber ties in anywhere from 25 to 50 feet from an end of the rope; then each carries a loose end on top of the pack or around the shoulders. This keeps the loose rope out of your way while you climb, but ready for use in a crevasse rescue.

Rope management

Keep the rope extended, without slack. This is the most important rule of rope management on a glacier. A rope that is fully extended between climbers is your insurance against taking a long plunge into a crevasse. A slack rope means you drop farther, increasing chances of hitting the sides or bottom or becoming wedged where the crevasse narrows. For the climbers on top, it can mean a much greater hit on the rope from the fallen climber and the danger of being pulled into the hole.

To help keep slack out of the rope, a rope leader needs to set a pace the others can follow for a long time. For their part, the second and third climbers must try to closely match the pace of the leader so the rope stays extended—but not taut. A taut rope is annoying because it pulls back on the climber ahead. You'll need to pay extra attention at turns, where the rope will start to go slack as the climber in front of you heads in a new direction, then tightens as you near the turn yourself. Throughout the turn, adjust speed as necessary, and avoid following the leader's footsteps; select an independent route that will keep the rope taut.

Don't forget safety when you reach a rest stop or campsite. The rope must stay extended and slack-free until the area has been thoroughly probed for crevasses. At a campsite, mark boundaries of the safe area with wands. Always belay climbers into and out of all rest and camp areas.

Another rope-management technique is to keep the rope running at right angles to crevasses. This makes it less likely that two climbers on the same rope will be walking dangerously near the edge of a particular crevasse at the same time. A rope team traveling in single file parallel to a crevasse runs the risk of one climber taking a long fall or of more than one climber tumbling in. Therefore, the second and third climbers on a rope should again avoid the footsteps of a leader who is walking parallel to a crevasse (perhaps looking for a snow bridge or for the end of the cavity). Instead, the followers should stay downhill of the leader and walk on their own separate courses, trying to keep the rope at a right angle to the crevasse.

The same technique is a good safety idea for traveling sideways across a glacier even if no crevasse is in sight. A sideways (traversing) route puts climbers parallel with the most likely direction of any hidden crevasse. Once again, the second and third climbers can blaze their own trail, staying downhill of the leader so the rope is at right angles to the most likely danger.

DETECTING CREVASSES

The first step in staying out of crevasses is to know where they are. Sometimes you can even get a head start before the trip by studying photos of the glacier, because crevasse patterns remain fairly constant from year to year.

On the approach hike, try for a good up-valley or cross-valley look at the glacier before reaching it. You may see an obvious route that would be impossible to discover once you're there. Consider making notes or sketches to help in remembering major crevasses, landmarks, and routes.

These distant views are useful, but prepare to be surprised. What appeared to be small cracks may be gaping chasms, and major crevasses may have been hidden from the angle of your view. Plan alternative routes if you can.

Once you're on the glacier, it's a continuous game of Find the Crevasse. Just because you can't see them doesn't mean they aren't there. Here are some important tips for detecting crevasses:

• Keep an eye out for sagging trenches in the snow that mark where gravity has pulled down on snow that covers a crevasse. The sags will be visible by their slight difference in sheen, texture, or color.
• Take advantage of the low-angle light of early morning and late afternoon to spot the characteristic shadows of sagging snow trenches. They may be impossible to detect in the flat light of a fog and difficult to see in the midafternoon sun.
• Be wary after storms in fall or late spring, when new snow can mask the thin sagging roof of a crevasse.
• Be especially alert in areas where you know crevasses form, such as around nunataks, at the sides of the glacier, and where slopes steepen.
• Check regularly to the sides of your route to determine whether open cracks to your left or right could possibly extend, beneath the snow, under your path.
• Remember that where there is one crevasse there are often many.

Snow probing is the technique to use if you have found a suspicious-looking area and want to search it for crevasses. If your probe locates a crevasse, continue probing to find its true lip.

Probe with your ice axe, thrusting the shaft into the snow a couple of feet ahead of the snow you are standing on. Keep the axe perpendicular to the slope and thrust it in with a smooth motion. You need an axe with a uniform taper from the spike to the shaft, because a blunt spike or jutting ferrule makes it hard to feel the snow.

If resistance to the thrust is uniform, you have established that the snow is consistent to at least the depth of your axe. If resistance lessens abruptly, you've probably found a hole. If your route must continue in the direction of this hole, use further axe thrusts to establish its extent. The leader should open up the hole and mark it with wands.

The value of probing depends on your skill and experience at interpreting the changes felt in the snow layers. An inexperienced prober may think the shaft broke through into a hole when all it really did was hit a softer layer of snow.

The length of the ice axe becomes a limiting factor in probing. The lead climber can also carry an avalanche probe ski pole, which is lighter, longer, and thinner than the axe for easier, deeper probes.

CROSSING CREVASSES

Climbers have a number of ways to get past a crevasse that lies across their route.

The end run

When a crevasse pinches to a close at one end, the safest and most dependable technique is the end run (fig. 13-3). A quarter-mile walk may gain you only 20 or 30 feet of forward progress, but it often beats a direct confrontation with the crevasse.

In late summer when the winter snow has melted down to the ice, you may be able to see the true end of the crevasse. But if fresh snow still blankets the glacier, the visible end of the crack is usually not its true end. Make a wide swing around the corner and probe carefully.

Snow bridges

If an end run is impractical, look for a bridge (fig. 13-4). Remnant snowcover sagging over the void forms one type of bridge. Other, sturdier bridges are really thin isthmuses between two crevasses, with foundations that extend deep into the body of the glacier.

Study a bridge carefully—try for a side view—before putting any faith in it. If you're in doubt, belay the leader in for probing and a close-up look. After the leader gets across, you can follow exactly in the original tracks, belayed from both sides of

Fig. 13–3. End run around a crevasse, keeping the rope taut by not following in the leader's footsteps

Fig. 13–4. Crossing a bridged crevasse under belay

the crevasse if you're the middle person on a three-person rope. Then belay the third climber across.

The strength of a snow bridge varies tremendously with temperature. An arch that might support a truck in the cold of winter or early morning may collapse under its own weight during an afternoon thaw. Cross every bridge with caution every time. Don't assume that because it held in the morning during the ascent that it's safe as you head down in the afternoon.

Jumping

Jumping is the final common tactic for crossing a crevasse (fig. 13-5). Most jumps across crevasses are short, simple leaps. If you're planning a desperate lunge, be sure you've ruled out all the alternatives and see that you are well belayed.

Before any significant jump, remove your pack. While belayed, probe to find the true edge of the crevasse. If you need a running start, tramp down the snow for better footing. As final preparation, put on parka, mittens, and hat, check prusiks and harness, and spool out the amount of rope slack needed from the belayer. Then jump—with your ice axe in the self-arrest position, ready to help you claw over the edge if you're shy of a clean landing.

With the rope now linked to the landing side, the other climbers have a less dangerous job ahead. The belay rope can help pull up on any jumper who falls just short of the target.

Use caution and common sense if the leap is from the high lip of a crevasse over to a lower side.

Fig. 13–5. Jumping a crevasse (belay not shown)

(Bergschrunds, for example, often have a high overhanging wall on the uphill side.) You can be injured in a long, hard leap. If you go for it, keep your feet slightly apart for balance, knees bent to absorb shock, and ice axe held ready for a quick self-arrest.

CREVASSE RESCUE

The depths of a great crevasse exhibit an awful beauty, both enticing and repellent. On a fine day, the walls are a sheen of soft blue ice in the filtered light from high above, and the cavern is cool and still as a church, or a tomb. It's a place every climber should visit once in a lifetime—for crevasse rescue practice. But if there's a second time, we hope it will be in the company of climbers who know the rescue techniques spelled out in the rest of this chapter.

RESCUE RESPONSE

You're the middle person on a three-person rope team traveling up a moderately angled glacier. The climber walking 50 feet in front of you suddenly disappears beneath the snow. What do you do?

Do not stop and think. Your immediate reflex must be to drop into self-arrest in the snow (facing away from the direction of pull) and hold the fall.

The climber at the end of the rope will be doing the same thing. (Chapter 12 details all the steps in self-arrest with the ice axe.)

After that, you and your ropemate topside, along with any other climbers in the neighborhood, get started on the rescue operation, working together with your fallen friend. The principal steps you will take (fig. 13-6), starting right from the instant of the fall, are:

1. Arrest the fall.
2. Set up an anchor.
3. Attach the rope to the anchor.
4. Check the fallen climber.
5. Devise a rescue plan.

Set up an anchor

Once the fall is stopped (fig. 13-6a), the middle climber on the three-person rope stays in self-arrest to support the weight of the fallen climber. The end climber slowly gets out of self-arrest, making sure the middle climber can hold the weight alone, then sets to work establishing an anchor (fig. 13-6b). However, if another rope team is on hand, both climbers can stay in self-arrest while the other team sets up the anchor.

The anchor goes between the middle climber and the lip of the crevasse. (If it's placed instead on the other side of the climber, eventual tension on the rope could make it impossible for that person to untie.) It takes a bombproof anchor because at least one life will be riding on it. Whoever establishes the anchor must work quickly, but without taking shortcuts.

Solid anchors can be made from the following types of protection: pickets pounded into firm snow; ice screws placed in ice; or snow flukes, ice axes, or skis buried as deadmen in soft snow. Ideally, put in two independent anchor placements (or more), with slings to equalize the load. A solitary ice axe driven vertically into the snow is not a good candidate as an anchor to carry the loads of a rescue.

Attach the rope to the anchor

The climber who set up the anchor now attaches a short sling to the climbing rope with a prusik knot, Bachmann knot, or mechanical ascender, and clips the sling to the anchor (fig. 13-6b). The knot or ascender is then slid down the rope, toward the crevasse, until the sling is tight. Now anyone who is still in self-arrest can ease the load off the ice axe and onto the anchor. Do it slowly to confirm that the anchor is solid and that the ascender or friction knot is gripping the climbing rope tightly. (Keep in mind that if you choose to use a prusik knot, one rescuer will have to tend the knot later to keep it open any time the fallen climber is being pulled up. The Bachmann knot and ascenders, on the other hand, usually require less tending.)

Check the fallen climber

Belay one rescuer to the edge of the crevasse to check out the climber's situation closely (fig. 13-6c). The rescuer can be belayed from the anchor by a teammate. Or the rescuer can operate with a self-belay—attaching a prusik loop to the rope that runs from the anchor to the fallen climber, then sliding this prusik along the rope as the rescuer moves toward the crevasse edge. On the way, the rescuer can probe the area and check for any other hazards that might endanger the rescue.

The rescuer will try to talk with the fallen climber. If there is no response, one person can rappel or be lowered on belay into the crevasse to help the fallen climber. But if there is a response, the rescuer can ask if the climber needs clothing, is injured, is able to get into prusik slings, and so forth. The person who fell in should be able to say whether self-rescue is a good possibility—by ice-climbing out or prusiking out—or whether a hoist from above will be needed.

Devise a rescue plan

With all the groundwork out of the way, it's time to get the climber out of the crevasse. There are a lot of methods to choose from, as you will see later in this chapter. Just use the one that looks the best for this particular case, depending on the condition of the climber, the number of rescuers, the equipment available, and any other variables.

a

b

c

Fig. 13–6. Rescue response: a, arresting the fall;
b, setting up the anchor and attaching the rope to
the anchor; c, checking on the fallen climber
(anchor of the climber giving a boot-axe belay not
shown for clarity).

Look for the best method that combines simplicity, speed, and safety.

First of all, a climber who falls into a crevasse doesn't necessarily have to come back up at the same spot. Sometimes there's another way out. Check the possibility of lowering or swinging the fallen climber to a ledge. It might be a good spot to rest and perhaps a gateway to a different part of the crevasse where rescue will be easier. Consider whether the bottom of the crevasse looks solid. This could offer another resting spot and a possible path to a climbing route or a snow ramp to the surface.

Whatever the rescue method, be sure the rope is padded to keep it from digging into the lip of the crevasse. A buried rope will sabotage either the rescuers' efforts to hoist the climber up over the lip or the climber's own attempts to prusik out. For padding, slide an ice-axe shaft, a ski, an ensolite pad, or even a pack under the rescue rope at the edge of the crevasse. (Anchor the padding so it can't fall into the crevasse.)

Throughout the rescue, everyone on top must be tied to the anchor or clipped into a prusik sling tied to an anchored rope or on belay at all times. If your party is large enough, assign one climber to brace and guard the anchor. Establish additional anchors if necessary.

Always remember who you're trying to help. Avoid knocking snow or ice down on the person in the crevasse. Keep talking to the fallen climber. Give reassurance and information about what's going on and enlist ideas for making the rescue go more smoothly.

INSIDE THE CREVASSE

While rescuers are busy topside, the person down below has work to do. Here's how you can prepare for rescue if you are the fallen climber:

Set up your prusik slings on the climbing rope so you can alternate between standing and sitting as you dangle. You will be a lot more comfortable, and will be ready to climb up the rope using the slings if that seems the best way out. (The next section in this chapter outlines self-rescue using prusik slings.)

Clip the climbing rope through a carabiner at your chest harness, if you didn't do so earlier. It will help you maintain an upright position.

Get your pack and ice axe out of the way. You may be able to send them up on a rope from the rescuers. You can also clip the axe to your seat harness, letting it hang so it doesn't interfere with your movement. For the pack, you have the option of attaching a sling to its haul loop and clipping the sling onto the climbing rope with a carabiner, just above your seat harness (but below the prusik attachments). Then the pack will just hang below you. Later, if you climb up the rope using a friction knot or ascenders, the hanging pack will slide freely along the bottom of the loop of climbing rope and weight the rope, making it easier to climb.

Keep warm. Close your parka, put on the hat and gloves you had stuffed in your pockets, and try to put on additional layers of clothing.

SELF-RESCUE

Self-rescue is often the easiest and fastest form of crevasse rescue. This is especially true for small parties that lack the muscle power to hoist you out or that may be pinned down holding the rope. It may be the only practical rescue method for a two-person party. Self-rescue has the added advantage of keeping the fallen climber active and warm.

In some cases, you may be able to climb the crevasse wall to safety, while on belay. Or you can climb back up the rope that held your fall. Two good self-rescue methods of ascending the rope are the stair-step prusik and the Texas prusik. They both use slings of accessory cord attached to the climbing rope with a prusik knot. However, they also work well if they are attached with the Bachmann knot, which incorporates a carabiner that makes a good handhold for loosening and sliding the slings. Mechanical ascenders also can be used instead of the friction knots.

If you ever use slings made of tubular webbing rather than accessory cord, the Klemheist knot is a better friction knot to use than the prusik or Bachmann.

Don't start up the rope until you get an OK from topside. Your movement could interfere with the work of rescuers who may be struggling to hold the fall and set up an anchor.

The stair-step prusik

This system of climbing the rope uses a separate sling for each leg. You can make a set of slings for yourself, and 25 feet (about 8 meters) of 6-millimeter accessory cord is plenty of material for both of them. Getting the size right requires some experimentation. When all the work is done, you should end up with two slings—one as long as the distance from your foot to your ears, the shorter one as long as from foot to elbow.

Each sling consists basically of a single strand of cord, tied with equal-sized loops (1 foot long or so) at each end. One will be the prusik loop, used in attaching the sling to the climbing rope with a prusik or Bachmann knot. The other is a foot loop, large enough to fit over any footwear, including crampons and overboots. Add a slip knot to this loop to prevent tightening down on the boot and cutting off circulation (fig. 13-7a-c).

You need to incorporate one little difference in the longer sling. Leave a 5-foot tail after you tie the loop that will be used for creating the prusik. Tie a small overhand loop at the end of this tail. When you use the slings, clip this small loop to your seat harness as a safety strap to catch you in case both feet slip out of the slings.

Before you head out onto a glacier, attach the prusik loops to the climbing rope so the slings are ready for immediate use in an emergency (fig. 13-7d,e). Attach them at a point beyond where the climbing rope leaves the carabiner at your chest harness, the longer sling attached beyond the shorter. (Pass the long sling through the chest carabiner as well.) Shove the other end of the long sling under the belt of your seat harness. Put the

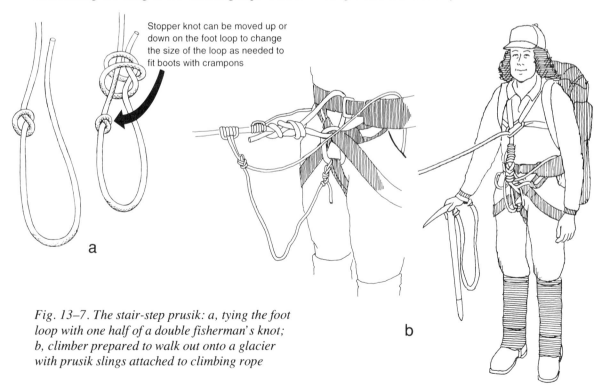

Stopper knot can be moved up or down on the foot loop to change the size of the loop as needed to fit boots with crampons

Fig. 13–7. The stair-step prusik: a, tying the foot loop with one half of a double fisherman's knot; b, climber prepared to walk out onto a glacier with prusik slings attached to climbing rope

Fig. 13–8.
Ascending a rope
using the stair-step
prusik

ends of both slings into your pockets, ready to be pulled out and slipped onto your feet when needed.

(If you are using mechanical ascenders instead of prusik loops to hold the sling to the rope, carry the ascenders on your seat harness and the slings in your pockets. After a crevasse fall, attach the ascenders to the rope.)

This is the sequence to follow if you need to climb the rope (fig. 13-8):

1. Take the foot loops from your pockets and slip them over your boots, cinching up on the slip knots.
2. Stand up in the short prusik sling, putting all your weight onto it.
3. Lift the leg attached to the long prusik sling, then loosen the knot attached to that sling and slide it up the rope some 18 inches.
4. Stand up in the long sling, shifting all your weight to it.
5. Lift the leg attached to the short sling, then loosen the knot attached to that sling and slide it about 18 inches up the rope.
6. Stand up again in the short sling.
7. Keep repeating the process and you'll walk up the rope, somewhat as if it were a flight of stairs.

The Texas prusik

This alternative method of ascending the rope also uses two slings, but this time only one goes to the feet while the other attaches directly to the seat harness (fig. 13-9). The foot sling has a separate loop for each foot (though an option is to provide just a single loop used by only one foot.)

As with the stair-step method, attach the slings to the climbing rope before you start walking on the glacier. The seat sling should extend to head level when you slide the prusik knot upward. The prusik for the foot loops should be tied below the seat prusik, with the knot at waist level when you are standing on the sling. (Attach a safety loop from the top of the leg sling to the locking carabiner at your seat harness.) Experiment to find the sling lengths that are best for you.

Fig. 13–9. Texas prusik dimensions

This is how to use the Texas prusik after a fall into a crevasse (fig. 13-10):

1. Remove the foot loops from your pocket and slip one over each boot, cinching up on the slip knots. (If you have a sling with just a single foot loop, slip it over one boot.)
2. Stand up in the foot slings.
3. Loosen the prusik knot attached to the seat sling and slide it up the rope until it is taut.
4. Sit down in the waist harness, putting all your weight on the seat sling.
5. Loosen the prusik knot attached to the foot slings and slide it up the rope (18 to 24 inches, if the sling is adjusted properly).
6. Once again, stand up in the foot slings.
7. Keep repeating the process.

Fig. 13–10. Ascending a rope using the Texas prusik: a, leg-raise position; b, stand-up position; c, rest position.

The Texas prusik is a simple system that permits more progress per cycle and more comfortable rests than with the stair-step prusik. A climber with an injured leg can still ascend the rope because only one leg is required if you choose to make use of only one foot loop. This method is harder to perform than the stair-step in very narrow crevasses.

With either the stair-step or the Texas prusik, some climbers attach etriers rather than conventional slings. The steps in these ladder-like slings can help you climb up and over a crevasse lip if the rope is entrenched in the snow.

TEAM RESCUES

All rescues are team rescues to some degree, because the fallen climber needs some help even for a self-rescue. However, a full team rescue usually involves hauling the climber to safety. Following are the principal team-rescue methods.

Brute force

Here's a technique we can all understand. Just grab the rope and pull. This is an excellent method for large groups because it's fast, uncomplicated, uses minimal equipment, and requires little or no help from the fallen climber. It works best when perhaps half a dozen strong rescuers can haul on the rope and when the working platform for the pullers is flat or downhill.

After the rescuers have established an anchor, checked the fallen climber, and padded the rope at the lip of the crevasse, they line up along the accident rope and grasp it. They haul by pulling on the rope hand over hand or by moving step by step away from the crevasse.

One rescuer tends the anchor and its tie-in point to the accident rope (where it is attached with a prusik knot, Bachmann knot, or a mechanical ascender). As the rope is pulled up, this rescuer sees that it moves smoothly through the tie-in point. The knot or ascender is then in position to grip and hold the rope if the rope is dropped or the pullers need a rest.

Rescuers should pull the rope at a slow, steady pace, especially when the fallen climber reaches the crevasse lip. If the rope has cut into the lip, the climber could be hurt by being pulled into the wall. At this point, rescuers may ask the climber to scramble over the lip while they hoist.

The single pulley (C-pulley)

Smaller groups without enough muscle to pull the climber out by brute force need a more sophisticated system. The single pulley gives rescuers a 2-to-1 mechanical advantage, doubling the amount of weight that each puller can raise (although friction somewhat lowers this ratio).

Several considerations enter into a decision to use the single-pulley (also known as the C-pulley). The fallen climber must be conscious in order to help by clipping into the rescue pulley. A separate length of rope is needed, either an unused end of the accident rope or another rope entirely. This method is, in fact, a good alternative to consider if the accident rope itself is embedded in the edge of the crevasse and won't move.

To carry out a single-pulley rescue (fig. 13-11), follow these steps:

1. Find a rescue rope. It must be at least twice as long as the distance from the anchor to the fallen climber.
2. Attach one end of the rescue rope to the existing anchor or to a new rescue anchor. (If the unused end of the accident rope is long enough to be used, tie a figure-8 loop in it a few feet beyond the rope's attachment to the anchor. Clip this loop into the anchor.)
3. Double the rescue rope into a big loop and attach a pulley with a locking carabiner.
4. Lower the loop with the pulley and carabiner down to the fallen climber. Tell the climber to clip the carabiner into the seat harness. Confirm that this has been done. Then tell the climber to take the strand of rescue rope that you will be pulling on and to run it through the carabiner at the chest harness, to help stay upright. Tell the climber *precisely* what to do.
5. Be sure the rescue rope runs over an ice axe or

Fig. 13–11. Setting up and raising a climber with the single pulley (rescuer's personal anchors omitted for clarity)

other padding at the crevasse edge to keep it from digging in.

6. Haul on the unanchored end of the lowered loop. As you haul, the climber can grab the anchored half of the loop and pull up. This relieves weight on the rope and makes hauling much easier.

7. A rescuer must attend to the original accident rope at the anchor and pull slack through the friction knot or ascender as the climber is raised. This keeps the accident rope ready at any time to accept the climber's weight again, in case of emergency or if the pullers need a rest.

The Z-pulley

The Z-pulley (fig. 13-12) magnifies the muscle power of small climbing parties by offering a 3-to-1 theoretical mechanical advantage through the use of two pulleys. It can be set up and operated with no help from the fallen climber, making it valuable in rescuing an unconscious person.

Fig. 13–12. Raising a climber with the Z-pulley

The Z-pulley system, which uses the accident rope, requires more equipment and is somewhat more complicated than the C-pulley.

You can get to work on the Z-pulley as soon as you have set up the anchor that is established after any crevasse fall. As usual, the accident rope will be secured to this anchor via a sling tied to the rope with a friction knot (prusik or Bachmann) or an ascender.

Take the loose end of the accident rope and lay out a long loop on the snow, in front of the anchor, so that the loop and the taut line leading to the fallen climber form a giant flat Z.

At the first bend in the Z (by the anchor), place a rescue pulley. Clip a locking carabiner through the pulley and attach the carabiner to the anchor with a short sling. (Some climbers prefer to establish a second anchor to secure this pulley.) The pulley will be located on the climbing rope, between the friction knot and the anchor.

At the second bend in the Z (closer to the crevasse lip), place a second pulley on the rope. Clip this ''floating'' pulley into a short sling that also is attached with a friction knot to the taut rope going to the fallen climber. You may have to see it to believe it, but you now have a Z-pulley setup, ready for use.

To work the system:

1. Pull hand over hand on the free end of the rope, hauling the climber upward.
2. Be sure the rope slides freely through the friction knot or ascender that is linked to the climbing rope near the anchor. This will be the friction brake that holds the accident rope whenever you reset the pulley. If it's a prusik knot, one rescuer needs to help keep it in the open, sliding position. If it's a Bachmann knot or mechanical ascender, it should be able to tend itself.
3. As the floating pulley is hauled in close to the other pulley, slowly relax your pull on the rope in order to let the friction brake take the weight of the climber. Don't let the two pulleys touch because that will undo the Z con-

figuration and convert your system to a direct pull—the old brute-force method.
4. Reset the Z-pulley by loosening the friction knot that is attached to the floating pulley and sliding it way out toward the crevasse lip once again.
5. Haul again on the free end of the rope.
6. Keep repeating the process.

Remember that in any rescue system calling for pulleys, you can substitute carabiners if necessary. However, they create far more friction and the rope will be much harder to pull.

Piggyback systems

To get even more mechanical advantage out of a rescue hauling setup, you can piggyback two systems. For example, establish a separate single-pulley setup to haul on the rope coming from a Z-pulley system. This now gives you a 6-to-1 theoretical mechanical advantage. Or set up a single pulley to haul on another single-pulley system for a 4-to-1 advantage.

To piggyback two systems, set up your initial hoist to the fallen climber, either a single pulley or a Z-pulley. Now establish a second anchor some distance behind the main one, to anchor the second system. Attach the second hoist, again either a single pulley or a Z-pulley, to the accident rope at the point where the rescuers would normally pull.

As you might guess, piggyback systems require an ample supply of slings, pulleys, carabiners, anchor material, and rope.

The Bilgeri rescue

The Bilgeri (fig. 13-13) is a sort of ''team self-rescue.'' It involves the rope-climbing techniques used in the stair-step prusik and the Texas prusik—except that the friction knots or ascenders are operated by a rescuer topside, not by the fallen climber.

Here's how to do it:

1. Secure the accident rope to an anchor with a friction knot or ascender—the standard procedure after any crevasse fall.

Climber is facing outward to
show rope detail. In actual
rescue situations the climber
would be faced inward *toward*
the crevasse wall.

*Fig. 13–13. Climber
ascending using the Bilgeri*

2. Tie a foot loop in the end of a length of rope (either a spare rope or the loose end of the accident rope).

3. Lower this loop to the climber.

4. Attach the upper end of this rope to the anchor with a friction knot or ascender.

5. Tell the climber to put one foot in the foot loop you lowered and the other foot in a prusik sling attached to the accident rope. The climber should now be standing in two foot loops—each on a separate strand of rope that is secured topside by separate friction-knot slings clipped to the anchor.

(To complete the picture, the fallen climber should take all the precautions associated with self-rescue: thread the foot loops through the seat harness and then down to the feet; run the ascent ropes through the chest carabiner to help maintain an upright position; clip a safety loop from the prusik sling to the seat harness.)

Everything is now ready for the ascent:

6. Shout ''Right,'' and the climber lifts (unweights) the right foot. You pull in 12 to 18 inches of slack through the friction knot anchoring that rope.

7. Next, shout ''Left.'' The climber lifts (unweights) the left foot while transferring all weight to the opposite rope. You pull in 12 to 18 inches of slack through the friction knot anchoring that rope.

8. Repeat the sequence until the climber is up and out.

This version of the Bilgeri is similar to the stair-step prusik. There's also a ''Texas prusik'' variation, useful for a person with an injured leg. The climber puts a boot into the foot loop that is lowered from above. The other foot is left free. To ascend, the climber alternates standing in the foot loop on one rope with sitting in the seat harness attached to the accident rope.

The Bilgeri can be a good idea if the fallen climber is in pretty good shape and can communicate readily with rescuers, but isn't particularly adept at working prusik slings. The Bilgeri rescue has an advantage over prusiking methods when the crevasse lip is reached. Because the knots are being handled up top, the fallen climber does not have to force prusik knots up a rope burrowed in the snow. If either of the Bilgeri ropes digs into the crevasse lip, you can free it from up top while the climber's weight is on the opposite line.

SPECIAL SITUATIONS

The realities of a rescue are bound to bring a few snags and surprises on the way to a successful conclusion. You may need to improvise on the basic techniques of rescue. The following are some special situations you could encounter and ideas on how to deal with them.

The middle person

It's an awkward situation when the middle person on a three-person rope team falls in a crevasse, and there are no other teams around to help. The fallen climber is temporarily left hanging while the only two people who can help are separated by the crevasse, each in self-arrest.

To get out of this fix, the climbers start by deciding which side of the crevasse is the rescue side; that is, which side should the fallen climber come out on? Usually, one of the two rescuers in self-arrest is holding more weight than the other. The one holding the least weight usually has the best chance to get up and establish an anchor while the rescuer on the other side stays in self-arrest to hold the fall.

With the anchor set up, the rescuer in self-arrest is ready to get free. This rescuer can ease back until the fallen climber's weight is on the anchor (keeping alert to the danger of also being pulled into the crevasse). Or this rescuer can try to set up a temporary anchor that will take the weight being held by the self-arrest.

Next step: the climber at the anchor tries to belay the climber on the wrong side over to the rescue side, if that person is needed to help in the operation. The loose end of the rope on the rescue side can be used for belaying, if it happens to be long enough. Or if they thought to bring along a lightweight 100-foot accessory line (a good precaution for a rope team traveling alone), this can provide the belay.

However, the climber on the wrong side could be stuck there if no belay or safe route is available. This climber should then set up an anchor and stay put.

On the rescue side, the ideal option now is for the fallen climber to ascend the rope on prusik slings. The rescuer can also use the Bilgeri technique, providing there's enough rope. If a hoist is necessary, the single rescuer can try a Z-pulley or a piggyback system. (For the friction brake at the anchor, be sure to use a Bachmann knot or an ascender, which require less tending than a prusik knot.)

In case one of the two middle members of a four-person rope team falls into a crevasse, conduct the rescue from the side that has two climbers topside.

Two-person rope team

Glacier climbers on a two-person rope team traveling alone really need to know their stuff when it comes to crevasse rescue. Each climber must carry enough equipment for an anchor and a hauling system. The topside climber not only stops the fall but must set up the anchor while staying in self-arrest.

As the sole rescuer, first secure your arrest position by digging in your feet and pressing the ice axe firmly into the snow.

Try to free one hand by rotating the upper half of your body—but keep leaning on the axe. Use your free hand to place a fluke, picket, or ice screw. At this point, you'll see the value of keeping the anchors easily accessible.

Then attach the rope to the anchor with a prusik sling. Ease the weight onto the anchor, keeping ready to resume self-arrest if the anchor doesn't hold. Once you're safely out of self-arrest, back up the anchor.

Now the fallen climber can ascend on prusik slings. Another option for the fallen climber is to work with the rescuer on a Bilgeri ascent—pro-

vided the rescuer is carrying enough spare rope (either extra line, or the coiled and unused rope end carried by climbers in a two-person team). If neither of these methods works in this particular situation, the rescuer will set up a hoist, either a Z-pulley or a piggyback system, using the extra rope resulting from tying in 25 to 50 feet from the rope end. The climbing rope must have a self-tending attachment to the anchor (either a Bachmann knot or an ascender). The rescuer can lighten the hoisting job by first pulling up the fallen climber's pack.

If the rescuer isn't able to set up an anchor in the first place, the fallen climber has no choice but to ascend on prusik slings while the rescuer remains in self-arrest.

Special rescues

New considerations come into the picture when you have to deal with an unconscious victim or with more than one fallen climber at a time.

To help an unconscious climber, first send someone down by rappelling or being lowered on belay. The helper can administer first aid and also get a fallen climber right-side up if necessary. The unconscious climber can be pulled up by brute force or with the Z-pulley. To help get the unconscious climber over the lip of the crevasse, a rescuer may have to work right at the edge or from inside the crevasse.

To rescue more than one fallen climber, assess each person's condition and the best method for getting each one out, and then decide the order of rescue. Be sure each fallen climber is given warm clothing, if needed, and keep them informed of rescue plans as they develop.

Working space

Rescue procedures can be modified to help give you the working space needed to carry out a successful operation.

Temporary anchor

This is a solution to a situation where there is very little working space between the edge of the crevasse and the person who is in self-arrest position to hold the fall. Normally, the anchor and then the Z-pulley would be set up in this space. But now there's not enough room.

The answer is simply to set up the main anchor *behind* the climber in self-arrest (instead of between the climber and the crevasse). Attach the climbing rope to the main anchor with a friction knot or ascender—but at this point, leave a couple of feet of slack between the main anchor and the climber in self-arrest, so that this climber isn't trapped in the system by tension on the rope.

This is where a temporary anchor comes in. Between the climber and the crevasse, set up a temporary anchor and use a prusik sling to secure the rope to it. This permits the climber to ease off from the self-arrest position, let the temporary anchor take over the weight, and untie from the climbing rope.

Now the rescuers can set up a normal Z-pulley in front of the main anchor. They now have plenty of working space. Once hauling begins, the prusik attached to the temporary anchor can be untied.

Difficult areas

Rescuers trying to work in a very narrow area between two crevasses can consider moving the operation. The rescue might proceed better if it is run from the opposite side of either crevasse.

Another option in a tight spot is to change the direction of pull on a Z-pulley system. Hook another pulley to the anchor and run the hauling end of the rope through it. Now the rescuers can pull in a direction more parallel to the crevasses.

Rescues from the uphill side of a crevasse are harder than those from the downhill side. If possible, move the operation to the lower side, where it will be easier for rescuers to haul and for the fallen climber to get over the lip of the crevasse.

Entrenched ropes

The upward progress of a person climbing out or being pulled out of a crevasse can be stopped cold by a rope that has dug itself into the lip.

The situation calls for some improvisation. For instance, a rescuer can attach prusik slings or etriers above the entrenched portion of the rope and drop them down for the climber to step into.

Another option is to switch to a new rescue rope. A rescuer can lower a new rope to the climber. Or the fallen climber can, in effect, provide a new rope by tossing the loose end of the climbing rope up to the rescuers. This is done by prusiking up to the lip, untying from the end of the climbing rope (after first tying in higher up), and throwing the loose end up to the rescuers.

A new rescue rope, carefully padded at the lip of the crevasse so it doesn't also get entrenched, opens up several rescue possibilities. The climber can switch prusik slings from the original climbing rope to the new free rope. Or the rescuers can haul the climber up and out on the new rope. Or the climber can merely transfer all weight to the new rope to give rescuers a much better chance of freeing the entrenched line.

Roofed crevasses

Wide roofed crevasses present special problems. The fallen climber may be hanging free, without a stabilizing wall for support, and the accident rope typically entrenches itself deeply into the snow of the crevasse roof. The climber may be bombarded by snow and ice dislodged by the rescuers above, who will be working in an area of proven instability.

Sometimes it's necessary for a well-belayed rescuer to take a shovel or axe and enlarge the hole the climber fell through. Do your best to keep snow and ice from hitting the climber.

Knowledge and preparation will minimize the hazards of roofed crevasses and the other problems of traveling near crevasses. Glacier travelers who learn about crevasses and regard them with a healthy respect may never fall in. If they do, they will know the techniques that give them the best chance to get back out.

• 14 •

ICE CLIMBING

The world of the ice climber embraces all the forms in which ice exists. In the high mountains, snow and other frozen precipitation endures pressure and heat over time to become the *alpine ice* of glaciers, icefields, and couloirs. This alpine ice is sometimes seen as *blue ice*, a hue born of its exposure to very low temperatures during formation. Blue ice is good for climbing and placing protection. *Black ice* is another alpine variation— old, hard ice, mixed with dirt, pebbles or other debris, often found in gullies and couloirs, and very difficult to climb.

When water freezes, the result is *water ice*. It can be as dramatic as a frozen waterfall or as common as *verglas*, the thin, clear coating that forms when rainfall or melting snow from upper cliffs freezes on rock. Verglas is difficult to climb because crampons have little to penetrate. Water ice is usually harder, steeper, and more brittle than alpine ice, but at high altitudes and low temperatures, the two may be indistinguishable.

Rock also comes in various forms, but is very stable when compared with ice. Yesterday's crack and slab problem will likely be there next year, but this morning's ice route may be only wet rock by afternoon. The ice climber learns to anticipate the ever-changing character of the climbing medium.

Ice-climbing techniques vary depending on steepness of the slope. You can walk without crampons on flat ice fairly easily, especially if rocks are embedded in the surface. On short slopes, you can use an ice axe to chop steps, but longer sections call for crampons. French technique—"flat-footing"—works well on steepening ice, up to a limit. But the steepest routes require the German technique of front-pointing.

This chapter will use some descriptive terms in referring to the approximate steepness of ice slopes. Here's roughly what they mean, in degrees of angle:

- Gentle: Up to 30 degrees
- Moderate: 30 to 45 degrees
- Steep: 45 to 60 degrees
- Extremely steep: 60 degrees and over
- Vertical: 80 to 90 degrees
- Overhanging: Over 90 degrees

EQUIPMENT

Ice climbers refine and expand their techniques and use them on greater climbing challenges with the help of modern equipment. Manufacturers offer a steady stream of specialized clothing, boots, crampons, ice tools, and ice anchors. Review Chapter 12 for a good general rundown on gear such as crampons and ice axes. Building on Chapter 12, this chapter will outline equipment features that are especially important for ice climbing.

CLOTHING

Clothes for ice climbing should offer a combination of comfort and function. In choosing a jacket or anorak, check to see that you can reach high and not have the anorak or jacket bottom rise above your waist. You don't want your waist exposed to the elements as you're reaching up to make a high ice placement. Reinforce the knees and ankles of rain pants or bibs.

Some climbers wear bibs or a body suit as an alternative to the conventional outfit of jacket (or anorak) and pants. A one-piece body suit of synthetic material retains warmth and rebuffs debris. For ventilation, it needs zippers that open from elbow to ankle, and another that opens the suit from stomach to back via the crotch. The body suit should not be confused with the expedition suit, essentially an insulated body suit.

For the hands, mittens with rubberized palms can help in gripping the bare-metal shaft of an ice tool—a tough job with a snow-coated nylon mitten. One option for covering your hands is high-density wool mittens (such as Dachsteins), which are not only warm but offer an unusual secondary feature. If you hit a difficult section of climbing and have only one ice tool, you can temporarily freeze a mittened hand to the ice for help through a move. For safekeeping, always attach wrist loops to your mittens and gloves.

BOOTS

Ice climbers use plastic (synthetic) boots more commonly than leather footwear. The plastic boots are warmer than leather and provide a rigid platform for crampons, which is especially important for front-pointing. Many plastic boots have indented toes and heels that help keep step-in/clamp-on crampon bindings securely attached.

Three-quarter-shank leather boots usually are adequate for general alpine ice climbing. However, leather boots used for extensive front-pointing should have a full shank.

Because ankle rotation is so important in French technique (flat-footing), you need a boot that permits good rotation. Leather boots often are better in this regard. And like any boots, you want ice-climbing footwear to fit well: snug in the heel and instep, and with room for toes to wiggle.

Make sure your gaiters fit your boots. You'll need full-length gaiters that extend from your foot to just beneath the knee. Insulated gaiters are available for added warmth.

CRAMPONS

Properly fitted hinged crampons are adequate for most alpine ice climbing. They work well with most types of climbing boots and are less expensive than rigid-frame designs. They should have medium-length points and require front points for ice climbing.

Climbers who do a lot of front-pointing (especially waterfall climbing) prefer rigid-frame crampons, which vibrate less than hinged crampons when kicked into water ice. Most rigid crampons should be worn with full-shank or plastic (synthetic) boots to prevent over-stressing the frame, although some newer models are strong enough to be worn with boots having less than full shanks. (For a fuller discussion of crampons, see Chapter 12.)

Crampon points must be sharp, and the harder the ice, the sharper the points need to be. Check the points before each climb and sharpen them if they need it.

The angle of the front points and of the first row of downward points is critical in determining the best penetration. For regular ice, the front points are shaped straight but bent slightly downward, and the first row is angled slightly forward (fig. 14-1a).

For waterfall ice, the front points are curved downward, and the ends of the first row are angled more forward than those used for regular ice (fig. 14-1b).

Some waterfall climbers prefer crampons with

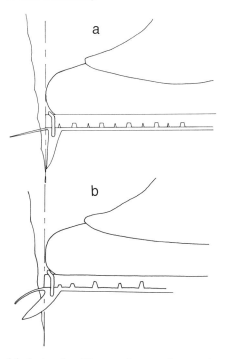

Fig. 14–1. Angle of front points: a, for regular ice; b, for waterfall ice.

just a single front point, which makes for easy placement (fig. 14-2). However, the single front point has more tendency to rotate than the normal double front points.

ICE TOOLS

Part of the fun of ice climbing is experimenting with the large variety of ice-climbing hand tools and learning how to use them. You can borrow, rent, or buy ice tools in order to discover which ones work best in your own climbing.

Most ice tools have shorter shafts than the standard axes used in snow climbing. The short shaft, commonly 50 to 60 centimeters, helps in accurate placement of the pick and reduces the shaft vibration that can fatigue arm muscles. Ice tools that feature a hammer in place of the adze (fig. 14-3) often have a shaft length even shorter than other tools (as short as 35 centimeters).

Many alpine ice climbers use a full-length ice axe partnered with a shorter hand tool. On more technical ice routes, many climbers choose to use two shorter hand tools. A versatile combination is to use one tool that has an adze and one that has a

Fig. 14–2. Rigid crampon with interchangeable single front point

Fig. 14–3. Typical ice hammers

hammer. The adze chops and scrapes ice for steps, belay positions, or ice bollards; the hammer pounds in pieces of protection. Some climbers prefer to hold the ice hammer in their dominant hand, which makes it easier to use in starting ice screws or placing ice and rock pitons.

For a long and demanding ascent, some climbers bring along a third tool. It can be used as an anchor at belay points, as a protection placement, or to replace a lost or broken tool. If your hand tools feature replaceable picks, you can carry a lightweight spare as insurance against a broken pick.

To help in gripping the ice tools, you can wear gloves with rubberized palms or use tools with a covering on the shaft that improves the grip. Inspect your tools before each outing to see that adzes, picks, and spikes are as sharp as possible. Keep these sharp edges covered with guards when they're not in use.

There is great variety in the styles of ice tools. Following are the principal design variations, categorized by the parts of the tool: pick, adze, shaft, and spike.

Picks

The job of the pick is to penetrate the ice, hold against a pull along the shaft, and release easily when its grip is no longer needed. The holding and releasing characteristics of a pick are determined by its weight and shape and by its teeth.

A tool with a relatively heavy head cuts and penetrates most readily, but may be difficult to extract because of its greater penetration. Removable weights can be added to the head to help balance your swing and give better ice penetration.

The steeper the droop of a pick and the sharper, deeper, and more frequent the teeth, the better the pick will hold; but the smoother the pick, the easier it is to remove. The teeth should be shaped to bite into the ice as you pull on the end of the shaft. Although thin, sharp edges penetrate and hold best, they are especially vulnerable to damage when they hit rock. A thin pick may place well, but is more prone to break from the twisting that often occurs when a climber tries to extract the tool. A thick-bladed pick, on the other hand, requires more force to place and is more likely to chip out plates

Fig. 14–4. Ice tools with various pick designs

of ice, but is less prone to break as you work to remove it.

With the conflicting demands on an ice tool, it's no wonder there is wide variation in pick design (fig. 14-4). Many tools are available with interchangeable picks, so you can choose the right one for a particular climb and replace a broken pick instead of discarding the tool. Talk to experienced ice climbers for help in choosing pick designs suitable for you. Here are the principal pick designs you will encounter.

Technically curved: The pick on a standard ice axe used in snow climbing curves slightly downward. But many of the shorter axes used in ice climbing feature a pick that curves down more sharply and holds better in ice. This technically curved pick is most often used on alpine and glacial ice. A good choice is an ice tool with a pick whose curvature matches your natural swing. The angle at the very end of the pick (which determines whether it has negative or positive clearance) is not a major consideration. The main thing is to keep the pick sharp.

Reverse curved: The ease of removal of a drooped pick that has some reverse curve (an upward curve) makes it a frequent choice for waterfall and other steep ice routes.

Straight drooped: An ice tool with a straight but sharply down-angled pick penetrates well in soft to hard ice.

Tubular: Tubular-nosed picks—thin and sharp—are popular for hard water ice because the tube shatters the ice less than a conventional pick.

Adzes

With the adze of an ice tool, you can chop steps, clear ice to make a good surface for screw placement, and cut footholds at belays. As with picks, adzes come in an array of shapes and sizes (fig. 14-5). Many ice tools accept interchangable adzes, letting you replace a broken adze or change adzes depending on ice conditions. You can even

Fig. 14–5. Side and end views of three adze designs

replace an adze with a hammer head.

The most common adze is straight, extending perpendicular to the shaft or drooping somewhat downward. The straight adze is excellent for cutting steps with sharp corners. Some adzes curve downward like the technically curved pick. The very end—the working edge—of some adzes curves slightly inward, although this impedes step-cutting because the full force of a swing is diffused. Tubular adzes are available, mainly for use on waterfall ice.

Shafts

The shafts of most ice tools are straight, but a few designs feature curved shafts (fig. 14-6). Be sure the curve of the shaft complements your natural swing. Curved shafts are designed to keep your knuckles from banging against the ice, aiding in a better placement.

Spikes

To penetrate ice, the spike on an ice tool must be sharp, and the joint between spike and shaft must be smooth. Spikes are solid or tubular. Solid spikes consist of a flat plate or a cone-shaped tip, and cone-shaped spikes point either straight down

Fig. 14–6. Curved-shaft ice tool

Fig. 14–7. Various ice-tool spike designs

or somewhat forward. Most spikes have carabiner holes, which you can clip to as a temporary anchor when setting up a belay anchor (fig. 14-7).

Attachment

A wrist leash from you to each ice tool serves several purposes. The leash secures a dropped tool, helps in the work of swinging the tool, and lets you rest your grip by hanging your weight from it.

A wrist leash is an energy-saving necessity on extremely steep or vertical ice. The leash attached through the carabiner hole at the head of the tool should be just long enough to let you grasp the shaft near the spike. The leash needs an end loop to slip your hand through. You may tie or tape the loop to the shaft at the desired hand position, to help hold your hand in the right spot at all times and direct the downward pull straight along the shaft (fig. 14-8). Used like this, the leash shares in the work of holding and swinging the axe.

The wrist leash also makes it possible to hang from an ice tool without maintaining a forearm-killing grip. To do this, let your arm hang straight, with hand and arm relaxed and body weight on your skeleton.

You can also rest by hanging from a tether that runs from the carabiner hole in the spike to your harness or gear sling. Make the tether long enough that it won't hinder your swing but short enough

Fig. 14–8. Wrist leash for ice tools

that it doesn't get in the way (perhaps catching on a crampon). Put an ice tool in a holster or tool loop when it's not needed.

ICE SCREWS

Ice screws evolved from ice pitons, which were extra-long, blade-type rock pitons with holes, notches, or bulges to increase their grip in ice. After World War II, climbers experimented with new designs that featured a greater shaft area to decrease the load per square inch on the ice and more holes to help the shaft freeze into the slope.

When ice screws first appeared in the early 1960s, enthusiasts claimed they would revolutionize ice climbing, bringing security to the slopes. Critics scoffed that the screws weren't much better than the older ice pitons. This proved particularly true of the lightweight, relatively weak "coat-hanger" ice screw, rarely used today. But ice screws continued to improve and now are considered reliable leader protection (fig. 14-9).

The modern tubular ice screw is the strongest and most reliable design. Commonly 7 to 9 inches long (18 to 23 centimeters), this screw works well in temperatures of both winter and summer. It is relatively easy to screw in and to screw out, with some models including a built-in ratchet for faster placement and removal. The hollow design minimizes fracturing of the ice by allowing the displaced ice to work itself out through the core of the screw.

After the screw is removed, ice inside the core must be cleaned out immediately or it may freeze to the interior, making the screw temporarily useless. The interior of some ice screws is slightly conical, permitting easier ice removal. If ice freezes to the inside, push it out with a length of stiff wire.

The shape and size of an ice screw have a great bearing on its strength. A large-diameter screw supports more weight than a smaller-diameter screw of the same length. A tubular screw holds a greater load than a solid one.

Another type of ice screw is hammered into place, but screwed back out. This type—developed in an attempt to make an easy-to-place and easy-to-remove screw—is available in both solid and tubular versions.

The solid versions can offer good protection in water ice at temperatures below freezing, but are less effective in other forms of ice and at higher temperatures. Melt-out is sometimes rapid because of limited thread displacement and, under load, they tend to shear through the ice. They can break

Fig. 14–9. Types of ice screws

if they aren't hammered in all the way, and they are sometimes tough to remove.

Hollow-core versions of pound-in, screw-out designs have the advantage of allowing the displaced ice to come out through the core instead of being forced aside by a solid screw. This design, with its small threads, can be placed with a series of light blows and removed relatively easily by unscrewing or by levering out with an axe pick. It works best in hard ice, but can be unreliable in temperatures above freezing.

OTHER GEAR

Holsters

You can add two holsters or a double-size holster to your seat harness for carrying ice tools. Try out the tools in the holster before you use it. The tools may be hard to remove if the holster was designed for small rock-climbing implements.

Ropes

Standard 10- to 11-millimeter climbing ropes are the most commonly used for ice climbing, though this depends on the type of climb and the preference of the climbers. Some ice climbers use a rope longer than the standard 50 meters (165 feet) to permit longer pitches. Some use double-rope or twin-rope techniques (outlined in Chapter 10).

Water-repellent ropes may be worth the extra cost because they won't freeze like regular ropes (though they can still become ice-coated). However, experience indicates the water repellency may not last the lifetime of the rope.

Head and eye protection

Your head and eyes need protection from the chunks of ice that start flying when climbers begin swinging their tools into ice. Helmets and goggles are both strongly recommended. The helmet, which also protects from rockfall, must adjust enough to make room for a stocking cap or balaclava. The goggles must fit when your helmet is on, provide protection from ultraviolet rays, and have adequate ventilation to minimize fogging. Sunglasses with side shields are an acceptable substitute.

TECHNIQUES OF ICE CLIMBING

A rock climber taking up ice climbing may find some striking similarities in the two pursuits. In both, climbers progress by moving their weight from one point of balance to another, support themselves as much as possible on their legs, and plan several moves in advance, climbing "with their eyes." On ice, as on rock, climbers use surface features, seeking out buckets and protrusions for handholds, footholds, and ice-tool placements. Of course, the differences are at least as striking. Ice climbers must rely on hand tools and on crampons. They learn to make do with anchors that can be uncertain, and they work in a medium that changes throughout the day and throughout the season.

TECHNIQUE OVERVIEW

Ice climbers usually employ features of two basic techniques, depending on steepness of the slope, conditions of the ice, and their ability and confidence level. They are known as the French and German techniques. The techniques are not mutually exclusive, and most climbers use aspects of both in working out the best way to handle a climb.

French technique (flat-footing)

French technique is the easiest and most efficient method of climbing gentle to steep ice and hard snow—once you learn how to do it. Good French technique demands balance, rhythm, and the confident use of crampons and axe.

French climbers developed the flat-footing technique, thus their terminology is commonly used. Terms using the French word *pied* refer to the feet; terms using *piolet* refer to the ice axe. *Pied à plat*, for example, is French for flat-footing. The name describes the technique: you must keep your feet as flat against the ice as possible at all times to keep all crampon points on the ice. It can be a difficult style to master because it requires severe rotation of the ankle on steep slopes.

The various French placements will be detailed later in this chapter. For now, here is an abbreviated directory of French ice-climbing terms, along with the approximate steepness of slope for each type:

For the feet:

- *Pied marche* (marching) Gentle, 0 to 15 degrees
- *Pied en canard* (duck walk) Gentle, 15 to 30 degrees
- *Pied à plat* (flat-footing) Moderate to steep, 30 to 65 degrees and higher

For the ice axe:

- *Piolet canne* (cane) Gentle to moderate, 0 to 40 degrees
- *Piolet ramasse* (cross-body) Moderate, 35 to 50 degrees
- *Piolet ancre* (anchor) Steep, 45 to 65 degrees and higher

German technique (front-pointing)

Developed by the Germans and Austrians for climbing the harder snow and ice of the eastern Alps, front-pointing can take an experienced ice climber up the steepest and most difficult ice slopes. With this technique, even average climbers can quickly overcome sections that would be difficult or impossible with French technique.

Front-pointing, in contrast to the choreography of flat-footing, is straightforward and uncomplicated. The technique is much like step-kicking straight up a snow slope, but instead of kicking your boot into the snow, you kick your front crampon points into the ice and step directly up on them.

Just as in French technique, however, good front-pointing is rhythmic and balanced, with the weight of your body over the crampons. Efficiency of movement is essential, whether it's planting your front points, placing your hand tools, or moving on the ice.

Although the Germans and Austrians developed it, German technique is frequently described with the general vocabulary of the French technique. Here is a brief directory of German technique, with approximate slope angles for each type. As you can see, aspects of French and German technique overlap in the steepness of slopes for which they are recommended. The proper technique to use depends on ice conditions and the preference of the climber.

For the feet:

- Front-pointing For all angles from 45 degrees through vertical and overhanging

For the ice tools:

- *Piolet panne* (low dagger) Steep, 45 to 55 degrees
- *Piolet poignard* (high dagger) Steep, 50 to 60 degrees
- *Piolet ancre* (anchor) Steep, 45 to 60 degrees
- *Piolet traction* (traction) Extremely steep, 60 degrees through vertical and overhanging

CLIMBING WITHOUT CRAMPONS

Climbing gentle ice slopes without crampons is balance climbing, moving up from one position of balance to the next. At each point of balance, your inside (uphill) foot is in front of and above the trailing outside (downhill) leg, which is fully extended so you can put most of your weight on the bone of that leg, minimizing muscular effort. The axe, in your uphill hand, moves only after your body and feet are in balance, and your feet move only after the axe has been moved forward. As you climb, look for irregularities in the surface of the ice to use as footholds.

Step-cutting

The earliest method of ascending steep ice was simply to cut steps. The invention of crampons reduced the need for step-cutting, but never eliminated it. Climbers still encounter sections of ice when they are not carrying crampons or face short ice problems that may not merit taking the time to put on crampons. A broken crampon, or an injured or inexperienced climber, may be reason enough to cut steps. Even if you're wearing crampons, you might welcome a slight step chipped out by the axe for added security or to serve as a small platform to rest on.

A stairway chopped up an ice slope will consist of steps cut diagonally up the hill or of "pigeonhole" steps cut straight up the slope. In either case, the steps are cut from a position of balance. The usual sequence is to cut two steps from a position of balance, place the axe for security, move up to a new position of balance, cut two more steps, and so on.

A single line of diagonal steps is usually cut up gentle slopes, while a double parallel line of diagonal steps is put in on moderate slopes where balance is more of a problem. Pigeonhole steps are used on steeper slopes.

To make diagonal steps in relatively soft ice, such as summer serac ice, stand in a position of balance with the axe in your outside (downhill) hand (fig. 14-10). Swing the axe from your shoulder, cutting with the adze and letting the weight of the axe do most of the work. On harder ice, this takes extra muscle, and two hands may be necessary. With successive swings, slice ice out of the step. The swings cut away from your body, starting at the heel-end of the new step and working toward the toe. Scoop out chunks of ice with the adze and use the adze and pick to finish the step. (On steeper sections, you can cut small fingerholds to use while you are cutting steps.)

On hard ice that fractures easily, swing the pick horizontally into the ice to define the bottom of the step so that vertical chopping doesn't destroy the

Fig. 14–10. Cutting diagonal steps

foothold. If you jerk outward on the axe just as the pick penetrates the ice, the pick should chip out the ice successfully rather than sticking in it. Make the step slope slightly inward to help keep your boot from slipping out. On gentle slopes, it may be OK if it holds only a small part of the boot, but steps on steeper slopes should be roomy enough for the entire boot. Space the steps so they are convenient for all members of your party.

When you're ready to change the direction of a series of diagonal steps, chop a hold large enough for both feet as a secure position for turning and for switching hands on the axe. For all step-cutting, you must attach the ice axe to your wrist with a leash to help support your hard-working hand and to prevent loss of the axe if you drop it.

Pigeonhole steps for the direct ascent of steep ice are placed about shoulder-width apart and within easy stepping distance of each other (fig. 14-11). Each step functions as both a handhold and foothold, so each should be large enough to hold the front half of a boot and should have a small lip to serve as a handhold. Cut the step, then create the lip with small chops of the adze.

If you decide to chop steps down an ice slope, the easiest method is to cut ladder steps that descend straight down the hill (fig. 14-12). To cut two steps in sequence, start in a position of balance, facing down the slope. Chop two steps directly below the ones you are standing in. When they are ready, step down with the outside (downhill) foot, and then the inside (uphill) foot. To cut just one step at a time, again start in a position of balance. Cut the step for the outside (downhill) foot and move that foot down into the step. Then cut the step for the inside (uphill) foot and move that foot down into it.

The step-cutter works at a tiring, difficult job on a slippery surface, often in an exposed location,

Fig. 14–12. Cutting steps on descent

Fig. 14–11. Cutting pigeonhole steps

and therefore usually needs to be belayed. The only way to be ready for that emergency when the skill of step-cutting can be a life-saver is to take the time once in a while to practice using your axe to chop steps.

CLIMBING WITH CRAMPONS

Modern crampon technique, evolving from the French and German styles, moves an ice climber efficiently upward with minimum fatigue. Flat-footing is generally used on lower-angle slopes and where point penetration is easy; front-pointing is most common on slopes steeper than 45 degrees and on very hard ice. In practice, most climbers blend them into a combination technique. In any technique, the most important element is confident use of the crampons. Practice on gentle and moderate slopes helps develop skill, confidence, and the aggressive approach needed at steeper angles.

A skilled ice climber, whether flat-footing or front-pointing, displays the same deliberate movement as a skilled rock climber on a difficult slab. The crampon points must be carefully and deliberately placed on the ice, the weight transferred from one foot to the other smoothly and decisively.

Boldness is essential to skillful cramponing. Exposure must be disregarded and concentration focused solely on the climbing. But boldness is not blind bravado. It is confidence and skill born of time and enthusiasm, nurtured in many practice sessions on glacial seracs and on ice bulges in frozen gullies, and matured by ascents of increasing length and difficulty. (See Appendix 2 for an explanation of rating systems that are used in assessing the difficulty of ice climbs.)

Fig. 14–13. French technique: duck walk combined with ice axe in cane position (pied en canard/piolet canne).

Gentle to moderate slopes

French technique (flat-footing)

Many climbers find flat-footing awkward and needlessly complicated when they first try it. Once mastered, however, it provides great security because it keeps you in balance over your feet, with maximum penetration of all vertical crampon points.

Ankle strain can be eased by pointing your boots downhill more and more as the slope steepens, so the flex needed to keep your feet flat comes from the more normal forward flex of the ankle and from the knees, which are bent away from the slope and spread well apart. Boots that are flexible at the ankle help. In addition, unlacing the upper part of the boot may permit more ankle flex.

Walking on gentle slopes with crampons requires little more technique than walking anywhere else. Keep your feet slightly farther apart than normal to avoid snagging a crampon point on clothing or on a crampon strap on your other foot. Press all bottom points of each crampon firmly into the ice and walk straight forward (in the manner known as *pied marche*, or marching). Use the ice axe in the cane position (*piolet canne*), holding the axe in the self-belay grasp, with the pick forward and your palm on top of the adze.

As the slope steepens slightly, it will begin to get awkward to keep your toes pointing directly uphill. So splay them outward, duck fashion (*pied en canard*). Continue to use the axe as a cane, in *piolet canne* (fig. 14-13).

As the slope gets steeper still, heading straight upward in pied en canard causes severe ankle strain. Then it's time to turn sideways to the slope and ascend diagonally for a more relaxed, comfortable step. Keep the feet flat (*pied à plat*), with all bottom crampon points stamped into the ice (fig. 14-14). Don't try to edge with crampons. Start with your feet pointed in the direction of travel. As the slope steepens, you'll have to rotate your feet more and more downward in order to keep them flat on the ice. On the steepest slopes they may be pointing downhill.

As the slope angle changes from gentle to mod-

Fig. 14–14. French technique, on a diagonal ascent: flat-footing combined with ice axe in cane position (pied à plat/piolet canne).

erate, using the axe in the cane position becomes awkward. You can now get greater security by holding the axe in the cross-body position (*piolet ramasse*), as shown in figure 14-15. Grip the shaft just above the spike with the inside hand and hold the head of the axe in the self-belay grasp, pick pointing forward, with the outside hand. Drive the spike into the ice, the shaft perpendicular to the slope and roughly horizontal across your waist.

In the cross-body position, most of the force on the axe should be at the hand on the shaft. The hand on the head stabilizes the axe and is a reminder not to lean into the slope. You need a full-length ice axe, rather than a shorter ice tool, to keep your body from leaning into the ice. Even experienced ice climbers have difficulty maintaining proper French technique with a short axe.

Move diagonally upward in a two-step sequence, much the same as ascending a snow slope without crampons. Remember to keep your feet flat at all times (fig. 14-15). Start from a position of balance, your inside (uphill) foot in front of

Fig. 14–15. French technique, on a diagonal ascent: flat-footing combined with ice axe in cross-body position (pied à plat/piolet ramasse).

and above the trailing outside (downhill) leg. From this in-balance position, bring the outside foot in front of and above the inside foot, into the out-of-balance position. The outside leg crosses over the knee of the inside leg, because if the cross is made at the ankle, stability is compromised and the next step will be difficult to make. To return to a position of balance, bring the inside foot up from behind and place it again in front of the outside foot. Keep the weight of your body over the crampons. Avoid leaning into the slope and creating the danger of crampon points twisting out of the ice. Step on lower-angled spots and natural irregularities in the ice to ease ankle strain and conserve energy.

During this diagonal ascent, plant the axe about an arm's length ahead of you each time before moving another two steps. Whether you're using the axe in the cane or the cross-body position, plant it far enough forward so that it will be near your hip after you move up to the next in-balance position.

To change direction (switchback) on a diagonal ascent of an ice slope, use the same technique as on a snow slope where you aren't wearing crampons, but keep your feet flat (fig. 14-16). From a position of balance, place the axe directly above your location. Move your outside (downhill) foot forward, into the out-of-balance position, to about the same elevation as the other foot and pointing slightly uphill. Grasping the axe with both hands, turn into the slope, moving your inside (uphill) foot to point in the new direction and slightly uphill. You are now facing into the slope, standing with feet splayed outward. (If the splayed-foot position feels unstable, you can front-point.) Return to the in-balance position by turning your attention to the foot that is still pointing in the old direction. Move this foot above and in front of the other foot. Reposition your grasp on the ice axe, depending on whether you are using the cane or cross-body method. You're now back in balance and facing the new direction of travel.

Fig. 14–16. French technique, changing direction on a diagonal ascent: flat-footing combined with ice axe in cross-body position (pied à plat/piolet ramasse).

Fig. 14–17. French technique, on a diagonal ascent: flat-footing combined with ice axe in anchor position (pied à plat/piolet ancre).

Moderate to steep slopes

With steeper ice, other variations of the French technique are called for. At some point, the German technique of front-pointing comes into play.

French technique (flat-footing)

On moderate to steep slopes, you can switch the axe from the cross-body position (*piolet ramasse*) to what is known as the anchor position (*piolet ancre*) for more security. Your feet remain flat, with all bottom crampon points stamped into the ice at each step.

To place the axe in *piolet ancre*, begin in a position of balance. Grip the ice-axe shaft just above the spike with your outside (downhill) hand. Swing the axe so that the pick sticks into the ice in front of and above your head, with the shaft parallel to the slope (fig. 14-17a). With your other hand, take hold of the axe head in a self-arrest grasp. Now pull on the axe as you move two steps forward to a new position of balance (fig. 14-17c). A gentle and constant outward pull sets the teeth and keeps the axe locked into the ice. When you're ready to release it, push the shaft toward the ice as

you lift the pick up and out.

In order to keep your feet flat at these angles, your body must lean farther away from the slope, knees and ankles flexed, and the toes of your boots will increasingly point downhill. Try to continue advancing upward in the standard sequence, moving two steps at a time. At the steepest angles, however, your feet will be pointing downhill, and you will have to begin shuffling your feet instead, moving backward up the slope. But continue to plant and remove the pick from a position of balance. The foot that is on the same side as your direction of travel should be at least slightly higher than the other foot, allowing the upper body to rotate for a smooth, strong swing of the axe.

You can change diagonal direction when the axe is in the anchor position by using the same sequence as with the cane or cross-body positions. However, on the steepest slopes, where you are shuffling backward, you can change direction simply by switching hands on the axe and planting it on your other side. There won't be much diagonal movement at this point, because you'll mainly be moving backward straight up the slope.

The French also devised a position—called *pied assis*—that gives leg muscles a rest and provides more security for replanting the axe (fig. 14-18). From a position of balance, bring your outside (downhill) foot up and beneath your buttocks, with the boot (flat as always) pointing straight downhill. Then sit down on that foot. You'll discover a balanced position, a relatively comfortable one.

The invaluable technique of flat-footing, used with the ice axe in the cane or cross-body positions, will serve an experienced climber for many alpine routes. For short stretches of steeper ice, flat-footing combined with the ice axe in anchor position will often work, but this marks the upper limit of French technique.

German technique (front-pointing)

On moderate to steep ice slopes, use of the French and German techniques begins to overlap. They both have a place on these slopes.

The French technique (flat-footing) takes a lot of practice to perfect, but most people pick up front-pointing quickly because it feels natural and secure. Unfortunately, this encourages climbers to use it excessively on moderate slopes where flat-footing would be more efficient and just as secure. In flat-footing, most of the stress is on the thigh muscles, where people usually have more strength than in the calf muscles strained by front-pointing. Even climbers who strongly prefer front-pointing would benefit from alternating the techniques to give calf muscles a rest.

Front-pointing uses not only the two forward points of each crampon, but also the two vertical points immediately behind them. These four points, properly placed, provide a platform to stand on.

Synthetic (plastic) boots provide a firm base for crampons and make front-pointing easiest. Full-shank stiff-soled leather boots also are good. Three-quarter-shank boots can be used in some cases, but require more muscular effort, while soft-soled boots are not suitable at all (fig. 14-19).

The best placement of the boot is straight into the ice, avoiding the splayed feet that tend to rotate the outside front points out of the ice. Boot heels need to be level in order to push the first set of vertical points into the ice and complete the four-point platform for standing (fig. 14-20).

Fig. 14–18. French technique: pied assis. The ice climber is using this position for rest and balance.

Fig. 14–19. Problems of trying to front-point with soft-soled boots

Resist the temptation to raise your heels higher. This pulls the stabilizing vertical points from the ice, endangering placement of the front points and fatiguing calf muscles. Your heels will normally feel lower than they really are, so if you think your heels are too low, the odds are that they are in the correct horizontal position. This is especially important coming over the top of steep ice onto a gentler slope, where the natural tendency is to raise your heels, relax your level of concentration, and hurry. This is a formula for trouble because it could cause the crampon points to shear from the ice.

Except in extremely hard ice, a firm, deliberate kick is usually enough to make sharp points bite. Kicking too hard or too often wastes energy and may shatter the ice. After placing the points, avoid foot movement because it can make them rotate out of the ice.

Front-pointing encompasses a selection of ice-axe positions.

Low-dagger *(piolet panne)*: This position is helpful in tackling a short, relatively steep section that requires only a few quick front-pointing moves. For *piolet panne*, hold the axe by the adze in the self-belay grasp and push the pick into the ice near your waist, to aid balance (fig. 14-21). This position tends to hold you away from the

Fig. 14–20. Correct boot position in front-pointing

Fig. 14–21. Front-pointing, with axe in low-dagger position (piolet panne)

Fig. 14–22. Front-pointing, with axe in high-dagger position (piolet poignard)

slope and out over your feet, the correct stance for front-pointing.

High-dagger *(piolet poignard):* If the slope is a bit too steep to insert the pick effectively into the ice at waist level, in low-dagger, move it into the high-dagger position (fig. 14-22). For this method, hold your hand on the axe head the same as if you were in self-arrest and jab the pick into the ice above your shoulder. Use the high-dagger in hard snow or relatively soft ice that the pick can penetrate easily.

Anchor position *(piolet ancre):* For harder ice or a steeper slope, you can abandon the high-dagger position for the anchor position that is also used in flat-footing. As you stand on front points, hold the axe shaft near the end and swing the pick in as high as possible (fig. 14-23). Front-point upward, holding on higher and higher on the shaft as you progress, adding a self-arrest grasp on the adze with the other hand when you get high enough. Finally, switch hands on the adze, converting to the low-dagger position. When the adze is at waist level, it's time to remove it from the ice and replant it higher.

Piolet traction: The steepest and hardest ice calls for piolet traction (fig. 14-24). The axe is held near the spike and planted high; the ice is then climbed by pulling down on the axe as you front-point up.

It becomes necessary to use a second ice tool on very hard or extremely steep ice when it gets too difficult to balance on your front points while re-planting the axe. It's possible to use two tools at the same time because, except for the anchor position, all ice-axe techniques associated with front-pointing require only one hand.

Using two tools provides three points of support—two crampons and one ice tool—as you re-plant the other tool. The placements must be secure enough that if one point of support fails, the other two will hold you until the third point is replaced. The legs carry most of the weight, but the arms help with both weight and balance.

In double-tool technique, you can use the same ice-axe method for both hands or a different method for each. For instance, you can climb with

Fig. 14–23.
Front-pointing, using axe in anchor position (piolet ancre)

Fig. 14–24. *Front-pointing with axe in piolet traction*

both tools in low-dagger (*piolet panne*), as shown in figure 14-25. Or you can place one tool in high-dagger (*piolet poignard*) and the other in *piolet traction*, as shown in figure 14-26. The upcoming section on vertical ice spells out details of double-tool technique using traction with both tools.

Combination techniques

One fast and powerful technique combines flat-footing and front-pointing. It's called the three-o'clock position because as one foot is front-pointing, the other is flat and points to the side (to three o'clock if it's your right foot, or nine o'clock if it's your left). The French term for the position is *pied troisiéme* (fig. 14-27), literally "third foot."

Pied troisiéme is a potent resource for a direct line of ascent, much less tiring than front-pointing alone. The position lets you distribute the work over more muscle groups by alternating techniques with each leg. As you climb, seek out irregular flatter spots and any nooks or crannies for flat-foot-

Fig. 14–26. Front-pointing, using piolet traction with the tool in the left hand and high-dagger (piolet poignard) with the tool in the right hand

ing, allowing you to rest calf muscles. With the ice axe, use whatever position is appropriate to the situation.

Climbers alternate crampon techniques depending on ice conditions. Flat-footing is usually more secure on frozen snow, ice crust over snow, and soft or rotten ice, because more crampon points dig into the surface. For soft snow over ice or hard snow, front-pointing or the three-o'clock position lets you blast through the surface to get points into the firmer layer beneath. Front-pointing is often the most secure technique for the average climber to use with very hard ice on all but gentle slopes. If you are having serious problems on a climb with flat-footing—perhaps due to fatigue, winds, high altitude, or fear—switch to front-pointing or the three-o'clock position.

Fig. 14–25. Front-pointing, using low-dagger position (piolet panne) with two tools

Fig. 14–27. Three-o'clock position (pied troisiéme)

Vertical ice

The basic method of climbing vertical ice is front-pointing combined with use of two ice tools in piolet traction, in which you pull down on both tools as you ascend (fig. 14-28).

The standard position for the feet is about shoulder width apart and level with each other, a stable and relatively comfortable stance. Reach up and plant the pick of one ice tool as high as possible—but off to the side a bit so you're not hit by dislodged ice or by a tool that comes loose. Then plant the other tool, in the same manner.

From the back, your body at this point resembles an "X" against the ice wall. Your feet are level with each other, heels slightly down, and your arms are straight. As you pull down on the tools, also pull slightly outward to keep their teeth set in the ice and apply inward pressure on the

Fig. 14–28. Front-pointing on vertical ice, piolet traction with two tools

crampon points. You can liken this to a mild lie-back on rock. To conserve energy, you can now hang your weight from the wrist loops rather than gripping the tools tightly.

To ascend, grasp the tools and pull yourself higher as you step upward on the front points to a new level position. You're now ready to replant the ice tools higher, one at a time, returning you to the X body position. Repeat this sequence. Concentrate on efficient, methodical placement of crampon points and hand tools. Rhythm is as important as balance.

To overcome ice bulges and small overhangs, you can try the monkey hang (fig. 14-29). Starting from the X body position, walk your front points up the ice without raising your body. Loosen—but do not remove—one of the hand tools. Rise to a standing or nearly standing position by pushing with your feet and pulling on the tools, and in one smooth, continuous motion, remove and replant the loosened tool. Quickly rest that arm by relaxing the hand and letting the arm hang from the tool's wrist loop. Loosen and replant the other

Fig. 14–29. The monkey hang

tool. You're now back in the X body position, ready to repeat the sequence.

Traversing steep to vertical ice

The principles for traversing are much the same as for front-pointing up steep ice. However, because you're moving to the side instead of straight up, it's more difficult to keep one foot perpendicular to the ice as you replace the front points of the other foot. If the heel rotates, the front points will also rotate and come out of the ice. Hand tools also tend to rotate out in sideways travel.

Start from a secure position—feet on the same level, with front points and hand tools in place (fig. 14-30). Replant the leading tool in the ice at about a 45-degree angle from your body. This puts it lower than if you were ascending, but not so far to the side that it causes your body to rotate out from the wall as soon as you remove the trailing tool. With the leading tool in place, you can shuffle sideways on front points. You also have the option of making a two-step move, crossing the trailing foot over the leading foot, and then bringing the other foot back into the lead. Most climbers prefer the shuffle, which is less awkward and feels more secure. After moving your feet, replant the trailing tool closer to your body. In good ice, the trailing tool can often be securely planted in a hole left by the leading tool—especially if the first tool leaves a small hole that can serve as a starter for a larger-nosed second tool.

Descending

Flat-footing

To descend gently sloping ice, simply face directly downhill, bend the knees slightly, and walk firmly downward (*pied marche*). Plant all bottom crampon points into the ice with each step. Hold the axe in the cane position (*piolet canne*).

As the descent angle steepens, bend your knees more and spread them apart, with body weight over your feet so all crampon points bite securely (fig. 14-31). Thigh muscles do the bulk of the work. For greater security, plant the axe perpendicular to the slope in the cross-body position (*piolet ramasse*), as shown in figure 14-32.

Fig. 14–30. Traversing vertical ice

Fig. 14–31. Flat-footing on descent, with ice axe in cane position (piolet canne)

Fig. 14–32. Flat-footing on descent, with ice axe in the cross-body position (piolet ramasse)

For the next level of security, use the axe in the support position (*piolet appui*), as shown in figure 14-33. Here's how to do it: grasp the axe near the middle of the shaft and hold it beside you as you descend. The axe head points uphill, with the pick down and the spike downhill.

As the slope steepens, switch the axe to the bannister position (*piolet rampe*), as shown in figure 14-34. To do this, grasp the axe near the end of the shaft. Swing the axe to plant the pick as far below as possible. Walk downward, sliding your hand along the shaft toward the head of the axe. It's important to maintain a slight outward pull on the shaft to keep the pick locked in the ice. Keep moving down until you are below the axe head.

Then push the shaft against the ice to help release the pick, and replant the axe farther down.

On a slope too steep to safely descend facing outward, turn sideways and descend diagonally. Your footwork changes to the same flat-foot technique used to ascend diagonally. Use the axe in the anchor position (*piolet ancre*), as shown in figure

Fig. 14–34. Flat-footing on descent, with ice axe in the bannister position (piolet rampe)

Fig. 14–33. Flat-footing on descent, with ice axe in the support position (piolet appui)

14-35. With your outside arm, swing the axe out in front and plant the pick in the ice, take hold of the head with the other hand in the self-arrest grasp, and then flat-foot diagonally down below the axe. The shaft rotates as you pass below it.

Front-pointing

It's often tiring and ineffective to try front-pointing down a gentle to moderate slope. A climber tends to be bent over, facing the moderate slope, and to vacillate between flat-foot and front-point technique.

On steep slopes, front-point and hand-tool techniques are generally the same for going down as for going up. But just as on rock, downclimbing is more difficult. There is a tendency to step too low, which keeps the heel too high, so front points may

Fig. 14–35. Flat-footing on descent, with ice axe in the anchor position (piolet ancre)

shear out or fail to penetrate in the first place. It's awkward to plant the ice tools because they must be placed closer to your body, so you lose the power of a good full swing. You don't get a good view of the route on a descent (although descending on a slight diagonal will help).

Climbers don't often front-point a descent, but it's still a valuable skill for occasions such as retreating from a route. Downclimbing ability also builds confidence in ascending.

Rappelling

Ice climbers often descend on rappel, sliding down a doubled rope attached through an anchor, just as in rock climbing. They use natural anchors whenever possible, of course, because snow flukes or other manufactured anchors used for rappelling usually must be left behind, a costly way to go.

PLACING ICE TOOLS

With any ice tool, the goal is accuracy and a solid placement—the first time. One or two swings saved at the bottom of a pitch mean that much more energy at the top. It takes a lot of practice to learn pinpoint placement. But with a combination of proper technique and equipment, you should be able to place a tool easily and precisely, keep it secure for as long as it's needed, and extract it with less effort than you took to place it (fig. 14-36).

Study the ice for a good placement. A slight depression above and slightly to the side is likely to be good. Ice is more compact and holds the pick better in depressions than in bulges, which shatter or break off under the impact of an ice tool. Try to make placements in opaque ice, less brittle than clear ice because it has more air trapped inside. Minimize the number of placements by planting the axe as high as possible and by moving upward as far as you can with each placement.

Different climbers will have different experiences, though they may be using identical tools on the same climb, because of differences in ability and climbing background. The more experienced climber, for instance, may climb confidently with only a small bite of the pick into the ice, while another climber might not feel comfortable without

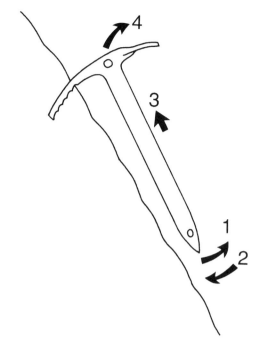

Fig. 14–36. How to remove an ice tool

slamming the tool deep. On most tools, only the first few teeth provide any useful bite in the ice, and the upward angle of the pick in the ice provides most of the holding power. (On an ice tool, small teeth often perform better than large teeth.) Keep your tools sharp.

Placement and removal techniques will vary somewhat, depending on the type of pick that is on the ice tool:

Technically curved: These picks result in an ice tool that is most like a standard ice axe. However, the picks are curved more than on a regular axe to hold better in ice, and the shaft is shorter to permit an easier swing on steep surfaces. A tool with a technically curved pick requires a natural swing, from the shoulder. The first swing should result in a satisfying, solid "thunk"—the sound and feel of a well-placed ice tool. This tool is used in conditions ranging from soft serac ice to hard water ice, though you may need to weight a lighter tool (perhaps with lead sheet taped to the head) for good penetration on hard ice. The pick is usually removed from the ice by lifting straight up on the shaft.

Reverse curved: While technically curved picks take a natural swing, the sharp angles of the reverse-curved and straight-drooped picks require a shorter, choppy swing. A reverse-curved pick, featuring a drooped pick with a slight upward curve, penetrates waterfall ice with a straight, downward hooking motion. It is usually easy to remove.

Straight drooped: This sharply angled pick re-quires a decisive downward flick at the end of a short swing, making it penetrate well in ice from soft to hard. It is fairly easy to remove by using an up-and-down levering motion. Avoid sideways twisting.

Tubular: A tubular-nosed tool works best with a short-arc swing and often grips securely on the first try. A tubular pick is moderately easy to remove by twisting sideways while holding the head (up-and-down levering can fracture the nose). The nose dents easily and is particularly vulnerable if the climb involves ice with sand or rocks close to the surface.

ROPED CLIMBING TECHNIQUES

Climbers usually rope up on ice. The principal exception comes when they decide that overall team safety is served best by climbing unroped. Late on a stormy day, for example, or while ascending a couloir threatened by rockfall, the greater speed of unroped travel might offer relatively more safety than continuing on the rope. It is also sensible to unrope through a section so difficult to protect that a fall by one roped climber would sweep them both away.

Ice climbers can get a measure of protection that is somewhere between climbing on belay and climbing unroped by setting up a running belay. It's another way for a team to move faster when storms or avalanches threaten and, more than ever, speed is safety. It can also be useful on gentle to moderate terrain where danger of falling is minimal and actual belays would be too time-consuming.

A running belay on ice is created very much the same as a running belay on rock (described in Chapter 10) or snow (described and illustrated in Chapter 12). Team members move simultaneously. The leader places protection as they climb and clips the rope through it; the follower removes the protection. The idea is to keep at least two points of protection between them at all times to hold the rope in case of a fall. Because this technique sacrifices much of the safety of true belaying, the decision to use it takes fine judg-ment, based on extensive experience.

Full belaying on ice requires a belayer, belay anchor, and intermediate points of protection, just as it does on snow or rock. A belay anchor is set up and the leader climbs the pitch on belay, sets up another anchor, and then belays the follower up the route. The climbers can either swing leads or have a single climber continue as the leader.

PROTECTION ON ICE

Modern ice screws offer dependable security on ice climbs. However, there is some sacrifice of safety in the time and energy it takes to put them in place. Leaders, therefore, commonly place fewer points of protection in a rope length on ice than they would in a rock pitch of the same length. Ice climbers also make some use of natural protection.

Natural protection

Ready-made natural protection is hard to come by on an alpine ice route, although climbers make use of the medium to fashion ice bollards. Good natural protection may be available not on the ice itself, but in rock bordering the route or protruding through the ice.

Natural protection is often found on frozen waterfalls, where runners can be placed around ice columns. Climbers also devise some slightly unconventional protection points. On frozen waterfalls or high alpine routes, where large ice columns may form only an inch or two apart, an ice screw tied off with webbing can be inserted behind the columns and turned sideways as a deadman. You may find a sheet of ice separated from the underlying rock by an inch or two, leaving a slit that can be enlarged enough to insert a screw tied off with webbing; again, turn the screw sideways to function as a deadman. You can also punch two holes in the sheet of ice, thread a runner through them, and clip the rope into it. On mixed rock and ice climbs, rock-climbing chocks may be wedged into ice holes.

Ice bollards

A bollard can be among an ice climber's most useful anchors. It can be used for rappelling or belaying. By linking together two bollards, one cut for an upward pull and the other for a downward pull, you have a multidirectional anchor. The strength of a bollard is proportional to its size and the hardness of the ice. Made of hard, solid ice, it can be stronger than the rope.

A completed ice bollard is teardrop-shaped when viewed from above, and horn-shaped when viewed from the side (fig. 14-37). All you need for a bollard is an ice axe and good ice, uniform and without cracks or holes. Cut the outline of the bollard with the axe pick. In hard ice, give it a diameter of 12 to 18 inches (30 to 45 centimeters) across the wide end of the teardrop. Cut a trench around the bollard at least 6 inches (15 centimeters) deep, working outward from the outline with both the pick and the adze.

Undercut the sides and top half of the bollard to form a horn that prevents the rope from popping off over the top. This is the most sensitive part of the construction because you can easily fracture or break the bollard if you're careless with the axe.

Ice screws

A favorable location for an ice-screw placement is the same as for an ice tool. A good choice is a natural depression, where fracture lines caused by the screw are not as likely to reach the surface (fig. 14-38a).

A screw placed into a bulge in the ice, on the other hand, can cause serious fracturing that weakens the placement or makes it useless. If this happens, move the screw a foot or two and try again. Generally keep screw placements at least 2 feet apart—more in rotten ice—to reduce chances that fracture lines from one placement could reach the other, weakening both.

The procedures for placing a screw vary somewhat with ice conditions, but the basic routine is

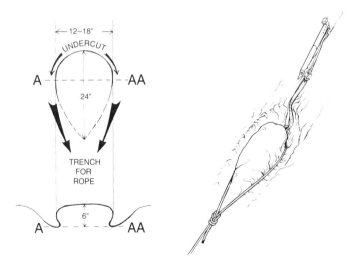

Fig. 14–37. Ice bollard: a, diagram; b, with backup ice-tool anchor.

much the same in any case: punch out a small starting hole with the pick or spike of a hand tool, to give a good grip for the starting threads or teeth of the screw. Make the hole gently, with light taps, to avoid fracturing the ice. Start the screw in the hole, angled uphill 45 to 60 degrees against the anticipated direction of pull. (On hard ice, it may take a few light taps to make the threads catch.)

On ice topped with a layer of soft snow or rotten ice, scrape down with the adze to get to a hard, trustworthy surface before making the starting hole (fig. 14-38b). In extremely rotten ice, make a large horizontal step with a hand tool and place the screw vertically at the back of the step, in a starting hole (fig. 14-38c). Press the screw firmly and twist it into the ice at the same time.

When glacier ice fractures and shatters at the surface, you may still be able to get a secure placement by continuing to install the screw and gently

Fig. 14–39. Screwing in an ice screw with an ice tool

chopping out the shattered ice with sideways strokes of the pick.

A screw with sharp cutting teeth can sometimes be screwed in all the way by hand. If not, do it with the help of a lever through the screw eye; another ice screw or the pick of a hand tool works well (fig. 14-39). Some screws provide a kind of built-in ratcheting capability, simplifying the work of screwing them in.

Twist the screw all the way until the eye is against the ice, tight and solid. Clip a carabiner into the eye, with the carabiner gate down and out. To slow melt-out in soft summer ice or direct sun, pack ice around the screw head. If the screw doesn't go in all the way, reduce leverage on it by tying it off at the surface of the snow with a runner, and then clipping into the runner.

Climbing extremely steep ice is fatiguing, physically and mentally. To conserve energy and keep moving upward efficiently, climbers work to minimize the number of screw placements. If the ice is hard and solid, or the slope not extremely steep, only one or two protection points may be placed on an entire pitch. Unless the ice is rotten, only one screw is placed at each protection point.

It usually takes two hands to place an ice screw, ticklish business on extremely steep, exposed ice. For extra support, you can slip one arm through the

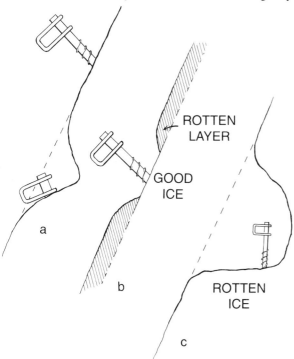

ROTTEN LAYER

GOOD ICE

ROTTEN ICE

a

b

c

Fig. 14–38. Ice-screw placements: a, in solid surface; b, with soft or rotten surface layer; c, in extremely rotten ice.

Fig. 14–40. Support from hand tools while placing an ice screw: a, through wrist leashes; b, from runners between tools and seat harness.

wrist loop of a solidly planted hand tool (fig. 14-40a). Or clip a runner from your seat harness to one or two securely placed hand tools (fig. 14-40b).

On a moderate to steep slope, it may help to chop a step for standing in as you place the screw. On extremely steep ice, however, it's too difficult a job, so save your energy. When it's time to place an ice screw, do it from your front points, and then continue climbing.

BELAYING ON ICE

Near the end of a pitch that you are leading, keep an eye out for a good belay spot, perhaps at a slight depression or where the ice is not so steep. Place a hand tool off to one side and clip in for temporary protection while you chop a step large enough to permit you to stand facing the ice with both feet flat and splayed.

Belay anchors

A standard anchor set-up for an ice belay takes two ice screws. Place the first screw in the ice in front of you, a bit to one side, at about waist to chest level. Clip in a carabiner and tie into it with the climbing rope as it comes from your seat harness. Use a clove hitch or figure-8 knot.

Unclip from the hand tool that was placed as a temporary anchor and replant that tool above and to the outside of the ice screw. Clip the tool to the screw (via the wrist leash or a runner) as a backup to the anchor. Then tell your belayer down below that you are off belay.

Now you can place the second ice screw. Put it

Fig. 14–41. Anchor set-up for an ice belay

above you and about 2 or 3 feet higher than the first one. Extend the climbing rope from the first screw to the second screw and tie in with a clove hitch. There should be little or no slack between the two screws. This completes the anchor set-up (fig. 14-41).

The next step in establishing your belay is to clip another carabiner into the second ice screw and clip the belay rope through the carabiner. This directs the pull from the climber through this screw. And after the follower ascends to the belay station and starts upward to take the lead, that screw becomes the first piece of protection on the new pitch.

Belay methods

You have the choice of using a mechanical belay device, a Münter hitch, or a hip belay. The anchor set-up is the same in any case. Your choice will probably depend on what you're accustomed to and on your degree of confidence in the anchor. The hip belay tends to be somewhat dynamic, with a bit of movement at the belay—resulting in a slower stop to a fall but less force on the anchor and intermediate protection points. Belay devices and the Münter hitch, on the other tend, tend to be less dynamic, stopping a fall faster but putting more force on the anchor and intermediate protection points. (See Chapter 7 for details on the various belay methods.)

Mechanical devices

A Münter hitch, or a belay device such as a slot, tube, or Bachli, is easy to set up and efficient in use. Many ice climbers use such a method as standard procedure. The mechanism is usually situated at your seat harness (fig. 14-42), though you also have the option of belaying directly from the anchor.

Fig. 14–42. Ice belay set-up for a mechanical belay device or Münter hitch at the climber's seat harness

Fig. 14–43. Ice belay set-up for a hip belay

Fig. 14–44. Boot/ice-screw belay

Hip belay

You can establish a hip belay as you stand facing the ice by running the belay rope through a control carabiner at your waist, around your back, through an extra carabiner on the first screw, and then into your braking hand (fig. 14-43). This arrangement is especially favored when the rope is stiff and frozen and could jam in belay devices.

Boot/ice-screw belay

For flat or gentle ice slopes, the boot/ice-screw belay is very useful (fig. 14-44). Here's how to do it: start by twisting an ice screw into place, then clip in a carabiner and run the belay rope through the carabiner. Plant your uphill boot over the screw, perpendicular to the direction of pull. Place the boot so that the inside point of your mid-boot row of crampons goes through the carabiner. Don't

jab the rope. Bring the belay end of the rope over your instep, around the back of your boot ankle, and into your uphill hand.

You control friction on the rope by the amount of wrap on the ankle, much as in a boot-axe belay. You can also adjust the space between the edge of the boot and the outside edge of the carabiner. If the climber falls, slowly tighten the rope low against the ankle with your uphill hand.

Helpful variations of the boot/ice-screw belay include two that utilize the Münter hitch. Use a large pear-shaped carabiner, which has the correct diameter for the Münter, instead of a standard carabiner. In one method, simply use a Münter hitch at the carabiner instead of running the belay rope around your ankle (fig. 14-45). Another method permits you to operate the belay while standing (fig. 14-46).

Fig. 14–45. Boot/ice-screw belay using Münter hitch

Fig. 14–46. Boot/ice-screw belay using Münter hitch while standing

THE ICE CLIMBER

To climb steep ice, you'll use a lot of what you learned in rock and snow climbing and add in the special tools and techniques for ice. As an ice climber, you will especially share the joys of snow climbing, along with its perils: avalanches, hazardous couloirs, and unstable cornices, ice blocks, and icefalls. (Chapter 12 provides a full catalog of snow-climbing dangers and how to avoid them.) You can find climbing opportunities year-around, from the winter challenge of waterfall ice on short dark days in cold weather to the summer experience of alpine ice on days that are long and warm.

Skill and confidence in ice climbing comes from long practice. If you can link up with a steady partner, so much the better. Practice together often. Work on pinpoint ice-tool and crampon placement, which conserves energy so you can meet the rigors of serious routes. Also work to increase the speed and efficiency of your climbing, gearing it to the conditions of the ice and the current strength of your body. Learn to determine when you and your partner should rope up for protection—and when it's safer not to. An experienced ice climber learns these skills and applies them with confidence and good judgment.

· 15 ·

WINTER AND EXPEDITION CLIMBING

Climbers enter a new world of effort and commitment when they take on winter or expedition climbing. There are big differences between the weekend alpine climbing practiced by most climbers and the winter and expeditionary mountaineering of the serious amateur climber or the professional alpine mountaineer. Winter climbing brings severe conditions that require specialized equipment, a high level of skill, and a tremendous will to succeed. Expedition climbing demands the skills of winter climbing in addition to the logistics of an extended trip, often in a foreign country.

The weather takes on a new importance during winter and on expeditions. On a typical weekend summer climb, weather is seldom a big issue. If the weather is poor, you can cancel the climb and try again when it gets better. If the weather turns poor on the climb, a bit of unpleasantry usually gets climbers down from the route and a wet walk brings them back to the trailhead. In the winter, however, good weather is harder to come by and frustrated climbers may give it a try despite a marginal forecast. If the weather does turn poor, descending the route and returning to the cars may become a mini-epic, with routefinding difficulties and increased danger from cornices and avalanches. On expeditions, the climbing team rarely has the luxury to pick and choose the weather. Once the team leaves town, the trip schedule grinds on inexorably and weather be-

comes a condition that must be dealt with like any other obstacle on the trip.

Extremes of hot and cold are common. You expect low temperatures during the winter, but it can get hot, too. On windless, cloudless days the temperature soars as sunlight reflects from the snow. Then, as quickly as a cloud can sail across the sky, the temperature plummets. At night, radiative cooling into a cloudless sky can create temperatures that test the mettle of the finest sleeping bag.

The shorter length of day is another obvious challenge of winter climbing. At the winter solstice, in the higher latitudes, the hours of daylight may be only half the hours available in summer. This means fewer hours for climbing and more hours of sack time in camp waiting for daylight. The winter camp must be made more comfortable for the long hours of waiting, and goals must be scaled back from summer expectations. You may decide to put off the most challenging climbs until late winter, when the day is longer. On expeditions, especially at higher latitudes during the summer, the shortness of day isn't usually a problem. However, climbers often adjust their own internal clocks, traveling in the cooler hours of early morning, late day, or even at night to reduce the problems of soft snow, rockfall, or avalanche.

If your goal is one of the high mountains of the world, acclimatization to the altitude is essential.

Schedules must match not only your ability to climb the route but the ability of your body to meet the rigors of living at high altitudes. More than one climber on the ''dog'' route of a high peak has turned back not because of weather or technical difficulties but because of too rapid an ascent.

To pull off a successful winter climb or expedition, it often takes a lot of extra gear. For a one-day summer rock climb, you may need little more than a rope, rack, lunch, water bottle, and windbreaker. But the pack for even the simplest winter climb is heavier, with more equipment and clothing. The pack for an overnight trip must accommodate a warm sleeping bag for the low temperatures, a comfortable four-season tent for the long nights and more severe weather, and an ample stove and cook kit. An expedition multiplies the amount of food and fuel by the length of the trip. The expedition also may require extra climbing equipment for ''fixing'' parts of the route, leaving ropes in place for the safety of climbers and porters.

Looking at all the special demands of winter and expedition climbing, it's no surprise you need exceptional endurance. This is different than the intense short-term effort made by weekend climbers, who are accustomed to the early Saturday morning drive to the trailhead and the bleary-eyed drive back home Sunday night or early Monday morning. It's the marathon run compared with the 100-yard dash. On an expedition, bursts of intense effort cannot be sustained, as the body does not heal or recover quickly at high altitudes. Team members need to find levels of physical and mental effort they can sustain for the entire trip. Save the climbing ''burnout'' of the weekend climb for the final summit push, and don't waste it on hauling a load between base camp and Camp 1.

Winter travelers often find the season's solitude a virtue of their adventures. Likewise, the expedition climber may cite the distance from civilization as a benefit. With this remoteness comes the need for self-sufficiency. The climbing team must rely on its own resources to get out of a jam because self-rescue is the only option when the nearest help is days or weeks away.

Winter mountaineering and expedition climbing have much in common. Most expeditions are to places where the climbing is decidedly wintery, such as Mount McKinley or the Himalaya. The best way to learn winter climbing is through multiday trips in your own part of the world. These climbs are obviously cheaper and easier to schedule than trips to Alaska or Nepal, but they get you fit and skilled for expedition climbing.

WINTER MOUNTAINEERING

Climbing in winter is a natural extension of climbing at other times of the year, with a lot of similar techniques and equipment and many of the same goals and rewards. It's just more complicated. This chapter goes into a number of topics that were taken up in earlier chapters, such as clothing, tents, and routefinding—but covers them in the specific detail needed to help you stay safe and comfortable in winter.

CLOTHING

Climb often enough in the mountains, and even in the summer you will encounter winterlike conditions. Likewise, many of the best winter climbs are done when the weather resembles spring. Your clothing and equipment must be prepared to accommodate both extremes.

For winter, summer clothing serves as the starting point. Begin with a wicking layer of underwear, followed by whatever layers of insulating clothing the weather dictates, topped off by a windbreaking layer. How much extra clothing you bring, and what kind, depends on the type of winter you can expect at your destination. Additional layers of synthetics work best in the cold damp of maritime climates. Where winter is drier and colder, you can take advantage of the lightness and compactness of down, which must be kept dry.

The dangerous chilling effect of wind means you must always pack a complete layer of windproof clothing during the winter. The wind layer needs to fit over all the insulating layers you are likely to wear at one time, and should overlay or tuck together for a solid shield against the wind. If you've left any chinks in the armor, the wind will find them. Fabrics vary in their windproofness so get recommendations from other climbers and from the people at outdoors stores. Laminated materials such as Gore-Tex are among the most windproof. (Chapter 2 has more information on clothes for mountaineering.)

Keeping dry

On a hot summer day, a sweaty shirt dries quickly in the sun and heat after you've stopped working. But in winter, there is little warmth from the sun to dry out wet clothing. The only other source of heat to dry a shirt is your own body, and tremendous amounts of energy are necessary to evaporate water. Wearing damp clothing is the quickest way to chill yourself.

Avoid dampness by regulating your pace and not allowing yourself to overheat. If clothes get damp, either from perspiration or precipitation, change as soon as camp is reached. If several layers of clothing are damp, at least change the layer closest to your skin.

CARE OF THE FEET

Because of their distance from the body core, extremities have the poorest circulation. To make matters worse for your feet in winter, they are always close to snow or ice. The same factors that keep your body warm—adequate insulation and staying dry—will also warm your feet.

The advent of plastic double boots made it much easier than before to keep your feet warm and dry. The plastic shell is an absolute barrier to snow and water, while the inner boot provides the insulation.

In some circumstances, bunny (or mouse) boots are an option. Developed originally for the military for arctic conditions, bunny boots rely on felt insulation sandwiched between airtight and watertight rubber inner and outer boots. The boot is not rigid and is best suited for non-technical routes. Because the rubber serves as a vapor barrier, keeping perspiration inside, it's necessary to dry your feet and change damp socks daily.

Gaiters are needed for keeping snow from entering the boot from the top. Standard gaiters cover the boot top and lower leg, while supergaiters add an additional layer over the entire boot. Overboots go one step further by including a layer, which quickly sheds snow, below the boot as well. Various brands of supergaiters and overboots offer insulation as well as a snow barrier.

Inside the boot, a vapor barrier sock will keep your foot warmer by preventing perspiration from evaporating. The energy required by evaporation robs warmth from your feet. The vapor barrier also keeps outer socks and boots drier. The sock is worn over a light pair of liner socks and beneath a heavier pair of insulating socks. The major disadvantage to vapor barrier socks is the necessity to change the liner socks and dry your feet each night. Apply foot powder and a strong anti-perspirant (not merely a deodorant) to help keep feet dry and comfortable—and watch out for blisters on the soft, moist skin.

The right socks are important in keeping your feet warm, but too many socks can do just the reverse. They can make the boot tight, restricting circulation and causing cold feet.

HEALTH

Surprisingly, dehydration is a winter hazard. Sweat may not pour from your brow the way it does in summer, but depending on your level of exertion and the dryness of the air, significant moisture loss occurs. Also, fluid intake normally drops because people don't crave cold drinks during the winter. Make a conscious effort to drink enough fluids to keep your urine output copious and clear. This need for fluids highlights the importance of a stove that can dependably melt plenty of snow for drinks.

Hypothermia and frostbite are more traditional winter health hazards. Both can be prevented by awareness of the hazards and by adequate clothing, food, and water. Avoid chills by staying as dry as possible and eating and drinking adequately. If you become chilled, do something about it. Put on more clothes or change damp clothes. If your feet are numb, wiggle your toes vigorously in the boot. If these actions don't work, it may be necessary to take a break to warm the numb body parts. When camp is established, inspect feet and fingers for frostbite and treat as necessary. (There is some general information on frostbite later in this chapter, but be sure to consult a first-aid text for details.)

As a member of a climbing party, you're responsible for taking good care of your own health and guarding against problems that could jeopardize the climb or endanger fellow climbers. At the same time, keep alert to any health problems of other team members.

WINTER CAMPING

Winter camping, more so than summer camping, demands well-developed rituals and habits. Efficiency and safety get a boost if everyone is familiar with their assignments. A tent goes up quickly and easily if two or three members of the party know exactly who does what: who holds the tent to keep it from blowing away, who threads poles through the sleeves, and who pushes the poles. Here's a look at the principal techniques and equipment that go into successful winter camping.

Snow shovels

The snow shovel (fig. 15-1) is a fundamental piece of equipment for the winter mountaineer, used to excavate climbers from avalanche debris, dig emergency shelters, prepare tent platforms, and—in some conditions—clear a climbing route. In choosing a shovel, a climber is torn between the heavy, bulky grain scoop, ideal for moving large amounts of snow quickly, and the compact folding or collapsing shovel, convenient to carry and therefore less likely to be left at home. A large party has the strength to carry both types. A small party will want to examine the route and expected uses before deciding which type or how many to take. If you expect to cut any sort of snow blocks for snow constructions, you will also need a snow saw.

Shelters

For overnight winter trips, you can stay in a tent or in a snow shelter. Tents are much easier to set up, but a good snow shelter is much sturdier. Both

Fig. 15–1. Snow construction tools

have their virtues depending on the situation, and you should know how to set up either one.

Snow shelters

A well-made snow shelter is far more secure than a tent. In a storm, as the snow piles up, the snow shelter becomes even more secure while the tent must be continually cleared of snow. Sometimes a snow shelter is the only possibility, such as on a narrow, windy ridge with no space for a tent. A snow shelter requires no special equipment other than a shovel and, sometimes, a snow saw.

Even if you use tents for sleeping, a snow shelter is a useful addition for an extended stay in one spot. The snow shelter can be the communal hall where cooking and socializing take place without fear of spilling soup on a sleeping bag or tearing a hole in a tent wall. The extra shelter also serves as a warehouse for equipment and a place of refuge if a tent fails in extreme conditions.

On the negative side, snow shelters take time to build; 2 to 3 hours is common. If you'll only be there one night, it may not be worth the effort. Building a snow shelter is hard work and may leave the building crew wet from perspiration and from the snow. In some circumstances a snow shelter is warmer than a tent. But if it's midday and the sun is out, the inside of a tent can be 40 or 50 degrees warmer than the outside air, and makes a great place for drying sleeping bags and clothing.

There are pluses and minuses to a number of snow-shelter designs. Check back to Chapter 3 for a look at how to build some of them.

Snow caves require both adequate snow depth and the right topography. Look for a fairly steep slope to dig into; it's much easier than trying to dig a cave into a shallow slope. The snow must be deep enough so you won't hit ground before you can excavate a cave that's large enough.

With igloos, the depth of the snow is not as critical because they are constructed of snow blocks. Therefore it's usually easier to build an igloo with lots of space and headroom than a roomy snow cave. In addition to a shovel, igloo construction requires a snow saw, experience in the art of igloo building, and good block-cutting

snow. If the snow isn't just right, and the snow blocks fall apart as you move them, forget about building an igloo.

You can also create hybrid snow shelters, combining igloo and snow-cave techniques. To make a typical hybrid shelter, dig into a snow slope through a relatively large opening; this makes it easy to excavate snow. When the cave is big enough, close the opening over with snow blocks. Then dig a smaller entrance for access to the shelter. Various types of trenches also provide shelter in the snow. (Chapter 3 also has details on snow trenches.)

Snow-shelter construction is a useful skill and it can be fun, but for short winter trips these shelters are not usually practical to build. It is on longer trips, where the investment in the snow shelter can be amortized over several nights or where conditions are too extreme for a tent, that snow shelters are most valuable.

Tents

Tents are the first choice in shelters for the typical weekend winter outing. A quality winter tent must be sturdy enough to withstand high winds and snow dumped during the night. Steep side walls aid in clearing snow off the tent, and an aerodynamic shape helps outwit the wind. Free-standing dome-type tents work well, and so do the tunnel-style (hoop) tents, which require a few stakes (fig. 15-2). Every winter tent, free-standing or not, needs multiple lashing points for tying into anchors to keep it from taking off like a box kite in a strong gust. The considerations that go into selecting and using a good winter tent apply likewise to tents used for expeditions.

Size: For extreme routes, where flat real estate is rare and weight is a supreme consideration, consider the compact and lightweight "wedge" tent, a free-standing design with two poles that go from corner to corner and cross in the middle. On most winter trips, however, you will want a tent that is roomy, though heavy. The extra room is used to store packs and personal gear as well as reduce feelings of claustrophobia during 15-hour nights in the tent.

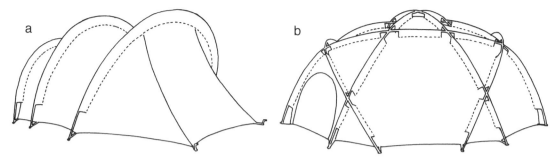

Fig. 15–2. Winter-quality tents: a, hoop style; b, dome.

Construction: Although single-walled tents of rainproof, breathable fabric are lighter, double-walled tents (with an integral or separate rain fly) are somewhat warmer and less subject to icing on the inside wall. Aluminum tent poles are usually stronger than fiberglass poles. High-tech poles of such materials as Kevlar or carbon fiber may someday supplant aluminum.

Features: Certain conveniences simplify wintertime tent living. These include multiple entrances (in case one entrance bears the brunt of the weather), a vestibule for cooking or storage, gear pockets inside the tent for organizing small items, and inside loops for hanging clothes or a lantern.

You can't pitch a tent without giving some thought first to selecting and preparing a site. Some tips:

Use the terrain to your advantage. Select a spot that is as near to flat as possible to make site preparation easier. Watch out for hazards such as crevasses, avalanche paths, and cornices. Observe the local wind patterns: a rock-hard or sculpted snow surface indicates frequent wind, while a loose powdery area indicates a zone where wind-transported snow is deposited. Keep in mind that although the powdery area may be protected from the direct wind, the tent may have to be cleared of snow frequently.

Compact a large-enough area for the tent and for movement around the tent to check tie lines or clear snow. Flatten and smooth the tent platform thoroughly to keep you from sliding toward one wall or the other during the night and to get rid of any uncomfortable lumps. This is especially important if you're staying for several nights, because the entire tent platform becomes rock hard with all features cast in ice after the first night. A ski does a great job of smoothing the tent platform.

Dig an entrance pit 1 foot or so deep once the tent is erected. The pit in front of the main tent door makes entering and leaving easier, as you can sit comfortably in the doorway and place your feet in the pit.

Build snow walls around the tent if the site is exposed to winds. The walls can be anywhere from about 3 to 6 feet high and will deflect some of the wind away from the tent (fig. 15-3). Keep the walls as far away from the tent as they are high (a 3-foot wall, for example, should be 3 feet away from the tent), because wind will deposit snow on the leeward side of the walls and fill this area quickly. Blocks cut by a snow saw make the easiest, quickest walls, though you can also just shovel snow into a pile to serve as a wall.

A number of special items are useful in winter camping. Each tent should have a snow brush—a small broom with synthetic bristles to sweep snow from boots, packs, clothing, and the tent. Each tent also needs a sponge for cleaning up cooking or drinking-cup spills and removing condensation from the inside tent walls. A cheery addition to a tent, especially during the long nights near the winter solstice, is a candle lantern. You might even consider a gas lantern, which can repay its price in weight and bother by bringing tremendous brightening and warming to a tent.

For anchoring a tent, you can use wide-profile stakes, mini snow flukes, or regular snow anchors.

Fig. 15–3. Typical winter camp: kitchen area, snow walls, and well-placed tent.

Skis, ski poles, ice axes, and such also work well. Of course, whatever you use to hold down the tent won't be available for other uses. Tie the tent to a tree if there is one nearby.

To help make your winter tent-bound hours more pleasant, you need some house rules. They will depend on the weather, the size of the tent, and the experience of the occupants. For example, a small tent may mean that packs stay outside. If the tent is large enough and packs are brought inside, they should be thoroughly brushed of snow first. House rules may dictate that boots be taken off outside, brushed of snow, and placed in a waterproof boot bag inside the tent. Boots can bring in snow, and they also can cut or tear holes in the tent floor. Use stuff sacks or a large personal tent sack to help you organize and protect personal gear and keep it out of the way of your tentmates. It often helps to have one person enter the tent first to lay sleeping pads and organize gear before others enter.

During a storm, you'll face the necessary chore of keeping snow cleared away from the tent. In most storms, it isn't the snow falling from the sky that creates the problem, but rather the snow carried by the wind. Nature desires a smooth snow surface with minimal obstructions to impede the wind. When the wind encounters an obstruction, such as your tent or snow wall, wind-transported snow will be deposited in a way that minimizes its impact on the wind. Snow is deposited on the leeward side of tents and snow walls, and the tent begins to be buried. Even a partially buried tent poses the risk of asphyxiation, especially if you are cooking in the tent. Clear the snow regularly from around the tent. (Avoid cutting the tent with the shovel. Nylon cuts easily when it is tensioned by a snow load.)

In a severe or prolonged storm, your tent may begin to disappear into the hole created by neighboring snowdrifts. You may need to move the tent up on top of the new snow surface.

Stoves

As with winter tents, a stove suitable for winter must be tougher and more capable than a stove relegated to summer use. In addition to heating food, it is used to melt pots full of snow, providing your only reliable source of water. The stove must have a high heat output in order to melt snow quickly, stability so that it supports a full pot of snow, and relative ease of repairing when this becomes necessary. It also must operate well at low temperatures (which pretty much rules out self-pressurizing white gas stoves, which do not have a pump).

The most popular stove fuels are white gas, kerosene, or pressurized butane cartridges (see Chapter 3 for more details on stoves and fuels). White gas or its close equivalents, such as Coleman fuel or Chevron Blazo, are readily available in the United States, while kerosene is usually more common in other countries. Both fuels are inexpensive and efficient. Kerosene's lower volatility is both a virtue and a drawback. It necessitates priming your stove with something more volatile, such as alcohol or stove preheating paste. On the other hand, it lessens the chance of stove flare-up, a serious hazard if you're cooking in the tent.

A multifuel stove is useful for foreign travel, letting you burn such fuels as Stoddard solvent, stove oil, and alcohol when white gas or kerosene aren't available. Follow the manufacturer's instructions for using the selected fuel, as it may require changing fuel jets or burner heads.

Stoves that use pressurized gas cartridges are easy to use—just turn the valve and light—and there is less chance of a fuel flare-up. But these cartridges react to the lower temperatures of winter by putting out less heat, because the butane then does not vaporize as well. You can help out by prewarming the cartridge next to your body. Newer models burn a mixture of butane and propane, or isomers of butane, and do somewhat better at low temperatures. The problem is not as bad at greater altitudes, where lower atmospheric pressures mean higher relative pressure inside the cartridge to help vaporize the fuel. The disposable gas cartridges are expensive and heavy, and spent cartridges must be packed out. Another disadvantage of some cartridge stoves is poor stability because

of a high stance and relatively narrow base. A cook set that suspends the stove and pot combination from the tent ceiling can solve this problem.

The snow that you melt for drinking water should come from a "drinking snow" pit, well away from the designated toilet and cleaning areas. Be sure everyone understands where it is and what it is for. Collect the snow as small pot-size chunks rather than as loose snow in order to make stoking the melting pot simpler and neater. If you are cooking in the tent, the process also is easier and cleaner if you collect the snow in a sack and then just bring the sack into the tent.

Cooking in the tent

Cooking in the tent is risky; it's also a convenience and at times a necessity. The risks go from the relatively minor ones of spilling pots onto sleeping bags or increasing condensation inside the tent, to the deadly dangers of tent fires or carbon monoxide poisoning. Nevertheless, cooking inside may be required if it's so windy the stove will not operate outside, or if it's so cold the cook risks frostbite. A tent vestibule is a big advantage because it provides the protection of cooking inside, with fewer risks.

Inside or out, your stove must be set on a stable platform to insulate the tent floor or snow from the heat of the stove, and to keep it from tipping over. A fallen stove is more than a nuisance, as it may spill fuel over gear or even set a tent on fire. Also, some stoves work significantly better if the fuel is insulated from the snow. A piece of $1/4$-inch plywood is a good stove pad. A snow shovel or snow fluke also may be pressed into service as a platform.

Here are some additional tips on inside cooking:
• Light the stove outside (or near an opening so it can be tossed outside if it flares) and bring it inside only after it is running smoothly.
• Cook near the tent door or in the tent vestibule. This puts the stove near the best ventilation and lets you throw the stove outside quickly in an emergency.
• Provide plenty of ventilation. This is critical. Carbon monoxide is colorless and odorless, so you

can't detect it. It is better to err on the conservative side by cooling off the tent with too large a ventilation hole rather than risk carbon monoxide poisoning with too small an opening.

Sleeping bags

A comfortable sleeping system is critical for winter trips, when the climber may spend the greater part of each day in the sack. It's colder than summer, so you need more insulation. This can come from a heavier sleeping bag or an overbag with additional insulation. An overbag must be large enough that it does not restrict the loft of the insulation in the inner bag. A non-insulating overbag, such as a bivouac sack, provides some extra warmth and protects the main bag from spills, condensation, and snow. If you don't use any kind of overbag, it may be helpful to have a sleeping bag with a cover made of material such as Gore-Tex to help keep the bag dry and windproof.

The type of insulation you want in your sleeping bag can depend on how wet the climate is. In the mild damp cold of coastal areas, synthetic bags work well as they absorb little or no moisture. As the temperature drops, there is less moisture in the air and the high loft of down clearly excels.

A vapor-barrier liner inside the sleeping bag adds to the sleeping system's warmth, especially in cold, dry environments. As with vapor-barrier clothing, the liner adds warmth by halting evaporative heat loss from your body. Less evaporation means less water vapor condensing on the sleeping bag and, therefore, a drier bag. The liner reduces your perspiration during the night and the subsequent necessary drinking the next morning to replace the lost fluid. The liner may feel clammy next to your skin so wear a single layer of synthetic underwear, which retains very little moisture and dries quickly in the morning. As an alternative to the liner, you can wear a vapor-barrier suit (shirt and bottom). The suit provides advantages similar to the liner, but it can also be worn when you're not in the sleeping bag.

An insulated pad is a critical component of the sleeping system, as the snow is virtually an infinite heat sink held at a constant 32 degrees. Inflatable foam pads such as the Therm-a-Rest are an excellent choice. You can add a closed-cell foam pad beneath the inflatable pad for added comfort, warmth, and reliability. Two foam pads or an extra-thick foam pad are good but somewhat bulky. (Take a look at Chapter 3 for additional general information on sleeping systems.)

WINTER CLIMBING

Winter makes just about every route harder to climb than in the summer. The first winter outing is usually a humbling experience in comparison to summer expectations. The days are shorter, travel is slower, and routine tasks take more time. Allow for the short days: scale down your goals, get under way at first light, and carry a good head lamp.

You will need skis or snowshoes for support, except during the low snow of early season or the firm snow of late season. Whether you choose skis or snowshoes depends on your ability and the route. Are you a diehard skier who loves skis even if conditions are poor? Are you good enough to ski virtually any slope? Will you be moving along a broad ridge or logging road, which is good terrain for skis, or will you be traveling through forest and brush? Is the approach long but easy, where the speed of skis is a benefit? Will you encounter technical climbing, where skis would be more cumbersome to carry than compact snowshoes? Consult specialized texts on skiing or snowshoeing for details on equipment and techniques.

For additional information applicable to mountaineering in snow, see Chapters 4, 12, and 14.

Routefinding

Winter routefinding gets challenging when bad weather hides the destination or landmarks along the way. Study the map ahead of time and become familiar with the terrain you will cross. Note broad features such as ridges, ravines, streams, and changes in steepness of the slope so that when you encounter them, you'll have an idea where you are. An altimeter is a vital companion to a compass for routefinding. If you cross an obvious ravine, for example, an altimeter should be able to pinpoint your position in the ravine by giving you an elevation to check on the map.

When the visibility is good, route features often stand out more clearly than in the summer. Ledges and couloirs hold snow and show up sharply against dark surrounding rock features. Ridges or arêtes blown free of snow stand out against the white of a snow face.

Avalanche hazard often dictates changes in the usual summer route, which may lead through an active avalanche path. Heavy snowfall, warm temperatures, or wind can increase the hazard of slab and loose-snow avalanches. Ridges are safer from avalanche than gullies and broad open slopes; windward slopes are safer than leeward. Never underestimate the danger of avalanche.

Wands are a big help in finding the return route during winter's poor weather and limited visibility, and when wind-driven snow covers your tracks. (For more details on routefinding on snow, see Chapter 12.)

Climbing mixed terrain

If your winter goal is normally a summer rock climb, be prepared to climb in crampons. Although considerable rock may be showing, the surface could be slick with a thin veneer of snow or ice. Even more than in the summer, climb deliberately. Search for small holds or level spots on which the crampon points can rest. This mixed climbing rapidly dulls crampon points, but they should be able to withstand the abuse. Consider carrying a small file to sharpen points if difficult ice climbing is required after the mixed terrain.

An ice tool (axe or hammer) is useful even on a rock route. The tool can be placed in occasional ice or snow pockets and can even be hooked over the edge of rock holds. When it is not needed, holster the tool on your harness (be sure the tool is secured, perhaps by its own leash) or sling it between your back and the pack.

Protection for mixed terrain

Previous chapters have detailed the types of protection used on rock, snow, and ice. Mix them all together, however, for winter climbing and there are some additional considerations.

Given a choice between a rock anchor and a snow anchor, the rock anchor is usually the one to use. It's relatively easy to check the soundness of rock anchors; not so with most snow or ice anchors. Even a good anchor in snow or ice has less strength than one well-placed in rock.

You may have to do a good bit of digging and grooming to clear away snow and ice in order to place a piece of protection in the rock. Your hands can knock off powdery snow, but it will probably take an ice axe to clear hard snow or ice. If a crack is filled with ice, a piton may be the only possible method of protection. But keep in mind that a piton scar made in winter is just as damaging as one made in summer. Always use the least damaging yet secure anchor.

Ice screws and pickets used for protection in mixed terrain sometimes go in only partway because the snow or ice is shallow. In this situation, tie off to the protection at the surface of the snow or ice to minimize the danger that the protection will be levered out (fig. 15-4). Don't try to force an ice screw farther in than it can go, because this useless effort could shatter the ice.

Fig. 15–4. Ice screw placement in thin ice over rock

Deep snow

The conventional wisdom is that loose snow will not stay long on a steep surface. But occasionally you encounter circumstances that seem to defy the rules, such as a short slope with snow well-anchored by boulders or by a wind-sculpted snow trough. Normal step-kicking won't work because the snow is too loose, nor is delicate footwork the answer. You must use your whole body to flail your way up the slope. An ice axe placed horizontally may be the only handhold, and you move upward on your knees rather than your feet. Rarely is the effort graceful.

At times, it takes a snow shovel to literally dig a path through the snow. Alternatively, teammates may pool their energies and toss the smallest member ahead in order to consolidate the path.

EXPEDITION CLIMBING

Expedition climbing does not represent a different type or standard of climbing as much as an expansion of the time scale for a climb. A weekend trip may involve several hours or a day for the approach to the peak, while an expedition can require two or three days of air travel followed by a day or two of land travel, followed by a ten-day hike into base camp. A rest break is not a 10- or 15-minute sit down, but may be an entire day spent lounging. The actual climbing is much the same as discussed in earlier chapters and in the winter climbing section of this chapter. The main differences between expedition climbing and other mountaineering come in the logistics of tackling a remote peak, the more severe weather likely to be encountered, and the challenge of climbing at high altitude.

The scope of this chapter is expeditions of three to four weeks, on relatively accessible 20,000- to 23,000-foot peaks, such as Alaska's Mount McKinley or Peru's Huascaran. Many of the techniques and considerations are similar to those of longer expeditions to higher peaks. However, there also are major differences in permits, hiring of porters, medical requirements, extremes of altitude and cold, use of oxygen, and so forth, that are beyond the scope of this chapter.

PLANNING AND PREPARATION

In deciding what peak to try and which route to climb, you will take a lot of factors into account:

Difficulty of the route: It's generally best to choose a route well within your climbing ability because the challenges of remoteness, changeable weather, and routefinding will add to the difficulties. Until you have gone on a few expeditions, think of the trip as an opportunity to apply well-practiced climbing skills in a new environment, rather than to push the limits of your ability.

Duration of the climb: Again, be realistic. Don't try to cram a twenty-five-day route into two weeks of annual leave.

Time of year: Study information on seasonal temperatures, winds, storms, rains, and amount of daylight. Your trip will be planned far in advance, so in choosing your dates you'll have to deal with probabilities and likelihoods, and hope that the realities will measure up when the time comes.

Costs: Major costs are equipment for the climb, transportation, and other expenses on the way to the peak, and hiring porters and pack animals to haul gear to base camp. In many cases, expenses within a country are minor compared with the cost of getting there. Estimate your costs based on research about the peak and/or area.

Location: Where to go? Alaska, Mexico, the Andes of South America, Europe, Nepal, Pakistan, India, the Soviet Union, and areas of Africa all boast difficult, remote peaks. The experience of traveling in a remote or foreign land is often one of the most enjoyable and rewarding aspects of an expedition.

After choosing your peak, research the mountain and its routes. Talk to climbers who have been there, look for write-ups in the journals of the American Alpine Club and of climbing organizations in Canada and Europe, and seek out guidebooks and stories in climbing magazines. Get all possible details on logistics, potential problems, where to buy fuel, what foods are available, objective hazards on the mountain, and so forth.

Have a backup route in mind in case the main objective is scratched because of avalanche hazard, bad weather, inability of some party members to continue, or any other reason. If you've chosen a highly technical route up your mountain, consider acclimating by climbing the standard route first, then taking on the tougher challenge.

Find out what permits and approvals are necessary. It helps to have typewritten itineraries, climbing resumes of party members, equipment lists, and medical information in hand ahead of time and while traveling to the peak. The appearance of good organization impresses bureaucrats the world around.

Choosing the team

Choosing a compatible team is the first step toward an enjoyable experience. Expedition climbing is full of stress, and climbers can be taxed to their physical and mental limits. Climbing literature abounds with "climb and tell" accounts of expeditions in which, it seems, team members despised their fellow climbers; you don't want your expedition to end up being another.

The skill of your team must, of course, be equal to the demands of the climb. Climbing with people of similar technical ability may improve compatibility. Team members need personalities that are compatible with each other, and must be able to live harmoniously with others in close quarters under stressful conditions. The climbers should agree on the philosophy of the trip in terms of climbing style, environmental impact, and degree of acceptable risk.

It's important to agree on leadership before the trip gets under way. If all climbers are of roughly equal experience, democratic decision-making usually works well. If one climber is clearly more experienced, that person can be given the leadership role. Even with a single leader, functional areas such as finance, food, medicine, and equipment should be delegated to others to lessen the leader's load and to keep everyone involved and

informed. This also helps build expedition leaders for the future. (You might consider taking a guided climb if this is your first expedition or if you lack capable partners.)

The number of climbers in the expedition depends partly on what route you've chosen. A party of two or four climbers may be best on technically difficult routes because of the efficiency of two-person rope teams and the limited space at bivouac sites. However, climbing with a very small team means that if one person becomes ill or cannot continue, the entire team may have to abandon the climb.

When the route itself does not determine the optimum party size, logistics becomes the deciding factor. As the number of climbers increases, issues of transportation, food, lodging, and equipment become more complicated. The advantage is that parties of six or eight have strength and reserve capacity. If one climber doesn't continue, the rest of the party has a better chance to go on with the expedition. And larger parties usually are better able to carry out self-rescue than smaller teams. However, the logistics of an expedition with more than eight members can become more burdensome than many climbers are willing to accept.

Establishing a climbing style

Do you plan to climb "expedition style" or "alpine style" or somewhere in between? There's a big difference, and it's a question you need to resolve early, based on the route, the size and strength of your party, and the preference of the climbers.

Traditional expedition climbing style involves multiple carries between camps, during which food, fuel, and supplies are ferried to higher camps. Technically difficult sections of the route are often protected with fixed lines—ropes anchored in place to minimize danger during repeated trips up and down. It's a slow and measured campaign for the summit.

Alpine climbing style usually means moving camps up the mountain in a continuous push, so that the route is climbed only once. All equipment and supplies are carried with the team at all times.

It's a light, quick bid for the top.

Expedition-style ascents take longer because more time is spent hauling loads between camps. They are heavier because more food, fuel, and perhaps fixed line must be carried, and more costly because of the greater time, equipment, and food. Alpine-style trips tend to be riskier as there is less margin of safety in case of bad weather or injury.

The climbing itinerary

Once you've researched your mountain, you can set up an itinerary that makes a good estimate of the number of days to allow for the approach to the peak, for carrying loads up the mountain, for climbing, for sitting out storms and for resting. An average elevation gain of 1,000 feet per day is good for acclimatization, and this figure should be correlated where possible with good campsites. Rest days built into the schedule provide time for mental and physical recuperation, equipment sorting, and such. They can also serve as a time buffer for unplanned delays caused by storms, illness, or other problems. If a storm hits, try to reschedule a rest period for the same time, making the best of a bad day.

For moving camps expedition-style up the mountain, double carries are generally adequate on a three-week climb. The first carry hauls food, supplies and equipment to the site of the next camp. The second carry involves tearing down the current camp and resetting it at the next site. On bigger mountains, camps may need to be stocked pyramid style, with many carries between camps early in the trip and few if any carries between later camps.

When repeated carries are necessary, each load is usually cached at the next camp while the climbers go back down for more. Plan to set up a protected cache to avoid damage from the elements and from animals. Dig a hole, cover it with something an animal can't get through, such as a sled or snowshoes, and pile snow on top. Mark the cache with long wands. But beware. Ravens on popular peaks have learned to identify caches, so place the wands a little distance away and smooth the surface above the cache.

Food and equipment

On expeditions to the remote mountains of the world, you either take it with you or you do without it. Having the necessary equipment, in working order, is much more critical than on a weekend climb where home is a short drive away. Your expedition needs a complete equipment list, both group and personal, worked out in discussions with all team members. (See the sample equipment list at the end of this chapter.)

Supplies for the group

• Food

Food constitutes the heaviest single category of weight carried by an expedition. But who's complaining? Food provides the necessary fuel for your body to carry loads and climb the route, and it also can serve as one of the great pleasures of the trip.

Every climber has preferences in food, so conduct a team survey of strong food likes and dislikes before planning menus. Combat the danger of carrying unpopular foods by providing lots of variety. If some team members don't like one item, there should be several others they will find tasty, or at least palatable. A condiment and seasoning kit with the likes of Tabasco sauce, spices, soy sauce, margarine, and mustard will add interest to bland packaged foods and perhaps salvage the unpopular foods.

Although fats have the highest caloric density (9 calories per gram), carbohydrates (4.1 calories per gram) are easiest to digest and provide the quickest energy. Proteins have about the same caloric density as carbohydrates, but are not as easy to digest and are usually accompanied by substantially more fat. A reasonable expeditionary diet has about 50 percent of its calories from carbohydrates, 30 percent from fat, and 20 percent from protein.

Plan to provide about 35 ounces (roughly 2 1/4 pounds) of food per person per day. With no waste, 35 ounces would provide more than 5,000 calories. In reality—because of packaging, non-nutritive fiber, and the food's irreducible water—the food will provide only about 3,900 calories per day. Experience will tell whether this is just right, too much, or not enough. Too much food means extra-heavy loads between camps and possibly a slower trip. Too little means you will begin losing weight. On a trip of three or four weeks, weight loss shouldn't cause a problem. But on longer expeditions, too much weight loss may effect the team's strength and endurance.

Food is your major controllable weight factor. As you sit at home planning menus and calculating energy expenditures, you'll be tempted to throw into the menu an extra cracker at breakfast, an extra candy bar during the day, or an extra cocoa at dinner. Resist this temptation at all cost. Unless the extra food never gets past base camp, it will eventually find its way onto the climbers' backs or into their sleds, slowing their pace while fatiguing them faster. If you are planning a twenty-day trip, take food for twenty days, not twenty-one. On unplanned storm days, you will simply have to stretch your rations. Food can always be stretched on an expedition, and it's easier than suffering the consequences of overloaded packs.

You can plan foods for early in the trip that are different from those for later as you get up on the mountain. Candidates for lower elevations and warmer climes are foods that are time-consuming to prepare, such as pancakes; items that suffer from freezing, such as cheese and peanut butter; and canned foods. Foods carried to higher altitudes should be very light and require a minimum of preparation, such as freeze-dried items, instant noodles, instant rice, and potatoes. Try to eat local food on approach marches and at base camp so you don't tire too early of expedition food.

Packaging and organizing food is an important element of planning. Take the food you've bought for the expedition and get rid of as much of the commercial packaging as possible. Repackage the food to minimize this packaging, reducing the weight you have to carry in and the garbage to be carried out. Keep the preparation instructions from the packaging material. You should prepackage rations into person-days (put in one bag the food for one person for one day), or into group-days (put in one bag the food for the entire group for one day), or into tent-days (put in one bag the food for one tent for one day). However you do it, measure the food into the correct portions and label it. Clear plastic sacks help organize the food while keeping the contents visible.

Adequate hydration is the first line of defense against altitude sickness. Bring lots of soups, hot drinks, and cold-drink mixes to help motivate you into drinking the necessary fluids. Contaminated water plagues nearly every part of the world. The expedition kitchen must be able to furnish adequate water for everyone through chemical decontamination, filtering, or boiling.

• Fuel

Fuel cannot be carried on airlines so it must be available at your destination. Multifuel stoves may be good insurance in foreign countries where white gas is not readily available. Even with a multifuel stove, check the fuel's compatibility with the stove before heading into the mountains. If you're using kerosene or a similar low-volatility fuel, be sure to buy alcohol or gas for priming the stove. The cleanliness of fuel in foreign countries is always questionable. Bring a filter and filter all fuel before using, and clean the stove often. Plan on using between $1/4$ pint and $1/2$ pint of fuel per person per day, depending on how much water must be boiled for purification or melted from snow.

Fuel containers are usually supplied in Alaska or Canada, but you must provide your own elsewhere. Aluminum containers as small as 1 liter are fine if you don't need to carry much fuel. For larger quantities, bring 1-gallon gas cans or sturdy approved plastic fuel containers. They should be new, as airlines object to containers with residual fuel vapors. Plastic bottles sold in foreign countries have a reputation for leaking.

• Community equipment

For communal cooking, take pots large enough for the group meal courses and for melting large amounts of snow. Filling water bottles is a common activity, so pots must be easy to pour from (a 2-quart coffee pot works well). Bring at least one cook pot per stove. Bring a metal gripper to use on pots that lack handles or bails, or use wool gloves as potholders. (Be careful using synthetic gloves, which will melt if they get too hot.)

To save a bit of weight, the party can carry an altimeter and a compass as pieces of group equipment rather than having each climber carry separate ones. Also among group equipment are wands, used for marking routes, camp perimeters, gear caches, and snow shelters. Carry long wands if there's a chance of significant snowfall. Tents are also community equipment. See the section on winter camping earlier in this chapter for guidelines on tents.

The party may carry radios to get weather information, call for emergency help, or communicate between climbers at different locations. The main choices are citizens' band, marine band, or FM. You'll have to do some investigating to determine both the technical feasibility and the legality of their use.

- Community climbing gear

The route determines the climbing gear you need. A route that involves only glacier travel may require just the basics: rope, crampons, and ice axe. Technical routes can take the whole gamut of equipment, from ice screws, snow flukes, and pickets to nuts and pitons.

Depending on the style and organization of the trip, climbing gear can be personal or community. On a technical route where climbers operate in self-sufficient pairs, climbing gear should be personal or left to each rope team to work out. In other cases, virtually all climbing gear—carabiners, runners, screws, and so forth—can be treated as group equipment. The choice is up to the team. Certain pieces of climbing gear, such as crampons and ice axes, are indispensable, and a large party may want to carry spares as insurance against equipment failure or loss.

The decision on what ropes to take also depends on the route and its difficulty. For technical pitches, you'll use use either a single rope (10.5 or 11 millimeters in diameter) or double or twin ropes (each 8 or 9 millimeters). On a glacier route, a single 9-millimeter rope may be adequate. Keep in mind, however, that an expedition puts extraordinary wear and tear on the rope because of its daily

use in bright sunlight. The team also needs to decide how much rope to bring for fixed line along the route. Fixed line is usually a polypropylene braided rope or a nylon kernmantle rope. Polypro is lightest and cheapest, but kernmantle is better for areas of high use.

- Repair kit

Equipment failure is common under the prolonged and rugged demands of an expedition, so count on needing to repair or substitute for failed gear. Put together a comprehensive repair kit, keeping in mind the relative importance of each piece of equipment to the progress of the group.

Among the repair-kit items should be:

- Tape. Gray duct tape seems to be the universal repair favorite, but other tapes, such as ripstop fabric tape or filament tape, are useful.
- Sewing kit for permanent repairs or those beyond the capability of tape.
- Extra stove parts and the tools to disassemble the stove.
- Tent-pole splices or extra tent poles. While the tent body or fly can be patched with tape, broken tent poles must be repaired or replaced.
- Extra crampon parts, such as screws, nuts, and connecting bars, and the necessary tools.
- Patch kit for inflatable foam pads that spring leaks.
- Also: crampon file, pliers, wire, accessory cord, pack buckle.

- First-aid kit

An expedition usually carries a comprehensive first-aid kit, which is assembled after everyone in the party has had input into the selections. Keep in mind the isolation of the peak, the specific medical conditions of team members, and their medical knowledge. Discuss your group's medical needs with a doctor who is familiar with mountaineering.

The first-aid kit may include such specialized or prescription items as a strong painkiller, antibiotics, a dental repair kit, and a suture kit. Be sure to carry a first-aid manual.

Personal gear

Expedition climbers need clothing and sleeping

bags that can stand up to prolonged use under severe conditions. The clothing and equipment suitable for winter climbing, outlined earlier in this chapter, works well for expeditions. The desired comfort rating for your sleeping system varies with the climate and season, but a good general rating for expeditions is about –30 degrees Fahrenheit (about –35 degrees Celsius).

Every person on an expedition team needs a big pack, with a capacity between 5,500 and 7,000 cubic inches, because there are times you will be called on to carry ''impossible'' loads. The pack also must be comfortable while you are wearing a climbing harness.

You may want mechanical ascenders, rather than prusik slings, both for crevasse rescue and for protection while climbing with a fixed line. The ascenders permit one-way movement by gripping or squeezing the line when your weight is on them but letting you move move them when they are unweighted. The ascenders, under such brand names as Jumar, Clog, and Gibbs, are necessary to handle the large, heavy expedition loads involved in any crevasse rescue. On fixed line, the prusik knots are unsafe because of the time required to unfasten and reattach them past each anchor you encounter on the way up or down.

Although two ascenders are the norm, one plus a prusik sling can work if you need to cut down on weight. Regardless of the choice, make sure the system can be operated while you're wearing bulky gloves or mittens.

Other items of personal gear to consider:

• Prescription glasses. Carry an extra set of prescription sunglasses.
• Journal. An expedition can make you introspective. A journal made of waterproof paper (look under surveyor supplies at a book store or stationery supply store) and some pencils can help pass the time.
• Books. You can catch up on reading while waiting for flights, or during rest days and storm days in the field. Coordinate your selection of books with other team members to avoid repetition and provide variety.

• Personal hygiene. On cold-weather trips where water is at a premium, chemical wash/wipes can provide a refreshing sponge bath.
• Pee bottle. During storms and cold nights, the pee bottle eliminates those unpleasant traipses to the latrine. Be sure the bottle has a secure top.

Physical and mental conditioning

Training for an expedition involves both physical and mental preparation. For the body, emphasize cardiovascular training and strength training equally. Cardiovascular conditioning is important for physical activity at high altitudes. Powerful leg muscles are needed to walk heavy loads up the mountain, and upper-body strength is needed to hoist and carry the large expeditionary packs.

Climbing itself is the best training. Climb often and in all weather conditions, carrying a heavy pack. If you can go on a typical two- to three-day climb packing gear for camping and climbing, gaining 3,000 to 5,000 feet per day, and feel you still have plenty of physical reserves, you're probably sufficiently fit for an expedition. An expedition climber needs the endurance to carry packs of 40 to 60 pounds (sometimes in addition to pulling a sled) for an elevation gain of 2,000 to 3,000 feet every day, day after day.

Your mind and spirit also need to get into shape for the rigors of an expedition. Learn about the special challenges of expedition travel and prepare yourself to accept them. Otherwise, you can be overwhelmed by the size and remoteness of the climbing area or lose your good spirits during a long storm or a bout with the flu.

Success on an expedition often goes to the person who has a greater desire or will to succeed, even though he or she may be physically weaker than another climber. It takes more than physical strength to deal with extreme cold, sickness, cramped quarters, poor food, conflict with teammates, the stress of technical climbing, and the lethargy brought on by high altitude.

You can work on both your physical and mental conditioning by seeking out experiences that come as close as possible to what you expect on the expedition. Prepare for the expedition by going on winter climbs and on longer trips. You may not be able to alter such objective conditions as cold or illness, but you can learn to exercise a great deal of mental control over your response and attitude toward them.

Before you leave home

Food and gear must be packed and frequently repacked to accommodate the various transportation modes used to get to the mountain. Become familiar with the requirements that face your expedition, such as airline regulations on bag sizes and weights, or muleteer requirements on load balancing. Keep lists of what went into each bag so any item can be retrieved readily. Before leaving home, plan travel arrangements for each leg of the journey and make reservations where possible. Try to work with a travel agent who has booked trips to the region before.

Be as healthy as possible when you leave town because, in all likelihood, you won't get better while traveling. For foreign travel, find out well in advance what inoculations are needed. Have a dental exam and leave no dental care pending. To stay healthy once you get to your destination, plan on purifying all water and be cautious about eating unpeeled fresh vegetables or fruit, dairy products, and uncooked food. And through all the complicated hurry and scurry of getting ready for a big expedition, try to remember that your goal is to get away from it all and climb a mountain.

EXPEDITIONARY CLIMBING TECHNIQUES

Expedition mountaineering calls for the rock, snow, ice, and winter climbing techniques that have been covered throughout this book. An expedition can add a couple of new techniques to your climbing repertoire: hauling sleds and using fixed lines.

Haul sleds

Expedition members often pull sleds or haul bags behind them on long glacier approaches as a way to move the loads of gear and supplies (fig. 15-5). A climber can transport a normal load in a backpack in addition to pulling a sled with another pack's worth of gear. Commercial haul sleds are available, with zippered covers to hold the load, a waist harness for you to wear, and rigid aluminum poles connecting the sled to the harness. These

Fig. 15–5. Sled and climber rigged for glacier travel

poles help control the sled when traversing or going downhill.

A cheaper but usable alternative is a plastic children's sled, with holes punched in the sides as rope attachment points. Load your gear into a duffel bag and tie it to the sled. Perlon (5 to 7 millimeters) is used to pull the sled, and most climbers prefer to attach the perlon to their pack, not their climbing harness. A final alternative is to drag a haul bag, constructed of durable, slick material to help it slide over the snow. A swivel connecter attaching the haul line to the haul bag will keep the rolling of the bag from putting twists in the line.

As the route steepens, the amount of weight you can pull in a sled decreases, and it can't be used at all on steep technical climbing terrain. Haul bags may then be what you need. (See Chapter 11 for techniques for using haul bags on technical routes.)

No special trick is involved in towing a sled behind you. It simply takes steadfast pulling. Where it can get complicated is during roped travel on glaciers, where any fall into a crevasse is made more treacherous by having the sled plunge down behind you. Even if you aren't injured by the plummeting sled, rescue is more difficult with the need to deal with you, your pack (perhaps weighing 60 pounds) and the sled (carrying another 50 pounds or so).

You can minimize the danger of getting hit by the sled during a crevasse fall with a simple preventive technique. Just take your climbing rope where it runs past the sled and tie it snugly with a clove hitch to a carabiner at the rear of the sled. In a crevasse fall, you will drop in, followed by the sled. But the sled will be stopped above you by the tie-in to the climbing rope. If you are using a hauling tether to the sled (instead of rigid aluminum poles), be sure the tether is long enough so you are well beyond the reach of the sled as it hangs from the climbing rope. This technique depends on having a team member behind you on the rope to arrest the fall of both you and the sled, so it won't work for the last climber on a rope. The last person either assumes the extra risk, or the team can decide to haul only two sleds for each three climbers.

Crevasse rescue

It takes some special procedures for crevasse rescue if you are hauling a sled (fig. 15-6), beyond those methods spelled out in Chapter 13. Imagine you have just fallen into a crevasse. The sled, attached to the climbing rope, dangles above you. Here is how you can help yourself get out.

First of all, get your weight onto the climbing rope. As you dangle in the crevasse, your weight may be on the sled haul line (or towing poles, if you are using a commercial sled). Transfer your weight to the climbing rope by standing in slings attached to your ascending system (mechanical ascenders, prusik slings, or a combination).

Then disconnect the attachment from you to the sled. If you are using a haul line attached to your pack, simply take off the pack and let it hang from the line.

Once free of the sled, you can try to rescue yourself or wait for your climbing mates to get you out. If you start up the climbing rope on your own, the sled probably will cause some complication. You may need to ascend around the climbing-rope knot that holds the sled. In this case, remove and reattach your ascenders above the knot, one at a time.

You may also need to untie from the climbing rope in order to move past the sled and reach the lip of the crevasse. To make it easier to disconnect from the climbing rope, many sled-pullers travel with the rope clipped to a locking carabiner on their harness, rather than tying directly to the harness itself. If you must unclip from the climbing rope, use extreme caution to ensure that the ascenders are secure.

Your fall into the crevasse can also mean extra effort for your teammates if they must pull you out. If you can't disconnect yourself from the sled or if there is no extra rescue rope available, they must haul both you and the sled at the same time. They will have to use a Z-pulley system to get the most mechanical advantage in pulling on the climbing rope. Far preferable is to use a spare rope to pull you out, and to then pull the sled out on the climbing rope it is already attached to.

Fig. 15–6. Crevasse self-rescue with sled

Fixed lines

A fixed line is simply a rope that is anchored to the route and left in place. It allows safe, quick travel up and down a difficult stretch. Climbers protect themselves by tying into a mechanical ascender on the fixed line, eliminating the need for time-consuming belays. If you fall while climbing next to the fixed line, the ascender cam locks onto the line and holds the fall.

It's also possible in some cases to climb a fixed line directly by hanging from slings attached to two ascenders and moving them methodically upward. However, fixed lines are not generally used for direct aid in the situations discussed in this chapter.

The fixed line simplifies the movement of people and equipment, especially when numerous trips are required, and permits less-experienced climbers to follow a route. Fixed lines have been common on large expeditions to major peaks to provide protection on long stretches of exposed climbing or to protect porters while they make carries from camp to camp in the face of such obstacles as icefalls, glaciers, and steep rock or ice. The lines make it possible for climbers and porters to carry heavier loads than they could safely carry without them.

Fixed lines are sometimes used as a siege tactic on difficult rock and ice faces, with climbers retreating down the lines each night to a base camp, then reascending the next day to push the route a little farther. They also come into play on continuous multiday aid climbs of big walls, where the second climber follows on the line, removing protection and hauling up equipment. The climbers do not retreat down this line, but move it upward as they go. Thus it becomes a "moving" fixed line, only one rope length long.

Some climbers argue that fixing ropes is an outmoded technique, no longer required to climb any mountain or route. This is not the majority view, but the technique should not be abused. Fixed lines should not be used to supplement the climbing ability of an expedition team. If many of the climbers don't have the ability to climb a route without help from a fixed line, find an alternate route.

Fixed lines should not be added on popular routes or in regions where they are not normally used.

In the past, climbers often abandoned fixed lines when a climb was done. It was not uncommon to find several lines, one on top of the next, frozen into a route. This is no longer acceptable in a time of increasing environmental awareness, and each party needs to make a commitment to remove its fixed lines.

Equipment for fixed lines

To set up and use fixed lines, you need rope, anchors, and ascenders. Climbing ropes don't make good fixed lines because they are designed to stretch under a load, an undesirable characteristic in a fixed line. What you want is a more static rope, one with low elongation under load. Nylon is the most common material for fixed lines, though polypropylene and Dacron also are used. Kernmantle construction is best, though braided ropes can be used.

The diameter of fixed lines usually varies between 7 and 10 millimeters, with the size depending on the terrain and the amount of use the line is expected to get. Try to carry your fixed line in long lengths. The ropes are usually manufactured in lengths of somewhere between 300 and 1,000 feet, depending on rope diameter.

To anchor the fixed line to the mountain, employ any attachment points that are normally used in belaying and climbing on rock or ice: pitons, chocks, natural outcrops, ice screws, pickets, and snow flukes or other deadman anchors.

A mechanical ascender attached from your harness to the fixed line is the most efficient means of protecting you from a fall as you climb next to the line. Prusik knots can be dangerous because it is so time-consuming to untie and retie them as you move past an anchor, especially while wearing mittens. Prusiks are OK in an emergency or on very short sections of rope.

Anchors for fixed lines

Every fixed line needs an anchor at the bottom to hold the rope in place while climbers ascend, and a bombproof anchor at the top. Mark the location of the anchors with wands so you can find them after a snow storm.

Place a series of intermediate anchors between the bottom and top of the fixed line. The fixed line is tied off at each anchor so that every section of line is independent of the others. This permits more than one climber at a time on the line. In deciding where to place the intermediate anchors, take several considerations into account. Place an anchor at points where you would like to change direction of the line or prevent pendulum falls. An anchor at the top of difficult sections of the route is helpful. If possible, place the intermediate anchors at natural resting spots, making it easier to stand and move the ascenders past the anchor.

Always bury or cover snow and ice anchors and inspect them regularly for possible failure from creep or melting. Also keep a close eye on any rock anchors capable of creeping or loosening. Place anchors at locations that help keep the line from rubbing on rough or sharp surfaces, or pad the line at points of abrasion. Even small amounts of wear can multiply into dangerous weak spots on fixed lines, which usually use lightweight rope. Falls will also damage the line. After any fall on the line, inspect it for damage and check the anchors for any indications of possible failure.

How to set up fixed lines

There are many variations in how to set fixed line, each appropriate for certain conditions, climber preferences, types of line and so forth. The key is to think through a system prior to starting out and if possible test and refine it before you actually need it. Here are three possible methods:

1. The most common way is for two or three climbers to ascend the route—using a standard climbing rope to belay one another or to establish a running belay—and setting the fixed line as they climb. They can carry the whole spool of line with them and let it out as they ascend, tying it off at each intermediate anchor along the way. Or they can just pull the end of the line up with them as they ascend, clipping the line into each anchor with carabiners. Then after anchoring the top, they can go back down, tying off the line at each anchor as they

go. In either case, it can be a big job. Carrying the spool of line is difficult, but so is pulling up on the end of the line and trying to overcome the tremendous friction that develops as it travels through carabiners and over the route.

2. The entire fixed line also can be set on descent. The material for the fixed line must first be carried to the top of the route, of course. Tie the line into a bombproof anchor at the top. Then rappel or downclimb to tie the line off at intermediate anchors. These anchors can be the ones that were placed on the earlier ascent of the route, although new ones can be added just for the fixed line.

3. You can also use the fixed line as your climbing rope at the same time you are setting it in place. Use the line just as you would a normal climbing rope, clipping it into anchors as you climb, belayed from below. At the top, tie the fixed line into a bombproof anchor, and then it is ready to be tied off at each intermediate anchor. The problem with this method is that fixed line is usually thinner and has less stretch than climbing ropes. If you fall, there's a bigger chance the line could break. Even if it holds, the limited stretch in the line would make for a hard fall. An additional drawback is that the friction on the line as you pull it up through more and more carabiners will probably limit the maximum length of the run. This method is best saved for short sections of fixed line or for instances where a standard climbing rope is being used as a fixed line.

Attaching fixed line to anchors

For the final tie-off of the fixed line at each intermediate anchor, use a clove hitch or figure-8 knot in the line. Tie a sling directly to the anchor and clip a figure-8 loop or clove hitch into a carabiner attached to that sling (fig. 15-7a). Or better yet, minimize use of carabiners and have one less link in the system by retying the sling directly through the figure-8 loop (fig. 15-7b).

Ascending

Ascending with a fixed line simply involves

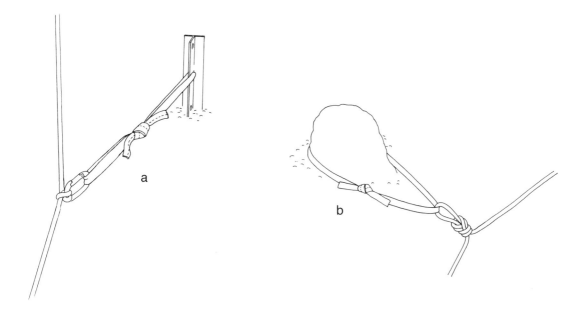

Fig. 15–7. Intermediate, fixed anchors: a, anchor with carabiners in system; b, anchor without carabiners.

climbing as usual, except that your harness is attached by a sling to the mechanical ascender on the line in case you fall (fig. 15-8).

Start by tying a sling from the ascender to your seat harness where you normally tie in with the climbing rope. (A less desirable way is to clip the sling into a locking carabiner attached to the harness.) Make the sling short so the ascender won't be out of reach if you fall. If you're climbing a near-vertical section or have a heavy pack, you may want to pass the sling through your chest harness as well to prevent tipping upside down in a fall.

Then attach the ascender to the fixed line, following the specific directions for your brand of ascender. The ascender should be oriented so that a fall will cause it to clamp the rope. It should slide easily up the line, but lock tight when pulled down. Test it before starting upward and also check the fittings on your seat harness.

You should attach a carabiner from the ascender sling or a separate sling to the fixed line to serve as a safety link as you move upward. If you fall and

the ascender fails, the safety carabiner will slide down the rope but stop at the next anchor below and arrest your fall.

At each intermediate anchor, you have to remove the ascender from the fixed line and reattach it beyond the knot. This is the most dangerous moment in fixed-line travel, particularly if conditions are severe and you are exhausted. Be sure the safety carabiner stays on the line while the ascender is detached. Some ascenders can be configured so the safety carabiner can be moved and reattached above the anchor first, followed by the ascender. This order offers more security than moving the ascender first. Another safety option is to briefly clip yourself into the anchor as you relocate the ascender.

Whatever your procedure, it's urgent that you think it through in advance and practice it on a good day so you can perform it reliably under the worst possible conditions.

More than one climber can use a fixed line at the same time as long as there is at least one anchor between each climber. Also be sure that a fall by

Fig. 15–8. Mechanical ascender attachment to fixed line: a, set up for normal movement; b, passing an anchor, move ascender separately from safety carabiner.

any climber would not cause rope movement, rockfall, or other activity that could endanger anyone else.

Descending

Climbing down with a fixed line is similar to climbing up. Again attach the ascender sling to your harness, then attach the ascender to the fixed line exactly the same as for ascending. Double-check that the ascender locks onto the rope when you pull down on it, and that it will be within reach if you end up hanging from it after a fall. Attach the safety carabiner.

Begin your descent. As you climb downward, you will be moving the ascender down the rope to stay with you. Use a light grip on the ascender release so that you can let go of it instantly to permit the ascender to grab the rope if you fall. It's natural to try to hang onto something if you lose your balance, but the last thing you want to grab hold of at that moment is the ascender release.

Take extreme care as you climb past anchors, removing and reattaching the ascender. As in climbing up, never detach the ascender and the safety carabiner at the same time. Again, you can temporarily clip into the anchor while you relocate the ascender. On steep sections of fixed line, rappelling the fixed line may be a good alternative to downclimbing.

Removing fixed lines

Exhausted mountaineers at the end of a grueling climb often find it easier to abandon gear, garbage, and fixed line to the mercies of the mountain. This kind of behavior has become less and less acceptable, and expeditions now are learning to approach their climbs with a commitment to removing all signs of their passage.

Removing fixed lines will be easier if you keep it in mind as you plan where to put them up in the first place. In some cases you may be able to use a ''moving'' fixed line, removing it and moving it higher as you ascend the mountain, then descending via a safer route. If you are leaving the mountain and going down a fixed route for the last time, plan a downclimbing or rappelling procedure, or a combination of the two, that will permit the party to remove the fixed line.

What applies to fixed line also applies to all the other odds and ends of the expedition. Everything that goes in has got to come back out. Crevasses can't be used as garbage dumps because between wind and hungry ravens, the contents can end up strewn up and down the glacier. You can set fire to burnable garbage, but haul the ashes out. For human waste, set up a group latrine at each camp. In an exception to the use of crevasses, you can line the latrine with plastic garbage bags and then dispose of the waste in a deep crevasse.

EXPEDITION WEATHER

You need to become something of an amateur weather forecaster on an expedition because your safety and success are so closely bound to nature's moods. When you get to the climbing area, add to your knowledge of local weather patterns by talking to other climbers and to people who live there. Find out the direction of the prevailing winds. Ask about rain and storms. On the mountain, become a student of weather patterns. Your altimeter can serve as a barometer to signal weather changes.

Take clues from the clouds. Cirrus clouds (mare's tails) warn of a front bringing precipitation within the next 24 hours. Lenticular clouds (cloud caps) mean high winds. A rapidly descending cloud cap signals that bad weather is coming. And if you climb into a cloud cap, expect high winds and poor visibility. Be prepared for the fact that big mountains typically have storms and winds to match. Wait storms out if you can because of the risk inherent in descending under bad conditions. If it looks like you'll be stuck for some time, start

rationing food.

Fair weather poses problems too. If it's hot and solar radiation is intensified by protected glaciers, the result can be collapsing snow bridges, crevasse movement, and increased icefall. Then it's best to climb at night, when temperatures are lowest and snow and ice are most stable.

MEDICAL CONDITIONS RELATED TO HIGH ALTITUDE

Expedition climbing and a great deal of other mountaineering takes you to altitudes where your body no longer feels at home. Every climber is affected to one degree or other by the reduced oxygen of higher elevations. It often causes acute mountain sickness, and it can lead to the life-threatening conditions of high altitude pulmonary edema and high altitude cerebral edema. Frostbite is another danger, though it's not limited to high altitudes. It's important to learn how to prevent these conditions, and how to recognize and treat them when they occur. This chapter offers some general guidelines on these maladies, but consult your first-aid book, specialized texts, or physicians familiar with mountaineering for detailed information.

Altitude sickness (acute mountain sickness)

When you ascend rapidly to an altitude you're not accustomed to, your system works to adjust to the new conditions. Breathing becomes more rapid to extract enough oxygen from the thinner air, and the blood increases its proportion of oxygen-carrying red corpuscles. Climbing slowly and steadily upward, climbers routinely suffer uncomfortable symptoms from moving into this new environment. First comes a general malaise and loss of appetite, then headache, followed by increasing weakness and lessening of interest in the climb. If you continue on at that point, there's often increased apathy, nausea, dizziness, and sleepiness. A retreat to lower elevations usually brings about rapid improvement.

Symptoms of altitude sickness (mountain sickness) can occur at relatively low altitudes. Some people feel dizzy or tired or experience palpitations when riding in a car at 8,000 feet or so. Climbers generally have more time to acclimatize and, except for shortness of breath, usually feel only minor effects until after they reach 12,000 feet or more. In regions such as the Pacific Northwest, where climbers live at sea level yet ascend to over 14,000 feet for a weekend climb of Mount Rainier, altitude sickness of greater or lesser severity is the rule rather than the exception.

You can help moderate the more severe symptoms of altitude sickness by some relatively simple techniques. In ascending, use the rest step to give your leg muscles mini-rests all the way up the mountain and help you maintain measured, methodical breathing. Take occasional full rest stops with forced deep breathing. Drink lots of water and keep nourishment up by snacking often. Follow a program of careful acclimatization (outlined later in this chapter).

Medical experts and specialized texts can provide information on the current use of drugs in combatting altitude sickness. Two prescription drugs—Diamox and dexamethasone—are commonly used to aid in prevention and treatment of altitude sickness. They are not a substitute for proper acclimatization, or for immediate descent if you get sick.

High-altitude pulmonary edema and cerebral edema

High-altitude pulmonary edema is the leakage of blood into the lungs, which restricts the air sacs (alveoli) in exchanging oxygen and carbon dioxide in the blood. Pulmonary edema rarely occurs in healthy people below 9,000 feet. The average elevation at which it strikes in the United States is 12,000 feet, and the level of onset varies for mountain ranges in other parts of the world.

Early symptoms of pulmonary edema are similar to those of pneumonia, although it is not precipitated by an infection and there is no fever. Within 12 to 36 hours after reaching high altitude, the victim of pulmonary edema experiences extreme

weakness, shortness of breath, nausea, vomiting, very rapid pulse (120 to 160), cyanosis (bluish color) of the fingernails, face and lips, noisy breathing which progresses to moist crackling breath sounds, and irritative coughing which produces a frothy white or pink sputum and later blood.

If untreated, the victim rapidly moves into the final phase characterized by unconsciousness and bubbles in the mouth or nose, and death will follow. The early symptoms may be mistaken for mountain sickness or fatigue, or may pass unnoticed during the night, with the morning finding the victim unconscious and in the final phase.

High-altitude cerebral edema is the accumulation of fluid in the brain. Symptoms begin with a severe, relentless headache resulting from pressure due to the swelling of brain tissue. They advance to difficulties with physical coordination, slurred speech, irrational behavior, collapse, and eventually death.

For both pulmonary and cerebral edema, you need to be alert to symptoms in yourself and others. The most effective first aid is rapid evacuation to lower altitude or constant administration of oxygen. Descending is the only way to recover, with a rapid descent of 3,000 feet usually bringing marked improvement. If the victim exhibits only minor symptoms, it may be OK to spend a few days at lower elevations and then go back up. But a climber who demonstrates advanced signs should not return to high altitude, as it takes weeks to recover from edemas.

Frostbite

Frostbite is a concern at high altitudes because of the cold environment and because reduced oxygen means your body is less efficient at generating internal warmth, making hands and feet more susceptible to freezing.

Frostbite is freezing of the tissues, and most commonly affects toes, fingers, and face. It occurs when an extremity loses heat faster than it can be replaced by the circulating blood, or it may result from direct exposure to extreme cold or high wind. Damp feet can freeze when moisture conducts heat away from the skin and destroys the insulating value of socks and boots. With continued cold or inactivity, circulation to the extremities is steadily reduced, accelerating the freezing process. If you're using good mountaineering clothing and equipment, frostbite is not likely to occur.

An area of superficial frostbite looks white or gray. Surface skin feels hard, but the underlying tissue will be soft. As the frostbite intensifies, the affected area becomes hard, cold, and insensitive.

You can warm superficially frostbitten areas by placing them against warm skin. Put your feet against a companion's abdomen or armpits. Warm your fingers in your own armpits. During rewarming, large blisters may appear on the surface, as well as in the underlying tissue. Two important cautions. You must not raise the temperature of the frostbitten area much above body temperature, such as by warming near a fire. And never rub the injured part, especially not with snow. The additional cooling and the abrasive action further damage devitalized tissues. Misguided efforts to give speedy relief invariably increase the injury.

You can thaw extensive or deep frostbite, in which the affected area is white, has no feeling, and appears deeply frozen. Immerse the damaged area in water that is at a temperature between 99 and 104 degrees Fahrenheit until it is thawed. But do not start the thawing unless you are sure you can thaw the part completely and without interruption. It's better to wait for medical help than risk incomplete thawing or refreezing. Sometimes it's better to make no attempt to thaw frozen feet until after you retreat from the mountains and can get transportation and medical aid. If you leave your feet frozen, it's still possible to walk on them and suffer little or no additional tissue damage. But once your feet are thawed, you won't be able to walk and you will probably experience severe pain.

ACCLIMATIZATION

The body needs time to acclimate to higher altitude. However, the time it takes to adapt varies from person to person.

Ascend at a moderate rate, averaging 1,000 feet a day in net elevation gain. If you are doing double carries, this may mean establishing camps at 2,000-foot intervals so that you carry one day and move camp the next, for a net gain of 2,000 feet every two days. If the suitable campsites are 3,000 feet apart, you can carry one day, move camp the next, and rest the third day, for a net gain of 3,000 feet every three days. Try not to overdo your efforts until you've become well acclimated, and schedule rest days after big pushes.

Hydration is critical in avoiding altitude sickness. Rather than relying on a figure for daily liquid consumption, such as 4 quarts per person, monitor your urine output and color. A good rule of thumb is that urine should be copious and clear, while dark urine indicates you're not drinking enough water.

Above 18,000 feet, most people begin to deteriorate physically regardless of acclimatization. Minimize the stays at high altitudes and periodically return to lower altitudes to recover. The old advice is good: Climb high, sleep low. The body acclimates much faster during exertion than during rest, and recovers more quickly at a lower altitude. Expedition-style climbing takes advantage of these concepts in carrying loads to a high camp, returning to lower altitude to recover, then ascending again.

AN EXPEDITION PHILOSOPHY

Members of an expedition need a common code to live by during the weeks they struggle together. A good one is summed up in three promises you and your teammates can make: To respect the land, to take care of yourselves, and to come home again.

Every day, your expedition will have the chance to put the health and beauty of the land ahead of your immediate comfort. The easy way out might be to burn wood fires or set up camp in a virgin meadow or abandon heavy gear. But if you've promised to respect the land, you'll be able to do the right thing.

If you and your partners have promised to take care of yourselves, you've made a commitment to group self-reliance. You may have no choice in the matter, anyway, as you will likely be a long way from rescuers, helicopters, hospitals, or even other climbers. You can prepare by thinking through the emergencies the expedition could face and laying plans for saving the day. You'll be happy the plans are ready if you have to use them, and grateful if you don't.

The third promise might be the hardest to keep because it can conflict with that burning desire for the summit. It's really a promise to climb safely and to sacrifice dreams of the summit before laying your life on the line. But expedition climbing is, after all, about pushing limits and testing yourself in a very tough arena. Each person and each team must decide what level of risk they wish to accept. Out of that flows daily decisions on how fast to ascend, what gear to carry, when to change routes, when to back off. Most climbers would rather return home safely than push for the summit under unsafe conditions. But how do you define "unsafe"? You'll keep the third promise by being sure you find the definition that is just right for your expedition.

A SAMPLE EXPEDITION EQUIPMENT LIST
GROUP GEAR

Shelter
- ☐ Expedition-quality tent
- ☐ Snow stakes and/or tent flukes
- ☐ Sponge and whisk broom
- ☐ Snow shelter construction tools: large snow shovel (for moving lots of snow); small snow shovel (for delicate trimming); snow saw (for cutting blocks)

Group climbing gear
- ☐ Ropes
- ☐ Hardware: snow and ice gear (pickets, flukes, ice screws); rock gear (pitons, spring-loaded camming devices, chocks); carabiners; runners; fixed line; extra climbing equipment (spare ice axe or tool, spare crampons)

Kitchen
- ☐ Stove gear: stove; wind screen and stove pad; fuel containers and fuel filter; matches and/or butane lighters
- ☐ Cook gear: pots; pot gripper, sponge/scrubber; dip cup and cooking spoon; snow sack

Repair kit
- ☐ Tent repair kit (pole splices, spare pole)
- ☐ Stove repair kit
- ☐ Crampon repair kit (extra screw, connecting bars, straps)
- ☐ Tape (duct, filament, ripstop fabric repair tape)
- ☐ Tools (standard, Phillips, and Allen screwdrivers, small pliers, small wire cutter/shear)
- ☐ Sewing kit: assorted needles and thread; assorted buttons, snaps, buckles, and "D" rings; Velcro (hook and rug); fabric (cordura, ripstop); flat webbing
- ☐ Miscellaneous: extra ski pole basket; wire and cord

First-aid kit

- [ ] Most expeditions will have a comprehensive group first-aid kit. In addition to the normal first-aid items, the kit should include the following drugs, plus others recommended by a physician.
- [ ] Prescription drugs. This will vary with the destination but should include antibiotics, strong analgesics, anti-diarrhetic, laxatives, and altitude medication (Diamox, dexamethasone).
- [ ] Non-prescription drugs. This will vary with the destination but should include a cough suppressant, decongestant, and mild analgesic (aspirin, ibuprofen).

Miscellaneous group gear

- [ ] Altimeter and compass
- [ ] Radio transceiver
- [ ] Latrine equipment (plastic sacks, rubber gloves)

PERSONAL GEAR

Clothing

- [ ] Synthetic fabric underwear
- [ ] Insulating layers
- [ ] Down clothing
- [ ] Wind protection garments (top and bottom)
- [ ] Extremities: hands (liner gloves, insulating gloves, and mittens); feet (liner socks, insulating socks, vapor-barrier socks); head (balaclavas, sun hats, face masks)
- [ ] Miscellaneous: bandannas; sun shirt; plastic double boots; supergaiters and/or overboots

Sleeping

- [ ] Sleeping bag
- [ ] Bivouac sack
- [ ] Vapor-barrier liner
- [ ] Inflatable foam pad
- [ ] Closed-cell foam pad

Climbing

- [ ] Ice axe
- [ ] Second ice tool
- [ ] Ski pole
- [ ] Seat harness with ice tool holsters
- [ ] Chest harness
- [ ] Crampons
- [ ] Personal carabiners
- [ ] Personal runners
- [ ] Ascenders and/or prusiks
- [ ] Helmet
- [ ] Large-volume pack
- [ ] Snowshoes or skis
- [ ] Sled with associated hardware (haul lines, carabiners, prusiks)

Miscellaneous gear

- [ ] Avalanche beacon
- [ ] Sunglasses and goggles
- [ ] Spare prescription glasses
- [ ] Personal hygiene: toilet paper; pee bottle; toothbrush; comb; chemical wash/wipes; sunscreen; lip balm; foot powder; ear plugs
- [ ] Personal recreation: camera and film; books; journal (waterproof paper); personal stereo

◆ 16 ◆

SAFETY AND LEADERSHIP

Mountaineering is a sport of controlled risk. Climbers deal with the hazards of nature and their own shortcomings by cultivating knowledge, skill, and good judgment. A list of dangers in the wilderness reads like a catalog of disaster unless you've studied the hazards and know how to avoid them in order to establish control over your own safety. Climbers also need to develop leadership ability to help promote their group's safety, comfort, and success.

ACCIDENTS

One way to prevent accidents is to study incidents that have happened and try to learn from them. The American Alpine Club does just that in its annual publication "Accidents in North American Mountaineering." The publication includes only actual climbing accidents, as distinguished from other mishaps that occur in mountainous regions. It describes only those accidents that are voluntarily reported, so it doesn't include numerous unpublicized incidents. The accidents represent only a fraction of those in mountaineering areas throughout the world.

More than 1,100 climbers have been killed in North American mountaineering accidents since 1947, when the American Alpine Club began its annual reports. Despite advances in equipment, skills, and techniques, a number of climbers are killed or injured each year. Every accident is a little different from every other, but there are many common causes and most involve human error. For example, modern gear rarely breaks by itself. Equipment failure is usually related to improper use or to poor placement of protection. Climbers also cause accidents when they try to exceed their climbing abilities by relying on incompletely learned techniques.

There are some limitations to the American Alpine Club statistics because the types of causes change as climbing practices evolve, and the classification of accidents is a difficult judgment call, especially in deciding the relationship of immediate and contributing causes. But in spite of these limitations, the annual reports roughly indicate the elements of danger in climbing by showing recurring patterns.

The most common immediate causes of accidents reported were (1) fall or slip on rock, (2) slip on snow and ice, and (3) falling rock or other object. The most common contributing causes were (1) climbing unroped, (2) attempting a climb that exceeded abilities (inexperience), and (3) being inadequately equipped for the conditions or climbing situation.

An accident victim may feel that a mishap occurred "like a bolt out of the blue." But it's clear, in retrospect, that many accidents moved step by step toward an almost predictable incident. The climber who takes off on an ascent without an ice axe because it was forgotten in the rush of leaving home may do fine all day in soft snow. If this climber slips during the descent on the firmer snow of evening and is injured, it's an accident—but it's no "bolt out of the blue." An alert leader tries to spot potential accidents, and takes such precautions as turning back a minimally equipped party in the face of worsening weather.

CLIMBING HAZARDS

Mountaineers face hazards of two sorts: the objective dangers of the mountain environment, and the subjective factors that are dependent on the climber. The objective, physical hazards of the mountains—the storms, the cold, the high altitude—are easy to recognize. No less important, but far harder to evaluate, are the subjective factors involving the climber's knowledge, skill, and judgment.

OBJECTIVE HAZARDS: THE MOUNTAIN ENVIRONMENT

Objective hazards are the natural processes that exist whether humans are involved or not. Darkness, storms, lightning, cold, precipitation, high altitude, avalanches, and rockfall are powerful, impersonal environmental conditions that can easily overwhelm humans. These objective hazards of the mountains are eternally persistent and changeable. We cannot control these forces, but we can learn to recognize them and act to minimize their dangers.

You will find detailed information throughout this entire book on dealing with objective hazards, especially in the chapters on wilderness travel and on the various types of climbing—rock, snow, ice, winter, and aid. They spell out ways to confront objective hazards ranging from fearsome exposure and rotten rock to avalanches and steep snow slopes with poor runout. They give advice on avoiding rockfall, icefall, cornices, crevasses, and other environmental dangers.

Many of the hazards of the terrain are relatively easy to spot, such as rotten rock or a steep cliff. The hazards of weather can be somewhat more difficult to identify because they change so quickly. When they do, it often adds significant risk to the climb. Rain or snow turns warm, dry rock into wet or icy surfaces difficult to climb. Wind blows ropes around and also makes communication more difficult. Fog or whiteout obscures the route, forcing you to rely on compass and altimeter for navigation and increasing the danger of falling into a crevasse or off of a cornice.

Cold weather, especially if it is abetted by wind and rain, can bring deadly hypothermia. Hot weather, on the other hand, poses the dangers of dehydration and hyperthermia. (Specialized courses and publications on mountaineering first aid provide information for diagnosis and treatment of these conditions.) Lightning, although not one of the principal hazards of mountaineering, has caused a number of serious accidents. The peaks and ridges that climbers seek generate the vertical updrafts and rain-cloud conditions that generate lightning.

Reducing the risk

To reduce risk, you need to recognize objective hazards and learn how to avoid them. If you recognize the possibility of rockfall, for instance, you will wear a hard hat and take extra care to prevent knocking rock loose with the rope or with your body. If you recognize an avalanche-prone slope, you will follow the correct procedures to avoid it and will know what to do in the event you or someone in your party is caught in a slide. If you see a white-out or other extremes of weather developing, you will have the training and equipment to deal with it.

It's simple to recognize the objective hazard of high exposure—that is, being in a steep and exposed place. There are exposed places where you can sit or stand without serious danger, but loose footing or a moment of inattention can bring tragedy. The safest response to exposure is to rope up so you are on belay or tied into the mountain. If you are the belayer, estimate the direction and magnitude of any force you may have to absorb if your partner falls and set up an anchored belay station where you can handle such a fall.

It's not so easy to recognize the hazard of a crevasse that is hidden beneath a layer of snow. But if you have studied glacier travel and learned the external signs of hidden crevasses, you will know when to rope up and how to choose routes that minimize the danger of falling into one. You and your companions also will have the training and equipment to carry out a safe, efficient crevasse rescue if that becomes necessary.

Help fortify yourself against objective hazards by always carrying the proper clothing, food, and equipment, because any trip can bring unexpected danger or an emergency bivouac. Protective gear, whether it's for technical climbing or bivouac survival, doesn't do any good if it is left at home, and it cannot often be replaced merely by nerve or skill.

You can use this book as a basic guide to proven gear and techniques, by studying the chapters on the various types of climbing and wilderness travel in addition to the specialized chapters on clothing, equipment, camping, navigation, knots, belaying, and rappelling. Then work to develop the experience and judgment to make the right decisions at the right time in order to avoid what are generally called accidents.

SUBJECTIVE FACTORS: THE CLIMBER

Subjective human factors share the blame for many accidents along with the objective physical hazards of the mountain. The climber without a bivy sack or extra clothes wouldn't have become hypothermic if it were not for that unexpected snowstorm. Conversely, the snowstorm wouldn't have caused any grief if it had not crossed paths with the climber.

The natural forces constantly at work on a mountain are usually harmless unless a human being is in their way at a critical instant. Then a small mistake—the subjective human factor—can cost dearly. A slope may be ripening to an avalanche tomorrow, but a climber ignorant of snow structure can trigger it today. A rock weakened by natural processes may be preparing to fall next week, but the weight of a climber can pull

it loose today. This subjective factor, which brings a particular climber to a given danger point at just the perilous moment, is nearly always at the root of a climbing accident.

Although we can't alter the objective hazards, we have considerable control over the subjective factors that can reduce their risk. These subjective elements affect every phase of a climb, including choice of route, skill of the climbers, equipment quality, physical conditioning, leadership, and climbing techniques. In the final analysis, everything goes back to a climber's knowledge, skill, and judgment. Any shortcomings will eventually show up in the reality of a climb.

Knowledge

A beginner ignorant of mountaineering gains knowledge from books, courses, mountain climbers—and from climbing. At the start, beginners won't even know they don't know: a novice might look at an avalanche-prone slope warming in the sun and not even be aware the party needs to ask itself whether there is a risk. But as they study and as they climb, beginners can add to their knowledge by keeping alert and asking questions.

A climber won't learn much by simply tagging along without paying attention to the climb, relying on others to make all the decisions and ending the day with not much more mountaineering knowledge than at the start. A climber with inadequate knowledge can mean danger to a climbing party, which may need to count on every member in an emergency—a poor time to have to unmask a climber's failings.

Skill

A great many climbers are skilled, but some are more skilled than others. The point is that it's important to match a climber's skill level with the particular climb. A good match and you have a safe, satisfying climb. A poor match and you could have disaster. An excellent climber trying to raise a personal level of skill faces increased risk; so does a novice moving up to an intermediate-level climb. A climber who does well on warm, dry rock may be in trouble if the rock is wet.

It takes practice and more practice to raise your level of skill. Practice under forgiving conditions. Try making those harder moves first at a practice area with a top rope, rather than on a long run-out at the end of a strenuous pitch. Keep working at it. A great part of climbing safety lies in competence that embraces a commitment to better methods, an eagerness to study and to learn, and a determination to practice and perfect the skills of mountaineering.

Judgment

Good judgment can be a climber's most valuable ally. Good judgment is the quality of using knowledge gained from study and experience to make sound decisions. Your mountaineering judgment should get better and better as you read and as you climb. Watch experienced climbers at work and try to determine what decision they will reach in a particular situation, and why. Learn to think, question, and reach informed decisions.

Experienced climbers won't always agree on what constitutes good judgment in a particular case. Some climbers demand a conservative high level of safety and would consider a decision that results in moderate risk to be evidence of poor judgment. Others would find the decision correct based on all the conditions of the climb and the abilities of the climbers. Each person has an individual definition of an acceptable level of risk, so climbers need to discuss this question with their teammates before a climb. The start of good judgment is to decide on an acceptable level of risk for yourself and to match your known skills with the difficulties of the climb.

A common form of poor judgment is underestimating the skills needed for an objective, whether it's a single move or a major mountain ascent. It's poor judgment to climb beyond your present ability and knowledge during a demanding climb. Try new moves and techniques in a practice situation. But if they come during a climb, be sure you have extra protection—good enough to prevent injury in case you fall and to permit you to get back on route afterward.

It's also poor judgment to let desire for the objective overwhelm an accurate assessment of the risk. Desire is a very useful element in climbing; it helps you forget weariness and calls forth your best efforts. But if it's not restrained, it can end in disaster. It can delude you into thinking that a faraway summit is close, that a questionable placement will hold, that a weakened team is strong enough. This is wishful thinking. Be rigorous in making a rational evaluation of weather, party strength, and other factors in deciding whether or not to turn back.

Good judgment in mountaineering also means acknowledging when you or your team are having a bad day. All experienced mountaineers remember days when their climbing lacked the usual feel; when easy pitches felt hard. Take any bodily limitations into account, such as fatigue, cramps, blisters, altitude sickness, or poor conditioning. If you're honest with yourself, you'll recognize that occasional bad day and scale back your plans accordingly.

LEADERSHIP

The safety, success, and fun of a climb depend in large part on leadership and organization. These formal concepts may sound a bit stuffy for the out-of-doors, but they exist in any successful climbing party. A small group of longtime climbing companions probably incorporates all the elements of leadership and organization with no conscious thought or effort because they have become habit over the years. It's a different matter with a party that includes beginners and whose members have never climbed together.

Leadership starts with each individual. Individual leadership means being aware of the group and its progress, whether or not you are the formal climb leader. Assume responsibility for your own knowledge and skill, and make personal judgments based on how they can support the group's objective. Be willing to speak up when you feel the risks of the climb may exceed the abilities of the party. Don't be deterred by fears that others know more than you and may consider you weak. By asserting personal leadership, you can contribute to group decision-making within the framework of the established organization.

The complexities of leadership grow as party size and trip length increase. On a weekend climb by two close friends, it's possible for one of them to take on all the organization and leadership chores: planning the menu, selecting the route, supplying the gear, and so forth. In a group of several friends, leadership may be by consensus. As the trip becomes more complex, one person may be designated the formal leader, charged with coordinating the group's activities.

The leader of a climb cannot do everything, nor is that desirable. A leader delegates duties and responsibilities in order to maintain an overview of the trip and ensure that all tasks are carried out. This also helps build morale as party members become more involved in the climb by taking on specific jobs such as planning meals, arranging transportation, or coordinating equipment. In a group that is large or in which the members are not well acquainted, the leader should appoint an assistant who can assume the role of leader if that becomes necessary.

A leader is also a teacher. Beginning mountaineers need help with climbing techniques, and experienced mountaineers may appreciate help in learning leadership. The best leaders exhibit the patience, empathy, and generosity that it takes to give members of their party experience in all phases of leadership.

Leaders prepare carefully to meet any major disaster that could befall their party. But the most common, and the most vexing, problems of leadership are the less dramatic, exasperating little mishaps that arise at the most inopportune moments—a lagging, footsore climber who is breaking in new boots, or another too ill or fatigued to continue the climb. There is no set answer for these trying situations. The leader is called on to use good judgment in evaluating the predicament, and then make a decision firmly and

unequivocally. An effective leader recognizes the potential for serious consequences in such seemingly trivial problems.

Mountaineering trips bring a rich spectrum of choices and make continual demands on a climber's will. Without leadership, even a strong party may wander aimlessly or sit paralyzed with indecision. But with good leadership, even a relatively weak party may achieve its goals.

THE STRENGTH OF THE CLIMBING PARTY

Whether a party is up to the challenges of a particular climb depends on its overall strength, which in turn involves the proficiency of the climbers, the size and speed of the group, and other important factors. Good leadership is central to maintaining a party's morale and making the most of its attributes.

Mountaineering proficiency

The strongest party consists of several climbers with a high degree of mountaineering proficiency—experienced, well-equipped, in good physical condition, with every skill for the climb at hand. What constitutes a weak party is not so easy to define. In some cases, a party is strong enough if it has only two strong climbers in addition to many weak members. In other situations, a group of ten strong climbers and one ineffective climber is too weak a party. A group with no experienced members is a weak party in any case.

The leader should be familiar with the climbers' abilities in order to know how to assign them. The leader may need a patient, reliable climber to encourage slow members at the rear of the group, or a pair of sharp routefinders to scout out the way ahead. If the leader is traveling near one end of a large party, an assistant should be assigned to help near the other end.

The leader also uses knowledge of the climbers' skills in setting up rope teams. In small parties, rope teams are usually formed by tacit agreement among members of the group. But in larger parties or in groups where the people are relative strangers, the leader may set up teams based on the climbers' experience, speed, and personality. Each team of experienced climbers should have enough strength to rotate the lead, sharing the work and giving less proficient climbers a chance to expand their experience.

Size of the climbing party

The minimum size for a mountaineering party is considered to be the number of people who can handle an accident situation adequately. Traditionally, a minimum party of three has been standard. Thus, if one climber is hurt, the second can stay with the victim while the third goes for help.

Variations from the basic unit of three depend on the situation. On difficult terrain or in adverse weather, when it would be dangerous for one person to go alone for help, four may be the safe minimum. On the other hand, the complexity of the route may make more then a single rope team of two a liability.

A glacier climb calls for four to six people, divided into two rope teams, in order to carry out an efficient crevasse rescue. A climb in a remote area where there may be no help within 100 miles must be planned for complete self-sufficiency and, therefore, may become an expedition of relatively large numbers. A small party in a remote area must consciously accept an increased level of risk.

It's a mistake, however, to believe that a larger party is always a safer party. A larger party can start bigger avalanches and kick down more loose rock. It will generally be slower and more unwieldy, both in camping and climbing. A party of ten to twelve is considered the largest that can impose itself on the wilderness without serious damage to the ecosystem—and even this is too large a group for some areas.

Backup support

A party gains in strength if it has a support team nearby or if there are other climbers in the area. To be useful, a support team must be willing and able to come to your aid, and ready to initiate rescue automatically at a prearranged time. Then, if your party doesn't report in by a certain time, a rescue

effort will get under way.

At the very least, be sure to leave a written description of your plans with a responsible person who will dispatch help if you don't return on time. Leave enough information so rescuers have a fair idea where to look, but there's no need to make it so detailed that you limit your own choices when you get to the area. If you do deviate from the schedule you left behind, keep in mind that you may be complicating any rescue effort. Give an estimated time of return, but build in enough leeway so that a few hours' delay from a routefinding error or other minor problem won't result in having the rescuers called out. Don't forget to check in when you return.

Keeping the party together

A critical responsibility of leadership is keeping the party together in order to concentrate strength and maintain communication. It's easy to divide up in the course of the trip, drifting into weak splinter groups. Some parties are large enough to divide into self-sufficient subgroups, but each subgroup must have adequate strength and leadership to meet its goals.

In small parties of equally proficient climbers, it's fairly simple to keep people together; if one lags, the others usually recognize the problem and slow their pace. In larger parties, the leader and assistants must work together to keep their group from splitting into independent fragments. This situation arises most often within organized club outings and climbing courses. Leaders of these groups may need to exert considerable control to keep the lead rope team from charging ahead, losing contact with climbers on the last rope.

It's even harder to keep a party together on the descent than it is on the way up. The leader, normally the last person off the mountain, must lay out crystal-clear instructions for where and when the party will meet in case of a separation. Glissading often results in breaking up parties. The fast, experienced glissaders are off the bottom of the run and on their way long before the last members of the group can overtake them. The leader should require a rendezvous of the entire party reasonably near the end of any major glissade. If the leader can hold the group to a pace everyone can maintain, there's little danger the party will be weakened by fragmentation or by having to search for a missing climber.

Time management

Speed is often equated with safety, and this can be true in crossing an area of rockfall hazard or trying to reach camp before dark. Speed also has its dangers. A quick, hard push can get climbers to a place where retreat is difficult in the face of deteriorating conditions, whereas a more measured, cautious approach would have left them with an easier withdrawal. Speed for its own sake can be a hazard if it comes at the expense of proper technique or safety precautions. The important thing is not how fast you go, but how wisely and well you use your time.

A climbing party's use of time should be planned out in advance, at least roughly. You can figure out the best time to get under way in the morning by mentally working through the various sections of the climb and estimating how long each will take. It's a good idea to set a time for turning back even if the summit hasn't been reached. The turn-around time will help prevent the party from pushing onward after it's too late to reach the summit and still get back to the camp or trailhead in daylight.

BECOMING A LEADER

Becoming a leader is a do-it-yourself project, requiring desire and initiative. The best way to become a good leader is to lead and to watch others lead, to organize informal private trips with friends on short, familiar climbs, and to gradually work up to more ambitious projects. Climb with experienced leaders and observe how they plan and how they work with their teams. Ask for assistant-leader positions on these climbs and become involved in the planning and decision-making.

Self-appraisal is a big part of becoming a good leader. Effective leaders take the time to assess their own performance, asking themselves: Did I do as well as I could? What went right? Why? What went wrong? Why? How could things have been improved?

Leadership brings pleasures as well as burdens. As awesome as the duty may appear, the exercise of competent leadership can become surprisingly easy if you prepare for it, fully accept the responsibility, and use common sense and good judgment to deal with rapidly changing situations.

⋄ 17 ⋄

ALPINE RESCUE

Mountaineer training emphasizes techniques for staying safe and healthy. But when injury or illness strikes, it's likely to be a long way from professional medical aid or rescue. Climbers are usually rescued by other climbers, often at great risk and sacrifice. So high a degree of mutual responsibility requires that every mountaineer be able to help in a rescue. This chapter focuses on efforts that can be mounted by a small climbing party without specialized equipment.

SEARCH

Searching for a missing person is one of the most common rescue activities. Start a search only if you can answer "yes" to this question: "Does the missing person need help?" If the person is healthy, well-equipped, traveling where injury is unlikely, and experienced in climbing and route-finding, there's a good chance he or she will find the way back to the party within a few hours. You may decide to defer a search until the next morning to give the missing person time to return.

Start the search immediately if the missing person might have wandered onto steep rock or a crevassed glacier, or is fatigued, inexperienced, or poorly equipped. Also get the search started right away if a physical problem, such as diabetes, is a factor, or if the missing person is a child. Search immediately if an entire rope team is missing after a severe storm, or in avalanche conditions, or on difficult terrain.

The thoroughness of a search will depend partly on how many searchers are available. A small party may be able to mount no more than a narrow search along a limited track. With a half dozen people, there probably can be a perimeter search. A large group can thoroughly comb a considerable area.

Regardless of the method, each person must know the full plan before the search begins. If the party decides to split up, each group must know where the others are. Arrange signals ahead of time: sounds such as yodels, yells or whistles, or visible signs with mirrors or lights. Establish a time and place for everyone to meet, whether or not they have found anything.

For safety, searchers should travel in pairs or remain within earshot of one another. Of course, this means that a search party of only two or three people can cover no more than a narrow strip of ground at a time. The best chance in this situation is to outguess the missing person. Put yourself in that person's place and visualize errors that might logically have been made. Check likely places such as the exits of off-route gullies and ridges.

If that doesn't work, retrace your party's original trail, searching all the way for tracks that indicate where the missing person wandered off. When such a point is found, proceed along the most likely path, watching for more footprints in snow, mud, sand, or on foot logs. In the absence of frequent footprints, searchers must fan out at broad intervals, calling to each other regularly and paus- ing frequently to listen for calls from the missing person. If no clues turn up after several hours of searching, it's probably time to go for outside help.

WHEN AN ACCIDENT HAPPENS

Leadership and discipline are key elements of success in alpine rescue. If your party has no recognized leader, select one to take charge in an emergency. The leader should consider suggestions from other members of the party, but the leader's decisions must be accepted without argument.

Go to the aid of an injured climber quickly—but move carefully to avoid any further accidents. On difficult terrain, dispatch only one or two rescuers, who are on belay and packing all the needed aid and rescue gear. As you climb or rappel down to an injured climber, keep to one side to avoid the danger of knocking rocks onto the victim. Stay calm; frenzied activity only complicates the rescue.

Urgent first aid should be rendered as soon as possible: bleeding stopped, breathing restarted, shock relieved, fractures immobilized. If it becomes necessary to move the victim to another spot because the accident site is too hazardous, use methods that will not compound the injuries.

It's important to keep close watch over the injured climber. A victim who is left unguarded, even for a few moments, must be tied to the mountain to prevent the danger of falling or wandering off, perhaps due to confusion or irrationality. Design the tie-in so that the climber cannot unfasten it.

In dealing with an emergency, swift action may be less effective than correct action. A hasty splitting up of the climbing party or any other spontaneous but shortsighted effort has less chance of ultimate success than one more deliberately considered. Therefore, after the initial demands of safety and first aid are satisfied, the leader and party sit down to plan. Everything must be thought through to the very end, everything prearranged, including what each person is to do under all circumstances throughout the rescue operation.

Every aspect of the situation needs cool analysis. How serious are the injuries? What measures are necessary to sustain the victim during evacuation? What is the terrain like and how far is it to the road? What are the strengths and resources of the party? Only after careful analysis of such questions should your party select a course of action.

EVACUATION BY THE CLIMBING PARTY

A climbing party can sometimes evacuate an ill or injured party member with no outside help. If the injured person can walk and the injuries are relatively minor, a lightened pack and moral support may be all that is needed. The party also may be able to evacuate a climber who has minor but disabling injuries such as a sprained ankle or injured knee.

An injured person generally benefits from a period of rest following an accident. Because the further trauma of immediate evacuation is seldom justified, postpone the move until the victim's condition has stabilized. The injured person can probably offer the best indications of when to begin the evacuation. Consult the victim and monitor the injuries closely, before and during the evacuation, and always keep the person's comfort in mind.

Some medical conditions require immediate evacuation: pulmonary edema, cerebral edema, unconsciousness for unknown cause, diabetic coma, and progressively deteriorating conditions such as appendicitis. Immediate evacuation also is necessary if circumstances of weather or terrain are life-threatening. Certain other conditions require that evacuation be delayed until trained medical help arrives (unless it will be more than 24 hours): head injuries, neck and spinal fractures, heart attack, apoplexy (stroke), and internal injuries. Evacuation is required but not urgent for all other serious injuries and illnesses.

OUTSIDE HELP

There are times a party can't cope with its own emergency. Outside help probably will be needed if a climber's injuries are severe, if the evacuation requires long stretches of lifting or lowering, or when circumstances—party size, condition of party, terrain, and distance to the trailhead—combine to make transport difficult. Thirty or more rescuers may be needed to carry a disabled victim for more than 2 or 3 miles on even the best of trails.

After your party decides that outside aid is needed, send for help as soon as the victim is stabilized and the persons going for aid are no longer needed at the accident site. In many areas, help by helicopter is usually no more than 3 hours away once word gets to the proper authorities, though this will depend on weather, terrain, and local politics. Ground rescuers often can be at the scene in 8 to 16 hours. If the climbing party is in a sheltered area accessible by helicopter and the weather is good, don't move the victim unless the injuries require doing so.

If your party needs help, don't hesitate in asking it from climbers on nearby peaks, from people living or working in the region, or from local authorities. A climbing party should know in advance where to turn for help if its own efforts fail and how to cooperate with rescuers and authorities.

It is sometimes not possible to send anyone from your group for help. Your only alternative then is to try to signal rescuers with noise or visual signals. Such a situation dramatizes the need to leave information about your intended route and estimated time of return with a responsible person, who will notify authorities if you don't show up.

GOING FOR HELP

If possible, send two climbers out together for help—partly for safety and partly because two people can do a better job of obtaining aid. Be sure they have a clear understanding of the party's situation and requirements so they will know exactly what aid to seek. They should take with them a list of the names and phone numbers of everyone in the party, a completed accident report form, and a map that pinpoints the accident site. Fill out an accident report form (fig. 17-1) for each injured person, with one copy going out with the messengers and the other being kept by the party leader.

Messengers need to carry enough gear to handle their own emergencies but not so much that they cannot move swiftly. However, the certainty, not the swiftness, of getting the message out is the most important consideration. The messengers must travel in a safe manner. The victim and other members of the party are relying solely on them, assuming authorities will get the word and that help will soon be on its way. The messengers should mark the route to help in finding the way back.

The messengers have several vital responsibilities once they get out of the wilderness. First of all, they contact the appropriate local authorities, such as the county sheriff or park personnel. They ask them to help in a rescue, or to relay the need for help to the local Mountain Rescue organization. If evacuation will take place over technical terrain, the authorities must know this so they will dispatch rescuers with the proper training.

The messengers' job is not ended at this point. They must make certain that messages are sent at once, accurately, and that they reach their destination. Often the organization of a rescue depends upon a chain of communication, messages relayed from person to person via telephone and radio, until finally a rescue leader is reached. Along the way, vital information may be ignored by non-mountaineers who do not understand the words they are asked to convey. The messengers should talk directly with a trusted fellow climber so that the line of communication is not broken. If the messengers can't speak personally to the rescue leader, they must be insistent with intermediaries—perhaps to the point of being obnoxious—to assure that a garbled message does not result in a tragic rescue failure.

The messengers then wait by the telephone at a meeting point, where they will get together with the rescue party. The messengers turn the accident report, map, and list of names over to the rescue leader and assist in devising a rescue plan. Unless

Fig. 17–1. Accident report form

FIRST AID REPORT FORM

© The Mountaineers

RESCUE REQUEST
Fill Out One Form Per Victim

TIME OF INCIDENT
AM PM DATE

NATURE OF INCIDENT
FALL ON: ☐ ROCK ☐ SNOW ☐ FALLING ROCK
☐ CREVASSE ☐ AVALANCHE
☐ ILLNESS EXCESSIVE ☐ HEAT ☐ COLD

BRIEF DESCRIPTION OF INCIDENT

INJURIES
(List Most Severe First)

FIRST AID GIVEN

SKIN TEMP/COLOR:

STATE OF CONSCIOUSNESS:

PAIN (Location):

RECORD:
Time
Pulse
Respiration
INITIAL   WHEN LEFT SCENE

VICTIM'S NAME   AGE

ADDRESS

NOTIFY (Name)

RELATIONSHIP   PHONE

DETACH HERE – SEND OUT WITH REQUEST FOR AID

- -

TEAR HERE – KEEP THIS SECTION WITH VICTIM

FINDINGS — FIRST AID GIVEN

START HERE
AIRWAY, BREATHING, CIRCULATION

INITIAL RAPID CHECK
(Chest Wounds, Severe Bleeding)

ASK WHAT HAPPENED:

ASK WHERE IT HURTS:

TAKE PULSE & RESPIRATIONS | PULSE | RESPIRATIONS

HEAD-TO-TOE EXAMINATION

HEAD: Scalp — Wounds
Ears, Nose — Fluid
Eyes — Pupils
Jaw — Stability
Mouth — Wounds

NECK: Wounds, Deformity

CHEST: Movement, Symmetry

ABDOMEN: Wounds, Rigidity

PELVIS: Stability

EXTREMITIES: Wounds, Deformity
Sensation & Movement
Pulses Below Injury

BACK: Wounds, Deformity

SKIN: Color
Temperature
Moistness

STATE OF CONSCIOUSNESS

PAIN (Location)

LOOK FOR MEDICAL ID TAG

ALLERGIES

VICTIM'S NAME   AGE

COMPLETED BY   DATE   TIME

VITAL SIGN RECORD

Record TIME	BREATHS		PULSE		PULSES BELOW INJURY	PUPILS	SKIN	STATE OF CONSCIOUS-NESS	OTHER
	Rate	Character	Rate	Character					
		Deep, Shallow, Noisy, Labored		Strong, Weak, Regular, Irregular	Strong Weak Absent	Equal Size, React To Light, Round	Color Tempera-ture Moistness	Alert, Confused, Unresponsive	Pain, Anxiety, Thirst, Etc.

TEAR HERE – KEEP THIS SECTION WITH THE VICTIM

DETACH HERE – SEND OUT WITH REQUEST FOR AID

SIDE 2 RESCUE REQUEST

EXACT LOCATION (Include Marked Map If Possible)

QUADRANGLE: SECTION:

AREA DESCRIPTION:

TERRAIN: □ GLACIER □ SNOW □ ROCK
□ BRUSH □ TIMBER □ TRAIL
□ FLAT □ MODERATE □ STEEP

ON SITE PLANS:
□ Will Stay Put
□ Will Evacuate To
Can Stay Overnight Safely □ Yes □ No
On Site Equipment: □ Tent □ Stove □ Food
□ Ground Insulation □ Flare □ CB Radio

LOCAL WEATHER

EVACUATION: □ Carry-Out □ Helicopter
□ Lowering □ Raising

EQUIPMENT: □ Rigid Litter
□ Food □ Water □ Other

PARTY MEMBERS REMAINING:
Beginners _____ Intermediate _____ Experienced _____

NAME _____ NOTIFY (Name) _____ PHONE

NOTIFY:
IN NATIONAL PARK: Ranger
OUTSIDE NATIONAL PARK: Sheriff/County Police, RCMP (Canada)

they are injured or extremely fatigued, they lead the rescuers back to the climbing party.

The messengers also have the job of seeing that information gets to relatives of people in the climbing party. Because of the urgency of seeking aid and the need to keep phone lines available, this job may have to await arrival of the rescue leader, who probably has had considerable experience in working with concerned relatives and with the news media.

TRANSPORT ON TECHNICAL TERRAIN

On steep terrain that demands technical climbing, even a minor illness or injury can make a person unable to travel without help. A large, well-equipped rescue party has a lot of options for safe and efficient evacuation of the victim. A small climbing party, however, will find it difficult to take any route that involves much raising or traversing. The small party usually will take an evacuation route straight down the fall line, which uses the least energy and equipment. Rescue on class 4 and 5 terrain usually requires more equipment than on the easier class 2 or 3 ground, where people rather than gear can provide most of the help.

Raising or lowering an injured person on technical terrain is a serious undertaking, with any number of things that can go wrong. A small climbing party should be prepared with prior training in rescue techniques and their complications, in order to avoid errors that make matters worse. A rescue is inherently more dangerous than a normal climb over the same ground because attention is focused on the victim instead of on the climbing. Often, the climbers must descend by a route unknown to them.

The prime object—moving the victim without further injury—is naturally uppermost in everyone's mind, yet the safety of each individual must never be forgotten. Solidly anchored belays may be required both for the victim and for the rescuers, even if they wouldn't be set up under ordinary climbing conditions. If ropes are in short supply, rescuers can be safeguarded by a fixed line to which they attach themselves with prusik slings.

A small party uses its available climbing hardware for rescue work and must think through the limitations of this equipment. Be sure the equipment can safely do what you plan to ask of it. The party's standard 11-millimeter climbing rope is usually adequate for rescue raising and lowering of single-person loads, although keep in mind that it will stretch. If the rope was involved in the accident, check it carefully for damage before using it in the rescue. Climbers in small parties often carry emergency items to help in a rescue. Depending on the climb, such items might include extra slings and carabiners, a pulley, folding saw, snow shovel, whistle, plastic tarp, and emergency smoke.

THE RESCUE BELAY

The belay is an important component of the system of raising and lowering persons who are ill or injured. Whenever possible, the person being moved should be on a belay that is independent of the mechanism that is being used for raising or lowering (fig. 17-2). With this independent belay, the victim is safeguarded in case of any disaster to the raising/lowering system, such as failure of the main anchor, rockfall damage to the rope, loss of the lowering brake or of the raising pulley, or injury to anyone operating the system. The belay anchor, independent of the main system anchor, should be constructed of multiple self-equalizing placements.

For belaying one person who is being raised or lowered, the belayer can use any standard belay device, maintaining it in a position that ensures maximum friction. Do not use a hip belay. For belaying two people at once, only the Münter hitch provides a safe enough degree of friction. (For a review of the Münter hitch, see Chapter 6.) The belayer should have the ability to continue lowering the victim if the original descent system fails. The belayer also should be able to safely carry out a knot bypass of the belay device (described later

Fig. 17–2. Typical lower with belay

in this chapter) if two or more ropes must be tied together for lowering.

LOWERING THE VICTIM

Before deciding to lower a victim, be sure that's exactly what you want to do. Once started, it's very hard to reverse. It can be especially tricky with a small party, in which there are not enough people to provide an independent belay or help out if complications arise. If you go ahead with lowering, watch that the rope doesn't dislodge dirt or rocks.

There are several possibilities for getting the affected person down the mountain, depending on the extent of illness or injuries:

Downclimbing: A person with slight injuries can climb down under tension from a tight belay, assisted by a companion who helps with placement of hands and feet. On snow or ice, large platform steps can be prepared.

Rappelling: If the victim has no head injury or symptoms of shock and is not seriously hurt, a rappel is possible. You can belay the rappel from above with a separate rope. Alternatively, you can offer a belay from below by holding onto the rope strands from the victim's rappel device. (However, don't pull down on the strands unless the injured person loses control of the rappel. Otherwise, you could interfere with the rappel, especially if the person is using a hip wrap for additional friction.)

Lowering in the seat harness: You may be able to lower the injured climber by the seat harness if neither downclimbing nor rappelling is possible. The victim must have no serious leg or upper-body injuries. Use a rope with a lowering device (described in the next section) to lower the victim, who uses hands and feet against the terrain to help guide the way down. The person will stay upright more easily by wearing a chest harness with the rescue rope going up through a carabiner at the harness. The injured person should be on an independent belay.

Back carry: This is a good technique if the victim has a minor but disabling lower body injury or is uneasy about rappelling or being lowered. Keep in mind that the rescuer must be strong enough to take the weight of the other person and still be able to maneuver. This will be especially difficult on low-angle rock. Connected like this to the victim, the rescuer will find it almost impossible to give first aid if medical problems arise. Do not use the back carry in cases that involve back or neck injuries, suspected internal injuries, serious head injuries, or other conditions requiring constant monitoring. For these, a rigid stretcher must be used.

Two common methods of back carry are the coil carry and the nylon-webbing carry. If possible, have the rescuer and victim on an independent belay, regardless of the method.

In the coil carry, the rescuer slips half the loops of a coiled rope over one shoulder and half over the other, with the coils looping down the back to form a seat for the injured climber (fig. 17-3). Tie a short piece of webbing around both loops over the rescuer's sternum to keep the coils from slipping off the shoulders. Run a prusik loop from the lowering rope to the injured person's chest harness to take some weight off the rescuer's shoulders and help keep the victim upright.

Another method of back carry employs nylon webbing to support and distribute the victim's weight (fig. 17-4). The webbing should be extremely well padded, especially under the victim's thighs, to prevent concentrated pressure that will cause a loss of circulation.

Fig. 17–3. Rope coil carry

Fig. 17–4. Nylon webbing carry

Fig. 17–5. Passing the knot in a two-rope lower through a doubled carabiner brake system

The lowering device

The best lowering device for use by a small party without specialized rescue gear is the standard carabiner brake system, as used in rappelling—but doubled (fig. 17-5). Simply construct two carabiner brakes, and join them with a locking carabiner. (Chapter 8 gives details on putting together a carabiner brake.) Each brake should include two braking carabiners (the crosswise carabiners).

The rescue rope runs through both brakes, providing increased friction for holding weight during lowering. The use of a standard belay device for technical lowering is not recommended because these devices were designed for single-person loads and may not provide sufficient friction for all the conditions of lowering. A doubled carabiner brake, on the other hand, provides enough friction for lowering two people at once.

Please note that the doubled brake system calls for a locking carabiner—not a pair of opposed regular carabiners—to join the two carabiner brakes. The single locking carabiner eliminates the possibility the rope could be pinched between a pair of carabiners. For the brakes themselves, standard symmetric oval carabiners work best.

Passing the knot

On a long pitch, you may want to tie two or more ropes together to permit a long uninterrupted descent for the injured person. As the knot approaches the lowering device (the doubled carabiner brake), it's necessary to stop lowering and perform a careful procedure to pass the knot safely through the device (fig. 17-5). Otherwise, the knot would jam.

It usually takes two people to carry out this procedure. Stop the descent when the knot gets to within 2 or 3 feet of the braking device. One person holds the lowering rope while the other attaches a prusik sling to the rope just below the brake, and then wraps this sling several times around one side of a carabiner that is anchored above the brake. (You can also connect to this carabiner with a Münter hitch if you wish.) The second person holds tight to the loose end of the sling while the first person gently eases the load onto the prusik by slacking off the lowering rope. The first person then passes the knot through the braking system one brake at a time: the upper brake is disassembled, the knot brought through, and the brake reassembled; then the same procedure follows with the bottom brake.

Once the knot has been passed through the entire system and the brakes are reset, the second person loosens the hold on the sling that is wrapped around the carabiner (or connected with a Münter hitch). This allows the load to slowly transfer back to the lowering rope, so the descent can continue. (The prusik sling must be long enough to allow for the slack introduced into the system when passing the knot.)

RAISING THE VICTIM

Lowering a person puts the force of gravity on the side of the rescuers, and therefore it's the preferred way to go, but sometimes there's no alternative to raising a victim up a steep face. Rescuers then have a choice of two general methods: the prusik system, which depends upon the victim's own efforts, and the pulley system, in which rescuers do the lifting.

These systems work on steep rock, snow, or ice, but they are usually associated with crevasse rescue. (Several versions of these systems are described in full in Chapter 13.) The same safety precautions that apply to lowering injured climbers apply to raising them. Whenever possible, safeguard the injured person with the use of backup anchors, safety prusiks, independent belays, and with padding or other measures to prevent ropes from being cut on sharp edges.

In the prusik system, the climber carries out a self-rescue by ascending in slings that are tied to the rope with prusik knots or other friction knots or that are attached with mechanical ascenders. This is an exhausting technique and has limited use in evacuating a seriously ill or injured person.

For a pulley system, rescuers usually use the Z-pulley, the most mechanically efficient of the basic pulley methods. There are some precautions to observe in using the Z-pulley: establish a main anchor that is bombproof. Keep extra prusik slings handy for replacements if a prusik in the system jams—and have a knife ready to cut away the jammed sling. (Caution: ropes and slings under tension cut very easily, so always cut away from other ropes.) Keep in continuous communication with the person you are raising.

Also be careful that the haulers don't pull too zealously on the rope. The Z-pulley is a powerful multiplier of forces, and it's possible to yank out an anchor, break a rope, or further injure the climber by pulling too hard against excessive friction or an unexpected obstruction.

Many rescuers prefer prusik knots to mechanical ascenders in a Z-pulley, because of the possibility the ascender could fail or could damage the rope. Give the prusik at least three wraps around the rescue rope. Each time you reset the Z-pulley, check that the prusik is holding securely.

TRAVERSING

If the descent deviates much from a route that is straight down the fall line, moving an injured person becomes very difficult. Try to avoid highly technical, exposed traverses, using them only as a last resort.

A pendulum technique is useful on terrain where rescuers can traverse overhead. For this method, suspend the injured person from an anchored rope. With a second rope, also anchored above, pull the victim sideways. Gradually release tension on the first rope as the victim pendulums to a position beneath the anchor of the second rope. Repeat the procedure if you need to traverse farther. As you pull on the pendulum rope, remember that ropes stretched horizontally have a tendency to snag and to knock rocks loose, and that they develop high stress under load. Victim and rescuers alike should be wearing helmets.

HAZARDS

Rescuers face the same hazards as climbers in general—hazards from objective environmental conditions such as storms, rockfall, cold, and high altitude, or from subjective human factors such as inadequate training and poor judgment. Dealing with any of these hazards greatly complicates a high-angle rescue.

Rescuers and climbers can minimize the impact of a storm or other objective hazard with proper equipment and contingency training. Ask the big "What if" questions before you leave on a trip, to be sure you have thought through the possible consequences of cold weather or high altitude or other hazards and are ready for them.

Take every possible precaution to guard against hazards as you raise or lower a person. If there is any doubt, confusion, or major disagreement on what is to be done, stop and reconsider the entire situation. Be especially wary of rockfall during raising and lowering operations. Wear helmets.

Subjective hazards exist when a person's skill, conditioning, or other qualities fall short of what is needed for safety on a particular climb. You can exercise a good deal of control over subjective hazards through planning and training before a climb, and by keeping alert during a climb to such hazards in yourself or others in the party. Dealing with the subjective hazards at the start of a rescue can minimize problems from objective hazards.

TRANSPORT ON NON-TECHNICAL TERRAIN

In many rescues the hardest job begins when the steep terrain is past and the ropes are put away. No longer aided by gravity, the party must carry its burden, very fatiguing work on rough ground. Under some conditions, however, a few simple techniques extend the capacity of the small party so that it need not call for help.

SHORT-DISTANCE CARRIES

Four-hand seat: This technique, useful for very short distances, requires two carriers who are the same height. The carriers grasp their own right wrist with their left hand, palms down. With the right hand, they grasp their partner's left wrist, forming a seat for the incapacitated person (fig. 17-6).

Ice-axe carry: This method permits longer carries than the four-hand seat. Carriers wearing rucksacks stand side by side, with the bundled shafts of two long-shaft ice axes supported between them in their pack straps. The person being carried sits on the padded shafts, arms over the carriers' shoulders (fig. 17-7).

Back carries: A strong climber can carry a person on his back for a considerable distance if the weight is distributed properly. The two back carries described earlier in this chapter—using webbing or a coiled rope—work well. The rucksack carry is another useful type of back carry. In this method, a large backpack is slit on the sides near the bottom so the carried person can step into it like a pair of shorts.

Fig. 17–6. Four-hand seat carry

Fig. 17–7. Ice-axe carry

LONG-DISTANCE CARRIES

A stretcher improvised from rope can make it possible to carry a person long distances over non-technical ground. But before doing this, carefully consider the fact that evacuation on an improvised stretcher is usually very rough on the victim. If there is a chance that further injury will result, wait until trained rescuers with proper equipment get there.

Here is how to make a stretcher from a climbing rope, as shown in figure 17-8: Place the rope (150 feet is best) on the ground. From its exact center, make sixteen 180-degree bends, eight extending on each side of the center. The distance between bends should be about as wide as the person who will be carried, with the full sixteen bends approximately as long as that person.

Bring one rope end around each side of the stretcher, next to the bends. Tie a clove hitch in the rope section adjacent to each bend; insert the bend through the loops of the clove hitch. Continue tying clove hitches and inserting bends until all the bends are bound within clove hitches. Leave a small loop between the apex of each bend and the knot; insert the remaining rope through these loops until the entire remainder is strung around the stretcher. Snug up the knots, tie off the rope ends, and pad the area that will support the person from neck to hips.

Have one of the rescuers try out any improvised stretcher to decide if it needs more padding or support, keeping the victim's comfort in mind.

EVACUATION ON SNOW

On snow, it's particularly urgent to protect an injured person from heat loss while you give first aid and plan the evacuation. Wrap the person in

Fig. 17–8. Climbing rope stretcher

extra clothing. Use pads, packs, or ropes as insulation from the snow. If the victim cannot be moved quickly, build a trench or low wall as a temporary wind shield. Of course, if you must stay overnight, the party will put up a tent or dig a snow cave.

If possible, move the victim to a sheltered location, preferably below timberline. Do this as soon as you have given first aid and prepared the person for travel.

An ill or injured climber may be able to get down a snow slope by using some form of assisted sitting glissade. Sometimes the climber can be lowered in a sitting glissade position. Or a rescuer can sit in front of the victim, smoothing the track, the two tied together and on belay. A victim in relatively good condition can be roped in with two or three companions who then glissade slowly as a team, constantly under control.

Rescuers can set up anchors for belays and for braking devices by using pickets, bollards, or deadman anchors such as snow flukes or buried ice axes. (Chapter 12 gives the details on setting up these anchors.) The boot-axe belay usually is not strong enough for use in rescues. Moats often provide superb anchor positions for lowering.

Snow evacuations often involve climbers rescued from an avalanche or a crevasse. (Techniques of avalanche rescue are covered in Chapter 12, and crevasse rescue is explained in Chapter 13.)

ORGANIZED RESCUE OPERATIONS

Mountain rescues are often mounted by professional rescue agencies or by highly trained volunteers. This chapter has emphasized rescue efforts that can be undertaken by climbing parties themselves. Organized rescue groups bring the benefits of wide experience and training, plus specialized equipment and techniques, including air rescue.

RESCUE ORGANIZATIONS

In the Alps, with its large corps of professional guides, organized rescue is all part of the business. In North America, mountain rescues are commonly carried out by volunteer organizations. The volunteers use their rescue training and knowledge of the local mountains to analyze a situation, decide a course of action and carry it through. They round up the needed equipment and rescuers from among local climbers who are on call for emergencies. In the state of Washington, for example, Mountain Rescue units are headquartered in the major cities. Rescue evacuations usually require a leader and from eighteen to twenty-four stretcher bearers, unless a helicopter does the job.

In most areas, official responsibility for rescue rests with an agency such as the county sheriff's department or the National Park Service, and volunteer rescue units work closely with these authorities.

SPECIALIZED EQUIPMENT

Rescue organizations use equipment specially designed to make their task easier. Although these items are not standard climbing gear, every climber should know what they are and what can be done with them.

Most important is a rigid stretcher of fiberglass or metal. A well-known design is the Stokes litter, which has a framework of metal tubing and a wire-mesh basket that closely fits the outlines of a person's body. The Stokes, although heavy, works well on technical evacuations and general carryouts. Fiberglass stretchers with a metal framework are lighter and can be broken down into sections for ease of carrying, especially valuable attributes for technical rescues. They are widely used on snow because they slide easily. Many stretchers permit attachment of a wheel for trail or snow carryouts.

For raising and lowering, rescuers sometimes employ hand-operated or engine-powered portable winches with wire cables or non-stretch ropes that are several hundred feet long. The ropes are lighter than wire cable and require no specialized equipment to use other than standard climbing gear.

Two-way radio communication greatly facilitates mountain rescue, if the gear is lightweight and efficient. However, it can be difficult to get reliable transmission and reception through heavy timber, intervening ridges, long distances, and bad weather.

HELICOPTER RESCUE

Climbers can communicate with air rescuers by constructing international ground symbols, which are familiar to most pilots (fig. 17-9). The symbols, signaling such information as the need for a doctor, should be 8 to 12 feet high with lines 1 foot wide. It's a good idea to keep a copy of the symbols in your first-aid kit.

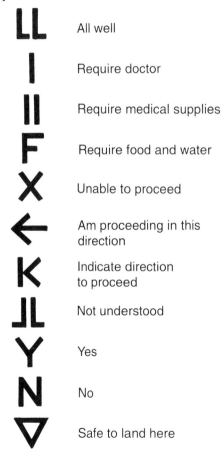

LL — All well

I — Require doctor

II — Require medical supplies

F — Require food and water

X — Unable to proceed

← — Am proceeding in this direction

K — Indicate direction to proceed

⊥ — Not understood

Y — Yes

N — No

▽ — Safe to land here

Fig. 17–9. Ground-to-air signals

The helicopter revolutionized mountain rescue. It can pluck climbers from cliffs and glaciers and get them to hospitals in hours rather than the days sometimes required by ground transport, often meaning the difference between life and death. A helicopter takes on a load by landing, or by hovering and lowering a sling or a stretcher on a cable attached to a power winch. Climbers need to know some of the requirements and limitations of helicopter operation.

The most important factors governing a helicopter's ability to evacuate are visibility, wind velocity and turbulence, and air density. In mountain flight, continual visual contact with the ground is essential, so a helicopter can't operate in poor weather. It can maneuver safely in winds up to about 35 miles per hour, with a wind of about 10 miles per hour being better than still air. A dangerous turbulence usually accompanies high wind. The altitude to which a helicopter can fly depends on air density, which decreases as either altitude or temperature increases. Thinner air reduces the lifting force of the rotor blades.

The people on the ground should try to prepare a helicopter landing zone that has a 360-degree choice of landing and takeoff direction, so the pilot can land or take off into the prevailing wind. Clear an area at least 100 feet in diameter around the touchdown pad, removing obstacles such as brush and loose objects. Make the area as level as possible, with a slope of not more than 8 percent. Try to establish a landing zone where the helicopter can drop downward as it takes off rather than having to fly upward.

Mark the landing area with colored tape or brightly colored objects, and use streamers, plastic ribbon, or smoke to indicate wind direction. Put the wind indicators at the edge or downwind of the landing area so they don't obstruct the pilot's vision. It is urgent that all loose items near the landing zone be well secured, especially those used to mark the boundaries. If the helicopter lowers equipment, allow it to touch ground first to dissipate static electricity.

A couple of arm signals can be important. If there is a last-minute danger to the helicopter, signal "do not land" by holding your arms straight out horizontally from your sides and moving them to over your head several times. If your party has been unable to mark wind direction or landing site, members of the group should stand with arms extended toward the landing area and the wind at their backs. This signals to the pilot: "Land where we are pointing; our backs are into the wind."

Several safety precautions will minimize hazards from a helicopter. Stay away from cliff edges or anywhere else where you might be injured if you are knocked over by the helicopter rotor's powerful down-wash winds. Watch out for flying debris, use eye protection, and have all gear safely secured. Approach the helicopter only after signalled to do so by the pilot or a crew member, and then duck down and approach or leave from near the front so the pilot can always see you. Don't

approach or leave the helicopter from any side where the ground is higher than where the helicopter is standing, and beware of the rear rotor, which is nearly invisible when spinning. If you're not needed near the helicopter, stay at least 75 feet away from the landing area.

Keep the victim's safety in mind as you prepare for the helicopter evacuation. Secure the person and any gear so there are no loose straps, ropes, or clothing; shield the person's face and eyes from flying debris and assure proper respiration. It takes time to secure an ill or injured climber to a stretcher. Remember that the person's safety is at stake and don't be rushed into this critical job just because the helicopter is waiting. Rescuers who put their training to use in a caring and efficient manner can often bring a happy ending to what may have been a long and difficult rescue effort.

◆ Appendix 1 ◆
THE CYCLE OF SNOW

Snow crystals form in the atmosphere when water vapor is precipitated at temperatures below freezing. They form around centers of foreign matter, such as microscopic dust particles, and grow as more ice formed from atmospheric water vapor is deposited on them. Tiny water droplets may also contribute to snow crystal growth. The crystals generally are hexagonal, but variations in size and shape are almost limitless and include plates, columns, and needles. The particular shape depends on the air temperature and the amount of water vapor available.

When a snow crystal falls through air masses with different temperature and water-vapor conditions, more complex or combined types may develop. Crystals in air that has a temperature near freezing stick together to become snowflakes, aggregates of individual crystals. When snow crystals fall through air that contains water droplets, the droplets freeze to the crystals, forming the rounded snow particles called graupel (soft hail).

The density of new-fallen snow depends on weather conditions. The lowest-density snow (lightest, driest) falls under moderately cold and very calm conditions. At extremely low temperatures, the new snow is fine and granular, with somewhat higher densities. The general rule is that the higher the temperature, the more dense (heavier, wetter) the snow, though density varies widely in the range of 20 to 32 degrees Fahrenheit (–7 to 0 degrees Celsius). The very highest densities are associated with graupel or needle crystals falling at temperatures near freezing. The percentage of water in new-fallen snow ranges from 1 to 30 percent, sometimes even higher, with the average for mountain snowfall being 7 to 10 percent. Wind affects snow density, for high winds break up falling crystals into fragments that pack together to form dense, fine-grained snow. The stronger the wind, the denser the snow.

Two types of snow form right at ground level.

Rime is the dull white, dense deposit formed from the freezing of droplets of water on trees, rocks, and other objects exposed to the wind. Rime deposits build up toward the wind. Rime may form large feathery flakes or a solid incrustation, but

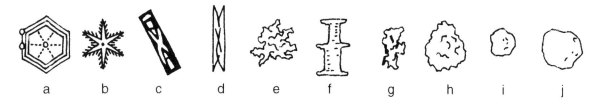

a   b   c   d   e   f   g   h   i   j

Fig. App. 1–1. Snow crystal forms: a, plates; b, stellar crystals; c, columns; d, needles; e, spatial dendrites (combinations of feathery crystals); f, capped columns; g, irregular particles (compounds of microscopic crystals); h, graupel (soft hail); i, sleet (icy shell, inside wet); j, hail (solid ice).

lacks regular crystalline patterns.

Hoarfrost, on the other hand, displays distinct crystalline shapes: blades, cups, and scrolls. Hoarfrost forms on solid objects by the process of sublimation—the direct conversion of atmospheric water vapor to a solid. Deposited on top of snow, it is known as surface hoar and is generally produced during a cold, clear night. The crystals appear fragile and feathery, and sparkle brilliantly in sunlight. A heavy deposit of surface hoar makes for fast, excellent skiing.

AGING OF THE SNOWCOVER

Snow that remains on the ground changes with time. The crystals undergo a process of change—metamorphism—that results in smaller, simpler forms and a snowpack that shrinks and settles. Because the snowpack generally becomes more stable over time, mountaineers find it useful to know the recent history of weather and snow conditions in an area.

Metamorphism begins the moment that snow falls and lasts until it melts. The equilibrium growth process gradually converts the varied original forms of the crystals into homogeneous rounded grains of ice (old snow). Both temperature and pressure affect the rate of change. When temperature within the snow is near the freezing point (32 degrees Fahrenheit; 0 degrees Celsius), change is rapid. The colder it gets, the slower the change, and it virtually stops below –40 degrees Fahrenheit (–40 degrees Celsius). Pressure from the weight of new snowfall over an older layer speeds changes within the layer. Snow that has reached old age—surviving at least one year and with all original crystals now converted into grains of ice—is called firn (or névé). Any further changes to firn snow lead to formation of glacier ice.

Another type of metamorphism takes place when water vapor is transferred from one part of the snowpack to another by vertical diffusion and is deposited in the form of ice crystals with different characteristics than those of the original snow. This kinetic growth process produces faceted crystals. When the process is carried to completion, the crystals often have a scroll or cup shape, appear to be layered, and may grow to considerable size. They form a fragile structure that loses all strength when crushed, and becomes very soft when wet. This weak and unstable snow form is known as depth hoar, popularly referred to as sugar snow. The necessary conditions for its formation are a large difference in temperature at different depths in the snow and sufficient air space so that water vapor can diffuse freely. The conditions are most common early in winter when the snowpack is shallow and unconsolidated.

As the snowpack on a slope moves very slowly downhill under the influence of gravity, the upper layers travel faster than those next to the ground. This internal deformation, called creep, proceeds most rapidly at the freezing point and diminishes with decreasing snow temperature. The entire snowpack also glides on the ground when

| 0 DAYS | 1 DAY | 5 DAYS | 15 DAYS | 25 DAYS | 50 DAYS |

Fig. App. 1–2. Destructive metamorphism of a snow crystal

the interface between snow and earth is at the melting point. If the ground is smooth (covered with grass, for instance), gliding is the dominant form of snow motion. The slow combined motions of creep and glide are so unhurried that they can't be noticed by the casual observer, but they cause the snowcover to exert enormous forces on obstacles in its path. The stresses produced by uneven snow creep are an important factor in avalanche formation.

Variations in the strength of snow are among the widest found in nature, with strength continually changing due to metamorphism, temperature differences, and wind. The hardness of wind-packed old snow may be fifty thousand times that of fluffy new snow. An increase in hardness is always associated with wind-drifted snow, or snow mechanically disturbed in any fashion, which undergoes a process known as age-hardening for several hours after it is disturbed.

SURFACE FORMS OF SNOWCOVER

Snow and ice undergo endless surface changes as they are worked on by wind, temperature, sun, freeze-and-thaw cycles, and rain. Following is a rundown on most of the surface permutations mountaineers typically encounter.

Powder snow: This is a popular term for light, fluffy new-fallen snow. However, powder snow is more specifically defined as new snow that has lost some of its cohesion due to the recrystallizing effects of steep temperature differences in the surface layers. These changes occur only during periods of persistent low temperatures. The changed snow is loose and powdery, commonly affords good skiing, and may form dry loose-snow avalanches.

Corn snow: After the advent of melting in early spring, a period of fair weather may be followed by formation of coarse, rounded crystals on the snow surface, often called corn snow. The crystals are formed from the daily melting and refreezing of the snow. Only when the same surface layer continues to melt and refreeze does true corn snow develop. When corn snow thaws each morning after the nighttime freeze, it's great for skiing and step-kicking.

Rotten snow: Rotten snow is a spring condition characterized by soft, wet layers that offer little support to the firmer layers above. In its worst forms, it will not support even the weight of a skier. Snow that promises good spring skiing in the morning, while there's some strength in the crust, may deteriorate to rotten snow later in the day. Rotten snow forms when lower layers of depth hoar become wet and lose what little strength they

have. It's a condition that often leads to wet loose-snow or slab avalanches running clear to the ground. Continental climates, such as those of the American Rockies, often produce rotten snow, which is much less likely to occur in the more stable maritime snowcovers of the Pacific coastal ranges of the United States and Canada.

Meltwater crust: This is a snow crust formed when water melted at the surface is refrozen and bonds snow crystals into a cohesive layer. A common variety is sun crust, so called because the source of heat for melting is solar radiation. Heat to permit meltwater crusts also comes from warm air or condensation at the snow surface. In winter and early spring the thickness of a sun crust is usually determined by the thickness of the surface layer where meltwater is formed in otherwise dry snow. In later spring and summer when free water is found throughout the snowcover, the thickness depends on how cold it gets at night.

Wind crust: In contrast to meltwater crust is the crust caused by action of the wind. After the surface snow layers are disturbed by the wind, age-hardening takes place. Fragments of snow crystals broken by the wind are compacted together when they come to rest, adding to the process. The hardening is compounded when the wind provides heat, particularly through water vapor condensation. Even when there is not enough heat to cause melting, the warming of the disturbed surface layer, followed by cooling when the wind dies, provides additional metamorphic hardening.

Firnspiegel: The thin layer of clear ice some-

Fig. App. 1–3. Surface features on snow: left, suncups; center, sastrugi; right, nieve penitentes.

times seen on snow surfaces in spring or summer is called firnspiegel. In the right conditions of sunlight and slope angle, its reflection produces the brilliant sheen of ''glacier fire.'' Firnspiegel forms when solar radiation penetrates the snow and causes melting just below the surface at the same time that freezing conditions prevail at the surface. Once formed, it acts like a greenhouse, bringing melting of the snow beneath while the transparent ice layer remains frozen at the surface.

Verglas: This is a layer of thin, clear ice formed from water freezing on rock. It is most commonly encountered at higher elevations in the spring or summer when a freeze follows a thaw. The water comes from rainfall or melting snow. Verglas may also be formed directly by supercooled raindrops freezing as they fall onto exposed objects (''freezing rain,'' also sometimes inaccurately called ''silver thaw'').

Drainage patterns: After melting has begun in spring, drainage patterns formed by the runoff of

water appear on snowfields. However, the actual flow takes place within the snowpack, not on the surface. As snow melts at the surface, the water formed percolates downward until it encounters impervious layers, which deflect its course, or highly permeable layers, which it can easily follow. Much of the water also reaches the earth beneath. The water that flows along within the snow often causes a branching pattern of channels on the surface. This happens because the flowing water accelerates the snow settlement around its channels, which are soon outlined by depressions at the surface. The dirt that collects in these depressions absorbs solar radiation and accentuates them further by differential melting.

Suncups: Suncups are depressions in the surface of summer snowfields, and they can vary in depth from 1 inch to 2 feet or more. They always occur as an irregular pattern covering an entire snowfield and form whenever weather conditions combine to accentuate surface irregularities. There must be motion of air to cause greater heat and mass transfer at high points of the snow than at the hollows. The air must be dry enough to favor evaporation, and there must be an additional source of external heat, usually the sun.

Under these circumstances, more heat reaches the points than the hollows but a larger proportion causes evaporation rather than melting. Because evaporation of snow demands more than seven times as much heat as melting, less snow is lost from the high points in the form of vapor than is lost from the hollows in the form of meltwater. The hollows melt faster than the points evaporate, and suncups form. They are enhanced by differential melting when dirt in the hollows absorbs solar radiation. The suncups also melt faster on the south (sunny) side in the Northern Hemisphere, so the whole suncup pattern gradually migrates northward across its snowfield.

Warm, moist winds tend to destroy suncups by causing faster melt at the high points and edges. A prolonged summer storm accompanied by fog, wind, and rain will often erase a suncup pattern completely, but they start to form again as soon as dry, fair weather returns.

Nieve penitentes: When suncups grow up, they become nieve penitentes (Spanish for "penitent snow"). They are the pillars produced when suncups intersect to leave columns of snow standing between the hollows. They are peculiar to snowfields at high altitudes, where radiation and atmospheric conditions conducive to suncups are intense. Nieve penitentes reach their most striking development among the higher peaks of the Andes and the Himalaya, where they may get several feet high and make mountain travel very difficult. The columns often slant toward the midday sun.

Wind and erosional features: The surface of dry snow develops a variety of erosional forms from the scouring of wind, such as the small ripples and irregularities on winter snowcover. On high ridges and treeless arctic territory, under the full sweep of the wind, these features attain considerable size. Most characteristic are the wavelike forms, with sharp prows directed toward the prevailing wind, known as sastrugi. A field of sastrugi—hard, unyielding, and as much as several feet high—can make for tough going. High winds over featureless snow plains also produce dunes similar to those found in desert sand, with the crescent-shaped dune, or barchan, being most common.

Cornices: Cornices are deposits of wind-drifted snow on the lee edge of ridges or other features. They offer a particular hazard as they overhang, forming an unstable mass that may break off

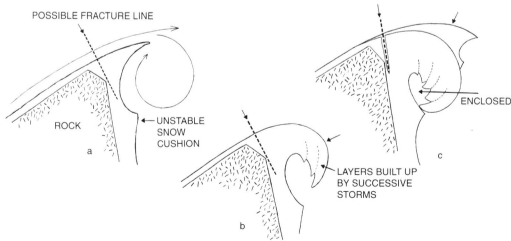

Fig. App. 1–4. Formation of cornices

from human disturbance or natural causes. Falling cornices are dangerous in themselves and also can set off avalanches.

During storms the precipitated snow furnishes material for cornice formation. Cornices also are formed or enlarged by material blown in from snowfields that lie to windward. As a general rule, cornices formed during snow storms are softer than those produced by wind drift alone.

THE FORMATION OF GLACIERS

Glaciers form for a rather simple reason. Snow that does not melt or evaporate during the year is carried over to the next winter. If snow continues to accumulate year after year, eventually consolidating and beginning a slow downhill movement, a glacier is formed.

Within the old snow (the firn, or névé), the metamorphic conversion of snow crystals into grains of ice has been completed. Now the grains of ice are changed into glacier ice in a process called firnification. Firn turns into glacier ice when the air spaces between the grains become sealed off from each other so that the mass becomes airtight.

Part of the glacier ice is formed by refreezing of percolating meltwater each spring when the lower snow layers are still at temperatures below freezing. This refrozen meltwater forms ice layers within the firn. Therefore, by the time compaction and metamorphism have prepared an entire area of firn for conversion to glacier ice, it may already contain irregular bodies of ice.

Once glacier ice has formed, metamorphism does not cease. Through crystallographic changes, some of the ice grains packed in the glacier continue to grow at the expense of their neighbors, and the average size of the ice crystals increases with age. Large glaciers, in which the ice takes centuries to reach the terminus, may produce crystals more than 1 foot in diameter, gigantic specimens grown from minute snow particles.

In our imagination, we can follow the birth of a simple valley-type alpine glacier. Picture a mountain in the Northern Hemisphere that has no glaciers. Now suppose climatic changes that cause snow to persist from year to year in a sheltered spot on a northern exposure.

From the first, snow starts to flow toward the valley in the very slow motion called creep. New layers are added each year, the patch of firn snow grows deeper and bigger, and the amount of snow in motion increases. The creeping snow dislodges soil and rock, while the melting, refreezing, and flow of water around and under the snow patch add to impact on the surroundings. This small-scale process of erosion eventually leads to formation of a hollow where the winter snows are deposited in deeper drifts. The snow gets to be 100 feet deep or so. The lower layers have nearly turned to glacier ice, while the increasing pressure of the many upper layers of firn causes the flow to accelerate. A glacier is born.

With continued nourishment from heavy winter snows, the glacier flows toward the valley as a stream of ice. At some point in its descent, the glacier reaches an elevation low enough and warm enough that no more new snow accumulates. The glacier ice begins to melt. Eventually the glacier reaches the point, even lower and warmer, at which all ice carried down from above melts each year. This is the lower limit of the glacier.

Glaciers vary from stagnant masses with little motion to vigorously flowing rivers of ice that transport large masses each year from higher to lower elevations. Glaciers in relatively temperate climates flow both by internal deformation and by sliding on their beds. Differences in speed within the glacier are somewhat like that in a river, fastest at the center and surface and slower at the sides and bottom where bedrock creates a drag. Small polar glaciers present a striking difference in appearance from their temperate cousins, for they are frozen to their beds and can flow only by internal deformation. The polar glaciers look much like flowing molasses, while temperate glaciers are rivers of broken ice.

◆ Appendix 2 ◆
RATING SYSTEMS

The development of rating systems began in the late-nineteenth and early-twentieth centuries in Britain and Germany. In the 1920s, Willo Welzenbach defined a rating system, using Roman numerals and the British adjectival system to compare and describe the routes in the Alps, which today forms the basis of the UIAA rating system. Today there are more than seven major rock, four alpine, four ice, and two aid-climbing rating systems used worldwide. This appendix will briefly describe some of these.

A rating system is a tool that helps a climber choose a climb that is within his or her abilities or presents a desirable level of challenge. The rating of a climb also reflects the type of equipment needed for the climb.

Rating climbs is a subjective task, which makes consistency between climbing areas elusive. The rating of climbs assumes good weather and the best equipment available. Variables that affect the rating of climbs include: how the local climbers who put up the routes interpret the rating system, how they want the area to be recognized, the type of rock or ice, and the type of climbing (e.g. face, crack, or friction rock climbing; front pointing or French technique ice climbing). The physical size and strength of the climber also affects how he or she thinks a climb should be rated. Ideally, a route is rated by consensus. A guidebook author typically has not climbed every route described and therefore has to rely on the opinions of others. In some cases, a route may have been done only once. When climbing in an area for the first time it is best to start at a lower level than normal in order to become familiar with the rock or ice, the type of climbing, and how the rating system reflects the qualities of the climbing.

NORTH AMERICAN RATING SYSTEMS

Rock climbing

Free climbing

In 1937, a modified Welzenbach rating system was introduced in America as the Sierra Club System. In the 1950s this system was modified to more accurately describe the technical climbing that was being done at Tahquitz Rock in California by adding a decimal figure to class 5 climbing. This has become known as the Yosemite Decimal System (YDS). This system categorizes terrain according to the techniques and equipment required to travel that terrain.

Class 1: A hiking scramble to a rocky gradient; generally hands are not needed.
Class 2: Involves some scrambling and likely use of hands; all but the most inexperienced and clumsy will not want a rope.
Class 3: Moderate exposure may be present; simple climbing or scrambling with frequent use of hands. A rope should be available.
Class 4: Intermediate climbing is involved and most climbers want a rope because of *exposure*. A fall could be serious or fatal. Another definition is that it begins when all beginners and most average climbers will want and should have a *belay*. Usu-

ally natural protection is easily found.

Class 5: Climbing involves use of a rope and natural or artificial protection by the leader to protect against a serious fall.

The extension of fifth-class climbing originally was meant to be a closed-ended scale of 5.0–5.9. The rising standards in the 1970s, however, led to a need for an open-ended scale. Strict decimal protocol was abandoned and 5.10 (pronounced ''five ten'') was adopted as the next highest class. Classes 5.10–5.14 (as of 1991) have been subdivided into four parts, a–d. (See Table 1.) A (+) or (–) is sometimes used as a rougher means to refine a classification. For example, 5.12(+) equates to 5.12c or 5.12d. It also can be used to indicate a sustained pitch (+) or a pitch of one or two moves of a given rating (–) (e.g. 5.8(–)).

The extension of fifth-class climbing cannot be defined accurately, either quantitatively or qualitatively. The following general guidelines to the extension of fifth-class climbing will aid the climber who is unfamiliar with the YDS descriptions.

5.0–5.4: A physically fit climber can usually climb at this level with little or no rock climbing skills, using only natural ability.
5.4–5.7: Requires use of rock-climbing techniques such as hand jamming and/or strength.
5.7–5.9: Rock-climbing shoes, good skills, *and* some strength are usually necessary at this level.
5.10 and above: Beyond rock shoes, excellent skills, and strength, this level requires training for climbing techniques and commitment of time to maintain that level.

The YDS rates only the hardest move on a pitch. The YDS gives no indication of overall difficulty, protection opportunity, exposure, runout, or strenuousness. Some guidebooks, however, will rate a pitch harder than the hardest move if it is very sustained at a lower level. A guidebook's introduction should explain any variation of the YDS used. Some guidebooks give routes two ratings, one for the hardest move and one for the overall difficulty of the pitch.

Because the standard use of the YDS defines only the hardest move, a *seriousness rating* was introduced by James Erickson in 1980 to indicate relative danger of a climb:

PG-13: Protection is considered adequate, and if properly placed, a fall would not likely be long or of consequence.
R: Protection is commonly considered inadequate. The possibility exists of a long fall onto good protection or a shorter fall onto poor protection, which may pull. A falling leader will probably suffer injuries.
X: Protection is commonly considered extremely poor. There exists the possibility of long falls, pulling several pieces of protection and causing serious injury or death.

Quality ratings are common in many guidebooks. The number of stars indicates the aesthetics of a particular climb. No standard has been set, so each area and guidebook have their own definitions. These star ratings are useful in guiding a climber who is new to the area to the quality routes.

The National Climbing Classification System (NCCS) for rating free climbing proposed in 1963, and using F1–F10, is largely out of use. Many old guidebooks used this system (see Table 1).

Aid climbing

Rating aid moves or climbs is different than rating free climbing in that it is not an open-ended system, nor do the ratings change with improved technology. The aid-climbing rating system indicates quality of protection and the difficulty of placing that protection. The scale is A0 or C0–A5 or C5, with A referring to the use of pitons and/or chocks, and C referring to clean aid climbing (chocks only), although the use of C has not been universally accepted. This system is used throughout the world except in Australia, which uses M0 (mechanical) to M8, with similar definitions as A0–A5.

A0 or C0: Aid points are fixed.
A1 or C1: Aid placements are solid and easily placed.
A2 or C2: Placements are awkward to place and

Fig. App. 2–1. Comparison of rock classification systems

UIAA	French	YDS	Australian	E. German	Brazilian	NCCS	British
I	1	5.2		I		F4	3a
II	2	5.3	11	II		F5	3b
III	3	5.4	12	III	II		3c
IV	4	5.5		IV	IIsup	F6	4a
V-		5.6	13	V	III		
V		5.7	14	VI	IIIsup	F7	4b
V+	5		15				4c
VI-		5.8	16	VIIa	IV	F8	
			17	VIIb			5a
VI	6a	5.9	18		IVsup	F9	
VI+	6a+	5.10a	19	VIIc	V	F10	
VII-	6b	5.10b	20	VIIIa	Vsup		5b
VII	6b+	5.10c	21	VIIIb	VI	F11	
		5.10d	22	VIIIc	VIsup		5c
V11+	6c	5.11a	23	IXa	VII	F12	
	6c+	5.11b	24	IXb			6a
VIII-	7a	5.11c			VIIsup	F13	
VIII	7a+	5.11d	25	IXc	VIII		6b
VIII+	7b	5.12a		Xa		F14	
	7b+	5.12b	26		VIIIsup		6c
IX-	7c	5.12c		Xb		F15	
IX		5.12d	27				
	7c+	5.13a	28	Xc		F16	7a
IX+	8a	5.13b	29				
X-	8a+	5.13c	30				
			31				
X	8b	5.13d	32				
	8b+						
X+	8c	5.14a	33				

British grades (right column annotations): VD, HVD, MS, S, HS, VS, HVS, E1, E2, E3, E4, E5, E6, E7 holds less.

A3 or C3: Aid placements will hold a short fall.

A4 or C4: Aid placements hold only body weight.

A5 or C5: Entails enough A4 placements to risk a very substantial fall.

Bouldering

Bouldering has its own rating system. It is a floating scale that moves upward as the standards rise. B1 is always the hardest YDS classification in existence, and B3 is always a climb that has never been repeated. In 1991, the bouldering ratings could be compared to the YDS as follows:

B1: 5.14

B2: above 5.14

B3: the climb is unrepeated

Alpine climbing

The National Climbing Classification System (NCCS) describes the overall difficulty of a multi-pitch alpine climb in terms of time and technical rock difficulty. It takes the following factors into account: length of climb, number of hard pitches, average pitch difficulty, difficulty of hardest pitch, commitment, routefinding problems, ascent time, rockfall, icefall, and weather problems. The approach and remoteness of an area also influence the grade of a climb, which will be regional and, thus, guidebook-dependent. It should be emphasized that with increasing grade an increasing level of psychological preparation and commitment is necessary. This system assumes a competent party for the level of climbing expected.

Grade I: Normally requires only several hours to do the technical portion; can be of any technical difficulty.

Grade II: Normally requires a half day for the technical portion; can be of any technical difficulty.

Grade III: Normally requires a full day for the technical portion; can be of any technical difficulty.

Grade IV: Expected to take one long hard day of technical climbing (longer on the first ascent); the hardest pitch is usually no less than 5.7.

Grade V: Expected to take an average one-and-a-half days; the hardest pitch is rarely less than 5.8.

Grade VI: Usually takes two or more days; generally includes considerably difficult free climbing and/or aid climbing.

The times given do not especially apply to glacier/snow/ice climbs. The type of climb affects which factors are emphasized. It is important to study a route description to understand which factors make it the grade that it is.

Ice climbing

The variable conditions of snow and ice climbing make rating climbs difficult. The only two factors that do not vary greatly from year to year are length and steepness of the ice. Snow depth, thickness of ice, and temperature affect the condition of the route; these factors plus the nature of the ice and whether or not it offers good protection affect its difficulty.

Three rating systems have been introduced in North America: the New England Ice Rating System, first described in the early 1970s by Rick Wilcox, another in 1979 by Jeff Lowe, and the third in 1988 by Albi Sole. All use a modified version of the Scottish system (composed of Grades 1–6), which consists of two elements referred to as the *seriousness grade* (or *overall grade* [Lowe] or *commitment rating* [NEI]) and the *technical grade*.

Depending on the terrain being rated, water or alpine ice may be denoted as WI or AI, respectively. *Water ice* may be a seasonal frozen water-fall or nonporous ice found in the alpine environment. *Alpine ice* is permanent ice of a porous nature generally in the form of consolidated snow such as that usually found in glaciers.

The *technical grade*, as defined by Sole, rates the single most difficult pitch, taking into account the sustained nature of the climbing, ice thickness, and natural ice features, such as chandeliers, mushrooms, or overhanging bulges.

Grade 1: Walking up ice with only the use of crampons.

Grade 2: A pitch of 60–70 degree ice, reasonably

consistent, with few short, steep steps. Good protection and belays.

Grade 3: Sustained 70–80 degree ice, usually thick and solid. May contain short, steep section, but will have good resting places and offer good protection and belays.

Grade 4: Sustained 75–85 degree ice, separated by good belays or a less steep pitch with significant vertical sections. Generally good-quality ice, offering satisfactory protection.

Grade 5: A noticeably more strenuous pitch of good but steep (85–90 degree) ice. May be considered the equivalent of 5.9 rock in terms of relative technical ability required.

Grade 6: A very steep, strenuous pitch with few resting places and often a hanging belay. The ice may not be of top quality and protection may be dubious.

Grade 7: A pitch of near vertical ice, which may be thin, of poor quality, and doubtful adhesion to the rock. Protection difficult or nonexistent.

The *Seriousness grade*, as defined by Sole, takes into account the length, continuity, remoteness, hazards, and difficulty of descent; it is not, however, totally unaffected by technical difficulty.

Grade I: A short climb close to the road with bombproof belays and an easy descent.

Grade II: A 1- or 2-pitch climb within easy reach of a vehicle, little objective danger, and easy descent by rappel or downclimbing.

Grade III: A multipitch route at low elevation, which may take several hours, or a route with a long approach on foot or ski, demanding good winter travel skills, or a route subject to occasional winter hazards. Descent usually by rappelling.

Grade IV: A multipitch route at higher elevations or in a remote region requiring mountaineering and winter travel skills. May be subject to objective hazards such as avalanches or rockfall. Descent may present difficulties and usually involves rappelling from bolts.

Grade V: A long climb on a high mountain face requiring a high level of competence and commitment. Subject to hazards of bad weather and avalanches. May have long approach or difficult descent.

Grade VI: A long multipitch route on a high alpine face, which only the best climbers will complete in a day. May include the logistical problems of winter alpine climbing.

Grade VII: The biggest and hardest Himalayan alpine-style climbs (Lowe definition).

The *New England Ice Rating System* is used extensively in New England and was developed for the water-ice climbing found there. This system applies to a normal winter ascent of the route in moderate weather conditions.

NEI 1: Low-angle water ice of 40–50 degrees, or long, moderate snow climbs requiring a basic level of technical expertise for safety.

NEI 2: Low-angle water-ice routes with short bulges up to 60 degrees.

NEI 3: Steeper water ice of 50–60 degrees with 70–90 degree bulges.

NEI 4: Short, vertical columns, interspersed with rests, on 50–60 degree ice; fairly sustained climbing.

NEI 5: Generally multipitch ice climbs with sustained difficulties and/or strenuous vertical columns, with little rest possible.

NEI 5 +: Multipitch routes with a heightened degree of seriousness, long vertical sections, and extremely sustained difficulties—the hardest ice climbs in New England to date.

The *commitment rating* shows the time and logistical requirements of the climb.

I: Up to several hours.

II: About half a day.

III: A full day, up to 7 or 8 hours.

IV: A substantial undertaking; a very long day, possibly including a bivouac.

V: A big-wall climb of one and a half to two days. Could be done in a single day by a very fit team.

VI: Multiday big-wall climbs requiring more than two days.

VII: Big-wall ascents in remote alpine situations.

Ice climbing is relatively new in America so standards vary from area to area and guidebook to guidebook. Some guidebooks define their own rating system: *Bob's Route* IV, 5 (indicating seriousness and technical grade), *Bob's Route* (5) (indicating technical grade), and *Bob's Route* IV, WI5 (indicating overall grade, technical grade, and water ice). Most guidebooks do give the length of the technical ice climbing.

OTHER MAJOR RATING SYSTEMS

Many of the rating systems used throughout the world are very similar to one another, especially in Europe. Table 2 indicates which rating systems are used in which country.

Rock climbing

Australian

The Australian system uses open-ended numerics 1–33. See Table 1.

Brazilian

The rating of climbs in Brazil is composed of two parts. The first number gives the general level of difficulty of the route ranging from first to eighth grade (or degree), which is written as grade 5°. There is no comparison to the YDS for this part of the system. The second part gives the difficulty of the hardest free move (or sequence of moves

Fig. App. 2–2. Rating systems used throughout the world

COUNTRY	RATING SYSTEM
Australia	Australian
Brazil	Brazilian
Britain	British, IFAS
Canada	YDS, NCCS
East Germany	E. German, IFAS
France	French, IFAS
West Germany	W. German = "UIAA," IFAS
Italy	French, IFAS
Japan	UIAA, "NCCS"
Spain	"French," IFAS
United States	YDS, NCCS

Quotation marks denote that only slight modifications have been made to the system indicated.

without a natural rest) in roman numerals with sup (superior) added for greater accuracy. See Table 1 for comparison to the YDS. Ratings of climbs are written as 5° VI.

British

The British classification system is comprised of two elements, the adjectival grade and the technical grade, and is expressed as, for instance, HVS 5a.

The *adjectival grade* describes the overall difficulty of a route, including factors such as exposure, how sustained the route is, seriousness, strenuousness, protection opportunities, and runout. Acronyms are used up to Extremely Severe. The need for an open-ended, less cumbersome system led to an alphanumeric adaptation, hence E1, E2, E3, etc.

Easy	E
Moderate	M
Difficult	Diff
Very Difficult	V. Diff
Hard Very Difficult	HVD
Mild Severe	MS
Severe	S
Hard Severe	HS
Very Severe	VS
Hard Very Severe	HVS
Extremely Severe	ES
subdivided as:	E1, E2, E3, etc.

The *technical grade* is defined as the hardest move on a particular route. This numeric component of the British system is also open-ended and is subdivided into a, b, and c (see Table 1).

The two grades are linked to each other. For example, the standard adjectival grade for a well-protected 6a, which is not particularly sustained, is E3. If the route is a bit run out then it would be E4; if it is really run out then it would be E5.

French

The French open-ended rating system currently extends from 1–8c. Starting at level 6, the ratings are subdivided a, a(+), b, b(+), c, and c(+). See Table 1.

Soviet Union

Currently, there is no rock-climbing classification system used in the Soviet Union. First ascents are often done by climbers from other countries who rate the climb according the rating system used in his or her own country.

UIAA

The UIAA rating system currently extends from I–X(+) with levels V–X subdivided into (–), (nought), and (+). It does not express length, time, seriousness, and dangers of the climb. See Table 1.

West German

The same as UIAA except uses arabic numbers (see Table 1).

Alpine climbing/ice climbing

Europe

The International French Adjectival System (IFAS) is an overall rating of alpine and ice climbs used primarily in the Alps. It expresses the seriousness of the route, including factors such as length, objective danger, how sustained it is, commitment, altitude, runouts, descent, and technical difficulty in terms of *terrain*. It has six categories that are symbolized by the first one or two letters of the French adjective used. It is further subdivided with the use of (+) or (–) or sup (superior) or inf (inferior).

F: *Facile* = easy. Steep walking routes, rock scrambling, and easy snow slopes. Crevasses possible on glaciers. Rope not always necessary.
PD: *Peu difficile* = moderate. Rock climbing with some technical difficulty, snow and ice slopes, difficult glaciers, and narrow ridges.
AD: *Assez difficile* = fairly hard. Fairly difficult and serious climbs, steep rock climbing, long snow/ice slopes above 50 degrees.
D: *Difficile* = hard. Sustained hard rock and snow/ice climbing.
TD: *Trés difficile* = very hard. Very difficult technical climbing on all kinds of terrain.
ED: *Extrêmement difficile* = extremely difficult. Extremely serious climbs with long sustained difficulties of the highest order.
ABO: *Abominable*

Soviet Union

The Soviet Union has an alpine rating system somewhat comparable to the NCCS system used in the United States. The scale is 1–6, with a and b subdivisions.

◆ Appendix 3 ◆
LIGHTNING

Though not one of the principal perils of moun- taineering, lightning has caused a number of serious—and mostly avoidable—accidents. The very nature of their sport places climbers on or near the most frequent targets: peaks and ridges produce the vertical updrafts and raincloud conditions that generate lightning; the prominences serve to trig- ger the strokes. Climbers therefore should under- stand the basic mechanisms involved and fix in their minds the fundamentals of evasive action.

For all practical purposes the hazards are three: (1) a direct strike, (2) ground currents, and (3) induced currents in the immediate vicinity of a strike.

Electrical potential builds up in a cloud in some- what the same manner one's body picks up an elec- trical charge on a dry day. Air is normally a very poor conductor (good insulator) of electricity; trees, rock, or earth are better conductors, more so when wet; the human body is still better; and most metals are best of all. Lightning seeks the path of least total resistance between the cloud and earth— the shortest possible line through the air. Ordi- narily the closest ground point is directly below the cloud, but a summit off to one side can be closer and become the bull's-eye.

Air ceases to be a good insulator when sub- jected to a sufficiently high electrical pressure; it *ionizes* and thereupon loses its insulating quality and becomes a conductor. The ionizing breakdown around a conducting projection often gives off a crackling noise (notorious in the Alps as the "buzzing of bees") caused by small sparks. The distinctive odor of ozone is usually noted. A bluish glow or *corona* (St. Elmo's fire) may be seen. If a person's head is the projection, the hair (if any) crackles and stands on end. Corona discharges have often been observed when the nearest cloud seemed too far away to be at all relevant. The sound or sight of corona does not necessarily indi- cate danger, but lacking more precise indication should be regarded as a warning, especially when thunderclouds are nearby. Additonally, any atmo- spheric activity symptomatic of commotion should stir suspicion. A sudden rush of cold air perhaps announces a strong cold front with possible lightning. A cloudburst of enormous raindrops or monster snowflakes or huge hailstones almost cer- tainly means a cumulonimbus is overhead.

Lightning is, of course, electricity, which is a stream of electrons. When the more than 100 bil- lion billion electrons in an average bolt strike a peak or a tree they do not just lie there in a puddle, but immediately spread out in all directions. In the process considerable damage can result. Two fac- tors determine the extent of human injury: the quantity of current, and the part of the body af- fected.

The worst threat is the passage of electricity *through* the body in a way which impairs some vital function such as heart, brain, or breathing action. A current from one hand to the other through the heart and lungs, or from head to foot through virtually all organs, is most dangerous, even if relatively small; one can survive a larger current from one foot to the other through the legs.

437

Climbers face other potential hazards: large currents can cause deep burns at points of entry and exit; a mild shock may momentarily startle them or set off muscular spasms, or they may move about in semiconsciousness, and in either case may fall off a cliff.

First thought should be given to avoiding areas which might be hit. The governing rule is to seek a location with nearby projections or masses that are somewhat closer than one's own head to any clouds which may drift by. In a forest the safest shelter is amid the shorter trees. The middle of a ridge is preferable to the ends; avoid shoulders.

An electrical discharge at a strike point instantly radiates outward and downward, with the intensity of the flow, and consequently the danger to climbers, decreasing rapidly as the distance from the strike increases. On firm rock, especially when wet, the major path in most cases is along the surface. Lichen patches, cracks, or soil may hold moisture and thus provide easy paths. High-voltage currents tend to jump across short gaps, as in a spark plug, rather than take a longer path around.

Current flows because of a voltage difference between two points along its path. A person bridging two such points with some part of his or her body presents a second and probably better path for the current, some portion of which is therefore diverted through his or her body. The wider the span, the greater the voltage difference and the greater the flow through the body.

With this background, several precepts can be listed:

1. Avoid moist areas, including crevices and gullies.
2. Span as small a distance (occupy as little area) as possible. Keep the feet close together; keep the hands off the ground.
3. Sit, crouch, or stand on insulating objects if possible—a coiled rope or a sleeping bag, preferably dry.
4. Stay out of small depressions; choose instead a narrow slight rise. A small detached rock on a scree slope is excellent.
5. Stay away from overhangs and out of small caves. Large caves are very good if one keeps clear of the walls and entrance. However, a cave might well be the lower terminus of a drainage crevice, and in such case should be avoided.
6. When on a ledge, crouch at the outer edge, at least 4 feet from the rock wall if possible. If there is danger of falling off in event of a shock, tie in *crosswise* to the prospective flow of current. Make the tie short and avoid placing the rope under the armpits.
7. Rappelling when lightning is imminent should be avoided, but may be a valid calculated risk if it is the quickest way to escape a danger zone. Dry synthetic rope presents the minimum hazard.
8. Contrary to popular belief, metal objects do not attract lightning as such. However, in the immediate vicinity of a strike, metals in contact with one's person may augment the hazard from *induced currents*. Induced currents usually are quite small, but when added to ground currents may mean the difference between life and death. Thus it is best to set aside all metals, but to keep them close by (don't worry about an article buried in the pack). A metal pack frame might well be positioned to provide a more attractive path for ground currents beside and past one's body. At distances greater than 100 feet from a possible strike there is no need to divest oneself of metal objects.

◆ Appendix 4 ◆
SUPPLEMENTARY READING

Chapter 3: Camping and food

American Heart Association. *Nutrition, Health and Athletic Performance*. Seattle: AHM, 1986.

Axcell, Claudia, Diana Cooke, and Vikki Kinmont. *Simple Foods For The Pack*. San Francisco: Sierra Club Books, 1986.

Berglund, Berndt and Clare Bolsby. *Wilderness Cooking*. New York: Charles Scribner's Sons, 1973.

Bergstrom, J., E. Hultman, L. Hermansen, and B. Saltin. "Diet, Muscle Glycogen and Physical Performance." Acta Physiol. Scand. 71:140, 1967.

Dairy Council. *Nutrition and Athletic Performance*. 46(2), March/April, 1975.

Fleming, June. *The Well-Fed Backpacker*. Portland, Oregon: Victoria House, 1978.

Food and Nutrition Board. *Recommended Dietary Allowances*, 19th ed. Washington, D.C.: 1980.

Gunn, Carolyn. *The Expedition Cookbook*. Denver: Chockstone Press, 1988.

McHugh, Gretchen. *The Hungry Hiker's Book of Good Cooking*. New York: Alfred A. Knopf, 1982.

Peterson, M. S. and C. M. Martinsen. *The Athlete's Cookbook*. Seattle: Smuggler's Cove Press, 1980.

Peterson, M. S. and K. Peterson. *Eat to Compete*. Chicago: Year Book Medical Publishers, Inc., 1988.

Prater, Yvonne and Ruth Dyar Mendenhall. *Gorp, Glop & Glue Stew: Favorite Foods from 165 Outdoor Experts*. Seattle: The Mountaineers, 1981.

SCAN. *Sports Nutrition*. Chicago: American Dietary Association, 1986.

Wallace, Aubrey. *Natural Foods for the Trail*. Yosemite, California: Vogelsang Press, 1977.

Chapter 4: Routefinding and navigation

Carrington, David and Richard Stephenson. *Map Collections in the United States and Canada—A Directory*, 4th ed. New York: Special Libraries Association, 1985.

Cobb, David. *Guide to U.S. Map Resources*. Chicago: American Library Association, 1986.

Dodd, K. *Guide to Obtaining USGS Information*, U.S. Geological Survey Circular 900. Washington, DC: U.S. Geological Survey, 1986.

Fleming, June. *Staying Found*. New York: Vintage Books, 1982.

Kals, W. *Land Navigation Handbook*. San Francisco: Sierra Club Books, 1983.

Makower, Joel, ed. *The Map Catalog*. New York: Vintage Books, 1986.

Miller, Victor C. and Mary E. Westerback. *Interpretation of Topographic Maps*. Columbus, OH: Merrill Publishing Company, 1989.

Moore Moffat, Riley. *Map Index to Topographic Quadrangles of the United States 1882–1940*.

Nicholson, N and L. Sebert. *The Maps of Canada*. Hamden, CT: Archon Press, 1981.

Parry, R. and C. Perkins. *World Mapping Today*. London: Butterworths, 1987.

Thompson, M. *Maps for America*, 3d ed. Washington, DC: U.S. Geological Survey, 1987.

Chapter 7: Belaying

Leeper, Ed. "Belaying: The European Connection." *Summit*, 25, no. 4 (August–September 1979): pp. 11–29.

——. "Belaying: Forces and Stopping Distances." *Summit*, 25, no. 6 (December–January 1980): pp. 6–13.

——. "Belaying: The Occupational Hazards." *Summit*, 26, no. 3: pp. 20–27.

Loughman, Michael. "Ropes, Anchors and Belayers." In *Learning to Climb*, pp. 64–104. San Francisco: Sierra Club Books, 1981.

Steele, George. "Equipment Notes: Some Thoughts on Belaying." *Mountain*, 32 (February 1974): pp. 35–37.

Chapter 8: Rappelling

Martin, Tom. *Rappelling*, 2d ed. Sterling, Kentucky: Search, 1988.

Chapters 9 and 10: Rock climbing and Leading and placing protection

Long, John. *How to Rock Climb*. Evergreen, Colorado: Chockstone Press, 1989.

Loughman, Michael. *Learning to Rock Climb*. San Francisco: Sierra Club Books, 1981.

March, Bill. *Modern Rope Techniques in Mountaineering*. Manchester/Milnthorpe, England: Cicerone Press, 1985.

Ontario Rock Climbing Association. *Rock Climbing Safety Manual*. Toronto: Ontario Rock Climbing Association, 1985.

Robbins, Royal. *Basic Rockcraft*. Glendale, California: La Siesta Press, 1971.

Chapters 12, 13, 14, and 15: Snow travel and climbing, Glacier travel and crevasse rescue, Ice climbing, and Winter and expedition climbing

Barry, John. *Alpine Climbing*. Seattle: Cloudcap Press, 1988.

——. *Snow and Ice Climbing*. Seattle: Cloudcap Press, 1987.

Chouinard, Yvon. *Climbing Ice*. San Francisco: Sierra Club Books, 1978.

Cliff, Peter. *Ski Mountaineering*. Seattle: Pacific Search Press, 1987.

Collister, Rob. *Lightweight Expeditions*. Seattle: Cloudcap Press, 1989.

Daffern, Tony. *Avalanche Safety for Skiers and Climbers*. Seattle: Rocky Mountain Books, 1983.

Everett, Boyd. *Organization of an Alaskan Expedition*. Pasadena, California: Gorak Press, 1984.

Fawcett, Ron, Jeff Lowe, Paul Nunn, and Alan Rouse. *The Climber's Handbook*. San Francisco: Sierra Club Books, 1987.

Houston, Charles. *Going Higher: The Story of Man and Altitude*. Burlington, Vermont: self-published, 1983.

LaChapelle, Edward. *ABC of Avalanche Safety*, 2d ed. Seattle: The Mountaineers, 1985.

Lowe, Jeff. *The Ice Experience*. Chicago: Contemporary Books, 1979.

March, Bill. *Modern Snow and Ice Techniques*. Manchester, England: Cicerone Press, 1973.

Prater, Gene. *Snowshoeing*, 3d ed. Seattle: The Mountaineers, 1988.

Selters, Andy. *Glacier Travel and Crevasse Rescue*. Seattle: The Mountaineers, 1990.

Chapter 17: Alpine Rescue

May, W. G. *Mountain Search and Rescue Techniques*. Boulder, Colorado: Rocky Mountain Rescue Group, 1973.

Padgett, Allen and Bruce Smith. *On Rope*. Huntsville, Alabama: National Speleological Society, 1987.

Setnica, Tim. *Wilderness Search and Rescue*. Boston: Appalachian Mountain Club, 1980.

Appendix 2: Rating systems

Fawcett, R., J. Lowe, P. Nunn, and A. Rouse. *Climbing*. London: Bell and Hyman Limited, 1986.

Lowe, Jeff. "Rate Your Turn, A System for Grading Ice Climbs." *Climbing*, no. 51 (November–December 1978): pp. 14–17.

Roberts, Eric. *Welzenbach's Climbs*. Seattle: The Mountaineers, 1980, pp. 38–41.

Smith, Craig. "Twigging the Grades." *Climbing*, 109 (August 1988): pp. 38–41.

Wiessner, Fritz. "UIAA Grading." *AAJ*, 16, no. 2 (1969).

Index